Study Guide

Psychology
Modules for Active Learning

TWELFTH EDITION

Dennis Coon

John O. Mitterer
Brock University

Prepared by

Jeannette Murphey

WADSWORTH
CENGAGE Learning™

Australia • Brazil • Japan • Korea • Mexico • Singapore • Spain • United Kingdom • United States

ISBN-13: 978-1-111-34357-6
ISBN-10: 1-111-34357-8

Wadsworth
20 Davis Drive
Belmont, CA 94002-3098
USA

Cengage Learning is a leading provider of customized learning solutions with office locations around the globe, including Singapore, the United Kingdom, Australia, Mexico, Brazil, and Japan. Locate your local office at: **www.cengage.com/global**

Cengage Learning products are represented in Canada by Nelson Education, Ltd.

To learn more about Wadsworth, visit **www.cengage.com/wadsworth**

Purchase any of our products at your local college store or at our preferred online store **www.cengagebrain.com**

Printed in the United States of America
1 2 3 4 5 6 7 15 14 13 12 11

CONTENTS

How to Use This Study Guide

This Study Guide for *Psychology: Modules for Active Learning, Twelfth Edition* is designed to help you learn more, study efficiently, and hopefully get better grades. The exercises in this guide are closely coordinated with text chapters so that you can practice and review what you've read. This twelfth edition has been completely revised from the previous edition in format and in questions. Each module within the study guide is now divided into major headings with each of these sections having its own language development guide to facilitate reading the textbook and its own set of completion, matching, and true-false questions to answer. New questions have been added to this edition with the final survey section now having matching and true-false questions as well as the completion type questions. The questions have also been revised to make them more like the test questions the student will encounter on their classroom tests.

Each Study Guide chapter contains the following:
- Chapter Overview
- Language Development Guide
- Recite and Review
- Connections
- Check Your Memory
- Critical Thinking Questions
- Final Survey and Review (completion, matching, and true-false questions)
- Mastery Test (40 multiple choice questions)

Solutions to the questions are provided in the back section of the Study Guide.

A brief description of each section follows, along with suggestions for how to use them.

Chapter Overview

The Chapter Overview summarizes major ideas in the text. By boiling chapters down to their essence, the Chapter Overview will give you a framework to build on as you bring in additional ideas, concepts, and facts. Read this section first, before doing the exercises, to remind you of what you've read in your text.

For each major heading under each Module, students will find a review section consisting of a language development guide, recite and review, connections, and check your memory. Critical thinking questions are provided in the modular sections in which they appeared within the textbook.

Language Development Guide

Each chapter contains idioms, special phrases, historical and cultural allusions, and challenging vocabulary that might be unfamiliar to you. The guide will give you simple definitions for these words and phrases. You may want to keep the guide open beside your textbook as you read each chapter. When you come to a word or phrase that is unfamiliar, look for a definition in the guide. It has been divided up into the same sections as the major headings within a module to help you follow along.

Recite and Review

This section is a completion question (fill-in-the-blank) review of major ideas in your text. This exercise will help you actively process information, so that it becomes more meaningful. It also gives you a chance to practice recalling ideas from your reading after you've closed the book. As you work through this section, don't worry if you can't fill in all the blanks. Do what you can, then fill in the rest using the answer key in the back of the Study Guide. Focus your attention on gaps in your knowledge and return to the text to clarify any points that you missed.

Connections

This section provides matching of concepts or terms with their definitions. Where appropriate, art is reproduced from the text so that you can match to images rather than words. This is a good way to add links to your memory. Again, check your answers to correct errors and fill in any concepts you may have missed.

Check Your Memory

This section provides sample true-false questions about the textbook material. It's easy to fool yourself about how much you are remembering as you read, so these questions help highlight facts and details you may have overlooked. If you answer any of these questions wrong, return to the textbook to figure out why the answer was the way it was.

Critical Thinking

This section provides short answer questions to help you process your textbook on a deeper level. They come in a variety of formats, but require that you go beyond the textbook material, or integrate information you've learned with information you know. You should always be able to back up your thoughts and opinions with research evidence from your text or other sources.

Final Survey and Review

This section consists of completion, matching, and true-false questions covering the entire chapter. The Final Survey and Review challenges you to consolidate earlier learning and to master key concepts from the text. It's not a test, so if you still can't fill in all the blanks it can direct you about what ideas might still be missing and needing extra practice. Every time you do an exercise in the Study Guide, try to learn a little more and rely on the answers in the back less and less. Go back and reread sections of your textbook if you need to do so.

Mastery Test

These multiple-choice questions are similar to those found on typical in-class exams. If you aren't doing so well on the Mastery Test, it is a clear sign that more study and review are needed. Don't expect perfect scores on the Mastery Test; the questions are designed to be difficult, and may cover material from your text that was not reviewed in the preceding *Study Guide* sections. The Mastery Tests are designed to continue the learning process and give you feedback about your progress.

Solutions

Answers are found in a separate section, by chapter, at the back of the *Study Guide*.

Additional Study Tips:

SQ4R: Use the process described in your text—look over the chapter, make note of the survey questions or create your own, read the section, try to answer the survey questions as well as the Knowledge Builder section in your text, and then give yourself another quiz when you are done with the entire chapter, and again as test time approaches.

Spread it out: DON'T CRAM! Your memory will be best if you read a little at a time, some every day in short stints, rather than trying to read one chapter (or several chapters) all at once. Waiting to read your text or to do all the study guide exercises until right before an exam is a recipe for disaster.

Read before class: You will remember more if you read the relevant sections of the text, and attempt some of the *Study Guide,* prior to addressing the material in class time. This allows you to have some knowledge going in, provides an aid for memory, makes lectures easier to understand, and enables you to ask more useful questions.

Make it personal: Memory is best when it is relevant and useful for you. Define concepts in your own words, think up examples of concepts from your own life, and relate this class' information to information you already know. That will make it much easier to remember than rote memorization will.

Time on Task: There's no substitute for taking your time. "Rushing through" leads to sloppy and incomplete learning. Most instructors assume two to three hours of studying per week for every hour in class or every hour of credit. Most students spend less time on class studying than they should. Hopefully, using this *Study Guide* will not only help you increase your time spent wrestling with the material, but help you be more efficient and productive in how that time is spent.

Be aware of your learning style: Visit your local career services or learning center, or one of several online sources to take a learning style inventory. Different people process information in different ways, and so should take notes and study in different ways. Some people learn best using different colors, drawing pictures, or using graphs and diagrams. Others learn by taking notes or underlining in their textbook; others by reading their notes out loud or explaining concepts to a classmate, significant other, or a pet. Adapt your note-taking and studying style to match the way you learn best, and your time will be easier and more productive.

A Five-Day Study Plan

There is no single "best" way to use this guide. Getting the most out of the *Study Guide* depends on your learning style and study habits. Nevertheless, as a starting point, you might consider using the following plan:

Day 1: Read the first Module in the textbook using the SQ4R method and using the language development guide in your study guide. Make notes of the major points or concepts as you read. Complete the Knowledge Builder at the end of this module in your textbook. Then, complete the parts of the first module in your study guide (Recite and Review, Connections, Check Your Memory, and Critical Thinking Question), checking your answers in the Solutions section. Return to the textbook to make sure you understand why any items you missed were wrong.

Note: If you have not completed at least a fourth of the chapter after reading the first module, you will need to read one or more sections of the second Module and complete the above steps for these sections.

For Days 2, 3, and 4:
Now read the next module(s) in your textbook using the SQ4R method and the language development guide and making notes of the major concepts. After each module, complete the knowledge builder in the textbook and complete the sections in the study guide (Recite and Review, Connections, Check your Memory, and Critical Thinking Question) that pertain to the module you just read. Take a short break. Now take 30 to 45 minutes and review all of your notes and completed study guide sections from the previous day(s) and ending with the sections you completed today.

Day 5:   Read the Chapter Overview in the Study Guide. Review all of your notes and your answers to the previous study guide questions. Take a short break. Now do the Final Survey and Review section and check your answers. If you miss any, review appropriate sections of the textbook again. Then take the Mastery Test, and go back to the textbook to fill in any gaps in your learning.

Note: You may wish to modify this plan to a Seven- or Ten-Day Plan if your professor allots more than a
       week per chapter. The key is to study and review each day rather than cramming for the
exam.

Summary

The close ties between *Psychology: Modules for Active Learning* and the Study Guide make it possible for the Study Guide to be used in a variety of ways. You may prefer to use it as you read each module as suggested in the Five-Day Plan or use the study guide to review after reading the whole chapter. Either way, if you use the Study Guide conscientiously, you will retain more, learn more, and perform better on tests. Enjoy your journey into the fascinating realm of human behavior.

About the Author

Jeannette Murphey is the author of this study guide for the twelfth edition of *Psychology, A Modular Approach to Mind and Behavior*. Dr. Murphey is also the author of the previous and current test banks for the Coon/Mitterer textbooks: *Psychology, A Modular Approach to Mind and Behavior; Psychology, A Journey,* and *Introduction to Psychology, Gateways to Mind and Behavior.* Dr. Murphey recently retired after over 30 years of educational experience, including 20 years as a psychology instructor at Meridian Community College. She also taught at Clarke College and Mississippi State University, was a mental health counselor, and a psychological examiner for the State Department of Education, She earned her Ph.D. in Educational Psychology from MSU in 1986 and became a nationally certified school psychologist in 1989. While at MCC, Dr. Murphey received several local, state, and national teaching awards. Since her retirement, she has been writing and helping her husband and two sons in the family businesses.

Introduction: The Psychology of Studying— Reflective Learning

Chapter Overview

When students read an assigned chapter, it is better for them to study the textbook rather than just read it. Those students who get better grades learn to work smarter, not just harder and longer. They also tend to understand and remember more of what they've learned long after their exams are over.

Experiential cognition refers to the style of thinking that occurs during passive experience, while reflective cognition involves actively thinking about an experience, such as mindfully reflecting on what one reads. Two powerful ways to be more reflective when reading the textbook include self-reference, a form of self-reflection, and critical thinking, which involves evaluating, comparing, analyzing, critiquing, and synthesizing what one reads. These ways to improve learning can be combined into the reflective SQ4R method.

SQ4R stands for *survey, question, read, recite, reflect,* and *review.* **S** equals *Survey* and involves students skimming through a chapter before they begin reading it. **Q** equals *Question,* with students turning each topic heading into one or more questions. The first R in SQ4R stands for *read.* After reading a small amount, the students should pause and recite (**R2** equals *Recite)* or rehearse, trying to mentally answer their questions. **R3** equals *Reflect,* which is the most important step in the SQ4R method and involves self-reference and critical thinking. **R4** equals *Review* with the students skimming back over a module or the entire chapter after they are done reading. Although the reflective SQ4R method can be applied to any text, this psychology textbook has been specifically designed to help students actively learn psychology. For example, each chapter opens with a chapter survey (S) with dialogue questions (Q) presented throughout the chapter. Terms are printed in boldface type and defined in a running glossary to aid reading (R1). Each module in this textbook ends with a study guide called a *Knowledge Builder that has Recite* questions (R2) as well as *Critical thinking and Relate questions (R3). Students are also encouraged to reflect more deeply through the Psychology in Action* modules and through the boxes in the textbook entitled *Discovering Psychology, Critical Thinking, Human Diversity, Brainwaves*, and *The Clinical File.* Each module concludes with a point-by-point *Summary* to help you identify important ideas to remember (R4).

Like effective reading, good notes come from actively seeking information. A listening/note-taking plan that works for many students is referred to as LISAN. **L** equals *Lead, Don't follow* and encourages students to read assigned materials before coming to class. **I** stands for *Ideas* and reminds students that every lecture is based on a core of ideas. **S** equals *Signal words, which are* words that tell students what direction the instructor is taking in the lecture, such as "the three main ideas are." **A** stands for *Actively listen,* encouraging students to sit where they can get involved and ask questions. **N** equals *Note taking,* reminding students to be selective and take good notes, but not be a tape recorder. Students must also remember to use and review their notes often.

Many study practices are notoriously unreflective, such as recopying lecture notes, studying class notes but not the textbook (or the textbook but not class notes), outlining chapters, answering study questions with the book open, and "group study" (which often becomes a party). The best students use reflective study strategies, such as attending class regularly, studying in a specific place without distractions, using spaced study sessions rather than massed practice (cramming), using mnemonics (memory aids), self-testing, and overlearning (studying past mastery).

1

Students should engage in self-regulated learning, which involves first setting specific, objective learning goals and then, making daily, weekly, and monthly plans for learning. Learners must also be their own teachers, giving themselves guidance, asking themselves questions, and rewarding themselves when their goals are reached. As the students evaluate their progress and goals, they must also take corrective action if they fall short of reaching their goals, adjusting how they budget their time or changing their learning environments.

A tendency to procrastinate is almost universal with procrastinators working only under pressure, skipping classes, giving false reasons for late work, and feeling ashamed of their last-minute efforts. Procrastination often occurs because students equate grades with their personal worth and would rather blame poor work on a late start, rather than a lack of ability. Perfectionism is also related to procrastination because students with high stands often end up with all-or-nothing work habits. Most students who procrastinate can improve by learning study skills and better time management, which as making weekly time schedules and a term schedule for quizzes, tests, and reports. Students who are reflective, active learners set specific goals for studying as well as finding ways to make schoolwork interesting and enjoyable.

It is also important for students to be able to show what they know on tests. The authors of the textbook provide general test-taking skills, such as surveying the test before you begin, reading all directions and questions carefully, using time wisely, and asking for clarification from the teacher. Specific recommendations are also given for taking objective tests, such as multiple choice and true-false. For example, answers that include superlatives, such as most, least, best, worse, largest, or smallest are often false. In addition, if a person changes his answers, research has determined that he or she is more likely to gain points than to lose them, especially if the person were uncertain of their first choice. Recommendations for taking essay tests include listing the main points of the answer before one begins writing, answering the question directly without "padding one's answer," and checking spelling and grammar last. For short answer tests that require students to fill in a blank, define a term, or list specific items, the best advice is to overlearn the details of the course, paying special attention to lists of related terms.

Digital media offer another way to be more reflective, although students should be aware that information on the Internet is not always accurate. Websites that will be helpful to students as they study psychology include the Book Companion Website, which has on-line quizzes, web links to the interesting websites listed after each module, flash cards, and crossword puzzles. *CengageNOW* provides a web-based, personalized study system that includes a pretest and a posttest for each chapter, while Cengage's Psychology Resource Center has a full library of original and classic video clips. The American Psychological Association (APA) offers summaries of scientific and scholarly literature in psychology at PsycINFO as well as providing an online library of general interest articles and career information at its organizational website.

Preview and Reflective Reading—How to Tame a Textbook
Survey Question: What's the difference between reading a textbook and studying it?

Language Development Guide
Preview
plough through a textbook: to forcefully work through the assigned pages
nada or zilch: nothing

Reflective Reading—How to Tame a Textbook
mindlessly: involuntarily, unconsciously
special effects: illusions and other tricks used in movies
extravaganza: amazing, exciting show
subsequent: later

2

passive: inactive
global warming: increase in the average temperature of Earth's near-surface air
skeptical: unconvinced
googling: using a search engine to obtain information from the Internet
mindfully: being aware
going beyond the information given: imagining possible solutions
self-reflection: examining one's inner thoughts
critique: review, evaluate, appraise
synthesize: create
figure: technical term for graphs, charts, drawings, and pictures
caption: title or description placed under a figure in text
read in short "bites": read in small amounts
cycle: series
module: unit or section
mindfulness: present-centered awareness
genuine: real and true
You bet!: "of course!" or "surely"
enhanced: improved
intellectual indigestion: mental confusion
digest information: to grasp and process information
preview: a sample
mental map: model of events in one's mind
dialogue questions: questions like those used in conversing with others
anticipate: expect
interact: work together; relate
boldface type: thick heavy type
glossary: word list; dictionary
practical: realistic
intriguing: very interesting
sharpen your skills: improving one's abilities
rich variability: great unpredictability

Recite and Review

1. Students who get good grades do not just work longer or harder, they work _____.
2. Studying psychology is not just important for exams, it is good to apply to one's _____.
3. Psychologist Donald Norman refers to the style of thinking that occurs during passive experience as _____ cognition.
4. When one actively thinks about something, reacting "mindfully," and "going beyond the information given," the person is exhibiting _____ cognition.
5. If you attempt to listen to your instructor's lecture while texting on your cell phone and then tell a friend that you cannot remember what the teacher said, you were most likely engaged in _____ cognition during the lecture.
6. You see a news program about the oil spill in the Gulf after the program ended you spend an hour googling articles about the oil rig explosion and oil spill. Your actions exhibit what is referred to as _____ cognition.
7. One powerful way to be more reflective is through a form of self-reflection called _____.
8. In order to be more reflective when you read your textbook, new facts, terms, and concepts should be _____ to your own experiences and information you already know well.

3

9. When you are reflective in your reading, new ideas are more personally _____ and easier to remember.
10. As Jermaine reflexively reads, he pauses to evaluate, compare, analyze, critique, and synthesize what he is reading. Jermaine would be described as a(n) _____ thinker.
11. The six steps of the SQ4R method include survey, question, read, recite, reflect, and _____.
12. As Ana opens her psychology textbook to begin reading her assignment, she starts by looking at topic headings, figure captions, and summaries. Ana is engaging in the SQ4R step called _____.
13. To accomplish the second step in using the SQ4R method, Tia turns every bold face heading into a(n) _____.
14. The first R in SQ4R stands for _____.
15. After reading a small amount in your textbook, you should pause rehearse or _____ what you have read.
16. The most important step in the SQ4R method is the step known as _____.
17. Each chapter in your psychology textbook opens with a chapter _____ that includes a *Preview* as well as a list of *Modules* and *Survey Questions* that will be covered.
18. In addition to the survey questions, there are questions that appear throughout each chapter, usually at the beginning of a paragraph, that are similar to questions that students like to ask themselves as they read. These questions are called _____ questions.
19. As students are reading the textbook, they can find the meanings of the technical terms listed in boldface type in the lower right-hand corner of each page. These definitions in the corner of the textbook pages are called a running _____.
20. To help you study in smaller "bites," each module in this textbook ends with a study guide called a(n) _____.
21. Each chapter in your textbook ends with a module that is filled with practical ideas about how you can relate various psychology topics to your own life. This ending module is called _____.
22. In each chapter there are boxes, such as *Discovering Psychology* that invites you to relate psychology to your own behavior and a box that encourages you to reflect on the rich variability of human experience entitled *Human* _____.
23. Eli is reading one of the boxes in his psychology textbook that explains how the brain relates to psychology. These boxes about the brain are called _____.
24. Amir, who plans to become a psychologist, is fascinated by the boxes in his textbook that explain how psychology can be applied to help people suffering from mental illness. Amir is most likely reading a box called *The _____ File*.
25. In order to help you identify important ideas to remember, each module concludes with a point-by-point _____, which is organized around the same *Survey Questions* you read at the beginning of the module.

Connections

1. ___ experiential cognition
2. ___ reflective cognition
3. ___ self-reference
4. ___ critical thinking
5. ___ SQ4R

6. ___ glossary

7. ___ Knowledge Builder

a. study guide at the end of each chapter
b. one of the interesting boxes in each chapter
c. active study-reading technique
d. "mini-dictionary"
e. style of thought arising during passive experience
f. ability to evaluate, compare, analyze, critique, and synthesize information
g. ending module of each chapter

4

8. ___ Brainwaves
9. ___ Psychology in Action

    h. style of thought arising while actively thinking about an experience
    i. practice of relating new information to prior life experience

Check Your Memory

1. TRUE or FALSE   Reading is the same as studying.
2. TRUE or FALSE   If you are actively thinking about an experience or what you are reading, you are exhibiting experiential cognition.
3. TRUE or FALSE   The style of thinking that occurs during passive experience is referred to as reflective cognition.
4. TRUE or FALSE   If you relate new facts, terms, and concepts to your own experiences and to information you already know well as you are reading, you are using self-reference.
5. TRUE or FALSE   As a critical thinker is reading, he or she pauses to evaluate, compare, analyze, critique, and synthesize what is being read.
6. TRUE or FALSE   The SQ4R method is an experiential listening/note-taking plan.
7. TRUE or FALSE   The **S** in the SQ4R method stands for *synthesize*.
8. TRUE or FALSE   Looking through the chapter at the headings and pictures before reading a chapter for the first time illustrates the review step of the SQ4R method.
9. TRUE or FALSE   When using the SQ4R, the student is encouraged to turn each topic heading into one or more questions.
10. TRUE or FALSE   The first R in SQ4R stands for *reflect*.
11. TRUE or FALSE   The second R in the SQ4R stands for *recite*.
12. TRUE or FALSE   The most important step in the SQ4R method is the *review*.
13. TRUE or FALSE   Using a reflective reading strategy has been shown to improve learning and course grades and to enhance long-term understanding.
14. TRUE or FALSE   The SQ4R method can be applied to any textbook.
15. TRUE or FALSE   Each chapter in your psychology textbook begins with a module entitled *Psychology in Action*.
16. TRUE or FALSE   Dialogue questions are similar to questions that students like to ask themselves as they read their psychology textbook.
17. TRUE or FALSE   Technical terms in the textbook are defined in a "thesaurus box" that is found in the upper left-hand corner of a page.
18. TRUE or FALSE   Each module in this textbook ends with a study guide called a Knowledge Builder.
19. TRUE or FALSE   *Human Diversity* and *Brainwaves* are two of the interest boxes found within each chapter of the psychology textbook.
20. TRUE or FALSE   Each module concludes with a point-by-point *Summary* that is organized around the *Survey Questions*.

Critical Thinking

1. How are the reflective SQ4R method and the LISAN method related?

Reflective Note Taking—LISAN UP!

Survey Question: Reading strategies may be good for studying, but what about taking notes in class?

Language Development Guide

strategies: plans

distractions: interruptions; disruptions

assigned materials: work/readings given and required of students

lecture based on core of ideas: the most essential aspects of the concepts/theories presented

on the contrary: in opposition to something that has been stated or expected

active: energetic, full of life

alert: aware, watchful, prepared

engaged: absorbed, connected

selective: choosy, discriminating

notes...seem like chicken scratches: very messy handwriting that is hard to read

Recite and Review

1. Jonas, who avoids distractions and skillfully gather ideas, would be described as a(n) _____ listener.
2. The authors of your textbook recommend a listening/note-taking plan called _____.
3. Before going to class, Carol completes the reading assignment and looks over the PowerPoint overheads provided by the instructor. By anticipating what her instructor will be discussing in class, Carol is demonstrating the step in the listening/note-taking plan known as _____.
4. According to the second step in the listening/note-taking plan, every lecture is based on a core of _____.
5. When your teacher says, "Most important is…." or "As an example," you should pay attention and listen carefully to these _____ words.
6. The letter A in the listening/note-taking plan stands for _____.
7. When you take notes during class, you should not try to be a tape recorder, taking down every word, but rather be _____ and write down only key points.
8. As soon as you can, reflexively improve your notes by filling in gaps, completing thoughts and looking for _____ among ideas.
9. In summarizing their notes, students should boil them down and _____ them.
10. After each class session, write down several major ideas, definitions, or details that are likely to become _____.

Connections

1. ___ lead, don't follow
2. ___ core of ideas
3. ___ signal words
4. ___ actively listen
5. ___ selective note-taking
6. ___ LISAN

a. writing down only key points
b. indicating the direction of the instructor's lecture
c. involves reading assigned materials before the lecture
d. listening/note-taking plan
e. every lecture is based on this
f. sitting where you can get involved in class

Check Your Memory

1. TRUE or FALSE   Like effective reading, good notes come from actively seeking information.
2. TRUE or FALSE   People who are active listeners are more prone to distractions and have trouble gathering and organizing their ideas.
3. TRUE or FALSE   The SQ4R is a listening/note-taking plan.
4. TRUE or FALSE   Reading assigned materials before going to class are part of the *Lead, Don't Follow* step of the listening/note-taking plan
5. TRUE or FALSE   Every lecture is based on a core of ideas with an idea usually being followed by examples or explanations.
6. TRUE or FALSE   When a teacher says, "On the contrary," he or she is using a signal word to indicate that an opposite idea is about to be presented.
7. TRUE or FALSE   When students actively listen, they are usually engaged in multi-tasking by both listening to the lecture and doing at least one other activity, such as completing homework, searching the internet on their laptop, or texting their friends.
8. TRUE or FALSE   Students who take accurate lecture notes tend to do well on tests
9. TRUE or FALSE   When taking notes in class, students should take down the instructor's lecture, word-for-word.
10. TRUE or FALSE   Most students take reasonably good notes, but then don't use them.
11. TRUE or FALSE   If students don't want their notes to seem like "chicken scratches," they should review them daily
12. TRUE or FALSE   After each class session, students should write down several major ideas, definitions, or details that are likely to become test questions.
13. TRUE or FALSE   Successive students must review, organize, reflect, extend, and think about new ideas.

Reflective Study Strategies—Making a Habit of Success

Language Development Guide

intelligence: refers to brainpower, how smart one is
efficiently: ably, economically, resourcefully
notoriously: being well-known
motivated: to be caused to act
MP3 player: digital audio player; consumer electronic device that stores, organizes, and playing audio files
MSN Messenger: provides instant messaging both text messaging and voice calling
YouTube: a video-sharing website on which users can upload, share, and view videos
cramming: trying to learn new information right before an exam; intensive memorization
massed up your studying: using "cramming" or massed practice
mnemonic: memory aid
exaggerated: overstated; larger-than-life
bizarre: strange; odd; unusual
vivid: clear, brilliant
interactive: acting on each other
practice tests: tests taken not for a grade to prepare for future exam on that material
self-testing: posing questions to yourself
substitute: replacement
overlearning: continuing to study the material even after you believe that you know it
you really know your stuff: capable; well-informed

Recite and Review

1. Regarding whether a study method is reflective or unreflective, recopying one's notes and outlining chapters would be considered _____.
2. When Jarrod reads his textbook and studies his notes, he always sits at his desk, turns his cell phone, TV, and the music off. In this way, Jarrod is developing a habit of studying that will become strongly linked with a specific _____.
3. Tawanda usually only studies intensely the night before a major exam and tries to learn a great deal of information at the last minute, a practice commonly called _____.
4. Hector has a major exam in three weeks and has begun studying about an hour each day. Hector is using _____ practice.
5. Long, uninterrupted study sessions are termed _____ practice.
6. A memory aid that links new information to ideas or images that are easy to remember is called _____.
7. Dela is trying to remember the Spanish word for *pen*, which is *la pluma*. So, she pictures a pen with a large feather plume. Dela is using a(n) _____.
8. A great way to improve grades is to take _____ tests before the real one in class.
9. A good way to reflectively study is to pose questions to yourself, which is called _____.
10. Trying to learn from quizzes alone will probably _____ your grades.
11. Regarding preparation for tests, many students _____ for exams.
12. If Carlos is like most students when estimating how well he will perform on the upcoming test, he will _____ how well he will perform.
13. Continuing to study beyond your initial mastery of a topic is called _____.
14. One way for students to make sure they have studied enough for tests is to always approach every test as if it were a(n) _____ test.
15. Regarding whether a study method is effective or not effective, overlearning the material for a test would be classified as _____.

Connections

1. ___ outlining chapters
2. ___ studying in a specific place
3. ___ spaced practice
4. ___ massed practice
5. ___ mnemonic
6. ___ self-testing
7. ___ overlearning

a. continue studying beyond your initial mastery of a topic
b. posing questions to yourself
c. memory aid
d. strongly links habit of studying
e. consists of long, uninterrupted study sessions
f. consists of a large number of relatively short study sessions
g. unreflective study strategy

Check Your Memory

1. TRUE or FALSE   Grades depend as much on effort as they do on "intelligence."
2. TRUE or FALSE   Recopying one's notes and outlining chapters are two reflective-type study strategies that can improve one's grades.
3. TRUE or FALSE   The best students emphasize quality by studying their books and notes in depth and attending classes regularly.
4. TRUE or FALSE   For most students getting poor grades is usually due to events beyond their control.
5. TRUE or FALSE   Students who are motivated to succeed usually get better grades.

6. TRUE or FALSE   Studying only in one specific place strongly links the habit of studying to that specific place, making it easier to start studying.

7. TRUE or FALSE   Long, uninterrupted study sessions are referred to as spaced practice.

8. TRUE or FALSE   Usually, you shouldn't try to learn anything new about a subject during the last day before a test.

9. TRUE or FALSE   Most mnemonics link new information to ideas or images that are easy to remember.

10. TRUE or FALSE   For best results, mnemonic images should be simple and realistic rather than exaggerated or bizarre.

11. TRUE or FALSE   Reflective studying should include self-testing, in which you pose questions to yourself.

12. TRUE or FALSE   Practice quizzes are available on the *Book Companion Website*.

13. TRUE or FALSE   Trying to learn from practice quizzes alone will probably lower your grades.

14. TRUE or FALSE   Practice quizzes can help students find out what topics they need to study more.

15. TRUE or FALSE   Most student overprepare for tests and underestimate how well they will perform on the test.

16. TRUE or FALSE   Overlearning is defined as continuing to study beyond your initial mastery of a topic.

17. TRUE or FALSE   Overlearning is an inefficient study strategy that causes excessive nervousness in students.

18. TRUE or FALSE   To make sure one has studied completely, it is best to approach every test as if it were a multiple choice test.

Self-Regulated Learning—Academic All-Stars

Language Development Guide

academic all-stars: students who make good grades and understand the class material

voluntary: action that is chosen and under one's own control

deliberately: on purpose; intentionally

goal-oriented: directed and guided by a purpose

specific (learning goal): clear-cut; precise

objective (learning goal): factual

monitor: to watch and check

progress: improvement

exceptional: excellent; outstanding

downloading: transferring information from a remote source, such as a website, to your computer

self-praise: verbally rewarding one's self, such as saying to oneself "Hey, I did it!" or "Good work!"

performance records: a collection of written details concerning measures of a student's functioning with a   course

long-range goals: what you aim to accomplish over a long period of time, such as a semester

(p. 13) *short-term targets*: goals to be reached in the near future

(p. 13) *revise*: adjust; change

(p. 13) *corrective:* action taken to improve

(p. 13) *budget your time*: setting time limits for various activities

(p. 13) *iPod:* a pocket-sized device used to play music files

(p. 13) *tutoring programs*: additional teaching sessions that provide individual instruction to students

9

(p. 13) *enrichment*: improvement
(p. 13) *personal empowerrment*: having control over all aspects of one's life

Recite and Review

1. Connor's study strategies would be described as a deliberately self-reflective and active self-guided study. Connor is exhibiting what is called _____ learning.
2. Each learning session should have specific, _____ learning goals.
3. In order to accomplish these learning goals, students should make daily, weekly, and monthly _____ for learning and put them into action.
4. Effective learners silently give themselves _____ and ask themselves questions.
5. Self-regulated learning depends on learners keeping records of their progress toward learning goals, a strategy known as _____.
6. Exceptional students quiz themselves, use study guides, and make sure they follow the reflective system for reading their textbooks known as the _____ method.
7. When you meet your daily, weekly, or monthly goals, it is important to _____ your efforts in some way.
8. When Terri meets her weekly goals in completing reading assignments, she tells herself, "This is great! I'm really getting things done." Terri is rewarding herself by using _____.
9. In order to determine if there are any specific areas that need improvement, it is a good idea to frequently evaluate your _____ records and goals.
10. If you fall short of your goals, you may need to adjust how you budget your _____.
11. When Joe fell short of his learning goals, he changed his _____ in order to deal with distractions.
12. If you discover that you lack necessary knowledge or skills, ask for help, take advantage of _____ programs, or look for information beyond your courses and textbooks

Connections

1. ___ self-regulated learning
2. ___ specific, objective learning goals
3. ___ learning strategy plans
4. ___ being your own teacher
5. ___ self-monitoring
6. ___ self-praise
7. ___ corrective actions
8. ___ tutoring programs

a. silently giving yourself guidance and asking yourself questions.

b. involves keeping records of one's progress toward learning goals (pages read, hours of studying, assignments completed)

c. helpful if you discover that you lack necessary knowledge or skills

d. deliberately self-reflective and active self-guided study

e. improving the way you budget your time. and changing your learning environment

f. should be made daily, weekly, and monthly and then put into action

g. a way to reward your efforts

h. should begin each learning session with these in mind.

Check Your Memory

1. TRUE or FALSE   Self-regulated learning is deliberately self-reflective and involves active self-guided study.
2. TRUE or FALSE   It is important to set specific, objective learning goals before beginning each learning session.

10

3. TRUE or FALSE   Plans for learning should be made on a weekly basis rather than on a daily or monthly basis.
4. TRUE or FALSE   To be most effective, learners should silently give themselves guidance and ask themselves questions.
5. TRUE or FALSE   Self-monitoring may involve keeping track of the number of pages read, the hours one has studied, and/or the assignments completed.
6. TRUE or FALSE   Exceptional students tend to quiz themselves, use study guides, and follow the reflective SQ4R system for reading the textbook.
7. TRUE or FALSE   When students meet their learning goals, it is not necessary for them to actually reward these efforts.
8. TRUE or FALSE   When students think to themselves, "Hey, I did it!" or "Good work!" they are engaging in egocentric delusional thought, which is harmful to their learning.
9. TRUE or FALSE   In the long run, success, self-improvement, and personal satisfaction are the real payoffs for learning.
10. TRUE or FALSE   It is a good idea for students to frequently evaluate their performance records and goals.
11. TRUE or FALSE   Falling short of one's learning goals is rarely caused by how a student budgets his or her time.
12. TRUE or FALSE   When students fall short of their learning goals, they may need to change their learning environment to deal with distractions.
13. TRUE or FALSE   If a student discovers that he or she lacks the necessary knowledge or skills, the students should ask for help from the teacher and take advantage of tutoring programs.

Procrastination—Avoiding the Last-Minute Blues

All these study techniques are fine. But what can I do about procrastination?

Language Development Guide

procrastination: delaying or putting off the performance of certain tasks
frustrated: feeling that results from your goals being blocked
equate: associate; connect
personal worth or self-worth: an evaluation of one's self
perfectionism: unhealthy belief that anything less than perfect is unacceptable
all-or-nothing work habits: tendency to not start a task unless everything about the task is perfect; seeing situations as completely acceptable or unacceptable
time management: techniques for scheduling one's time in order to better accomplish tasks
allocates: assigns or gives out
committed: dedicated; devoted to
checklist: items arranged as a reference to guide a person's actions, ex. study skills checklist
at a glance: looking quickly
measurable: being able to assess or calculate how much
challenging: demanding, not easy
virtually: almost
fascinated: captivated; engrossed
missing the point: getting the wrong idea; being confused
attitude: a learned tendency to respond to people, objects, or institutions in a positive or negative way

Recite and Review

1. Tim works only under pressure, skip classes, give false reasons for late work, and feel ashamed of his last-minute efforts. Tim would be described as a(n) _____.
2. Mary acts as if her grades tell whether she is a good person who will succeed in life. Mary is equating her grades with her _____.
3. By waiting to the last minute to complete his term paper, Owen can blame his poor work on a late start, rather than a lack of _____.
4. Perfectionist students often end up with _____ work habits
5. People who have a tendency to procrastinate can alleviate this problem by learning study skills and through better _____.
6. Amira is making a chart showing all the hours in each day of the week. She then fills in all the times for sleep, meals, classes, and work; then all her study times; and labels the remaining hours as free times. Amira is making a(n) _____ schedule.
7. After making a chart showing the hours devoted to classes, work, meals, sleep, and study, Hannah used this schedule as a(n) _____, so that she'd know at a glance which tasks were done and which still needed attention.
8. Hope is making a chart in which she lists the dates of all quizzes, tests, reports, papers, and other major assignments for each class. Hope is making a(n) _____ schedule.
9. The beauty of sticking to a schedule is that it will help you avoid feeling bored while you are working or _____ when you play.
10. Students who study hard and practice _____ management do get better grades
11. Students who are reflective, active learners set specific goals for studying, which are clear-cut and _____.
12. Zeb's history professor expects his students to read a chapter per week with a test once a month. Since his professor does not give frequent assignments, Zeb should set his own _____ goals.
13. You are most likely to procrastinate if you think a task will be _____.
14. The best educational experiences are _____, yet fun
15. You should not wait for teachers to "make" their courses interesting since interest is really a matter of your _____.

Connections

1. ___ procrastinators
2. ___ personal worth
3. ___ perfectionism
4. ___ weekly time schedule
5. ___ term schedule
6. ___ specific goals
7. ___ student's attitude

a. evaluation of one's self
b. lists the dates of all quizzes, tests, reports, papers, and other major assignments for each class.
c. work only under pressure, give false reasons for late work, and feel frustrated much of the time
d. having impossibly high standards
e. determines if a topic or class will be interesting
f. should be clear-cut and measurable
g. written plan to allocate time for study, work, and leisure activities for each hour in a day

12

Check Your Memory

1. TRUE or FALSE   A tendency to procrastinate is a rare problem for most people.
2. TRUE or FALSE   Even when procrastination doesn't lead to failure, it can cause much suffering.
3. TRUE or FALSE   Procrastinators give false reasons for their late work.
4. TRUE or FALSE   People who procrastinate typically feel less frustrated, bored, or guilty than do people who do not procrastinate.
5. TRUE or FALSE   Many students equate grades with their personal worth.
6. TRUE or FALSE   By procrastinating students can blame poor work on a late start, rather than a lack of ability.
7. TRUE or FALSE   People who are perfectionistic rarely procrastinate.
8. TRUE or FALSE   Students with extremely high standards often end up with all-or-nothing work habits.
9. TRUE or FALSE   Students who procrastinate can reduce this problem by learning study skills and better time management.
10. TRUE or FALSE   A written plan that allocates the time you will spend for study, work, and leisure activities each week is called a term schedule.
11. TRUE or FALSE   Sticking to a schedule often makes a person feel bored when they are working and guilty when they play.
12. TRUE or FALSE   Specific goals should be broad and very flexible.
13. TRUE or FALSE   More effort early in a course can greatly reduce the "pain" and stress you will experience later.
14. TRUE or FALSE   If your professors don't give frequent assignments, students should set their own day-by-day goals.
15. TRUE or FALSE   You are most likely to procrastinate if you think a task will be unpleasant.
16. TRUE or FALSE   The best educational experiences are courses that are easy and require the least amount of study time and effort.
17. TRUE or FALSE   Virtually, every topic is interesting to someone, somewhere.
18. TRUE or FALSE   If a student does not find a course interesting, it is because the teacher did not make the course interesting.

Reflective Test Taking—Are You "Test Wise"?

Survey Question: If I read and study effectively, is there anything else I can do to improve my grades?

Language Development Guide

test wise: understanding the characteristics of various test item types, which gives one an advantage when taking a test
clarification: explanation; clearing up any misunderstanding
objective tests: test that gives the same score when different people correct it
partial match: answer does not correspond exactly
finding free information in later questions: answer to an early test item is given in the question portion of another test item
eliminate: get rid of
alternatives: choices or options
your guessing odds: your chance or probability of correctly choosing the outcome
50-50: each of the two events has an equal chance of occurring

penalty for guessing: a test in which points are taken off from the final score based on the number of wrong answers is said to have a penalty for guessing, while a test that only considers the number of correct answers has no penalty for guessing

automatically: routinely; without thinking

random guessing: making choices by chance

folk wisdom: traditional beliefs that may or may not be based in fact

flawed: faulty

rating: placing an event in a position higher or lower on a scale

circumstances: situations; conditions

superlatives: adjectives or adverbs that describe an extreme degree when used in comparisons, such as "smallest" and "largest"

essay tests: tests that require students to answer questions by writing organized paragraphs that often involve explanations, comparisons, or drawing conclusions

half marks: partial credit is given for an answer

extra marks: additional or bonus points are added

logical: drawing conclusions based on formal principles of reasoning

elaborate: complex; detailed

grammar: a set of rules for combining language units into meaningful speech or writing

short-answer tests: tests that ask the student to fill in a blank, define a term, or list specific items

Recite and Review

1. In taking any test, it is important to read all directions and questions carefully because they may give you good advice or _____ to an answer.
2. Before a student begins a test, he or she should quickly _____ the test.
3. When taking a test, one should answer the _____ questions first.
4. Carolyn is taking a multiple choice test, while April is taking a true-or-false test. Both students are taking a(n) _____ test.
5. In taking a multiple choice test, you should relate the question to what you know about the topic, read the alternatives, and look for a match. If none matches, then reexamine the choices and look for a(n) _____ match.
6. When taking a test, later questions may help you answer some of the earlier more difficult question because theses later questions may provide _____.
7. With a four-choice multiple-choice test, you have one chance in _____ of guessing right.
8. On a four-response multiple choice item, if you can eliminate two alternatives, your guessing odds improve to _____.
9. On a test, it is best to go back and answer any skipped items unless there is a penalty for _____.
10. If you are forced to guess on a test item, do not choose the longest answer or the letter you have used the least, since both strategies lower scores more than _____ guessing does.
11. On multiple choice tests if you change answers, you are _____ likely to gain points than to lose them.
12. If you are uncertain of your first choice on an objective item or if it was a hunch, then your second choice is often more _____.
13. Since some answers may be partly true, yet flawed in some way, it is important to remember when taking a multiple choice test that you are searching for the one _____ answer to each question.
14. If you are uncertain when choosing among the different responses, try _____ each multiple- choice alternative on a 1–10 scale.
15. There are few circumstances that a response that includes the words *always* or _____will be the correct answer.

14

16. Regarding whether a response is likely to be true or false, answers that include superlatives, such as *most, least, best, worst, largest, or smallest* are often _____.

17. Essay questions are a weak spot for students who lack _____, don't support their ideas, or don't directly answer the question, or who lack _____.

18. In answering an essay question, it is important to read the question carefully and to note key words, such as *compare, contrast, discuss, evaluate, analyze,* and *describe* because these words all demand a certain _____ in your answer.

19. If the essay question asks for a definition and an example, make sure you provide both since providing just a definition or just an example will get you _____ marks.

20. Before you begin writing your essay answer, you should reflect on your answer for a few minutes and list the _____ you want to make, writing them as they come to mind, rearranging them in a logical order, and then writing your answer.

21. After you finish your answer, look over it for errors in spelling and _____.

22. Short answer tests require the student to define a term, list specific items, or to _____.

23. The best way to prepare for short-answer tests is to _____ the details of the course.

24. To help in answering short-answer questions, students should pay special attention to lists of related _____ as they study.

25. The type of test item that gives little information in the question itself that can help the student answer the question is the _____.

Connections

1. ___ "test wise"
2. ___ objective tests
3. ___ essay tests
4. ___ short answer tests
5. ___ superlatives
6. ___ "free information" on a test

a. require test takers to fill in a blank, define a term, or list specific items

b. answer to an early test item is given in the question portion of another test item

c. examples are most, least, best, worst, largest, or smallest

d. understanding the characteristics of various test types, giving one an advantage in taking a test

e. examples are multiple-choice and true-false items

f. require test takers to compare, contrast, discuss, evaluate, analyze, and describe

Check Your Memory

1. TRUE or FALSE   It is best not to look through a test when you first receive it but immediately start answering the first question.

2. TRUE or FALSE   When taking a test, it is better to answer the more difficult items before answering the easy questions.

3. TRUE or FALSE   Multiple choice and true-false test items are classified as subjective measures.

4. TRUE or FALSE   If you are taking a multiple choice test and do not find the answer you expect among the alternatives, then you should reexamine the responses and look for a partial match.

5. TRUE or FALSE   One should read all the choices for each multiple choice question before making a decision.

6. TRUE or FALSE   On a multiple choice test, you may find "free information" in later questions that will help you answer earlier items.

7. TRUE or FALSE   With a four-choice multiple-choice test, you have one chance in two of guessing correctly.

15

8. TRUE or FALSE   If you can eliminate two alternatives on a four-choice multiple-choice test, your guessing odds improve to 50-50.

9. TRUE or FALSE   Unless there is a penalty for guessing, you should be sure to answer all items on an objective test.

10. TRUE or FALSE   If you have to guess on a multiple choice test, you should choose the longest answer among the alternatives, since it is usually the correct one.

11. TRUE or FALSE   When you go back to answer skipped multiple choice items, you should choose the letter you've used the least, since it is most likely to be correct.

12. TRUE or FALSE   Don't change your answers on a multiple-choice test, since your first choice is usually right.

13. TRUE or FALSE   A good way to find the *best* answer to a multiple choice test question is to rate the choices on a 1-10 scale with the highest rating being the *best* answer.

14. TRUE or FALSE   Responses on a test that include superlatives, such as *most, least, largest,* or *smallest* are most often true.

15. TRUE or FALSE   Students who lack organization in their writings and do not answer questions directly often have trouble with essay questions.

16. TRUE or FALSE   Key words in essay questions, such as *compare, contrast, discuss, evaluate, analyze,* and *describe* must be emphasized within the essay answer.

17. TRUE or FALSE   If the essay question asks for a definition and an example, a student will often receive only half marks if they provide just a definition or just an example.

18. TRUE or FALSE   If you are asked to give two examples on an essay question and you give three examples, you will most likely earn extra marks.

19. TRUE or FALSE   Before you begin to write your answer to an essay question, you should construct an elaborate plan or outline of your answer.

20. TRUE or FALSE   In writing essay answers, students should look over these answers for errors in spelling and grammar last.

21. TRUE or FALSE   Tests that ask you to fill in a blank, define a term, or list specific items are referred to as short answer questions.

22. TRUE or FALSE   The best way to prepare for short-answer tests is to overlearn the details of the course.

23. TRUE or FALSE   If you don't know the answer to a fill-in-the-blank question, you rarely get any clues from the question itself.

Using Digital Media—Netting New Knowledge

Language Development Guide

digital media: any information, such as text, audio, video, or graphics that is transferred or stored in digital form

amnesia: loss of memory

zoophobia: fear of animals

vast array: huge range

authoritative: reliable

websites: subpart of the Internet involving an interlinked system of information "sites" or "pages."

American Psychological Association (APA): scientific and professional organization of psychologists in the United States

Wikipedia: a web-based collection of encyclopedic articles that allows visitors to the site to contribute and edit the information provided

entries: items, statements, submissions

personal blogs: website in which an individual regularly submits descriptions or comments regarding events

healthy dose of skepticism: a sizeable amount of doubt

Book Companion Website: a web-based collection of online quizzes, links to web sites, flash cards, and crossword puzzles to help students as they study

launching pad: a good starting point

flash cards: set of two-sided cards usually with a term or question on one side and the definition or answer on the other and are used as a study aid

appreciation (of psychology): understanding

CengageNOW: a web-based, personalized study system that provides a pretest and a posttest for each chapter

animations: cartoon-like presentations

eBook: an electronic textbook

simulations: an imitation of real situation

Cengage's Psychology Resource Center: web-based, personalized study system that provides a pretest and a posttest for each chapter

classic: memorable; lasting

log in: to enter your user name and password when using a computer

PsycINFO: made available by the APA and provides summaries of the scientific and scholarly literature in psychology

scholarly: academic, educated, learned

abstract: short summary of the scholarly article

indexed: filed (usually by key terms)

drug abuse: excessive misuse of a psychoactive substance

postpartum depression: a mild to moderately severe depression that begins within three months following childbirth

creativity: a form of thinking that involves originality, flexibility, and fluency (ready flow of ideas)

subscribes: purchases

terminal: refers to a computer within the college network that students can use

accessed: right to use; admitted to

digital journeys: taking an information trip through the Internet

Zen: a school of Buddhism that advocates that personal enlightenment through meditation

live words: words come from personal experience, according to Zen Buddhism

dead words: according to Zen Buddhism, words that just tell "about" a subject rather than coming from personal experience

Recite and Review

1. When Gary uses the Internet to conduct research for his term paper, he is using what is referred to as digital _____.
2. Websites provided by the American Psychological Association would be considered _____ sources, while Wikipedia entries and personal blogs would not.
3. Since the Internet is not always accurate, it is wise to approach all websites with a healthy dose of _____.
4. Students using this psychology textbook can find online quizzes, web links, flash cards, and crossword puzzles at The _____ Website.
5. Susie is using the web-based, personalized study system that provides a pretest and a posttest for each chapter of her psychology textbook. This web-based system is called _____.
6. Psychology is brought to life with a full library of original and classic video clips plus interactive learning modules tied to all of the topics covered in your introductory psychology course at the _____ Center.

17

7. Students can find the titles of interesting websites they may want to explore at the end of each module in the textbook with the best way to reach these sites being through the _____ website.
8. One of the best specialized online databases is offered by the American Psychological Association and provides summaries of the scientific and scholarly literature in psychology. This database is called _____.
9. Each record in the specialized database offered by the APA consists of a(n) _____, which is a short summary, plus notes about the author, title, source, and other details with all entries being indexed using key terms.
10. The APA maintains an online library of general interest _____ on aging, anger, children and families, depression, divorce, emotional health, kids and the media, sexuality, stress, testing issues, women and men, and other topics.
11. For links to recent articles in newspapers and magazines, students should check the APA's _____ page
12. According to Zen Buddhists, _____ words are "about" a subject.
13. If students reflect on what they read, their books will be collections of what Zen Buddhists call _____ words, which come from personal experience.

Connections

1. ___ authoritative
2. ___ The Book Companion Website
3. ___ CengageNOW
4. ___ Cengage Psychology Resource Center
5. ___ PsycINFO
6. ___ The APA Website
7. ___ APA's PsycPORT page
8. ___ abstract
9. ___ "live words"
10. ___ "dead words"

a. come from personal experience
b. maintains an online library of general interest articles on psychological topics
c. short summary
d. provides summaries of the scientific and scholarly literature in psychology
e. links to recent articles in newspapers and magazines
f. provide online quizzes, web links, flash cards, and crossword puzzles
g. are "about" a subject
h. reliable, dependable source
i. has a full library of original and classic video clips plus interactive learning modules
j. web-based, personalized study system

Check Your Memory

1. TRUE or FALSE   When students are taking online quizzes, they are using what is called analog media.
2. TRUE or FALSE   According to your textbook, Wikepedia is considered an authoritative source.
3. TRUE or FALSE   Students using this psychology textbook can find online quizzes, web links, flash cards, and crossword puzzles at the PsycPORT page.
4. TRUE or FALSE   *CengageNOW* creates personalized study plans, which include media such as videos, animations, learning modules, and links to the eBook.
5. TRUE or FALSE   A full library of original and classic video clips plus interactive learning modules tied to all of the topics covered in the introductory psychology course can be found at the Cengage Psychology Resource Center.
6. TRUE or FALSE   The best way to reach the interesting websites listed at the end of each module in the textbook is through the book companion website.

18

7. TRUE or FALSE   PsycINFO is provided by the National Institute of Mental Health.
8. TRUE or FALSE   Each record in PsycINFO consists of a method, results, and discussion section.
9. TRUE or FALSE   Almost every college and university subscribes to PsycINFO so that students can search PsycINFO through their college library or computer center for free.
10. TRUE or FALSE   The American Psychological Association maintains an online library of general interest articles on psychological topics.
11. TRUE or FALSE   Zen Buddhists define "live words" as "about" a subject.
12. TRUE or FALSE   Since books are related to one's personal experience, Zen Buddhists would describe them as "dead words."

Final Survey and Review--Completion

Preview and Reflective Reading—How to Tame a Textbook
1. Experiential cognition refers to the style of thinking that occurs during _____ experience.
2. One powerful way to be more reflective is through self-reference, which is a form of _____.
3. As you read your textbook, you should pause to evaluate, compare, analyze, critique, and synthesize this material, which will help you to become a(n) _____ thinker.
4. Before you begin reading a module in your textbook, you should look at topic headings and figure captions to help you build a "mental map" of upcoming topics. By doing so you are engaging in the SQ4R step called _____.
5. The 3rd R in the SQ4R method stands for _____.
6. Students do not have to guess about the meaning of technical terms because in the lower right-hand corner of textbook pages, they will find a(n) _____.
7. In each chapter there are boxes, such as *Human Diversity*, which encourages students to reflect on the rich variability of human experience, while the box that invites students to relate psychology to their own behavior is entitled _____.

Reflective Note Taking—LISAN Up!
8. If you avoid distractions and skillfully gather information, you would be described as a(n) _____ listener.
9. If you read the chapter before your instructor lectures on this material, you are demonstrating the step in the LISAN method called _____.
10. When you hear your professor state "Three reasons for…," you immediately play attention to these _____ words that indicate the direction of the professor's lecture.
11. The letter N in the LISAN method stands for _____.

Reflective Study Strategies—Making a Habit of Success
12. Ideally, a student should study in one specific _____.
13. When a student uses a large number of relatively short study sessions, it is called _____.
14. Bonnie uses exaggerated, bizarre, and sometimes funny images to remember the names of the parts of the brain. Bonnie is using _____.
15. Posing questions to yourself as you study is called _____.
16. Wanda has decided that she does not need to read her textbook if she thoroughly studies the online quizzes. Wanda's method of study will most likely result in _____ grades.

19

17. Students should plan to do extra study and review after they think they are prepared for a test in order to _____ the class material.

Self-Regulated Learning—Academic All-Stars

18. Tomas engages in active, deliberately self-reflective study, which is called _____ learning.
19. Exceptional learners keep records of their progress toward learning goals, such as pages read and hours of studying, a process called _____.
20. When you meet your daily, weekly, or monthly goals, you should reward your efforts in some way, such as going to a movie or through _____, which involves telling yourself, "Hey, I did it!"
21. Students who fall short of their learning goals may need to change their learning environments to prevent spending so much time watching TV, daydreaming, or talking to friends, which can be _____ to studying.

Procrastination—Avoiding the Last-Minute Blues

22. Students who often end up with all-or-nothing work habits are the ones who set excessively _____ for themselves.
23. Learning study skills and developing better time management can help students who have a tendency to wait to the last minute to complete their work, that is, students who _____.
24. A chart that lists the times you sleep, eat, study, and go to class each day is called a(n) _____ schedule.
25. A good way for students to keep up with the dates of all their tests, reports, and other major assignments is to make a chart called a(n) _____ schedule.
26. To avoid feeling bored while you are working or guilty when you play, it is important to stick to a(n) _____.
27. Students who are reflective, active learners set specific, clear-cut, measurable _____ for studying.

Reflective Test Taking—Are You "Test Wise"?

28. Tests that contain only true-false or multiple choice questions are classified as _____ tests.
29. Fill-in-the-blank and define the term questions are considered _____ questions.
30. On a four-response multiple choice item, if you can eliminate _____ alternatives, your guessing odds improve to 50-50.
31. On multiple choice tests if you change answers, you are more likely to _____ points.
32. On objective test items, a response is often false if it contains _____, such as *most, least, best, worst, largest, or smallest*.
33. Students who lack organization in their writing, don't support their ideas, or don't directly answer the question usually have difficulty in answering _____ questions.
34. Since these types of questions give little information within the question itself, the best way to overlearn the details of the course when preparing for _____ tests.

Using Digital Media—Netting New Knowledge

35. Sources on the Internet that students can use for research and study are collectively known as _____ media.
36. The Book Companion Website has online quizzes, web links, flash cards, and _____.
37. The Cengage Psychology Resource Center has a full library of original and classic _____ plus interactive learning modules tied to all of the topics covered in your introductory psychology course.

38. Each record in PsycINFO consists of a short summary called a(n) _____, plus notes about the author, title, source, and other details

39. An online library of general interest articles on aging, anger, children and families, depression, divorce, emotional health, kids and the media, sexuality, stress, testing issues, women and men, and other topics is maintained at the _____.

40. If students reflect on what they read, their books will be collections of what Zen Buddhists call live words, which come from _____.

Final Survey and Review--Matching

Part 1

1. ___ experiential cognition
2. ___ reflective cognition
3. ___ self-reference
4. ___ critical thinking
5. ___ mnemonic
6. ___ self-testing
7. ___ overlearning
8. ___ self-regulated learning
9. ___ self-praise
10. ___ self-monitoring

a. involves keeping records of one's progress toward learning goals
b. self-reflective and active self-guided study
c. style of thought arising while actively thinking about an experience
d. practice of relating of new information to prior life experience
e. continuing to study beyond your initial mastery of a topic
f. ability to evaluate, compare, analyze, critique, and synthesize information
g. memory aid
h. evaluating learning by posing questions to yourself
i. style of thought arising during passive experience
j. a way to reward your efforts

Part 2

1. ___ SQ4R
2. ___ LISAN
3. ___ signal words
4. ___ weekly time schedule
5. ___ term schedule
6. ___ spaced practice
7. ___ massed practice
8. ___ Book Companion Website
9. ___ *CengageNOW*
10. ___ PsycINFO

a. web-based, personalized study system that provides a pretest and a posttest for each chapter
b. provides online quizzes, web links, flash cards, and crossword puzzles
c. searchable, online database that provides brief summaries of the scientific and scholarly literature in psychology
d. listening/note-taking plan
e. long, uninterrupted study sessions
f. active study-reading technique
g. lists the dates of all quizzes, tests, reports, papers, and other major assignments for each class
h. tells the direction of the instructor's lecture
i. written plan that allocates time for study, work, and leisure activities for each day
j. large number of relatively short study sessions.

Final Survey and Review—True or False

Preview and Reflective Reading—How to Tame a Textbook

1. TRUE or FALSE   When you are reacting "mindfully" and "going beyond the information given," you are exhibiting reflective cognition.
2. TRUE or FALSE   An intuitive thinker pauses to evaluate, compare, analyze, critique, and synthesize what they are reading.
3. TRUE or FALSE   The S in the SQ4R method stands for survey.
4. TRUE or FALSE   Students do not have to guess about the meaning of technical terms because there is a knowledge building box that defines these terms in the upper left-hand corner of the textbook pages.
5. TRUE or FALSE   The most important step in the SQ4R method is reflect.
6. TRUE or FALSE   Each chapter in the textbook ends with The Clinical File module.

Reflective Note Taking—LISAN Up!

7. TRUE or FALSE   The LISAN is an active study-reading technique that aids reading comprehension.
8. TRUE or FALSE   The I in the LISAN method stands for *inquiry*.
9. TRUE or FALSE   Words that tell you which direction the instructor is taking in his or her lecture are called signal words.
10. TRUE or FALSE   When taking notes, students should be selective, not taking down the lecture word-for-word.

Reflective Study Strategies—Making a Habit of Success

11. TRUE or FALSE   Group study and outlining chapters are considered reflective study strategies.
12. TRUE or FALSE   Massed practice consists of a large number of relatively short study sessions.
13. TRUE or FALSE   Making mnemonic images exaggerated or bizarre is more effective than using simple, realistic images.
14. TRUE or FALSE   The online practice quizzes can serve as a substitute for studying the textbook and lecture notes.
15. TRUE or FALSE   Overlearning involves continuing to study until you achieve initial mastery of a topic and then stopping.
16. TRUE or FALSE   One way to overlearn is to approach all tests as if they will be true-false tests.

Self-Regulated Learning—Academic All-Stars

17. TRUE or FALSE   Self-regulated learning depends on self-monitoring.
18. TRUE or FALSE   When students meet their daily, weekly, or monthly goals, they should reward their efforts in some way, including self-praise.
19. TRUE or FALSE   If students fall short of your learning goals, they should adjust how they budget their time and change their learning environment to eliminate distractions.

Procrastination—Avoiding the Last-Minute Blues

20. TRUE or FALSE   People who procrastinate often blame their poor work on a lack of ability rather than a late start.
21. TRUE or FALSE   Many times students who are perfectionistic procrastinate because they have all-or-nothing work habits.

22

22. TRUE or FALSE   Better time management and learning study skills can help alleviate the problem of procrastination.
23. TRUE or FALSE   A term schedule is a written plan that allocates time for study, work, and leisure activities for each day of the week.
24. TRUE or FALSE   Sticking to a schedule will help you avoid feeling bored while you are working or guilty when you play.
25. TRUE or FALSE   Specific goals for studying should be clear-cut and measurable.
26. TRUE or FALSE   Whether you find a course interesting is dependent on your own attitude, not whether the teacher made the course interesting.

Reflective Test Taking—Are You "Test Wise"?

27. TRUE or FALSE   When taking a test, it is better to answer the easy questions before answering the difficult ones.
28. TRUE or FALSE   Essay and short answer questions are classified as objective measures.
29. TRUE or FALSE   When you are forced to guess on multiple choice items, you should choose the longest answer or the letter you've used the least in order to gain the most points.
30. TRUE or FALSE   If you are unsure about and answer and change it, you are more likely to lose points than if you stayed with your first choice.
31. TRUE or FALSE   Answers that include superlatives such as *most, least, best, worst, largest,* or *smallest* are most often false.
32. TRUE or FALSE   In writing essay answers, elaborate plans or outlines are not necessary.
33. TRUE or FALSE   Tests that ask you to fill in a blank, define a term, or list specific items are referred to as essay questions.

Using Digital Media—Netting New Knowledge

34. TRUE or FALSE   Websites provided by the American Psychological Association would be considered authoritative sources.
35. TRUE or FALSE   *Cengage's Psychology Resource Center* is a web-based, personalized study system that provides a pretest and a posttest for each chapter.
36. TRUE or FALSE   Students using this psychology textbook can find online quizzes, web links, flash cards, and crossword puzzles at the Book Companion Website.
37. TRUE or FALSE   A full library of original and classic video clips plus interactive learning modules tied to all of the topics covered in the introductory psychology course can be found at the *CengageNOW*.
38. TRUE or FALSE   Each record in PsycINFO consists of an abstract (short summary), plus notes about the author, title, source, and other details
39. TRUE or FALSE   Students can find links to recent articles in newspapers and magazines at the APA's PsycPORT page.
40. TRUE or FALSE   Seeing books as just "about a subject" would be described by Zen Buddhists as seeing books as "live words."

Mastery Test

1. Last night you looked through several magazines and skimmed several articles while watching the TV. When a friend asks you what programs you watched on TV or what articles you were reading, you could not tell her anything specific about these activities. According to Donald Norman, this passive experience last night is an example of
    a. reflective cognition.
    b. self-referencing.
    c. experiential cognition.
    d. depersonalization.

2. As Emma reads her psychology textbook, she tries to relate the terms and concepts to her own life experiences. Emma is exhibiting the process known as
   a.   self-referencing.
   b.   self-monitoring.
   c.   self-testing.
   d.   self-projection.

3. Dr. Morgan encourages his students to analyze, compare, synthesize, and evaluate the research studies he presents in class. Dr. Morgan wants his students to become _____ thinkers.
   a.   animistic
   b.   experiential
   c.   critical
   d.   intuitive

4. As Simon begins his reading assignment in psychology, he first looks at the Preview section and the list of questions and modules on the first page of the chapter. He then looks through the rest of the chapter at the topic headings and reads under the pictures. According to the SQ4R method, Simon is exhibiting the step known as
   a.   question.
   b.   recite.
   c.   review.
   d.   survey.

5. Juanita reads the chapter in small "bites," stopping after she reads to look for the main idea of the passage and then rehearses it. Juanita is exhibiting the step in the SQ4R method known as
   a.   survey.
   b.   recite.
   c.   review.
   d.   reflect.

6. Two powerful ways to reflect on what one has read are
   a.   spaced practice and massed practice.
   b.   self-praise and self-monitoring.
   c.   self-reference and critical thinking.
   d.   recopying one's notes and outlining the chapter.

7. Anya noticed that many of the paragraphs in the psychology chapter start with questions similar to questions that she would "ask" herself as she reads. These questions are called
   a.   dialogue questions.
   b.   sequential reflections.
   c.   keyword questions.
   d.   mnemonics.

8. In your psychology textbook, each module ends with a study guide called
   a.   discovering psychology.
   b.   the knowledge builder.
   c.   the running glossary.
   d.   the clinical file.

9. Jake's favorite part of each psychology chapter is the end module that is filled with practical ideas about how psychology relates to his own life. This end module is called
    a. Psychology in Action.
    b. Brainwaves.
    c. Human Diversity.
    d. Knowledge Builder.

10. Jeffrey knows how to maintain his attention during the instructor's lecture and to avoid distractions. Jeffrey would be described as a(n)
    a. knowledge builder.
    b. experiential learner.
    c. intuitive thinker.
    d. active listener.

11. Tam is using a reflective note-taking strategy that has been shown to improve listening as well as helping him to take more accurate notes during his teachers' lectures. Tam is most likely using
    a. NAMI.
    b. LISAN.
    c. SQ4R.
    d. ALCO.

12. Before going to class, Anita reads her assignment as well as reading through the notes that her teacher has posted online. In this way, Anita will be able to anticipate what her teacher will say and to take better notes. Anita is illustrating which step in the reflective note-taking strategy?
    a. Ideas.
    b. Attention, please.
    c. Reflect.
    d. Lead, don't follow.

13. The second step in the reflective note-taking strategy emphasizes that every lecture is composed of a core of
    a. ideas.
    b. illustrations.
    c. communications.
    d. signal words.

14. During a lecture when an instructor says, "as an example," he or she is stating support for an idea, while "on the contrary" is the instructor's way of pointing out an opposite idea. According to the note-taking strategy, students should listen for these
    a. reflective signposts.
    b. illustrations.
    c. signal words.
    d. mnemonics.

15. The "A" step in the reflective note-taking strategy stands for
    a. accurate notes.
    b. apply knowledge.
    c. analyze content.
    d. actively listen.

16. Which of the following statements would NOT be good advice to help a student to take good notes in class?
    a. Try to be like a tape recorder in class, taking down what the teacher says word-for-word.
    b. Summarize your notes, boiling them down and organizing them.
    c. Link new ideas to information you already know.
    d. Make up questions from your notes and be sure you can answer them.

17. According to your textbook, which of the following would be considered a GOOD study strategy?
    a. massed practice
    b. overlearning
    c. outlining your chapters
    d. group study sessions

18. Armand's method of studying for a test is to study for six to eight hours the day before the test, "cramming" as much new material as he can. This inefficient method of studying is known as
    a. spaced practice.
    b. massed practice.
    c. experiential study.
    d. overlearning.

19. To remember that *lapin* is the French word for rabbit, you imagine "a rabbit jumping in your lap." To remember this French word, you are using a(n)
    a. mnemonic.
    b. cue analyzer.
    c. localizer.
    d. lisan device.

20. When Toni studies for a multiple choice test, she studies her notes as if she is taking an essay test, studying long past initial mastery of the concepts. Toni is using
    a. the LISAN method.
    b. the SQ4R method.
    c. overlearning.
    d. an ineffective, unreflective study strategy.

21. Darrian uses the study strategies that his instructor has recommended, sets specific learning goals, and budgets his time well among all of his activities. When he has difficulty with course, he seeks out the help of the tutors in the learning center at the college. Darrian would be described as a(n)
    a. a student with all-or-nothing work habits.
    b. experiential learner.
    c. compulsive student.
    d. self-regulated learner.

22. Keeping a record of the number of pages you have read, hours studied, and assignment completed as part of evaluating your progress toward your learning goals is known as
    a. self-referencing.
    b. self-monitoring.
    c. self-testing.
    d. self-knowledge.

23. Sara equates her grades with her personal worth and often waits until the last minute to complete an assignment. In this way, if she makes a poor grade on the assignment, she can blame it on getting a late start rather than her lack of ability. Sara is exhibiting the characteristics of a person who
    a. is a self-regulated learner.
    b. uses spaced practice.
    c. procrastinates.
    d. overlearns.

24. Students who are perfectionists often have trouble starting an assignment and end up
    a. overlearning.
    b. using spaced practice.
    c. setting weekly time schedules.
    d. with all-or-nothing work habits.

25. During the first week of classes, Philippe takes a calendar and jots down all the dates of tests, reports, papers, and other assignments that are listed in all of his course syllabi. Philippe is making a(n)
    a. term schedule.
    b. weekly time schedule.
    c. SQ4R plan.
    d. LISAN plan.

26. Specific goals should be clear-cut and
    a. experiential.
    b. broad-based.
    c. flexible.
    d. measureable.

27. Palo tells a friend that he just can't pay attention in his history class because it is not an interesting course. Whether Palo finds history interesting or not is determined by
    a. his major in college.
    b. his own attitude.
    c. how interesting his history classes were in high school.
    d. the effort his college teacher puts into making the history class interesting.

28. The best educational experiences one has in college are the classes that
    a. were easy and required little out-of-class work.
    b. fun and challenging.
    c. involved hands-on tasks and little lecture.
    d. had lots of group discussions.

29. Mara is taking a test with multiple choice items and true-false items. Mara is taking a(n) _____ test.
    a. objective
    b. subjective
    c. projective
    d. short-answer

30. Abbot is taking a multiple choice test and is unsure about the answer he has chosen on four of the questions. So, he goes back and rereads each question. Abbot is more likely to gain points if he _____ on these questions.
    a. changes his answers
    b. sticks with his original answers
    c. chooses the longest response
    d. chooses the least used letter

31. Which of the following would NOT be a good test-taking strategy?
    a. Quickly survey the entire test before you begin.
    b. Answer the more difficult questions before the easy ones.
    c. Remember that answers that include superlatives, such as *most, least, best, worst, largest,* or *smallest* are often false.
    d. Be sure to answer all questions, if there is no penalty for guessing.

32. On a test, Jordan is asked to compare and contrast two psychological theories and to evaluate their usefulness in treating a particular mental disorder. Jordan is most likely taking a(n) _____ test.
    a. projective
    b. objective
    c. essay
    d. short-answer

33. Petra is taking a test in which there are define-the-term items and fill-in-the-blanks. Petra is most likely taking a(n) _____ test.
    a. projective
    b. mnemonic
    c. essay
    d. short-answer

34. Margo is taking an essay test. She should
    a. make a specific and detailed outline for each question on scratch paper before writing the actual answer.
    b. pad her answer in order to fill up the available space on the test page since most teachers do not read the entire answer but look at the amount written.
    c. give additional examples than the number requested in order to earn additional marks.
    d. wait until last to check for spelling and grammar because the ideas presented are usually more important.

35. Which test item type gives little information in the question itself with the best way to prepare for it being to overlearn the details of the course?
    a. multiple choice
    b. true-false
    c. short answer
    d. matching

28

36. Carmen is using Wikepedia and personal blogs as her sources for her psychology term paper. Carmen's sources
    a. would be less authoritative than websites provided by the APA.
    b. would be more authoritative than websites provided by the APA.
    c. would be equal in authoritativeness to websites provided by the APA.
    d. should be used regardless of their authoritativeness.

37. To study for her psychology test, Margo uses online quizzes, crossword puzzles, and flash cards that are located at
    a. PsycINFO.
    b. PsycPORT.
    c. The APA Website.
    d. the Book Companion Website.

38. *CengageNOW* provides the student with
    a. an online library of psychology articles.
    b. flash cards and crossword puzzles.
    c. a personalized study plan.
    d. full library of original and classic video clips.

39. Almost every college and university subscribes to a specialized online database provided by the American Psychological Association called
    a. NIMH.
    b. PsycINFO.
    c. PsycTREK.
    d. LISAN.

40. There is a distinction in Zen between "live words" and "dead words." Live words are defined as
    a. secular.
    b. spiritual.
    c. about a subject.
    d. coming from personal experience.

Chapter 1: Discovering Psychology and Research Methods

Chapter Overview

The field of psychology is an ever-changing panorama of people and ideas that can help us understand ourselves and one another better. Psychology is defined as the scientific study of behavior and mental processes. Some major areas of research in psychology are comparative, learning, sensation and perception, personality, biopsychology, social, cognitive, developmental, forensic, the psychology of gender, cultural psychology, and evolutionary psychology. Psychologists may be directly interested in animal behavior, or they may study animals a models of human behavior. As a science, psychology's goals are to describe, understand, predict, and control behavior.

Critical thinking is central to the scientific method, to psychology, and to effective behavior in general. Critical thinking is a type of reflection that involves evaluating comparing, analyzing, critiquing, and synthesizing information. To judge the validity of a claim, it is important to gather evidence for and against the claim and to evaluate the quality of the evidence. Unlike psychology, pseudopsychologies, such as phrenology, palmistry, graphology, and astrology, have changed little over time because their followers seek evidence that appears to confirm their beliefs and avoid evidence that contradicts their beliefs. Belief in pseudopsychologies is based in part on uncritical acceptance, confirmation bias, and the Barnum effect. The scientific method consists of highly refined procedures for observing the world, testing hypotheses, and drawing valid conclusions. Important elements of a scientific investigation include observing, defining a problem, proposing a hypothesis, gathering evidence/testing the hypothesis, forming a theory, and publishing results. Before they can be investigated, psychological concepts must be given operational definitions.

Psychology evolved from philosophy to become a unique discipline. Wilhelm Wundt, who studied conscious experience, established the first psychological lab in 1879 in Germany. The first school of thought in psychology was structuralism, a kind of "mental chemistry" based on introspection. Structuralism was followed by functionalism, behaviorism, and Gestalt psychology. Radical behaviorists only studied overt behavior, although the cognitive behaviorists saw the importance of thinking and expectations in determining one's behavior. Psychodynamic approaches, such as Freud's psychoanalytic theory, emphasize the unconscious origins of behavior. Humanistic psychology accentuates subjective experience, human potentials, and personal growth. Three complementary perspectives in modern psychology are the biological perspective, including biopsychology and evolutionary psychology; the psychological perspective, including behaviorism, cognitive psychology, the psychodynamic approach, and humanism; and the sociocultural perspective.

Although psychologists, psychiatrists, psychoanalysts, and counselors all work in the field of mental health, their training and methods differ considerably. Clinical and counseling psychologists, who do psychotherapy, represent only two of dozens of specialties in psychology.

31

Other representative areas of specialization are industrial-organizational, educational, consumer, school, developmental, engineering, medical, environmental, forensic, community, psychometric, and experimental psychology. Psychological research may be either applied (to answer an immediate problem) or basic (to seek knowledge for its own sake).

Experimentation is the most powerful way to identify cause-and-effect relationships. In an experiment, two or more groups of subjects are formed with these groups differing only with regard to the independent variable (condition of interest as a cause in the experiment). Effects on the dependent variable are then measured with all other conditions (extraneous variables) being held constant. In their research, investigators must follow ethical principles with both human and animal subjects. Research participant bias arises when participants' expectations influence their behavior in an experiment with the placebo effect being a source of research participant bias in experiments involving drugs. To alleviate research participant bias, a single-blind experiment can be used in which the participants are unaware of which group is the experimental group and which is the control group. A related problem is researcher bias. Researcher expectations can create a self-fulfilling prophecy, in which a participant changes in the direction of the expectation. In a double-blind experiment, neither the research participants nor the researchers collecting data know who was in the experimental group or the control group, which controls for both researcher bias as well as research participant bias.

Psychologists use several specialized research methods. Each method has strengths and weaknesses, but all are needed to fully investigate human behavior. Unlike controlled experiments, nonexperimental methods usually cannot demonstrate cause-and-effect relationships. Naturalistic observation is a starting place in many investigations. Three problems with naturalistic observation are the effects of the observer on the observed, observer bias, and an inability to explain observed behavior. Researchers using naturalistic observation of animals, other than humans, must also be careful of the anthropomorphic error. In the correlational method, relationships between two traits, responses, or events are measured with a correlation coefficient being computed to gauge the strength of the relationship. Correlations allow prediction, but they do not demonstrate cause-and-effect connections. The clinical method employs case studies, which are in-depth records of a single subject. Case studies provide insights into human behavior that can't be gained by other methods, such as the occurrence of rare events or disorders. In the survey method, people in a representative sample are asked a series of carefully worded questions.

The popular media are filled with inaccurate information about psychological topics, so it is essential to critically evaluate this information. Problems in media reports are often related to biased or unreliable sources of information, uncontrolled observation, misleading correlations, false inferences, oversimplification, use of single examples, and unrepeatable results.

Preview: Why, Oh Why, Do They Do That?

Language Development Guide

eclectic: drawing from many sources
unique: one of a kind
revelers: those engaged in the celebration
riotous: wild and unruly
climaxes: the high point (of the festival)
wicker: hard woven fiber usually used for baskets
hippies: counterculture originating in the U.S. in the 1960s
rednecks: slang term originally used to refer to poor white farmers in the southern part of the U.S.
of every stripe: of every kind
monasteries: place where monks or nuns live and work

panorama: wide view
envy: be jealous of
ultimate: the last; the greatest

Module 1.1 The Science of Psychology
Behave Yourself!
Survey Question: What is psychology and what are its goals?

Language Development Guide
conformity: bringing one's behavior into agreement with behavior of others in a group
profession: job, work, career
commonsense: long-held beliefs, most of which have not undergone scientific observation
physiological: related to biological functioning of the body
potential: possible
sensitive: precise
memory traces: physical changes in nerve cells or brain activity that takes place when memories
    are stored
psychotic: having severe mental disorder that involves delusions (strongly-held false beliefs)
    and/or hallucinations (hearing, seeing, feeling things that are not there)
lost touch with reality: lack of awareness of present reality due to delusions and/or hallucinations
    (see above definition of *psychotic*)
motives: needs
reflective: to think deeply
logical: reasonable
flawed: faulty; unsound
objective: neutral; unbiased; impartial
draw valid conclusions: reaching well-founded reasons for an event by using the scientific
    method
absence makes the heart grow fonder: the lack of something, such as a particular person, makes
    the person or object more desirable or loved
boiling hot: very hot, as if one is in boiling water
aggravated assaults: an aggressive action toward another person with the intent to injure (usually
    with a deadly weapon)
in parallel: occurring in the same direction (as one event increases so does the other)
hot under the collar: irritable
interpersonal: between persons
outcome: result
predictable: expected
suspicions: thoughts and feelings regarding an event
confirmed: established
hostile: aggressive; unfriendly
physical exertion: using one's muscles and energy
systematically: carefully planned
sluggish: slow-moving
impractical: unreasonable
unethical: immoral; unprincipled; wrong
vividly: clearly
personality trait: a stale, enduring quality that a person shows in most situations
motivation: internal processes that initiate, maintain, and direct activities
personality profile: usually a graph of the scores obtained on several personality traits

creative: inventive, original, resourceful

course: path

conception: fertilization; mother's egg and father's sperm unite

transitions: changes

learning: any relatively permanent change in behavior brought about by experience

punishment: any event that follows a response and decreases its likelihood of occurring again

sensation: the process of detecting physical energies, such as light or sound, with the sensory organs that are found in the eye, ear, tongue, skin, and nose.

perception: the mental process of organizing sensations into meaningful patterns, such as visual images into words.

discern: tell the difference

species: types; classes; varieties

fascinated: absorbed; captivated

porpoises: mammal that lives in the ocean; related to whales and dolphins, but smaller than dolphins

primarily: mainly

nervous system: network of specialized cells that sends and receives messages throughout the body to control the body's responses to stimuli; made up of brain, spinal cord, and all nerve cells throughout the body

gender stereotypes: oversimplified and widely held beliefs about the basic characteristics of human males and females

persuasion: a deliberate attempt to change attitudes or beliefs with information and arguments

interpersonal attraction: social attraction to another person

evolved: developed; changed

trends: tendencies

culture: an ongoing pattern of life, characterizing a society at a given point in history

disciplined: how parents teach their children self-control

legal: related to the law and established rules in society

reliability: dependability; consistency

eyewitness testimony: someone who saw an event occur giving evidence in court

flatworms: one of the simplest type of animals; tiny soft-bodied worms, includes tapeworms and Planaria (used in some of the research studies in the textbook)

domestic animals: animals that are tame, not wild; are accustomed to being under human control and depend on humans for basic needs; common examples are farm animals (livestock) and pets

conserve: save

endangered species: at risk of the entire population of this type of animal dying out

classifying: placing in a category; organizing; grouping

suicide: deliberately killing oneself; "permanent solution to a temporary problem"

bystander apathy: lack of interest or concern among witnesses to an accident or crime

diffusion of responsibility: responsibility for action is spread out among those present and is lessened

obligated: forced; duty-bound; required

perplexing: confusing; puzzling

forecast: guess

aptitude: capacity to learn a skill

guarantee: assurance; promise

valid: legitimate; justifiable

fatal: deadly

humanely: kindly

outgrowth: result; product

boil down: summarize

34

Recite and Review

1. To achieve the goals of psychology, psychologists use scientific investigation and _____ thinking.
2. The word *psychology* comes from the ancient Greek roots *psyche,* which means "_____," and *logos,* meaning "knowledge or study."
3. Today, psychology is now defined as the scientific study of behavior and _____.
4. Directly observable actions and responses are considered _____ behaviors.
5. Remembering your vacation last year would be considered a(n) _____ behavior.
6. Today, psychology is considered both science and a(n) _____.
7. Although many people regard themselves as expert "people watchers" and form their own theories of behavior, these self-appointed authorities and their long-held _____ beliefs about human behavior are often wrong.
8. Scientific observation is based on gathering _____ evidence, which consists of information gained from direct observation.
9. Scientific observation is carefully planned, or _____.
10. When scientific observations are confirmed by more than one observer, they are said to be _____.
11. When psychologists gather observed facts, they are said to be collecting _____.
12. Dios, a developmental psychologist, uses a systematic process for answering scientific questions called a(n) _____ method.
13. Glynnis is a psychologist who is studying the motivation and traits of freshmen college students. Glynnis is most likely a(n) _____ theorist.
14. Amos is studying the physical and mental changes that individuals make as they grow from infancy to adulthood. Amos is most likely a(n) _____ psychologist.
15. Tia is interested in the reward and punishment patterns used in discipline for preschoolers. Tia is most likely a(n) _____ theorist.
16. A psychologist that studies how our five senses help us adapt to the world would be a sensation and _____ psychologist.
17. Arnie is a psychologist who has devoted his life to the study of reptiles and amphibians. Arnie would be considered a(n) _____ psychologist.
18. Reasoning, problem solving, memory, and other mental processes would be of most interest to a(n) _____ psychologist.
19. Biological processes, especially activities in the nervous system, would most likely be studied by a type of psychologist known as a(n) _____.
20. Marilyn studies the differences in how males and females manage people in the work settings and compares this behavior to how female and male children engage in play activities. Marilyn is most likely a(n) _____ psychologist.
21. Leadership, friendship, and conformity are topics of interest for _____ psychologists.
22. Jerome is interested in how food preparation has changed through the history of humankind. Jerome would be considered a(n) _____ psychologist.
23. The foods you eat, the way you were reared by your parents, and the laws you obey would all be of interest to a(n) _____ psychologist.
24. Studies of the "criminal mind" and the behavior of juries during a trial would most interest a(n) _____ psychologist.
25. If Amir uses rats to study the connections between diet and exercise and weight reduction in humans, Amir is using a(n) _____ model in his research.
26. The goal of psychology that involves naming and classifying behaviors is called _____.
27. In answering the "why" questions regarding the aging process, Tatum has met the goal of psychology known as _____.

35

28. The ability to forecast behavior defines the goal of _____ in psychology.
29. When a therapist helps a client to overcome a fear of flying, this therapist is illustrating the psychological goal of _____.

Part 1: Connections

1. ___ psychology
2. ___ covert behavior
3. ___ empirical evidence

4. ___ systematic
5. ___ intersubjective
6. ___ animal model
7. ___ goal of description
8. ___ goal of understanding
9. ___ goal of prediction

10. ___ goal of control

a. answers the "why" questions
b. carefully planned
c. scientific study of behavior and mental processes
d. altering conditions that affect behavior
e. naming and classifying behaviors
f. forecasts behavior
g. private, internal activities
h. confirmed by more than one observer
i. discovering principles that apply to humans by using other species
j. information gained from direct observation

Part 2: Connections

1. ___ personality theorist

2. ___ developmental psychologist

3. ___ learning theorist

4. ___ sensation and perception psychologist

5. ___ comparative psychologist
6. ___ cognitive psychologist

7. ___ biopsychologist

8. ___ gender psychologist

9. ___ social psychologist

10. ___ evolutionary psychologist
11. ___ cultural psychologist

12. ___ forensic psychologist

a. study reasoning, problem solving, memory, and other mental processes
b. apply psychological principles to legal issues
c. primarily study animal species other than humans
d. study how behavior has changed during the long history of humankind
e. study such topics as reward and punishment
f. study how individuals change throughout their life span
g. study topics, such as attitudes, persuasion, racism, and friendship
h. study how behavior relates to biological processes, such as the nervous system.
i. study traits, motivation, and individual differences in people
j. study differences in females and males
k. study how meaning is attached to information gained through vision, hearing, touch, etc.
l. study differences in language, foods, parenting, and laws among different groups around the world

Check Your Memory

1. TRUE or FALSE   Psychology can help you better understand yourself and others.

2. TRUE or FALSE   The Greek roots of the word *psychology* consist of *psyche,* which means "mind," and *logos,* meaning "knowledge or study."
3. TRUE or FALSE   The modern definition of psychology is the study of the brain, personality, and abnormal behavior.
4. TRUE or FALSE   Although it is a hidden activity, dreaming would be classified as a behavior.
5. TRUE or FALSE   Psychology can best be described as a profession, not a science.
6. TRUE or FALSE   Commonsense beliefs are often wrong.
7. TRUE or FALSE   Most humans use only 10 percent of their potential brainpower.
8. TRUE or FALSE   The more motivated you are, the better you will do at solving a complex problem.
9. TRUE or FALSE   To change people's behavior toward members of ethnic minority groups, we must first change their attitudes.
10. TRUE or FALSE   The term empirical evidence refers to the opinion of an acknowledged expert.
11. TRUE or FALSE   Scientific observation is both systematic and intersubjective.
12. TRUE or FALSE   It may be impractical or unethical to study some topics in psychology.
13. TRUE or FALSE   Through scientific research it was found that people who said they "never dream" actually dream frequently.
14. TRUE or FALSE   Learning theorists study personality traits, motivation, and individual differences.
15. TRUE or FALSE   Topics such as prejudice, leadership, conformity, and persuasion would most likely be studied by developmental psychologists.
16. TRUE or FALSE   Cognitive psychologists are interested in researching memory, reasoning, and problem solving.
17. TRUE or FALSE   Comparative psychologists study and compare the differences between human males and females.
18. TRUE or FALSE   Forensic psychologists apply psychological principles to legal issues.
19. TRUE or FALSE   Some psychologists use animal models to discover principles that apply to humans.
20. TRUE or FALSE   When psychologists name and classify behaviors based on a detailed record of scientific observations, they are meeting the goal of understanding.
21. TRUE or FALSE   The goal of psychology called prediction involves the ability to forecast behavior accurately.
22. TRUE or FALSE   The psychology goal of control involves a threat to the personal freedom of both research participants and clients in therapy.

Critical Thinking Question

1. All sciences are interested in controlling the phenomena they study. True or false?

Module 1.2 Critical Thinking and the Scientific Method in Psychology

Critical Thinking—Take It with a Grain of Salt

Survey Question: What is critical thinking?

Language Development Guide

take it with a grain of salt: consider, think about it
skeptical: doubtful; unconvinced
genuine: real; authentic
Rolex watch: expensive watch

designer: expensive, trendy, stylish

eBay: online shopping and auction website

ignorance: lack of knowledge

subatomic particles: smaller parts of atoms, such as protons, neutrons, and electrons

"buy": accept; believe

outrageous: disgraceful

"healing" crystals: the belief that quartz crystals contain energy that speeds can cure various physical or mental problems

miraculous: unbelievable; amazing

remedies: cures

"channeling" dead people: the claimed ability to transmit messages from the dead to the living

critiquing: reviewing; assessing critically

synthesizing: creating

challenge: question; oppose

conventional wisdom: ideas that are generally accepted within a society

probing: examine, look closely, investigate

transcend: go beyond or above, avoid

matters of faith: with conviction; total belief

authority: expert; specialist

guru: leader or teacher, usually a spiritual one

convinced: sure; confident; certain

sincere: earnest; honest

automatically: unconsciously; involuntarily; robotically

self-demeaning: to degrade or disresepect oneself

credible: believable

open-minded: flexible; tolerant; unbiased

gullible: easy to fool; overly trusting

astronomer: scientist who studies the formation and movement of stars, planets, moons, comets, etc.

Carl Sagan: famous American astronomer, who popularized the study of the stars and planets through his books and television series *Cosmos*.

exquisite: delicate

scrutiny: inspection; study; search

hypothesis: educated guess; predicted outcome

implications: the possible importance

nature: make-up; characteristics

conflicts of interest: having a personal interest in a situation that interferes with one's objective, impartial view of this situation

independent researcher: one who is impartial, nonbiased; free from conflicts of interest

provisional: temporary

enriches: improves; enhances

tackle: begin; undertake

lively: active

Recite and Review

1. Critical thinking is a type of reflection that involves evaluating comparing, analyzing, critiquing, and _____ information.

2. Critical thinkers are willing to challenge _____ wisdom by asking the hard questions.

3. The heart of critical thinking is a willingness to actively _____ on ideas.

4. Critical thinkers recognize that true knowledge comes from constantly _____ our understanding of the world.
5. One of the principles of critical thinking is that few truths transcend the need for logical analysis and _____ testing.
6. Critical thinkers do not always know what is true; and therefore they question their beliefs and are willing to admit they were _____.
7. An idea is not automatically true if it comes from claimed expertise or from a(n) _____.
8. Critical thinkers do not just look at the amount of evidence, but instead evaluate the _____ of the evidence.
9. Critical thinking requires a(n) _____ mind.
10. Questions that critical thinkers should ask themselves when evaluating new information include: Are the claims understandable? Do they make logical sense? Is there another possible _____ or a simpler one?
11. Critical thinkers should also ask these questions about the investigators: How reliable and trustworthy were the investigators? Do they have any _____ of interest?

Check Your Memory

1. TRUE or FALSE   Critical thinking is another name for commonsense reasoning.
2. TRUE or FALSE   Critical thinkers recognize that true knowledge comes from holding a constant and consistent view of the world.
3. TRUE or FALSE   Most ideas can be evaluated by applying the rules of logic, evidence, and the scientific method.
4. TRUE or FALSE   Critical thinkers do not question their beliefs and rarely admit they are wrong.
5. TRUE or FALSE   Authority or claimed expertise should automatically make an idea true.
6. TRUE or FALSE   Being a critical thinker requires one to give more weight to the quantity of evidence rather than the quality of evidence.
7. TRUE or FALSE   Critical thinking requires an open mind.
8. TRUE or FALSE   Questions that a critical thinker should ask him or herself include: "What was the nature and quality of the tests?" and "Can they be repeated?"

Critical Thinking Question

Can you think of some "commonsense" statements that contradict each other?

Module 1.2 Critical Thinking and the Scientific Method in Psychology
Pseudopsychologies—Palms, Planets, and Personality
Survey Question: How does psychology differ from false explanations of behavior?

Language Development Guide

resembles: looks like
contradictions: disagreements
popularized: to make something acceptable or interesting to the general public
nineteenth century: 1801-1900
anatomy: study of the organs and systems of the human body
revealed: to make known; disclose
so far off: very wrong
combativeness: eager to fight
overwhelming: great amount; overpowering
forgeries: fake; phony; counterfeit
arguably: maybe; perhaps

validity: logical truth

devastating: overwhelmingly damaging

vague: unclear; imprecise; fuzzy

tragedy: disaster

by chance: occur accidentally

compatibility: match, similarity

touchy: awkward; delicate

zodiac: an arrangement in the shape of a wheel that shows the twelve astrological signs, which are based on twelve constellations (groups of stars)

constellation: grouping of stars

Scorpio: astrological sign of person born between October 23 – November 21; means the Scorpion

Libra: astrological sign of person born between September 23 – October 22; means the Scales

horoscope: astrological predictions

uncannily: strangely; mysteriously

flattering: pleasing

desirable: sought after

ring of truth: sounds like it could be true

birth sign: astrological sign based on the day one was born

Virgo: astrological sign of person born between August 23 – September 22; The Virgin

nitpicking: criticizing about small or unimportant things

unbearable: awful; intolerable

make a good doorstop: very stiff and dull personality

compensate: make up for

disciplined: closely controlled

worrisome: troublesome; irritating

insecure: unsure of oneself

hemmed in: surrounded by; severely restricted or limited

independent thinker: using your own observations in understanding the world

frank: open, honest

extroverted: bold and outgoing

affable: friendly

introverted: shy; not outgoing

wary: cautious; careful

reserved: distant; shy

aspirations: goals

classic: memorable; lasting

(personality) dimensions: factors; aspects; components

illusion: deception

thrive: succeed; prosper

Aquarius: astrological sign of person born between January 20 – February 18; means the Water bearer

Gemini: astrological sign of person born between May 21- June 20; means the Twins

ironic twist: strange outcome

psychic mediums: person who claims to be able to communicate with the dead

edited: altered; revised

all-purpose: broad; general

fortunes: predictions of the future

clarify: make clear

emphasis: place importance

scholastic: academic; educational
prominently: importantly
nuisance: irritation; annoyance

Recite and Review

1. A pseudopsychology is any unfounded system that resembles _____.
2. Many pseudopsychologies give the appearance of science but are actually _____.
3. Pseudopsychologies change little over time because their followers avoid evidence that _____ them.
4. Franz Gall, a German anatomy teacher, claimed that personality traits were revealed by the shape of one's skull, a pseudopsychology known as _____.
5. The pseudopsychology that claims that lines on the hand reveal personality traits and predict the future is called _____.
6. Although people's personalities cannot be revealed through an analysis of their handwriting, the pseudopsychology called _____ can be used to detect forgeries.
7. The most popular pseudopsychology holds that the positions of the stars and planets at the time of one's birth determine personality traits and affect behavior and is called _____.
8. When Janae had her palm "read," she believed the flattering statements made about her personality, a tendency known as _____.
9. When Charles consulted a medium who claimed she could contact his dead uncle, Charles tended to remember the few bits of correct information and forgot the incorrect information she provided. Charles' experience illustrates the _____.
10. The fact that horoscopes present general information that would be equally for all 12 signs takes advantage of the _____ effect to keep people reading their forecasts each day.

Connections

1. ___ pseudopsychology
2. ___ phrenology
3. ___ palmistry
4. ___ graphology
5. ___ astrology
6. ___ uncritical acceptance
7. ___ confirmation bias
8. ___ Barnum effect

a. lines on hand reveal personality traits and predict the future
b. tendency to consider personal descriptions accurate if they are stated in general terms
c. tendency to believe positive or flattering descriptions of yourself
d. personality traits revealed by shape of skull
e. tendency to remember things that match our expectations and forget the rest
f. any unfounded system that gives the appearance of science
g. personality determined by positions of the stars and planets at the time of one's birth
h. personality traits revealed by handwriting

Check Your Memory

1. TRUE or FALSE   A pseudopsychology is any unfounded system that resembles psychology.
2. TRUE or FALSE   Phrenology was popularized in the eighteenth century by Fritz Perls.
3. TRUE or FALSE   Phrenology claimed that personality traits were revealed by the lines on one's palms.
4. TRUE or FALSE   Graphology holds that the positions of the stars and planets at the time of one's birth determine personality traits and affect behavior.

41

5. TRUE or FALSE   Graphologists do no better than untrained college students in rating personality and job performance.
6. TRUE or FALSE   A study of more than 3,000 predictions by famous astrologers found that only a small percentage were fulfilled.
7. TRUE or FALSE   Research has shown a significant association between the "compatibility" of couples' astrological signs and their marriage and divorce rates.
8. TRUE or FALSE   Research has found no connection between people's astrological signs and their intelligence.
9. TRUE or FALSE   Although the zodiac has shifted in the sky by one full constellation since astrology was first set up, contemporary astrologers ignore this shift.
10. TRUE or FALSE   The tendency to believe the positive or flattering descriptions given you by pseudopsychologists is called uncritical acceptance.
11. TRUE or FALSE   When we remember the few correct predictions made by a psychic but forget the incorrect ones, we are exhibiting the Barnum effect.
12. TRUE or FALSE   The confirmation bias is the tendency to consider personal descriptions accurate if they are stated in general terms.
13. TRUE or FALSE   Astrology's popularity shows that many people have difficulty separating valid psychology from systems that seem valid but are not.
14. TRUE or FALSE   Pseudopsychologies tend to be just a nuisance and rarely do any harm.
15. TRUE or FALSE   Valid psychological principles are based on opinions and wishful thinking.

Critical Thinking Question

Try constructing a few "Barnum statements," personality statements that are so general that virtually everyone will think they apply to themselves. Can you string them together to make a "Barnum personality profile"? Can you adapt the same statements to construct a "Barnum horoscope"?

Module 1.2 Critical Thinking and the Scientific Method in Psychology

Scientific Research—How to Think Like a Psychologist

Survey Question: How is the scientific method applied in psychological research?

Language Development Guide

opposites attract: persons with different personalities will like each other

birds of a feather flock together: persons with similar personalities will like and maintain a relationship with each other

every cloud has a silver lining: each bad event has a benefit

where there's smoke, there's fire: if something appears to be wrong, it probably is

heart (of all sciences): central part

systematic: orderly

haphazard: random; disorganized

precise: exact; specific

chatty: talkative

stereotype: overgeneralized label

biasing: prejudicing; prejudging, without fairness

tentative: not final; unconfirmed

frustration: negative emotional state that occurs when one's goals are blocked

disconfirm: prove false

operationally: stated specifically

concept: generalized idea representing a category of related objects or events

covert: hidden, secret, unobserved

iPhone: cell phone that has multi-media capabilities

overt: observable; not hidden

estimate: approximate

stress: mental and physical condition that occurs when a person must adjust or adapt to the environment

professional journal: a scholarly magazine that presents articles on current research that have been reviewed by experts in that field of study

prior: previous; earlier

statistically analyzed: interpreting the numerical data collected in research studies

proposed: suggested

Recite and Review

1. "Opposites attract" and "Birds of a feather flock together" are two contradictory _____ statements.
2. To be scientific, your observations must be planned and _____.
3. The scientific method is a form of critical thinking based on careful collection of evidence, accurate description and measurement, precise definition, controlled observation, and _____ results.
4. The first step in the scientific method is for the research to make _____.
5. The second step in the scientific method involves _____ a problem.
6. A tentative statement about, or explanation of, an event or relationship is called a(n) _____.
7. Unobservable ideas, such as covert behaviors, can be tested in real-world terms by using _____ definitions, which state the exact procedures used to represent a concept.
8. To find out about the conversations students have between classes, researchers used an electronically activated recorder to track the student's conversations, which illustrates the step in the scientific method known as Gathering evidence/Testing the _____.
9. A system of ideas designed to interrelate concepts and facts in a way that summarizes existing data and predicts future observations is referred to as a(n) _____.
10. Because scientific information must always be publicly available, the results of psychological studies are usually published in professional _____.
11. The results of a study will be more credible if other researchers are able to repeat, or _____ the results.
12. Research reports begin with a very brief summary of the study and its findings called a(n) _____, which allows you to get an overview without reading the entire article.
13. In a research article, the question to be investigated as well as background information on prior studies and related topics are presented in the _____ section of the report.
14. When Barry wanted to replicate a particular study, he paid careful attention to the _____ section of the research article that described the specific procedures used to gather data.
15. Statistical data, including graphs and tables, of the results of an experiment would be found in the _____ section of a research report.
16. Implications of the study just completed and future studies to be conducted would be found in the _____ section of a research report.

Connections

1. ___ scientific method
   a. part of research report that describes the specific procedures used to gather the data

43

2. ___ hypothesis	b. brief summary of the study and its findings
3. ___ operational definition	c. implications of the study are explained and further studies proposed
4. ___ replicate	d. repeating an experiment
5. ___ theory	e. educated guess about the relationship between variables
6. ___ abstract	f. system of ideas designed to interrelate concepts and facts
7. ___ introduction	g. data may be graphed, summarized in tables, or statistically analyzed in this section
8. ___ method	h. provides background information by reviewing prior studies on the same topic
9. ___ results	i. form of critical thinking based on careful measurement and controlled observation
10. ___ discussion	j. allows unobservable ideas to be tested in real-world terms

Check Your Memory

1. TRUE or FALSE   Much of what passes for common sense is vague and inconsistent.
2. TRUE or FALSE   To be scientific, your observations must be planned and systematic.
3. TRUE or FALSE   The scientific method is a form of critical thinking based on careful measurement and controlled observations.
4. TRUE or FALSE   Proposing a hypothesis is the first step in the scientific method.
5. TRUE or FALSE   Theory building is one of the steps in the scientific method.
6. TRUE or FALSE   A hypothesis is a system of ideas designed to interrelated concepts and facts to summarize existing data.
7. TRUE or FALSE   If you define "sleep deprivation" as "the number of hours of without sleep," you are using an operational definition.
8. TRUE or FALSE   Scientific information must always be publicly available so that other researchers can read about the results and make their own observations if they doubt the study's findings.
9. TRUE or FALSE   If you wanted to get an overview of a study and its findings without reading the entire article, one should read the brief summary called the abstract.
10. TRUE or FALSE   In the discussion section, the researcher provides background information by reviewing prior studies on the same or related topics.
11. TRUE or FALSE   In the introduction part of a research report, the author describes the specific procedures used to gather data for the research.
12. TRUE or FALSE   In the results section of a research report, data may be graphed, summarized in tables, or statistically analyzed.

Module 1.3 History and Contemporary Perspectives
A Brief History of Psychology—Psychology's Family Album
Survey Question: How did the field of psychology emerge?

Language Development Guide

philosophy: study of problems related to values, knowledge, reason, and existence
contemporary: modern; current
informally: casually; off the record

in contrast: quite the opposite

"father of psychology": started the scientific study of psychology

laboratory: a place in which studies can be conducted under controlled conditions

conscious: aware

evokes: bring to mind

"looking inward": stopping to focus on something and think about it deeply

time perception: being aware of the passage of time

insisting: not taking "no" for an answer

"elements": parts

chemical compound: substance that is made up of two or more elements

settle: come to agreement

despite: even though

insight: sudden mental reorganization of a problem that makes the solution obvious

(separate) discipline: branch of learning

deduced: figured out; realized

evolution: changes that take place in inherited physical features over several generation

retained: kept

habits: deeply ingrained learned behavior pattern

classroom dynamics: the relationship and interactions of classroom members

spurred: encouraged

objected: opposed; protested

subjective (experience): personal experience

objectivity: act of being impartial or independent

adopted: accepted; took on

well-formed: mentally and physically healthy

determined: caused by

overstatement: exaggeration

just the same: nonetheless; nevertheless

natural science: a field of study that uses the scientific method in research

conditioning chamber: apparatus used to study animal behavior, particularly as it relates to classical and operant learning (conditioning)

pigeons: a type of bird that is also called a dove

"radical behaviorist": strict behaviorists that study only overt behavior and discount the role of covert mental activities in determining behavior

"designed culture": a planned society (Skinner's version would have it based on behavioral principles, especially the use of reinforcement)

misguided: mistaken; unwise

streaming videos: a media delivery system, such as how Internet television is provided

principles: theories

"low-pitched": tone of sound is low or deep

tuba: largest brass musical instrument with the lowest pitch

"high-pitched": tone of sound is high or shrill

flute: narrow-tube-like woodwind instrument with a high pitch

melody: tune; song

relationship: association

perceptually: in understanding something experienced through the senses

launched: began

school of thought: group of people who share similar beliefs or theories

to advance: to spread

inspired: brought about; started

psychotherapy: a psychological technique used to help make positive changes in a person's personality, behavior, or adjustment

45

hysteria: old term for a mental disorder in which physical complaints have
  emotional causes; now called somatoform disorders

new horizons: new possibilities

mental life is like an iceberg: only aware of a small bit of one's mental life (tip of iceberg) with
  the largest amount being out of your awareness (hidden below the surface, like the largest
  part of the iceberg

impulses: urges; wishes

threatening: frightening

"Freudian slips": the mistake of saying what you really feel (it slips out)

humorous: funny

tardy: late

probe: search

"the child is father to the man": means one's childhood affects one's adulthood (Freud's idea);
  line from a poem by William Wordsworth

modified: change; alter

social motives: learned needs, such as the need for achievement or power

legacy: something that is handed down from the past

evident: obvious; apparent

spirituality: one's deepest values; a religious or inner aspect one's being

deprived: denied; something taken away

initially: to begin with

descent: parentage; ancestry

contributed: a part of the cause

Caucasian: describes race of European ancestry; white

awarded: presented; granted

Ph.D.: doctor of philosophy; highest academic degree to be earned

diversity: range; variety

persons of color: American term used to describe all persons who are not white (Caucasian)

offered: presented

founded: set up; started

inauguration: swearing in (of the President)

Recite and Review

1. The first laboratory to study conscious experience was set up in Leipzig, Germany, in 1879
   by _____, who became known as the "father of psychology."
2. In this first psychological laboratory, the scientists had their subjects probe the sensations
   created by various stimuli through a process of "looking inward" called _____.
3. Wundt's ideas were carried to the United States by _____, who called these ideas
   structuralism.
4. The field of psychology was broadened to include animal behavior, religious experience, and
   abnormal behavior by _____, who wrote *Principles of Psychology* (1890), which also
   helped to establish psychology as a separate discipline.
5. Functionalism was concerned with how the mind helps us _____ to our environments.
6. The behaviorist John B. Watson adopted the concept of conditioning from the Russian
   physiologist _____.
7. "Give me a dozen healthy infants, well-formed, and my own special world to bring them up
   in and I'll guarantee to take any one at random and train him to become any type specialist I
   might select—doctor, lawyer, artist, merchant-chief, and yes, beggarman and thief" was the
   famous claim of psychologist _____.

8. The psychologist who believed that our actions are controlled by rewards and punishments and who developed a conditioning chamber that bears his name was _____.

9. A psychologist who believes that behavior can be explained through conditioning but who also believes thinking and expectations play an important role ascribes to the view known as _____.

10. Max Wertheimer was the first to advance _____ psychology, whose slogan is "The whole is greater than the sum of its parts."

11. Psychoanalytic psychology was developed by Austrian physician _____.

12. According to psychoanalytic psychology, threatening thoughts are held out of awareness through a process known as _____.

13. Alfred Adler, Karen Horney, Carl Jung, and Erik Erikson accepted much of Freud's theory but revised parts of it and became known as _____.

14. Any theory that emphasizes internal motives, conflicts, and unconscious forces is referred to as a(n) _____ theory.

15. Carl Rogers and Abraham Maslow would be considered _____ psychologists.

16. Since both behaviorism and psychoanalytic psychology view behavior as being governed by forces beyond a person's control, these types of psychology would be described as having a strong undercurrent of _____.

17. A psychologist who believe that his or her clients can freely choose to live more creative, meaningful, and satisfying lives would be considered a(n) _____ psychologist.

18. If you try to fully develop your potentials and become the best person you can be, you are exhibiting _____.

19. Humanists stress subjective factors, such as self-image, self-evaluation, and frame of _____.

20. The first psychology course was taught by _____ in 1875.

21. In 1886, the first American psychology textbook was written by _____.

22. Having been the first woman to be awarded a Ph.D. in psychology _____ published an influential textbook on animal behavior, titled *The Animal Mind*.

23. In 1920, the first African American man to earn a doctoral degree in psychology was _____.

24. The first African-American female to be awarded a Ph.D. in psychology was _____ with this event occurring in 1933.

25. Of all undergraduate and graduate degrees awarded in psychology since 2000, approximately _____ percent have to women

Connections

1. ___ Wundt
2. ___ Titchener
3. ___ James
4. ___ Wertheimer
5. ___ Skinner
6. ___ Freud
7. ___ Maslow
8. ___ Prosser
9. ___ Jung
10. ___ Dewey

a. functionalist
b. neo-Freudian
c. first African-American woman to be awarded a Ph.D. in psychology
d. father of psychology
e. wrote first American psychology textbook
f. created a conditioning chamber that bears his name
g. known for creating psychoanalysis
h. brought structuralism to America
i. humanist that developed the concept of self-actualization
j. first to advance the Gestalt viewpoint

Check Your Memory

1. TRUE or FALSE   Sigmund Freud developed the first psychological lab in 1866 in the city of Vienna, Austria.
2. TRUE or FALSE   Edward Titchener brought the psychological ideas of Wilhelm Wundt to American and called these ideas structuralism.
3. TRUE or FALSE   The behaviorists utilized a technique known as introspection.
4. TRUE or FALSE   William James broadened psychology to include animal behavior, religious experience, and abnormal behavior.
5. TRUE or FALSE   The functionalists' ideas were influenced by Darwin's principle of natural selection.
6. TRUE or FALSE   The ideas of the humanists gave rise to the fields of educational psychology and industrial psychology.
7. TRUE or FALSE   John B. Watson adopted Ivan Pavlov's concept of conditioning to explain most behavior.
8. TRUE or FALSE   B. F. Skinner would be considered a cognitive behaviorist because he believed that the role of thinking placed a major role in determining one's behavior.
9. TRUE or FALSE   Skinner opposed the use of punishment because it does not teach correct responses.
10. TRUE or FALSE   Max Wertheimer was the first to advance the humanistic viewpoint.
11. TRUE or FALSE   Gestalt psychologists studied thinking, learning, and perception as whole units, not by analyzing experiences into parts.
12. TRUE or FALSE   Abraham Maslow created the first fully developed psychotherapy called transactional analysis.
13. TRUE or FALSE   Sigmund Freud believed that repressed thoughts were revealed by dreams, emotions, or slips of the tongue.
14. TRUE or FALSE   Carl Jung and Erik Erikson modified Freud's ideas and became known as Neo-Freudians.
15. TRUE or FALSE   Humanistic psychologists believe that our behavior is determined by forces beyond our control.
16. TRUE or FALSE   Humanists are interested in psychological needs for love, self-esteem, belonging, self-expression, creativity, and spirituality.
17. TRUE or FALSE   One's frame of reference refers to the on-going process of fully developing one's personal potential and becoming the best person one can be
18. TRUE or FALSE   The first psychology textbook was written by John B. Watson.
19. TRUE or FALSE   The first psychology course was taught by William James.
20. TRUE or FALSE   Francis Sumner was the first woman to be awarded a Ph.D. in psychology.
21. TRUE or FALSE   Margaret Washburn was the first African-American woman to be awarded a Ph.D. in psychology in America.
22. TRUE or FALSE   In recent years, one quarter of all undergraduate degrees and 16 percent of doctorates in psychology have been awarded to persons of color.

Critical Thinking Question

Modern sciences like psychology are built on observations that can be verified by two or more independent observers. Did structuralism meet this standard? Why or why not?

Module 1.3 History and Contemporary Perspectives
Psychology Today—Three Complementary Perspectives on Behavior
Survey Question: What are the contemporary perspectives in psychology?

Language Development Guide

fierce: intense; forceful

clashes: disagreements; quarrels

prominence: importance

genetics: study of inherited characteristics

biochemists: scientists who study the chemical elements and processes within living plants and animals

refuted: disproved

pressing: urgent; critical

well-being: combination of health, happiness, security, and comfort

achievement: meeting one's internal standard of excellence

virtues: qualities

optimal: best possible; most favorable

ideally: preferably; in a perfect world

fulfilling: satisfying; accomplishing

multicultural: acceptance of many different cultures

gospel choir: musical group that sings music that expresses Christian beliefs

Oshogatsu: Japanese New Year

archers: use of bow and arrows

ward off: defend against; hold off

new social reality: new rules of society; new customs

norm: standard; average

"minority groups": social groups that make up a smaller portion of the population

invalid: untrue

universal: worldwide

Native American: groups of people whose ancestors were original to the Americas; did not immigrate; some group members prefer to be referred to as American Indians

delusion: strongly-held false beliefs

mental health: emotional and cognitive fitness

take…into account: to consider

diagnosis: identifying aspects of a condition or disorder

ethnicity: a group who have shared beliefs and customs

eclectic: diverse; use of a variety of sources

complement: balances; goes together

physiology: study of the functioning and make-up of living creatures

neutral: not a positive nor negative view

reductionistic: explaining a complex subject by breaking it down into its simpler parts

mechanistic: impersonal view of humans; viewing causes of the behavior of humans, much like one would view the actions of a machine

information-processing: theory that the human mind solves problems and stores data much like the processing of a computer: input, processing, output

computer-like: view of the human mind as operating similar to how a computer operates

negative: downbeat view

pessimistic: gloomy; negative

positive: upbeat view

philosophical: dealing with deeper, more theoretical views of life; rather than a objective, scientific view

interactionist: based more on social forces (arising from the social contact between people)

49

Recite and Review

1. The three broad areas that shape modern psychology are the biological, psychological, and _____ perspectives.
2. Biopsychologists and others who study the brain and nervous system, such as biologists and biochemists, are part of the broader field known as _____.
3. The part of the biological perspective that seeks to explain behavior through the activity of the brain and nervous system, physiology, genetics, the endocrine system, and biochemistry is the _____ view.
4. Natural selection is used to explain behavior in the _____ view of behavior.
5. As researchers in recent years have devised ways to study covert behaviors, such as problem-solving and memory, the view of behavior that has gained greater prominence is _____ psychology.
6. The part of the psychological perspective that sees behavior as shaped and controlled by one's environment is the _____ view.
7. A somewhat negative and pessimistic view of human nature is seen in the _____ view of behavior.
8. The part of the psychological perspective that emphasizes that behavior is guided by one's self-image, by subjective perceptions of the world, and by needs for personal growth is the _____ view.
9. A neutral, interactionist view of human nature that emphasizes that behavior is related to the environment that a person is born, grows up, and lives from day to day is the _____ view.
10. The study of human strengths, virtues, and optimal behavior is called _____ psychology.
11. The idea that behavior must be judged relative to the values of the culture in which it occurs is referred to as _____.
12. Rules that define the behavior that is acceptable and expected within your social group are called _____.
13. Because they realize that a single perspective is unlikely to fully explain complex human behavior, most contemporary psychologists would be considered _____ in their viewpoint and use of approaches.

Connections

1. ___ biopsychological view
2. ___ evolutionary view
3. ___ behavioristic view
4. ___ cognitive view

5. ___ psychodynamic view
6. ___ sociocultural view

7. ___ positive psychology

8. ___ cultural relativity
9. ___ social norms

10. ___ eclectic

a. studies observable behaviors and effects of learning
b. behavior directed by hidden, unconscious forces
c. drawing from many perspectives and approaches
d. explains behavior through principles based on natural selection
e. study of human strengths, virtues, and optimal behavior
f. explains behavior through activity of nervous system, endocrine system, and genetics
g. rules that define acceptable and expected behavior for members of a group
h. involves considering the values of the group being observed
i. human behavior understood in terms of the mental processing of information
j. interactionist view that sees behavior as being influenced by the environment in which a person grows up

Check Your Memory

1. TRUE or FALSE   Early systems, such as structuralism, have disappeared entirely from psychology, except as historical notes.
2. TRUE or FALSE   Functionalism and Gestalt psychology have blended into newer, broader perspectives in psychology.
3. TRUE or FALSE   The three broad perspectives that shape modern psychology are the genetic, behavioral, and environmental perspectives.
4. TRUE or FALSE   Those who take a biopsychological view explain behavior through the activity of the brain and nervous system, not the actions of genetics or the endocrine system.
5. TRUE or FALSE   The humanistic view seeks to explain behavior through the evolutionary principles based on natural selection.
6. TRUE or FALSE   The behavioristic view takes a neutral, scientific, somewhat mechanistic view of human nature.
7. TRUE or FALSE   Cognitive psychology has gained greater prominence in recent years as researchers have devised ways to objectively study covert behaviors, such as thinking and problem-solving.
8. TRUE or FALSE   Psychodynamic psychologists continue to trace human behavior to unconscious processes.
9. TRUE or FALSE   Inspired by the humanists, positive psychology is a new area of study that focuses on human strengths, virtues, and effective functioning.
10. TRUE or FALSE   A client's cultural beliefs have not been shown to affect his or her diagnosis and treatment for mental disorders.
11. TRUE or FALSE   Cultural diversity is becoming the norm with some large cities' "minority" groups being the majority.
12. TRUE or FALSE   Rules that define acceptable and expected behavior for members of various groups are referred to as cultural stereotypes.
13. TRUE or FALSE   Today many psychologists would be considered eclectic in their viewpoints.

Module 1.4 Psychologists and Their Specialties

Psychologists—Guaranteed Not to Shrink

Survey Question: What are the major specialties in psychology?

Language Development Guide

postgraduate: education beyond a bachelors degree
bumbling: awkward; clumsy
buffoon: fool; clown
intimate: private, personal
distort: misrepresent
ethical code: guidelines for proper behavior
dignity: self-respect
confidentiality: right to have information about self kept private
welfare: one's interests and well-being
misconceptions: mistaken belief; false impression
clinicians: professional working in the physical or mental health field, ex. doctor, nurse, psychologist
emotionally stable: being able to control and regulate one's moods
keen: highly sensitive

privileges: the right to perform certain services, such as prescribing medicine

moustache and goatee: facial hair on the upper lip and chin

spectacles: glasses

(German) accent: tone and pronunciation of words; reference to the accent of many of the first psychoanalysts, who were trained in Austria/Germany by Sigmund Freud

well-padded couch: reference to the couch on which Freud had his patients recline during therapy

supervised counseling experience: part of training that involves counseling under the guidance of a licensed professional

practical helping skills: counseling skills that are important regardless of the client's problems, such as building trust, not being judgmental, using open-ended questions (requires more than yes or no)

hang a shingle: begin or open a professional business

rigorous: demanding; thorough

state examining board: evaluates and licenses individuals in various professions

rebirther: a person who helps you imagine the experience of your birth

primal feeling facilitator: a person who helps you express your anger

cosmic aura balancer: a person who tries to align unseen energy forces around the body

life skills coach: usually serves as a paraprofessional (does not have academic degree, but has some training) to help people with various life's problems, such as resisting drugs or dealing with stress

self-proclaimed titles: not a formal title conferred, but one given to oneself

honorable: praiseworthy; principled

solely: only

specialty: area in which one is an expert

subculture: smaller part of the larger cultural group that differentiates itself from the through dress, music, religion, politics, etc.

disturbed: troubled

urban noise: noise pollution found in many large cities

crowding: the feeling of overstimulation caused by a loss of privacy or by the nearness of others

environmental issues: include concerns, such as crowding, littering, noise pollution, and energy and resource conservation

rehabilitation: treatment; remedy

acquisition: gaining

gender identity: one's personal, private sense of maleness or femaleness

skills analysis: process of determining the abilities of an applicant for a particular job

compliance (in taking medicine): following the directions

vocational counseling: helping individuals to develop career goals

learning disabilities: having difficulty in reading, math, or other academics due to perceptual or processing problems, but not due to intellectual, physical, sensory, or emotional problems

Recite and Review

1. "Shrink" is the slang term for a(n) _____.
2. A professional who is highly trained in the methods, knowledge, and theories of psychology and who has a master's degree or a doctorate in one of many specialties, including clinical, counseling, educational, social, gender, and personality would be a(n) _____.
3. Santos is a psychologist who treats the most severe mental disorders, such as schizophrenia and bipolar disorder. Santos is most likely a(n) _____ psychologist.
4. Maria is a psychologist who treats clients who have adjustment problems at work or at school. Maria would most likely be a(n) _____ psychologist.

52

5. Most clinical psychologists have a Ph.D. degree and follow a(n) _____ model, which means they are trained to do either research or therapy with many doing both.
6. Some clinicians earn a degree, which emphasizes therapy skills rather than research. This degree is called a(n) _____.
7. To embark on a career in psychology, a person should be sensitive to the feelings of others, find theories and complex projects interesting, have good communication skills, and be emotionally _____.
8. Timothy, a medical doctor who treats mental disorders by doing psychotherapy, is also licensed to legally prescribe drugs in all 50 states of the U.S. Timothy is a(n) _____.
9. Psychologists in the U.S. states of New Mexico and _____ can now legally prescribe drugs.
10. A person with an M.D. or Ph.D. degree who also has further training in Freudian psychoanalysis would be referred to as a(n) _____.
11. David earned a master's degree in counseling and then underwent two years of full-time supervised counseling experience as a marriage and family counselor. The master's degree and the supervised experience were required for David to become a(n) _____ counselor.
12. Margo is a mental health professional who is trained to apply social science principles to help patients in clinics and hospitals and whose typical duties include evaluating patients and families, conducting group therapy, or visiting a patient's home, school, or job to alleviate problems. Margo is most likely a psychiatric _____.
13. High levels of competence, integrity, and responsibility; respect for people's rights to privacy, dignity, confidentiality, and personal freedom; and protection of the client's welfare are all part of the professional code of _____ followed by psychologists.
14. Clinical and counseling psychologists make up _____ percent of all psychologists.
15. Those psychologists who are employed full-time at colleges or universities, where they teach and do research, consulting, or therapy make up _____ percent of all psychologists.
16. While an educational psychologist is more likely to investigate classroom dynamics and evaluate educational programs, a(n) _____ psychologist typically conducts psychological testing, treats learning disabilities, and provides emotional and vocational counseling for students.
17. Dr. Shettra is a psychologist who selects job applicants, does skills analysis, evaluates on-the-job training, and improves work environments and human relations in work settings. Dr. Shettra is a(n) _____ psychologist.
18. Dr. Cicero is conducting research regarding how packaging, advertising, and marketing methods affects the buying habits of different ages. Dr. Cicero is a(n) _____ psychologist.
19. When a psychologist studies memory simply to understand how memory works, this psychologist is conducting _____ research.
20. Dr. Reed is studying how to improve the exercise and eating habits of children in order to decrease childhood obesity. Dr. Reed's study would be considered _____ research.

Connections

1. ___ psychologist

   a. studies conducted to solve immediate practical problems

2. ___ psychiatrist

   b. Ph.D. or M.D. with additional training in Freudian techniques

3. ___ psychoanalyst

   c. types of this profession include forensic, school, comparative, and industrial-organizational

4. ___ licensed counselor

   d. emphasizes therapy skills rather than research

5. ___ psychiatric social worker

   e. medical doctor with additional training in diagnosis and treatment of mental disorders

53

6. ___ shrink

    f. trained to apply social science principles to help patients in clinics and hospitals, and may conduct home visits

7. ___ scientist-practitioner model

    g. studies conducted to seek knowledge for its own sake

8. ___ Psy.D.

    h. trained to do either research or therapy, but may do both

9. ___ basic research

    i. slang term for a psychiatrist

10. ___ applied research

    j. has master's degree and supervised experience in practical helping skills, but does not treat serious mental disorders

Check Your Memory

1. TRUE or FALSE   "Shrink" is the slang term for any mental health professional.
2. TRUE or FALSE   Psychologists are often inaccurately portrayed in the media.
3. TRUE or FALSE   Most psychologists are therapists in private practice.
4. TRUE or FALSE   The differences between clinical and counseling psychology are beginning to fade.
5. TRUE or FALSE   The Psy.D. degree emphasizes scientific research skills rather than therapy skills.
6. TRUE or FALSE   A person who would enjoy becoming a psychologist is emotionally stable, has good communication skills, and is good at recognizing patterns and evaluating evidence.
7. TRUE or FALSE   A psychiatrist is a medical doctor who treats mental disorders through psychotherapy and can also prescribe medication.
8. TRUE or FALSE   Psychologists in New York, Nevada, and Illinois can now legally prescribe drugs.
9. TRUE or FALSE   To become a psychoanalyst, you must have an M.D. or Ph.D. degree plus further training in Freudian psychoanalysis.
10. TRUE or FALSE   The typical duties of a psychiatric social worker include evaluating patients and families; conducting group therapy; and/or visiting a patient's home, school, or job to alleviate problems.
11. TRUE or FALSE   To work as a clinical or counseling psychologist, you must have a license issued by a state examining board.
12. TRUE or FALSE   High levels of competence, integrity, and responsibility are part of the professional code of ethics that psychologist follow.
13. TRUE or FALSE   About 75 percent of psychologists are clinical and counseling psychologists.
14. TRUE or FALSE   At present, the American Psychological Association (APA) consists of more than 50 divisions.
15. TRUE or FALSE   Thirty percent of all psychologists are employed full-time at colleges or universities, where they teach and do research, consulting, or therapy.
16. TRUE or FALSE   Specialties in psychology include community, consumer, engineering, and school psychology.
17. TRUE or FALSE   Comparative psychologists study and compare the behavior of different species, especially animals.
18. TRUE or FALSE   A psychologist who studies urban noise, crowding, and human use of space would most likely be an environmental psychologist.
19. TRUE or FALSE   Studying how the two hemispheres of the brain transmit information to each other would be considered applied research.
20. TRUE or FALSE   Studying ways to improve the memories of eyewitnesses to crimes would be an example of basic research.

54

Critical Thinking Question

If many psychologists work in applied settings, why is basic research still of great importance?

Module 1.5 The Psychology Experiment
The Psychology Experiment—Where Effect Meets Cause
Survey Question: How is an experiment performed?

Language Development Guide

formal trial: under controlled conditions
directly: completely; precisely
vary: change; alter
suspected: supposed; assumed
legally drunk: .08 blood alcohol limit or greater which equals .08 milliliters or grams per liter of blood or exhaled breath
point of reference: a position with which to compare
dunces: slang for an unintelligent person
hungover: physical effects of alcohol withdrawal usually the morning after heavy alcohol consumption
deception: trickery
ethics committee: group appointed at a college or university to oversee the research conducted in order to protect the rights of research subjects
debate: discussion; argument
risks: dangers
ensure: make certain
debrief: to provide information about the research to the participants after the study is completed
with respect to: regarding
equated: made equal

Recite and Review

1. A formal trial undertaken to confirm or disconfirm a hypothesis about the causes of behavior is called a(n) _____.
2. Animals or people whose behavior is being investigated are referred to as experimental subjects, while human subjects may also be referred to as _____.
3. Any condition that changes or can be made to change is called a(n) _____.
4. The control group and the experimental group are treated exactly alike except for the _____ variable.
5. In an experiment, the condition being investigated as a possible cause of some change in behavior and whose value is chosen by the experimenter is the _____ variable.
6. The results of the experiment, which are often revealed by measures of performance, such as test scores would be the _____ variable.
7. Conditions that a researcher wishes to prevent from affecting the outcome of the experiment are called _____ variables.
8. In an experiment to determine whether listening to music while studying affects learning, listening to music while studying would be the _____ variable.
9. In an experiment to determine whether the use of a hands-free cell phone affects driving ability, the scores achieved on a test of driving ability would be the _____ variable.
10. In an experiment to determine whether the use of a hands-free cell phone affects driving ability, the person's familiarity with the car used in the experiment would be a(n) _____ variable.

55

11. In an experiment to determine whether listening to music while studying affects learning, the group that would study in a quiet room would be the _____ group.
12. Dr. Grace is conducted an experiment to determine whether exercise decreases depression symptoms. The group that would exercise would be the _____ group.
13. Extraneous variables that involve personal characteristics, such as age or intelligence, can be controlled through a(n) _____ of the subjects to the two groups.
14. Conditions other than the independent variable, such as the amount of study time, the temperature in the room, the time of day, the amount of light are prevented from affecting the outcome of the experiment by making all these conditions _____ for both the experimental and control groups.
15. Three areas of ethical concern in behavioral research are the invasion of privacy, the risk of lasting harm, and the use of _____.
16. Investigators are expected to "ensure the welfare of animals and treat them _____."
17. To oversee research, most university psychology departments have _____ committees.
18. Basic ethical guidelines for psychological researchers include to accurately describe risks to potential participants, to maintain confidentiality, and to ensure that participation in the research is _____.
19. The results of an experiment are considered to be statistically _____ when they would occur very rarely by chance only.
20. Research findings become more convincing when they can be repeated, or _____ by other researchers.

Connections

1. ____ independent variable
2. ____ dependent variable
3. ____ extraneous variable
4. ____ random assignment
5. ____ experimental group
6. ____ control group
7. ____ statistically significant
8. ____ ethical guidelines for research

a. conditions excluded from affecting the outcome of the experiment
b. evenly balances the personal differences in the two research groups
c. provides point of reference for comparison between the two groups in an experiment
d. would occur by chance in less than 5 experiments out of 100
e. helps minimize risk to the subjects
f. altered by the experimenter and is the suspected cause for difference in behavior
g. group of subjects exposed to the condition being investigated
h. the results of the experiment

Check Your Memory

1. TRUE or FALSE   As a method of research, an experiment only allows us to describe and predict behavior, but does not meet the goal of understanding behavior.
2. TRUE or FALSE   Animals or humans whose behavior is investigated during research are referred to as experimental subjects, while human subjects are also called participants.
3. TRUE or FALSE   Extraneous variables measure the results of the experiment.
4. TRUE or FALSE   Dependent variables are conditions that the researcher wishes to prevent from affecting the outcome of the experiment.
5. TRUE or FALSE   In an experiment to test whether hunger affects memory, hunger is the dependent variable.

6. TRUE or FALSE   In an experiment to test whether cell phone use affects driving ability, previous driving experience would be an extraneous variable.

7. TRUE or FALSE   In an experiment to test whether a new medication decreases the symptoms of ADHD, the symptoms of ADHD would be the independent variable.

8. TRUE or FALSE   In an experiment to test whether listening to music while studying improves test grades, the experimental group would study in a quiet room without music.

9. TRUE or FALSE   In an experiment to test whether cell phone use affects driving ability, the group that would drive the obstacle course while talking on a cell phone would be the control group.

10. TRUE or FALSE   The control group provides a point of reference for comparison with the scores in the experimental group.

11. TRUE or FALSE   Random assignment evenly balances personal differences in the experimental and control groups.

12. TRUE or FALSE   Extraneous variables, such as the amount of study time, the temperature in the room, and the amount of light can be prevented from affecting the outcome of experiment by making all these extraneous conditions exactly alike for both groups

13. TRUE or FALSE   According to the ethical guidelines, deception is never to be used within an experiment.

14. TRUE or FALSE   According to the ethical guidelines, psychological researchers must accurately describe risks to potential participants and must ensure that participation is voluntary.

15. TRUE or FALSE   According to the ethical guidelines, psychological researchers must provide results and interpretations to the participants after the research is concluded.

16. TRUE or FALSE   Although the American Psychological Association has set up ethical guidelines for human research, there are no ethical guidelines for research with other animal species.

17. TRUE or FALSE   Most university psychology departments have ethics committees that oversee research.

18. TRUE or FALSE   In a carefully controlled experiment, the independent variable is the only possible cause for any effect noted in the dependent variable.

19. TRUE or FALSE   To be statistically significant, a difference must be large enough so that it would occur by chance in less than 20 experiments out of 100.

20. TRUE or FALSE   Research findings become more convincing when they can be replicated by other researchers.

Critical Thinking Question

There is a loophole in the statement, "I've been taking vitamin C tablets, and I haven't had a cold all year. Vitamin C is great!" What is the loophole?

Module 1.5 The Psychology of Experiment
Double Blind—On Placebos and Self-Fulfilling Prophecies
Survey Question: What is a double-blind experiment?

57

Language Development Guide

stimulant: a substance that increases activity in the body and nervous system

assesses: measures; evaluates

flawed: damaged

injection: "a shot in the arm;" substance is put into the body through a needle

morphine: psychoactive drug classified as a depressant-narcotic; pain reliever

basis: source; origin

inert: inactive, powerless

blind (as to the hypothesis): unaware

arrangement: plan; procedure

biased: partial; influenced; predisposed

in essence: basically; in actual fact

hints: tips-off; suggests; implies

preparatory school: secondary school (high school) designed to prepare students for college or specific training, such as the military

airmen: person enlisted in military air force of a particular country

subtly: faintly

body language: non-verbal communication through facial expressions, gestures, body movements, and posture

underestimate: undervalue; take too lightly

prophesy: predict; forecast

live up or down: to act according to what people expect of you, whether they expect good or bad

antidepressant drugs: mood-elevating drugs that counteract depression

"wonder drug": seen as a miracle cure

herbal health remedies: the use of substances found in nature, such as herbs, to treat various physical and mental complaints

Recite and Review

1. Changes in the behavior of research participants caused by the unintended influence of their own expectations are referred to as _____ bias.
2. An inactive substance given in the place of a drug in psychological research or by physicians who wish to treat a complaint by suggestion is called a(n) _____.
3. When participants who are given a pill during an experiment unconsciously expect to feel or perform better, which leads to a change in their behavior, this is referred to as the _____ effect.
4. After a person takes a sugar pill or a saline injection, there is a reduction in _____ activity linked with pain, so the effect is not imaginary
5. When researchers know who is in the experimental and control group, but the participants do not, this is called a(n) _____-blind experiment.
6. Dr. Samson is conducting a drug study on the effects of a new antidepressant in controlling depression symptoms. The new antidepressant pill will be given to the participants in the _____ group.
7. Dr. Bahar is conducting a drug study involving a new antipsychotic medication given in injection form. The group that will receive the inactive, saline injection will be the _____ group.
8. When a researcher subtly communicates his expectations to his subjects, this is referred to as a(n) _____ bias.
9. A teacher expects her minority students to underachieve in her classes and subtly communicates these expectations to her students. If the minority students then "give up" and do underachieve in her class, then a(n) _____ prophecy has taken place.

58

10. Dr. Imes is conducting a drug study in which one group of participants will receive the real drug and the other group will be given a placebo. Dr. Imes has his assistant prepare the drug packets, so that neither he nor his participants will know until the end of the experiment who received the real drug and who received the placebo. Dr. Imes is conducting a(n) _____-blind experiment.

Connections

1. ___ research participant bias
2. ___ researcher bias
3. ___ experimental group
4. ___ control group
5. ___ single-blind experiment
6. ___ double-blind experiment
7. ___ placebo
8. ___ self-fulfilling prophecy

a. changes in behavior due to the research subjects' expectations that treatment will have some effect
b. neither subjects nor experimenter know who is in which research group
c. inactive substance given in the place of a drug in psychological research
d. prediction that prompts people to act in ways that make the prediction come true
e. subjects do not know which research group they are in, but experimenter does
f. unintended influence of a researcher's actions, such as subtly communicating his or her expectations
g. group of subjects who receive the inert substance in place of the real drug
h. group of subjects who receive the real drug in an experiment

Check Your Memory

1. TRUE or FALSE   If the experimental group knows they will be receiving study skills training and the control group knows that they won't be trained, knowing this difference can create expectations and result in the research participant bias regarding any differences in performance that may result between the two groups.
2. TRUE or FALSE   The placebo effect is a form of research participant bias.
3. TRUE or FALSE   Placebos are used on in research but are never used by medical doctors with actual patients.
4. TRUE or FALSE   Placebo effects can be quite powerful with a saline injection being 70 percent as effective as morphine in reducing pain.
5. TRUE or FALSE   In a typical drug study the control group is given the real drug, while the experimental group gets a placebo.
6. TRUE or FALSE   To help control for research participant bias, a single-blind experiment can be used.
7. TRUE or FALSE   Placebos have been shown to affect depression, alertness, tension, sexual arousal, and cravings for alcohol.
8. TRUE or FALSE   After a person takes a placebo, there is a reduction in brain activity linked with pain, so the effect is not imaginary.
9. TRUE or FALSE   If the experimenter unintentional hints to the participants what he or she expects to occur within the experiment, the experimenter has set up the Barnum effect.
10. TRUE or FALSE   A prediction that prompts people to act in ways that make the prediction come true is known as uncritical acceptance.
11. TRUE or FALSE   When the research subjects nor the experimenters with direct contact with the subject know who is in the experimental or control group, the arrangement is called a double-blind experiment.

12.TRUE or FALSE   Making both the research subjects and the researchers with direct contact to the subjects "blind" to who is in the experimental and control group controls for both research participant bias and researcher bias.

Critical Thinking Question
People who believe strongly in astrology have personality characteristics that actually match, to a degree, those predicted by their astrological signs. Can you explain why this occurs?

Module 1.6 Nonexperimental Research Methods
Nonexperimental Psychological Research—Different Strokes
Survey Question: What nonexperimental research methods do psychologists use?

Language Development Guide
nonexperimental: research methods that provide information but cannot establish true cause-and-effect relationships
technique: method
depression: mental disorder characterized by feelings of powerlessness and hopelessness
psychosis: withdrawal from reality marked by delusions and hallucinations, disturbed thoughts and emotions, and personality disintegration
clinical settings: places in which one-on-one therapy or medical care is given
questionnaires: series of questions presented in written or oral form to obtain information from people
poll: interview; ask questions

Recite and Review
1. Because it is not always possible to conduct experiments, psychologists gather evidence and test hypotheses using _____ methods.
2. Psychologists who want to study behavior in natural settings use a technique called

   _____.
3. In order to study mental disorders, such as depression or psychosis, psychologists often use the _____ method.
4. Psychologists who are looking for interesting relationships between events often rely on the _____ method.
5. Questions about the behavior of large groups of people are often best answered with the _____ method.

Connections
1. ___ non-experimental methods
2. ___ experimental method
3. ___ naturalistic observation
4. ___ correlational method
5. ___ clinical method
6. ___ survey method

a. used to look at the relationships between events
b. usually used to study mental disorders
c. involves asking questions about the behavior of large groups of people
d. studying the behavior of humans and other animals in their natural settings
e. research method that can show cause-and-effect relationships
f. group of research methods that cannot show cause-and-effect

60

Check Your Memory

1. TRUE or FALSE The best way to identify cause-and-effect relationships is to use the clinical method.
2. TRUE or FALSE The study of mental disorders and therapies used to treat them are usually conducted using the survey method.
3. TRUE or FALSE When psychologists poll large groups of people, they are using the case study method.
4. TRUE or FALSE If you wanted to describe the behavior of squirrels, rabbits, and other wildlife as it unfolds in the forest and meadows in your area, you would most likely use naturalistic observation.
5. TRUE or FALSE Psychologists make measurements to discover relationships between events when they are using the correlational method.

Module 1.6 Nonexperimental Research Methods
Naturalistic Observation

Language Development Guide

tool-making: constructing any device that makes work easier, including animals that use twigs to get food

tampered (with): interfered; meddled

naturalists: biologist and other scientists who observe animals where they normally live

minimized: reduced; decreased

concealing: hiding

miniaturized: made smaller

"critter cams": video/audio recorders worn by wild animals so information can be gained about their behavior and environment

New Caledonian crows: tool-making birds (crows) that live on islands in the South Pacific

forage: hunt; look for

clever: smart

primates: classification (order) that includes humans, monkeys, and apes

selected: chosen; preferred

labeled: placed in a particular category

"mentally retarded": seen by many as an offensive term for individuals that have an intellectual disability

"normal": having no intellectual, learning, or emotional disability; being average or typical in all respects

ratings: scores along a scale

consequences: end result; effect; outcome

attributing: assigning; attaching

temptation: attraction to; being drawn in

cologne: scent for the body that is not as long-lasting or as strong as perfume

irritates: stings

Recite and Review

1. Jane Goodall discovered that chimpanzees use grass stems as tools to obtain termites as food. Her discovery was made using naturalistic observation, which is a(n) _____ research method.
2. Naturalistic observation allows us to study behavior that has not been _____ with by outside influences.
3. Regarding the goals of psychology, the naturalistic observation method allows us to only meet the goal of _____.

4. Since participants who know they are being observed tend to change their behavior, a researcher may choose to use a hidden video camera to record the participants behavior and, thus, minimize the observer _____.
5. During observational studies, the tendency for some observers to see what they expect to see or to record only selected details is called the observer _____.
6. Your cat has just jumped up on your table and drank your milk. You scold your cat, and then tell your friend that you can tell that your cat feels "guilty" about drinking your milk because of the "sad" look on his face. Your statement about the "guilt" of your cat illustrates a limitation in observation known as the _____ error.
7. Psychologists doing naturalistic studies make a special effort to minimize bias by keeping a detailed summary of data and observations known as a(n) _____.

Connections

1. ___ naturalistic observation
2. ___ observer effect
3. ___ observer bias
4. ___ anthropomorphic error
5. ___ observational record
6. ___ natural setting

a. typical environment in which a person or animal lives
b. changes in a subject's behavior brought about by an awareness of being observed
c. allows descriptions of behavior as it unfolds naturally
d. attributing human thoughts, feelings, and motives to animals as a way to explain their behavior
e. detailed summary of data and observations
f. observer distorts perceptions to match expectations

Check Your Memory

1. TRUE or FALSE Naturalistic observation allows us to meet the goal of understanding in psychological research.
2. TRUE or FALSE Jane Goodall's study of chimpanzees made use of the correlational method.
3. TRUE or FALSE Naturalistic observation allows us to study behavior that has not been tampered with or altered by outside influences.
4. TRUE or FALSE Concealing the observer helps to reduce the observer effect.
5. TRUE or FALSE The observer bias is a problem in which observers see what they expect to see or record only selected details.
6. TRUE or FALSE An error in attributing human thoughts, feelings, or motives to animals as a way of explaining their behavior is referred to as the Barnum effect.
7. TRUE or FALSE An observational record is a detailed summary of data and observation with the most objective record being the use of video recording.

Critical Thinking Question

Attributing mischievous motives to a car that is not working properly is a thinking error similar to anthropomorphizing. T or F?

Module 1.6 Nonexperimental Research Methods
Correlational Studies

Language Development Guide

social popularity: being well-liked and admired by one's peers
degree: extent; amount; level of

coefficient (of correlation): a number showing the extent of the relationship
nonexistent: absent
zombie: mind-less
confident: sure
reiterate: repeat; say again

Recite and Review

1. A psychologist who studies the association between the IQs of parents and their children or between anxiety and test performance is using a(n) _____ method.
2. The coefficient of correlation indicates the strength and _____ of the relationship.
3. A +1.00 or -1.00 would both be described as _____ correlations.
4. Regarding its strength, a correlation coefficient of -.89 would be described as _____.
5. A correlation coefficient of _____ indicates that no relationship exists between the two events.
6. A correlational study found that as one's exercise time increases, one's stamina increases. This relationship illustrates a(n) _____ correlation.
7. A correlational study found that students who had poor grades in high school tended to have poor grades in college. This relationship illustrates a(n) _____ correlation.
8. As unauthorized cell phone usage by students increases in a classroom, attention to the teacher's lecture decreases. This relationship illustrates a(n) _____ correlation.
9. Correlations cannot demonstrate causation, but they do allow us to make _____.
10. If a psychologist discovers that the blood of patients with schizophrenia contains a certain chemical not found in the general population, it does not automatically mean that the chemical causes schizophrenia or having schizophrenia causes the chemical to form. It could be some unknown _____, such as the typical diet in mental hospitals.
11. The scatterplot at the right indicates a strong _____ correlation.

Connections

1. ___ correlated
2. ___ coefficient of correlation
3. ___ positive correlation
4. ___ negative correlation

5. ___ zero correlation

6. ___ third factor

7. ___ perfect correlation

a. only describes a +1.00 or a -1.00
b. increases in one measure are matched by decreases in the other
c. linked together in an orderly way
d. increases in one measure matched by increases in the other with decreases corresponding with decreases
e. sometimes the cause of an association between two events is really this
f. scatterplot:

g. expresses the strength and direction of the relationship between two events

Check Your Memory

1. TRUE or FALSE   A psychologist who found an association between beauty and social popularity most likely used an experimental method to show this cause-and-effect.
2. TRUE or FALSE   When two observations or events are correlated, this means they are linked together in an orderly way.
3. TRUE or FALSE   Coefficients of correlation express both the strength and the direction of the relationship between the two events.
4. TRUE or FALSE   Coefficients of correlation range from a +3.00 to a -3.00.
5. TRUE or FALSE   A correlation coefficient of +2.5 indicates a mathematical error has been made.
6. TRUE or FALSE   A correlation coefficient of -1.00 would indicate a very weak relationship between events.
7. TRUE or FALSE   In a negative correlation, decreases in one measure are matched by decreases in the other.
8. TRUE or FALSE   In a positive correlation, decreases in one measure are matched by increases in the other.
9. TRUE or FALSE   If you obtained a moderately negative correlation between the number of hours that students play computer games and their grades, this would indicate that playing computer games causes student's grades to decrease.

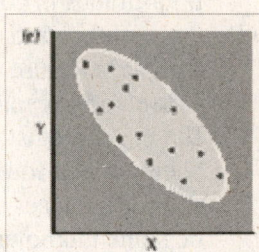

10. TRUE or FALSE   Correlational studies help us make predictions.
11. TRUE or FALSE   The scatterplot at the right indicates a strong positive correlation.

Module 1.6 Nonexperimental Research Methods

The Clinical Method

Language Development Guide

"genius": having very high IQ (greater than 140) and/or those who are exceptionally creative
rampage: wild, chaotic destructive activity
in-depth: thorough; very detailed
foreman: person in charge of a construction crew
impaled: run through; speared
surly: grumpy, irritable
foul-mouthed: crude; uses very offensive language
quadruplets: multiple births consisting of four babies born at the same time, often non-identical, but can be identical, or a combination of identical and non-identical offspring

Recite and Review

1. Many useful ideas about how to treat emotional problems have been provided by _____ studies of psychotherapy.
2. Since case studies are often thought of as accidents or natural events that provide psychological data, they are sometimes referred to as natural _____.
3. One remarkable case from the history of psychology was reported by Dr. J. M. Harlow in 1868 of a young foreman on a work crew, who had a 13-pound steel rod impaled into the front of his brain by a dynamite explosion. This young foreman's name was _____.

4. When Michael Melnick suffered a similar injury in 1981 to that experienced by the foreman in 1868, Melnick recovered completely, with no lasting ill effects, which shows why psychologists prefer controlled _____ and often use lab animals for studies of the brain.
5. The study of the Genain quadruplets, who all developed schizophrenia before age 25, is a classic _____ study in psychology that could only have been studied in this way.
6. The conclusions drawn from clinical observations are limited because case studies lack formal _____ groups.

Connections

1. ___ case study
2. ___ natural clinical tests
3. ___ Phineas Gage

4. ___ Michael Melnick
5. ___ Genain sisters

6. ___ formal control groups

a. what is lacking in the clinical method
b. developed schizophrenia before age 25
c. foreman in 1868 who experienced destruction of frontal brain matter with personality changes
d. in-depth focus on all aspects of a single person
e. accidents or other natural events that provide psychological data
f. carpenter in 1981 who experienced destruction of frontal brain matter with no personality changes

Check Your Memory

1. TRUE or FALSE   The clinical method would be used to study rare events, such as childhood "genius" and "rampage" school shootings.
2. TRUE or FALSE   Phineas Gage is remembered as the first psychologist to use the clinical method in research.
3. TRUE or FALSE   Case studies may sometimes be thought of as natural clinical tests, which are accidents or other natural events that provide psychological data.
4. TRUE or FALSE   Because case studies of individuals with the same brain injury have shown different reactions, psychologists prefer controlled experiments and often use lab animals for studies of the brain.
5. TRUE or FALSE   The case study of the four Genain sisters determined that their schizophrenia was completely caused by environmental influences.
6. TRUE or FALSE   Case studies lack formal control groups.

Module 1.6 Nonexperimental Research Methods
Survey Method—Here, Have a Sample

Language Development Guide
proportion: quantity; amount
blue-collar workers: non-professional workers, laborers, factory workers, service workers
ultimately: in the end
erred: made a mistake
fortunately: luckily
recruited: signed up; taken from
further: additionally
invalidate: cancel; undo
exaggerate: overstate
vulnerability: weakness; defenselessness

terrorist: a radical or fanatic who uses violence for political purposes

staged: set up in a certain way

natural event: something that happens without warning or influence by humans

artificial: an imitation; man-made, not natural

field experiments: experiments conducted outside the laboratory in as natural a setting
    as possible while still maintaining controlled conditions, ex. experiments conducted in schools

objection: protest; opposition to

conclusively: with certainty; definitely

coincidental: by accident; just two events occurring at the same time

Recite and Review

1. Public polling techniques are used to answer psychological question in the _____ method.
2. A small part of a larger population that accurately reflects the characteristics of the whole population is known as a representative _____.
3. When a representative part of a larger population is selected for a nation-wide study, it must include the same _____ of men, women, young, old, professionals, blue-collar workers, Republicans, Democrats, whites, African Americans, Native Americans, Latinos, Asians, and so on, as found in the population as a whole.
4. The best way to get a representative part of the larger population is to use _____ selection.
5. In the study you are conducting, the population was defined as all the students on your college campus, but you surveyed only the students in an honors section of college algebra. Your findings will not be representative of your population because your survey was based on a(n) _____ sample.
6. Today, a cost-effective way to reach very large groups of people is to use _____-based research.
7. The tendency for people to give "polite" or socially desirable answers to survey questions is called the _____.

Connections

1. ___ survey method

a. a smaller part of the larger group that accurately reflects characteristics of the whole group

2. ___ population

b. tendency to give "polite" or socially desirable answers

3. ___ representative sample

c. use of public polling techniques to answer psychological questions

4. ___ biased sample

d. smaller part of the group that does not accurately reflect the larger group from which it was drawn

5. ___ random selection

e. an entire group of animals or people belonging to a particular category

6. ___ courtesy bias

f. each member of the larger group has an equal chance of being in the representative smaller group

Check Your Memory

1. TRUE or FALSE   In the survey method, people in a representative sample are asked a series of carefully worded questions.
2. TRUE or FALSE   Representative samples are often obtained by randomly selecting who will be included as participants.

3. TRUE or FALSE   A good sample must include the same proportion of men, women, young, old, professionals, blue-collar workers, Republicans, Democrats, whites, African Americans, Native Americans, Latinos, Asians, and so on, as found in the population as a whole.
4. TRUE or FALSE   Modern surveys like the Gallup and Harris polls have not been very accurate erring on the average of 10 percent per poll since 1954.
5. TRUE or FALSE   Surveys conducted by popular magazines that require their readers to cut out the surveys in the magazine and mail them in to the magazine have been shown to be surprising accurate.
6. TRUE or FALSE   Biased samples can limit web-based research because it is not easy to control who actually answers online questionnaires.
7. TRUE or FALSE   Many people show a distinct courtesy bias when answering questions concerning sex, drinking or drug use, income, and church attendance.

Critical Thinking Question

A psychologist conducting a survey at a shopping mall (The Gallery of Wretched Excess) flips a coin before stopping passersby. If the coin shows heads, he interviews the person; if it shows tails, he skips that person. Has the psychologist obtained a random sample?

Module 1.7 Psychology in Action: Psychology in the Media

Psychology in the Media—Seeking Klingon Interpreter

Survey Question: How good is psychological information found in the popular media?

Language Development Guide

fiction: invented stories

"echo chamber": repeated sounds; real echo chambers are often used in audio recording for television programs

hoaxes: untrue stories or cheating schemes

half-truths: misinformation

urban legends: folklore; myths

Klingon: a warrior race in the science fiction series *Star Trek*

psychiatric patients: persons hospitalized for severe mental disorders

fluent: to speak effortlessly

incredible: hard to believe

astonishing: amazing; surprising

biofeedback: devices used to measure physical arousal responses, or the training therapy which uses biofeedback equipment to train control over one's arousal level

sleep-learning devices: tapes or CDs which play spoken language to you while you are sleeping

subliminal: stimuli presented outside of conscious awareness, below or above a perceptual threshold

extrasensory perception (ESP): purported ability to perceive events in ways that cannot be explained by known capacities of the sensory organs

testimonials: statements from individuals about their first-hand experience

preliminary: first round

stage mentalists: performances of purported ESP abilities for entertainment

charlatans: impostor; con artist

promoters: advertisers

corollary: the content of this statement follows from (is a result of) a previous statement

anecdotes: a brief story that is usually presented as a real event (but may not be)

relevant: important; significant

unsophisticated: simple, naïve (inexperienced)

susceptible: at risk

"neurolinguistic programming": technique used in a controversial large group awareness program that is purported to help people face fearful events, such as firewalking.

physicist: a scientist who studies matter and energy (physics)

callused: rough; hardened

transmits: passes on; conveys

presume: suppose; guess

foundation: basis; groundwork

lunar cycles: phases or changes in the moon's appearance

lunar effect: the false belief that the phases of the moon affect one's behavior

moonstruck: one's behavior being supposedly affected by the moon's phases (affected by a "bad moon rising")

bombarded: flooded; overrun by

comprehend: understand

Recite and Review

1. Psychology is a popular topic in contemporary media, but unfortunately, much of what you will encounter is based on _____ value rather than critical thinking or science.

2. Because the Internet is awash with rumors, hoaxes, half-truths, and urban legends, the authors of your textbook recommend that you "be _____" when you read these "incredible" and "astonishing stories."

3. Since information used to sell a product often reflects a desire for profit rather than the objective truth, it is always important to consider the _____ of information related to this advertised claim.

4. Magician James Randi is offering $1,000,000 to anyone who can demonstrate _____ abilities under controlled conditions, but as yet no one has passed the preliminary tests.

5. Jessica called an "advisor" who created the illusion that she knew private information about Jessica and could predict her future. Jessica believed these personal descriptions because the "advisor" stated these descriptions in vague, general terms, a tendency known as the _____ effect.

6. Advertisements that promise to reveal "the secret to unlimited joy" or "create a new personality in three sessions" are excellent examples of _____.

7. You caution your friend about the dangers of smoking, but he reminds you that his grandfather smoked from the time he was a young teen and lived to be 89 years old. Your friend has based his belief about smoking on a(n) single _____.

8. It is important to beware of the findings of "experiments" that were performed without _____ groups.

9. Your friend believes that crime rates are directly influenced by the rising and falling of the lunar cycles. However, your friend has failed to distinguish between correlation and _____.

10. You observe that your best friend is looking your way and is frowning. From this observation, you believe your friend is angry with you about something. You later find that she did not notice you were standing there and was frowning because she has a headache. In this case, you have failed to distinguish between observation and _____.

Connections

1. ___ importance of being skeptical

2. ___ consider the source of the information

3. ___ Barnum effect

4. ___ oversimplification

5. ___ individual cases

6. ___ importance of a control group

7. ___ distinguish correlation from causation

8. ___ distinguish observation from inference

a. You see a sign about a seminar on the "Three Steps to Love and Fulfillment in Marriage."

b. You know a life-long smoker who lived to be 95 years old.

c. An infomercial recommends a sleep-learning device that improves grades

d. You see an article about a special diet that was found to control hyperactivity in a group of 25 children.

e. Your personality description from the telephone psychic is surprising accurate.

f. If an increase in births occurs with the full moon, then lunar cycles affect birth rates.

g. If you observe a person laughing, then he or she must be happy.

h. You read on the internet that giant alligators are living in the sewers of New York.

Check Your Memory

1. TRUE or FALSE   Regarding psychology in the media, a critical thinker should be skeptical of "astonishing" findings and should consider the source of the information.

2. TRUE or FALSE   At least some psychic ability is necessary to perform as a stage mentalist.

3. TRUE or FALSE   The personality descriptions and predictions made by psychic advisors on the telephone are often believed by their customers due to the Barnum effect.

4. TRUE or FALSE   An example of oversimplification is provided by websites devoted to videos that promises to reveal "the secret to good health" or the "the secret to wealth."

5. TRUE or FALSE   Individual cases described in the media or testimonials cannot establish proof of what is true in general.

6. TRUE or FALSE   Successful fire walking requires the person to be trained in neurolinguistic programming.

7. TRUE or FALSE   If a horticulture class reported that they increased the growth rate of plants by playing classical music in the greenhouse 24 hours a day, this would be considered a valid experiment.

8. TRUE or FALSE   Violent crime has been shown to rise and fall with lunar cycles.

9. TRUE or FALSE   If you see a person laughing, it would be accurate and appropriate to infer that this person is happy.

10. TRUE or FALSE   The inferences, opinions, and interpretations of an expert on the causes of mental illness have no value.

Critical Thinking Question

Many parents believe that children become "hyperactive" when they eat too much sugar, and some early studies seemed to confirm this connection. However, we now know that eating sugar rarely has any effect on children. Why do you think that sugar appears to cause hyperactivity?

Final Survey and Review—Completion

Module 1.1 The Science of Psychology
Psychology—Behave Yourself!
Survey Questions: What is psychology and what are its goals?

1. Psychology is the scientific study of mental processes and _____.
2. Remembering what you did last weekend would be considered a(n) _____ behavior.
3. Psychologists engage in critical thinking as they gather and analyze _____ evidence to answer   questions about behavior.
4. Anna is studying the physical and mental changes that occur in children as they mature into adolescents. Anna is most likely a(n) _____ psychologist.
5. Persuasion, interpersonal attraction, and obedience are topics of interest for _____ psychologists.
6. If Juan uses rats to study how humans might react to a particular drug to treat Parkinson's disease, Juan   is using a(n) _____ model in his research.
7. As a science, psychology's goals are to describe, understand, _____, and control behavior.

Module 1.2 Critical Thinking and the Scientific Method in Psychology
Critical Thinking—Take It with a Grain of Salt
Survey Question: What is critical thinking?

8. Critical thinking involves evaluating comparing, analyzing, critiquing, and synthesizing information and is a type of _____.
9. Critical thinking requires an open _____.

Module 1.2 Critical Thinking and the Scientific Method in Psychology
Pseudopsychologies—Palms, Planets, and Personality
Survey Question: How does psychology differ from false explanations of behavior?

10. Brian believes that his personality is revealed by the shape of his skull and the bumps on his head. Brian believes in the pseudopsychology known as _____.
11. Although handwriting analysis cannot be used to determine personality traits, it can be used to detect   _____.
12. When Terrence had consulted a telephone "psychic advisor," he believed the flattering statements made about his personality, a tendency known as _____.

Module 1.2 Critical Thinking and the Scientific Method in Psychology
Scientific Research—How to Think Like a Psychologist
Survey Question: How is the scientific method applied in psychological research?

13. Dr. Sanchez is using a form of critical thinking based on careful collection of evidence, accurate description and measurement, precise definition, controlled observation, and repeatable results. Dr. Sanchez is using the _____.
14. The exact procedures used to represent a concept are referred to as the concept's _____ definition.
15. Darra is getting an overview of the entire article by reading the brief summary at the beginning of the article known as the _____.

70

Module 1.3 History and Contemporary Perspectives
A Brief History of Psychology—Psychology's Family Album
Survey Question: How did the field of psychology emerge?

16. The first school of thought in psychology was a kind of "mental chemistry" based on introspection and was called _____.
17. John B. Watson and B.F. Skinner belonged to the school of thought in psychology known as _____.
18. Threatening thoughts are held out of awareness through a process known as repression, according to _____ psychology.
19. Subjective factors, such as self-image, self-evaluation, and frame of reference would be emphasized by _____ psychologists.
20. The first woman to be awarded a Ph.D. in psychology was _____.

Module 1.3 History and Contemporary Perspectives
Psychology Today— Three Complementary Perspectives on Behavior
Survey Question: What are the contemporary perspectives in psychology?

21. The biopsychology view seeks to explain behavior through activity of the brain and nervous system, physiology, genetics, biochemistry, and the _____ system.
22. As a counselor, Joshua uses many different psychological perspectives and techniques to help his clients. Joshua would be considered a(n) _____ psychologist.

Module 1.4 Psychologists and Their Specialties
Psychologists—Guaranteed Not to Shrink
Survey Question: What are the major specialties in psychology?

23. While severe mental disorders would most likely be treated in a hospital setting by a clinical psychologist, milder adjustment problems would most likely be treated by a(n) _____ psychologist.
24. Rather than emphasizing research, a Psy.D. degree emphasizes _____ skills.
25. Psychologists in the U.S. states of Louisiana and _____ can now legally prescribe drugs.
26. Dr. Javis is studying how to help patients in the early stages of Alzheimer's disease retain their memory skills. Dr. Javis is conducting _____ research.

Module 1.5 The Psychology Experiment
The Psychology Experiment—Where Effect Meets Cause
Survey Question: How is an experiment performed?

27. You are conducting an experiment to determine if a new math tutorial increases math scores in fifth graders. The math tutorial is the _____ variable.
28. In an experiment to determine whether the LISAN method improves students' grades, the intelligence and motivation of the students would be _____ variables.
29. In an experiment to determine if the use of time-out decreases oppositional behavior in preschoolers, the time-out procedure would be not be used with the _____ group.

Module 1.5 The Psychology Experiment
Double Blind—On Placebos and Self-Fulfilling Prophecies
Survey Question: What is a double-blind experiment?

30. The placebo effect is an example of the _____ bias.

71

31. You are conducting an experiment to determine if a new drug controls the mood swings of people with bipolar disorder. Your assistant prepares the packets containing the real drug and the placebo, but neither you nor the participants know who will be receiving the real drug. You are conducting a(n) _____-blind study.

32. Three areas of ethical concern in behavioral research are the invasion of privacy, the use of deception, and the risk of lasting _____.

Module 1.6 Nonexperimental Research Methods
Nonexperimental Psychological Research—Different Strokes
Survey Question: What nonexperimental research methods do psychologists use?

33. Dr. Omar is studying the schizotypal personality disorder. He will most likely use a nonexperimental method known as the _____ method to study this rare condition.

34. For his doctoral research, Tony plans to conduct a nation-wide poll of the opinions of people regarding off-shore oil drilling. Tony will be using the nonexperimental method known as the _____ method.

Module 1.6 Nonexperimental Research Methods
Naturalistic Observation

35. Naturalists must be careful to keep their distance and avoid "making friends" with the animals they are watching, since this could change the animal's behavior, leading to a form of bias known as the _____.

36. The temptation to assume that an animal is "angry," "jealous," "bored," or "guilty" known as the _____ error.

Module 1.6 Nonexperimental Research Methods
Correlational Studies

37. The coefficient of correlation indicates the direction and _____ of the relationship.

38. A correlational study found that as one's exercise time increases, one's depressive symptoms decrease. This relationship illustrates a(n) _____ correlation.

Module 1.6 Nonexperimental Research Methods
The Clinical Method

39. The case study method was used to study the brain injury of _____ in 1868 and Michael Melnick in 1981.

40. A case study was used to study the Genain quadruplets, who all developed the mental disorder called _____ before the age of 25.

Module 1.6 Nonexperimental Research Methods
Survey Method—Here, Have a Sample

41. A representative sample accurately reflects the characteristics of the larger group known as the _____.

42. People often give socially desirable answers to questions, such as how often they give money to charities. This tendency is known as the _____ bias.

Module 1.7 Psychology in Action: Psychology in the Media
Psychology in the Media—Seeking Klingon Interpreter
Survey Question: How good is psychological information found in the popular media?

43. Tyron is very skeptical of an article that describes "Four Short Steps to Happiness" because this is a(n) _____ of a very complex subject.

72

44. Your friend tells you that her brother increased his grades by a grade level by listening to a motivational tape once a week. You question this grade-improvement method because a(n) _____ does not tell what is true in general.

45. You observe what looks like a man attacking a woman; and then you realize that he is performing the Heimlich Maneuver because she is choking. This illustrates that one must distinguish between observation and _____.

Final Survey and Review—Matching

Module 1.1 The Science of Psychology

1. ___ overt behavior
2. ___ research method
3. ___ biopsychologists
4. ___ description
5. ___ prediction
6. ___ forensic psychologists
7. ___ cognitive psychologists
8. ___ social psychologists
9. ___ animal model
10. ___ control

a. interested in the topics of interpersonal attraction, leadership, and attitudes
b. goal of psychology that involves classifying and naming behaviors
c. interested in problem-solving and memory
d. goal of psychology that involves altering conditions that affect behavior
e. interested in how behavior relates to the activities of the nervous system
f. systematic approach to answering scientific questions
g. discovering principles that apply to humans by using other species
h. directly observable actions and responses
i. apply psychological principles to legal issues
j. goal of psychology involved in accurately forecasting behavior

Module 1.2 Critical Thinking and the Scientific Method in Psychology

1. ___ critical thinking
2. ___ phrenology
3. ___ graphology
4. ___ uncritical acceptance
5. ___ confirmation bias
6. ___ Barnum effect
7. ___ hypothesis
8. ___ theory
9. ___ operational definition
10. ___ abstract

a. brief summary of the study and its findings
b. remember information that fits one's expectations while forgetting discrepancies
c. system of ideas designed to interrelate concepts and facts
d. claimed personality traits revealed by the shape of one's skull
e. tendency to consider a personal description accurate if it is stated in very general terms
f. allows unobservable ideas to be tested in real-world terms
g. to reflect on, evaluate, compare, analyze, critique, and synthesize information
h. tendency to believe generally positive or flattering descriptions of oneself
i. educated guess about the relationship between variables
j. claimed handwriting reveals personality traits

73

Module 1.3 History and Contemporary Perspectives

1. ____ Gestalt psychology
2. ____ behaviorism
3. ____ psychodynamic

4. ____ humanistic psychology
5. ____ functionalism
6. ____ structuralism
7. ____ social norms
8. ____ positive psychology
9. ____ sociocultural view
10. ____ women and minorities in psychology
11. ____ eclectic

a. Watson, Skinner, and conditioning
b. Freud and the Neo-Freudians
c. interactionist view that sees behavior as being influenced by the environment in which a person grows up
d. "mental chemistry" and introspection
e. drawing from many perspectives and approaches
f. Washburn, Sumner, and Prosser
g. "the whole is greater than the sum of its parts"
h. Maslow, Rogers, and self-actualization
i. influenced by the work of Charles Darwin
j. study of human strengths, virtues, and optimal behavior
k. rules that define acceptable and expected behavior for members of a group

Module 1.4 Psychologists and Their Specialties

1. ____ psychologist

2. ____ psychiatrist

3. ____ psychoanalyst

4. ____ licensed counselor

5. ____ psychiatric social worker

6. ____ basic research

7. ____ applied research

a. medical doctor with additional training in diagnosis and treatment of mental disorders
b. has master's degree and supervised experience in practical helping skills, but does not treat serious mental disorders
c. studies conducted to solve immediate practical problems
d. Ph.D. or M.D. with additional training in Freudian techniques
e. studies conducted to seek knowledge for its own sake
f. types of this profession include forensic, school, comparative, and industrial-organizational
g. trained to apply social science principles to help patients in clinics and hospitals, and may conduct home visits

Module 1.5 The Psychology Experiment

1. ____ independent variable

2. ____ dependent variable

3. ____ extraneous variable

4. ____ control group

5. ____ statistically significant

6. ____ random assignment

7. ____ placebo effect

a. evenly balances the personal differences in the two research groups
b. would occur by chance in less than 5 experiments out of 100
c. prediction that prompts people to act in ways that make the prediction come true
d. changes in behavior due to participant's expectations that drug will have some effect
e. provides point of reference for comparison with the scores of the experimental group
f. subjects do not know which research group they are in, but experimenter does
g. conditions excluded from affecting the outcome of the experiment

8. ___ self-fulfilling prophecy
9. ___ single-blind experiment
10. ___ double-blind experiment

h. neither subjects nor experimenter know who is in which research group
i. the results of the experiment
j. altered by the experimenter and is the suspected cause for difference in behavior

Module 1.6 Nonexperimental Research Methods /
Module 1.7 Psychology in Action: Psychology in the Media

1. ___ observer effect
2. ___ observer bias
3. ___ anthropomorphic error
4. ___ positive correlation
5. ___ negative correlation
6. ___ case study
7. ___ survey method
8. ___ population
9. ___ courtesy bias
10. ___ inference
11. ___ causation

a. critical thinkers must distinguish between observation and this
b. critical thinkers must distinguish between correlation and this
c. an entire group of animals or people belonging to a particular category
d. attributing human thoughts, feelings, and motives to animals as a way to explain their behavior
e. increases in one measure matched by increases in the other with decreases corresponding with decreases
f. observer distorts perceptions to match expectations
g. in-depth focus on all aspects of a single person
h. increases in one measure are matched by decreases in the other
i. use of public polling techniques to answer psychological questions
j. changes in a person's behavior brought about by an awareness of being observed
k. tendency to give socially desirable answers

Final Survey and Review—True or False

Module 1.1 The Science of Psychology
Psychology—Behave Yourself!
Survey Questions: What is psychology and what are its goals?

1. TRUE or FALSE   Daydreaming would be classified as a covert behavior.
2. TRUE or FALSE   Through scientific research it was found that almost half of the human population never dream.
3. TRUE or FALSE   Cognitive psychologists are interested in studying personality traits, motivation, and individual differences.
4. TRUE or FALSE   Forensic psychologists study and compare the behavior of different species, especially animals.
5. TRUE or FALSE   Only a small percentage of psychological studies involve animals.
6. TRUE or FALSE   The goal of prediction refers to altering conditions that affect behavior.
7. TRUE or FALSE   The naming and classifying of a behavior meets the goal of description in psychology.

75

Module 1.2 Critical Thinking and the Scientific Method in Psychology
Critical Thinking—Take It with a Grain of Salt
Survey Question: What is critical thinking?

8. TRUE or FALSE   Authority or claimed expertise does not automatically make an idea true.
9. TRUE or FALSE   One of the principles of critical thinking is that few truths transcend the need for commonsense reasoning.

Module 1.2 Critical Thinking and the Scientific Method in Psychology
Pseudopsychologies—Palms, Planets, and Personality
Survey Question: How does psychology differ from false explanations of behavior?

10. TRUE or FALSE   Phrenology claimed that personality traits are revealed through handwriting analysis.
11. TRUE or FALSE   Research has found no association between the "compatibility" of couples' astrological signs and their marriage and divorce rates.
12. TRUE or FALSE   When we remember the few correct predictions made by a psychic but forget the incorrect ones, we are exhibiting the confirmation bias.

Module 1.2 Critical Thinking and the Scientific Method in Psychology
Scientific Research—How to Think Like a Psychologist
Survey Question: How is the scientific method applied in psychological research?

13. TRUE or FALSE   Making observations is the first step in the scientific method.
14. TRUE or FALSE   A theory is a testable hunch or educated guess about behavior.
15. TRUE or FALSE   If you wanted to get an overview of a study and its findings without reading the entire article, one should read the discussion part of article.

Module 1.3 History and Contemporary Perspectives
A Brief History of Psychology—Psychology's Family Album
Survey Question: How did the field of psychology emerge?

16. TRUE or FALSE   Carl Rogers brought the psychological ideas of Wilhelm Wundt to American and called these ideas functionalism.
17. TRUE or FALSE   Skinner advocated the use of punishment because it teaches correct responses.
18. TRUE or FALSE   Ivan Pavlov and Max Wertheimer modified Freud's ideas and became known as humanists.
19. TRUE or FALSE   Inez Beverly Prosser was the first African-American woman to be awarded a Ph.D. in psychology in America.

Module 1.3 History and Contemporary Perspectives
Psychology Today—Three Complementary Perspectives on Behavior
Survey Question: What are the contemporary perspectives in psychology?

20. TRUE or FALSE   The humanistic view takes a neutral, scientific, somewhat mechanistic view of human nature.
21. TRUE or FALSE   Psychodynamic psychologists see behavior as being controlled by conditioned responses to external stimuli.
22. TRUE or FALSE   Rules that define acceptable and expected behavior for members of various groups are referred to as social norms.

Module 1.4 Psychologists and Their Specialties
Psychologists—Guaranteed Not to Shrink
Survey Question: What are the major specialties in psychology?
23. TRUE or FALSE   "Shrink" is the slang term for psychiatrists, but not for psychologists.
24. TRUE or FALSE   Presently, psychologists are not allowed to prescribe medication in any of the 50 states of the United States.
25. TRUE or FALSE   Studying ways to improve the memories of eyewitnesses to crimes would be an example of applied research.

Module 1.5 The Psychology Experiment
The Psychology Experiment—Where Effect Meets Cause
Survey Question: How is an experiment performed?
26. TRUE or FALSE   In an experiment to test whether cell phone use affects driving ability, previous driving experience would be a dependent variable.
27. TRUE or FALSE   In an experiment to test whether listening to music while studying improves test grades, the control group would study in a quiet room without music.
28. TRUE or FALSE   To be statistically significant, a difference must be large enough so that it would occur by chance in less than 5 experiments out of 100.

Module 1.5 The Psychology Experiment
Double Blind—On Placebos and Self-Fulfilling Prophecies
Survey Question: What is a double-blind experiment?
29. TRUE or FALSE   After a person takes a placebo, the effect created is an imaginary one, since there is no reduction in brain activity linked to taking the placebo.
30. TRUE or FALSE   A prediction that prompts people to act in ways that make the prediction come true is known as the Barnum effect
31. TRUE or FALSE   When the research subjects nor the experimenters with direct contact with the subject know who is in the experimental or control group, the arrangement is   called a single-blind experiment.

Module 1.6 Nonexperimental Research Methods
Nonexperimental Psychological Research—Different Strokes
Survey Question: What nonexperimental research methods do psychologists use?
32. TRUE or FALSE   The best way to identify cause-and-effect relationships is to use a correlational method.
33. TRUE or FALSE   When psychologists poll large groups of people, they are using the survey method.

Module 1.6 Nonexperimental Research Methods
Naturalistic Observation
34. TRUE or FALSE   Naturalistic observation only allows us to meet the goal of description in psychological research.
35. TRUE or FALSE   Concealing the observer helps to reduce the observer bias.
36. TRUE or FALSE   An error in attributing human thoughts, feelings, or motives to animals as a way of explaining their behavior is referred to as the anthropomorphic error.

Module 1.6 Nonexperimental Research Methods
Correlational Studies

37. TRUE or FALSE   Coefficients of correlation range from a +1.00 to a -1.00.

38. TRUE or FALSE   In a negative correlation, decreases in one measure are matched by increases in the other.

39. TRUE or FALSE   The scatterplot to the right shows a very strong positive correlation.

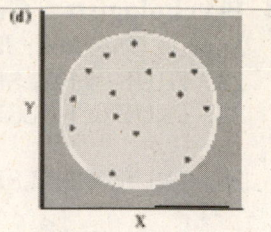

Module 1.6 Nonexperimental Research Methods
The Clinical Method

40. TRUE or FALSE   The case study of the Genain brothers was conducted because all of them had experienced frontal lobe damage due to work-related injuries.

41. TRUE or FALSE   The clinical method is the only nonexperimental method that has a formal control group.

Module 1.6 Nonexperimental Research Methods
Survey Method—Here, Have a Sample

42. TRUE or FALSE   The Gallup poll has erred in its election predictions by only 1.5 percent since 1954.

43. TRUE or FALSE   The population is defined as the a smaller group that is randomly selected so that it accurately reflects the entire representative sample.

Module 1.7 Psychology in Action: Psychology in the Media
Psychology in the Media—Seeking Klingon Interpreter
Survey Question: How good is psychological information found in the popular media?

44. TRUE or FALSE   Examples, anecdotes, single cases, and testimonials are all potentially deceptive because they do not tell us what is true in general.

45. TRUE or FALSE   Anybody with reasonably callused feet can walk over a bed of coals without being burned.

Mastery Test

1. Mental processes, such as thinking and daydreaming, would be considered _____ behavior.
   a. anterograde
   b. retrograde
   c. covert
   d. overt

2. Who among the following would most likely study the behavior of elephants and gorillas?
   a. developmental psychologist
   b. comparative psychologist
   c. environmental psychologist
   d. forensic psychologist

78

3. Dr. Alejaro studies how people conform in group settings and obey authorities. Dr. Alejaro is most likely a(n) _____ psychologist.
    a. comparative
    b. environmental
    c. social
    d. developmental

4. An engineering psychologist helps redesign an airplane to make it safer to fly. The psychologist's work reflects which of psychology's goals?
    a. understanding
    b. control
    c. prediction
    d. description

5. When critically evaluating claims about behavior it is important to also evaluate the
    a. source of anecdotal evidence.
    b. credentials of an authority.
    c. quality of the evidence.
    d. strength of one's intuition.

6. Which of the following pairs is most different?
    a. pseudo-psychology — critical thinking
    b. graphology — pseudo-psychology
    c. palmistry — phrenology
    d. psychology — empirical evidence

7. The German anatomy teacher Franz Gall popularized
    a. palmistry.
    b. phrenology.
    c. graphology.
    d. astrology.

8. A tendency to believe flattering descriptions of oneself is called
    a. the Barnum effect.
    b. the astrologer's dilemma.
    c. the confirmation bias.
    d. uncritical acceptance.

9. In an experiment, hunger is described as the subject having had no food or beverage, except water, for eight hours. This description is referred to as a(n)
    a. estimated value.
    b. theoretical element.
    c. operational definition.
    d. hypothesis.

10. In his research report, Dr. Bradford provided background information and all prior research done on his subject in the _____ part of the research report.
    a. results
    b. discussion
    c. abstract
    d. introduction

11. Who among the following placed the greatest emphasis on introspection?
    a. Watson
    b. Wertheimer
    c. Washburn
    d. Wundt

12. Which pair of persons had the most similar ideas?
    a. Titchener — Skinner
    b. James — Darwin
    c. Watson — Rogers
    d. Wertheimer — Maslow

13. The behaviorist definition of psychology clearly places great emphasis on
    a. unconscious conflicts.
    b. free will.
    c. psychodynamic responses.
    d. conditioned responses.

14. Appreciating an orchestra playing Mozart's fifth symphony more than a musician playing a solo on a clarinet reflects _____ psychology.
    a. Gestalt
    b. cognitive
    c. behavioral
    d. biopsychology

15. The first African American man and woman to be awarded a Ph.D. in psychology in America were
    a. Sumner and Prosser.
    b. Rogers and Maslow.
    c. Rank and Erikson.
    d. Perls and Milgram.

16. The idea that threatening thoughts are sometimes repressed would be of most interest to a
    a. structuralist.
    b. psychoanalyst.
    c. humanist.
    d. Gestaltist.

17. "A neutral, reductionistic, mechanistic view of human nature." This best describes which viewpoint?
    a. psychodynamic
    b. humanistic
    c. psychoanalytic
    d. biopsychological

18. Depending on what will work best with his clients, Dr. Carlson may use behavioral, cognitive, or humanistic techniques. By drawing from these many sources, Dr. Carlson would best be described as a(n) _____ psychologist.
   a. psychodynamic
   b. eclectic
   c. comparative
   d. sociocultural

19. Rather than treating people for severe mental disorders, Mara is a psychologist who treats people for milder adjustment disorders on an out-patient basis. Mara is most likely a(n) _____ psychologist.
   a. counseling
   b. clinical
   c. social
   d. developmental

20. Who among the following is most likely to treat the physical causes of psychological problems and is able to prescribe medication in all 50 states of the United States?
   a. counseling
   b. psychoanalyst
   c. forensic psychologist
   d. psychiatrist

21. If you are conducting research to determine how sensitive newborns are to various smells, you would be conducting _____ research.
   a. applied
   b. basic
   c. archetypal
   d. humanistic

22. Experiments show cause-and-effect relationships with the cause being the _____ variable.
   a. extraneous
   b. dependent
   c. independent
   d. control

23. In an experiment on the effects of sleep deprivation on the reading scores of elementary school children, reading scores are the _____ variable.
   a. control
   b. independent
   c. dependent
   d. reference

24. In an experiment on the effects of exercise on adolescents' mood levels, the group that would not exercise would be the _____ group.
   a. control
   b. independent
   c. dependent
   d. extraneous

25. Dr. Raymond is conducting an experiment on a new tutorial for psychology students. One group will be complete the tutorial, while another group of students will not. To equalize the intelligence and motivation of the psychology students in the two groups, Dr. Raymond should use
   a. extraneous selection.
   b. random assignment.
   c. independent control.
   d. participant replication.

26. In Dr. Shay's experiment, she obtained results that would occur by chance in less than five experiments out of 100. Dr. Shay's results
   a. are invalid.
   b. are statistically significant.
   c. cannot be replicated.
   d. allow prediction but do not causation.

27. Claire was given a sugar pill by her doctor for back pain. Soon after taking this pill, Claire stated that she was experiencing no pain. Claire is experiencing a(n)
   a. anthropomorphic error.
   b. placebo effect.
   c. somatization bias.
   d. psychosomatic complication.

28. In testing the effectiveness of a new medication, Dr. Amos as well as his participants will be unaware of who received the real medication and the inactive substance in this study. Dr. Amos is using a _____-blind experiment.
   a. zero
   b. single
   c. double
   d. control

29. Jake is conducting a study using naturalistic observation, while Kelly is using the clinical method in her research. Both Jake and Kelly are using _____ methods.
   a. experimental
   b. nonexperimental
   c. correlational
   d. survey

30. Terri attaches miniature "critter cams" to 10 stray cats in order to study their behavior. The use of these miniature cameras will minimize the
   a. confirmation bias.
   b. Barnum effect.
   c. observer effect.
   d. placebo effect.

31. A psychologist studying lowland gorillas should be careful to avoid the
   a. anthropomorphic error.
   b. placebo effect.
   c. confirmation bias.
   d. Barnum effect.

32. The graph at the right shows a _____ correlation.
   a. zero
   b. positive
   c. negative
   d. causal

33. Which of the following is the STRONGEST correlation?
   a. +1.35
   b. -.93
   c. +.32
   d. -.02

34. As the temperature increases in the classroom, the sleepiness of the students increases. This illustrates a _____ correlation.
   a. zero
   b. positive
   c. negative
   d. causal

35. Which of the following correlation coefficients indicates a perfect relationship?
   a. -1.00
   b. 100.0
   c. +2.00
   d. 0.00

36. Which method would most likely be used to study the effects of tumors in the frontal lobes of human subjects?
   a. sampling method
   b. correlational method
   c. clinical method
   d. experimental method

37. You are conducting a survey of the voters in your state or province. You will be randomly selecting 200 registered voters to contact by phone. These 200 voters would be considered the
   a. population.
   b. representative sample.
   c. control group.
   d. extraneous group.

38. You are conducting a survey regarding the type and amount of alcohol people consume on a weekly basis. Replies to questions, such as this one, are not always truthful due to the
   a. confirmation bias.
   b. Barnum effect.
   c. courtesy bias.
   d. halo effect.

39. A teacher reports to her principal that the new note-taking strategy that she taught increased the students' test grades on the World War II exam. Her principal reminds the teacher that you cannot conclude that the new note-taking strategy affected the students' grades because
    a. the placebo effect was not considered.
    b. only a correlation can establish causation.
    c. no correlation was computed.
    d. there was no control group.

40. A person who is observed crying may not be sad. This suggests that it is important to distinguish between
    a. individual cases and generalizations.
    b. correlation and causation.
    c. control groups and experimental groups.
    d. observation and inference.

Chapter 2: Brain and Behavior

Chapter Overview

Ultimately, all behavior can be traced to the activity of neurons. Sensations, thoughts, feelings, motives, actions, memories, and all other human capacities are associated with brain activities and structures. The firing of an action potential (nerve impulse) is basically an electrical event. Communication between neurons is chemical: Neurotransmitters cross the synapse, attach to receptor sites, and excite or inhibit the receiving cell. Chemicals called neuropeptides appear to regulate activity in the brain. By combining information, neurons act as simple computers, which become very powerful when they operate in parallel as neural networks. The brain's circuitry is not static. The brain can "rewire" itself and even grow new neurons in response to changing environmental conditions.

The nervous system can be divided into the central nervous system and the peripheral nervous system, which includes the somatic (bodily) and autonomic (involuntary) nervous systems. The brain carries out most of the "computing" in the nervous system. The spinal cord connects the brain to the peripheral nervous system and can process simple reflex arcs. The peripheral nervous system carries sensory information to the brain and motor commands to the body. "Vegetative" and automatic bodily processes are controlled by the autonomic nervous system, which has a sympathetic branch and a parasympathetic branch. Neurons and nerves in the peripheral nervous system can often regenerate. At present, damage in the central nervous system is usually permanent, although scientists are working on ways to repair damaged neural tissue.

Brain structure is investigated though dissection and less intrusive CT scans and MRI scans. A major brain research strategy involves localization of function to link specific structures in the brain with specific psychological or behavioral functions. Brain function is investigated through clinical case studies, electrical stimulation, ablation, deep lesioning, electrical recording, and microelectrode recording, as well as less intrusive EEG recording, PET scans, and fMRI scans.

The human brain is marked by advanced corticalization, or enlargement of the cerebral cortex. The left cerebral hemisphere contains speech or language "centers" in most people. It also specializes in writing, calculating, judging time and rhythm, and ordering complex movements. The right hemisphere is largely nonverbal. It excels at spatial and perceptual skills, visualization, and recognition of patterns, faces, and melodies. The left hemisphere is good at analysis and it processes small details sequentially. The right hemisphere detects overall patterns; it processes information simultaneously and holistically. "Split brains" can be created by cutting the corpus callosum. The split-brain individual shows a remarkable degree of independence between the right and left hemispheres.

The most basic functions of the lobes of the cerebral cortex are as follows: frontal lobes (motor control, speech, abstract thought, and sense of self); parietal lobes (bodily sensation); temporal lobes (hearing and language); occipital lobes (vision). Damage to any of these areas will impair the named functions. Primary sensory and motor areas are found on the lobes of the cerebral cortex. Association areas on the cortex are neither sensory nor motor in function. They are related to more complex skills such as language, memory, recognition, and problem solving. Damage to either Broca's area or Wernicke's area causes speech and language problems known as aphasias.

The brain can be subdivided into the forebrain, midbrain, and hindbrain. The subcortex includes hindbrain and midbrain brain structures as well as the lower parts of the forebrain, below the cortex. The medulla contains centers essential for reflex control of heart rate, breathing, and other "vegetative" functions. The cerebellum maintains coordination, posture, and muscle tone. The reticular formation directs sensory and motor messages, and part of it, known as the RAS, acts as an activating system for the cerebral cortex. The thalamus carries sensory information to the cortex. The hypothalamus exerts powerful control over eating, drinking, sleep cycles, body temperature, and other basic motives and behaviors. The limbic system is strongly related to emotion. It also contains distinct reward and punishment areas and an area known as the hippocampus that is important for forming memories.

Endocrine glands serve as a chemical communication system within the body. The hormones from the endocrine glands entering the bloodstream affect behavior, moods, and personality. Many of the endocrine glands are influenced by the pituitary (the "master gland"), which is, in turn, influenced by the hypothalamus. Thus, the brain controls the body through both the fast nervous system and the slower endocrine system.

The vast majority of people are right-handed and therefore left-brain dominant for motor skills. Over 90 percent of right-handed persons and about 70 percent of the left-handed also produce speech from the left hemisphere. Brain dominance and brain activity determine if you are right-handed, left-handed, or ambidextrous. Most people are strongly right-handed. A minority are strongly left-handed. A few have moderate or mixed hand preferences or they are ambidextrous. Thus, handedness is not a simple either/or trait. Left-handed people tend to be less strongly lateralized than right-handed people (their brain hemispheres are not as specialized).

Preview: Finding Music in Walnut-Grapefruit Tofu

Language Development Guide

flamenco: musical and dance style of Spain

passionate: fiery

"in the zone": experience felt during a peak performance of an activity; consists of full involvement in the activity; also called flow

classical: style of instrumental music that originated in Europe in the ninth century

jazz: style of music that originated in the early 1900s in the U.S. south

hip-hop: involves music including rap in which verse is spoken to a particular beat

duplicate: copy

Coldplay: an alternative rock band from England

Taylor Swift: country singer and songwriter

tofu: soft, white food made from soy milk (bean curd)

squishy: spongy; soggy

blob: a drop; a dot

exquisite: extreme, perfect

network: system; set of connections

immense: vast; great

undeniably: definitely

realm: area; field

Module 2.1 Neurons and the Nervous System
Neurons—Building a "Biocomputer"
Survey Question: How do neurons operate and communicate?
Language Development Guide
spidery: composed of thin threads like a spider's web or spider's legs

input: put in; enter (information)

process: deal with; sort

output: communicate processed information

cross section: side view

probes: device used to obtain electrical measurements

generate: produce

renews: refreshes; restarts

Bruce Springsteen: rock musician

riff: fast series of musical notes

cables: wires braided together

metaphor: a phrase or image used to represent the nature or characteristics of something else

trigger point: the point of no return, when a gun goes off

dominoes: flat, rectangular game pieces that have two squares of dots numbering zero (no dots) to
        12 (six dots on each square)

a wave of falling blocks will zip rapidly to the end of the line: when one block (domino) falls, it
        falls into the next block, causing it to fall, and so on, continuing down the row

dips: drop down

model: representation

immune system: protects the body against disease

bullring: arena in which bull fighting occurs

retreated: move away

"control centers": areas of the brain that manage vital functions, such as movement, breathing, etc.

microscopic: very tiny

squirt gun: toy gun that shoots water

interlink: connect

"speaks" dopamine: is only affected by dopamine

temperament: hereditary physical core of personality

outright: entire

mimic: imitate

in the short run: short-term (use)

in the long run: long-term (use)

recreational drugs: using a psychoactive drug for fun, not for a medical use

drug addiction: involves the person building up a tolerance to the drug and having withdrawal
        symptoms when without the drug

paralysis: a complete loss of muscle function

jerk: pull; yank

opiate-like: pain-relieving substances

runner's high: rush of pleasure during a marathon race

masochism: having pleasure from experiencing pain

acupuncture: Chinese medical art of relieving pain and illness by inserting thin needles into the
        body

euphoria: joy and excitement

initiation rites: ceremonies that are used to mark the passage of a young person into adulthood

induce: bring about; cause

hardy: strong and lasting

souls: persons

saunas: small room designed for wet or dry heat

"decides": in the case of neurons, the result of the combined excitatory and inhibitory messages

on balance: overall effect

"listens": neuron receives input

in the meantime: time period between two events

shoebox: about 6 inches tall, 8 inches wide, 12 inches long

Fear Factor: TV reality show that involved contestant teams performing various fear-producing
stunts *compensate*: make up for

Recite and Review

1. Weighing three pounds, wrinkled like a walnut, the size of a grapefruit, the texture of tofu, and able to process immense amounts of information are characteristics of the human _____.

2. An individual nerve cell is called a(n) _____.

3. The 100 billion individual nerve cells are supported in a variety of ways by an equal number of _____ cells.

4. The part of an individual nerve cells that looks like tree roots and receive messages from other neurons are the _____.

5. The soma is also known as the _____.

6. Altogether, the human brain contains about 3 million miles of miniature cable-like structures that carry messages through the brain and nervous system called _____.

7. The bulb-shaped structures at the end of axons that form synapses with the dendrites and somas of other neurons are called _____.

8. When a neuron is inactive, its electrical charge is said to be in a(n) _____ potential.

9. If the electrical charge rises to a minus 50 millivolts, the neuron will reach its trigger point for firing, also called its _____:

10. When this trigger point is reached, a nerve impulse will sweep down the axon at up to 200 miles per hour with nerve impulse being referred to as a(n) _____ potential.

11. The axon membrane is pierced by tiny tunnels or "holes," called _____.

12. During the nerve impulse, the "gates" to the tiny tunnels in the axon membrane "pop" open and allow _____ ions to rush into the axon.

13. Because a nerve impulse will occur completely or not at all, it is said to be a(n) _____ event.

14. After each nerve impulse, the cell briefly dips below its resting level and it becomes less willing to fire, a state known as a(n) _____ after-potential.

15. A fatty layer that coats some axons and aids the conduction of a nerve impulse is called _____.

16. When a nerve impulse is conducted down an axon, it tends to jump from gap to gap in the fatty layer coating the axon. This process is known as _____ conduction.

17. The disease involving numbness, weakness, and paralysis that occurs when the immune system attacks and destroys the fatty layer covering some axons is called _____.

18. When an action potential reaches the tips of the axon terminals, the chemicals that are released into the synaptic gap are called _____.

19. When chemical molecules cross over a synapse, they attach to special receiving areas on cell bodies and dendrites known as _____.

20. The shaking and muscle tremors of Parkinson's disease are caused by too little of the neurotransmitter known as _____.

21. Involved with mood, appetite, and sleep, the inhibitory neurotransmitter that can lead to depression if one has too little of it is the neurotransmitter _____.

22. A person or animal given curare cannot move because curare competes with the neurotransmitter _____.
23. Brain chemicals that do not carry messages directly, but instead regulate the activity of other neurons are called _____.
24. Involved with learning and memory, the excitatory neurotransmitter that can cause neuron death and autism if an excess is present is the neurotransmitter _____.
25. The painkilling effects of acupuncture and the "runner's high" are explained by the release of _____ from the pituitary gland.
26. Interlinked collections of neurons that process information in the brain are known as neural _____.
27. Through one's experiences, new synapses may form between neurons or synaptic connections may grow stronger or grow weaker and die. This capacity of the brain to change in response to experiences is known as _____.

Part 1: Connections

1. _____ soma
2. _____ dendrites
3. _____ axon terminals
4. _____ axon

Part 2: Connections

1. ___ axon
2. ___ dendrite
3. ___ ions
4. ___ myelin
5. ___ soma
6. ___ synapse
7. ___ neurotransmitter
8. ___ salutatory conduction
9. ___ negative after-potential
10. ___ threshold
11. ___ neuroplasticity

a. a fatty insulating coating on some axons that speeds conduction
b. microscopic space between two neurons over which messages pass
c. neuron fiber that looks like a tree branch and receives incoming messages
d. any chemical released by a neuron that alters the activity in other neurons
e. a drop in electrical charge below the resting potential
f. electrically charged particles
g. main body of a neuron
h. the point at which a nerve impulse is triggered
i. the capacity of our brains to change in response to experience
j. fiber that carries information away from the cell body of a neuron
k. the process by which nerve impulses conducted down the axons of neurons coated with a fatty layer jump from gap to gap in this layer

Part 3: Connections

1. ___ acetylcholine

a. excitatory neurotransmitter involved in arousal and vigilance, and mood with an excess leading to anxiety

89

2. ___ serotonin

     b. deficiency of this neurotransmitter leading to Parkinson's disease and an excess to schizophrenia

3. ___ dopamine

     c. has major inhibitory effect in the central nervous system; participates in moods; deficiency may lead to anxiety

4. ___ norepinephrine

     d. excitatory neurotransmitter involved in learning and memory with excess leading to neuron death and autism

5. ___ GABA

     e. deficiency of this neurotransmitter playing a role in Alzheimer's disease

6. ___ glutamate

     f. inhibitory neurotransmitter involved in moods, appetite, and sleep with a deficiency leading to depression and/or anxiety

Check Your Memory

1. TRUE or FALSE   Another name for the cell body is soma.
2. TRUE or FALSE   Looking like tree roots, the axon specializes in receiving information from other neurons.
3. TRUE or FALSE   Human axons may be up to a meter long.
4. TRUE or FALSE   When a neuron reaches threshold, an action potential, or nerve impulse, sweeps down the axon at up to 200 miles per hour
5. TRUE or FALSE   During an action potential, the ion channels pop open and allow oxygen ions (O+) to rush into the axon.
6. TRUE or FALSE   The ion channels first open near the axon terminal and then continue opening down the length of the axon until it reaches the soma.
7. TRUE or FALSE   A negative after-potential occurs because potassium ions (K^+) flow out of the neuron while the membrane gates are open.
8. TRUE or FALSE   The gaps in the myelin that coats some axons act to slow down a nerve impulse and prevent repeated firings of the same neuron.
9. TRUE or FALSE   If the myelin layer is damaged, a person will suffer from schizophrenia.
10. TRUE or FALSE   An action potential is primarily a chemical process, while communication between neurons is electrical.
11. TRUE or FALSE   The microscopic space between two neurons, over which messages pass, is called a synapse.
12. TRUE or FALSE   Receptor sites that are sensitive to neurotransmitters are found in large numbers on the axons and axon terminals.
13. TRUE or FALSE   Too little acetylcholine can cause Parkinson's disease, while too much can cause autism.
14. TRUE or FALSE   Too little serotonin may underlie depression.
15. TRUE or FALSE   GABA has an excitatory effect on the central nervous system, while glutamate has an inhibitory effect.
16. TRUE or FALSE   Neuropeptides do not carry messages directly, but instead regulate the activity of other neurons, affecting memory, pain, emotion, pleasure, hunger, and sex.
17. TRUE or FALSE   Endorphins are released from the pituitary gland and underlie the painkilling effects of placebos and acupuncture.
18. TRUE or FALSE   The overuse of recreational drugs like cocaine overstimulates the reward system in the brain and disturbs dopamine function, resulting in drug addiction.

90

19. TRUE or FALSE   Rats raised in a complex environment have more synapses and longer dendrites in their brains than rats raised in a simpler environment.
20. TRUE or FALSE   Every time you learn something, you are reshaping your living brain, a process termed neurogenic ablation.

Critical Thinking Question

What effect would you expect a drug to have if it blocked passage of neurotransmitters across the synapse?

Module 2.1 The Nervous System—Wired for Action
Survey Question: What are the major parts of the nervous system?

Language Development Guide

playing catch with a football: a game where a ball is tossed back and forth
ablaze: as if on fire, rapid, active
wiring diagram: picture representation of an electrical pathway
computing: performing operations; processing
intricate: complex
magnification: enlargement
"tunnel": passageway
regain: get back
severed: cut off
skeletal muscles: tissues that move and support the body structure of the body
voluntary behavior: chosen with intent
Derek Jeter: professional baseball player with the New York Yankees
vegetative: keeping you alive even when one is not conscious
eyes to dilate: pupils enlarge
flash of anger: brief burst of irritation
coordinate: match; manage
snarling: growling
lunges: leaps toward (as in an attack)
involuntary: reflexive; done without your control
emergency: crisis; urgent situation
"fight or flight": in stress situation, animals either prepare to attack or to run
in essence: essentially; basically
arouses: stirs up; stimulates
synapses: passing a message to another nerve cell
contract: tighten
adaptive: being able to adjust to situations
grandstand catches: in sports, to catch a ball dramatically to impress observers
coaxing: "persuading"; carefully and gradually bringing out
grafting: new tissue joined to older tissue, mending, connecting
trials: tests; experiments
confined: limited to; restricted to
false hopes: illusion that something will occur
emerge: to appear
optimistic: positive; hopeful
slowly go downhill: reduce, decline
careening: going very fast
simultaneously: at the same time

originate: begin
stunning: amazing; surprising
transplants: moving nerve tissue from one body to another
restrained: held down
Parkinson's disease: disorder of the central nervous system that progressively impairs motor movements

Recite and Review

1. The brain and spinal cord make up the _____ nervous system.
2. Large bundles of neuron axons that can be seen without magnification are called _____.
3. Damaged nerve fibers in the peripheral nervous system can be repaired because they are covered by _____.
4. The somatic and autonomic systems are the two major parts of the _____ nervous system.
5. When Jason tosses a football, this voluntary action is under the control of a part of the peripheral system known as the _____ nervous system.
6. Digestion and endocrine secretion are under the control of a part of the peripheral system known as the _____ nervous system.
7. You see the neighborhood bully coming toward you. Your pulse begins to race and your breathing comes in short, fast gasps because of the activation of the _____ branch of the autonomic nervous system.
8. After a car narrowly misses hitting your car at an intersection, you notice that your heart is racing, and you are sweating profusely. However, by the time you get home, your heart rate has returned to normal, and you are no longer sweating. This calming of your body occurred because of the _____ branch of the autonomic nervous system.
9. Connecting the brain to other parts of the body is the spinal cord, which is made up of columns of _____ (bundles of axons covered with myelin).
10. Carrying sensory and motor messages to and from the spinal cord are _____ pairs of spinal nerves.
11. Leaving the brain directly are 12 pairs of _____ nerves.
12. If you step on a tack, you automatically jerk your foot away due to a simple behavior known as a(n) _____, which arises within the spinal cord.
13. Information from your senses are carried toward the central nervous system by a(n) _____ nerve.
14. Inside the spinal cord, linking other neurons together are the _____ neurons.
15. A cell that carries commands from the central nervous system to muscles and glands is called a(n) _____ neuron.
16. Muscle fibers are made up of cells that are capable of producing a response, which are called _____ cells.
17. Research strategies that have shown promise in repairing cut spinal cords include grafting nerve fibers to fill the gap and injecting _____ cells (immature cells that can mature into a variety of specialized cells).
18. The production of new brain cells is known as _____.
19. Due to a stroke, Bobby's left arm is partially paralyzed. So, doctors restrain his good right arm, forcing his impaired arm to be more active and increase the growth of new neurons in his brain. This procedure is known as _____ movement therapy.
20. A theory proposed by neuroscientists Toro and Deakin states that the brains of individuals with a particular mental disorder are unable to create new neurons to replace old ones that have died, leaving their brains with fewer neurons and smaller than normal. Their theory relates to the mental disorder known as _____.

92

Part 1: Connections

1. _____ spinal cord
2. _____ autonomic system
3. _____ parasympathetic branch
4. _____ peripheral nervous system
5. _____ central nervous system
6. _____ somatic system

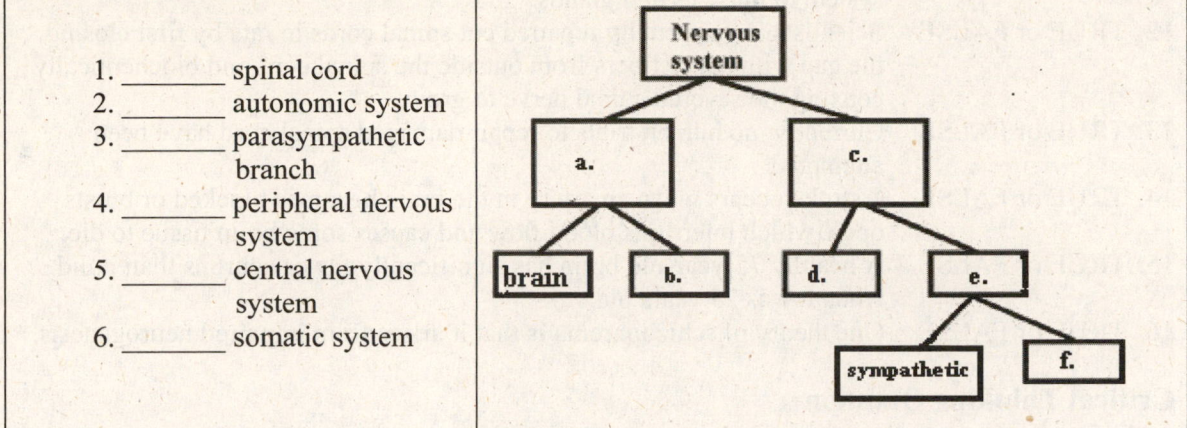

Part 2: Connections

1. ___ central nervous system
2. ___ somatic nervous system
3. ___ sympathetic nervous system
4. ___ parasympathetic nervous system
5. ___ neurilemma
6. ___ cranial nerves
7. ___ reflex arc
8. ___ motor neurons
9. ___ effector cells
10. ___ neurogenesis

a. the simplest behavior in which a stimulus provokes an automatic response
b. the "fight-or flight" system
c. calms the body
d. the production of new brain cells
e. twelve pair leave the brain directly
f. brain and spinal cord
g. system that controls voluntary movement
h. cells that make up muscle fibers and are capable of producing a response
i. cells that carry commands from the CNS to muscles and glands
j. layer of cells on axons in the peripheral system that aids in the repair of damaged nerve cells

Check Your Memory

1. TRUE or FALSE   The peripheral nervous system is made up of the brain and spinal cord.
2. TRUE or FALSE   A high-powered microscope is needed to see nerves.
3. TRUE or FALSE   Neurilemma forms a "tunnel" that damaged nerve fibers can follow as they repair themselves.
4. TRUE or FALSE   The axons of most neurons in the brain and spinal cord are covered by neurilemma.
5. TRUE or FALSE   When you kick a soccer ball, this voluntary movement is under the control of the somatic nervous system.
6. TRUE or FALSE   Heart rate, digestion, and perspiration are under the control of the autonomic nervous system.
7. TRUE or FALSE   The parasympathetic nervous system prepares the body for "fight or flight" during times of danger or high emotion.
8. TRUE or FALSE   If you were to cut through the spinal cord, you would see columns of white matters, which are bundles of axons covered with myelin.
9. TRUE or FALSE   Thirty-one pairs of cranial nerves leave the brain directly.
10. TRUE or FALSE   Reflex arcs are simple behaviors that arise within the spinal cord, without any help from the brain.

11. TRUE or FALSE   A sensory neuron is one that carries messages from the central nervous system to muscles and glands.

12. TRUE or FALSE   Scientists have partially repaired cut spinal cords in rats by first closing the gap with nerve fibers from outside the spinal cord and biochemically coaxing the severed spinal nerve to grow.

13. TRUE or FALSE   Currently, no human trials to repair damaged spinal cord have been attempted.

14. TRUE or FALSE   A stroke occurs when an artery in the brain becomes blocked or bursts open, which interrupts blood flow and causes some brain tissue to die.

15. TRUE or FALSE   A healthy 75-year-old brain has significantly fewer neurons than it did when it was 25 years old.

16. TRUE or FALSE   One theory of schizophrenia is that it arises from impaired neurogenesis.

Critical Thinking Question

Where in all the brain's "hardware" do you think the mind is found? What is the relationship between mind and brain?

Module 2.2 Brain Research
Mapping Brain Structure—Pieces of the Puzzle
Survey Question: How are different parts of the brain identified?

Language Development Guide

anatomists: study the structure of living things

autopsied: surgery performed on dead bodies to yield information

dissection: process of taking apart and observing various structures within dead animals or humans

anatomically distinct: well-defined parts of the total structure (of the brain)

revolutionized: updated; modernized

conventional: standard; regular

shadowy: unclear; indistinct

specialized: very specific

visible: able to be seen

angles: viewpoints

magnetic field: a force created by the differing charges within electric currents

slice: a small segment of the tissue can be viewed

peer: examine

transparent: clear; see-through

Recite and Review

1. Dr. Merra is a psychologist who studies how biological processes, especially those of the nervous system, relate to behavior. Dr. Merra is a(n) _____.

2. Anatomists have learned much about brain structure by cutting apart autopsied human and animal brains and examining them under a microscope. This procedure of cutting apart brain parts is called _____.

3. A computer-enhanced X-ray image of the brain or body is called a(n) _____ scan.

4. Jared was in a car accident and was taken to the hospital and placed inside a magnetic field so that the doctors could see a three-dimensional model of his body and brain. Jared underwent a procedure called a(n) _____ scan.

94

Connections

1. ___ biopsychology
2. ___ dissection
3. ___ CT scan
4. ___ MRI scan

a. specialized type of X-ray
b. study of how biological process, such as the nervous system are related to behavior
c. use of a magnetic field to provide a three-dimensional image
d. cutting apart autopsied body parts

Check Your Memory

1. TRUE or FALSE   A biopsychologist would most likely study how people's nervous systems are related to their behavior.
2. TRUE or FALSE   Anatomists have learned much about brain structure by dissecting autopsied human and animal brains and examining them under a microscope.
3. TRUE or FALSE   In an EEG scan of the brain, X-rays taken from a number of different angles are collected by a computer and formed into an image of the brain.
4. TRUE or FALSE   During an MRI scan, the body is placed inside a magnetic field.
5. TRUE or FALSE   CT scans produce more detailed images than are possible with MRI scans.

Module 2.2 Mapping Brain Function—Figuring Out What the Parts Do
Survey Question: What do the different parts of the brain do?

Language Development Guide

localize: identify, specify
capacities: abilities
consistently: every time
presumably: most likely
stroke: brain damage often caused by a blood clot in the brain
brainstem: the lowest portions of the brain, including the cerebellum, medulla, pons, and reticular formation
brain dead: irreversible end to all brain activity needed to sustain life without life support machines
receptors: any structure that receives stimuli from the environment
scalp: area of the head bordered by the face and neck and consists of skin (on which hair grows) and connective tissue
insulated wire: coated with a nonconductive material
target area: the small spot that will receive the electrical stimulation
astonishing: surprising; amazing
euphoria: extreme happiness
against his or her will: without a person's consent
control a person like a robot: controlling a person's actions and movements
elicited: draw out; bring forth
modified: toned down; moderated
circumstances: situations
Sci-Fi movies: science fiction movies that depict fantasy and futuristic situations, such as space aliens and deep space travel
ruthless: cruel; brutal
enslave: to make a person into a slave or property of another person

radio controlling: directing a toy's actions from a distance
alternate: different; substitute
glimpse: quick look
origins: beginnings
invasive: breaks the skin and enters the body (a less invasive procedure would not)
amplifies: increases; strengthens
epilepsy: brain disorder that causes seizures
hypnosis: altered state of consciousness characterized by narrowed attention and an increased
   openness to suggestion
detects: identifies; distinguishes
emitted: produced
radioactive glucose: sugar with unstable nuclei that emit particles that can be traced (radioactivity
   marks the substance)
consumed: used
brain efficiency: effective and successful use of the thinking capacity of the brain
brain scans: visual imaging of the structure and functioning of the brain
innate: born with it
untapped: unused
reserves: supplies; stockpile
to deceive: mislead; trick
"atlases": charts
*It is just a matter of time until even brighter beacons are flashed into the shadowy inner world of
   thought*: new discoveries about the brain will occur soon

Recite and Review

1. When a research links specific structures in the brain with specific psychological or
  behavioral functions, the researcher is _____function.
2. Doctors kept careful detailed records of Phineas Gage's behaviors and personality changes
  after his traumatic head injury. The doctors were using a(n) _____ study.
3. The surface of the brain can be "turned on" by stimulating it with a mild electrical current
  delivered through a thin insulated wire, or electrode, with the procedure being known as
  _____.
4. Surgical removal of parts of the brain is called _____.
5. A strong electric current can be used to destroy a small amount of brain tissue when delivered
  to a target area inside the brain during a procedure known as _____.
6. The electrical activity of a single neuron can be detected by using the tip of a(n) _____,
  which is an extremely thin glass tube filled with a salty fluid.
7. As part of sleep study, small disk-shaped metal will be placed on Parnell's scalp to record his
  brain waves onto a moving sheet of paper. These researchers are using a(n) _____.
8. A PET scan detects subatomic particles emitted by weak radioactive _____ as it is
  consumed by the brain.
9. The brains of people who perform well on a difficult reasoning test were found to consume
  less energy than those of poor performers by psychologist Richard Haier and his colleagues,
  who used a(n) _____ scan to determine this difference.
10. To tell if a person was lying, psychiatrist Daniel Langleben and his colleagues used
  _____ scan.
11. Langleben and associates found that when a person is lying, the area of the brain that was the
  most active was the _____ of the brain.

Connections

1. ___ localization of function
2. ___ clinical case study

3. ___ ESB

4. ___ ablation

5. ___ deep lesioning

6. ___ EEG
7. ___ PET scan

8. ___ fMRI

a. detailed investigation of a single person
b. provides structural and functional imaging of the brain and has been used to detect lying
c. computer-generated image of brain activity based on glucose consumption in the brain
d. removal of a small amount of brain tissue using an electrode
e. device that detects, amplifies, and records brain waves on a moving sheet of paper or a computer screen
f. surgical removal of large parts of the brain
g. research strategy of linking specific structures in the brain to specific psychological or behavioral responses
h. "turning on" the brain by stimulating it with a mild electric current

Check Your Memory

1. TRUE or FALSE   If damage to a particular part of the brain consistently leads to a particular loss of function, then we say the function is localized in that structure.
2. TRUE or FALSE   The clinical case study of Kate Adamson's locked-in syndrome illustrated that the brainstem controls vital functions, such as movement and breathing.
3. TRUE or FALSE   When ESB is used during brain surgery, the patient, who is awake during the surgery, will be able to describe what effect the stimulation is having.
4. TRUE or FALSE   Although ESB can call forth behaviors, such as aggression, alertness, eating, tearing, and sleeping, it cannot control a person like a robot.
5. TRUE or FALSE   Both ablation and deep lesioning destroy brain tissue.
6. TRUE or FALSE   The tip of a microelectrode is small enough to detect the electrical activity of a single neuron.
7. TRUE or FALSE   EEGs are used to measure the waves of electrical activity produced near the surface of the brain.
8. TRUE or FALSE   A PET scan detects neutrons emitted by weak radioactive iodine as it is utilized by the brain.
9. TRUE or FALSE   Haier and his associates found that the brains of people who perform well on a difficult reasoning test consume more energy than those of poor performers.
10. TRUE or FALSE   Most people use only 10 percent of their brain capacity.
11. TRUE or FALSE   In their studies, psychiatrist Daniel Langleben and his colleagues used ESB to distinguish between lies, false statements made with the intention to deceive, and confabulations.
12. TRUE or FALSE   A person who is lying will show less activity in the front of the brain than a person who is telling the truth.

Critical Thinking Question

Deep lesioning is used to ablate an area in the hypothalamus of a rat. After the operation, the rat seems to lose interest in food and eating. Why would it be a mistake to automatically conclude that the ablated area is a "hunger center"?

Module 2.3 Hemispheres and Lobes of the Cerebral Cortex
The Cerebral Cortex—My, What a Wrinkled Brain You Have!

Survey Questions: How do the left and right hemispheres differ? What are the different functions of the lobes of the cerebral cortex?

Language Development Guide

superior: better
pretty unimpressive: rather average; nothing special
surpass: outdo
mammalian record holders: refers to the mammal with the largest brain by size or weight
that honor: the winner of
tip the scales: to weigh a certain amount
puny: small, weak
noteworthy: remarkable
absolute weight: actual weight
relative weight: weight as a comparison
sets you apart: what makes you different from the others
mantle: cloak, covering
(Albert) Einstein: theoretical physicist and intellectual
spatial reasoning: ability to visualize patterns in space, such as rotating geometric shapes in one's mind or solving 3-D puzzles
acknowledge: recognize
"alien" arm: unfamiliar; strange
resumed: return to
like a thunderbolt: quickly
subtle: faint; slight; understated
clumsiness: awkward; lack of coordination in movements
awkward gait: lack of coordination in the way one walks
hand-eye coordination: to be able to use the information from the eye to guide the movements of the hand (for example in picking up an object seen)
fine muscle control: small, precise movements of the hand, fingers, and thumb
telltale signs: revealing indicators or warnings
full-blown: advanced; fully developed
Nobel Prize(s): international awards given annually for scientific discoveries and societal advances, such as for peace or for medicine (named after Alfred Nobel, who invented dynamite)
concepts: ideas; views
dilemmas: problem
gallantly: like a hero or protector
overrides: takes priority over
ultimate: final; last
right hand not knowing what the left hand is doing: each hand acting independently; comes from a Biblical reference about being generous without public recognition
irony: when a speaker says one thing but means another
sarcasm: a sharp, bitter, or cutting expression

implications: inferences; consequences

nuances: tone; fine degrees of

overall context: the entire situation

simultaneously: at the same time

coherent: logical; consistent; reasoned

wide-angle view: taking an overall look at something, not narrow

zooms in on: looks closely at

local focus: narrow view

global focus: large-scale, overall view

make love: sex

drastically: considerably; significantly

fissures: cracks; splits; little gaps

sense of self: understanding one's personal identity

twitch: little jerks; trembles

dexterity: skillful movement, not clumsy

agile: responsive and coordinated

devoted: committed to; assigned to

incidentally: by the way; before I forget; while we're on the subject

"motor maps": representation of which movements would occur if a particular area was
        stimulated in the motor cortex

violin: smallest and highest pitched stringed instrument; sound produced by drawing a bow across
        the four strings; informally may be referred to as a "fiddle"

viola: stringed instrument with size and pitch between a violin and a cello; also played with a bow

cello: stringed instrument played with a bow; larger than a viola, but smaller than the bass

"hand maps": shows areas on the motor and sensory maps of the cortex devoted to the hand

merely: just; simply

obligingly: cooperatively; willingly

intuitively: naturally without thinking

underlie: bring about

imitation: to repeat the actions of others

triggered: set off

flood of interest: a great deal of attention

speculate: think; reason that

partially: partly; to a degree

spectrum: range; variety

restrictive (behavior): limiting

repetitive (behavior): recurring

impaired: weakened; damaged

reflecting: imitating; mirroring

empirical confirmation: to prove through direct observation

portion: section

fluently: easily; effortlessly

utter: say, speak

grammar: set of rules for making sounds into words and words into sentences

pronunciation: way a word is spoken

labored: difficult; awkward

generates: creates; produces

get "stuck": fixed; trapped

somatic: of the body

register: be aware of projects: is sent to; propelled to

MP3: format for music downloads (of favorite songs)
light up on PET scan: indicates that energy is being used in this area of the brain
TV-like image: the process of vision does not occur like having a TV screen in one's occipital lobe
evolutionary standpoint: looking at the situation using the theories of evolutionary psychology
social animals: animals that interactive often with other members of its species
organ of consciousness: the human brain
"I have half a mind to tell you what I think": considering doing or saying something
sounding out words: attempting to pronounce words, usually using phonics
routes: ways; paths
brain-bearing species: humans
"biocomputer": human brain
awe: wonder

Recite and Review

1. The area of the brain that is responsible for the human intellectual superiority within the animal kingdom is the _____.
2. The outer layer of the brain consists of spongy tissue made up mostly of cell bodies and is referred to as _____ matter.
3. The two hemispheres of the brain are divided into smaller areas known as _____.
4. There is an increased size and wrinkling of the cortex of the brain in higher animals that is referred to as _____.
5. The two hemispheres of the brain are connected by a thick band of fibers called the _____.
6. After having a stroke that damaged his right hemisphere, Tomas will not eat food on the left side of a plate and refuses to acknowledge his paralyzed left arm as his own. Tomas is showing symptoms of a condition known as _____.
7. When Paula visited her elderly grandfather, she noticed that one of his eyelids was drooping, and he was walking awkwardly and showing poor hand-eye coordination. She immediately took him to his doctor because these subtle behavioral signs, called _____ signs, may indicate that her grandfather has had a stroke.
8. Roger Sperry discovered that the right and left hemispheres perform differently on tests of language, music, and other capabilities because of his work with people who had undergone the "_____" operation.
9. During a research study, Bob, a patient whose two hemispheres were separated, had a dollar sign flashed to his right brain and a question mark to his left brain. He was then asked to draw what he saw, using his left hand, out of sight. Bob's left hand would draw a _____.
10. The hemisphere that is superior at math, judging time and rhythm, and coordinating the order of complex movements is the _____ hemisphere
11. Amanda is an artist and is also very good at detecting the emotions that other people are feeling. Her superior perceptual skills are mainly the function of the _____ hemisphere.
12. People lose their ability to understand jokes, irony, sarcasm, implications, and other nuances of language, if damage occurs to the _____ hemisphere.
13. Connie tends to focus on small details and deal with information in a sequential fashion, which are both characteristics of the _____ hemisphere of the brain.
14. In solving a problem, Justin tends to "look at the big picture" and processes information simultaneously, which are characteristics of the _____ hemisphere of the brain.
15. Some of the lobes of the cerebral cortex are regarded as separate areas because their functions are different with other lobes being defined by the presence of larger _____ on the surface of the cortex.
16. The primary motor area of the brain that directs our muscles is located in the _____ lobes of the brain.

17. The motor cortex is one brain area that contains neurons, which become active when we perform an action and when we merely observe someone else carrying out the same action. These special neurons are called _____ neurons.

18. A person with damage to association areas in the left hemisphere may suffer an impaired ability to use language called _____.

19. After a motorcycle accident, Parker has shown labored speech and problems with his grammar and pronunciation. Parker most likely has damage to an area located on the left frontal lobe known as _____ area.

20. If a person's personality changes drastically after suffered brain damage, he or she most likely damaged the _____ cortex, which generates a sense of self and an awareness of one's current emotional state.

21. The primary somatosensory area is located on the _____ lobes.

22. The primary auditory area is the main site where hearing first registers and is located in the _____ lobes.

23. Jamie had a stroke and is now experiencing difficulty understanding the meaning of words. Jamie most likely had damage to an area located on the left temporal lobe known as _____ area.

24. An impaired mirror neuron system, which causes a child to have problems interacting and communicating with other people, may underlie the serious childhood disorders known as _____ spectrum disorders.

25. Patients will experience blind spots in their vision if there are tumors in the primary visual area located in the _____ lobes of the brain.

26. A fascinating form of "mindblindness" in which the person is unable to identify and perceive familiar faces is called _____.

27. In studies of how men and women's brains function during a language task, it was found that both sides of the brain were activated in more than half of the _____ tested.

28. In studies of men and women's brains, it was found that women had more gray and white matter concentrated in their _____ lobes than the men did.

Part 1: Connections

1. _____ Wernicke's area
2. _____ temporal lobe
3. _____ cerebellum
4. _____ Broca's area
5. _____ parietal lobe
6. _____ frontal lobe
7. _____ occipital lobe

Part 2: Connections

1. ____ corticalization   a. area of the parietal lobe that senses touch, temperature, and pressure

101

2. ___ corpus callosum

    b. area of the temporal lobe related to the understanding of language

3. ___ mirror neurons

    c. sensory area of the temporal lobe related to hearing

4. ___ primary motor cortex

    d. area of the occipital lobe

5. ___ prefrontal cortex

    e. area in the frontal lobe involved in one's sense of self, reasoning, and planning

6. ___ Broca's area

    f. area of the frontal lobe related to one's control of movement

7. ___ Wernicke's area

    g. area of the frontal lobe associated with speech production, grammar, and pronunciation

8. ___ primary somatosensory cortex

    h. an increase in the size and wrinkling of the cerebral cortex

9. ___ primary auditory area

    i. band of fibers that connects the two hemispheres

10. ___ primary visual area

    j. impairment of this system may be the cause of autism spectrum disorders

Check Your Memory

1. TRUE or FALSE   Animals surpass humans in strength, speed, and sensory sensitivity.
2. TRUE or FALSE   The ratio of brain weight to body weight in humans is 1 to 20.
3. TRUE or FALSE   While a small positive correlation exists between intelligence and brain size, overall size alone does not determine human intelligence.
4. TRUE or FALSE   The cerebral cortex covers most of the brain with a mantle of white matter, which is made up primarily of axons covered with neurilemma.
5. TRUE or FALSE   The increase in the size and wrinkling of the cortex is referred to as lateralization.
6. TRUE or FALSE   The cerebral cortex contains 70 percent of the neurons in the central nervous system.
7. TRUE or FALSE   The two hemispheres of the cerebral cortex are connected by a bridge of nerve tissue called the corpus callosum.
8. TRUE or FALSE   If a person has damage to the right hemisphere due to a stroke or tumor, they may show spatial neglect for their left visual field.
9. TRUE or FALSE   Although major brain injuries are easy enough to spot, psychologists also look for more subtle signs that the brain is not working properly called neurological soft signs.
10. TRUE or FALSE   "Split-brain" operations are rare surgeries that were performed to control severe epilepsy.
11. TRUE or FALSE   "Split-brain" operations caused such severe conflicts between the actions of the two hemispheres that people who underwent these surgical procedures were unable to function without 24-hour assistance within institutions.
12. TRUE or FALSE   If we flash a picture of a cat to the right brain of a split-brain patient and a picture of a basketball to his left brain and then ask him to draw what he saw using his left hand (out of sight), the patient will draw a basketball.
13. TRUE or FALSE   The left brain is especially good at recognizing patterns, faces, and melodies; putting together a puzzle, or drawing a picture.

102

14. TRUE or FALSE   Information is processed simultaneously and holistically in the right hemisphere.
15. TRUE or FALSE   People normally use both sides of the brain at all times.
16. TRUE or FALSE   Some of the lobes of the cerebral cortex are defined by larger fissures on the surface of the cortex, while others are regarded as separate areas because their functions are quite different.
17. TRUE or FALSE   The primary motor area is located in the temporal lobes of the brain.
18. TRUE or FALSE   More of the motor cortex is devoted to the hands than to the feet.
19. TRUE or FALSE   Human empathy as well as the ability to imitate others may arise from activation of mirror neurons.
20. TRUE or FALSE   Damage to Wernicke's area causes motor (or expressive) aphasia.
21. TRUE or FALSE   Dramatic personality changes can occur when there is damage to the prefrontal cortex, which generates our sense of self.
22. TRUE or FALSE   Patients with damage to the frontal lobes often get "stuck" on mental tasks and repeat the same wrong answers over and over.
23. TRUE or FALSE   The lips and hands take up more area of the somatosensory cortex than do the back and trunk of the body.
24. TRUE or FALSE   The sensory area for hearing is located in the front area of the parietal lobes.
25. TRUE or FALSE   When a person has receptive or fluent aphasia, he or she can hear speech, but has difficulty understanding the meaning of words.
26. TRUE or FALSE   The visual area in the brain acts like a little TV screen in the brain.
27. TRUE or FALSE   Areas devoted to recognizing faces lie in association areas on the underside of the occipital lobes.
28. TRUE or FALSE   Visual agnosia is sometimes referred to as "mindblindness."
29. TRUE or FALSE   When Broca's area is damaged some women can use the right side of their brains to compensate for the loss.
30. TRUE or FALSE   Regarding brain differences in men and women, women have more gray matter, while men have more white matter.

Critical Thinking Questions

1. If you wanted to increase the surface area of the cerebral cortex so that more would fit within the skull, how would you do it?

2. If your brain were removed, replaced by another, and moved to a new body, which would you consider to be yourself, your old body with the new brain, or your new body with the old brain?

Module 2.4 Subcortex and Endocrine System
The Subcortex—At the Core of the (Brain) Matter
Survey Question: What are the major parts of the subcortex?

Language Development Guide
survive: to live on
fatal: deadly
vital: critical; very important
solely: only
communication system: means of transferring information
disrupt: upset
endanger: put in danger
karate chop: hit with the side of the hand

posture: position in which one hold his or her body upright against gravity

crippling: unable to use arms and/or legs

tremor: shaking

priority: main concern

commands: instructions

limbs: arms and legs

vigilant: watchful

branch: split; divide; separate

bombards: showers; floods

snaps to attention: quickly becomes alert

averting: preventing

momentarily: briefly

like buried treasure: like precious objects hidden underground, important and secret

switching stations: place where trains change to different tracks

master control center: main, centralized area that regulates emotions and basic needs

diverse: varied

crossroads: place where highways meet

reproduction: creating offspring; breeding

backfire: car tailpipe makes a loud bang

phobias: extreme fear

outburst: sudden occurrence; to explode

startled: alarmed; frightened

primitive: ancient; prehistoric

navigate through space: move around in our surroundings

dose: amount

overlap: intersect

amphetamine: synthetic stimulant drugs

heroin: narcotic; powerful pain reliever

nicotine: natural stimulant found in tobacco

"thrilling": exciting

appeal: attraction

shivers down your spine: to make one feel excited

"aversive": something, such as pain or discomfort, that causes avoidance

striking (rattlesnake): attacking

journey: trip; tour

magic: powerful mystery

for the sake: in the interest of

half-truth: somewhat deceptive statement that contains an element of truth

scatters: spread out

converges: comes together

implies: means

practicing cultural knowledge: studying subjects; acquiring information and skills

virtuoso: expert

interface: the crossing point; the point of interaction

access: get into and use

Recite and Review

1. The hindbrain, midbrain, and parts of the forebrain, excluding the cerebral cortex, make up the _____.
2. The midbrain forms a link between the brainstem and the _____.

3. The part of the brainstem that is important for the reflex control of vital functions, including heart rate, breathing, and swallowing is the _____.
4. The crippling disease called spinocerebellar degeneration is caused by damage to the part of the brainstem known as the _____.
5. Giving priority to some messages entering the brain and turning other away is a network of fibers and cell bodies that lie within the medulla and brainstem called the _____.
6. The area of the brain that looks like a small bump on the brainstem, acts as a bridge to other brain areas, and influences sleep and arousal is called the _____.
7. As Jethro plays his guitar, these motor skills will be stored in a part of the hindbrain called the _____.
8. You are driving at night when suddenly you round a bend and see a deer standing in the road. You snap to attention and apply your brakes in time so avoid hitting the deer. You were able to avert the accident because your brain was aroused by the _____ system.
9. Vision, hearing, taste, and touch all pass through a small, football-shaped structure in the forebrain that acts as a final "switching" station for sensory messages. This structure is the

   _____.
10. The part of the brain that acts as a master control center for emotion and many basic motives and can affect behaviors as diverse as sex, rage, body temperature, hormone release, eating and drinking, sleep, and waking is the _____.
11. Playing a major role in producing emotion and motivated behavior is a group of structures, including the hypothalamus, parts of the thalamus, the amygdala, and the hippocampus with this grouping being known as the _____ system.
12. People who suffer from phobias and disabling anxiety often feel afraid without knowing why
12. because of a part of the forebrain associated with fear responses known as the _____.
13. Memory-like or dream-like experiences can be produced by stimulating the _____ lobes because the hippocampus lies inside them.
14. Many commonly abused drugs activate reward, or "pleasure" pathways within the _____ system.
15. Researchers have developed a way in which a completely paralyzed person can control a computer through brain–computer interfaces that translates the patient's _____ recordings into commands for the computer.

Part 1: Connections

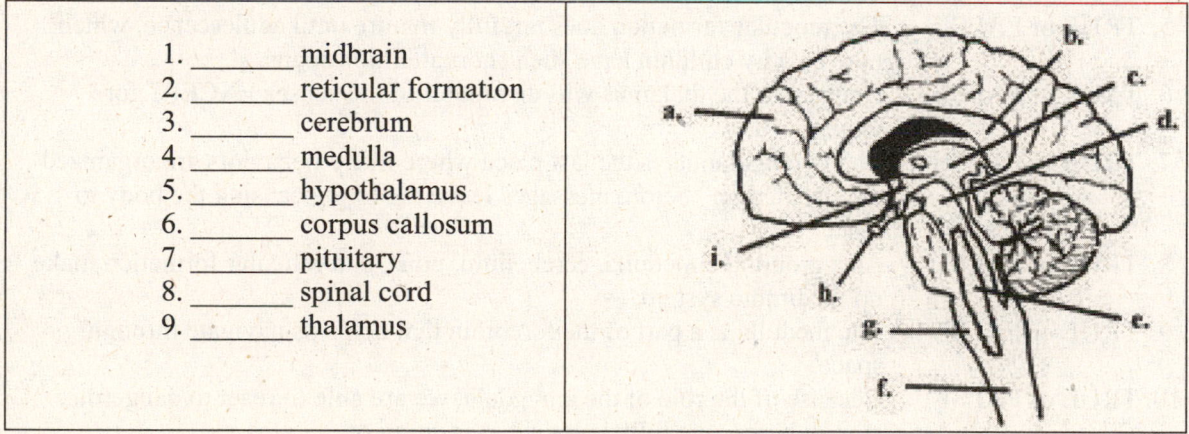

1. _____ midbrain
2. _____ reticular formation
3. _____ cerebrum
4. _____ medulla
5. _____ hypothalamus
6. _____ corpus callosum
7. _____ pituitary
8. _____ spinal cord
9. _____ thalamus

105

Part 2: Connections

1. ___ midbrain
2. ___ medulla
3. ___ pons
4. ___ cerebellum
5. ___ reticular formation
6. ___ thalamus
7. ___ hypothalamus
8. ___ amygdala
9. ___ hippocampus
10. ___ limbic system

a. a part of the forebrain that serves as a "crossroads" to connect many areas of the brain and which acts as a master control center for emotion and many basic motives

b. looks like a small bump on the brainstem and influences sleep and arousal

c. several parts of the brain in this region act as "pleasure" and "aversive" pathways

d. regulates posture, muscle tone, and muscular coordination and stores memories related to skills and habits

e. link between forebrain and brainstem

f. part of the forebrain that is important in forming long-term verbal memories

g. influences attention by giving priority to some incoming messages while turning others aside

h. small football-shaped structure in the forebrain that acts as a final "switching station" for sensory messages on their way to the cortex

i. connects brain with the spinal cord and controls vital life functions

j. provides a primitive, "quick pathway" to the cortex, particularly for fear responses

Check Your Memory

1. TRUE or FALSE   Serious damage to the subcortex can be fatal.
2. TRUE or FALSE   The brainstem consists mainly of the thalamus and hypothalamus.
3. TRUE or FALSE   Musicians, who practice special motor skills throughout their lives, have larger than average midbrains.
4. TRUE or FALSE   The first symptoms of spinocerebellar degeneration are tremors, dizziness, and muscular weakness.
5. TRUE or FALSE   The reticular formation does not fully mature until adolescence, which may be why children have such short attention spans.
6. TRUE or FALSE   Damage to the thalamus will disrupt all of the senses EXCEPT for vision.
7. TRUE or FALSE   The hypothalamus is the last place where many behaviors are organized or "decided on" before messages leave the brain, causing the body to react.
8. TRUE or FALSE   As a group, the medulla, cerebellum, pons, and reticular formation make up the limbic system.
9. TRUE or FALSE   The medulla is a part of the forebrain that helps us navigate through space.
10. TRUE or FALSE   Because of the role of the amygdala, we are able to react to dangerous stimuli before we fully know what is going on.
11. TRUE or FALSE   The hippocampus lies inside the occipital lobes, which is why stimulating the occipital lobe creates dream-like sensations.

12. TRUE or FALSE   During evolution, the limbic system was the earliest layer of the forebrain to develop

13. TRUE or FALSE   Animals will learn to press a lever to deliver a dose of electrical stimulation to the limbic system.

14. TRUE or FALSE   Many of the pleasure pathways in the brain are found in the pons, where they overlap with areas that control reflexes and sleep.

15. TRUE or FALSE   Researchers have developed brain-computer interfaces that translate a patient's EEG recordings into commands that can be used to control a computer.

Critical Thinking Question

Subcortical structures in humans are quite similar to corresponding lower brain areas in animals. Why would knowing this allow you to predict, in general terms, what functions are controlled by the subcortex?

Module 2.4 The Endocrine System—My Hormones Made Me Do It

Survey Question: Does the glandular system affect behavior?

Language Development Guide

parallel: similar; matching; corresponding

secrete: produce and emit

lymph system: a pathway for immune cells that protect the body

puberty: biologically defined period during which a person matures sexually and becomes capable of reproduction

dwarfism: disease causing people to be abnormally small

jet lag: having difficulty adjusting one's body clock when traveling to different time zones

seldom: not often; hardly ever

maternal behavior: caring; protective actions of a mother toward her offspring

turmoil: unrest; instability; confusion

elevated: raised; increased

prevail: exist

(hormonal) irregularities: abnormal (incorrect) levels or amounts

routine: everyday; usual

boosted: increased

globe: ball; round shape

base (of the brain): lower center

perfectly proportioned: ideal balance

prominent: standing out; readily noticeable

character actors: plays a particular role, not a leading one; easily recognizable

wrestlers: athletes engaged in a hand-to-hand combat sport consisting of throws and holds with professional wresting also involving more sports entertainment with wrestlers playing character heroes and villains

metabolism: the rate at which energy is produced and used in the body

remnant: remains of

"third-eye": refers to an inner eye (since it is light-sensitive)

coming to light: being discovered

so to speak: in a manner of speaking; sort of

variations: differences

dusk: sunset

expended: burned up

sizeable: large
tense: uptight; anxious
intellectual disability: formal IQ below 70 and a significant impairment in adaptive functioning
clot: thicken
bark: the outermost layers, like of a tree
deficiency: lack of
evoke: cause
craving: want, wish
Peruvian: person born in the South American country of Peru
issue: topic; subject
"bulk up": to gain weight
synthetic: artificial; not naturally-occurring
versions: types; kinds
side effects: by-products of; additional results of
shrinkage: reduction; decrease in size
sexual impotence: sexual dysfunction now referred to as male erectile disorder; inability to
       maintain an erection for sexual intercourse
hostility: unfriendliness; lack of sympathy; resentment; aggression
"roid rage": uncontrollable violent behavior resulting from the use of anabolic steroids
stunted: delayed, shortened
ban: disallow; forbid
ebb and flow: decreasing and increasing

Recite and Review

1. Glands that secrete chemicals directly into the bloodstream or lymph system are part of the
    _____ system.
2. The chemicals that are related to neurotransmitters but are secreted by the glands are called
    _____.
3. In both males and females, androgens are related to their _____.
4. If persons receive too little growth hormone during their growth period, they will have
    _____ dwarfism.
5. Too much growth hormone late in the growth period causes a condition in which the arms,
    hands, feet, and facial bones become enlarged called _____.
6. The hypothalamus in the forebrain directs the master gland in the body called the
    _____ gland.
7. A gland found in humans but which is associated with a well-developed light-sensitive organ,
    or third-eye, in certain fishes, frogs, and lizards is the _____ gland.
8. In women, milk output during breast-feeding is controlled by the _____ gland.
9. In the last few months, Marta has been very tense, excitable, and nervous and has lost weight.
    It was found that the gland that regulates metabolism was overactive. This gland is the
    _____ gland.
10. In response to daily variations of light, the pineal gland releases a hormone called
    _____.
11. In infancy, hypothyroidism limits development of the nervous system, leading to severe
    _____.
12. The source of epinephrine and norepinephrine is the inner core of the adrenal glands known
    as the adrenal _____.
13. Regulating the salt balance in the body is a set of hormones called the corticoids, which are
    produced by the outer "bark" of the adrenal glands known as the adrenal _____.

108

14. An oversecretion of the adrenal sex hormones can cause a condition characterized by exaggerated male characteristics called _____.
15. Although this synthetic form of testosterone can have serious side effects, many athletes will take _____ to "bulk up" their muscles.

Connections

1. ___ endocrine system

2. ___ hypothalamus

3. ___ pituitary gland

4. ___ acromegaly

5. ___ pineal gland

6. ___ thyroid gland
7. ___ adrenal medulla

8. ___ adrenal cortex

9. ___ virilism

10. ___ anabolic steroids

a. located in the neck and regulates metabolism

b. made up of glands that secrete chemicals directly into the bloodstream or lymph system

c. secretes melatonin in response to daily variations in light

d. regulates growth and controls milk output during breast-feeding

e. the source of epinephrine and norepinephreine

f. synthetic versions of testosterone

g. a part of the forebrain that directs the "master gland"

h. exaggerated male characteristics due to over-secretion of the adrenal sex hormones

i. a condition in which the arms, hands, feet, and facial bones become enlarged

j. produces a set of hormones called corticoids that regulate salt balance in the body and serve as a secondary source of sex hormones

Check Your Memory

1. TRUE or FALSE   Hormones are related to neurotransmitters because they can both activate cells in the body and require receptor sites.
2. TRUE or FALSE   Hormones secreted during times of high emotion tend to interrupt and interfere with memory formation.
3. TRUE or FALSE   The same hormones prevail when you are angry as when you are fearful.
4. TRUE or FALSE   Disturbing personality patterns may be linked to hormonal irregularities
5. TRUE or FALSE   After watching violent scenes from *The Godfather,* men had lower levels of the male hormone testosterone.
6. TRUE or FALSE   If too little growth hormone is secreted, the child will develop acromegaly.
7. TRUE or FALSE   The pituitary gland is directed by the hippocampus, which lies directly below the pituitary in the brain.
8. TRUE or FALSE   Melatonin levels in the bloodstream rise at dusk and peak around midnight and fall again as morning approaches.
9. TRUE or FALSE   Symptoms of hyperthyroidism include sleepiness, obesity, depression, and inactivity.
10. TRUE or FALSE   The sympathetic branch of the autonomic nervous system causes the hormones epinephrine and norepinephrine to be released by the adrenal glands.
11. TRUE or FALSE   The adrenal medulla produces a set of hormones called corticoids.

12. TRUE or FALSE   An oversecretion of the adrenal sex hormones can cause a woman to grow a beard or cause a man's voice to become so low it will be difficult to understand.

13. TRUE or FALSE   Oversecretion of the adrenal sex hormones early in life can cause premature puberty.

14. TRUE or FALSE   Dangerous increases in hostility and aggression have been linked with anabolic steroid use.

15. TRUE or FALSE   Almost all major sports organizations have banned the use of anabolic steroids.

Module 2.5 Psychology in Action: Handedness—Are You Dexterous or Sinister?

Are You Right- or Left-Handed?

Survey Question: In what ways do right- and left-handed individuals differ?

Language Development Guide

frowned upon: to wrinkle one's eyebrows as a sign of disapproval

insincere: dishonest; deceitful

sinister: evil, manipulative

paragon of virtue: a perfect example or model for good qualities

dexterity: skill using one's hands

coordinated: movements of limbs and muscles are in step and in time; lack of clumsiness

just: fair; honest

agility: nimbleness; dexterity

dominant (hand): main; leading

literally: exactly; factually

preceding: earlier; just prior

matter of degree: relative intensity

adapted from: taken from

spin a top: a toy that is balanced on its end point while turning rapidly on its axis; one of the oldest toys

flip pancakes: turning the pancake on the other side to cook

insert: put or place into

inconsistency: changeability

(hand) preference: first choice; favorite

two left feet: clumsy, uncoordinated

behavioral indicator: a sign that a specific behavior exists

hooked hand: the hand is bent around the pen and above the writing line

hand gestures: using the hands to signal or communicate emphasis

leap to any conclusions: make a decision before knowing enough

foolproof: perfect

inherited: through one's parents' genes

apparent: obvious

fetal ultrasound image: 3-D picture of developing baby through the use of high-frequency sound waves *dictated*: taught, forced upon

identical twins: develop from the same egg and same sperm; have exactly the same genetic make-up *to date*: so far

birth traumas: prematurity (born early and/or small), low birth weight, and breech birth

breech birth: baby enters birth canal buttocks or feet first rather than head first

110

social pressure: influence exerted by one's peer group
favoring: preferring
collectivist cultures: place importance on being a part of a group
individualistic cultures: importance of personal success and individual accomplishments
accident-prone: having a greater than average number of mishaps
right-handed world: most tools and other household devices designed for right-handed people
masquerading as: pretending to be
notable: famous; important
Leonardo da Vinci: famous Italian Renaissance painter, sculptor, and inventor whose paintings
          include the *Mona Lisa* and *The Last Supper*
Michelangelo: famous Italian Renaissance sculptor and painter whose most famous works
          include the paintings on the Sistine Chapel and the sculpture of David
Pablo Picasso: 20th century Spanish painter and sculptor whose style cubism gave rise to abstract
          art
M. C. Escher: famous 20th century Dutch graphic artist
conceivably: possibly
imagery: mental representations
visualizing: picture in one's mind
fencing: combat sport in which participants fight using long, light mental sword
striking: dramatic
take pride: rejoice
lopsided: out of balance
symmetrical: evenly balanced or proportioned
ambidextrous: able to use both hands equally well
pitch memory: ability to recognize or produce a tone relative to other tones
correspondingly: also; likewise

Recite and Review

1. The Latin word for right is _____.
2. To better assess whether one is strongly right-handed, strongly left-handed, or shows an inconsistency, a person can take the _____ Questionnaire.
3. The single most important behavioral indicator of sidedness is _____.
4. Lefties who write with a hooked hand are usually _____-brain dominant for language processing.
5. Many left-handed children are still forced to use their right hand for writing, eating, and other skills, especially in India and Japan, which are both _____ cultures, unlike the U.S. and Canada, which would be described as individualist.
6. People may be at risk for more immune-related diseases if they show _____ handedness.
7. Derrick is especially good at visualizing three-dimensional objects. He is most likely _____- handed.
8. A psychologist is studying the differences between the two sides of the body, especially differences in the abilities of each brain hemisphere. This psychologist is studying _____.
9. Individuals who have better than average pitch memory are most likely left-handed or _____.
10. Edgar experienced less language loss and recovered more quickly from his stroke than his brother Jon. Edgar is most likely _____-handed.

Connections

1. ___ righties
2. ___ lefties
3. ___ ambidextrous
4. ___ sideness
5. ___ lateralization
6. ___ handedness
7. ___ dominant hemisphere

a. a term usually applied to the side of a person's brain that produces language
b. able to use either hand with equal skill
c. a combination of preferences for hand, foot, eye, and ear
d. preference for which hand one uses
e. were often referred to as dexterous, coordinated, skillful, and just
f. specialization in the abilities of the brain hemispheres
g. were often characterized as clumsy, awkward, unlucky, or insincere

Check Your Memory

1. TRUE or FALSE   Righties are more likely to be referred to as clumsy, awkward, unlucky, or insincere.
2. TRUE or FALSE   If you are left-handed, there is literally more area on the right side of your brain devoted to controlling your left hand than vice versa.
3. TRUE or FALSE   People generally prefer breathing through one nostril over the other and even have a preference for which direction they lean their head when kissing.
4. TRUE or FALSE   Only 19 percent of all lefties and 3 percent of all righties use their right brain for language.
5. TRUE or FALSE   Gesturing more with your right hand is associated with right-brain language processing
6. TRUE or FALSE   Clear hand preferences are apparent before birth with prenatal hand preferences persisting for at least 10 years after birth.
7. TRUE or FALSE   Studies of twins show that hand preferences are directly inherited like eye color and skin color.
8. TRUE or FALSE   The proportion of left-handers in collectivist countries is only about half that found in individualist countries, such as the United States and Canada.
9. TRUE or FALSE   A small minority of lefties owe their hand preference to birth traumas with this group also having higher rates of allergies and learning disorders.
10. TRUE or FALSE   There are more left-handed architects, artists, and chess players than would be expected
11. TRUE or FALSE   In general, right-handers are more symmetrical in almost everything including eye dominance, fingerprints, and even foot size.
12. TRUE or FALSE   Right-handed individuals typically experience less language loss after damage to either brain hemisphere and recover more easily.

Critical Thinking Question

News reports that left-handed people tend to die younger have been flawed in an important way: The average age of people in the left-handed group was younger than that of subjects in the right-handed group. Why would this make a difference in the conclusions drawn?

Final Survey and Review--Completion

Module 2.1 Neurons and the Nervous System
Neurons—Building a "Biocomputer"
Survey Question: How do nerve cells operate and communicate?

1. Information enters the neuron at the dendrite, is processed by cell body, also known as the _____.
2. The electrical charge of an inactive neuron is called its _____ potential.
3. After each nerve impulse, the neuron becomes less willing to fire, a state known as a negative _____.
4. Multiple sclerosis is a disease involving numbness, weakness, and paralysis that occurs when the immune system attacks and destroys the _____ layer.
5. An excess of dopamine is believed to cause the mental disorder known as _____.
6. Alzheimer's disease is believed to result from a lack of the neurotransmitter _____.
7. Enkephalins and endorphins do not carry messages directly, but, instead, regulate the activity of other neurons and are, therefore, classified as _____.
8. Every time you learn something, you are reshaping your living brain, a process described as self-directed _____.

Module 2.1 Neurons and the Nervous System
The Nervous System—Wired for Action
Survey Question: What are the major parts of the nervous system?

9. The central nervous system is made up of the brain and _____.
10. Nerves can be seen without magnification and consist of large bundles of neuron _____.
11. Neurilemma allows damaged nerve fibers in the _____ nervous system to be repaired.
12. Messages are carried to and from the sense organs and skeletal muscles in the _____ nervous system.
13. The sympathetic and parasympathetic branches make up the _____ nervous system.
14. The body is prepared for "fight or flight" during times of danger or high emotion by the _____ branch.
15. Information is transferred from a sensory neuron to a connector neuron in the spinal cord and back through a motor neuron during a(n) _____.
16. Although the brain loses cells daily, it simultaneously grows new neurons to replace them through a process known as _____.

Module 2.2 Brain Research
Mapping Brain Structure—Pieces of the Puzzle
Survey Question: How are different parts of the brain identified?

17. Biopsychology is the study of how biological processes, especially those occurring in the nervous system, are related to _____.
18. When Terrence suffered a stroke, his doctor used a specialized type of X-ray called a(n) _____ scan to view the damage to his brain.
19. The type of scan that uses a very strong magnetic field to produce an image of the body's interior is the _____ scan.

113

Module 2.2 Brain Research
Mapping Brain Function—Figuring Out What the Parts Do
Survey Question: What do the different parts of the brain do?

20. The detailed symptoms of Kate Adamson's locked-in syndrome was extensively studied by doctors using a(n) _____ study.

21. To treat his severe obsessive-compulsive disorder, Brad's doctor used a strong electric current to destroy a very small amount of brain tissue in a target area of Brad's brain. The doctor was using a procedure known as deep _____.

22. The technique that amplifies very weak signals (brain waves) and records them on a moving sheet of paper or a computer screen is called _____.

23. Using PET scans, psychologist Richard Haier and his colleagues found that the brains of people who perform well on a difficult reasoning test consume _____ energy than those of poor performers.

24. To tell if a person was lying, psychiatrist Daniel Langleben and his colleagues looked at brain activity in the front of the brain using a technique known as _____.

Module 2.3 Hemispheres and Lobes of the Cerebral Cortex
The Cerebral Cortex—My, What a Wrinkled Brain You Have!
Survey Questions: How do the left and right hemispheres differ? What are the different functions of the lobes of the cerebral cortex?

25. There are four lobes in each of the two hemispheres making up the _____.

26. Tia had a stroke that damaged her right hemisphere. She sometimes looks at her left arm and says that it does not belong to her. Tia is experiencing a condition known as _____.

27. When a "split-brain" operation is performed, the doctor sever the connection between the two hemispheres by cutting the _____.

28. If we flash a dollar sign to the right brain and a question mark to the left brain of a split-brain patient and then ask the patient to tell us what he saw, he would say a _____.

29. The hemisphere that helps us express emotions and detect the emotions that other people are feeling is the _____ hemisphere.

30. In general, the hemisphere that tends to process information sequentially and to focus on details is the _____ hemisphere.

31. The lobes of the brain that are associated with higher mental abilities, play a role in your sense of self, and are responsible for the control of movement are the _____ lobes.

32. Motor (or expressive aphasia) is caused by damage to _____ area in the left frontal lobes.

33. Touch, temperature, pressure, and other somatic sensations flow into the primary somatosensory area of the _____ lobes.

34. At the back of the brain, the areas of the cortex concerned with vision are the _____ lobes.

35. In a study of men and women with similar IQ scores, brain images revealed men's gray matter was split between their frontal and parietal lobes, while their white matter was mostly in the _____ lobes.

Module 2.4 Subcortex and Endocrine System
The Subcortex—At the Core of the (Brain) Matter
Survey Question: What are the major parts of the subcortex?

36. The subcortex is made up of the hindbrain, midbrain, and parts of the forebrain, excluding the _____.

114

37. A karate chop to the back of the neck can be extremely dangerous because it could damage the part of the brain that controls heart rate and breathing. This part is called the _____.

38. The part of the brainstem that lies at the base of the brain and primarily regulates posture, muscle tone, and muscular coordination is the _____.

39. One reason that children have such short attention spans is that a part of the hindbrain does not fully mature until adolescence. This part is the _____.

40. The system in lower animals that helps organize basic survival responses and in humans has a clear link to emotions is the _____ system.

41. A "quick pathway" to the cortex that enables us to react to dangerous stimuli before we fully know what is going on is the part of the brain known as the _____.

42. Many of the pleasure centers in the brain overlap with areas in a brain part that controls thirst, sex, and hunger called the _____.

Module 2.4 Subcortex and Endocrine System
The Endocrine System—My Hormones Made Me Do It
Survey Question: Does the glandular system affect behavior?

43. The sex drive in both males and females is related to male sex hormones known as _____.

44. Dwarfism, giantism, and acromegaly are three conditions resulting from an incorrect amount of growth hormones being released from the _____ gland. hands, feet, and facial bones become enlarged known as _____.

45. In response to daily variations in light, melatonin is released by the _____ gland.

46. Secreted by the adrenal medulla, the hormone that arouses the body, is linked with anger, and also functions as a neurotransmitter is _____.

47. Younger adolescents are at increased risk of heart attack and stroke, liver damage, or stunted growth if they try to improve their athletic ability by taking _____.

Module 2.5 Psychology in Action: Handedness—Are You Dexterous or Sinister?
Are You Right- or Left-Handed?
Survey Question: In what ways do right- and left-handed individuals differ?

48. A psychologist asks Simone to throw a ball, to kick a football, to look through a telescope, and to listen to a conversation on her cell phone. This psychologist is assessing Simone's hand, foot, eye and ear preference, which is known as _____.

49. Left-handed individuals who write with a straight hand and righties who write with a hooked hand are usually _____-brain dominant for language processing.

50. The proportion of left-handers in collectivist societies, such as India and Japan, is only about half that found in _____ cultures such as the United States and Canada

51. People with inconsistent handedness as opposed to consistent left-handers may be at risk for more _____-related diseases

52. The physical size and shape of the cerebral hemispheres are more alike in people who are _____ handed.

Final Survey and Review—Matching

Module 2.1 Neurons and the Nervous System

1. ___ axon   a. a fatty insulating coating on some axons that speeds conduction

2. ___ dendrite   b. the production of new brain cells

115

3. ___ soma
c. neuron fiber that looks like a tree branch and receives incoming messages

4. ___ synapse
d. deficiency of this neurotransmitter plays a role in Alzheimer's disease

5. ___ myelin
e. layer of cells that aids in the repair of damaged nerve cells

6. ___ acetylcholine
f. made up of brain and spinal cord

7. ___ dopamine
g. main body of a neuron

8. ___ neurilemma
h. the simplest behavior in which a stimulus provokes an automatic response

9. ___ neurogenesis
i. controls voluntary movement

10. ___ autonomic nervous system
j. fiber that carries information away from the cell body of a neuron

11. ___ central nervous system
k. deficiency of this neurotransmitter leads to Parkinson's disease and an excess to schizophrenia

12. ___ somatic nervous system
l. microscopic space between two neurons over which messages pass

13. ___ reflex arc
m. made up of the sympathetic and parasympathetic branches

Module 2.2 Brain Research

1. ___ CT scan
a. a device that detects, amplifies, and records brain waves on a moving sheet of paper or a computer screen

2. ___ MRI scan
b. a detailed investigation of a single person

3. ___ clinical case study
c. provides structural and functional imaging of the brain and has been used to detect lying

4. ___ ESB
d. a computer-generated image of brain activity based on glucose consumption in the brain

5. ___ localization of function
e. "turning on" the brain by stimulating it with a mild electric current

6. ___ ablation
f. removal of a small amount of brain tissue using an electrode

7. ___ deep lesioning
g. a three-dimensional image of the brain or body based on the response to a magnetic field

8. ___ EEG
h. surgical removal of larger parts of the brain

9. ___ PET scan
i. the research strategy of linking specific structures in the brain to specific psychological or behavioral responses

10. ___ fMRI
j. a computer-enhanced X-ray image of the brain or body

Module 2.3 Hemispheres and Lobes of the Cerebral Cortex

1. ___ corticalization
a. location of Broca's area and motor cortex

2. ___ corpus callosum
b. location of primary visual area

3. ___ mirror neurons
c. location of Wernicke's area and primary auditory area

4. ___ frontal lobes
d. impairment of this system may be the cause of autism spectrum disorders

116

5. ___ parietal lobes
6. ___ temporal lobes

7. ___ occipital lobes

e. location of primary somatosensory area
f. increase in the size and wrinkling of the cerebral cortex
g. connects right and left hemispheres

Module 2.4: Subcortex and Endocrine System

1. ___ medulla

2. ___ cerebellum

3. ___ reticular formation

4. ___ thalamus

5. ___ hypothalamus

6. ___ amygdala

7. ___ hippocampus

8. ___ pituitary gland

9. ___ pineal gland

10. ___ thyroid gland

11. ___ adrenal medulla

12. ___ adrenal cortex

a. control center for emotion and many basic motives and directs the "master gland"
b. secretes melatonin in response to daily variations in light
c. the source of epinephrine and norepinephreine
d. regulates posture, muscle tone, and muscular coordination and stores memories related to skills and habits
e. located in the neck and regulates metabolism
f. part of the forebrain that is important in forming long-term verbal memories
g. produces a set of hormones called corticoids that regulate salt balance in the body and serve as a secondary source of sex hormones
h. small football-shaped structure in the forebrain that acts as a final "switching station" for sensory messages on their way to the cortex
i. connects brain with the spinal cord and controls vital life functions
j. influences attention by giving priority to some incoming messages while turning others aside
k. secretes growth hormones and controls milk production during breastfeeding
l. provides a primitive, "quick pathway" to the cortex, particularly for fear responses

Module 2.5 Psychology in Action: Handedness—Are You Dexterous or Sinister?

1. ___ right-handed persons

2. ___ left-handed persons
3. ___ ambidextrous

4. ___ sideness

5. ___ lateralization

6. ___ dominant hemisphere

a. a term usually applied to the side of a person's brain that produces language
b. able to use either hand with equal skill
c. a combination of preferences for hand, foot, eye, and ear
d. physical size and shape of their cerebral hemispheres are more alike
e. experience more language loss after brain damage and recover more slowly
f. specialization in the abilities of the brain hemispheres

117

Final Survey and Review—True or False

Module 2.1 Neurons and the Nervous System
Neurons—Building a "Biocomputer"
Survey Question: How do nerve cells operate and communicate?

1. TRUE or FALSE   During an action potential, the ion channels pop open and allow potassium ions (K+) to rush into the axon from outside the membrane.
2. TRUE or FALSE   If the myelin layer is damaged, a person will suffer from multiple sclerosis.
3. TRUE or FALSE   An action potential is primarily an electrical process, while communication between neurons is a chemical process.
4. TRUE or FALSE   The microscopic space between two neurons, over which messages pass, is called a soma.
5. TRUE or FALSE   Too little acetylcholine may play a role in Alzheimer's disease.
6. TRUE or FALSE   An excess of serotonin has been implicated in neuron death and autism
7. TRUE or FALSE   Every time you learn something, you are reshaping your living brain, a process termed self-directed neuroplasticity.

Module 2.1 The Nervous System—Wired for Action
Survey Question: What are the major parts of the nervous system?

8. TRUE or FALSE   The central nervous system is made up of the brain and spinal cord.
9. TRUE or FALSE   The axons of neurons within the peripheral nervous system are covered by neurilemma, which aids in their repair.
10. TRUE or FALSE   When you ride a bicycle, this voluntary movement of your leg muscles is under the control of the autonomic nervous system.
11. TRUE or FALSE   "Vegetative" functions, such as heart rate, digestion, and perspiration are under the control of the somatic nervous system.
12. TRUE or FALSE   Thirty-one pairs of spinal nerves carry sensory and motor messages to and from the spinal cord.
13. TRUE or FALSE   A connector neuron is one that carries messages from the central nervous system to muscles and glands.
14. TRUE or FALSE   A healthy brain will have significantly fewer neurons when it is 75 years old than when it is 25 years old.

Module 2.2 Brain Research
Mapping Brain Structure—Pieces of the Puzzle
Survey Question: How are different parts of the brain identified?

15. TRUE or FALSE   Dissection reveals that the brain is made up of many anatomically distinct areas or "parts."
16. TRUE or FALSE   A CT scan utilizes a very strong magnetic field to produce an image of the body's interior.
17. TRUE or FALSE   MRI scans produce more detailed images than are possible with CT scans.

Module 2.2 Mapping Brain Function—Figuring Out What the Parts Do
Survey Question: What do the different parts of the brain do?

18. TRUE or FALSE   Electrical stimulation of the brain (ESB) could be used to control a person like a robot.

118

19. TRUE or FALSE   An electroencephalograph (EEG) uses microelectrodes to measure the brain waves deep inside the human brain.

20. TRUE or FALSE   Using PET scans, Haier and his associates found that the brains of people who perform well on a reasoning test consume less energy than those of poor performers.

21. TRUE or FALSE   Langleben demonstrated that a person who is lying will show more activity in the front of the brain than a person who is telling the truth.

Module 2.3 Hemispheres and Lobes of the Cerebral Cortex
The Cerebral Cortex—My, What a Wrinkled Brain You Have!

Survey Questions: How do the left and right hemispheres differ? What are the different functions of the lobes of the cerebral cortex?

22. TRUE or FALSE   The cerebral cortex covers most of the brain with a mantle of gray matter, which is spongy tissue made up mostly of cell bodies.

23. TRUE or FALSE   Failing to notice objects in one's left visual field after brain damage to the right hemisphere would be referred to as spatial neglect.

24. TRUE or FALSE   "Split-brain" operations rarely cause conflicts between the actions of the two hemispheres because both halves of the brain normally have about the same experience at the same time.

25. TRUE or FALSE   If we flash a picture of a cat to the right brain of a split-brain patient and a picture of a basketball to his left brain and then ask him to draw what he saw using his left hand (out of sight), the patient will draw a basketball.

26. TRUE or FALSE   The right hemisphere is superior at math, judging time and rhythm, and coordinating the order of complex movements, such as those needed for speech.

27. TRUE or FALSE   The left hemisphere appears to process information simultaneously and holistically.

28. TRUE or FALSE   The primary motor area is located in the frontal lobes of the brain.

29. TRUE or FALSE   Damage to Wernicke's area causes receptive (or fluent) aphasia.

30. TRUE or FALSE   The somatosensory area is located on the temporal lobes of the brain.

31. TRUE or FALSE   Damage to mirror neurons may partially explain the occurrence of autism spectrum disorders.

32. TRUE or FALSE   Broca's aphasia is an inability to identify seen objects and is caused by damage to the association areas on the occipital lobes.

33. TRUE or FALSE   In a study of men and women with similar IQ scores women had more gray and white matter concentrated in their frontal lobes than the men did.

Module 2.4 Subcortex and Endocrine System
The Subcortex—At the Core of the (Brain) Matter

Survey Question: What are the major parts of the subcortex?

34. TRUE or FALSE   You could lose large portions of your cerebral cortex and still survive.

35. TRUE or FALSE   The medulla contains centers important for the reflex control of vital life functions, including heart rate, breathing, swallowing

36. TRUE or FALSE   Musicians tend to have smaller than average cerebellums, since they need fewer neurons to practice their special skills.than average cerebellums.

37. TRUE or FALSE   The amygdala looks like a small bump on the brainstem and acts as a bridge between the medulla and other brain areas.

38. TRUE or FALSE   Incoming messages from the sense organs branch into a part of the hippocampus called the hippocampal activating system, which bombards the cortex with stimulation, keeping it active and alert.
39. TRUE or FALSE   Damage to the thalamus will disrupt all of the senses EXCEPT for hearing.
40. TRUE or FALSE   Laughter has its origins in the limbic system

Module 2.4 The Endocrine System—My Hormones Made Me Do It

Survey Question: Does the glandular system affect behavior?

41. TRUE or FALSE   For both men and women, watching a romantic film boosted a hormone that's linked to relaxation and reproduction.
42. TRUE or FALSE   In women, the pineal gland controls milk output during breast-feeding.
43. TRUE or FALSE   A person suffering from hypothyroidism (an underactive thyroid) tends to be thin, tense, excitable, and nervous.
44. TRUE or FALSE   An oversecretion of adrenal sex hormones early in life causes premature puberty and enabled a five--year-old Peruvian girl to give birth to a son.
45. TRUE or FALSE   The use of anabolic steroids can cause voice deepening or baldness in women and shrinkage of the testicles, sexual impotence, or breast enlargement in men.

Module 2.5 Psychology in Action: Handedness—Are You Dexterous or Sinister? Are You Right- or Left-Handed?

Survey Question: In what ways do right- and left-handed individuals differ?

46. TRUE or FALSE   The Latin word for left is sinister.
47. TRUE or FALSE   Forcing a left-handed child to use his right-hand has not been shown to create speech or reading problems.
48. TRUE or FALSE   Gesturing more with your left-hand is associated with left-brain language processing.
49. TRUE or FALSE   Most left-handed persons produce speech from their right hemispheres.
50. TRUE or FALSE   The only sure way to check brain dominance is to do medical tests that involve assessing one cerebral hemisphere at a time.
51. TRUE or FALSE   Two left-handed parents are more likely to have a left-handed child than two right-handed parents are.
52. TRUE or FALSE   More musicians are ambidextrous than would normally be expected

Mastery Test

1. Information in neurons usually flows in what order?
    a. soma, dendrites, axon
    b. dendrites, soma, axon
    c. dendrites, myelin, axon terminals
    d. axon, soma, axon terminals

2. When the axon's ion channels pop open and allow sodium ions to rush into the axon, a(n)
    a. action potential is occurring.
    b. neuron is in a resting potential.
    c. neuron is in a negative after-potential.
    d. synaptic transmission has been completed.

120

3. Saltatory conduction is the process by which nerve impulses conducted down the axons of neurons and jump from gap to gap within the _____ layer.
   a. myelin
   b. acetylcholine
   c. neuropeptide
   d. neurilemma

4. Neurotransmitters are released from the axon terminal of one axon and bind to the receptor sites on another neuron by crossing the
   a. myelin sheath.
   b. synapse.
   c. neurilemma.
   d. mitochondria.

5. People with Parkinson's disease lack or have very little of the neurotransmitter
   a. dopamine.
   b. GABA.
   c. epinephrine.
   d. serotonin.

6. South American Indians of the Amazon River Basin use curare as an arrow poison for hunting because it competes with the neurotransmitter
   a. acetylcholine.
   b. serotonin.
   c. enkephalin.
   d. dopamine.

7. Regulating the activity of other neurons is most characteristic of
   a. negative after-potentials.
   b. reflex arcs.
   c. acetylcholine.
   d. neuropeptides.

8. Research has shown that our brains have the capacity to change in response to experiences, such as therapy and training. This ability is called
   a. synaptic malleability.
   b. neuroresilency.
   c. neuroplasticity.
   d. neurilemmic potential.

9. The axons of most neurons outside the brain and spinal cord are covered by a thin layer of cells that forms a "tunnel" that damaged fibers can follow as they repair themselves. This layer of cells is called
   a. myelin.
   b. acetylcholine.
   c. neuropeptide.
   d. neurilemma.

121

10. When you toss a ball or ride a bicycle, the voluntary muscles you used are under the control of the
    a. central nervous system.
    b. somatic nervous system.
    c. sympathetic branch of the autonomic nervous system.
    d. parasympathetic branch of the autonomic nervous system.

11. At times of emergency, which of the following prepares the body for "fight-or flight"?
    a. central nervous system
    b. somatic nervous system
    c. sympathetic branch of the autonomic nervous system
    d. parasympathetic branch of the autonomic nervous system

12. You are reaching into the stove with a pot holder when your little finger touches the hot baking sheet. You immediately jerk your hand back, spilling some of the cookies in the stove. This automatic action of your hand to the pain is called a(n)
    a. reflex arc.
    b. somatic reflex.
    c. cranial arc.
    d. synaptic reflex.

13. Which of the following is a specialized type of X-ray?
    a. PET scan
    b. CT scan
    c. MRI scan
    d. EEG scan

14. After Joshua fell down a set of stairs and was knocked unconscious, he was examined at the hospital using a procedure in which he was placed in a magnetic field that generated a three-dimensional image of his body and brain. The procedure being utilized is a(n)
    a. EEG.
    b. PET scan.
    c. CT scan.
    d. MRI scan.

15. The level of activity in various parts of Tia's brain will be determined by measuring the amount of radioactive glucose used by her brain cells in these areas. Tia's brain activity will be measured by a(n)
    a. EEG.
    b. PET scan.
    c. CT scan.
    d. ESB.

16. When medications and therapy are ineffective with severe obsessive-compulsive disorder, a strong electric current can be used to destroy a small of amount of brain tissue by lowering an electrode into a target area inside the brain. This procedure is known as
    a. EMDR.
    b. neuroplasticity.
    c. deep lesioning.
    d. electroconvulsive therapy.

17. Upon waking, Natasha experienced difficulty with her eye-hand coordination and exhibited an awkward gait when she walked. Natasha is exhibiting neurological _____ of a stroke.
    a. soft signs
    b. behavior markers
    c. aphasic symptoms
    d. episodic precursors

18. In the past, some people with severe epilepsy underwent a "split-brain" operation in which the
    a. amygdala was removed.
    b. connection between the hypothalamus and pituitary gland was severed.
    c. corpus callosum was cut.
    d. prefrontal cortex was separated from the rest of the brain.

19. Dinah's ability to work as a commercial artist would be most impaired if she damaged which area?
    a. Broca's area
    b. corpus callosum
    c. left cerebral hemisphere
    d. right cerebral hemisphere

20. Speech, language, calculation, and analysis are special skills of the
    a. right cerebral hemisphere.
    b. limbic system.
    c. left cerebral hemisphere
    d. reticular activating system.

21. Which of the following brain areas tends to focus on small details and process information sequentially?
    a. amygdala
    b. hippocampus
    c. left cerebral hemisphere
    d. right cerebral hemisphere

22. Electrically stimulating a portion of which brain lobe would produce muscle movements?
    a. occipital lobe
    b. frontal lobe
    c. parietal lobe
    d. temporal lobe

23. Damage to the mirror neurons may play a role in which of the following disorders?
    a. autism spectrum disorders
    b. schizophrenia
    c. bipolar disorders
    d. multiple sclerosis

24. You feel an insect crawling on your arm. The sensation of the insect's movement on your arm is being processed in which lobe of your brain?
    a. parietal lobe
    b. frontal lobe
    c. temporal lobe
    d. occipital lobe

25. After a stroke, Jasmine was able to speak but had difficulty understanding the meaning of words. The stroke most likely damaged which area?
    a. amygdala
    b. Broca's area
    c. Wernicke's area
    d. occipital lobe

26. A tumor in which brain area would most likely cause blind spots in a person's vision?
    a. frontal lobe
    b. parietal lobe
    c. temporal lobe
    d. occipital lobe

27. Which of the following is a part of the hindbrain?
    a. pons
    b. hypothalamus
    c. hippocampus
    d. amygdala

28. Tony is a skilled musician as well as an expert tennis player. Many would say it is due to his excellent muscular coordination, which is directed by which part of the hindbrain?
    a. medulla
    b. hippocampus
    c. hypothalamus
    d. cerebellum

29. Which part of the brain is associated with attention, alertness, and some reflexes, such as sneezing and coughing?
    a. hippocampus
    b. medulla
    c. cerebellum
    d. reticular formation

30. Which part of the brain acts as a final switching station for all incoming sensory information, except for smell?
    a. amygdala
    b. pons
    c. thalamus
    d. reticular activating system

31. Many of your emotions as well as your basic motives, such as hunger, thirst, and sex, are directed by the
    a. hypothalamus.
    b. hippocampus.
    c. reticular formation.
    d. midbrain.

32. Electrically stimulating which part of the limbic system would most likely elicit fear responses in a person?
    a. amygdala
    b. cerebellum
    c. thalamus
    d. reticular formation

33. When you remember the places and events of previous vacations, these lasting memories were stored by which part of the brain?
    a. amygdala
    b. hypothalamus
    c. thalamus
    d. hippocampus

34. Which of the following pairs contains the "master gland" and its master?
    a. pineal—thalamus
    b. thyroid—RAS
    c. pituitary—hypothalamus
    d. adrenal—cerebellum

35. Jed is a professional wrestler, who has prominent facial features and large hands and feet that were caused by an overproduction of growth hormone late in his growth cycle. This condition is known as
    a. hyperthyroidism.
    b. hypothyroidism.
    c. acromegaly.
    d. virilism.

36. Which hormone is released by the pineal gland with the levels of this hormone rising in the bloodstream at dusk, peaking around midnight, and falling again as morning approaches?
    a. thyroxin
    b. melatonin
    c. dopamine
    d. acetylcholine

37. Which gland if underactive in infancy can limit the development of the child's nervous system and cause severe intellectual disability?
    a. thyroid gland
    b. adrenal gland
    c. pituitary gland
    d. pineal gland

38. Which of the following is produced by the adrenal medulla, tends to arouse the body, and is linked with anger?
    a. serotonin
    b. norepinephrine
    c. acetylcholine
    d. dopamine

39. Which of the following indicates right-brain language processing?
    a. A person who gestures with his or her right hand.
    b. A left-handed person who writes with a hooked left hand.
    c. A right-handed person who writes with a straight hand.
    d. A right-handed person who writes with a hooked position.

40. Which of the following statements about handedness is FALSE?
    a. Hand preferences are directly inherited like eye color or skin color.
    b. A majority of left-handers produce speech from the left hemisphere.
    c. Left-handers are less lateralized than the right-handers.
    d. Left-handers are more symmetrical in eye dominance, fingerprints, and foot size than right-handers.

Chapter 3: Human Development

Chapter Overview

Heredity (nature) and environment (nurture) are interacting forces that are both necessary for human development. However, caregivers can only influence environment. The chromosomes and genes in each cell of the body carry hereditary instructions. Most characteristics are polygenic and reflect the combined effects of dominant and recessive genes. Maturation of the body and nervous system underlies the orderly development of motor skills, cognitive abilities, emotions, and language. Many early skills are subject to the principle of readiness. Prenatal development is influenced by environmental factors, such as various teratogens, including diseases, drugs, and radiation, as well as the mother's diet, health, and emotions. During sensitive periods in development, infants are more sensitive to specific environmental influences. Early perceptual, intellectual, or emotional deprivation seriously retards development, whereas deliberate enrichment of the environment has a beneficial effect on infants. In general, environment sets a reaction range within which maturation unfolds. Temperament is hereditary. Most infants fall into one of three temperament categories: easy children, difficult children, and slow-to-warm-up children. A child's developmental level reflects heredity, environment, and the effects of the child's own behavior.

The human neonate has a number of adaptive reflexes, including the grasping, rooting, sucking, and Moro reflexes. Neonates begin to learn immediately, and they appear to be aware of the effects of their actions. The rate of maturation varies from person to person. Also, learning contributes greatly to the development of basic motor skills. Tests in a looking chamber reveal a number of visual preferences in the newborn. The neonate is drawn to bright lights and circular or curved designs. Infants prefer human face patterns, especially familiar faces. In later infancy, interest in the unfamiliar emerges. Emotions develop in a consistent order, starting with generalized excitement in newborn babies. Three of the basic emotions—fear, anger, and joy— may be unlearned.

Emotional attachment of human infants is a critical early event. Infant attachment is reflected by separation anxiety. The quality of attachment can be classified as secure, insecure-avoidant, or insecure-ambivalent. Secure attachment is fostered by consistent care from parents who are sensitive to a baby's signals and rhythms. Secure attachment is fostered by consistent care from parents who are sensitive to a baby's signals and rhythms. Meeting a baby's affectional needs is as important as meeting needs for physical care.

Studies suggest that parental styles have a substantial impact on emotional and intellectual development. Three major parental styles are authoritarian, permissive, and authoritative (effective). Authoritative parenting appears to benefit children the most. Whereas mothers typically emphasize care giving, fathers tend to function as playmates for infants. Both care-giving styles contribute to the competence of young children. The ultimate success of various parenting styles depends on what culture or ethnic community a child will enter. Parenting styles vary across cultures.

Learning to use language is a cornerstone of early intellectual development. Language development proceeds from crying to cooing, then babbling, the use of single words, and then to telegraphic speech. The underlying patterns of telegraphic speech suggest a biological predisposition to acquire language. This innate tendency is augmented by learning. Prelanguage communication between parent and child involves shared rhythms, nonverbal signals, and turn-taking. Motherese or parentese is a simplified, musical style of speaking that parents use to help their children learn language.

The intellect of a child is less abstract than that of an adult. Jean Piaget theorized that intellectual growth occurs through a combination of assimilation and accommodation. Piaget also held that children go through a fixed series of cognitive stages. The stages and their approximate age ranges are sensorimotor (0–2), preoperational (2–7), concrete operational (7–11), and formal operations (11–adult). Learning principles provide an alternate explanation that assumes that cognitive development is continuous and does not occur in stages. Recent studies of infants under the age of one year suggest that they are capable of thought well beyond that observed by Piaget. Similarly, children begin to outgrow egocentrism as early as age 4. Lev Vygotsky's sociocultural theory emphasizes that a child's mental abilities are advanced by interactions with more competent partners. Mental growth takes place in a child's zone of proximal development, where a more skillful person may scaffold the child's progress.

The timing of puberty can complicate the task of identity formation, a major task of adolescence. Identity formation is even more challenging for adolescents of ethnic descent. In Western industrialized societies, the transition into adulthood is further complicated as it is increasingly delayed well into the twenties. Lawrence Kohlberg identified preconventional, conventional, and postconventional levels of moral reasoning. Developing mature moral standards is also an important task of adolescence. Most people function at the conventional level of morality, but some never get beyond the selfish, preconventional level. Only a minority of people attain the highest, or postconventional level, of moral reasoning. Carol Gilligan distinguished between Kohlberg's justice perspective and a caring perspective. Mature adult morality likely involves both.

Erik Erikson identified a series of specific psychosocial dilemmas that occur as we age. These range from a need to gain trust in infancy to the need to live with integrity in old age. Successful resolution of the dilemmas produces healthy development, whereas unsuccessful outcomes make it harder to deal with later crises. Well-being during adulthood consists of six elements: self-acceptance, positive relations with others, autonomy, environmental mastery, having a purpose in life, and continued personal growth. Physical aging starts early in adulthood. Every adult must find ways to successfully cope with aging. Only a minority of people have a midlife crisis, but midlife course corrections are more common. Intellectual declines associated with aging are limited, at least through one's seventies. This is especially true of individuals who remain mentally active. Successful lives are based on happiness, purpose, meaning, and integrity. Ageism refers to prejudice, discrimination, and stereotyping on the basis of age. It affects people of all ages but is especially damaging to older people. Most ageism is based on stereotypes, myths, and misinformation. Typical emotional reactions to impending death include denial, anger, bargaining, depression, and acceptance, but not necessarily in that order or in every case. Death is a natural part of life. There is value in understanding it and accepting it.

Effective parental discipline tends to emphasize child management techniques (especially communication), rather than power assertion or withdrawal of love. Consistency is also an important aspect of effective parenting. Effective parents allow their children to express their feelings but place limits on their behavior. Much misbehavior can be managed by use of I-messages and the application of natural and logical consequences.

Preview: It's a Girl!

Language Development Guide
glimpse: quick look
frankly: truthfully
prune: wrinkly dried fruit
pudgy: fat
stubby: short
unfold: develop
instructive: useful; informative
take for granted: undervalue
literal: exact words
tracing: mapping out; outlining

Module 3.1 The Interplay of Heredity and Environment
Nature and Nurture—It Takes Two to Tango
Survey Question: How do heredity and environment affect development?

Language Development Guide
human growth sequence: pattern of physical development from conception to death.
prenatal: time between conception and birth
deprivation: the loss or withholding of normal stimulation, nutrition, comfort, and love; a
       condition of lacking
enrichment: intentionally making an environment more stimulating, nutritional, comforting, and
       loving
ultimately: finally; at last
interplay: interaction; a relationship between
nature: due to genetic make-up
nurture: due to the environment
inborn: hereditary
progressive: advancing; increasing
conception: fertilization; sperm and egg unite
from the womb to the tomb: from birth to death
heredity: the transmission, or passing on, of physical and psychological characteristics from
       parents to offspring through genes
governed: directed; managed; controlled
analogy: comparison based on similar characteristics
dimensions: factors; aspects
essential: necessary
prominent: well-known; important
potentials: possibilities
limitations: weak points
nutrition: food
transmission: passing on
incredible: huge
nucleus: control center
code: set of instructions
record: detailed information

room left over to spare: extra space
milestone: high point
sequencing: determining the order
heritage: inheritance
segments: parts; sections
in actuality: in real life
expression (of genes): instructions or information from the genes are used
susceptibility: weakness to
genes can switch on (or off) at certain ages: genes can be activated to produce an effect
exert: put forth
sexual orientation: one's degree of emotional and erotic attraction to members of the same sex,
     opposite sex, or both sexes
host: multitude; large number
climax: peak
duration: length of time
senescence: biological process of going old; aging
physiological: study of the biological functioning of the body
deterioration: decline; weakening
approximate: rough estimate; near
say goodbye to diapers: to have bladder and bowel control; to be toilet-trained
overeager: demanding
"trying": difficult
false alarms: a warning that was untrue (in toilet training, a child "thinking" he or she has to use
     the bathroom but really does not)
"accidents": mistakes in toileting
dictate: order; command
so why fight nature?: there is no reason to try to change one's inborn maturational schedule
the wet look is in: a phrase that originally referred to damp hair style as being popular, but in this
     case it refers to toddlers' wet panties when they have a toileting "accident"
profound: great; intense
blooming and pruning: dendrites growing when used and reducing in complexity and number
     when unused
evolving: changing; advancing
cave dwellers: refers to prehistoric humans
gangsta rapper: a recording artist/musician that performs a particular style of rap music
characterizing the
     experiences of urban (city) street gangs
Upper Paleolithic: late Stone Age; beginning of a variety of humans (Cro-Magnon man) that are
     more similar to modern day humans
a hunter or food gatherer: obtaining food in the wild through the killing of animals or gathering
     foods that grow wild; food not obtained through agriculture
womb: uterus; part of a woman's body in which the unborn baby grows
penetrated: entered
German measles: contagious infection that causes a rash; also called rubella
syphilis: a bacterial sexually transmitted disease that can be cured in its early stages
HIV: Human immunodeficiency virus causes acquired immunodeficiency syndrome (AIDS) and is
     incurable
radiation: energy in waves
congenital: present at birth
defects: flaws, errors

fetus: term for the unborn baby during the period from the end of the eighth week after conception until birth

apparent: visible; obvious

sickle-cell anemia: genetic blood disease occurs more in Black people of African descent

hemophilia: inherited bleeding disorders in which the ability of blood to clot is impaired; occurs more inmales

cystic fibrosis: inherited disease that affects the lungs, digestive system, and sweat glands; occurs more in white people of northern-European descent

muscular dystrophy: group of genetic diseases that cause increasing weakness of the voluntary muscles controlling movement

albinism: genetic disorder in which there is a partial or total lack of pigment; occurs in plants and animals

intellectual disabilities: developmental disability characterized by a significant impairments in mental ability (IQ below 70) and adaptive (self-care) abilities

embryo: term for the unborn baby during the period from the end of the second week after conception through the eighth week (after conception)

pesticides: any substance used to kill or repel insects

polychlorinated biphenyls (PCBs): group of man-made oily liquid compounds used in coolants, insulation, flame retardant materials, and other uses; banned in 1970s because of its harmful effects

affected: changed by

miscarrying: spontaneous loss of a pregnancy before 24 weeks (before fetus has a change of survival)

premature: birth before fetus has been in the womb 37 weeks

"up in smoke": to be destroyed

poor start in life: growing up being deprived of normal care and nutrition

alter: change

crucial: essential; very important

optimal: best; most favorable

impaired: harmed

deliberately: intentionally; on purpose

stimulating: interesting; motivating

tragically: sadly

mute: voiceless; silent

fortunately: luckily; happily

milder (deprivation): less; minor

cope: deal with

poverty: shortage of necessities; neediness

resources: possessions and assets

impoverished: poor

lags: delays

turmoil: unrest; confusion

socioemotional: involves the development of self and interactions with others

in the extreme: in the worst possible situation

delinquent: young person under the age of 18 who frequently breaks the law

vicious cycle: repeating never-ending sequence

poverty line: minimum level of income set by each country that a person needs in order to live adequately

grim: harsh

enhance: improve

novel: unusual; different; new

"soil": materials in which to grow
wonderland: playground
platforms: raised areas
cubbyholes: little compartments
long leap: quite a distance
lowly: simple
exploration: looking at
"child-proof": making areas of the home so children cannot break things as they play and explore
not vegetables: persons are reactive and alert to the environment
responsive: reactive and alert
in light of this: because of certain information presented
child prodigy: young child who can perform adult skills at a high level
reciprocal: give-and-take; joint
distractibility: attention can be easily diverted
a dynamic relationship blossoms: social bonds form
elicit: bring out, cause
dynamically: forcefully; vigorously
tightly interwoven: closely mingled or linked

Recite and Review

1. Ultimately, the person you are today reflects a continuous interplay between the forces of nature and _____.
2. The study of progressive changes in behavior and abilities that involves every stage of life from conception to death is called _____ psychology.
3. The genetic transmission of physical and psychological characteristics from parents to their children refers to _____ (or "nature").
4. The nucleus of every human cell contains a long, ladder-like chain of pairs of chemical molecules that is called _____.
5. In 2003, a major scientific milestone was reached when the sequencing of all three billion chemical base pairs making up our human genes was completed by the _____ Project.
6. Each cell of the human body, with the exception of the sperm cells and ova, has a total of _____ chromosomes.
7. Sperms cells and ova each contain only _____ chromosomes.
8. Small areas of DNA that affect a particular process or personal characteristics are called _____.
9. A particular characteristic will appear every time the gene is present, if the gene is _____.
10. A particular trait will only be expressed if it is paired with a second gene of the same kind, when the genes are _____.
11. Samantha inherited a blue-eyed gene from her mother and a brown-eyed gene from her father. Samantha will have _____ eyes.
12. If each parent has one brown-eye gene and one blue-eye gene, the chance that a child will have blue eyes is one in _____.
13. Most of our characteristics are controlled by many genes working in combination with this effect being referred to as _____.
14. The physical growth and development of the body, brain, and nervous system is referred to as _____.
15. The prenatal period, the neonatal period, infancy, early childhood, middle childhood, pubescence, puberty, adolescence, adulthood, and senescence make up the human _____.

132

16. Before Zelda is able to walk, minimum levels of maturation must occur before these walking skills can be learned, a condition known as _____.

17. Although girls are toilet trained a little earlier than average and boys a little later, the average age for completed toilet training is about _____ year(s).

18. The sum of all external conditions that affect a person is referred to as the environment or "_____."

19. Compared to the adult brain, the brain of a newborn baby has fewer of the nerve cell branches that receive information called _____.

20. In comparison to the adult brain, newborn babies have fewer connections between nerve cells with these connections called _____.

21. Its capability to be altered by experience means that the newborn brain is highly _____.

22. Early learning experiences literally shape the developing brain with new connections being formed and unused ones disappearing, a process called "_____."

23. During prenatal development, some diseases and environmental toxins can affect the unborn baby inside the womb, also called the _____ environment.

24. Environmental problems that affect the developing fetus and that become apparent at birth are called "birth defects" or _____ problems.

25. Problems, such as sickle-cell anemia, hemophilia, albinism, cystic fibrosis, and muscular dystrophy are examples of _____ disorders.

26. German measles, X-rays, drugs, or anything that is capable of directly causing a birth defect is referred to as a(n)_____.

27. Tessa's baby has a small head, bodily defects, and facial malformations due to her heavy drinking while she was pregnant. Terra's baby has a condition known as _____.

28. Smoking during pregnancy greatly reduces the amount of _____ to the fetus.

29. The times when children are more susceptible to particular types of environmental influences are called _____ periods.

30. Peter grew up in a home environment which was lacking in normal nutrition, stimulation, comfort, and love. Peter's childhood environment would be described as one of _____.

31. Alanna grew up in a home environment in which her parents deliberately made it more stimulating and loving, a condition referred to as _____.

32. In Benloucif, Bennett, and Rosenzweig's experiment in which young rats were placed in stimulating environments with objects to manipulate, these rats as adults were found to be superior at learning mazes and had larger, heavier brains, with a thicker _____.

33. The limits that one's environment places on the effects of heredity are referred to as the _____.

34. Newborn babies' sensitivity, irritability, distractibility, and typical moods reflect the inherited, physical core of their personalities, which is called their _____.

35. Juanita's baby would be described as moody, intense, and easily angered. Juanita has one of the 10 percent of newborns described as _____ children.

36. A child that is relaxed and agreeable much of the time would be called a(n) _____ child.

37. Becca would be described as a very timid, unexpressive child most of the time. Her temperament would be classified as _____.

38. When growing infants influence their parents' behavior, while at the same time being influenced themselves, we call these _____ influences.

39. A person's current state of physical, emotional, and intellectual development is called his or her _____.

40. The three factors combine to determine your current state of physical, emotional, and intellectual development are heredity, environment, and _____.

Connections

1. ___ "nature"

2. ___ DNA

3. ___ chromosomes

4. ___ polygenic characteristics

5. ___ readiness

6. ___ congenital problems

7. ___ sensitive period
8. ___ deprivation

9. ___ enrichment

10. ___ reaction range
11. ___ temperament

12. ___ developmental level

a. when maturation has advanced enough to allow rapid acquisition of a particular skill

b. a time during which certain events must take place for normal development to occur

c. the physical core of personality including emotional sensitivity and energy level

d. deliberately making an environment more stimulating, nutritional, and loving

e. thread-like "colored bodies" in the nucleus of each cell

f. an individual's current state of physical, emotional, and intellectual development

g. traits that are influenced by many genes

h. a long, ladder-like chain of pairs of chemical molecules

i. the loss or withholding of normal stimulation, nutrition, comfort, or love

j. birth defects

k. the limits environment places on the effects of heredity

l. genetic transmission of physical and psychological characteristics from parents to their children

Check Your Memory

1. TRUE or FALSE   Developmental psychology is the study of the physical changes that occur from infancy through adolescence.
2. TRUE or FALSE   The person one is reflects a continuous interaction between the forces of nature and nurture.
3. TRUE or FALSE   The order of organic bases in DNA acts as a genetic code.
4. TRUE or FALSE   The complete sequencing of all 6 billion chemical pairs in human DNA was completed in 1965 by the Manhattan Project.
5. TRUE or FALSE   Each cell of the human body, except for the sperms and ova, has a total of 28 chromosomes.
6. TRUE or FALSE   When a gene is dominant, the feature it controls will appear every time the gene is present.
7. TRUE or FALSE   If both parents have brown eyes all of their children must have brown eyes.
8. TRUE or FALSE   Most of our characteristics are controlled by single genes.
9. TRUE or FALSE   Genes can switch on (or off) at certain ages or developmental stages.
10. TRUE or FALSE   The germinal period, pubescence, and senescence make up the human growth sequence.
11. TRUE or FALSE   The average age for completed toilet training is about 20 months.
12. TRUE or FALSE   The brain of a newborn baby has fewer dendrites and synapses than an adult brain.
13. TRUE or FALSE   Modern humans are still genetically quite similar to cave dwellers who lived 30,000 years ago.

134

14. TRUE or FALSE   Albinism, sickle-cell anemia, hemophilia, and cystic fibrosis are examples of congenital problems.
15. TRUE or FALSE   No direct intermixing of blood takes place between a mother and her unborn child.
16. TRUE or FALSE   Anything capable of directly causing birth defects is called a teratogen.
17. TRUE or FALSE   Infants affected by fetal alcohol syndrome have low birth weight, a small head, bodily defects, and facial malformations.
18. TRUE or FALSE   If a mother is addicted to morphine, heroin, or methadone, her baby may be born with an addiction.
19. TRUE or FALSE   Children of mothers who smoked during their pregnancies score lower on tests of language and mental ability.
20. TRUE or FALSE   The time when children are more susceptible to particular types of environmental influences is called their developmental level.
21. TRUE or FALSE   Impoverished children tend to be sick more often, their cognitive development lags, and they do poorly at school.
22. TRUE or FALSE   Adults who grew up in poverty often remain trapped in a vicious cycle of continued poverty.
23. TRUE or FALSE   Rats that were placed in enriched environments developed smaller, lighter brains with thinner cortex.
24. TRUE or FALSE   The limits environment places on the effects of heredity is called the reaction range.
25. TRUE or FALSE   Temperament is the inherited, physical core of personality.
26. TRUE or FALSE   About 20 percent of children would be classified as difficult children, who are restrained, unexpressive, or shy.
27. TRUE or FALSE   Good parenting can reciprocally influence a very shy child to become progressively less shy.
28. TRUE or FALSE   The current state of one's physical, emotional, and intellectual development is referred to as "nurture."

Critical Thinking Question

Environmental influences can interact with hereditary programming in an exceedingly direct way. Can you guess what it is?

Module 3.2 The Neonate
The Newborn—More Than Meets the Eye
Survey Question: What can newborn babies do?
Language Development Guide
contrary to common belief: the opposite of what is usually believed
oblivious: unaware
emergence: appearance
timetable: schedule
inert: lifeless; passive
unfeeling: no emotions
acute: sharp; finely tuned
adaptive: useful, functional
reflex: inborn, automatic response to a stimulus
elicit: bring forth
trapeze artists: high-flying, swinging circus performers
nursing: babies being breast-feed

rhythmic: occurring in regular measured intervals, like a musical beat

abruptly: suddenly

cling: hang on; hug

rate: speed

universal: worldwide

weird: odd; strange

rolling: movement by turning over front to back

creeping: moving by wriggling forward on the stomach, using arms and dragging feet behind them

shuffling: moving by scooting on one's bottom using a hand behind to push and feet in front to scoot or scooting on one's bottom using a rocking motion and leg movements to move forward

orderly: arranged; logical; organized

extremities: furthest point, which are the hands and feet

flunked: got a failing grade

standard: typical; normal

impact: influence; effect

flawed: faulty; imperfect

wobbly: unstable

"tune": adjust

evident: obvious

mere: simply

mimics: imitators; copycats

purses (lips): lips form a rounded shape as if one is about to whistle or blow out a candle

facial gestures: movement of facial muscles as in winking, smiling, frowning, etc.

mimicry: imitation

agitated: troubled; restless; nervous

challenge: difficult task

imagine: to picture in one's mind

chamber: compartment

images: representations; figures

reflect: mirrored

sharper: clearer, in focus

checkerboards: grids with boxes of alternating colors

bull's-eyes: concentric circles

a person inside that little body: that babies are responsive and have a personality and preferences

fascinated: captivated

gazing: looking

scrambled: mixed-up, rearranged

make sense: to understand

general excitement: enthusiastic; pleasurably thrilled; not bored

blossomed: develops

consistent: dependable; regular

abundant: many

hardwired: fixed, determined

haphazard: random; disorganized

baby buggy: stroller or small wheeled cart in which a baby rides and parents push

dazzling: amazing

transformed: changed

unique: one of a kind

Recite and Review

1. A newborn human infant is referred to as a(n) _____.
2. Helping the newborn in its environment are reflexes, such as the sucking, rooting, and Moro reflexes, which together are referred to as _____ reflexes.
3. You place your finger into a newborn infant's palm, and this baby holds on to your finger with surprising strength, illustrating the _____ reflex.
4. When newborns' cheeks are touched, they will turn toward the touch as if searching for the nipple to feed, which illustrates the _____ reflex.
5. You accidentally drop a pan in the kitchen and notice that your baby who is in the high chair make a hugging motion with his arms because the loud noise elicited the _____ reflex.
6. The rate of maturation varies from child to child, but the _____ of maturation is almost universal.
7. Your child first raises his head, then his chest, then crawls, stands, and eventually walks. This head-to-toe progression of motor control would be described as _____.
8. Your child first uses his arms and then his hands to grasp an object, then just the palm, and eventually uses his fingers and thumb. This progression of motor control from the center of the body to the extremities is called _____.
9. The earliest age at which babies can imitate actions a day after seeing them is _____ months old.
10. To find out what infants prefers to look at and what holds their attention, Robert Fantz invented a device called a(n) _____.
11. Babies are able to recognize categories of objects that differ in shape or color by _____ months old.
12. According to Jerome Kagan's research, unusual objects, like scrambled faces, begin to interest a young child at about the age of _____ years.
13. According to Bridges and others, the only emotion a newborn infant clearly expresses is _____.
14. Unlike Bridges, Carroll Izard believes that the most common infant expression was _____.
15. In addition to the most common infant expression, Carroll Izard stated that there were three other common infant expressions, which are sadness, joy, and _____.
16. Bridges found that emotions appear in a consistent order and that the first basic split is between _____ and _____ emotions.
17. When a 10-month-old sees his mother, he begins to smile. Ian's smile at this age would be considered a(n) _____ smile.

Connections

1. ___ neonate
2. ___ rooting reflex
3. ___ Moro reflex
4. ___ grasping reflex
5. ___ sucking reflex
6. ___ looking chamber
7. ___ cephalocaudal

8. ___ proximodistal
9. ___ interest

a. device used to find out what infants can see and what holds their attention
b. most common emotion according to Bridges
c. most common emotion according to Izard
d. rhythmic nursing
e. newborn human infant
f. elicited by seeing a parent's face
g. searching behavior elicited by touching the newborn's cheek
h. pattern of motor control from head to toe
i. pattern of motor control from the center of the body to the extremities

10. ___ general excitement

11. ___ social smile

j. elicited by pressing an object into a newborn's palm

k. elicited by loud noise

Check Your Memory

1. TRUE or FALSE Newborn babies can lift their heads and turn over.
2. TRUE or FALSE Newborn babies tend to be oblivious to their surroundings.
3. TRUE or FALSE Although their senses are less acute, neonates can see, hear, smell, taste, and respond to pain and touch.
4. TRUE or FALSE If you touch an infant's cheek, the infant will turn away from your touch, which illustrates the Moro reflex.
5. TRUE or FALSE If an infant's position is changed abruptly or if he or she is startled by a loud noise, the infant will exhibit the Babinski reflex.
6. TRUE or FALSE The order of maturation varies from child to child, but the rate of maturation is almost universal.
7. TRUE or FALSE Muscular control that spreads in a pattern from head to toe is called proximodistal.
8. TRUE or FALSE Babies as young as three months can imitate actions a day after seeing them.
9. TRUE or FALSE Babies who are three to eight weeks old seem to understand that a person's voice and body should be connected.
10. TRUE or FALSE Researchers have found that three-day-old babies prefer to look at simpler colored objects like rectangles rather than more complex patterns.
11. TRUE or FALSE When shown different face masks, infants under the age of one prefer unfamiliar, scrambled face masks, while two-year-old babies prefer the familiar-looking face.
12. TRUE or FALSE According to Bridges and others, the only emotion a newborn infant clearly expresses is fear, while Izard found that the most common infant expression was anger.
13. TRUE or FALSE Bridges observed that all the basic human emotions appear before age two.
14. TRUE or FALSE Bridges found that emotions appear in a consistent order and that the first basic split is between pleasant and unpleasant emotions.
15. TRUE or FALSE According to Izard, emotions are "hardwired" by heredity and related to evolution, such as the smile helping babies to survive by inviting parents to care for them.

Critical Thinking Question

If you were going to test newborn infants to see if they prefer their own mother's face to that of a stranger, what precautions would you take?

Module 3.3 Social Development in Childhood

Social Development—Baby, I'm Stuck on You

Survey Question: Of what significance is a child's emotional bond with adults?

Language Development Guide

rooted: has its origin; cause by

physical contact: closeness in space between people, includes touch

emotional bond: close relationship; attachment

significance: importance

social creatures: animals that prefer to be in groups rather than alone

lays a foundation: activities or knowledge that comes before and sets the base or groundwork for the next step

siblings: brothers and sisters

core: important aspect

primary caregivers: those people who take care of the child on a daily basis, ex. mothers and fathers

cuddly: appearance invites one to hug the object

replicas: copies; imitations

security: safety

reassuring: comforting; restores confidence

optimal: ideal, desirable, best

"home base": a place to run back to in order to feel safe

miserable: very unhappy

be a serious handicap: cause trouble or problems in daily living

professional help: mental health professionals, such as counselors, psychologists, etc.

quality: the level of excellence

stable: constant; durable; lasting

mixed feelings: partly positive and partly negative emotions regarding a situation ("want something" but "don't want it")

resist: refuse something; oppose it

resiliency: ability to recover after problems or difficulties

plight: suffering

remote: distant; withdrawn; detached

intentioned: kindly purpose

relying on: depending on for support

abandoned: left or discarded by others

skeptical: doubtful

commitment: complete dedication; devotion

unappreciated: one's worth is not recognized

preceding: previous; earlier

intimacy: ability to care about others and to share experiences with them

rhythms: individual pattern and pace as set by one's biological clock

intrusive: interfering; meddling; pushy

overstimulating: excessive excitement

rejecting: refuse to accept

drowsy: sleepy

vocalizing: to express with one's voice

outgoing: friendly

adversely affect: hurt, damage

reversed: undone; switched

beforehand: earlier; previously

monitor: check; watch

insist: not take no for an answer

(staff) turnover: rate at which an employer replaces their staff

menagerie: wild animal collection

stockade: enclosed or fenced in area (usually for protection)

"spoiling": overindulging children to the point that lack control and frequently misbehave

Recite and Review

1. The foundation for one's relationships with other people occurs through _____ development.
2. The close emotional bond that babies form with their primary caregivers is called an emotional _____.
3. To investigate mother-infant relationships, Harry Harlow separated baby rhesus monkeys from their mothers at birth with the real mothers being replaced with _____.
4. Harlow's studies illustrated that primate infants become attached to the object that provides _____.
5. It is evident that emotional bonds have formed around eight to 12 months of age when children will cry and show signs of fear when left alone or with someone unfamiliar. This behavior is referred to as _____.
6. Ana has a fear that she will get lost and never see her parents again. She clings to her parents, following them around when she is home with it being a constant struggle to get her to go to school. Ana is suffering from _____ disorder.
7. The psychologist that identified three attachment styles in young children was _____.
8. During an attachment study, Jimmy becomes upset when his mother leaves and runs to her when she reenters the room. Jimmy would be classified as having a(n) _____ attachment.
9. In an attachment study, Mara did not become upset when her mother left the room and turned away and continued playing when her mother reentered the room. Mara would be classified as having a(n) _____ attachment.
10. During an attachment study, Hannah became very upset when her mother left the room and ran to her when she returned but then angrily resisted her mother hugging her and pulled away from her mother. Hannah would be classified as having a(n) _____ attachment.
11. Adults who get nervous if anyone gets too close to them emotionally would be classified as having a(n) _____ attachment style.
12. Adults who love their romantic partners but worry constantly that they cannot trust their partners or that their partners do not really love them would be classified as having a(n) _____ attachment style.
13. If a mother tries to play with a drowsy infant or ignores a baby who is looking at her and vocalizing, her baby may not develop a secure attachment because of this lack of _____ caregiving.
14. Children tend to have better relationships with their mothers and fewer behavior problems as well has better cognitive skills and language abilities if they attend _____ day cares.
15. A baby's needs for love, warmth, and care, are every bit as important as more obvious needs for food, water, and physical care. These needs for love and care are referred to as _____ needs.

Connections

1. ___ social development
2. ___ surrogate mothers
3. ___ contact comfort
4. ___ separation anxiety
5. ___ securely attached

a. inanimate dummies used in Harlow's attachment study
b. includes attachment to parents and relationships with other children and adults
c. emotional needs for love and affection
d. distress displayed by infants when away from their primary caregiver
e. anxious emotional bond marked by a tendency to look away from parent or caregiver upon their return

140

6. ___ insecure-avoidant

7. ___ insecure-ambivalent

8. ___ affectional needs

f. reassuring feeling human and animal infants get from touching or clinging to something soft and warm

g. stable and positive emotional bond in which infant seeks out mother upon her return

h. anxious emotional bond marked by both a desire to be with a parent and some resistance to being reunited

Check Your Memory

1. TRUE or FALSE   In his study, Harry Harlow separated baby rhesus monkeys from their mothers at birth with the real mothers being replaced with mother dogs.

2. TRUE or FALSE   Harlow's studies confirmed that attachment occurs to the object that is the food source for the infant.

3. TRUE or FALSE   There is a sensitive period during the first year of life in which attachment must occur for optimal development.

4. TRUE or FALSE   Mothers usually begin to feel attached to their baby before birth.

5. TRUE or FALSE   For the first few months of life, babies respond more or less equally to everyone, but by two or three months, most babies prefer their mothers to strangers.

6. TRUE or FALSE   Separation anxiety in children first appears between 18 to 24 months of age.

7. TRUE or FALSE   About 1 in 20 children suffer from separation anxiety disorder in which they are miserable when they are separated from their parents with many refusing to go to school.

8. TRUE or FALSE   The psychologist that classified attachment styles as secure, insecure-avoidant, and insecure-ambivalent was Carol Gilligan.

9. TRUE or FALSE   An insecurely-ambivalent infant tends to turn away from the mother when she returns.

10. TRUE or FALSE   Infants who are securely attached at the age of one year show resiliency, curiosity, problem-solving ability, and social skills in preschool.

11. TRUE or FALSE   Many of the children raised in the overcrowded Romanian orphanages and adopted by North American families were poorly attached to their new parents with some wandering off with strangers and others being anxious and remote.

12. TRUE or FALSE   An adult with an ambivalent attachment style would most likely feel misunderstood and unappreciated in their romantic relationships and would long to be close to others but would not sure if they can be trusted.

13. TRUE or FALSE   Fathers of securely attached infants tend to be outgoing, agreeable, and happy in their marriage.

14. TRUE or FALSE   Even high quality day cares have been shown to weaken children's relationships to their mothers and to increase behavior problems in the children.

15. TRUE or FALSE   Children in high-quality day cares have better cognitive skills and language abilities.

16. TRUE or FALSE   The overall group size for a quality day care should be between 20 and 28 children.

17. TRUE or FALSE   During the first year of life it is nearly impossible to "spoil" a baby.

Critical Thinking Question

Can emotional bonding begin before birth?

Module 3.3 Parental Influences—Life with Mom and Dad

Survey Question: How important are parenting styles?

Language Development Guide

rigid: firm and unbending; inflexible

strict: harsh; severe

obedience: complying with the demands of person with power

authority: person with power; an expert

be emotionally stiff: unexpressive

withdrawn: quiet, remote

apprehensive: anxious; nervous

curiosity: interested in knowing and learning

accountable: held responsible

enforced: insisted on; compelled to follow

his or her own way: being able to do whatever one wants to

dependent: needy; relying on others for support

aimless: purposeless; directionless

run amok: to act crazy with rage

nonauthoritarian: not harsh; guides with reasoning

thrive: succeed

competent: capable; knowledgeable

assertive: standing up for one's rights without hurting others

inquiring: interested in; curious

nurturing: caring and taking care of

tactile: touch

rough-and-tumble play: physical playing that is noisy and slightly violent, such as wrestling

conventional: traditional

peekaboo: baby game where parent hides their face behind their hands, and then surprises the child by opening their hands quickly and saying, "peekaboo"

affectionate: loving

risk-taking: actions that may be dangerous or unpleasant

prevail: exist

it's no wonder: it's hardly surprising

gender role: pattern of behaviors that are regarded as "male" or "female" by one's culture

ethnic: characteristics of a large group of people who share such cultural aspects as language, religion, customs, etc.

distinctiveness: unique (one of a kind); individuality

summary: overall review of information

valid: suitable; applicable

roots lie in: ancestors from

child-rearing: raising children, parenting

customs: traditions; practices

generalizations: overviews of situations rather than very detailed and specific

interdependence: relying or needing one another; mutual dependence

adversity: hardship

elders: older persons

necessity: essential

142

urban: inner-city
self-reliance: independence; able to care for oneself
resourcefulness: imagination and inventiveness in dealing with situations
promote: encourage
indulgent: tolerant; not strict
courteous: polite; considerate
cooperation: teamwork; assisting one another
competition: seeing each other as rivals; in opposition
obliged: required; made to
greater good: setting aside individual wants in favor of the overall needs of a larger group, such as family
at stake: in danger; at risk
lenient: easygoing; not strict
permissive: tolerant; lax
conforming: bringing behavior in agreement with the norm or with members of a group
teasing: making fun of; laughing at
shaming: embarrassing or humiliating
generosity: kindness; giving aid and contributions
hospitality: welcoming others with warmth
pursuit: search; quest
thrift: being careful with one's money; saving
conservatism: maintain existing or traditional values and behaviors
welfare: well-being; happiness
extended family: grandparents, aunts, uncles, cousins, in-laws, etc.

Recite and Review

1. The three major parental styles were studied by the psychologist _____.
2. A child who is expected to stay out of trouble and to accept, without question, what his or her parents regard as right or wrong most likely has parents who have a(n) _____ parenting style.
3. Parents who give little guidance, allow too much freedom, and who do not hold their children accountable for their actions would be classified as having a(n) _____ parenting style.
4. Sara's parents supply firm and consistent guidance combined with love and affection. Sara's parents would be classified as having a(n) _____ parenting style.
5. Daniel would be described as emotionally stiff, withdrawn, apprehensive, lacking in curiosity, but obedient and self-controlled. Daniel's parents most likely used a(n) _____ parenting style.
6. As a child, Cora was dependent and immature and misbehaved frequently. Her misbehavior escalated as a teenager and included truancy from school, shoplifting, and drug use. Cora's parents most likely used a(n) _____ parenting style.
7. Children who are competent, self-controlled, independent, assertive, and inquiring and who use positive coping skills most likely had parents who used a(n) _____ parenting style.
8. The parent who is more likely to play with their children and tell them stories is the _____.
9. The parent who speaks to infants more and plays more conventional games, such as peekaboo, is the _____.

143

10. Tim was raised by parents who emphasized loyalty and interdependence among family members, security, developing a positive identity, and not giving up in the face of adversity. His parents also stressed obedience and respect for elders with his parents being fairly strict in their discipline style. Tim's parents emphasize the cultural values of traditional _____ families.

11. Parents who are affectionate and indulgent toward younger children, but expect their older children to be calm, obedient, courteous, and respectful and who stress cooperation over competition and social skills over cognitive skills are most likely of the _____ culture.

12. Lee's parents tend to act as teachers who encourage hard work, moral behavior, and achievement and tend to emphasize interdependence among group members. Lee and his parents are most likely of the _____-American culture.

13. The father in this culture tends to be a strong authority figure who demands obedience from his children so that the family will not be shamed by the child. He also emphasizes to his children the importance of success, generosity, and hospitality. This culture is most likely the _____ American culture.

Connections

1. ___ authoritarian parents
   a. parent who pays more visual attention and engages in unusual play

2. ___ overly permissive parents
   b. culture that values social skills over cognitive skills and cooperation over competition

3. ___ authoritative parents
   c. culture that values individual effort and independence and are more likely to force young children to sleep alone

4. ___ maternal influences and characteristics
   d. parents in this culture act as teachers, are group-oriented, and lenient in their parenting until age five when they expect children to show obedience and self-control

5. ___ paternal influences and characteristics
   e. parenting style that supplies firm and consistent guidance combined with love and affection

6. ___ African-American families
   f. culture that emphasizes loyalty, security, the development of a positive identity, and resourcefulness with discipline being fairly strict

7. ___ Hispanic families
   g. parenting style that gives little guidance, too much freedom, or does not require the child to take responsibility

8. ___ Asian-American families
   h. culture that emphasizes welfare of family over individual identity; values success, generosity, hospitality, and conservatism with punishment involving spankings or shaming in front of others

9. ___ Arab-American families
   i. parent who speaks more to the child and plays more conventional games

10. ___ Western culture families
   j. parenting style that enforces rigid rules and demands strict obedience

Check Your Memory

1. TRUE or FALSE   Psychologist Diana Baumrind studied the effects of three major parental styles.
2. TRUE or FALSE   Because Laura's parents demand complete obedience to their rigid rules without question or explanation, they would be classified as authoritative parents.
3. TRUE or FALSE   Overly permissive parents give the child rights similar to an adult's but few responsibilities.
4. TRUE or FALSE   Children of authoritarian parents are competent, self-controlled, independent, assertive, and inquiring and use positive coping skills.
5. TRUE or FALSE   Mothers pay more visual attention to their children as well as engaging in more unusual play with the children than fathers do.
6. TRUE or FALSE   Fathers can be as affectionate, sensitive, and responsive as mothers are.
7. TRUE or FALSE   Traditional African-American values emphasize loyalty and interdependence among family members, security, developing a positive identity, and resourcefulness.
8. TRUE or FALSE   In the Hispanic culture, social skills, such as being calm, obedient, courteous, and respectful, may be valued more than cognitive skills.
9. TRUE or FALSE   Asian cultures tend to value individual effort and independence.
10. TRUE or FALSE   The Asian culture tends to be lenient and permissive in their parenting of children under the age of five years.
11. TRUE or FALSE   Punishment for children in Middle Eastern cultures generally consists of spankings, teasing, or shaming in front of others.
12. TRUE or FALSE   Many of the parenting practices in North America, such as forcing young children to sleep alone, would be considered odd or wrong in other cultures.

Critical Thinking Question

Which parenting style is most likely to lead to eating disorders in children?

Module 3.4 Language Development in Childhood
Language Development—Who Talks Baby Talk?
Survey Question: How do children acquire language?

Language Development Guide
miraculous: magical
carry them out: to follow or obey them
assert: declare; state
intently: closely; carefully
mischief: getting into trouble
temper tantrum: anger expressed in uncontrollable behavior - screaming, hitting, crying, etc.
stubborn: unwilling to change
this, too, shall pass: this situation will soon be over
comprehension: understanding
leap forward: great improvement
phenomenal: unusual; exceptional
truly entered the world of: can use
accounts: explains
explosion of: great increase

linguist: studies language
long (claimed): has stated for a long time
predisposition: natural tendency or inclination
limited: restricted; reduced
part of the story: partly explains
underestimates: not placing enough value on
contexts: situations; backgrounds
clarifying: making clear
inborn language recognition: the inherited ability to identify language sounds
go to a great deal of trouble: put forth a lot of effort
arousal: excitement; stimulation
optimal: most favorable; best
expectations: beliefs
signals: signs; indicators
"conversational": informal; everyday
exchanges: talks
unmistakably: obviously; definitely
exaggerated: overstated; inflated
voice inflections: rising and falling in tone of voice
apparently: obviously
switch: change
distinct: well-defined; noticeable
"musical" quality: has characteristics of music
melodies: musical tunes
universal: worldwide
"Nein! Nein!": German word for "no!"
"Basta! Basta!" Spanish word meaning "Enough" and meaning "Stop!"
"Not! Dude!": English slang telling a person (dude) not to do something
"Oooh pobrecito": means "poor little thing" in Spanish
prompt: encourage; bring about
nevertheless: however; even so
sophisticated: highly developed; refined; complicated
full flowering: complete development
cultivation: nurturing, care

Recite and Review

1. From age one month on, babies use a vocalization known as _____ to gain attention.
2. Around six to eight weeks of age, babies begin a repetition of vowel sounds called

   _____.
3. The consonants *b*, *d*, *m*, and *g* are combined with vowel sounds to produce meaningless language sounds during the _____ stage of language development.
4. Marta is 20 months old and communicates with her mother using one word at a time, such as "go," "juice," or "up." Maria is in the _____ stage of language development.
5. Connie is 26 months old and talks in simple two-word sentences called _____ speech.
6. During their second year of life, children become increasingly capable of mischief and temper tantrums, a phase known as "the _____."
7. Noam Chomsky believed that humans have a hereditary readiness, or biological _____ to develop language.
8. Children around the world use a limited number of patterns in their first sentences with the typical pattern of "Mama give" being classified as _____.

146

9. When a child says "See kitty," he or she is using the typical pattern of a simple sentence known as _____.
10. Little Tanya says "Allgone milk." She is using the typical pattern of a simple sentence known as _____.
11. Specialists in the psychology of language are called _____.
12. Many psychologists feel that Chomsky underestimates the importance of social contexts and _____ that shape language development.
13. In early language development, any behavior, such as touching, vocalizing, gazing, or smiling, that allows nonverbal interaction makes up a system of shared _____.
14. Parent and child alternate sending and receiving messages in a pattern of "conversational" _____.
15. Alfred is talking to his infant using an exaggerated pattern of speaking in which he uses short, simple sentences, repeats them frequently, and raises the tone of his voice. Alfred is speaking to his child using _____.
16. Leesa is talking to her baby using a rising, then falling pitch. Mothers around the world usually use this pattern of pitch when they want to _____ their baby.
17. A short, sharp rhythm is used to convey a(n) _____ to a baby.
18. The sensitive period in language learning involves the first _____ years of a child's life.

Connections

1. ___ crying
2. ___ cooing
3. ___ babbling
4. ___ single-word stage
5. ___ telegraphic speech
6. ___ biological predisposition
7. ___ psycholinguist
8. ___ signals
9. ___ turn-taking
10. ___ parentese

a. use to gain attention starting at one month of age
b. specialist in the psychology of language
c. two-year-olds using words arranged in two-word sentences, such as "want juice"
d. consonants *b, d, m,* and *g* are combined with vowel sounds to produce meaningless language sounds
e. an 18-month-old baby using one word at a time, such as "go" or "kitty"
f. touching, vocalizing, gazing, or smiling that allows nonverbal interaction
g. presumed hereditary readiness to learn certain skills, such as how to use language
h. repetition of vowel sounds, such as "oo" and "ah"
i. pattern of speech used when talking to infants, marked by exaggerated voice inflections
j. the alternate sending and receiving of messages

Check Your Memory

1. TRUE or FALSE   Language development is closely tied to maturation.
2. TRUE or FALSE   Babies coo from the moment of birth and use it to gain attention from one month on.
3. TRUE or FALSE   At first babbling is the same around the world with all babies babbling the same meaningless language sounds.
4. TRUE or FALSE   At about one year of age children respond to real words, such as no or hi.

5. TRUE or FALSE   When children speak in simple two-word sentences it is referred to as binary speech.
6. TRUE or FALSE   The mischief, stubbornness, and temper tantrums of "the terrible twos" are simply the child becoming more independent.
7. TRUE or FALSE   By first grade, a child will be able to understand around 8,000 words and use about 4,000 words.
8. TRUE or FALSE   Noam Chomsky claims that a child's language patterns are not innate but are the result of learning and the social context that the learning takes place.
9. TRUE or FALSE   If a child says "My doll," she is using an agent-action pattern of speech.
10. TRUE or FALSE   If a child says "See kitty," he is using a pattern of speech known as possession.
11. TRUE or FALSE   Specialists in the psychology of language are called psycholinguists.
12. TRUE or FALSE   Babies actively participate in language learning by asking questions, such as "What dis?"
13. TRUE or FALSE   When a child makes a language error, parents typically repeat the child's sentence, with needed corrections or ask a clarifying question to draw the child's attention to the error.
14. TRUE or FALSE   To help lay a foundation for later language use, parents and child develop a system of shared signals that include touching, gazing, and smiling.
15. TRUE or FALSE   Infants as young as four months engage in vocal turn-taking with adults.
16. TRUE or FALSE   When a baby is still babbling, parents tend to use parentese, but as soon as the baby says its first word, they switch to using long, adult-style sentences.
17. TRUE or FALSE   Mothers around the world use a high-pitched, rising melody with their babies when they want to call attention to objects.
18. TRUE or FALSE   To give comfort, parents use low, smooth, drawn-out tones.
19. TRUE or FALSE   Our inherited tendency to learn language determines whether a baby will speak English, Vietnamese, Spanish, or Russian.
20. TRUE or FALSE   The first seven years of life are a sensitive period in language learning.

Critical Thinking Question

The children of professional parents hear more words per hour than the children of welfare parents, and they also tend to score higher on tests of mental abilities. How else could their higher scores be explained?

Module 3.5 Cognitive Development in Childhood
Cognitive Development—Think Like a Child
Survey Question: How do children learn to think?

Language Development Guide
insights: understandings
proposed: put forth
update: bring up to date; revise
tutor: teacher; coach
philosopher: studies reason, existence, knowledge, truth, etc.
generally speaking: commonly said
abstract: more theoretical; not concrete
base: establish
categories: groupings; types

principles: rules
tempting: appealing
illustrious: famous
launched: started
watch the children: take care of the children; baby-sit
deeply: greatly
convinced: sure; certain
pounds: hits
wrench: tool for gripping and turning objects such as bolts
a dime is worth less than a (larger) nickel: dimes ($0.10) are smaller in size than nickels ($0.05).
"mind's eye": imagination
nonintellectual: lacking understanding
nonverbal: not involving language or words
anticipate: expect; predict
tunnel: covered passageway
conceptions: ideas
perched: hanging out on the edge; suspended from
operated on: organized; managed
transforming: changed
think symbolically: think in representative images
irrelevant: not important; unrelated
bothered: upset; worried
fooled: tricked
"age of reason": able to reason; refers to time that church doctrine specifies children as being morally responsible for their actions as well as the movement in Europe during the 1700s when scientists and philosophers advocated using reason and thinking rather than established traditions to make decisions
trend: tendency
logical: rational; reasonable; sound
ego: sense of self
center of his or her world: point of focus
to illustrate: to show; to demonstrate
exasperatingly: annoyingly
selfish: self-centered
uncooperative: unhelpful; stubborn
in the ordinary sense: in the usual way
to underlie: the cause of
preoccupation: absorbs one's attention
name-calling: form of verbal abuse and involves referring to a person by an insulting name
retaliate: fight back, seek revenge
foe: enemy
panty-girdle: women's undergarment to make women look slimmer
"street smarts": slang term for knowledge one gains through experience, not from books (such as riding a bicycle on the streets and looking for cars)
hallmark: the main characteristic
"snake": a shape that is long and slender like a snake
despite: even though
believing in Santa Claus: Christmas gift-giver, Saint Nicholas bringing presents down the chimney on Christmas Eve
break away: separate from
democracy: considered a rule by the people, rather than a monarchy (kings and queens)

honor: good reputation

hypothetical possibilities: theoretical; supposed

suppositions: guesses; speculations

projections: predictions

attained: reached

inductive reasoning: going from specific facts or observations to general principles

deductive reasoning: going from general principles to specific situations

physics: science of matter and energy

wisdom: a mixture of reasoning ability, openness, intelligence, and creativity

ideal: perfect

novel: different

accelerated: speed up

oppress: worry; distress

pressured: forced

Monopoly: popular board game where players buy properties, charge rent, build hotels, and try to end the game owning everything or having the most money

"road map": a drawing of pathways or roads to particular areas

on a broad scale: to a large extent

stage-like leaps: changes taking place in phases or steps; not continuously

waves: in a series

parallel: similar

adept: skillful

mistook: make an error

incompetence: lack of skill

"magic shows": demonstrations of illusions

"theater": place where presentation occurs

duplicate: copies

perspectives: viewpoints

except perhaps early on Monday morning: joke - referring to early week sleepiness

exclaimed: yelled

endearing: charming

proposed: put forth

false-belief: mistake made due to incorrect reasoning

in the meantime: for now

sarcastic: ironic; cynical

figures of speech: words and phrases that are not used in a literal way

underestimated: not placing enough value on

master the intellectual tools: develop reasoning skills

too little credit: not placing enough value on

dialogues: discussions; conversations

A Child's Guide to Life on Earth: referring to the need for an instruction manual for raising kids

version: type

"discoveries": breakthroughs

jigsaw puzzle: game where you must reassemble a picture that has been divided up into small pieces

gets the hang of it: succeed in learning something

tailored: fit, made, gave, matched

bridges: connections

mental territory: new level of reasoning

collaborations: teamwork; group effort

baseball cards: information about professional athletes on cards that children trade with each other

150

decipher: make sense of
unconsciously: without knowing or being aware of it

Recite and Review

1. The Swiss psychologist and philosopher who believed that all children mature through a series of distinct stages in intellectual development was _____.
2. Tyron pounds the pegs into the holes of the toy workbench using a toy hammer. He later picks up the toy wrench and pounds on the pegs. By using the wrench like the hammer, Tyron is using an existing mental pattern in a new situation, which illustrates the process known as _____.
3. As Tyron gets older, he only uses the hammer for pounding and the wrench for loosing bolts. Thus, he has modified his existing mental patterns to fit new demands through a process known as _____.
4. Five-month-old Asma wants her mother's car keys. Her mother slips the keys into her pocket, and Asma behaves as if the keys do not exist and turns her attention back to her toy. Asma did not continue crying because she does not understand that the keys continue to exist even after her mother hid them. Asma lacks _____.
5. Babies begin to actively pursue disappearing objects and spend much of their time coordinating information from their senses with their muscle movements during the _____ stage of cognitive development.
6. Although Kenny can form mental images or ideas, he cannot easily transform those images or ideas in his mind. Kenny is in the _____ stage of cognitive development.
7. Children that think that the sun and moon follow them when they are walking or engage in thinking that makes little use of reasoning or logic, which is called _____ thought.
8. Five-year-old Santana thinks that a nickel is "more" because it is bigger than a dime. Santana is in the _____ stage of cognitive development.
9. Because children engage in more logical, adult-like thought at age seven, this age has been called the "age of _____."
10. Juan's mother is looking at herself in a mirror when little Juan steps in front of her, blocking her view of her dress. Juan's mother asks him to move so she can see better, but Juan just moves closer to the mirror, so he can see better. Juan's inability to take his mother's viewpoint illustrates _____ thought.
11. When Darnell is asked if he has a brother, he says "Yes, Terrence is my brother." Then, when Darnell is asked if Terrence has a brother, Darnell says, "No." Darnell's thinking lacks _____.
12. The period of cognitive development during which children begin to use concepts of time, space, volume, and number, but in simplified ways is the _____ stage.
13. A researcher has two balls of clay and asks a child if there is the same amount of clay in the two balls. When the child says, "Yes," the researcher rolls one of the balls of clay into a "snake" and asks the child if there is the same amount of clay in the ball as in the "snake." The child says, "Yes, it's the same clay. You just changed its shape." This child has developed the concept of _____.
14. Children who can reverse thoughts but are not yet able to handle abstract principles are in the _____ stage of cognitive development.
15. Children who are able to consider hypothetical possibilities are most likely in the _____ stage of cognitive development.
16. To encourage a child's intellectual development, Piaget believed that teaching efforts should be aimed at just beyond the child's current level of comprehension, an approach called the _____ strategy.

151

17. Piaget suggested that parents and teachers provide experiences that are only slightly novel, unusual, or challenging since a child's intellect develops mainly through the process of _____.

18. Parents should avoid "hothousing," or _____, which involves "pushing" children to learn reading, math, gymnastics, swimming, or music at an accelerated pace that can bore or oppress them.

19. In attempting to play the Monopoly game, children would most likely put the houses, hotels, and dice in their mouths if their cognitive development is in the _____ stage.

20. A child attempts to play Monopoly by rolling the dice and moving her game piece, but she continually makes up her own rules and does not appear to understand the basic rules of the game. This child is most likely in the _____ stage of cognitive development.

21. In playing the game of Monopoly, Erin understands basic instructions and will play by the rules but is not capable of hypothetical transactions dealing with mortgages, loans, and special pacts with other players. Erin is most likely in the _____ stage of cognitive development.

22. Children do not undergo stage-like leaps in general mental ability, but continuously gain specific knowledge through their experiences, according to the _____ theorists.

23. Between the ages of seven and 15, peak synaptic growth shifts to the parietal lobes and the _____ lobes of the brain.

24. Some of the three-month-old infants in Renee Baillargeon's study showed that they could make mental representations because they acted surprised and gazed longer at _____ events presented in the "baby theater."

25. The understanding that people have mental states, such as thoughts, beliefs, and intentions, and that other people's mental states can be different from one's own is referred to as _____.

26. When shown their image on a television, most infants will not recognize their image until they are at least _____ months old.

27. If you wanted to assess whether a child understood that other people can have mental states different from one's own, you would use the false-_____ task.

28. While Piaget stressed the role of maturation in cognitive development, the Russian scholar who focused on the impact of sociocultural factors was _____.

29. According to the sociocultural theory, the range of tasks a child cannot yet master alone but that he or she can accomplish with the guidance of a more capable partner is referred to as the zone of _____.

30. The process of adjusting instruction so that it is responsive to a beginner's behavior and supports the beginner's effort to understand a problem or gain a mental skill is called _____.

Connections

1. ___ assimilation
2. ___ accommodation

3. ___ object permanence

4. ___ theory of mind

5. ___ intuitive thought

6. ___ egocentric thought

a. forced teaching
b. type of thinking that makes little or no use of reasoning or logic

c. stage that children coordinate information from eyes and ears with muscle movements

d. range of tasks a child cannot yet master alone, but that can be accomplished with the guidance of a more capable partner

e. stage that children think abstractly and theoretically

f. stage that children begin to use language and think symbolically but illogically

152

7. ___ conservation

g. thought that fails to consider the viewpoints of others

8. ___ "hothousing"

h. process of modifying existing mental patterns to fit new demands

9. ___ zone of proximal development

i. stage that children think logically but not abstractly

10. ___ scaffolding

j. concept that weight, mass, and volume of matter remain unchanged even when the shape or appearance of the object changes

11. ___ sensorimotor stage

k. understanding that people have mental states and that other people's mental states can be different from one's own

12. ___ preoperational stage

l. temporary support given to a child to help him or her learn how to think

13. ___ concrete operational stage

m. concept that objects continue to exist even when they are hidden from view

14. ___ formal operations stage

n. process of using existing mental patterns in new situations

Check Your Memory

1. TRUE or FALSE   Children tend to base their understanding on particular examples and use fewer generalization and categories than adults do.
2. TRUE or FALSE   Many of Piaget's ideas came from observing his own children as they solved various thought problems.
3. TRUE or FALSE   Assimilation refers to modifying existing ideas to fit new situations or demands.
4. TRUE or FALSE   Cognitive development during the sensorimotor stage is mostly nonverbal.
5. TRUE or FALSE   Age five is referred to as the "age of reason" because children at this age are beginning to exhibit intuitive thinking.
6. TRUE or FALSE   Because preoperational children are egocentric, they cannot understand why the driver of a car cannot see them if they can see the car.
7. TRUE or FALSE   Children usually stop believing in Santa Claus when they reach the preoperational stage because they have developed inductive and deductive reasoning.
8. TRUE or FALSE   To preoperational children, the name of an object is as much a part of the object as its size, shape, and color and underlies their preoccupation with name-calling.
9. TRUE or FALSE   Reversibility of thought and conservation both appear during the concrete operational stage.
10. TRUE or FALSE   An understanding of hypothetical possibilities develops during the formal operations stage.
11. TRUE or FALSE   Formal thinking may be more a result of culture and learning than maturation.
12. TRUE or FALSE   It is recommended that forced teaching be used to accelerate the intellectual development of children and prevent boredom and apathy.
13. TRUE or FALSE   Piaget believed that a child's intellect develops mainly through assimilation.
14. TRUE or FALSE   According to the learning theorists, children continuously gain specific knowledge from their experience and do not undergo stage-like leaps in general mental ability.

15. TRUE or FALSE   In the late teens, the brain actively destroys unneeded connections, especially in the frontal lobes.
16. TRUE or FALSE   Playing peak-a-boo is a good way to establish the permanence of objects for children in the sensorimotor stage.
17. TRUE or FALSE   In playing Monopoly, a child in the preoperational stage would be able to easily understand and follow the basic instructions and rules of the game.
18. TRUE or FALSE   Baillargeon found that infants as young as three months of age show signs of forming mental representations of the world.
19. TRUE or FALSE   Current research indicates that children as young as four can understand that other people's mental states differ from their own.
20. TRUE or FALSE   Most infants recognize themselves in a mirror at the age of nine months.
21. TRUE or FALSE   Available evidence suggests that children with autism spectrum disorders have not developed an adequate theory of mind.
22. TRUE or FALSE   A criticism of Piaget's theory of cognitive development is that he underestimated the impact of cultural influences on children's mental development.
23. TRUE or FALSE   Vygotsky's key insight was that children's thinking develops through dialogues with more capable persons.
24. TRUE or FALSE   Learning experiences are most helpful when they take place outside of a child's zone of ultimate development.
25. TRUE or FALSE   Vygotsky introduced a process of temporary support given to a child as they solved problems, which he called "hothousing."

Critical Thinking Question

Using Piaget's theory as a guide, at what age would you expect a child to recognize that a Styrofoam cup has weight?

Module 3.6 Adolescence, Young Adulthood, and Moral Development
Adolescence and Young Adulthood—The Best of Times, the Worst of Times
Survey Question: Why is the transition from adolescence to adulthood especially challenging?

Language Development Guide
exuberance: energy and enthusiasm
youthful searching: exploring the world
"the best of times, the worst of times": quote from Charles Dickens' *A Tale of Two Cities* about that time period of the French Revolution, but which is used in this case to illustrate the ups and downs of adolescence
status: position; rank
criterion: factor in deciding
taking a job: being hired
reproductive maturity: capable of producing an offspring
weather: go through, experience
beneficial: helpful
dominant: forceful; bossy
clear-cut: obvious, straightforward
body image: a person's perception of his or her own physical appearance
prestige: popularity, recognition
counterparts: corresponding members

costs and benefits: disadvantages and advantages
distorted: unclear; vague
in a very real sense: actually
signals: indicates
autonomous: independent; self-directed
ambiguities: uncertainties
spurred: encouraged
contemplate: consider
ethnic heritage: cultural group to which you are born
ethnic minorities: cultural groups in an area that lack the wealth or political power of the more
     numerous cultural groups
prominence: importance
excluded: left out
degrading: humiliating; demeaning
stereotypes: labels based on oversimplified concepts
multicultural: equal status, recognition, and acceptance given to different ethnic and cultural
     groups
Latino: Latin American; of Hispanic descent
Chicano: of Mexican descent
tolerant: open-minded; understanding
range of options: many alternatives; wide selection
prolong: lengthen
extended adolescence: lengthen the number of years adolescence lasts
engaged: planning to get married
dual degree: two majors in college
ambiguous: unclear; vague
impractical: unusable
at worst: most awful situation
political science: the study of government and politics
no ring on my finger: not married
having nothing ahead to count on: no plans or career or marriage
no direction: no goals
forging: building
trapped in a "maturity gap": not an adolescent and not an adult
affluent: rich
alternatively: then again
regardless: in any case
turbulent: restless; confusing

Recite and Review

1. Amanda is presently in the culturally defined period between childhood and adulthood, which
    is called _____.
2. A person matures sexually and becomes capable of reproduction during the biologically
    defined period known as _____.
3. The most widely accepted standards for adult status in North America are (1) taking
    responsibility for oneself, (2) making independent decisions, and (3) becoming _____
    independent.
4. In elementary school, Lindsay was less popular and had a poorer self-image, while she had a
    more positive body image and greater peer prestige in junior high and high school. Regarding
    the onset of her sexual maturation, Lindsay is most likely a(n) _____-maturing girl.

155

5. Regarding the onset of sexual maturation, the boys who are most likely to get into trouble with drugs, alcohol, and antisocial behavior are the _____-maturing boys.

6. A key task in adolescence is _____ formation.

7. Adolescents are better able to ask questions about their place in the world and about morals, values, politics, and social relationships after they have attained the cognitive stage of _____.

8. Juanita is an adolescent who not only contemplates the question, "Who am I?" but also the questions of "Who am I at home?", "Who am I at school?" and "Who am I with friends in my neighborhood?" Juanita is experiencing the powerful influence that her _____ heritage has on her personal identity.

9. Adolescents from minority cultures may experience lowered self-esteem and confusion regarding their roles, values, and personal identities because they often face degrading _____ concerning their intelligence, sexuality, social status, manners, and so forth.

10. The confusion felt by minority teens could be alleviated with positive models, a more tolerant society, and having group _____.

11. According to sociologist James Côté, the societies that are the most tolerant of young people extending their adolescence and prolonging their identity explorations into their 20s are the _____ societies, such as the United States and Canada.

12. Jeffrey Arnett refers to an extended adolescent period in which individuals who are in their 20s live at home with their parents, are not yet married, have no children, and no settled career as _____ adulthood.

13. The "kippers" in England, the "boomerang kids" of Australia, and the "nesthockers" of Germany are called _____ in the United States.

14. In a comparison of adolescence, midlife, and old age, the more emotionally turbulent of the three, according to your textbook, would be _____.

Connections

1. ___ adolescence

2. ___ puberty

3. ___ emerging adulthood

4. ___ criterion for adult status in North America

5. ___ early maturation for boys

6. ___ early maturation for girls

7. ___ kippers

8. ___ boomerang kids

9. ___ nesthockers

10. ___ twixters

a. Arnett's term for the period in which individuals take longer to find their identity and to establish themselves as adults

b. generally beneficial in both elementary, junior high, and high school

c. slang term in Germany for extended adolescence

d. slang term in Australia for extended adolescence

e. slang term in England for extended adolescence

f. slang term in the United States for extended adolescence

g. biologically defined period during which a person matures sexually and becomes capable of reproduction

h. culturally defined period between childhood and adulthood

i. taking responsibility for oneself, making independent decisions, and becoming financially independent

j. less popular and poorer self-image in elementary school with benefits and risks in junior high and high school

Check Your Memory

1. TRUE or FALSE   Puberty is the culturally defined period between childhood and adulthood.
2. TRUE or FALSE   Almost all cultures recognize the transitional status of adolescence, but the length of adolescence varies greatly from culture to culture.
3. TRUE or FALSE   The most widely accepted standards for adult status in North America includes graduation from high school or having a child.
4. TRUE or FALSE   Most people reach reproductive maturity in their early teens.
5. TRUE or FALSE   For boys, reaching sexual maturation later than average is generally more beneficial than early maturation.
6. TRUE or FALSE   Fast-maturing girls usually have a better self-image and are more popular during late elementary school, while becoming less popular and having a poorer self-image during junior high and high school.
7. TRUE or FALSE   One added cost of early maturation for both boys and girls is that it may force premature identity formation.
8. TRUE or FALSE   As ethnic minorities in America continue to grow in status and prominence, adolescents are less likely to feel rejected or excluded because of their ethnic heritage.
9. TRUE or FALSE   Teens who take pride in their ethnic heritage have lower self-esteem, a poorer self-image, and a weaker sense of personal identity.
10. TRUE or FALSE   Teens who take pride in their ethnic heritage are more likely to engage in drug use or violent behavior.
11. TRUE or FALSE   Many of the problems in adolescent identity formation stem from unclear standards about the role adolescents should play within society.
12. TRUE or FALSE   Twixters is a nickname for young adolescents who spend all of their free time socializing online.
13. TRUE or FALSE   The period of extended adolescence often seen in affluent Western societies is referred to as "emerging adulthood."
14. TRUE or FALSE   In less affluent countries and in poorer parts of America, most adolescents continue to "become adults" at much younger ages.
15. TRUE or FALSE   In many ways adolescence and young adulthood are more emotionally turbulent than midlife or old age.

Critical Thinking Question

Are labels like "adolescent" or "young adult" reflective of heredity or environment?

Module 3.6 Moral Development—Growing a Conscience

Survey Question: How do we develop morals and values?

Language Development Guide

terminal illness: a sickness that will cause the death of the person
pleading: begging
extraordinary: special
desperately: urgently; greatly
conscience: sense of right or wrong
influential: important
account: explanation
posed: asked
dilemma: problems; predicament
broke into: entered illegally

consequences: outcomes; results
intermediate: in-between; middle
justify: give a good reason for
comprehensive: complete, overall, all-inclusive
universal: complete
dignity: self-respect
penalty: punishment
advance: develop
getting away with the crime: not be punished
moral compass: personal standard for making ethical decisions
fundamental: basic
ethic: moral value
refuge: shelter
porcupine: animal classified as a rodent that is covered in long quills (sharp shines)
mole: small animal that is blind with most burrowing underground
opt: chose; selected
moral yardstick: set of ethical rules

Recite and Review

1. The development of values, beliefs, and thinking abilities that act as a guide regarding what is acceptable behavior is referred to as one's _____ development.
2. In order to study how children of different ages develop their values and beliefs about acceptable behavior, psychologist Lawrence Kohlberg used _____.
3. According to Kohlberg, moral thinking based on the consequences of one's choices or actions is called _____ moral reasoning.
4. According to Kohlberg, moral thinking based on a desire to please others or to follow accepted rules and values is called _____ moral reasoning.
5. According to Kohlberg, moral thinking based on carefully examined and self-chosen moral principles is called _____ moral reasoning.
6. If you do not steal because you do not want people to think that you are a thief, your moral thinking in this situation would be at the _____ level of moral reasoning.
7. People place a high value on justice, dignity, and equality when they are at the _____ level of moral reasoning.
8. If you do not steal because you do not want to go to jail, your moral thinking in this situation would be at the _____ level of moral reasoning.
9. According to Kohlberg, the level of moral reasoning that is most characteristic of young children and delinquents is the _____ level.
10. Older children and most adults reason at the _____ level of moral thinking.
11. Kohlberg estimated that only about 20 percent of the adult population achieves the _____ level of moral reasoning.
12. Carol Gilligan pointed out that Kohlberg's system is concerned mainly with the ethic of _____.
13. When women are faced with real-life dilemmas, Carol Gilligan believes that they tend to move toward an ethic of _____.
14. A woman who is concerned about what pleases or helps others would be placed at the _____ level in Kohlberg's system.
15. Current research has found that both men and women use both ethics described by Gilligan with the choice depending on the _____.

158

Connections

1. ___ moral development
2. ___ moral dilemmas
3. ___ preconventional level
4. ___ conventional level
5. ___ postconventional level
6. ___ ethic of justice
7. ___ ethic of caring

a. moral thinking based on carefully examined and self-chosen moral principles
b. moral thinking based on the consequences of one's choices
c. Kohlberg's system for assessing moral reasoning is based on this concept
d. Gilligan identified this concept through her studies of women who faced real-life dilemmas
e. moral thinking based on a desire to please others or to follow accepted rules
f. assessment technique used by Kohlberg
g. process by we acquire values, beliefs, and thinking patterns that guide responsible behavior

Check Your Memory

1. TRUE or FALSE   Moral development starts in childhood and continues into adulthood.
2. TRUE or FALSE   Moral values are especially likely to come into sharper focus as capacities for self-control and abstract thinking increase.
3. TRUE or FALSE   To study moral development, Lawrence Kohlberg used a mail-out survey which was sent out to 10,000 adults throughout the United States and Canada.
4. TRUE or FALSE   At the conventional level, moral thinking is guided by the consequences of one's actions.
5. TRUE or FALSE   Persons at the postconventional level of moral reasoning would most likely say that they would not speed on the highway because everyone should obey the law.
6. TRUE or FALSE   One English survey revealed that 11 percent of men and three percent of women would commit murder for one million dollars if they could be sure of getting away with the crime.
7. TRUE or FALSE   When presented with the druggist dilemma, if a person says, "It won't do him any good to steal the drug because his wife will probably die before he gets out of jail," this person is exhibiting the postconventional level of moral reasoning.
8. TRUE or FALSE   Regarding the druggist dilemma, if the person says that the man should steal the drug but then turn himself into the police, the person would be exhibiting the preconventional level of moral reasoning.
9. TRUE or FALSE   People who wish to avoid the disapproval of others or follow a traditional morality of authority would be functioning at the conventional level of moral reasoning.
10. TRUE or FALSE   The conventional level of moral reasoning is most characteristic of young children and delinquents.
11. TRUE or FALSE   Kohlberg estimated that only about 45 percent of the adult population achieves postconventional morality.
12. TRUE or FALSE   Carol Gilligan pointed out that Kohlberg's system of classifying moral reasoning was based on the ethic of caring, while women are more likely to use an ethic of justice in making moral decisions.

159

13. TRUE or FALSE   From Gilligan's perspective, a woman's concern with relationships could look like a weakness rather than a strength within the Kohlberg moral level classification.

14. TRUE or FALSE   Several studies have found little or no difference in men's and women's overall moral reasoning abilities.

15. TRUE or FALSE   Whether a person bases his or her moral decision on the ethic of caring or the ethic of justice appears to depend on the situation being faced.

Module 3.7 Challenges Across the Lifespan
The Story of a Lifetime—Rocky Road or Garden Path?
Survey Question: What are the typical tasks and dilemmas through the lifespan?

Language Development Guide
overview: summary
mortality: death
inevitable: certain
Rocky Road or Garden Path: difficult or easy time
markers: signs
turning points: defining moment; decision point
perhaps: maybe
preview: sample of what is to come
encounter: meet
confronts: challenges
mastered: accomplished
vocation: career
resolving: solving; settling the issue
a string of: a series of
stunted: held back; slowed down
crude: simple and rough
ridiculed: teased, made fun of
overprotected: indulge by doing things for the child
initiative: resourcefulness
fateful: significant; important
dizzying speed: very fast
"entrance into life": learning what is required in the real world outside one's family
industry: productiveness; hard work
inferiority: weakness; inadequacy
adequacy: competence
integrated: included
unified: combined; fused
intimacy: an ability to care about others and to share experiences with them
isolation: loneliness
in line: in agreement
guarantee: assure
shallow: superficial
unfulfilling: unrewarding
next generation: next age group
stagnant: inactive
bitter: resentful
dreary: miserable
trouble spots: difficulty times

Recite and Review

1. Graduating from high school, voting for the first time, and getting married are notable events and are referred to as developmental _____.
2. For optimal development at each stage of life, a person must master a new development _____.
3. According to Erik Erikson, a conflict between one's personal impulses and the social world is known as a(n) _____ dilemma.
4. Erikson believed that during the first year of life if a baby is given warmth, touching, love, and predictable physical care, he or she will develop _____.
5. Inadequate or unpredictable care or parents who are cold, indifferent, or rejecting can lead to basic _____, which can later cause insecurity, suspiciousness, or an inability to relate to others.
6. From ages one to three, children express their growing self-control by climbing, touching, exploring, and trying to do things for themselves in a stage Erikson called _____ versus shame and doubt.
7. If parents give their preschooler the freedom to play, ask questions, use his or her imagination, and choose activities, the child will develop _____, according to Erikson.
8. If parents criticize their preschooler, prevent their play, or discourage the child from asking questions, the preschooler is likely to experience feelings of _____.
9. The elementary school years make up Erikson's stage of industry versus _____.
10. According to Erikson, adolescents who fail to develop a sense of identity will suffer from an uncertainty about who they are and where they are going, a state known as _____.
11. According to Erikson, the major conflict in young adulthood involves intimacy versus _____.
12. Jan is a middle-aged woman, who is helping to guide her children and grandchildren as well as the students in her classes. According to Erikson, Jan is expressing _____.
13. Failure to broaden one's concerns and energies to include the welfare of others and society as a whole during midlife results in what Erikson referred to as _____.
14. When 75-year-old Doug looks back over his life, he is satisfied that his life had meaning and that he lived responsibly. According to Erikson, Doug is exhibiting _____.
15. According to Erikson, a person in old age who sees their life as a series of missed opportunities will experience _____.

Connections

1. ___ developmental milestone
2. ___ developmental task
3. ___ psychosocial dilemma
4. ___ trust versus mistrust
5. ___ generativity versus stagnation
6. ___ identity versus role confusion
7. ___ industry versus inferiority

a. young adult challenge to develop meaningful friendships or remain in shallow, unfulfilling ones
b. conflict in the first year of life over being given predictable or inadequate care
c. any conflict that occurs between one's personal impulses and the social world
d. adolescence crisis to develop a unified sense of self
e. conflict created as toddlers' express their growing self-control
f. notable event or turning point in one's life, such as having a child or retirement
g. conflict in middle adulthood in which self-interest is countered by an interest in guiding the next generation

8. ___ integrity versus despair

    h. conflict of preschoolers as they ask questions, use their imaginations, and choose play activities

9. ___ intimacy versus isolation

    i. teachers, classmates, and events in middle childhood shape one's attitude during this conflict

10. ___ autonomy versus shame and doubt

    j. developing self-respect for the life one has lived or seeing life as a series of missed opportunities

11. ___ initiative versus guilt

    k. any skill, such as reading, that must be mastered for optimal development

Check Your Memory

1. TRUE or FALSE   Notable events or turning points, such as getting married, are called developmental tasks.
2. TRUE or FALSE   Any skill that must be mastered or personal change that must take place for optimal development to occur is called a developmental milestone.
3. TRUE or FALSE   Erik Erikson suggested that we face a specific psychosocial dilemma at each stage of life.
4. TRUE or FALSE   Erikson's concept of "trust" during the first year of life comes from the same conditions that help babies become securely attached to their parents.
5. TRUE or FALSE   From ages one to three, children face the crisis of industry versus inferiority.
6. TRUE or FALSE   The freedom to play, use one's imagination, and ask questions are important in the development of initiative during the preschool years.
7. TRUE or FALSE   Erikson's stage of generativity versus stagnation is the first time that teachers, classmates, and adults outside the home become as important as parents in shaping attitudes toward oneself.
8. TRUE or FALSE   According to Erikson, adolescents face the important task of forming deep friendships or remaining isolated.
9. TRUE or FALSE   Seventy-five percent of college-age men and women ranked a good marriage and family as important adult goals.
10. TRUE or FALSE   Persons who fail to develop a sense of autonomy during young adulthood suffer from role confusion, an uncertainty about who they are and where they are going.
11. TRUE or FALSE   Marriage and sexual involvement guarantees intimacy and allows one to overcome isolation.
12. TRUE or FALSE   Productive and creative work can be used to express generativity.
13. TRUE or FALSE   Failure to achieve industry during middle adulthood leads to feelings of despair.
14. TRUE or FALSE   Developing a sense of integrity in old age allows one to face aging and death with dignity.
15. TRUE or FALSE   Knowing about Erikson's eight stages allows one to anticipate typical trouble spots in one's life and to understand the problems and feelings of friends and relatives at various points in the life cycle.

Critical Thinking Question

Trying to make generalizations about development throughout life is complicated by at least one major factor. What do you think it is?

162

Module 3.7 Middle and Late Adulthood: Will You Still Need Me When I'm 64?

Survey Question: What is involved in well-being during later adulthood?

Language Development Guide

strife: difficulty, fighting

legal conflicts: issues dealing with the law or involving crimes

run the gauntlet: phrase refers to a challenge; comes from a punishment in ancient times in which a person was forced to run between two rows of soldiers that each strike the person as he runs by

environmental mastery: being able to manage one's life circumstances to meet one's needs and values

personal growth: includes self-awareness, setting goals, and developing one's strengths

offset: balanced; compensated

midlife crisis: psychological distress and self-doubt experienced by some people during middle age due; occurs more in Western societies

midcourse correction: milder adjustments made in middle age that would not be considered a "crisis"

reworking old identities: altering aspects of one's life to better meet one's new needs in middle age

taking stock: evaluating, looking over, examining

"wake-up calls": refers to awaken one from inactivity in order to make needed changes

complicated: made more difficult

sickly: unhealthy

infirm: in poor health; weak

senile: mental impairment due to diseases and problems that occur during old age

wholeheartedly: entirely

nursing homes: facility that cares for the elderly individuals who are not physically or mentally able to care for themselves

silver-haired stars: successful older people

intact family: family that is unbroken by divorce

flexible personality: person who is adaptable

spouse: husband, wife, or partner

perceptual processing speed: the rate at which one can utilize information in thinking to solve a problem

"those who live by their wit die with their wits": keeping oneself mental active allows one to live out their late adulthood years mentally sharp

optimism: hopefulness

gratitude: thankfulness

empathy: capacity for taking another's point of view and being ability to feel what another is feeling

enlightened: open-minded

obsolescence: being unnecessary, thrown away or discarded, been replaced by something new

cast aside: ignore, reject

discrimination: treating member of various social groups differently in circumstances where their rights or treatment should be identical

prejudice: negative emotional attitude held against members of a particular group of people

patronizing: demeaning a person usually by talking to individual in overly polite and simple way

"dirty old man": stereotype of an elderly man who acts in a lewd (sexually vulgar) manner toward young women

"meddling old woman": stereotype of an elderly woman who intrudes into other people's personal business

"senile old fool": stereotype of elderly people being mentally impaired and acting silly
perpetuate: keep alive; spread
myths: falsehood
diversity: variety
aerobic-dancing: exercise routine
expertise: knowledge or skill in a particular area

Recite and Review

1. Well-being during adulthood has the six elements of self-acceptance, positive relations with others, autonomy, environmental mastery, a purpose in life, and continued personal growth, according to psychologist _____.
2. The percentage of men and women who believe they have experienced a midlife crisis is _____ percent.
3. At midlife, you are less likely to go through a "crisis," and more likely to make a(n) "midcourse _____."
4. A midlife transition usually consists of achieving valued goals, finding one's own truths, preparing for old age and reworking old _____.
5. For some people, difficult turning points in life can create opportunities for personal growth because they can serve as "_____."
6. After the late 50s, personal development is complicated by _____.
7. The percentage of people older than 65 who are in a nursing home is _____ percent.
8. You are most likely to stay mentally sharp in old age if you remain healthy, live in a favorable environment, are involved in intellectually stimulating activities, have a flexible personality, married to a smart spouse, maintain your perceptual processing speed, and are satisfied with your accomplishments in midlife, according to gerontologist _____.
9. Four psychological characteristics shared by the healthiest, happiest older people are optimism, gratitude, connection with others, and _____.
10. If you are not promoted in your job because your boss thinks you are "too old" or "too young," the boss is exhibiting discrimination or prejudice based on age called _____.
11. People do experience a gradual loss of skills that require speed or rapid learning, which are called _____ abilities.
12. Deitra is 65 years old and has an excellent vocabulary and memory for facts about many subjects. These skills of Deitra are known as _____ abilities.

Connections

1. ___ Ryff's elements of well-being in adulthood
2. ___ midlife transition
3. ___ gerontologist
4. ___ Schaie's ways to stay mentally sharp in old age
5. ___ ageism
6. ___ fluid abilities
7. ___ crystallized abilities

a. skills involving learned knowledge, such as vocabulary
b. skills requiring speed and rapid learning
c. discrimination or prejudice based on a person's age
d. be healthy, have flexible personality, marry a smart spouse, maintain perceptual processing speed, and be satisfied with accomplishments
e. reworking old identities, achieving valued goals, finding one's own truths
f. self-acceptance, positive relations with others, autonomy, environmental mastery, purpose in life, and continued personal growth
g. psychologist who studies aging and the aged

Check Your Memory

1. TRUE or FALSE   Financial security is one of the six elements that Carol Ryff believes contributes to well-being during adulthood.
2. TRUE or FALSE   Ryff found that for many older adults, age-related declines are offset by positive relationships and greater mastery of life's demands.
3. TRUE or FALSE   Eighty percent of men and women believe they have experienced a midlife crisis.
4. TRUE or FALSE   People are more likely to survive a "crisis" at midlife than to make a "midcourse correction."
5. TRUE or FALSE   Ideally, the midlife transition involves reworking old identities, achieving valued goals, finding one's own truths, and preparing for old age.
6. TRUE or FALSE   After the late 50s, personal development is complicated by physical aging.
7. TRUE or FALSE   About 20 percent of those people older than 65 are in nursing homes.
8. TRUE or FALSE   On intellectual tests, top scorers over the age of 65 matched the average for men younger than 35.
9. TRUE or FALSE   A psychologist who studies aging and the aged is called a thanatologist.
10. TRUE or FALSE   Schaie found that people were more likely to stay mentally sharp in old age if they had flexible personalities.
11. TRUE or FALSE   Schaie found that people were more likely to stay mentally sharp if they were married to a smart spouse.
12. TRUE or FALSE   Four psychological characteristics shared by the healthiest, happiest older people are optimism, gratitude and forgiveness, empathy, and a connection with others.
13. TRUE or FALSE   Ageism can oppress the young as well as the old.
14. TRUE or FALSE   Ageism is often expressed through patronizing language with the older person being spoken to in an overly polite, slow, loud, and simple way.
15. TRUE or FALSE   People do experience a gradual loss of crystallized abilities as they age with their fluid abilities remaining strong or improving into their 60s.

Module 3.7 Death and Dying—The Final Challenge

Survey Question: How do people typically react to death?

Language Development Guide

statistics: numerical data

convincing: show proof

in spite of this: but; yet

"that's all folks": means something is ending; it was the famous sign-off (ending) to many Warner Brothers cartoons, featuring the characters Bugs Bunny and Porky Pig with their voices being provided by Mel Blanc

circumstances: conditions

denial: refusing to acknowledge

"passed away," "expired," "gone to God," or "breathed one's last": slang expression for death

impending: coming; approaching

isolate: separate; detach

confirming: proving

initially: at first

reminder: cue

165

ultimate: final
threat: danger
having life torn away: dying
spill over: leak out; be expressed as
rage: extreme anger
evoked: called to mind
envied: jealous of
bargain: make a deal; negotiate
granted: permitted; allowed
dedicate: give; devote; commit
futility: hopelessness
exhaustion: overtiredness
routines: everyday habits and schedules
profound: great; intense
come to terms: begin to accept a situation that is not of your liking
at peace: calm
inevitable: something you can't escape or avoid
companionship: friendship
styles: approaches
eventual: final
conversely: equally likely
survivors: those who live longer than others
"freeze up": unable to speak or move because of one is anxious
genuine: sincere; honest
hospice: facility or program that helps terminally ill patients and their families by offering
        support, guidance, pain relief, and companionship

Recite and Review

1. Compared to younger people, older persons have _____ death fears.
2. Older people more often fear the _____ of dying.
3. When we speak of a dead person as having "passed away, "expired," "gone to God," or "breathed one's last," this language illustrates the reaction of _____.
4. A direct and highly influential account of the emotional responses to death comes from the work of a researcher named _____.
5. Joshua's field of study involves studying the emotional and behavioral responses of people regarding death. Joshua would be referred to as a(n) _____.
6. Regarding the five basic emotional reactions to impending death, the typical first reaction involves _____ and isolation.
7. The reaction that may be evoked when a terminally ill person envies the health of their friends is _____.
8. Arnold is praying to God to allow him to live until his daughter graduates from college. If he is granted this request from God, Arnold promises to right all of his past wrongs in his business career. Arnold is exhibiting the emotional reaction to death known as _____.
9. As death draws near and the person begins to recognize that death cannot be prevented, feelings of futility and exhaustion set in during the emotional reaction known as _____.
10. A person is neither happy nor sad, but at peace with the inevitable during the emotional reaction to impending death known as _____.
11. Today, many terminally ill individuals benefit from a program, which typically offers support, guidance, pain relief, and companionship and is referred to as _____ care.

166

Connections

1. ___ thanatologist
2. ___ anger
3. ___ acceptance
4. ___ bargaining
5. ___ denial and isolation
6. ___ depression
7. ___ hospice care

a. provides support, pain relief, and companionship for the terminally ill
b. feelings of futility, exhaustion and profound sadness regarding one's impending death
c. attempting to "buy" more time from God
d. specialist who studies emotional and behavioral reactions to death and dying
e. struggle with death has been resolved
f. often expressed as rage toward the living
g. attempts to avoid any reminder of one's death

Check Your Memory

1. TRUE or FALSE   Most people are poorly informed about the process of dying.
2. TRUE or FALSE   Older persons actually have fewer death fears than younger people do.
3. TRUE or FALSE   Christine Ladd-Franklin was a thanatologist who postulated the five basic emotional reactions to impending death.
4. TRUE or FALSE   A typical first reaction to impending death is bargaining with God for more time.
5. TRUE or FALSE   The "Why me" reaction to impending death is an expression of anger.
6. TRUE or FALSE   Trying to be "good" in order to live longer is characteristic of the denial reaction to impending death.
7. TRUE or FALSE   Not all terminally ill persons display all five of the emotional reactions to impending death nor do the emotional reactions always occur in the same order.
8. TRUE or FALSE   The same emotional reactions shown in death can also be seen when people are going through a divorce or the loss of a job.
9. TRUE or FALSE   In order to help the dying, it is important to recognize that dying persons do not want to discuss their impending death openly.
10. TRUE or FALSE   Adults tend to "freeze up" when they are around someone who is dying.
11. TRUE or FALSE   Hospices typically offer support, guidance, pain relief, and companionship for the dying.

Module 3.8 Psychology in Action: Effective Parenting—Raising Healthy Children

Survey Question: How do effective parents discipline and communicate with their children?

Language Development Guide

effective: successful; useful
capacity: ability
mutually: jointly
count on it: believe it
smear: spread
antisocial: lacking guilt or remorse; no conscience
insecure: unsure of oneself; lacking confidence
authoritative: firm, dependable, and respectful
socializes: learning to interact and be around other people

destroying: tearing down; breaking up
boundaries: limits
spontaneity: being able to act naturally, unplanned, unprompted
spanking: punishment involving a slap on the child's rear (buttock)
minimize: reduce
model: perfect
big plus: major advantage
empower: give power or strength to
imposing: requiring; enforcing
backfire: go wrong; fail
artificially: insincere, false; not natural
sense of entitlement: believing one has the right to certain privileges not given to others
bully: frighten; torment; harass; intimidate
enhance: increase
eating disorders: usually refers to anorexia (self-starvation) and bulimia (vomiting to rid self of excessive food) in order to be thinner
stability: being constant; permanence
overlooked: ignored; fail to see
mode: form; type
caution: watchfulness; carefulness
scolding: yelling at
humiliate: disgrace; demean; make a person feel unworthy
breed: produces
resentment: hate
reserve: set aside; keep back
pose: cause
creative: inspired; imaginative; resourceful
distinction: difference
have no brains: slang for lacking intelligence
debating: arguing
conclude: end; finish off
progress: steps forward; improvement
lecturing: reprimanding; scolding
intrinsic: based on internal motivations, not on external rewards or punishments
clash: conflict; disagreement
averted: prevented
live the message: be an example of

Recite and Review

1. Children grow up with a capacity for love, joy, fulfillment, responsibility, and self-control when parents use a(n) _____ parenting style.
2. When parents spend enjoyable time encouraging their children in a loving and mutually respectful fashion, these are referred to as _____ interactions.
3. Guidance regarding acceptable behavior is referred to as _____.
4. If a parent spanks a child or takes away his toys for misbehavior, the parent is using the discipline method known as _____
5. When a parent punishes a child by refusing to speak to the child or rejecting the child, the parent is using the discipline method known as _____.
6. A discipline method that combines praise, recognition, approval, rules, and reasoning to encourage desirable behavior is called _____ techniques.

168

7. Fear and hatred of parents as well as the child lacking spontaneity and warmth are common reactions to the discipline method known as _____.

8. Jessie would be described as self-disciplined and a "model child" with a good conscience. However, she is also anxious, insecure, and dependent on adults for approval. Jessie was most likely disciplined by parents who used the method known as _____.

9. High self-esteem in children tends to be promoted by parents who use the discipline method known as _____ techniques.

10. Low self-esteem is related to the use of physical punishment and the discipline method known as _____.

11. According to Maggie Mamen, spoiled, self-indulgent children with a sense of entitlement and a lack of self-control occur when parents use a(n) _____ parenting style.

12. Children feel angry and confused because they cannot predict the consequences of their own behavior when discipline is _____.

13. Punishment, such as scolding or taking away privileges, is most effective when done _____, especially for younger children.

14. Spanking and other forms of physical punishment are not particularly effective for children younger than age _____.

15. Physical punishment is less effective with children after age _____ and can breed resentment.

16. The child expert who believed that the key to clear communication between parent and child involved making a distinction between feelings and behavior was _____.

17. The child psychologist who believed that parents should send *I-messages* to their children, rather than *you-messages* was _____.

18. Accusing, lecturing, bossing, or criticizing are examples of _____-messages.

19. Messages that tell children what effect their behavior had on you are _____-messages.

20. When a child refuses to eat dinner and then gets uncomfortably hungry, the child is experiencing a(n) _____ consequence.

21. When a mother tells her daughter that she can play with her dolls as soon as she takes a bath, the mother has used a(n) _____ consequence.

Connections

1. ___ power assertion
2. ___ withdrawal of love
3. ___ management techniques
4. ___ consistency
5. ___ You-messages
6. ___ I-messages
7. ___ natural consequences
8. ___ logical consequences

a. combining praise, recognition, approval, rules, and reasoning to enforce child discipline

b. communication that involves threatening, accusing, bossing, lecturing, or criticizing another person

c. with respect to child discipline, the maintenance of stable rules of conduct

d. intrinsic effects that tend to follow a particular behavior

e. communication that states the effect someone else's behavior has on you

f. withholding affection to enforce child discipline

g. reasonable effects that are defined by the parents for a particular behavior

h. use of physical punishment or coercion to enforce child discipline

169

Check Your Memory

1. TRUE or FALSE   Authoritarian parents typically use positive parent-child interactions to help their children develop responsibility and self-control.
2. TRUE or FALSE   When parents fail to provide discipline, children become antisocial, aggressive, and insecure.
3. TRUE or FALSE   Effective discipline allows children to feel free to express their deepest feelings.
4. TRUE or FALSE   When a child misbehaves, a parent using power assertion discipline will refuse to speak to the child, threaten to leave, or act as if the child is temporarily unlovable.
5. TRUE or FALSE   As a discipline method, management techniques involve physical punishment or a show of force, such as taking away toys or privileges.
6. TRUE or FALSE   Most children show no signs of long-term damage from spanking, if spanking is backed up by supportive parenting.
7. TRUE or FALSE   Frequent spankings tend to decrease the children's aggressiveness and lead to fewer problem behaviors.
8. TRUE or FALSE   The withdrawal of love method of discipline tends to produce children who are self-disciplined but who also tend to be anxious, insecure, and dependent on adults for approval.
9. TRUE or FALSE   In elementary school, children with high self-esteem tend to be more popular, cooperative, and successful in class.
10. TRUE or FALSE   Low self-esteem is related to the use of the management techniques style of discipline.
11. TRUE or FALSE   Clinical psychologist Maggie Mamen believes that many modern parents, who tried to "empower" their children by imposing few limits and giving them everything they wanted actually created children with an artificially high level of self-esteem.
12. TRUE or FALSE   As adults, children who had a sense of entitlement now place excessive importance on being physically attractive, which leads to stress, drug and alcohol use, and eating disorders.
13. TRUE or FALSE   Inconsistency in discipline makes children feel angry and confused because they cannot control the consequences of their own behavior.
14. TRUE or FALSE   Parents should make sure there is a connection between disapproval of the behavior and disapproval of the child, such as saying "I'm going to punish you because you are bad."
15. TRUE or FALSE   Punishment, such as a scolding or taking away privileges, is most effective when postponed a few hours to give children time to think about their misbehavior.
16. TRUE or FALSE   Spanking and other forms of physical punishment are not particularly effective for children younger than age two.
17. TRUE or FALSE   Spankings become less effective after age five because they tend to humiliate the child and breed resentment.
18. TRUE or FALSE   Physical punishment should be reserved for situations that pose an immediate danger to younger children, such as a child running into the street.
19. TRUE or FALSE   It is usually more effective to reward children when they are being good than it is to punish them for misbehavior.
20. TRUE or FALSE   After age five, the withdrawal of love method is the most effective form of discipline.

21. TRUE or FALSE   According to Haim Ginott, parents should teach their children that all feelings are appropriate with only actions being subject to disapproval.
22. TRUE or FALSE   I-messages typically take the form of threats, name-calling, accusing, bossing, lecturing, or criticizing.
23. TRUE or FALSE   If a child throws a temper tantrum and gains nothing but a sore throat because the tantrum is ignored by the parents, then it is a logical consequence has automatically discouraged the child's misbehavior.

Critical Thinking Question

Several Scandinavian countries have made it illegal for parents to spank their own children. Does this infringe on the rights of parents?

Final Survey and Review—Completion

Module 3.1 The Interplay of Heredity and Environment
Nature and Nurture—It Takes Two to Tango
Survey Question: How do heredity and environment affect development?

1. Karra is a psychologist who is interested in studying the progressive changes in behavior and abilities that occur at each stage of the life span. Karr is most likely a(n) _____ psychologist.
2. Hank has a condition called albinism in which he lacks skin pigmentation. He received this gene for albinism from both of his parents, although neither of them has the condition. The gene for albinism must be a(n) _____ gene.
3. In order not to harm her unborn child, Tanya avoids alcohol, tobacco products, and X-rays, which are all considered _____, since they can cause birth defects.
4. When young rats were placed in "rat wonderlands" with many objects to manipulate, the adult   rats were found to have larger, heavier brains. The researchers of this experiment deliberately made the rats' environment more stimulating, a condition referred to as _____.
5. Soon after Ben was born, his mother noticed that he was a timid, restrained, unexpressive child, which describes a temperament known as _____.

Module 3.2 The Neonate
The Newborn—More Than Meets the Eye
Survey Question: What can newborn babies do?

6. Baby Jo is sitting in her swing when her older brother runs through the house and slams a door, making a loud noise. Baby Jo will most likely react to this noise by showing the _____ reflex.
7. Baby Arnold was first able to raise his head, then his chest, then crawled using his hands and feet, and then stood upright. Baby Arnold is showing motor development known as _____.
8. The looking chamber used in visual perceptual research was developed by _____.
9. Carroll Izard believes that the most common infant expressions, in order, are interest, joy, anger, and _____.

Module 3.3 Social Development in Childhood
Social Development—Baby, I'm Stuck on You
Survey Question: Of what significance is a child's emotional bond with adults?

10. The researcher who investigated mother-infant relationships by taking infant monkeys from their biological mothers and replacing them with wire and terry cloth surrogates was _____.

11. Ten-month-old Libba cried whenever her mother left her with the new babysitter. Libba's crying demonstrates that Libba has formed an emotional bond with her mother. Libba's crying behavior in this situation is referred to as _____.

12. Delbert thinks that most people are well intentioned, and he is comfortable relying on others and having others depend on him. Delbert most likely has a(n) _____ attachment style.

13. Researchers have found that children placed in poor quality day cares are likely to develop _____ problems that did not exist before.

Module 3.3 Parental Influences—Life with Mom and Dad
Survey Question: How important are parenting styles?

14. Twelve-year-old Greg is described by his teachers as competent, assertive, inquiring, and self- controlled. His parents most likely used a(n)_____ parenting style.

15. The parent that tends to tell stories to the child and is the child's playmate is most likely the _____.

16. The culture in which parents are fairly strict in their discipline style, emphasize loyalty and interdependence among family members, and encourage their children to not give up in the face of adversity is the traditional _____ -American family.

Module 3.4 Language Development in Childhood
Language Development—Who Talks Baby Talk?
Survey Question: How do children acquire language?

17. Little Melanie has just begun to add the consonants of *b, d, m,* and *g* to the vowel sounds she was already making. Melanie is now exhibiting the stage in language development known as _____.

18. Kerry has been especially mischievous lately with "No" being her favorite answer to all of her mother's requests. Kerry is showing signs of entering a phase in child development known as the "_____."

19. The psycholinguist who believed that humans have a biological predisposition to learn language was _____.

20. When parents and infant communicate through touching, vocalizing, gazing, and smiling, they are using a system of shared _____.

Module 3.5 Cognitive Development in Childhood
Cognitive Development—Think Like a Child
Survey Question: How do children learn to think?

21. When you modify your ideas to fit new requirements, you are using the process Piaget called _____.

22. Babies develop object permanence during the stage of cognitive development .known as _____.

23. Children are egocentric, cannot mental transform images, and lack reversibility during the _____ stage.

24. Individuals are capable of inductive and deductive reasoning and can comprehend physics, philosophy, psychology, and other abstract systems when they develop _____ operational thought.

172

25. In Baillargeon's studies, three-month-old infants acted surprised and gazed longer at _____ events.
26. In order to appreciate that other people may lie, be sarcastic, make jokes, or use figures of speech, a child must have developed theory of _____.
27. While Piaget stressed the role of maturation in cognitive development, Russian scholar Lev Vygotsky focused on the impact of _____ factors.
28. According to Vygotsky, children should be taught within their zone of _____.

Module 3.6 Adolescence, Young Adulthood, and Moral Development
Adolescence and Young Adulthood—The Best of Times, the Worst of Times
Survey Question: Why is the transition from adolescence to adulthood especially challenging?
29. The biologically defined period of the life span in which a person matures sexually and becomes capable of reproduction is called _____.
30. Simon would be described as relaxed, dominant, self-assured, and popular but is more at risk for getting into trouble with drugs, alcohol, and antisocial behavior. Simon is most likely a(n) _____ boy.
31. Teens who take pride in their ethnic heritage have higher self-esteem, a better self-image, and a stronger sense of their personal _____.
32. The "twixters," the "kippers," the "Nesthockers," and "the boomerang kids" are all slang expressions for what Jeffrey Arnett refers to as _____ adulthood.

Module 3.6 Moral Development—Growing a Conscience
Survey Question: How do we develop morals and values?
33. The psychologist that developed the three levels of moral reasoning was _____.
34. Regarding the druggist dilemma, if the person says that the man should steal the drug but then turn himself into the police, the person would be exhibiting the _____ level of moral reasoning.
35. When presented with the druggist dilemma, if a person says, "It won't do him any good to steal the drug because his wife will probably die before he gets out of jail," this person is exhibiting the _____ level of moral reasoning.
36. Delinquents and young children are most likely functioning at the _____ level of moral reasoning.
37. Carol Gilligan pointed out that women are more likely to use an ethic of caring, while male psychologists have, for the most part, defined moral maturity in terms of autonomy and _____.

Module 3.7 Challenges Across the Lifespan
The Story of a Lifetime—Rocky Road or Garden Path?
Survey Question: What are the typical tasks and dilemmas through the lifespan?
38. Learning to read in childhood, adjusting to sexual maturity in adolescence, and establishing a vocation as an adult are examples of developmental _____ and must be mastered for optimal development.
39. Babies become securely attached to their parents if their parents provide them with predicable care, which is the same criterion for developing basic _____ in Erikson's theory.
40. During the second of Erikson's stages, if parents ridicule or overprotect their toddlers and do not let them try their new skills, the child may not develop _____.

41. Cara is an adolescent whose conflicting experiences as a student, friend, athlete, worker, daughter, and girlfriend must be integrated into a unified sense of self during Erikson's stage known as _____.
42. According to Erikson, an ability to care about others and to share experiences with them is known as _____.

Module 3.7 Middle and Late Adulthood: Will You Still Need Me When I'm 64?
Survey Question: What is involved in well-being during later adulthood?
43. According to Carol Ryff, well-being in adulthood includes the six elements of self-acceptance, positive relations with others, autonomy, a purpose in life, continued personal growth, and environmental _____.
44. Tamara is a psychologist who studies aging and the aged. Tamara is a(n) _____.
45. According to Warner Schaie, you are most likely to stay mentally sharp in old age if you remain healthy, live in a favorable environment, are involved in intellectually stimulating activities, are married to a smart spouse, maintain your perceptual processing speed, and are satisfied with your accomplishments in midlife, and have a flexible _____.
46. Speaking to older people in an overly polite, slow, loud, and simple way implying that they are infirm, even when they are not is an example of the prejudice known as _____.
47. Sixty-year-old Ralph can expect to experience a gradual decline on tasks requiring speed and rapid learning, which are called _____ abilities.

Module 3.7 Death and Dying—The Final Challenge
Survey Question: How do people typically react to death?
48. Eighty-year-old Amy has greater fears about the _____ of death rather than death itself.
49. Elisabeth Kübler-Ross studied the process of death and identified the five reactions to impending death. Regarding her expertise, Kübler-Ross' profession would best be described as a(n) _____.
50. Kübler-Ross' five reactions to impending death include denial and isolation, anger, bargaining, depression, and _____.
51. Marta is terminally ill and is receiving support from an in-home service that will help relieve her pain and provide companionship. This service is known as _____ care.

Module 3.8 Psychology in Action: Effective Parenting—Raising Healthy Children
Survey Question: How do effective parents discipline and communicate with their children?
52. When her child misbehaves, Tonya refuses to speak her child and acts as if the child is temporarily unlovable. Tonya is using a discipline approach known as _____.
53. After age five, the most effective form of discipline that combines praise, recognition, rules and reasoning is _____.
54. Changing *no* to *yes,* especially to quiet a nagging child is an example of _____ discipline.
55. Child expert Haim Ginott believed that the key to clear communication between parent and child involved the parent making a distinction between behavior and _____.
56. According to psychologist Thomas Gordon, the type of messages that force children to accept responsibility for the effects of their actions are _____-messages.
57. In situations that don't produce natural consequences, parents can set up rational and reasonable effects known as _____ consequences.

174

Final Survey and Review—Matching

Module 3.1 The Interplay of Heredity and Environment

1. ___ DNA
2. ___ chromosomes
3. ___ recessive trait
4. ___ dominant trait
5. ___ maturation
6. ___ congenital problems
7. ___ sensitive period
8. ___ enrichment
9. ___ reaction range
10. ___ temperament

a. the limits environment places on the effects of heredity
b. a time during which certain events must take place for normal development to occur
c. the physical core of personality including emotional sensitivity and energy level
d. deliberately making an environment more stimulating, nutritional, and loving
e. thread-like "colored bodies" in the nucleus of each cell
f. birth defects
g. requires two genes to produce the effect
h. a long, ladder-like chain of pairs of chemical molecules
i. physical growth and development of the body and nervous system
j. requires only one gene to produce the effect

Module 3.2 The Neonate

1. ___ rooting reflex
2. ___ Moro reflex
3. ___ grasping reflex
4. ___ cephalocaudal
5. ___ proximodistal
6. ___ interest
7. ___ general excitement

a. elicited by pressing an object into a newborn's palm
b. most common emotion according to Bridges
c. most common emotion according to Izard
d. pattern of motor control from the center of the body to the extremities
e. elicited by loud noise
f. searching behavior elicited by touching the newborn's cheek
g. pattern of motor control from head to toe

Module 3.3 Social Development in Childhood

1. ___ securely attached
2. ___ insecure-avoidant
3. ___ insecure-ambivalent
4. ___ authoritarian parents
5. ___ overly permissive parents
6. ___ authoritative parents

a. parents in this culture act as teachers, are group-oriented, and lenient in their parenting until age five when they expect children to show obedience and self-control
b. anxious emotional bond marked by both a desire to be with a parent and some resistance to being reunited
c. culture that values individual effort and independence and are more likely to force young children to sleep alone
d. culture that values social skills over cognitive skills and cooperation over competition
e. anxious emotional bond marked by a tendency to avoid reunion with a parent or caregiver
f. parenting style that supplies firm and consistent guidance combined with love and affection

175

7. ___ African-American families

    g. culture that emphasizes loyalty, security, the development of a positive identity, and resourcefulness with discipline being fairly strict

8. ___ Hispanic families

    h. parenting style that gives little guidance, too much freedom, or does not require the child to take responsibility

9. ___ Asian-American families

    i. culture that emphasizes welfare of family over individual identity; values success, generosity, hospitality, and conservatism with punishment involving spankings or shaming in front of others

10. ___ Arab-American families

    j. stable and positive emotional bond in which infant seeks out mother upon her return

11. ___ Western culture families

    k. parenting style that enforces rigid rules and demands strict obedience

Module 3.4 Language Development in Childhood

1. ___ cooing

    a. pattern of speech used when talking to infants, marked by exaggerated voice inflections

2. ___ babbling

    b. specialist in the psychology of language

3. ___ telegraphic speech

    c. two-year-olds using words arranged in two-word sentences, such as "want juice"

4. ___ signals

    d. consonants *b*, *d*, *m*, and *g* are combined with vowel sounds to produce meaningless language sounds

5. ___ parentese

    e. repetition of vowel sounds, such as "oo" and "ah"

6. ___ biological predisposition

    f. presumed hereditary readiness to learn certain skills, such as how to use language

7. ___ psycholinguist

    g. touching, vocalizing, gazing, or smiling that allows nonverbal interaction

Module 3.5 Cognitive Development in Childhood

1. ___ assimilation

    a. stage that children think abstractly and theoretically

2. ___ accommodation

    b. concept that weight, mass, and volume of matter remain unchanged even when the shape or appearance of the object changes

3. ___ object permanence

    c. stage that children coordinate information from eyes and ears with muscle movements

4. ___ theory of mind

    d. range of tasks a child cannot yet master alone, but that can be accomplished with the guidance of a more capable partner

5. ___ egocentric thought

    e. stage that children begin to use language and think symbolically but illogically

6. ___ conservation

    f. thought that fails to consider the viewpoints of others

7. ___ zone of proximal development

    g. stage that children think logically but not abstractly

176

8. ___ sensorimotor stage
h. understanding that people have mental states and that other people's mental states can be different from one's own

9. ___ preoperational stage
i. process of modifying existing mental patterns to fit new demands

10. ___ concrete operational stage
j. concept that objects continue to exist even when they are hidden from view

11. ___ formal operational stage
k. process of using existing mental patterns in new situations

Module 3.6 Adolescence, Young Adulthood, and Moral Development

1. ___ adolescence
a. period in which individuals take longer to find their identity and to establish themselves as adults

2. ___ puberty
b. moral thinking based on the consequences of one's choices

3. ___ emerging adulthood
c. moral thinking based on carefully examined and self-chosen moral principles

4. ___ preconventional level
d. Kohlberg's system for assessing moral reasoning is based on this concept

5. ___ conventional level
e. Gilligan identified this concept through her studies of women who faced real-life dilemmas

6. ___ postconventional level
f. moral thinking based on a desire to please others or to follow accepted rules

7. ___ ethic of justice
g. biologically defined period during which a person matures sexually and becomes capable of reproduction

8. ___ ethic of caring
h. culturally defined period between childhood and adulthood

Module 3.7 Challenges Across the Lifespan

1. ___ developmental milestone
a. conflict of preschoolers as they ask questions, use their imaginations, and choose play activities

2. ___ industry versus inferiority
b. skills involving learned knowledge, such as vocabulary

3. ___ initiative versus guilt
c. discrimination or prejudice based on a person's age

4. ___ trust versus mistrust
d. feelings of futility, exhaustion and profound sadness regarding one's impending death

5. ___ generativity versus stagnation
e. psychologist who studies aging and the aged

6. ___ integrity versus despair
f. conflict in middle adulthood in which self-interest is countered by an interest in guiding the next generation

7. ___ gerontologist
g. specialist who studies emotional and behavioral reactions to death and dying

8. ___ thanatologist
h. provides support, pain relief, and companionship for the terminally ill

9. ___ ageism

10. ___ fluid abilities

11. ___ crystallized abilities

12. ___ denial and isolation

13. ___ depression
14. ___ hospice

i. developing self-respect for the life one has lived or seeing life as a series of missed opportunities

j. notable event or turning point in one's life, such as having a child or retirement

k. typical first emotional reaction to impending death

l. conflict in the first year of life over being given predictable or inadequate care

m. skills requiring speed and rapid learning

n. teachers, classmates, and events in middle childhood shape one's attitude during this conflict

Module 3.8 Psychology in Action: Effective Parenting—Raising Healthy Children

1. ___ logical consequences

2. ___ natural consequences

3. ___ management techniques

4. ___ power assertion

5. ___ withdrawal of love

6. ___ I-messages

7. ___ you-messages

a. communication that involves threatening, accusing, bossing, lecturing, or criticizing another person

b. combining praise, recognition, approval, rules, and reasoning to enforce child discipline

c. use of physical punishment or coercion to enforce child discipline

d. intrinsic effects that tend to follow a particular behavior

e. communication that states the effect someone else's behavior has on you

f. withholding affection to enforce child discipline

g. reasonable effects that are defined by the parents for a particular behavior

Final Survey and Review—True or False

Module 3.1 The Interplay of Heredity and Environment
Nature and Nurture—It Takes Two to Tango
Survey Question: How do heredity and environment affect development?

1. TRUE or FALSE   A human sperm cell has a total of 46 chromosomes in its nucleus.
2. TRUE or FALSE   The brain of a newborn baby has a greater number of dendrites and synapses than an adult brain.
3. TRUE or FALSE   Exposure of a fetus to alcohol, drugs, or X-ray could result in what is known as a congenital problem.
4. TRUE or FALSE   The time when children are more susceptible to particular types of environmental   influences is called their reaction range.
5. TRUE or FALSE   More children have an easy temperament than a difficult temperament.

Module 3.2 The Neonate
The Newborn—More Than Meets the Eye
Survey Question: What can newborn babies do?

6. TRUE or FALSE   If you touch an infant's cheek, the infant will turn toward your touch, which illustrates the rooting reflex.

7. TRUE or FALSE   Muscular control that spreads in a pattern from head to toe is called cephalocaudal.

8. TRUE or FALSE   Babies at about two years of age will show more interest in familiar objects than unusual objects, such as scrambled faces.

9. TRUE or FALSE   At first, a baby's smiling is haphazard, but by the age of eight to 12 months, infants smile more frequently when another person is nearby

Module 3.3 Social Development in Childhood
Social Development—Baby, I'm Stuck on You
Survey Question: Of what significance is a child's emotional bond with adults?

10. TRUE or FALSE   Babies show a strong attachment to their mothers from birth, showing separation anxiety during the first month of life.

11. TRUE or FALSE   Infants who are securely attached at the age of one year show a lack of social skills and are overly dependent on their teachers during preschool.

12. TRUE or FALSE   An adult with an avoidant attachment style is skeptical about the idea of true love, has difficulty trusting his or her partner, and tends to pull back when things do not go well in a relationship.

13. TRUE or FALSE   The overall group size for a quality day care should be between 12 to 15 children.

Module 3.3 Parental Influences—Life with Mom and Dad
Survey Question: How important are parenting styles?

14. TRUE or FALSE   Because Ned's parents demand complete obedience to their rigid rules without question or explanation, they would be classified as authoritarian parents.

15. TRUE or FALSE   Fathers pay more visual attention to their children, are more tactile, and are more likely to engage their children in unusual play.

16. TRUE or FALSE   Western cultures tend to be more group-oriented and emphasize interdependence among individuals.

Module 3.4 Language Development in Childhood
Language Development—Who Talks Baby Talk?
Survey Question: How do children acquire language?

17. TRUE or FALSE   The correct sequence in the language development of children is cooing, crying, telegraphic speech, babbling, and one-word utterances.

18. TRUE or FALSE   Noam Chomsky underestimated the roles that learning and the social context play in language development.

19. TRUE or FALSE   The exaggerated pattern of speaking in which parents typically raise the tone of their voices, use short, simple sentences, and repeat themselves is known as transformational speech.

20. TRUE or FALSE   Parents usually warn their infants through a rising, then a falling pitch in their voices.

Module 3.5 Cognitive Development in Childhood
Cognitive Development—Think Like a Child
Survey Question: How do children learn to think?

21. TRUE or FALSE   Children tend to use more generalizations and categories in their thinking than adults do.
22. TRUE or FALSE   Accommodation refers to using existing mental patterns in new situations.
23. TRUE or FALSE   An understanding of hypothetical possibilities develops during the preoperational stage.
24. TRUE or FALSE   Children develop object permanence during the concrete operational stage.
25. TRUE or FALSE   If Benjamin blocks your view by standing in front of the TV because he assumes that you can see it if he can see, then Benjamin is exhibiting egocentric thinking.
26. TRUE or FALSE   The concept that mass, weight, and volume remain unchanged when the shape of objects changes is called theory of mind.
27. TRUE or FALSE   Contemporary cognitive researchers now believe that Piaget mistook babies' limited physical skills for mental incompetence in his testing of the infants' abilities.
28. TRUE or FALSE   Vygotsky believed that adults help children learn how to think by "scaffolding," or supporting, their attempts to solve problems or discover principles.

Module 3.6 Adolescence, Young Adulthood, and Moral Development
Adolescence and Young Adulthood—The Best of Times, the Worst of Times
Survey Question: Why is the transition from adolescence to adulthood especially challenging?

29. TRUE or FALSE   The biologically defined period during which a person matures sexually and becomes capable of reproduction is called adolescence.
30. TRUE or FALSE   Late-maturing boys are usually more popular and have a better self-image in elementary school as well as junior high and high school.
31. TRUE or FALSE   Ethnic adolescents have often faced degrading stereotypes concerning their intelligence, sexuality, social status, and manners.
32. TRUE or FALSE   Emerging adulthood is much less common in affluent Westernized cultures.

Module 3.6 Moral Development—Growing a Conscience
Survey Question: How do we develop morals and values?

33. TRUE or FALSE   In order to study how children of different ages develop their values and beliefs about acceptable behavior, psychologist Lawrence Kohlberg asked people questions regarding various moral dilemmas.
34. TRUE or FALSE   Persons at the conventional level of moral reasoning would most likely say that they would not speed on the highway because everyone should obey the law.
35. TRUE or FALSE   Moral thinking based on a desire to please others is characteristics of the postconventional level.
36. TRUE or FALSE   Kohlberg estimated that only about 20 percent of the adult population achieves the postconventional level of moral reasoning.
37. TRUE or FALSE   The psychologist that deserved credit for identifying the ethic of caring, which is second major way in which moral choices are made, was Elisabeth Kübler-Ross.

180

Module 3.7 Challenges Across the Lifespan
The Story of a Lifetime—Rocky Road or Garden Path?
Survey Question: What are the typical tasks and dilemmas through the lifespan?

38. TRUE or FALSE   According to Erikson, a child who is given inadequate or unpredictable care during the first year of life is likely to develop feelings of despair rather than integrity.

39. TRUE or FALSE   If parents criticize their preschooler, prevent their play, or discourage the child from asking questions, the preschooler is likely to experience feelings of mistrust rather than trust.

40. TRUE or FALSE   Erikson's stage of industry versus inferiority is the first time that teachers, classmates, and adults outside the home become as important as parents in shaping attitudes toward oneself.

41. TRUE or FALSE   Marriage or sexual involvement is no guarantee of developing intimacy.

42. TRUE or FALSE   To be generative, a person must broaden his or her concerns and energies to include the welfare of others and society as a whole.

Module 3.7 Middle and Late Adulthood: Will You Still Need Me When I'm 64?
Survey Question: What is involved in well-being during later adulthood?

43. TRUE or FALSE   Sharing life's joys and sorrows with others and having a better understanding of how the world works can help carry people through midlife and into their later years.

44. TRUE or FALSE   On intellectual tests, top scorers over the age of 65 scored significantly below the average for men younger than 35

45. TRUE or FALSE   In Japan, ageism is expressed as respect for the elderly and is seen as positive.

46. TRUE or FALSE   Popular representations of the elderly as "dirty old men," "meddling old women," and "senile old fools" were once thought to be stereotypes but are now found to be accurate descriptions of this age group.

47. TRUE or FALSE   Skills, such as the knowledge of history facts and psychology concepts are examples of fluid abilities.

Module 3.7 Death and Dying—The Final Challenge
Survey Question: How do people typically react to death?

48. TRUE or FALSE   Compared to adolescents, an elderly person has more death fears.

49. TRUE or FALSE   A typical first reaction to impending death is denial and isolation.

50. TRUE or FALSE   In general, one's approach to dying will mirror his or her style of living.

51. TRUE or FALSE   To help reduce the feeling of isolation, Kirsti Dyer suggests that family members or friends should try to be respectful, genuine, aware of nonverbal cues, or just be there for the dying person.

Module 3.8 Psychology in Action: Effective Parenting—Raising Healthy Children
Survey Question: How do effective parents discipline and communicate with their children?

52. TRUE or FALSE   Frequent spanking tends to increase aggression and leads to more problem behaviors, not fewer.

53. TRUE or FALSE   Low self-esteem is related to physical punishment and the withholding of love.

54. TRUE or FALSE Parents should separate disapproval of the act from disapproval of the child by saying "I'm upset about what you did" rather than saying "You are bad."

55. TRUE or FALSE It is usually more effective to punish children for misbehavior than to reward children when they are being good.

56. TRUE or FALSE After age five, management techniques are the most effective form of discipline.

57. TRUE or FALSE Ginott encouraged parents to teach their children that both feelings and actions are subject to disapproval.

Mastery Test

1. In most areas of development, "nature" and "nurture"
   a. act independently of each other.
   b. often conflict with each other, thereby canceling out the effects of the other.
   c. are responsible for most genetic disorders by acting together.
   d. are continuously interacting.

2. Genetic information is coded in long, ladder-like chains consisting of pairs of chemical molecules, which are referred to as one's
   a. reaction range.
   b. teratogenic level.
   c. MSG.
   d. DNA.

3. Kendra has sickle-cell anemia, which is a recessive genetic disorder. To have this condition, Kendra must have received
   a. two recessive genes from her mother.
   b. two recessive genes from her father.
   c. one recessive gene from her mother and one from her father.
   d. a recessive gene from one parent and a dominant gene from the other parent.

4. If a trait is polygenic, this means that this characteristic is controlled by
   a. two dominant genes.
   b. two recessive genes.
   c. many genes working in combination.
   d. environmental teratogens.

5. The broad, universal patterns of the human growth sequence can be attributed to
   a. motor primacy.
   b. the environment.
   c. congenital imprinting.
   d. heredity.

6. Parents who begin toilet training their child at 18 months of age will most likely be in for 10 trying weeks of false alarms and "accidents" because
   a. they were not consistent in their training techniques.
   b. maturation controls when toilet training will be completed.
   c. the child has a common congenital disorder that delays the completion of toilet training.
   d. the child was a girl and girls tend to complete toilet training later than boys.

182

7. Fetal alcohol syndrome (FAS) is caused by a(n)
   a. polygenic interaction.
   b. recessive gene.
   c. teratogen.
   d. incompatible blood types of the parents.

8. Early childhood stimulation is to enrichment as poverty is to
   a. polygenic interaction.
   b. sensitive period.
   c. reaction range.
   d. deprivation.

9. Since she was born, Samantha has been a fussy child, who reacts intensely and angrily to most situations. Thomas and Chess referred to children with this moody temperament as
   a. easy children.
   b. difficult children.
   c. slow-to-warm-up children.
   d. the most common temperament.

10. An infant startled by a loud noise will typically display a(n) _____ reflex.
    a. Moro
    b. rooting
    c. Meltzoff
    d. imprinting

11. To find out what infants can see and what holds their attention, Robert Fantz invented a device known as the
    a. visualization box.
    b. perceptual apparatus.
    c. looking chamber.
    d. attentional mirror.

12. At what age do babies become interested in unusual objects, such as scrambled faces, and seem to want to understand why this unusual object differs from what they have come to expect?
    a. nine months
    b. one year
    c. 15 months
    d. two years

13. An infant's muscular control develops from the center of the body outward toward the extremities in a pattern known as the
    a. zone of proximal development.
    b. proximodistal pattern.
    c. cephalocaudal pattern.
    d. scaffolding principle.

14. Which of the following emotions do many researchers believe is the only emotion that newborn infants clearly express?
    a. anger
    b. fear
    c. joy
    d. general excitement

15. When frightened by the wind-up toys, the baby monkeys, who had been separated from their real mothers at birth,
    a. clung to the wire surrogate mother with the milk bottle.
    b. clung to the terry cloth surrogate mother that had no bottle.
    c. showed no consistency in which surrogate mother it clung to for security.
    d. clung to neither surrogate but instead cowered in the corner and displayed a disturbed rocking behavior.

16. An insecure-ambivalent attachment is revealed by
    a. social referencing by the child.
    b. the child turning away and avoiding contact with the parent.
    c. the child seeking contact but then pulling away from the parent.
    d. a child needing a security blanket when the parent is not present.

17. Infants who are securely attached at the age of one year tend to be
    a. anxious and remote with others.
    b. resilient and curious.
    c. dependent and immature.
    d. lacking in social skills.

18. Children in high-quality day cares tend to exhibit
    a. increased behavior problems.
    b. poorer relationships with their mothers.
    c. poorer cognitive skills.
    d. none of these.

19. In which parental style are the parents firm and consistent in their discipline and teach their children to manage and control their emotions and to use positive coping skills?
    a. authoritative
    b. authoritarian
    c. overly permissive
    d. power assertion

20. Fathers are more likely than mothers to
    a. play conventional games, such as peekaboo with their infants.
    b. provide verbal stimulation.
    c. pay visual attention to their children.
    d. offer comfort and emotional care to their children.

21. Families in which culture are typically affectionate and indulgent toward younger children, stress cooperation more than competition, and tend to value social skills, such as obedience and respect, more than cognitive skills?
    a. African-American families
    b. Asian-American families
    c. Hispanic families
    d. Middle Eastern families

22. A child combines the consonants *b, d, m,* and *g* with vowel sounds to produce meaningless language sounds during the _____ stage of language development.
    a. "terrible twos"
    b. babbling
    c. cooing
    d. telegraphic

23. Which of following claimed that our language patterns are inborn much like our ability to coordinate walking?
    a. Mary Ainsworth
    b. B. F. Skinner
    c. Noam Chomsky
    d. John Watson

24. When she speaks to her baby, Antonia raise the tone of her voice, uses frequent gestures, and repeats short, simple sentences. Antonia is using _____ in speaking with her baby.
    a. semantic decoding
    b. transformations
    c. babbling
    d. parentese

25. Eighteen-month-old Timmon loves to bang on things with his toy hammer. His mother hands him a small toy guitar and shows him how to pluck the strings. However, Timmon proceeds to bang on things with the toy guitar as if it is a hammer. Timmon is exhibiting
    a. transformation.
    b. assimilation.
    c. accommodation.
    d. conservation.

26. It is dangerous for a preoperational child to cross a busy street because they are unable to understand that a driver may not see them even if the child can see the car, a cognitive limitation known as
    a. egocentric thought.
    b. object permanence.
    c. conservation.
    d. reversibility.

27. In playing the game of Monopoly, if a child understands the basic instructions and plays by the rules but does not understand hypothetical transactions dealing with mortgages and loans, the child is most likely in the _____ stage of cognitive development.
    a. sensorimotor
    b. formal operations
    c. concrete operational
    d. preoperational

28. Jerry able to understand sarcasm and figures of speech and even understands his older brother's weird jokes and that his brother may lie to him sometimes. Jerry has developed
    a. egocentric thought.
    b. animism.
    c. conservation.
    d. theory of mind.

29. Russian scholar Lev Vygotsky focused on the impact of _____ on cognitive development.
    a. heredity
    b. sociocultural factors
    c. humanistic needs and drives
    d. reinforcement and punishment

30. Premature identity formation is one of the risks of
    a. early generativity.
    b. egocentric thought.
    c. an inability to resolve the trust versus mistrust crisis.
    d. early puberty.

31. A period of prolonged identity exploration that extends from the late teens to at least the mid 20s is called
    a. "childhood revisited."
    b. elongated adolescence.
    c. emerging adulthood.
    d. arrested puberty.

32. Seeking approval and upholding law, order, and authority are characteristics of which level of moral development?
    a. preconventional
    b. conventional
    c. postconventional
    d. postformal

33. Carol Gilligan stated that Kohlberg's system of classifying moral development was based on the ethic of justice, while she believed women were more likely to use an ethic of
    a. caring.
    b. intuition.
    c. logic.
    d. autonomy.

34. According to Erikson, the dilemma faced by preschoolers of four or five years of age would be
    a. trust versus mistrust.
    b. identity versus role confusion.
    c. initiative versus guilt.
    d. industry versus inferiority.

35. According to Erikson, developing a sense of integrity is a special challenge in
    a. adolescence.
    b. young adulthood.
    c. middle adulthood.
    d. late adulthood.

36. Regarding middle age and late adulthood, which of the following statements is FALSE?
    a. Only about 25 percent of men and women believe they have experienced a midlife crisis.
    b. People tend to experience a gradual loss of crystallized abilities as they age, which can be offset by their fluid abilities.
    c. In Japan, ageism is expressed as respect for the elderly, while ageism tends to have a negative impact on individuals in Western nations.
    d. Only about 5 percent of those older than 65 are in nursing homes.

37. Which of the following individuals is best known for conducting research in the area of death and dying and describing the five emotional reactions to impending death?
    a. Carol Ryff
    b. Elisabeth Kübler-Ross
    c. Maggie Mamen
    d. Mary Ainsworth

38. The thought "It's all a mistake" would most likely occur as part of which emotional reaction to impending death?
    a. anger
    b. freezing up
    c. denial and isolation
    d. bargaining

39. Maggie and Tim set rules for their children and use reasoning combined with praise. Maggie and Tim's style of child discipline is known as
    a. the power assertion method.
    b. overly permissive parenting.
    c. management techniques.
    d. authoritarian discipline.

40. One thing that all forms of effective child discipline have in common is that they
    a. are consistent.
    b. make use of punishment.
    c. involve a temporary withdrawal of love.
    d. emphasize you-messages.

Chapter 4: Sensation and Perception

Chapter Overview

The senses act as selective data reduction systems in order to prevent the brain from being overwhelmed by sensory input. Sensation begins with transduction in a receptor organ with other data reduction processes being sensory adaptation, analysis, and coding. Sensation can be partially understood in terms of sensory localization in the brain.

The eye is a visual system, not a photographic one. The entire visual system is structured to analyze visual information. Four common visual defects are myopia, hyperopia, presbyopia, and astigmatism. The rods and cones are photoreceptors in the retina of the eye. The rods specialize in peripheral vision, night vision, seeing black and white, and detecting movement. The cones specialize in color vision, acuity, and daylight vision. Color vision is explained by the trichromatic theory in the retina and by the opponent-process theory in the visual system beyond the eyes. Total color blindness is rare, but 8 percent of males and 1 percent of females are red-green color-blind or color-weak. Dark adaptation is the dramatic increase in retinal sensitivity to light that occurs after a person enters the dark with maximum visual sensitivity occurring after being in complete darkness for 30 to 35 minutes.

Sound waves are the stimulus for hearing. They are transduced by the eardrum, auditory ossicles, oval window, cochlea, and ultimately the hair cells. Frequency theory explains how we hear tones up to 4,000 hertz, while place theory explains tones above 4,000 hertz. Two basic types of hearing loss are conductive hearing loss and sensorineural hearing loss. Noise-induced hearing loss is a common form of sensorineural hearing loss caused by exposure to loud noise.

Olfaction (smell) and gustation (taste) are chemical senses that respond to airborne or liquefied molecules. The lock and key theory of olfaction partially explains smell. In addition, the location of the olfactory receptors in the nose helps identify various scents. Sweet and bitter tastes are based on a lock-and-key coding of molecule shapes. Salty and sour tastes are triggered by a direct flow of ions into taste receptors.

The somesthetic senses include the skin senses, vestibular senses, and kinesthetic senses (receptors that detect muscle and joint positioning). The skin senses are touch, pressure, pain, cold, and warmth. Sensitivity to each is related to the number of receptors found in an area of skin. Distinctions can be made between warning pain and reminding pain. Selective gating of pain messages takes place in the spinal cord, as explained by gate control theory. Pain can be reduced through counterirritation and by controlling anxiety and attention. According to sensory conflict theory, motion sickness is caused by a mismatch of visual, kinesthetic, and vestibular sensations. Motion sickness can be avoided by minimizing sensory conflict.

Perception is an active process of constructing sensations into a meaningful mental representation of the world. Perceptions are based on simultaneous bottom-up and top-down processing. Complete percepts are assembled out of small sensory features in "bottom-up" fashion, while preexisting knowledge guide "top-down" processing as features are organized into a meaningful whole. Separating figure and ground is the most basic perceptual organization. The

189

following Gestalt principles also help organize sensations: nearness, similarity, continuity, closure, contiguity, and common region. A perceptual organization may be thought of as a hypothesis held until evidence contradicts it. In vision, the image projected on the retina is constantly changing, but the external world appears stable and undistorted because of size, shape, and brightness constancy.

Incoming sensations are affected by selective attention, a brain-based process that allows some sensory inputs to be selected for further processing while others are ignored. Selectively attending to one's text message while driving can be a dangerous combination.

A basic, innate capacity for depth perception is present soon after birth. Depth perception depends on binocular cues of retinal disparity and convergence. Depth perception also depends on the monocular cue of accommodation. Monocular "pictorial" depth cues also underlie depth perception. They are linear perspective, relative size, height in the picture plane, light and shadow, overlap, texture gradients, aerial haze, and motion parallax. The moon illusion can be explained by the apparent-distance hypothesis, which emphasizes that many depth cues are present when the moon is near the horizon, and few are present when it is overhead.

Suggestion, motives, emotions, attention, and prior experience combine in various ways to create perceptual sets, or expectancies. Personal motives and values often alter perceptions by changing the evaluation of what is seen or by altering attention to specific details. Perceptual learning influences the top-down organization and interpretation of sensations. One of the most familiar of all illusions, the Müller-Lyer illusion, seems to be related to perceptual learning, linear perspective, and size–distance invariance relationships.

Parapsychology is the study of purported psi phenomena, including telepathy (including mediumship), clairvoyance, precognition, and psychokinesis. Research in parapsychology remains controversial because of a variety of problems and shortcomings. The bulk of the evidence to date is against the existence of ESP. The more carefully controlled an ESP experiment is, the less likely it is to produce evidence that ESP occurs.

Eyewitness testimony is surprisingly unreliable. Eyewitness accuracy is further damaged by weapon focus, and a number of similar factors. When a stimulus is repeated without change, our response to it undergoes habituation. Perceptual accuracy is enhanced by reality testing, dishabituation, and conscious efforts to pay attention. It is also valuable to break perceptual habits, to broaden frames of reference, to beware of perceptual sets, and to be aware of the ways in which motives and emotions influence perceptions.

Preview: The Two Step: Bats and Murder

Language Development Guide

bathed in a swirling kaliedoscope: surrounded by many colors

electromagnetic radiation: waves given off by electrically charged particles, ex. microwaves, radio waves

molecules: make up all matter with each molecule consisting of at least two atoms of one or more chemicals

mechanical forces: application of energy to bend or compress a substance

void: emptiness

drink in the beauty: to appreciate or enjoy

every bat was "shouting": bats make high-pitched screeches that reflect (echo) off objects to help them navigate through the air

colliding: smashing into

passed out: unconscious

loosing his collar: unbuttoning top button and also undoing tie

illusions: misleading or misconstructed perceptions of events that are real

raw material: basic, natural, unprocessed substance

Module 4.1 Sensory Processes

Sensory Systems—The First Step

Survey Question: In general, how do sensory systems function?

Language Development Guide

strikes: arrives at
whiz: speed; zoom
catchy: likable and memorable
transpired: happened
convert: change
translates: changes, converts
light years: very, very far away (one light year equals 10 trillion kilometers)
peer: look closely; stare
dewdrop: a drop of water from the moisture that occurs on outside objects in the morning and evening
might get quite loud: showing anger by shouting and yelling
bioelectric fields: the electromagnetic fields produced by living things
visible spectrum: spread of electromagnetic energies to which the eyes respond
echolocation: process used by various animals in which they emit sounds and listen for the
        sound reflections, or echoes, to determine their distance from objects when they are
        navigating and looking for food
pitch darkness: extremely dark, such as a night with no or little moonlight
sauerkraut: sour cabbage (made so through a fermenting process)
head cheese: sausage made from the head, feet, and sometimes tongue and heart of a pig
attuned or "tuned": structured to receive; adjusted to
sufficiently: adequately; suitably
squash: squeeze; flatten
crude: basic, simple, unfinished
raw data: basic information, uninterpreted
jumbled: messy; disorderly; cluttered

Recite and Review

1. Because they convert one kind of energy to another, sensory receptors, such as your eyes and ears, are referred to as biological _____.
2. The process of detecting physical energies with the sensory organs is called _____.
3. When we interpret and organize the sounds we hear into meaningful patterns, we are using the process known as _____.
4. Because our senses select, analyze, and filter information until only the most important information remains, our senses act as a(n) _____ system.
5. A great deal of selection occurs before information is sent to the brain because the sensory receptors do not change, or _____ all of the energies they encounter.
6. Although humans lack this ability, sharks have special organs that can sense the _____ fields of other living creatures.
7. Brian measures the physical energies of sound waves and electromagnetic radiation and relates these measures to the sensations experienced by human observers. Brian's field of study is called _____.
8. Human eyes can transduce only a tiny fraction of the entire range of electromagnetic energies, the part we call the _____.
9. The ears of bats can transduce echoing sound waves that we humans can't hear. This ability that allows them to fly in extreme darkness is called _____.

10. The minimum amount of physical energy necessary to produce a sensation is called the _____ threshold.
11. Sensory adaptation involves the sense receptors responding less to _____ stimuli.
12. Sensory adaptation occurs quickly within the human sense of _____.
13. The separation of sensory information into its important elements is known as sensory _____.
14. As our visual sense processes information, it divides the world into basic stimulus patterns, such as lines, shapes, edges, or colors, which are important _____ features.
15. Our visual system is attuned to these basic stimulus patterns because it has a set of _____ detectors.
16. Because our visual system is highly sensitive to line orientation, a single vertical line placed among a group of slanted lines in a drawing will create an effect called _____.
17. A frog's eyes are basically "tuned" to detect bugs nearby, but the frog's "bug detectors" won't work if the "small, black dots" are not _____.
18. In the experiment in which some kittens were raised in rooms with vertical strips and some in rooms with horizontal strips, the cats were able to jump onto a chair and walk on the floor but bumped into chair legs if they were raised in the _____-striped room.
19. In experiments similar to the kittens raised in rooms with missing features, researchers found an actual _____ in brain cells tuned to the missing features.
20. Our sensory systems change important features of the world into messages that can be understood by the brain through a process referred to as sensory _____.
21. A change in stimulus intensity that is detectable to an observer is called the _____ threshold.
22. If you take your fingertips and press firmly on your eyelids, this pressure will create visual sensations known as _____.
23. The type of sensation one experiences depends on which brain area is activated, a process known as sensory _____.
24. Blind individuals have been able to "see" large objects, such as furniture and doorways through a technique in which electrical signals are sent to the brain using a miniature television _____.

Connections

1. ____ sensation
2. ____ perception
3. ____ psychophysics
4. ____ biological transducer
5. ____ absolute threshold
6. ____ difference threshold
7. ____ sensory analysis
8. ____ perceptual features
9. ____ sensory coding

a. a change in stimulus intensity that is detectable to an observer
b. basic elements of a stimulus, such as the lines, shapes, edge, or colors of a visual stimulus
c. devices, such as the sense organs, that convert one kind of energy into another
d. visual sensations caused by the mechanical excitation of the retina
e. separation of sensory information into important elements
f. the minimum amount of physical energy necessary to produce a sensation
g. the type of sensation one experiences depends on which brain area is activated
h. the mental process of organizing sensations into meaningful patterns
i. the study of the relationship between physical stimuli and the sensations they evoke in a human observer

10. ___ sensory localization

       j.   the process of detecting physical energies with the sensory organs

11. ___ phosphenes

       k.   process by which the sense organs change important features of the world into messages that can be understood by the brain

Check Your Memory

1. TRUE or FALSE   The primary function of the senses is to act as biological transducers, devices that convert one kind of energy into another.

2. TRUE or FALSE   As you read this statement, your brain interprets these black lines and shapes into meaningful patterns known as "words" through a process known as sensation.

3. TRUE or FALSE   The field of study that looks at the relationship between physical stimuli and the sensations they evoke in human observers is called sensory phrenology.

4. TRUE or FALSE   Our senses limit what we can experience because they do not transduce all the physical energies surrounding us.

5. TRUE or FALSE   Humans can sense the bioelectric fields of other living things.

6. TRUE or FALSE   The parts of the electromagnetic spectrum that humans can transduce include infrared and ultraviolet light and gamma rays.

7. TRUE or FALSE   The absolute threshold is defined as a change in stimulus intensity that is detectable to an observer.

8. TRUE or FALSE   We do not notice the pressure from a wristwatch, waistband, ring, or glasses because of sensory adaptation.

9. TRUE or FALSE   The visual sense shows the quickest and most long-lasting sensory adaptation.

10. TRUE or FALSE   Separation of sensory information into important perceptual features is called sensory localization.

11. TRUE or FALSE   A single vertical line placed among a group of slanted lines will produce the pop-out effect because the human visual system is highly sensitive to perceptual features, such as line orientation.

12. TRUE or FALSE   An insect has to be moving for the feature detectors in a frog's eyes to work.

13. TRUE or FALSE   In Blakemore and Cooper's experiment with kittens raised in either vertically-stripped rooms or horizontally-striped rooms, the "vertical" cats could easily jump onto a chair but would bump into chair legs.

14. TRUE or FALSE   Sensory coding refers to changing important features of the world into messages understood by the brain.

15. TRUE or FALSE   If you press firmly on your eyelids, you will produce visual sensations called pheromones.

16. TRUE or FALSE   Sensory localization makes it possible to artificially restore varying degrees of sight and hearing to individuals who are blind or deaf.

Critical Thinking Question

William James once said, "If a master surgeon were to cross the auditory and optic nerves, we would hear lightning and see thunder." Can you explain what James meant?

Module 4.2 Vision
Vision—Catching Some Rays
Survey Question: How does the visual system function?

Language Development Guide

visual richness: detail

ease: no effort

wavelength: distance between the peaks of two consecutive waves

indigo: between a blue and purple

violet: purple

illumination: lighting

drab: plain, boring, off-white color

pixels: smallest picture (screen) unit

membrane: thin covering; film

focal point: central, main, crucial distance

image sensor: part of a digit camera that converts an optical image into electric signals

misshapen: deformed; distorted

fuzzy: blurry; unclear

"behead": person's head will appear to disappear when the image of the head is on one' blind spot

sharpness (of vision): in focus; clear

high-resolution: a very detailed image

blur: distorted; unclear

blinders: device used to restrict side vision, usually used with horses

fatigue: tiredness; exhaustion

flashbulb: produces light to take photographs in darkness

pigment: color (light-sensitive) chemical

hoots of laughter: to be teased with loud, jeering shouts of laughter

clashing: conflicting; not matching

sheepishly: awkwardly; guiltily

jumble: mix-up; cluster

replica: copy; imitation

definitive: best; ultimate

embedded: implanted, set into

xenon: a colorless, odorless gas used in headlights of cars; emits a bright blue light when electrically stimulated

ready rooms: used for preflight briefings for fighter pilots

Recite and Review

1. The narrow spread of electromagnetic energies to which the eyes respond is called the
   _____.

2. Visible light starts at "short" wavelengths of 400 nanometers, which we see as _____.

3. The basic color categories of red, orange, yellow, green, blue, indigo, and violet are referred to as _____.

4. A mixture of many wavelengths forms _____ light.

5. Compared to a muddy "brick" red, an intense "fire-engine" red is said to be more
   _____.

6. The dimension of vision that corresponds roughly to the amplitude, or height of the light waves is _____.

7. To focus images on the light-sensitive layer, both digit cameras and your eyes have a(n)
   _____.

8. In the eye, the light-sensitive cells are collectively known as _____.

9. These light-sensitive cells are located in an area about the size and thickness of a postage stamp called the _____.

194

10. Most focusing is done at the front of the eye by a clear membrane that bends light inward called the _____.
11. Your eye's focal point changes when muscles attached to the lens alter it shape through a process called _____.
12. If your eyeball is too short, nearby objects will be blurred, but distant objects will be sharp, resulting in farsightedness, also called _____.
13. When your eyeball is too long and images fall short of the retina, nearsightedness, also called _____ results.
14. When the cornea or the lens is misshapen, the eye will have more than one focal point with part of vision being focused and part being fuzzy, a problem known as _____.
15. Margo is in her late 40s and the lens of her eyes have become less flexible and less able to accommodate, which results in a condition known as _____.
16. Pia currently wears glasses for nearsightedness but now has developed the farsightedness that comes with age. In order to correct both vision problems, Pia will most likely have to wear a special type of glasses known as _____.
17. The visual receptors that work best in bright light and produce color sensations and fine details are the _____.
18. The visual receptors for dim light that produce only black and white sensations are the _____.
19. The area of the retina that has no receptors and where the optic nerve passes out of the eye and blood vessels enter is called the _____.
20. A small cup-shaped area in the middle of the retina that contains only cones is called the _____.
21. Normal visual acuity is designated as _____ vision.
22. The test for visual acuity that requires a person to read rows of letters of diminishing size until he or she can no longer distinguish them is called the _____ chart.
23. A test of visual acuity that requires no familiarity with letters, but instead requires the person to report which side of each figure has a break in it is the _____.
24. You are running down the field for a touchdown when you notice "out of the corner" of your eye an opposing player coming up behind you. You were able to see this other player because of your side vision, also called _____ vision.
25. A person who has lost his or her "side vision" sees the world as if wearing blinders, a condition known as _____ vision.
26. Because most rods are 20 degrees to each side of the fovea, looking next to an object you wish to see will give you the best _____ vision.
27. The theory of color vision, which holds that there are three types of cones, each more sensitive to either red, green, or blue, is the _____ theory.
28. The theory of color vision, which states that vision analyzes colors into "either-or" messages, is the _____ theory.
29. Visual sensations that persist after a stimulus is removed much like seeing a spot after a flashbulb goes off are called _____.
30. The theory of color vision that explains what happens in the optic pathways and the brain after information leaves the eye is the _____ theory.
31. Leonard is totally colorblind and sees the world as if it were "a black-and-white movie" because he lacks _____ in his retina or these structures do not function normally.
32. Peter can see most colors but sees both the colors "red" and "green" as a yellowish brown. Peter has partial colorblindness, or a color _____.
33. The percentage of Caucasian males are unable to see the colors "red" and "green" normally is _____ percent.
34. If you have normal color vision, you can detect the numbers or designs on the _____ test.

35. To help people who have problems seeing "red" and "green" on traffic lights, the red light is mixed with _____ light.
36. The green light on a traffic light is really a(n) _____-green light.
37. The dramatic increase in retinal sensitivity to light that occurs after a person enters the dark is referred to as _____.
38. When struck by light, visual pigments break down chemically, or _____.
39. To restore light sensitivity, the visual pigments in the rods must _____, which takes time.
40. Submarines, airplane cockpits, and ready rooms for fighter pilots are often illuminated with an extremely _____-colored light because the rods are insensitive to it.

Part 1: Connections

1. _____ ciliary muscle
2. _____ retina
3. _____ iris
4. _____ blind spot
5. _____ lens
6. _____ optic nerve
7. _____ pupil
8. _____ cornea

Part 2: Connections

1. ___ retina
2. ___ lens
3. ___ cornea
4. ___ rod
5. ___ cone
6. ___ blind spot
7. ___ fovea
8. ___ hue
9. ___ brightness
10. ___ afterimage

a. light-sensitive layer of cells at the back of the eye
b. color sensations or categories
c. visual receptor for dim light
d. small cup-shaped area in the back of the eye made up of only color receptors
e. muscles attached to it alter its shape to change the eye's focal point
f. where the optic nerve leaves the eye
g. visual sensations that persist after a stimulus is removed
h. corresponds to amplitude of light waves
i. visual receptor for color
j. clear membrane at the front of the eye that bends light inward

Part 3: Connections

1. ___ acuity
2. ___ accommodation
3. ___ hyperopia
4. ___ myopia

a. defects in the cornea or lens that cause some areas of vision to be out of focus
b. sharpness of one's vision
c. inability to distinguish red-green or to distinguish blue-yellow
d. eyeball is too short with nearby objects being blurred

196

5. ___ astigmatism   e. loss of side vision
6. ___ presbyopia   f. eyeball is too long causing distant objects to be blurred

7. ___ tunnel vision   g. increased retinal sensitivity to light
8. ___ trichromatic theory   h. farsightedness caused by aging of lens
9. ___ opponent-process theory   i. color vision is based on three cone types: red, green, and blue

10. ___ color weakness   j. eye's focal point changes as the muscles attached to the lens alter its shape

11. ___ dark adaptation   k. color vision based on three coding systems (red or green, yellow or blue, black or white)

Check Your Memory

1. TRUE or FALSE   Longer light waves of 700 nanometers produce visible light that we sense as purple or violet.
2. TRUE or FALSE   White light is a mixture of many wavelengths.
3. TRUE or FALSE   Hues from a narrow band of wavelengths are very saturated, or "pure."
4. TRUE or FALSE   Waves of greater amplitude are "taller," carry more energy, and cause the colors we see to appear brighter or more intense.
5. TRUE or FALSE   The layer of light-sensitive cells in the back of the eye is called the cornea.
6. TRUE or FALSE   Your eye's focal point changes when the muscles attached to the lens alter its shape through a process known as assimilation.
7. TRUE or FALSE   If your eyeball is too long, images fall short of the retina, resulting in hyperopia.
8. TRUE or FALSE   Farsightedness due to aging is known as myopia.
9. TRUE or FALSE   When the cornea or the lens is misshapen, part of the vision will be focused and part will be fuzzy, a problem known as presbyopia.
10. TRUE or FALSE   Bifocal lenses correct near vision and distance vision.
11. TRUE or FALSE   The eye has more cones than rods.
12. TRUE or FALSE   The cones are the visual receptors for dim light that produce only black and white sensations, while the rods are the receptors for color.
13. TRUE or FALSE   The optic nerve passes out of the eye in an area where there are no photoreceptors.
14. TRUE or FALSE   The blind spot does not cause a gap in one's vision because the visual cortex fills in the "gap" with patterns from surrounding areas.
15. TRUE or FALSE   The fovea contains only cones.
16. TRUE or FALSE   Normal visual acuity is designated as 20/40 vision.
17. TRUE or FALSE   The Landolt rings test visual acuity requires no familiarity with letters.
18. TRUE or FALSE   The rods are quite sensitive to movement in one's peripheral vision.
19. TRUE or FALSE   People who suffer from tunnel vision are experiencing a loss of peripheral vision.
20. TRUE or FALSE   The best night vision comes from looking next to the object you wish to see.
21. TRUE or FALSE   The trichromatic theory of color vision is based on three coding systems: red or green, yellow or blue, and black or white.
22. TRUE or FALSE   According to the opponent-process theory of color vision, fatigue caused by making one response produces an afterimage of the opposite color as the system recovers.

23. TRUE or FALSE   The opponent-process theory of color vision explains what happens in the eye itself, while the trichromatic theory of color vision explains how colors are analyzed after messages leave the eye.
24. TRUE or FALSE   A color-blind person either lacks rods or has rods that do not function normally.
25. TRUE or FALSE   Partial color blindness is known as color weakness.
26. TRUE or FALSE   An inability to distinguish the colors "red" and "green" occurs more often among Asian American males than Caucasian males.
27. TRUE or FALSE   Women cannot be color blind.
28. TRUE or FALSE   Blue-yellow color blindness occurs more often than red-green color blindness.
29. TRUE or FALSE   To help red-green color-blind individuals with traffic lights, blue light is added to the red light and yellow light is mixed with the green light.
30. TRUE or FALSE   The Snellen test is used to assess one's degree of color blindness.
31. TRUE or FALSE   Increased retinal sensitivity to light is known as dark adaptation.
32. TRUE or FALSE   It takes about 30 to 35 minutes of complete darkness to reach maximum visual sensitivity.
33. TRUE or FALSE   When struck by light, visual pigments bleach, or break down, chemically.
34. TRUE or FALSE   The rods are insensitive to extremely blue light, so submarines and airplane cockpits are illuminated with blue lights.

Critical Thinking Question

Sensory transduction in the eye takes place first in the cornea, then in the lens, then in the retina. True or false?

Module 4.3 Hearing, the Chemical Senses, and the Somesthetic Senses

Hearing—Good Vibrations

Survey Question: What are the mechanisms of hearing?

Language Development Guide

neglect: ignored; overlooked
tremors: vibrations
intuitively: instinctively, automatically
riches of sound: treasures produced by sound
shades: sunglasses
realm: territory
titanic: very big
elaborate: complex; complicated
balance pencils: putting pencil behind one's external ear
collide: run into
link: connect
snail-shaped: spiral wound tube
organ: collection of tissues that serves as a tool or instrument
bristles: spikes or quill (part of hair that stiffly stands up)
brush against: sweep across
tectorial membrane: gel-like surface layer that covers organ of Corti
triggered: activate; set off
pitch: tone of a sound (high-pitched or low-pitched)
corresponding: matching

fed into: supplied to
excite: stimulate
register: expressed
base: bottom
signaled: indicated
notch: gap or groove
afflict: cause problems
immobilized: stop; put out of action
hobbies: leisure pursuit
pastimes: leisure; amusement
cobweb: spider web
fragile: easily broken
abuse: misuse
download: transferring a file from one computer to another
ring tones: sound that indicates an incoming telephone call
amplified: enlarged; made greater (louder)
iPod-style earbuds: headphones that fit inside ear
boombox car stereos: larger and louder car stereo systems
intact: undamaged
spurred: encouraged
cochlear implants: device surgically implanted near auditory nerve that allows individuals with
        severe deafness to "hear" sounds
bypass: go around
coil: loop
channels: pathways
crude: simple; rough
"like a radio that isn't quite tuned in": sound not clear; has static
enthusiasts: fan
siren: warning sound

Recite and Review

1. The peaks of the invisible waves that make up sound are called _____.
2. The valleys of sound waves are referred to as _____.
3. Any vibrating object, such as a tuning fork, the string of a musical instrument, or your vocal cords, will produce a rhythmic movement of air molecules called _____.
4. Movies that show the characters reacting to the "roar" of alien starships in deep space are in error because sound does not travel within a(n) _____.
5. The number of waves per second is referred to as the _____ of sound waves.
6. The number of waves per second corresponds to the perceived tone or _____ of a sound.
7. The physical "height" of a sound wave that tells how much energy the wave contains is called its _____.
8. Psychologically, the "height" of a sound wave corresponds to its sound intensity called _____.
9. The external part of the ear that acts like a funnel to concentrate sounds is called the _____.
10. After sound waves are guided into the ear canal, they collide with the eardrum, also called the _____, which is set in motion.
11. When the eardrum vibrates, it causes three small bones called the auditory _____ to vibrate.
12. The three small bones in the middle ear are the malleus (hammer), the _____ (anvil), and the stapes (stirrup).

13. The stapes is attached to a membrane on the cochlea, which moves back and forth making waves in the fluid inside the cochlea. This membrane is called the _____;

14. The center part of the cochlea that contains the tiny hair cells that detect waves in the fluid is called the _____.

15. Atop each hair cell are "bristles" that brush against the tectorial membrane when waves ripple through the cochlear fluid. These "bristles" are called _____.

16. An 800-hertz tone will produce 800 nerve impulses per second, according to the _____ theory of hearing.

17. The theory of hearing that states that higher and lower tones excite specific areas of the cochlea is the _____ theory.

18. The theory that explains how sounds up to about 4,000 hertz reach the brain is the _____ theory of hearing.

19. High tones register most strongly at the _____ of the cochlea.

20. Lower tones move hair cells near the narrow _____ of the cochlea.

21. The reason that hunters sometimes lose hearing in a narrow pitch range is best explained by the _____ theory of hearing.

22. Because of an injury, Jonah's eardrums and ossicles were damaged, causing a(n) _____ hearing loss.

23. Because of an illness, Armand's auditory nerve was damaged, causing a(n) _____ hearing loss.

24. Hearing aids, which make sounds louder and clearer can improve the hearing of individuals who have a(n) _____ hearing loss.

25. By the time a person is 65, more than 40 percent of his or her inner ear hair cells will be gone, mainly those that transduce _____ pitches.

26. The Hunter's notch is an example of a common form of sensorineural hearing impairment called a(n) _____ hearing loss.

27. A permanent hearing loss may be caused by daily exposure to _____ decibels or more.

28. With every 20-decibels increase, the sound pressure increases by a factor of _____.

29. A permanent hearing loss may be caused by a brief exposure to sounds, such as the loudness of a nearby jet airplane, which registers at _____ decibels.

30. Terrell lost his hearing because his job in construction caused severe damage to his inner ear hair cells. Because his auditory nerve was intact, Terrell was able to regain some of his hearing through a device which bypasses his hair cells and stimulates the auditory nerve directly. This device is called a(n) _____.

Part 1: Connections

1. _____ vestibular system
2. _____ cochlea
3. _____ round window
4. _____ auditory canal
5. _____ stapes
6. _____ auditory nerve
7. _____ incus
8. _____ oval window
9. _____ malleus
10. _____ tympanic membrane

Part 2: Connections

1. ___ stereocilia
2. ___ tympanic membrane
3. ___ auditory ossicles
4. ___ oval window
5. ___ pinna
6. ___ organ of Corti

a. eardrum
b. malleus, incus, and stapes
c. external part of ear
d. membrane on the cochlea attached to stapes
e. center part of cochlea
f. "bristles" atop each hair cell

Part 3: Connections

1. ___ compression
2. ___ rarefaction
3. ___ pitch
4. ___ loudness
5. ___ frequency theory of hearing
6. ___ place theory of hearing
7. ___ conductive hearing loss
8. ___ sensorineural hearing loss
9. ___ hearing aids
10. ___ cochlear implants

a. can improve hearing if eardrums or ossicles are damaged
b. explains how sounds up to about 4,000 hertz reach the brain
c. tone of a sound
d. can improve hearing by directly stimulating the auditory nerve
e. states that higher and lower tones excite specific areas of the cochlea
f. peaks of a sound wave
g. occurs when the transfer of vibrations from the outer ear to the inner ear is weak
h. valleys of a sound wave
i. caused by damage to the inner ear hair cells or the auditory nerve
j. sound intensity corresponding to amplitude

Check Your Memory

1. TRUE or FALSE — Unlike vision, which is limited to stimuli in front of the eyes, hearing collects information from all around the body.
2. TRUE or FALSE — The peaks of sound waves are referred to as rarefaction, while the valleys are referred to as compression.
3. TRUE or FALSE — Sound waves can travel in a vacuum.
4. TRUE or FALSE — The frequency of sound waves corresponds to perceived loudness.
5. TRUE or FALSE — The amplitude of a sound wave corresponds to perceived pitch.
6. TRUE or FALSE — The external parts of your ears that act as funnels to concentrate sounds are technically referred to as the auditory ossicles.
7. TRUE or FALSE — The name of the three small bones in the middle ear are the iris, the ampullae, and otolith.
8. TRUE or FALSE — The membrane on the cochlea that vibrates and make waves in the cochlear fluid is called the tympanic membrane.
9. TRUE or FALSE — The center part of the cochlea is called the organ of Corti.
10. TRUE or FALSE — When the stereocilia, or "bristles," atop each hair cell are bent, transduction takes place and nerve impulses are triggered, which then flow to the brain.
11. TRUE or FALSE — According to the frequency theory, an 800-hertz tone will produce 1600 nerve impulses per second.
12. TRUE or FALSE — According to the place theory, low tones register most strongly at the base of the cochlea near the oval window.

13. TRUE or FALSE The place theory explains how sounds up to about 4,000 hertz reach the brain.
14. TRUE or FALSE The "Hunter's notch" occurs when hair cells are damaged in the area affected by the pitch of gunfire.
15. TRUE or FALSE If the eardrums or ossicles are damaged or immobilized by disease or injury the person will have a sensorineural hearing loss.
16. TRUE or FALSE Noise-induced hearing loss is a common form of conductive hearing loss.
17. TRUE or FALSE By the time people are 65, more than 40 percent of their hair cells will be gone, mainly those that transduce high pitches.
18. TRUE or FALSE Dead hair cells in the inner ear are never replaced.
19. TRUE or FALSE Hearing aids are used to treat sensorineural hearing losses, while cochlear implants are used to treat conductive hearing losses.
20. TRUE or FALSE Daily exposure to 85 decibels or more may cause permanent hearing loss.
21. TRUE or FALSE Brief exposure to 150 decibels can cause permanent hearing loss.
22. TRUE or FALSE Normal conversation is around 60 decibels in loudness.
23. TRUE or FALSE With every 20-decibel increase, the sound pressure will increase by a factor of 10.
24. TRUE or FALSE Those who receive a cochlear implant before age 2 learn spoken language at a near normal rate.

Critical Thinking Question

Why do you think your voice sounds so different when you hear a tape recording of your speech?

Smell and Taste—The Nose Knows When the Tongue Can't Tell
Survey Question: How do the chemical senses operate?

Language Development Guide
Ramsay: British chef Gordon Ramsay, seen on TV cooking shows
gourmet: someone who enjoys eating and tasting food
minor: lesser; secondary
deceived: misled; misinformed
unfolding mystery: developing situation that is yet unknown
hint: suggestion; indication
camphor: produced from wood; smells like a moth repellent
musk: sweaty mammal smell
etherish: dry cleaning fluid smell
"holes" or "pockets": pouches; compartments
like a piece fits into a puzzle: an exact fit
distinctive: unique; individual
solvents: substance that dissolves another substance
potions: chemical mixes, brews
poisonings: toxic, fatal substances if eaten
foraging: searching, hunting (for food)
inedible: unfit for eating
extracts: small specific substance taken out of a material
kelp: seaweed
monosodium glutamate (MSG): food additive; sodium salt
subjective: personal

flavor enhancer: added to food to make them taste better

savory: salty, spicy; not sweet

"comfort food": simple, familiar foods that lead one to "feeling good," often foods associated with one's home or culture

intricately: with small details, delicately

Recite and Review

1. The sense of smell is known as _____.
2. The sense of taste is called _____.
3. Both taste and smell are considered _____ senses.
4. Smell receptors respond to _____ molecules.
5. Because of an injury, Theresa has lost her ability to smell a particular odor, a condition known as _____.
6. Specifically-shaped molecules produce the odors of floral, camphoric, musky, minty, and _____.
7. Different shaped "holes" exist on the surface of the smell receptors with the chemicals that produce odors matching a hole of the same shape. This is the _____ theory of olfaction.
8. The strength of an odor is determined by the _____ of activated receptors.
9. Due to a severe infection, Jackie now has a total loss of smell, which is called _____.
10. A loss of smell, either partial or total, can occur due to exposure to chemicals, infection, allergies, or a blow to the head that tears the _____.
11. Regarding the four basic tastes, we are most sensitive to _____.
12. Of the four basic tastes, people are least sensitive to _____.
13. The order of taste sensitivity may have helped prevent poisonings when most humans foraged for food, because foods are more likely to be inedible if they taste bitter or _____.
14. Most experts now believing that a fifth taste quality exists called _____.
15. The receptors for this "brothy" fifth taste are sensitive to a substance found in MSG called _____.
16. Flavors seem varied because we tend to include sensations of texture, temperature, smell, and, in the case of "hot" chili peppers, _____ along with taste.
17. Mainly located on the top side of the tongue, especially around the edges, are the receptors known as _____.
18. Regarding the basic tastes, the lock-and-key theory best explains how we taste sweet and _____.
19. Regarding the basic tastes, a direct flow of charged atoms into the tips of taste cells triggers the tastes of saltiness and _____.

Connections

1. ___ olfaction
2. ___ gustation
3. ___ dysosmia
4. ___ lock-and-key theory

5. ___ anosmia

6. ___ umami
7. ___ taste bud
8. ___ sweet

9. ___ bitter

a. fifth taste quality described as savory
b. sense of smell
c. sense of taste
d. holds that odors are related to the shapes of chemical molecules
e. of the four basic tastes, humans are most sensitive to this taste
f. receptor cell for taste
g. total loss of the sense of smell
h. of the four basic tastes, humans are least sensitive to this taste
i. "smell blindness" for a particular odor

Check Your Memory

1. TRUE or FALSE   Gustation is the term for one's sense of smell.
2. TRUE or FALSE   Smell and taste are both considered to be chemical senses.
3. TRUE or FALSE   As air enters the nose, it flows over roughly five million nerve fibers embedded in the lining of the upper nasal passages.
4. TRUE or FALSE   If a person has "smell blindness" for a particular odor, the person has the condition known as agnosia, with a total loss of smell called aphasia.
5. TRUE or FALSE   The lock and key theory holds that odors are related to the shapes of chemical molecules.
6. TRUE or FALSE   Scents are, in part, identified by the location of the receptors in the nose that are activated by a particular odor.
7. TRUE or FALSE   The number of activated receptor cells tells the brain how strong an odor is.
8. TRUE or FALSE   Twenty people out of 100 experience some degree of "smell blindness."
9. TRUE or FALSE   "Smell blindness" may occur because of infections, allergies, and blows to the head, which tear the nerves for the sense of smell.
10. TRUE or FALSE   Regarding the four basic tastes, we are most sensitive to sweet tastes.
11. TRUE or FALSE   The fifth taste quality is umami and is described as a savory or "brothy" taste.
12. TRUE or FALSE   The receptors for the fifth taste quality are sensitive to glutamate, a substance found in monosodium glutamate (MSG).
13. TRUE or FALSE   Flavors include sensations of texture, temperature, smell, and even pain.
14. TRUE or FALSE   If you plug your nose and eat small bits of apple, potato, and onion, they will "taste" almost exactly alike.
15. TRUE or FALSE   The taste buds are mainly located on the underside of the tongue, especially in the middle.
16. TRUE or FALSE   The tastes of sweet and bitter are triggered by a direct flow of charged atoms into the tips of taste cells.

Critical Thinking Question

Smell and hearing differ from vision in a way that may aid survival. What is it?

The Somesthetic Senses—Flying by the Seat of Your Pants
Survey Question: What are the somesthetic senses?

Language Development Guide

flying by the seat of your pants: doing an activity by intuition, or "by how it feels" rather than by following instructions, such as flying a plane intuitively, not using instruments

gymnast flying through a routine: going through the well-practiced gymnastics presentation quickly

sobriety test: having a person walk a straight line to prove the person is not drunk from alcohol

acceleration: going faster

plight: situation, predicament

"mapped": recorded in a chart or diagram

density: concentration; thickness

jab: poke or stab

insensitivity: do not feel

empathy: understanding and compassion for others

nagging: annoying repeating

204

aching: dull pain; throbbing
agony: extreme pain
terminal: deadly; incurable
"gate": opening; entry way
tingling: tickle, soft throbbing
twirled: spinning or turning (needle between fingers)
chronic: long-lasting
debatable: doubtful; questionable
phantom: ghost
matrix: a created environment
farfetched: unbelievable; unlikely
amputation: loss of body part, usually refers to an arm or leg
encounter: meet
inadvertently: unintentionally; unconsciously; by mistake
shrink: get smaller; reduce in size
vividly: clearly; plainly
constructed: built; created; made
futuristic: advanced; ahead of their time
counterirritation: creating minor pain to alleviate more severe pain
strategy: plan
generations: age groups throughout history
take the edge off: originally meant to dull the edge of a blade on a knife but now means to dull or
         decrease the effect of something, such as pain
endure: bear; tolerate
apparent: obvious; noticeable
anticipate: expect
principle: rule
body piercer: person who punctures the skin to attach the jewelry
distraction: diverting one's attention
whirr: whine and buzz
roar of the surf: the load, constant sound of the waves breaking on shore
crank up: make louder
throw up: to vomit; expel contents of stomach through one's mouth
orbit: to travel around the earth or moon
weightlessness: lightness due to lack of gravity
motion sickness: dizziness and nausea that occurs when one's balance is disrupted due to constant
         movement
gravity: the pull of the earth's mass on other objects
gelatin-like: consistency of a soft gel or jelly
swirl: spin; churn
"flap" or "float": a valve opening
heaving: raising
pitching: swaying, lurching
disorientation: confusion
heaving of another kind: vomiting
"green": felt sick with nausea
miserable: very unhappy
fix your vision: focus your visual attention
immobile: motionless; stationary

Recite and Review

1. Collectively, the sensations produced by the skin, muscles, joints, and organs of balance make up the _____ senses.
2. Specifically, the receptors in the muscles and joints that detect body position and movement make up the _____ sense.
3. The skin receptors produce at least five different sensations: light touch, pain, cold, warmth, and _____.
4. The skin receptors that can produce all five sensations are the _____.
5. Compared to other areas of the body, important areas such as the lips, tongue, face, hands, and genitals have a higher _____ of receptors.
6. When pain is carried by large nerve fibers, it is sharp, bright, fast, and seems to come from specific body areas. This is the body's _____ system.
7. Children who repeatedly burn themselves, break bones, bite off parts of their tongues, become ill without knowing it, and have difficulty in showing empathy for the pain of others are born with a congenital _____.
8. Pain that is carried by small nerve fibers is slower, nagging, aching, widespread, and very unpleasant. This is the body's _____ system.
9. Melzack and Wall's theory that some pain messages can block other pain messages is called the _____ theory.
10. According to Melzack and Wall's theory, messages carried by large, fast nerve fibers seem to close the _____ pain gate directly.
11. According to Melzack and Wall's theory, messages from small, slow fibers go through the pain gate and then pass on to a(n) _____ system in the brain.
12. The Chinese medical art of relieving pain and illness by inserting thin needles into the body is called _____.
13. Months or years after losing a limb, most amputees have _____ sensations.
14. Although amputation may remove a limb, the limb still exists as far as the brain-generated internal model of the body is concerned. This internal model is called the _____.
15. By applying a mild current to a patient's skin and causing a slight pain, the patient's chronic pain will be blocked in a procedure known as _____.
16. In general, unpleasant emotions tend to _____ pain.
17. Being fully informed about a painful procedure before undergoing it tends to _____ your anxiety.
18. If you arrange a signal with your dentist so that you can raise your hand and the dentist will stop drilling, you are using the principle of _____ to decrease your pain.
19. You are having a tooth filled and you dig your fingernail into your knuckle while the dentist is working. You are using a procedure known as _____.
20. To reduce fear and pain during a medical procedure, a doctor has his patient watch a funny movie on a small screen mounted above the patient's head. To reduce his patient's pain, the doctor is using _____.
21. Weightlessness and space flight often cause severe motion sickness because they affect the _____ system.
22. The structures in the inner ear that contain tiny crystals in a soft, gelatin-like mass and are sensitive to movement, acceleration, and gravity are the _____ organs.
23. The sensory organs for balance are three fluid-filled tubes called the _____.
24. As fluid moves through these tubes in the inner ear, movement is detected when the fluid bends a small "flap," or "float," called the _____.
25. Motion sickness results from a mismatch between information from vision, the vestibular system and kinesthesis, according to the _____ theory.

26. Scientists believe that we may evolved to react to sensory conflict with vomiting because the vestibular system and vision are disturbed when one consumes a(n) _____.

27. Lying down, closing your eyes or fixating on an unmoving distant point will help to minimize _____.

Connections

1. ___ skin senses
2. ___ kinesthetic senses
3. ___ vestibular senses
4. ___ warning system
5. ___ reminding system
6. ___ gate-control theory
7. ___ sensory conflict theory
8. ___ acupuncture
9. ___ phantom limb sensations
10. ___ neuromatrix
11. ___ distraction
12. ___ counterirritation
13. ___ otolith organs
14. ___ semicircular canals

a. explains why motion sickness occurs
b. Chinese medical art of relieving pain and illness by inserting thin needles into the body
c. the sense of balance, position in space, and acceleration
d. sense that detects light touch, pressure, pain, cold, and warmth
e. the illusory sensation that an arm or leg still exists after it is lost through accident or amputation
f. using any mild pain, like pinching yourself, to block more intense or long-lasting pain
g. pain carried by large nerve fibers that lets the body known that damage may be occurring
h. sense organ for balance
i. the sense involving body movement and positioning
j. sense organ that detects movement, acceleration, and gravity
k. internal model of the body generated by the brain
l. theory that proposes that pain messages pass through neural openings in the spinal cord
m. pain is carried by small nerve fibers
n. method of pain reduction that involves voluntarily focusing on an alternative stimulus rather than on the pain

Check Your Memory

1. TRUE or FALSE   Somesthetic sensitivity includes the skin senses, the kinesthetic senses, and the vestibular senses.
2. TRUE or FALSE   When you demonstrate how to tie your shoe, you will be activating receptors in your muscles and joints that are part of the kinesthetic system.
3. TRUE or FALSE   The receptors for the vestibular senses are found in the inner ear.
4. TRUE or FALSE   The skin has more nerve endings for touch and pressure than for pain.
5. TRUE or FALSE   The skin receptor known as the Pacinian corpuscle is highly sensitive to all five skin sensations.
6. TRUE or FALSE   Important areas, such as the lips, tongue, face, hands, and genitals have a higher density of skin receptors than do less important areas.

7. TRUE or FALSE The tip of your nose has more pain receptors per square centimeter than are found in the skin behind the knee.

8. TRUE or FALSE Children who are born with a rare inherited insensitivity to pain repeatedly burn themselves, break bones, bite off parts of their tongues, and become ill without knowing it.

9. TRUE or FALSE The reminding system can cause agony long after an injury has healed.

10. TRUE or FALSE According to the opponent-process theory, if the "gate" in the spinal cord is "closed" by one pain message, other messages may not be able to pass through.

11. TRUE or FALSE Messages carried by the small, slow nerve fibers seem to close the spinal pain gate directly.

12. TRUE or FALSE Messages from the large, fast nerve fibers seem to pass on to a "central biasing system" in the brain.

13. TRUE or FALSE The acupuncturist's needles are used to activate the large pain fibers.

14. TRUE or FALSE Studies have shown that acupuncture produces short-term pain relief for 40 to 80 percent of patients tested.

15. TRUE or FALSE Most amputees have phantom limb sensations, including pain, for months or years after losing a limb.

16. TRUE or FALSE Phantom limb pain can be explained by the gate control theory.

17. TRUE or FALSE Phantom limb pain occurs because the brain creates a body image called the neuromatrix in which the missing limb still exists.

18. TRUE or FALSE Functional magnetic resonance imaging (fMRI) confirms that sensory and motor areas of the brain are more active when a person feels a phantom limb.

19. TRUE or FALSE A person who loses an arm may at first have a phantom arm and hand, but after many years, the phantom may shrink so that only a hand is felt at the shoulder.

20. TRUE or FALSE If you pinch yourself while having a root canal procedure on a tooth, you are using a pain relieving procedure known as counterirritation.

21. TRUE or FALSE In general, unpleasant emotions, such as anger, decrease pain, while pleasant emotions increase pain.

22. TRUE or FALSE The more control you feel you have over a painful stimulus, the less pain you will experience.

23. TRUE or FALSE Being fully informed about a painful medical procedure tends to dramatically increase one's anxiety and, thus, increases one's pain.

24. TRUE or FALSE Research has shown that listening to music at home can be a good distractor from chronic pain.

25. TRUE or FALSE Within the vestibular system the fluid-filled sacs that detect movement, acceleration, and gravity are called sensory ossicles.

26. TRUE or FALSE The fluid-filled tubes called the organ of Corti within the cochlea are the sensory organs for balance.

27. TRUE or FALSE As fluid moves through the tubes, it bends a small "flap" called the crista that detects movement within these tubes.

28. TRUE or FALSE According to the sensory conflict theory, dizziness and nausea occur when sensations from the vestibular system do not match sensations from the eyes and body.

29. TRUE or FALSE Since many poisons disturb the vestibular system, we may have evolved to react to sensory conflict by vomiting to expel the poison.

30. TRUE or FALSE If you experience motion sickness as a passenger in a car, it is best to keep your eyes wide open and focus on a moving point like another car.

Critical Thinking Question

1. What measures would you take to ensure that an experiment involving pain is ethical?

2. Drivers are less likely to become carsick than passengers are. Why do you think drivers and passengers differ in susceptibility to motion sickness?

Module 4.4 Perceptual Processes
Perception—The Second Step
Survey Question: In general, how do we construct our perceptions?

Language Development Guide

slams on: forcefully steps on the brakes of the car to try to stop quickly

skids: slides

welter: chaos; confusion

constancies: free from change

newfound: brand new

cataract: a clouding of the lens of the eye that causes degrees of blindness

struggling: stressed

misconstructed: developed or interpreted incorrectly

filtered: sorted or categorized by

vicious: mean; cruel; violent

habitually: usually; customarily

assumption: guess; notion

lopsided: irregular; uneven; unbalanced

distorting: misrepresenting; twisting it

proportions: relationship between (the walls)

magically: produced by unexplained or supernatural powers

external reality: the real or actual world; not fantasy

engaging: using

element of doubt: small amount of uncertainty

confirm: prove

straight-edge: ruler or other tool to determine if lines are straight, not curved

spontaneously: of their own accord; done instinctively

mentally disturbed: significant impairment in psychological functioning

dementia: serious mental impairment in old age caused by deterioration (weakening, decline) of the brain

"lost touch with reality": thinking is irrational; usually accompanied by hallucinations and/or delusions (strongly held false beliefs)

full-blown: total; full-scale; advanced case

curiously: oddly

leukemia: cancer of the blood

painstakingly: carefully

emerge: to appear; come into view

proposed: put forth

plainer: undecorated; simple

background: surroundings

inborn: inherited; innate

adjacent: next to

"birds of a feather flock together": those who are similar in characteristics, ideas, etc. tend to group together

uniforms: costume worn as part of a team or distinct group

continuation or continuity: the act of continuing such that there is an uninterrupted connection

squared-off: trimmed until it looks like a square having right angles

implied: indirectly means

bounded: bordered; enclosed by

despite: even though

minimal: smallest amount

cues: sign; indication

state or province: areas of some countries like U.S. are divided into states and some areas like in Canada are divided into provinces

geographic region: area defined by its land features or the people that live there

camouflaged: hidden away; disguised

detectives: investigator (seeking answers)

constructive: useful; productive

ambiguous: confusing; vague; unclear

contours: shapes; curves

fanciful: imaginary

scenes: pictures; settings

actively: energetically; enthusiastically

passively: without interest

three-pronged: having three points or spiked parts

widget: object, thing, tool

stable: constant; permanent

hurdles: problems; obstacles

traffic: movement of large number of cars on streets and people walking on sidewalks in an area

curiosity: interest in

restrained: held back; confined

rescue: save

neon lamps: lights that become bright slowly and fade slowly

Recite and Review

1. Your ability to sense the world does not guarantee that you can attach meaning, or _____ it correctly.

2. A mental model of an event that is actively created by your brain is known as a(n) _____.

3. Length, position, motion, curvature, or direction is consistently misjudged in a(n) _____.

4. A person will seem to "magically" grow larger as he or she walks from the left to the right corner in the _____ room.

5. An imaginary sensation, such as seeing, hearing, or smelling something that does not exist in the external world is called a(n) _____.

6. The Fraser's spiral is an example of a(n) _____.

7. Obtaining additional information to check on the accuracy of one's perceptions is known as _____.

8. A major symptom of psychosis, dementia, epilepsy, migraine headaches, alcohol withdrawal, and drug intoxication is the presence of _____.

9. The famous mathematician John Nash suffered from schizophrenia and eventually learned sort out which of his experiences were real and which were imaginary by using his ability to engage in _____.

10. Persons may "see" people, animals, buildings, plants, and other objects appear and disappear in front of their eyes if they have a rare condition that afflicts mainly older people who are partially blind but not mentally disturbed. This rare condition is called _____ syndrome.

11. When people with this rare condition "see" these people and objects appear and disappear, the experiences are called "_____."

12. When we begin constructing our perception from small features until we have a complete perception, this is known as _____ processing.

13. If we use pre-existing knowledge to rapidly organize features into a meaningful whole, then we are using _____ processing.

14. If you put together a puzzle that you have never seen before and start matching the colors and looking for the corner pieces, then you are using _____ processing.

15. If you look at the picture of the completed puzzle on the front of the puzzle box before you begin, then you are using _____ processing.

16. The first perceptual ability to appear after cataract patients regain sight and is believed to be an inborn perception is _____ organization.

17. The figure and ground can be switched in _____ figures.

18. The psychologists who identified several principles, including closure and similarity that bring some order to our perceptions, were the _____ psychologists.

19. If three people stand close to each other and a fourth person stands 10 feet away, the adjacent three will be seen as a group and the distance person as an outsider, which illustrates the principle of perception known as _____.

20. A group of basketball players are standing together but you tend to group them into two teams based on the colors of their uniforms, which illustrates the principle of perception known as _____.

21. We tend to perceive a simple pattern, such as two wavy lines intertwined rather than a complex pattern of lines. This simplicity in perception illustrates the principle of perception known as _____.

22. The tendency to complete a figure so that it has a consistent overall form is called _____.

23. Our tendency to form shapes, even with minimal cues is shown in the implied shapes that are not actually bounded by an edge or an outline and called _____ figures.

24. For the talent show, a group of football players dress up as girls and lip sync to a pop tune sung by female singers. Their lip syncing makes it appear that these young men are actually "singing like the ladies" and illustrates the principle of perception know as _____.

25. Our tendency to mentally group together people from a particular country or state is based on the principle of perception known as _____.

26. The principles of perception offer us some basic "plans" for organizing parts of our day-to-day perceptions, thus illustrating the use of _____ processing.

27. Camouflage patterns break up _____ organization.

28. Carol makes a guess regarding the type of animal standing beneath the tree at the top of the hill. Carol's guess is referred to as a perceptual _____.

29. Since clouds allow one to see more than one shape or interpretation, they would be considered _____ stimuli.

30. The Necker's cube is a good example of a(n) _____ stimulus.

31. A pattern, such as the "three-pronged widget," which cannot be organized into stable, consistent, or meaningful perceptions, is called a(n) _____ figure.

32. In order to use objects' size to judge distances, you must become visually _____ with the objects.

33. Knowing that the perceived size of an object remains the same, even though the size of its image on the retina changes refers to _____.

34. Some of our perceptual abilities would be considered inborn, or _____.
35. Many of our perceptions are based on prior experiences, or are _____ ones.
36. If you hold your left hand a few inches in front of your nose and your right hand at arm's length, your right hand should appear to be about half the size of your left hand, but you still know your right hand did not suddenly shrink, because of size _____.
37. If you look at this page from directly overhead and then from an angle, the page will still look like a rectangle, which illustrates _____.
38. You are standing outside with your friend who is wearing a white shirt. When a cloud shades the sun, your friend's white shirt still appears white because it continued to reflect a larger proportion of light than nearby objects, which illustrates _____.

Part 1: Connections

1. ___ perceptual construction
2. ___ illusions
3. ___ hallucinations
4. ___ "sane hallucinations"

5. ___ reality testing

6. ___ bottom-up processing

7. ___ top-down processing
8. ___ perceptual hypothesis

9. ___ native
10. ___ empirical

a. symptom of Charles Bonnet syndrome
b. initial guess regarding how to organize a stimulus pattern
c. term means based on prior experience
d. applying pre-existing knowledge to rapidly organize sensory information into a meaningful perception.
e. imaginary sensations, such as seeing, hearing, or smelling something that does not exist in the external world
f. distorted perceptual constructions of stimuli that actually exist
g. term refers to perceptions that are inborn
h. obtaining additional information to check on the accuracy of perceptions
i. mental model of external events
j. organizing perceptions by beginning with low-level features

Part 2: Connections

1. _____ continuity
2. _____ common region
3. _____ closure
4. _____ nearness
5. _____ reversible figure
6. _____ similarity

Part 3: Connections

1. ___ figure-ground organization

2. ___ nearness

3. ___ similarity

a. perceptions that tend toward simplicity and continuity
b. implied shapes that are not actually bounded by an edge or an outline
c. patterns which cannot be organized into stable, consistent, or meaningful perceptions

4. ___ continuation

d. explains why we tend to mentally group together people from a particular country, state, or province

5. ___ closure

e. for example, the page of a book will still be a rectangle whether it is viewed from overhead or from an angle

6. ___ illusory figures

f. this nearness in time and space is often responsible for the perception that one thing has caused another

7. ___ contiguity

g. perceived size of an object remains the same despite changes in its retinal image

8. ___ common region

h. tendency to fill gaps and complete a figure so that it has a consistent overall form

9. ___ ambiguous stimuli

i. stimuli that are alike in size, shape, color, or form tend to be grouped together

10. ___ impossible figures

j. stimuli that is close in distance to each other tend to be grouped together

11. ___ size constancy

k. only holds true if objects are all illuminated by the same amount of light

12. ___ shape constancy

l. patterns allowing more than one interpretation

13. ___ brightness constancy

m. part of a stimulus appears to stand out as an object against a less prominent background

Check Your Memory

1. TRUE or FALSE   Newly sighted persons must learn to identify objects, to read clocks, numbers, and letters, and to judge sizes and distances.
2. TRUE or FALSE   A mental model of an event that is actively created by your brain is known as a perceptual construction.
3. TRUE or FALSE   The Skinner room is a lopsided space that appears square when viewed from a certain point, creating the illusion of people "magically" growing as they walk from one corner to the other.
4. TRUE or FALSE   A major symptom of psychosis and dementia is the presence of illusions.
5. TRUE or FALSE   When people trace their figure around a circle in the Fraser's spiral, they are using reality testing to confirm what is "real" in the design.
6. TRUE or FALSE   Perceptual misconstruction is responsible for many illusions
7. TRUE or FALSE   People with Charles Bonnet syndrome have "sane hallucinations."
8. TRUE or FALSE   Hallucinations are one of the clearest signs that a person has "lost touch with reality."
9. TRUE or FALSE   People with Charles Bonnet syndrome are usually severely mentally disturbed and lack the ability to do reality testing.
10. TRUE or FALSE   Bottom-up processing uses preexisting knowledge to rapidly organize features into a meaningful whole.
11. TRUE or FALSE   Top-down processing is like putting together a puzzle you have solved many times.
12. TRUE or FALSE   The behaviorists proposed several perceptual principles that organize our view of the world, including closure, contiguity, and common region.
13. TRUE or FALSE   Nearness is the first perceptual ability to appear after cataract patients regain their sight.

14. TRUE or FALSE   In a figure-ground organization, the part of the stimulus that stands out as an object is called the ground.
15. TRUE or FALSE   In reversible figures, figure and ground can be switched.
16. TRUE or FALSE   According to the principle of perception known as closure, if four people are standing close together and one person is standing 10 feet away, we have a tendency to group the four people in a group with the distant person being an outsider.
17. TRUE or FALSE   Continuity refers to the tendency to fill in the gaps in order to complete a figure so that it has a consistent overall form.
18. TRUE or FALSE   Implied shapes that are not actually bounded by an edge or an outline are known as illusory figures.
19. TRUE or FALSE   Contiguity is often responsible for the perception that one thing has caused another.
20. TRUE or FALSE   The principle of common region explains why we tend to mentally group together people from a particular country, state, province, or geographic region.
21. TRUE or FALSE   Because the principles of perception offer us some basic "plans" for organizing parts of our day-to-day perceptions, using them would be an example of bottom-up processing.
22. TRUE or FALSE   Camouflage patterns break up figure-ground organization.
23. TRUE or FALSE   An initial guess regarding how to organize a stimulus pattern is referred to as a perceptual hypothesis.
24. TRUE or FALSE   Since people can have more than one interpretation of a Rorschach inkblot, these shapes would be considered ambiguous stimuli.
25. TRUE or FALSE   The Necker's cube is an example of an impossible figure.
26. TRUE or FALSE   You must be visually familiar with objects to use their size to judge distance.
27. TRUE or FALSE   If one's perceptions are not inborn, but are based on prior experience, we say these perceptions are empirical.
28. TRUE or FALSE   Newborn babies show some evidence of size constancy.
29. TRUE or FALSE   On the highway, alcohol intoxication impairs size and shape constancy, adding to the accident rate among drunk drivers.
30. TRUE or FALSE   Brightness constancy holds true only if all the objects are illuminated by the same amount of light.

Critical Thinking Question

People who have taken psychedelic drugs, such as LSD or mescaline, often report that the objects and people they see appear to be changing in size, shape, and brightness. This suggests that such drugs disrupt what perceptual process?

Selective Attention—Tuning In and Tuning Out

Survey Question: Why are we more aware of some sensations than others?

Language Development Guide

manageable: controllable
to handle: to deal with
"seat-of-the-pants phenomenon": unaware of the touch and pressure of your pants on your skin because one is not selectively attending to it
divert: redirect; reroute
"tune in on": focus attention on

214

excluding: leaving out; not including

"cocktail party effect": in a group, you can focus and listen to which every conversation around you that you choose

dull: boring, uninteresting

eavesdrop: listen in; overhear something

nod your head: moving head up and down to show you agree

companion: person you are in the presence of, usually a friend or acquaintance

vividly: clearly, with detail

thumped: pound; beat like a drum

striking: remarkable; unusual

pedestrian: person walking

texting: exchanging brief written messages through one's cell phone

bottleneck: refers to the amount of water that can come out of a bottle is limited by the width of the bottle's neck and opening and as a metaphor refers to the amount of information is limited by the broadness or narrowness of our attention

command: controls; dominates

hot-air balloon: a vehicle consisting of a large air bag, with a passenger basket hanging underneath

repetitious: something repeated over and over again

dripping faucet: a tiny amount water dropping from a spout continuously

contrasting: different from the other

preceding: earlier; previous

feats: accomplishments

retinal images: picture formed in the retina of the eye

rehearse: practice; review

Recite and Review

1. As you sit reading this page, receptors for touch and pressure in the seat of your pants are sending nerve impulses to your brain but you were unaware of them until just now because of _____ attention

2. When you are in a group of people, surrounded by voices, you can still select and attend to the voice of the person you are facing, which illustrates the "_____ effect".

3. You are so focused on reading your psychology textbook that you do not notice that it has begun to rain until it thunders. Your intense focus on your textbook would be an example of _____.

4. In a study, participants were asked to watch a video and count how many times a basketball passed between the members of the team wearing black shirts. While they were watching, a man in a gorilla costume walked onto the court. The fact that half of the participants failed to notice the "gorilla" illustrates the effect known as _____.

5. Voluntarily focusing on a specific sensory input is called _____.

6. A failure to notice a stimulus because attention is focused elsewhere is called _____.

7. Like a bottleneck, the information channel linking the senses to perception becomes narrower due to _____.

8. Intense and contrasting stimuli tend to command one's _____.

9. A dripping faucet at night makes little noise by normal standards, but may become as attention getting as a single sound many times louder because of its _____.

10. Attention is also frequently related to a change in stimulation, also referred to as _____.

215

Connections

1. ____ selective attention
2. ____ inattentional blindness
3. ____ "cocktail party effect"
4. ____ bottleneck

5. ____ contrast

6. ____ repetitious stimuli

7. ____ intense stimuli

a. narrowing of a channel, such as for information
b. change in stimulation
c. a dripping faucet would be an example
d. stimuli that is large, loud, bright, and colorful
e. when in a group of people, surrounded by voices, one can attend to the voice of the person he or she is facing
f. failure to perceive a stimulus that is in plain view, but not the focus of attention
g. voluntarily focusing on a specific sensory input

Check Your Memory

1. TRUE or FALSE   Selective attention is like a bottleneck, or narrowing, in the information channel linking the senses to perception.
2. TRUE or FALSE   If you are not aware of the traffic sounds outside your apartment because you are focusing on studying your textbook, then you are exhibiting selective attention toward your textbook reading.
3. TRUE or FALSE   Voluntarily focusing on a specific sensory input is known as perceptual habituation.
4. TRUE or FALSE   The "cocktail party effect" is an example of inattentional blindness.
5. TRUE or FALSE   Inattentional blindness probably explains why fans of opposing sports teams often act as if they had seen two completely different games.
6. TRUE or FALSE   Stimuli that are brighter, louder, larger, or unexpected tend to capture attention.
7. TRUE or FALSE   A person who fails to perceive a stimulus that is in plain view, but not the focus of attention is exhibiting dishabituation.
8. TRUE or FALSE   The more engaged you are with your cell phone while driving, such as texting instead of just having a conversation, the greater the problem of inattentional blindness to traffic hazards.
9. TRUE or FALSE   Repetitious stimuli, such as advertising jingles, tend to greatly decrease one's attention.
10. TRUE or FALSE   The use of contrast is an effective attention-getting device.

Module 4.5 Depth Perception

Depth Perception—What If the World Were Flat?

Survey Question: How is it possible to see depth and judge distance?

Language Development Guide

cross your eyes: focusing each eye inward as if looking at the tip of one's nose
two-dimensional: seeing only width and height of a scene; without depth
three-dimensional: seeing width, height, and depth of a scene
playing catch: throwing a ball back and forth between two people
shoot baskets: play basketball
navigating: finding one's way
restored: brought back; fixed
innate: born with it

checkered: plaid; looks like the game board used in checkers

drop-off: steep decline that one might fall from

shallow: low; not deep

"skydiving": falling through the air

coordination: use one's muscles during movement in a skillful, efficient, effective way

"crash landings": slang for falling and coming to rest on one's rear end or bumping into objects

discrepancy: difference

fused: merged; brought together

parallel: equal; matching; two adjacent lines or planes that do not meet

shoot trash can hoops: tossing paper wads at the trash can across the room

feed: supply

exaggerating: overstating; inflating

"But officer, my psychology text said to . . .": getting a driving ticket for your poor driving (braking too soon, etc.) while having one eye closed as the demonstration in the textbook suggests

As their name implies: the description is in the name itself

flow back: go to

limited: narrow; small amount

impart: pass on

trace: draw; outline; sketch

horizon: noticeable line that appears to separate the earth from the sky

special effects: illusions used in films and television programs

receding: moving back; withdrawing

shadow: darkness or shade

removes any doubt: completely sure

texture: feel of surface

cobblestone: rounded stones used in paving streets before asphalt and concrete

coarse: rough; uneven

finer: more even and smoother

aerial: above the ground

perspective: viewpoint

smog: air pollution; combination of smoke and fog

haze: mist combined with dust and smoke

crystal clear: like glass

strictly speaking: to be completely accurate

scenery: landscape; surroundings

your gaze at a right angle to the road: looking directly at the road, not parallel with it

stroll: leisurely walk

intriguing: interesting

silver dollar: coin approximately 1.5 inches in diameter

magnified: enlarged

atmosphere: layer of gases surrounding the earth

telescope: instrument used to view distant objects

Recite and Review

1. The ability to see three-dimensional space and to accurately judge distances is called _____ perception.

2. One way of studying the depth perception of infants is to use a glass-topped table with one side appearing to be a "drop-off," an apparatus known as the _____.

3. When tested for depth perception, six- to 14-month-old infants were given a choice of crawling to one of two sides of the glass-topped table. Even when their mothers tried to call them toward it, most infants refused to crawl to the _____ side of the table.

4. The most recent research shows that depth perception begins to develop as early as _____ weeks of age.

5. Evidence that depth perception depends on both brain maturation and individual experience comes from the observation that the development of depth perception is not complete until about _____ months of age.

6. When babies after the age of four months fall, it probably has less to do with depth perception and more to do with a lack of _____.

7. Perceptual features that require two eyes and impart information about distance and three-dimensional space are called _____ depth cues.

8. Perceptual features that require just one eye and impart information about distance and three-dimensional space are called _____ depth cues.

9. The most basic source of depth perception is the discrepancy in the images that reach the right and left eyes, which is called _____.

10. When the image from each eye is fused into one overall image, three-dimensional sight, also called _____ vision, occurs.

11. Director James Cameron developed especially for his film *Avatar* a stereoscopic camera that creates a sensation of depth by simulating retinal _____.

12. Whenever you estimate a distance under 50 feet such as when you play catch or "shoot hoops," you are using the process known as _____.

13. Compared to perception based on just one eye, judging depth using stereoscopic vision is _____ times better.

14. The process that helps us judge distances within about four feet of the eyes and involves the bending of the lens of the eyes to focus on nearby objects and is called _____.

15. Regarding the use of one or two eyes, convergence is classified as a(n) _____ depth cue.

16. Regarding the use of one or two eyes, accommodation is classified as a(n) _____ depth cue.

17. Features found in paintings, drawings, and photographs that impart information about space, depth, and distance are known as _____ depth cues.

18. If you stand between two railroad tracks, they appear to meet near the horizon, even though they actually remain parallel. This effect is known as _____ perspective.

19. When an artist makes the more distant objects in his painting smaller than the objects that are near, he is using _____ to create depth.

20. Special effects in films create sensational illusions of depth by rapidly changing the image _____ of planets, airplanes, monsters.

21. Objects that are placed closer to the horizon line in a drawing tend to be perceived as more distant, according to the cue known as _____.

22. Most objects are lighted within a painting in order to create clear patterns of light and _____.

23. In Petra's drawing, the tree partially blocks the house, indicating that the tree is closer than the house. This pictorial depth cue is called overlap, or _____.

24. If you stand in the middle of a gravel road, the rocks will look coarse near your feet and smaller and finer if you look at the gravel at a distance. These changes that contribute to depth perception are referred to as _____ gradients.

25. Distant objects tend to be hazy, washed out in color, and lacking in detail with _____ perspective.

218

26. You are riding in a car and notice that nearby objects appear to move a sizable distance, while objects farther away appear to move more slightly in relation to the background. This noticed difference is an example of relative motion, also called _____.

27. Much of the apparent depth of a good movie comes from the pictorial depth cue known as _____.

28. Perceiving the moon as larger when it is low in the sky is referred to as the _____.

29. The explanation for the moon appearing larger when it is low in the sky is referred to as the _____ hypothesis.

30. If you remove depth cues by looking at a horizon moon through a rolled-up paper tube, the moon will appear _____.

Part 1: Connections

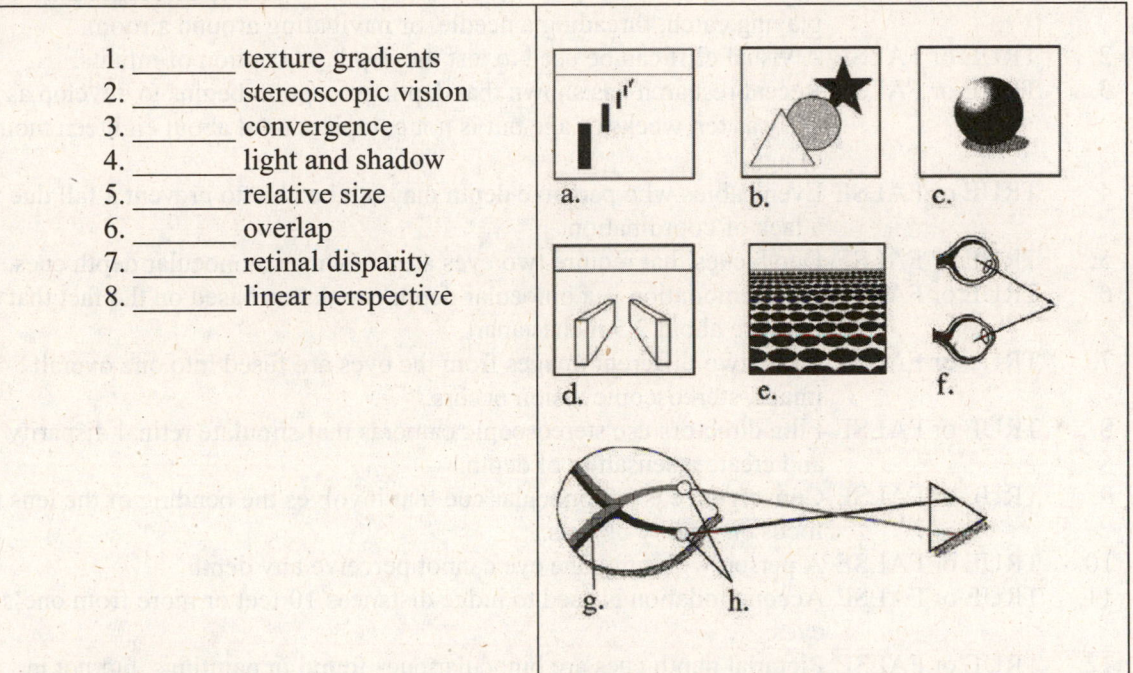

1. _____ texture gradients
2. _____ stereoscopic vision
3. _____ convergence
4. _____ light and shadow
5. _____ relative size
6. _____ overlap
7. _____ retinal disparity
8. _____ linear perspective

Part 2: Connections

1. ___ visual cliff
2. ___ retinal disparity
3. ___ convergence
4. ___ accommodation
5. ___ linear perspective
6. ___ relative size
7. ___ height in the picture plane
8. ___ light and shadow

a. more distant objects appear smaller and nearby objects larger

b. binocular cue based on the fact that the eyes are about 2.5 inches apart

c. distant objects tend to be hazy

d. means of testing the depth perception of infants

e. near objects look coarse, while distance objects appear smaller and finer

f. nearby objects appear to rush backward with remote objects moving in the same direction and slower

g. apparent meeting of parallel lines in the environment

h. depth created because we assume that objects are lighted from one direction, usually from above

9. ___ overlap or interposition

10. ___ texture gradients

11. ___ aerial perspective

12. ___ relative motion or motion parallax

13. ___ apparent-distance hypothesis

i. binocular cue that allows one to estimate distance under 50 feet

j. explanation for the moon illusion

k. occurs when one object partially blocks another object

l. monocular cue that involves the bending of the lens to focus on nearby objects

m. objects placed closer to the horizon line in a drawing tend to be perceived as more distant

Check Your Memory

1. TRUE or FALSE Without depth perception, you would have difficulty driving a car, playing catch, threading a needle, or navigating around a room.

2. TRUE or FALSE A visual cliff can be used to test the depth perception of infants.

3. TRUE or FALSE Recent research has shown that depth perception begins to develop as early as ten weeks of age but is not complete until about eighteen months of age.

4. TRUE or FALSE Even babies who perceive depth may not be able to prevent a fall due to a lack of coordination.

5. TRUE or FALSE Depth cues that require two eyes are known as monocular depth cues.

6. TRUE or FALSE Accommodation is a binocular depth cue that is based on the fact that the eyes are about 2.5 inches apart.

7. TRUE or FALSE When two different images from the eyes are fused into one overall image, stereoscopic vision occurs.

8. TRUE or FALSE Film directors use stereoscopic cameras that simulate retinal disparity and create a sensation of depth.

9. TRUE or FALSE Convergence is a monocular cue that involves the bending of the lens to focus on nearby objects.

10. TRUE or FALSE A person with only one eye cannot perceive any depth.

11. TRUE or FALSE Accommodation is used to judge distances 10 feet or more from one's eyes.

12. TRUE or FALSE Pictorial depth cues are binocular cues found in paintings, but not in movies.

13. TRUE or FALSE The pictorial cue called interposition is based on the apparent convergence of parallel lines in the environment.

14. TRUE or FALSE Special effects in films create sensational illusions of depth by rapidly changing the image size of planets, airplanes, and monsters.

15. TRUE or FALSE Objects that are placed higher in a drawing tend to be perceived as more distant.

16. TRUE or FALSE The pictorial cue of retinal disparity occurs when one object partially blocks another object.

17. TRUE or FALSE If you stand in the middle of a cobblestone street, the texture of the street will be small and fine near your feet and coarser as you look into the distance.

18. TRUE or FALSE If you look at a mountain range on a crystal-clear day, it might look like it was only a few miles away when, in reality, the mountain range could be 50 miles away.

19. TRUE or FALSE Much of the apparent depth of a good movie comes from the motion parallax, or relative motion, captured by the camera.

20. TRUE or FALSE If you are riding on a bus and watching the scenery pass, nearby objects will seem to move very little or not at all, while more remote objects will appear to rush backward.
21. TRUE or FALSE When the moon is on the horizon, it looks like a dime, but when it is directly overhead, it looks like a silver dollar.
22. TRUE or FALSE The moon illusion is caused by the moon being magnified by the atmosphere.

Critical Thinking Question

1. What hearing ability would you say is most closely related to stereoscopic vision?

2. What size object do you think you would have to hold at arm's length to cover up a full moon?

Module 4.6 Perception and Objectivity

Perceptual Learning—Believing is Seeing

Survey Question: How is perception altered by expectations, motives, emotions, and learning?

Language Development Guide

split second: a moment, a very short time
lag: delay
pop of a flashbulb: old flashbulbs used provide light for taking photographs would flash or "pop" when it was activated
common: universal
car backfires: unburned fuel in the exhaust system causes the sound like "gunfire"
jump the gun: rush, start early
as a matter of fact: actually; in fact
in essence: basically
flashing light: usually means the flashing of a police car
"rats": exclamation instead of using an expletive (bad language)
"busted": being arrested for breaking the law
wine snobs: a person who believes he or she is very knowledgeable about wines
twist: misrepresentation; distortion
gang members: group of youths that typically engage in criminal activities
queers: slang term for homosexual persons
bitches: slang term for cold or mean females
merchandised: sell
pushed in ads: promoted for consumers to buy
"sex appeal": physical attractiveness
"spotlight": focus
scope: range; extent of
bias: prejudice; unfairness
moods: low-intensity, long-lasting emotional states
expertise: very knowledgeable
in-group: group to which one feels loyalty and a part of
social context: environmental circumstances
apparently: in fact
alterations: changes; modifications
monitored: checked; observed
indeed: certainly

aesthetic: dealing with the nature of beauty and art

impact: influence; effect

percepts: representation of what has been perceived

icons and cursors: small computer pictures and pointers

novice: beginner

dried basil, oregano, and tarragon: Italian spices

linebacker: defensive football player

a run: opposing team will be running with the football in player hand

a pass: opposing team will be throwing the football to a receiver

ingrained: firmly established

grotesque: ugly

inverted: turned upside down

habitual: normal; usual

deceptively: misleadingly

invariance: property of objects that remain unchanged when something about the object is altered

compensate: balance; offset

presumes: guesses; supposes

pretty safe: sure it is true

mounds: small hills

at most: as a rule; generally

Recite and Review

1. A readiness to perceive in a particular manner, induced by strong expectations, is referred to as a(n) _____.

2. In one study, participants were told that they were tasting a $90 wine and a $10 wine, although the same wine was served both times. Because the participants stated that the $90 wine tasted better than the $10 wine, this illustrates that suggestion frequently create perceptual _____.

3. If you are hungry, food-related words are more likely to gain your attention than nonfood words, which illustrates how _____ play a role in shaping our perceptions.

4. In constructing their ads, advertisers take advantage of two motives that are widespread in our society, sex and _____.

5. According to psychologist Barbara Frederickson, our perceptual focus will be narrowed when we are experiencing _____ emotions.

6. Frederickson found that one's scope of attention is broadened by _____ emotions.

7. The difficulty in recognizing faces of people from different races than our own, which is known as the _____ effect.

8. We are much better at recognizing faces of people from our own race than from others with this effect being diminished if we are in a(n) _____ mood.

9. Members of different races or ethnic groups are led to see in-group faces differently because they have developed perceptual expectancies, or perceptual _____.

10. Since European Americans tend to focus on themselves and their sense of personal control, they are characterized as a(n) _____ culture.

11. East Asians tend to focus on their personal relationships and social responsibilities and would be considered a(n) _____ culture.

12. European Americans tend to explain actions in terms of _____ factors.

13. East Asians tend to explain actions in terms of their _____ context.

14. In an experiment in which American and Japanese participants were shown scenes in which the figure and the ground were both altered, the American participants were better at detecting changes in the _____.

222

15. In the experiment in which the figure and the ground were both altered, the Japanese participants were better at finding alterations in the _____.
16. Regarding their focus of attention, Westerners typically have a relatively _____ focus.
17. Regarding their focus of attention, Easterners tend to have a(n) _____ focus.
18. Because England is one of the few countries in the world where people drive on the left side of the road, it is not unusual for visitors to step off curbs in front of cars, after carefully looking for traffic in the wrong direction, which shows that prior experience has a powerful impact on _____ processing in perception.
19. Changes in how we construct sensory information into percepts that can be attributed to prior experience are called perceptual _____.
20. A linebacker in football may be able to tell if the next play will be a run or a pass by watching one or two key players, rather than the entire opposing team. This illustrates the importance of _____.
21. Ingrained patterns of perceptual organization and attention are called _____.
22. In general, illusions are produced by combining habitual eye movements, continuity, perceptual habits, and size and shape _____.
23. The illusion in which the horizontal line with arrowheads appears shorter than the line with Vs is called the _____ illusion.
24. If two objects make images of the same size, the more distant object must be larger. This is known formally as _____.
25. A group of people in South Africa, who live in a "round" culture and lack experience with straight roads or square buildings, are the _____.

Connections

1. ___ perceptual set
2. ___ motives
3. ___ emotions
4. ___ other-race effect
5. ___ individualists
6. ___ collectivists
7. ___ perceptual learning
8. ___ perceptual habits
9. ___ size-distance invariance

a. changes in how we construct sensory information into percepts that can be attributed to prior experience
b. seeing in-group faces differently
c. focus on personal relationships and social responsibilities
d. positive ones broaden one's focus of attention; negative ones narrow one's focus
e. anxiety and sex are two of the ones used in advertising
f. well-established patterns of perceptual organization and attention
g. focus on themselves and their sense of personal control
h. explains the moon illusion and the *Müller-Lyer* illusion
i. readiness to perceive in a particular manner, induced by strong expectations

Check Your Memory

1. TRUE or FALSE   Past experiences, motives, context, and suggestions can create a perceptual expectancy that prepares you to perceive in a certain way.
2. TRUE or FALSE   A perceptual expectancy is a perceptual hypothesis that we are very likely to apply to a stimulus, even if applying it is inappropriate.
3. TRUE or FALSE   In the experiment in which participants were told they were tasting an "expensive wine" and a "less expensive" wine when, in reality, they

were tasting the same wine, the reason the participants thought the "more expensive" wine tasted better was due to dishabituation.

4. TRUE or FALSE   In the experiment in which participants thought they were tasting an "expensive wine" and a "less expensive" wine when they were tasting the same wine, functional MRI images confirmed that brain areas related to pleasure were more active when participants thought they were tasting the more expensive wine.

5. TRUE or FALSE   Labeling people as "gang members," "mental patients," and "illegal immigrants," tends to distort perceptions.

6. TRUE or FALSE   If you are hungry, food-related words will have no more effect on your attention than nonfood words do.

7. TRUE or FALSE   An advertisement that plays on one's desire to be attractive and to avoid embarrassment is utilizing the motives of "sex" and "anxiety."

8. TRUE or FALSE   Positive emotions generally narrow our perceptual focus and increase the likelihood of inattentional blindness.

9. TRUE or FALSE   In recognizing faces, a consistent "other-race effect" occurs in which people are better at identifying individuals from their own race and ethnic group than from other races and ethnic groups.

10. TRUE or FALSE   When people are in negative moods, their ability to recognize people from other races improves.

11. TRUE or FALSE   European Americans are individualistic people who tend to focus on themselves and their sense of personal control.

12. TRUE or FALSE   East Asians tend to explain actions in term of internal factors, while European Americans tend to explain actions in terms of their social context.

13. TRUE or FALSE   When the figure and background are slightly changed in drawings, it was found that Japanese participants were better at finding alterations in the figure, while Americans were better at finding alterations in the background.

14. TRUE or FALSE   People from Eastern cultures have a relatively narrow focus of attention, while Western cultures have a broader focus of attention.

15. TRUE or FALSE   Learning has a powerful impact on top-down processing in perception.

16. TRUE or FALSE   Perceptual learning helps us to tell the difference between stimuli that seemed identical at first.

17. TRUE or FALSE   Ingrained patterns of organization and attention are called dishabituations.

18. TRUE or FALSE   In the demonstration of the face presented in the upright position and the upside-down face, perceptual learning had more impact on how one perceives the upside-down face.

19. TRUE or FALSE   Size and shape constancy, habitual eye movements, continuity, and perceptual habits combine in various ways to produce the illusions.

20. TRUE or FALSE   The Müller-Lyer illusion consists of seven concentric circles that appear to radiate.

21. TRUE or FALSE   The Müller-Lyer illusion and the moon illusion can both be explained by size-distance invariance.

22. TRUE or FALSE   The Zulus are a group of people in South Africa that live in a "square" culture, so that they do not have any experience with curved or rounded surfaces.

23. TRUE or FALSE   Because of their prior experiences, the Zulus do not experience the Müller-Lyer illusion.

Critical Thinking Question

Cigarette advertisements in the United States are required to carry a warning label about the health risks of smoking. How have tobacco companies made these labels less visible?

Module 4.7 Extrasensory Perception

Extrasensory Perception—Do You Believe in Ghosts?

Survey Question: Is extrasensory perception possible?

Language Development Guide

general public: ordinary people
paranormal: beyond the range of normal experience
astound: amaze; surprise
impulse: urge; compulsion
purported: supposed
defy: challenge
prophetic: predictive
foretell: predict
toss in: add
exert: apply; bring to bear
inanimate: non-living
willpower: determination; drive
skeptical: disbelieving
shuffled: mixed up; rearranged
fraud: a con; swindle
chance: luck
plague: afflict; cause trouble
deception: trickery; dishonesty
"for profit": to make money
enterprises: business undertaking
convicted: found guilty in a court of law
felony: serious crime
accent: the inflection and pronunciation of words common to a region
"reading": information provided by the psychic
reliance: dependence on
"hot and cold": listening for whether answers given are close to correct or far from the truth
"leakage": the escape of information unintentionally
meticulous: careful; thorough; detailed
premonition: a feeling or suspicion that something is not right; a forewarning
coincidence: occurred by accident or by chance
hunch: guess; gut feeling
spectacular: amazing; impressive
sustained: maintained; continued; to keep going
"decline effect": psychic ability fading in and out
subsequent: following; later
conclusively: decisively; convincingly
rigor: thoroughness; precision
competent: capable; knowledgeable
unbiased: fair; impartial; neutral
google: conduct an internet search
undoubtedly: certainly; definitely

intrepid: bold; daring
irrefutable: convincing; certain
inconclusive: open to doubt; unconvincing
"true believers": person who is extremely devoted to a cause or idea
beyond debate: clear, undisputed
zero, zip, nada: nothing
probed: searched; explored

Recite and Review

1. The purported ability to perceive events in ways that cannot be explained by known sensory capacities is known as _____.
2. Darrin is interested in studying ESP and other psi phenomena. This study is called _____.
3. Events that seem to defy accepted scientific laws are called _____ phenomenon.
4. Telepathy, clairvoyance, and precognition make up the three basic forms of _____.
5. Rose believes that she can communicate directly with another person's mind, which is the purported psi ability known as _____.
6. On a television program, the main character is able to solve crimes by discussing the case with his deceased father who was a famous detective. This main character is demonstrating the purported ability known as _____.
7. If a person is able to gain information in ways that are unaffected by distance or normal physical barriers, the person is exhibiting _____.
8. Prophetic dreams that foretell the future are one example of the ESP ability called _____.
9. Wendy believed when she was angry with the teacher that she could concentrate on the teacher's desk and mentally "push" objects off the desk. Wendy believed that she had the psi ability known as _____.
10. The first researcher who conducted a formal investigation of psi events and tried to study ESP objectively was _____.
11. ESP researchers often use a deck of 25 cards that have five symbols, star, wavy lines, plus, circle and square, printed on them with these cards called _____ cards.
12. In a typical test, a receiver tries to guess the correct symbol on a card by reading the mind of a sender looking at the card with pure guessing in these tests producing an average score of _____ "hits" out of 25 cards.
13. Jed believes that he has precognition because he predicted that the stock market would be down at the end of the week. Although Jed is convinced, one cannot rule out _____ as the cause.
14. Examples of demonstrations of ESP that are based on deception and tricks are "for profit" enterprises, such as telephone psychics and _____ demonstrations of ESP.
15. Telephone psychics often use a set of techniques that lead people to believe in the truth of what they are saying called _____ readings.
16. Telephone psychics often rely on the same techniques as practitioners of the horoscope, including uncritical acceptance, the confirmation bias, and the _____ effect.
17. Early ESP experiments were plagued by poorly printed cards, accidental "leakage" of helpful information, and deliberate _____.
18. Modern parapsychologists are now well aware of the need for security, accuracy in record keeping, meticulous control, the repeatability of experiments, and the _____-blind experiments.
19. If, by coincidence, a person's hunch turns out to be correct, it may be _____ as precognition or clairvoyance

20. Even when the same researchers use the same subjects, many of the most spectacular findings in parapsychology simply cannot be _____.
21. Improved ESP research methods have resulted in _____ positive results.
22. When a person in an ESP experiment temporarily scores above chance, this statistically unusual outcome that could occur by chance alone is referred to as a(n) "_____."
23. The inability of a person to maintain psi ability over any sustained period of time is called the "_____."
24. The ESP researchers who support the existence of ESP believe that this inability to maintain the psi ability over time indicates that parapsychological skills are very _____.
25. Edgar Mitchell referred to below-chance trials on his ESP experiments as intentional "_____.".
26. The professional magician and skeptic who is offering a $1,000,000 prize to anyone who can demonstrate evidence of psi events under standardized conditions is _____.
27. A person who is unconvinced is referred to as a(n) _____.
28. The results of more than 1.5 million ESP trials done through the mass media found an ESP effect that was _____ significant.

Connections

1. ____ ESP
2. ____ psi phenomena
3. ____ parapsychology
4. ____ telepathy
5. ____ mediumship
6. ____ clairvoyance
7. ____ precognition
8. ____ psychokinesis
9. ____ Zener cards
10. ____ stage ESP
11. ____ cold readings
12. ____ run of luck
13. ____ "decline effect"

a. purported ability to perceive events at a distance or through physical barriers
b. purported ability to mentally alter or influence objects or events
c. purported ability to directly know another living person's thoughts
d. set of techniques used to lead people to believe in the truth of what a psychic is saying about them
e. statistically unusual outcome that could still occur by chance alone
f. study of extranormal psychological events
g. purported ability to communicate with a person who is dead
h. simulation of ESP for the purpose of entertainment
i. purported ability to perceive events in ways that cannot be explained by known capacities of the sensory organs
j. inability of a person to maintain psi ability over a sustained period
k. events that seem to lie outside the realm of accepted scientific laws
l. used by J.B. Rhine in his experiments
m. purported ability to accurately predict future events

Check Your Memory

1. TRUE or FALSE   About half the general public believes in the existence of ESP, while very few psychologists share this belief.
2. TRUE or FALSE   Parapsychology is the study of ESP and other psi phenomena.
3. TRUE or FALSE   The three basic forms of ESP include mediumship, telepathy, and psychokinesis.

4. TRUE or FALSE   If you believe that you can accurately predict future events, you believe you have the purported ability known as telepathy.

5. TRUE or FALSE   If you think you can concentrate and mentally alter traffic lights so that they will immediately turn "green," you believe that you have the purported ability called psychokinesis.

6. TRUE or FALSE   The late J. B. Rhine was one of the first investigators who tried to study ESP objectively.

7. TRUE or FALSE   Pure guessing in the ESP tests that use Zener cards will produce an average score of 15 "hits" out of 25 cards.

8. TRUE or FALSE   Stage demonstrations of ESP are based on deception and tricks.

9. TRUE or FALSE   The TV-psychic "Miss Cleo", who was supposedly a Jamaican psychic, was actually an actress from Los Angeles.

10. TRUE or FALSE   The paranormal expectancy is a group of techniques that are used by psychics to lead people to believe in the truth of what a psychic is saying about them.

11. TRUE or FALSE   Early ESP experiments were plagued by cheating as well as accidental "leakage" of helpful information.

12. TRUE or FALSE   Modern studies of ESP now utilize double-blind experiments, meticulous control, and replication.

13. TRUE or FALSE   When people think that they have had a prophetic dream that comes true, it is difficult to exclude coincidence as the cause.

14. TRUE or FALSE   For every ESP study with positive results, there are many others that fail and are never published.

15. TRUE or FALSE   Improved research methods in studying ESP have resulted in more positive results.

16. TRUE or FALSE   A statistically unusual outcome that could occur by chance alone is called a "decline effect."

17. TRUE or FALSE   Some ESP researchers believe that the "run of luck" shows that parapsychological skills are very fragile.

18. TRUE or FALSE   Edgar Mitchell reinterpreted below-chance trials in his ESP experiments as "successes," claiming they represented intentional "psi missing."

19. TRUE or FALSE   According to the evidence collected over the last 130 years researchers cannot conclusively say whether or not psi events actually occur.

20. TRUE or FALSE   Professional magician and skeptic James Randi is offering a $1,000,000 prize to anyone who can demonstrate evidence of psi events under standardized conditions.

21. TRUE or FALSE   Being a skeptic means that a person is against something.

22. TRUE or FALSE   The 1.5 million ESP trials done through the mass media found a significant ESP effect.

Critical Thinking Question

1. What would you estimate is the chance that two people will have the same birthday (day and month, but not year) in a group of 30 people?

2. A "psychic" on television offers to fix broken watches for viewers. Moments later, dozens of viewers call the station to say that their watches miraculously started running again. What have they overlooked?

228

Module 4.8 Psychology in Action: Becoming a Better Eyewitness to Life

Survey Question: How can I learn to perceive events more accurately?

Language Development Guide

lot of weight: very influential
infallible: never makes mistakes
vulnerable: at risk
overoptimism: excessive confidence
bluntly: directly, without diplomacy
sworn: pledge; claim
"instant replay": exact copy of an event
prone: inclined to
revealing: disclosing
prey: victim
culprit: criminal
monochromatic light: of one color or shade
unreliable: undependable
exonerated: declared innocent, set free
cleared: record is now blank
bearing: being influenced by
tolerant: open-minded; understanding
objectivity: being impartial; not biased
subtle: sly; clever
trap: trick; con; snare
elusive: hard to pin down; vague
styles: approaches; methods
immersion: completely in
surrender: giving in
cease: stop
restriction: limitation; constraint
"if you've seen one tree, you've seen them all": no need to see more than one of the same thing
variety: range; selection
appreciating: being thankful for
miracle: wonder
clarity: clearness
avenue: method
maxims: proverbs; truths; guidelines
irritably: impatiently; angrily
cleansed: purified; washed
infinite: endless
interrupt: disrupt; break up
routes: paths; roads
routines: habits; customs
nonpreferred hand: one that you usually do not use to do most jobs
pigeonhole: categorize
wary: careful
stereotypes: oversimplified images of people
swayed: influenced
disputes: disagreement; quarrel
drift: float; coast

Recite and Review

1. A study of real eyewitness cases found that the wrong person was chosen from police lineups _____ percent of the time.
2. An eyewitness's confidence is not a good predictor of the _____ of the testimony.
3. An eyewitness's testimony about an event can be affected by how the questions put to that witness are _____.
4. Regarding eyewitness perceptions, very high levels of stress tend to _____ accuracy.
5. Compared to a person who only witnessed the crime, the eyewitness accuracy of the victim is _____.
6. If the culprit of a crime used a knife or a gun, victims often fall prey to the _____.
7. Eyewitnesses sometimes identify as a culprit someone they have seen in another situation or context, which is known as unconscious _____.
8. Identifying the color what the perpetrator was wearing can be highly unreliable if the judgments of color were made under _____ light, such as an orange street light.
9. More than 200 people who were convicted of murder, rape, and other crimes in the United States mainly based on eyewitness testimony have been exonerated through _____ testing.
10. To maintain personal objectivity requires frequent _____ testing.
11. The humanistic psychologist who believed that some people perceive themselves and others with unusual accuracy and characterized these people as especially alive, open, aware, and mentally healthy was _____.
12. People who are unusually accurate in their perceptions about themselves and others have perceptual styles marked by a lack of self-consciousness, a freedom from criticizing, a general "surrender" to experience, and an immersion in the _____.
13. A type of learning in which the person responds less to predictable and unchanging stimuli is called _____.
14. When people reverse this tendency to respond less to stimuli, and they begin to attend more to everyday stimuli, we refer to this reversal as _____.
15. Creative people tend to _____ more slowly than average to stimuli.
16. To enhance perceptual awareness, we must try to get away from habitual, _____ processing.
17. In enhancing one's awareness, he or she must beware preexisting categories that distort your perceptions, which are known as perceptual _____.
18. When you actively look for additional evidence to verify the accuracy of your perceptions, you are using _____.
19. In a dispute or argument, it is especially valuable to take the other person's _____.
20. The key to being a good "eyewitness" to life is not to drift through life in a haze, but instead make a conscious effort to _____ to other people and your surroundings.

Connections

1. ___ weapon focus
2. ___ unconscious transference
3. ___ habituation
4. ___ dishabituation
5. ___ Maslow's description of perceptive people

a. actively looking for additional evidence to check accuracy of perceptions
b. identifying as a culprit someone they have seen in another situation or context
c. attending to the gun or knife impairs an eyewitness's ability to identify the culprit's face
d. key to this process is to pay attention
e. expectations and pre-existing categories

230

6. ___ perceptual sets
7. ___ reality testing

f. responding less to predictable and unchanging stimuli
g. immersed in the present and lacking self-consciousness

Check Your Memory

1. TRUE or FALSE Eyewitness testimony is frequently wrong.
2. TRUE or FALSE The more confident an eyewitness is regarding their testimony, the more accurate the testimony is.
3. TRUE or FALSE Very few U.S. judges trust the accuracy of eyewitness testimony
4. TRUE or FALSE Impressions formed when a person is surprised, threatened, or under stress are especially prone to distortion.
5. TRUE or FALSE One study of eyewitness cases found that the wrong person was chosen from police lineups 25 percent of the time.
6. TRUE or FALSE The eyewitness testimony of a victim is more accurate than an observer's testimony.
7. TRUE or FALSE The presence of a weapon tends to improve an eyewitness's ability to accurately identify the culprit's face.
8. TRUE or FALSE An eyewitness's testimony about an event can be affected by how the questions are worded.
9. TRUE or FALSE Eyewitness testimony about an event often reflects not only what was actually seen but also information obtained later on.
10. TRUE or FALSE Eyewitnesses have sometimes incorrectly identified someone they have seen in another situation or context as a culprit.
11. TRUE or FALSE Judgments of clothing color by witnesses are best made under monochromatic light.
12. TRUE or FALSE An eyewitness's perception and memory for an event may be affected by his or her attitudes and expectations.
13. TRUE or FALSE When identifying the culprit of a crime, eyewitnesses are better at identifying members of other races than in identifying members of their own race.
14. TRUE or FALSE Personal objectivity requires frequent reality testing to maintain.
15. TRUE or FALSE Creative people habituate more quickly than average.
16. TRUE or FALSE According to Maslow, people who perceive themselves and others with unusual accuracy have perceptual styles marked by self-consciousness, the ability to evaluate others directly and accurately, and an immersion in past experiences.
17. TRUE or FALSE To become more perceptual aware, we must utilize habituation in everyday life.
18. TRUE or FALSE Utilizing perceptual sets and top-down processing will help a person to become more perceptually aware.
19. TRUE or FALSE Taking the other person's perspective is especially valuable in disputes or arguments.
20. TRUE or FALSE The key to being a better "eyewitness" to life is to pay attention.

Critical Thinking Question

Return for a moment to the incident described at the beginning of this chapter. What perceptual factors were involved in the first version of the "murder"? How did the girl affect what was seen?

231

Final Survey and Review—Completion

Module 4.1 Sensory Processes
Sensory Systems—The First Step
Survey Question: In general, how do sensory systems function?

1. As you read this statement, your brain interprets these black lines and shapes into meaningful patterns known as "words" through a process known as _____.
2. Smokers often do not get how much nonsmokers are bothered by the smell of tobacco smoke because the smoker's smell receptors have undergone sensory _____.
3. In Blakemore and Cooper's experiment with kittens raised in either vertically-stripped rooms or horizontally-striped rooms, the cats that could easily avoid chair legs, but missed when they tried to jump onto a chair were the ones raised in the _____-stripped rooms.
4. As you rub your eyes, you exert pressure and cause visual sensations, called _____ to appear.

Module 4.2 Vision
Vision—Catching Some Rays
Survey Question: How does the visual system function?

5. Tabitha's cornea is misshapen so that part of her vision will be focused while a part will be fuzzy. This vision problem is called _____.
6. Carlton is having his vision checked at his doctor's office and is asked to read rows of letters of diminishing size until he can no longer distinguish them. Carlton's vision is being checked using the _____ chart.
7. The area where the optic nerve leaves the eye is called the _____.
8. Afterimages are best explained by the _____ theory of color vision.
9. Submarines, airplane cockpits, and ready rooms for fighter pilots are often illuminated with an extremely red-colored light because the visual receptors called the _____ are insensitive to it.

Module 4.3 Hearing, the Chemical Senses, and the Somesthetic Senses
Hearing—Good Vibrations
Survey Question: What are the mechanisms of hearing?

10. Maria has several pierced earrings in the external part of her ear, which is technically called the _____.
11. Another name for the tympanic membrane is the _____.
12. Tiny hair cells are located in the organ of Corti, which is the center part of the _____.
13. The Hunter's notch is a noise-induced hearing loss that damages the hair cells and is, thus, classified as a(n) _____ hearing impairment.

Module 4.3 Smell and Taste—The Nose Knows When the Tongue Can't Tell
Survey Question: How do the chemical senses operate?

14. Floral, camphoric, musky, minty, and etherish are odors that are each produced by molecules with specific _____.
15. Because of a blow to the head that tore his olfactory nerve, Tim has a completely loss his ability to smell any odor, a condition known as _____.
16. Umami is sensitive to a substance found in MSG called _____.
17. The theory that best explains how we taste sweet and bitter is the _____ theory.

Module 4.3 The Somesthetic Senses—Flying by the Seat of Your Pants

Survey Question: What are the somesthetic senses?

18. Body position and movement are detected by receptors in the muscles and joints and make up the _____ sense.
19. Dorothea has a chronic nagging lower back ache. The pain she feels is being carried by small nerve fibers that are part of the body's _____ system.
20. Little Tony is getting an injection at the doctor's office. Just before, he is given the injection, Tony pinches the top of his hand, creating a "little" pain to counteract the "larger" injection pain. Tony is using a pain-relieving technique known as _____.
21. The structure called the crista is found inside each fluid-filled tube that makes up the sensory organ for balance called the _____.

Module 4.4 Perceptual Processes
Perception—The Second Step

Survey Question: In general, how do we construct our perceptions?

22. Gina is looking into what appears to be a regular room. However, a small person begins to walk from one side of the room to the other and "magically" grows larger. Gina is experiencing the illusion created by the _____ room.
23. Briana suffers from schizophrenia in which she often "hears" voices that are not there. These "voices" are called auditory _____.
24. Lindy is looking at an unusual picture and cannot seem to figure out what it is. So, Lindy begins looking at each of features until she discovers that the picture is "the letter K." In discovering the meaning of this picture, Lindy used _____ processing.
25. Our tendency to see illusory figures as whole figures with borders is an example of the Gestalt principle of _____.
26. April and Arnold are looking at a huge fluffy cloud. April thinks it looks like a "bear climbing a tree," while Arnold sees a "rocket ship blasting off." This cloud is an example of a(n) _____ stimulus.
27. On the highway, alcohol intoxication increases the accident rate among drunk drivers because it impairs size and shape _____ .

Module 4.4 Selective Attention—Tuning In and Tuning Out

Survey Question: Why are we more aware of some sensations than others?

28. You are so focused on watching your favorite reality TV show that you do not even hear your roommate in the room until he puts a bowl of popcorn on the table next to you. Your intense focus on your TV program would be an example of _____.
29. A person who fails to perceive a stimulus that is in plain view, but not the focus of attention is exhibiting _____.
30. The use of contrast tends to _____ your attention.

Module 4.5 Depth Perception
Depth Perception—What If the World Were Flat?

Survey Question: How is it possible to see depth and judge distance?

31. A glass-topped table that is used to test depth perception in infants is called the _____.
32. Depth cues that require two eyes are known as _____ depth cues.
33. The depth cue that is based on the fact that the eyes are about 2.5 inches apart is called _____.
34. The pictorial cue based on the apparent convergence of parallel lines in the environment is called _____.

233

35. Smog, fog, dust, and haze make distant objects look washed out in color and lacking in detail, while a crystal-clear day without the haze will make distant objects look closer. This illustrates the pictorial cue known as _____.

36. Because of depth cues, the moon on the horizon tends to look _____ than the moon overhead.

Module 4.6 Perception and Objectivity
Perceptual Learning—Believing is Seeing

Survey Question: How is perception altered by expectations, motives, emotions, and learning?

37. Jasmine is in a good mood and is happy and optimistic. According to Barbara Frederickson, Jasmine's scope of attention will most likely be _____.

38. Cultures, such as the United States and Canada, in which the people tend to focus on themselves and their own sense of personal control are classified as _____ countries.

39. A novice chef who discovers how to tell the difference between dried basil, oregano, and tarragon has altered how she constructs sensations into perceptions through a process known as perceptual _____.

40. Lance draws two horizontal lines the same length and then places an arrowhead at each end of one of the lines and Vs on each end of the other. Lance has just drawn the _____ illusion.

Module 4.7 Extrasensory Perception
Extrasensory Perception—Do You Believe in Ghosts?

Survey Question: Is extrasensory perception possible?

41. Rosita believes that she can communicate with relatives who have died. Rosita believes that she has the psi ability known as _____.

42. Tawana is being assessed for psychic abilities using a deck of 25 cards having five symbols, star, wavy lines, plus, circle and square. Tawana is being assessed using _____ cards.

43. Brenda is playing "psychic" at the school carnival. She was able to lead people to believe in the truth of what she was saying by being very good at what are known as "_____ readings."

44. Although Tawana scored above chance on one of the tests, she was unable to sustain this "ability," a situation known as the "_____ effect."

Module 4.8 Psychology in Action: Becoming a Better Eyewitness to Life

Survey Question: How can I learn to perceive events more accurately?

45. Marcia's purse was snatched. Compared to a person who merely observed the purse-snatching, Marcia's eyewitness testimony as the victim will be _____ as far as accuracy.

46. Eve unintentionally identified a person she had seen earlier in class as the person who stole her computer from the campus bench. This is known as unconscious _____.

47. If you have learned to respond less to predictable and unchanging stimuli, you are exhibiting _____.

48. Tia is in a "fun house" in which water seems to run uphill and the floor and ceiling are inverted. In order to verify the accuracy of her perceptions in this unusual place and walk around, she must utilize _____ testing.

234

Final Survey and Review—Matching

Module 4.1 Sensory Processes

1. ___ sensation

2. ___ perception

3. ___ biological transducer

4. ___ absolute threshold

5. ___ difference threshold

6. ___ sensory localization

7. ___ perceptual features

a. devices, such as the sense organs, that convert one kind of energy into another

b. basic elements of a stimulus, such as the lines, shapes, edge, or colors of a visual stimulus

c. the process of detecting physical energies with the sensory organs

d. a change in stimulus intensity that is detectable to an observer

e. the minimum amount of physical energy necessary to produce a sensation

f. the type of sensation one experiences depends on which brain area is activated

g. the mental process of organizing sensations into meaningful patterns

Module 4.2 Vision

1. ___ cornea

2. ___ rod

3. ___ cone

4. ___ blind spot
5. ___ fovea

6. ___ astigmatism

7. ___ hyperopia
8. ___ myopia

9. ___ presbyopia
10. ___ trichromatic theory
11. ___ opponent-process theory

a. color vision based on three coding systems (red or green, yellow or blue, black or white)

b. small cup-shaped area in the back of the eye made up of only color receptors

c. defects in the cornea or lens that cause some areas of vision to be out of focus

d. where the optic nerve leaves the eye

e. eyeball is too long causing distant objects to be blurred

f. clear membrane at the front of the eye that bends light inward

g. visual receptor for dim light

h. eyeball is too short with nearby objects being blurred

i. visual receptor for color

j. farsightedness caused by aging of lens

k. color vision is based on three cone types: red, green, and blue

Module 4.3 Hearing, the Chemical Senses, and the Somesthetic Senses

1. ___ tympanic membrane

2. ___ auditory ossicles
3. ___ pinna
4. ___ organ of Corti
5. ___ otolith organs
6. ___ semicircular canals

7. ___ neuromatrix

a. the sensory organ for movement, acceleration, and gravity

b. "smell blindness" for a particular odor
c. center part of cochlea
d. eardrum
e. the sensory organ for balance
f. explains how sounds up to about 4,000 hertz reach the brain

g. explains why motion sickness occurs

235

8. ___ umami

9. ___ dysosmia

10. ___ olfaction

11. ___ gustation
12. ___ kinesthetic

13. ___ frequency theory
14. ___ sensory conflict theory
15. ___ gate-control theory
16. ___ place theory
17. ___ lock-and-key theory

h. internal model of the body generated by the brain
i. theory that proposes that pain messages pass through a neural opening in the spinal cord
j. states that higher and lower tones excite specific areas of the cochlea
k. external part of ear
l. receptors for this sense are in muscles and joints
m. malleus, incus, and stapes
n. fifth taste quality described as savory
o. sense of smell
p. sense of taste
q. holds that odors are related to the shapes of chemical molecules

Module 4.4 Perceptual Processes

1. ___ illusions

2. ___ hallucinations

3. ___ "sane hallucinations"

4. ___ top-down processing

5. ___ bottom-up processing

6. ___ figure-ground organization

7. ___ closure

8. ___ contiguity

9. ___ ambiguous stimuli

10. ___ impossible figures

11. ___ shape constancy

12. ___ selective attention
13. ___ inattentional blindness

a. voluntarily focusing on a specific sensory input
b. patterns which cannot be organized into stable, consistent, or meaningful perceptions
c. this nearness in time and space is often responsible for the perception that one thing has caused another
d. imaginary sensations, such as seeing, hearing, or smelling something that does not exist in the external world
e. distorted perceptual constructions of stimuli that actually exist
f. patterns allowing more than one interpretation
g. for example, the page of a book will still be a rectangle whether it is viewed from overhead or from an angle
h. failure to perceive a stimulus that is in plain view, but not the focus of attention
i. tendency to fill gaps and complete a figure so that it has a consistent overall form
j. organizing perceptions by beginning with low-level features
k. part of a stimulus appears to stand out as an object against a less prominent background
l. symptom of Charles Bonnet syndrome
m. applying pre-existing knowledge to rapidly organize sensory information into a meaningful perception

Module 4.5 Depth Perception

1. ___ visual cliff
2. ___ retinal disparity
3. ___ convergence
4. ___ accommodation
5. ___ linear perspective
6. ___ height in the picture plane
7. ___ texture gradients
8. ___ interposition
9. ___ aerial perspective
10. ___ motion parallax

a. nearby objects appear to rush backward with remote objects moving in the same direction and slower
b. binocular cue based on the fact that the eyes are about 2.5 inches apart
c. distant objects tend to be hazy
d. means of testing the depth perception of infants
e. near objects look coarse, while distance objects appear smaller and finer
f. apparent meeting of parallel lines in the environment
g. objects placed closer to the horizon line in a drawing tend to be perceived as more distant
h. binocular cue that allows one to estimate distance under 50 feet
i. occurs when one object partially blocks another object
j. monocular cue that involves the bending of the lens to focus on nearby objects

Module 4.6 Perception and Objectivity

1. ___ perceptual set
2. ___ other-race effect
3. ___ individualists
4. ___ collectivists
5. ___ perceptual habits
6. ___ size-distance invariance

a. focus on themselves and their sense of personal control
b. focus on personal relationships and social responsibilities
c. seeing in-group faces differently
d. well-established patterns of perceptual organization and attention
e. explains the moon illusion and the *Müller-Lyer* illusion
f. readiness to perceive in a particular manner, induced by strong expectations

Module 4.7 Extrasensory Perception

1. ___ telepathy
2. ___ precognition
3. ___ clairvoyance
4. ___ psychokinesis
5. ___ cold readings
6. ___ run of luck
7. ___ decline effect

a. set of techniques used to lead people to believe in the truth of what a psychic is saying about them
b. statistically unusual outcome that could still occur by chance alone
c. inability of a person to maintain psi ability over a sustained period
d. purported ability to accurately predict future events
e. purported ability to perceive events at a distance or through physical barriers
f. purported ability to mentally alter or influence objects or events
g. purported ability to directly know another living person's thoughts

237

Module 4.8 Psychology in Action: Becoming a Better Eyewitness to Life

1. ___ weapon focus

2. ___ unconscious transference

3. ___ habituation

4. ___ dishabituation
5. ___ reality testing

a. actively looking for additional evidence to check accuracy of perceptions

b. identifying as a culprit someone they have seen in another situation or context

c. attending to the gun or knife impairs an eyewitness's ability to identify the culprit's face

d. key to this process is to pay attention
e. responding less to predictable and unchanging stimuli

Final Survey and Review—True or False

Module 4.1 Sensory Processes
Sensory Systems—The First Step
Survey Question: In general, how do sensory systems function?

1. TRUE or FALSE   The field of study that looks at the relationship between physical stimuli and the sensations they evoke in human observers is called psychopsychics.

2. TRUE or FALSE   Our senses acts a data reduction system, selecting and sending only the most important data to the brain.

3. TRUE or FALSE   Sensory receptors generally respond best to unchanging stimuli.

4. TRUE or FALSE   Sensory adaptation is the process that makes it possible to artificially restore varying degrees of sight and hearing to individuals who are blind or deaf.

Module 4.2 Vision
Vision—Catching Some Rays
Survey Question: How does the visual system function?

5. TRUE or FALSE   The basic color categories of red, orange, yellow, green, blue, indigo, and violet are referred to as saturation.

6. TRUE or FALSE   Farsightedness due to aging is known as presbyopia.

7. TRUE or FALSE   The fovea contains only rods.

8. TRUE or FALSE   The trichromatic theory of color vision explains what happens in the eye itself, while the opponent-process theory of color vision explains how colors are analyzed after messages leave the eye.

9. TRUE or FALSE   Regarding dark adaptation, it takes about 10 to 15 minutes of complete darkness to reach maximum visual sensitivity.

Module 4.3 Hearing, the Chemical Senses, and the Somesthetic Senses
Hearing—Good Vibrations
Survey Question: What are the mechanisms of hearing?

10. TRUE or FALSE   Sound waves cannot travel in a vacuum.

11. TRUE or FALSE   Psychologically, the "height" of a sound wave corresponds to its pitch.

12. TRUE or FALSE   According to the place theory, high tones register most strongly at the base of the cochlea near the oval window.

13. TRUE or FALSE   If the eardrums or ossicles are damaged or immobilized by disease or injury the person will have a conductive hearing loss.

238

Module 4.3 Smell and Taste—The Nose Knows When the Tongue Can't Tell
Survey Question: How do the chemical senses operate?

14. TRUE or FALSE   The sense of smell is known as gustation, while the sense of taste is known as olfaction.
15. TRUE or FALSE   If a person has "smell blindness" for a particular odor, the person has the condition known as dysosmia.
16. TRUE or FALSE   Regarding the four basic tastes, we are most sensitive to bitter tastes.
17. TRUE or FALSE   Salt and sour tastes appear to be based on a lock-and-key match between molecules and receptors.

Module 4.3 The Somesthetic Senses—Flying by the Seat of Your Pants
Survey Question: What are the somesthetic senses?

18. TRUE or FALSE   The receptors for the vestibular senses are found in the muscles and joints.
19. TRUE or FALSE   The skin receptors produce at least five different sensations that include light touch, pain, warmth, and pressure.
20. TRUE or FALSE   The painkilling effects of acupuncture can be explained by the sensory conflict theory.
21. TRUE or FALSE   To minimize motion sickness, you should try to keep your head still and fix your vision on a distant immobile object.

Module 4.4 Perceptual Processes
Perception—The Second Step
Survey Question: In general, how do we construct our perceptions?

22. TRUE or FALSE   Charles Bonnet syndrome is a psychotic condition that involves mental deterioration and auditory hallucinations.
23. TRUE or FALSE   Carmen is visiting a modern art gallery and reads that the first painting in the gallery is entitled "The Letter K." Knowing the title of the painting gives Carmen knowledge that will allow her to use top-down processing in perceiving the painting.
24. TRUE or FALSE   The psychodynamic psychologists identified several principles that bring some order to our perceptions.
25. TRUE or FALSE   Lip syncing and ventriloquism both illustrate the perception principle known as common region.
26. TRUE or FALSE   Camouflage patterns break up the perceptual organizations known as contiguity.
27. TRUE or FALSE   When perceptions are based on prior experiences, we refer to them as native ones.

Module 4.4 Selective Attention—Tuning In and Tuning Out
Survey Question: Why are we more aware of some sensations than others?

28. TRUE or FALSE   The "cocktail party effect" is an example of selective attention.
29. TRUE or FALSE   Using a cell phone while driving can cause inattentional blindness.
30. TRUE or FALSE   Stimuli that are brighter, louder, or larger tends to decrease one's attention.

Module 4.5 Depth Perception
Depth Perception—What If the World Were Flat?

Survey Question: How is it possible to see depth and judge distance?

31. TRUE or FALSE   The discrepancy in the images that reach the right and left eyes is known as interposition.
32. TRUE or FALSE   Convergence is used to estimate distances under 50 feet from one's eyes.
33. TRUE or FALSE   Objects that are placed higher in a drawing tend to be perceived as nearer.
34. TRUE or FALSE   If you are riding on a bus and watching the scenery pass, nearby objects will appear to rush backward, while more remote objects seem to move very little or not at all.
35. TRUE or FALSE   Stereoscopic vision is 10 times better for judging depth than perception based on just one eye.
36. TRUE or FALSE   If you remove depth cues by looking at a horizon moon through a rolled-up paper tube, the moon will appear larger.

Module 4.6 Perception and Objectivity
Perceptual Learning—Believing is Seeing

Survey Question: How is perception altered by expectations, motives, emotions, and learning?

37. TRUE or FALSE   In the experiment in which participants were told they were tasting an "expensive wine" and a "less expensive" wine when, in reality, they were tasting the same wine, the reason the participants thought the "more expensive" wine tasted better was due to perceptual expectancy.
38. TRUE or FALSE   When people are in positive moods, their ability to recognize people from other races improves.
39. TRUE or FALSE   East Asians tend to be individualistic people who look for internal factors to explain people's actions and tend to have a narrower focus of attention.
40. TRUE or FALSE   The Zulus of South Africa live in a "round" culture and have rarely encountered buildings that utilize a straight line or a square shape.

Module 4.7 Extrasensory Perception
Extrasensory Perception—Do You Believe in Ghosts?

Survey Question: Is extrasensory perception possible?

41. TRUE or FALSE   About half of all psychologists believe in the existence of ESP.
42. TRUE or FALSE   If you believe that you can accurately predict future events, you believe you have the purported ability known as psychokinesis.
43. TRUE or FALSE   Improved research methods in studying ESP have resulted in fewer positive results.
44. TRUE or FALSE   A statistically unusual outcome that could occur by chance alone is called a "run of luck."

Module 4.8 Psychology in Action: Becoming a Better Eyewitness to Life

Survey Question: How can I learn to perceive events more accurately?

45. TRUE or FALSE   The presence of a weapon impairs an eyewitness's ability to accurately identify the culprit's face.
46. TRUE or FALSE   Judgments of color made under monochromatic light are highly unreliable.

47. TRUE or FALSE   The key to being a better "eyewitness" to life is to become more self-conscious.

48. TRUE or FALSE   To become more perceptually aware, one must create perceptual sets and utilize habituation.

Mastery Test

1. You are attending a concert. The process of interpreting the sounds as a particular melody is called
   a. auditory assimilation.
   b. auditory accommodation.
   c. sensation.
   d. perception.

2. The fact that the eyes are only sensitive to a narrow band of electromagnetic energies shows that vision acts as a(n) _____ system.
   a. opponent-process
   b. gate-control
   c. central biasing
   d. data reduction

3. You enter a newly painted room and are overwhelmed by the paint smell. After several minutes, the paint smell seems to have disappeared, but what has really happened is that your olfactory receptors have experienced
   a. sensory gating.
   b. dysosmia.
   c. sensory adaptation.
   d. counterirritation.

4. Which of the following processes has made it possible to artificially restore sight and hearing through implants that send messages to various areas of the brain?
   a. perceptual accommodation
   b. subliminal perception
   c. somesthetic coding
   d. sensory localization

5. Sara has farsightedness due to her eyeball being too short, while Beatrice is farsightedness due to the lens of her eye becoming less flexible due to aging. Which statement is TRUE?
   a. Sara has myopia, and Beatrice has hyperopia.
   b. Sara has presbyopia, and Beatrice has astigmatism.
   c. Sara has hyperopia, and Beatrice has presbyopia.
   d. Sara has astigmatism, and Beatrice has myopia.

6. The blind spot in the eye occurs because this area of the retina lacks
   a. rhodopsin.
   b. photoreceptors.
   c. sensory gate.
   d. dorsal pathways.

7. Which theory of color vision best explains the fact that we do not see yellowish blue?
   a. trichromatic
   b. chromatic gating
   c. Ishihara hypothesis
   d. opponent-process

8. Submarine and airplane crewmen are able to move from a well-lit room to a dark room without having to undergo dark adaptation because of the use of _____ lights in the lighted room.
   a. red
   b. green
   c. blue
   d. yellow

9. The center part of the cochlea is called the
   a. pinna.
   b. organ of Corti.
   c. ampullae.
   d. otolith organ.

10. Rods and cones are to vision as _____ are to hearing.
    a. auditory ossicles
    b. vibrations
    c. pinnas
    d. hair cells

11. High tones register at the base of the cochlea with lower tones near the narrow outer tip of the cochlea, according to the _____ theory of hearing.
    a. place
    b. sensorineural
    c. conductive
    d. frequency

12. Your mother is a hairdresser and, because she has been around ammonia and other hairdressing potions, her olfactory sense has been impaired. This condition is known as
    a. agnosia.
    b. aphasia.
    c. somesthesia.
    d. dysosmia.

13. Your sense of smell and your sense of taste for sweet and bitter are both based on the _____ theory.
    a. trichromatic
    b. gate control
    c. lock-and-key
    d. opponent-process

14. Regarding gustation of the four basic tastes, we are least sensitive to
    a. sour.
    b. bitter.
    c. sweet.
    d. salt.

15. A gymnast "flying" through a routine on the uneven bars must rely on her skin senses, her kinesthetic senses, and her vestibular senses, which together make up the _____ senses.
    a. somesthetic
    b. audition
    c. peripheral
    d. gustation

16. If you jab yourself with a pin, you will feel a sharp pain. This pain message is carried by large nerve fibers that are part of the body's _____ system.
    a. reminding
    b. vestibular
    c. warning
    d. kinesthetic

17. According to Melzack, the neuromatrix explains why many amputees experience
    a. physiological nystagmus.
    b. physical dysosmia.
    c. post-traumatic scarring.
    d. phantom limb sensations.

18. When a mild electric current is applied to the skin to create mild tingling, agonizing pain can be greatly reduced. This procedure is known as
    a. selective distraction.
    b. reinterpretation.
    c. counterirritation.
    d. sensory conflict.

19. Within the inner ear is the sensory organ for balance called the
    a. organ of Corti.
    b. semicircular canals.
    c. vomeronasal organ.
    d. auditory ossicles.

20. Which theory explains how a mismatch between information from vision, the vestibular system, and kinesthesis causes motion sickness?
    a. sensory conflict theory
    b. gate control theory
    c. opponent-process theory
    d. cognitive dissonance theory

21. Megan, a young woman, screams out loud saying "Insects are crawling everywhere!" when none are present. Hilda, who is an elderly woman and partially blind, claims that people are disappearing and appearing in front of her eyes. Which statement is TRUE?
    a. Megan is experiencing hallucinations, while Hilda is experiencing "sane hallucinations."
    b. Megan is experiencing illusions, while Hilda is experiencing inattentional blindness.
    c. Megan is experiencing tinnitus; while Hilda is experiencing dementia.
    d. Megan is experiencing "sane hallucinations," while Hilda is experiencing delusions.

22. You are putting a puzzle together. After only a few pieces are in place, your past experience gives you the plan to rapidly fill in the final picture. In completing this familiar puzzle, you have used
    a. bottom-up processing.
    b. top-down processing.
    c. perceptual habituation.
    d. perceptual dishabituation.

23. Which group of psychologists identified several principles, including nearness and similarity that bring order to our perceptions?
    a. Gestalt psychologists
    b. psychodynamic psychologists
    c. cognitive-behavioral psychologists
    d. structuralists

24. An artist manages to portray a face with just a few unconnected lines. Apparently the artist has capitalized on
    a. closure
    b. contiguity
    c. shape constancy.
    d. figure-ground.

25. The camouflaged insect known as the giant walking stick insect is able to hide among the leaves and twigs because camouflage patterns break up
    a. brightness constancy.
    b. figure-ground organization.
    c. shape constancy.
    d. common region organization.

26. One reason for the increased accident rate among drunk drivers is that alcohol intoxication
    a. impairs size and shape constancies.
    b. increases bottom-up processing.
    c. leads to "sane hallucinations."
    d. causes stereoscopic vision.

27. While your friend is driving, you are looking at the street signs so you can tell him where to turn. Your ability to focus on the street signs and not on all the advertising signs and road signs that are at each intersection illustrates
    a. perceptual expectancy.
    b. selective attention.
    c. sensory localization.
    d. sensory gating.

28. You are focusing so intently on texting your friend during class that you fail to notice the professor walking toward your desk until she is standing in front of you and calling your name. Your failure to notice the movement of your instructor or the giggles of your classmates while concentrating on your cell phone texting, illustrates the effect known as
    a. sequential attention.
    b. dishabituation.
    c. sensory gating.
    d. inattentional blindness.

244

29. You are "shooting hoops" at the gym. The binocular cue that you use to judge the distance of the basketball hoop is
    a. accommodation.
    b. convergence.
    c. linear perspective.
    d. interposition.

30. Amanda is painting a desert scene with a winding road that goes off into the mountains. One way Amanda is creating depth in her painting is to make the parallel lines of this road converge as it gets closer to the distant mountains. Amanda is using the pictorial cue known as
    a. accommodation.
    b. interposition.
    c. linear perspective.
    d. aerial perspective.

31. In a drawing, a cat partially blocks part of the girl's legs, which shows that the cat is nearer than the girl to the observer and illustrates the pictorial depth cue of
    a. accommodation.
    b. interposition.
    c. texture gradient.
    d. aerial perspective.

32. Which of the following explains that the moon illusion occurs because the presence of depth cues on the horizon makes the horizon seem more distant than the night sky?
    a. apparent-distance hypothesis
    b. opponent-process theory
    c. figure-ground organization
    d. contiguity theory

33. An American visiting England, where they drive on the left side of the road, will have to be especially careful crossing the street because in looking for oncoming traffic, Americans have developed a(n) _____ to look in the opposite direction.
    a. linear perspective
    b. perceptual habit
    c. orientation response
    d. habituation

34. According to research by Barbara Frederickson, which of the following was found to broaden our scope of attention so that we can more readily recognize people from other races?
    a. perceptual expectancies
    b. perceptual habituation
    c. negative emotions
    d. positive emotions

35. When American and Japanese participants were shown drawings of everyday scenes and later saw a version in which changes were made to the figure and to the background, the Americans
    a. paid more attention to the figure.
    b. paid more attention to the background.
    c. paid equal attention to both figure and background.
    d. did not notice any changes to either the figure or the ground.

36. Several TV shows have a main character that is able to communicate with a person who is dead. This purported psi ability would be called
    a. precognition.
    b. psychokinesis.
    c. mediumship.
    d. transcendental messaging.

37. Some of the earliest objective experiments of psi events were conducted using Zener cards by
    a. B. F. Skinner.
    b. J.B. Rhine.
    c. Carl Jung.
    d. Max Wertheimer.

38. You see a poster announcing an ESP show by a famous psychic. During this show, this psychic will perform feats of telepathy, psychokinesis, and precognition. You can be assured that the psychic will most likely
    a. experience a run of luck.
    b. experience the "decline effect."
    c. use cold readings, deception, and a sleight of hand.
    d. be able to demonstrate telepathy and precognition, but not psychokinesis.

39. Regarding eyewitness testimony, which of the following statements is TRUE?
    a. Very high levels of stress increase the accuracy of eyewitness perceptions.
    b. The more confident the eyewitness, the more accurate his or her testimony will be.
    c. Eyewitness accuracy is virtually the same for witnessing a crime as it is for being a victim.
    d. Judgments of color are more accurate if they are made under monochromatic light.

40. Perceiving the world more accurately can be achieved through
    a. dishabituation.
    b. the use of perceptual habits.
    c. developing perceptual sets.
    d. top-down processing.

Chapter 5: States of Consciousness

Chapter Overview

Consciousness is a core feature of mental life consisting of sensations and perceptions of external events as well as self-awareness of mental events including thoughts, memories, and feelings about experiences and the self. States of awareness that differ from normal, alert, waking consciousness are called altered states of consciousness (ASCs). Altered states are especially associated with sleep and dreaming, hypnosis, sensory deprivation, and psychoactive drugs. Cultural conditioning greatly affects what altered states a person recognizes, seeks, considers normal, and attains.

Sleep is an innate biological rhythm essential for survival. Moderate sleep loss affects mainly vigilance and performance on routine or boring tasks. Higher animals and people deprived of sleep experience involuntary microsleep. Sleep patterns show some flexibility, but 7 to 8 hours remains average. The amount of daily sleep decreases steadily from birth to old age.

Sleep occurs in four stages. Stage 1 is light sleep, and stage 4 is deep sleep. The sleeper alternates between stages 1 and 4 (passing through stages 2 and 3) several times each night. According to the dual process hypothesis, sleep "refreshes" the body and brain and helps form lasting memories. The two most basic sleep states are rapid eye movement (REM) sleep and non-REM (NREM) sleep. REM sleep is strongly associated with dreaming. NREM sleep brings overall brain activation levels down, "calming" the brain. REM sleep and dreaming help us store important memories.

Insomnia may be temporary or chronic. Behavioral approaches to managing insomnia, such as sleep restriction and stimulus control, are quite effective. Sleepwalking, sleeptalking, and sleepsex occur during NREM sleep. Night terrors occur in NREM sleep, whereas nightmares occur in REM sleep. Sleep apnea (interrupted breathing) is one source of insomnia and daytime hypersomnia (sleepiness). Apnea is suspected as one cause of sudden infant death syndrome (SIDS). With only a few exceptions, healthy infants should sleep face up or on their sides. Narcolepsy (sleep attacks) and cataplexy (a sudden temporary paralysis of the muscles) are caused by a sudden shift to stage 1 REM patterns during normal waking hours.

The Freudian, or psychodynamic, view is that dreams express unconscious wishes, frequently hidden by dream symbols. Many theorists have questioned Freud's view of dreams. For example, the activation-synthesis model portrays dreaming as a physiological process. The neurocognitive view of dreams holds that dreams are continuous with waking thoughts and emotions. Most dream content is about familiar settings, people, and actions.

Hypnosis is an altered state characterized by narrowed attention and increased suggestibility. (Not all psychologists agree that hypnotic effects require an alteration of consciousness.) Hypnosis appears capable of producing relaxation, controlling pain, and altering perceptions. Hypnosis alters perceptions and behavior, but it is more capable of changing subjective experiences than habits, such as smoking. Stage hypnotism takes advantage of typical stage behavior and uses deception to simulate hypnosis.

Meditation and sensory deprivation are beneficial ways to alter consciousness through relaxation. Concentrative meditation can be used to focus attention, alter consciousness, and reduce stress. Major benefits of meditation are its ability to interrupt anxious thoughts and to elicit the relaxation response. Brief exposure to sensory deprivation can also elicit the relaxation response. Under proper conditions, sensory deprivation may help break long-standing habits.

Psychoactive drugs affect the brain in ways that alter consciousness. Most psychoactive drugs can be placed on a scale ranging from stimulation to depression. Drugs may cause a physical dependence (addiction) or a psychological dependence, or both. The physically addicting drugs are alcohol, amphetamines, barbiturates, cocaine, codeine, GHB, heroin, methadone, morphine, nicotine, and tranquilizers. Drug use can be classified as experimental, recreational, situational, intensive, and compulsive. Drug abuse is most often associated with the last three. Polydrug abuse is also a problem.

Stimulant drugs are readily abused because of the period of depression that often follows stimulation. The greatest risks are associated with amphetamines (especially methamphetamine), cocaine, MDMA, and nicotine, but even caffeine can be a problem. Nicotine includes the added risk of lung cancer, heart disease, and other health problems.

Barbiturates and tranquilizers are depressant drugs whose action is similar to that of alcohol. The overdose level for barbiturates and GHB is close to the intoxication dosage, making them dangerous drugs. Mixing barbiturates, tranquilizers, or GHB and alcohol may result in a fatal drug interaction. Alcohol is the most heavily abused drug in common use today. Binge drinking is a problem among college students. It is possible to pace the consumption of alcohol. Marijuana is subject to an abuse pattern similar to alcohol. Studies have linked chronic marijuana use with lung cancer, various mental impairments, and other health problems.

Collecting and interpreting your dreams can promote self-awareness. Freud held that the meaning of dreams is hidden by condensation, displacement, symbolization, and secondary elaboration. Hall emphasizes the setting, cast, plot, and emotions of a dream. Cartwright's view of dreams as feeling statements and Perls's technique of speaking for dream elements are also helpful. Dreams may be used for creative problem solving, especially when dream awareness is achieved through lucid dreaming.

Preview: Bending Your Mind

Language Development Guide

bending your mind: altering one's consciousness
mindfulness meditation: mental exercise based on widening attention to become aware of
   everything experienced at any given moment
a joint: marijuana
spare change: coins rather than paper money
ritual: ceremony
mythical: legendary; fabled
Aborigines: first or earliest people to inhabit a place
aspiring: hoping; seeking; desiring
consults: seeks advice or help from
elder: senior; leader
congregation: people attending worship
peyote tea: contains mescaline derived from the peyote cactus
sacrament: religious ritual or ceremony
resounds: echoes; booms
convent: community of priests or nuns
contemplation: thought

flotation chamber: one floats in a dark chamber of water; see description later in the chapter
resuming: starting again
brews: prepares
cappuccino: Italian coffee drink consisting of espresso, hot milk, and steamed-milk foam
exotic: rare, special

Module 5.1 States of Consciousness and Sleep
States of Consciousness—The Many Faces of Awareness
Survey Question: What is consciousness?

Language Development Guide

unconscious: in a comatose state
crucial: essential; critical
rim: edge
insignificance: unimportance
awe: mixture of wonder and fear
phenomena: occurrences
fatigue: tiredness; exhaustion
delirium: confusion; disorientation
euphoria: mixture of excitement and joy
time sense: perceiving the passage of time
suggestibility: readily accepting the suggestions of others
sensory overload: senses are overwhelmed in processing sensory information leading to a lack of focus
rave: dance party
Mardi Gras: festival party 40 days before Easter in New Orleans
mosh pit: dance area where dancers jump and bump into each other
monotonous stimulation: repetitive stimulation that is very boring
"highway hypnotism": being able to drive and respond to external events without consciously being aware of them due to a divided state of consciousness; usually occurs with routine tasks (ex. making turns that you don't remember making on your way home)
hyperventilation: breathing rapidly
dehydration: the body needing water
near-death experiences: people claiming to have died and then brought back to life
sweat lodge: Native American meditation building
sage: small evergreen shrub-like plant that has grayish leaves and is used as a spice that has an earthy, wild taste and smell
chant: reciting words in a song-like manner
yoga: a meditative physical and mental exercise that originated in India
Whirling Dervishes: dancers who spin
revelation: the revealing or disclosing of information that usually results from a religious experience
intoxification: being "drunk;" being mentally and physically impaired usually after overconsuming a substance or from being poisoned
enlightenment: gaining insight or an understanding into the true nature of something

Recite and Review

1. All of your sensations, perceptions, memories, and feelings that you are aware of at any given moment make up your _____.
2. You are the expert on what it feels like to be you, which referred to the _____ experience.

249

3. The difficulty of knowing other minds is one reason why the early behaviorists distrusted the research technique of the structuralists known as _____.
4. In order to understand the minds and behavior of other people and of animals, psychologists must adopt an objective, _____ point of view.
5. We spend most of our lives in a state of clear, organized alertness known as _____.
6. Distinct shifts in our perceptions, emotions, memories, time sense, thoughts, feelings of self-control, and suggestibility occur during a(n) _____ of consciousness.
7. During a Sioux Indian ceremony, several men sit in total darkness inside a small chamber heated by coals, and chanting rhythmically. This ceremony is known as the _____ ceremony.
8. The yoga practices of Hindu mystics and the dances of the Whirling Dervishes of Turkey are regarded by these cultures as pathways to personal enlightenment and produce _____ of consciousness.
9. You experienced sensory overload while you were in a mosh pit at the concert. Then, you experienced a monotonous 400-mile drive back home after the concert. Both of these situations could produce a(n) _____ of consciousness.
10. What altered states are recognized and considered normal are the result of _____ conditioning.

Connections

1. ___ consciousness
2. ___ waking consciousness
3. ___ altered state of consciousness (ASC)
4. ___ first-person experience
5. ___ third-person point of view

a. objective viewpoint
b. based on one's own subjective experience
c. state of clear, organized alertness
d. consists of all the sensations, perceptions, memories, and feelings one is aware of at any given moment
e. occurs from delirium, hypnosis, drugs, and sensory overload

Check Your Memory

1. TRUE or FALSE   To be conscious means to be aware.
2. TRUE or FALSE   It is possible to know the first-person experience of other people.
3. TRUE or FALSE   It is not possible to know the first-person experience of lower animals, such as dogs, cats, or bats.
4. TRUE or FALSE   The early behaviorists utilized introspection to understand the mind and consciousness.
5. TRUE or FALSE   We spend most of our lives in waking consciousness.
6. TRUE or FALSE   During an altered state of consciousness, there are changes in the quality and pattern of mental activity.
7. TRUE or FALSE   Heightened self-awareness is an important feature of many ASCs.
8. TRUE or FALSE   The Sioux Indians use the sweat lodge ceremony to cleanse the mind and soul and lead to personal enlightenment.
9. TRUE or FALSE   People rarely seek an altered state of consciousness for pleasure.
10. TRUE or FALSE   Cultural conditioning affects what altered states we recognize and consider normal.
11. TRUE or FALSE   The most common altered state is "highway hypnotism" that occurs on long monotonous drives.

Sleep—Catching a Few ZZZ's
Survey Question: What are the effects of sleep loss or changes in sleep patterns?

Language Development Guide

ZZZ's: refers to sound people make when they are asleep; snoring
thundering: rumbling; roaring
whimper: sob; cry
eventually: in the end
impose: force
snooze: nap
stupor: a daze; trance; state of unconsciousness
coma: loss of consciousness
become hell: horrible experience
"official": certified and recorded
slurred: words running together; garbled; inaudible
drooping: baggy; sagging
susceptible: prone to; at risk; vulnerable
treadmill: exercise machine for walking or running in place
drift: flow; coast
spell: lead to; mean
necessity: required; essential
luxury: treat; extra
macro-accidents: large accidents
struggling: involving great effort
delusions: a false belief
hallucinations: false sensory experience of something that does not exist
"crazy": having a mental illness; not acting rationally or reasonable
sleep debt: an accumulated sleep deficiency
steady: fixed; stable; firm
light-dark cycles: day and night
external time markers: cues within the environment that indicate what time it is
tie: bind; link
on the other end of the scale: the opposite of
doze: sleep lightly; nap
urging: advising; insisting on
"siesta": Spanish word for midday sleep
hospital interns: doctors who are in their first year in a university or public hospital and are
      expected to put in numerous hours of work with very little sleep
tempted: attracted; enticed; persuaded
astronauts: a person in U.S. who is trained for space flight
tailored: modified; adapted
yield: give way; give in
whims: impulse; sudden desire

Recite and Review

1. If Santos is like most people, he will spend approximately _____ years of life asleep.
2. Sleep is an innate, repeating cycle of physiological activity called a(n) _____.
3. A rare disease that prevents sleep always ends with _____.
4. According to *The Guinness Book of Records*, the person who holds the world record for going without sleep for 264 hours is _____.

5. This record of 264 hours will remain intact since *The Guinness Book of Records* no longer recognizes competitions involving sleep _____.

6. Sleep loss typically causes trembling hands, drooping eyelids, inattention, irritability, staring, general discomfort, and _____ pain sensitivity.

7. Ryan is a teenager who stays up late and gets up early to go to school. At school, he shows a common problem among adolescents, which is excessive daytime sleepiness known as _____.

8. Most people who have not slept for a day or two can still do interesting or _____ mental tasks.

9. Santos has not been getting enough sleep. On his way to work, he almost had a car accident when he momentarily "fell" asleep for a few seconds and swerved into the other lane of traffic. Santos experienced what is known as a(n) _____.

10. Jake is a truck driver who has been awake about 60 hours. Besides being "cranky" and feeling disoriented, Jake actually thought he saw something "move" beside him in the cab. Jake appears to be in the initial stages of temporary _____.

11. By picking a day when you feel well rested, sleeping that night until you wake without an alarm clock, and awaken feeling rested, you have determined your natural _____.

12. If clocks and light-dark cycles were removed as cues, humans eventually would shift to a sleep-waking cycle that averages slightly more than _____ hours.

13. Clocks as well as light and darkness help tie our sleep rhythms to days that are exactly 24 hours long with these environmental indicators being called _____.

14. The small percentage of the population who average five hours of less per night are classified as _____.

15. Marian sleeps between nine and ten hours every night. She would be considered a(n) _____.

16. Sid is 60 years old. If he is like a majority of people over 50, his average amount of sleep per night will be _____ hours.

17. Sleeping in two-to four-hour cycles, infants spend up to _____ hours sleeping.

18. The natural sleep pattern between time awake and time asleep is a ratio of _____ to one.

Connections

1. ___ biological rhythm
2. ___ sleep deprivation

3. ___ hypersomnia
4. ___ microsleep
5. ___ sleep-deprivation psychosis

6. ___ sleep pattern

a. order and timing of daily sleep periods
b. being prevented from getting desired or needed amounts of sleep
c. any repeating cycle of biological activity
d. excessive daytime sleepiness
e. temporary state brought about by severe sleep loss; includes confusion, disorientation, delusions, and hallucinations
f. brief shift in brain-wave patterns to those of sleep

Check Your Memory

1. TRUE or FALSE   You are totally unresponsive during sleep.
2. TRUE or FALSE   While you are asleep, it is possible to learn many complex skills, including mathematics or a foreign language.
3. TRUE or FALSE   A good sleep can help you remember what you learned the day before.
4. TRUE or FALSE   Sleep is an innate biological rhythm that can be bent or stretched but not ignored.

5. TRUE or FALSE   A rare disease that prevents sleep always ends in death.
6. TRUE or FALSE   If you go without sleep for three days, you will have to sleep at least 30 hours to reverse the effects of the sleep deprivation.
7. TRUE or FALSE   The Guinness Book of Records no longer recognizes sleep deprivation competitions because of possible health risks.
8. TRUE or FALSE   Sleep loss causes decreased pain sensitivity.
9. TRUE or FALSE   Excessive daytime sleepiness is called narcolepsy.
10. TRUE or FALSE   Rapid physical changes during puberty increase the need for sleep.
11. TRUE or FALSE   Most people who have not slept for a day or two can still do simple or boring routines, but have trouble working on complex mental tasks.
12. TRUE or FALSE   Brief shifts in brain-wave patterns to those of sleep are called microsleeps and have been the cause of thousands of car accidents.
13. TRUE or FALSE   Sleep helps keep the brain healthy by regulating its temperature, conserving energy, and aiding brain development and repair.
14. TRUE or FALSE   Severe sleep loss can cause a temporary sleep-deprivation psychosis with hallucinations and delusions appearing after 60 hours of wakefulness.
15. TRUE or FALSE   Your natural sleep need is shown when you do not feel disoriented upon awakening to an alarm clock set one hour earlier than normal waking time.
16. TRUE or FALSE   If external time markers are removed for four to six weeks humans will eventually shift to a sleep-waking cycle that averages slightly less than 20 hours.
17. TRUE or FALSE   Short sleepers average five hours or less of sleep per night, while long sleepers doze nine hours or more per night.
18. TRUE or FALSE   Persons older than 50 average about nine hours of sleep per night.
19. TRUE or FALSE   Infants spend up to 20 hours a day sleeping, usually in two- to four-hour cycles.
20. TRUE or FALSE   Midafternoon sleepiness is a natural part of the sleep cycle.
21. TRUE or FALSE   Natural sleep patterns have a ratio of 3 to 1 between time awake and time asleep.

Critical Thinking Question

Why might it be better for the unscheduled human sleep-waking cycle to average more than 24 hours, instead of less?

Stages of Sleep—The Nightly Roller-Coaster

Survey Question: Why do we sleep?

Language Development Guide

roller-coaster: amusement park ride in which a car carrying several people travels rapidly on a track that has peaks and valleys and now even loops
network: complex arrangement of connections
seesaw: going up and down; also a playground apparatus that goes up and down
generated: produced
amplified: enlarged; intensified; strengthened
descend: go down
distinctive: distinguishing
boundary: margin; border line
oblivion: state of unconsciousness

253

fluctuations: variations; rising and falling

recurring: returning

spouse: wife, husband, or partner

physical exertion: work out of one's muscles in which much energy is used

bombarded: attacked; overrun with

neural: pertaining to the nerves, neurons, and nervous system

jumble: clutter; mess; mixed up

fade: weaken; disappear gradually

doesn't "sweat the small stuff": not worrying about or focusing on trivial things

"sharpen": to make more precise

dramatically: noticeably; considerably; significantly

sort: arrange; organize; classify

retain: hold on to

strategies: plans; approaches

pulling an all-nighter: working or studying all night without any sleep

hearty: substantial; plentiful; filling

vivid: bright, clear; dramatic

correspond: match

iguana: large lizard

bizarre: strange; odd

imagery: mental pictures

speaking very loosely: not a precise, scientific explanation

streaming: flowing

efficiently: in a well-organized way

"offline": when a computer is not connected to another outside source, such as the internet; thus, when one is asleep one's brain is not connected to the world, its working "offline"

waver: get weak or unstable

erotic: arousing sexual desire

paralyzed: unable to move

hilarious: very funny

escapades: an adventure; antics; incidents

thrash: beat or flail one's limbs or body

dawn: sunrise

sinister: evil; creepy; threatening

lurking: prowling; creeping around; hanging around in a threatening manner

suffocating: smothering; choking

vanish: disappear

terrified: frightened; scared

episodes: periods; occurrences

alien being: a life form from another world

shrug off: make a gesture of doubt or indifference

weird: strange; odd

intruders: an uninvited visitor; trespasser

angels: kind beings that act as messengers from Heaven

demons: evil spirits

witches: possessing magical or supernatural powers, which can be used to inflict harm on others

out-of-body experiences: feeling of being detached from one's body and observing oneself and one's surroundings from nearby

abducted: kidnapped; taken against one's will

space aliens: life forms not from Earth

folklore: traditional beliefs and stories handed down orally within a culture

254

legends: story handed down throughout history that may or may not be true
supernatural: existence beyond the visible observable world
paranormal: beyond the range of normal human experiences or beyond scientific explanation

Recite and Review

1. Whether you are awake or asleep right now depends on the _____ between separate sleep and waking systems.
2. The brain does not "shut down" during sleep, rather, the_____ of activity changes
3. Changes in the tiny electrical signals generated by the brain can be amplified and recorded with a(n) _____.
4. Marta is awake and alert in her psychology class. If we could look at her brain waves right now, we would see a pattern of small fast waves called _____ waves.
5. You are watching TV when your thoughts begin to drift and you close your eyes. As you doze off, your brain waves would be larger, slower waves known as _____ waves.
6. The four levels of sleep identified by brain-wave patterns and behavior changes are known as _____.
7. Stage 1 sleep, when your heart rate slows, your breathing is irregular, and your muscles relax, would best be described as _____ sleep.
8. Dara has just dozed off while studying when she experiences a muscle twitch that awakens her. This muscle twitch occurring during stage 1 sleep is known as a(n) _____.
9. During stage 2 sleep, the short bursts of distinctive brain-activity that mark the true boundary of sleep are called _____.
10. In stage 3 sleep, a new brain wave that is very large and slow begins to appear. This new wave is called a(n) _____ wave.
11. Reached by most people about one hour after they go to sleep is stage 4 slow-wave sleep, which would be considered _____ sleep.
12. Sleep that involves a return to stage 1 brain wave patterns and is associated with dreaming is called _____ sleep.
13. Dream-free about 90 percent of the time, stages 1, 2, 3, and 4, collectively, make up _____ sleep.
14. According to the dual process hypothesis, the basic state of sleep that "calms" the brain is _____ sleep.
15. The basic state of sleep that appears to "sharpen" our memories of the previous day's more important experiences is _____ sleep.
16. After hearing the rumor about the company downsizing, LaShonda has been worrying all day about whether she will be laid off from her job. Tonight as she sleeps, LaShonda will most likely experience an increased amount of _____ sleep.
17. Juanita has worked hard in her garden all day and is very fatigued when she goes to bed. Because of all this physical exertion, Juanita will most likely experience increasing amounts of _____ sleep.
18. Newborn babies have lots of new experiences to process so they spend eight to nine hours a day, or 50 percent of their total sleep time in _____ sleep.
19. Brain areas associated with imagery and emotion become more active during _____ sleep.
20. When he is dreaming, Aaron tends to thrash around and leap out of bed. Aaron's lack of muscle paralysis during REM sleep is called _____ disorder.
21. Mara is just waking up and is still experiencing sleep paralysis. While in this state, she senses that something, an alien being, is in her bedroom and is pressing down on her chest trying to suffocate her. Mara is experiencing _____.

255

Connections

1. ___ EEG

2. ___ alpha waves

3. ___ beta waves

4. ___ delta waves

5. ___ hypnic jerk

6. ___ sleep spindles

7. ___ sleep stages

8. ___ REM sleep

9. ___ non-REM (NREM) sleep

10. ___ dual process hypothesis

11. ___ REM behavior disorder

12. ___ hypnopompic hallucinations

a. distinctive bursts of brain wave activity that indicate a person is asleep

b. reflex muscle twitch that occurs as your muscles relax during stage 1 sleep

c. caused by a lack of muscle paralysis during REM sleep

d. sleep that occurs during stages 1, 2, 3, and 4 and "calms" the brain

e. device designed to detect, amplify, and record electrical activity in the brain

f. large, slow brain waves associated with relaxation and falling asleep as seen in stage 1 sleep

g. sleep that is associated with dreaming, "sharpens" our memories, and is increased by daytime stress

h. caused by sleep paralysis occurring just before you wake up with person feeling like they are suffocating, floating, or that an alien being is in their bedroom

i. small, fast brain waves associated with being awake and alert

j. large, slow brain waves that occur in deeper sleep stages 3 and 4

k. levels of sleep identified by brain-wave patterns and behavioral changes

l. explains that sleep "refreshes" the brain and stores memories

Check Your Memory

1. TRUE or FALSE Whether you are awake or asleep right now depends on the balance between separate sleep and waking systems.
2. TRUE or FALSE The brain literally "shuts down" during sleep.
3. TRUE or FALSE Changes in tiny electrical signals generated by the brain can be amplified and recorded with an electroencephalograph.
4. TRUE or FALSE When one is awake and alert, a pattern of fast brain waves called alpha waves are present.
5. TRUE or FALSE Immediately before sleep, as one becomes relaxed and during stage 1 sleep, one's brain waves are predominantly made up of delta waves.
6. TRUE or FALSE During stage 1 sleep, as one's muscles relax, a person may experience a reflex muscle twitch known as cataplexy.
7. TRUE or FALSE During stage 3 sleep distinctive bursts of brain wave activity called hypnic jerks occur.
8. TRUE or FALSE Stage 4 brain waves are almost pure beta waves with people experiencing rapid eye movement sleep.
9. TRUE or FALSE NREM sleep is dream-free about 90 percent of the time.
10. TRUE or FALSE Physical exertion tends to increase the amount of REM sleep, while daytime stress tends to increase the amount of NREM sleep.

256

11. TRUE or FALSE   According to the opponent process hypothesis, REM sleep "calms" the brain, while NREM sleep appears to "sharpen" our memories of the previous day's more important experiences.

12. TRUE or FALSE   REM sleep may stimulate the developing brain with newborn babies spending eight or nine hours a day in REM sleep.

13. TRUE or FALSE   People who are born blind do not show rapid eye movements during sleep and do not dream.

14. TRUE or FALSE   All mammals show REM sleep, while reptiles show no signs of REM sleep.

15. TRUE or FALSE   REM sleep is a time of high emotion with the heart beating irregularly and the blood pressure and breathing wavering.

16. TRUE or FALSE   During NREM sleep, both males and females appear to be sexually aroused with no sexual arousal being shown during REM sleep.

17. TRUE or FALSE   A person with REM behavior disorder lacks muscle paralysis during REM sleep and will often thrash around violently, leaping out of bed, or attacking his or her bed partner.

18. TRUE or FALSE   When sleep paralysis occurs just as one begins to wake up, a person may experience hypnopompic hallucinations in which the person may sense that alien beings are in the bedroom.

Critical Thinking Question

In addition to helping store memories, what biological advantages might sleeping provide?

Module 5.2 Sleep Disturbances and Dreaming

Sleep Disturbances—The Sleepy Time Blues

Survey Question: What are some sleep disorders and unusual sleep events?

Language Development Guide

beating: pounding; thrashing
frenetic: busy; intense; hectic
epidemic: widespread outbreak
intriguing: fascinating
sleepy time blues: unhappiness related to the quality of one's sleep
sleep clinics: diagnostic and treatment centers for sleep disturbances
complaints: ailment; problem conditions
sleep attacks: sudden sleepiness
pretty low: near the bottom
pastimes: activities done in one's spare time
chronic: continuing, unrelieved condition
self-defeating cycle: repeating activities that will continue to hurt you
excess: surplus; overload of
heightened arousal: increased stimulation
block: stop; prevent
delays: postpones; puts off
beat this cycle: defeat this repetitive series of activities
withdrawal (from sleeping pills): physical illness and discomfort that occurs when one stops using an addictive psychoactive substance
irony: incongruity; absurdity; clash
nonprescription: medicine obtained with a doctor's approval

sleep-inducing: to cause sleep

drastically: significantly; hugely

"sleeping-pill junkies": people that abuse sleep pills

painstakingly: carefully

weaned: removed from

rebound: returning again, bounce back

drawbacks: disadvantages; problems

amnesia: loss of memory

remedy: cure; solution

lifestyle: way of life; everyday routines

fragmenting: breaking up

paradoxical: containing a contradiction or inconsistency

progressive muscle relaxation: an approach to relaxation that involves tightening and loosing
   muscles throughout the body in sequence

blotting out: erasing

strenuous: demanding; exhausting

starchy foods: break down quickly into sugar; include breads, cereals, potatoes, rice, pasta

drop the bomb: destroy

stimulants: substances that increases activity in the body and nervous system

eerie: strange; scary

obstacles: barriers

shuffling: rearranging

brandishing: waving; showing off

shuffling feet: quick, dragging footsteps

immobilized: unable to move

startled: surprised; alarmed

realm: area

drenched: soaked

vaguely: dimly; unclearly

plague: trouble; afflict

horror movie: film meant to produce fear, shock, and disgust

banished: gotten rid of; removed

"re-programs": to rewrite or revise

sage: wise person

"Laugh and the whole world laughs with you; snore and you sleep alone": a joke on the saying
"Laugh and the whole world laughs with you, cry and you cry alone" but referring to snorers
   annoying their spouse

wood sawing: like sawing logs, meaning snoring

gulps: swallow quickly

diaphragm: sheet of muscle tissue across the bottom of lower ribs important in respiration

obstructions: barriers; obstacles

monitor: device that continually checks bodily functions, such as an infant's breathing

shrill: piercing high-pitched scream

pediatrician: doctor who specializes in the medical care of infants, children, and adolescents

"back to sleep": slogan that helps people remember that infants should sleep on their backs

eliminating: getting rid of

irresistible: overpowering; uncontrollable

triggers: causes; sets off

collapse: fall down

devastate: destroy; ruin; wreck

intrudes: breaks into; interfere

breeding: selective reproduction of offspring by genetics
outstanding: great; excellent
roll over and play dead: trick involving a dog turning on his back and being still as if dead

Recite and Review

1. Hypersomnia, narcolepsy, and sleep apnea are all types of _____.
2. Difficulty in getting to sleep or staying asleep and not feeling rested describes _____.
3. At night, Kenny tends to have muscle twitches, primarily in his legs that occur every 20 to 40 seconds and severely disturb his sleep. Kenny is suffering from periodic _____ syndrome.
4. When Elena goes to bed, her legs begin to cramp, ache, and tingle to the point that she must move her legs in order to relieve these constant sensations. Elena would be diagnosed with _____ syndrome.
5. No matter how much sleep, Tom has had, he always has trouble waking up and is often very irritable and sometimes verbally aggressive with anyone that tries to awaken him. Tom's slow transition to clear consciousness after awakening from sleep is called _____.
6. Amad is an adult who has experienced repeated occurrences of night terrors throughout his life. Amad's condition is referred to as _____ disorder.
7. Sara has been transferred to the night shift at work and is having difficulty falling asleep during the daytime. This mismatch between when her body wants to sleep and the demands of her job has resulted in Sara experiencing a(n) _____ disorder.
8. Worry, stress, and excitement are the most common causes of _____ insomnia.
9. If insomnia lasts for more than three weeks, then doctor will most likely make the diagnosis of _____ insomnia.
10. Every time Lindsey stops taking her sleeping pills, she has extreme trouble going to sleep or she dozes off and wakes up several times during the night. Lindsey is experiencing _____ insomnia.
11. Prescription sedatives drastically lower sleep quality by decreasing both REM sleep and NREM stage _____ sleep.
12. A behavioral approach to treating insomnia involves linking sleep with a specific bedtime and a specific place, the bed. This approach is known as _____.
13. Even if you miss an entire night of sleep, it is important not to sleep late in the morning or to nap more than an hour. In other words, limit sleep only to your normal bedtime hours. This behavioral approach is called _____.
14. In order to get to sleep quickly on a business trip, Lori keeps her eyes wide open in the dark hotel room until her eyes become so tired that they close, and sleep comes unexpectedly. Lori has used the the approach to getting to sleep known as the _____.
15. Sonya meditates each night before she goes to bed to blot out worries and induce _____ before sleep.
16. Six hours before bedtime, Terrence works out in his home gym because sleep is promoted by engaging in strenuous _____ during the day.
17. Eating a starchy snack, such as cookies, bread, pasta, oatmeal, pretzels, or dry cereal, can promote sleep because it increases the amount of an amino acid called _____ that reaches the brain.
18. Eating starchy foods increases an amino acid in the brain, which, in turn, increases the level of the neurotransmitter associated with relaxation, a positive mood, and sleepiness. This neurotransmitter is _____.
19. Caffeine, which is found in colas and coffee, and nicotine in cigarettes can prevent sleep because they are both classified as _____ drugs.
20. People who sleepwalk are referred to as _____.

21. EEG studies have shown that sleepwalking occurs during stages 3 and 4 of _____ sleep.
22. The official name for sleepsex, a disorder in which a sleeping person attempts to have sex with his or her bed partner, is _____.
23. Maya has been having vivid, recurrent bad dreams of running from a tall stranger through a deserted city street. Since she does not move in her sleep during these bad dreams and can remember the details of them, Maya would most likely be diagnosed with a(n) _____ disorder.
24. Timmy is four years old and has been awakening in a panic a couple of times a week for the last month. When his parents hear his screams, they run to his room and find Timmy sitting up in bed and drenched in sweat. The next morning Timmy does not remember what happened. Timmy is most likely experiencing a(n) _____.
25. A bad dream that occurs during REM sleep is called a(n) _____.
26. One technique for eliminating bad dreams involves making these bad dreams more familiar while you are awake as well as mentally "reprogramming" future dreams so that they are less frightening. This technique is known as _____.
27. Benjamin snores loudly during sleep with his breathing stopping for periods of 20 seconds to two minutes numerous times a night. Benjamin has the sleep disorder known as _____.
28. For people who experience repeated interruptions to their breathing during sleep, treatments include weight loss, surgery for breathing obstructions, and the use of a breathing mask to aid breathing during sleep called a(n) _____ mask.
29. Sleep apnea is suspected as one cause of "crib death," also known as _____.
30. To help prevent "crib death," healthy infants are better off sleeping on their sides or on their _____.
31. Parents sharing their beds with infants may accidentally suffocate their infants when they roll over on top of the infant, which is referred to as _____.
32. Aaron has suddenly fallen asleep while standing and talking. Emotional excitement, especially laughter, commonly triggers these sudden sleep attacks. Aaron has _____.
33. More than half of all individuals who have irresistible sleep attacks also experience sudden temporary paralysis of their muscles called _____.
34. The sudden sleep attacks and paralysis appear to occur when one's waking state is intruded on by _____ sleep.
35. The disorder that involving sudden, irresistible sleep attacks is rare, but runs in families. This disorder has also been bred through several generations of dogs, which indicates that this condition is _____.
36. Although there is no known cure for this sleep attack disorder, the frequency and intensity of these attacks can be reduced by using a drug named _____.

Part 1: Connections

1. ___ insomnia
2. ___ hypersomnia

3. ___ periodic limb movement disorder
4. ___ restless legs syndrome
5. ___ sleep drunkenness
6. ___ somnambulism

7. ___ nightmare disorder

a. excessive daytime sleepiness
b. muscle twitches, primarily affecting the legs, that occur every 20 to 40 seconds and severely disturb sleep
c. state of panic during NREM sleep
d. sudden, irresistible sleep attack
e. difficult in getting to sleep or staying asleep
f. sudden temporary paralysis of the muscles, leading to complete body collapse
g. slow transition to clear consciousness after awakening sometimes associated with irritable or aggressive behavior

260

8. ___ night terror
9. ___ sleep apnea
10. ___ narcolepsy
11. ___ cataplexy

h. repeated interruption of breathing hundreds of times a night
i. irresistible urge to move the legs to relieve sensations of cramping, tingling, prickling, aching, or tension
j. vivid, recurrent bad dreams that occur during REM sleep and significantly disturb sleep
k. sleepwalking that occurs during NREM stages 3 and 4

Part 2: Connections

1. ___ temporary insomnia
2. ___ chronic insomnia
3. ___ drug-dependency insomnia
4. ___ stimulus control
5. ___ sleep restriction
6. ___ paradoxical intention
7. ___ tryptophan
8. ___ imagery rehearsal
9. ___ CPAP (continuous positive airway pressure) mask
10. ___ "back to sleep"
11. ___ overlaying

a. sleep loss caused by withdrawal from sleeping pills
b. amino acid that increases the amount of serotonin in brain and helps one sleep
c. helps prevent SIDS
d. occurs when a sleeping adult rolls over on top of an infant
e. used to treat sleep apnea in adults
f. linking a particular response with specific stimuli, such as sleep with the bed
g. usually caused by worry, stress and excitement and happens to everyone
h. used to eliminate nightmares
i. only sleeping during normal bedtime hours to avoid fragmenting sleep rhythms
j. an inability to sleep lasting for more than three weeks
k. by trying to keep eyes open as long as possible allows sleep to come unexpectedly

Check Your Memory

1. TRUE or FALSE   Artificial lighting, frenetic schedules, exciting pastimes, smoking, drinking, and overstimulation have contributed to a new epidemic of sleep problems.

2. TRUE or FALSE   If you have muscle twitches, especially of the legs that occur every 20 to 40 seconds and severely disturb sleep, you may have the sleep disturbance known as NREM behavior disorder.

3. TRUE or FALSE   Restless legs syndrome involves an irresistible urge to move one's legs to relieve sensations of cramping, tingling, aching, or tension.

4. TRUE or FALSE   If a person makes a slow transition to clear consciousness after awakening and is often irritable and aggressive when awakened, the person has a sleep disorder known as hypersomnia.

5. TRUE or FALSE   People who sometimes work days and then rotate to an evening shift may experience sleep-wake schedule disorder in which there is a mismatch between their bodily rhythm and the demands of their work environment.

6. TRUE or FALSE   Insomnia includes difficulty in going to sleep, frequent nighttime awakenings, waking too early, or a combination of these problems.

261

7. TRUE or FALSE   Worry, stress, and excitement can common reasons for temporary insomnia.

8. TRUE or FALSE   When you are experiencing temporary insomnia, it is best to get up and do something like reading and return to bed only when you begin to feel that you are struggling to stay awake.

9. TRUE or FALSE   If sleeping problems last for more than one week, then a diagnosis of chronic insomnia can be made.

10. TRUE or FALSE   Nonprescription sleeping pills, such as Sominex, Nytol, and Sleep-Eze have little sleep-inducing effects.

11. TRUE or FALSE   Barbiturates tend to increase both stage 4 sleep and REM sleep.

12. TRUE or FALSE   People who have taken barbiturates for insomnia must be painstakingly weaned from their sleep medicines, otherwise terrible nightmares and "rebound insomnia" may drive them back to drug use.

13. TRUE or FALSE   Sleep loss caused by withdrawal from sleeping pills is called sleep terror disorder.

14. TRUE or FALSE   Newer drugs, such as Ambien and Lunesta, which induce sleep, have possible side effects, which include amnesia, increased appetite, decreased sex drive, depression, and sleepwalking.

15. TRUE or FALSE   The behavioral remedy for insomnia that involves linking sleep with being in bed and linking sleep with a particular time of day is referred to as the paradoxical intention.

16. TRUE or FALSE   If an entire night's sleep is missed, one should either go to bed immediately and sleep late the next day or nap several hours that afternoon in order to regain the sleep lost.

17. TRUE or FALSE   A behavioral technique in which a person keeps their eyes open in the dark and stays awake as long as possible, allowing sleep to come unexpectedly, is called sleep restriction.

18. TRUE or FALSE   Eating starchy foods increase the amount of tryptophan, which increases the amount of serotonin in the brain and promotes relaxation and sleep.

19. TRUE or FALSE   People who sleepwalk are called somnambulists.

20. TRUE or FALSE   Sleepwalkers usually have their eyes open when they are "walking."

21. TRUE or FALSE   No sleepwalker has ever driven a car or played a musical instrument while asleep.

22. TRUE or FALSE   Sleepwalking and sleeptalking both occur when the person is in REM sleep.

23. TRUE or FALSE   Sexsomnia is a sleep disorder in which a sleeping person attempts to have sex with his or her bed partner.

24. TRUE or FALSE   When a person has a night terror, they usually remember this dream very vividly, while a person who has a nightmare disorder rarely remembers the dream.

25. TRUE or FALSE   Nightmares occur during NREM stage 4, while night terrors occur during REM sleep.

26. TRUE or FALSE   Night terrors are most common in childhood, but they continue to plague about two out of every 100 adults.

27. TRUE or FALSE   Imagery rehearsal can be used to eliminate nightmares.

28. TRUE or FALSE   A person who snores loudly, with short silences and loud gasps or snorts, is likely to be suffering from sleep drunkenness.

29. TRUE or FALSE   Narcolepsy is suspected as one cause of sudden infant death syndrome (SIDS), or "crib death."

30. TRUE or FALSE   Babies at risk for SIDS are often premature, have a shrill, high-pitched cry, engage in breath-holding, breathe mainly through an open mouth, or remain passive when their face rolls into a pillow or blanket.
31. TRUE or FALSE   To prevent SIDS, healthy babies are better off sleeping on their stomachs.
32. TRUE or FALSE   People with sleep apnea tend to fall directly into REM sleep.
33. TRUE or FALSE   Some cases of sleep apnea occur because the brain stops sending signals to the diaphragm to maintain breathing, while another cause is blockage of the upper air passages.
34. TRUE or FALSE   Treatments for sleep apnea include weight loss, surgery for breathing obstructions, and the use of the CPAP mask.
35. TRUE or FALSE   Research has indicated that narcolepsy is hereditary.
36. TRUE or FALSE   There is no known cure for narcolepsy, but a drug named sodium oxybate reduces the frequency and intensity of attacks.

Critical Thinking Question

Even without being told that somnambulism is an NREM event, you could have predicted that sleepwalking doesn't occur during dreaming. Why?

Dreams—A Separate Reality?

Survey Question: Do dreams have meaning?

Language Development Guide

ushered in: lead the way; guided
"golden era": period of great discovers
inquiry: investigation; study; analysis
"nondreamers": people who do not think they dream (but they do)
real time: actual seconds and minutes
"flashes" (of time): instances; the tiniest portion of a second
urgent: more critical; a more pressing need
suppressing: restraining; holding back
memory lapses: temporary failure to remember something
anxiety: dread, uneasiness based on an unclear threat
regard: consider; think
fantasies: daydreams; imagination
emphasize: call attention to; point out
unconscious: region of the mind that is beyond awareness
landmark: breakthrough; revolutionary
advanced: developed
proposals: offerings or suggestions
disguised: hidden, distorted
symbolic: stands for or represents something
manifest: obvious; visible
latent: hidden; covered
journey: trip; travels
trivial: minor; unimportant
"day residues": remains of the day's events
carryovers: leftovers; something remaining
radically: completely; totally
random: by chance

primitive: simple; crude; unsophisticated
classic: typical; usual
feedback: information returned about a response
reflect: show; reveal
perspective: point of view
continuity: connection; link
exotic: unusual; out of the ordinary
trapeze artist: a performer, usually in a circus, that swings on bars or ropes suspended high above
     the ground
exquisite: wonderful
relief: removal of something distressing or painful
reborn: revived; undergone a spiritual or emotional regeneration

Recite and Review

1. REM sleep was discovered in the year _____.
2. Dreams are usually spaced about _____ minutes apart.
3. To determine how important REM sleep is, a dream researcher awakened volunteers each time they entered REM sleep. This dream researcher was _____.
4. When the volunteers who were prevented from having REM sleep were finally allowed to sleep undisturbed, they dreamed extra amounts, an effect called a(n) _____.
5. In general, daytime disturbances are not related to the type of sleep lost but to the _____ of sleep lost.
6. Alcohol reduces sleep quality by suppressing _____ sleep
7. Internal conflicts and unconscious forces are emphasized in the _____ theories of dreaming.
8. The idea that dreams are expressions of unconscious desires, or wish fulfillment, first appeared in the landmark book entitled *The Interpretation of Dreams* (1900), which was written by _____.
9. Images in dreams that serve as visible signs of hidden ideas, desires, impulses, emotions, and relationships are called _____.
10. Bob has a dream that he is at his office, but he is in his underwear. This remembered part of Bob's dream is known as the _____ content.
11. Bob's dream of wearing his underwear at his office might be interpreted as Bob feeling vulnerable and unprepared for his new job. This interpretation would be considered the _____ content.
12. An attempt to explain how random activity in the lower brain centers results in the manufacture of relatively bizarre dreams by higher brain centers is called the _____ hypothesis.
13. The hypothesis that the lower brain centers are randomly "turned on" during REM sleep with higher brain areas trying to interpret this random activity was postulated by psychiatrists Alan Hopson and _____.
14. The theory that explains that our dreams are a conscious expression of REM sleep processes that are sorting and storing daily experiences is the _____ theory.
15. This theory that views dreams as reflecting everyday waking thoughts and emotions was proposed by _____.
16. According to Hopson, dreams tend to be more primitive and more bizarre than daytime thoughts because parts of the cortex are mostly shut down during REM sleep. The areas of the cortex that are shut down are the _____ areas.

17. Compared to dreams of flying, floating, and falling, the dream actions of running, jumping, riding, sitting, and talking occur _____ often.
18. Although each dream theory has strengths and weaknesses, studies of dream content tend to support the _____ theory.

Connections

1. ____ REM rebound
2. ____ wish fulfillment
3. ____ dream symbols
4. ____ manifest content
5. ____ latent content
6. ____ psychodynamic dream theory
7. ____ activation-synthesis hypothesis
8. ____ neurocognitive dream theory

a. hidden meaning content of a dream as revealed by dream interpretation and analysis
b. proposal that dreams reflect everyday waking thoughts and emotions
c. explains that random activity in lower brain centers results in the manufacture of relatively bizarre dreams by higher brain centers
d. the unconscious desire expressed in a dream
e. surface or "visible" content of a dream as remembered by the dreamer
f. images in dreams that serve as visible signs of hidden ideas, emotions, and relationships
g. explanation of dreaming that emphasizes internal conflicts and unconscious forces within the dreamer
h. occurrence of extra rapid eye movement sleep following sleep deprivation of this stage

Check Your Memory

1. TRUE or FALSE   REM sleep was discovered in 1898 by William Domhoff.
2. TRUE or FALSE   Most people dream four or five times a night, but not all people remember their dreams.
3. TRUE or FALSE   Dreams are usually spaced about 30 minutes apart with the first dream lasting about 30 minutes and the last one lasting about 10 minutes.
4. TRUE or FALSE   When William Dement deprived the participants in his experiment of REM sleep they developed a temporary sleep deprivation psychosis and exhibited psychotic behaviors, including hallucinations and paranoid delusions.
5. TRUE or FALSE   Alcohol reduces sleep quality by suppressing REM sleep, thus setting up a powerful REM rebound effect when the alcohol is withdrawn.
6. TRUE or FALSE   Missing any sleep stage can cause a rebound for that stage.
7. TRUE or FALSE   In general, daytime disturbances are related to the type of sleep lost rather than the total amount of sleep lost.
8. TRUE or FALSE   The psychodynamic theories of dreaming emphasize internal conflicts and unconscious forces.
9. TRUE or FALSE   Freud believed that dreams were based on wish fulfillment with these unconscious desires being expressed as disguised dream symbols.
10. TRUE or FALSE   The obvious, visible portion of a dream that the dreamer remembers is called the latent content, while the hidden, symbolic meaning is called the manifest content.
11. TRUE or FALSE   Freud did not believe that all dreams have a deeper meaning but that some dreams are trivial "day residues" or carryovers from ordinary waking events.

12. TRUE or FALSE   The activation-synthesis hypothesis explains that during REM sleep several lower brain centers are "turned on" in a random fashion with the higher brain centers manufacturing bizarre dreams as they interpret this random brain activity.

13. TRUE or FALSE   According to the neurocognitive dream theory, dreams reflect ordinary waking concerns because many brain areas that are active when we are awake remain active during dreaming.

14. TRUE or FALSE   Of the three main dream theories, recent studies of dream content tend to support the psychodynamic theory's emphasis on unconscious conflicts and desires being expressed as dream symbols.

15. TRUE or FALSE   Dreams tend to be more primitive and more bizarre than daytime thoughts because the frontal areas of the cortex, which control higher mental abilities, are mostly shut down during REM sleep.

16. TRUE or FALSE   The favorite dream setting is a faraway place that you may have never visited.

17. TRUE or FALSE   The action in dreams usually takes place between the dreamer and two or three other emotionally important people whether friends, enemies, loved ones, or employers.

18. TRUE or FALSE   Most people have unusual dreams of flying, floating, or falling rather than ones with common themes, such as running, sitting, or talking.

19. TRUE or FALSE   About half of all dreams have sexual elements.

Module 5.3 Hypnosis, Meditation, and Sensory Deprivation

Hypnosis—Look into My Eyes

Survey Question: What is hypnosis?

Language Development Guide

myths: falsehoods

centuries-old: 100's of years old

master: to meet the challenge of learning something well

circumstances: conditions

beneficial: helpful

heavy: tiring

magnets: substances or objects that produce a magnetic field (attract and repel objects)

relied: to depend on

magnetism: force of attraction or repulsion between various substances, such as iron

"animal magnetism": Mesmer's name for the mysterious force that he created with magnets to cure people of disease

rejected: discarded; cast off

branded: identified

coined: created; made up

surgeon: doctor that specializes in operations that cut and remove parts of the human body

proposed: suggested; put forth

dissociative: division or disruption of one's awareness

plunge: force; thrust; push

detached: separated

merely: just; only

blend: mixture; combination

conformity: bringing one's behavior into agreement with the behavior of others by choice

obedience: bringing one's behavior into agreement to the demands of an authority

266

autosuggestion: process of influencing one's own behavior in subtle (less obvious) ways

gain insight: obtain a clear understanding

metal nut: small block of metal with a central, threaded hole designed to fit around a bolt or screws (small bars of metal)

mental force: using the energy of one's mind

subtle: slight; less obvious

micromuscular movements: tiny changes in the positions and motion of muscles

automatic: happen without effort

intentionally: on purpose

voluntary intent: chosen purpose

incidentally: by the way

underlies: causes

Ouija boards: flat boards supposedly used to communicate with spirits and are marked with letters, numbers, and other symbols that spell out words as the pointer device (with the person's fingers resting on top) moves to a letter

self-therapy: making positive changes in oneself usually through reading self-help books

prevails: succeeds, wins

principles: theories and rules

mysterious: puzzling; unexplained

"magical": supernatural; paranormal

stage hypnotists: those who use hypnosis to entertain; often performing only a simulation of hypnosis

"let go": give permission to oneself to relax and not try to maintain control

vivid: detailed

basically: mainly; essentially

cooperate: to work with and comply with their requests

anesthesia: loss of sensation in an area of the body

lethargic: tired; sluggish

contrary: the opposite of

portrayed: represented; shown

immoral: morally wrong; wicked

repulsive: disgusting

disrobing: take clothing off

prone to: are likely to; have a tendency to

responsive: open; receptive

faking: pretending; acting

rigid: unable to bend; stiff

conclusions: findings; deductions

enhance: improve

false memories: when thoughts, inferences, and mental associations are mistaken for true memories

bar: forbid; prevent

testifying: give evidence; state under oath

claim: state; say; declare

"regress": going back to one's childhood

"age-regressed": procedure used in hypnosis that supposedly results in a person going back in their mind and reliving an actual event from sometime in their past, such as their childhood.

subjective experience: how one is personally encountering an event

intones: says

giggle: laugh nervously; silly laugh

squirm: twist and fidget in a sitting place

circus: performance involving wild animals, acrobats, aerial artists, clowns, etc.

simulation: imitation
"spoil the act": ruin the show
readily: willingly
disinhibits: lack of control or restraint
"director": manager; leader
loosen up: relax
stars of the show: main performers; center of attention
antics: actions involving clowning around
"ham": person who exaggerates their performance
taking advantage of the situation: having a favorable position because of these particular conditions
deception: trickery; fraud; con
impressive: remarkable; extraordinary
suspend: hang; dangle
astounding: amazing
nightclubs: establishments that are open late at night and provide alcoholic drinks, food, and
      entertainment

Recite and Review

1. Interest in hypnosis began in the 1700s when Austrian doctor believed that he could cure disease with magnets when, in reality, his treatments relied more on the power of suggestion. This Austrian doctor was _____.
2. The term *hypnosis* was coined by English surgeon _____.
3. The Greek word *hypnos* means "_____."
4. When EEG patterns recorded during hypnosis were compared to the EEG patterns of people who are asleep and to people pretending to be hypnotized, these patterns were found to be _____.
5. Hypnosis is often defined as an altered state of consciousness, characterized by narrowed attention and an increased openness to _____.
6. The best-known state theory of hypnosis was proposed by _____.
7. According to this state theory, hypnosis causes a "split" in awareness, called a(n) _____ state.
8. In a demonstration, hypnotized subjects who were told to feel no pain when they plunged one hand into a painful bath of ice water said they felt no pain and acted like they felt no pain, but with their free hand wrote, "It hurts." According to the state theory, the part of the hypnotized person that was aware of the pain but remained in the background is the _____.
9. Hypnosis is merely a blend of conformity, relaxation, imagination, obedience, and role-playing, according to the _____ theory of hypnosis.
10. Many theorists believe that all hypnosis is really self-hypnosis in which a person influences his or her own behavior in subtle ways, a behavior referred to as _____.
11. Ouija boards appear to answer questions without any conscious movements by the person. This can be explained by _____.
12. All techniques encourage a person (1) to focus attention on what is being said, (2) to relax and feel tired, (3) to "let go" and accept suggestions easily, and (4) to use vivid _____.
13. The tendency of hypnotized persons to carry out suggested actions as if they were involuntary is called the _____ effect.
14. Most people will not act out hypnotic suggestions that they consider repulsive or _____.
15. About eight people out of 10 can be hypnotized, but good hypnotic subjects occur in only _____ people out of 10.

16. How easily a person can become hypnotized is referred to as hypnotic _____.
17. A hypnotic test that includes such suggested behavior as the postural sway, eye closure, finger lock, and the hand lowering is called the _____.
18. Regarding its effects on memory, hypnosis frequently increases the number of _____ memories.
19. Given the proper instructions, a person can be made to smell a small bottle of ammonia and respond as if it were a wonderful perfume, illustrating how hypnosis can produce _____ changes.
20. A simulation of hypnosis for entertainment purposes is called _____.

Connections

1. ___ "animal magnetism"   a. explanation of hypnosis as a blend of conformity, relaxation, imagination, obedience, and role-playing

2. ___ hypnosis   b. tendency for hypnotized persons to carry out requested actions as if they were involuntary

3. ___ hidden observer   c. altered state of consciousness characterized by narrowed attention and increased suggestibility

4. ___ state theory of hypnosis   d. detached part of the hypnotized person's awareness that silently views the events happening

5. ___ nonstate theory of hypnosis   e. simulation of hypnosis for entertainment
6. ___ autosuggestion   f. one's capacity to become hypnotized
7. ___ basic suggestion effect   g. proposes that hypnosis causes dissociation, or "split" in awareness

8. ___ hypnotic susceptibility   h. influencing one's own behavior in subtle ways as in self-hypnosis

9. ___ stage hypnosis   i. treatment to cure diseases developed by Franz Mesmer

Check Your Memory

1. TRUE or FALSE   Interest in hypnosis began in the 1700s with Fritz Perls, who thought he could cure disease by putting people into an altered state of consciousness using magnets.

2. TRUE or FALSE   A surgeon named Stephen LaBerge coined the term "hypnosis," which comes from the Latin word for "trance."

3. TRUE or FALSE   EEG patterns recorded during hypnosis look the same as the EEG patterns of a person who is asleep or those of a person pretending to be hypnotized.

4. TRUE or FALSE   Hypnosis is often defined as an altered state of consciousness, characterized by narrowed attention and an increased openness to suggestion.

5. TRUE or FALSE   The best-known state theory of hypnosis was proposed by James Braid and explains that hypnosis is a blend of conformity, relaxation, imagination, obedience, and role-playing.

6. TRUE or FALSE   According to the state theory, the hidden observer is a detached part of the hypnotized person's awareness that silently observes events.

7. TRUE or FALSE   Many theorists believe that all hypnosis is really self-hypnosis or autosuggestion.

8. TRUE or FALSE   Autosuggestion is probably the reason that Ouija boards answer questions without any conscious movement by the person using the pointer.

9. TRUE or FALSE   All techniques for inducing hypnosis encourage a person (1) to focus attention on what is being said, (2) to relax and feel tired, (3) to "let go" and accept suggestions easily, and (4) to use vivid imagination.

10. TRUE or FALSE   The tendency of hypnotized persons to carry out suggested actions as if they were involuntary is called the mesmerism effect.

11. TRUE or FALSE   Most people will involuntarily act out hypnotic suggestions that they consider immoral or repulsive, such as disrobing in public or harming someone.

12. TRUE or FALSE   About three out of 10 people can be hypnotized, but only one out of 10 will be a good hypnotic subject.

13. TRUE or FALSE   Hypnosis depends more on the skills of the hypnotist than on the efforts or abilities of the hypnotized person.

14. TRUE or FALSE   Hypnotic susceptibility is measured by giving a series of suggestions and counting the number of times a person responds.

15. TRUE or FALSE   Some of the items found on the Stanford Hypnotic Susceptibility Scale are the amnesia test, the finger lock, and the postural sway.

16. TRUE or FALSE   While under hypnosis people will exhibit superhuman strength for a short time.

17. TRUE or FALSE   Many states now bar persons from testifying in court if they were hypnotized to improve their memory of a crime they witnessed.

18. TRUE or FALSE   Hypnosis can relieve pain especially in situations, such as phantom limb pain, where painkillers are ineffective.

19. TRUE or FALSE   Most theorists now believe that hypnotic subjects who are "age-regressed" are only acting out a suggested role.

20. TRUE or FALSE   Given the proper instructions, a hypnotized person can be made to smell a small bottle of ammonia and respond as if it were a wonderful perfume.

21. TRUE or FALSE   Hypnosis can alter color vision, hearing sensitivity, and one's time sense.

22. TRUE or FALSE   Hypnosis has been shown to be highly effective in helping people to stop smoking, drinking, and overeating.

23. TRUE or FALSE   Most instances of stage hypnosis are merely simulations of hypnosis for the purpose of entertainment.

24. TRUE or FALSE   During a stage performance, being labeled "hypnotized" takes away the personal responsibility of the volunteer who can then act silly without fear or embarrassment.

25. TRUE or FALSE   In order to suspend a person between two chairs (head on one chair and feet on the other), the person would have to be hypnotized.

Critical Thinking Question

What kind of control group would you need in order to identify the true effects of hypnosis?

Meditation—Chilling, the Healthy Way

Survey Question: Do meditation and sensory deprivation have any benefits?

Language Development Guide

focal point: main spot of one's attention
"open": receptive

270

expansive: large, wide
embrace: accept; adopt
nonjudgmental: tolerant; lenient
self-consciousness: awareness of one's thoughts and actions and how others might view them
wilderness: in areas away from civilization
core: main aspect
physiological: normal biological functioning
mechanisms: systems
pace: speed
distracting: diverting one's attention
immune system: protects the body from infections and foreign objects that enter it
foster: promote
clarity: clearness
concentration: attention
psychotherapy: any psychological method used to bring about positive changes in a person's personality, behavior, or adjustment
hint: clue
solitary confinement: in prison, being locked up by yourself
arctic: A region between the North Pole and the northernmost line of timber lands of North America, Europe, and Asia
high-altitude pilots: these pilots must wear confining pressurized space suits to fly this high
long-distance truck drivers: drive the interstate across the country almost continually
radar operators: focus on the movement of lighted dots on a screen in complete darkness
monotonous: boring, repetitive
distorted: unclear; fuzzy
prolonged: extended; made longer
isolation tanks: one floats in a dark chamber of water; see description and picture in this textbook section
habitual: usual; routine
"loosen" belief systems: weaken one's tendency to stick to one viewpoint
skilled sports: sports that have specific rules and require training and physical talent; not a leisure activity
marksmanship: skill at accurately shooting at a target with a gun of some type
elicit: draw out
leisure: free time; time off from work
fast-paced society: busy, hectic schedules; people are under time pressure at work
"space out": slang for disoriented; not thinking clearly or in an organized way
occasional: not often; infrequent; every now and then
mindless: not thinking clearly or in an organized way
attuned: adjusted or used to; aware of
sleepwalk through life: person is not aware of his or her surroundings; not thinking

Recite and Review

1. Meditation and sensory deprivation have been widely used as a means of altering consciousness through deep _____.
2. Meditation may be a distinct state of consciousness as evidenced by PET and fMRI scans, which show changes in the activity of the _____ lobes.
3. Petra is using the form of meditation in which she attends to a single focal point, such as an object, a thought, or her own breathing. Petra is using _____ meditation.
4. Roberto is using a type of meditation in which he widens his attention so that he becomes aware of everything around him. Roberto is using _____ meditation.

271

5. In comparing the two forms of meditation, the form that is the most difficult to attain is _____ meditation.
6. As part of her meditation exercise, Jane uses a smooth flowing word or sound, such as "om" to help her concentrate. This word is known as a(n) _____.
7. Medical researcher Herbert Benson believes that the core of meditation is an innate physiological pattern that opposes your body's fight-or-flight mechanisms called the _____ response.
8. The physical benefits of meditation include lowered heart rate, blood pressure, muscle tension, and other signs of stress as well as improved _____ system activity.
9. Research has shown that a variety of psychological disorders, from insomnia to excessive anxiety can be relieved and aggression and the illegal use of psychoactive drugs can be reduced through the use of _____ meditation.
10. Any major reduction in the amount or variety of sensory stimulation is called _____.
11. People sometimes have bizarre sensations, dangerous lapses in attention, and wildly distorted perceptions when faced with limited or _____ stimulation.
12. A form of mild sensory restriction that results in a variety of psychological benefits is called _____.
13. A small floatation tank in which people float in darkness and silence and can bring about deep relaxation is called a(n) _____ chamber.
14. Sensory restriction interrupts habitual behavior patterns, while deep relaxation makes people more open to _____.
15. If you are the type of person who finds it difficult to ignore upsetting thoughts, then the best way to promote relaxation would be through _____ meditation.
16. A state of open, nonjudgmental awareness of current experience is called _____.
17. Cancer patients have lower levels of distress and a greater sense of well-being when they are taught _____ meditation.

Connections

1. ___ concentrative meditation
2. ___ mindfulness meditation
3. ___ mantra
4. ___ relaxation response
5. ___ sensory deprivation (SD)

a. innate physiological pattern that opposes your body's fight-or-flight mechanisms
b. word used as the focus of attention in concentrative meditation
c. any major reduction in the amount or variety of sensory stimulation
d. mental exercise based on widening attention to become aware of everything experienced at any given moment
e. mental exercise based on attending to a single object or thought

Check Your Memory

1. TRUE or FALSE   Meditation and sensory deprivation have been widely used as a means of altering consciousness through deep relaxation.
2. TRUE or FALSE   During meditation, PET and fMRI scans reveal activity changes in the subcortical areas of the brain, but not within the cerebral cortex regions.
3. TRUE or FALSE   In mindfulness meditation, you attend to a single focal point, such as an object, a thought, or your own breathing.
4. TRUE or FALSE   A mantra is a word used in mindfulness meditation.
5. TRUE or FALSE   Mindfulness meditation is more difficult to attain than concentrative meditation.

272

6. TRUE or FALSE   During concentrative meditation, a person widens his or her attention to become aware of everything experienced at any given moment.

7. TRUE or FALSE   Medical researcher Herbert Benson believes that the core of meditation is the relaxation response, which is an innate physiological pattern that opposes the body's fight-or-flight mechanisms.

8. TRUE or FALSE   Research has shown that mindfulness meditation relieves a variety of psychological disorders, including insomnia and anxiety disorders.

9. TRUE or FALSE   Mindfulness mediation has been shown to reduce aggression and the illegal use of psychoactive drugs.

10. TRUE or FALSE   Sensory deprivation (SD) refers to any major reduction in the amount or variety of sensory stimulation.

11. TRUE or FALSE   Intense or prolonged sensory deprivation has been shown to be very relaxing.

12. TRUE or FALSE   Mild sensory deprivation has been shown to help people to quit smoking, lose weight, and reduce their use of alcohol and drugs.

13. TRUE or FALSE   Psychologist Peter Suedfeld calls the psychological benefits of mild sensory deprivation Restricted Environmental Stimulation Therapy (REST).

14. TRUE or FALSE   REST has shown promise in stimulating creativity and enhancing performances in skilled sports.

15. TRUE or FALSE   If a person finds it difficult to ignore upsetting thoughts, then mindfulness meditation may be the best solution to help the person relax.

16. TRUE or FALSE   A state of mindfulness involves allowing one's self to "space out" and have one's thoughts wander aimlessly.

17. TRUE or FALSE   Cancer patients who are taught mindfulness meditation have lower levels of distress and a greater sense of well-being.

Critical Thinking Question

Regular meditators report lower levels of stress and a greater sense of well-being. What other explanations must we eliminate before this effect can be regarded as genuine?

Module 5.4 Psychoactive Drugs

Drug-Altered Consciousness—The High and Low of It

Survey Question: What are the effects of the more commonly used psychoactive drugs?

Language Development Guide
Module 5.4

persistent: enduring; lasting; continuing
prescription: approved and given by a doctor to treat a specific condition
ease: relieve; lessen
induce: bring on; cause
potential: likelihood
illicit: unlawful
menu: lost of choices
overview: summary
abused: misused and overused
administer: give out
capable: able to
mimicking: imitating

273

circuitry: system of pathways

addictive: habit-forming, either physically or psychologically

nucleus accumbens: part of the forebrain found in the limbic system near hypothalamus, releases the neurotransmitter dopamine that increases pleasure

fool: trick; deceive

compulsion: very strong urge to engage in a particular activity

hook: curved or bent piece of metal used to catch something, such as a fish

snares: traps; catches

risk-taking: tendency to engage in harmful or dangerous behaviors

controlled substances: chemicals or drugs which are regulated by the government of a country regarding their production, purchase, or use

curiosity: interest in learning or finding out more about something

feelings of inadequacy: feeling unworthy; feeling like a failure

cope: deal with

consequences: results or outcomes

on demand: whenever needed or wanted

compulsive: habitual; uncontrollable

exceed: go beyond; surpass

predictors: cues that forecast what will occur in the near future

peers: people of equal status, age, etc.; friends

delinquency: a young person who frequently breaks the law

maladjustment: inability to emotionally deal with situations in one's environment

nonconformity: refusal to change one's behavior to go along with a social group

alienated: separated from others

impulsive: responding quickly without thinking; reckless

distressed: suffering; in pain

antisocial: not socialized; acting without a conscience; no remorse; no guilt

symptom: warning sign

dependencies: state of relying on and being controlled by this situation

cramps: painful contractions and spasms

crave: to want or yearn for something

social drinkers: those who casually drink small amounts of alcohol only at group gatherings

polydrug abuse: the abuse of two or more psychoactive drugs in combination

intravenously: drug administered using a needle into a blood vein

hepatitis: condition in which the liver becomes inflamed (swollen) and damaged

AIDS: acquired immunodeficiency syndrome, caused by the HIV virus transmitted through the exchange of blood and other fluids (sexually-transmitted); very serious and often fatal; no cure

Recite and Review

1. A substance capable of altering attention, judgment, memory, time sense, self-control, emotion, or perception is a(n) _____.
2. A substance that increases activity in the body and nervous system is called an "upper," or a(n) _____.
3. Greg is taking a drug that will decrease activity in his body and nervous system. Greg is taking a "downer," or _____.
4. Typically, drugs imitate or alter the effects of the chemicals that carry messages between brain cells called _____.
5. Some drugs block incoming messages by filling _____ sites on brain cells.
6. Nearly all addictive drugs produce feelings of pleasure by stimulating the brain's _____ circuitry.

274

7. Addictive drugs increase dopamine activity in the medial forebrain bundle and a brain region called the _____.
8. Because the brain systems that restrain their risk-taking are not as mature as those that reward pleasure seeking, the age group that are especially susceptible to addiction are _____.
9. Because drugs that can ease pain, induce sleep, or end depression have a high potential for abuse, the more powerful psychoactive drugs are _____ substances.
10. All the frequently abused drugs produce immediate feelings of pleasure, but with delayed _____.
11. Tia has built up a tolerance to alcohol and experiences withdrawal symptoms when she doesn't drink every day. Tia is exhibiting a(n) _____ dependence to alcohol.
12. Physical illness that follows removal of a drug is called _____.
13. A drug user is experiencing a reduced response to a drug and must take larger and larger doses to get the desired effect. This part of a physical addiction is called a(n) _____.
14. Michael feels that he must take Ecstasy on a regular basis in order to maintain emotional comfort and well-being. Michael has a(n) _____ dependence on Ecstasy.
15. Some psychologists define addiction as any _____ habit pattern.
16. Short-term drug use based on curiosity is referred to as _____ drug use.
17. Brent only uses Ecstasy when he is at a "rave" party. Brad's drug-taking behavior would be considered _____.
18. Andy is a long-haul trucker and uses amphetamines to stay awake for long periods of time. Andy's use of amphetamines would be considered _____ drug use.
19. Anna uses tranquilizers daily and is showing some elements of dependence. Anna's drug use would be considered _____.
20. If a person exhibits intense use of a drug and extreme dependence, he or she is exhibiting _____ drug use.
21. The abuse of more than one drug at the same time is called _____ abuse.
22. When one drug enhances the effect of another, drug _____ have occurred.
23. Alcohol, amphetamines, barbiturates, morphine, and nicotine are drugs that are most likely to lead to a (n)_____ dependence.
24. Using just about any psychoactive drug can lead to a(n) _____ dependence.
25. People are at high risk for developing hepatitis and AIDS if they take drugs _____.

Connections

1. ____ stimulant (upper)
2. ____ depressant (downer)
3. ____ psychological dependence
4. ____ withdrawal symptoms
5. ____ drug tolerance
6. ____ nucleus accumbens
7. ____ experimental drug use
8. ____ social-recreational drug use
9. ____ situational drug use

a. short-term use of drugs based on curiosity
b. abuse of more than one drug at the same time
c. addictive drugs increase the dopamine activity in this brain region
d. drug-taking behavior characterized by the daily use of the drug with some elements of dependence
e. drug-taking behavior characterized by extreme dependence on the drug
f. use of drugs for a specific problem, such as needing to stay awake
g. drug is necessary to maintain emotional comfort or well-being
h. one drug enhances the effect of another
i. occasional use of drugs for pleasure, relaxation, or when interacting with other people

10. ___ intensive drug use

j. substance that increases activity in the body and nervous system

11. ___ compulsive drug use

k. physical illness and discomfort following removal of a drug

12. ___ drug interactions

l. reduction in the body's response to a drug

13. ___ polydrug abuse

m. substance that decreases activity in the body and nervous system

Check Your Memory

1. TRUE or FALSE   Prescription drugs that can ease pain, induce sleep, or end depression have a high potential for abuse.

2. TRUE or FALSE   The most common way to deliberately alter human consciousness is to administer a psychoactive drug.

3. TRUE or FALSE   Caffeine, alcohol, and nicotine are considered psychoactive drugs.

4. TRUE or FALSE   Psychoactive drugs can be placed on a scale ranging from stimulation to hallucinogenic to narcotic to no effect.

5. TRUE or FALSE   The most powerful psychoactive drugs are known as controlled substances.

6. TRUE or FALSE   Some drugs, such as Ecstasy, amphetamines, and some antidepressants directly stimulate brain cells by mimicking neurotransmitters.

7. TRUE or FALSE   Cocaine causes more neurotransmitters to be released, increasing the activity of the brain cells.

8. TRUE or FALSE   Addictive drugs increase acetylcholine activity in the midbrain bundle and the medulla oblonga, which, in turn, stimulates the parietal cortex.

9. TRUE or FALSE   Addictive drugs physically change the brain's reward circuitry, making it harder for the addict to overcome his or her addiction.

10. TRUE or FALSE   Adolescents are especially susceptible to addiction because brain systems that restrain their risk-taking are not as mature as those that reward pleasure-seeking.

11. TRUE or FALSE   All of the frequently abused drugs produce immediate pleasure with delayed punishment.

12. TRUE or FALSE   Taking drugs is a symptom, rather than a cause, of personal and social maladjustment.

13. TRUE or FALSE   The best predictors of adolescent drug use and abuse are drug use by peers, parental drug use, delinquency, parental maladjustment, poor self-esteem, social nonconformity, and stressful life changes.

14. TRUE or FALSE   Persons who develop a psychological dependence on a drug experience drug tolerance and physical withdrawal symptoms.

15. TRUE or FALSE   The physical illness that follows removal of a drug is referred to as a drug tolerance.

16. TRUE or FALSE   Some psychologists define addiction as any compulsive habit pattern, which means that if a person has lost control over his or her drug use, for whatever reason, the person is addicted.

17. TRUE or FALSE   Some people remain social drinkers for life, whereas others become alcoholics within weeks of taking their first drink.

18. TRUE or FALSE   A person whose use of drugs is short-term and based on curiosity would be classified as a social-recreational user.

19. TRUE or FALSE   A person who uses drugs to cope with a specific problem, such as needing to stay awake, would be classified as an intensive user.

20. TRUE or FALSE   The abuse of more than one drug at the same time is called multimodal drug use.
21. TRUE or FALSE   The drugs that are most likely to lead to physical dependence are the hallucinogens, such as LSD, mescaline, and psilocybin.
22. TRUE or FALSE   When one drug enhances the effect of another, it is called a multiplicative combination.
23. TRUE or FALSE   Using just about any drug can result in psychological dependence.
24. TRUE or FALSE   People who take drugs intravenously are at high risk for developing hepatitis and AIDS.

Uppers—Amphetamines, Cocaine, MDMA, Caffeine, Nicotine

Language Development Guide

synthetic: artificial; man-made
street names: slang terms for objects, such as drugs
legitimate: lawful; rightful; valid
hyperactivity: excessive movement and restlessness
"study drugs": drugs taken to focus better while doing school work
offset: counteracted; made up for
worrisome: troublesome; causes one to worry
potent: powerful; strong
variation: alternative; option
snorted: inhaled
injected: put into a vein with a needle
backyard labs: illegal production of an illicit drug
massive: huge; large
fueled: increased; added to
subculture: a social group that is part of a larger culture and is distinguished by its status, religion, behavior, or other factors
speed freaks: a person who has reached a high level of addiction to amphetamines
binge: rapid or continuous use
"crash": the extreme tiredness and depression that follows several days of continued amphetamine
pose: cause; establish
crippling: disabling; impairing
irritability: being touchy and in a bad mood
paranoid delusions: being overly suspicious of others with false beliefs that someone is out to harm you
extracted: take out; remove from
coca plant: South American shrub from which cocaine is extracted
euphoria: feeling very happy and excited; overjoyed
boundless: unlimited; endless
potions: tonic; liquid remedy; medicine
cure-alls: a remedy or medicine that supposedly can be effectively used to treat any illness
"real thing": a joke about Coca-Cola's ad campaign that called this soft drink, the "real thing"
metabolized: chemically broken down and used by the body
rivals: competes with; challenges
access: right to use
irresistible: uncontrollable; overpowering
convulsions: seizures; tremors; spasms

"rush": intense pleasurable sensation

jarring: jolting; shocking

paranoia: extreme suspicion and mistrust

boredom: dullness; monotony

pattern: design; model

ripe: ready

progress: develop; advance

endangered: put in danger

Cocaine Anonymous: twelve-step program involving support group meetings that help people to recover from a drug addiction

on the horizon: a development that is soon to occur

vaccine: injection given to a person to prevent the occurrence of an illness or, in this case, an addiction

clinical trials: experiment to determine the safety and effectiveness of a drug

serotonin: neurotransmitter important in mood regulation

dilated: open, widen

elevated: raise; make higher

jaw clenching: tightening of jaw muscles that bring the top and bottom teeth very tightly together

appetite: desire for food

diminishes: reduces

retarding: slowing, delaying

orgasm: climax and release of sexual excitement

publicity: information in the media

arrhythmias: out of normal rhythm

"rave" parties: dance parties in which Ecstasy is often used

impact: effect

and that's not counting Seattle!: joke, Seattle is known for its frequent coffee drinking

inhibit: hold back; slow down

apparent: obvious; evident; visible

breast cysts: tiny rounded sac found in the breast that is filled with fluid or semisolid substances

miscarriage: spontaneous loss of an unborn embryo or fetus before 24 weeks of gestation

modest: fairly small

toxic: poisonous; deadly

chain-smoking: smoking one cigarette after another for pleasure

array: collection; display

relapse: go back to

abstinence: self-denial

bronchitis: inflammation of the larger breathing tubes within the lungs

fertility: the degree to which one is capable of producing offspring

urban cowboys: person who grew up in a city but displays the behaviors, customs, and dress thought to be a part of a rural culture

Skol bandits: small amount of tobacco (snuff) in a small tea bag-like pouch that is placed in mouth with the nicotine being absorbed through the skin of the mouth

chewing tobacco: shredded strands of tobacco leaves placed between the cheek and gum or chewed with the nicotine absorbed through the skin in the mouth

snuff: ground, powdery tobacco, which can be sniffed through the nose as a dry powder or as a moist powder placed on the gum or put in pouches to be absorbed through the skin of the mouth

pinch: a small amount, referring to the amount of snuff or chewing tobacco put into the mouth

smokeless tobacco: chewing tobacco and snuff

equivalent: the same as

278

secondary smoke: also called second-hand smoke; passive smoking; inhaling the smoke of tobacco products used by other people

irresponsible: careless; reckless; neglectful

expose: subjecting or placing one in a situation, usually a harmful one, such as exposing children to secondary smoke

taper: shrink; decrease

cold turkey: stopping use all at once

advocates: supporters; believers

resume: restart

nicotine patches: a nonprescription stick-on patch that gradually releases nicotine through the skin to help tobacco-users gradually give up tobacco

nicotine gum: an nonprescription chewable product containing nicotine used to help tobacco users gradually give up tobacco

Recite and Review

1. Synthetic stimulants that have common street names such as "speed," "bennies," or "dexies" are called _____.

2. Once widely prescribed for weight loss or depression, today the main legitimate medical use for these synthetic stimulants is to treat childhood hyperactivity and overdoses of _____ drugs.

3. Adderall and Ritalin are mixtures of these synthetic stimulants and are frequently used to treat _____.

4. The illegal use of Adderall and Ritalin by normal college students to improve their focus while doing school work has produced only slight improvement in problem-solving performance, which has been offset by a slight loss of _____.

5. The more potent variation of these synthetic stimulants, which is made cheaply in backyard labs and can be snorted, injected, or eaten is _____.

6. Most abusers of this potent variation of synthetic stimulants end up taking ever-larger doses to get the desired effect, which illustrates that this drug rapidly produced a(n) drug _____.

7. True speed freaks typically go on binges lasting several days, and then afterwards due to a lack of food and sleep, they "_____."

8. These synthetic stimulants can also cause a loss of contact with reality with affected users having paranoid delusions and often becoming violent toward themselves or others. This condition is known as _____.

9. A powerful central nervous system stimulant extracted from the leaves of the coca plant is _____.

10. This stimulant derived from the leaves of the coca plant increases the chemical messengers dopamine, which produces a "rush" of pleasure, and _____, which arouses the brain.

11. Coca-Cola now contains caffeine, but from 1886 until 1906, Coca-Cola contained small amounts of _____.

12. During the withdrawal from the more potent stimulant drugs, persons may experience an inability to feel pleasure called _____.

13. A vaccine is currently undergoing clinical trials that would prevent the stimulation of the nervous system by the drug _____.

14. The drug that produces a rush of energy with users saying it makes them feel closer to others and heightens sensory experiences is Ecstasy, also known as _____.

15. Ecstasy causes brain cells to release extra amounts of the neurotransmitter _____.

16. Emergency room doctors see many Ecstasy cases, including Ecstasy-related deaths caused by heart arrhythmias and elevated body temperature known as _____.

17. Ecstasy diminishes sexual performance, impairing erection in 40 percent of men and in both men and women it retards _____.
18. Ecstasy use at "rave" parties actually does intensify the impact of the music, but the end result is often overstimulation of the brain, which can result in a "rebound" _____.
19. The most frequently used psychoactive drug in North America is _____.
20. Edna drinks about 15 to 20 cups of coffee a day. She has been experiencing insomnia, irritability, loss of appetite, chills, racing heart, and elevated body temperature, which are all signs of _____.
21. The natural stimulant that is found mainly in tobacco and is so toxic that it is sometimes used to kill insects is _____.
22. The average age that a person smokes their first cigarette is _____.
23. The percent of people who relapse within one year of quitting smoking is _____ percent.
24. A burning cigarette releases a large variety of potent cancer-causing substances, or _____.
25. Chewing tobacco and snuff are referred to as _____ tobacco.
26. Along with the other types of cancers, users of chewing tobacco and snuff run a higher risk of developing _____ cancer.
27. It is particularly irresponsible of smokers to expose young children, who are especially vulnerable, to _____ smoke
28. It becomes an all-or-nothing proposition when people quit smoking by going _____.
29. The best way to taper off on one's smoking is by using a method known as _____.
30. During the process of quitting smoking, many people find that using nicotine patches or gum helps them get through the _____ period

Connections

1. ___ amphetamines
2. ___ amphetamine psychosis
3. ___ cocaine
4. ___ anhedonia
5. ___ MDMA ("Ecstasy")
6. ___ caffeine
7. ___ caffeinism
8. ___ nicotine
9. ___ carcinogens

a. inability to feel pleasure, often seen in withdrawal

b. most frequently used psychoactive drug in North America

c. chewing tobacco and snuff with users having a higher risk of developing oral cancer

d. natural stimulant found mainly in tobacco; so toxic sometimes used to kill insects

e. drug often used a "rave" parties; causes brain cells to release extra serotonin with users saying it makes them feel closer to others and heightens sensory experiences

f. method of quitting a drug by tapering off, delaying, or stretching one's use of the drug

g. loss of contact with reality with paranoid delusions that often result in the abuser becoming violent to self or others

h. unhealthy dependence with numerous physical and psychological complaints; often seen in people who drink 15 or more cups of coffee a day

i. method of quitting a psychoactive drug by stopping the drug abruptly and completely

280

10. ___ smokeless tobacco

11. ___ secondhand smoke

12. ___ "cold turkey"

13. ___ scheduled gradual reduction

j. synthetic stimulants that go by the street names of "speed," "bennies," and "dexies"

k. cancer-causing substances, many of which are released in burning cigarettes

l. passive exposure to tobacco smoke which can result in lung cancer for the victims

m. powerful central nervous system stimulant extracted from the leaves of the coca plant

Check Your Memory

1. TRUE or FALSE   Amphetamines are synthetic stimulants.
2. TRUE or FALSE   Today, the main legitimate medical uses of amphetamines are to encourage weight loss and treat depression.
3. TRUE or FALSE   Drugs used to treat attention deficit/hyperactivity disorder (ADHD) consist of mixtures of tranquilizers.
4. TRUE or FALSE   When normal college students have taken Adderall and Ritalin as "study drugs," they may see a slight increase in creativity with a slight decrease in problem-solving performance.
5. TRUE or FALSE   Methamphetamine is a more potent variation of amphetamine and can be snorted, injected, or eaten.
6. TRUE or FALSE   Amphetamines rapidly produce a drug tolerance.
7. TRUE or FALSE   Amphetamines supply energy by decreasing the body's use of its resources.
8. TRUE or FALSE   Amphetamines can cause a loss of contact with reality called cataplexy.
9. TRUE or FALSE   The smokable form of crystal methamphetamine is known as "crack" on the street.
10. TRUE or FALSE   Although the rumor still persists, the soft drink Coca-Cola never contained even small amounts of cocaine.
11. TRUE or FALSE   At the turn of the twentieth century, dozens of nonprescription potions and cure-alls (medicines) contained cocaine.
12. TRUE or FALSE   The main difference between the effects of amphetamines and cocaine is that cocaine lasts several hours, while amphetamines are quickly metabolized.
13. TRUE or FALSE   Cocaine tends to decrease the chemical messengers acetylcholine and adrenaline.
14. TRUE or FALSE   A person who stops using cocaine experiences heroin-like withdrawal symptoms.
15. TRUE or FALSE   An inability to experience pleasure is called anhedonia and is experienced by cocaine users when cocaine is withdrawn.
16. TRUE or FALSE   Signs of cocaine abuse include compulsive use, loss of control, and disregarding consequences.
17. TRUE or FALSE   A vaccine is currently undergoing clinical trials that prevents cocaine from stimulating the nervous system.
18. TRUE or FALSE   The drug MDMA, or Ecstasy, is chemically similar to benzodiazepine tranquilizers.
19. TRUE or FALSE   Ecstasy causes brain cells to decrease the amount of serotonin present.
20. TRUE or FALSE   MDMA tends to decrease body temperature, heart rate, and blood pressure.
21. TRUE or FALSE   Ecstasy does intensify the music at "rave" parties, which can result in overstimulation and a "rebound" depression that can persist for months.

281

22. TRUE or FALSE   Heavy users of Ecstasy typically do not perform well in tests of learning and memory and show some signs of underlying brain damage.

23. TRUE or FALSE   Caffeine stimulates the brain by blocking chemicals that normally inhibit or slow nerve activity.

24. TRUE or FALSE   Overuse of caffeine may result in an unhealthy dependence known as caffeinism.

25. TRUE or FALSE   Caffeine encourages the growth of breast cysts in women, and may contribute to bladder cancer, heart problems, and high blood pressure.

26. TRUE or FALSE   People who drink two or three cups of coffee a day will not experience any withdrawal symptoms if they stop using caffeine.

27. TRUE or FALSE   The most frequently used psychoactive drug in North America is nicotine.

28. TRUE or FALSE   Nicotine is so toxic that it is sometimes used to kill insects.

29. TRUE or FALSE   The average age of a person trying their first cigarette is 11, and it takes five years before dependence sets in.

30. TRUE or FALSE   The symptoms of nicotine withdrawal may last from two to six weeks and may be worse than heroin withdrawal.

31. TRUE or FALSE   Up to 90 percent of people who quit smoking relapse within a year.

32. TRUE or FALSE   A burning cigarette releases a large variety of carcinogens, which harm nearly every organ of the body.

33. TRUE or FALSE   The combined health risks of smoking reduce the life expectancy of the average smoker by 10 to 15 years.

34. TRUE or FALSE   Smokeless tobacco, such as chewing tobacco and snuff, are considered safe alternatives to smoking cigarettes because they release smaller amounts of nicotine and do not appear to cause cancer.

35. TRUE or FALSE   Secondary smoke has not been shown to cause lung cancer or heart disease.

36. TRUE or FALSE   Quitting cigarettes cold turkey tends to work better for most people than gradually quitting.

Critical Thinking Question

The U.S. government, which helps fund antismoking campaigns and smoking-related health research, also continues to subsidize tobacco growers. Can you explain this contradiction?

Downers—Sedatives, Tranquilizers, and Alcohol

Language Development Guide

"solid alcohol": effects of barbiturates are similar to "liquid alcohol"
properties: characteristics
sedative: drug that calms the body
on the street: when sold illegally "on the street"
degreasing solvent: substances that clean surfaces by dissolving the oil, grease, other particles
drain cleaner: substance used to dissolve the solid clogs, such as hair, within a drain
get high: experience a drug intoxication
mini-epidemic: small outbreak
socialize: meet and hang out with other people
margin: space; leeway
gag reflex: contraction in the back of the throat that helps prevent chocking agitation
leery: doubtful; distrustful

degrease your brain: jokingly pointing out that the drug GHB made from a degreasing solvent can damage your brain

alleviate: lessen

spike drinks: when substances are illegally placed into people's drinks without their knowledge with the intention of harming them

unwary: unsuspecting

"date rape" drug: Rohypnol is referred to by this name because it has been used in numerous rapes of both women and men

prelude: lead into; comes before

learned the hard way: learning by an actual bad experience

gulped: drank and swallowed quickly; swallowing a mouthful

brew: mixture

fermented: conversion of grain, fruit, potatoes, etc. (carbohydrates) to alcohol by using yeasts

distilled: heating the fermented liquid and condensing or concentrating it

animation: liveliness; enthusiasm

aphrodisiac: substance that supposedly increases sexual desire

drink "provokes the desire, but it takes away the performance": alcohol is thought to increase sexual arousal, but causes problems during sexual intercourse

alarming: shocking; upsetting

wasted: unable to think, speak, or move normally

trips to the ER: situations that require medical assistance at the emergency room of a hospital

brain power: ability to think

wit: a comic; a clever person

the conscience dissolves in alcohol: alcohol causes bad moral or ethical decisions

temptation: appeal; attraction; enticement

overestimate: misjudge; miscalculate; expecting the number to be greater

lured: drawn in; tempted

sobering up: being without alcohol, so one is clear-headed

"dried out": cutting off the person's supply of alcohol

mutual-help approach: participants help each other and in doing so help themselves

premise: idea; principle

stay "dry": not drink alcohol

hit rock bottom: lose everything, be at the worst time of your life

rational: based on logic and reason

deny: reject; disagree with

Recite and Review

1. Barbiturates and tranquilizers are sometimes referred to as "solid _____."
2. Sedative drugs that depress the nervous system and go by the street names of "blue heavens," "yellow jackets," "goof balls," or "pink ladies" are called _____.
3. A central nervous system depressant that is a mixture of degreasing solvent and drain cleaner and goes by the street name of "scoop" is _____.
4. Compared to the amount typically taken by users, potentially fatal doses of "scoop" are only _____ times that amount.
5. Some users of "scoop" choke to death on their own vomit because this drug inhibits the _____ reflex.
6. Valium is the best known example of the drugs that lower anxiety and reduce tension and called _____.

7. A drug that is odorless and tasteless, lowers inhibitions, produces intoxication, induces short-term amnesia, and has been used as a "date rape" drug is sold under the trade name of _____.
8. It is especially risky to combine barbiturates or tranquilizers with _____.
9. Alcohol is classified as a(n) _____ drug.
10. At a party, Greg downs five alcoholic drinks in a short period of time, while his girlfriend Anna has four alcoholic drinks during this same period. The term for this type of drinking is called _____ drinking.
11. Research has shown that the percent of brain power (memory capacity) lost by teenagers and young adults who drink too much alcohol is as much as _____ percent.
12. What sets alcohol abusers apart from social drinkers is that alcohol abusers also drink to cope with _____.
13. Regulating one's drinking in social situation involves such things has limiting drinking to the first hour of a social event and practicing how to refuse drinks politely but firmly. This approach is known as _____ drinking.
14. Research has shown that college students are often lured into overdrinking because they often _____ how much their fellow students are drinking.
15. Treatment for alcohol dependence begins with sobering up the person and cutting off his or her supply during the phase referred to as _____.
16. One mutual-help approach that has been fairly successful takes a spiritual approach while acting on the premise that it takes a former alcoholic to understand and help a current alcoholic. This approach is known as _____.
17. Other group approaches to treating alcohol abuse offer a rational, nonspiritual approach and include Secular Organizations for Sobriety (SOS) and _____.
18. There is a strong tendency for abusive drinkers to _____ they have a problem.

Connections

1. ___ barbiturates
2. ___ GHB
3. ___ tranquilizers
4. ___ alcohol
5. ___ binge drinking
6. ___ paced drinking
7. ___ detoxification
8. ___ Alcoholics Anonymous (AA)
9. ___ Rational Recovery

a. intoxicating element in fermented and distilled liquors
b. withdrawal of person from alcohol during alcohol treatment
c. sedative drugs that depress brain activity; used to calm patients or induce sleep
d. mutual-help group for treating alcohol abuse that takes a spiritual approach
e. depressant that is a mixture of degreasing solvent and drain cleaner
f. non-spiritual group approach for treating alcohol abuse
g. drugs that lower anxiety and reduce tension and include Valium and Xanax
h. consuming five or more alcoholic drinks in a short time for men; four drinks for women
i. regulating drinking during social situations so that one remains comfortable, pleasant, and coherent

Check Your Memory

1. TRUE or FALSE   Barbiturates are sedative drugs that are medically used to calm patients or to induce sleep.

2. TRUE or FALSE At mild dosages, barbiturates have an effect similar to alcohol intoxication.

3. TRUE or FALSE Barbiturates are often taken in excess amounts because a first dose may be followed by others, as the user becomes uninhibited or forgetful.

4. TRUE or FALSE Mild GHB intoxication can produce anxiety, social phobia, and low-level hallucinations.

5. TRUE or FALSE No deaths from overdoses of GHB have been reported.

6. TRUE or FALSE Currently, GHB is not classified as a controlled substance.

7. TRUE or FALSE GHB is often manufactured in homes by combining degreasing solvent with drain cleaner.

8. TRUE or FALSE Valium and Xanax are classified as benzodiazepine tranquilizers.

9. TRUE or FALSE Rohypnol can induce short-term amnesia and sleep and has been used as a "date rape" drug in the spiked drinks of unsuspecting victims.

10. TRUE or FALSE Since they have the same effect on the nervous system, combing barbiturates or tranquilizers with alcohol is rarely a problem.

11. TRUE or FALSE Alcohol is classified as a stimulant drug and an aphrodisiac.

12. TRUE or FALSE One American dies every 20 minutes in an alcohol-related car crash.

13. TRUE or FALSE Binge drinking is defined as three or more drinks in a short time for men and two or more drinks in a short time for women.

14. TRUE or FALSE Research has shown that teenagers and young adults who drink too much may lose as much as 10 percent of their brain power.

15. TRUE or FALSE What sets alcohol abusers apart from social drinkers is that alcohol abusers also drink to cope with negative emotions, such as anxiety and depression.

16. TRUE or FALSE In paced drinking, a person limits their drinking primarily to the last hour of a social event or party.

17. TRUE or FALSE Research has shown that college students tend to underestimate how much their fellow students at a party are drinking.

18. TRUE or FALSE The phase of alcohol treatment known as detoxification consists of restoring the person's health and the use of antidepressants and psychotherapy to treat the addiction.

19. TRUE or FALSE The mutual help group known as Rational Recovery takes a spiritual approach, while Alcoholics Anonymous (AA) takes a nonspiritual approach.

20. TRUE or FALSE Eighty percent of those who remain in AA for more than one year get through the following year without a drink.

Hallucinogens—Tripping the Light Fantastic

Language Development Guide

psychotic-like: having characteristics of a person who has lost touch with reality
anesthetic: drug that produces loss of awareness and feeling; used to put person to sleep (for surgery)
incidentally: by the way
tragedy: disaster; heartbreaking misfortune
derived: resulting from; made from
resinous: like the sap or plant secretions; yellowish-brown and the consistency of tar
scraped: rubbed; scratched; grated
subtle: faint; slight
despite this: even with
hazardous: dangerous; risky

as a matter of fact: actually; really

accumulates: builds up

seat: center; headquarters

realm: area, domain

people who smoke dope may act like dopes: joke stating that people who smoke marijuana act like stupid people

regain: recover; get back

hydrocarbons: organic compounds of hydrogen and carbon (many harmful), such as benzene and methane found in tobacco smoke

tar: dark, oily substance containing hydrocarbons

prostate: gland within the male reproductive system

cervical: pertaining to the lower narrow end of the uterus (the cervix) in the woman's reproductive system

marginally: slightly, just barely

ovulation: release of the woman's egg or ovum from the ovaries

detrimental: harmful

"what's in the pot": joke referring to the harmful contaminants often found in marijuana

ebb and flow: to going out and coming in, like a wave that flows into the beach and returns back to sea; to increase and then decrease

Recite and Review

1. Substances that alter or distort sensory impressions are called _____
2. The most popular illicit drug in America is _____.
3. Reggie is taking a drug that can produce hallucinations and psychotic-like disturbances even when taken in small amounts. Reggie is "dropping acid," also known as _____.
4. The main active chemical in marijuana is _____.
5. Van is taking a hallucinogenic drug derived from the peyote cactus. This drug is _____.
6. The drug known as "magic mushrooms" or "shrooms" is _____.
7. An anesthetic known as "angel dust, that has stimulant, depressant, and hallucinogenic effects is _____.
8. The dried leaves and flowers of the hemp plant are known as _____.
9. When Cannabis leaves are scraped, they yield a resinous material called _____.
10. THC accumulates in the body's fatty tissues, especially in the brain and _____ organs.
11. Although both types of dependence are possible, marijuana's potential for abuse lies primarily in the realm of _____ dependence.
12. For about a day after people smoke marijuana, there is impairment in their attention, coordination, and _____ memory.
13. Compared to the amount of cancer-causing hydrocarbons in tobacco smoke, marijuana smoke has _____.
14. Regarding sperm production in males, marijuana temporarily _____ it.
15. THC can increase the risk of disease because it suppresses the body's _____ system.
16. Activity levels in the part of the brain that controls coordination, are lower than normal in marijuana abusers. This part of the brain is the _____.

Connections

1. ____ hallucinogen

   a. main active chemical in marijuana; accumulates in body's fatty tissues, especially brain and reproductive organs

2. ____ LSD

   b. also known as "magic mushrooms" or "shrooms"

286

3. ___ mescaline

4. ___ psilocybin

5. ___ PCP

6. ___ marijuana

7. ___ hashish

8. ___ THC

c. classification of substances that alter or distort sensory impressions

d. anesthetic with hallucinogenic effects; also known as "angel dust"

e. consists of the dried leaves and flowers of the hemp plant

f. also known as "acid"; in small amounts can produce hallucinations and psychotic-like disturbances

g. consists of the resinous material scraped from Cannabis leaves

h. hallucinogen derived from peyote cactus

Check Your Memory

1. TRUE or FALSE   Marijuana is the most popular illicit drug in America.
2. TRUE or FALSE   THC, which is the main active chemical in marijuana, is classified as a mild hallucinogen.
3. TRUE or FALSE   When taken in tiny amounts, LSD can produce hallucinations and psychotic-like disturbances in thinking and perception.
4. TRUE or FALSE   Psilocybin is derived from the peyote cactus, while mescaline comes from mushrooms.
5. TRUE or FALSE   The anesthetic, which has hallucinogenic, stimulant, and depressant effects is PCP.
6. TRUE or FALSE   Hashish consists of the dried leaves and flowers of the hemp plant, while marijuana is the resinous material scraped from Cannabis leaves.
7. TRUE or FALSE   At high dosages, marijuana can produce paranoia, hallucinations, and delusions.
8. TRUE or FALSE   No overdose deaths from marijuana have been reported.
9. TRUE or FALSE   THC accumulates in the body's fatty tissues, especially the brain and reproductive organs.
10. TRUE or FALSE   Naturally occurring chemicals similar to THC may help the brain cope with pain and stress.
11. TRUE or FALSE   Although both types of dependence are possible, marijuana's potential for abuse lies primarily in the realm of physical addiction, not psychological dependence.
12. TRUE or FALSE   Frequent marijuana users show small declines in learning, memory, attention, and thinking abilities.
13. TRUE or FALSE   When surveyed at age 29, nonusers are healthier, earn more, and are more satisfied with their lives than people who smoke marijuana regularly.
14. TRUE or FALSE   Tobacco smoke contains 50 percent more cancer-causing hydrocarbons and 16 times more tar than marijuana smoke.
15. TRUE or FALSE   Marijuana lowers sperm production in males, and users produce more abnormal sperm.
16. TRUE or FALSE   THC can actually enhance the body's immune system, decreasing one's risk of disease.
17. TRUE or FALSE   Activity levels in the cerebellum are lower than normal in marijuana abusers, which explain why chronic marijuana users tend to show some loss of coordination.
18. TRUE or FALSE   Children whose mothers smoked marijuana during pregnancy show lowered ability to succeed in challenging, goal-oriented activities.

287

Critical Thinking Question

Why do you think there is such a contrast between the laws regulating marijuana and those regulating alcohol and tobacco?

Module 5.5 Psychology in Action: Exploring and Using Dreams

Survey Question: How can dreams be used to promote personal understanding?

Language Development Guide

acquainted: familiar; aware
catch a dream: remember your dream
disrupt: interrupt; upset
recall: remember
plot: story line
diary: journal; record; log
enrichment: enhancement; improvement
pioneering: ground-breaking; new; original
literal: meaning exactly what they say
exhibitionist: person who displays his or her genitals to unwilling viewers; "flashing"
vulnerable: helpless; weak
playwright: author of the play
primitive: simple, basic
comical: funny; amusing
would be blind: did not see
puns: a witty play on words
pinned: held down; restrained
"twisting your arm": pressuring someone
mythical: fabled; fairy-tale
striving: determined; motivated
apprehension: uneasiness; dread
originator: inventor; creator
"re-owned": to take responsibility for one's own feelings
waking fantasy: daydream
paradoxes: contradictions, confusing problems
pharmacologist: scientist who researches the effects of drugs
tremendous: great; wonderful
breakthrough: advancement; step forward
scribbled: writing quickly; jotting down
"set": position; fix yourself
steep: soak; saturate
"workshop": educational class or work session
engulfed: swallowed up; overwhelmed
enlightening: making clear; increasing one's knowledge

Recite and Review

1. When "catching a dream" in order to remember it, natural awakening almost always follows soon after a(n) _____ period.
2. During the process of "catching a dream", it is important upon awakening, to lie still and review the dream images with your eyes _____.

288

3. In "catching a dream," you should record your dreams in chronological order in a permanent dream _____ .

4. Regarding whether they increase or decrease dreaming, alcohol, amphetamines, cocaine, and valium have all been found to _____ REM sleep.

5. Regarding its effects on dreaming, LSD tends to slightly _____ REM sleep.

6. Mabel drinks three or four cola drinks during the day. Regarding REM sleep, we would expect the caffeine to have _____ effect.

7. To unlock dreams, Freud identified four mental filters that disguise the meanings of dreams. These filters are called _____ .

8. According to Freud, a dream character that looks like a teacher, acts like your father, talks like your mother, and is dressed like your employer might represent all the authority figures in your life. This one dream character representing many people in your life illustrates the mental filter known as _____ .

9. A student angry at his parents might dream of accidentally wrecking their car instead of directly attacking them. This redirection toward safer images would be an example of the dream filter known as _____ .

10. The nonliteral expression of the dream content that Freud interpreted represents the dream filter known as _____ .

11. When we remember a dream, we have a tendency to make the dream more logical and to add details, which is the dream filter known as _____ .

12. A dream should be thought of as a play with a setting, cast, and plot and the dreamer as the playwright, according to dream theorist _____ .

13. Dreams are primarily "feeling statements" with the overall emotional tone of a dream being the major clue to its meaning, according to dream theorist _____ .

14. The originator of Gestalt therapy considered most dreams a special message about what's missing in our lives or feelings that need to be "renowned." This dream theorist was

_____ .

15. An approach to dream analysis that some find helpful is to "take the part of" or "speak for" each of the characters and objects in the dream. This approach was developed by

_____ .

16. In order to conclude a dream or carry it to a more meaningful ending, a person can continue the dream as a(n) _____ .

17. Nightmare sufferers can use an approach to "reprogram" their own nightmares called

_____ .

18. The story of Dr. Otto Loewi dreaming about an experiment that he later performed is an example of using dreams to produce _____ solutions.

19. Dreaming can be especially useful in solving problems that require a fresh point of view, since dreaming reduces your _____ .

20. Being able to take advantage of dreams for problem solving is improved if you visualize or think intently about a problem, reviewing all relevant information before you go to bed. In other words, you have "_____" yourself before retiring.

21. Camden is dreaming when she begins to feel that she is really awake during this dream and is capable of normal thought and action. Camden is experiencing a(n) _____ dream.

22. In an experiment at the Stanford University Sleep Research Center, participants gave prearranged signals, such as a clenched fist, when they became aware they are dreaming. This research was conducted by dream researcher _____ .

23. Because the dream participants in the Stanford research were able to clench their fists when they knew they were dreaming illustrates that in this state, dreamers can partially overcome REM sleep _____ .

24. Sleeping in a hammock, a boat, or a waterbed may increase the number of _____ dreams.

289

25. These dreams in which the dreamer feels awake are increased when sleeping in a hammock because this swaying motion stimulates the _____ system.

Connections

1. ___ Freud's dream processes
2. ___ condensation
3. ___ displacement
4. ___ symbolization
5. ___ secondary elaboration
6. ___ Hall's approach to dream analysis
7. ___ Cartwright's approach to dream analysis
8. ___ Perls' approach to dream analysis
9. ___ lucid dreaming

a. mental filters that hide the true meanings of dreams
b. directing emotions or actions toward safe or unimportant dream images
c. dreams are a special message about what's missing in one's life; helpful for person to "speak for" each character and object in the dream
d. the nonliteral expression of dream content
e. dreams are plays; dreamer is playwright; consider setting, cast of characters, plot, and emotions portrayed in a dream
f. combining several people, objects, or events into a single dream image
g. dreamer feels awake and capable of normal thought and action
h. making a dream more logical and complete while remembering the dream
i. the overall emotional tone of a dream is the major clue to its meaning

Check Your Memory

1. TRUE or FALSE   Natural awakening almost always follows soon after a REM period.
2. TRUE or FALSE   To "catch a dream," it is important, upon awakening, to sit up in bed immediately with your eyes wide open and say the dream details out loud.
3. TRUE or FALSE   Dream memories disappear quickly, so to "catch a dream" you have to review the dream and preserve it by writing about it or by recording it.
4. TRUE or FALSE   Amphetamines and cocaine increase REM sleep.
5. TRUE or FALSE   Alcohol, barbiturates, and Valium decrease REM sleep.
6. TRUE or FALSE   LSD tends to decrease REM sleep slightly, while marijuana slightly increases REM sleep.
7. TRUE or FALSE   Caffeine has no effect on REM sleep.
8. TRUE or FALSE   To unlock dreams, Otto Loewi identified six dream processes that disguise the meaning of dreams.
9. TRUE or FALSE   When several people, objects, or events are combined into one dream image, the dream process is known as displacement.
10. TRUE or FALSE   Directing emotions or actions toward safer or unimportant dream images is known as secondary elaboration.
11. TRUE or FALSE   While remembering a dream, if the person makes the dream more logical and complete, then condensation has taken place.
12. TRUE or FALSE   Dream theorist Calvin Hall preferred to think of dreams as plays with a setting, cast of characters, and a plot and the dreamer as a playwright.
13. TRUE or FALSE   Dream theorist Rosalind Cartwright takes a psychodynamic approach to dream analysis and believes one must look for the symbolic meaning of each person, place, or situation that is present in the dream.

290

14. TRUE or FALSE Describing your dream to family members and friends can be harmful because their interpretations are based on their experiences, not yours.
15. TRUE or FALSE Fritz Perls considers most dreams as special messages about what's missing in our lives, what we avoid doing or feelings that need to be "re-owned."
16. TRUE or FALSE An approach that Perls found helpful was to "take the part of" or "speak for" each of the characters or objects in the dream.
17. TRUE or FALSE Dreamers can also gain insight through a dream exercise in which one continues a dream as a waking fantasy so that the dream may be concluded or carried on to a more meaningful ending.
18. TRUE or FALSE Nightmare sufferers can use a technique known as the paradoxical intention to modify their own nightmares.
19. TRUE or FALSE Although experiments are being conducted, there has been no research findings to date that has shown that dreams can be used to enhance creativity.
20. TRUE or FALSE The dreams of nonimaginative people tend to be less vivid and can rarely be used for personal growth.
21. TRUE or FALSE During a sleep spindle episode, a person feels as if she or he is fully awake within the dream world and capable of normal thought and action.
22. TRUE or FALSE Persons in a lucid state of dreaming can partially overcome REM sleep paralysis.
23. TRUE or FALSE Sleeping in a hammock, a boat, or on a waterbed tends to decrease the number of lucid dreams a person has.

Critical Thinking Question

The possibility of having a lucid dream raises an interesting question: If you were dreaming right now, how could you prove it?

Final Survey and Review—Completion

Module 5.1 States of Consciousness and Sleep
States of Consciousness—The Many Faces of Awareness
Survey Question: What is consciousness?
1. The only way that you can understand what your best friend is thinking is through an objective, _____ point of view.
2. You are in your college class and are presently in a state of clear, organized alertness, which is known as _____ consciousness.
3. A high fever, dehydration, and sleep loss can all produce a(n) _____ of consciousness.

Module 5.1 Sleep—Catching a Few ZZZ's
Survey Question: What are the effects of sleep loss or changes in sleep patterns?
4. Ted is trying to go to college during the day and then work late at night. Due to this schedule, he experiences excessive daytime sleepiness which is known as _____.
5. Sleep-deprived Ted is sitting in class with his head leaning on his hand when suddenly Ted momentarily falls asleep with his head slipping off his hand. Ted has just experienced a(n) _____.
6. Pia only requires four to five hours of sleep per night to feel refreshed. Pia is one of a small percentage of people who are referred to as _____.

291

Module 5.1 Stages of Sleep—The Nightly Roller-Coaster

Survey Question: Why do we sleep?

7. The true boundary of sleep occurs when a sleeper exhibits sleep spindles during stage _____.

8. During one's deepest sleep, an EEG will show a preponderance of slow _____ waves.

9. If you are worried about two upcoming tests and a report that are due, you will most likely show an increase in the basic state of sleep known as _____ sleep.

10. Clancy is convinced that she has been abducted by space aliens and undergone their horrible medical tests because she has awakened several mornings unable to move, felt electrical sensations going through her body, heard buzzing sounds, and felt the presence of others in the room. Clancy is most likely experiencing a sleep disturbance known as _____.

Module 5.2 Sleep Disturbances and Dreaming

Sleep Disturbances—The Sleepy Time Blues

Survey Question: What are some sleep disorders and unusual sleep events?

11. LaTonya has been having trouble going to sleep for over a month. She is experiencing _____ insomnia.

12. Eating a few cookies or some pretzels before going to bed always makes Marty sleep. This is because these starchy snacks increase an amino acid known as _____.

13. A preschooler who sits up in bed and screams out in his sleep in a state of panic but does not remember the incident in the morning most likely had a(n) _____.

14. Tony snores very lightly when he sleeps with moments of silence that are immediately followed by Tony gasping for air. Tony most likely has a sleep disorder known as _____.

15. Sudden, irresistible sleep attacks in which the person falls directly into REM sleep characterizes a sleep disorder known as _____.

Module 5.2 Dreams—A Separate Reality?

Survey Question: Do dreams have meaning?

16. Because of his overuse of alcohol over the last few weeks, Don's REM sleep has been suppressed. After he stops drinking, Don may experience extra amounts of dreaming, particularly nightmares, due to a condition known as _____.

17. You dream that you are sitting in a coffee shop with three of your friends. These literal, remembered details about your dream make up the _____ content.

18. The dream theorist that believed that dreams express unconscious desires and conflicts as disguised dream symbols was _____.

19. The dream theory that explains that dreams reflect your waking concerns, such that an athlete would dream about winning the game is the _____ theory.

Module 5.3 Hypnosis, Meditation, and Sensory Deprivation

Hypnosis—Look into My Eyes

Survey Question: What is hypnosis?

20. Hypnosis is often defined as an altered state of consciousness, characterized by an increased openness to suggestion and narrowed _____.

21. According to the state theory, hypnosis causes a dissociative state in which one part of the person's awareness silently views the events as they transpe. This detached part of awareness is known as the _____.

22. Both Carol and Petra have their fingers on the pointer of the Ouija board and are asking "it" questions. The pointer seems to move without any conscious effort by either girl. This situation is best explained by the concept of _____.

23. Bart is taking a test that will determine if he would make a good hypnotic subject. The test, which includes such items as the finger lock and the postural sway is called the _____.
24. During stage hypnosis, volunteers are unusually cooperative because they don't want to "spoil the act," so they readily follow almost any instruction given by the hypnotist-entertainer. This is referred to as _____ suggestibility.

Module 5.3 Meditation—Chilling, the Healthy Way
Survey Question: Do meditation and sensory deprivation have any benefits?
25. If Joan uses a mantra during her meditation exercise, she is most likely using the form known as _____ meditation.
26. The core of meditation, according to Herbert Benson, is the relaxation response, which opposes the body's _____ mechanisms.
27. Carmen spends an hour in darkness and silence in a small floatation tank. She is achieving deep relaxation through a brief form of _____.

Module 5.4 Psychoactive Drugs
Drug-Altered Consciousness—The High and Low of It
Survey Question: What are the effects of the more commonly used psychoactive drugs?
28. Alana is taking a substance that increases activity in the body and nervous system. This substance would be described as an "upper," or a(n) _____.
29. Ecstasy, amphetamines, and some antidepressants increase the activity of brain cells by causing more _____ to be released.
30. When Leon stops administering heroin, he experiences violent flu-like symptoms of nausea, vomiting, diarrhea, chills, sweating, and cramps, which are referred to as _____ symptoms.
31. Darby is using amphetamines as well as tranquilizers and alcohol. Darby is exhibiting _____ abuse.

Module 5.4 Uppers—Amphetamines, Cocaine, MDMA, Caffeine, Nicotine
32. Once widely prescribed for weight loss or depression, today the main legitimate medical use for amphetamines is to treat overdoses of depressant drugs and childhood _____.
33. Carlo has been abusing amphetamines to the extent that he has a loss of contact with reality and is having paranoid delusions and has become violent towards his family. Carlo's condition is known as _____.
34. From 1886 until 1906, Coca-Cola contained small amounts of cocaine, which was replaced with a stimulant called _____.
35. Several dancers at a "rave" party have been brought to an emergency room because of heart arrhythmias and elevated body temperature. The stimulant drug that these dancers most likely consumed was _____.
36. Denise is a frequent user of the most used psychoactive drug in North America, which is _____.
37. Jay has decided to quit smoking cigarettes "cold turkey," when a more effective way to quit smoking would be to use the method known as _____.

Module 5.4 Downers—Sedatives, Tranquilizers, and Alcohol
38. Regarding how they affect the nervous system, alcohol, barbiturates, GHB, and benzodiazepine tranquilizers are all considered _____ drugs.

293

39. Sera has been prescribed a drug to help her sleep. She will need to be careful when taking this drug since it is often taken in excess amounts because a first dose may be followed by others, as the user becomes uninhibited or forgetful. Sera has most likely been prescribed a(n) _____.

40. A mini-epidemic of a drug made from a mixture of degreasing solvent and drain cleaner has taken place, especially at nightclubs and raves with this drug producing euphoria, a desire to socialize, and a mild loss of inhibitions. This drug is _____.

41. Valium and the "date rape" drug called Rohypnol are examples of a class of drugs known as _____.

42. Carrie is at a party and has consumed four mixed alcoholic drinks within a two-hour period. Carrie's alcohol intake would be considered _____ drinking.

43. Due to his alcohol addiction, Willard was taken to a medical facility in which he was sobered up and his supply of alcohol was cut off. This phase of rehab is referred to as _____.

Module 5.4 Hallucinogens—Tripping the Light Fantastic

44. Kelsey is using a drug that is classified as an anesthetic, but which has stimulant, depressant, and hallucinogenic properties. Kelsey is most likely using the drug known as "angel dust," or _____.

45. Barbara and her friends are using a hallucinogen referred to as "magic mushrooms" or "shrooms." They are using the drug known as _____.

46. The THC in marijuana accumulates in the body's fatty tissues, especially in the reproductive organs and the _____.

47. Garth, who frequently smokes marijuana, seems to be constantly sick. Garth's numerous illnesses may be due to marijuana's tendency to suppress the body's _____ system.

Module 5.5 Psychology in Action: Exploring and Using Dreams

Survey Question: How can dreams be used to promote personal understanding?

48. Regarding increases or decreases in REM sleep, Brian's use of cocaine will most likely _____ his REM sleep.

49. You are angry with your roommate and dream that you "accidentally" lose a message from her boyfriend. This redirection toward a safer alternative for your anger would be an example of the dream filter known as _____.

50. In analyzing her client's dreams, Dr. Able concentrates only on the emotional tone of the dream rather than the actions that take place. Dr. Able is utilizing the dream analysis technique of _____.

51. When Tori dreams, she often realizes while she is still asleep that she is dreaming and can change the dream. Tori is experiencing _____ dreaming.

Final Survey and Review—Matching

Module 5.1 States of Consciousness and Sleep

1. ___ altered state of consciousness (ASC)

    a. distinctive bursts of brain wave activity that indicate a person is asleep

2. ___ microsleep

    b. reflex muscle twitch that occurs as your muscles relax during stage 1 sleep

3. ___ sleep-deprivation psychosis

    c. caused by a lack of muscle paralysis during REM sleep

4. ___ alpha waves

    d. sleep that occurs during stages 1, 2, 3, and 4 and "calms" the brain

5. ___ beta waves

6. ___ delta waves

7. ___ hypnic jerk

8. ___ sleep spindles

9. ___ REM sleep

10. ___ non-REM (NREM) sleep

11. ___ REM behavior disorder

12. ___ hypnopompic hallucinations

e. temporary state brought about by severe sleep loss; includes confusion, disorientation, delusions, and hallucinations

f. large, slow brain waves associated with relaxation and falling asleep as seen in stage 1 sleep

g. sleep that is associated with dreaming, "sharpens" our memories, and is increased by daytime stress

h. caused by sleep paralysis occurring just before you wake up with person feeling like they are suffocating, floating, or that an alien being is in their bedroom

i. small, fast brain waves associated with being awake and alert

j. large, slow brain waves that occur in deeper sleep stages 3 and 4

k. brief shift in brain-wave patterns to those of sleep

l. states of consciousness that occur from delirium, hypnosis, drugs, and sensory overload

Module 5.2 Sleep Disturbances and Dreaming

1. ___ insomnia
2. ___ hypersomnia
3. ___ somnambulism
4. ___ nightmare disorder

5. ___ night terror

6. ___ sleep apnea

7. ___ narcolepsy

8. ___ paradoxical intention

9. ___ REM rebound

10. ___ psychodynamic dream theory

11. ___ activation-synthesis hypothesis

12. ___ neurocognitive dream theory

a. excessive daytime sleepiness
b. sudden, irresistible sleep attack
c. state of panic during NREM sleep
d. explains that random activity in lower brain centers results in the manufacture of relatively bizarre dreams by higher brain centers

e. repeated interruption of breathing hundreds of times a night

f. difficulty in getting to sleep or staying asleep

g. explanation of dreaming that emphasizes internal conflicts and unconscious forces within the dreamer

h. occurrence of extra rapid eye movement sleep following sleep deprivation of this stage

i. by trying to keep eyes open as long as possible allows sleep to come unexpectedly

j. proposal that dreams reflect everyday waking thoughts and emotions

k. vivid, recurrent bad dreams that occur during REM sleep and significantly disturb sleep

l. sleepwalking that occurs during NREM stages 3 and 4

Module 5.3 Hypnosis, Meditation, and Sensory Deprivation

1. ____ hidden observer
2. ____ state theory of hypnosis
3. ____ nonstate theory of hypnosis
4. ____ basic suggestion effect
5. ____ hypnotic susceptibility
6. ____ concentrative meditation
7. ____ mindfulness meditation
8. ____ mantra
9. ____ relaxation response
10. ____ sensory deprivation (SD)

a. mental exercise based on attending to a single object or thought
b. tendency for hypnotized persons to carry out requested actions as if they were involuntary
c. innate physiological pattern that opposes your body's fight-or-flight mechanisms
d. any major reduction in the amount or variety of sensory stimulation
e. word used as the focus of attention
f. mental exercise based on widening attention to become aware of everything experienced at any given moment
g. proposes that hypnosis causes dissociation, or "split" in awareness
h. one's capacity to become hypnotized
i. explanation of hypnosis as a blend of conformity, relaxation, imagination, obedience, and role-playing
j. detached part of the hypnotized person's awareness that silently views the events happening

Module 5.4 Psychoactive Drugs

1. ____ marijuana
2. ____ caffeine
3. ____ LSD
4. ____ barbiturates
5. ____ MDMA ("Ecstasy")
6. ____ psilocybin
7. ____ cocaine
8. ____ GHB
9. ____ PCP
10. ____ amphetamines
11. ____ alcohol
12. ____ nicotine
13. ____ mescaline
14. ____ tranquilizers

a. drugs that lower anxiety and reduce tension and include Valium and Xanax
b. powerful central nervous system stimulant extracted from the leaves of the coca plant
c. intoxicating depressant in fermented and distilled liquors
d. natural stimulant; so toxic sometimes used to kill insects
e. anesthetic with hallucinogenic effects; also known as "angel dust"
f. hallucinogen derived from peyote cactus
g. also known as "magic mushrooms" or "shrooms"
h. synthetic stimulants that go by the street names of "speed," "bennies," and "dexies"
i. also known as "acid"; in small amounts can produce hallucinations and psychotic-like disturbances
j. depressant that is a mixture of degreasing solvent and drain cleaner
k. sedative drugs that depress brain activity; used to calm patients or induce sleep
l. hallucinogen derived from the dried leaves and flowers of the hemp plant
m. stimulant often used a "rave" parties; causes brain cells to release extra serotonin
n. most frequently used psychoactive drug in North America

296

Module 5.5 Psychology in Action: Exploring and Using Dreams

1. ___ Freud's dream analysis
2. ___ Hall's dream analysis
3. ___ LaBerge's dream research
4. ___ Perls' dream analysis
5. ___ Cartwright's dream analysis

a. use of dream processes, such as condensation and displacement
b. the overall emotional tone of a dream is the major clue to its meaning
c. dreams are a special message about what's missing in one's life; helpful for person to "speak for" each character and object in the dream
d. use of lucid dreaming
e. dreams are plays; dreamer is playwright; consider setting, cast of characters, plot, and emotions portrayed in a dream

Final Survey and Review—True or False

Module 5.1 States of Consciousness and Sleep
States of Consciousness—The Many Faces of Awareness
Survey Question: What is consciousness?

1. TRUE or FALSE   It is not possible to know the first-person experience of other people.
2. TRUE or FALSE   Sleep, dreaming, and daydreaming are three examples of altered states of consciousness.
3. TRUE or FALSE   Altered states of consciousness are due to innate biological rhythms and cannot be environmentally-caused.

Module 5.1 Sleep—Catching a Few ZZZ's
Survey Question: What are the effects of sleep loss or changes in sleep patterns?

4. TRUE or FALSE   While you are asleep, it is possible to learn a simple skill, but not a complex one, such as mathematics.
5. TRUE or FALSE   Rapid physical changes during puberty increase an adolescent's need for sleep.
6. TRUE or FALSE   If you go for more than 60 hours without sleep, you may experience REM behavior disorder.

Module 5.1 Stages of Sleep—The Nightly Roller-Coaster
Survey Question: Why do we sleep?

7. TRUE or FALSE   When you are relaxed and allowing our thoughts to drift, an EEG would show that you have a preponderance of beta brain waves.
8. TRUE or FALSE   Dreamless slow-wave NREM sleep increases after physical exertion.
9. TRUE or FALSE   REM sleep helps us sort and retain memories, especially memories about strategies for solving problems.
10. TRUE or FALSE   Amy's muscles do not paralyze when she is in REM sleep, which indicates that she has a condition known as hypersomnia.

Module 5.2 Sleep Disturbances and Dreaming
Sleep Disturbances—The Sleepy Time Blues
Survey Question: What are some sleep disorders and unusual sleep events?

11. TRUE or FALSE   An irresistible urge to move one's legs to relieve sensations of cramping, tingling, aching, or tension is known as somnambulism.

12. TRUE or FALSE   Nonprescription sleep aids have been shown to be very effective in treating temporary and chronic insomnia.

13. TRUE or FALSE   A behavioral technique in which a person keeps their eyes open in the dark and stays awake as long as possible, allowing sleep to come unexpectedly, is called the imagery rehearsal.

14. TRUE or FALSE   Both sleepwalking and night terrors occur during NREM sleep.

15. TRUE or FALSE   Treatments for narcolepsy include weight loss, surgery for breathing obstructions, and the use of the CPAP mask.

Module 5.2 Dreams—A Separate Reality?

Survey Question: Do dreams have meaning?

16. TRUE or FALSE   Dreams occur in a "flash" with no dream lasting longer two minutes.

17. TRUE or FALSE   The psychodynamic theories of dreaming emphasize that dreams are continuations of our waking concerns and do not have deep symbolic meanings.

18. TRUE or FALSE   The activation-synthesis hypothesis states that when the forebrain is activated, it creates the manifest content of dreams, which is then synthesized into the deep latent content of dreams by the lower more primitive brain regions.

19. TRUE or FALSE   The action in dreams usually takes place between you and stranger in an unfamiliar place.

Module 5.3 Hypnosis, Meditation, and Sensory Deprivation

Hypnosis—Look into My Eyes

Survey Question: What is hypnosis?

20. TRUE or FALSE   The term *hypnosis* was coined by an English doctor named Ernest Hilgard.

21. TRUE or FALSE   EEG patterns recorded during hypnosis are different from those observed when a person is asleep or pretending to be hypnotized.

22. TRUE or FALSE   Most people will not act out hypnotic suggestions that they consider immoral or repulsive.

23. TRUE or FALSE   No state in the United States bars persons from testifying in court if they were hypnotized to improve their memory of a crime they witnessed.

24. TRUE or FALSE   Generally, hypnosis is more successful at changing subjective experience than it is at modifying behaviors such as smoking or overeating.

Module 5.3 Meditation—Chilling, the Healthy Way

Survey Question: Do meditation and sensory deprivation have any benefits?

25. TRUE or FALSE   Mindfulness meditation is easier to attain than concentrative meditation.

26. TRUE or FALSE   If a person finds it difficult to ignore upsetting thoughts, then concentrative meditation may be the best solution to help the person relax.

27. TRUE or FALSE   Although mild sensory deprivation can be very relaxing, it has not been shown to be effective in helping people to quit smoking, lose weight, and reduce their use of alcohol and drugs.

298

Module 5.4 Psychoactive Drugs
Drug-Altered Consciousness—The High and Low of It
Survey Question: What are the effects of the more commonly used psychoactive drugs?

28. TRUE or FALSE   Nicotine and opiates directly stimulate brain cells by mimicking neurotransmitters.
29. TRUE or FALSE   Addictive drugs intensify feelings of pleasure by stimulating a brain region called the corpus callosum.
30. TRUE or FALSE   Drug tolerance and withdrawal symptoms define the development of a psychological dependence.
31. TRUE or FALSE   A person who uses drugs to cope with a specific problem, such as needing to stay awake, would be classified as a compulsive user.

Module 5.4 Uppers—Amphetamines, Cocaine, MDMA, Caffeine, Nicotine

32. TRUE or FALSE   When normal college students have taken Adderall and Ritalin as "study drugs," they may see a slight increase in problem-solving performance and a slight decrease in creativity.
33. TRUE or FALSE   The main difference between the effects of amphetamines and cocaine is that the effects of amphetamines last several hours, while cocaine is quickly metabolized.
34. TRUE or FALSE   The inability to experience pleasure after cocaine withdrawal is known as cataplexy.
35. TRUE or FALSE   MDMA, also called Ecstasy, is chemically similar to amphetamines.
36. TRUE or FALSE   Moderate caffeine use of up to three cups of coffee per day has not been shown to be harmful to a woman's pregnancy or to her unborn child.
37. TRUE or FALSE   The average age of a person trying their first cigarette is 15, and it takes about a year before dependence sets in.

Module 5.4 Downers—Sedatives, Tranquilizers, and Alcohol

38. TRUE or FALSE   GHB is classified as a controlled substance, which makes its possession a felony.
39. TRUE or FALSE   Some abusers of barbiturates suffer severe emotional depression that may end in suicide.
40. TRUE or FALSE   The noisy animation at drinking parties is due to alcohol's effect as a stimulant drug.
41. TRUE or FALSE   Binge drinking is a serious sign of alcohol abuse.
42. TRUE or FALSE   In paced drinking, a person limits their drinking primarily to the first hour of a social event or party.
43. TRUE or FALSE   Only twenty percent of those who remain in AA for more than one year get through the following year without a drink.

Module 5.4 Hallucinogens—Tripping the Light Fantastic

44. TRUE or FALSE   The hallucinogen mescaline is derived from the peyote cactus.
45. TRUE or FALSE   Marijuana smoke contains 50 percent more cancer-causing hydrocarbons and 16 times more tar than tobacco smoke.
46. TRUE or FALSE   Marijuana has not been shown to cause either physical or psychological dependence.
47. TRUE or FALSE   The loss of coordination shown by chronic marijuana users is caused by the activity levels in the limbic system of the brain being lowered by the THC in the marijuana.

Module 5.5 Psychology in Action: Exploring and Using Dreams

Survey Question: How can dreams be used to promote personal understanding?

48. TRUE or FALSE   Caffeine tends to significantly increase REM sleep.
49. TRUE or FALSE   While remembering a dream, if the person makes the dream more logical and complete, then, according to Freud, secondary elaboration has occurred.
50. TRUE or FALSE   Dream theorist Fritz Perls preferred to think of dreams as plays with a setting, cast of characters, and a plot and the dreamer as a playwright.
51. TRUE or FALSE   Sleeping in a hammock, a boat, or on a waterbed tends to increase the number of lucid dreams a person has.

Mastery Test

1. Delirium, euphoria, fatigue, and daydreaming all have in common the fact that they are
   a. forms of normal waking consciousness.
   b. caused by sensory deprivation.
   c. perceived as subjectively real.
   d. altered states of consciousness (ASCs).

2. The difficulty of knowing other minds is why the early behaviorists distrusted
   a. the use of introspection.
   b. objective studies of humans.
   c. stimulus-response explanations for behavior.
   d. the natural sciences.

3. The sweat lodge ceremony of the Sioux Indians is used to create altered states as a
   a. source of pleasure and recreation.
   b. form of punishment.
   c. pathway to personal enlightenment.
   d. test of courage and a rite of passage for the males of the tribe.

4. Which of the following statements about sleep is FALSE?
   a. Humans spend approximately 25 years of their life asleep.
   b. Not all animals sleep.
   c. If a person does not eventually sleep, he or she will go into a stupor, a coma, and then die.
   d. Humans are able to learn complex skills, such as mathematics or a foreign language, while asleep.

5. Rapid physical changes during puberty increases an adolescent need to sleep, but the quality and quantity of their sleep tends to decrease during the teen years, resulting in excessive daytime sleepiness known as
   a. insomnia.
   b. narcolepsy.
   c. hypersomnia.
   d. sleep apnea.

6. Persons who have not slept for a day or two are susceptible to brief shifts in brain activity to the pattern normally recorded during sleep, which is referred to as
   a. microsleep.
   b. sleep apnea
   c. the hypnopompic state.
   d. lucid sleeping.

7. Which of the following statements about sleep and sleep patterns is TRUE?
   a. If light-dark cycles are removed, humans eventually shift to a sleep-waking cycle that averages 22 hours.
   b. People older than 50 average nine hours of sleep a night.
   c. Natural sleep patterns have a ratio of three to one between time awake and time asleep.
   d. Most people who have not slept for a day or two can still do interesting or complex mental tasks.

8. Becca is awake and alert in psychology class. Her EEG would most likely show a preponderance of which brain wave pattern?
   a. alpha
   b. beta
   c. theta
   d. delta

9. Jai is entering light sleep; his heart rate is slowing; his breathing is irregular; and the muscles of his body are relaxing, when Jai is suddenly awakened by a reflex muscle contraction called a
   a. hypnic jerk.
   b. microsleep.
   c. hypnopompic reflex.
   d. cataplexy contraction.

10. The two most basic states of sleep that make up the dual process hypothesis are
    a. stage 1 sleep and stage 2 sleep.
    b. alpha wave sleep and delta wave sleep.
    c. non-REM sleep and REM sleep.
    d. narcoleptic sleep and cataplexic sleep.

11. Newborn babies have lots of new experiences to process so they spend eight to nine hours a day, or 50 percent of their total sleep time in
    a. non-REM sleep.
    b. sleep marked by sleep spindles.
    c. delta wave sleep.
    d. REM sleep.

12. Sleep paralysis, which normally prevents people from moving during REM sleep, can also occur just as they begin to wake up. During such episodes, these people may feel like they are floating out of their bodies or feel like they are suffocating, experiences which are symptoms of
    a. hypnopompic hallucinations.
    b. REM behavior disorder.
    c. narcolepsy.
    d. non-REM nightmares.

13. Using the paradoxical intention and eating a starchy snack before bedtime are two behavioral remedies used to treat
    a. narcolepsy.
    b. insomnia.
    c. sleep apnea.
    d. REM behavior disorder.

301

14. Leo is a four-year-old who is experiencing night terrors, while his 11-year-old brother sleepwalks. Both of the night-time activities of these two brothers occur during
    a. REM sleep.
    b. NREM sleep.
    c. cataplexic sleep.
    d. the lightest stage of sleep.

15. Which of the following sleep disorders is suspected as one cause of sudden infant death syndrome?
    a. narcolepsy
    b. cataplexy
    c. sleep apnea
    d. somnambulism

16. Tamara was awakened throughout the night for a sleep study and did not get enough REM sleep. The next night, she was allowed to sleep without interruption. Tamara would be likely to experience
    a. insomnia.
    b. REM rebound.
    c. somnambulism.
    d. REM behavior disorder.

17. Which theory of dreaming states that one must analyze the dream's manifest content in order to uncover its latent, symbolic meaning?
    a. activation-synthesis hypothesis
    b. neurocognitive dream theory
    c. lucid dream theory
    d. psychodynamic dream theory

18. According to which dream theory are dreams viewed as conscious expressions of the REM sleep processes that sort and store daily experiences so that a hungry person would be more likely to dream of food?
    a. activation-synthesis hypothesis
    b. neurocognitive dream theory
    c. hypnopompic dream analysis
    d. psychodynamic dream theory

19. Which of the following believed he could cure diseases with magnets but whose strange "treatments" are related to hypnosis because they actually relied on the power of suggestion, not magnetism?
    a. Ernest Hilgard
    b. James Braid
    c. Franz Mesmer
    d. William Domhoff

20. Peta is participating in a hypnosis experiment in which she is hypnotized, then her left arm is placed in ice water. Although she says that she feels no pain when asked, her right hand wrote, "It hurts." The part of Peta's awareness that "felt" the pain is called the
    a. hidden observer.
    b. latent reporter.
    c. phobic partner.
    d. overlay.

21. To impress his friends of his ability, Brad held a string with a ring attached and mentally made the ring swing back and forth. What really happened was that as Brad thought about moving the ring, his fingers made micromuscular movements that made the string sway. This is known as
    a. autosuggestion.
    b. telekinesis.
    c. hypnotic susceptibility.
    d. stimulus control.

22. Which of the following most clearly occurs under hypnosis?
    a. superhuman acts of strength
    b. genuine instances of age regression
    c. altering color vision and hearing sensitivity
    d. memory enhancement through the reduction of false memories

23. Amir is using a mental exercise in which he will widen his attention to embrace a total, nonjudgmental awareness of the world. Amir is engaging in _____ meditation.
    a. hypnogogic
    b. perceptive
    c. mindfulness
    d. concentrative

24. The REST technique makes use of
    a. sensory deprivation.
    b. hypodynamic imagery.
    c. hallucinogenic drugs.
    d. A CPAP mask.

25. Alcohol, amphetamines, MDMA, caffeine, GHB, mescaline, and LSD have in common the fact that they are all
    a. physically addicting.
    b. psychoactive drugs.
    c. classified as stimulants.
    d. classified as hallucinogens.

26. Addiction is often accompanied by a reduced response to a drug, which leads the user to take larger and larger doses of the drug to get the desired effect. This effect is referred to as
    a. compulsive binging.
    b. psychological dependence.
    c. drug withdrawal.
    d. drug tolerance.

27. By definition, compulsive drug use involves
    a. intense use and extreme dependence.
    b. short-term use based on curiosity.
    c. experimental use.
    d. use of the drug to cope with a specific problem.

28. Nicotine and opiates stimulate the brain by
    a. causing more neurotransmitters to be released.
    b. slowing the removal of neurotransmitters after they are released.
    c. mimicking the neurotransmitters.
    d. eliminating certain neurotransmitters.

29. Adderall and Ritalin, two popular "study drugs", are both mixtures of
    a. tranquilizers.
    b. barbiturates.
    c. hypnotics.
    d. amphetamines.

30. Elaine has taken a stimulant drug that will cause her brain cells to release extra amounts of serotonin, will produce a rush of energy, and elevate her body temperature. Under this drug's influence, Elaine may feel closer to others with the impact of the music and other sensory experiences being intensified. Elaine most likely consumed which drug?
    a. GHB
    b. MDMA
    c. alcohol
    d. marijuana

31. Which of the following is currently the most frequently used psychoactive drug in North America?
    a. caffeine
    b. marijuana
    c. alcohol
    d. nicotine

32. Which of the following is an addictive stimulant drug that, in large doses, causes stomach pain, vomiting, diarrhea, cold sweats, dizziness, confusion, and muscle tremors and is so toxic that it is sometimes used to kill insects?
    a. MDMA
    b. GHB
    c. mescaline
    d. nicotine

33. The street drug GHB is
    a. similar in its effects on the central nervous system to crystal meth.
    b. classified as a hallucinogenic drug.
    c. not physically addicting, but can create a psychological dependence.
    d. made from a mixture of degreasing solvent and drain cleaner.

34. Mickey is drinking alcohol at a party. During the first two hours at the party, he consumes three mixed drinks and three beers, which he alternates. Mickey is engaging in
    a. binge drinking.
    b. paced drinking.
    c. situational drinking.
    d. polydrug abuse.

35. Ina has entered an alcohol treatment center and is presently going through detoxification, which involves
    a. intensive individual counseling and use of sedative drugs.
    b. sobering her up and cutting off her supply of alcohol.
    c. an extensive medical and nutritional workup to restore her health.
    d. group counseling within the 12-step program.

36. According to your textbook, which of the following drugs is NOT classified as a hallucinogen?
    a. Rohypnol
    b. mescaline
    c. LSD
    d. marijuana

37. Which of the following drugs has been shown to slightly increase REM sleep?
    a. alcohol
    b. caffeine
    c. cocaine
    d. LSD

38. Garrett dreams of a gruesome monster that is chasing him. As he is hiding behind a rock looking at the monster, he notices that it has the face of his boss and the hair color and style of his mother's. The monster's voice even sounds like his girlfriend's when she is angry. All of Garrett's fears being rolled up into one package illustrates which of the dream processes?
    a. displacement.
    b. sublimation.
    c. condensation.
    d. secondary elaboration.

39. When Dr. Morrison analyzes his clients' dreams, he usually looks at the dream as a special message telling people what is missing in their lives. To help his clients' work through these messages, he has his clients speak for each character or object within the dream. Dr. Morrison is following the dream analysis approach of
    a. Rosalind Cartwright.
    b. Stephen LaBerge.
    c. Calvin Hall.
    d. Fritz Perls.

40. Deanna feels awake and capable of normal action while she is sleeping. Deanna is experiencing
    a. lucid dreaming.
    b. the basic suggestion effect.
    c. sleep drunkenness.
    d. REM rebound.

Chapter 6: Conditioning and Learning

Chapter Overview

Learning is a relatively permanent change in behavior due to experience. Associative learning is a simple type of learning that affects many aspects of daily list. Cognitive learning involves making use of information-rich higher mental processes. Learning resulting from conditioning depends on reinforcement. Reinforcement increases the probability that a particular response will occur. Classical (or respondent) conditioning and instrumental (or operant) conditioning are two basic types of associative learning. In classical conditioning, a neutral stimulus is followed by an unconditioned stimulus. With repeated pairings, the neutral stimulus begins to elicit a response. In operant conditioning, responses that are followed by reinforcement occur more frequently.

Classical conditioning, studied by Pavlov, occurs when a neutral stimulus (NS) is associated with an unconditioned stimulus (US). The US causes a reflex called the unconditioned response (UR). If the NS is consistently paired with the US, it becomes a conditioned stimulus (CS) capable of producing a conditioned (learned) response (CR). When the conditioned stimulus is followed by the unconditioned stimulus, conditioning is reinforced (strengthened).

From an informational view, conditioning creates expectancies, which alter response patterns. In classical conditioning, the CS creates an expectancy that the US will follow. Higher order conditioning occurs when a well-learned conditioned stimulus is used as if it were an unconditioned stimulus, bringing about further learning. When the CS is repeatedly presented alone, conditioning is extinguished (weakened or inhibited). After extinction seems to be complete, a rest period may lead to the temporary reappearance of a conditioned response. This is called spontaneous recovery. Through stimulus generalization, stimuli similar to the conditioned stimulus will also produce a response. Generalization gives way to stimulus discrimination when an organism learns to respond to one stimulus but not to similar stimuli.

Conditioning applies to visceral or emotional responses as well as simple reflexes. As a result, conditioned emotional responses (CERs) also occur. Irrational fears called phobias may be CERs. Conditioning of emotional responses can occur vicariously (secondhand) as well as directly.

To understand why people behave as they do, it is important to identify how their responses are being reinforced. Operant conditioning occurs when a voluntary action is followed by a reinforcer (which increases the frequency of the response) or a punisher (which decreases the frequency of the response). Delaying reinforcement greatly reduces its effectiveness, but long chains of responses may be maintained by a single reinforcer. Superstitious behaviors often become part of response chains because they appear to be associated with reinforcement. By rewarding successive approximations to a particular response, behavior can be shaped into desired patterns. If an operant response is not reinforced, it may extinguish (disappear). But after extinction seems complete, it may temporarily reappear (spontaneous recovery). Both positive reinforcement and negative reinforcement increase the likelihood that a response will be repeated. Punishment decreases the likelihood that the response will occur again.

Operant learning may be based on primary reinforcers (which are rooted in biology), secondary reinforcers (such as tokens and social reinforcers), and feedback (knowledge of results). Primary reinforcers are "natural," physiologically based rewards. Intracranial stimulation of "pleasure centers" in the brain can also serve as a primary reinforcer. Secondary reinforcers are learned. They typically gain their reinforcing value by direct association with primary reinforcers or because they can be exchanged for primary reinforcers. Tokens and money gain their reinforcing value in this way. Feedback aids learning and improves performance. It is most effective when it is immediate, detailed, and frequent. Programmed instruction breaks learning into a series of small steps and provides immediate feedback. Computer-assisted instruction (CAI) does the same but has the added advantage of providing alternative exercises and information when needed.

Reward or reinforcement may be given continuously (after every response) or on a schedule of partial reinforcement. Partial reinforcement produces greater resistance to extinction. The four most basic partial schedules of reinforcement are fixed ratio, variable ratio, fixed interval, and variable interval. Each produces a distinct pattern of responding.

Stimuli that precede a reinforced response tend to control the response on future occasions (stimulus control). Two aspects of stimulus control are generalization and discrimination. In generalization, an operant response tends to occur when stimuli similar to those preceding reinforcement are present. In discrimination, responses are given in the presence of discriminative stimuli associated with reinforcement and withheld in the presence of stimuli associated with nonreinforcement.

Punishment decreases response frequency. Punishment occurs when a response is followed by the onset of an aversive event or by the removal of a positive event (response cost). Punishment is most effective when it is immediate, consistent, and intense. Although severe punishment can virtually eliminate a particular behavior, mild punishment usually only temporarily suppresses responding. Reinforcement must be used to make lasting changes in the behavior of a person or an animal. The undesirable side effects of punishment include the conditioning of fear to punishing agents and situations associated with punishment, the learning of escape and avoidance responses, and the encouragement of aggression.

Cognitive learning involves higher mental processes, such as understanding, knowing, or anticipating. Even in relatively simple learning situations, animals and people seem to form cognitive maps (internal representations of relationships). In latent learning, learning remains hidden or unseen until a reward or incentive for performance is offered. Discovery learning emphasizes insight and understanding, in contrast to rote learning.

Learning can occur by merely observing and imitating the actions of another person or by noting the consequences of the person's actions. Observational learning is influenced by the personal characteristics of the model and the success or failure of the model's behavior. Studies have shown that aggression is readily learned and released by modeling. Media characters can act as powerful models for observational learning. Media violence increases the likelihood of aggression by viewers.

By applying operant conditioning principles, it is possible to change or manage your own behavior. When managing behavior, self-reinforcement, self-recording, feedback, and behavioral contracting are all helpful. Four strategies that can help change bad habits are reinforcing alternative responses, promoting extinction, breaking response chains, and avoiding antecedent cues.

Module 6.1 Learning and Classical Conditioning
Preview: Rats!

Language Development Guide
vividly: clearly
terrified: scared
scamper: runs; darts

shivered: trembled
rodent: group of mammals that include rats, mice, squirrels, beavers, and guinea pigs
respected: appreciated for some skill or ability
shrieking: screaming
good-naturedly: cheerfully
ribbed: made fun of; teased
vicarious classical conditioning: learning brought about by observing another person react to a particular stimulus
dread: fear; be afraid of
newfound: recently obtained
abstract: based on theory; not concrete or literal
chastened: to correct by punishment
reach into every corner of our lives: are continually present in every aspect of our lives

What Is Learning—Does Practice Make Perfect?
Survey Question: What is learning?

Language Development Guide
bassoon: woodwind instrument
"party": have a good time with friends
needless to say: obviously; of course
incapacitated: out of action; harmed
dull: uninteresting
fundamental: basic; important; essential
excludes: rules out; leaves out
qualifies: is eligible; meets the requirements
association: connection
species: part of biological classification that can interbreed and produce fertile offspring
unique: exclusive; only one of its kind
probability: likelihood; odds
identifiable: certain; expressed
unlocking the secrets: understanding
noting: observing; being aware of
precede: comes before
reliably: dependably; consistently
triggers: causes
consequences: results; outcomes; effects
compliments: praise; saying nice things about
snicker: quietly laugh
insult: put you down; say offensive; degrading things about you

Recite and Review
1. Six-year-old Lana listens to her mother vividly describe how a large rat had terrified her. Although Lana has never seen a live rat, she becomes visibly upset if someone even talks about a rat. Lana developed her fear of rats through _____ classical conditioning.
2. If you make a relatively permanent change in your behavior due to experience, you are exhibiting _____.
3. Whenever a person or an animal forms a simple connection among various stimuli and/or responses, _____ learning occurs.
4. Classical conditioning and operant conditioning are two types of _____ learning.

5. Higher-level learning that involves thinking, knowing, understanding, and anticipation is called _____ learning.
6. Learning from written language is unique to humans and is one reason why our species is called *Homo Sapiens* from the Latin word for man and _____.
7. Any event that increases the probability that a response will occur again is the key to associative learning and is called _____.
8. Any identifiable behavior whether an observable action, or an internal one is called a(n) _____.
9. Events that precede a response are called _____.
10. Effects that follow a response are called _____.
11. A form of learning in which reflex responses are associated with new stimuli is called _____ conditioning.
12. A puff of air will elicit an eye blink, which is an automatic, nonlearned response called a(n) _____.
13. If we sound a horn just before each puff of air hits your eye several times, the horn alone will eventually make you blink. This illustrates _____ conditioning.
14. When an antecedent stimulus that does not produce a response is linked with one that does, _____ conditioning will occur.
15. Learning is based on the consequences of responding in the form of learning known as _____ conditioning.
16. If you wear a particular shirt and get lots of compliments, you will probably wear this shirt again because wearing the shirt has received the consequence known as _____.
17. If you wear a particular shirt and you get laughed at or insulted about your "taste" in clothes, then you will probably stop wearing this shirt because you received the consequence known as _____.

Connections

1. ___ learning
2. ___ associative learning
3. ___ cognitive learning
4. ___ reinforcement
5. ___ response
6. ___ antecedent
7. ___ consequence
8. ___ reflex
9. ___ classical conditioning
10. ___ operant conditioning

a. any identifiable behavior that can be an observable action or an internal behavior
b. learning based on the consequences of responding
c. any relatively permanent change in behavior that can be attributed to experience
d. effect that follows a response, such as reinforcement or punishment
e. event that precedes a response
f. higher-level learning involving thinking, knowing, understanding, and anticipation
g. innate, automatic response to a stimulus; for example, an eye blink
h. form of learning in which reflex responses are associated with new stimuli
i. formation of simple connections between various stimuli and/or responses and includes both classical and operant conditioning
j. any event that increases the probability that a particular response will occur

Check Your Memory

1. TRUE or FALSE   Learning includes both temporary changes in behavior as well as more permanent changes in behavior caused by motivation and maturation.
2. TRUE or FALSE   If you see someone get shocked by touching a particular light fixture and you avoid this light fixture, then you learned to avoid the light fixture through vicarious classical conditioning.
3. TRUE or FALSE   Two types of associative learning are classical conditioning and operant conditioning.
4. TRUE or FALSE   Some animals do engage in simpler forms of cognitive learning.
5. TRUE or FALSE   Repeating a response many times produces learning.
6. TRUE or FALSE   The key to associative learning is reinforcement.
7. TRUE or FALSE   Responses include observable actions but not internal actions, such a faster heartbeat.
8. TRUE or FALSE   If you are stung by a bee and associate the pain with bees, then learning has occurred.
9. TRUE or FALSE   Events that come before a response are called consequences, while the effects that follow a response are the antecedents.
10. TRUE or FALSE   Classical conditioning is based on the consequences of our actions.
11. TRUE or FALSE   An automatic, nonlearned response is called a reflex.
12. TRUE or FALSE   Operant conditioning is a form of learning in which reflex responses are associated with new stimuli.
13. TRUE or FALSE   Reinforcement and punishment are two types of consequences.
14. TRUE or FALSE   When four-year-old Juan tried to pick a rose and got pricked by a thorn, he associated the rose with pain and is now afraid of roses, which illustrates classical conditioning.
15. TRUE or FALSE   When Emil added lots of different spices to his meat loaf and created an excellent meal, he continued to use these spices whenever he made the meat loaf, which illustrates operant conditioning.

Classical Conditioning—Does the Name Pavlov Ring a Bell?

Survey Question: How does classical conditioning occur?

Language Development Guide

Does the name Pavlov Ring a Bell?: Is Pavlov familiar to you?

twentieth century: generally refers to the 1900s; specifically 1901-2001

physiologist: scientist who studies the functioning of living things; a part of biology

Nobel Prize: international award presented annual in several areas, such as medicine (or physiology), *physics*; literature, chemistry, peace, etc.

drooled: salivated

digestion: how the body breaks down food

salivation: process of producing and secreting fluid from the mouth as a part of the digestive process

tidbit: small piece

neutral: does not cause a change

sequence: series; arrangement

evoke: bring about

elicit: bring forth; draw out

trivial: unimportant; minor

suspecting: thinking; assuming

cerebellar dysfunction: abnormal functioning of the cerebellum

311

autism: severe disorder that involves impaired communication and social interaction that is usually evident during the first three years of life

obsessive-compulsive disorder: extreme preoccupation with certain thoughts that the person attempts to control by performing repetitive behaviors, such as controlling thoughts of germs with repetitive handwashing

fetal alcohol syndrome: condition caused by the mother drinking alcohol while pregnant resulting in low birth weight, small head, body defects, facial malformations, and intellectual and emotional disabilities

dementia: serious mental impairment in old age caused by wear and tear and weakening of the brain over time

diagnoses: determining the cause of a problem through an analysis or examination of the symptoms

disordered: not functioning normally

minimally conscious: have suffered brain damage, but can make a deliberate cognitive response, such as responding to his or her own name (not in a coma)

vegetative state: have suffered brain damage to the point that the person lacks cognitive awareness; can make reflexive responses, and have their eyes open (not in a coma)

misdiagnosed: incorrect determination regarding the cause of a problem

Recite and Review

1. Pavlovian conditioning and respondent conditioning are two other names for _____ conditioning.
2. Pavlov was originally studying salivation as it related to the bodily process of _____.
3. In his original experiment Pavlov noticed something unusual, which was that the dogs were salivating before he gave them the _____.
4. At the beginning of Pavlov's learning experiment, the stimulus that was original a neutral stimulus (NS) was the _____.
5. In Pavlov's learning experiment, the food the dogs were given was the _____ stimulus.
6. The food elicited salivation in Pavlov's experiment, with this salivation to the food being the unconditioned _____.
7. After the bell was paired with the food, the bell was referred to as a(n) _____ stimulus.
8. Classical conditioning had occurred when the dog made the new response of salivating to the _____.
9. A puff of air to the eye will cause anyone to blink their eye. If you blow a horn and then immediately blow a puff of air into the person's eye, this pairing of the horn with the puff of air will eventually lead to the person blinking to the sound of the horn, which would be considered the _____ response.
10. When a child undergoing chemotherapy, they become nauseated due to the chemotherapy. If the child then becomes nauseated at the sight of the treatment room, the treatment room would be the _____ stimulus.
11. The main part of the brain that is involved in eye blink conditioning is the _____.
12. Eye blink conditioning may be useful for distinguishing severely brain-damaged individuals who are in a vegetative state and cannot be conditioned from those who can be conditioned and are considered _____.

Connections

1. ___ respondent conditioning

2. ___ unconditioned stimulus (US)

a. innate reflex response, such as the salivation to the food in Pavlov's experiment

b. stimulus that evokes a response because of its pairing, such as the bell in Pavlov's experiment

3. ___ unconditioned response (UR)

4. ___ neutral stimulus (NS)

5. ___ conditioned stimulus (CS)
6. ___ conditioned response (CR)

7. ___ eye blink conditioning

c. another name for classical or Pavlovian conditioning
d. learned response, such as salivation to the bell in Pavlov's experiment
e. stimulus that does not evoke a response
f. involves the cerebellum with dysfunction indicating the possibility of autism
g. stimulus innately capable of eliciting a response, such as the food in Pavlov's experiment

Check Your Memory

1. TRUE or FALSE Pavlov was originally studying the process of digestion when he made his dogs salivate, but switched to a learning experiment when he noticed that the dogs salivated before he placed the food in their mouths.
2. TRUE or FALSE Another name for Pavlovian conditioning is instrumental learning.
3. TRUE or FALSE Originally in Pavlov's experiment, the food was considered a neutral stimulus (NS) in regards to salivation.
4. TRUE or FALSE In Pavlov's classical conditioning experiment, the dog's salivation to the food was classified as a conditioned response.
5. TRUE or FALSE After the bell was paired with the food in Pavlov's experiment, the bell became known as a conditioned stimulus.
6. TRUE or FALSE In Pavlov's experiment, the dog's salivation to the bell would be classified as the unconditioned stimulus.
7. TRUE or FALSE If one sounds a horn and then blows a puff of air into a person's eye, the horn is considered the conditioned stimulus and will eventually cause the person to blink without the puff of air.
8. TRUE or FALSE If you have a virus that causes you to get nauseated after you eat a big plate of spaghetti, the next time you are served spaghetti you may feel nauseated because the spaghetti has become an unconditioned stimulus for the nausea.
9. TRUE or FALSE Researchers have found that the amygdala is the main brain part involved in eye blink conditioning.
10. TRUE or FALSE Psychologist Joseph Steinmetz found that people with autism, obsessive-compulsive disorder, fetal alcohol syndrome, and dementia all show unusual eye blink conditioning.
11. TRUE or FALSE Brain-damaged patients who are in a vegetative state can be conditioned using the eye blink response and may recover, while people who are minimally conscious cannot be conditioned using the eye blink response and will most likely not recover.

Principles of Classical Conditioning—Here's Johnny

Language Development Guide

squirt: spray
optimal: best
clap: put your hands together
a real hit: a successful performance
extends: expands, continues; stretches
celebrities: famous people

313

advertisers: one whose job is to promote a product
origins: sources; causes
interconnected: being linked
shot: an injection of a substance under the skin
hypodermic: a hollow needle
poked: jabbed, stuck, pricked
adaptable: flexible; able to adjust to change
acquired: obtained; gained
imitations: fakes
knockoffs: imitations; fakes
buzzer: noisemaker
in essence: basically; really
dreaded: feared
put-away-that-PlayStation-controller tone: you are in trouble and about to be punished
PlayStation-controller: device that directs the movements on a video game

Recite and Review

1. The period in conditioning during which a response is reinforced is called _____.
2. Because the unconditioned stimulus brings forth a response, which becomes associated with the conditioned stimulus, the process is referred to as _____ reinforcement.
3. If we pair the sound of a bell with lemon juice placed in a person's mouth, the salivation to the lemon juice would be the _____ response.
4. In pairing the sound of a bell with lemon juice being placed in a person's mouth, the sound of the bell would be the _____ stimulus.
5. For classical conditioning to occur, the optimal delay between the conditioned stimulus and the unconditioned stimulus is from a half second to _____ seconds.
6. Classical conditioning in which a conditioned stimulus (CS) is used to reinforce further learning; that is, a CS is used as if it were a US (unconditioned stimulus) is referred to as _____ conditioning.
7. If you have been classically conditioned to salivate to the sound of a bell and this response is well-learned, we could clap our hands and then sound the bell, and you would eventually salivate to the clap of our hands, a process known as _____ conditioning.
8. Today, many psychologists think that classical conditioning does have mental origins because we tend to look for associations among events that could aid our survival, a perspective called the _____ view.
9. Thoughts about how events are interconnected are referred to as mental _____.
10. When you are about to get an injection, your muscles tighten because your body is preparing for the pain that will reliably follow the injection, which illustrates the _____ view of classical conditioning.
11. Classical conditioning can be weakened by removing the connection between the conditioned and unconditioned stimulus, a process called _____.
12. The reappearance of a learned response after it has been apparently extinguished is called a(n) _____.
13. A cat has learned to "come running" when you shake the cat food box. If the cat also "comes running" when you shake your cereal box, the cat is demonstrating stimulus _____.
14. A person has been classically conditioned to blink each time you play a particular note on the piano. However, if you play higher or lower notes, the person's blinking will _____.
15. The reason that many stores carry imitations of nationally known products is most likely due to stimulus _____.

314

16. A person who is fearful of large dogs but is not afraid of small or medium-sized dogs is exhibiting stimulus _____.
17. A child who responds differently to the voice tones of his parents that are associated with punishment from those voice tones associated with praise or affection is illustrating stimulus _____.

Connections

1. ____ acquisition
2. ____ respondent reinforcement
3. ____ higher order conditioning
4. ____ informational view
5. ____ expectancy
6. ____ extinction
7. ____ spontaneous recovery
8. ____ stimulus generalization
9. ____ stimulus discrimination

a. the training period during conditioning when a response is strengthened by reinforcement
b. learned ability to respond differently to similar stimuli
c. classical conditioning in which a conditioned stimulus is used to reinforce further learning, that is, a CS is used as if it were a US
d. the anticipation concerning future events or relationships
e. reappearance of a learned response after it has been extinguished
f. the perspective that explains that we look for associations among events
g. reinforcement that occurs when an unconditioned stimulus closely follows a conditioned stimulus
h. weakening of the conditioned response by removing the connection between the conditioned and unconditioned stimulus
i. other stimuli similar to the conditioned stimulus tend to trigger a response

Check Your Memory

1. TRUE or FALSE   During acquisition, a conditioned response must be reinforced.
2. TRUE or FALSE   Classical conditioning is reinforced when the unconditioned stimulus is followed by the conditioned stimulus in a process known as instrumental reinforcement.
3. TRUE or FALSE   If we ring a bell and then squirt lemon juice into a person's mouth, the person will salivate to the lemon juice and eventually to the sound of the bell only with the unconditioned stimulus being the lemon juice.
4. TRUE or FALSE   For classical conditioning to occur, the optimal delay between the conditioned stimulus and the unconditioned stimulus is from six seconds to 15 seconds.
5. TRUE or FALSE   When a well-learned conditioned stimulus is used to reinforce further learning, the process is known as the method of successive approximations.
6. TRUE or FALSE   Advertisers are using stimulus discrimination when they pair images that evoke good feelings with pictures of their products.
7. TRUE or FALSE   Unlike psychologists today, Pavlov believed that classical conditioning involved higher mental processes.

8. TRUE or FALSE The informational view of classical conditioning explains that we look for associations among events and in doing so we create new mental expectancies or thoughts about how events are interconnected.

9. TRUE or FALSE Because the conditioned stimulus (CS) reliably precedes the unconditioned stimulus (US), we can say that the conditioned stimulus predicts the occurrence of the US.

10. TRUE or FALSE Classical conditioning can be weakened by removing the connection between the conditioned and unconditioned stimulus through a process known as extinction.

11. TRUE or FALSE The reappearance of a learned response after its apparent extinction is called vicarious conditioning.

12. TRUE or FALSE A child who is burned by a match and also shows fear to similar objects with flames, such as candles, fireplaces, and gas stoves is exhibiting response chaining.

13. TRUE or FALSE Stimulus generalization explains why many stores carry imitations of nationally known products, hoping that customers conditioned to the real products will generalize these feelings to the cheaper knockoffs.

14. TRUE or FALSE If you can distinguish between your boss's good mood and his bad mood and act accordingly, then you are exhibiting stimulus discrimination.

Critical Thinking Question

Lately you have been getting a shock of static electricity every time you touch a door handle. Now there is a hesitation in your door-opening movements. Can you analyze this situation in terms of classical conditioning?

Classical Conditioning in Humans—An Emotional Topic

Survey Question: Does conditioning affect emotions?

Language Development Guide

bakery: a store where bread, cookies, and cakes are made
"gut": instinctual
blush: face redden due to feelings of shame
embarrassed: felt self-conscious and humiliated
heart pounds: to feel as if heart is beating rapidly
belittle: tease or criticize
persists: continues; refuses to go away
realistic: reasonable; practical
bugs: insects
previously: beforehand
trace: track down
disgusted: sickened
limited: partial
disabling: put out of action
readily: easily; effortlessly
eased: reduced; relieved
merely: just; simply
elevations: heights
undoubtedly: certainly
undergone: experienced
traumatized: disturbed and troubled

terrorist: radical; fanatic; extremist who intimidates, threatens, and harms others
counsel: advise and support
vicarious: experiencing through one's imagination the feelings and actions of others
"secondhand": received through another
escalators: moving staircase
prejudiced: having a negative emotional attitude toward members of other groups
"picked up": got; developed; gained

Recite and Review

1. A dependable, inborn stimulus-and-response connection, such as a bright light causing the pupil of the eye to narrow is called a(n) _____.

2. If your face reddened when you were punished as a child, you may blush now when you are embarrassed or ashamed, which illustrates that blushing can be considered a(n) _____ response.

3. Through classical conditioning, new stimuli and situations are linked with many involuntary, _____ nervous system responses.

4. One of the most common mistakes people make with pets (especially dogs) is hitting them if they do not come when called. Thus, calling the animal gets associated with the pain of being hit, which makes calling the dog the _____ stimulus for fear and withdrawal.

5. Even though she realizes that people fly in airplanes every day, Marta either finds an excuse not to go to the company sales meeting across country or else drives all weekend to get to the meeting on Monday morning. Marta's fear would be classified as an extreme fear, or _____.

6. Many psychologists believe that extreme disabling fears begin as learned emotional reactions to a previously neutral stimulus, which are called _____ responses.

7. These classically-conditioned, extreme emotional fears can be spread to other stimuli by higher order conditioning and stimulus _____.

8. During a conditioned emotional response, the part of the limbic system in the brain that becomes more active and produces feelings of fear is the _____.

9. Merely reading about how to control fears will not alleviate them, because the lower brain areas are not significantly affected by _____ learning.

10. Conditioned fears do respond to a therapy in which a person is gradually exposing to the feared stimuli while remaining calm and relaxed. This therapy is called _____.

11. In order to get Courtney to like him on their first date, Lamar plays her favorite music in the car and then takes her out for her favorite Mexican food. Because Lamar is paired with these pleasant images, Courtney may develop a favorable conditioned _____ response toward him.

12. Children who learn to fear thunder by watching their parents react to it have undergone _____ classical conditioning.

13. The emotional attitudes we develop toward foods, political parties, and ethnic groups were probably conditioned not only by direct experiences but through _____ conditioning as well.

Connections

1. ___ conditioned emotional responses (CERs)

2. ___ phobia

a. reducing fear or anxiety by repeatedly exposing a person to emotional stimuli while the person is deeply relaxed

b. emotional response that has been linked to a previously nonemotional stimulus by classical conditioning

3. ___ amygdala

    c. classical conditioning brought about by observing another person react to a particular stimulus

4. ___ desensitization

    d. fear that persists even when no realistic danger exists

5. ___ vicarious classical conditioning

    e. part of the brain that becomes active during a CER

Check Your Memory

1. TRUE or FALSE   At its simplest, classical conditioning depends on unconditioned reflex responses

2. TRUE or FALSE   Many involuntary, autonomic nervous system, responses are linked with new stimuli and situations by operant conditioning.

3. TRUE or FALSE   Conditioned emotional responses (CERs) occur in humans but not lower animals, such as dogs or cats.

4. TRUE or FALSE   Psychologists believe that many phobias begin as conditioned emotional responses (CERs).

5. TRUE or FALSE   Stimulus generalization and higher order conditioning can spread conditioned emotional responses (CERs) to other stimuli.

6. TRUE or FALSE   During a conditioned emotional response (CER), an area of the brain called the pons becomes more active and produce feelings of fear.

7. TRUE or FALSE   Cognitive learning plays a large role in controlling the lower brain regions and conditioned emotional responses (CERs).

8. TRUE or FALSE   Conditioned fears have been shown to respond well to a therapy called desensitization, which is done by gradually exposing the person to feared stimuli while she or he remains calm and relaxed.

9. TRUE or FALSE   Children who learn to fear thunder by watching their parents react to it have undergone spontaneous recovery conditioning.

10. TRUE or FALSE   People who counsel traumatized victims of sexual abuse can themselves develop vicarious trauma.

11. TRUE or FALSE   Developing a fear of spiders from watching a TV show about human deaths due to spider bites illustrates vicarious classical conditioning.

12. TRUE or FALSE   The emotional attitudes we develop toward foods, political parties, and ethnic groups can only be conditioned directly, not through vicarious, or secondhand conditioning.

Module 6.2 Operant Conditioning

Operant Conditioning— Ping-Pong Playing Pigeons?

Survey Question: How does operant conditioning occur?

Language Development Guide

regret: feel sorry
ping-pong: table tennis
pigeons: type of bird; doves
pioneer: leads the way
satisfying: pleasing; enjoyable
frown: glare; scowl; sulk
actively: vigorously; energetically
"operates on": to work on something

refers: pertains to; involves
voluntary: chosen; deliberate
muting: silencing; quieting
obnoxious: annoying
passive: inactive; being acted on rather than acting
"happens to": being passive; being acted on
as a practical rule of thumb: general principle or way of doing things developed through real-world experience
chamber: enclosed space; compartment
clarify: to make clear; explain
snags: catches
grooms: cleans oneself
sniffs: smells
lever: bar; pedal
click!: sound made when lever or bar is pressed
depresses: pushes down
food pellet: small pill-sized bits of food
scurries: rushes; scampers; darts about
molded: changed; created
further: in addition
severely disturbed: with a behavior disorder
courteous: polite; well-mannered
dog agility: a competitive sport in which dogs quickly move around a number of barriers or obstacles to achieve the fastest time.
navigate: find the way
obstacles: barrier; blockage
hurdles: barrier that is jumped over
seesaws: long, narrow board attached to a structure in the middle so that, as one end of the board goes up while the other end is down
inclined: leaning
taps: very lightly knock on something; pat or rap
shot: attempt, try in golf
superstitions: irrational belief, usually about luck
athletic supporter: protective undergarment for male athletes
phew!: reaction of disgust
rituals: customs; cultural practices
ward off: to hold or fight something off
abundant: plentiful
faith: confident belief and trust
barren: empty
complicated: complex; difficult
gradual: slow and ongoing
bores: not interesting
lottery tickets: a type of gambling in which people buy tickets and there is a drawing for a monetary prize
tempted: attracted; enticed
withheld: refuse to give
spontaneous: impulsive; unplanned; natural
marked: noticeable; obvious
misbehavior: mischief; acting up
tantrums: fit of temper; outburst

show off: try to make an impression; brag; boast
granted: admittedly; it is true
scolding: yelling at; reprimanding
nevertheless: yet; but
dramatic: remarkable; impressive
constructively: usefully
disruptive: unruly; troublesome; upsetting
stressed: emphasized; highlighted; underscored
fooled: tricked
negating: opposing
backpack: cloth sack held onto one's back by two straps that the person's arms go through
state of affairs: the overall present situation and conditions
irritates: annoys; aggravates; bothers
channels: the designated pathways for specific television signals to be transmitted to homes
stereo: music player
blasting: being sent out very loudly
pound on: hit with the side of your fist
radar trap: police hide and wait to catch drivers in the act of speeding
henceforth: from now on
fine: penalty; punishment
cold: unfeeling
distant: isolated
rejection: receiving a negative response; dismissed
denied: refused; disallowed; turned down

Recite and Review

1. Operant conditioning is also known as _____ learning.
2. In operant conditioning, we associate responses with the events that come after the response called _____.
3. Responses that lead to desirable outcomes are repeated, while those that produce undesirable results are not. This is a statement of the law of _____.
4. This law that explains that desirable outcomes are repeated and those with undesirable results are not was proposed by learning theorist _____.
5. The learning of voluntary responses occurs through _____ conditioning.
6. Involuntary responses are learned through _____ conditioning.
7. The reinforcement in classical conditioning occurs _____ the response.
8. In operant conditioning the reinforcement occurs _____ the response.
9. The learner tends to be passive in _____ conditioning.
10. The role of the learner is active during _____ conditioning.
11. In classical conditioning, the response is elicited, while in operant conditioning, the response is _____.
12. A positive event that may increase responding but does not always increase responding is referred to as a(n) _____.
13. Any event that reliably increases the probability or frequency of responses it follows is called a(n) operant _____.
14. An operant conditioning chamber is also known as a(n) _____ box.
15. The learning theorist who invented the operant conditioning chamber and proposed many of the principles of operant conditioning was _____.
16. We learn to expect that a certain response will have a certain effect at certain times, according to the _____ view of operant conditioning.

17. Operant reinforcement works best when it is given only after a desired response has occurred. Thus, we say that the operant reinforcement is response _____.

18. For rats in an operant conditioning chamber, little or no learning occurs if the delay between bar pressing and receiving food exceeds _____ seconds.

19. In agility training, dogs are taught to navigate a variety of obstacles with the trainer only being able to reinforce the dog after he completes the entire sequence. This learning of a series of events took place through a process known as response _____.

20. A golfer taps her club on the ground three times and then hits a great shot. If she continues to tap the ground three times before each subsequent shot, she is illustrating _____ behavior.

21. The long series of events necessary to prepare a meal is rewarded by the final eating. This illustrates the process of _____.

22. Behaviors repeated because they seem to produce reinforcement even though they are actually unnecessary are called _____ behaviors.

23. Gradually molding responses to a final desired pattern is called _____.

24. Jake has hired a tennis instructor to help improve his serve as well as other aspects of his game. To improve Jake's serve, his instructor reinforces ever-closer matches to the final goal of a "perfect" tennis serve. These ever-closer matches to the final goal are known as _____.

25. If you are no longer reinforced with laughs when you tell a joke, you will probably, over time, tell fewer and fewer jokes. This illustrates operant _____.

26. A few weeks after they give up on buying state lottery tickets, many people are tempted to buy another one as if they are "just checking to see if their luck has changed." This brief return of the operant response is called a(n) _____.

27. When parents pay attention to their children's misbehavior but ignore them when they are playing quietly, they are unknowingly reinforcing their children for negative _____.

28. After you shovel the snow, your mother gives you a hug and fixes you a hot chocolate. The consequences provided by your mother would be considered _____.

29. A politician who irritates you is being interviewed on the evening news. When you change the channels so you won't have to listen to him, you have removed this unpleasant image and been _____ reinforced for your action.

30. Any event that follows a response and decreases its likelihood of occurring again is referred to as _____.

31. Darin insults his little brother, and his mother scolds him for this misbehavior. This scolding is a painful, unpleasant event, or _____ stimulus.

32. After Darin's mother scolded him for insulting his little brother, this misbehavior decreased. Thus, the scolding served as a(n) _____.

33. Response cost is considered a type of _____.

34. When children are removed from situations that normally allow them to gain reinforcement, they are undergoing a response cost strategy known as _____.

35. If you receive a parking ticket for staying too long in a parking spot, you will be less likely to repeat this behavior because a positive reinforcer (money) has been removed after your undesirable parking response. Thus, the parking fine illustrates the use of a type of punishment known as _____.

36. Regarding the amount of responding that takes place, negative reinforcement _____ responding.

37. Regarding the amount of responding that takes place, punishment _____ responding.

38. Regarding the amount of responding that takes place, nonreinforcement _____ responding.

Connections

1. ___ instrumental learning
2. ___ law of effect
3. ___ operant reinforcer
4. ___ reward
5. ___ operant conditioning chamber
6. ___ response contingent
7. ___ response chaining
8. ___ superstitious behavior
9. ___ shaping
10. ___ operant extinction
11. ___ negative reinforcement
12. ___ punishment (aversive type)
13. ___ response cost

a. any event that reliably increases the probability or frequency of responses it follows
b. occurs when a response is followed by an end to discomfort or by the removal of an unpleasant event
c. behavior repeated because it seems to produce reinforcement, even though it is actually unnecessary
d. reinforcement is given only after a desired response has occurred
e. gradually molding responses to a final desired pattern
f. pleasant event that does not always increase responding
g. following a response with an unpleasant consequence, which decreases the likelihood of the response occurring again
h. another name for operant conditioning
i. weakening or disappearance of a nonreinforced operant response
j. removal of a positive state of affairs that decreases the response, such as the procedure known as time out
k. another name for a Skinner box
l. responses that lead to a satisfying state of affairs are repeated, while those that lead to undesirable results are not
m. assembly of separate responses into a series of actions that lead to reinforcement

Check Your Memory

1. TRUE or FALSE   Operant conditioning applies to all living creatures and explains much day-to-day behavior.
2. TRUE or FALSE   Operant conditioning is also known as respondent learning.
3. TRUE or FALSE   The law of effect was proposed by psychologist Albert Bandura.
4. TRUE or FALSE   The law of effect states that responses that lead to desirable effects are repeated, while those that produce undesirable results are not.
5. TRUE or FALSE   Operant conditioning refers mainly to learning involuntary responses with reinforcement occurring before the response.
6. TRUE or FALSE   Responses are elicited in operant conditioning, while they are voluntarily emitted during classical conditioning.
7. TRUE or FALSE   Rewards do not always increase responding.
8. TRUE or FALSE   An operant reinforcer is any event that reliably increases the probability or frequency of responses it follows.
9. TRUE or FALSE   Another name for an operant conditioning chamber is a Thorndike shaping box.
10. TRUE or FALSE   In operant conditioning, new behavior patterns are molded by changing the probability that various responses will be made.

11. TRUE or FALSE   According to the information view of operant conditioning, we come to expect that the unconditioned stimulus will follow the conditioned stimulus and produce an effect.

12. TRUE or FALSE   Operant reinforcement works best when it is response contingent, which means that it must be given only after a desired response has occurred.

13. TRUE or FALSE   For rats in an operant conditioning chamber, little or no learning occurs if the delay between bar pressing and receiving food exceeds 50 seconds.

14. TRUE or FALSE   The long series of events, such as studying for quizzes, taking tests, and writing reports, that are necessary to pass a college course are rewarded at the end of the semester with an A, which illustrates the concept of response chaining.

15. TRUE or FALSE   A baseball player who draws four lines in the dirt before getting in the batter's box is illustrating the concept of successive approximations.

16. TRUE or FALSE   During operant training, animals often show unnecessary responses, such as scratching an ear before pressing the lever, that are similar to the superstitious behaviors exhibited by humans.

17. TRUE or FALSE   The gradual molding of responses to a final desired pattern is known as latent learning.

18. TRUE or FALSE   Through shaping, animals have been taught to play Ping-Pong, to play a toy piano, and to do other tricks.

19. TRUE or FALSE   The weakening or disappearance of a nonreinforced operant response is referred to as operant extinction.

20. TRUE or FALSE   The brief return of an operant response after it has been extinguished is called counterconditioning.

21. TRUE or FALSE   Negative attention seeking occurs when parents give their attention for playing quietly, but ignore the annoying behaviors, such as whining and temper tantrums.

22. TRUE or FALSE   Both positive and negative reinforcement increase responding.

23. TRUE or FALSE   If you are working outside and get cold and you put your coat on, putting on the coat is being reinforced through response cost.

24. TRUE or FALSE   Negative reinforcement is a mild type of punishment.

25. TRUE or FALSE   Punishment occurs when there is a decrease in responding due to the response being followed by an aversive consequence or by the removal of a positive state of affairs.

26. TRUE or FALSE   If you take cough syrup to stop your coughing, taking the cough syrup has been negatively reinforced.

27. TRUE or FALSE   The best known form of response cost is time out, in which children are removed from situations that normally allow them to gain reinforcement.

28. TRUE or FALSE   Parking tickets and other fines are based on response cost.

29. TRUE or FALSE   As a consequence, nonreinforcement increases responding.

Operant Reinforcers—What's Your Pleasure?

Survey Question: Are there different kinds of operant reinforcement?

Language Development Guide

categorizing: classifying; sorting
distinction: difference
distinguish: tell apart
exerts: uses; puts forth
feedback: information about the effect a response had

examine: look at

rooted in: caused by

double latte: a strong coffee drink with milk

iPod-style controller: click wheel, or touch-sensitive ring that quickly locates the desired song (discussed in Chapter 16)

twirl: spin; whirl; rotate

implants: devices fixed or set deeply (into a part of the brain or body)

"wired for pleasure": has electrodes inserted into the brain's pleasure centers

collapse: fall down

exhaustion: overtiredness

revive: recover; restore

in favor: preferring it

activate: turn on

sensitivity: responsiveness to

shudders: shake; tremble

Playboy: American men's magazine

Microsoft: American computer technology company

politicians: elected officials

tied: joined; attached

"heel": command for a dog to walk beside the handler's knee

skip: omit; leave out

exchanged: swapped; switched; replaced

sleep with: have sex with

token: symbol

gold stars: small, adhesive-backed stars that are stuck on a child's school work to reward excellence

poker chips: small disk-shaped objects used to represent the money one bets when playing this card game

"Chimp-O-Mat": vending-like machine that provides food treats to chimpanzees when they place poker chips in the slot; developed for a study of operant conditioning

dispensed: give out

developmentally disabled: having life-long mental and/or physical impairments

privileges: special benefit

"grab bag": a container that has an assortment of items that can be used as rewards

mischievous: a playful trick

participate: take part in

target behavior: specific action to be changed

split ends: the protective outer layer of each hair strand becomes dry and damaged and the hair tears into

graduate students: college students seeking advanced degrees, such as a masters, specialist, or doctoral degrees

decades: a decade is a period of 10 years; so several 10-year periods; a long time

toying: dealing with something lightly, not with purpose

cords (on the window shades): strings that move shades up or down and open or shut

coworkers: people who work at the same place you do

driven and blazing: strong, intense

dart: move quickly

contorts: twist the body

furiously: rapidly, quickly

depicts: shows

Wii game: video game that involves a wireless motion sensing controller that allows person to imitate the movement of various sports, exercise and get feedback on the television screen

animated: energetic; enthusiastic; excited

snowboarding: sport in which one goes down snow covered slopes on a surf board-like object with bindings to hold it to the feet and no ski poles

excel at: be the best

virtual: an artificially created environment that tries to comes close to the real thing

flow: stream; course

absence: without

darts: small pointed missiles thrown at the round board hanging on the wall

explicitly: clearly

video replays: to repeat a recorded version of an event

tennis serves: player tosses ball up and hits it with a tennis racket toward his or her opponent who will try to hit it (return the ball)

pick-off moves: strategy in baseball to throw to particular bases to strike players out

it pays: it is a good thing

practical: realistic; helpful

"throw-away" society: country that buys many disposable goods that are discarded with no regard for the damage to the planet

fossil fuels: energy sources made from the decomposition of dead organisms millions of years ago, such as oil, natural gas, and coal

strip, clear, and farm the land: removing too many trees to farm the land and causing erosion

very face of the Earth: the surface of this planet

wasteful: careless in the use of resources

polluting: contaminate; spoil

and the like: and other similar examples

energy taxes: tax on an energy source to discourage environmentally damaging sources and encourage energy conservation or use of alternative sources

rebates: refunding or returning some of the money one paid for a product as an incentive to purchase the product in the first place

offered: put forth

installing: put in

insulation: material used as a temperature barrier, such as to keep the cold or heat out

energy-efficient appliances: stoves, refrigerators, dishwashers, etc. that use less electricity and gas while still functioning at high level

tax breaks: allowed to pay less tax as a reinforcement for protecting the environment

preserve: protecting; conserving

recycling: collecting and processing discarded materials for use in creating new products

prompt: timely; without delay

dorms: housing for college students

basis: source on which something is established

resource consumption: use of natural resources

public concern: awareness of the problem by the country

global warming: increase in the average temperature of the earth's land and oceans believed to be caused by the greenhouse effect (gases forming a blanket-like covering that allows sunlight in but does not let the heat rays go out)

calculating: computing; determining

volume: amount; quantity

greenhouse gases: chemical compound gases that trap heat, such as water vapor, carbon dioxide, ozone, methane, nitrous oxide, and others

atmosphere: mixture of gases surrounding the Earth
applied: used
makes sense: wise; reasonable; practical
learning aids: devices to help improve or make learning easier
supply: provide; furnish
format: design; arrangement
to get a sense: to understand
encounter: meet; come across
right?: isn't this correct?
via: through; by means of
drill-and-practice: structured, repetitive review of information
affectionately: warmly
drill-and-kill: joke about the repetitive nature of drill-and-practice can "bore one to death"
increasingly: more and more
rich: intense; powerful
computer graphics: visual images and data generated or utilized by the computer
simulations: imitations of the real event
"microworld": simulated learning environment created by the computer
real-world: actual situations that occur
pause: stop temporarily; take a break
remember?: did you remember to complete the knowledge builder section
mastery: accomplishment of a skill

Recite and Review

1. Reinforcement tends to exert its effect on voluntary behavior through _____ conditioning.
2. Feedback is a key component of _____ learning.
3. The type of reinforcers that are natural, nonlearned, and fill an immediate physical need are called _____ reinforcers.
4. Psychoactive drugs, intracranial stimulation, and the avoidance of pain are all examples of _____ reinforcers.
5. Intracranial stimulation (ICS) involves the activation of pleasure pathways in the _____ system of the brain.
6. In experiments with rats, alcohol and cocaine were found to increase the sensitivity of the pleasure pathways in the brain. Another psychoactive drug that also increased the sensitivity of these pleasure pathways and to also increase the rats' tendency to engage in intracranial stimulation was the drug _____.
7. Money, attention, approval, success, affection, and grades all serve as learned or _____ reinforcers.
8. Learned reinforcers, such as praise, often gain their reinforcing properties by being associated with a(n) _____ reinforcer.
9. Since printed money, which has little or no value of its own, can be exchanged for food, water, and lodging, printed money is an example of a secondary reinforcer known as a(n) _____ reinforcer.
10. Tangible secondary reinforcers, such as money, have the advantage of not losing their reinforcing value as quickly as _____ reinforcers do.
11. Systems for managing and altering behavior through reinforcement of selected responses that have been used with troubled children and adults in special programs and in ordinary elementary school classrooms are called _____.
12. Reinforcement based on receiving attention, approval, or affection from another person is called a(n) _____ reinforcer.

326

13. Students have decided to shape their teacher's behavior. Every time their teacher moves to her right, the students lean forward, make eye contact, and look "really" interested in the teacher's lecture. However, when she moves to her left, the students lean back and generally look bored. To shape their teacher's behavior, the students are using _____ reinforcers.

14. Every time a player moves, a video game responds instantly with sounds, animated actions, and a higher or lower score. Regarding the player's progress, this video game is providing _____.

15. Knowledge of results (KR) is another name for _____.

16. An approach to help increase conservation of energy and decrease polluting involves individuals and companies receiving a different set of _____ for these actions.

17. If energy taxes are used to increase the cost of using fossil fuels, this would be an example of a type of punishment known as _____ to decrease fuel consumption.

18. If rebates are offered for buying energy-efficient appliances, this would be a use of _____ to increase conservation.

19. When entire families recycle, the family member that reinforces the recycling behavior of the other family members is usually the _____.

20. When families, work groups, or factories recycle, they typically recycle more when they receive weekly information about how much they recycled. This is an example of _____.

21. The new tool that makes it easier for individuals to get information about their individual resource consumption is called the _____ calculator.

22. Many people are now calculating the volume of greenhouse gases that their individual consumption adds to the atmosphere, which is called their _____.

23. Feedback is most effective when it is frequent, immediate, and _____.

24. Any learning format that presents information in small amounts, gives immediate practice, and provides continuous feedback to learners is called _____ instruction.

25. Besides giving continuous feedback, students can receive hints about why an answer was wrong and what is needed to correct when they use a drill-and-practice formats on computer, which are referred to as _____.

26. Some types of learning formats on computers make use of instructional games in which stories, competition with a partner, sound effects, and game-like graphics increase interest and motivation. These types of formats are known as _____ games.

27. Students can explore an imaginary situation or "microworld" that imitates real-world problems in computer learning formats known as educational _____.

Connections

1. ___ primary reinforcers

   a. information returned to a person about the effects a response has had; also known as knowledge of results

2. ___ secondary reinforcers

   b. involves stimulation of the pleasure centers of the brain; considered a primary reinforcer

3. ___ intracranial self-stimulation (ICS)

   c. learning is aided by computer-presented information, exercises, games, and simulations

4. ___ token reinforcers

   d. specific type of instructional media that makes use of competition with a partner, sound effects, and entertainment

5. ___ social reinforcers

   e. allows students to explore an imaginary situation or "microworld" that imitates real-world problems

327

6. ___ feedback

    f. any learning format that presents information in small amounts, gives immediate practice, and provides continuous feedback to learners

7. ___ programmed instruction

    g. tool used to give feedback regarding individual resource consumption

8. ___ CAI (computer-assisted instruction)

    h. reinforcement based on receiving attention, approval, or affection from another person

9. ___ serious games

    i. tangible secondary reinforcers, such as money, gold stars, poker chips, etc.

10. ___ educational simulations

    j. nonlearned reinforcers, usually those that satisfy physiological needs

11. ___ carbon footprint calculator

    k. any learned reinforcers which gain reinforcing properties by association with primary reinforcers

Check Your Memory

1. TRUE or FALSE   Primary reinforcers are natural and nonlearned and fill an immediate physical need.
2. TRUE or FALSE   Money, praise, and affection are examples of primary reinforcers.
3. TRUE or FALSE   Intracranial self-stimulation (ICS) that involves the direct activation of the hindbrain would be considered a secondary reinforcer.
4. TRUE or FALSE   The very few humans who have ever had a chance to try direct brain stimulation report feeling intense pleasure that is better than food, water, sex, or drugs.
5. TRUE or FALSE   Many natural primary reinforcers activate the same pleasure pathways in the brain as intracranial self-stimulation (ICS).
6. TRUE or FALSE   When rats are allowed to self-administer nicotine, they were less likely to engage in intracranial self-stimulation because nicotine decreases the sensitivity of pleasure pathways in the brain.
7. TRUE or FALSE   Secondary reinforcers are learned reinforcers that often gain their reinforcing properties through their association with primary reinforcers.
8. TRUE or FALSE   A tangible secondary reinforcer that can be exchanged for primary reinforcers is referred to as a token reinforcer.
9. TRUE or FALSE   Token reinforcers tend to lose their reinforcing value more quickly than primary reinforcers do.
10. TRUE or FALSE   Token economies have been used successfully with troubled children and adults in special programs.
11. TRUE or FALSE   Token economies have not been found to be effective in reducing discipline problems of young children at home or in elementary school classrooms.
12. TRUE or FALSE   Reinforcement based on receiving attention, approval, or affection from another person is known as a social reinforcer.
13. TRUE or FALSE   Every time a player moves, a video game responds instantly with sounds, animated actions, and a higher or lower score, illustrating the reinforcing power of feedback.
14. TRUE or FALSE   Another name for feedback is latent reinforcement.
15. TRUE or FALSE   When energy taxes are used to increase the cost of using fossil fuels, this is an example of negative reinforcement being used to decrease consumption of these fuels.

16. TRUE or FALSE   Rebates for installing insulation and buying energy-efficient cars are examples of the use of reinforcement to increase conservation.

17. TRUE or FALSE   When recycling is done within families, it is usually the father that encourages and reinforces the other family members' efforts.

18. TRUE or FALSE   Giving work groups, families, or factories weekly feedback regarding how much they have recycled has not been shown to either increase or decrease people's recycling efforts.

19. TRUE or FALSE   The carbon recycling adjuster is a tool that makes it easier for individuals to get feedback about their individual resource consumption.

20. TRUE or FALSE   Feedback is most effective when it is broad-based, intermittent, and general.

21. TRUE or FALSE   Any learning format that presents information in small amounts, gives immediate practice, and provides continuous feedback to learners is known as guided discovery learning.

22. TRUE or FALSE   When compared to non-CAI approaches, computer-assisted instruction (CAI) has not been shown to save any time or effort.

23. TRUE or FALSE   CAI learners exhibit a higher final level of skill or knowledge than do learners using non-CAI methods.

24. TRUE or FALSE   People often do better with feedback from a computer because they can freely make mistakes and learn from them.

25. TRUE or FALSE   Some CAI programs, called cognitive maps, make use of stories, competition with a partner, sound effects, and game-like graphics.

26. TRUE or FALSE   Educational simulations allow students to explore an imaginary situation or "microworld" that mimics real-world problems.

Critical Thinking Question

Can you imagine different forms of feedback?

Module 6.3 Partial Reinforcement and Stimulus Control

Partial Reinforcement—Las Vegas, a Human Skinner Box?

Survey Question: How are we influenced by patterns of reward?

Language Development Guide

ill equipped: unprepared
imagine: picture in your mind
contrary: opposite
would be well advised to: should
stop-and-go fashion: series of stopping and starting; not in a continuous manner
Las Vegas: city in Nevada that has numerous places to gambling (casinos)
curiously: strangely; oddly
shift: change to
resistant: opposed to; against
obscure: difficult to understand
lost in the lore of: now unknown
habit: a very established, deeply-rooted learned pattern of behavior
casino: a place in which legal gambling takes place
slot machines: gambling machine with three or more wheels or reels which spin or computer graphics which move when a lever is pulled or a button is pushed
spills: falls; drops
payoff: win money

329

"get hooked": addicted

retirement: giving up work

alas: sadly

contrast: compare; make a distinction

Bingo!: in this case and expression of "I won!" (Bingo is a board game where the winner yells "Bingo!")

"the one": the winning one

hard to resist: difficult to fight against; easy to give in

nonreward: response not followed by reinforcement

exaggeration: overstatement

penniless: without any money

cleaned out: lose all your money

cumulative recorder: machine that measures number of responses over time

tick marks: small diagonal lines

fixed: set; unchanging

piecework: per item made

output: amount produced

varied: mixed; assorted

interval: time period

keen: exact, expert

spurts: brief but fast

zooming: going fast

famous: well-known

"stuck in time": being able to be only in the present time

pecking key: object in the Skinner box that the pigeon or other animal touches with its beak or nose in order to receive a food reinforcer

scrub jays: bird found in southwestern United States, Mexico, and Central America

hoarders: people or animals who store, collect, save large amounts of various objects

decay: rot; decompose

edible: safe to eat

debate: dispute; discussion; question

beloved: much-loved

settle: to decide on; agree to accept it

flip-flops: simple sandal shoe in which a strap is usually between first and second toe

parallel: similarity; comparison

busy signal: telephone indicator that the person you wish to speak to is already talking to someone and your call cannot go through to him or her

doggedly: determinedly; stubbornly

bulldog tenacity: bulldogs were bred to hold on to an angry bull; so extreme stubbornness, refusal to give up

anglers: people who like to fish

Recite and Review

1. A rule or plan for determining which responses will be reinforced is called a(n) _____ of reinforcement.
2. If a reinforcer follows every correct response, then the person is receiving _____ reinforcement.
3. Reinforcers do not follow every correct response in the four plans of reinforcement known as _____ reinforcement.

330

4. Responses acquired through reinforcement that do not follow every correct response are highly resistant to extinction. This principle is known as the _____ effect.

5. When reinforcement does not follow every correct response it makes it harder for the learner to distinguish between periods of reinforcement and periods of _____.

6. Edgar is teaching his son how to use a new wood carving tool. During these initial stages of teaching, Edgar should reinforce his son using _____ reinforcement.

7. After his son has been working with the new wood carving tool for awhile, Edgar should maintain this behavior using one of the four schedules of _____ reinforcement.

8. In order to collect the data regarding an animal's responses within a Skinner box, scientists use a device that consists of a moving strip of paper and a mechanical pen that jumps upward each time a response is made. This device is called a(n) _____ recorder.

9. When responses are recorded in a Skinner box, rapid responding by the animal causes the mechanical pen on the recorder to draw a(n) _____ line.

10. When an animal in a Skinner box makes no response, the recorder on the box indicates this with a(n) _____ line.

11. When reinforcers are being given to the animal in the Skinner box, this will be indicated on the recorder by small _____ on the lines.

12. You are hired to clean the large windows in a building. For your labor, you will be paid $150 for every ten windows you clean. You are receiving this monetary reinforcement on a(n) _____ schedule of partial reinforcement.

13. If a reinforcer is given after three to seven correct responses with the actual number of responses needed for reinforcement changing randomly, then the type of partial reinforcement schedule being used is a(n) _____.

14. A set number of correct responses must be made to get a reinforcer in the type of partial reinforcement known as _____.

15. Playing a slot machine is an example of the type of partial reinforcement known as _____.

16. The ratio schedule that tends to produce the greater resistance to extinction is the _____ ratio schedule.

17. Golf, tennis, and baseball are reinforced on the partial reinforcement schedule known as _____.

18. If a reinforcer is given for a correct response only after a set amount of time has passed since the last reinforced response, then the type of partial reinforcement schedule being used is a(n) _____.

19. As a college student you are able to think about your high school graduation as well as think about your future graduation from college. Being able to move back and forth through time in your mind makes you a(n) _____ traveler.

20. Pigeons and rats show that they are sensitive to a passage of time because they stop responding immediately after receiving a reinforcer and do not start again until just before the next scheduled reinforcement when they are placed on a(n) _____ schedule of partial reinforcement.

21. In an experiment, birds called scrub jays were allowed to hoard some nuts in one location and some worms in another and then were confined. When they were released after different time periods, the birds went to the location with the freshest food rather than their favorite food, which showed that they were aware of the _____ of time.

22. Getting paid every other week for work done comes closest to the schedule of partial reinforcement known as _____.

23. Success in fishing would be an example of the partial schedule of reinforcement called _____.

24. If a reinforcer is given for the first correct response made after a random amount of time has passed since the last reinforced response, then the partial reinforcement schedule being used is _____.

Connections

1. ___ schedule of reinforcement

2. ___ continuous reinforcement

3. ___ partial reinforcement effect

4. ___ fixed ratio (FR) schedule

5. ___ variable ratio (VR) schedule

6. ___ fixed interval (FI) schedule

7. ___ variable interval (VI) schedule

8. ___ cumulative recorder

9. ___ cognitive time travelers

a. reinforcer given for the first correct response after a varied amount of time has passed

b. reinforcer given for the first correct response after a set amount of time has passed

c. device consisting of a moving strip of paper and a mechanical pen that records responses in a Skinner box

d. schedule in which every correct response is followed by a reinforcer

e. varied number of correct responses must be made to get a reinforcer

f. set number of correct responses must be made to get a reinforcer

g. rule or plan for determining which responses will be reinforced

h. when only a portion of all responses are reinforced, the responses acquired will be more resistant to extinction

i. being able to move back and forth through time in one's mind

Check Your Memory

1. TRUE or FALSE   Continuous reinforcement means that you reinforce every correct and incorrect response made.
2. TRUE or FALSE   Partial reinforcement is better to use during initial learning, while continuous reinforcement is more resistant to extinction.
3. TRUE or FALSE   Partial reinforcement includes long periods of nonreward making it harder to distinguish between periods of reinforcement and extinction.
4. TRUE or FALSE   The partial reinforcement effect states that responses acquired by partial reinforcement are easier to extinguish than responses acquired through continuous reinforcement.
5. TRUE or FALSE   Schedules of reinforcement are plans for determining which responses will be reinforced.
6. TRUE or FALSE   A cumulative recorder is a device that consists of a moving strip of paper and a mechanical pen that is connected to a Skinner box to record the animal's rate of responding.
7. TRUE or FALSE   In response recordings, rapid responding is indicated by a horizontal line being drawn by the recording device, while no response is indicated by a vertical line.
8. TRUE or FALSE   A child who received a gold star for every 10 problems he completes correctly is being reinforced on a fixed interval (FI) schedule of reinforcement.

9. TRUE or FALSE   Factory or farm workers who are paid on a piecework basis would be on a fixed ratio (FR) schedule of reinforcement.
10. TRUE or FALSE   Golf, tennis, baseball, and many other sports are reinforced on a variable ratio basis.
11. TRUE or FALSE   Playing a slot machine is an example of a variable interval (VI) schedule of reinforcement.
12. TRUE or FALSE   Being paid every other week at your employment is similar to a fixed ratio (FR) schedule of reinforcement.
13. TRUE or FALSE   Success in fishing is on a variable ratio (VR) schedule of reinforcement.
14. TRUE or FALSE   Fixed ratio (FR) and variable ratio (VR) schedules produce high response rates.
15. TRUE or FALSE   Fixed ratio (FR) schedules tend to produce greater resistance to extinction than variable ratio (VR) schedules.
16. TRUE or FALSE   In interval schedules, the time interval that must pass before reinforcement is given is measured from the last reinforced response with any responses made during the time interval not being reinforced.
17. TRUE or FALSE   Fixed interval (FI) schedules produce moderate response rates with few responses occurring just after a reinforcement is delivered and a spurt of activity occurring just before the next reinforcement.
18. TRUE or FALSE   Variable interval (VI) schedules produce slow, steady response rates and tremendous resistance to extinction.
19. TRUE or FALSE   Humans are cognitive time travelers, who regularly zoom back and forth through time in their minds.
20. TRUE or FALSE   Conditioning studies have repeatedly shown that animals are "stuck in time" and are not sensitive to its passage.

Critical Thinking Question

A business owner who pays employees an hourly wage wants to increase productivity. How could the owner make more effective use of reinforcement?

Stimulus Control—Red Light, Green Light

Language Development Guide

intersections: crossroads; junction
in similar fashion: in a like way
formally: official
illuminated: lighted
basically: in the end; essentially
meanwhile: for now
back at the table. . . .: joking way to say going back to the dog and table example
aptly: appropriately; rightly
"sniffer" dogs: dogs trained to discriminate the smell of drugs or other articles and indicate to their handlers when and where they have located the drugs
border crossings: checkpoint at a country's boundary with another country used to monitor individuals entering the country
contraband: illegal items
tremendous: great; huge
impact: influence
brands: trade names of products
freeway: a wide highway designed for high speed traffic and/or a large number of cars

333

contingencies: eventuality; possible events
tailgating: driving too closely behind someone
ringtone: sound made by a phone to indicate an incoming call

Recite and Review

1. When you are driving, your behavior at intersections is controlled by the red or green light, which illustrates the behavioral effect of _____.
2. When stimuli that consistently precede a rewarded response tend to influence when and where the response will occur, the effect is known as _____.
3. The reason that young children may temporarily call all men "daddy," much to the embarrassment of their parents is due to operant stimulus _____.
4. The tendency to respond to stimuli similar to those that preceded operant reinforcement is known as operant stimulus _____.
5. The tendency to make an operant response when stimuli previously associated with reward are present and to withhold the response when stimuli associated with nonreward are present is known as operant stimulus _____.
6. Stimuli that precede reinforced and nonreinforced responses are known as _____ stimuli.
7. The presence of a police car on the side of the road tends to bring about rapid reductions in driving speed, lane changes, and tailgating because the police car serves as a(n) _____ stimulus.
8. Because you fed your dog scraps from the kitchen table, your dog now jumps whenever you are at the kitchen table. If your dog now jumps when you are sitting at any table in the house, the dog is showing operant stimulus _____.
9. Your dog is jumping every time you sit at a table in the house because you originally fed him from the kitchen table. However, since you will not be feeding him at any of tables in the house (except the kitchen table), your dog's jumping should extinguish at these tables due to _____.
10. The "sniffer" dogs that locate drugs and explosives at airports and border crossings are trained to recognize these substances through operant stimulus _____.
11. Learning to recognize different automobile brands and different types of music are examples of operant stimulus _____.
12. If you use one ring tone for people you want to speak to, one for people you don't, and yet another for calls from strangers, then your ring tones are serving as _____ stimuli.

Connections

1. ___ stimulus control

2. ___ operant stimulus generalization

3. ___ operant stimulus discrimination

4. ___ discriminative stimuli

5. ___ nonreinforcement

a. tendency to respond to stimuli similar to those that preceded operant reinforcement

b. the stimuli that precede reinforced and nonreinforced responses

c. tendency to make an operant response when stimuli associated with reward are present and to withhold the response when stimuli associated with nonreward are present

d. consequence that leads to the extinction of the response

e. stimuli present when an operant response is acquired tend to determine when and where the response is made

Check Your Memory

1. TRUE or FALSE   Stimuli that consistently precede a rewarded response tend to influence when and where the response will occur, an effect known as stimulus control.
2. TRUE or FALSE   Two important aspects of stimulus control are generalization and discrimination.
3. TRUE or FALSE   Operant stimulus discrimination explains why children may temporarily call all men daddy, much to the embarrassment of their parents.
4. TRUE or FALSE   Learning to recognize different type of music involves operant stimulus discrimination.
5. TRUE or FALSE   A police car on the side of the road would be an example of a stimulus generalizer that signals drivers to slow down.
6. TRUE or FALSE   The "sniffer" dogs that locate drugs and explosives at airports and border crossings are trained to recognize these substances through operant stimulus generalization.
7. TRUE or FALSE   Stimulus control explains why we pick up phones that are ringing, but rarely answer phones that are silent.
8. TRUE or FALSE   If you started using the SQ4R method to study in psychology class and then start using this method in your other classes, you are exhibiting operant stimulus generalization.
9. TRUE or FALSE   Although your cat meows to the sound of the can opener because his canned food was opened this way, this response of meowing to the can opener will be extinguished if you switch to dry food due to nonreinforcement.
10. TRUE or FALSE   If you use one ring tone for people you want to speak to, one for people you don't, and yet another for calls from strangers, then your ring tones are serving as discriminative stimuli.

Critical Thinking Question

How could you use conditioning principles to teach a dog or a cat to come when called?

Module 6.4 Punishment

Punishment—Putting the Brakes on Behavior

Survey Question: What does punishment do to behavior?

Language Development Guide

reprimands: scoldings, warnings
unfinished: incomplete
starved: hungry for; wants something badly
onset: start
humanely: kindly; caringly
haphazardly: at random; irregularly
"Wait 'til your father comes home, then you'll be sorry": the father will punish the child with a spanking when he gets home from work
feared brute: monster
light socket: electrical connector
suppresses: reduces, holds back
slapping: hitting
sneaks: steals

snack: item of food eaten between meals; usually involving cookies or salted chips

sneaky snacking: funny way of saying "to steal a snack"

but seriously: honestly; in reality

to reiterate: to repeat; to say again

drawbacks: disadvantages

resented: bear a grudge; feel bitter about; hate

obnoxious: unbearable; horrible; intolerable

relief: feeling of a burden as been removed; getting a break from something horrible

dodge: move away; avoid; get out of the way

postpone: put off; delay

sidestep: avoid; get out of the way

nips: small bites

veterinarian: doctor of animals other than humans

lash out: to verbally or physically attack another

frustrated: blocked from reaching one's goal; irritated

hostile: showing ill will; very unfriendly

antisocial: without a conscience; without guilt or remorse

punitive: penalizing; punishing

humiliation: shame; disgrace; embarrassment

quell: suppress or put down completely

defiance: disobedience; uncooperativeness

in light of: considering

liberal: generous; large amounts

harsh: cruel; severe

sparing the rod: part of a Biblical saying, used to suggest that if a child is not physically punished, he or she will behave badly and have a bad character

minimize: reduce; decrease

backed up: supported or assisted with

coupled: joined with

antispanking laws: prohibiting or banning the use of physical punishment with children by adults

poses: establishes

incompatible: that oppose; that conflict with

withdrawn: removed; pulled away

rebuke: scolding; reprimand

bridge: link; connect

explode: get very angry; fly into a rage

offense: wrong-doing

counter: opposite; offsets

acknowledge: recognize; allow

carried away: to get so excited that one will overdo a behavior

abusive: cruel; vicious

guard against: protect against; ward off; resist

retain: keep; hold on to

ideally: in a perfect world

"habit forming": addicting; becoming well-established

disrespectful: rude; impolite; bad-mannered

temptation: attraction; the pull

silence may be golden: the common saying "silence is golden" means that quiet moments are special and should be enjoyed

Recite and Review

1. Within instrumental learning, spankings, reprimands, fines, and failing grades are all examples of the consequence that suppresses responses called _____.

2. Any consequence that reduces the frequency of a target behavior is referred to as a(n) _____.

3. If Chris is starved for attention, a reprimand or a spanking could _____ his misbehavior.

4. To be most effective, reinforcement and punishment must be given only after a response occurs, which means it is response _____.

5. Punishment involves either the onset of an unpleasant event or the removal of a positive state of affairs, which is called _____.

6. The effectiveness of punishers as well as reinforcers depends on when they are presented, whether immediately or delayed, which refers to the importance of _____.

7. Research shows that punishment works best when the punisher is presented _____ after the response.

8. Another variable that influences the effectiveness of punishment is whether the punishment is given each time the response occurs, which refers to the importance of _____.

9. Whether the punishment is mild or severe refers to the variable affecting punishment called _____.

10. In looking at the effects of mild versus severe levels of punishment, research has found that a response will only be temporarily suppressed if one uses _____ punishment.

11. The permanent suppression of actions as basic as eating has occurred when people have used _____ punishment.

12. When people and situations are associated with punishment, they tend to become feared, resented, or disliked through _____ conditioning.

13. Learning to make a response in order to end an aversive stimulus is called _____ learning.

14. Learning to make a response in order to postpone or prevent discomfort describes _____ learning.

15. The new employee at your office is a loud and obnoxious person, who tends to want to engage you in numerous conversations throughout the day. If you were able to end your conversation with this person by telling him that you needed to return a phone call to a client before a particular time, you will probably use this excuse again, which illustrates _____ learning.

16. Lately, every time you see the loud and obnoxious person coming down the hall at your office, you tend to duck into the restroom or another cubicle. Each time you sidestep this person, you are again reinforced, illustrating _____ learning.

17. Children who run away from their parents when they are being punished are illustrating _____ learning.

18. Often, children who have been frequently punished will learn to lie about their behavior and will spend as much time away from home as possible, which illustrates _____ learning.

19. When spanked, a child may feel angry and frustrated. If that child then goes outside and hits his brother or sister, the danger is that this act may feel good to the child because it releases anger and frustration. Thus, the child is rewarded for this act of _____.

20. Classroom disruptions, defiance, and inattention are more likely to be controlled by using praise, approval, and tangible rewards, which are examples of _____ reinforcement.

21. Regarding the three basic tools for controlling simple learning, responses are strengthened by _____.

22. Responses are suppressed by the basic tool of _____.

23. In controlling simple learning, responses are extinguished through _____.
24. The basic tools for controlling simple learning work best when they are used in _____.
25. When trying to change a child's misbehavior, it is usually best to begin by trying to encourage good behavior by making liberal use of _____.
26. In addition to encouraging good behavior, parents should try to eliminate misbehavior by ignoring the problem behavior, which involves the process known as _____.
27. Negative emotional reactions, avoidance and escape behaviors, and increased aggression occur when parents use harsh or excessive _____.
28. If punishment is used at all, it should be mild and used in situations that pose immediate _____.
29. Punishment can be used to suppress a response if the punishment produces actions _____ with that response.
30. Taking away privileges works best for older children and adults and is an example of the punishment known as _____.
31. When using mild punishment, such as reprimanding a child for taking away her sister's toys, it is best to also reward an alternate, desired response that is in direct opposition to the unacceptable behavior, such as rewarding her for sharing her toys with her sister. This reinforcement of an alternate, desired response illustrates the use of _____-conditioning.
32. Two-thirds of child abuse cases start out as parents attempting to discipline using _____.
33. It is important to never punish a person in front of other people. This will allow the person to maintain his or her dignity and self-_____.
34. A common error in parenting is to rely too much for training or discipline on the consequence of _____.
35. The overall emotional adjustment of a child or pet is significantly better if the child is disciplined mainly by _____.
36. Using punishment can become "habit forming" because the punishment brings a sudden end to the adult's irritation, which acts as _____ reinforcement for the adult.

Connections

1. ___ punisher
2. ___ contingently
3. ___ consistency
4. ___ timing
5. ___ intensity
6. ___ escape learning
7. ___ avoidance learning
8. ___ reinforcement
9. ___ nonreinforcement
10. ___ counter-conditioned

a. refers to when the consequence is given, such as immediately or delayed
b. learning to make a response in order to end an aversive stimulus
c. any event that decreases the probability or frequency of a response it follows
d. learning to make a response in order to postpone or prevent discomfort
e. causes responses to extinguish
f. rewarded for displaying any behavior that is in direct opposition to the unacceptable behavior
g. means that the consequence is only given after the person or animal makes the response
h. refers to whether the consequence is given each time the response occurs
i. refers to the strength of the consequence, such as mild or severe
j. consequence that strengthens or increases responding

338

Check Your Memory

1. TRUE or FALSE   Punishment lowers the probability that a response will occur again.
2. TRUE or FALSE   To be most effective, punishment must be given contingently.
3. TRUE or FALSE   A reprimand or a spanking is always considered a punisher whether it reduces the frequency of the behavior or not.
4. TRUE or FALSE   Delaying the punishment long enough for the child to think about his or her misbehavior, such as "waiting until your father gets home," is an effective way to punish an undesirable response.
5. TRUE or FALSE   Mild punishment only temporarily suppresses a response.
6. TRUE or FALSE   Severe punishment may permanently suppress responding, even for actions as basic as eating.
7. TRUE or FALSE   Punishment is an effective and efficient means of toilet training and teaching children to eat politely.
8. TRUE or FALSE   In the experiment in the Skinner box in which one group of rats was punished with a slap for each bar press and the other group was not, the punishment of the slap led to rapid extinction of the bar pressing.
9. TRUE or FALSE   People and situations associated with punishment tend, through classical conditioning, to become feared, resented, or disliked.
10. TRUE or FALSE   Aversive stimuli encourage escape and avoidance learning.
11. TRUE or FALSE   Escape learning is based on negative reinforcement.
12. TRUE or FALSE   A child who runs from his parents when they are punishing him is exhibiting escape learning.
13. TRUE or FALSE   A teen who lies about her behavior and spends as much time away from home as possible is exhibiting avoidance learning.
14. TRUE or FALSE   Studies have found that children who are physically punished are less likely to engage in aggressive, impulsive, or antisocial behavior.
15. TRUE or FALSE   Positive reinforcement is much less likely to decrease classroom disruptions, defiance, and inattention than punishment.
16. TRUE or FALSE   A classic study of angry adolescent boys found that if they were severely punished at home, they suppressed their misbehavior at home but were more aggressive elsewhere, such as school.
17. TRUE or FALSE   Reinforcement strengthens responses, while nonreinforcement causes responses to extinguish.
18. TRUE or FALSE   Reinforcement, nonreinforcement, and punishment work best when used in combination.
19. TRUE or FALSE   It is much more effective to strengthen and encourage desirable behaviors than it is to punish unwanted behaviors.
20. TRUE or FALSE   Most children show no signs of long-term damage from spanking if it is backed up by supportive parenting.
21. TRUE or FALSE   Currently, there have been no antispanking laws passed in any country.
22. TRUE or FALSE   If punishment is used at all, it should be mild and used in situations that pose immediate danger, such as running into the street.
23. TRUE or FALSE   "Sparing the rod" (failing to use physical punishment) has been shown to spoil a child, to encourage increased aggression, and to lead to long-term mental health problems.
24. TRUE or FALSE   Taking away privileges or other positive reinforcers has not been shown to be effective with older children and adults.
25. TRUE or FALSE   If you cannot punish an animal or young child immediately, wait for the next instance of misbehavior.

26. TRUE or FALSE   Both parents should try to punish their children for the same things and in the same way.

27. TRUE or FALSE   A child who is reprimanded for taking toys from a sibling should be counter- conditioned, or rewarded for displaying any behavior that is opposite to the unacceptable behavior, such as sharing toys with the sibling.

28. TRUE or FALSE   Since punishment indicates what the "right" response is, punishment can be used to teach new behaviors.

29. TRUE or FALSE   It is important for parents to be willing to admit their mistake if they wrongfully punish the child or if they punish too severely.

30. TRUE or FALSE   When possible, it is recommended that a person receive his or her punishment in front of others, so that the punishment will be remembered longer.

31. TRUE or FALSE   Two-thirds of child abuse cases start out as attempts at physical punishment.

32. TRUE or FALSE   The overall emotional adjustment of a child or pet disciplined mainly by reward has been shown to be much worse than those disciplined mainly by punishment.

33. TRUE or FALSE   When children are noisy or disrespectful and are punished, this sudden end to the adult's irritation acts as negative reinforcement and encourages the adult to use punishment more often in the future.

Critical Thinking Question

1. Using the concept of partial reinforcement, can you explain why inconsistent punishment is especially ineffective?

2. Escape and avoidance learning have been applied to encourage automobile seat belt use. Can you explain how?

Module 6.5 Cognitive Learning and Imitation
Cognitive Learning—Beyond Conditioning
Survey Question: What is cognitive learning?

Language Development Guide

accordingly: for that reason
realm: area
dimension: aspect; factor
loosely speaking: in an informal way
maze: puzzling pathway
lowly: humble; simple
mental giant: genius; very intelligent
in a sense: sort of
diagrams: drawings; charts; graphs
envision: imagine
"uneducated": lacking specific knowledge
remote: distant
mechanical: proceeding automatically by habit; like a machine
parallelogram: four-sided figure with opposite sides parallel to each other and equal in length
"piece": a section
rectangle: parallelogram with four right angles

formula: rule; procedure
implies: indicates; suggests
stumble: proceed unsteadily; trip up

Recite and Review

1. Learning that extends learning beyond basic conditioning into the realms of memory, thinking, problem solving, and language is called _____ learning.
2. People develop an overall mental picture of how their town is laid out and use it as a guide even when they must detour or take a new route. This mental picture is called a(n) _____.
3. Learning that occurs without obvious reinforcement and remains hidden until reinforcement is provided is referred to as _____ learning.
4. Finding your way through the many levels found in many video games requires that you develop an internal representation of these levels called a(n) _____.
5. In humans, learning that is related to higher-level abilities, such as making a mental note regarding information that might come in handy in the future, is called _____ learning.
6. Many psychologists believe that learning is more lasting and flexible when people learn facts and principles through _____.
7. Learning that takes place mechanically, through repetition and memorization, or by learning rules is called _____ learning.
8. Learning based on insight and understanding is called _____ learning.
9. Learning that can lead to a better understanding of new or unusual problems is _____ learning.
10. The best teaching strategies occur when students are given enough freedom to actively think about problems and enough direction so that they gain useful knowledge, a teaching strategy known as _____.

Connections

1. ___ cognitive learning
2. ___ cognitive map
3. ___ latent learning
4. ___ rote learning
5. ___ discovery learning
6. ___ guided discovery

a. any learning strategy based on insight and understanding
b. learning that takes place mechanically, through repetition and memorization, or by learning rules
c. internal images or other mental representations of an area that underlie an ability to choose alternative paths to the same goal
d. refers to understanding, knowing, anticipating, and making use of information-rich higher mental processes
e. students are given enough freedom to actively think about problems and enough direction so that they gain useful knowledge
f. learning that occurs without obvious reinforcement and that remains unexpressed until reinforcement is provided

Check Your Memory

1. TRUE or FALSE   Cognitive learning refers to understanding, knowing, anticipating, or otherwise, making use of information-rich higher mental processes.

341

2. TRUE or FALSE   Learning your way around your hometown illustrates the formation of a cognitive map.

3. TRUE or FALSE   Latent learning occurs without obvious reinforcement and remains hidden until reinforcement is provided.

4. TRUE or FALSE   In a classic animal study in which the first group of rats was rewarded for completing the maze and the second group was not rewarded, the second group never ran the maze as quickly as the first group even after the second group was rewarded for completing it.

5. TRUE or FALSE   When students draw pictures or diagrams to help them envision how concepts fit together, the students are developing an eidetic map.

6. TRUE or FALSE   In humans, latent learning is related to higher-level abilities, such as anticipating future reward.

7. TRUE or FALSE   Just satisfying curiosity can be enough to reward learning.

8. TRUE or FALSE   If students, who have ridden the school bus for six months, are able to direct the new bus driver on where to turn and when to stop to let students off, the students' knowledge was most likely due to latent learning.

9. TRUE or FALSE   Although discovery learning can be efficient, most psychologists believe that rote learning is more lasting and flexible and leads students to a better understanding of new or unusual problems.

10. TRUE or FALSE   The best teaching strategies are based on guided discovery, in which students are given enough freedom to actively think about problems and enough guidance so that they gain useful knowledge.

Critical Thinking Question

Draw a map of your school's campus as you picture it now. Draw a map of the campus as you pictured it after your first visit. Why do the maps differ?

Modeling—Do as I Do, Not as I Say
Survey Question: Does learning occur by imitation?

Language Development Guide

Do as I do, not as I say: a play on the phrase "Do as I say, not as I do"
tedious: tiring, boring or repetitive work
trial-and-error: way of learning by trying something; if in error, trying again until you succeed
tuneup: minor car maintenance
feats: achievements; accomplishments
world-class: first-rate; outstanding
gymnasts: sport involving flexibility and balance; tumblers
status: position; standing; rank
thereafter: from then on
punch: hit with fist
cartoon: humorous short film with characters' actions drawn; a drawing
duplicate: copy
tragically: sadly; unfortunately
domestic violence: physical abuse toward a spouse or domestic partner
commit: do it
swats: hits; slaps
promptly: quickly; without delay

"this will teach you…": this will show you that what you did was wrong
unrealistic: not practical; unworkable
so why does everybody love Raymond, anyway?: joke, reference to the television show title, 'Everybody Loves Raymond'
print media: newspapers and magazines
lion's share: majority
countless: numerous
torture: to make suffer; cruelty
G-rated: appropriate for the general audience, including young children, to view
in short: in summary; briefly
massive dose: very large amount
conclusively: convincingly; decisively
prone: likely; have a tendency to
ominously: threatening; worrisome
contacted: gotten in touch with; spoken to
professional wrestling: sport in which two unarmed people are paid to compete in hand-to-hand battles
rap music: type of music that involves rhythmic talking that rhymes
gore: blood and extreme physical injury
military combat: battles and fighting during war
flamethrower: weapon that sends out ignited fuel for several yards
writhe: squirm; thrash about; twist and turn
Mortal Kombat: best-selling violent fighting video game
retaliation: revenge; responding in anger to an offense against you
competitor: opponent; challenger
don't mess with: don't bother; leave that person alone
exposure: contact with; experience with
desensitizes: less sensitive; less responsive to
fair to say: it is only right to say
consumers: users or viewers of
invariably: always
identify with: feeling emotionally connected; wanting to be like this person
copy: imitate
heroes: persons that display exceptional courage in helping others; good guys
villains: bad guys; evil characters
restricted: limited; controlled
permissible: allowable
apparent: obvious

Recite and Review

1. Watching and imitating the actions of another person or noting the consequences of the person's actions can lead to _____ learning, or modeling.
2. The theorist that said that many of our behaviors are learned through modeling was _____.
3. If you learned a new dance step by watching some of your peers dancing at the prom, you learned the dance step through _____ learning.
4. When we learn a skill through modeling, it often allows us to skip the tedious _____ stage of learning.
5. Greg watched his guitar instructor finger the strings to make various chords. Thus, during this learning process, Greg's instructor is serving as an example, or _____.

343

6. For observational learning to take place, the learner must remember what was done by first paying _____ to the model.

7. You long to be a world class ice skater and have carefully observed televised ice skating tournaments and can remember all the jumps and spins. However, you will not be able to become that level of skater if you cannot _____ the modeled behavior.

8. A learner is more likely to imitate a modeled behavior if the model was successful at a task or if the model was _____ for making the response.

9. In general, models who are attractive, trustworthy, capable, admired, powerful, or high in status tend to be _____.

10. A learner will repeat the modeled behavior if he or she, upon making this new response, receives either normal reinforcement or informational _____.

11. In a classic experiment on modeling, children watched an adult attack a large blow-up "_____" doll.

12. When three groups of children watched a live adult model, a filmed model, and a cartoon model, respectively, physically attack a doll, most of the children in all three groups imitated the attack on the doll when allowed to play with it. Of the three model types, the one that was slightly less effective in encouraging aggression was the _____ model.

13. Since actual imitation of a response depends on whether the model was rewarded or punished, we can say that observational learning only _____ a person to duplicate a response.

14. When a parent says one thing but does a completely different behavior, children tend to do what the parent _____.

15. Of the various types of media, including video games, television, movies, the Internet, music, and print media, the one that consumes a majority of young people's media attention is _____.

16. Studies show conclusively that if children watch a great deal of televised violence, they will be more prone to behave _____.

17. One possibility of how video game violence increases aggressive behavior is that repeated exposure to violence makes the players less likely to react negatively to violence, or _____ them to violence.

18. By playing violent video games, the players may learn to be aggressive in real life because they have _____ being violent against other people.

19. In general, media violence can make aggression more likely, but in any given child, it does not invariable "_____" the aggression to occur.

20. Youngsters are more likely to copy televised violence if they believe that aggression is an acceptable way to _____.

21. Young people are also more likely to copy televised violence if they believe that TV violence is _____.

22. Children are more likely to imitate violent TV characters if they _____ with these characters.

23. Very young children, in particular, are more likely to be influenced by TV violence because they do not fully recognize that media characters and the stories are _____.

24. According to your textbook, the amount of permissible violence on television has been restricted by the countries of Norway, Switzerland, and _____.

Connections

1. ___ observational learning
   a. person who serves as an example in observational learning

2. ___ Bo-Bo the Clown
   b. nonviolent video game used in an aggression-retaliation study

3. ___ Mortal Kombat

4. ___ PGA Tournament Golf

5. ___ desensitization

6. ___ model

c. violent video game used in an aggression-retaliation study

d. part of a classic study involving violent live, filmed, and cartoon models

e. learning achieved by watching and imitating the actions of another or noting the consequences of those actions

f. being less likely to react negatively to violence

Check Your Memory

1. TRUE or FALSE   The psychologist who conducted research on modeling and believed that anything that could be learned from direct experience could be learned by observation was Carl Rogers.

2. TRUE or FALSE   Humans are the only mammals that can learn through observational learning.

3. TRUE or FALSE   Learning a skill through observational learning allows a person to skip the tedious trial-and-error stage of learning.

4. TRUE or FALSE   Through observational learning, a person can learn new responses and to carry out or avoid previously learned responses.

5. TRUE or FALSE   Observational learning is not helpful in learning general rules that can be applied to various situations,

6. TRUE or FALSE   For observation learning to occur, the learner must pay attention to the model, remember what was done, and be able to reproduce the modeled behavior.

7. TRUE or FALSE   If a model is successful at a task or rewarded for a response, the learner is more likely to imitate the behavior.

8. TRUE or FALSE   In general, models who are attractive, powerful, or high in status are less likely to be imitated since they are not similar to the observer.

9. TRUE or FALSE   Once people try the new response they saw modeled, normal reinforcement or feedback determines whether the response will be repeated thereafter.

10. TRUE or FALSE   Most of the participants in the "Bo-Bo the Clown" doll experiment did not imitate the aggression they had seen.

11. TRUE or FALSE   In the "Bo-Bo the Clown" doll experiment, the cartoon aggression was slightly more effective than the filmed and live models.

12. TRUE or FALSE   When parents tell a child to do one thing but model a completely different response, the children tend to imitate what the parents do, and not what they say.

13. TRUE or FALSE   Through modeling, children learn attitudes, gestures, emotions, personality traits, fears, anxieties, and bad habits.

14. TRUE or FALSE   Children who witness domestic violence are more likely to commit it themselves when they become adults.

15. TRUE or FALSE   Of the various media formats, including television, video games, movies, the Internet, music, and print media, the Internet consumes the majority of young people's media attention.

16. TRUE or FALSE   There are no studies that demonstrate that children who watch a great deal of televised violence are more prone to behaving aggressively.

17. TRUE or FALSE   Studies have shown that watching violence on television as a child as no effect on one's behavior as a young adult.

345

18. TRUE or FALSE   G-rated cartoons average 10 minutes of violence per hour.

19. TRUE or FALSE   In a study of college students who played violent and nonviolent video games, the students who played the violent Mortal Kombat did not show any more aggression on later tasks than those who had played the nonviolent PGA Tournament Golf.

20. TRUE or FALSE   Repeated exposure to video game violence tends to oversensitize players, making them more likely to react negatively to violence and, thus, less prone to engage in it.

21. TRUE or FALSE   Children tend to imitate what they observe in all media both good and bad behaviors.

22. TRUE or FALSE   Youngsters who believe that aggression is an acceptable way to solve problems are most likely to copy televised aggression.

23. TRUE or FALSE   Children who identify with violent TV characters are most likely to model their aggressive acts.

24. TRUE or FALSE   Young children are less likely to be influenced by media violence because they fully recognize that media characters and stories are fantasies.

25. TRUE or FALSE   Media heroes tend to behave as aggressively as the villains.

26. TRUE or FALSE   Countries like Canada, Norway, and Switzerland have restricted the amount of permissible violence on television.

Critical Thinking Question

Children who watch many aggressive programs on television tend to be more aggressive than average. Why doesn't this observation prove that televised aggression causes aggressive behavior?

Module 6.6 Psychology in Action: Behavioral Self-Management—A Rewarding

Survey Question: How does conditioning apply to everyday problems?

Language Development Guide

successive: the following
iPod: small music player
Guitar Hero: series of music video games that simulate the playing of guitar and bass
fall short: fail
systematically: methodically; scientifically
cappuccino: strong coffee drink
swear: use bad language; curse
tally: count, total
expense: cost
sharp-edged: cutting; satirical
junk food: snack foods that lack nutritional value
cravings: desiring; longing for
lounge: a place to relax and take a break at work
sticking: continuing to do them till the end
forfeit: give up, lose
dissertation: a lengthy research report written as a requirement for an advanced degree, usually a doctoral degree
deadline: end of the time limit; ending date

346

postdated: check that becomes payable on a future date
despised: hated
Ku Klux Klan and American Nazi Party: extreme racist organizations

Recite and Review

1. If you would like to exercise more, read more books, and attend more classes, it can be helpful to us behavioral _____.
2. To help people manage their own behavior, they can adapt and use the principles of _____ conditioning.
3. The first step in managing your own behavior involves choosing a(n) _____.
4. In setting up a plan to manage one's own behavior, the second step involves recording how much time you currently spend performing the specific behavior or counting the number of desired or undesired responses you make each day, which is called recording a(n) _____.
5. In setting realistic goals for gradual improvement on each successive week, it is important to remember the principle of _____.
6. If Artee meets her daily goal for exercise, she will watch an hour of television at night; and if she reaches her weekly goal, she will treat herself to a movie. The hour of television and the movie are serving as _____ for meeting her goals.
7. Any high-frequency response can be used to reinforce a low-frequency response, according to the _____ principle.
8. You like to watch TV, but hate to study. So, you make it a rule not to turn on the TV until you have studied for an hour. You are using the principle popularized by psychologist David _____.
9. Keeping records of response frequencies, or self-recording, is a form of informational _____.
10. Self-recording is helpful because you are more likely to engage in desired behaviors and less likely to perform undesired behaviors when you systematically _____ yourself.
11. Jon often makes jokes at the expense of others and gets reinforced for this behavior through the attention of his classmates. If Jon is able to get the same amount of attention by giving other people praise and compliments, he can break this habit of being hurtful to others by using the strategy that involves _____.
12. By discovering what is reinforcing an unwanted response and removing, avoiding, or delaying the reinforcement, one would be using the strategy of _____.
13. If you are in the habit of coming home from work, eating a lot of junk food while watching TV and spoiling your dinner, then one way to stop this bad habit is to scramble the sequence of events, such as taking a shower, studying, eating dinner, and then watching TV. This illustrates the strategy of breaking up _____.
14. Bob wants to stop smoking, so he removes ashtrays, matches and extra cigarettes from his house, car, and office. Bob has removed cues or _____ stimuli for smoking.
15. Kendra is using a formal agreement stating behaviors she will change and the consequences, both reinforcers and mild punishment, that will be applied. Kendra is using a(n) _____.

Connections

1. ____ target behavior
    a. strategy for change that involves trying to get the same reinforcement with a new response

2. ____ baseline
    b. self-management based on keeping records of response frequencies

3. ____ Premack principle
    c. strategy for change that involves discovering what is reinforcing an unwanted response and removing it

347

4. ___ self-recording
5. ___ alternate responses

d. record of current behavior before the change
e. strategy for change that involves removing stimuli that elicit the bad habit

6. ___ extinction
7. ___ response chains

f. activity you want to change
g. formal agreement stating behaviors to be changed and consequences that apply

8. ___ cues and antecedents

h. any high-frequency response can be used to reinforce a low-frequency response

9. ___ behavioral contract

i. strategy for change involving scrambling the sequence of events that leads to an undesired response

Check Your Memory

1. TRUE or FALSE   The principles of classical conditioning can be adapted to manage one's own behavior, such as learning to exercise or to cut down on smoking.
2. TRUE or FALSE   The first step in a behavioral self-management program is to record a baseline.
3. TRUE or FALSE   Establishing goals and choosing reinforcers are two of the steps in a behavioral self-management program.
4. TRUE or FALSE   Using a high-frequency response to reinforce a low-frequency response is called the Thorndike principle.
5. TRUE or FALSE   If you systematically observe yourself, you will be more likely to engage in desired behaviors and less likely to perform undesired behaviors.
6. TRUE or FALSE   Self-recording helps break patterns with the feedback providing motivation as you begin to make progress.
7. TRUE or FALSE   The strategy for change that involves trying to get the same reinforcement with a new response is referred to as stimulus control.
8. TRUE or FALSE   If you try to discover what is reinforcing an unwanted response and remove, avoid, or delay the reinforcement, you are using extinction.
9. TRUE or FALSE   Breaking up response chains that precede an undesired behavior will help break a bad habit.
10. TRUE or FALSE   If you want to stop smoking and remove matches, cigarettes, and ashtrays that elicit smoking, you are using the change strategy known as vicarious conditioning.
11. TRUE or FALSE   A formal agreement stating behaviors to be changed and consequences that apply is a behavioral contract.

Critical Thinking Question
How does setting daily goals in a behavioral self-management program help maximize the effects of reinforcement?

Final Survey and Review—Completion

Module 6.1 Learning and Classical Conditioning
What Is Learning—Does Practice Make Perfect?
Survey Question: What is learning?
1. The simple connection formed between two stimuli or the connection between a response and consequence are both examples of _____ learning.

2. Antecedents occur _____ a response.
3. If you tell a joke and most of the people that hear it laugh, you have received the consequence called _____.

Module 6.1 Classical Conditioning—Does the Name Pavlov Ring a Bell?
Survey Question: How does classical conditioning occur?

4. Classical conditioning is also called Pavlovian conditioning and _____ conditioning.
5. In Pavlov's experiment, the dogs learned to salivate to a bell because the bell was associated with food. Therefore, the unconditioned stimulus in this experiment was the _____.
6. Little Katy is scratched by a cat and becomes afraid of cats. Because the cat was associated with pain, the cat would be considered a(n) _____ stimulus.
7. The reflex conditioning that may be useful for distinguishing severely brain-damaged individuals who are in a vegetative state and those who are minimally conscious is the _____ conditioning.

Module 6.1 Principles of Classical Conditioning—Here's Johnny

8. According to this informational view, we look for associations among events and by doing so we create new mental _____.
9. Your dog has learned to bark when he hears the can opener open his canned dog food. However, you have now switched your dog to dry food. Your dog will eventually stop barking to the sound of the can opener because you have broken the association between the can opener and the food, which illustrates the process of _____.
10. Tom is afraid of snakes. When he walks by a garden hose in his friend's yard, he jumps out of the way. Tom is exhibiting stimulus _____.
11. Janine is afraid of rats, but enjoys playing with her friend's guinea pig. Janine is exhibiting stimulus _____.

Module 6.1 Classical Conditioning in Humans—An Emotional Topic
Survey Question: Does conditioning affect emotions?

12. Abby's face reddens whenever she feels ashamed just like it did when she was a child. Abby's blushing would be considered a(n) conditioned _____.
13. In order to alleviate her fear of insects, Carmen is undergoing a therapy in which she will be gradually exposed to the feared stimuli. This therapy is called _____.
14. Five-year-old Geordi observes his mother's fear of heights; and subsequently he, too, shows the same fear. Geordi developed this fear through _____ classical conditioning.

Module 6.2 Operant Conditioning
Operant Conditioning—Ping-Pong Playing Pigeons?
Survey Question: How does operant conditioning occur?

15. The law of effect was developed by psychologist _____.
16. The learner tends to be active in emitting voluntary responses in _____ conditioning.
17. Eric will only receive money for painting the fence when he finishes the job and it has been inspected by the owner. Thus, Eric's monetary reinforcement is said to be response _____.
18. The long series of events, such as studying for quizzes, taking tests, and writing reports, that are necessary to pass a college course are rewarded at the end of the semester with an A, which illustrates the concept of response _____.

349

19. A baseball player who has come to believe that he must eat chicken before every game is exhibiting _____ behavior.
20. You have a bad cough, so you put a cough drop (lozenge) in your mouth, which relieves your cough. The next time you have a cough, you reach for a cough drop because of the consequence called _____.
21. Time-out is an example of a type of punishment known as _____.

Module 6.2 Operant Reinforcers—What's Your Pleasure?

Survey Question: Are there different kinds of operant reinforcement?

22. Food, water, psychoactive drugs, and the absence of pain would all be considered _____ reinforcers.
23. Lisa attends an elementary school class in which the students receive gold stars for "good behavior," such as turning in homework, being cooperative, etc. When the students have collected a certain number of gold stars, they can exchange them for special privileges or various items. Lisa's classroom appears to operate as a(n) _____.
24. If a child's behavior is being shaped by attention, praise, and approval, then the adult is using the secondary reinforcers known as _____ reinforcers.
25. Another name for informational feedback is _____.
26. Feedback is most effective when it is detailed, immediate, and _____.

Module 6.3 Partial Reinforcement and Stimulus Control

Partial Reinforcement—Las Vegas, a Human Skinner Box?

Survey Question: How are we influenced by patterns of reward?

27. When a person is first learning a new skill, the person should be reinforced on a(n) _____ schedule of reinforcement.
28. One's performance in a sport, such as tennis or soccer, as well as forms of gambling are reinforced on a partial schedule of reinforcement known as _____.
29. Brides-to-be are famous for planning their weddings down to the last detail, and most people are able to remember detailed situations from their childhoods, which illustrates that we are cognitive _____.
30. Your teacher gives a psychology quiz every Friday, so you usually study on Thursday night and do not look at your psychology book until the next Thursday night. This illustrates a partial schedule of reinforcement known as _____.

Module 6.3 Stimulus Control—Red Light, Green Light

31. We pick up phones that are ringing, but rarely answer phones that are silent, which illustrates the behavioral effect of _____.
32. Alisa uses one ring tone for people she wants to speak to, one for people she doesn't, and yet another for calls from strangers. Thus, Alisa's ring tones are serving as _____ stimuli.
33. Your young child calls every woman he sees with gray hair and glasses, "grandma," since they look like your mother. Your young child is exhibiting operant stimulus _____.

Module 6.4 Punishment

Punishment—Putting the Brakes on Behavior

Survey Question: What does punishment do to behavior?

34. The consequence that involves either the onset of an unpleasant event or the removal of a positive state of affairs is called _____.
35. The three basic tools used to control simple learning are reinforcement, punishment, and _____.

36. Choosing not to go to the restaurant where your ex-boyfriend works illustrates _____ learning.
37. Lana's two children are fighting over toys, so Lana decides to reward them for the response of sharing toys, which is a behavior that is in direct opposition to fighting over toys. Lana is using _____.
38. Whenever Jeffrey gets too loud, his mother gives him a swat on the rear end, and he gets quiet for awhile. This "quiet" that occurs after she spanks Jeffrey acts as _____ for Jeffrey's mother.

Module 6.5 Cognitive Learning and Imitation
Cognitive Learning—Beyond Conditioning
Survey Question: What is cognitive learning?
39. Learning your way around your college campus illustrates the formation of a(n) _____.
40. You are listening to a very interesting speaker at a workshop. If you make mental notes about some of ways she maintains the audience's attention, you are exhibiting _____ learning.
41. Dr. Hopewell is using a teaching strategy that gives students enough freedom to actively think about problems and enough guidance so that they gain useful knowledge. Dr. Hopewell is using _____.

Module 6.5 Modeling—Do as I Do, Not as I Say
Survey Question: Does learning occur by imitation?
42. Another name for modeling is _____ learning.
43. A learner will repeat the modeled behavior if he or she, upon making this new response, receives either feedback or _____.
44. Your five-year-old brother watches you carefully as you type your term paper on the computer, but he will not be able to model your actions because he cannot _____ this modeled behavior.
45. Repeated exposure to violence in video games can make the players less likely to react negatively to violence, or _____ them to violence.
46. Five-year-old Timmy never misses his favorite superhero on television, and he even has pajamas with this superhero on them. Thus, Timmy is more likely to imitate this superhero's aggressive actions because he _____ him.

Module 6.6 Psychology in Action: Behavioral Self-Management—A Rewarding
Survey Question: How does conditioning apply to everyday problems?
47. Carol wants to exercise more and eat healthier food, so she will be using behavioral _____.
48. You have made a rule not to turn on the TV until you have studied for an hour. Thus, by using TV viewing as reinforcement for studying, you are illustrating the _____ principle.
49. Judith is in the habit of reaching for a bag of chips when she is hungry. To satisfy her afternoon hunger, Judith decides to substitute an apple or a handful of grapes for the chips. Judith is illustrating the use of _____ in changing this habit.
50. In order to finish his dissertation, Graham has written out an agreement that states the number of pages he will write each week, the rewards for meeting this goal and the punishments for not reaching his goal. Graham has set up a(n) _____.

351

Final Survey and Review—Matching

Module 6.1 Learning and Classical Conditioning

Part 1:

1. ___ learning
2. ___ classical conditioning
3. ___ operant conditioning
4. ___ response
5. ___ antecedent
6. ___ consequence
7. ___ reflex
8. ___ vicarious classical conditioning
9. ___ acquisition

a. any identifiable behavior that can be an observable action or an internal behavior
b. learning based on the consequences of responding
c. any relatively permanent change in behavior that can be attributed to experience
d. the training period during conditioning when a response is strengthened by reinforcement
e. event that precedes a response
f. learning that takes place from observing another person react to a particular stimulus
g. innate, automatic response to a stimulus; for example, an eye blink
h. form of learning in which reflex responses are associated with new stimuli
i. effect that follows a response, such as reinforcement or punishment

Part 2:

1. ___ unconditioned stimulus (US)
2. ___ unconditioned response (UR)
3. ___ neutral stimulus (NS)
4. ___ conditioned stimulus (CS)
5. ___ conditioned response (CR)
6. ___ extinction
7. ___ spontaneous recovery
8. ___ stimulus generalization
9. ___ stimulus discrimination

a. learned response, such as salivation to the bell in Pavlov's experiment
b. learned ability to respond differently to similar stimuli
c. stimulus innately capable of eliciting a response, such as the food in Pavlov's experiment
d. innate reflex response, such as the salivation to the food in Pavlov's experiment
e. reappearance of a learned response after it has been extinguished
f. stimulus that does not evoke a response
g. stimulus that evokes a response because of its pairing, such as the bell in Pavlov's experiment
h. weakening of the conditioned response by removing the connection between the conditioned and unconditioned stimulus
i. other stimuli similar to the conditioned stimulus tend to trigger a response

Module 6.2 Operant Conditioning

1. ___ law of effect

a. removal of a positive state of affairs that decreases the response, such as the procedure known as time out

352

2. ___ positive reinforcement

b. occurs when a response is followed by the removal of an unpleasant event and increases responding

3. ___ negative reinforcement

c. weakening or disappearance of a nonreinforced operant response

4. ___ punishment, aversive type

d. reinforcement is given only after a desired response has occurred

5. ___ response cost

e. gradually molding responses to a final desired pattern

6. ___ operant extinction

f. pleasant event that follows a response and increases responding

7. ___ response chaining

g. unpleasant event that follows a response and decreases the likelihood of the response occurring again

8. ___ shaping

h. responses that lead to desirable effects are repeated; those that produce undesirable results are not

9. ___ response contingent

i. assembly of separate responses into a series of actions that lead to reinforcement

Module 6.3 Partial Reinforcement and Stimulus Control

1. ___ continuous reinforcement

a. reinforcer given for the first correct response after a set amount of time has passed

2. ___ fixed ratio (FR) schedule

b. schedule in which every correct response is followed by a reinforcer

3. ___ variable ratio (VR) schedule

c. varied number of correct responses must be made to get a reinforcer

4. ___ fixed interval (FI) schedule

d. set number of correct responses must be made to get a reinforcer

5. ___ variable interval (VI) schedule

e. stimuli present when an operant response is acquired tend to determine when and where the response is made

6. ___ stimulus control

f. tendency to respond to stimuli similar to those that preceded operant reinforcement

7. ___ operant stimulus generalization

g. reinforcer given for the first correct response after a varied amount of time has passed

8. ___ operant stimulus discrimination

h. tendency to make a response when stimuli associated with reward are present and to withhold the response when stimuli associated with nonreward are present

Module 6.4 Punishment

1. ___ escape learning

a. causes responses to extinguish

2. ___ avoidance learning

b. any event that decreases the probability or frequency of a response it follows

3. ___ reinforcement

c. learning to make a response in order to postpone or prevent discomfort

4. ___ nonreinforcement

d. rewarded for displaying any behavior that is in direct opposition to the unacceptable behavior

353

5. ___ punishment

 e. learning to make a response in order to end an aversive stimulus

6. ___ counter-conditioned

 f. consequence that strengthens or increases responding

Module 6.5 Cognitive Learning and Imitation

1. ___ cognitive learning

 a. learning that takes place mechanically, through repetition and memorization, or by learning rules

2. ___ cognitive map

 b. learning achieved by watching and imitating the actions of another or noting the consequences of those actions

3. ___ latent learning

 c. person who serves as an example in observational learning

4. ___ rote learning

 d. refers to understanding, knowing, anticipating, and making use of information-rich higher mental processes

5. ___ discovery learning

 e. students are given enough freedom to actively think about problems and enough direction so that they gain useful knowledge

6. ___ guided discovery

 f. learning that occurs without obvious reinforcement and that remains unexpressed until reinforcement is provided

7. ___ observational learning

 g. any learning strategy based on insight and understanding

8. ___ model

 h. internal images or other mental representations of an area that underlie an ability to choose alternative paths to the same goal

Module 6.6 Psychology in Action: Behavioral Self-Management—A Rewarding

1. ___ Premack principle

 a. strategy for change that involves discovering what is reinforcing an unwanted response and removing it

2. ___ alternate responses

 b. strategy for change that removing stimuli that elicit the bad habit

3. ___ extinction

 c. strategy for change that involves trying to get the same reinforcement with a new response

4. ___ response chains

 d. formal agreement stating behaviors to be changed and consequences that apply

5. ___ cues and antecedents

 e. any high-frequency response can be used to reinforce a low-frequency response

6. ___ behavioral contract

 f. strategy for change involving scrambling the sequence of events that leads to an undesired response

Final Survey and Review—True or False

Module 6.1 Learning and Classical Conditioning
What Is Learning—Does Practice Make Perfect?
Survey Question: What is learning?

1. TRUE or FALSE   Two types of associative learning are latent and discovery learning.
2. TRUE or FALSE   Responses include both observable actions as well as internal actions, such a faster heartbeat.
3. TRUE or FALSE   When four-year-old Sam catches a bee in his hand and gets stung, he associates the bee with pain and is now afraid of bees, which illustrates operant conditioning.

Module 6.1 Classical Conditioning—Does the Name Pavlov Ring a Bell?
Survey Question: How does classical conditioning occur?

4. TRUE or FALSE   In Pavlov's experiment, the dog's salivation to the bell would be classified as the unconditioned response.
5. TRUE or FALSE   If you have a virus that causes you to get nauseated after you eat a big plate of spaghetti, the next time you are served spaghetti you may feel nauseated because the spaghetti has become an conditioned stimulus for the nausea.
6. TRUE or FALSE   If a puff of air directed at your eye will cause you to blink, then blinking to the puff of air would be a conditioned response.
7. TRUE or FALSE   Researchers have found that the cerebellum is the main brain part involved in eye blink conditioning.

Module 6.1 Principles of Classical Conditioning—Here's Johnny

8. TRUE or FALSE   For classical conditioning to occur, the optimal delay between the conditioned stimulus and the unconditioned stimulus is from ½ second to five seconds.
9. TRUE or FALSE   In higher order conditioning, the unconditioned response becomes strong enough to be used like conditioned response.
10. TRUE or FALSE   Removing the connection between the conditioned and unconditioned stimulus will produce a spontaneous recovery.
11. TRUE or FALSE   The reason that many stores carry imitations of nationally known products is most likely due to stimulus discrimination.

Module 6.1 Classical Conditioning in Humans—An Emotional Topic
Survey Question: Does conditioning affect emotions?

12. TRUE or FALSE   Emotional conditioning can occur in animals, such as dogs and cats.
13. TRUE or FALSE   During a conditioned emotional response (CER), an area of the brain called the amygdala becomes more active and produce feelings of fear.
14. TRUE or FALSE   Developing a fear of air travel from watching a plane crash on the news illustrates response chaining.

Module 6.2 Operant Conditioning
Operant Conditioning— Ping-Pong Playing Pigeons?
Survey Question: How does operant conditioning occur?

15. TRUE or FALSE   In operant conditioning, the learners tend to be passive with their responses being involuntarily elicited.

16. TRUE or FALSE   Albert Bandura invented the operant conditioning chamber and proposed many of the principles of operant conditioning.

17. TRUE or FALSE   The gradual molding of responses to a final desired pattern is known as shaping.

18. TRUE or FALSE   The weakening or disappearance of a nonreinforced operant response is referred to as response cost.

19. TRUE or FALSE   Negative attention seeking occurs when parents ignore their children when they are playing quietly, but pay attention to the annoying behaviors, such as whining and temper tantrums.

20. TRUE or FALSE   Negative reinforcement decreases the probability of a response being repeated.

21. TRUE or FALSE   Parking tickets and other fines are based on the process known as escape learning.

Module 6.2 Operant Reinforcers—What's Your Pleasure?

Survey Question: Are there different kinds of operant reinforcement?

22. TRUE or FALSE   Money, praise, and affection are examples of secondary reinforcers.

23. TRUE or FALSE   Primary reinforcers tend to lose their reinforcing value more quickly than token reinforcers do.

24. TRUE or FALSE   Rebates for installing insulation and buying energy-efficient cars are examples of the use of response cost to increase conservation.

25. TRUE or FALSE   Any learning format that presents information in small amounts, gives immediate practice, and provides continuous feedback to learners is known as programmed instruction.

26. TRUE or FALSE   Computer-assisted instruction (CAI) learners have not been shown to achieve a higher final level of skill or knowledge than do learners using non-CAI methods.

Module 6.3 Partial Reinforcement and Stimulus Control

Partial Reinforcement—Las Vegas, a Human Skinner Box?

Survey Question: How are we influenced by patterns of reward?

27. TRUE or FALSE   Continuous reinforcement is better to use during initial learning, while partial reinforcement is more resistant to extinction.

28. TRUE or FALSE   Factory or farm workers who are paid on a piecework basis would be on a variable interval (VI) schedule of reinforcement.

29. TRUE or FALSE   Playing a slot machine is an example of a variable ratio (VR) schedule of reinforcement.

30. TRUE or FALSE   Conditioning studies have shown that animals are sensitive to the passage of time.

Module 6.3 Stimulus Control—Red Light, Green Light

31. TRUE or FALSE   Two important aspects of stimulus control are shaping and response chaining.

32. TRUE or FALSE   A police car on the side of the road would be an example of a discriminative stimulus that signals drivers to slow down.

33. TRUE or FALSE   The "sniffer" dogs that locate drugs and explosives at airports and border crossings are trained to recognize these substances through operant stimulus discrimination.

Module 6.4 Punishment

Punishment—Putting the Brakes on Behavior

Survey Question: What does punishment do to behavior?

34. TRUE or FALSE   Punishment should not be used in toilet training or in teaching children to eat politely.

35. TRUE or FALSE   In the experiment in the Skinner box in which one group of rats was punished with a slap for each bar press and the other group was not, the punishment of the slap temporarily slowed responding, but it did not cause more rapid extinction.

36. TRUE or FALSE   Tara has learned to be quiet when her boss gets angry because this response tends to end his tirades and illustrates escape learning.

37. TRUE or FALSE   A classic study of angry adolescent boys found that if they were severely punished at home, they tended to continue misbehaving at home but suppressed their misbehavior in other places, such as school.

38. TRUE or FALSE   It is much more effective to punish unwanted behaviors than to strengthen and encourage desirable behaviors.

Module 6.5 Cognitive Learning and Imitation

Cognitive Learning—Beyond Conditioning

Survey Question: What is cognitive learning?

39. TRUE or FALSE   Finding your way through your home in the dark illustrates that you have developed a cognitive map of your house.

40. TRUE or FALSE   In a classic animal study in which the first group of rats was rewarded for completing the maze and the second group was not rewarded, the second group ran the maze as quickly as the rewarded group when they were given food, illustrating that latent learning had taken place.

41. TRUE or FALSE   Learning that can lead to a better understanding of new or unusual problems is rote learning.

Module 6.5 Modeling—Do as I Do, Not as I Say

Survey Question: Does learning occur by imitation?

42. TRUE or FALSE   The theorist most associated with the study of observational learning was Abraham Maslow.

43. TRUE or FALSE   In general, models who are attractive, powerful, or high in status are more likely to be imitated.

44. TRUE or FALSE   Tony's dad tells him that smoking is bad, but Tony's dad smokes. When Tony becomes a teenager, he is more likely to do what his dad told him to do than to imitate his dad's smoking behavior.

45. TRUE or FALSE   Studies show conclusively that if children watch a great deal of televised violence, they will be more prone to behave aggressively.

46. TRUE or FALSE   Younger children, in particular, are more likely to be influenced by the violence on TV and video games because they don't fully recognize that media characters and stories are fantasies.

Module 6.6 Psychology in Action: Behavioral Self-Management—A Rewarding

Survey Question: How does conditioning apply to everyday problems?

47. TRUE or FALSE   The principles of operant conditioning can be adapted to manage one's own behavior, such as learning to exercise or to cut down on smoking.

357

48. TRUE or FALSE   Observing your own behavior without the help of other objective observers has not been shown to prevent you engaging in undesirable behaviors or engaging in desired ones.

49. TRUE or FALSE   If you want to stop smoking, and you remove ashtrays, matches and extra cigarettes from your house, car, and office, then you are using a method of changing bad habits known as breaking response chains.

50. TRUE or FALSE   A formal written agreement stating behaviors to be changed, goals to be met, and rewards and punishments to be applied is called a Premack principle.

Mastery Test

1. Respondent conditioning and instrumental learning are two types of
   a. associative learning.
   b. respondent conditioning.
   c. cognitive learning.
   d. vicarious conditioning.

2. Tanya hears the doorbell and goes to the door to find that the package she has been expecting has finally arrived. Hearing the doorbell would be considered a(n) _____ to her response.
   a. antecedent
   b. consequence
   c. primary event
   d. type of feedback

3. When Jack sings, his friends applaud and compliment his wonderful singing voice, but when Jack tells jokes his friends usually either groan or roll their eyes. Jack now sings more, but does not tell any jokes. This change in Jack's behavior is due to _____ conditioning.
   a. classical
   b. operant
   c. respondent
   d. vicarious

4. In Pavlov's famous classical conditioning experiment, the bell served as the
   a. unconditioned response (UR).
   b. conditioned stimulus (CS).
   c. unconditioned stimulus (US).
   d. conditioned response (CR).

5. Before going in for his first chemotherapy session, Barry had fried chicken at the hospital cafeteria. After his chemotherapy session, he becomes nauseous and vomits as a result of the chemotherapy. Since then, Barry cannot eat or even smell fried chicken. In this example, the unconditioned stimulus is the
   a. fried chicken.
   b. hospital cafeteria.
   c. chemotherapy.
   d. act of becoming nauseous.

6. Advertisers often pair images that evoke good feelings with pictures of their products so that you will also learn by association to feel good when you see their products. In doing so, these advertisers have extended the learning beyond the original conditioned stimulus, which illustrates
    a. instrumental conditioning.
    b. observational learning.
    c. vicarious learning.
    d. higher order conditioning.

7. The information view of learning places emphasis on the creation of mental
    a. expectancies.
    b. reinforcement schedules.
    c. contracts.
    d. approximations.

8. In classical conditioning, if we remove the connection between the conditioned stimulus and unconditioned stimulus, which of the following will occur?
    a. higher order conditioning
    b. stimulus generalization
    c. extinction
    d. spontaneous recovery

9. If Serra is afraid of mice and also shows fear when presented with gerbils and hamsters, she is exhibiting
    a. extinction.
    b. stimulus generalization.
    c. stimulus discrimination.
    d. instrumental conditioning.

10. Although the chairs are very similar, six-year-old Tina shows fear when sitting in the dentist's chair, but not when she is sitting in the hairdresser's chair to get her hair cut. Which of the following is Tina exhibiting regarding the two chairs?
    a. extinction
    b. stimulus generalization
    c. stimulus discrimination
    d. vicarious conditioning

11. Which area of the brain becomes more active and produces feelings of fear when a person is experiencing a conditioned emotional response?
    a. amygdala
    b. medulla
    c. cerebellum
    d. corpus callosum

12. Many people were traumatized by watching media coverage of the aftermath of Hurricane Katrina. This is an example of
    a. avoidance learning.
    b. escape learning.
    c. negative reinforcement.
    d. vicarious conditioning.

13. Responses that lead to desirable effects are repeated, while those that produce undesirable results are not. Edward Thorndike called this the law of
    a. association.
    b. effect.
    c. responding.
    d. generalization.

14. An involuntary response is said to be elicited during _____ conditioning.
    a. instrumental
    b. operant
    c. insight
    d. classical

15. To teach the students in a class to raise their hand before being "called on," the teacher should make "getting called on"
    a. the unconditioned response.
    b. a primary reinforcer.
    c. conditionally-programmed.
    d. response-contingent.

16. In making a sculpture, the artist uses her hands to make thousands of manipulations to the clay before she can admire her finished product. This is an example of
    a. stimulus generalization.
    b. vicarious conditioning.
    c. response chaining.
    d. conditioned emotional responses.

17. As Mena begins this year's soccer competitions, she makes sure that she is wearing the little necklace she wore when she won the state championship last year. Mena's wearing of this necklace during her soccer matches is an example of
    a. response chaining.
    b. vicarious conditioning.
    c. response cost.
    d. superstitious behavior.

18. A rat is placed in a Skinner box for the first time. In order to get the rat to press the lever at the other end of the box, we will have to reinforce successive approximations to his moving toward the lever and pressing it. The process of training we are using is called
    a. higher order conditioning.
    b. shaping.
    c. vicarious conditioning.
    d. operant extinction.

19. Although it used to be your favorite TV program, you now find that this program is not as interesting as it once was, and you watch it less and less until you do not even turn on your TV when you know the program is on. This process is known as
    a. operant extinction.
    b. stimulus generalization.
    c. negative reinforcement.
    d. response chaining.

360

20. When her daughter throws temper tantrums, Terri tends to drop what she is doing to try to console her daughter. However, when her daughter is playing quietly, Terri tends to focus on her housework and ignores her daughter. Terri should be advised that her parenting style may lead to which of the following?
    a. escape and avoidance learning
    b. respondent conditioning
    c. negative attention seeking
    d. vicarious conditioning

21. You are sitting in class near the air conditioning vents and are so cold you are shivering. Then, you remember your warm-up jacket is in your backpack. By putting on your jacket and ending this "frigid" situation, you have experienced
    a. positive reinforcement.
    b. negative reinforcement.
    c. response cost.
    d. response chaining.

22. You and your roommate have a long drive ahead of you. While your roommate drives and listens to the radio, you decide to read your new novel. However, after a few minutes of riding and reading, you get a terrible headache, so you stop reading. Which consequence did you receive for your act of riding and reading?
    a. latent chaining.
    b. negative reinforcement.
    c. punishment.
    d. nonreinforcement.

23. If you receive a parking ticket for parking your car in a "No Parking Zone," you are less likely to park in this zone again, which illustrates the effect of
    a. response chaining.
    b. negative reinforcement.
    c. latent learning.
    d. response cost.

24. Every time you fix yourself a snack while you are studying or turn up the air conditioning on a hot summer evening, your actions show the power of _____ reinforcers.
    a. primary
    b. secondary
    c. generalized
    d. vicarious

25. When you were little, your mother would give you a cookie for picking up your toys. Now when you do chores around the house, like mowing the lawn, you prefer to receive money and praise, which are both classified as _____ reinforcers.
    a. primary
    b. secondary
    c. latent
    d. vicarious

26. A researcher has implanted an electrode into a rat's limbic system. By pressing a lever, the rat can administer intracranial stimulation to its pleasure center. This intracranial self-stimulation (ICS) would be considered a(n)
    a. negative reinforcer.
    b. primary reinforcer.
    c. response cost.
    d. secondary punisher.

27. To help your daughter learn to pick up her toys, clean her room, feed her cat, and do other chores, you set up a chart on which you put a colorful "sticker" for each task she completes. When your daughter earns a whole row of stickers, she gets to choose a prize from the "grab bag." When the whole chart is full, your daughter will get to choose an activity, such as "going bowling" or "going to the movies." You are using
    a. primary reinforcers.
    b. response costs.
    c. token reinforcers.
    d. latent reinforcers.

28. You are attending a cooking school and are given the assignment to create an appetizer. Your cooking instructor will be evaluating your "dish" based on taste, appearance, and creativity, which will help you improve your performance in each of these areas. Your instructor's critique of your appetizer illustrates the importance of
    a. feedback.
    b. latent learning.
    c. discovery learning.
    d. negative reinforcement.

29. Introducing an energy tax to reduce people's tendency to waste energy would be an example of
    a. response cost.
    b. negative reinforcement.
    c. response chaining.
    d. higher-order conditioning.

30. In Stella's class, the students are using workbooks that teach mathematics in small units, require the students to practice each skill immediately, and then give the students immediate feedback regarding their answers. Stella's students are using
    a. discovery learning.
    b. vicarious instruction.
    c. programmed instruction.
    d. latent learning.

31. Six-year-old Carlos receives a dollar for every 20 weeds that he pulls up in his mother's flower garden. Carlos is being reinforced on a _____ schedule of reinforcement.
    a. fixed ratio
    b. fixed interval
    c. variable ratio
    d. variable interval

32. Ashad has an English report due every other Friday. Ashad tends to wait until the day before the due date and then works frantically to complete the report before the 3:00 p.m. Friday deadline. This type of responding will typically occur when a person is on which type of schedule of reinforcement?
    a. fixed ratio
    b. fixed interval
    c. variable ratio
    d. variable interval

33. You are in an elevator watching the numbers light up on the panel. The numbers "1," "2," and "3" light up but you make no response, since your room is on the fourth floor. However, when the panel light shows "4," you pick up your bag and prepare to get off when the doors open. This example illustrates that your response of picking up your bag and preparing to exit the elevator were under
    a. operant extinction.
    b. stimulus generalization.
    c. stimulus control.
    d. the partial reinforcement effect.

34. Which of the following usually only temporarily suppresses responses?
    a. response chaining
    b. negative reinforcement
    c. mild punishment
    d. stimulus control

35. Every time Jared is around his mother, they seem to get in an argument, so Jared tends to "stop by" the house to visit his father and siblings when he knows his mother will not be home. Jared is exhibiting _____ learning.
    a. avoidance
    b. latent
    c. place
    d. escape

36. Although you felt "lost" when you first came to campus, you now have little trouble getting from class to class or even giving directions to other students because you have developed a(n) _____ of the campus.
    a. mental operant
    b. latent image
    c. cognitive map
    d. iconic adaptation

37. A teaching strategy that gives students enough freedom to actively think about problems and enough teacher direction so that they gain useful knowledge is called
    a. latent discovery.
    b. vicarious learning.
    c. instrumental learning.
    d. guided discovery.

38. A learner must be able to attend to the model, remember what was done, be able to reproduce the modeled behavior, and be successful or rewarded for the response in order for which of the following to take place?
    a. operant shaping
    b. response chaining
    c. observational learning
    d. respondent conditioning

39. You enjoy playing videogames, but you want to practice piano more. So, you decide that you will not play any videogames when you get home from school until you have practiced piano for an hour. You are using which of the following to increase your time playing the piano?
    a. primary reinforcer
    b. response cost
    c. the partial reinforcement effect
    d. the Premack principle

40. Marie wants to lose weight, so she lists the number of pounds she will lose each month. She also states how she will be rewarded if she meets her goal, such as seeing a movie or getting a manicure. Marie also lists some unpleasant chores she will have to complete if she does not meet her goal. After writing this down, she enlists her best friend to help her carry out this plan, and they both sign the plan. Marie is using which of the following approaches to losing weight?
    a. operant extinction
    b. a behavioral contract
    c. a cognitive map
    d. observational learning

Chapter 7: Memory

Chapter Overview

Memory is an active, computer-like system that encodes, stores, and retrieves information. The three stages of memory (sensory memory, short-term memory, and long-term memory) hold information for increasingly longer periods. Sensory memories are encoded as iconic memories or echoic memories. Short-term memories tend to be encoded by sound, and long-term memories by meaning.

Selective attention determines what information moves from sensory memory, which is exact but very brief, on to short-term memory (STM). STM has a capacity of about five to seven bits of information, but this can be extended by chunking, or recoding. Short-term memories are brief and very sensitive to interruption, or interference; however, they can be prolonged by maintenance rehearsal.

Long-term memory (LTM) serves as a general storehouse for meaningful information. Elaborative encoding helps us form lasting, long-term memories. Long-term memories are relatively permanent. LTM seems to have an almost unlimited storage capacity. Constructive processing tends to alter memories. Remembering is an active process. Our memories are frequently lost, altered, revised, or distorted. LTM is highly organized. The structure of memory networks is the subject of current research. In redintegration, memories are reconstructed, as one bit of information leads to others, which then serve as cues for further recall. LTM contains procedural (skill) and declarative (fact) memories. Declarative memories can be semantic or episodic.

The tip-of-the-tongue state shows that memory is not an all-or-nothing event. Memories may therefore be revealed by recall, recognition, relearning, or priming. In recall, memories are retrieved without explicit cues, as in an essay exam. Recall of listed information often reveals a serial position effect. A common test of recognition is the multiple-choice question. In relearning, material that seems to be forgotten is learned again, and memory is revealed by a savings score. Recall, recognition, and relearning measure mainly explicit memories. Other techniques, such as priming, are necessary to reveal implicit memories.

Herman Ebbinghaus found that forgetting is most rapid immediately after learning, as shown by the curve of forgetting. Forgetting can occur because of failures of encoding, of storage, or of retrieval. Failure to encode information is a common cause of "forgetting." Forgetting in sensory memory and STM is due to a failure of storage through a weakening (decay) of memory traces. Decay of memory traces may also explain some LTM losses. Failures of retrieval occur when information that resides in memory is nevertheless not retrieved. A lack of memory cues can produce retrieval failure. State-dependent learning is related to the effects of memory cues. Much forgetting in STM and LTM is caused by interference. In retroactive interference, new learning interferes with the ability to retrieve earlier learning. Proactive interference occurs when old learning interferes with the retrieval of new learning. Memories can be consciously suppressed and they may be unconsciously repressed. Extreme caution is warranted when "recovered" memories are the only basis for believing that traumatic events, such as childhood sexual abuse, happened in the past.

Lasting memories are recorded by changes in the activity, structure, and chemistry of brain cells. It takes time to consolidate memories. In the brain, memory consolidation takes place in the hippocampus. Until they are consolidated, long-term memories are easily destroyed. Intensely emotional experiences can result in flashbulb memories. After memories have been consolidated, they appear to be stored in the cortex of the brain. Memories are recorded in the brain through nerve cells and how they interconnect.

Eidetic imagery (photographic memory) occurs when a person is able to project an image onto a blank surface. Eidetic imagery is rarely found in adults. However, many adults have internal memory images, which can be very vivid. Although it's true that some people have naturally superior memories, everyone can learn to improve his or her memory. Exceptional memory may be based on natural ability or learned strategies. Usually it involves both.

Excellent memory abilities are based on using strategies and techniques that make learning efficient and that compensate for natural weaknesses in human memory. Memory can be improved through better encoding strategies, such as elaborating, selecting and organizing information as well as whole learning, the progressive part method, encoding memory cues, overlearning, and spaced practice. Memory can also be improved through better retrieval strategies, such as using feedback, recitation, rehearsal, and active search strategies. When you are studying or memorizing, you should also keep in mind the effects of serial position, sleep, and hunger.

Memory systems (mnemonics) greatly improve immediate memory. However, conventional learning tends to create the most lasting memories. Mnemonic systems use mental images and unusual associations to link new information with familiar memories already stored in LTM. Effective mnemonics tend to rely on mental images and bizarre or exaggerated mental associations.

Module 7.1 Memory Systems
Preview: Fuhgeddaboudit

Language Development
fuhgeddaboudit: "forget about it"
automatically: involuntarily; robotically
burden: problem; a load; a weight
wowed: greatly impressed or excited
ease: not difficult; effortlessness
consonants: letters of the alphabet that are not vowel sounds
formulas: rules; principles
envy: be jealous of
trivia: collection of details and facts that are interesting but not very important

Stages of Memory—Do You Have a Mind Like a Steel Trap? Or a Sieve?
Survey Question: How does memory work?

Language Development Guide
mind like a steel trap: refers to sharpness or quickness of the mind (and memory)
(mind like) a sieve: refers to having a poor memory (running through the holes in the sifter)
instant messaged: direct text-based communication in real-time through a telephone network or
    Internet

memory as a dusty storehouse of facts: a long-forgotten, rarely used (dusty) collection of information

recovers: get back

trace: map out

fleeting: brief; momentary; passing

persist: endure; continue

flurry: rapid burst

announcer: presenter; broadcaster

portion: piece; part

subsequently: later

dumped: lost, thrown away

interruption: to stop the continuous action; disruption

interference: two items attempting to occupy the same space

dial: to put in the numbers to call someone on a telephone

notice: become aware of

scratchpad: notebook

transferred: passed on; moved to

from aardvark to zucchini: from the beginning to the end

math to Desperate Housewives: from a logical science to a romantic drama (soap opera-style) TV program

limitless: never ending; vast

"filled up": completely full; no space left

mistakenly: wrongly; incorrectly

hocked: sold

gems: jewels; precious stones

financing: put money into; pay for

bravely: fearlessly; having courage; boldness

defied: challenged; confronted; dared

scornful: mocking; showing disrespect

deceive: mislead; trick; lie to

an egg, not a table: refers to the Earth being rounded, not flat

typifies: describes

sturdy: strong; well-built

sought: hunted

proof: evidence

forging along: working continually

doubters: nonbeliever; skeptics

fearful: scary; awful

rumors: tales; stories

edge: rim; boundary (if the Earth was flat, one could sail off the edge)

at last: in the end

creatures: beings

signifying: suggesting; telling

momentous: historic; significant; important

emphasizes: calls attention to; points out

impact: influence

warehouse: building for storing a large number of items

filing cabinets: containers for keeping papers in order

tossed away: thrown away; discarded

ranch: very large farm usually seen in western United States on which herds of horses, sheep, or cattle graze (eat) over many acres of grass

feat: achievement
horsemanship: skill of riding horses
whereas: while; but
membership: association; relationship; connection
self-centered: selfish; concerned only with self
interactions: relations; contract
analogy: comparison
general picture: summary; overview
rehearse: go over; repeat; practice

Recite and Review

1. You are attending a performance at your college of a professional memorizer, or _____.
2. People with such amazing memories that they can't separate important facts from trivia or facts from fantasy have actually had to devise methods to _____ information.
3. In a very real sense, who we are is determined by what we remember and what we _____.
4. The active system that receives, stores, organizes, alters, and recovers information is called _____.
5. Sensory memory, short-term memory (STM), and long-term memory (LTM) are the three stages of memory as summarized by the _____ model of memory.
6. Converting information into a form in which it will be retained in memory is the process known as _____.
7. Holding information for later use refers to the process called _____.
8. When we recover information from memory storage, we are engaged in the process of memory known as _____.
9. The stage of memory that holds an exact record of incoming information for a few seconds or less is called _____ memory.
10. When you look at a rose, a fleeting visual image will persist for about one-half second with this visual image being an example of _____ memory.
11. During your professor's lecture, each word said by this professor will persist in your auditory system for up to two seconds with these sounds being a part of your _____ memory.
12. When you focus on a particular portion of sensory input, you are able to move this information from sensory memory to short-term memory through a process known as _____.
13. Regarding the form in which words and letters are stored, short-term memories will most often be stored _____.
14. Information will be quickly "dumped" from short-term memory unless you silently say it over and over to yourself, a process called _____.
15. You have looked up the phone number to a restaurant and are about to dial the number when your phone rings. After telling the person on the other end that they have the wrong number, you go to dial the number to the restaurant but cannot remember it and must now look the number up again. This situation illustrates that short-term memory is very sensitive to interruption, or _____.
16. When short-term memory is combined with other mental processes and is used for thinking and solving problems, it is called _____ memory.
17. The relatively permanent storage of important information describes _____ memory.
18. The more you know, the _____ it is to add new information.
19. Long-term memories are stored on the basis of _____.
20. When we want to use knowledge from long-term memory to answer a question, the information is returned to _____ memory.

21. Because horsemanship is very important to cowboys and horse ranchers, these people will be better prepared to _____ and store intricate information about horses.
22. In a comparison of American and Chinese adults, the adults who emphasized the importance of individuals were the _____ adults.
23. When American and Chinese adults were compared, the adults who emphasized the importance of being members of a group were the _____ adults.
24. When asked to recall 20 memories from any time in their lives, American memories tended to be _____ centered.
25. When Chinese adults were asked to recall 20 memories from any time in their lives, the Chinese adults remembered their own interactions with family and friends and important social or _____ events.

Part 1: Connections

1. _____ selective attention
2. _____ long-term memory
3. _____ incoming information
4. _____ encoding for LTM
5. _____ sensory memory
6. _____ short-term memory
7. _____ rehearsal buffer

Part 2: Connections

1. ____ memory
2. ____ encoding
3. ____ storage
4. ____ retrieval
5. ____ sensory memory
6. ____ iconic memory
7. ____ echoic memory
8. ____ selective attention
9. ____ short-term memory (STM)
10. ____ working memory
11. ____ long-term memory (LTM)

a. focusing on a selected portion of sensory input
b. recovering information from storage
c. brief continuation of sensory activity in the auditory system after a sound is heard
d. holding information within the system
e. when STM is being used for thinking and problem solving
f. first stage of memory that holds an exact record of incoming information for a few seconds or less
g. active mental system that receives, stores, organizes, alters, and recovers information
h. second stage of memory that holds small amounts of information for a short time
i. converting information into a usable form
j. mental image or visual representation
k. memory system used for relatively permanent storage of meaningful information

Check Your Memory

1. TRUE or FALSE A professional memorizer is called a mnemonist.
2. TRUE or FALSE Who we are is determined by what we remember and what we forget.
3. TRUE or FALSE Memory is a passive system in which information is automatically accumulated as a warehouse of facts.
4. TRUE or FALSE Converting information into a form in which it will be retained in memory is known as selective retrieval.

369

5. TRUE or FALSE The three stages of memory are summarized by the Hobson-McCarley model of memory.

6. TRUE or FALSE Short-term memory is the briefest stage of memory and holds an exact record of incoming information for a few seconds or less.

7. TRUE or FALSE When you first see the bird in the sky, an iconic memory, or visual image, will persist for about one-half second.

8. TRUE or FALSE After you hear a sound, there will be a brief continuation of this sensory activity in your auditory system for up to two seconds, which is known as echoic memory.

9. TRUE or FALSE Selective attention controls what information moves from working memory to long-term memory.

10. TRUE or FALSE Although short-term memories can be stored as images, they are most often stored phonetically.

11. TRUE or FALSE Because of the way information is stored in short-term memory, if you are introduced to a person named Bill and you forget his name, you are more likely to call him by the name Bob or Ben than Will or Phil.

12. TRUE or FALSE Unless we rehearse information, it will be quickly "dumped" from short-term memory and forever lost.

13. TRUE or FALSE Short-term memory prevents our minds from storing useless trivia.

14. TRUE or FALSE Unlike long-term memory, short-term memory is not very sensitive to interference.

15. TRUE or FALSE When short-term memory is combined with other mental processes, it acts more like a "mental scratchpad," or working memory, briefly holding the information we need when we are thinking and solving problems.

16. TRUE or FALSE Long-term memory holds nearly limitless amounts of important information in relatively permanent storage.

17. TRUE or FALSE The more information you know, the harder it becomes to add new information to memory.

18. TRUE or FALSE If you try to retrieve the word "barn" from long-term memory, you are more likely to remember a word with a similar meaning like "shed" than a word that sounds like barn, such as "yarn" or "darn."

19. TRUE or FALSE If you can link information in short-term memory to knowledge already stored in long-term memory, it gains meaning and makes it easier to remember.

20. TRUE or FALSE When we want to use knowledge from long-term memory to answer a question, the information is returned to the sensory memory stage.

21. TRUE or FALSE Because horses are very important to cowboys and ranchers, people in this subculture are better prepared to encode and store detailed information about horses than people from subcultures in which horses are not very important.

22. TRUE or FALSE Because the American culture emphasizes group membership, Americans will tend to remember important social or historical events and their own interactions with family members and friends.

23. TRUE or FALSE Since the Chinese culture places emphasis on the individual, people in that culture tend to have more self-centered memories.

Critical Thinking Question

Why is sensory memory important to filmmakers?

Module 7.2 STM and LTM
Short-Term Memory—Do You Know the Magic Number?
Survey Question: What are the features of short-term memory?

Language Development Guide
quirks: oddities; peculiarities
dig deeper: try especially hard
inner workings: mechanisms that function internally and are not outwardly visible
magic number: special amount
series: sequence; string of items
capacity: ability; amount; size
"slots": holes; openings
"bins": containers; holders
hostess: woman who organizes and is officially in charge of a social gathering
satisfied: contented; pleased
proper: correct
TV: television
IBM: International Business Machines, a computer company
USN: United States Navy
YMCA: Young Men's Christian Association, an international organization that promotes the spiritual, social, and physical welfare of young men
whatever: anything; no matter what
stack: pile
elusive: vague; indefinable; hard to create
artificial: unnatural; contrived
prolong: extend
maintenance: preservation; upholding; continuing; protection
repetition: saying or doing something over and over
elaborative: planned and detailed
far: much; a lot
elaborate: add details
reflect: think about
relate: associate; connect; link
recycled: recovered; reused
syllable: group of letters that form a unit of spoken language; usually one uninterrupted sound
awkward: uncomfortable; clumsy; embarrassed
unfortunately: unluckily; sorry to say
icy: cold; unfriendly
reply: answer; response

Recite and Review

1. A psychologist calls out six one-digit random numbers at one per second and then asks you to repeat these numbers. The psychologist is assessing your attention and your _____ memory.

2. A test in which one-digit random numbers are called out and then the person is asked to repeat them is called a(n) _____ test.

3. Psychologist George Miller found that short-term memory is limited to the "magic number" of _____ (plus or minus 2) informational units.

4. A meaningful unit of information, such as a number, a letter, or a word is called an informational _____.

371

5. If several numbers or words are grouped together, they will form a larger unit of information known as an informational _____.

6. The process that recodes or reorganizes information into units that are already in long-term memory is called _____.

7. Using the letters that correspond to each number on a telephone, you, as the head librarian, create the new telephone number for the library of "Great Books" by using the process called _____.

8. Unlike psychologist George Miller, some psychologists now believe that unless some recoding is involved, short-term memory may actually hold only _____ items.

9. You can prolong information in short-term memory by silently repeating it, a process called _____.

10. A short-term memory has a greater chance of being stored in long-term memory the more times it is _____.

11. If you learned your multiplication tables by repeating them over and over again, you learned them through _____ learning.

12. While reading your psychology textbook, if you try to relate the new concepts and ideas presented to your own experiences or to information learned in other classes, then you are making this new information more meaningful and lasting by using the process of _____.

13. Asking "why" questions as you read and relating new concepts to information you already know is similar to the advice given in the textbook introduction on study skills that explains _____ learning.

14. Experiments by Peterson and Peterson using nonsense syllables showed that after 12 to 18 seconds short-term memory for these syllables was gone forever without _____.

Connections

1. ____ digit-span test

2. ____ information bit

3. ____ information chunk

4. ____ recoding or "chunking"

5. ____ maintenance rehearsal

6. ____ rote learning

7. ____ elaborative encoding

a. silently repeating or mentally reviewing information to hold it in short-term memory

b. made up of bits of information grouped into larger units

c. learning that takes place mechanically through simple repetition and memorization

d. measure of attention and short-term memory

e. links new information to memories that are already in LTM

f. a single meaningful "piece" of information, such as a digit or letter

g. reorganizing or modifying information to assist storage in memory

Check Your Memory

1. TRUE or FALSE — The digit-span test is a measure of attention and short-term memory that involves the participants repeating a series of numbers presented to them.

2. TRUE or FALSE — Psychologist George Miller found that short-term memory is limited to the "magic number" 10 (plus or minus 2).

3. TRUE or FALSE — When all the "slots" in short-term memory are filled, there is no room for new information.

4. TRUE or FALSE — A meaningful unit of information, such as a number, a letter, or a word is called an information chunk.

5. TRUE or FALSE   If you are given the letters, I, B, M, Y, M, C, A, U, S, A and you reorganize them into the three larger units of IBM, YMCA, and USA, then you are using the process known as chunking.

6. TRUE or FALSE   Some psychologists believe that short-term memory holds only four items, unless some chunking has occurred.

7. TRUE or FALSE   If you silently repeat a phone number to yourself, you are using redintegration to keep this number in your short-term memory.

8. TRUE or FALSE   The more times a short-term memory is rehearsed, the greater its chances of being stored in long-term memory.

9. TRUE or FALSE   Learning by simple repetition is known as reflective learning.

10. TRUE or FALSE   Maintenance rehearsal is used to link new information to memories that are already in long-term memory.

11. TRUE or FALSE   Asking yourself "why" questions as you read your psychology book and relating the psychological concepts and theories to real-life examples from your own life are two ways of using elaborative encoding.

12. TRUE or FALSE   In an experiment using nonsense syllables, Peterson and Peterson found that after 12 to 18 seconds without rehearsal, the short-term memory for these syllables was gone forever.

Long-Term Memory—A Blast from the Past
Survey Questions: What are the features of long-term memory?

Language Development Guide

electrode: a small electronic that gives or measures electrical activity

neighborhood: area; region

patient: person who is under medical care

vivid: clear; dramatic; colorful; brilliant

permanently: enduring; everlasting

sound track: narrow strip at one side of a movie film that carries the sound portion

exaggeration: overstatement

resemble: look like

relatively: rather; fairly; somewhat

appreciate: understand; recognize the value of; be aware

slumber: sleep

bunk: narrow bed built like a shelf into or against a wall

groggy: sleepy, dull feeling; confused and unsteady

"smashed": shattered; to noisily break into pieces

"bumped": hit; strike; knock out of position

"contacted": coming together; touching of two items

constructive: combining materials as an improvement

logic: reason

indeed: in fact; certainly

Disney: U.S. film company that is known for the cartoon character of Mickey Mouse

Bugs Bunny: cartoon character created by the Warner Brothers film company

Warner Brothers: U.S. film company

Disneyland: large amusement park in California

manipulate: influence; control

jam: used in two ways in this text—a fruit spread and a clog or blockage

Bingo: "you've got it;" word shouted when a person has all the spaces filled on their bingo card and has won that game in which numbered balls are drawn at random

familiarize: make known; publicize
intent: aim; goal; plan; purpose
impressions: feelings; thoughts; reactions
beverage: a drink
cool: fun; awesome
hot: attractive
flashes: shows; displays
target: aim; goal; reference point
recollection: memory; recall
fiction: fantasy; falsehood
eventually: in the end; in time
in reality: in the real world; in fact
in effect: in fact
"brand": product name; identifying part
remarkably: surprisingly; amazingly
contrary: the opposite
overwrite: replace
attributed: assigned; credited it to
abducted: kidnapped
captive: confined; locked up; imprisoned
ransom: money demanded for the return of a kidnapped person
imply: mean; involve
suggestive: indicates
weave: intertwine; knot together; merge; unite
to make matters worse: to top it all off; additionally
confidence: self-belief; trust in self
unshakable: firm; sure; constant
corroborating: supporting; confirming; back up
jogging: stirring; causing to function with a jolt
recreating: restoring; re-establishing
revisit: return to
scene: site; place; location
aspects: features; parts
context: situation; environment; circumstances
standard: normal; typical; ordinary
elicited: drawn out; brought forth
joined at the hip: always together
"memory index": directory; file; guide
alphabetically: arranged in order by the letters of the language
not a chance!: not ever; no possibility
from aardvark to zebra: from the beginning to the end
Antarctic: continent at the South Pole
Voilá: French term whose literal meaning is "see there"; used to call attention, to express
        approval, or to suggest an appearance occurred by magic
penguin: aquatic, flightless bird that lives in the lower southern hemisphere
canary: birds that are yellowish-green with some brown striping on its back
network: system; net-like arrangement
unleashed: set free; let loose
flood: overflow; downpour; abundance
seemingly: apparently; on the face of it
"branches": divisions of some larger arrangement

374

touched off: begun
quite: fairly; very
sparse: thin; light; meager
reinforcements: support; back ups
senses: meanings
you bet: of course; yes; sure
to begin: first and most important
pops up: comes to mind quickly
sharp: definite; clear-cut
off-chance: a slight chance; very unlikely event
grounded: not allowed to go out (punishment)
well: favorably; highly; greatly
clear: apparent; obvious
curious: odd; strange; unusual
amnesia: loss of memory
conclude: decide; suppose
procedural: practical skills
declarative: making a statement
register: is recorded
Peter Jackson: film director, producer, and screenwriter from New Zealand; best known for
            directing the three
Lord of the Rings films
Lord of the Rings: three volumes of a fantasy tale written by J.R.R. Tolkien that includes hobbits,
            wizards, dwarfs and other creatures and was made into three films
trilogy: set of three literary, dramatic, or artistic works that are connected
Randy Jackson: singer, musician, record producer, and judge on *American Idol*
American Idol: reality television program that is a singing competition to find new solo artist
semantic: related to word meanings
episodic: significant incident
dictionary: reference book of word meanings
encyclopedia: reference book containing information on a wide range of subjects
immune: resistant; protected
impersonal: formal and objective
"autobiographical": the story of a person's life as written by that person
formation: development; creation
kindergarten: preschool, usually for ages between four and six years
posed: asked; put forward

Recite and Review

1. The neurosurgeon who electrically stimulated his patients' brains during brain surgery and
   found that the activation of some brain areas seemed to produce vivid memories of long-
   forgotten memories was _____.
2. Brain stimulation only produces memory-like experiences in only about three percent of
   cases with most of the experiences resembling _____ more than memories.
3. Reorganizing or updating memories on the basis of logic, reasoning, or the addition of new
   information is called _____.
4. According to economist Jesse Shapiro, when a company floods the television airways with
   numerous ads that try to create positive memories of their product, they are using "_____."
5. Elizabeth Loftus presented a video of a car accident to research participants and then used the
   words "smashed" or "bumped into" to describe the accident. When she used the word

"smashed," several of the participants remembered seeing "broken glass" when there was none in the accident. These students had created _____.

6. Because a hypnotized person is more likely than normal to use imagination to fill in gaps in memory, hypnosis is more likely to increase the occurrence of _____ memories.

7. When witnesses "remember" a face that they actually saw somewhere other than the crime scene, it is not due to this new information "overwriting" their existing memories. The real problem is that the witnesses often can't remember the _____ of their memory.

8. To help police detectives, R. Edward Geiselman and Ron Fisher created a technique for jogging the memory of eyewitnesses called the _____.

9. The key to Geiselman and Fisher's approach is recreating the crime scene, so that the sounds, smells, and objects, provide helpful stimuli known as retrieval _____.

10. Back in the context of the crime, the witness is encouraged to recall events from different viewpoints and in different _____.

11. Long-term memory stores huge amounts of information during a lifetime with each person's "_____" being highly organized.

12. The pattern of associations among items of information in one's memory is referred to as the memory _____.

13. If people are given the two statements: "A canary is an animal" and "A canary is a bird" to which they must answer yes or no, most people will say yes faster to the statement "A canary is a(n) _____."

14. Long-term memory is organized as a(n) _____ of linked ideas.

15. If ideas are "farther" apart, then, in order to connect them within your memory, it will take a longer chain of _____.

16. Every time Meg hears a particular song on the radio, she is transported back to the senior prom and memories of her old boyfriend. For Meg, an entire past experience was reconstructed from this one small auditory cue through the process known as _____.

17. Students can build more elaborate memory networks, which will provide more retrieval cues, if they use _____ when they study.

18. Students' memory and understanding tend to be weaker if they study using only _____ learning.

19. Skill memories and fact memories are two distinct categories of _____ memory.

20. Memories which include basic conditioned responses and learned actions, such as typing or driving are called known as skill memories, or _____ memories.

21. Skill memories register in "lower" brain areas, especially the part of the brain called the _____.

22. Specific fact memories, such as names, faces, words, dates, and ideas, which may be either of a personal or nonpersonal nature are part of the memory category known as _____ memory.

23. Fact memories can be further divided into episodic memory and _____ memory.

24. The names of objects, the days of the week or months of the year, simple math skills, and the seasons are all impersonal facts that make up a part of long-term memory called _____ memory.

25. An "autobiographical" record of personal experiences constitute the type of declarative memories known as _____ memories.

26. The type of declarative memories that serve as a mental dictionary or encyclopedia of the basic knowledge about the world are called _____ memories.

27. A specific time and place is re-experienced when one is remembering a(n) _____ memory.

28. Of the two types of fact memories, the one that is most easily forgotten is a(n) _____ memory.

Part 1: Connections

1. _____ procedural memory
2. _____ sensory memory
3. _____ episodic memory
4. _____ short-term memory
5. _____ declarative memory

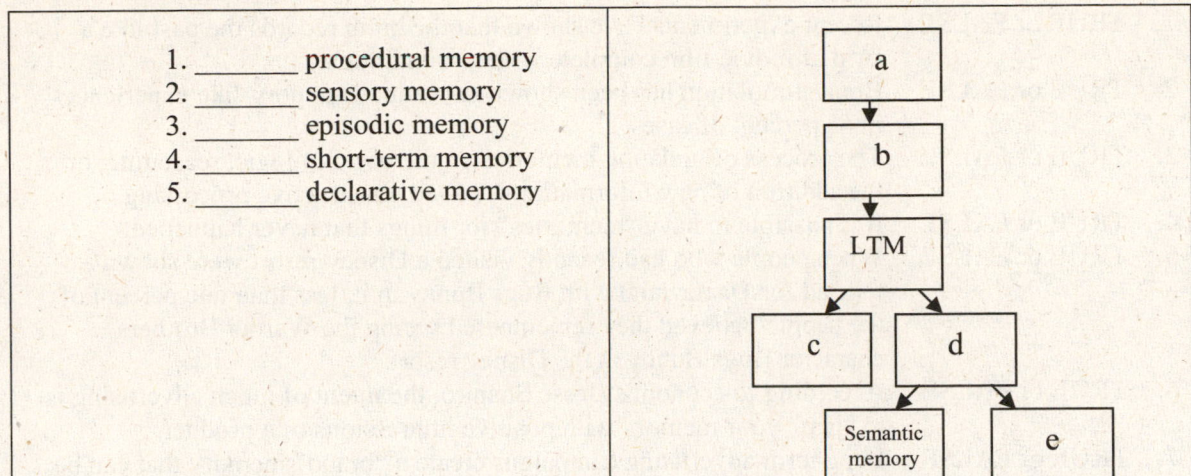

Part 2: Connections

1. ____ constructive processing

2. ____ "memory jamming"

3. ____ pseudomemories

4. ____ cognitive interview

5. ____ memory structure

6. ____ network model

7. ____ redintegration

8. ____ procedural memory

9. ____ declarative memory

10. ____ semantic memory

11. ____ episodic memory

12. ____ cerebellum

a. part of long-term memory containing specific factual information, both personal and impersonal

b. refers to the pattern of associations among items of information

c. process by which memories are expanded or reconstructed by starting with one memory and then following chains of association to other related memories

d. subpart of fact memory that records impersonal knowledge about the world

e. technique used by advertisers that involves adding numerous positive memories of their products in the consumers' memories

f. lower brain area where procedural memories are stored

g. subpart of fact memory that records personal experiences that are linked with specific times and places

h. use of various cues and strategies to improve the memory of eyewitnesses

i. views long-term memory as an organized system of linked information

j. reorganizing or updating memories on the basis of logic, reasoning, or the addition of new information

k. long-term memories of conditioned responses and learned skill

l. false memories

Check Your Memory

1. TRUE or FALSE   Recent experiments have shown that the brain records the past like a strip of movie film complete with a sound track.

2. TRUE or FALSE   Brain stimulation has been shown to produce memory-like experiences in 65 percent of cases.

3. TRUE or FALSE   The process of updating memories on the basic of logic, reasoning, or the addition of new information is called constructive processing.

4. TRUE or FALSE   It is possible to have "memories" for things that never happened.

5. TRUE or FALSE   When people who had recently visited a Disney resort were shown a fake ad for Disneyland with Bugs Bunny in it, less than one percent of the people believed they remembered seeing the Warner Brothers character Bugs Bunny at the Disney resort.

6. TRUE or FALSE   According to economist Jesse Shapiro, the intent of much advertising is to "jam" your memory with positive impressions of a product.

7. TRUE or FALSE   Long-term advertising campaigns create a "brand" memory that can be remarkably strong, especially when the ads were first viewed in early childhood.

8. TRUE or FALSE   The pseudomemories of eyewitnesses are a common problem in police work.

9. TRUE or FALSE   We often have trouble remembering the source of a memory.

10. TRUE or FALSE   Research has shown the hypnosis when used for crime investigation tends to increase the incidence of true memories, while decreasing the occurrence of false memories.

11. TRUE or FALSE   No matter whether a memory is true or false, a hypnotized person's confidence in the accuracy of the memory can be unshakeable.

12. TRUE or FALSE   The key to a cognitive interview is recreating the crime scene by having witnesses revisit the scene in their imaginations or in person so sounds, smells, and objects can provide retrieval cues.

13. TRUE or FALSE   During a cognitive interview, the witness is encouraged to recall events in different orders and from different viewpoints.

14. TRUE or FALSE   When used properly, the cognitive interview produces 75 percent more correct information than standard questioning.

15. TRUE or FALSE   The drawback to the cognitive interview is that it tends to elicit numerous false memories.

16. TRUE or FALSE   If people are given the two statements: "A canary is an animal" and "A canary is a bird" to which they must answer yes or no, most people will say yes to the statement "A canary is an animal" faster than to the other statement.

17. TRUE or FALSE   Information in long-term memory is arranged alphabetically, much like a dictionary or encyclopedia.

18. TRUE or FALSE   A model of memory that views memory as an organized system of linked information is known as the associative learning model.

19. TRUE or FALSE   When you look at a picture of your wedding and one memory after another comes flooding back, you are experiencing eidetic imagery.

20. TRUE or FALSE   One memory serves as a cue to trigger another memory in the process known as redintegration.

21. TRUE or FALSE   More elaborative encoding results in more confused and ineffective memory networks with fewer retrieval cues.

22. TRUE or FALSE   Students who study using rote rehearsal have stronger memories as well as showing a deeper understanding of the concepts studied.

23. TRUE or FALSE Long-term memories for conditioned responses and learned actions, such as those involved in typing, driving, or swinging a golf club are called semantic memories.

24. TRUE or FALSE Skill memories register in the "higher" brain areas, especially the hippocampus, while declarative memories register in the "lower" brain areas, especially the cerebellum.

25. TRUE or FALSE Declarative memory stores specific factual information, such as names, faces, words, dates, and ideas and can be personal or impersonal information.

26. TRUE or FALSE The category of declarative memories can be further subdivided into skill and procedural memories.

27. TRUE or FALSE A person with amnesia usually lacks procedural memories, but still has most of their episodic memories.

28. TRUE or FALSE You usually remember where you learned semantic memories, since they are linked with specific times and places.

29. TRUE or FALSE Episodic memories will be more accurate and more likely to be retained than semantic memories.

30. TRUE or FALSE It is the forgetting of episodic information that results in the formation of semantic memories.

Critical Thinking Question

Parents sometimes warn children not to read comic books, fearing that they will learn less in school if they "fill their heads up with junk." Why is this warning unnecessary?

Module 7.3 Measuring Memory
Measuring Memory—The Answer Is on the Tip of My Tongue
Survey Question: How is memory measured?

Language Development Guide

tested: assessed; how information or memory was measured
revealed: made known
partial: incomplete
stuck: caught; trapped
available: obtainable; existing
retrievable: capable of being regained; able to get back
"tip of your tongue": information on the verge (the edge, very close) of being recalled
sextant: navigational instrument used to find latitude and longitude and consists of a telescope and tool for measuring angles
sampan: small flat-bottomed wooden boat with two oars and may have a shelter in which the family lives; used in Southeast Asia for fishing and transportation in inland waters
ambergris: waxy grayish substance formed in the intestines of sperm whales; it is found floating at sea or washes ashore and is added to perfumes to slow down the rate of evaporation
drew a blank: could not remember
theme music: repeated melody (at the beginning and within a TV program)
induce: bring on; produce; cause
beforehand: ahead of time
illusion: false impression
World Series: baseball championship
Hamlet: play written by William Shakespeare
direct: exact; complete

memorized: learned by rote; remembered completely

lineup: group of people, including the crime suspect, are put together by police so that a witness to the crime can identify the person who committed the crime

basis: source

tragic: sad; terrible

culprit: offender; criminal

sequential: in consecutive (successive) order

It's all Greek to me: I don't understand

quotation: copying or repeating the words from a literary source or of an expert source

evident: obvious

wasted: of no useful purpose

half-pipe: usually refers to snowboarding; it is the smooth-surfaced, half-moon shaped chute on which snowboarders do their stunts

gold medal: circular disk made of gold that serves as the trophy for winning first place in a competition

Olympics: world sports competition that occurs in winter and summer every four years

Taylor Swift: American country-pop singer and songwriter

album: collection of song recordings on the same CD or vinyl record

explicit: overt; exact; definite

implicit: hidden; implied

to type: to use a computer keyboard to input data or write using a typewriter

"prime": prepare; get ready; set up

Recite and Review

1. If you know that you possess a memory, but you just can't seem to retrieve it, you are experiencing the _____ state.

2. People can often tell beforehand if they are likely to remember something. This is called the _____.

3. The illusion that you have already experienced a new situation that you are actually seeing for the first time is called _____.

4. The reason that people sometimes feel that they have already experienced a new situation when they are actually seeing it for the first time is that the new experience triggers vague memories of a past experience, without yielding any _____.

5. Tests of memory include recall, recognition, and _____.

6. A test of memory that involves a direct retrieval of information and often requires verbatim memory is _____.

7. When you are asked to memorize a list of items, you will most likely forget the items in the middle, which illustrates the _____ effect.

8. The last items in a list are remembered well because they are still in _____ memory.

9. The first items in a list are remembered well because they entered an "empty" short-term memory, which you could move into long-term memory through _____.

10. Sue is taking an essay test, while Jada is taking a fill-in-the-blank test. Both are taking a test of _____.

11. If you take a multiple choice test in your psychology test, you are being asked to identify previously learned material, which means that this test assesses your _____ memory.

12. According to research, you are most likely to be amazingly accurate in identifying pictures and photographs if your memory is measured for _____.

13. An eyewitness who is asked to give a detailed description of the suspect to a police artist must use _____.

14. An eyewitness who is asked to pick out the suspect from a group of "mug shots" is using _____.

15. On a multiple choice item, one of the listed responses is the correct answer while the others are called _____.

16. On a multiple choice item, if the correct answer and the incorrect responses are very similar, then your memory is likely to be _____.

17. If the correct answer and the incorrect responses on a multiple choice test are very different, you may experience a false sense of recognition known as a(n) _____.

18. To avoid identifying the wrong person in a police line-up, witnesses can be shown one photo at a time and decide whether the person is the culprit before another photo is shown in what is known as a(n) _____ lineup

19. You learned to conjugate Spanish verbs in high school. Now five years later, you are taking a Spanish course and are conjugating verbs again. You are able to complete this task much faster than the other students in your class who have never taken Spanish, which illustrates a test of memory known as _____.

20. Of the three memory tests, the most sensitive measure is typically _____.

21. In your on-line psychology class, it takes you 90 minutes to attain mastery on a module that teaches classical and operant conditioning concepts. Three months later as part of your review for the final exam, you redo this same learning module and are able to mastery the concepts in 40 minutes. Thus, the time difference between these two modules represents your _____ score.

22. A memory that a person is aware of having and can be consciously retrieved is called a(n) _____ memory.

23. A memory that a person does not known exists and must be retrieved unconsciously is called a(n) _____ memory.

24. Recall, recognition, and the tests you take in school rely on _____ memories.

25. Memories that lie outside of awareness, such as unconsciously knowing where the letters are on a keyboard, are considered _____ memories.

26. If you wanted to label a blank drawing of a computer keyboard with the letter, number, or symbol that goes on each key, you would most likely have to pretend you are typing and actually move your fingers as if spelling various words. This movement of your fingers would provide cues to these hidden memories through a process known as _____.

Connections

1. ___ tip-of-the-tongue (TOT) state
2. ___ feeling of knowing
3. ___ déjà vu
4. ___ recall
5. ___ recognition memory
6. ___ relearning
7. ___ serial position effect

a. learning again something that was previously learned

b. feeling that a memory is available but not quite retrievable

c. facilitating the activation and retrieval of hidden memories by using cues

d. memory that a person is aware of having and can be consciously retrieved

e. allows people to predict beforehand whether they will be able to remember something

f. false items included with an item to be recognized

g. illusion that you have already experienced a new situation that you are actually seeing for the first time

8. ___ distractors h. ability to correctly identify previously learned information

9. ___ false positive i. to supply or reproduce memorized information with a minimum of external cues

10. ___ savings score j. amount of time conserved when relearning information

11. ___ explicit memory k. memory that a person does not known exists and must be retrieved unconsciously

12. ___ implicit memory l. false sense of recognition

13. ___ priming m. tendency to make the most errors in remembering the middle items of an ordered list

Check Your Memory

1. TRUE or FALSE   Whether you have remembered something often depends on how you are tested.

2. TRUE or FALSE   You either remember something or you do not remember it with partial memories being a very rare occurrence.

3. TRUE or FALSE   The tip-of-the-tongue (TOT) state is the feeling that a memory is available but not quite retrievable.

4. TRUE or FALSE   The fact that people can often tell beforehand if they are likely to remember something is called the feeling of knowing.

5. TRUE or FALSE   Déjà vu is the illusion that you have already experienced a new situation that you are actually seeing for the first time.

6. TRUE or FALSE   When a new experience triggers vague memories of a past experience, without yielding any details, eidetic imagery is occurring.

7. TRUE or FALSE   Three commonly used tests of memory are serial position, priming, and consolidation.

8. TRUE or FALSE   To complete a fill-in-the-blank question on your psychology test, you must use recognition.

9. TRUE or FALSE   Tests of recall often require verbatim memory.

10. TRUE or FALSE   When you are asked to memorize a list of items, you will most likely forget the items in the middle, which illustrates the serial position effect.

11. TRUE or FALSE   The first items of a list are remembered well because they entered an "empty" short-term memory, which allows rehearsal of the items so that they move into long-term memory.

12. TRUE or FALSE   An ability to correctly identify previously learned information is called proactive consolidation.

13. TRUE or FALSE   Recall memory is usually superior to recognition memory.

14. TRUE or FALSE   If you take a multiple-choice test, you are using recognition memory.

15. TRUE or FALSE   Most people's recognition memory is usually very poor for pictures and photographs.

16. TRUE or FALSE   When you identify a person in a police line-up, you are using recall.

17. TRUE or FALSE   On a multiple choice test, the incorrect responses that are included along with the correct one are referred to as alternative correlates.

18. TRUE or FALSE   Having only one choice in the police line-up that looks like it could be correct can produce a false positive.

19. TRUE or FALSE   To prevent tragic eyewitness mistakes, police can use a sequential lineup in which a witness is shown one photo at a time and must decide whether the person is the culprit before another photo is shown.

20. TRUE or FALSE   Of the three measures of memory, recognition is the most sensitive measure.
21. TRUE or FALSE   Relearning is measured by a savings score.
22. TRUE or FALSE   If you studied algebra and a foreign language in high school, you will be able to relearn each of these subjects more quickly when you take them in college than if you were to learn these subjects for the first time in college.
23. TRUE or FALSE   Implicit memories are past experiences that can be consciously brought to mind.
24. TRUE or FALSE   Recall, recognition, and the tests you take in school rely on explicit memories.
25. TRUE or FALSE   Priming can be used to facilitate the retrieval of implicit memories.
26. TRUE or FALSE   Unconsciously knowing where the letters are on a keyboard is an example of an implicit memory.

Critical Thinking Question

When asked to explain why they may have failed to recall some information, people often claim it must be because the information is no longer in their memory. Why does the existence of implicit memories challenge this explanation?

Module 7.4 Forgetting
Forgetting—Why We, Uh, Let's See; Why We, Uh . . . Forget!
Survey Question: Why do we forget?

Language Development Guide

vexing: frustrating
hang on: retain
intervals: time periods
swayed: influenced
nonsense: meaningless
remote: distant; far away
detergent: soap
Slumdog Millionaire: British film set in India in which a person raised on the street makes it to the final question on the Indian version of the game show "Who Wants to Be a Millionaire?"
Academy Award: trophy given to the best in each film category, such as best picture of the year
Million Dollar Baby: American film about the relationship between a female boxer and her trainers
minimizes: reduces
cramming: intense studying shortly before an exam
lapse: delay; gap
conversely: in opposition; on the other hand
snap your finger: action to indicate that something will happen quickly or by magic
poof!: used to indicate that something has suddenly vanished
"card magic": a card trick
penny: one cent coin
overlooked: unnoticed; unseen
absent-mindedness: being so lost in one's own thoughts that one is unaware of one's surroundings; being forgetful
check it out: you have to look at it
approaches: comes up to; moves toward
switch: swap, trade, change

383

fooled: tricked

replacement: substitute; stand-in

ethnic: cultural

harsh: cruel; unkind

bias: partiality; unfairness

acquainted: familiar

initiate: start; set off

flurry: sudden burst

leaky bucket: a container with a crack or hole

pours: flows

account: explain

contradiction: disagreement; inconsistency

senile: loss of mental functioning due to old age

trivial: unimportant

"pops": bursts

Rats!: a cry of anger

for instance: for example

come on: really

visualize: imagine; picture it

lemon: citrus fruit with sour taste

lavender: purple flowering plant

get drunk: become intoxicated from alcohol

farfetched: unbelievable

prompt: bring about; trigger; encourage

rehashing: repeating

arguments: quarrels; disagreements

further: additional

insight: understanding

about business as usual: normal course of activity

inhibit: hinder; prevent

moral: lesson

procrastinate: put off; postpone

competing: battling; fighting

primarily: first and foremost

beneficial: helpful

disruptive: upsetting; troublesome

mandolin: a guitar-like stringed musical instrument

violin: stringed instrument with four strings and played with a bow; informally called a fiddle

trumpet: brass instrument with three valves that change the pitch as one blow air through closed lips into the instrument

all other things being equal: if things stay the same and there are no complications

initially: at first

intuitive: quick perceptive feeling

grasp: understanding

mastery: complete knowledge or skill in a certain area

motor scooter: usually a vehicle with two small wheels and a low-powered gasoline engine that turns the rear wheel

indeed: certainly; in fact

conflict: disagreement; clash

comical: funny

launching: act of moving a boat or other sea vessel into the water; act of sending out

384

on a more serious note: a crucially important point
standardization: consistency; sameness
cockpits: compartment on a plane where the pilots fly (control) the plane
scan: look quickly
irritations: annoyances; frustrations
horrors: awfulness; terrors
combat: battles; warfare
prone: tendency; inclined to
persist: endure; continue; refuse to go away
accusations: claims; blames; charges
alleged: suspected
molested: harmed through unwanted, improper sexual activity
twilight state: cloudy, disordered consciousness
sued: take legal action against
irresponsible: reckless; careless
accused: blamed; charged
innocence: blameless of the wrongdoing
implanted: inserted; placed
Alan Alda: TV and movie actor best known for the TV show "M*A*S*H"
genuine: real; true
verified: confirmed; proven
deaden: reduced; muffled
merely: just; only

Recite and Review

1. The early memory researcher who tested his own memory at various intervals after learning and was able to plot a graph that depicted the amount of memorized information remembered after these varying lengths of time was _____.
2. To prevent being swayed by prior learning, memory tests often use meaningless words called _____.
3. The graph that shows the amount of memorized information remembered after varying lengths of time is called the _____.
4. Research has shown that forgetting is rapid at first and is then followed by a(n) _____ decline.
5. Even if you do not have to remember the information for very long, you may not learn enough information in the first place if you use an ineffective study technique known as _____.
6. In the textbook, the card magic trick occurred due to _____ failure of the other cards.
7. After three years, students who took a university psychology course had forgotten about _____ percent of the facts they learned.
8. Failure to store sufficient information to form a useful memory is called _____.
9. In the experiment in which the participant was talking to a young college student when two workers carrying a door passed between them with the college student being switched with another young person, the age group that was least likely to notice the switch were _____.
10. Dividing your attention between studying and other activities, such as watching television, can lead to forgetting because a memory was never formed, a type of forgetting known as _____.

385

11. One of the reasons why eyewitnesses are better at identifying members of their own ethnic group than person from other groups is the tendency of people to categorize strangers in _____ terms.

12. A good way to prevent encoding failure is to actively think about the information you are learning, which is called _____ encoding.

13. Physical changes in nerve cells or brain activity that take place when memories are stored are called memory _____.

14. A major factor in the loss of sensory memories and short-term memories is memory _____.

15. Some long-term memories may fade from infrequent retrieval, or _____.

16. Although some unused memories fade, many others are carried for life, a fact that casts doubt on the theory of _____ as a major cause of forgetting.

17. Memories can be available and still not be _____ (capable of being retrieved when necessary).

18. People remember better if the same odor is present when they study and are tested, indicating that the odor is serving as a memory _____.

19. If stimuli associated with a memory are missing when the time comes to retrieve information, then you are experiencing what is called _____ forgetting.

20. If you are in a bad mood, you will tend to recall unpleasant memories, which illustrates _____ learning.

21. The tendency for new memories to impair retrieval of older memories and for older memories to impair the learning of new information is called _____.

22. In a classic experiment in which college students learned lists of nonsense syllables with one group studying then sleeping and the second group studying and staying awake, the group that remembered the most were the students who had _____.

23. When you began this psychology course, you believed a number of myths about human behavior. However, after studying psychology this semester, this new learning will inhibit your old memories regarding human behavior and illustrates how _____ interference occurs.

24. Your life-time use of English grammar is making it difficult to learn the grammar rules in Spanish, which illustrates _____ interference.

25. Your mastery of one task helps you to learn another similar skill. You are experiencing _____.

26. If your mastery of one task conflicts with the learning of another task, it is called _____.

27. The type of transfer that occurs less often than the other type with the conflict being relatively brief is _____ transfer.

28. Unconsciously pushing unwanted memories out of awareness is called _____.

29. The active, conscious attempt to put something out of mind is called _____.

30. Many sexually abused children develop problems that persist into adulthood with some vividly remembering the abuse, while others have no memory of the abuse due to _____.

31. When psychologists try to help an adult uncover hidden memories of a traumatic childhood, the memories that result whether true or false are called _____ memories.

32. A hypnotic drug that induces a twilight state of consciousness and has mistakenly been called a "truth drug" is _____.

33. When hypnosis, guided visualization, suggestion, age regression, and similar techniques elicit fantasies that are mistaken for real memories, the result may be the _____ syndrome.

Part 1: Connections

1. ____ encoding failure

2. ____ memory decay

3. ____ disuse

4. ____ memory cue

5. ____ state-dependent learning

6. ____ retroactive interference

7. ____ proactive interference

8. ____ repression

9. ____ suppression

a. fading or weakening of memories assumed to occur when memory traces become weaker; occurs in sensory memory and STM

b. memory influenced by one's bodily and emotional conditions at the time of learning and at the time of retrieval

c. tendency for new memories to inhibit the retrieval of old memories

d. failure to store sufficient information to form a useful memory

e. any stimulus associated with a particular memory and usually enhances retrieval

f. unconsciously pushing unwanted memories out of awareness

g. conscious effort to put something out of mind or to keep it from awareness

h. tendency for old memories to inhibit the retrieval of newer memories

i. theory that memory traces weaken when memories are not periodically used or retrieved

Part 2: Connections

1. ____ nonsense syllables

2. ____ curve of forgetting

3. ____ memory traces

4. ____ availability (in memory)

5. ____ accessibility (in memory)

6. ____ positive transfer

7. ____ negative transfer

8. ____ false memory syndrome

a. memories currently stored that can be retrieved when necessary

b. all memories currently stored

c. mastery of one task aids learning or performing another

d. graph that shows the amount of memorized information remembered after varying lengths of time

e. fantasies elicited during recovered memory procedures that are mistaken for real memories

f. mastery of one task conflicts with learning or performing another

g. physical changes in nerve cells or brain activity that takes place when memories are stored

h. meaningless three-letter words used in memory testing

Check Your Memory

1. TRUE or FALSE   An early memory researcher Herman Ebbinghaus tested his own memory at various intervals after memorizing nonsense syllables.

2. TRUE or FALSE   A graph that shows the amount of information remembered after varying lengths of time is known as an encoding histogram.

3. TRUE or FALSE   Forgetting tends to be slow at first and is then followed by a rapid decline.

4. TRUE or FALSE   In general, recent events are recalled more accurately than those from the remote past.

5. TRUE or FALSE   If you cram for an exam, you do not have to remember for very long, but you may not learn enough in the first place.

6. TRUE or FALSE   The failure to store sufficient information to form a useful memory defines forgetting due to disuse.

7. TRUE or FALSE   If you do not know what building is pictured on the back of a 20-dollar U.S. bill, it is probably due to retroactive interference.

8. TRUE or FALSE   In encoding failure, a memory was never formed in the first place.

9. TRUE or FALSE   In the experiment in which the participant is talking to a young college student when two workers carrying a door pass between them with the college student being switched with another young person, the people who were least likely to notice the switch were older adults.

10. TRUE or FALSE   A tendency to categorize people in general terms is one of the reasons why eyewitnesses are better at identifying members of their own ethnic group than persons from other groups.

11. TRUE or FALSE   Memory traces are physical changes in nerve cells or brain activity that take place when memories are stored.

12. TRUE or FALSE   Memory decay is the main factor in the loss of long-term memories, but does not cause memory loss for sensory or short-term memories.

13. TRUE or FALSE   Some long-term memory traces may fade from infrequent retrieval called disuse and eventually become too weak to retrieve.

14. TRUE or FALSE   Disuse explains the memory loss that occurs during redintegration, relearning, priming, and senility.

15. TRUE or FALSE   Even if memories are available in your memory, they may not be accessible.

16. TRUE or FALSE   One reason retrieval may fail is because memory cues are missing when the time comes to retrieve information.

17. TRUE or FALSE   Your memory will be better during testing if you visualize the room in which you will be tested while studying.

18. TRUE or FALSE   Your memory will be better during testing if you wear the same perfume when being tested that you wore while studying.

19. TRUE or FALSE   If you are in a happy mood, you are more likely to remember happy memories, which illustrates state-dependent learning.

20. TRUE or FALSE   Suppression refers to the tendency for new memories to impair retrieval of older memories and visa versa.

21. TRUE or FALSE   It is not completely clear to researchers whether new memories alter existing memories or whether they make it harder to retrieve earlier memories.

22. TRUE or FALSE   Proactive interference refers to the tendency for new learning to inhibit retrieval of old learning.

23. TRUE or FALSE   Sleeping after study can help you retain memories, while reading, writing, or even watching TV may cause interference.

24. TRUE or FALSE   Retroactive interference occurs when past learning inhibits the recall of new learning.

25. TRUE or FALSE   The greater the similarity between two subjects studied, the more interference that will take place.

26. TRUE or FALSE   If you learn Spanish and then you study French and the Spanish interferes with you learning French, then retroactive interference is occurring.

27. TRUE or FALSE   The interference effects apply primarily to memories of verbal information with similarity in learning skills sometimes being beneficial, rather than disruptive.
28. TRUE or FALSE   A skateboarder who takes up surfing will probably experience positive transfer.
29. TRUE or FALSE   Positive transfer of skills is usually brief and occurs less often than negative transfer.
30. TRUE or FALSE   Negative transfer is most likely to occur when a new response must be made to an old stimulus.
31. TRUE or FALSE   Through repression, painful, threatening, or embarrassing memories are held out of consciousness.
32. TRUE or FALSE   A conscious effort to put something out of mind or to keep it from awareness is known as displacement.
33. TRUE or FALSE   People prone to repression tend to be extremely sensitive to emotional events.
34. TRUE or FALSE   In time, active suppression of a memory may become true repression.
35. TRUE or FALSE   Under the influence of Amytal, patients with repressed memories will automatically tell the truth.
36. TRUE or FALSE   Hypnosis, guided visualization, suggestion, age regression, and similar techniques can elicit fantasies that are mistaken for real memories and result in the false memory syndrome.
37. TRUE or FALSE   False memories cannot be deliberately implanted.
38. TRUE or FALSE   No matter how real a recovered memory may seem, it could be false, unless it can be verified by others or by medical records.

Critical Thinking Questions

1. Based on state-dependent learning, why do you think that music often strongly evokes memories?

2. You must study French, Spanish, psychology, and biology in one evening (poor thing!). What do you think would be the best order in which to study these subjects so as to minimize interference?

Memory and the Brain—Some "Shocking" Findings
Survey Question: How does the brain form and store memories?

Language Development Guide

preceding: before; prior to
trauma: shock and distress
electroconvulsive: electric shocks that cause seizures or convulsions
intact: whole; unbroken
switching station: where a train changes directions to a different track
striking: surprising
eternally: forever
terrorist: radical; fanatic
9/11: the attack on the World Trade Center took place on September 11, 2001 (9/11)
frozen: stationary; unmoving
significant: important
assassinations: murder of a public official
John F. Kennedy: 35th President of the United States; assassinated by gunshot during a motorcade in Dallas, Texas on November 22, 1963

Martin Luther King, Jr.: African-American civil rights leader and Baptist minister; assassinated by gunshot on motel balcony in Memphis, Tennessee on March 29, 1968

Challenger space shuttle disaster: space vehicle with seven crew members exploded just after launch on January 28, 1986

Columbia space shuttle disaster: space vehicle with seven crew members exploded upon re-entry into the atmosphere on February 1, 2003

death of Princess Diana: popular British royal, Princess of Wales, ex-wife of Prince Charles, died in car accident in Paris, France on August 31, 1997

activate: turn on; set in motion; stimulate

heightened: to raise; to make more intense

intensify: strengthen; increase

tragedies: misfortune; disaster; human suffering

clarity: clearness in perceiving

prom: (short for promenade) formal dance for high schoolers at the end of the year

crystallize: come together into a definite shape

consistent: reliable; constant

landmarks: milestone; prominent marker

haunt: recur constantly; hang around

maltreatment: abuse

"flashbacks": episodes of reliving a trauma

handicapped: disabled

simplify: make things easier and shorter

coordination: skill

marine: sea

circuit: path

"reprograms": encodes new instructions

chemical "signature": unique pattern

potentiation: to make powerful; to enhance the effect

affected: acted on; influenced

Recite and Review

1. A football player is tackled and loses consciousness for a minute or so. When he comes to, he does not remember catching the football and being tackled. This football player is experiencing _____ amnesia.
2. After a brain injury, a woman is unable to store new memories, although everything that happened before the head injury is "crystal clear." This woman is experiencing _____ amnesia.
3. The process by which relatively permanent memories are formed in the brain is called _____.
4. If a person or animal received an electroconvulsive shock (ECS), this shock will prevent the process of _____.
5. A person who undergoes electroconvulsive shock therapy for severe depression will most likely have some degree of _____ amnesia.
6. Many parts of the brain are responsible for memory, but the part of the brain that acts as a "switching station" between short-term and long-term memory is the _____.
7. If this "switching station" between short-term memory and long-term memory is damaged, patients usually develop _____ amnesia.
8. If you studied, slept eight hours, and were then awake for eight hours, you would remember more than if you studied and stayed awake eight hours because more _____ would occur before interference begins.

390

9. Your vivid, emotional memory of the 9/11 terrorist attacks on the World Trade Center is called a(n) _____ memory.
10. Memory consolidation is intensified and vivid, emotional memories are produced when powerful experiences activate the _____ system of the brain.
11. More than anything else, what sets flashbulb memories apart from other memories is our tendency to place great _____ in them, even when they are wrong.
12. According to blood flow patterns, the type of long-term memories that appear to be stored in the cerebellum are the _____ memories.
13. Blood flow patterns reveal that the long-term memory stored in the front and back of the cerebral cortex are the fact, or _____ memories.
14. The front of the cerebral cortex is the storage area for the type of fact memories called _____ memories.
15. In the back of the cerebral cortex, one would find the type of fact memories known as _____ memories.
16. Eric Kandel and his colleagues studied learning in the *aplysia,* which is a type of marine _____.
17. In working with the aplysia, Kandel and his colleagues found that learning occurred when certain nerve cells in a circuit alter the amount of _____ they release.
18. The activity, structure, and chemistry of brain cells can also be altered through _____.
19. When two or more brain cells which are interconnected become very active at the same time, these connections will grow stronger through a process called _____.
20. If the hippocampus is electrically stimulated, this process of making memory connections stronger would be _____.

Connections

1. ___ retrograde amnesia
2. ___ anterograde amnesia
3. ___ consolidation

4. ___ electroconvulsive shock (ECS)
5. ___ flashbulb memory
6. ___ long-term potentiation

7. ___ aplysia

8. ___ hippocampus
9. ___ front of the cortex

10. ___ back of the cortex

11. ___ cerebellum

a. scientific name for a marine snail
b. process by which relatively permanent memories are formed in the brain
c. process that occurs when two or more interconnected brain cells become more active at the same time resulting in the connections between them growing stronger
d. storage place for procedural memories
e. storage place for episodic memories
f. forgetting the events that occurred before an injury or trauma
g. brain structure associated with emotion and the transfer of information from short-term memory to long-term memory
h. storage place for semantic memories
i. forgetting the events that follow an injury or trauma; inability to store new memories
j. memories created at times of high emotion that seem especially vivid
k. electric current passed directly through the brain that produces a seizure

391

Check Your Memory

1. TRUE or FALSE   Anterograde amnesia involves forgetting events that occurred before an injury or trauma, while retrograde amnesia involves forgetting events that follow an injury or trauma.

2. TRUE or FALSE   The process by which relatively permanent memories are formed in the brain is called redintegration.

3. TRUE or FALSE   An electroconvulsive shock (ECS) can produce retrograde amnesia, erasing the memory of the painful shock occurring.

4. TRUE or FALSE   If the hippocampus is damaged, patients usually develop anterograde amnesia and show an inability to consolidate new memories.

5. TRUE or FALSE   You would forget less if you studied, stayed awake eight hours, and then slept eight hours than you would if you studied, slept eight hours, and were awake for eight hours.

6. TRUE or FALSE   An eidetic image is an especially vivid image that seems to be frozen in memory at times of personal tragedy, accident, or other emotionally significant events.

7. TRUE or FALSE   Heightened activity in the limbic system of the brain appears to intensify memory consolidation.

8. TRUE or FALSE   Although people have great confidence in their vivid recollections of emotionally or historically significant events, these recollections are not always accurate.

9. TRUE or FALSE   Some memories go beyond flashbulb clarity and become so intense that they cause "flashbacks" and leave a person emotionally handicapped.

10. TRUE or FALSE   According to blood flow patterns, declarative memories appear to be stored in the cerebellum.

11. TRUE or FALSE   Procedural memories are stored in the cerebral cortex of the brain.

12. TRUE or FALSE   We use the front of the brain cortex for semantic memories, while the back areas are used for episodic memories.

13. TRUE or FALSE   Eric Kandel found that learning in sea snails occurred when certain nerve cells in a circuit alter the amount of transmitter chemicals they release.

14. TRUE or FALSE   Learning alters the activity, structure, and chemistry of brain cells with such changes determining which connections get stronger and which become weaker.

15. TRUE or FALSE   If two or more interconnected brain cells become more active at the same time, the connections between them grow stronger through a process called long-term potentiation.

16. TRUE or FALSE   Electrically stimulating parts of the brain involved in memory can increase and enhance long-term potentiation.

17. TRUE or FALSE   Drugs that increase long-term potentiation also tend to improve memory.

Module 7.5 Exceptional Memory and Improving Memory

Exceptional Memory—Wizards of Recall

Survey Question: What are "photographic" memories?

Language Development Guide

superior: exceptional; expert

treasure map: drawing or chart that marks the location of buried treasure or a secret passage; usually found as part of a fictional story; rarely used in real life

hut: simple, one-room shelter usually made of wood; a shack

eidetic: able to recall with amazing accuracy

"scanned": doing a quick thorough examination

"projected": causing an image to appear on a surface

neon sign: glowing colored light generated by a inert gas (does not react chemically with other substances), such as neon (orange-red glow), flowing through glass tubing

Alice's Adventures in Wonderland: a book written by Lewis Carroll about a little girl named Alice who follows a white rabbit down a rabbit hole and has many adventures in the strange land she finds there

apron: outer garment usually made of cloth that covers the clothes on the front of body, attached by strings tied around the neck and waist; usually worn by those cooking, cleaning, by nurses (sometimes) and lab workers working with chemicals (use rubber ones)

striking: remarkable; outstanding

disappointed: let down; upset; dissatisfied

attested: declared; confirmed

ingredients: parts; elements; components

scraps: bits; pieces

ultimately: in the end; finally

basically: on the whole; mostly

avid: keen; enthusiastic; devoted

feat: notable act or achievement; accomplishment

underlies: is the foundation, basis, cause

expertise: having exceptional skill or great deal of knowledge in a particular area

extension: lengthening; increasing; expansion of

phenomenal: extraordinary; exceptional; rare

diligent: hard-working; industrious

daunting: intimidating; overwhelming

persuaded: convinced

challenging: difficult; demanding

diabolical: showing a wicked ability

specialized: expert; specific

naturally: biologically; born with; innate

acquired: to develop or learn something

mnemonics: any kind of memory system or aid

contestant: competitor; contender; participant

exceedingly: very; extremely

excel: do extremely well in; to stand out

implies: suggests

"gift": special talent

conclude: to decide

Recite and Review

1. In your graphic design class, you are asked to draw the floor design of your apartment, depicting every door and window. To accomplish this, you must first create a(n) _____ of your apartment.

2. In the experiment by Kosslyn, Ball, and Reiser in which the participants memorized a treasure map and then pictured a black dot moving from one part of the island to another, the time it took for the participant to "move" the dot in their minds was directly related to the actual _____ on the map.

3. The ability to retain a "projected" mental image long enough to use it as a source of information is referred to as _____ imagery.

4. The images that are usually "viewed" mentally with the eyes closed are the _____ images.

5. The images that are best "seen" on a plain surface, such as a blank piece of paper, are _____ images.

6. "Photographic memory" is most often used to describe a mental ability called _____.

7. Although Mr. S, the mnemonist described at the beginning of the textbook chapter, could remember tremendous amounts of information, he could not separate important facts from trivia, such as the ingredients on the back of a cereal box. In other words, he lacked a(n) _____ memory.

8. In his study of a student volunteer named Steve who eventually memorized 80 digits, Ericsson found that Steve could still only memorize seven individual consonants, which showed that Steve's memory feats were not due to having a better _____ memory.

9. Ericcson found that Steve had learned new ways to store long lists of digits into long-term memory by grouping the digits into larger meaningful units through a process called _____.

10. Wilding and Valentine found that certain types of information were easier to encode and recall for the exceptional memorizers because they possessed specialized knowledge and _____.

11. At the World Memory Championships, many of the contestants used special memory "tricks" called _____.

12. Since several of the memory contestants were able to excel on tasks that prevented the use of learned strategies and techniques, Wilding and Valentine concluded that exceptional memory is usually based on both learned strategies and _____ ability.

Connections

1. ___ mental images
2. ___ eidetic imagery
3. ___ chunking
4. ___ selective memory
5. ___ mnemonics

a. organizing information into larger meaningful units

b. ability to retain a "projected" mental image long enough to use it as a source of information

c. internal images or visual depictions used in memory and thinking

d. any kind of memory system or aid that enhances memories

e. being able to separate important facts from trivia or facts from fantasy in encoding information

Check Your Memory

1. TRUE or FALSE   To answer a question of how many doors are in one's house or apartment, most people form mental images of each room and count the doorways they visualize.

2. TRUE or FALSE   In the experiment by Kosslyn, Ball, and Reiser in which the participants memorized a treasure map and then pictured a black dot moving from one part of the island to another, the time it took for the participant to "move" the dot in their minds was directly related to the actual distances on the map.

3. TRUE or FALSE   The ability to retain a "projected" mental image long enough to use it as a source of information is referred to as "flashbulb" memories.

4. TRUE or FALSE   "Photographic memory" is most often used to describe a memory ability called eidetic imagery.

5. 5. TRUE or FALSE   A child is more likely to have eidetic imagery than an adult.

6. TRUE or FALSE   Eidetic images are usually "viewed" mentally with the eyes closed, while internal mental images are best "seen" on a plain surface, such as a blank piece of paper.

7. TRUE or FALSE   Eidetic images have been described as being somewhat like the after-images a a person might have after looking at a flashbulb or a brightly lit neon sign.

8. TRUE or FALSE   The mnemonist Mr. S. described in the textbook had a very selective memory.

9. TRUE or FALSE   Exceptional memorizers tend to have specialized interests and use mnemonics.

10. TRUE or FALSE   The memory strategies uses by memory champions tend to double the capacity of the person's short-term memory, so that they have more than seven slots in their short-term memory.

11. TRUE or FALSE   Several of the memory contestants that Wilding and Valentine studied were able to excel on tasks that prevented the use of learned strategies and techniques.

12. TRUE or FALSE   Wilding and Valentine's research with exceptional memorizers showed that these people have superior intellectual abilities and somewhat different brain configurations.

Critical Thinking Question

Mr. S had great difficulty remembering faces. Can you guess why?

Improving Memory—Keys to the Memory Bank
Survey Question: How can I improve my memory?

Language Development Guide

the jury is still out: still don't know if
augment: supplement; add to
boil down: reduce
chores: tasks
manageable: controllable
marginal notes: writing on the side edges of your textbook page
going blank: forgetting
daunting: difficult
jog: assist
potent: strong; powerful; effective
knit: combine; unit; tie
code: system
bare: basic; simple
insurance: protection; assurance
boredom: dullness
fatigue: tiredness; exhaustion
superior: better
to schedule: to plan; to arrange
schedule: timetable; calendar; agenda; to-do list
designate: assign

treat: behave toward; regard; consider

proceeds: to go forward

progress: advancement; growth; improvement

prime: major; main; key

icing on your study cake: a pleasant extra

minimum: the smallest amount

realistic: practical; reasonable

cramming: studying large amounts of information in a short period of time

eluded: escaped

scarecrow: a figure made to resemble a man and placed in a field to scare away birds that would eat the crops

Judy Garland: American singer and actress during the 1920s to the 1960s

The Wizard of Oz: the classic 1939 American fantasy film based on a children's book by Frank Baum; girl by the name of Dorothy is transported by a tornado from Kansas to the land of Oz where she has adventures with characters such as the scarecrow, tin man, cowardly lion, wicked witch, and the wizard of Oz

Ray Bolger: American actor, dancer, and comedian in 1920s to the 1970s who is best known for his role as the scarecrow in the Wizard of Oz

impressions: vague ideas or feelings

recapturing: recalling; bringing back

context: circumstances; situations; surroundings (that can determine meaning)

impressed: deeply influenced or affected

flash cards: a study tool, small pieces of paper with a term or question on one side and its definition or answer on the other

"night person": person who tends to stay up late into the night

ample: plenty of

so Mother was right: advice from your mother was correct

inherent: built in naturally; inborn

TV dinners: frozen meals

Twinkies: yellow snack cake

Recite and Review

1. Rehearsal, selection, and organization are considered strategies that can be used when studying to improve the memory process of _____ .

2. Recitation and review are considered strategies that can improve one's performance on tests by improving the memory process of _____.

3. The best rehearsal strategy is to look for connections within existing knowledge, which is known as _____.

4. Too often, students underline too much in their textbook. Student should use marginal notes to summarize their ideas and practice very _____ marking.

5. If you have to memorize a rather difficult list of words, it is best to reorganize the words into larger units called _____.

6. Summarizing your class readings and your class notes so that the overall network of ideas becomes clearer and simpler illustrates how organization can encourage better _____ of information.

7. When you have to memorize fairly short, organized speech, it would be best for you to use _____ learning.

8. If you are learning a long complex speech, it would be best to study using _____ learning.

9. You have numerous lines and speeches to learn as the lead in a three act play. To learn this extremely long and complex material, you will need to break this learning task into a series

of short sections A, B, and C and learn A, then A and B together, and finally A, B, and C. This technique is called the _____ method.

10. To decide which learning approach to use, it is best to study the largest _____ amount of information you can at one time.

11. When you are learning a long list of items in order, you should give extra practice to the middle of the list because of the _____ effect.

12. When you break long lists of information into short sub-lists, it is best to make the _____ sublists the shortest of all.

13. Some of the most important stimuli to aid retrieval are the memory _____ present during encoding.

14. During study, one should try to use new names, ideas, or terms in several sentences and form images that include the new information because it involves _____ encoding.

15. Continuing to study beyond the point of bare mastery of facts is called _____.

16. The best insurance against going blank on a test because of being nervous is _____.

17. To keep boredom and fatigue to a minimum, students should alternate short study sessions with brief rest periods in a pattern called _____ practice.

18. A schedule in which studying continues for long periods, without interruption is called _____ practice.

19. Learning proceeds best when you check your progress by having a knowledge of results, or _____.

20. When you are reading a text, you should stop frequently and try to remember what you have just read by restating it in your own words, a technique known as _____.

21. You should hold the amount of new information you try to memorize to a minimum as you are _____ before a test.

22. Successful retrieval is usually the result of a planned _____ of memory.

23. One study found that students were most likely to recall names that eluded them if they made use of impressions about the length of the name, letter sounds within the name, similar names, and other types of _____ information.

24. A technique used in police work that can be modified to jog one's memory and involves recalling events in different orders and from different viewpoints is the _____.

25. When using flashcards, you look at the first card and then move this card a few cards back in the stack and then do the same with the next few cards. When you get to the first "old" card, you test yourself on it and move it even farther back in the stack. By going through your flashcards in this manner, you are _____ how long you remember.

26. Sleeping after studying _____ interference.

27. People who are hungry almost always score _____ on memory tests.

Connections

1. ___ elaborative encoding
2. ___ whole learning
3. ___ progressive-part method
4. ___ serial position effect
5. ___ memory cues

a. continuing to study beyond the point of bare mastery of facts
b. studying continues for long periods without interruption
c. involves summarizing aloud while learning which forces one to practice retrieving information
d. technique used by police that can be modified to jog your memory
e. looking for connections to existing knowledge

6. ___ overlearning

7. ___ spaced practice

8. ___ massed practice

9. ___ recitation

10. ___ cognitive interview

f. alternating short study sessions with brief rest periods

g. best method to use in memorizing a speech that is fairly short and organized

h. stimuli that aid retrieval with the best ones being those present during encoding

i. tendency to make the most errors in remembering the middle items of a list

j. breaking a learning task into a series of short sections and then learn part A; then A and B; then A, B, and C; and so forth

Check Your Memory

1. TRUE or FALSE   There is very little you can do to improve your brain's natural ability to store long-term memories.
2. TRUE or FALSE   Scientists are still unsure whether herbs, such as Ginkgo biloba, and vitamins, such as vitamin E, actually improve human memory.
3. TRUE or FALSE   Memory cues and organization are considered retrieval strategies, while recitation and review are considered encoding strategies.
4. TRUE or FALSE   The more you rehearse, or mentally review information as you read, the better you will remember it.
5. TRUE or FALSE   Maintenance rehearsal involves looking for connections to existing knowledge and is the best way to review information as you read.
6. TRUE or FALSE   Most students underline too little in their textbooks, rather than too much.
7. TRUE or FALSE   If you must memorize a difficult list of words, it is best to reorganize the items on the list into chunks.
8. TRUE or FALSE   Constructing summaries of what you read can improve memory by encouraging better encoding of information.
9. TRUE or FALSE   For extremely long, complicated information, it is still better to use whole learning rather than part learning.
10. TRUE or FALSE   If you break an extremely long and complex learning task into a series of short sections and then learn part A; then A and B; then A, B, and C; and so forth, you are using a technique known as the progressive-part method.
11. TRUE or FALSE   When you are learning a long list of items in order, you should give extra practice to the middle of the list because of the serial position effect.
12. TRUE or FALSE   When you break long lists of information into short sub-lists, it is best to make the ending sublists the shortest of all.
13. TRUE or FALSE   The best memory cues are those that were present during encoding.
14. TRUE or FALSE   When you study, it is best to try to use new names, ideas, or terms in several sentences and to form images that include the new information.
15. TRUE or FALSE   Overlearning tends to decrease one's memory for the material studied.
16. TRUE or FALSE   It is more effective to use massed practice when studying than spaced practice.
17. TRUE or FALSE   A good way to provide feedback for yourself while studying is recitation.
18. TRUE or FALSE   When reviewing right before a test, it is wise to hold the amount of new information you try to memorize to a minimum.

19. TRUE or FALSE   In one classic experiment, the best memory score was earned by a group of students who spent 20 percent of their time reciting and 80 percent reading.
20. TRUE or FALSE   Variations on the cognitive interview used in police work can be used to jog your memory when trying to recall information for a test.
21. TRUE or FALSE   An effective retrieval strategy is to go through the alphabet, trying each letter as the first sound of a name or word you are seeking.
22. TRUE or FALSE   When using flash cards to study terms and concepts, the best strategy is to go through all the cards in the same order at least three times.
23. TRUE or FALSE   Sleeping after studying reduces interference.
24. TRUE or FALSE   People who are hungry almost always score higher on memory tests.
25. TRUE or FALSE   Drinking a cup of coffee before a test has been shown to significantly lower one's performance on the test.

Critical Thinking Question

What advantages would there be to taking notes as you read a textbook, as opposed to underlining words in the text?

Module 7.6 Psychology in Action: Mnemonics—Memory Magic
Survey Question: Are there any tricks to help me with my memory?

Language Development Guide

pairs of cranial nerves:
olfactory nerves: sensory nerves from nose
optic nerves: sensory nerves from retina of eyes
oculomotor nerves: motor nerves to control eyeball and eyelid movement
trochlear nerves: motor nerves that move eyes upward or sideways
trigeminal nerves: sensory and motor nerves involved with touch and pain sensations of the face and head and chewing
abducens nerves: motor nerves that control eye movements
facial nerves: sensory and motor nerves involved in taste and facial expressions
vestibulocochlear nerves: sensory nerves of the vestibular system (balance and gravity)
glossopharyngeal nerves: sensory and motor nerves of the tongue
vagus nerves: very long sensory and motor nerves the control the ears, voice box, stomach, heart, lungs; sometime called the "wandering nerve"
spinal accessory nerves: motor nerves that control head movements and assist the vagus nerves
hypoglossal nerves: motor nerves that control tongue and swallowing
tempting: attractive; appealing
to resort: to turn to for relief
fortunately: luckily; happily
superiority: advantage; dominance
hath: old usage of to have
spectrum: ordered display of the components of an emission or wave, such as the visible spectrum
budding: up-and-coming; promising
port: left-hand side of a boat when one is facing forward
starboard: right-hand side of a boat when one is facing forward
musical staff: a set of five horizontal lines and four spaces, each of which represents a different musical pitch; used in musical notation
generation: entire group of individuals born and living at about the same time

acrostics: first letter of each word or line form a word or phrase when read together; used as a
     memory aid

encounter: meet

technical: scientific, industrial, or mechanical

clarified: to make clear

outrageous: shocking; extreme

exaggerated: overstated

bizarre: strange

ray gun: fictional type of gun that shoots an energy beam; used often in science fiction

outperformed: surpassed; outshined; did much better

sampling: group of examples

applications: uses

jam-packed: to crowd to capacity

flapping: flutter; shaking; flailing

chirping: tweeting; singing

as a matter of fact: actually; really

short run: over a small length of time

fragile: easily broken

conventional: usual; regular; normal

nibbling: taking small bites of something

dribbling: bouncing a ball by tapping it with one hand

ridiculous: absurd; silly

latissimus dorsi: large flat muscle on either side of the back

sigh: to exhale noisily

slightest: least; smallest amount

extensive: widespread; wide range; general

leaning: bending sideways; slanting

psst: sound used to get someone's attention and then whisper information to them

flexibility: easy to shape and adapt

Van Gogh: famous Dutch painter who is known for cutting his own ear off

dim past: long ago and forgotten

errands: tasks; chores

ancient: very old

orators: speakers; lecturers

statues: sculptures that represent people, animals, or events

bun: bread roll

hive: structure in which a colony of bees lives and makes honey

skeptical: cynical; doubtful

fair trial: try it out before criticizing it

worthwhile: valuable; useful

Recite and Review

1. Any kind of memory system or aid is called a(n) _____.
2. Remembering the colors of the spectrum in order by using the first letter of each color to form the name Roy G. Biv illustrates the use of a group of memory system known as _____.
3. In general, transferring information from short-term memory to long-term memory is aided by making the information _____.
4. In using memory aids, words tend to be harder to remember than memory aids that use _____.

5. Bizarre images make stored information easier to retrieve because they make the information more _____.
6. Bizarre images as memory aids mainly help improve one's immediate memory and tend to work best for fairly _____ information.
7. College students who used exaggerated mental associations to remember the names of unfamiliar animals outperformed students who used simple repetition, or _____ learning.
8. To remember the Spanish word "carta," which means "letter," you can link it to the familiar English word "cart" and visualize "a cart full of letters." You are using the _____ method.
9. Mnemonics work best during the _____ stages of learning.
10. Mnemonic memories tend to work in the short run and tend to be more _____ than conventional memories.
11. Mnemonics are not likely to be helpful unless you make extensive use of _____.
12. To remember lists of ideas, objects, or words in order, you can form an exaggerated association connecting the first item to the second, then the second to the third, and so on. This is known as forming a(n) _____.
13. Ancient Greek orators had an interesting way to remember ideas in order when giving a speech. Their method involved taking a(n) _____.
14. If you learn a standard ordered list of items, such as 1. is a bun, 2 is a shoe, 3 is a tree, 4 is a door, and 5 is a hive and then remember a list in order by forming an image associated with each item on this standard list, then you are using a mnemonic device known as a(n) _____.

Connections

1. ___ mnemonic

   a. remembered the notes represented by the lines and spaces of the musical staff by learning "F-A-C-E" and "**E**very **G**ood **B**oy **D**oes **F**ine"

2. ___ acrostics

   b. any kind of memory system or aid

3. ___ keyword method

   c. ancient Greek orators associated topics with the images of statues found along a familiar path in order to remember ideas in order

4. ___ forming a chain

   d. to remember the Spanish word *carta*, which means "letter", imagine a shopping cart filled with postal letters

5. ___ taking a mental walk

   e. remembering the list in order—elephant, doorknob, string, watch, rifle, oranges—by picturing a full-size elephant balanced on a doorknob playing with a string tied to him

6. ___ using a system

   f. using a standard list of numbered objects, such as: 1 is a bun, 2 is a shoe, 3 is a tree, 4 is a door, 5 is a hive; and then forming an image associating bun with the first item on your list and shoe with the second item, and so on

Check Your Memory

1. TRUE or FALSE   Rote learning has been shown to be superior to mnemonic learning.
2. TRUE or FALSE   Making a word from the first letter of each cranial nerve and stringing them together to make a nonsense sentence is an example of the keyword method.
3. TRUE or FALSE   If some facts or ideas in a chapter seem to stay in your memory easily, you should associate other more difficult facts with them.
4. TRUE or FALSE   Acrostics are more effective if you make up your own.
5. TRUE or FALSE   Visual pictures, or images, are generally easier to remember than words.
6. TRUE or FALSE   Bizarre images mainly help improve immediate memory, and they work best for fairly simple information.
7. TRUE or FALSE   In acrostics, a familiar word or image is used to link two other words or items.
8. TRUE or FALSE   An example of the keyword method would be to remember the Spanish word *pajaro* means bird by using the words "parked car-o" and visualizing a parked car filled with birds.
9. TRUE or FALSE   Mnemonic memories are more fragile than conventional memories.
10. TRUE or FALSE   If you have trouble remembering history, you should picture each historical personality as a part of the remote past and try to visualize their pictures from the textbook.
11. TRUE or FALSE   Mnemonics are not likely to be helpful unless you make extensive use of images.
12. TRUE or FALSE   Ancient Greek orators used to the keyword method to remember ideas in order when giving a speech.
13. TRUE or FALSE   A helpful strategy to remember lists of ideas is to make up a short story that links all the items on a list.
14. TRUE or FALSE   If you learn a standard ordered list of items, such as 1. is a bun, 2 is a shoe, 3 is a tree, 4 is a door, and 5 is a hive and then remember a list in order by forming an image associated with each item on this standard list, then you are using a mnemonic device known as a system.

Critical Thinking Question

How are elaborative encoding and mnemonics alike?

Final Survey and Review—Completion

Module 7.1 Memory Systems
Stages of Memory—Do You Have a Mind Like a Steel Trap? Or a Sieve?
Survey Question: How does memory work?

1. According to the Atkinson-Schiffrin model, the three stages of memory are sensory memory, long-term memory, and _____ memory.
2. When you look at a sunset and shut your eyes, the fleeting visual image that persists for about one-half second would be an example of the type of sensory memory known as_____ memory.
3. As you work on your homework, you are combining your short-term memory with other mental processes. This type of memory used for thinking and problem solving is referred to as _____ memory.

4. Americans tend to emphasize individualism when recalling memories, while the Chinese tend to emphasize their membership in groups, which illustrates how _____ affects our memories.

Module 7.2 STM and LTM
Short-Term Memory—Do You Know the Magic Number?
Survey Question: What are the features of short-term memory?

5. Angela is taking a test in which one-digit random numbers are called out, and then she repeats them back to the examiner. Angela is taking the _____ test.
6. Using the letters that correspond to each number on a telephone, you have created a new telephone number for your business called "Music Store" by using the process called _____.
7. If you learned the words to the Gettysburg Address by repeating them over and over again, you learned this famous speech through _____ learning.
8. Caleb is studying his economic terms and principles by relating them to current economic events he has seen on TV and also how they might be used in his father's business. Caleb is learning these terms by using _____ encoding.

Module 7.2 Long-Term Memory—A Blast from the Past
Survey Questions: What are the features of long-term memory?

9. In one study, people who had visited a Disney resort were shown several fake ads for Disney that featured Bugs Bunny. Later, about 16 percent of the people who saw these fake ads claimed that they had met Bugs at Disneyland, which is impossible because Bugs Bunny is a Warner Brothers character. These people had created memories through a process known _____.
10. Compared to standard police questioning, a technique developed by Geiselman and Fisher that can yield 35 percent more correct information when used properly is the _____.
11. Every time Stuart sees the leaves outside his window turn to red and gold, he is transported back to his fall hiking trip along the Appalachian Trail two years ago. For Stuart, an entire past experience was reconstructed from this one small visual cue through the process known as _____.
12. Although you have not been on a pair of roller skates in five years, you soon are skating around the rink with no trouble. These memories would be considered _____ memories.
13. Remembering your high school graduation and the dance afterward would be a type of fact memory known as a(n) _____ memory.

Module 7.3 Measuring Memory
Measuring Memory—The Answer Is on the Tip of My Tongue
Survey Question: How is memory measured?

14. You are listening to the radio when the theme music from a old TV program is played. The song is so familiar, and you know that you know it but you just can't think of the title, so you start going through the alphabet to try to trigger the memory. You are experiencing the _____ state.
15. You are playing a trivia game with friends at a party. As soon as your question is read, your best friend tells every one, "Look at her face, she knows the answer." What your best friend saw on your face is called the _____.
16. The serial position effect occurs when you are asked to memorize a list of items, and you tend to forget the items in the _____ position.

17. You are taking a test that asks you to write an essay comparing the three major schools of thought in psychology. Your memory is being tested by _____.

18. By giving a person the first letters of a word or a partial drawing, you are activating these hidden memories through a process known as _____.

Module 7.4 Forgetting
Forgetting—Why We, Uh, Let's See; Why We, Uh . . . Forget!
Survey Question: Why do we forget?

19. If you do not know what building is pictured on the back of a 20-dollar U.S. bill, it is probably due to the type of forgetting known as _____.

20. When you get angry at your girlfriend, you tend to remember the other arguments you have had over the past year, which illustrates how memories can be formed through _____ learning.

21. Although long-term memories are not loss in this manner, both sensory memory and short-term memory often fade away after a short time due to _____.

22. In a classic experiment in which college students learned lists of nonsense syllables with one group studying then sleeping and the second group studying and staying awake, the group that slept remembered the _____.

23. You have just moved to a new location. For the first month, every time you are asked to write your new address on a form, you inadvertently write the name of your old city. This error occurred due to _____ interference.

24. A skateboarder who takes up snowboarding will probably experience _____ transfer.

25. A friend of yours is seeing a therapist who is planning to use hypnosis and age regression to try to uncover some of your friend's repressed memories. Your friend should be advised that these procedures could result in the _____ syndrome.

Module 7.4 Memory and the Brain—Some "Shocking" Findings
Survey Question: How does the brain form and store memories?

26. You are in a car accident and are hit on the head by an object from your backseat and temporarily knocked unconscious. When you come to, you cannot remember anything about how the accident occurred. You are experiencing _____ amnesia.

27. After your grandmother's stroke, she had trouble storing new memories, although her memories before the stroke have remained intact. Your grandmother is experiencing _____ amnesia.

28. Electroconvulsive therapy tends to interrupt the process that forms memories called _____.

29. Your grandmother tells you about the vivid memories she has of the day that President John F. Kennedy was assassinated in Dallas, Texas. Your grandmother's memory of this event would be considered a(n) _____ memory.

30. According to blood flow patterns, long-term procedural memories appear to be stored in the _____.

Module 7.5 Exceptional Memory and Improving Memory
Exceptional Memory—Wizards of Recall
Survey Question: What are "photographic" memories?

31. You are describing the floor plan of your new house to a friend, so you shut your eyes and begin to walk through the rooms in "your head." You are using _____ images.

32. Your six-year-old nephew is able to look at a picture in his book and then look onto a blank sheet of paper and vividly describe the picture in extreme detail. Your nephew appears to have an ability known as _____ imagery.

33. If you remember everyone listed on the film credits from the main actors to the people who handle the lighting and props and every house and street number you saw on your way to the movie, then, regarding the information you encode, you are lacking a(n) _____ memory.

34. You have been practicing for the state memory championship. Although you are able to recall 40 digits, you are only able to repeat seven separate consonant back. This illustrates that your amazing ability is due to chunking and not due to having a better _____ memory.

Module 7.5 Improving Memory—Keys to the Memory Bank

Survey Question: How can I improve my memory?

35. During a class lecture, Millie tends to underline almost every line in her textbook. Millie should practice more _____ marking.

36. For the piano recital, Justin will be playing a very long, complex musical piece. So, he breaks this piece down into four sections and then learns to play part A; then parts A and B together; and then A, B, and C and so on. Justin is using the _____ method

37. Connie is learning a long list of words and will go over the middle items of the list several more times due to the _____ effect.

38. Mandy has learned that if she wants to do well on her tests she must study for multiple choice tests as if they were essay tests. This studying that continues beyond bare mastery of the facts is known as _____.

39. To keep boredom and fatigue to a minimum, Jay alternates short study sessions with brief rest periods in a pattern known as _____ practice.

40. When you go through the alphabet, trying each letter as the first sound of a name or word you are aiding retrieval by using _____ information.

41. In using a cognitive interview to jog your memory, you would recall events in different orders and from different _____.

Module 7.6 Psychology in Action: Mnemonics—Memory Magic

Survey Question: Are there any tricks to help me with my memory?

42. The keyword method and acrostics would be examples of _____.

43. Although forming images that make sense is better in most situations, stored information will become more distinctive and easier to retrieve if you use _____ images.

44. Joey is using a familiar word to link two other words or items. He is using the _____ method.

45. As Randy memorizes his lines for the play, he imagines himself in the different places he will be standing on stage. In remembering his lines, he is using a technique used by the Greek orators called taking a(n) _____.

Final Survey and Review—Matching

Module 7.1 Memory Systems

1. ___ encoding
2. ___ storage

3. ___ retrieval
4. ___ iconic memory

5. ___ echoic memory

a. recovering information from storage
b. brief continuation of sensory activity in the auditory system after a sound is heard
c. holding information within the system
d. memory system used for relatively permanent storage of meaningful information
e. mental image or visual representation

6. ___ selective attention
7. ___ long-term memory (LTM)
8. ___ working memory

f. when short-term memory is being used for thinking and problem solving
g. converting information into a usable form
h. focusing on a selected portion of sensory input

Module 7.2 STM and LTM

1. ___ constructive processing
2. ___ "memory jamming"

3. ___ pseudomemories

4. ___ cognitive interview

5. ___ elaborative encoding

6. ___ maintenance rehearsal

7. ___ redintegration

8. ___ chunking

9. ___ procedural memory

10. ___ semantic memory

11. ___ episodic memory

a. false memories
b. grouping information into larger units to assist storage in memory
c. process by which memories are expanded or reconstructed by starting with one memory and then following chains of association to other related memories
d. subpart of fact memory that records impersonal knowledge about the world
e. technique used by advertisers that involves adding numerous positive memories of their products in the consumers' memories
f. links new information to memories that are already in LTM
g. subpart of fact memory that records personal experiences that are linked with specific times and places
h. use of various cues and strategies to improve the memory of eyewitnesses
i. silently repeating or mentally reviewing information to hold it in short-term memory
j. reorganizing or updating memories on the basis of logic, reasoning, or the addition of new information
k. long-term memories of conditioned responses and learned skill

Module 7.3 Measuring Memory

1. ___ tip-of-the-tongue (TOT) state

2. ___ déjà vu

3. ___ recall

4. ___ recognition memory

5. ___ relearning

6. ___ serial position effect

7. ___ explicit memory

a. to supply or reproduce memorized information with a minimum of external cues
b. facilitating the activation and retrieval of hidden memories by using cues
c. memory that a person is aware of having and can be consciously retrieved
d. feeling that a memory is available but not quite retrievable
e. ability to correctly identify previously learned information
f. illusion that you have already experienced a new situation that you are actually seeing for the first time
g. memory that a person does not known exists and must be retrieved unconsciously

406

8. ___ implicit memory

    h. learning again something that was previously learned

9. ___ priming

    i. tendency to make the most errors in remembering the middle items of an ordered list

Module 7.4 Forgetting

1. ___ encoding failure

    a. fading or weakening of memories assumed to occur when memory traces become weaker; occurs in sensory memory and STM

2. ___ memory decay

    b. forgetting the events that occurred before an injury or trauma

3. ___ cue-dependent forgetting

    c. failure to store sufficient information to form a useful memory

4. ___ retroactive interference

    d. process by which relatively permanent memories are formed in the brain

5. ___ proactive interference

    e. conscious effort to put something out of mind or to keep it from awareness

6. ___ repression

    f. tendency for old memories to inhibit the retrieval of newer memories

7. ___ suppression

    g. inability to store new memories

8. ___ retrograde amnesia

    h. unconsciously pushing unwanted memories out of awareness

9. ___ anterograde amnesia

    i. tendency for new memories to inhibit the retrieval of old memories

10. ___ consolidation

    j. retrieval fails because the stimuli associated with a memory are missing

Module 7.5 Exceptional Memory and Improving Memory

1. ___ mental images

    a. continuing to study beyond the point of bare mastery of facts

2. ___ eidetic images

    b. internal images or visual depictions used in memory and thinking

3. ___ whole learning

    c. studying continues for long periods without interruption

4. ___ progressive-part method

    d. involves summarizing aloud while learning which forces one to practice retrieving information

5. ___ overlearning

    e. alternating short study sessions with brief rest periods

6. ___ spaced practice

    f. best method to use in memorizing a speech that is fairly short and organized

7. ___ massed practice

    g. breaking a learning task into a series of short sections and then learn part A; then A and B; then A, B, and C; and so forth

8. ___ recitation

    h. "projected" images retained long enough to use as a source of information

Module 7.6 Psychology in Action: Mnemonics—Memory Magic

1. ___ mnemonic
2. ___ acrostics
3. ___ keyword method
4. ___ forming a chain
5. ___ taking a mental walk
6. ___ using a system

a. the first letters of a list of words or ideas are formed into another word or sentence
b. any kind of memory system or aid
c. way ancient Greek orators remembered ideas in order
d. using a familiar word or image to link two items
e. forming bizarre associations to connect the first item on your list with the second item and the second with the third
f. using a standard list of numbered objects to associate each item of your ordered list

Final Survey and Review—True or False

Module 7.1 Memory Systems
Stages of Memory—Do You Have a Mind Like a Steel Trap? Or a Sieve?
Survey Question: How does memory work?

1. TRUE or FALSE   Converting information into a form in which it will be retained in memory is known as encoding.
2. TRUE or FALSE   Selective attention controls what information moves from sensory memory into short-term memory.
3. TRUE or FALSE   Although short-term memories can be stored phonetically, they are most often stored as meaningful visual images.
4. 4. TRUE or FALSE   It is easier to add new information to your memory if you already know a great deal of information.

Module 7.2 STM and LTM
Short-Term Memory—Do You Know the Magic Number?
Survey Question: What are the features of short-term memory?

5. TRUE or FALSE   Psychologist George Miller believed that short-term memory was limited to the "magic number" 4 (plus or minus 2).
6. TRUE or FALSE   A meaningful unit of information, such as a number, a letter, or a word is called an information bit.
7. TRUE or FALSE   Asking yourself "why" questions as you read your psychology book and relating the psychological concepts and theories to real-life examples from your own life are two ways of using maintenance rehearsal.
8. TRUE or FALSE   Learning by simple repetition is known as rote learning.

Long-Term Memory—A Blast from the Past
Survey Questions: What are the features of long-term memory?

9. TRUE or FALSE   Elizabeth Loftus is a neurosurgeon who believes that the brain records the past like a strip of movie film complete with a sound track.
10. TRUE or FALSE   According to Shapiro, the more positive fictional commercials we see, the more likely we are to remember an actual negative experience with a product.

408

11. TRUE or FALSE   Research has shown the hypnosis tends to increase the incidence of false memories..

12. TRUE or FALSE   If people are given the two statements: "A canary is an animal" and "A canary is a bird" to which they must answer yes or no, most people will say yes to the statement "A canary is a bird" faster than to the other statement.

13. TRUE or FALSE   Procedural memory stores specific factual information, such as names, faces, words, dates, and ideas that can be personal or impersonal information.

Module 7.3 Measuring Memory

Measuring Memory—The Answer Is on the Tip of My Tongue

Survey Question: How is memory measured?

14. TRUE or FALSE   Déjà vu is an example of partial retrieval.

15. TRUE or FALSE   When you take a multiple-choice test, your memory is being tested for recall.

16. TRUE or FALSE   If you were asked to identify a person in a police line-up, you would be using recognition memory.

17. TRUE or FALSE   Of the three measures of memory, relearning is the most sensitive measure.

18. TRUE or FALSE   Recall, recognition, and the tests you take in school rely on implicit memories.

Module 7.4 Forgetting

Forgetting—Why We, Uh, Let's See; Why We, Uh . . . Forget!

Survey Question: Why do we forget?

19. TRUE or FALSE   The early memory researcher who used nonsense syllable to test his own memory and constructed the curve of forgetting was Albert Bandura.

20. TRUE or FALSE   In the experiment in which the participant is talking to a young college student when two workers carrying a door pass between them with the college student being switched with another young person, the people who were more likely to notice the switch were older adults.

21. TRUE or FALSE   Disuse doesn't seem to account for our ability to recover seemingly forgotten memories through redintegration, relearning, and priming.

22. TRUE or FALSE   If you are studying two subjects, such as Spanish and French grammar, this greater similarity in the two subjects will create less interference than if the two subjects were extremely different, such as history and math.

23. TRUE or FALSE   Negative transfer of skills is usually brief and occurs less often than positive transfer.

24. TRUE or FALSE   False memories can be deliberately implanted.

25. TRUE or FALSE   Active suppression of a memory has not been shown to lead to the true repression of a memory.

Memory and the Brain—Some "Shocking" Findings

Survey Question: How does the brain form and store memories?

26. TRUE or FALSE   If the hippocampus is damaged, patients usually develop retrograde amnesia.

27. TRUE or FALSE   Electroconvulsive therapy tends to cause severe anterograde amnesia in many patients.

28. TRUE or FALSE   Flashbulb memories have been shown to be extremely accurate regarding the details of the particular historical event.

29. TRUE or FALSE   According to the blood flow patterns, semantic memories appear to be stored in the back of the cerebral cortex.

30. TRUE or FALSE   If two or more interconnected brain cells become more active at the same time, the connections between them grow stronger through a process called long-term redintegration.

Module 7.5 Exceptional Memory and Improving Memory

Exceptional Memory—Wizards of Recall

Survey Question: What are "photographic" memories?

31. TRUE or FALSE   When using mental images, people usually "view" them with their eyes closed.

32. TRUE or FALSE   Eidetic memory is most common during adolescence and young adulthood, and does not disappear until old age.

33. TRUE or FALSE   The mnemonist Mr. S. described in the textbook lacked a selective memory.

34. TRUE or FALSE   Wilding and Valentine's research with exceptional memorizers showed that these people did not have superior intellectual abilities or different types of brains.

Improving Memory—Keys to the Memory Bank

Survey Question: How can I improve my memory?

35. TRUE or FALSE   Scientists have recently discovered that herbs, such as Ginkgo biloba, and vitamins, such as vitamin E, actually can significantly improve human memory.

36. TRUE or FALSE   The use of memory cues, spaced practice, and organization are considered encoding strategies to improve memory.

37. TRUE or FALSE   For extremely long, complicated information, it is better to use part learning or progressive-part learning rather than whole learning.

38. TRUE or FALSE   When you break long lists of information into short sub-lists, it is best to make the middle sublists the shortest of all.

39. TRUE or FALSE   Overlearning is your best insurance against going blank on a test because of being nervous.

40. TRUE or FALSE   In one classic experiment, the best memory score was earned by a group of students who spent 80 percent of their time reciting and only 20 percent reading.

41. TRUE or FALSE   Sleeping after studying increases interference.

Module 7.6 Psychology in Action: Mnemonics—Memory Magic

Survey Question: Are there any tricks to help me with my memory?

42. TRUE or FALSE   Making a word from the first letter of each cranial nerve and stringing them together to make a nonsense sentence is an example of acrostics.

43. TRUE or FALSE   In using mnemonics, visual images are harder to remember than words.

44. TRUE or FALSE   If you have trouble remembering history, you should picture each historical personality as a person you know right now with this person doing whatever the historical figure did.

410

45. TRUE or FALSE   In order to remember the topics of their speech in order, the ancient Greek orators would take a mental walk along a familiar path and associate the topics in their speech with the images of statues found along the walk.

Mastery Test

1. In order for you to remember all the new terms in psychology this semester, three key processes in memory must occur. These processes are
   a. storage, organization, and recovery.
   b. attention, encoding, and decoding.
   c. encoding, storage, and retrieval.
   d. attention, storage, and recovery

2. A three-stage model of memory was proposed by
   a. Atkinson and Schiffrin.
   b. Hobson and McCarley.
   c. Cannon and Bard.
   d. Rosenthal and Jacobson.

3. A fleeting visual image is called an icon, while a brief flurry of activity in your auditory system is called an echo. Both types of brief memories are part of _____ memory.
   a. working
   b. short-term
   c. episodic
   d. sensory

4. As part of an experiment, you are asked to look at pictures flashed for a few seconds onto a computer screen and note the type of animal shown in each picture. In order for you to remember the animal, you will have to move this fleeting image of an animal into your short-term memory by using
   a. constructive processing.
   b. selective attention.
   c. consolidation.
   d. priming.

5. When you are introduced to Sonya, you later call her Tonya, which illustrates the type of mistake that usually occurs because short-term memories are encoded
   a. iconically.
   b. phonetically.
   c. episodically.
   d. semantically.

6. When you are putting together a puzzle, planning your term paper, or doing mental arithmetic, your short-term memory briefly holds the information you need for this problem-solving. In this capacity, short-term memory is called _____ memory.
   a. redintegrative
   b. procedural
   c. working
   d. implicit

7. You are asked to read a short story and then write a brief summary of it without referring back to the book. You may be incorrect on some of the trivial details of the story, but you will probably correctly describe the main character, setting, and plot, which illustrates that long-term memory is usually stored by
   a. sound.
   b. iconic imaging.
   c. implicit priming.
   d. meaning.

8. People from the United States tend to recall memories that focus on what they did in a particular event, while people from China tend to recall memories that focus on their interactions with family members and friends. This difference in the recalling of events is the result of
   a. cultural influence.
   b. mnemonic strategies.
   c. eidetic imagery differences.
   d. pseudo-memories.

9. Which psychologist proposed that short-term memory is limited to the "magic number" 7 (plus or minus two) information bits?
   a. George Miller
   b. Nelson Cowan
   c. Herman Ebbinghaus
   d. Karl Lashley

10. Chunking is especially helpful in extending the space capacity of _____ memory.
    a. sensory
    b. short-term
    c. procedural
    d. episodic

11. If you link the new information you are studying to memories that are already in long-term memory, you are using a process known as
    a. redintegration.
    b. rote learning.
    c. maintenance rehearsal.
    d. elaborative encoding.

12. Sixteen percent of the people shown the ad for the Disney resort featuring Bugs Bunny believed that they had seen this Warner Brothers character when they last visited Disneyland. These pseudo-memories resulted from
    a. redintegration.
    b. constructive processing.
    c. eidetic imagery.
    d. consolidation.

13. The more fictional positive commercials we see, the less likely we are to remember an actual negative experience with a product, which economist Jesse Shapiro called
    a. the "feeling of knowing."
    b. "recovered memory."
    c. "memory jamming."
    d. the "tip-of-tongue" (TOT) state.

14. You witnessed an assault outside the mall. It happened so fast and you were so scared that you are not sure you can remember any details. At the police station, the officer has you close your eyes and imagine that you are back at the mall where the crime took place. The officer encourages you to remember any sounds or smells present and to recall aspects of the event in a different order and from different viewpoints. To help trigger more details about this crime, this officer is using
    a. hypnosis.
    b. mindfulness meditation.
    c. the cognitive interview.
    d. the time regression technique.

15. You are able to agree that "a cat is an animal" faster than "a cat is a vertebrate" because the second phrase requires a longer chain of associations, according to the _____ model of memory.
    a. short-term potentiation
    b. network
    c. consolidation
    d. cue-dependent

16. Leeza is walking in the park when a little girl runs by carrying a blue snow cone. All at once Leeza remembers all the summers as a teenager that she worked at her uncle's snow cone stand in her hometown. This process that expanded Leeza's memory from seeing the blue snow cone is called
    a. redintegration.
    b. eidetic imagery.
    c. semantic processing.
    d. mnemonic encoding.

17. Skills are to procedural memories as facts are to _____ memories.
    a. implicit
    b. iconic
    c. eidetic
    d. declarative

18. Knowing the names of the four seasons would be a(n) _____ memory.
    a. semantic
    b. episodic
    c. implicit
    d. procedural

19. You have gone back to your hometown for a class reunion, when you see a familiar face walking toward you. You know you should know this person's name, and you even think her name begins with a D. You are experiencing what is known as
    a. encoding failure.
    b. the tip-of-the-tongue (TOT) state.
    c. the cocktail party effect.
    d. the serial position effect.

413

20. You are on vacation to a part of the country you have never visited. You are walking along a path in the national park when all at once you get the feeling that you've viewed this exact scene before. This feeling that occurs when a new experience triggers vague memories of past experiences, without yielding any details is known as
    a. a recovered memory.
    b. encoding failure.
    c. a feeling of knowing.
    d. déjà vu.

21. Taking an essay or fill-in-the-blank test requires a person to use
    a. recall.
    b. recognition.
    c. relearning.
    d. priming.

22. Middle items are neither held in short-term memory nor moved to long-term memory. This statement explains the
    a. semantic forgetting curve.
    b. serial position effect.
    c. tip-of-the-tongue (TOT) state.
    d. déjà vu.

23. You are given a box that contains photographs of your former teachers, persons from the community, and strangers. If you are asked to select the pictures of all your former teachers, you would be using
    a. recall.
    b. relearning.
    c. recognition.
    d. eidetic imagery.

24. To reduce false identification by eyewitnesses, the police should
    a. have witnesses view all the pictures of all the suspects at one time.
    b. have witnesses view the pictures of the suspects one at a time.
    c. use hypnosis since it has proven to be a reliable source of data collection.
    d. not use any eyewitness testimonies since they are not reliable.

25. Kirby's memory has been assessed using the most sensitive memory task. This task measures
    a. recall.
    b. recognition.
    c. relearning.
    d. repriming.

26. Past experiences that you can consciously bring to mind are known as _____ memories.
    a. explicit
    b. implicit
    c. echoic
    d. iconic

27. The researcher who is best known for using nonsense syllables to study memory and who constructed the curve of forgetting was
    a. Eric Kandel.
    b. Herman Ebbinghaus.
    c. Aleksandr Luria.
    d. R. Edward Geiselman.

28. Although you have seen hundreds of U.S. twenty dollar bills in your lifetime and even know that Andrew Jackson is the U.S. president on the front side of this bill, you have no idea what building is on the back of a twenty dollar bill. The reason you have forgotten this fact is most likely due to
    a. anterograde amnesia.
    b. proactive interference.
    c. encoding failure.
    d. retroactive interference.

29. The best explanation for the tendency of eyewitnesses to be better at identifying members of their own ethnic group than the members of other groups is
    a. the serial position effect.
    b. that heightened anxiety decreases memory consolidation.
    c. the tendency to categorize strangers in general terms.
    d. the tendency to repress traumatic experiences.

30. Research has shown that people remember better if the same odor, such as lemon or lavender, is present when they study and when they are tested. This finding illustrates that odors can enhance memory because they serve as
    a. mnemonics.
    b. eidetic imagery.
    c. distractors.
    d. memory cues.

31. If you are in a happy mood, you are more likely to remember recent happy events, while if you are in a bad mood, you will tend to have unpleasant memories. This finding is best explained by
    a. repression.
    b. the false memory syndrome.
    c. state-dependent learning.
    d. proactive interference.

32. You came into psychology class believing the word "negative" means "harmful." This past learning hinders your understanding of new terms, such as "negative correlation" and "negative reinforcement," in which "negative" has a different meaning and illustrates the cause of forgetting known as
    a. proactive interference.
    b. retroactive interference.
    c. state-dependent learning.
    d. encoding failure.

415

33. Having played the guitar for several years, Justin easily learned to play the banjo. This illustrates
    a. proactive processing.
    b. retroactive processing.
    c. positive transfer.
    d. negative transfer.

34. When making your first speech during speech class, you get flustered and forget most of your speech. During the next week, you try to put this embarrassing incident out of your mind. This conscious effort not to "think about" this first speech is called
    a. repression.
    b. suppression.
    c. positive transfer.
    d. negative transfer.

35. Lionel forgot the events that occurred before his head injury, which is characteristic of _____ amnesia.
    a. proactive
    b. retroactive
    c. anterograde
    d. retrograde

36. During times of high emotion, heightened activity in the limbic system of the brain intensify memory consolidation and produce vivid images that seem to be frozen in one's memory and are called
    a. flashbulb memories.
    b. eidetic imagery.
    c. implicit memories.
    d. echoic memories.

37. To form lasting memories, the brain appears to use a process in which two or more interconnected brain cells become more active at the same time and cause their connections to grow stronger. This process is called
    a. activation-synthesis consolidation.
    b. long-term potentiation.
    c. proactive transfer.
    d. acrostic processing.

38. After looking at a picture in a book, six-year-old Trina can see a visual image "projected" out in front of her for at least 30 seconds. The image is so clear and lasting that she can answer detailed questions regarding the picture or object. Trina appears to be experiencing
    a. eidetic imagery.
    b. flashbulb memories.
    c. sane hallucinations.
    d. lucid dreaming.

39. Petra wants to improve her study strategies and enhance her memory and performance on tests. Which of the following would be POOR advice for Petra?
    a. Petra should overlearn the class material.
    b. Petra should use massed practice when studying.
    c. Petra should sleep after studying to reduce interference.
    d. Petra should eat a good breakfast or lunch before taking tests at school.

40. The approach used by the ancient Greek orators to remember ideas in order when giving a speech involved
    a. acrostics.
    b. the keyword method.
    c. a mental walk.
    d. eidetic imaging.

Chapter 8: Cognition, Language, Creativity, and Intelligence

Chapter Overview

Thinking is an internal representation of external stimuli or situations. Three basic units of thought are images, concepts, and language (or symbols).

Images may be stored in memory or created to solve problems. Images can be three-dimensional, they can be rotated in space, and their size may change. Kinesthetic images are used to represent movements and actions. Kinesthetic sensations help structure the flow of thoughts for many people.

A concept is a generalized idea of a class of objects or events. Concept formation may be based on positive and negative instances or rule learning. In practice, concept identification frequently makes use of prototypes, or ideal models. Concepts may be conjunctive ("and" concepts), disjunctive ("either/or" concepts), or relational. The denotative meaning of a word or concept is its dictionary definition. Connotative meaning is personal or emotional.

Language encodes events into symbols, for easy mental manipulation. The study of meaning in language is called semantics. Bilingualism is a valuable ability. Two-way bilingual education allows children to develop additive bilingualism while in school. Language carries meaning by combining a set of symbols according to a set of rules (grammar), which includes rules about word order (syntax). True languages are productive and can be used to generate new ideas or possibilities. Complex gestural systems, such as American Sign Language, are true languages. Chimpanzees and other primates have been taught American Sign Language and similar systems. This suggests to some that primates are capable of very basic language use. Others question this conclusion.

The solution to a problem may be arrived at mechanically (by trial and error or by rote application of algorithmic rules), but mechanical solutions are often inefficient. Solutions by understanding usually begin with discovery of the general properties of an answer, followed by a functional solution. Problem solving is aided by heuristics, which narrow the search for solutions. When understanding leads to a rapid solution, insight has occurred. Three elements of insight are selective encoding, selective combination, and selective comparison. Insight can be blocked by fixations. Functional fixedness is a common fixation, but emotional blocks, cultural values, learned conventions, and perceptual habits are also problems.

To be creative, a solution must be practical and sensible as well as original. Creative thinking requires divergent thought, characterized by fluency, flexibility, and originality. Tests of creativity measure these qualities. Five stages often seen in creative problem solving are orientation, preparation, incubation, illumination, and verification. Not all creative thinking fits this pattern. Studies suggest that the creative personality has a number of characteristics, most of which contradict popular stereotypes. There is only a very small correlation between IQ and creativity. Some creative thinking skills can be learned.

Intuitive thinking can be fast and accurate but also often leads to errors. Wrong conclusions may be drawn when an answer seems highly representative of what we already believe is true. Emotions also lead to intuitive thinking and poor choices. A second problem is ignoring the base rate (or underlying probability) of an event. Clear thinking is usually aided by stating or framing a problem in broad terms.

Intelligence refers to the general capacity (or g-factor) to act purposefully, think rationally, and deal effectively with the environment. In practice, intelligence is operationally defined by intelligence tests, which provide a useful but narrow estimate of real-world intelligence. The first intelligence test was developed by Alfred Binet. The modern version of Binet's test is the *Stanford-Binet Intelligence Scale, Fifth edition* (SB5) and measures five cognitive factors: fluid reasoning, knowledge, quantitative reasoning, visual-spatial processing, and working memory. Another major intelligence test is the *Wechsler Adult Intelligence Scale, Fourth edition* (WAIS-IV). The original WAIS was the first adult IQ test. David Wechsler also developed an intelligence test for children with the current version being the *Wechsler Intelligence Scale for Children* (WISC-IV). Like the Stanford-Binet, the Wechsler tests are individual tests that yield a single overall intelligence score as well as measuring aspects of both verbal and performance intelligences. Some of the cognitive factors assessed by the WAIS-IV include verbal comprehension, perceptual reasoning, working memory, and processing speed. Group intelligence tests are also available. The well-known *SAT Reasoning Test* (SAT) is a group test that measures aptitudes for language, math, and reasoning and is used to predict one's chance for success in college. Intelligence was originally expressed as an intelligence quotient (IQ), defined as mental age divided by chronological age and then multiplied by 100. Currently, a deviation IQ is used and is based on the distribution of IQ scores that approximates a normal curve. Artificial intelligence refers to any artificial system that can perform tasks that require intelligence when done by people. Two principal areas of artificial intelligence research on particular human skills are computer simulations and expert systems.

Most people score in the mid-range on intelligence tests. Only a small percentage of people have exceptionally high and low IQ scores. People with IQs in the gifted or "genius" range of above 140 tend to be superior in many respects. However, by criteria other than IQ, many children can be considered gifted or talented in one way or another. The term intellectually disabled is applied to those whose IQ falls below 70 and who lack various adaptive behaviors. About 50 percent of the cases of intellectual disability are organic. Many of the remaining cases are thought to reflect familial intellectual disability.

Traditional IQ tests often suffer from a degree of cultural and racial bias. For this and other reasons, it is wise to remember that IQ is merely an index of intelligence and that intelligence is narrowly defined by most tests. Many psychologists have begun to forge new, broader definitions of intelligence. Howard Gardner's theory of multiple intelligences is a good example. Intelligence is partially determined by heredity. However, environment is also important, as revealed by IQ increases induced by education and stimulating environments.

Various strategies that promote divergent thinking tend to enhance creative problem solving. In group situations, brainstorming may lead to creative solutions. The principles of brainstorming can also be applied to individual problem solving.

Module 8.1 Imagery, Concepts, and Language
Preview: Homo Sapiens

Language Development Guide
adaptable: adjustable; flexible to change
creatures: beings
frenzied: busy; frantic; hyperactive

placid: calm, relaxed; peaceful

retreats: safe hideaways; refuges; removing oneself from the usual environment

Steven Hawking: well-known British theoretical physicist (who has a form of ALS or Lou-Gehrig's disease and is almost completely paralyzed)

Lou Gehrig's disease: is the name given to amyotrophic lateral sclerosis (ALS), which is a disease that damages the nerve cells of the spinal cord that control voluntary muscle movement; named after Lou Gehrig, a New York Yankees baseball player who was diagnosed with it in the late 1930s; the famous physicist Stephen Hawking has ALS.

short-circuiting: electrical malfunction

confined: restricted to; limited to; restrained by

manually: by hand; physically

speech synthesizer: artificial producing human speech using a computer

despite: even with

disabilities: a general term that covers many different impairments of body and mind

unaffected: unchanged

fiercely: intensely

theoretical physicist: explain physical phenomena using mathematical models

determination: willpower; strength of mind

advance: develop; move forward

wisdom: a mixture of intelligence, good judgment, reason, creativity, openness, and tolerance

What Is Thinking?—Brains over Brawn

Survey Question: What is the nature of thought?

Language Development Guide

brawn: strength; muscle

abstract: thinking in terms of concepts and generalizations, not concrete thinking

feats: accomplishments

Shakuntala Devi: female calculating prodigy (unusually gifted young person) from India who first exhibited her calculating gift at age three

"world's record": best performance of a particular skill

Miguel Najdorf: Polish-born chess grand master of Jewish descent who immigrated to Argentina before the World War II; most popular opening in modern chess is named after him (Najdorf Variation)

simultaneously: at the same time

notational: system of figures or symbols to represent numbers, quantities, or values

delve: look into

intuition: quick, impulsive thought

Recite and Review

1. Unlike other species who owe much of their success to strength or speed, humans owe their success more to _____ abilities.
2. Our species is called *Homo sapiens* from the Latin words for *man* and _____.
3. The process of thinking or mentally processing information is called _____.
4. When a person is daydreaming, problem solving or reasoning, he or she is engaged in a form of _____.
5. At its most basic, an internal representation or mental expression of a problem or situation is referred to as _____.
6. A chess player who mentally tries out several moves before actually touching a chess piece is able to avoid mistakes because she is able to _____ her moves.

421

7. Picture-like mental representations are known as _____.
8. Ideas that represent categories of objects or events are called _____.
9. The words or symbols, and rules for combining them make up a(n) _____.

Connections

1. ___ cognition	a. any type of internal representation of a problem or situation
2. ___ image	b. consists of words or symbols, and rules for combining them, that are used for thinking and communication
3. ___ concept	c. generalized idea representing a category of related objects
4. ___ language	d. an icon or any mental representation that has picture-like qualities
5. ___ thoughts	e. the mental processing of information

Check Your Memory

1. TRUE or FALSE   Humans owe most of their success to physical strength and speed than to their thinking abilities.
2. TRUE or FALSE   Our species is called *Homo sapiens* from the Latin words for *upright* and *animal*.
3. TRUE or FALSE   Cognition refers to mentally processing information.
4. TRUE or FALSE   Daydreaming is not considered a form of thinking.
5. TRUE or FALSE   Thoughts are internal representations of a problem or situation.
6. TRUE or FALSE   Thinking is not limited to humans.
7. TRUE or FALSE   The basic units of thought are phonemes, morphemes, and semantics.
8. TRUE or FALSE   Picture-like mental representations are called morphemes.
9. TRUE or FALSE   Concepts are ideas that represent categories of objects or events.
10. TRUE or FALSE   Language consists of words or symbols, and rules for combining them.

Mental Imagery—Does a Frog Have Lips?

Survey Question: In what ways are images related to thinking?

Language Development Guide

imagery: ability to mentally picture objects
bakery: place where baked goods, such as cakes, pies, doughnuts, are produced and sold
delicious: tastes good
cross: pass over
barriers: structures that stop free movement
spiced: use of seasoning that give off a strong smell and taste
"pointy": sharp; having many spikes or points
unleash: set free; allow to run free
variations: differences
tennis stroke: act of hitting a tennis ball
chef: professional cook
stubby: short, rounded, blunted
tackle: begin; attempt; undertake
rotate: turn around
"mind's eye": imagining a remembered or a created scene
specializes: focuses on; dedicated to

egg carton: container for transporting whole raw eggs

assembled: put together; built

proposed: future; planned

Albert Einstein: best known theoretical physicist of 20th century; known for his theories of relativity; Nobel Prize winner

Thomas Edison: American inventor; whose inventions include the light bulb, phonograph, and motion picture camera

Lewis Carroll: pen name of Charles Dodgson, English author of *Alice's Adventures in Wonderland* and *Through the Looking-Glass*

original: creative; imaginative; unique

intellects: minds; brain power

heavily: a great deal

"zoom in": examine closely

oversize: large, expand

electrons: subatomic particles of matter that has a negative charge

in a sense: a clear explanation

combination: code; number sequence that opens a lock or safe

twirling: spinning around quickly

clockwise: motion that proceeds in the same direction as the hands of a clock

counterclockwise: motion that proceeds in the opposite direction to the hands of a clock

faucet: water valve

martial arts: self-defense or fighting arts, now a sport; developed in Japan and Korea; such as judo and karate

movement-oriented: learning that involves motion

flawlessly: perfectly

Recite and Review

1. Almost every person has visual and _____ images.
2. More than half of individuals have imagery for touch, taste, smell, pain, and _____.
3. Some people have a rare form of imagery in which images cross normal sensory barriers, such as a person seeing pain as the color orange. This type of imagery is called _____.
4. When we make a decision, change our feelings, improve a skill, or need to aid our memory, we use mental _____.
5. Unlike photographs, mental images are not _____.
6. If you were asked "Do frogs have lips and a stubby tail?" you would first form a mental image and then mentally "_____" it.
7. Mentally "picking up" an object and turning it around is partly based on imagined movement and is referred to as mental _____.
8. When you see something, your eyes activate the brain's primary visual area. Then, when you form a mental image, the brain areas where memories are stored send signals back to the visual cortex, where once again, an image is produced through a process referred to as "_____."
9. Cara is applying past experiences to problem solving. Cara is using _____ images.
10. If you constructed an original piece of pottery for the art exhibit, you are using images that are different from anything in your memory. These are called _____ images.
11. People with good imaging abilities tend to score higher on tests of _____.
12. The number of people out of 100 who find it impossible to produce mental images is _____.
13. The number of people out of 100 who have very strong imagery is _____.

423

14. Stephen Kosslyn found that it is harder to "see" the details in our mental images when these mental images are _____.

15. Using Kosslyn's finding, the best way to understand the parts of the human ear would be to "see" the ear as a cave and explore its parts. Thus, you should form _____ images of the ear.

16. The type of images that are created from muscular sensations and are especially important when you play music, dance, or participate in sports are _____ images.

17. If you were asked "which direction do you turn the hot-water handle in your kitchen to shut off the water?" you would probably "turn" the faucet in your imagination before answering, which illustrates the use of _____ images.

18. The people who learn movement-oriented skills the fastest are those individuals who are high in _____ imagery.

Connections

1. ____ synaesthesia		a. information from memory
2. ____ mental rotation		b. image created from muscular sensations
3. ____ "reverse vision"		c. imagery that crosses normal sensory barriers
4. ____ stored image		d. formation of a mental image through the activation of brain areas
5. ____ created image		e. partly based on imaged movements and involves mentally "picking up" an object and turning it around
6. ____ kinesthetic image		f. image that is assembled or invented

Check Your Memory

1. TRUE or FALSE   Less than half of all humans have visual and auditory images.
2. TRUE or FALSE   About 95 percent of humans have imagery for movement, taste, smell, and pain.
3. TRUE or FALSE   If a person says that chicken tastes "pointy" or that pain is the color orange, this person is experiencing a rare form of imagery called sane hallucinations.
4. TRUE or FALSE   We can use mental images to change our feelings and to improve a skill.
5. TRUE or FALSE   Mental images appear flat, like photographs.
6. TRUE or FALSE   When asked, "Does a cat have eyelashes and does its tail curl at the tip end? a person will picture in their "mind's eye" a cat's eyes and then mentally "rotate" the cat in mental space to check its tail.
7. TRUE or FALSE   "Reverse vision" refers to the process that occurs in the brain to form a mental image.
8. TRUE or FALSE   If you are thinking about the first car you drove, you would using created images.
9. TRUE or FALSE   When you form the mental image of an original story you will be writing in English class, you are using a stored image.
10. TRUE or FALSE   People with good imaging abilities tend to score higher on tests of creativity.
11. TRUE or FALSE   Twenty-five out of 100 people find it impossible to produce mental images, while 25 out of 100 have very strong imagery.
12. TRUE or FALSE   Most artists, architects, designers, sculptors and filmmakers have excellent visual imagery.
13. TRUE or FALSE   Stephen Kosslyn found that the larger an image is, the harder it is to see its details.

424

14. TRUE or FALSE   Kinesthetic images are created from muscular sensations.
15. TRUE or FALSE   People with good kinesthetic imagery learn motor skills faster than those with poor kinesthetic imagery.

Concepts—I'm Positive, It's a Whatchamacallit

Survey Question: What are concepts?

Language Development Guide

whatchamacallit: what you may call it; used when the exact name for something cannot be remembered
experts: person who is skilled or knowledgeable regarding a particular subject; an authority
fanciers: person having a strong interest or liking for something
enthusiasts: person absorbed by a particular subject
literally: factually
Pekingese: breed of dog from China that is small, long-haired, and short-legged with a wide, flat nose
dust mop: a cleaning tool with a long handle and an end made of long stripes of absorbent material
Great Danes: large, muscular dog breed from Germany that has a short, smooth coat and a narrow head
Chihuahuas: very small breed of dog from Mexico that has pointed ears; a round head; a short, smooth coat; and large eyes
efficient: useful
rhythm and blues: music that blends blues (origin in southern African American music) and jazz; was the forerunner of rock 'n' roll
hip-hop: popular urban youth culture, closely associated with rap music and with the style and fashions of African-American inner-city residents
fusion: music that blends jazz music and rock rhythms
salsa: Latin-American music
metal: energetic rock music with loud electric guitars and drums
country: music usually involving a guitar that expresses personal emotions and is based on the music of the rural South and the cowboy music of the West
rap: characterized by lyrics that are spoken rather than sung
conjunctive: tending to connect
relation: significant association
disjunctive: presenting two or more alternatives; disjointed
pitch: throw or toss
foul ball: hitting a ball with a bat outside the lines that define the width of the playing field
prototypical: the standard or original form
vase: container for flowers
relevant: applicable; important to
inaccurate: wrong; incorrect
oversimplified: making something so simple that it becomes distorted or false due to ignoring important details
social stereotypes: oversimplified images of the traits of individuals who belong to a particular social group
conservatives: against abrupt change; in favor of preserving traditional values and customs and keeping the way things are now
liberals: broad-minded regarding different ideas and behavior in others; favor gradual reform; freely giving of one's money
muddle: confuse
prejudice: negative emotional attitude held against members of a particular group of people

discrimination: treating members of various social groups differently in circumstances where their rights or treatment should be identical

subtleties: finer points

generally speaking: mostly; in general

nudist: person who prefers to live life without wearing clothes

censor: job to find and remove objectionable or bad or damaging content

enhanced radiation device: small thermonuclear device that produces a smaller blast but releases large amounts of lethal energy waves

neutron bomb: nuclear device that kills all life through radioactive neutron energy but with very little blast damage

conscientious: thorough; careful; hard-working

nitpicky: too detail-focused; from finding and removing baby lice from hair

Recite and Review

1. As you see an apple, you categorize it as a type of fruit. In doing so, you are illustrating the use of _____ formation.
2. Bird watchers, tropical fish fanciers, and other experts all learn to look for identifying _____ that beginners tend to miss.
3. The process of classifying information into meaningful categories is referred to as _____.
4. At its most basic, this process of classifying information is based on experiences with positive and _____ instances.
5. As adults, we often acquire concepts by learning or forming conceptual _____.
6. A guideline for deciding whether objects or events belong to a concept class is called a(n) _____.
7. To be a psychometrist in most U.S. states, you must have masters' degree in psychology and specialized training in the administration and interpretation of psychological tests. According to this description, a psychometrist would be a(n) _____ concept.
8. A job announcement states that a person applying for the job must have a Masters' degree in Business Administration or a B.S. degree in business with five years work experience. This job announcement illustrates a(n) _____ concept.
9. For you to be a grandparent, one of your children must have a child. Being a grandparent would be a(n) _____ concept.
10. For a child to be able to ride the roller coaster, he or she must be taller than the horizontal line drawn on the board near the entrance to the ride. Thus, to be a passenger on this roller coaster is based on how one's height compares to the height of the horizontal line and makes this a(n) _____ concept.
11. If a majority of people would agree that a cow is a good example of a farm animal, then a cow would be considered an ideal model of a farm animal and is referred to as a(n) _____.
12. Categorizing people into oversimplified concepts would be an example of a thinking error caused by using a(n) _____ concept.
13. These oversimplified concepts of groups of people are called social _____.
14. When we classify people, objects or events as absolutely right or wrong, good or bad, or fair or unfair, we are exhibiting a one-dimensional thought process called _____ thinking.
15. The exact definition of a word or concept, such as found in a dictionary, is known as its _____ meaning.
16. If you are using the subjective, personal, or emotional meaning of a word or concept, then you are utilizing its _____ meaning.

426

17. A technique that could be used to rate words or concepts on dimensions, such as good/bad, strong/weak, and active/passive would be assessing the _____ meaning of the word or concept.

18. Kip is rating different musical types, according to active/passive, smooth/rough, good/bad, etc. Kip is most likely rating these types of music using a technique known as the _____.

Connections

1. ___ concept formation	a.	"and" concept in which the class of objects has two or more features in common
2. ___ conceptual rule	b.	oversimplified concepts of groups of people
3. ___ conjunctive concept	c.	process of classifying information into meaningful categories
4. ___ relational concept	d.	subjective, personal, or emotional meaning of a word or concept
5. ___ disjunctive concept	e.	one-dimensional thought
6. ___ prototype	f.	ideal model used as a prime example of a particular concept
7. ___ social stereotypes	g.	"either/or" concept in which the concept is defined by the presence of at least one of several possible features
8. ___ all-or-nothing thinking	h.	technique used for measuring subjective meanings by rating concepts good/bad, active/passive, etc.
9. ___ denotative meaning	i.	guideline for deciding whether objects or events belong to a concept class
10. ___ connotative meaning	j.	concept defined by the association between features of an object or between an object and its surroundings
11. ___ semantic differential	k.	exact dictionary definition of a word or concept or its objective meaning

Check Your Memory

1. TRUE or FALSE   A transformation is an idea that represents a category of objects or events.

2. TRUE or FALSE   If you are an expert on a topic, such as horses, flowers, or football, you literally see things differently than less well-informed people do.

3. TRUE or FALSE   Young children usually use conceptual rules in concept formation, while adults usually use positive and negative instances.

4. TRUE or FALSE   A conceptual rule is a guideline for deciding whether objects or events belong to a concept class.

5. TRUE or FALSE   If a motorcycle must have two wheels and an engine and handlebars, then it would be considered a disjunctive concept.

6. TRUE or FALSE   To be diagnosed with a psychotic disorder, a person must either show delusions or hallucinations or both, making a psychotic disorder a conjunctive concept.

7. TRUE or FALSE   In giving directions to the ball field, you say that it is two blocks north of city hall, making the ball field in your description a relational concept.

8. TRUE or FALSE   Defining "siblings" as individuals with the same parents makes "siblings" a relational concept.

9. TRUE or FALSE   If a rose is an ideal model of a flower, then a rose would be called a stereotype.
10. TRUE or FALSE   Using oversimplified concepts often leads to thinking errors.
11. TRUE or FALSE   Oversimplified concepts of groups of people are called social stereotypes.
12. TRUE or FALSE   Classifying things as absolutely right or wrong, good or bad, or fair or unfair is referred to as prototypical thinking.
13. TRUE or FALSE   The connotative meaning of a word or concept is its exact definition, while the denotative meaning is the emotional or personal meaning of the word or concept.
14. TRUE or FALSE   Connotative meaning can be measured with a technique called the semantic differential.
15. TRUE or FALSE   When we rate words or concepts, most of their subjective meaning boils down to the dimensions of good/bad, strong/weak, and active/passive.

Critical Thinking Question

A Democrat and a Republican are asked to rate the word *democratic* on the semantic differential. Under what conditions would their ratings be most alike?

Language—Don't Leave Home Without It

Survey Question: What is the role of language in thinking?

Language Development Guide

don't leave home without it: refers to the slogan spoken in the American Express credit card commercial
vague: unclear, fuzzy
nevertheless: yet; on the other hand
manipulate: use
skyscraper: very tall building
cathedral: large religious building of the Christian faith
temple: religious building for various faiths, including Jewish, Hindu, Buddhist, etc.
subtly: delicately; cleverly
alters: changes
context: surroundings; situation; framework
marksmanship: skill at shooting at a target
bartending: mixing and serving alcoholic drinks
likewise: in a similar way
invaded: marches into; occupies; overruns
liberated: set free
martini: alcoholic drink made of gin (or vodka) and vermouth
prime beef: first-class quality meat from cattle
slab: large flat, thick piece
bridge: link; connection
barrier: obstacle
cause a rash: result in many
banner: sign
circumcised: removal of foreskin from the penis
international: worldwide
diplomacy: negotiation; mediation; international relations
semantic: meaning

vital: very important; critical

Si o No, Oui ou Non: Yes or No (Spanish); Yes or No (French)

definitely: certainly; without a doubt

flexibility: able to adapt

immersed: completely covered; (only this language used in class)

sink or swim: try and either succeed or fail

competent: capable

grasp: understanding

in short: to summarize

poses no threat: does not damage

variety: assortment

drawbacks: disadvantages

fluent: express oneself easily

politically: dealing with the structures within government

dominant: forceful; influential

immigrants: people who leave one country (usually of their birth) and go to another country to live permanently

foreign languages: languages not spoken by the majority of the people in a certain area

eroding: damaging

regardless: in spite of

fostering: promoting; nurturing

competitiveness: engaging in a contest with another in order to measure one's abilities against others

globalizing: the connection and interdependence of the countries around the world regarding business and social issues

information economy: importance of the Internet and online services in today's business throughout the world

mbwa: dog in Swahili

Swahili: official language of Kenya and Tanzania and widely used in east and central Africa

linguist: specialist in the study of language

core: central; main

transformation: change; conversion

universal: worldwide; found in all languages

declarative: sentence that makes a statement

voices: forms of verbs

past tense: verbs that express an action or state occurring in the past (at an earlier time)

passive voice: form of verb used to indicate that the subject of the verb is receiving the action

irregular verb: verbs that do not follow the standard rules when changing tenses; ex. run becomes ran, not runned

true: real; actual; valid

infinite: endless; countless; unlimited

profound: deep; philosophical; great

"We hold these truths, that all men are created equal": quote from the U.S. Declaration of Independence, 1776

gestural: moving the hand, arm, or other part of the body to communicate or express a thought

mime: acting without words

breakthrough: productive discovery; overcoming an obstacle

magic moment: unmistakable, special point in one's life

pantomime: to act out using gestures and without words

code: systematic set of rules

Old Kentish: Old English language spoken before 1100 A.D.

spatial: relating to space or location

evolved: developed by gradual changes

string: extend together in a line

remnant: small part that remains

origins: source from which something arises

embody: represent; express

rich: full; of great value

flee: run away; escape

distress: danger; trouble

sucker: a general term referring to someone or something

primitive: simple; crude

gimme: slang for give me

peak: maximum degree

chips: small round disks; tokens

magnetized: will attract and hold objects made of iron or steel

compound sentences: has two or more independent clauses (have a subject and predicate)

qualification: a standard must be met before the act can occur; ex. if this is met; then that will happen.

certainty: firmness; confidence

interchanges: give-and-take communications

spontaneous: original, by oneself without instruction

wet: urinated

annoyance: irritation; frustration

glancing: quickly looking

exasperated: frustrated; annoyed

idiot: being uneducated; stupid

plagued: afflicted; troubled by

grammarless: without proper word order

pygmy: very small

geometric: shapes, such as used in math; examples include circles, squares, triangles

prompt: cue, signal

consistently: reliably; every time

on a par: equal

roots: origins; beginnings

on the other hand: instead

insists: is firm in the claim; maintains

issue: subject; question

resolved: settled; determined

unravel the mysteries: help understanding

Recite and Review

1. Most thinking relies heavily on language, because words allow the world to be translated or _____ into mental symbols that are easy to manipulate.

2. If Jabar studies the meaning in words and language, his field of study is referred to as _____.

3. The word "shot" means different things when we are thinking of marksmanship, bartending, medicine, photography, or golf, which illustrates that words get much of their meaning from _____.

4. Most people have difficulty ignoring the color word and focusing on the color of the ink in which the word is printed on the illustration known as the _____ task.

5. Numerous semantic problems between cultures can occur due to the inaccurate translation of _____.

6. The ability to speak two languages is known as _____.

7. Immersed in English-only classrooms, where they are expected to "sink or swim," millions of minority American children who do not speak English at home experience _____ bilingualism.

8. For the majority of children who speak English at home, learning a second language usually results in _____ bilingualism.

9. Juanita is attending a program in which English-speaking children and children with limited English proficiency are taught half the day in English and half in a second language. Juanita is in a program known as _____ bilingual education.

10. One property of language is it must provide _____ that stand for objects and ideas.

11. The basic speech sounds of a language are called _____.

12. A word or a syllable constitutes the smallest meaningful unit in a language and is known as a(n) _____.

13. A language must have a set of rules for making sounds into words and words into sentences, which is called _____.

14. If a child has trouble with the order of words within a sentence, then the child has problems, specifically, with the rules of word order, which are called _____.

15. "Dog bites man" is different from "Man bites dog," which illustrates that the meaning of a sentence is changed by its word order, or _____.

16. The linguist who stated that we do not learn all the sentences we might ever say but rather actively create them by applying unspoken rules to change core ideas into various sentences was _____.

17. Rules by which a simple declarative sentence may be changed to other voices or forms, such as past tense or passive voice are called _____ rules.

18. When a child applies the normal past tense to the verb "to run" and says "runned," this child is using _____ rules.

19. A true language is able to generate new thoughts or ideas, which means that a true language must be _____.

20. American Sign Language (ASL) is considered a true language and is classified as a(n) _____ language.

21. The grammar, syntax, and semantics of American Sign Language (ASL) is considered a(n) _____ type of grammar, etc.

22. Sign languages define a distinct community and embody a personal _____.

23. Animal communication lacks the ability to generate new thoughts and ideas; therefore, we say that animal communication lacks the _____ quality of human language.

24. Beatrix and Allen Gardner taught a female chimp named Washoe to use American Sign Language through imitation and _____ conditioning.

25. A chimp named Sarah was taught to utilize 130 "words" by using plastic chips arranged on a magnetized board by researcher _____.

26. One of the chimp Sarah's top achievements was her use of statements, which contain a qualification, often in the if/then form called _____ statements.

27. Untrained chimps have communicated with humans using simple _____.

28. Almost all animal language studies have been plagued by problems with word order, or _____.

29. Kanzi, a pygmy chimpanzee studied by Duane Rumbaugh and Sue Savage-Rumbaugh, learned to communicate by pushing buttons on a computer keyboard with each of the 250 buttons marked with geometric word-symbol called a(n) _____.

30. Researchers stated that Kanzi's grammar was equal to that of a(n) _____-year-old child.

Connections

1. ___ semantics	a.	language that has a spatial grammar, syntax, and semantics
2. ___ Stroop interference task	b.	learning a second language results in reduced competency in both first and second language
3. ___ bilingualism	c.	basic speech sounds of a language
4. ___ subtractive bilingualism	d.	study of meanings in words and language
5. ___ additive bilingualism	e.	learning a second language increases competence in both languages and in cognitive skills
6. ___ two-way bilingual education	f.	set of rules for combining language units into meaningful speech or writing, such as sounds into words and words into sentences
7. ___ phonemes	g.	rules by which a simple declarative sentence may be changed to other voices or forms, such as past tense or passive voice
8. ___ morphemes	h.	rules for ordering words when forming sentences and is one part of grammar
9. ___ grammar	i.	contains a qualification, often in the if/then form
10. ___ syntax	j.	ability to speak two languages
11. ___ transformation rules	k.	geometric word-symbol that was used in animal communication studies
12. ___ gestural language	l.	involves naming the color of the ink in which the word is printed
13. ___ conditional statement	m.	smallest meaningful units in a language, such as syllables or words
14. ___ lexigram	n.	program in which English-speaking children and children with limited English proficiency are taught half the day in English and half in a second language

Check Your Memory

1. TRUE or FALSE   Thinking may occur without language.
2. TRUE or FALSE   Words encode or translate the world into mental symbols that are easier to manipulate.
3. TRUE or FALSE   The study of meaning in words and language is known as phonetics.
4. TRUE or FALSE   Words get much of their meaning from context.
5. TRUE or FALSE   The words we use can greatly affect our thinking.
6. TRUE or FALSE   The serial position task involves a person naming the color ink in which a color word is printed.
7. TRUE or FALSE   Language plays a major role in defining ethnic communities and other social groups and can be either a bridge or a barrier between cultures.
8. TRUE or FALSE   The ability to speak two languages is known as multiculturalism.
9. TRUE or FALSE   Studies have found that students who learn to speak two languages well have better mental flexibility, general language skills, control of attention, and problem-solving abilities.
10. TRUE or FALSE   Minority American children who do not speak English at home and are immersed in English-only classrooms usually experience additive bilingualism.

11. TRUE or FALSE   The majority of children who speak English at home and learn a second language almost always experience subtractive bilingualism.

12. TRUE or FALSE   A program in which English-speaking children and children with limited English proficiency are taught half the day in English and half in a second language is known as bidirectional language immersion education.

13. TRUE or FALSE   Bilingual education tends to be politically unpopular among majority language speakers with some individuals feeling that recent immigrants and "foreign languages" are eroding their culture.

14. TRUE or FALSE   A property of a true language is that it must provide symbols that stand for objects and ideas.

15. TRUE or FALSE   The smallest meaningful units in a language, such as syllables or words are known as phonemes.

16. TRUE or FALSE   A set of rules for combining language units into meaningful speech or writing is called grammar.

17. TRUE or FALSE   If a child says, "to town went you," he or she is exhibiting a problem with syntax.

18. TRUE or FALSE   The linguist who believed that we do not learn all the sentences we might ever say but actively create them was Hans Selye.

19. TRUE or FALSE   Rules by which we change a simple declarative sentence to other tenses or voices are called pragmatic rules.

20. TRUE or FALSE   When a child applies the normal past tense rule to "eat" and says "I eated the cookie," this child is using transformation rules.

21. TRUE or FALSE   A property of a true language is that it must be productive, which means it can generate new thoughts or ideas.

22. TRUE or FALSE   A true language must be verbally spoken.

23. TRUE or FALSE   American Sign Language (ASL) is classified as a pantomimed code and not a true language.

24. TRUE or FALSE   If a person understands American Sign Language (ASL), he or she can understand French Sign, Chinese Sign, or any other sign language.

25. TRUE or FALSE   Signing children pass through the stages of language development at about the same age as speaking children do.

26. TRUE or FALSE   Some psychologists now believe that speech evolved from gestures, far back in human history.

27. TRUE or FALSE   Completely different brain areas become active when a person speaks than when they use sign language.

28. TRUE or FALSE   Sign languages not only are a means of communication but also embody a personal identity and define a distinct community.

29. TRUE or FALSE   Animal communication lacks the productive quality of human language.

30. TRUE or FALSE   Beatrix and Allen Gardner used classical conditioning to teach a female chimp to communicate using lexigrams.

31. TRUE or FALSE   David Premack taught a chimp named Sarah to use plastic chips arranged on a magnetized board to answer questions; label things as "same" or "different;" classify objects by color, shape, and size; form compound sentences; and use conditional statements.

32. TRUE or FALSE   Even untrained chimps use simple gestures to communicate with humans.

33. TRUE or FALSE   Duane Rumbaugh and Sue Savage-Rumbaugh taught Kanzi, a pygmy chimpanzee, to use a computer keyboard with geometric word-symbols and to follow correct word order in her sentences.

34. TRUE or FALSE   Researchers estimated that Kanzi's grammar was equal to that of a two-year-old child.

Critical Thinking Question

Chimpanzees and other apes are intelligent and entertaining animals. If you were doing language research with a chimp, what major problem would you have to guard against?

Module 8.2 Problem Solving
Problem Solving—Getting an Answer in Sight
Survey Question: What do we know about problem solving?

Language Development Guide

commonplace: usual; routine, everyday; simple

nonpoisonous: safe

leftovers: uneaten meal portions

significant: important

ocean liner: large commercial ship that carries many passengers and cargo

deck: level area aboard a ship

port: harbor; area where a ship can land

speedboat: small, fast motorized boat that carries only a very few passengers

rote: memorization through repetition, without thought

era: period of time

generate: produce; create

split second: an instant; in a flash

background: training; education; experience

comprehension: understanding

inoperable: cannot be surgically removed

tumor: growth; lump; swelling

diseased: unhealthy

classic: memorable; timeless

properties: qualities; features

requirements: conditions

intensity: strength; power

phase: stage; period

proposed: suggested; put forward

exposure: contact

Texas Hold'em: poker game in which players each receive two cards and share five other cards

odds tables: list of the probabilities for each event occurring, such as each poker hand

persist: continue; keep on

You can't get there from here: no way to solve it; phrase originated in the U.S. state of Maine in trying to explain directions to a far off spot and giving up trying to describe how to get there

strategy: plan; approach

alternatives: options

"rule of thumb": easily learned and easily applied shortcuts to the solution of new problems by using experience with similar problems in the past and understanding that this shortcut might not work in all situations

odds: chances; probability

guarantee: promise; assure

state of affairs: general set of conditions that exist at any point in time

intermediate: in-between; transitional

analogies: comparisons, similarities

eliminate: get rid of

434

clarify: make clear; simplify

novices: beginner

acquired: obtained; learned

fluid: smooth; graceful; flowing

tactic: method; approach

mind you: you should notice this

"Genius is one percent inspiration and ninety-nine percent perspiration": what appears to be all intelligence is usually the result of a lot of hard work or effort

distractions: something that diverts or interrupts one's attention

ensure: make certain

irrelevant: not important; not applicable

hourglass: a time instrument where sand falls from one glass ball to another

hat rack: an upright stand that holds hats or hats and coats

overcoat: a long coat for the rain, generally would go over a suit jacket

C-clamp: a tool for holding pieces of wood together while glue sets

clamp: hold tightly together; fasten

wedged: squeezed, fit

pole lamp: a rod with lights on each side that is wedged between the ceiling and floor to provide light

Hansel and Gretel: German folk tale written by the Grimms Brothers about children who are abandoned in the forest and find their way home by leaving bread crumbs, but later outsmart a witch

sacred: holy; blessed

hanging balance: an instrument used for weighing that has a container hanging from either end of a horizontal bar, so that equal weight in each container occurs when the two containers are level with each other

resourceful: inventive; imaginative; creative

that's no fairy tale: meaning it is not false or a lie; a fairy tale is a fictional, highly fanciful story intended for children

tendency: predisposed to; inclined to

hung up: delayed, slowed; stuck

unnecessary: needless; pointless

restrictions: limits; constraints

prime: main; key

dime: 10 cent coin

screwdriver: tool for tightening or loosening screws

overcome: defeated; beat; rose above

mount: hang

thumbtacks: short pins with flat heads used for attaching papers to a corkboard by pressing the flat head with one's thumb or fingers

facilitated: made possible; assist; helped

apparently: it seems that; obviously

preconceptions: biases, previous knowledge or beliefs

mental blocks: something that prevents one from carrying out a mental task

precariously: unstable, likely to fall

toppling: bringing down

hinder: delay; hold back; get in the way

inhibition: prevented from acting due to feeling self-conscious

making a fool of oneself: behaving in such a way that people think you are stupid

tolerate: permit; accept

ambiguity: vagueness; uncertainty

excessive: too much
self-criticism: focusing on one's own faults
architect: person who designs building and other living spaces
unconventional: different from the usual or normal way of doing things
frivolous: silly; something not to be taken seriously
stern: strict; harsh; demanding
marketing: area of business involved in the advertising and selling of products
conventions: customs, standards, rules
taboos: restrictions imposed by social custom
habits: long-standing, learned patterns of behavior
elements: parts; aspects; factors
composition: work of art

Recite and Review

1. Solutions that are achieved by trial and error or by rote are called _____ solutions.
2. Tony is solving a problem by rote. Thus, his thinking will be guided by a learned set of rules called a(n) _____.
3. If you were asked to divide a two-digit number into a five-digit number without a calculator, you would using a(n) _____.
4. In problem solving, a deeper comprehension of the nature of the problem is referred to as _____.
5. In the first phase of problem solving, the type of solution the defines the requirements for success but not in enough detail to guide further action is called a(n) _____ solution.
6. In the second phase of problem solving, a person often proposes a number of workable, or _____ solutions.
7. Almost everyone who tries to play a poker game like Texas Hold 'Em begins at the mechanical, _____ level.
8. If you used instructions and the printed odds tables available for every stage of playing Texas Hold 'Em, you would be learning by _____.
9. In time, those who practice playing Texas Hold 'Em will begin to understand the _____ of the game.
10. In finding the right key among ten keys, you randomly try one key and then another. To find the correct key, you are using a(n) _____ strategy.
11. A "rule of thumb" approach that reduces the number of alternatives that thinkers must consider in solving a problem is called a(n) _____.
12. Working backward from the desired goal to the starting point is one example of the use of a(n) _____.
13. Research has shown that expert skills are based on specialized organized knowledge, or systematic information and acquired strategies, or learned _____.
14. Compared to novice chess players, master players quickly see what lines of play should be explored next because they have the ability to intuitively recognize _____.
15. The fast, fairly effortless thinking based on experience with similar problems that experts often show is referred to as _____.
16. Many areas of expertise, including chess, take about _____ years to develop.
17. If a person experiences a sudden mental reorganization of a problem that makes the solution obvious, this person has experienced _____.
18. Psychologist Janet Davidson believes that this sudden mental reorganization involves three selective combination, selective comparison, and selective _____.
19. The ability to relate new problems with old information or with problems already solved is known as selective _____.

20. Being able to select information that is relevant to a problem, while ignoring distractions is called selective _____.

21. When you bring together seemingly unrelated bits of useful information, you are using selective _____.

22. You are asked the question: "If you have nine red socks and six blue socks in your drawer, how many socks will you have to take out to ensure you have a pair of the same color?" You will be able to give the correct answer of "three," if you ignore the irrelevant information of the number of socks in the drawer, which is an ability known as selective _____.

23. You were able to solve the murder mystery at the dinner theatre because you related this story to similar ones you had read in mystery novels. You solved this mystery due to selective _____.

24. On a TV show, a man was able to utilize his belt, his shoelaces, dental floss, and his shirt tied in knots to escape from the roof of a building. To make his escape, this character used selective _____.

25. American college students were able to solve the cave problem because they related this story to the story of Hansel and Gretel that they heard when they were children. They used selective _____.

26. The reason that more Chinese students were able to solve the problem of how to weigh the gold coins and more American students were able to solve the cave problem was due to their remembering a story from their childhood. This illustrates that people are prepared to solve some types of problems more easily than others because of the experiences provided by their particular _____.

27. The tendency to get "hung up" on wrong solutions or to become blind to alternatives is called _____.

28. Rigidity in problem solving caused by an inability to see new uses for familiar objects is known as _____.

29. We can avoid many fixations by categorizing the world in a more _____ way.

30. To be more creative, one should try to see the world as if through the eyes of a child, without any _____.

31. You come up with a unique idea to introduce your topic in your next speech, but you are afraid that everyone will laugh at you and think you are a silly fool, so you start your speech out in a more conventional manner. This barrier to your creative problem solving would be classified as a(n) _____ barrier.

32. In the company meeting, your boss gets angry every time anyone uses humor in discussing an idea. Your boss thinks that only reason and logic are "good" and humor and playfulness are "bad." Your boss is exhibiting a(n) _____ barrier to problem solving.

33. If you cannot see that your coffee mug could be used as a cereal bowl when all the bowls are dirty, then you are exhibiting a(n) _____ barrier to problem solving

34. Habits that lead to a failure to identify important elements of a problem are called _____ barriers to problem solving.

35. Your friend places a stack of objects on top of a $20 bill and tells you that you can have the money if you can get the bill out without touching or moving the objects. Your failure to see the solution of splitting the bill and pulling it out from each side was due to the taboo of not destroying money, which would be classified as a(n) _____ barrier to problem solving.

Part 1: Connections

1. ___ mechanical solution	a. sudden mental reorganization of a problem that makes the solution obvious
2. ___ algorithm	b. rigidity in problem solving caused by an

437

			inability to see new uses for familiar objects
3. ___ understanding (of a problem)		c.	fast, fairly effortless thinking based on experience with similar problems
4. ___ general solution		d.	tendency to repeat wrong solutions or faulty responses, especially as a result of becoming blind to alternatives
5. ___ functional solution		e.	detailed, practical, and workable solution
6. ___ random search strategy		f.	one who intuitively recognizes patterns
7. ___ heuristic		g.	learned set of rules that always leads to the correct solution of a problem
8. ___ expert		h.	having a deeper comprehension of the nature of the problem
9. ___ automatic processing		i.	"rule of thumb" strategy that reduces the number of alternatives thinkers must consider
10. ___ insight		j.	trying possible solutions to a problem in a more or less haphazard manner
11. ___ fixation		k.	problem solution achieved by trial and error or by a fixed procedure based on learned rules
12. ___ functional fixedness		l.	solution that correctly states the requirements for success but not in enough detail for further action

Part 2: Connections

1. ___ selective encoding	a.	conventions about uses (functional fixedness), meanings, possibilities, taboos
2. ___ selective combination	b.	inability to tolerate ambiguity and fears of making a mistake or of being embarrassed
3. ___ selective comparison	c.	habits leading to a failure to identify important elements of a problem
4. ___ emotional barrier to problem solving	d.	ability to bring together seemingly unrelated bits of useful information
5. ___ cultural barrier to problem solving	e.	values that hold that feelings, intuitions, pleasure and humor are bad and should not be a part of problem solving
6. ___ learned barrier to problem solving	f.	ability to select information that is relevant to a problem, while ignoring distractions
7. ___ perceptual barrier to problem solving	g.	ability to relate new problems to old information or to problems already solved

Check Your Memory

1. TRUE or FALSE   Mechanical solutions are achieved by trial and error or by rote.
2. TRUE or FALSE   When a problem is solved by rote, thinking is guided by a heuristic.
3. TRUE or FALSE   Many problems cannot be solved mechanically.
4. TRUE or FALSE   Understanding in problem solving refers to having a deeper comprehension of the nature or general properties of the problem.
5. TRUE or FALSE   A functional solution defines the requirements for success but not in enough detail to guide further action.

438

6. TRUE or FALSE   If you used the written instructions for the card game of Texas Hold 'Em and the printed odds tables available for every stage of play, you would be learning this card game by rote learning.

7. TRUE or FALSE   If the number of alternatives is small, a random search strategy may work in solving a problem.

8. TRUE or FALSE   An algorithm is a "rule of thumb" that reduces the number of alternatives thinkers must consider.

9. TRUE or FALSE   If you represent the problem in other ways, such as graphs or analogies, you are using a heuristic strategy to solve the problem.

10. TRUE or FALSE   Research has shown that expert skills are based on acquired strategies and specific organized knowledge.

11. TRUE or FALSE   Chess experts are better than novice chess players in their ability to intuitively recognize patterns that suggest what lines of play should be explored next.

12. TRUE or FALSE   Becoming a star performer in chess comes from having an inborn superior memory and from a general strengthening of the mind.

13. TRUE or FALSE   Experts show more sequential processing, which is a slow, methodical effortful thinking based on intense focus and concentration.

14. TRUE or FALSE   Expertise, such as that of expert chess players, takes about 10 years to build up.

15. TRUE or FALSE   A thinker who suddenly solves a problem has experienced insight.

16. TRUE or FALSE   Psychologist Janet Davidson believes that insight involves random search strategies, rote learning, and functional fixedness.

17. TRUE or FALSE   The ability to select information that is relevant to a problem and ignore distractions is known as selective encoding.

18. TRUE or FALSE   Bringing together seemingly unrelated bits of useful information is known as selective comparison.

19. TRUE or FALSE   The ability to relate new problems to old information and problems already   solved is known as selective combination.

20. TRUE or FALSE   A tendency to get "hung up" on wrong solutions or to become blind to possible alternatives is known as fixation.

21. TRUE or FALSE   If you have ever used a plastic garbage bag as a make-shift rain coat, you have overcome functional fixedness.

22. TRUE or FALSE   Since every culture prepares it members to solve some types of problems more easily than others, learning about other cultures could make us more resourceful thinkers.

23. TRUE or FALSE   If you are flexible in categorizing the world, you will have a tendency to exhibit more fixations.

24. TRUE or FALSE   Because young children have less experience with the use of various objects, they are less likely than adults to show functional fixedness.

25. TRUE or FALSE   Excessive self-criticism and an inability to tolerate ambiguity are classified as perceptual barriers to problem solving.

26. TRUE or FALSE   Values that hold that fantasy is a waste of time and playfulness is just for children would be cultural barriers to problem solving.

27. TRUE or FALSE   Functional fixedness is classified as an emotional barrier to problem solving.

28. TRUE or FALSE   A person putting together a poster who focuses so much on the content boxes that he or she forgets that the "empty spaces" surrounding the boxes are also important parts of the poster is illustrating a learned barrier to creative problem solving.

439

Critical Thinking Questions

1. Do you think that it is true that "a problem clearly defined is a problem half solved"?

2. Sea otters select suitably sized rocks and use them to hammer shellfish loose for eating. They then use the rock to open the shell. Does this qualify as thinking?

Module 8.3 Creative Thinking and Intuition

Creative Thinking—Down Roads Less Traveled

Survey Question: What is creative thinking?

Language Development Guide

the course of human history: over time

take for granted: expect something to always be available; valuing someone or something too lightly

technology: application of science to achieve productivity

regarded: looked upon

radical: revolutionary; major

realms: areas; fields

promote: encourage; support

roads less traveled: areas less used; also a reference to the line about the road less traveled in Robert Frost's poem "The Road Not Taken" as well as a reference to psychiatrist M. Scott Peck's book
The Road Less Traveled about the attributes that lead to human fulfillment

proceeding: going on

explicit: exact; precise; specific

discarded: thrown away

shift: change; swing

novel: fresh; different; innovative; unusual

tap: utilize; bring forth

practical: useful; functional

sensible: reasonable; sane

"harebrained scheme": foolish plan; originally meant having no more sense than a hare (rabbit)

"stroke of genius": a very clever and innovative idea

brings...to bear: uses those aspects mentioned to influence and change his or her ideas

orientation: defining the direction

dimensions: aspects; features

preparation: getting ready; putting things in order

saturate: flood; oversupply

incubation: growth under conditions that encourage development

attempted: to try to perform

futile: useless; unsuccessful

at this point: at this time

subconscious: operating beyond consciousness

set aside: not focused on; temporarily forgotten

"cooking": developing

illumination: enlightened; gaining knowledge

"Aha!" experience: moment of creative insight

depicted: shown, drawn

verification: gaining additional proof

critically: careful and exact

evaluate: assess
faulty: incorrect
reverts: goes back
neat: tidy; orderly
sequence: order
legend has it: there was a story
suspected: believed likely
goldsmith: a person who makes and sells jewelry and other articles made from gold
substituted: replacing one thing with another
Archimedes: Greek scientist, mathematician, and inventor who lived between around 287 BC to
         212 BC
cheated: something of value taken through deception, fraud, lying
"Eureka, eureka!": used to express success upon discovering or finding something; comes from
         Greek word "heureka," which mean "I have found it"
displace: cause to move from its original position
brass: yellow metal alloy (mixture) of zinc and copper
denser: thicker
unfortunately: sadly
purity: free from any different substances; made only of this one material
fate: future; outcome for
springing: moving forward quickly
incremental: increasing gradually by degrees
giants: persons of great importance in their field; major figure in their field
Mozart: eighteenth-century Austrian composer of classical music; was a child prodigy
Picasso: famous twentieth century Spanish painter and sculptor
eccentric: strangely playful
introverted: shy, unsocial, interested in one's own mental life
neurotic: emotionally unstable or anxious
inept: failure, awkward, unskilled
unbalanced in their interests: one-sided; narrow interests
edge of madness: close to being insane
cultivate: nurture, use, encourage
public image: side of one's personality that is shown to others
paint: depict; portray
metaphors: figures of speech in which a word or phrase is used to represent another, such as
         "rolling in dough"; metaphors can be extended into parables
irrational: illogical; unreasonable
uninhibited: outgoing; unrestrained
assumptions: guesses; hypotheses
mental sets: readiness to perceive and act in a particular manner
chaos: complete disorder
mystical: supernatural; spiritual
symbolic thought: representing reality in abstract concepts
form: shape and structure of things; all the visible elements
fame: being very well known
an end in itself: existing for its own sake
nonconforming: not going along with established group expectations
primarily: mainly
otherwise: if not; or else
outlandish: different, strange, weird
in particular: especially

441

taking risks: taking chances; ventures

Recite and Review

1. The laws of gravity were developed through observations of specific examples. Thus, the thinking that led to these laws would be considered _____ thought.
2. Using the laws of gravity to predict the behavior of a single falling object requires _____ thought.
3. If one proceeds from given information to new conclusions on the basis of explicit rules, one is using _____ thought.
4. Thought that is intuitive, haphazard, or irrational is called _____ thought.
5. Fluency, flexibility, and originality are used to rate one's _____.
6. If you were asked to come up with new ways to use billions of discarded plastic containers, the total number of solutions you produced would indicate your _____.
7. In coming up with new ideas for using discarded plastic containers, the number of times you shift from one class of possible uses to another would indicate your _____.
8. How novel or unusual your ideas are for using the billions of plastic containers indicates your _____.
9. Creativity is often defined by your capacity for _____ thinking.
10. Thinking directed toward the discovery of a single established correct answer is called _____ thinking.
11. Thinking that produces many ideas or alternatives is called _____ thinking.
12. A creativity test that asks you to come up with as many uses as possible for various common objects is called the _____ Test.
13. If you are given a word, such as "creativity," and are asked to make as many new words as possible by rearranging the letters, you are taking the creativity test known as the _____ Test.
14. "If all the cars stopped running on earth, what changes would occur?" might be a question on the creativity test known as the _____ Test.
15. To be creative, a solution to a problem must be more than novel, unusual, or original. If the solution is an idea, it must be sensible; and if it is an invention, it must be _____.
16. The first stage of creative thought in which a person defines the problem and identifies its most important dimensions is referred to as the _____ stage.
17. Creative thinkers saturate themselves with as much information about the problem as possible during the _____ stage.
18. Most major problems produce a period during which all attempted solutions will be futile and problem solving must proceed on a subconscious level. This third stage of creative thought is called _____.
19. The "Aha!" experience that is often depicted in cartoons as a light bulb appearing over the thinker's head illustrates the fourth stage of creative thought known as _____.
20. The final step in creative thought in which the thinker tests and critically evaluates the solution is called the _____ stage.
21. If a solution proves faulty, the thinker reverts back to the stage of creative thought called _____.
22. In the legend about Archimedes determining if a goldsmith had substituted cheaper metals for the gold in the crown, the stage of creative thought in which Archimedes asked himself the question "How can I tell what metals have been used in the crown without damaging it?" would be the stage called _____.
23. When Archimedes stepped into his bath and suddenly knew the solution to the problem of the gold crown, he ran naked through the streets shouting, "Eureka, eureka!" which illustrates the stage of creative thought known as _____.

24. Rather than springing from sudden insights, much creative problem solving is the end result of many small steps, which means creative problem solving is _____.
25. Some authors believe that truly exceptional creativity requires a rare combination of thinking skills, a supportive social environment, and _____.
26. The correlation between creativity and IQ would be described as a small _____ correlation.
27. Creative people's range of knowledge and interest would be described as _____ than average.
28. Creative people question assumptions and break mental _____.
29. Creative people are more likely to have vivid dreams, mystical experiences, and other unusual states of _____.
30. You can become more creative by taking risks, analyzing ideas, seeking unusual connections between ideas, and practicing _____ thinking.

Part 1: Connections

1. ___ inductive thought	a. thought that is intuitive, haphazard, or irrational
2. ___ deductive thought	b. drawing conclusions on the basis of formal principles of reasoning
3. ___ logical thought	c. refers to how novel or unusual one's ideas are
4. ___ illogical thought	d. thought that goes from specific facts or observations to general principles
5. ___ fluency	e. conventional thinking directed toward the discovery of a single established correct answer
6. ___ flexibility	f. refers to the number of times a person shifts from one class of possible ideas to another
7. ___ originality	g. thought that applies a general set of rules to specific situations
8. ___ convergent thinking	h. thinking in which many possibilities are developed from one starting point
9. ___ divergent thinking	i. refers to the total number of suggestions one is able to make in solving a problem

Part 2: Connections

1. ___ Unusual Uses Test	a. test of creativity that asks you to rearrange the letters of a word to make as many new words as possible
2. ___ Consequences Test	b. stage of creative thought in which problem solving proceeds on a subconscious level
3. ___ Anagrams Test	c. test of creativity that asks you to list the results following a basic change in the world
4. ___ orientation (in creative thought)	d. stage of creative thought in which rapid insight into the solution occurs
5. ___ preparation (in creative thought)	e. stage in creative thought in which the person tests and critically evaluates the solution

6. ___ incubation (in creative thought)	f. test of creativity that involves finding original ways to utilize common objects
7. ___ illumination (in creative thought)	g. stage in creative thought when the person defines the problem and identifies its most important dimensions
8. ___ verification (in creative thought)	h. stage in creative thought in which the person saturates themselves with as much information about the problem as possible

Check Your Memory

1. TRUE or FALSE   If you infer the laws of gravity from observing many falling objects, then you are using deductive thought.
2. TRUE or FALSE   Using the laws of gravity to predict the behavior of a single falling object requires inductive thought.
3. TRUE or FALSE   Logical thought involves drawing conclusions on the basis of formal principles of reasoning.
4. TRUE or FALSE   Thought that is intuitive, personal, and haphazard is called creative thinking.
5. TRUE or FALSE   On tests of creativity, the number of times you shift from one class of possible uses to another is called fluency.
6. TRUE or FALSE   Your total number of suggestions on a creativity test indicates your flexibility.
7. TRUE or FALSE   Originality refers to how novel or unusual your ideas are on the creativity test.
8. TRUE or FALSE   Thinking directed toward the discovery of a single established correct answer is called divergent thinking.
9. TRUE or FALSE   Your creativity is indicated mainly by your capacity for convergent thinking.
10. TRUE or FALSE   Rather than repeating learned solutions, divergent thinking produces new answers, ideas, or patterns.
11. TRUE or FALSE   The items on a creativity test called the *Anagrams Test* asks the test taker to use the letters in a word like "imaginative" and make as many words as possible from it.
12. TRUE or FALSE   The *Unusual Uses Test* and the *Consequences Test* are two tests of creativity.
13. TRUE or FALSE   To be creative, the solution to a problem must be practical if it is an invention or sensible if it is an idea.
14. TRUE or FALSE   The first step in the creative process involves the creative thinker saturating themselves with as much information about the problem as possible.
15. TRUE or FALSE   The point at which problem solving must proceed on a subconscious level is called the illumination stage.
16. TRUE or FALSE   The final step in which a solution is critically evaluated is called the orientation stage of creative thought.
17. TRUE or FALSE   If a solution proves faulty, the thinker reverts to the stage of incubation.
18. TRUE or FALSE   When Archimedes was asked to find a way to tell if cheaper metals had been used in the king's crown, the stage of creative thought in which he checked all known methods of analyzing metals would be the preparation stage.

444

19. TRUE or FALSE The stage of creative thought in which Archimedes placed a pound of gold in a tub of water and marked the level of the water and then took the gold out and put the crown in the tub of water would be the incubation stage.

20. TRUE or FALSE Much of creative thought is incremental, or the end result of many small steps.

21. TRUE or FALSE Some authors believe that truly exceptional creativity requires a rare combination of thinking skills, personality, and a supportive social environment.

22. TRUE or FALSE Research has shown that highly creative people are eccentric, introverted, neurotic, socially inept, unbalanced in their interests, and on the edge of madness.

23. TRUE or FALSE There is a small positive correlation between creativity and IQ.

24. TRUE or FALSE Creative people are good at using mental images and metaphors in thinking.

25. TRUE or FALSE Creative people tend to use broad categories, question assumptions, break mental sets, and find order in chaos.

26. TRUE or FALSE Creative people tend to very interested in fame and being known for their successes.

27. TRUE or FALSE Creative people experience more unusual states of consciousness, such as vivid dreams and mystical experiences.

28. TRUE or FALSE Research has shown that creative thinking cannot be learned.

Intuitive Thought—Mental Shortcut? Or Dangerous Detour?

Survey Question: How accurate is intuition?

Language Development Guide

detour: alternative route; indirect route
identical: the same
contradictory: conflicting
disastrous: seriously damaging results
star teachers: teachers who are effective in helping students to learn
intriguing: fascinating; interesting
amazingly: remarkably
course evaluations: paper or electronic questionnaires used to assess instruction factors in each course at the end of each semester
mere: simple; sheer
hurried: quick; rushed
slivers: thin slice; splinter
testament: proof
trick: special skill
noted: famous
face of uncertainty: when we are in doubt
seriously: badly
flawed: containing errors or mistakes
pitfall: hidden danger or difficulty
probable: likely
Shaun White: American snowboarder; two-timed gold medalist
halfpipe: U-shaped, high-walled ramp used in snowboarding and skateboarding
likelihood: chance; possibility

profile: summary of a person's personality
commit: carried out
theft: stealing
affluent: rich
suburb: residential area bordering a city
hot cognition: refers to how emotions affect thinking
cloud: confuse
underlying: present but not obvious
motivation: internal processes that initiate, sustain, and direct activities
perhaps: maybe; possibly
fortunate: lucky
skip: omit; leave out
exception: not included
framing: way something is stated
custody: legal home and care, right to primary parenting
granted: given to; approved
award: give
rapport: friendly relationship
drawbacks: disadvantages; problems
denied: refused
disqualify: throw out, eliminate from consideration
channel us down a narrow path: restrict our list of choices
weighing: considering; pondering
pros and cons: advantages and disadvantages
broadest: very wide
outlook: likely future
journalist: writer or editor for a newspaper, magazine, television, or radio regarding current events
short-circuit: disrupt, break

Recite and Review

1. Although it can lead to thinking errors, irrational, intuitive thought may actually contribute to _____ problem solving.
2. Dinah is introduced to her new boss. In the first few seconds of this meeting, Dinah thinks, "I'm not going to like this person very much." This quick, impulsive thought regarding her boss that is not based on any formal logic is called _____.
3. Nalini Ambady asked people to watch three 10-second video clips of teachers they did not know and to rate the teachers. The correlation between these participants' ratings and the year-end course evaluations made by actual students would be described as a(n) _____ positive correlation.
4. Malcolm Gladwell in his book *Blink* called these immediate, intuitive reactions to small bits of experience, "_____."
5. The part of the brain that does automatic, unconscious processing is referred to as the _____.
6. The two noted psychologists who studied how people make decisions in the face of uncertainty and found that human judgment is often seriously flawed were Amos Tversky and _____. .
7. If you often select wrong answers because these answers seem to match preexisting mental categories, you are utilizing a(n) _____.

446

8. In courtrooms, jurors are more likely to think a defendant is guilty if the person appears to fit the profile of a person likely to commit a crime, which illustrates the faulty thinking caused by the _____ heuristic.

9. Rather than comparing candidates' records and policies, Jake tends to vote for the person he likes rather than the person who is most qualified for the job, which illustrates that one's good judgment can be affected by _____.

10. People would probably not get married in the face of a 50 percent divorce rate, if they did not ignore the _____.

11. Even though he has heard the warnings many times, Guy continues to smoke two packs of cigarettes a day. Regarding his likelihood of having lung cancer or heart disease, Guy is ignoring the _____.

12. One's decisions can be affected by the way a problem is stated or structured, which is referred to as _____.

13. Usually, the best decisions are produced when a problem is stated in the _____ way.

14. If you ask the question "Should Parent A be awarded custody?" you will most likely get a different answer than if you asked "Should Parent A be denied custody?" This illustrates how decisions are affected by _____.

Connections

1. ____ intuition	a. underlying probability of an event
2. ____ "thin-slicing"	b. quick, impulsive thought that does not make use of formal logic or clear reasoning
3. ____ cognitive unconscious	c. terms in which a problem is stated or the way that it is structured
4. ____ representativeness heuristic	d. tendency to select wrong answers because they seem to match preexisting mental categories
5. ____ base rate	e. part of the brain that does automatic processing without our being aware of it
6. ____ framing	f. quickly making sense of thin slivers of experience

Check Your Memory

1. TRUE or FALSE   Irrational, intuitive thought may contribute to creative problem solving, but it can also lead to thinking errors.

2. TRUE or FALSE   A quick, impulsive thought that does not make use of formal logic or clear reasoning is called originality.

3. TRUE or FALSE   When Nalini Ambady asked people to watch three 10-second video clips of teachers they did not know and to rate the teachers, their ratings correlated highly with year-end course evaluations made by actual students.

4. TRUE or FALSE   According to Malcolm Gladwell, "thin-slicing" is a case of hurried irrationality that can almost always lead to errors in judgment.

5. TRUE or FALSE   The part of the brain that does the automatic, unconscious processing involved in "thin-slicing" is called the cognitive unconscious.

6. TRUE or FALSE   Quick impressions are most valuable when you take the time to verify them through further observation.

7. TRUE or FALSE   A tendency to select wrong answers because they seem to match preexisting mental categories is known as the representative algorithm.

447

8. TRUE or FALSE   In courtrooms, jurors are more likely to think a defendant is guilty if the person appears to fit the profile of a person likely to commit a crime.

9. TRUE or FALSE   For many people, choosing which political candidate to vote for is a good example of how emotions can cloud clear thinking.

10. TRUE or FALSE   In decision-making, emotions such as fear, hope, anxiety, liking, or disgust can eliminate possibilities from consideration or promote them to the top of the list

11. TRUE or FALSE   People who smoke, drink and then drive, or skip wearing auto seat belts are ignoring the base rate for injury or illness for these situations.

12. TRUE or FALSE   If you ask the question "Should Parent A be awarded custody?" most people would look for the negative qualities of the parent, while if the question were stated "Should Parent A be denied custody?" a person is most likely to look for positive qualities in the parent.

13. TRUE or FALSE   The narrowest way of framing, or stating a problem usually produces the best decisions.

14. TRUE or FALSE   The way a question is framed can channel one down a narrow path so he or she attends to only part of the information provided, rather than weighing all the pros and cons.

Critical Thinking Question

A coin is flipped four times with one of the following results: (a) H T T H, (b) T T T T, (c) H H H H, (d) H H T H. Which sequence would most likely precede getting a head on the fifth coin flip?

Module 8.4 Intelligence
Human Intelligence—The IQ and You
Survey Question: How is human intelligence defined and measured?

Language Development Guide

"smart": clever; intelligent; bright

debated: argued; discussed; questioned

astounded: surprised

encyclopedia: reference book with comprehensive information on many topics

breezed: to move quickly through

genius: someone who has an extremely high IQ or is highly creative and who gains worldwide recognition for their achievements

flash of brilliance: a highly creative idea

potential: capacity for development; possible ability

launched: introduced; unleashed

ongoing: continuing

accepted: established; standard

broadly speaking: generally; loosely

global: universal

core: central part; foundation

adaptation: successful adjustment to environmental conditions; effective functioning

beyond this: except for this

operational: able to be used

verbal fluency: ability to use words quickly and accurately

grip: ability to grasp or hold with hand

Guitar Hero: musical video game

revised: modified

age-ranked: categorized according to the age of the person who should be able to answer them

naturally: of course

fluid reasoning: ability to think logically and to problem solve

quantitative reasoning: application of mathematical concepts and skills to real-life problems

visual-spatial processing: ability to perceive the location of objects in relation to others

reproduce: duplicate; make a copy

estimate: calculate approximately

brighter: smarter; has higher IQ

exceeds: surpasses; goes above

supplied: made available for use

convert: translate; change

relative standing: numbers which indicate where a score is in comparison to the rest of the scores in a set of data

percentile: percentage of a distribution having a lower score than the person's percentile in question, such that a person that scored at the 70th percentile has a score at or higher than 70% of those taking that test

boast: brag

losers: one who fails consistently or one who is disliked and unpopular

minimal: the least amount

supervision: management; direction; guidance

aptitudes: ability, likely future success

don't work by magic: there are mental processes that occur that can be understood and duplicated

robot: mechanical device capable of performing a variety of complex human tasks; often made to look like a human figure

spiffy: smart; unique; amusing

Rubik's Cube: three-dimensional mechanical puzzle with six sides and nine different colored stickers on each side

exchanging: sending back and forth

qualify: meets the requirements

face: confront

"shift gears": to suddenly change what you are doing

incredible: hard to believe

"blind": unable to see or recognize

literal: adhering to the actual meaning or spelling of a word

stymied: thrown off, distracted, prevented from a solution

harmonizing: to bring into agreement so they go together

diagnosing: identifying the cause

vast: large

persistence: continuing and refusing to give up

"laboratory": workplace in which to conduct scientific research

demystified: understood, explained

geological formations: physical features of the earth

Recite and Review

1. The modern testing movement was born when the minister of education in Paris asked a psychologist in 1904 to find a way to distinguish slower students from the more capable ones. This psychologist was _____.

2. The accepted definition of intelligence is the global capacity to act purposefully, to deal effectively with the environment, and to think _____.

3. The core of intelligences consists of general mental abilities called the _____.

4. Many psychologists simply spell out the procedures they use to measure intelligence, which is referred to as a(n) _____ definition of intelligence.

5. In 1916, the first French intelligence test was revised for use in North America and was called the Stanford-Binet Intelligence Scale. This revision was conducted at Stanford University by psychologist _____.

6. Today's Stanford-Binet (SB-5) is still primarily made up of _____ questions that get harder at each level.

7. The Stanford-Binet (SB-5) is appropriate for people from age _____ to 85+ years.

8. The Stanford-Binet (SB-5) measures five cognitive factors with each factor being measured with questions that involve words and numbers called _____ questions.

9. Each cognitive factor of the Stanford-Binet (SB-5) is also measured with questions that use pictures and objects called _____ questions.

10. Jane is being administered the Stanford-Binet (SB-5) and is presented with analogy questions and with items that ask her to fill in the missing shape in a group of objects. These types of items are measuring the cognitive factor called _____.

11. While taking the Stanford-Binet (SB-5), Ana is asked a variety of questions on a wide range of topics, such as "Why is yeast added to bread dough?" and "What does "cryptic" mean?" Ana is taking items on the SB-5 that assess the cognitive factor called _____.

12. Fanta is taking the Stanford-Binet (SB-5) and is presented with word problems that require her to do mathematical computations in her head. Fanta is completing items on the SB-5 that assess the cognitive factor called _____.

13. Tim is reproducing patterns of blocks and choosing the picture that shows how a piece of paper would look if it were folded. Tim is completing the Stanford-Binet (SB-5) items that assess _____.

14. Sara is asked to correctly remember the order of colored beads on a stick and to repeat a series of digits forward and backward. Sara is completing the items on the Stanford-Binet (SB-5) that assess the cognitive factor called _____.

15. If you were to take the SB5, it would yield a score for general intelligence, for each of the five cognitive factors, for verbal intelligence, and for _____ intelligence.

16. The first IQ test to assess adult intelligence was developed by psychologist _____.

17. The factors of verbal comprehension, perceptual reasoning, working memory, and processing speed are measured by the adult intelligence test known as the _____-IV.

18. On this adult intelligence test, questions on subtests, such as Block Design, Matrix Reasoning, and Visual Puzzles measure the factor known as _____.

19. On a widely used adult intelligence test, Marta is completing the tasks on subtests called Digit Span and Arithmetic, which will measure the cognitive factor known as _____.

20. Keith is completing the tasks on the subtests of Symbol Search and Coding on a widely used adult intelligence test. These two subtests are measuring the factor known as _____.

21. The average mental ability that a person displays at a given age on the IQ test is referred to as the person's _____.

22. If you subtract a person's birth date from the current calendar date, you are calculating the person's _____.

23. The level of age-ranked questions a person can answer on an IQ test would be used to determine the person's _____ age.

24. When a person's mental age is divided by his or her chronological age and multiplied by 100, it yields a(n) _____.

25. If ten-year-old Paula has a mental age of nine, her IQ score will be _____.

26. If ten-year-old Miguel completes all the 13-year-old items on the IQ test, his IQ score will be _____.

27. If seven-year-old Banta's IQ is 100, then her mental age would be _____ years.

28. Average intelligence is usually defined as any IQ score from 90 to _____.

29. When a person's mental age is higher than their chronological age, the IQ score will be _____ 100.
30. When a person's chronological age is higher than their mental age, the IQ score will be _____ 100.
31. Barry's chronological age and his mental age are the same; therefore his IQ score will be _____.
32. Modern tests have tables supplied with the test that are used to convert a person's relative standing in the group to an IQ score and tell how far above or below average the person's score falls. This type of IQ based on a person's relative standing in his or her age group is called a(n) _____ IQ.
33. If half the people your age who take a test score higher than you and half the people score lower than you, then you scored on this test at the _____ percentile.
34. If your IQ score was 100 on an intelligence test, then your score would be at the _____ percentile.
35. Since the SB5 and the Wechsler scales must be administered by a trained specialist to only a single person at a time, they are classified as _____ intelligence tests.
36. When tests are administered to large numbers of people at the same time with little supervision, the tests are classified as _____ tests.
37. Armando is taking a test in a room with his classmates. On this test, Armando will be required to read, to follow instructions, and to solve problems of logic, reasoning, mathematics, or spatial skills. Based on the way it is being administered, Armando's test would be classified as a(n) _____ intelligence test.
38. Administered to large numbers of people at the same time, the well-known test that measures aptitudes for language, math, and reasoning and was designed to predict one's chances for success in college is the _____.
39. Unlike computers, humans can "shift gears" from one topic to another, which is referred to as being mental _____.
40. Any computer program that is capable of human-like problem solving or intelligent responding is referred to as _____ intelligence.
41. Computers have been able to harmonize music and diagnose diseases because these tasks can be reduced to a set of _____ the computer can apply.
42. In situations where speed, vast memory, and persistence are required, the best option is to use _____ intelligence.
43. Computer programs that attempt to duplicate specific human behaviors, especially thinking, decision making, or problem solving are known as computer _____.
44. Computer programs that have been used to predict the weather, analyze geological formations, diagnose disease, play chess, read, and tell when to buy or sell stocks are known as _____ systems.

451

Part 1: Connections

1. ____ intelligence	a. index of intelligence defined by MA / CA x 100
2. ____ Stanford-Binet (original and SB-5)	b. type of artificial intelligence that attempts to duplicate specific human behavior, such as thinking, decision making, or problem solving
3. ____ mental age	c. first developed by Lewis Terman with newest edition being appropriate for people age two to 85+
4. ____ chronological age	d. group test that was designed to predict one's chances for success in college
5. ____ intelligence quotient (IQ)	e. person's age in years
6. ____ deviation IQs	f. first "adult" IQ test and first test to yield separate scores for verbal and performance intelligences
7. ____ WAIS	g. overall capacity to think rationally, act purposely, and deal effectively with the environment
8. ____ SAT Reasoning Test (SAT)	h. type of artificial intelligence that responds as a (human) specialist in that field would
9. ____ computer simulations	i. average mental ability people display at a given age
10. ____ expert systems	j. IQ obtained statistically from a person's relative standing in his or her age group

Part 2: Connections

1. ____ g-factor	a. test items assess the extent to which a person is acquainted with facts and information over a wide range of topics
2. ____ operational definition of intelligence	b. items ask test takers to reproduce patterns of blocks or to show how a piece of paper would look if it were folded or cut
3. ____ fluid reasoning (on SB-5)	c. test that must be given to a single person by a trained specialist
4. ____ knowledge factor (on SB-5)	d. uses analogy items and items that ask people to fill in the missing shape or tell a story that explains what is going on in a series of pictures
5. ____ quantitative reasoning (on SB-5)	e. measures ability to use short-term memory
6. ____ visual-spatial processing (on SB-5)	f. consists of general mental abilities that make up the core of intelligence
7. ____ working memory (on SB-5)	g. test given to large groups of people with minimal supervision
8. ____ individual intelligence tests	h. defined by procedures used to measure it
9. ____ group intelligence tests	i. measures a person's ability to solve problems involving numbers

452

Check Your Memory

1. TRUE or FALSE   Intelligence cannot be observed directly.
2. TRUE or FALSE   In 1904, the minister of education in Paris asked Alfred Binet to find a way to distinguish slower students from the more capable.
3. TRUE or FALSE   The accepted definition of intelligence is the global capacity to think both convergently and divergently.
4. TRUE or FALSE   The core of intelligence consists of general mental abilities called the g-factor.
5. TRUE or FALSE   Many psychologists simply accept an operational definition of intelligence by spelling out the procedures they use to measure it.
6. TRUE or FALSE   The French IQ test was revised for use in North America by Louis Stanford in 1910.
7. TRUE or FALSE   The Stanford-Binet (SB5) is still primarily made up of age-ranked questions and is appropriate for people from ages two to 85+.
8. TRUE or FALSE   On the SB5, if a person is asked to tell a story that explains what is going on in a series of pictures, the cognitive factor being assessed is called working memory.
9. TRUE or FALSE   SB5 items that assess the cognitive factor of fluid reasoning require the test taker to reproduce block patterns and to answer questions regarding directions.
10. TRUE or FALSE   Items on the SB5 that require the test taker to repeat a series of digits forward or backward after hearing them once are assessing quantitative reasoning.
11. TRUE or FALSE   The Stanford-Binet (SB-5) yields a score for general intelligence, verbal intelligence, nonverbal intelligence, and each of the five cognitive factors.
12. TRUE or FALSE   Unlike today's SB-5, the original Stanford-Binet was better suited for use with children and adolescents, not adults.
13. TRUE or FALSE   The WAIS was the first adult IQ test.
14. TRUE or FALSE   On the WAIS-IV, the subtests of Similarities, Vocabulary, and Information measure the factor known as Perceptual Reasoning.
15. TRUE or FALSE   On the WAIS-IV, the subtests of Digit Span and Arithmetic are used to measure the factor known as Processing Speed.
16. TRUE or FALSE   Mental age is based on the level of age-ranked questions a person can answer correctly.
17. TRUE or FALSE   One's chronological age is one's birth age in years.
18. TRUE or FALSE   A mental age by itself cannot indicate whether a person's overall intelligence is high or low.
19. TRUE or FALSE   The formula for IQ is chronological age divided by mental age and multiplied by 100.
20. TRUE or FALSE   If an adolescent is 15 years old and has a mental age of 12, his IQ would be 120.
21. TRUE or FALSE   If a six-year-old child has a mental age of eight, then her IQ is 80.
22. TRUE or FALSE   If a 12-year-old child has a mental age of 12, then his IQ is 100.
23. TRUE or FALSE   Average intelligence is usually defined as any IQ score from 90 to 109.
24. TRUE or FALSE   IQ scores below 100 occur when mental age is higher than one's age in years.
25. TRUE or FALSE   IQ scores will be over 100 when one's chronological age is greater than one's mental age.

26. TRUE or FALSE   An IQ obtained statistically from a person's relative standing in his or her age group is called a deviation IQ.

27. TRUE or FALSE   If you score at the fiftieth percentile, then half the people your age who took the test scored higher than you and half scored lower.

28. TRUE or FALSE   If you scored at the 97th percentile on an IQ test, your IQ would be 100.

29. TRUE or FALSE   The SB5 and the Wechsler tests are individual intelligence tests, while the SAT Reasoning Test is an example of a group test.

30. TRUE or FALSE   The SAT Reasoning Test was designed to predict a person's chances for success in college.

31. TRUE or FALSE   Because the SAT Reasoning Test measures a number of different mental aptitudes, it can be used to estimate general intelligence.

32. TRUE or FALSE   During instant message exchanges, computer programs have been able to easily fool humans into thinking there was another "person" e-mailing them rather than a computer program.

33. TRUE or FALSE   Computer are more mentally flexible than humans and can "shift gears" from one topic to another, while humans are very literal and "blind" outside of a set of rules.

34. TRUE or FALSE   Artificial intelligence (AI) refers to computer programs capable of doing things that require intelligence when done by people.

35. TRUE or FALSE   AI programs are valuable in situations where speed, vast memory, and persistence are required.

36. TRUE or FALSE   Computer simulations are computer programs that respond as a human expert would and have been used to predict the weather and diagnose diseases.

Critical Thinking Question

Is it ever accurate to describe a machine as "intelligent"?

Variations in Intelligence—Curved Like a Bell

Survey Question: How much does intelligence vary from person to person?

Language Development Guide

vary: differ

approximates: comes close; estimated to be

exceptionally: very; extremely

advanced: higher

professional positions: jobs requiring advanced college degrees, such as doctors, lawyers, etc.

sizable: considerable; significant

dramatics: acting in plays; participation in theatrical productions

blossom: develop; grow

nurtured: cared for; supported

spot: identify

purely: entirely; completely

possession: owning

precocious: early, advanced

shortchange: to treat unfairly

Rain Man: nickname of the autistic character played by actor Dustin Hoffman in the 1988 film of the same name that was inspired by the life of Kim Peek, who had extraordinary memory talents but had extreme difficulty with abstract thinking, tests of general intelligence, and adaptive living skills *calendar calculations*: for any date on a past or future calendar, the person can accurately tell what day of the week it falls

mental powers: special mental states and abilities

crystal clarity: clear precision

prime numbers: any whole number greater than one that can only be evenly divided by itself and one

harbors: holds; conceals

embers: sparks; small glowing coals

fan: stir up; encourage

into full flame: to become more intense, brighter

offensive: insulting; impolite

adaptive: useful for survival, health, or effective functioning

figures into: plays a part; is included

rejection: refusing to accept

teasing: playfully making fun of

ridicule: mocking and humiliating

defective: flawed, broken, damaged

delivery: birth

metabolic: biochemical processes that take place in living things; how the body breaks down food and other substances

malnutrition: insufficient diet; lack of food

PCBs: PolyChlorinated Biphenyls that were once used extensively in electrical devices, coolants, and lubricants but which contaminated the environment to a degree and caused cancers and other health problems

toxins: poisons and pollutants

degree: level of

impoverished: below standard, lacking, poor

enrichment: deliberately making an environment more intellectually stimulating, nutritional, and supportive

Recite and Review

1. The distribution of IQ scores approximates a bell shape known as a(n) _____ curve.
2. In the distribution of IQ scores, most scores fall close to the _____ of the curve.
3. Only two people out of 100 score above 130 on IQ tests with these bright individuals usually described as "_____."
4. For people with extremely high IQs or for those who are exceptionally creative, psychologists usually reserve the term "_____."
5. The psychologist who selected 1,500 children with IQs of 140 or more and followed this group into adulthood was _____.
6. Regarding their use of their talents and their careers, most of the 1,500 intellectually gifted children studied from childhood through adulthood were found to be _____ in these areas.
7. The correlation between IQ scores and school grades has been calculated to be a correlation of _____.
8. IQ is not good at predicting success in art, music, writing, dramatics, science, and leadership with these skills being more strongly related to _____.
9. Although it does not guarantee success, a high IQ reveals one's _____.
10. In the study of the 1,500 children with high IQs, the difference in the ones who were successful as adults and those who were not was due to the successful ones having a desire to know, to excel, and to persevere, which is called _____.
11. A person is usually described as gifted if he or she has either a high IQ or special aptitudes or _____.

12. Early signs of giftedness include children talking in complete sentences by the age of two or three, reading by age three, and typically an unusually good _____.

13. Seeking out older children and adults and showing kindness, understanding, and cooperation toward others at an early age are signs of _____.

14. Because they may be the victims of subtle biases in standardized intelligence tests, the groups less ikely to be recognized as gifted are the physically disabled and _____ children.

15. When a person of limited intelligence shows exceptional mental ability in one or more narrow areas, such as mental arithmetic, calendar calculations, art, or music, the person is said to have _____ syndrome.

16. One theory of why persons of limited intelligence can show an exceptional ability in some area, such as music or art, is that these people are freed from the "distractions" of language and other higher-level thought due to suffering some form of damage to their _____ hemispheres.

17. Another theory of why persons of limited intelligence can show an exceptional ability in some area, such as mental arithmetic, is that it results from intense _____.

18. Intellectual disability begins at an IQ of approximately _____ or below.

19. In diagnosing an intellectual disability, one must also evaluate the person's ability to perform basic skills, such as dressing, eating, communicating, shopping, and working, which are called _____ behaviors.

20. It is important to realize that intellectually disabled persons can be easily hurt by rejection and have no handicap where _____ are concerned.

21. With an IQ of 45 and an educational classification of trainable, Mary's degree of intellectual disability would be classified as _____.

22. A person with an IQ below 20 and needing an all-encompassing and persistent level of physical care would have a degree of intellectual disability that would be classified as

_____.

23. About half of all cases of intellectual disability are related to physical disorders and are considered to have a(n) _____ cause.

24. Fetal damage can cause intellectual disability and include damage from disease, infection, or drugs, which are collectively known as _____.

25. A lack of oxygen during delivery can result in _____ injuries that can cause intellectual disabilities.

26. Intellectual disabilities can be caused by disorders, which affect the production and use of energy in the body, and are referred to as _____ disorders.

27. Cases of intellectual disability in which no known biological cause can be identified, but which often occur in very poor households are referred to as _____ intellectual disability.

28. In these cases of intellectual disability in which no known biological problem can be identified, the degree of intellectual disability is usually in the 50 to 70 IQ range and classified as _____.

Connections

1. ___ normal curve	a. desire to know, to excel, and to persevere
2. ___ giftedness	b. possession of a high IQ typically of 130 or higher or special talents or aptitudes
3. ___ intellectual determination	c. lack of oxygen during delivery is one example
4. ___ savant syndrome	d. prenatal damage from teratogens

5. ___ organic intellectual disability	e. disability consisting of lowered intelligence related to all types of physical disorders or damage
6. ___ familial intellectual disability	f. bell-shaped curve characterized by a large number of scores in a middle area, tapering to very few extremely high and low scores
7. ___ fetal damage	g. problems that affect energy production
8. ___ birth injuries	h. disability consisting of lowered intelligence that is related to growing up in an impoverished environment
9. ___ metabolic disorders	i. person of limited intelligence shows exceptional mental ability in one or more narrow areas, such as mental arithmetic, calendar calculations, art, or music

Check Your Memory

1. TRUE or FALSE   The distribution of IQ scores approximates a normal curve.
2. TRUE or FALSE   In a normal curve, most of the scores fall at the extreme ends with very few being in the middle area.
3. TRUE or FALSE   About 15 out of 100 people score above 130 on an IQ test, while five out of 100 people score above 140.
4. TRUE or FALSE   Some psychologists reserve the term "genius" for people with extremely high IQs or those who are exceptionally creative.
5. TRUE or FALSE   Lewis Terman selected 1,500 children with IQs of 140 or more and followed their progress through adulthood.
6. TRUE or FALSE   Research by Terman and others have shown that the majority of children with IQs over 140 are mentally unstable and usually unsuccessful in their adult careers.
7. TRUE or FALSE   In general, the correlation between IQ scores and school grades is almost a zero correlation, showing virtually no relationship between the two.
8. TRUE or FALSE   IQ has been shown to be good at predicting success in art, music, writing, dramatics, science, and leadership.
9. TRUE or FALSE   A high IQ reveals one's potential and does not guarantee success.
10. TRUE or FALSE   The desire to know, to excel, and to persevere is called intellectual determination and is important in one's success.
11. TRUE or FALSE   Giftedness refers to having a high IQ, not to having special talents or aptitudes, such as creativity.
12. TRUE or FALSE   A gifted child usually speaks in complete sentences by age two or three and begins to read often by age three.
13. TRUE or FALSE   Gifted children tend to seek out older children and adults and show kindness, understanding, and cooperation toward others.
14. TRUE or FALSE   Ethnic minority children and children with physical disabilities are less likely to recognized as gifted.
15. TRUE or FALSE   A person with Klinefelter's syndrome has limited intelligence, but shows exceptional mental ability in one or more narrow areas, such as mental arithmetic, calendar calculations, art, or music.
16. TRUE or FALSE   Persons with limited intelligence but who have exceptional mental ability in some narrow area, such as music or art, are theorized to suffer from damage to the right hemisphere that helps increase their focus in this one area.

17. TRUE or FALSE   Another theory of how individuals with limited intelligence are able to perform extraordinary mental arithmetic and calendar calculations is that this ability is the result of intense practice.

18. TRUE or FALSE   Intellectual disability begins at an IQ of approximately 80 or below.

19. TRUE or FALSE   A person's ability to perform adaptive behaviors is a part of the evaluation for intellectual disability.

20. TRUE or FALSE   Intellectually disabled persons have no handicap where feelings are concerned and are easily hurt by rejection and teasing and respond warmly to love and acceptance.

21. TRUE or FALSE   With an IQ of 60 and the need for intermittent support, Morgan's degree of intellectual disability would be moderate with her educational classification being dependent.

22. TRUE or FALSE   Intellectual disability based largely on growing up in an impoverished environment is referred to as organic intellectual disability.

23. TRUE or FALSE   Metabolic disorders and birth injuries are the major causes of familial intellectual disability.

24. TRUE or FALSE   In most cases of familial intellectual disability, the degree of intellectual disability is mild, in the 50 to 70 IQ range.

25. TRUE or FALSE   About half of all cases of intellectual disability are organic, while 30 to 40 percent of cases are familial.

Questioning Intelligence—How Intelligent Is the Idea of Intelligence?

Survey Question: What are some controversies in the study of intelligence?

Language Development Guide

controversies: disagreements; debates

"culture fair": minimizes cultural bias (minimizes importance of skills and knowledge more common to some cultures than others)

implements: tools

piles: stacks; heaps

Kpelle culture in Liberia: largest ethnic group of the West African nation of Liberia

function: use; purpose

wise: intelligent

anecdote: short story of an incident

Cree of northern Canada: one of largest groups of Native Americans in North America

tundra: vast treeless plain with permanently frozen subsoil located in the Arctic regions

Puluwat people in the South Pacific: live on the numerous small islands in the Southwestern part of the Pacific near the Equator and are known for their navigational skills on the ocean

navigation: planning and directing the course of a boat or ship

translated: restated in another language

fault must lie: the error must be cause by

rural: countryside; away from a city

developing countries: countries in which a majority of the people have a low economic standard of living

diversity: variety

to stress: to emphasize; point out

truly: honestly

lie at the heart: are important to

intricate: with small or complex detail

traditional: customary; usual

autistic savants: person who has autism (disorder characterized by impaired social interaction and communication) but has exceptional ability in a specialized area, such as music or mathematical calculation

convinced: persuaded; influenced

forge ahead: move forward quickly

different mental "languages": differing thinking styles; different way of using words and language

pursuits: jobs, interests

medicine man: Native American healer

simplify: to make it easier

implication: something that is inferred or suggested

tied into: joined with

cultivate: develop; encourage

reared: raised, parented

roughly: about; more or less

gaps: differences

to inflate: exaggerate; overstate

take...into account: include as a cause

contribute: give; supply

resemble: be similar

degree: amount

orphanage: public facility in which children without parents are cared for

boosts: increases; improvements

reflect: show, reveal

technologically complex: the numerous scientific innovations in society

wireless network: any type of computer network that operates through radio waves rather than cables

popular culture: the attitudes, customs, viewpoints, and knowledge passed on through mass media

Pong: one of the earliest arcade video games that involved a simple table tennis game

Pac Man: one of the earlier video games that involved a yellow-dot character named Pac-Man that moved through a maze eating dots and prizes

The World of Warcraft: multiplayer online role-playing game based on a comic book series

Second Life: a virtual world that can be accessed on the Internet in which computer users interact with other people (residents) in this world by means of avatars (representation of himself/herself)

rich: vivid; powerful

intense: to an extreme degree

furthermore: in addition

fans: follower; devotee; enthusiast

prompt: encourage

(TV) dramas: fictional story depicted on television that follows the characters lives and adventures

weave: intertwine; united within

plot lines: story design

(TV) season: period of the year that involves a set number of episodes of a TV program being shown

persistent: continuing

claim: statement; declaration

"genetic heritage": biological inheritance

climbing out of poverty: increasing one's economic standard of living

counterarguments: line of reasoning that is offered in opposition to another claim

to begin: first

it is no secret: it is common knowledge; it is apparent

part of the equation: part of the cause
indeed: certainly; without a doubt
erased: removed; wiped away
tantalizing: exciting
Barack Obama: 44th and current president of the United States; first African-American to be
        elected U.S. president
counterparts: corresponding person with many of the same characteristics
role model: someone that is admired and imitated
blood group testing: genetically determined classes of blood; blood types
ethnic ancestry: origins of one's ethnic group or culture
does not even make genetic sense: not scientifically valid regarding DNA findings
external markers: specific physical features
in the final analysis: in truth when all the facts are known
fixed: set; permanent
a total mess: a complete disaster; unsuccessful
uninspired: boring; dull; bland
spiced: brighten up; jazzed up; made better by adding

Recite and Review

1. When members of the Kpelle culture in Liberia were asked to sort objects, they grouped them together by _____.
2. According to members of the Kpelle culture, the way Westerners group objects is how a(n) _____ would do it.
3. Among the Cree of Northern Canada, "smart" people are the ones who are able to find food on the frozen tundra because of their _____ skills.
4. For the Puluwat people in the South Pacific, being smart is being able to get from island to island using ocean-going _____ skills.
5. Psychologists have tried to create tests minimize the importance of skills and knowledge that may be more common in some cultures than in others. These tests are referred to as _____ tests.
6. Compared with children in developing countries, a child who grows up in the United States may be better prepared to take both nonverbal tests and traditional IQ tests because this culture is very "_____."
7. Many psychologists believe that it is time to forge new, broader definitions of intelligence since the basic goal of tests is not to predict the likelihood of success in school, but to better predict "_____" success.
8. The number of distinctly different kinds of intelligences postulated by Howard Gardner is _____.
9. Gardner's theory of distinctly different kinds of intelligences is called the theory of _____.
10. According to Gardner, traditional IQ tests measure only a part of real-world intelligence, namely, linguistic, logical-mathematical, and _____ abilities.
11. According to Gardner, a poet, actor, or minister, who has a great deal of self-knowledge would be strong in _____ intelligence.
12. According to Gardner, a psychologist, teacher, or a politician, who is strong in social skills, has a great deal of _____ intelligence.
13. Howard Gardner would say that a dancer, athlete, and surgeon are all strong in _____ intelligence.

14. A biologist, who understands animals and their habitat, and a organic farmer, who is able to produce fruits and vegetables from the land should a high ability in the intelligence Gardner referred to as _____.

15. Studies of twins reared together or separated at birth have been used to estimate how much the environment and _____ affect intelligence.

16. Twins who come from two separate eggs fertilized at the same time are called _____ twins.

17. Katie and Karen are twins, who developed from a single egg and have the same genes. Katie and Karen are _____ twins.

18. Josh and Jacob are twins, who are no more alike genetically than ordinary siblings, but have IQs that are more alike than the IQs of ordinary siblings. Josh and Jacob are _____ twins.

19. Psychologists who emphasize genetics believe that adult intelligence is roughly _____ percent hereditary.

20. A study that found that the IQs of biological and adopted children reared by the same mother were both similar to the mother's IQ provided strong evidence for the _____ view of intelligence.

21. When 25 intellectually disabled children were moved from an orphanage and given love and a more stimulating environment, these children gained an average of _____ IQ points.

22. The initially less "intellectually disabled" children, who stayed in the orphanage and were not moved to a more stimulating environment, lost an average of _____ IQ points.

23. A particularly dramatic environmental effect is the fact that Westernized nations have shown average IQ gains during the last 30 years of _____ points.

24. Stephen Johnson believes that the increase in IQ scores over the last 30 years is due to videogames, the Internet, computer software, and popular television becoming more _____ and requiring more cognitive effort.

25. Compared to the scores of European-American children on standardized IQ tests, African-American children score an average of about _____ points lower.

26. In a study in which poor African-American orphans were placed in better-off European-American adoptive families, their IQs increased by an average of _____ points.

27. Friedman and his colleagues administered a 20-item test to African-American and European-American students before and during the 2008 U.S. presidential election and found that the. African-   American students performed more poorly than European-American students before the election and performed just as well as their European-American counterparts during the election. Friedman referred to the cause of this change as the "_____."

28. According to Robert Sternberg, minority cultures view "book learning" as less important than "street smarts," or _____ intelligence.

29. Robert Sternberg refers to "book learning" as _____ intelligence.

30. In correlational studies of ethnic ancestry and IQ scores in which actual blood group testing was used, the researchers found _____ correlations.

31. In dealing with life problems, Melody uses a mixture of convergent thinking, intelligence, reason, creativity, and originality and approaches others with openness and tolerance. Melody would be described as having _____.

Connections

1. ___ multiple intelligences	a. test designed to minimize the importance of skills and knowledge that may be more common in some cultures than in others
2. ___ intrapersonal intelligence	b. mixture of convergent thinking, reason, intelligence, creativity, and originality
3. ___ interpersonal intelligence	c. what Sternberg called "street smarts"

4. ___ naturalist		d.	Gardner's term for the ability to understand one's own self
5. ___ practical intelligence		e.	role model inspired better academic performance in African-American students
6. ___ analytic intelligence		f.	Howard Gardener's theory that there are several specialized types of intellectual ability
7. ___ twin studies		g.	what Sternberg called "book learning"
8. ___ culture-fair test		h.	Gardner's term for the ability to understand others, or social abilities
9. ___ Obama effect		i.	ability possessed by biologists and organic farmers in understanding the environment
10. ___ wisdom		j.	research used to separate the relative impact of heredity and environment

Check Your Memory

1. TRUE or FALSE When tested, the Kpelle culture of Liberia sorted objects the same way as the technologically advanced Western cultures.

2. TRUE or FALSE The Cree of northern Canada believe that being smart means having navigational skills, while the Puluwat people in the South Pacific believe, "smart" people are the ones who have exceptional visual skills needed to find food.

3. TRUE or FALSE A culture-fair test is designed to minimize the importance of skills and knowledge that may be more common in some cultures than in others.

4. TRUE or FALSE Culture-fair rests are useful in testing children in the United States who come from poor communities, rural areas, or ethnic minority families.

5. TRUE or FALSE No intelligence test can be entirely free of cultural influences.

6. TRUE or FALSE Howard Gardner theorized that there are four distinctly different kinds of intelligence.

7. TRUE or FALSE According to Howard Gardner, a person who has a great deal of self-knowledge is high in interpersonal intelligence, while people high in social skills possess intrapersonal intelligence.

8. TRUE or FALSE According to Howard Gardner, dancers, athletes, and surgeons are high in bodily-kinesthetic intelligence.

9. TRUE or FALSE Most of us are probably strong in only a few types of multiple intelligences, while geniuses like Albert Einstein seem to be able to use nearly all of the multiple intelligences, as needed, to solve problems.

10. TRUE or FALSE Traditional IQ tests measure only a part of real-world intelligence, namely, linguistic, logical-mathematical, and spatial abilities.

11. TRUE or FALSE Some children might find it easier to learn math or reading if these topics were tied into art, music, dance, and drama.

12. TRUE or FALSE Twin studies have been used to estimate how much heredity and environment affect intelligence.

13. TRUE or FALSE Fraternal twins are twins that develop from a single egg and a single sperm and have identical genes.

14. TRUE or FALSE Parents treat fraternal twins more alike than ordinary siblings, resulting in a closer match in IQs.

15. TRUE or FALSE In general, the IQs of siblings having the same parents and reared in the same home are more similar than the IQs of identical twins separated at birth and reared in different homes.

462

16. TRUE or FALSE   Psychologists who emphasize genetics believe that adult intelligence is roughly 50 percent hereditary.

17. TRUE or FALSE   One study found that biological children and adopted children reared by the same mother tend to resemble her IQ to the same degree no matter whether or not they share her genes.

18. TRUE or FALSE   In the study in which 25 intellectually disable children were moved from an orphanage and placed in a loving, stimulating environment, these children gained only an average of five IQ points with the intellectual disabled children left in the orphanage losing no IQ points.

19. TRUE or FALSE   Westernized nations have shown average IQ gains of 30 points during the last 20 years.

20. TRUE or FALSE   Steven Johnson believes that video games, the Internet, and television are becoming more complex and are demanding greater cognitive effort from its viewers.

21. TRUE or FALSE   African-American children score an average of about 15 points lower on standardized IQ tests than European-American children.

22. TRUE or FALSE   One study found that placing poor African-American orphans into better-off European-American adoptive families increased the children's IQs by an average of 13 points.

23. TRUE or FALSE   Friedman and associates found that the "Obama effect" provided strong evidence that intelligence is strongly affected by the environment.

24. TRUE or FALSE   IQ tests do not predict school performance, but do predict later career success.

25. TRUE or FALSE   According to Robert Sternberg, analytic intelligence refers to "street smarts," while practical intelligence is defined by "book learning."

26. TRUE or FALSE   Most psychologists have concluded that there is no scientific evidence that group differences in average IQ are based on genetics.

27. TRUE or FALSE   Studies that used actual blood group testing found significant positive correlations between ethnic ancestry and IQ scores.

28. TRUE or FALSE   Intelligence reflects development as well as potential, nurture as well as nature.

29. TRUE or FALSE   Being intelligent means that you also have wisdom.

30. TRUE or FALSE   People who are wise approach life with openness and tolerance.

Critical Thinking Question

Some people treat IQ as if it were a fixed number, permanently stamped on the forehead of each child. Why is this view in error?

Module 8.5 Psychology in Action: Enhancing Creativity—Brainstorms

Survey Question: What can be done to improve thinking and promote creativity?

Language Development Guide

brainstorms: may refer to brainstorming, which is a group creativity technique designed to generate a large number of ideas in the solution of a problem

"eminence": distinction; fame; importance

inspiration: stimulated, motivated; encouraged

preconceived: formed in advance

impede: obstruct; hold back

forewarned: advise someone in advance regarding a danger

best of all: the most effective choice

wisely: showing good judgment

cross out: delete something with a line

edible: things that can be eaten

at the very least: one should at a minimum do this

jog: jerk; shake

modes: methods; approaches

time pressure: having a shortened amount of time to complete a task

embellish: enhance; elaborate

fruitful: productive

digging deeper: try harder

mental "prospecting": idea searching

trigger: set off; activate

open a new avenue: try a different way

skim: read quickly

old problems in new clothing: many problems have similarities to other problems you have solved in the past

add spice to life: to make something more interesting

sparks: inspires; triggers; sets off standardized: designed so that questions, conditions for administering, scoring, and procedures are administered the same way

canvas: piece of such fabric on which an oil painting is composed

Recite and Review

1. Thomas Edison explained his creativity by saying, "Genius is 1 percent inspiration and 99 percent _____."
2. Many studies of creativity show that "genius" and "eminence" involve inspiration as well as dedication and _____.
3. A major barrier to creative thinking that leads us to see a problem in preconceived terms that impede our problem-solving attempts is called a mental _____.
4. Fixations and functional fixedness are specific types of mental _____.
5. In order to design a better doorway, a supervisor gives his employees the task of "devising ways to better separate areas for living and working." The supervisor is encouraging creativity by defining the problem _____.
6. Creativity requires _____ thinking.
7. A sense of time pressure tends to _____ creativity.
8. Looking for analogies to your current problem tends to _____ creativity.
9. Regarding creativity, allowing time for incubation tends to _____ it.
10. To trigger a new perspective, the theorist who recommends randomly looking up words in the dictionary and relating them to the problem is _____.
11. Worrying about the correctness of solutions tends to _____ creativity
12. One of psychologist Mihalyi Csikszentmihalyi's recommendations for becoming more creative is to make a commitment to doing things _____.
13. One of Csikszentmihalyi's recommendations for becoming more creative is to start doing more of what you really _____.
14. According to Csikszentmihalyi, to be more creative, one should take time each day for thinking and _____.

Connections

1. ___ mental set	a. avoiding criticizing one's efforts in the initial stages of problem solving
2. ___ incubation	b. example would be randomly looking through a dictionary at the words

3. ___ time pressure	c. seeing similarities in old and new problems
4. ___ defining a problem broadly	d. tendency to perceive a problem in a way that blinds one to possible solutions
5. ___ seeking varied input	e. enlarging one's view of the problem
6. ___ delaying evaluation	f. problem solving proceeds at a subconscious level
7. ___ looking for analogies	g. shortened time to complete a task

Check Your Memory

1. TRUE or FALSE   Fixations and functional fixedness are specific types of mental sets.
2. TRUE or FALSE   Relying on mental sets aids problem-solving by increasing divergent thinking.
3. TRUE or FALSE   One way to restate a problem that will increase creativity is to imagine how another person would view it.
4. TRUE or FALSE   Creativity requires you to dig deeper with logic.
5. TRUE or FALSE   When trying to solve a new problem, looking for analogies or similarities to old problems will tend to confuse you and should be avoided.
6. TRUE or FALSE   When you are under a sense of time pressure, you are more likely to think creatively.
7. TRUE or FALSE   To help solve a problem more divergently, Edward de Bono recommends that you randomly look up words in the dictionary and relate them to the problem.
8. TRUE or FALSE   Representing a problem in a variety of ways is often the key to finding a solution to the problem.
9. TRUE or FALSE   In the first stages of creative thinking, it is important to systematically criticize your efforts.
10. TRUE or FALSE   One of psychologist Mihalyi Csikszentmihalyi's recommendations for becoming more creative is to find something that surprising you every day and try to surprise at least one person every day.
11. TRUE or FALSE   One of Csikszentmihalyi's recommendations for becoming more creative is to start doing more of what you really need to do even if you dislike rather than focusing so much on your enjoyment.
12. TRUE or FALSE   According to Csikszentmihalyi, if something sparks your interest, you should follow it.

Critical Thinking Question

Do you think there is any connection between your mood and your creativity?

Final Survey and Review—Completion

Module 8.1 Imagery, Concepts, and Language
What Is Thinking?—Brains over Brawn
Survey Question: What is the nature of thought?

1. Daydreaming, problem solving, and reasoning, all involve the mental processing of information known as _____.
2. Thinking often involves images, concepts, and _____.
3. When you categorize an event or an object, you are forming _____.

465

Module 8.1 Mental Imagery—Does a Frog Have Lips?

Survey Question: In what ways are images related to thinking?

4. If you normally see human voices as various colors as well as sounds, then you have a rare form of imagery known as _____.

5. You are shown a block design and then asked to select the picture of this block design in a different orientation from among four pictures. To accomplish this task, you must mentally _____ the image of this original design.

6. As you form a mental image of the beautiful river scene you saw on your vacation, your brain areas where memories are stored send signals back to the visual cortex, where an image is produced through a process referred to as "_____."

7. You are designing your new house and incorporating features that you have never seen in other houses. You will most likely use _____ images.

8. In order to learn climbing routes and plan their next few moves, rock climbers must use _____ imagery.

Module 8.1 Concepts—I'm Positive, It's a Whatchamacallit

Survey Question: What are concepts?

9. Jeffery is in college psychology and will most likely acquire the psychological concepts by learning conceptual _____.

10. If a "good teacher" is one that is fair, kind, knowledgeable, and presents interesting lectures, then your concept of a "good teacher" would be considered a(n) _____ concept.

11. If a "great weekend get-away" could be either a beach resort or hiking in the mountains or a listening to jazz in the French Quarter of New Orleans, then a "great weekend get-away" would be a(n) _____ concept.

12. If a majority of people would agree that a carrot is a good example of a vegetable, then a carrot would be considered an ideal model of a vegetable and would be called a(n) _____.

13. If you wanted the exact definition of the term "bipolar," you would most likely look in a medical dictionary to find what is known as its _____ meaning.

14. The semantic differential would most likely be used to find a word's _____ meaning.

Module 8.1 Language—Don't Leave Home Without It

Survey Question: What is the role of language in thinking?

15. Alton is conducting research in an area of study that looks at the meaning in words and language, which is called _____.

16. "Duck" can mean a type of bird or a warning "to put your head down to avoid being hit," which illustrates that words get much of their meaning from _____.

17. If Aria can speak both English and French fluently, we say she is _____.

18. A prefix, such as "un" and a suffix, such as "ful" would both be examples of small meaningful units known as _____.

19. When a young child says, "I goed to preschool," he is applying the normal past tense rule to the irregular verb to go, which actually illustrates the use of _____ rules.

20. Some psychologists now believe that far back in human history, speech evolved from _____.

21. Since animals can generate an infinite number of new ideas and thoughts by rearranging words, they lack the important property of language known as _____.

Module 8.2 Problem Solving

Problem Solving—Getting an Answer in Sight

Survey Question: What do we know about problem solving?

466

22. Mechanical solutions are achieved by rote or by _____.
23. Sanje is completing the addition and subtraction calculations by using the learned set of rules his teacher taught him. This learned set of rules is referred to as a(n) _____.
24. To solve a marketing problem for his company, Aaron is trying to identify how the current state of affairs differs from the desired goal and will also try to represent this problem in other ways with graphs, diagrams, or analogies. These would be considered _____ strategies.
25. Acquired strategies and specific organized knowledge have been shown by research to be the foundation for _____ skills.
26. Chinese students were able to solve the problem of how to weigh the gold coins by relating the problem in this story to a childhood story they remember about weighing an elephant. To solve this problem, the Chinese students used selective _____.
27. Joe has swept his house, but cannot find his dust pan to pick up the dirt. Unfortunately, Joe was not able to see that he could use an old magazine to sweep the dirt upon. Joe is exhibiting _____.
28. A colleague sees that your class is working in groups and displaying their ideas on colorful posters. She later criticizes your method of teaching, since she believes that only serious term papers and tests should be used to evaluate student with a course. This colleague is illustrating a(n) _____ barrier to problem solving.

Module 8.3 Creative Thinking and Intuition
Creative Thinking—Down Roads Less Traveled
Survey Question: What is creative thinking?

29. As an environmental psychologist, Josh has to take the general principles he has learned about conservation and apply these principles to specific situations. Josh is using _____ thought.
30. Amanda has been asked to list as many uses as possible for an empty shoe box. The number of times she shifts from one class of possible uses to another would be her _____ score.
31. If you are asked to come up with the one "best" answer to a question, you are being asked to use _____ thinking.
32. You are at a bridal shower, and one of the games involves coming up with as many words using the letters in "bridal shower." This game is similar to the creativity test called the _____ Test.
33. To be creative, a solution to a problem must be more than novel, unusual, or original. If the solution is an invention, it must be practical; and if it is an idea, it must be _____.
34. In the legend about Archimedes determining if a goldsmith had substituted cheaper metals for the gold in the crown, the stage of creative thought in which Archimedes collected all the information on known methods for analyzing metals would be the stage called _____.
35. In their thinking, creative people are good at using mental images and _____.

Module 8.3 Intuitive Thought—Mental Shortcut? Or Dangerous Detour?
Survey Question: How accurate is intuition?

36. Beth is introduced to her roommate's new boyfriend. In the first few seconds of this meeting, Beth thinks, "There is something about this person I don't like, and I think my roommate needs to be careful." This quick, impulsive thought regarding the roommate's new boyfriend that is not based on any formal logic is called _____.
37. According to Gladwell, the basis of more carefully reasoned judgments can result from quickly making sense of thin slivers of experience, also called "_____."
38. Giving greater weight to a choice if it seems to be representative of what we already know is known as the _____.

39. Even though Kim has be warned on numerous occasions not to text on her cell phone while she drives, she continues this danger practice because she is ignoring the _____.

Module 8.4 Intelligence
Human Intelligence—The IQ and You
Survey Question: How is human intelligence defined and measured?

40. Binet's IQ test was revised for use in North America and renamed the Stanford-Binet by psychologist _____.
41. By selecting items for an intelligence test, a psychologist is establishing a(n) _____ definition of intelligence.
42. If you are asked to fill in the missing shape in a group of objects and are presented with analogy questions, you are most likely completing the Stanford-Binet nonverbal and verbal items that measure the cognitive factor called _____.
43. On the WAIS-IV, the subtests of Similarities, Vocabulary, and Information measure the factor known as _____.
44. If 12-year-old Petra's IQ is 100, then her mental age would be _____ years.
45. Sanchez was administered an individual IQ test. The test examiner then looks on tables to see how far above or below average his score falls relative to his age group. The examiner is determining Sanchez's _____ IQ.
46. A group test designed to predict your chances for success in college and which measures aptitudes for language, math, and reasoning is the _____.
47. Greg works for a national weather service and uses a computer program to help him to analyze and predict the weather. This computer program is called a(n) _____ system.

Module 8.4 Variations in Intelligence—Curved Like a Bell (Module 8.4)
Survey Question: How much does intelligence vary from person to person?

48. The distribution of IQ scores is a normal curve and approximates a(n) _____ shape.
49. People are usually described as "gifted" if they are score above _____ on IQ tests.
50. A desire to know, to excel, and to persevere separates gifted individuals who are successful and those who are not. This quality is called _____.
51. Although Ian has a severe case of autism, he has the exceptional ability to be able to reproduce any musical composition after hearing it only a few times. Ian would be described as having _____ syndrome.
52. When diagnosing an intellectual disability, one considers the IQ as well as the person's ability to perform _____ behaviors.
53. When the cause of an intellectual disability is based largely on living in an impoverished environment, the intellectual disability is called _____.

Module 8.4 Questioning Intelligence—How Intelligent Is the Idea of Intelligence?
Survey Question: What are some controversies in the study of intelligence?

54. Regarding how Western cultures and the Kpelle culture of Liberia sort objects, a person that sorted objects into categories, such as clothes, containers, tools, and food, would be sorting like the _____ culture does.
55. Carmen is taking an intelligence test that was designed to minimize the importance of skills and knowledge that may be more common in some cultures than in hers. Carmen is taking a(n) _____ test.
56. April has exceptional skills in dealing with social interactions at work and at home. Gardner would say that she is high in _____ intelligence.
57. The fact that identical twins reared apart have very similar IQs provides evidence that intelligence is strongly affected by _____.

468

58. The "Obama effect" provides strong evidence that intelligence is strongly affected by the
_____.

59. According to Robert Sternberg, minority cultures often view practical intelligence as more important than _____ intelligence.

Module 8.5 Psychology in Action: Enhancing Creativity—Brainstorms
Survey Question: What can be done to improve thinking and promote creativity?

60. Midge has difficulty in problem solving because she often views the problem in a preconceived manner that blinds her to possible solutions. Midge's problem solving is being hindered by having a mental _____.

61. If your boss wants your group to design a new can opener, and you have your team to think about the idea of "opening" in general rather than about can openers specifically, then they are more likely to think creatively because you defined this problem _____.

62. Exposing yourself to a wide variety of information is a good way to encourage _____ thinking.

63. According to Csikszentmihalyi, to be more creative, one should take time each day for relaxing and _____.

Final Survey and Review—Matching

Module 8.1 Imagery, Concepts, and Language
Part 1:
1. ___ synaesthesia

2. ___ prototype
3. ___ conjunctive concept
4. ___ relational concept

5. ___ disjunctive concept
6. ___ stored image

7. ___ created image

8. ___ kinesthetic image
9. ___ denotative meaning

10. ___ connotative meaning

a. "and" concept in which the class of objects has two or more features in common
b. image that is assembled or invented
c. image created from muscular sensations
d. subjective, personal, or emotional meaning of a word or concept
e. image taken from memory of past experiences
f. exact dictionary definition of a word or concept or its objective meaning
g. "either/or" concept in which the concept is defined by the presence of at least one of several possible features
h. imagery that crosses normal sensory barriers
i. ideal model used as a prime example of a particular concept
j. concept defined by the association between features of an object or between an object and its surroundings

Part 2:
1. ___ semantics

2. ___ bilingualism
3. ___ phonemes

4. ___ morphemes

a. smallest meaningful units in a language, such as syllables or words
b. study of meanings in words and language
c. rules by which a simple declarative sentence may be changed to other voices or forms, such as past tense or passive voice
d. ability to speak two languages

469

5. ___ grammar

e. contains a qualification, often in the if/then form

6. ___ transformation rules

f. geometric word-symbol that was used in animal communication studies

7. ___ conditional statement

g. set of rules for combining language units into meaningful speech or writing, such as sounds into words and words into sentences

8. ___ lexigram

h. basic speech sounds of a language

Module 8.2 Problem Solving

1. ___ algorithm

a. ability to bring together seemingly unrelated bits of useful information

2. ___ heuristic

b. rigidity in problem solving caused by an inability to see new uses for familiar objects

3. ___ random search strategy

c. fast, fairly effortless thinking based on experience with similar problems

4. ___ automatic processing

d. tendency to repeat wrong solutions or faulty responses, especially as a result of becoming blind to alternatives

5. ___ selective encoding

e. inability to tolerate ambiguity and fears of making a mistake or of being embarrassed

6. ___ selective combination

f. values that hold that feelings, intuitions, pleasure and humor are bad and should not be a part of problem solving

7. ___ selective comparison

g. learned set of rules that always leads to the correct solution of a problem

8. ___ fixation

h. ability to select information that is relevant to a problem, while ignoring distractions

9. ___ functional fixedness

i. "rule of thumb" strategy that reduces the number of alternatives thinkers must consider

10. ___ emotional barrier to problem solving

j. trying possible solutions to a problem in a more or less haphazard manner

11. ___ cultural barrier to problem solving

k. ability to relate new problems to old information or to problems already solved

Module 8.3 Creative Thinking and Intuition
Part 1:

1. ___ inductive thought

a. quick, impulsive thought that does not make use of formal logic or clear reasoning

2. ___ deductive thought

b. drawing conclusions on the basis of formal principles of reasoning

3. ___ logical thought

c. underlying probability of an event

4. ___ intuition

d. terms in which a problem is stated or the way that it is structured

5. ___ convergent thinking

e. conventional thinking directed toward the discovery of a single established correct answer

6. ___ divergent thinking

    f. tendency to select wrong answers because they seem to match preexisting mental categories

7. ___ representativeness heuristic

    g. thought that applies a general set of rules to specific situations

8. ___ base rate

    h. thinking in which many possibilities are developed from one starting point

9. ___ framing

    i. thought that goes from specific facts or observations to general principles

Part 2:

1. ___ fluency

    a. refers to the total number of suggestions one is able to make in solving a problem

2. ___ flexibility

    b. stage of creative thought in which problem solving proceeds on a subconscious level

3. ___ originality

    c. refers to the number of times a person shifts from one class of possible ideas to another

4. ___ orientation (in creative thought)

    d. stage of creative thought in which rapid insight into the solution occurs

5. ___ preparation (in creative thought)

    e. stage in creative thought in which the person tests and critically evaluates the solution

6. ___ incubation (in creative thought)

    f. refers to how novel or unusual one's ideas are

7. ___ illumination (in creative thought)

    g. stage in creative thought when the person defines the problem and identifies its most important dimensions

8. ___ verification (in creative thought)

    h. stage in creative thought in which the person saturates themselves with as much information about the problem as possible

Module 8.4 Intelligence

Part 1:

1. ___ intelligence (general, accepted definition)

    a. index of intelligence defined by MA / CA x 100

2. ___ operational definition of intelligence

    b. mixture of convergent thinking, reason, intelligence, creativity, and originality

3. ___ practical intelligence

    c. desire to know, to excel, and to persevere

4. ___ analytic intelligence

    d. Gardner's term for the ability to understand one's own self

5. ___ intelligence quotient (IQ)

    e. what Sternberg called "book learning"

6. ___ deviation IQs

    f. defined by procedures used to measure it

7. ___ multiple intelligences

    g. overall capacity to think rationally, act purposely, and deal effectively with the environment

8. ___ artificial intelligence

    h. Gardner's term for the ability to understand others, or social abilities

9. ___ intrapersonal intelligence

    i. what Sternberg called "street smarts"

10. ___ interpersonal intelligence

j. Howard Gardener's theory that there are several specialized types of intellectual ability

11. ___ intellectual determination

k. computer programs capable of doing things that require intelligence when done by people

12. ___ wisdom

l. IQ obtained statistically from a person's relative standing in his or her age group

Part 2:

1. ___ normal curve

a. group test that was designed to predict one's chances for success in college

2. ___ culture-fair test

b. disability consisting of lowered intelligence that is related to growing up in an impoverished environment

3. ___ Stanford-Binet (original and SB-5)

c. possession of a high IQ typically of 130 or higher or special talents or aptitudes

4. ___ WAIS

d. test designed to minimize the importance of skills and knowledge that may be more common in some cultures than in others

5. ___ SAT Reasoning Test (SAT)

e. disability consisting of lowered intelligence related to all types of physical disorders or damage

6. ___ giftedness

f. first "adult" IQ test and first test to yield separate scores for verbal and performance intelligences

7. ___ savant syndrome

g. first developed by Lewis Terman with newest edition being appropriate for people age two to 85+

8. ___ organic intellectual disability

h. research used to separate the relative impact of heredity and environment

9. ___ familial intellectual disability

i. person of limited intelligence shows exceptional mental ability in one or more narrow areas, such as mental arithmetic, calendar calculations, art, or music

10. ___ twin studies

j. bell-shaped curve characterized by a large number of scores in a middle area, tapering to very few extremely high and low scores

Module 8.5 Psychology in Action: Enhancing Creativity—Brainstorms

1. ___ mental set

a. avoiding criticizing one's efforts in the initial stages of problem solving

2. ___ incubation

b. example would be randomly looking through a dictionary at the words

3. ___ looking for analogies
4. ___ defining a problem broadly

c. seeing similarities in old and new problems

d. tendency to perceive a problem in a way that blinds one to possible solutions

5. ___ seeking varied input
6. ___ delaying evaluation

e. enlarging one's view of the problem

f. problem solving proceeds at a subconscious level

472

Final Survey and Review—True or False

Module 8.1 Imagery, Concepts, and Language
What Is Thinking?—Brains over Brawn
Survey Question: What is the nature of thought?
1. TRUE or FALSE   Thinking is limited only to the human species.
2. TRUE or FALSE   Daydreaming is considered a form of thinking.
3. TRUE or FALSE   Language is defined as those ideas that represent categories of objects or events.

Module 8.1 Mental Imagery—Does a Frog Have Lips?
Survey Question: In what ways are images related to thinking?
4. TRUE or FALSE   More than half of us have regularly had images that cross normal sensory barriers and are referred to as sane hallucinations.
5. TRUE or FALSE   Mental images can be used to improve memory and to change one's feelings.
6. TRUE or FALSE   Mental images are not flat, like photographs.
7. TRUE or FALSE   The visual cortex is activated when a person has a mental image.
8. TRUE or FALSE   If you form a mental image of your kitchen in order to describe it for someone, you are using created images.

Module 8.1 Concepts—I'm Positive, It's a Whatchamacallit
Survey Question: What are concepts?
9. TRUE or FALSE   Lionel is four-years-old and will most likely acquire his concepts at this age through positive and negative instances of the object.
10. TRUE or FALSE   If you explain that city hall is two streets west of the mall, then you are using a conjunctive concept to provide directions.
11. TRUE or FALSE   If you tell someone that you are shorter than your older brother but taller than your younger brother, then you are using a relational concept.
12. TRUE or FALSE   Oversimplified concepts of groups of people are called prototypes.
13. TRUE or FALSE   When you put in a tremendous number of hours on your term paper, you describe yourself as "conscientious," while your friends describe you as a "perfectionist," which illustrates a difference in connotative meanings for "working hard."
14. TRUE or FALSE   Denotative meanings are usually measured with a technique called the semantic differential.

Module 8.1 Language—Don't Leave Home Without It
Survey Question: What is the role of language in thinking?
15. TRUE or FALSE   Thinking requires that you have language.
16. TRUE or FALSE   English-only instruction can leave minority students poorly prepared to succeed in the majority culture.
17. TRUE or FALSE   Basic speech sounds are known as morphemes.
18. TRUE or FALSE   The linguist who believed that we do not learn all the sentences we might ever say but actively create them was Noam Chomsky.
19. TRUE or FALSE   If a person understands American Sign Language (ASL), he or she will not automatically be able to understand other gestural languages, such as French Sign, Spanish Sign, or Chinese Sign.

20. TRUE or FALSE   Signing children do not pass through the same stages of language development as speaking children do.

21. TRUE or FALSE   No chimpanzee unless they were extensive trained has shown any inclination to communicate with humans using simple gestures.

Module 8.2 Problem Solving

Problem Solving—Getting an Answer in Sight

Survey Question: What do we know about problem solving?

22. TRUE or FALSE   When a problem is solved by rote, thinking is guided by an algorithm.

23. TRUE or FALSE   In solutions by understanding, functional solutions are usually discovered by use of a random search strategy.

24. TRUE or FALSE   Heuristics raise the odds of success, but do not guarantee a solution.

25. TRUE or FALSE   Automatic processing frees "space" in short-term memory, making it easier to work on the problem.

26. TRUE or FALSE   The ability to select information that is relevant to a problem and ignore distractions is known as selective comparison.

27. TRUE or FALSE   Because children have less experience with the use of various objects, they are more likely than adults to show functional fixedness.

28. TRUE or FALSE   When a person focuses so much on getting all the information on his PowerPoint slides that he does not realize that the colors chosen for the words and background make reading the slides very difficult, he is exhibiting a perceptual barrier to creative problem solving.

Module 8.3 Creative Thinking and Intuition

Creative Thinking—Down Roads Less Traveled

Survey Question: What is creative thinking?

29. TRUE or FALSE   Thinking in which a general rule or principle is gathered from a series of specific examples is known as deductive thinking.

30. TRUE or FALSE   Anthony has been asked to list as many uses as possible for an empty shoe box with his total number of answers being his flexibility score.

31. TRUE or FALSE   When your boss asks you to come up with as many possible ways to market a particular product as possible, she is asking you to use convergent thinking.

32. TRUE or FALSE   When Archimedes found that all known methods for analyzing metals would involve cutting or melting the crown, he was forced to temporarily set the problem aside, which illustrates the stage of creative thought known as verification.

33. TRUE or FALSE   There is a large positive correlation between IQ and creativity, which means that those with the highest IQs are also the ones that will show the most creativity.

34. TRUE or FALSE   Creative people value their independence and prefer complexity.

35. TRUE or FALSE   Some creative thinking skills can be learned.

Module 8.3 Intuitive Thought—Mental Shortcut? Or Dangerous Detour?

Survey Question: How accurate is intuition?

36. TRUE or FALSE   A quick, impulsive thought that does not make use of formal logic or clear reasoning is called inductive reasoning.

37. TRUE or FALSE   When Nalini Ambady asked people to watch three 10-second video clips of teachers they did not know and to rate the teachers, their ratings showed no correlation with the year-end course evaluations made by actual students.

38. TRUE or FALSE   In many high-risk situations, ignoring base rates is the same as thinking you are an exception to the rule.

39. TRUE or FALSE   The broadest way of framing, or stating a problem usually produces the best decisions.

Module 8.4 Intelligence
Human Intelligence—The IQ and You
Survey Question: How is human intelligence defined and measured?

40. TRUE or FALSE   In 1904, the minister of education in Germany asked Fritz Perls to find a way to distinguish slower students from the more capable and the first IQ test was devised.

41. TRUE or FALSE   The accepted definition of intelligence is the global capacity to act purposefully, to think rationally, and to deal effectively with the environment.

42. TRUE or FALSE   On the SB5, if a person is asked to tell a story that explains what is going on in a series of pictures, the cognitive factor being assessed is called fluid reasoning.

43. TRUE or FALSE   On the WAIS-IV, the subtests of Digit Span and Arithmetic are used to measure the factor known as Processing Speed.

44. TRUE or FALSE   Chronological age is based on the level of age-ranked questions a person can answer.

45. TRUE or FALSE   Average intelligence is usually defined as any IQ score from 70 to 90.

46. TRUE or FALSE   If you scored at the fiftieth percentile on an IQ test, your IQ would be 80.

47. TRUE or FALSE   During instant message exchanges, no computer program to date has been able to fool a human participant into thinking there was another "person" e-mailing them.

Module 8.4 Variations in Intelligence—Curved Like a Bell
Survey Question: How much does intelligence vary from person to person?

48. TRUE or FALSE   About two out of 100 people score above 130 on an IQ test, while less than one-half of one percent score above 140.

49. TRUE or FALSE   In general, the correlation between IQ scores and school grades is .50, which is a sizable association

50. TRUE or FALSE   Research by Terman and others have shown that the majority of children held professional positions and were successful in their adult careers.

51. TRUE or FALSE   Gifted children usually seek out younger children they can bully and often show spoiled, self-centered behavior regarding others.

52. TRUE or FALSE   Persons with savant syndrome are theorized to suffer from damage to the left hemisphere that freeing them from the "distractions" of language, concepts, and higher-level thought.

53. TRUE or FALSE   In most cases of familial intellectual disability, the degree of intellectual disability is severe, in the 25 to 45 IQ range.

Module 8.4 Questioning Intelligence—How Intelligent Is the Idea of Intelligence?

Survey Question: What are some controversies in the study of intelligence?

54. TRUE or FALSE   A test designed to minimize the importance of skills and knowledge that may be more common in some cultures than in others is known as a multicultural diversity test.

55. TRUE or FALSE   Howard Gardner theorized that there are eight distinctly different kinds of intelligence.

56. TRUE or FALSE   In general, the IQs of identical twins separated at birth and reared in different homes are more similar than the IQs of fraternal twins having the same parents and reared in the same home.

57. TRUE or FALSE   Psychologists who emphasize genetics believe that adult intelligence is roughly 75 percent hereditary.

58. TRUE or FALSE   Westernized nations have shown only average IQ gains of five points during the last 30 years.

59. TRUE or FALSE   People can be intelligent without being wise.

Module 8.5 Psychology in Action: Enhancing Creativity—Brainstorms

Survey Question: What can be done to improve thinking and promote creativity?

60. TRUE or FALSE   Looking for analogies to your current problem tends to inhibit creativity.

61. TRUE or FALSE   If you are feeling hurried by a sense of time pressure, you are less likely to think creatively.

62. TRUE or FALSE   In the first stages of creative thinking, it is important to avoid criticizing your efforts.

63. TRUE or FALSE   One of psychologist Mihalyi Csikszentmihalyi's recommendations for becoming more creative is to stop worrying about doing things well.

Mastery Test

1. If you describe the best friend's voice as a "burst of aqua" and the sunshine as smelling of "fresh baked bread," you are probably experiencing
   a. synaesthesia.
   b. "sane hallucinations."
   c. "thin-slicing."
   d. creative fluency.

2. You are asked to form an image of a pig in your mind and describe its nose. In order for you to describe its tail, your image will have to undergo a(n)
   a. conceptual recoding.
   b. mental rotation.
   c. algorithmic transformation.
   d. disjunctive conceptualization.

3. If you construct an original abstract painting, you would be using a _____ image.
   a. disjunctive
   b. prototypical
   c. created
   d. stored

4. If you are asked to describe the correct procedure for a "tennis serve," you would most likely use _____ imagery.
   a. synaesthesia
   b. conjunctive
   c. gustatory
   d. kinesthetic

5. During concept formation, children are more likely to use
   a. positive and negative instances.
   b. conceptual rules.
   c. disjunctive concepts.
   d. conjunctive concepts.

6. "Either-or" concepts, such as a pet can be either a cat or a dog or a bird, or a fish, etc., are referred to as _____ concepts.
   a. conjunctive
   b. disjunctive
   c. relational
   d. prototypical

7. If an apple is a prime example of the concept of fruit, then an apple would be considered a
   a. relational concept.
   b. connotation.
   c. denotation.
   d. prototype.

8. If you use a semantic differential to rate the word "politics," you are measuring this word's _____ meaning.
   a. disjunctive
   b. conjunctive
   c. connotative
   d. denotative

9. The difference between "rare prime beef" and a "bloody slab of dead cow" is primarily a matter of
   a. syntax.
   b. heuristics.
   c. semantics.
   d. transformation rules.

10. The majority of children who speak English at home and then learn a second language will most likely experience
    a. additive bilingualism.
    b. subtractive bilingualism.
    c. grammar and syntax problems with their native language.
    d. cognitive decline due to language confusion.

11. Carol is training to become a speech pathologist and is asked to list all of the basic speech sounds of the English language on a test. Carol is being asked to list all of the
    a. phonemes.
    b. morphemes.
    c. lexigrams.
    d. transformations.

12. The mark of a true language is that is must
    a. be spoken.
    b. be productive.
    c. involve intuitive encoding.
    d. involve selective comparisons.

13. Among the primates described in the animal language studies, Kanzi, a pygmy chimpanzee trained by Rumbaugh and Rumbaugh, was most successful at
    a. uttering four spoken words.
    b. using lexigrams to form sentences in correct word order.
    c. using plastic chips on a magnetized board to express conditional statements.
    d. using American Sign Language to construct six-word sentences.

14. Random search strategies are most similar to
    a. selective encoding.
    b. automatic processing.
    c. trial-and-error problem solving.
    d. the orientation phase of problem solving.

15. If you cannot reach a goal directly, you should try to identify an intermediate goal or sub-problem that at least gets you closer. This strategy will help reduce the number of alternatives you have to consider and is called
    a. an algorithm.
    b. a heuristic
    c. intuitive processing.
    d. automatic processing.

16. Amy is taking a math reasoning test. As she is reading one of the word problems on the test, Amy suddenly realizes that this problem, although new, is very similar to one of the problems she solved in the textbook while studying for this test. Amy's insight into the similarity of the two problems illustrates selective
    a. encoding.
    b. combination.
    c. elaboration.
    d. comparison.

17. Leeza has a job interview, but she has cat hair all over her black jacket. She searches and searches for her lint brush, but cannot find it. Her failure to realize that tape could be used to remove the cat hair illustrates which type of barrier to problem solving?
    a. emotional
    b. learned
    c. cultural
    d. perceptual

18. As a psychology intern, you use the standard criteria for psychoses to diagnose specific cases and to predict each client's behavior. In this situation, your thinking would best be described as
    a. intuitive.
    b. inductive.
    c. deductive.
    d. divergent.

478

19. You are taking a creativity test in which you are asked to draw as many pictures as you can in 10 minutes using a tiny square in each section as a part of your picture. Your total number of drawings would indicate your _____ regarding this creative task.
    a. originality
    b. flexibility
    c. fluency
    d. elaborative skills

20. While trying to solve a problem, Kal generates as many possible solutions as he can think of. Kal is using _____ thinking.
    a. intuitive
    b. divergent
    c. convergent
    d. transformational

21. Fiona is working on her term paper for English class. She has gathered a tremendous amount of research and is trying to organize it. However, her attempts at organizing the data seem futile. So, Fiona sets the paper aside and let this problem with organization proceed in her mind at a subconscious level. According to the stages of creative thought, Fiona is currently in the stage called
    a. illumination.
    b. incubation.
    c. verification.
    d. orientation.

22. Avery is a very creative person. We can expect Avery to
    a. also be highly intelligent.
    b. be eccentric, introverted, and socially inept.
    c. have a greater-than-average range of interests.
    d. be interested in fame and success.

23. In the study by Ambady in which participants rated 10-second video clips of teachers they did not know, these participants were making sense of these small bits of experience by using
    a. synaesthesia.
    b. algorithms.
    c. transformation patterns.
    d. thin-slicing.

24. When people think they are an exception to the rule and continue to drink and drive, these individuals are exhibiting the intuitive thinking error known as
    a. the representativeness heuristic.
    b. ignoring the base rate.
    c. broad-based framing.
    d. the gambler's fallacy.

25. You are trying to eat healthier and are reading the labels on the food packages. One package says that each serving of their frozen entree is 90 percent fat-fee, while another brand states that their frozen entree only contain 10 percent fat per serving. Even though both products contain the same amount of fat, you may intuitively find one brand's statement more appealing due to
    a. framing.
    b. ignoring the base rate.
    c. the representativeness heuristic.
    d. "thin-slicing."

26. Creating an intelligence test provides a(n) _____ definition of intelligence.
    a. analytical
    b. reliable
    c. operational
    d. valid

27. Which of the following psychologists revised Binet's intelligence test for use in North America and called it the *Stanford-Binet Intelligence Scale*?
    a. Lewis Terman
    b. Howard Gardner
    c. Robert Sternberg
    d. David Wechsler

28. Which of the five cognitive factors measured by the Stanford-Binet (SB-5) involves a person determining their location by imagining that they are facing in one direction and then making various right and left turns?
    a. fluid reasoning
    b. knowledge
    c. visual-spatial processing
    d. working memory

29. A nine-year-old child with an IQ of 100 would have a mental age of _____ years.
    a. seven
    b. nine
    c. 10
    d. 12

30. A person's relative intellectual standing in his or her age group is revealed by the
    a. mental age.
    b. g-factor.
    c. chronological age.
    d. deviation IQ.

31. Marial is taking the SAT Reasoning Test (SAT). Which of the following statement about the SAT is FALSE?
    a. The SAT will measure her aptitudes for math, language, and reasoning.
    b. The SAT will be used to predict her chances for success in college.
    c. The SAT can be used to estimate her general intelligence.
    d. The SAT will be administered to her individually with an examiner presenting each task to her.

32. The distribution of IQ scores approximates a(n)
    a. U-shaped curve with most scores at the extreme ends and few in the middle.
    b. bell-shaped curve with most scores in the middle and few at the extreme ends.
    c. horizontal line with scores being evenly-distributed.
    d. diagonal line with most scores clustering at the top end of the scale.

33. From his study of the gifted, Lewis Terman found that the gifted students who were successful as adults possessed
    a. creativity.
    b. leadership abilities.
    c. intellectual determination.
    d. emotional intelligence.

34. A type of intellectual disability that appears to be based largely on the effects of a poor environment, in which nutrition, intellectual stimulation, and emotional support are inadequate is called
    a. savant syndrome.
    b. familial intellectual disability.
    c. post-organic intellectual disability.
    d. metabolic-intellectual disorder.

35. According to the multiple intelligences theory, a person with a high degree of self-knowledge, such as an actor, a poet, and a minister, would excel in _____ intelligence.
    a. naturalist
    b. linguistic
    c. interpersonal
    d. intrapersonal

36. Computer programs that can duplicate specific human behavior, such as problem solving and programs that can predict the weather, play chess, and diagnose diseases are applications of
    a. artificial intelligence.
    b. computer proxemics.
    c. framing modules.
    d. executive processing.

37. The greatest similarity in IQs would be expected between
    a. identical twins reared apart.
    b. fraternal twins reared together.
    c. siblings of the same sex reared together.
    d. parents and children.

38. Westernized nations have shown a 15-point average IQ gain in the last 30 years. These findings support the idea that intelligence is greatly influenced by
    a. nature.
    b. the environment.
    c. genetics.
    d. the broader definition of intelligence.

39. Sera is being administered an individual test in which her intelligence will be assessed without being affected by her verbal skills, cultural background, and educational level. Sera is taking
    a. the SAT Reasoning Test.
    b. an anagrams test.
    c. a culture-fair test.
    d. a multi-cultural test.

40. Which of the following would most likely increase one's creativity?
    a. utilizing mental sets
    b. defining problems narrowly and specifically
    c. having a sense of time pressure
    d. looking for analogies

Chapter 9: Motivation and Emotion

Chapter Overview

Motives initiate, sustain, direct, and terminate activities. Motivation typically involves the sequence: need, drive, goal, and goal attainment (need reduction). Behavior can be activated either by needs (push) or by goals (pull). The attractiveness of a goal and its ability to initiate action are related to its incentive value. Three principal types of motives are biological motives, stimulus motives, and learned motives. Most biological motives operate to maintain homeostasis. Circadian rhythms are closely tied to sleep, activity, and energy cycles. Time zone travel and shift work can seriously disrupt motivation, sleep, and bodily rhythms.

Hunger is influenced by a complex interplay between fullness of the stomach, blood sugar levels, metabolism in the liver, and fat stores in the body. The most direct control of eating is affected by the hypothalamus, which has areas that act like feeding and satiety systems. The hypothalamus is sensitive to both neural and chemical messages, which affect eating. Other factors influencing hunger are the body's set point, external eating cues, the attractiveness and variety of diet, emotions, learned taste preferences and aversions, and cultural values. Obesity is the result of internal and external influences, diet, emotions, genetics, and exercise. The most effective way to lose weight is behavioral dieting, which is based on techniques that change eating patterns and exercise habits. Anorexia nervosa and bulimia nervosa are two prominent eating disorders. Both tend to involve conflicts about self-image, self-control, and anxiety.

Like hunger, thirst and other basic motives are primarily under the central control of the hypothalamus. Thirst may be either intracellular or extracellular. Pain avoidance is unusual because it is episodic as opposed to cyclic. Pain avoidance and pain tolerance are partially learned. The sex drive is also unusual because it is nonhomeostatic.

Drives for stimulation are partially explained by arousal theory, which states that an ideal level of bodily arousal will be maintained if possible. The desired level of arousal or stimulation varies from person to person. Optimal performance usually occurs at moderate levels of arousal, as described by an inverted U function. The Yerkes-Dodson law states that for simple tasks, the ideal arousal level is higher; and for complex tasks it is lower.

Social motives are learned through socialization and cultural conditioning and account for much of the diversity of human motivation. People high in need for achievement (n-Ach) are successful in many situations due to their perseverance, passion, and self-confidence. Self-confidence greatly affects motivation in everyday life.

Maslow's hierarchy of motives categorizes needs as either basic or growth oriented. Lower needs are assumed to be prepotent (dominant) over higher needs. Self-actualization, the highest and most fragile need, is reflected in meta-needs. Meta-needs are closely related to intrinsic motivation. In some situations, external rewards can undermine intrinsic motivation, enjoyment, and creativity.

An emotion consists of physiological changes, adaptive behavior, emotional expressions, and emotional feelings. The primary emotions of fear, surprise, sadness, disgust, anger, anticipation, joy, and acceptance can be mixed to produce more complex emotional experiences. The left hemisphere of the brain primarily processes positive emotions. Negative emotions are processed in the right hemisphere. The amygdala provides a quick pathway for the arousal of fear that bypasses the cerebral cortex.

Physical changes associated with emotion are caused by the hormone adrenaline and by activity in the autonomic nervous system (ANS). The sympathetic branch of the ANS is responsible primarily for arousing the body; the parasympathetic branch, for quieting it. The polygraph, or "lie detector," measures emotional arousal (rather than lying) by monitoring heart rate, blood pressure, breathing rate, and the galvanic skin response (GSR). The accuracy of the lie detector can be quite low. Newer brain imaging methods, such as fMRI, are showing great promise in lie detection.

Basic facial expressions of fear, anger, disgust, sadness, and happiness are universally recognized. Facial expressions reveal pleasantness versus unpleasantness, attention versus rejection, and a person's degree of emotional activation. The formal study of body language is known as kinesics. Body gestures and movements (body language) also express feelings, mainly by communicating emotional tone rather than specific universal messages. Body positioning expresses relaxation or tension and liking or disliking.

Contrary to common sense, the James-Lange theory says that emotional experience follows bodily reactions. In contrast, the Cannon-Bard theory says that bodily reactions and emotional experiences occur at the same time. Schachter's cognitive theory emphasizes that labeling bodily arousal can determine what emotion you feel. Appropriate labels are chosen by attribution (ascribing arousal to a particular source). Contemporary views of emotion place greater emphasis on the effects of emotional appraisals. One of the best ways to manage emotion is to change your emotional appraisal of a situation. The facial feedback hypothesis holds that facial expressions help define the emotions we feel. Contemporary views of emotion emphasize that all of the elements of emotion are interrelated and interact with each other.

Emotional intelligence is the ability to consciously make your emotions work for you in a wide variety of life circumstances. People who are emotionally smart are able to perceive, use, understand, and manage emotions. They are self-aware and empathetic; know how to use emotions to enhance thinking, decision making, and relationships; and have an ability to understand and manage emotions. Positive emotions are valuable because they tend to broaden our focus and they encourage personal growth and social connection.

Preview: Are You Moved by the Music of Life?

atmosphere: surroundings; environment
emotion is the "music" that enriches the rhythms of our lives: emotions make life better
vaguely: dimly; hazily
suspect: guess
empathize: be sensitive to, emotionally understand
the drumbeat of human behavior: the pace or pattern
color: affect; influence
derive: come from
solely: only
the music of death: can cause one to die

Module 9.1 Overview of Motivation
Motivation—Forces that Push and Pull
Survey Questions: What is motivation? Are there different types of motives?

484

Language Development Guide

pursue: follow
satisfied: content; fulfilled
dynamics: energies; forces
initiated: begun
sustained: kept going; continued
terminated: ended
clarify: make it clear
growl: rumble; make noises
restless: on edge; impatient
resumes: starts again
deficiency: lack, absence
energized: strengthened; boosted
activate: set in motion; turn on
exclaims: shouts out
pie lust: desire for sweets
"pull": being drawn toward
"push": forced to
incentive: encouragement
silkworms: larvae or caterpillar of the silk moth raised for the silk it produces and as an Asian
　　　snack food
aspiring: hopeful
pretty horrible: very bad
leftovers: uneaten edible remains of a meal that can be eaten as a snack or as another meal
bare: empty
motive: need; aim
survival: continued life
elimination: removal
wastes: parts of food not used by the body
innate: born with
express: make known
manipulation: doing things, changing one's surroundings
not strictly: not exactly
in nature: characteristically
standing for election: taking a chance on running for elected position with the possibility of
　　　winning or losing
auditioning: presenting one's talent, such as singing, to be judged for inclusion on a show
American Idol: reality TV competition show involving new individual singers
status: ranking; standing
security: feeling safe
achievement: success
regulation: controlled
rest room: bathroom
routine: usual; everyday
exaggerate: inflate; overstate
famine: food shortage; starvation
poverty: lack of basic necessities
grip: hold
evident: obvious; clear
essential: necessary

equilibrium: balance

optimal: best possible

deviates: differs from; departs from

restore: bring back

thermostat: a control for room temperature, turning on and off the furnace or air conditioning

exceeds: goes beyond

hovering: being near

diminish: lessen; reduce

amino acid levels: nutrients in the body that come from protein rich foods

shift: change

peak: reach the highest point

time zones: regions on the earth each having a different standard time schedule

disturbed: upset

resynchronize: get back into a normal rhythm

relative to: in comparison to

jet lag: physical symptoms (fatigue, sleepiness) that result from altering one's circadian rhythm usually by traveling to other time zones

intermittent: irregular; not steady

burned the midnight oil: stay up late at night to work or study (refers to using an oil lamp to see late at night)

destination: where you are going

Recite and Review

1. Simon has an inability to name emotions, while being only vaguely aware of his own emotions and those of others. Simon suffers from _____.
2. The words "motivation" and "emotion" both derive from the Latin word *movere*, which means to _____.
3. Motivation refers to the ways in which our actions are initiated, sustained, directed, and _____.
4. Many motivated activities begin with an internal deficiency called a(n) _____.
5. The psychological expression of internal needs or valued goals is called a(n) _____.
6. If you are studying and become hungry, your action of going to your refrigerator for food is referred to in the model of motivation as a(n) _____.
7. The target or objective of motivated behavior is called a(n) _____.
8. According to the model of motivation, a need causes a drive, which activates a(n) _____, designed to attain a goal.
9. It is not uncommon for older people to suffer from dehydration despite experiencing a lack of thirst, which means that they have a need for water but not a(n) _____.
10. You have eaten a hearty meal and are "too full." However, your mother brings out cheesecake, your favorite dessert, and you eat two pieces. Although you were not hungry, you were motivated to eat the cheesecake because of its _____ value.
11. If you were very hungry, you would probably reject fresh, live grub worms as a meal because for most people they are low in _____ value.
12. Our actions are energized by a mixture of internal needs and external _____.
13. Hunger, thirst, and pain avoidance are innate and necessary for one's survival and are, thus, classified as _____ motives.
14. The needs for activity, exploration, manipulation, and physical contact appear to be innate, but are not necessary for one's survival and are, thus, classified as _____ motives.
15. The needs for approval, status, power, and achievement are examples of _____ motives.

486

16. Biological drives are essential because they maintain our bodily equilibrium, which is called _____.
17. When you become too hot, more blood will flow through your skin and you will begin to perspire, which illustrates that the body's first reaction to disequilibrium is _____.
18. The regulation of your body's equilibrium works similar to the _____ in your house.
19. Every 24 hours, our bodies undergo a cycle of biological changes called _____ rhythms.
20. Body temperature, blood pressure, and amino acid levels shift from hour to hour with a person feeling more motivated and alert once a day when these levels are at their_____.
21. Jet lag and shift work both can cause fatigue, irritability, upset stomach, and depression because there is a mismatch between the sun and clocks and your _____ .
22. If a person experiences a major time zone shift of five hours or more, the time it takes for the body to resynchronize can be up to _____ weeks.
23. Regarding directions, adaptation to time zone shifts is relatively easy if you fly _____.
24. Exposure to short periods of bright light early in the morning can reset one's biological clock because bright light reduces the amount of a brain chemical produced by the pineal gland called _____.
25. Gradually matching your sleep-waking cycle to a new time schedule is known as _____.

Part 1: Connections

1. ___ motivation
2. ___ alexithymia
3. ___ melatonin
4. ___ preadaptation
5. ___ incentive value
6. ___ biological motives
7. ___ stimulus motives
8. ___ learned motives

a. inability to name emotions with a lack of awareness of one's own emotions and those of others
b. the appeal of a goal above and beyond its ability to fill a need
c. innate needs for activity and information but not necessary for survival
d. needs that are not innate and explain many human activities, and include the need for achievement, power, and affiliation
e. internal processes that initiate, sustain, direct, and terminate activities
f. hormone produced by pineal gland that induces sleep
g. gradually matching one's sleep-waking cycle to a new time schedule
h. innate needs that must be met for survival

Part 2: Connections

1. ___ need
2. ___ drive
3. ___ response
4. ___ goal
5. ___ homeostasis
6. ___ circadian rhythms

a. any action, glandular activity, or other identifiable behavior
b. target or objective of motivated behavior
c. cyclical changes in bodily functions and arousal levels that vary on a schedule approximating a 24-hour day
d. psychological expression of internal needs or valued goals, such as hunger, thirst, or for success
e. internal deficiency that may energize behavior
f. steady state of bodily equilibrium

Check Your Memory

1. TRUE or FALSE   A person who is unable to name his emotions and is only vaguely aware of them has a condition known as aphasic agnosia.
2. TRUE or FALSE   Motivation consists of the internal processes that initiate, sustain, direct, and terminate behavior.
3. TRUE or FALSE   An internal deficiency is known as a drive, which causes an energized motivational state known as a need.
4. TRUE or FALSE   People can suffer a bodily need for water despite experiencing a lack of thirst.
5. TRUE or FALSE   Incentive value refers to the value of a goal above and beyond its ability to fill a need.
6. TRUE or FALSE   Although you are very hungry, you will probably not eat the liver and onions in your parents' refrigerator because this food dish has low incentive value.
7. TRUE or FALSE   The incentive value of goals helps explain motives that do not seem to come from internal needs, such as drives for success, status, and approval.
8. TRUE or FALSE   Stimulus motives are not innate, but they must be met for individual survival.
9. TRUE or FALSE   Pain avoidance, hunger and thirst are considered biological motives.
10. TRUE or FALSE   Stimulus motives include the needs for power, affiliation, approval, achievement, and security.
11. TRUE or FALSE   Biological drives are essential because they maintain homeostasis.
12. TRUE or FALSE   The first reactions to disequilibrium in the human body are automatic.
13. TRUE or FALSE   People are usually less motivated, less alert, and often sleepy at the peak of their circadian rhythm.
14. TRUE or FALSE   For major time zone shifts (five hours or more), it can take up to two weeks to resynchronize.
15. TRUE or FALSE   If you fly east, adapting in relatively easy, while flying west requires a much longer adaptation time.
16. TRUE or FALSE   Adjusting to jet lag is slowest when you stay indoors, where you can sleep and eat on "home time."
17. TRUE or FALSE   A 30-minute exposure to bright light late in the late afternoon is helpful for resetting one's circadian rhythm.
18. TRUE or FALSE   Bright light affects the timing of body rhythms by increasing the amount of acetylcholine produced by the pituitary gland.
19. TRUE or FALSE   If you can anticipate an upcoming body rhythm change, it is best to preadapt to your new schedule.
20. TRUE or FALSE   Gradually matching your sleep-waking cycle to a new time schedule is known as sleep restriction.

Critical Thinking Question

Many people mistakenly believe that they suffer from "hypoglycemia" (low blood sugar), which is often blamed for fatigue, difficulty concentrating, irritability, and other symptoms. Why is it unlikely that many people actually have hypoglycemia?

Module 9.2 Hunger, Thirst, Pain, and Sex
Hunger—Pardon Me, My Hypothalamus Is Growling
Survey Question: What causes hunger? Overeating? Eating disorders?

488

Language Development Guide
Module 9.2

instructive: something you can learn from

pardon me: I'm sorry

my hypothalamus is growling: a reference to the fact it is the hypothalamus in the brain that creates hunger, not a growling stomach

originate: begin

contractions: muscles get suddenly tighter and possibly painful

hunger pangs: extreme feeling of hunger

inflated conclusion: joke; inflated could mean filled with air, or in this context, an exaggeration

distended: swollen; inflated; bloated

remember last Thanksgiving?: asking if the person remembers overeating at Thanksgiving dinner

promote: encourage; advance

suppress: hold back

no single "hunger thermostat": not one part of body or brain that regulates hunger

satiety: signal that you are full, that you have eaten enough

balloon up: increase in weight

incidentally: before I forget; by the way

munchies: a craving for food

show promise: has the potential; looks good

spare tire is well-inflated: joke; normal reference is an extra wheel in your car has air in it - in this context a reference to extra fat around one's stomach or waist

radical: extreme

self-starvation: purposely denying oneself food

dramatic: remarkable

overtaking: out doing; leaving behind

stigma: rejected or criticized by society, perceived as a negative characteristic, mark or sign of shame

plentiful: plenty of; abundant

Frosh 15: slang for a 15 pound weight gain occurring during the first year of college

culprit: guilty party

dulls: reduces

"sweet tooth": a craving or fondness for sweets

cheese Danish: a sweet baked pastry (baked good)

delightful: wonderful

aversion: extreme dislike

fad diet: a food plan that is popular for a short time

grapefruit: citrus fruit; one fad diet was to eat only grapefruits to lose weight

prone: naturally inclined to do something

fat-conscious: an awareness of and focus on people's sizes and weights

revolting: disgusting; awful

delicacy: a special and often expensive food

by the same token: likewise

vegans: persons who avoid using or eating any animal products

vegetarians: persons eat a plant-based diet and no meat, but may or may not eat eggs or dairy products

barbaric: cruel and primitive

"supermarket" diet: a wide variety of foods, many of which are high in sugar, salt, fat, and calories

gross: very obvious; serious

fast food: usually refers to any food prepared at a quick service restaurant and usually consists of high-calorie foods, such as hamburgers and fries or to frozen microwaveable foods with precooked ingredients that take very little effort to prepare

"supersized" meals: ordering and eating larger portions of meals

paradox: a contradiction (refers to the paradox of dieting in which one initially loses weight but then gains back even more weight)

scarce: limited; in short supply

bouncing between feast and famine: sometimes eating a lot and sometimes not eating

overhaul: repair; fix; make major changes

committed: dedicated to

rebound: bounce back; returning

step counter: small device worn that records (counts) every step a person makes; also called a pedometer

vigorously: energetically; briskly

"diet diary": record of when, where, and what you eat and your feelings before and after eating

"dangerous" times and places for overeating: where and when you are most tempted to overeat

sip: drinking small amounts of a beverage

wary: careful

bouillon: a broth; a thin, watery, clear soup

chart: record

realistic: sensible; practical; reasonable

"threshold": upper limit; a maximum

devastating: shocking; upsetting; destructive

self-inflicted: damaging action done to oneself

malnutrition: body does not receive adequate nutrients either through a bad or unbalanced diet, or from not eating enough food

compulsive: uncontrollable and irrational

dominate: control; rule

debilitating: extreme weakening of the body

gorge: eat very large amounts

laxatives: medicines that cause diarrhea

bingeing: consuming a lot of something at one time

purging: causing oneself to vomit

spasms: tremors; contractions

muscle dysmorphia: disorder in which person is obsessed by thoughts of not being muscular enough

altering: changing

excessive exercise: exercising much more than you need to for basic health, such as walking for four hours a day when thirty minutes is recommended

unduly: overly

distorted: misrepresented

wasting away: getting thinner and thinner

idealized: seen as a perfect image

"fans": admirers

engaged in: a part of; participating in

pole vaulting: an Olympic sport to use a long rod to propel oneself over a high bar

ridding themselves: getting rid of

self-contempt: to hate oneself

self-monitoring: observing, recording, and checking on one's own behavior

perpetuate: to cause to continue

Recite and Review

1. In a classic experiment in which a swallowed balloon with an attached tube was inflated and contracted, the researchers incorrectly concluded that hunger was caused by the contractions of an empty stomach. These researchers were Washburn and _____.

490

2. The brain receives many signals from the tongue, stomach, intestines, and liver, which all make up a person's _____ system.
3. The hypothalamus is a small area at the base of the brain that regulates many aspects of motivation and emotion, especially hunger, thirst, and _____ behavior.
4. The hypothalamus is sensitive to levels of many substances in the blood, especially levels of _____.
5. The area of the brain that is referred to as the feeding system and initiates eating is the _____ hypothalamus.
6. The area of the brain known as the satiety system that acts as a "stop mechanism" for eating is the _____ hypothalamus.
7. An animal will never eat again, unless force fed, if something destroys its _____ hypothalamus.
8. A rat with hypothalamic hyperphagia is a very fat rat due to damage to its _____ hypothalamus.
9. When you are hungry your stomach lining produces a hormone that activates the feeding system in the brain. This hormone is called _____.
10. You should consider studying before your eat rather than immediately afterward because the part of the brain involved in learning is activated by the hormone _____.
11. The part of the hypothalamus that affects hunger by both starting and stopping eating is the _____ nucleus.
12. The part of the hypothalamus that is sensitive to a substance called neuropeptide Y (NPY) is the _____.
13. An animal will eat until it cannot hold another bite when NPY is present in _____ amounts.
14. The hypothalamus also responds to a chemical found in an illicit drug and produces an intense hunger, sometimes called the "munchies." This illicit drug is _____.
15. After you eat a meal, the drive to eat will cease because the intestines release a chemical called _____.
16. You are less likely to overeat if you eat slowly because the hypothalamus does not respond to the signals from the liver and other organs for at least _____ minutes.
17. Your brain controls your weight over the long term by monitoring the amount of _____ stored in your body in specialized cells.
18. The weight you maintain when you are making no effort to gain or lose weight is called your _____.
19. Fat cells release a substance that is carried in the bloodstream to the hypothalamus where it tells us to eat less. This substance released by the fat cells is called _____.
20. Radical diets may raise the set point for fat, resulting in _____ -induced obesity.
21. The percent of adults in the United States are overweight is roughly _____ percent.
22. As a cause of needless deaths, smoking is currently in first place but is being overtaken by _____.
23. Signs and signals linked with food are called _____ cues.
24. If you are well fed, the tongue's sensitivity to sweet tastes is dulled by the chemical _____.
25. If you eat too much of any particular food, it will become _____ appealing.
26. If you got sick after eating too much ice cream, you may never eat ice cream again because you have developed a(n) _____.
27. Your active dislike of a food because the food was paired with sickness is an example of _____ conditioning.
28. Barbara is an overweight teen, who tends to overeat when she is sad or anxious. This overeating often leads to more distress due to her weight gain, and the cycle continues, illustrating how _____ eating occurs.

29. In North America, we would probably never consider eating the eyes out of the steamed head of a monkey; but in other parts of the world, it is considered a delicacy, which illustrates how one's culture affects the _____ value of foods.

30. The types and amounts of foods you regularly eat define your current _____.

31. Jared is a college student who eats lots of cookies, cheese, peanut butter, bananas, salami, and other foods that are high in fat and sugar. Jared's diet can lead to obesity and is known as the "_____" diet.

32. Food portions at restaurants in the United States are larger than they are in France by at least _____ percent.

33. People often regain more weight after going on a radical diet because dieting tends to affect the body's rate of metabolism by _____ it.

34. Repeatedly losing and gaining weight is called "_____ dieting."

35. Repeatedly losing and gaining weight may make it harder and harder each time to lose weight because this type of dieting affects a person's set point for fat by _____ it.

36. Weight reduction based on changing exercise and eating habits, rather than temporary self-starvation is called _____ dieting.

37. To prevent rebound weight gain, a person needs to exercise and burn just _____ extra calories a day.

38. It is helpful to learn your eating habits by observing yourself and keeping a(n) "_____."

39. Deena is sixteen years old and thinks she is "fat," but she is currently below 85 percent of her normal body weight for her height and her menstrual periods have stopped. Deena most likely is suffering from _____.

40. Ayna is a college freshman, who tends to eat large amounts of food, but "controls her weight" by vomiting after these large meals or using laxatives. Ayna most likely is suffering from _____.

41. More and more men are experiencing excessive worry about not being muscular enough, a disorder known as muscle _____.

42. Girls who spend a lot of time reading fashion magazines are more likely to have distorted _____ images.

43. Mia is a teen girl who would be described as a "perfect" daughter, always helpful, considerate, conforming, and obedient. She appears to be seeking perfect control in her life by being perfectly slim. Mia is most likely suffering from _____.

44. Persons with bulimia often are obsessed with thoughts of weight and food and feel anxiety and guilt. The vomiting reduces this anxiety and guilt, which makes purging highly _____.

45. Treatment for anorexia and bulimia may include drugs to relieve obsessive fears, a medical diet, self-monitoring of food intake, and changing maladaptive thinking patterns and beliefs about weight and body shape through the use of a(n) _____ approach.

Part 1: Connections

1. _____ ventromedial hypothalamus
2. _____ lateral hypothalamus
3. _____ paraventricular nucleus

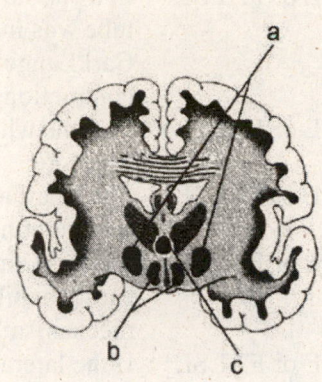

Part 2: Connections

1. ___ lateral hypothalamus
2. ___ ventromedial hypothalamus
3. ___ paraventricular nucleus
4. ___ ghrelin
5. ___ neuropeptide Y (NPY)
6. ___ glucagon-like peptide 1 (GLP-1)
7. ___ leptin
8. ___ set point

a. substance that affects the paraventricular nucleus and in large amounts will cause an animal to eat until it cannot hold another bite
b. part of brain that acts as a satiety system
c. part of brain that acts as feeding system
d. substance released by fat cells that signals the hypothalamus for the person to eat less
e. proportion of body fat that you tend to maintain when you are making no effort to gain or lose weight
f. part of brain that keeps blood sugar levels steady by both starting and stopping eating
g. chemical released by the intestines and ends one's desire to eat
h. hormone produced by stomach lining when hungry and also activates parts of the brain involved in learning

Part 3: Connections

1. ___ diet-induced obesity
2. ___ external eating cues
3. ___ taste aversion
4. ___ "supermarket" diet
5. ___ "Yo-yo dieting"
6. ___ behavioral dieting
7. ___ anorexia nervosa
8. ___ bulimia nervosa

a. diets with high fat and sugar content that encourage overeating
b. repeatedly losing and gaining weight
c. active self-starvation with body weight below 85 percent of normal
d. gorging on food, then vomiting or taking laxatives to avoid gaining weight
e. an active dislike for a particular food
f. results from radical diets raising one's set point for fat
g. weight reduction based on changing exercise and eating habits
h. signs and signals linked with food

493

Check Your Memory

1. TRUE or FALSE   In a classic experiment in which a swallowed balloon with an attached tube was inflated and contracted, the researchers William James and Carl Lange correctly concluded that hunger was caused by the contractions of an empty stomach.

2. TRUE or FALSE   Persons who have had their stomachs removed do not feel hunger anymore.

3. TRUE or FALSE   The small area in the forebrain known as the pons is especially important in regulating motives, including hunger, thirst, and the sex drive.

4. TRUE or FALSE   The ventromedial hypothalamus acts as a feeding system that initiates eating, while the lateral hypothalamus acts as a satiety system, or "stop mechanism" for eating.

5. TRUE or FALSE   If the lateral hypothalamus is destroyed, the animal may never eat again, unless force fed.

6. TRUE or FALSE   Damage to a rat's ventromedial hypothalamus can produce a very fat rat with a condition called hypothalamic hyperphagia.

7. TRUE or FALSE   Your stomach lining produces, neuropeptide Y, which activates the lateral hypothalamus and causes you to stop eating.

8. TRUE or FALSE   The paraventricular nucleus of the hypothalamus helps keep blood sugar levels steady by both starting and stopping eating.

9. TRUE or FALSE   Because of how hormones produced by the stomach act, it is best for students to study after they eat and not immediately before.

10. TRUE or FALSE   The hypothalamus responds to a chemical in marijuana, which can produce intense hunger (the "munchies").

11. TRUE or FALSE   After you eat a meal, glucagon-like peptide 1 (GLP-1) is released by the intestines and causes eating to cease.

12. TRUE or FALSE   It takes at least 10 minutes for the hypothalamus to respond after you begin eating.

13. TRUE or FALSE   Your set point is the weight you maintain when you are making no effort to gain or lose weight.

14. TRUE or FALSE   When your body weight goes below the set point, you will stop feeling hungry.

15. TRUE or FALSE   Fat cells release a substance called leptin, which is carried in the bloodstream to the hypothalamus, where it tells us to eat less.

16. TRUE or FALSE   There is currently no known way to lower your set point for fat, since the number of fat cells remains unchanged throughout adult life.

17. TRUE or FALSE   Radical diets can lower the set point for fat, resulting in diet-induced anorexia.

18. TRUE or FALSE   Roughly 65 percent of adults in the United States are overweight with more than one-third being obese.

19. TRUE or FALSE   Many college freshmen gain weight rapidly during their first three months on campus with all-you-can-eat dining halls in the dorms and nighttime snacking appearing to be the causes.

20. TRUE or FALSE   The presence of others can affect whether people overeat (or undereat) depending on how much everyone else is eating and how important it is to impress others.

21. TRUE or FALSE   If you are well fed, leptin tends to increase and enhance the tongue's sensitivity to sweet tastes.

22. TRUE or FALSE   If you eat too much of any particular food, it will become less appealing.

494

23. TRUE or FALSE   Taste aversion is a type of operant conditioning.
24. TRUE or FALSE   Taste aversions may help people avoid severe nutritional imbalances.
25. TRUE or FALSE   People with weight problems are prone to overeat when they are anxious, angry, or sad.
26. TRUE or FALSE   Cultural values greatly affect the incentive value of foods.
27. TRUE or FALSE   In general, sweetness, high fat content, and variety tend to discourage overeating and help one maintain a healthy weight.
28. TRUE or FALSE   Food portions in France are 25 percent larger than they are in the United States.
29. TRUE or FALSE   The French take longer to eat a meal, which discourages overeating.
30. TRUE or FALSE   Although dieters do lose weight, most regain it soon after they stop dieting.
31. TRUE or FALSE   Dieting speeds up the body's rate of metabolism, making the dieter's body less efficient in conserving calories and storing them as fat.
32. TRUE or FALSE   Weight reduction based on changing exercise and eating habits, rather than temporary self-starvation is known as "yo-yo dieting."
33. TRUE or FALSE   Burning just 200 extra calories a day through exercise can help prevent rebound weight gains.
34. TRUE or FALSE   To help weight reduction, you should eat in different rooms of the house to discourage eating cues and also do another activity while eating, such as reading, watching TV, studying, or talking on the phone.
35. TRUE or FALSE   People who diet moderately every day lose significantly more weight than a person who intensely diets every other day.
36. TRUE or FALSE   It is generally better to eat more small meals a day than fewer large ones because more calories are burned.
37. TRUE or FALSE   Even though, persons suffering from anorexia do not seek food, they often still feel physical hunger.
38. TRUE or FALSE   From five to eight percent of people with anorexia die of malnutrition.
39. TRUE or FALSE   About 10 percent of people with anorexia and 25 percent of people with bulimia are now males.
40. TRUE or FALSE   In a study by Zellner and associates, women with abnormal eating disorders chose an ideal figure that was much heavier than what they thought their current weights were.
41. TRUE or FALSE   People engaged in sports, such as wrestling, gymnastics, high jumping, and cycling are particularly likely to develop eating disorders.
42. TRUE or FALSE   Anorexic teen girls are usually described as "perfect" daughters and appear to be trying to gain some measure of control.
43. TRUE or FALSE   People suffering from bulimia often feel anxiety and guilt with the vomiting increasing this anxiety and guilt, thus making purging a form of severe punishment.
44. TRUE or FALSE   Most people suffering from eating disorders will not seek help on their own, especially men.
45. TRUE or FALSE   Treatment for anorexia usually begins with giving drugs to relieve obsessive fears of gaining weight.
46. TRUE or FALSE   Therapy for anorexia and bulimia most often involves a psychoanalytic approach, which focuses on their unconscious conflicts about weight and control.

Critical Thinking Question

Kim, who is overweight, is highly sensitive to external eating cues. How might her wristwatch contribute to her overeating?

Module 9.2 Hunger, Thirst, Pain, and Sex
Biological Motives Revisited—Thirst, Pain, and Sex

Survey Questions: Is there more than one type of thirst? In what ways are pain avoidance and the sex drive unusual?

Language Development Guide

retain: hold

nomadic: people who travel, who have no permanent home

prize: value; treasure

Gatorade: a drink taken especially after exercise to help restore minerals lost through perspiration

quenched: satisfied; reduced

"tough": strong

endure: bear; tolerate

cutting: body mutilation involving slashing one's own skin

agonize: hurt

apparently: it seems that; in fact

devotees: supporters; fans; people who enjoy

body art: tattoos and other permanent body decoration

contrary: the opposite

castration: surgical or chemical procedures that either remove or destroy the functioning of the sex organs

abolish: put an end to; eliminate

aroused: stimulated

primarily: mainly; for the most part

receptive: willing to mate

puberty: biologically defined period during which a person matures sexually and becomes capable of reproduction

corresponding: matching; related

supplements: additional substances

erotic: sexual

inhibitions: something that blocks or restrains behavior

no doubt: surely

accounts: explains

reputation: something a object or person is known for

seduction: luring or tempting someone into having sex

Ogden Nash: American humorist and poet

dandy: fine

Candy is dandy, but liquor is quicker: romance can be seductive, but a woman's defense to having sex can be lowered more rapidly by serving her alcohol

suppresses: holds back; blocks

orgasm: sexual climax

reputed: supposed; presumed

impair: harm

amyl nitrite: chemical that dilates blood vessels

virtually: almost; nearly

496

Recite and Review

1. Thirst is regulated by separate thirst and thirst satiety systems in the part of the brain called the _____.
2. When water is lost from the fluids surrounding the cells of your body, the result is a(n) _____ thirst.
3. When fluid is drawn out of cells due to an increased concentration of salts and minerals outside the cell, the thirst that is triggered is a(n)_____ thirst.
4. Bleeding, vomiting, diarrhea, sweating, and drinking alcohol cause _____ thirst.
5. If you eat a large bag of salty potato chips, you will most likely experience _____ thirst.
6. A beverage containing salts and minerals, like a sports drink will be most satisfying when you have a(n) _____ thirst.
7. Plain water would be the best beverage to satisfy a(n) _____ thirst.
8. Hunger, thirst, and sleepiness come and go in a fairly regular cycle each day, but pain avoidance, by contrast, is a(n) _____ drive.
9. Through observation of family members, friends, and other role models, a person's level of pain tolerance is _____.
10. The strength of one's motivation to engage in sexual behavior is referred to as the _____.
11. In lower animals, the motivation to engage in sexual behavior is directly related to the release of the male and female sex _____.
12. Female mammals (other than humans) are interested in mating only when their fertility cycles are in "heat," also called the stage of _____.
13. The "heat" cycle is caused by the release of a female hormone called _____ into the bloodstream.
14. In most animals, the sex drive can be abolished through a procedure known as _____.
15. The sex drive in men is related to the amount of male hormones, including testosterone, that are released from the testes. These male hormones are known as _____.
16. In addition to estrogen, a woman's body produces small amounts of other hormones that will affect her sex drive. These hormones are called _____.
17. In small doses, alcohol may stimulate erotic desire by lowering _____.
18. Getting drunk affects sexual desire, arousal, pleasure, and performance by _____ it.
19. Substances that increase sexual desire or pleasure are called _____.
20. Regarding the human sexual response, amphetamines, amyl nitrite, barbiturates, and cocaine tend to _____ it.
21. Regarding the human sexual response, Ecstasy, LSD, and marijuana tend to _____ it.
22. The human sex drive is relatively independent of bodily need states, which means that the human sex drive is largely _____.
23. The amount of time since the human sex drive was last satisfied does not seem to increase or decrease the sex drive, which means that no clear relationship exists between the human sex drive and _____.

Connections

1. ____ extracellular thirst

2. ____ intracellular thirst

3. ____ episodic drive
4. ____ sex drive

a. any of a number of male sex hormones, especially testosterone
b. strength of one's motivation to engage in sexual behavior
c. any of a number of female sex hormones
d. substances that increase sexual desire or pleasure

5. ___ estrus

6. ___ estrogens

7. ___ androgens

8. ___ non-homeostatic drive
9. ___ aphrodisiacs

e. any drive that is relatively independent of physical deprivation cycles or bodily need states

f. thirst triggered when fluid is drawn out of cells due to an increased concentration of salts and minerals outside the cell

g. stage of fertility cycle when female mammals (other than humans) are interested in mating; also referred to as "heat"

h. non-cyclical drive, such as pain avoidance

i. thirst caused by a reduction in the volume of fluids found between body cells

Check Your Memory

1. TRUE or FALSE   If you were to take a drug that made your mouth constantly wet, or dry, your water intake would remain normal.

2. TRUE or FALSE   Thirst is regulated by separate thirst and thirst satiety systems in the hypothalamus.

3. TRUE or FALSE   Intracellular thirst occurs when water is lost from the fluids surrounding the cells of your body.

4. TRUE or FALSE   Extracellular thirst occurs when excess salt causes fluid to be drawn out of cells.

5. TRUE or FALSE   Some nomadic peoples of the Sahara Desert prize blood as a beverage, probably because of its saltiness.

6. TRUE or FALSE   Bleeding, vomiting, diarrhea, sweating, and drinking alcohol cause intracellular thirst.

7. TRUE or FALSE   Extracellular thirst is usually quenched by drinking plain water, while a slightly salty beverage, such as a sports drink, will best satisfy an intracellular thirst.

8. TRUE or FALSE   Hunger, thirst, and sleepiness come and go on a fairly regular cycle each day, while pain avoidance, by contrast, is an episodic drive.

9. TRUE or FALSE   Pain tolerance is learned by observing family members, friends, and other role models.

10. TRUE or FALSE   In all mammals, sex is necessary for both individual survival and for group survival.

11. TRUE or FALSE   Female mammals (other than humans) are interested in mating only when their fertility cycles are in the stage of estrus, or "heat," which is caused by a release of estrogen into the bloodstream.

12. TRUE or FALSE   In most animals, castration will abolish the sex drive.

13. TRUE or FALSE   Hormones affect the human sex drive, but not as directly as in other animals.

14. TRUE or FALSE   Both men and women produce androgens, which affect their sex drives.

15. TRUE or FALSE   In large doses, alcohol increases sexual desire, arousal, pleasure, and performance.

16. TRUE or FALSE   Substances that are reputed to increase sexual desire or pleasure are called aphrodisiacs.

17. TRUE or FALSE   Amphetamines, amyl nitrite, barbiturates, cocaine tend to increase and enhance sexual response.

18. TRUE or FALSE   Ecstasy, LSD, and marijuana tend to impair sexual response.

498

19. TRUE or FALSE   The sex drive in humans is homeostatic and shows a clear relationship to deprivation.
20. TRUE or FALSE   People may seek to arouse the sex drive as well as to reduce it.

Module 9.3 Arousal, Achievement, and Growth Needs

Stimulus Drives—Skydiving, Horror Movies, and the Fun Zone

Survey Question: How does arousal relate to motivation?

Language Development Guide

skydiving: sport of parachuting out of a plane
"diet": routine; schedule
mere: simple
scan: search; examine; check
sheer: pure; total
surfing the web: going online, exploring on the Internet
cage diving: going under water in a safety cage to watch sharks feeding
bungee jumping: sport of jumping off a bridge with an elastic cord tied around one's ankles
white-water rafting: traveling on an inflatable boat down a fast and rocky river
bold: brave; daring; confident
bland: mild to tasteless
orderly: neat and organized
nurturant: caring
dark side: negative, hidden aspect
set aside: do not include
below par: poorly
inverted: overturned; reversed
sufficiently: adequately
drop off: decrease
frenzied: hyperactive; frantic
stalled: stuck
bearing down on you: coming at you
complexity: difficulty
sprinters: athlete who runs a short distance at his or her fastest speed
tournament-deciding: determines whether he or she will win the competition or not
putt: striking the golf ball lightly with the golf club so that it rolls directly into a small hole in the ground
antidote: cure
going blank: forgetting the information one should know
combat: fight; oppose; contend with
end of the world: the worst possible thing that could happen
testy: irritable; grumpy; bad-tempered

Recite and Review

1. The needs for information, exploration, manipulation, and sensory input are called _____ motives.
2. The activation of the body and nervous system is known as _____.
3. People try to maintain the activation of their bodies and nervous systems at ideal, or comfortable, levels, according to the _____ theory.
4. At death, it is zero, in sleep it is low, moderate during normal daily activities, and high during times of excitement, emotion, or panic. This is at description of one's usual levels of _____.
5. Sensation seeking is a trait of people who prefer high levels of _____.

6. People who tend to be bold and independent, value change, report more sex partners, are more likely to smoke, and prefer sour and crunchy foods are people who are _____ in sensation-seeking.
7. Mae would be described as orderly, nurturant, and giving, and she enjoys the company of others. Mae's level of sensation seeking is most likely _____.
8. People who engage in risky behaviors, such as substance abuse are more likely to be _____ sensation seekers.
9. If we set aside individual differences, most people perform best when their arousal level is _____.
10. The relationship between arousal and performance forms a(n) _____ function.
11. The ideal level of arousal depends on the _____ of a task.
12. When a task is relatively simple, it is best for arousal to be _____.
13. If the task is complex, it is best for arousal to be _____.
14. The relationships among arousal, task complexity, and performance are explained by the _____ law.
15. A golfer making a putt would probably perform best at a(n) _____ level of arousal.
16. A track star running in the 50 meter dash track would probably perform best at a(n) _____ level of arousal.
17. Test anxiety is a mixture of heightened physiological arousal and excessive _____.
18. The most direct antidote for test anxiety is _____.
19. By studying long before the test day, one's test anxiety can be reduced through _____.
20. One can lower the physiological symptoms of test anxiety by learning _____ techniques.
21. Test anxiety can also be lowered through one's friends providing _____.
22. To reduce nervousness from the possibility of going blank or running out of time, one should plan and _____ how to cope with these situations.
23. Another helpful strategy involves listing the upsetting thoughts you usually have during exams and then coming up with calming, rational replies, or _____ statements, for each one.

Connections

1. ___ arousal
2. ___ stimulus motives

3. ___ arousal theory

4. ___ high in sensation seeking

5. ___ low in sensation seeking

6. ___ inverted U function

7. ___ Yerkes-Dodson law

8. ___ test anxiety

9. ___ coping statements

a. activation of the body and the nervous system
b. tend to be bold, independent, value change, more likely to smoke, and prefer sour and crunchy foods
c. high levels of arousal and worry that seriously impair performance on assessments
d. explains the relationships among arousal, task complexity, and performance
e. based on needs for exploration, manipulation, curiosity, and stimulation
f. tend to be orderly, nurturant, and giving, and enjoy the company of others
g. calm, rational replies that are used to combat one's worries
h. states that people prefer to maintain ideal, or comfortable, levels of arousal and will seek ways to raise or lower it to maintain this optimal level
i. explains the relationship of arousal and performance with people performing best, in general, at a moderate level or arousal

Check Your Memory

1. TRUE or FALSE — Stimulus drives reflect needs for information, exploration, manipulation, and sensory input.
2. TRUE or FALSE — The drive for information and exploration does not occur until the child reaches approximately age four.
3. TRUE or FALSE — Stimulus drives occur in humans, but not in other animals.
4. TRUE or FALSE — According to the James-Lange theory, we try to keep our level of arousal at the highest level possible.
5. TRUE or FALSE — Arousal refers to the activation of the body and the nervous system.
6. TRUE or FALSE — Arousal is zero at death, low during sleep, moderate during normal daily activities, and high at times of excitement, emotion, or stress.
7. TRUE or FALSE — Whether you are high or low in sensation seeking is probably based on how your body responds to new, unusual, or intense stimulation.
8. TRUE or FALSE — People high in sensation seeking tend to be orderly, nurturant, and giving, and they enjoy the company of others.
9. TRUE or FALSE — People high in sensation seeking report having more sexual partners, are more likely to smoke, and prefer spicy, sour, and crunchy foods.
10. TRUE or FALSE — If individual differences are set aside, most people perform best when their arousal level is moderate.
11. TRUE or FALSE — The relationship between arousal and performance forms a U-shaped pattern, in which performance decreases as your arousal level increases, up to the middle of the curve then it improves as arousal decreases.
12. TRUE or FALSE — If a task is more complex, your best performance will occur at higher levels of arousal.
13. TRUE or FALSE — The relationships among arousal, task complexity, and performance is called the Yerkes-Dodson law.
14. TRUE or FALSE — Test anxiety is a mixture of heightened physiological arousal and excessive worry.
15. TRUE or FALSE — Hard work is the most direct antidote for test anxiety.
16. TRUE or FALSE — Overpreparing for a test usually increases one's test anxiety.
17. TRUE or FALSE — Self-relaxation skills can be learned and used to lower one's test anxiety.
18. TRUE or FALSE — To reduce nervousness before a test, you should rehearse how you will cope with upsetting events, such as going blank on a test or running out of time.
19. TRUE or FALSE — You can learn to combat worries that cause test anxiety by using calming, replies known as humorous irrational beliefs.
20. TRUE or FALSE — Becoming a more confident test taker can actually increase your test scores.

Module 9.3 Arousal, Achievement, and Growth Need

Learned Motives—The Pursuit of Excellence

Survey Questions: What are learned motives? Social motives? Why are they important?

Language Development Guide

pursuit: search
status: importance, rank, privilege
affiliation: being with people, having friends
strive: try hard
prestige: fame
relish: enjoy; take pleasure in

true grit: a phrase meaning to be brave and determined; also the name of a famous American western movie and its recent remake

perseverance: determination; persistent

passion: enthusiasm

when the going gets tough, high achievers (the tough) get going: phrase means when situations get difficult, those who are strong and determined continue to work hard.

elite: the best

reserved: set aside; kept back

dedicated: committed; devoted to a purpose

tackle: undertake; begin; deal with

attainable: within reach; possible

master: to become skilled in

emulate: try to be like; to imitate

regard it as a sign: recognize

cultivating: developing; working on

impact: influence; affect

prestigious: high-status; impressive; prominent

exploit: take advantage of; misuse; manipulate

dark side: hidden, negative aspect

American dream: to live better than their parents did

poorly adjusted: unable to deal with everyday demands and stresses

expose: to provide access to some influence

"just for fun": not for a grade or other external reward

"living" for their talent: enjoying an activity so much that it becomes the most important thing in one's life

heights of achievement: upper levels of skill and expertise

upshot: outcome; results

blossom: to develop and grow

prodigies: highly talented children

eminent: famous or important

ingredients: factors; parts; elements

pursuits: activities you wish to excel in or hobbies you enjoy

"talent will surface" on its own: the belief that talent is innate and natural and requires no practice or hard work

largely a myth: mostly false

Recite and Review

1. Acquired through cultural conditioning, success, achievement, status, grades, and power are all a type of learned needs known as _____ motives.
2. The desire to excel or to meet some internalized standard of excellence is referred to as the need for _____.
3. In general, exceptional success comes not from great natural talent, but from drive and _____.
4. College students high in the need for achievement attribute success to their own _____.
5. College students high in the need for achievement attribute failure to insufficient _____.
6. Students complete difficult tasks, earn better grades, renew their efforts when they perform poorly, and tend to excel in their occupations when they have a high need for _____.
7. Like elite athletes, people can improve their motivation by increasing their _____.

502

8. When tackling an important task, you should set goals that are specific and challenging, but _____.

9. When dealing with an important task, it is recommended that a person advance in small steps toward his or her goals and to _____ these steps.

10. When you first acquire a skill, your goal should be to make _____ in learning the skill.

11. The challenges you will undertake, the effort you will make, and how long you will persist when things don't go well are all affected by whether or not a person has _____.

12. Ira enjoys challenges, relishes the chance to test his abilities, and strives to do well any time he is evaluated. Ira has a strong need for _____.

13. Tyrone buys expensive possessions and wears prestigious clothes in order that others known how important he is. He likes to make an impact on other or to have control over them, often exploiting his relationships to his benefit. Tyrone has a strong need for _____.

14. People tend to be poorly adjusted and unhappy when their main goal in life is to make _____.

15. In fostering high achievement, Bloom found that the parents initially exposed their children to art or music or sports, etc. "just for fun'; but after the children began to actively cultivate their abilities, the parent provided a(n) _____.

16. Elite performance in music, sports, chess, the arts, and many other pursuits typically requires dedicated practice for at least _____ years.

Connections

1. ___ social motives
2. ___ need for achievement (nAch)
3. ___ need for power
4. ___ self-confidence

a. desire to excel or meet some internalized standard of excellence
b. believing that one can successfully carry out an activity or reach a goal
c. desire to have social impact and control over others
d. learned motives acquired as part of growing up in a particular culture

Check Your Memory

1. TRUE or FALSE   We acquire social motives, such as success, grades, money, and achievement through socialization and cultural conditioning.

2. TRUE or FALSE   The desire to meet an internal standard of excellence is referred to as the need for power.

3. TRUE or FALSE   A need for achievement is the same as having a need for power.

4. TRUE or FALSE   People with strong needs for achievement want their importance to be visible, so they buy expensive possessions, wear prestigious clothes, and exploit relationships.

5. TRUE or FALSE   Research has shown that drive and determination lead to exceptional success in most fields.

6. TRUE or FALSE   People who are high in the need for achievement earn better grades and excel in their occupations.

7. TRUE or FALSE   College students high in the need for achievement attribute success to their own ability and failure to insufficient effort.

8. TRUE or FALSE   People whose main goal in life is to make lots of money tend to be poorly adjusted and unhappy.

9. TRUE or FALSE   When you are first acquire a skill, you should concentrate on improving your performance by comparing yourself to how well other people are performing.

10. TRUE or FALSE   Self-confidence can be enhanced by setting goals that are specific and challenging, but attainable, and to advance toward these goals in small steps.

11. TRUE or FALSE   If you fail in meeting your goal, regard it as a sign that you need to find a different skill to learn.

12. TRUE or FALSE   Self-confidence affects motivation by influencing the challenges you will undertake, the effort you will make, and how long you will persist when things do not go well.

13. TRUE or FALSE   The first steps toward high achievement begin when parents expose their children to music, art, sports, scientific ideas, and so forth, "just for fun."

14. TRUE or FALSE   Those who became exceptional in their fields actually began with very ordinary skills as children.

15. TRUE or FALSE   Studies of child prodigies and eminent adults show that their talent just magically surfaced and was not the result of intensive practice or expert coaching.

Module 9.3 Arousal, Achievement, and Growth Need
Motives in Perspective—A View from the Pyramid
Survey Question: Are some motives more basic than others?

Language Development Guide

in perspective: taking a reasonable appraisal something
pyramid: structure or three-dimensional shape made of triangles (model for Maslow's theory)
proposed: suggested; put forward
potential: what one is capable of becoming
fragile: easily broken; delicate
life-enhancing: making life more enjoyable
personal growth: developing toward one's potential
actualizing: realizing; making it real
humanly: by all means
essence: core; real meaning
spontaneity: natural without constraints
benevolence: kindness; compassion
uniqueness: distinct; one of kind
ease: effortlessness
autonomy: independence
self-sufficiency: independent and self-supporting
syndrome of decay: poor psychological health
apathy: lack of interest
alienation: isolation
vitality: energy
documented: supported by
fasts: voluntarily does not eat
social protest: a strong reaction against perceived social injustices in an effort to change them
temporary: brief
self-imposed: voluntarily chosen to endure
objections: oppositions to; protests
uniformity: consistency; sameness
drudgery: dull and tiring work
opportunity: chance

504

stems from: comes from
obligations: duties; responsibilities
spontaneous: natural; unplanned
lavishly: richly, excessively
coerced: forced
bribed: paid for favors
faking it: acting a lie
initiative: being resourceful; inventive
bonuses: extra pay or extra benefits
innovative: inventive; original
phased out: to bring to an end in steps or stages

Recite and Review

1. The full use of one's personal potential is called _____.
2. The hierarchy of human needs depicted in the form of a pyramid was proposed by the humanistic psychologist _____.
3. At the base or bottom of the pyramid of human needs are the _____ needs.
4. Because the needs at the base of the pyramid must be met if we are to survive, they tend to be dominant over the higher needs and are said to be _____.
5. If you are feeling threatened, then you are lacking in the needs for _____.
6. The first four levels of the hierarchy of needs are called _____ needs.
7. The needs you have for your family and friends would be encompassed by the _____ needs.
8. The needs for recognition and self-respect make up the needs for _____.
9. Because these lower four levels of needs are activated by a lack of food, security, love, etc., they are also referred to as _____ needs.
10. At the top of the hierarchy are the needs that are expressed as the need for self-actualization. These needs are called _____ needs.
11. Wholeness, perfection, completion, justice, richness, simplicity, aliveness, beauty, goodness, uniqueness, playfulness, truth, autonomy, and meaningfulness make up the _____.
12. When the higher needs of the hierarchy go unfulfilled, people fall into a "syndrome of _____."
13. On ratings of vitality, self-actualization, and general well-being, college students who are primarily concerned with money, personal appearance, and social recognition tend to score _____ than average.
14. Few people are primarily motivated by needs for self-actualization with most being concerned with esteem, love, or _____.
15. Tamara reads numerous books because she enjoys reading and learning new information. Tamara's motivation for reading would be described as _____.
16. Mark studies in order to get good grades and to please his parents. Mark's motivation for studying would be described as _____.
17. When you freely choose to do something for enjoyment or to improve your abilities, your motivation is usually intrinsic, according to the _____ theory.
18. Most of the activities we think of as "work" are _____ rewarded.
19. Excessive rewards can decrease spontaneous interest and _____ motivation.
20. People are more likely to be creative when they are _____ motivated.
21. On the job, salaries and bonuses may increase the amount of work done, but work quality is affected more by personal interest and freedom of choice, which are _____ factors.

505

22. If basic skills are lacking in schools, a parent may wish to motivate the child with small rewards that would eventually be phased out. This would be a good use of _____ motivation.

Part 1: Connections

1. _____ safety and security
2. _____ basic needs
3. _____ love and belonging
4. _____ self-actualization
5. _____ physiological needs
6. _____ esteem and self-esteem
7. _____ growth needs

Part 2: Connections

1. ___ self-determination theory
2. ___ hierarchy of human needs
3. ___ prepotent
4. ___ basic needs
5. ___ meta-needs
6. ___ intrinsic motivation
7. ___ extrinsic motivation

a. motivation based on personal enjoyment of a task or activity
b. motivation based on obvious external rewards or obligations
c. theory that explains how doing things for enjoyment or to improve one's abilities can be motivating
d. needs associated with impulses for self-actualization
e. being dominant over other needs
f. Maslow's theory of motives based on their presumed strength
g. another name for the deficiency needs

Check Your Memory

1. TRUE or FALSE   Abraham Maslow called the full use of personal potential self-esteem needs.
2. TRUE or FALSE   At the base of the hierarchy of needs are the physiological needs, which are prepotent, or dominant over the higher needs.
3. TRUE or FALSE   Abraham Maslow described the first four levels of the hierarchy of needs as growth needs.
4. TRUE or FALSE   The needs for love and belonging and the needs for esteem and self-esteem are both considered basic needs.
5. TRUE or FALSE   The need for self-actualization is based on deficiencies in one's basic needs.
6. TRUE or FALSE   Maslow called the less powerful but humanly important actualization motives meta-needs.
7. TRUE or FALSE   Goodness, playfulness, beauty, perfection, and aliveness are examples of meta-needs.
8. TRUE or FALSE   When the meta-needs are unfulfilled, people fall into a "syndrome of decay" marked by despair, apathy, and alienation.
9. TRUE or FALSE   Maslow's hierarchy is well documented by scientific research.
10. TRUE or FALSE   Most people are more concerned with the needs for esteem, love, or security than the need for self-actualization.

11. TRUE or FALSE   Intrinsic motivation is based on the personal enjoyment of doing an activity or task, without any obvious external rewards.

12. TRUE or FALSE   If you study hard in order to get good grades or to get the approval of your parents or professors, then you are intrinsically motivated.

13. TRUE or FALSE   Most of the activities we think of as "work" are extrinsically motivated.

14. TRUE or FALSE   Excessive rewards can decrease intrinsic motivation and spontaneous interest.

15. TRUE or FALSE   People are more likely to be creative and their work quality improved when they receive extrinsic motivation.

16. TRUE or FALSE   In one classic study, children who were lavishly rewarded for drawing with felt-tip pens later showed little interest in playing with the pens again.

17. TRUE or FALSE   If a child has no intrinsic interest in reading, then extrinsic rewards can help increase his or her interest in reading.

18. TRUE or FALSE   If extrinsic rewards are used with children to help them improve their reading or math skills, etc., these rewards should be moderate to large and used on a continuous basis for as long as possible.

Critical Thinking Question

Many U.S. college freshmen say that "being well-off financially" is an essential life goal and that "making more money" was a very important factor in their decision to attend college. Which meta-needs are fulfilled by "making more money"?

Module 9.4 Emotion and Physiological Arousal

Inside an Emotion—How Do You Feel?

Survey Question: What happens during emotion?

Language Development Guide

terrified: scared; frightened; shocked

fleeing: running away; escaping

posture: arrangement of body, arms, and legs

stirrings: moving; strong feelings

stage fright: fear and nervousness associated with performing

choking: performing badly when normally you perform well

spoil: ruin

contempt: hatred

disrupt: upset

pounding: beating

butterflies: nervousness

contorts: twists

efficient: capable; well-organized

mutually exclusive: cannot occur at the same time

ticklish: sensitive to touch

willpower: self-control; determination

strikes: launches an attack

flinch: draw back; cringe

recoil: draw back

specializes: designed for a specific activity

bypassing: going around
phobias: intense, irrational fears
"blind": are unaware
"read": to perceive
conveyed: expressed

Recite and Review

1. Physiological arousal; changes in facial expressions, gestures, posture; and subjective feelings characterize a(n) _____.
2. The word *emotion* derives from the Latin word meaning to _____.
3. Emotions are linked to attacking, fleeing, seeking comfort, helping others, and reproducing, which are all behaviors that help us to survive and adjust to changing conditions and are known as basic _____ behaviors.
4. A major element of fear, anger, joy, and other emotions involves changes in heart rate, blood pressure, perspiration, and other bodily stirrings, which are collectively known as _____.
5. Most of the bodily changes that occur when we are fearful or angry are caused by activity in the branch of the autonomic nervous system called the _____ branch.
6. The bodily changes due to fear or anger are also due to the effects of the hormones produced by the _____ glands.
7. Outward signs of what a person is feeling, which serve to tell others what emotions we are experiencing are called _____.
8. We are usually most familiar with our own private emotional experience, which are referred to as _____.
9. When you are intensely afraid, your hands tremble, your face contorts, your posture becomes tense and defensive, and your voice changes. These are referred to as your _____.
10. Robert Plutchik has identified fear, surprise, sadness, disgust, anger, anticipation, joy, and trust (acceptance) as the eight _____ emotions.
11. When you're angry, you may feel anything from rage to simple annoyance, which shows that emotions can vary in _____.
12. Five-year-old Tupac feels both joy and fear as he eats a cookie he stole from his mom's cookie jar. Joy and fear can be mixed to yield the more complex emotion known as _____.
13. A mixture of love, anger, and fear yields the complex emotion of _____.
14. Low intensity emotional states that can last for many hours, or even days and prepare us to act in different ways are called _____.
15. You are likely to be more adaptable, make better decisions, and be more helpful, efficient, creative, and peaceful when you are in a(n) _____.
16. A person's mood fluctuates with whether his or her body temperature is at its daily low or high point, which shows that moods are closely linked to one's _____.
17. It is possible to experience both a positive and a negative emotion at the same time because positive and negative emotions are processed in different _____.
18. When you experience happiness, this positive emotion is being processed in the _____ of the brain's cerebral cortex.
19. Negative emotions, such as angry and sadness, are processed in the _____ of the brain's cerebral cortex.
20. Jermaine has a phobia of dogs and experiences disabling anxiety often without knowing why. This unexplained fear and anxiety is due to the action of the subcortex part of the brain called the _____.

508

21. Some people "blind" to emotions and are unable to "read" or understand other people's emotions when they experience damage to the part of the brain called the _____.
22. People, who are unable to "read" or understand other people's emotions have the most trouble "reading" the emotional expressions conveyed by the people's _____.

Connections

1. ___ emotion
2. ___ adaptive behaviors
3. ___ physiological changes (in emotion)
4. ___ adrenaline

5. ___ emotional expressions
6. ___ emotional feelings

7. ___ primary emotions

8. ___ moods

9. ___ left hemisphere

10. ___ right hemisphere

11. ___ amygdala

a. low-intensity, long-lasting emotional states
b. hormone that tends to arouse the body
c. part of the limbic system that produces fear responses
d. alterations in heart rate, blood pressure, perspiration, and other involuntary responses
e. includes eight identified by Robert Plutchik
f. private, subjective experience of having an emotion
g. part of the brain that processes positive emotions
h. actions that aid our attempts to survive and adjust to changing conditions
i. part of the brain that processes negative emotions
j. state characterized by physiological arousal, changes in facial expression, gestures, posture, and subjective feelings
k. outward signs that an emotion is occurring

Check Your Memory

1. TRUE or FALSE   The word *emotion* derives from the Latin word meaning "to emphasize."
2. TRUE or FALSE   Emotions are linked to many basic adaptive behaviors, such as attacking, seeking comfort, helping others, and reproduction.
3. TRUE or FALSE   Changes in heart rate, blood pressure, and perspiration are examples of emotional expressions.
4. TRUE or FALSE   The physiological changes of an emotion are caused by activity in the somatic nervous system and by the hormone serotonin, which is released by the pineal gland.
5. TRUE or FALSE   When you are intensely afraid, your hands tremble, your face contorts, your posture become tense and defensive, all of which are outward signs called subjective feelings.
6. TRUE or FALSE   The part of emotion with which we are usually most familiar is our own emotional feelings.
7. TRUE or FALSE   Robert Plutchik identified six primary emotions, which are fear, embarrassment, jealousy, joy, anger, and love.
8. TRUE or FALSE   The emotion known as guilt is a mixture of joy and fear.
9. TRUE or FALSE   A mood is the mildest form of emotion and can last for many hours, or even days.
10. TRUE or FALSE   Our moods are closely tied to circadian rhythms with our mood tending to be more positive at the peak of our circadian rhythm.
11. TRUE or FALSE   It is impossible to have both a positive and negative emotion occurring simultaneously.

12. TRUE or FALSE   The right hemisphere processes positive emotions, while the left hemisphere processes negative emotions.
13. TRUE or FALSE   Most people are more ticklish on their right sides.
14. TRUE or FALSE   The amygdala receives sensory information very directly and quickly, bypassing the cortex and allowing us to respond to potential danger before we really known what is happening.
15. TRUE or FALSE   People who suffer damage to the cerebellum become "blind" to emotion and are unable to "read" or understand other people's emotions.
16. TRUE or FALSE   People who have trouble "reading" emotions typically have the most trouble detecting the emotional expressions conveyed by people's posture and gestures.

Module 9.4 Emotion and Physiological Arousal
Physiology and Emotion—Arousal, Sudden Death, and Lying
Survey Questions: What physiological changes underlie emotion? Can "lie detectors" really detect lies?

Language Development Guide
Bushman: member of a tribe that live on the African plains
prowler: a person moving about secretly, as in search of things to steal
universal: worldwide
relative: comparative
inhibiting: stopping; obstructing
restricted: held back; controlled
conserve: save
collapse: breakdown; falling down
rebound: return; bouncing back
savage: cruel; inflicting much pain and suffering
literally: factually
civilian: nonmilitary
backwoods midwife: a person in a remote area who can assist with delivering a baby
criminals: those who commit a serious crime that could result in jail time
convictions: found guilty of breaking the law; guilty verdict or sentence
confession: the person's statement that he or she is guilty of the crime
if you can't count on someone's word: if you cannot believe what a person tells you is the truth
detecting: identifying; distinguishing; uncovering
falsehoods: lies
accompany: go together with
invasion of privacy: the wrongful probe or investigation of the private areas of a person's life by another individual, the government, or other institution
suspect: the person one thinks may have committed the crime
"hooked up": connected to
conductance: a substance's ability to conduct an electric current
violating: disobeying
restraining order: a written order preventing one person from coming near, threatening, or harming another person
harassing: intensely bothering someone through threats and/or stalking (following) someone
put yourself in her place: try to imagine that you are this other person
critical: serious; important
circumstances: situations; conditions

510

documented: recorded
evidence: proof; facts
elevated: higher
alternatives: options
proponents: supporters
irrelevant: unimportant; having no connection
screen: check out; select
despite: even with
flaws: errors; faults

Recite and Review

1. The reactions of the autonomic nervous system (ANS) are nearly universal because they are
   _____.

2. The autonomic nervous system (ANS) connects the brain with the internal organs and
   _____.

3. The branch of the ANS that activates the body for emergency action is the _____
   branch.

4. The branch of the ANS that quiets the body and conserves energy is the _____ branch.

5. The branch of the ANS that releases sugar into the bloodstream, makes the heart beat faster,
   temporarily slows digestion, and restricts blood flow in the skin is the _____ branch.

6. On your way home from work, you narrowly missed being hit by another car. It has now
   been 25 minutes since the near accident, and you are starting to feel "better" with your heart
   not pounding anymore and your muscles beginning to relax. These changes that occurred 25
   minutes after the accident are due to the _____ branch of the ANS.

7. The branch of the ANS that responds the slowest is the _____ branch.

8. After a strong emotional shock, the branch of the ANS that may overreact and lower blood
   pressure too much, causing you to become dizzy or faint is the _____ branch.

9. This overreaction of calming the body too much after a terrifying experience can sometimes
   cause death and is referred to as a(n) _____.

10. For older persons and those with heart problems, a heart attack may occur because of the
    person's initial stress-related reaction to the incident. In this case, the heart attack was caused
    by the _____ branch of ANS.

11. The percent of wrongful convictions that include false confessions as evidence has been
    documented to be around _____ percent.

12. The lie detector's real name comes from a word that means "many writings," which is
    _____.

13. The lie detector was invented in 1915 by a psychologist, who also created the comic book
    character *Wonder Woman*. This psychologist's name is _____.

14. The lie detector really does not detect lies, but instead measures general _____.

15. The lie detector records changes in heart rate, blood pressure, breathing, and the electrical
    conductance of the skin (sweating), which is called _____.

16. To minimize problem in using the lie detector, skilled examiners use a series of multiple
    choice questions when administering the lie detector. This series of multiple choice questions
    is known as the _____ test.

17. Supporters of the lie detector claim it to be _____ percent accurate.

18. The lie detector may be thrown off by tranquilizing drugs, by people who can lie without
    anxiety, and by _____.

19. In studies involving real crimes, the lie detector, on average, rated one innocent person guilty
    out of _____.

511

20. If you are tested for employment or for other reasons with a lie detector, the best advice is to remain calm; and if your honesty is wrongly questioned by the machine, you should _____ the results.

21. Newer methods for detecting lies involve directly measuring brain activity using the _____.

22. Psychiatrist Daniel Langleben theorizes that extra brain areas are activated when a person is telling _____.

Connections

1. ___ autonomic nervous system (ANS)

2. ___ sympathetic branch

3. ___ parasympathetic branch

4. ___ parasympathetic rebound

5. ___ polygraph

6. ___ galvanic skin response (GSR)

7. ___ guilty knowledge test

8. ___ functional MRI

a. change in the electrical conductance of the skin, due to sweating

b. brain scans used to detect lying

c. part of ANS that activates the body in times of stress

d. series of multiple choice questions used in combination with a lie detector

e. commonly called a "lie detector"

f. system of nerves that connects the brain with the internal organs and glands

g. part of ANS that quiets the body and conserves energy

h. severe lowering of the blood pressure due to the nervous system overreacting to an intense emotion

Check Your Memory

1. TRUE or FALSE   The reactions of the sympathetic and parasympathetic systems are innate, universal, and automatic.

2. TRUE or FALSE   The parasympathetic and sympathetic systems are the two branches of the somatic nervous system.

3. TRUE or FALSE   The parasympathetic branch activates the body at times of stress, while the sympathetic branch quiets the body and conserves energy.

4. TRUE or FALSE   When the sympathetic branch is activated, your digestion is temporarily slowed and the blood flow in the skin is restricted to reduce bleeding.

5. TRUE or FALSE   The sympathetic system responds much more slowly than the parasympathetic system.

6. TRUE or FALSE   After a strong emotional shock, the parasympathetic system may overreact and lower blood pressure too much, causing you to become dizzy or faint.

7. TRUE or FALSE   If the parasympathetic rebound is severe, it can sometimes cause death.

8. TRUE or FALSE   For older persons or those with heart problems, stress-related sympathetic effects may be enough to bring about heart attack and collapse.

9. TRUE or FALSE   In Asia where the number four is considered unlucky, more heart patients die on the fourth day of the month than any other day.

10. TRUE or FALSE   As many as 25 percent of all wrongful convictions include false confessions as evidence.

11. TRUE or FALSE   The word polygraph literally means "fountain of truth."

12. TRUE or FALSE   The lie detector, or polygraph, was invented in 1945 by psychologist Stanley Schachter, who also created the *Spiderman* superhero.

13. TRUE or FALSE   The polygraph is not a lie detector at all, but rather measures general emotional arousal.

14. TRUE or FALSE   One of the measures taken by a polygraph is skin conductance, or sweating.

15. TRUE or FALSE   The series of multiple choice questions that are used in combination with a polygraph examination are referred to as the criminal intent profiling test.

16. TRUE or FALSE   The polygraph can be thrown off by self-inflicted pain and by using tranquilizers.

17. TRUE or FALSE   The polygraph cannot be thrown off by a person thinking about past emotional experiences when being asked the irrelevant questions or by a person who can lie without anxiety.

18. TRUE or FALSE   The polygraph test is much more likely to label a guilty person innocent than an innocent person guilty.

19. TRUE or FALSE   The National Academy of Sciences recently recommended that polygraph tests be utilized to screen employees and to discover thefts within a company.

20. TRUE or FALSE   When a person tells a lie, extra brain areas must be activated to tell a lie, which can be seen in fMRI brain images.

Critical Thinking Question

Can you explain why people "cursed" by shamans or "witch doctors" sometimes actually die?

Module 9.5 Emotional Expression and Theories of Emotion

Expressing Emotions—Making Faces and Talking Bodies

Survey Question: How accurately are emotions expressed by the face and "body language"?

Language Development Guide

making faces and talking bodies: facial expressions and body language
bare their teeth: show teeth, snarl in threatening or menacing ways
scheming: being tricky or evil
neutral faces: no facial expression shown
presumably: most likely
Westerns: films with cowboys, cattle, horses, and ranches in it
"smile when you say that, pardner": by smiling you will be saying that you did not really mean the verbal insult; pardner is an western American (Texas) term for a friend or companion
context: situation
clarify: make clear
"natural": normal; common
harmony: in agreement
at odds: in opposition to
superiority: self-importance; dominance; authority
reputation: as characterized by
"toughen up": being strong; not show emotions
curtail: hold back; reduce
extent: degree or amount

barrier: obstacle; difficulty
blunted: made less intense or less strong
tragedies: disasters; events that cause human suffering
mass murder: many persons intentionally killed by another at one time
offended: upset; feel sad about what was said or done
informally: in every day language
masterful: shows excellent skill in an area
telegraphs: sends a message
casually: in a relaxed manner
positioning: placing
reveal: show
concealed: hidden
"lean toward": can mean either posture or preferring something

Recite and Review

1. After observing that angry tigers, monkeys, dogs, and humans all bare their teeth in the same way, the famous scientist that proposed that emotional expressions are a carryover from human evolution was _____.

2. Psychologists believe our survival is aided because we communicate our feelings to others through our _____.

3. When presented with sad, angry, and neutral faces, people in one study were able to more quickly detect the _____ faces.

4. The facial expressions that scientists agree are recognized around the world are fear, anger, disgust, sadness, happiness, and _____.

5. There are two facial expressions that scientists believe are probably universal, but the scientists are as yet unsure of them. They are contempt and _____.

6. The most universal and easily recognized facial expression of emotion is a(n) _____.

7. A mixture of two or more basic expressions is called a facial _____.

8. Facial expressions can be boiled down to three basic dimensions, which are pleasantness-unpleasantness, attention-rejection, and _____.

9. Some facial expressions are only found in specific cultures and are, thus, shaped by _____.

10. In North America, sticking out one's tongue is a sign of disrespect or teasing, while in China, sticking out the tongue is a gesture of _____.

11. To clarify the meaning of a facial expression, one must know the social _____.

12. The emotion that is very commonly expressed in Western cultures, but not in Asian cultures is the emotion of _____.

13. Positive feelings are linked to membership in groups and a high value is placed on group harmony in many _____ cultures.

14. Personal independence and a free expression of individual rights and needs are emphasized in _____ cultures.

15. In America, we tend to have positive feelings such as pride, happiness, and superiority, which emphasize our role as _____.

16. In a comparison of adult men and women in Western cultures, it was found that the persons that have the most difficulty expressing their emotions are _____.

17. Regarding male and female infants, the babies that start out life more emotionally expressive are the _____ babies.

18. Regarding the emotions of sadness, anger, fear, shame, and guilt, boys from grade school on are "allowed" to freely express only the emotion of _____.

514

19. Reginald studies "body language," including body movement, posture, gestures, and facial expressions. Reginald's field of study is known as _____.
20. Since the meaning of gestures and other aspects of body language are not universal, it is most realistic to say that body language reveals an overall _____.
21. The most general "messages" of body language involve liking or disliking, and relaxation or _____.
22. According to body language, casually positioning the arms and legs, leaning back (if sitting), and spreading the arms and legs indicates _____.
23. Madge is leaning toward Jeff, which body language experts would say means _____.
24. Body positioning indicates feelings that would normally be _____.

Connections

1. ___ basic (facial) expressions
2. ___ facial blend
3. ___ dimensions of facial expressions
4. ___ general messages indicated by body positioning
5. ___ Asian cultures
6. ___ Western cultures
7. ___ kinesics
8. ___ smile
9. ___ anger

a. most universal and easily recognized facial expression of emotion
b. relaxation or tension and liking or disliking
c. positive feelings emphasize role as individuals
d. study of communication through body movement, posture, gestures, and facial expressions
e. pleasantness-unpleasantness, attention-rejection, and activation (or arousal)
f. recognized around the world and include fear, anger disgust, sadness, surprise, and happiness
g. only emotion that American boys are "allowed" to express
h. mixture of two or more basic expressions
i. positive feelings linked with membership in groups

Check Your Memory

1. TRUE or FALSE   Charles Darwin observed that angry tigers, monkeys, dogs, and humans all bare their teeth in the same way.
2. TRUE or FALSE   Emotional expressions aided the survival of the human species by communicating emotional feelings to others.
3. 3. TRUE or FALSE People are able to detect happy, sad, or neutral faces much faster than they are able to detect angry and scheming faces.
4. TRUE or FALSE   Basic expressions appear to be fairly universal with the facial expressions of fear, anger, disgust, sadness, surprise, and happiness (enjoyment) being recognized around the world.
5. TRUE or FALSE   Because children who are born blind have little opportunity to learn emotional expressions from others, they do not display the basic expression in the same way as sighted people do.
6. TRUE or FALSE   A smile is the most universal and easily recognized facial expression of emotion.
7. TRUE or FALSE   Your face can produce some 20,000 different expressions with most of these being facial blends, or mixtures of two or more basic expressions.
8. TRUE or FALSE   The three basic dimensions of facial expressions are relaxation-tension, liking-disliking, and truth-lying.

515

9. TRUE or FALSE   To clarify the meaning of facial expressions, it is important to know its social context.

10. TRUE or FALSE   Sticking out one's tongue is considered a sign of disrespect in all cultures.

11. TRUE or FALSE   Anger is a very common emotion in Asian cultures because they emphasize personal independence and a free expression of individual rights and needs.

12. TRUE or FALSE   In America, positive feelings are most often linked with membership in groups, such as friendly feelings, closeness with others, and respect.

13. TRUE or FALSE   Compared with women, men in Western cultures are more likely to have difficulty expressing their emotions.

14. TRUE or FALSE   Female babies start out life more emotionally expressive than male babies.

15. TRUE or FALSE   While girls are encouraged to express sadness, fear, shame, and guilt, American boys are more likely to be allowed to express only anger and hostility.

16. TRUE or FALSE   Physical semantics is the study of communication through body movement, posture, gestures, and facial expressions.

17. TRUE or FALSE   When you touch your thumb and first finger together to form a circle, this means "Everything is A-okay" in all cultures.

18. TRUE or FALSE   Relaxation in body language is expressed by casually positioning the arms and legs, leaning back (if sitting), and spreading the arms and legs.

19. TRUE or FALSE   Liking is expressed mainly by leaning toward a person or object.

Module 9.5 Emotional Expression and Theories of Emotion

Theories of Emotion—Several Ways to Fear a Bear

Survey Question: How do psychologists explain emotions?

Language Development Guide

prominent: important; well-known
swerve: turn sharply
skid: slide; spin out
abrupt: sudden
halt: stop
simultaneously: at the same time
attribution: deciding about cause
sneaks: to move quietly
"boo!": phrase used to scare someone, but can be used to show displeasure toward a poor performance
slapstick: humor involving injury to others, such as falling down or getting hit with something
injection: a liquid substance, usually medicine, is put into body tissue using a needle
stirred-up: aroused; stimulated
amused: pleased; laughing; smiling
agitated: restless
shake your "paw": shake hands; a friendly gesture
relieved: put at ease
fear of bear bodies to an appreciation of bare bodies: a play on homonyms with the topic going from fear of an animal (a bear) to an experiment using pictures of naked bodies
guarantee: assurance; promise
amplified: louder than usual
in reality: in fact
slides: pictures projected on a screen

516

consistently: every time
persuaded: convinced
apparent: obvious
artificial: false; fake
stirred up emotionally: intensives or upsets one's feelings
formula: recipe; process
propose: suggest; offer
your intended: person you want to marry
suspension bridge: bridge hanging on wires
chasm: deep hole or crack in the earth
irresistible: appealing; overpowering
charms: attractive, pleasing features
conclude: decide
wow: word that means that you are very impressed or very pleased
preceding: that which comes before
farfetched: unbelievable; unlikely
ingenious: clever; original; creative
swaying: rocking; swinging
case of love at first fright: play on the saying, "Love at first sight," meaning developing romantic
        feelings instantly
restricted: limited
slighted: insulted
demeaned: humiliate; put down
ideals: values; principles
repulsive: disgusting
yearn: long for; desire; crave
cuts you off: moves suddenly into the road lane closely in front of you, often causing you to have
        to slow down
wear-and-tear: damage over time
the picture still seems incomplete: do not have the whole story or explanation yet
central: main; most important
"emotional billboard" (face): something that displays one's feelings
innately programmed changes: a genetic plan that directs these events to occur
"making faces": voluntarily changing one's facial expressions
monitored: observed
confirmed: proved
posed: created; positioned
crosswise: sideways, horizontally
"down": sad; depressed
suppressing: keep in check; hold back; hid
ups and downs: times one feels happy and times one feels sad
calm and collected: relaxed and in control of one's emotions
conversely: on the other hand
snarling: growling
lunges: jumps or dives, moves suddenly toward
teeth bared: teeth showing
"uh oh, big trouble!": you are in danger
twists into a mask of fear: face expression shows extreme fear
blossom: grow
change course: change directions; become different
proceeds: goes on

517

Recite and Review

1. If you are walking down the street and a large growling dog is staring at you several yards down the side walk, you will feel fear, become aroused, and then run and yell, according to the _____ theory of emotion.

2. Jeb saw a growling bear on his path through the woods. According to one theory of emotion, Jeb will first run, then become aroused, and then feel fear as he becomes aware of his bodily reactions. This explains the _____ theory of emotion.

3. The theory of emotion states that emotional feelings and bodily arousal occur simultaneously is the _____.

4. Emotional feelings and bodily arousal occur simultaneously because the cortex, which produces feelings and the hypothalamus, which arouses the body are alerted at the same time by the part of the brain called the _____.

5. An emotion occurs when we apply a particular label to general physiological arousal, according to Schachter's _____ theory.

6. By deciding which source led to our physiological arousal, we choose the appropriate label for an emotion through the process of _____.

7. In an experiment in which participants were injected either with adrenaline, a tranquilizer, or a placebo (salt water) and were shown a slapstick comedy film, the participants who were injected with the adrenaline found the film the funniest because the arousal of their body was _____ to the movie.

8. You are most likely to "love" someone who gets you stirred up emotionally because if you already care for this person, these added emotions of frustration, fear, and anger intensify your original caring. This intensification of "love" is explained by the _____ theory of emotion.

9. The emotions we experience are greatly influenced by how we think about an event in the first place, according to psychologist _____.

10. Evaluating the personal meaning of a stimulus or situation refers to _____.

11. According to Carrol Izard, emotions cause innately programmed changes in facial expression with the sensations from the face providing cues to the brain that help us determine what emotion we are feeling. This idea is known as the facial _____ hypothesis.

12. Psychologist Paul Ekman had people make different facial expressions while he monitored their heart rate and skin temperature. He found that when a person makes a different facial expression, there is a change in the _____ nervous system.

13. In an experiment, people rated how funny they thought cartoons were while holding a pen crosswise between their lips or between their teeth. The people who thought the cartoons were funnier were the people who held the pen in their _____.

14. Researchers have found that people tend to cope poorly with life, are prone to depression, and have impaired thinking and memory if they _____ their emotions.

15. Research has shown that feedback from arousal and from our behavior does add to our emotional experience, which was first explained by the _____ theory of emotion.

16. The timing of events within an emotion was correctly explained by the _____ theory.

17. The importance of emotional appraisal was correctly stressed by psychologist _____.

18. An emotional stimulus is appraised as a threat or other cause for emotion with your appraisal giving rise to ANS arousal and cognitive labeling and also releasing innate emotional expressions, which leads to adaptive behavior, according to the _____ theory of emotion.

19. A snarling dog is in your path. When you judge this emotional stimulus (dog) as a threat, you have exhibited _____.

20. After you judge the snarling dog to be a threat, you run from the animal. By running, you have exhibited _____ behavior.

21. The intensity of an emotional feeling is directly related to the amount of _____ nervous system arousal.

Connections

1. ____ commonsense theory of emotion
2. ____ James-Lange theory
3. ____ Cannon-Bard theory
4. ____ Schachter's cognitive theory
5. ____ attribution
6. ____ emotional appraisal
7. ____ facial feedback hypothesis
8. ____ suppressing emotion
9. ____ contemporary model of emotion

a. mental process of assigning causes to events, such as assigning arousal to a particular source
b. states that we behave (run), experience arousal, and then experience emotional feelings
c. states that sensations from facial expressions help define what emotion a person feels
d. states that we feel (fear, etc.), become aroused, and then respond (run, etc.)
e. appraisal gives rise to arousal and cognitive labeling, behavior, facial/postural expressions, and emotional feelings
f. states that emotions occur when physical arousal is labeled or interpreted on the basis of experience and situational cues
g. restraining one's emotions and appearing calm
h. states that activity in the thalamus causes emotional feelings and bodily arousal to occur simultaneously
i. evaluating the personal meaning of a stimulus or situation

Check Your Memory

1. TRUE or FALSE   The commonsense theory of emotion states that if you were to suddenly see a bear, you would run and then feel fear.
2. TRUE or FALSE   The Cannon-Bard theory states that emotional feelings and bodily arousal occur at the same time.
3. TRUE or FALSE   James and Lange believed that if you were faced with a snarling dog, you would first feel fear and then become aroused and then run and yell.
4. TRUE or FALSE   According to Schachter's cognitive theory, emotion occurs when we apply a particular label to general physiological arousal.
5. TRUE or FALSE   In an experiment in which participants were injected either with adrenaline, a tranquilizer, or a placebo (salt water) and were shown a slapstick comedy film, none of the participants found the film funny because they attributed the arousal of their bodies to the drugs they had been given.
6. TRUE or FALSE   In the experiment in which the male students were asked to rate the attractiveness of women in several photographs, the students who heard the false heartbeat attributed the heartbeat to being attracted to a particular photograph.
7. TRUE or FALSE   Attribution theory predicts that you are least likely to "love" someone who gets you stirred up emotionally, especially if the emotions are fear or frustration.
8. TRUE or FALSE   According to Richard Lazarus, the emotions you experience are greatly influenced by how you think about an event in the first place.

9. TRUE or FALSE   If you change your emotional appraisal of an event from evaluating it as disaster to a minor irritation, you can minimize emotional wear-and-tear.

10. TRUE or FALSE   According to the facial feedback hypothesis, emotions cause changes in facial expressions, which produce sensations that act as cues to help us determine what emotion we are feeling.

11. TRUE or FALSE   Paul Ekman believed that "making faces" can actually cause emotions.

12. TRUE or FALSE   In an experiment in which people rated how funny they thought cartoons were while holding a pen crosswise in their mouths, the ones that held the pen in their lips thought the cartoons were funnier than the people who held the pen between their teeth.

13. TRUE or FALSE   Suppressing emotions increases activity in the sympathetic nervous system.

14. TRUE or FALSE   Suppressing emotions can impair thinking and memory, as you devote energy to self-control.

15. TRUE or FALSE   People who consistently suppress their emotions generally experience better emotional and physical health.

16. TRUE or FALSE   Paying attention to our negative emotions can lead us to think more clearly about the positive and the negative and result in better decision making.

17. TRUE or FALSE   James and Lange were right that feedback from arousal and behavior adds to our emotional experiences.

18. TRUE or FALSE   Schachter and Valins were right about the timing of events when experiencing emotions.

19. TRUE or FALSE   The contemporary model of emotion does not include emotional appraisal or cognitive labeling.

20. TRUE or FALSE   The intensity of this emotional feeling is directly related to the amount of autonomic nervous system arousal taking place in your body.

Critical Thinking Question

People with high spinal injuries may feel almost no signs of physiological arousal from their bodies. Nevertheless they still feel emotion, which can be intense at times. What theory of emotion does this observation contradict?

Module 9.6 Psychology in Action
Emotional Intelligence—The Fine Art of Self-Control
Survey Question: What does it mean to have "emotional intelligence"?

Language Development Guide

recipe: plan
stifle: hold in
sustaining life rhythms: maintaining a happy life
mesh well: fit, match
sabotage: damage, undermine, disrupt
toll: tax; charge; payment
foundation: basis; base
tuned in to: aware of, notice
envious: jealous
disruptive: upsetting; troublesome
pinpoint: identify
"reading": interpreting the meaning of

amplify or restrain: make larger or smaller, enhance or hold back

misery: unhappiness

make no mistake: you can be certain; have no doubt about

constructive: helpful

persistent: constant; lasting

mend: repair; fix

new direction in life: to begin a new phase in life, such as a new career or a new way of dealing with life

save their skins: survive

expelling: getting rid of; forcing out; spitting out

savor: take pleasure in

integrate: put together; join together

side effect: by-product; added result

buffers: protections

take...into account: consider it

extremely rational: based only on objective information; on logic

sensible: reasonable

emotionally empty: lacking fulfillment and happiness

offer a toast: making a speech to honor a person and then drinking (champagne) to their health and success

roast: a party for a person where jokes or embarrassing stories are told about the person being honored

bereaved: person suffering from the death of a loved one

Recite and Review

1. A recipe for handling relationships smoothly states "Be angry with the right person, to the right degree, at the right time, for the right purpose, and in the right way." These words of wisdom were given to us by the Greek philosopher _____.

2. According to psychologists Peter Salovey and John Mayer, the ability to perceive, use, understand, and manage emotions is known as _____.

3. Careers and relationships can be ruined, one's achievement can be sabotaged, and depression can result if one lacks emotional _____.

4. Being tuned in to one's own feelings and being able to sense what others are feeling defines the ability to _____ emotions.

5. If you can remember how you reacted emotionally in the past, it can help you react better to new situations, which illustrates effectively _____ emotions.

6. If you realize that an emotion is a cue, such as anger being a cue that something is wrong or that depression means we feel helpless, then you are exhibiting the skill known as _____ emotions.

7. If you know how to calm down when you are angry and also know how to calm others, you are demonstrating your ability to _____ emotions.

8. The actions that probably helped our ancestors save their skins were probably most associated with _____ emotions.

9. Our focus tends to be broadened and personal growth and social connection encouraged by _____ emotions.

10. Extremely rational approaches to making choices can produce sensible but emotionally _____ decisions.

11. The ability to consciously make your emotions work for you describes _____.

12. By paying close attention to your emotions and the emotions of others, emotional skills can be _____.

521

Connections

1. ___ emotional intelligence
2. ___ perceiving emotions
3. ___ using emotions

4. ___ understanding emotions
5. ___ managing emotions
6. ___ empathy
7. ___ positive emotions
8. ___ negative emotions

a. emotions are seen as cues to what's is wrong
b. being able to feel what others are feeling
c. are most associated with our ancestors' survival
d. recognize emotions in self and others quickly
e. tend to broaden our focus
f. emotional competence
g. being able to calm oneself and others
h. remembering how one reacted emotionally in the past to help one react better in the future

Check Your Memory

1. TRUE or FALSE   Peter Salovey and John Mayer refer to the ability to perceive, use, understand, and manage emotions as emotional intelligence.
2. TRUE or FALSE   Emotionally intelligent people tend to be more combative and argumentative with others than those with low emotional skills.
3. TRUE or FALSE   Poor emotional skills can lead to marriage and parenting problems, ruined careers, sabotaged achievement, and poor physical and psychological health.
4. TRUE or FALSE   Emotionally intelligent people can accurately perceive their own emotions as well as being able to "read" facial expressions and tone of voice in others.
5. TRUE or FALSE   When good fortune comes their way, people who are emotionally smart do not share their accomplishments with others in order not to provoke envy and weaken their relationships.
6. TRUE or FALSE   People who are emotionally intelligent know what causes various emotions, what they mean, and how they affect behavior.
7. TRUE or FALSE   People who are emotionally intelligent have an ability to amplify or restrain emotions, depending on the situation.
8. TRUE or FALSE   Negative emotions tend to broaden our focus, while positive emotions tend to narrow our focus.
9. TRUE or FALSE   Negative emotions are associated with actions that probably helped our ancestors save their skins.
10. TRUE or FALSE   A capacity for having positive emotions is a basic human strength, and cultivating good feelings is a part of emotional intelligence.
11. TRUE or FALSE   Extremely rational approaches to making choices produce sensible and emotional intelligent decisions.
12. TRUE or FALSE   Emotional skills can be learned with many valuable lessons coming from paying attention to one's own emotions and the emotions of others.

Critical Thinking Question

You are angry because a friend borrowed money from you and hasn't repaid it. What would be an emotionally intelligent response to this situation?

Final Survey and Review—Completion

Module 9.1 Overview of Motivation
Motivation—Forces that Push and Pull
Survey Questions: What is motivation? Are there different types of motives?

1. The ways in which our actions are initiated, sustained, directed, and terminated is referred to as _____.
2. Your need to become the first chair violinist in your school's orchestra would be classified as a(n) _____ motive.
3. When your body deviates from the ideal levels of temperature, blood pressure, and nutrient levels, automatic reactions begin to restore bodily equilibrium through a process known as _____.
4. If you are experiencing jet lag and it is taking a long time for you to adapt to the new time zone, the direction in which you flew was most likely _____.
5. Exposure to short periods of bright light early in the morning can reset one's biological clock because bright light reduces the amount melatonin produced by the _____ gland.

Module 9.2 Hunger, Thirst, Pain, and Sex
Hunger—Pardon Me, My Hypothalamus Is Growling
Survey Question: What causes hunger? Overeating? Eating disorders?
6. In a classic experiment in which a swallowed balloon with an attached tube was inflated and contracted, the researchers incorrectly concluded that hunger was caused by the contractions of an empty stomach. These researchers were Cannon and _____.
7. The ventromedial hypothalamus acts as a "stop mechanism" for eating as is known as the _____ system.
8. The lateral hypothalamus is activated by a hormone produced by the stomach lining called _____.
9. Bart is using an illicit drug that has a chemical that will affect the hypothalamus and cause him to have an intense hunger. This illicit drug is most likely _____.
10. Diet-induced obesity occurs when radical diets raise one's _____ for fat.
11. An active dislike for a particular food that results from classical conditioning is called a(n) _____.
12. Karen is overhauling her regular diet so it is healthier and lighter and is increasing her exercise to a brisk 30-minute walk five times a week. Her plan is an approach known as _____ dieting.
13. After overeating, Dina purges the food by vomiting or using laxatives to control her weight. Dina appears to be suffering from the condition known as _____.

Module 9.2 Hunger, Thirst, Pain, and Sex
Biological Motives Revisited—Thirst, Pain, and Sex
Survey Questions: Is there more than one type of thirst? In what ways are pain avoidance and the sex drive unusual?
14. Mickey is hot and sweaty from exercising and prefers to drink a sports drink to quench his thirst. Mickey has a(n) _____ thirst.
15. Jeff's sleep occurs in a cyclic manner, while his avoidance of pain would be considered _____.
16. Both men's and women's sex drive is affected by a group of male hormones known as _____.
17. Since sex is not related to the amount of deprivation, we say that it is _____.

Module 9.3 Arousal, Achievement, and Growth Needs
Stimulus Drives—Skydiving, Horror Movies, and the Fun Zone
Survey Question: How does arousal relate to motivation?

18. Although no food treats or other external rewards are needed, monkeys will quickly learn to solve a mechanical puzzle made up of interlocking metal pins, hooks, and latches because this exploration and manipulation of their surroundings is a(n) _____ motive.
19. Jay smokes, prefers spicy chicken wings, and enjoys sky diving. Jay is most likely a high _____.
20. A swimmer competing in the 50 meter freestyle would probably perform best at a high level of arousal, while a person playing a complicated piano composition would perform better at a lower level. These situations illustrate the _____ law.
21. Whenever LaMicca thinks, "I'm going to fail this test and everybody will think I'm stupid," she has taught herself to think "If I prepare well and control my worries, I will probably pass the test; and even if I don't, it won't be the end of the world." To control her test anxiety, LaMica is using _____ statements.

Module 9.3 Arousal, Achievement, and Growth Needs
Learned Motives—The Pursuit of Excellence
Survey Questions: What are learned motives? Social motives? Why are they important?

22. Social motives are acquired through socialization and cultural _____.
23. It is very important for Tanya to meet her own standard of excellence and to do her best in situations in which she will be evaluated. Tanya has a high need for _____.
24. When tackling an important task, it is important that goals be challenging, attainable, and _____.
25. When a person has a desire to have impact or control over others, this person has a high need for _____.

Module 9.3 Arousal, Achievement, and Growth Needs
Motives in Perspective—A View from the Pyramid
Survey Question: Are some motives more basic than others?

26. The biological needs at the base of the Maslow's hierarchy are said to be prepotent, or _____ over the higher needs.
27. College students scored lower than average in vitality, self-actualization, and general well-being if they were primarily concerned with social recognition, money, and _____.
28. Maslow estimated that most people were more motivated by the needs for esteem, love, or security than they were by _____.
29. A certain amount of challenge, surprise, and complexity makes a task rewarding when a person is _____ motivated.

Module 9.4 Emotion and Physiological Arousal
Inside an Emotion—How Do You Feel?
Survey Question: What happens during emotion?

30. The sympathetic nervous system and the hormones of adrenaline and noradrenaline produce the _____ of an emotion.
31. Fear, surprise, sadness, disgust, anger, anticipation, joy, and trust (acceptance) are the eight primary emotions identified by _____.
32. The mildest forms of emotional states that are closely tied to circadian rhythms and affect our day-to-day behavior are our _____.

524

33. When an armed robber was robbing the store that Ted works in, he put a gun up to Ted's head and Ted showed no fear. In fact, Ted has trouble "reading" the emotions of other people as well because of damage to the part of the limbic system of the brain known as the _____.

Module 9.4 Emotion and Physiological Arousal
Physiology and Emotion—Arousal, Sudden Death, and Lying
Survey Questions: What physiological changes underlie emotion? Can "lie detectors" really detect lies?

34. On your way home from work, you narrowly missed being hit by another car. Your rapid heart beat, rapid breathing, and intense sweating are due to the reactions of the branch of autonomic nervous system called the _____ branch.
35. There have been instances in which military combat was so savage that some soldiers literally died of fear because their heart was slowed by an overreaction of the autonomic nervous system called a(n) _____.
36. William Marston, a psychologist who created the comic book character *Wonder Woman* also invented the _____.
37. Psychiatrist Daniel Langleben theorizes that extra brain areas are activated when a person is telling a lie that can be seen on brain scans using a(n) _____.

Module 9.5 Emotional Expression and Theories of Emotion
Expressing Emotions—Making Faces and Talking Bodies
Survey Question: How accurately are emotions expressed by the face and "body language"?

38. The facial expressions that scientists agree are recognized around the world are anger, disgust, sadness, happiness, surprise, and _____.
39. Facial expressions can be boiled down to three basic dimensions, which are pleasantness-unpleasantness, activation (or arousal), and _____.
40. Positive feelings are more often linked with membership in groups in _____ cultures.
41. In one of your psychology classes, you are studying body movement, posture, gestures, and facial expressions as a means of communication. You are studying _____.

Module 9.5 Emotional Expression and Theories of Emotion
Theories of Emotion—Several Ways to Fear a Bear
Survey Question: How do psychologists explain emotions?

42. Ned saw a growling bear on his path through the woods. According to one theory of emotion, Ned will feel fear, become aroused, and then run. This explains the _____ theory of emotion.
43. Emotional feelings and bodily arousal occur simultaneously because the thalamus alerts the parts of the brain that produce feelings and arousal at the same time with the feelings being produced by the cortex and the arousal of the body being produced by the _____.
44. You and a friend have gone to a horror movie. As the movie progresses and the "body count" increases, both of your hearts are racing and your palms are sweating. However, you label this physiological arousal as uncomfortable, while your friend considered it fun. Your difference in emotions is best explained by Schachter's _____ theory of emotion.
45. The psychologist who had people make various facial expressions while he measured their heart rate and skin temperature and discovered that "making faces" can actually cause emotion was _____.
46. The amount of autonomic nervous system arousal is directly related to the intensity of a(n) _____.

Module 9.6 Psychology in Action
Emotional Intelligence—The Fine Art of Self-Control
Survey Question: What does it mean to have "emotional intelligence"?

47. Emotional intelligence is the ability to perceive, use, understand, and manage emotions, according to psychologists Peter Salovey and _____.

48. Asma remembers that she was not as forceful at the last meeting when presenting her ideas, so she plans to use this past information about her emotions and reactions to improve her interactions at the next meeting. Asma is effectively _____ emotions.

49. Our focus of attention tends to be narrowed and our ideas about possible actions limited when we are experiencing _____ emotions.

50. Sensible but emotionally empty decisions are often produced when one makes choices using extremely _____ approaches.

Final Survey and Review—Matching

Module 9.1 Overview of Motivation

1. ___ motivation	a. the appeal of a goal above and beyond its ability to fill a need
2. ___ need	b. steady state of bodily equilibrium
3. ___ drive	c. examples are hunger, thirst, and "for success"
4. ___ incentive value	d. internal processes that initiate, sustain, direct, and terminate activities
5. ___ biological motives	e. cyclical changes in bodily functions and arousal levels that vary on a schedule approximating a 24-hour day
6. ___ stimulus motives	f. innate needs for information and activity that are not necessary for survival
7. ___ learned motives	g. innate needs that must be met for survival
8. ___ homeostasis	h. needs that are not innate, that explain many human activities, and include the need for achievement, power, and affiliation
9. ___ circadian rhythms	i. internal deficiency that may energize behavior

Module 9.2 Hunger, Thirst, Pain, and Sex
Part 1:

1. ___ lateral hypothalamus	a. repeatedly losing and gaining weight
2. ___ ventromedial hypothalamus	b. part of brain that acts as a satiety system
3. ___ paraventricular nucleus	c. an active dislike for a particular food
4. ___ taste aversion	d. active self-starvation with body weight below 85 percent of normal
5. ___ set point	e. weight reduction based on changing exercise and eating habits
6. ___ "Yo-yo dieting"	f. part of brain that keeps blood sugar levels steady by both starting and stopping eating
7. ___ behavioral dieting	g. non-cyclical drive, such as pain avoidance
8. ___ anorexia nervosa	h. thirst triggered when fluid is drawn out of cells due to an increased concentration of salts and minerals outside the cell

526

9. ___ bulimia nervosa
10. ___ extracellular thirst

11. ___ intracellular thirst

12. ___ episodic drive

13. ___ non-homeostatic drive

i. part of brain that acts as feeding system
j. any drive that is relatively independent of physical deprivation cycles or bodily need states
k. proportion of body fat that you tend to maintain when you are making no effort to gain or lose weight
l. gorging on food, then vomiting or taking laxatives to avoid gaining weight
m. thirst caused by a reduction in the volume of fluids found between body cells

Part 2:

1. ___ ghrelin

2. ___ estrogens

3. ___ leptin

4. ___ androgens
5. ___ aphrodisiacs

6. ___ glucagon-like peptide 1 (GLP-1)

7. ___ neuropeptide Y (NPY)

a. substance released by fat cells that signals the hypothalamus for the person to eat less
b. chemical released by the intestines and ends one's desire to eat
c. substance that affects the paraventricular nucleus and in large amounts will cause an animal to eat until it cannot hold another bite
d. any of a number of female sex hormones
e. hormone produced by stomach lining when hungry and also activates parts of the brain involved in learning
f. substances that increase sexual desire or pleasure
g. any of a number of male sex hormones, especially testosterone

Module 9.3 Arousal, Achievement, and Growth Needs

1. ___ Yerkes-Dodson law

2. ___ self-determination theory

3. ___ need for achievement (nAch)

4. ___ need for power

5. ___ test anxiety

6. ___ social motives

7. ___ meta-needs

8. ___ basic needs

9. ___ intrinsic motivation

10. ___ extrinsic motivation

a. motivation based on personal enjoyment of a task or activity
b. desire to have social impact and control over others
c. high levels of arousal and worry that seriously impair performance on assessments
d. explains the relationships among arousal, task complexity, and performance
e. needs associated with impulses for self-actualization
f. theory that explains how doing things for enjoyment or to improve one's abilities can be motivating
g. motivation based on obvious external rewards or obligations
h. desire to excel or meet some internalized standard of excellence
i. learned needs acquired as part of growing up in a particular culture
j. another name for the deficiency needs

527

Module 9.4 Emotion and Physiological Arousal

1. ___ adaptive behaviors
2. ___ emotional expressions
3. ___ emotional feelings

4. ___ primary emotions
5. ___ moods
6. ___ left hemisphere

7. ___ right hemisphere

8. ___ amygdala

9. ___ parasympathetic rebound

10. ___ polygraph
11. ___ guilty knowledge test

12. ___ functional MRI

a. low-intensity, long-lasting emotional states
b. brain scans used to detect lying
c. part of the limbic system that produces fear responses
d. resulted from the work of William Marston
e. resulted from the work of Robert Plutchik
f. private, subjective experience of having an emotion
g. series of multiple choice questions used in combination with a lie detector
h. actions that aid our attempts to survive and adjust to changing conditions
i. part of the brain that processes negative emotions
j. outward signs that an emotion is occurring
k. part of the brain that processes positive emotions
l. severe lowering of the blood pressure due to the autonomic nervous system overreacting to an intense emotion

Module 9.5 Emotional Expression and Theories of Emotion

1. ___ kinesics

2. ___ James-Lange theory

3. ___ Cannon-Bard theory

4. ___ Schachter's cognitive theory

5. ___ attribution

6. ___ emotional appraisal

7. ___ facial feedback hypothesis

a. mental process of assigning causes to events, such as assigning arousal to a particular source
b. states that we behave (run), experience arousal, and then experience emotional feelings
c. states that sensations from facial expressions help define what emotion a person feels
d. evaluating the personal meaning of a stimulus or situation
e. study of communication through body movement, posture, gestures, and facial expressions
f. states that emotions occur when physical arousal is labeled or interpreted on the basis of experience and situational cues
g. states that activity in the thalamus causes emotional feelings and bodily arousal to occur simultaneously

Module 9.6 Psychology in Action: Emotional Intelligence—The Fine Art of Self-Control

1. ___ emotional intelligence
2. ___ empathy

a. tend to broaden our focus
b. ability to perceive, use, understand, and manage emotions

528

3. ___ positive emotions

4. ___ negative emotions

c. are most associated with our ancestors' survival

d. being able to feel what others are feeling

Final Survey and Review—True or False

Module 9.1 Overview of Motivation
Motivation—Forces that Push and Pull
Survey Questions: What is motivation? Are there different types of motives?

1. TRUE or FALSE   A person who is unable to name his emotions and is only vaguely aware of them has a condition known as alexithymia.
2. TRUE or FALSE   People cannot suffer a bodily need for water without also experiencing a strong thirst drive.
3. TRUE or FALSE   A goal's appeal beyond its ability to fill a need is known as homeostasis.
4. TRUE or FALSE   Pain avoidance, hunger and thirst are considered stimulus motives.
5. TRUE or FALSE   For major time zone shifts (five hours or more), it usually takes about 12 hours to resynchronize one's biological rhythms.

Module 9.2 Hunger, Thirst, Pain, and Sex
Hunger—Pardon Me, My Hypothalamus Is Growling
Survey Question: What causes hunger? Overeating? Eating disorders?

6. TRUE or FALSE   Even though Alex had his cancerous stomach removed, he will still experience hunger.
7. TRUE or FALSE   If the ventromedial hypothalamus is destroyed, the animal may never eat again unless force fed.
8. TRUE or FALSE   Because the hormone ghrelin activates parts of the brain involved in learning, students should consider studying before they eat, not immediately after.
9. TRUE or FALSE   When your body weight goes below the set point, you will feel hungry.
10. TRUE or FALSE   If you are well fed, leptin tends to decrease and dull the tongue's sensitivity to sweet tastes.
11. TRUE or FALSE   Americans take longer to eat than the French do, which encourages overeating.
12. TRUE or FALSE   If Margo diets intensely every other day, research shows that she will lose as much weight as people who diet moderately every day.
13. TRUE or FALSE   Because Lance is an athlete in both gymnastics and track, he will be less susceptible to developing an eating disorder.

Module 9.2 Hunger, Thirst, Pain, and Sex
Biological Motives Revisited—Thirst, Pain, and Sex
Survey Questions: Is there more than one type of thirst? In what ways are pain avoidance and the sex drive unusual?

14. TRUE or FALSE   Extracellular thirst occurs when water is lost from the fluids surrounding the cells of your body.
15. TRUE or FALSE   Hunger and thirst are considered episodic drives.
16. TRUE or FALSE   Tolerance for pain is largely unaffected by learning.
17. TRUE or FALSE   Getting drunk decreases sexual desire, arousal, pleasure, and performance.

529

Module 9.3 Arousal, Achievement, and Growth Needs
Stimulus Drives—Skydiving, Horror Movies, and the Fun Zone
Survey Question: How does arousal relate to motivation?

18. TRUE or FALSE   Stimulus drives occur in both humans and other animals.
19. TRUE or FALSE   People low in sensation seeking tend to be orderly, nurturant, and giving, and they enjoy the company of others.
20. TRUE or FALSE   If we set aside individual differences, most people perform best when their arousal level is high.
21. TRUE or FALSE   If a task is more complex, your best performance will occur at lower levels of arousal.

Module 9.3 Arousal, Achievement, and Growth Needs
Learned Motives—The Pursuit of Excellence
Survey Questions: What are learned motives? Social motives? Why are they important?

22. TRUE or FALSE   People with strong needs for achievement want their importance to be visible, so they buy expensive possessions, wear prestigious clothes, and exploit relationships.
23. TRUE or FALSE   College students with a high need for achievement tend to blame others or circumstances for their failures.
24. TRUE or FALSE   When you first acquire a skill, your goal should be to make progress in learning, not comparing yourself to the performance of others.
25. TRUE or FALSE   Elite performance in music, sports, chess, the arts, and many other pursuits requires at least 10 years of dedicated practice.

Module 9.3 Arousal, Achievement, and Growth Needs
Motives in Perspective—A View from the Pyramid
Survey Question: Are some motives more basic than others?

26. TRUE or FALSE   At the top of Maslow's hierarchy are the deficiency needs.
27. TRUE or FALSE   Goodness, playfulness, beauty, perfection, and aliveness are examples of our basic needs, according to Maslow.
28. TRUE or FALSE   When you freely choose to do something for enjoyment or to improve your abilities, your motivation is considered extrinsic.
29. TRUE or FALSE   If extrinsic rewards are used with children to help them improve their reading or math skills, etc., these rewards should be small and phased out as soon as possible.

Module 9.4 Emotion and Physiological Arousal
Inside an Emotion—How Do You Feel?
Survey Question: What happens during emotion?

30. TRUE or FALSE   The physiological changes of an emotion are caused by activity in the sympathetic nervous system and by the hormones adrenaline and noradenaline.
31. TRUE or FALSE   The part of emotions with which we are usually most familiar are the emotional expressions of others.
32. TRUE or FALSE   Positive emotions are processed mainly in the left hemisphere of the brain.
33. TRUE or FALSE   People who suffer damage to the reticular formation become "blind" to emotion and are unable to "read" or understand other people's emotions.

Module 9.4 Emotion and Physiological Arousal
Physiology and Emotion—Arousal, Sudden Death, and Lying
Survey Questions: What physiological changes underlie emotion? Can "lie detectors" really detect lies?

34. TRUE or FALSE   The sympathetic branch activates the body at times of stress, while the parasympathetic branch quiets the body and conserves energy.
35. TRUE or FALSE   There have not been any recorded deaths due to parasympathetic rebound, only mild faintings and dizziness.
36. TRUE or FALSE   The National Academy of Sciences has concluded that polygraph tests should not be used to screen employees.
37. TRUE or FALSE   The polygraph is much more likely to label an innocent person guilty, rather than a guilty person innocent.

Module 9.5 Emotional Expression and Theories of Emotion
Expressing Emotions—Making Faces and Talking Bodies
Survey Question: How accurately are emotions expressed by the face and "body language"?

38. TRUE or FALSE   Children born blind express emotions with their faces in about the same ways as sighted people do.
39. TRUE or FALSE   People from Asian cultures are more likely to express anger in public than people from Western cultures.
40. TRUE or FALSE   Male babies start out life more emotionally expressive than female babies
41. TRUE or FALSE   The "A-okay" hand gesture has different meanings in different cultures.

Module 9.5 Emotional Expression and Theories of Emotion
Theories of Emotion—Several Ways to Fear a Bear
Survey Question: How do psychologists explain emotions?

42. TRUE or FALSE   The James-Lange theory states that emotional feelings and bodily arousal occur at the same time.
43. TRUE or FALSE   Attribution theory predicts that you are more likely to "love" someone who gets you stirred up emotionally, even if the emotions are fear, anger, or frustration.
44. TRUE or FALSE   In an experiment in which people rated how funny they thought cartoons were while holding a pen crosswise in their mouths, the ones that held the pen in their teeth thought the cartoons were funnier than the people who held the pen between their lips.
45. TRUE or FALSE   Suppressing emotions tends to decrease activity in the sympathetic nervous system.
46. TRUE or FALSE   The contemporary model of emotion includes both emotional appraisal and cognitive labeling in its explanation.

Module 9.6 Psychology in Action
Emotional Intelligence—The Fine Art of Self-Control
Survey Question: What does it mean to have "emotional intelligence"?

47. TRUE or FALSE   When good fortune comes their way, people who are emotionally smart share their accomplishments with others in order to strengthen relationships and increase emotional well-being.

48. TRUE or FALSE   Positive emotions tend to broaden our focus, while negative emotions tend to narrow our focus.

49. TRUE or FALSE   Positive emotions are the ones most associated with actions that probably helped our ancestors save their skins.

50. TRUE or FALSE   Emotional skills are innately programmed and cannot be learned.

Mastery Test

1. Gideon has a condition in which he has trouble empathizing with the feelings of others and is only vaguely aware of his own emotions. Gideon most likely has a condition known as
   a. agnosia.
   b. alexithymia.
   c. Wernicke's aphasia.
   d. dysgraphia.

2. Motivation refers to the ways in which activities are initiated and terminated as well as sustained and
   a. acquired.
   b. valued.
   c. aroused.
   d. directed.

3. Although both a chocolate sundae and a bowl of grub worms would satisfy your hunger drive, a chocolate sundae would have a higher
   a. biological motive.
   b. stimulus motive.
   c. homeostatic value.
   d. incentive value.

4. One's need for exploration and activity are categorized as _____ motives.
   a. biological
   b. learned
   c. stimulus
   d. extrinsic

5. Basic biological motives, such as hunger and thirst, are closely related to
   a. one's meta-needs..
   b. homeostasis.
   c. activity in the reticular formation.
   d. the levels of melatonin in the brain.

6. Regarding circadian rhythms and the occurrence of jet lag, which of the following statements is TRUE?
   a. If you fly east, it is easier to adapt to the time change.
   b. Adjusting to jet lag is fastest when you stay indoors and eat and sleep on your "home time."
   c. For major time zone shifts of five hours or more, it can take up to two weeks to resynchronize your biological clock.
   d. A 30-minute period of exposure to bright light late in the afternoon can help to reset your circadian rhythm.

532

7. An animal would dramatically overeat if which part of its hypothalamus was destroyed?
   a. lateral
   b. ventromedial
   c. parietal
   d. endometrial

8. It is better to study before you eat than immediately after because the same hormone that activates the lateral hypothalamus also activates parts of your brain involved in learning. This hormone is called
   a. serotonin
   b. melatonin
   c. leptin
   d. ghrelin

9. The weight you maintain when you are making no effort to gain or lose weight is called your
   a. set point.
   b. critical mass.
   c. satiety limit.
   d. homeostatic mass.

10. All-you-can-eat buffets, snack vending machines at work, and advertisements for conveniently fixed decadent desserts can lead to obesity because they all serve as
   a. set points.
   b. external eating cues.
   c. intrinsic eating cues.
   d. homeostatic incentives.

11. If you develop an active dislike for a food, this is called a taste aversion and was most likely acquired through
   a. classical conditioning.
   b. yo-yo dieting.
   c. operant conditioning.
   d. behavioral dieting.

12. Although in some parts of the world eating monkey eyes is considered a delicacy, to Americans it is not. This difference in preference is largely influenced by
   a. cultural values.
   b. sensation-seeking.
   c. genetic predispositions.
   d. biological motives.

13. Regular exercise, keeping a "diet diary," learning to weaken personal eating cues, and charting one's daily progress are all part of a weight reduction using
   a. "yo-yo dieting."
   b. behavioral dieting.
   c. the "supermarket diet."
   d. the homeostatic set point diet.

14. Binge eating is most associated with
    a. bulimia nervosa.
    b. alexithymia.
    c. behavioral dieting.
    d. anorexia nervosa.

15. You have just eaten a "very salty" meal prepared by your roommate. After a meal like this, you are most likely to have a(n) _____ thirst.
    a. extracellular
    b. intracellular
    c. hypothalamic
    d. homeostatic

16. Unlike hunger and thirst, pain avoidance is considered to be
    a. episodic.
    b. extrinsic.
    c. cyclic.
    d. unaffected by learning.

17. The sex drive in both men and women tends to increase with increasing levels of the hormones called
    a. androgens.
    b. serotonins.
    c. leptins.
    d. dopamines.

18. Because the human sex drive can be aroused at virtually any time and shows no clear relationship to deprivation, we say that the human sex drive is
    a. homeostatic.
    b. non-homeostatic.
    c. cyclic.
    d. extrinsically-motivated.

19. In our daily lives, we try to keep the activation of our body and nervous system at an optimal level, according to the _____ theory of motivation.
    a. attribution
    b. opponent-process
    c. drive reduction
    d. arousal

20. Maria would be described as a neat, orderly person, who is also giving and nurturing and enjoys the company of others. Maria's characteristics are those of a person who is
    a. self-actualized.
    b. low in the need for achievement.
    c. low in sensation-seeking.
    d. more extrinsically-motivated than intrinsically motivated.

21. When Connor is playing racquet ball, his arousal must be higher for him to play a good game, while his arousal must be lower to complete a delicate putt when playing golf. This difference is levels of arousal based on task complexity is best explained by the
    a. opponent-process theory.
    b. James-Lange theory.
    c. emotional appraisal hypothesis.
    d. Yerkes-Dodson law.

22. Regarding test anxiety, which of the following is a FALSE statement?
    a. Overpreparing for a test often leads to the occurrence of test anxiety.
    b. To reduce nervousness before a test, a student should rehearse how he or she will cope with upsetting events, such as running out of time on the test.
    c. A student should list the upsetting thoughts that occur during exams and write calming, rational replies to combat each one.
    d. Test anxiety is a mixture of heightened physiological arousal and excessive worry.

23. Marcus has a desire to have impact on others, so he buys expensive cars and clothes. However, he has also been known to exploit relationships for his personal gain. Marcus would be described as
    a. being emotional intelligence.
    b. being motivated by stimulus needs.
    c. having a high need for achievement.
    d. having a high need for power.

24. Juan is a top gymnastics performer and will be competing in the Summer Olympics. According to the research on top performers, the main reason that Juan is an exceptional success is
    a. his natural talent.
    b. luck and good fortune.
    c. his drive and determination.
    d. the timing of events that allows leaders in various fields to emerge.

25. In Maslow's hierarchy of needs, the physiological needs, needs for safety and security, needs for love and belonging, and needs for esteem and self-esteem are all considered
    a. deficiency motives.
    b. growth needs.
    c. stimulus motives.
    d. meta-needs.

26. Perfection, richness, beauty, autonomy, and aliveness are classified as
    a. individualistic needs for power.
    b. basic needs.
    c. meta-needs.
    d. deficiency motives.

27. Exercising to lose weight so you can buy new "skinny" clothes and be told you "look marvelous" involves _____ motivation.
    a. intrinsic
    b. extrinsic
    c. stimulus
    d. prepotent

28. Activity in the autonomic nervous system is directly responsible for which component of emotion?
    a. emotional feelings
    b. emotional expressions
    c. physiological changes
    d. stimulus motivation

29. The mildest form of emotion that affects day-today behavior and can last for many hours or even days is called a(n)
    a. primary emotion.
    b. secondary emotion.
    c. mood.
    d. physiological arousal state.

30. Positive and negative emotions can occur at the same time because positive emotions are processed in the
    a. amygdala, and negative emotions in the hypothalamus.
    b. hypothalamus, and negative emotions in the amygdala.
    c. right hemisphere, and negative emotions in the left hemisphere.
    d. left hemisphere, and negative emotions in the right hemisphere.

31. Which of the following is an overreaction to intense emotion that can lower blood pressure so much that it causing dizziness and fainting and in rare cases, even death?
    a. adrenaline poisoning
    b. sympathetic overload
    c. parasympathetic rebound
    d. opponent-process feedback

32. During a polygraph examination, a series of multiple choice questions are usually asked. These multiple choice questions make up the _____ test.
    a. guilty knowledge
    b. denotative meanings
    c. comparative guilt
    d. critical incidents

33. An alternative technique for detecting lies besides the polygraph involves the use of
    a. fMRI.
    b. biofeedback.
    c. an emotional intelligence test.
    d. a need for achievement test.

34. Activation and pleasantness-unpleasantness are two of the three basic dimensions of
    a. emotional feelings.
    b. voice inflections.
    c. body positioning.
    d. facial expressions.

35. Compared with people in Asian countries, people in North America are more likely to express which emotion?
    a. anger
    b. sadness
    c. interest
    d. fear

36. Which theory of emotion holds that emotional feelings and bodily arousal occur at the same time with the thalamus alerting the cortex and the hypothalamus?
    a. James-Lange theory
    b. Schachter's cognitive theory
    c. Cannon-Bard theory
    d. the facial feedback hypothesis

37. The theory of emotion that explains that emotions occur when physical arousal is labeled or interpreted is
    a. Schachter's cognitive theory.
    b. the Cannon-Bard theory.
    c. the facial-feedback hypothesis.
    d. the James-Lange theory.

38. People would think that cartoons are funnier if they see them while holding a pen crosswise in their teeth. This observation supports
    a. the James-Lange theory.
    b. the Cannon-Bard theory.
    c. Schachter's cognitive theory.
    d. the facial feedback hypothesis.

39. Empathy is a major characteristic of individuals who
    a. have a high need for achievement.
    b. are high sensation seekers.
    c. are emotionally intelligent.
    d. have alexithymia.

40. Regarding positive and negative emotions, which of the following statements is TRUE?
    a. Negative emotions are associated with actions that probably helped our ancestors survive.
    b. Positive emotions tend to narrow our focus and limit our ideas.
    c. Negative emotions tend to broaden our focus and make us look at many options.
    d. To be emotionally mature, one must learn to treat negative emotions as an unwelcome misery and try to suppress them as much as possible.

Chapter 10: Sex, Gender, and Sexuality

Chapter Overview

Male and female are not simple either/or categories. Sexual identity is complex, multifaceted, and influenced by biology, socialization, and learning. Biological sex consists of genetic sex, gonadal sex, hormonal sex, and genital sex. Sexual development begins with genetic sex (*XX* or *XY* chromosomes) and is then influenced by prenatal hormone levels. Androgen insensitivity, exposure to progestin, the androgenital syndrome, and similar problems can cause a person to be born with an intersexual condition. Estrogens (female sex hormones) and androgens (male sex hormones) influence the development of different primary and secondary sexual characteristics in males and females.

Sexual orientation refers to one's degree of emotional and erotic attraction to members of the same sex, opposite sex, or both sexes. A person may be heterosexual, homosexual, or bisexual. Similar factors (heredity, biology, and socialization) underlie all sexual orientations. As a group, homosexual men and women do not differ psychologically from heterosexuals. All three sexual orientations (heterosexual, homosexual, bisexual) are part of the normal range of sexual behavior.

Male and female behavior patterns are related to learned gender identity and gender role socialization. Many researchers believe that prenatal hormones exert a biological biasing effect that combines with social factors to influence psychosexual development. On most psychological dimensions, women and men are more alike than they are different. Gender identity usually becomes stable by age 3 or 4 years. Gender role socialization seems to account for most observed female–male gender differences. Parents tend to encourage boys in instrumental behaviors and girls in expressive behaviors. Gender role stereotypes often distort perceptions about the kinds activities for which men and women are suited.

People who possess both masculine and feminine traits are androgynous. Roughly one third of all persons are androgynous. Approximately 50 percent are traditionally feminine or masculine. Psychological androgyny is related to greater behavioral adaptability and flexibility.

Gender variant individuals experience a persistent mismatch between their biological sex and their experienced gender. Sex reassignment surgery may be undertaken to help resolve the discrepancy.

While "normal" sexual behavior is defined differently by various cultures, adults typically engage in a wide variety of sexual behaviors. However, coercive and/or compulsive sexual behaviors are emotionally unhealthy. Sexual arousal is related to the body's erogenous zones, but mental and emotional reactions are the ultimate source of sexual responsiveness. Evidence indicates that the sex drive peaks at a later age for females than it does for males, although this difference is diminishing. Castration may or may not influence sex drive in humans. Sterilization does not alter the sex drive. Frequency of sexual intercourse gradually declines with increasing age. However, many elderly persons remain sexually active, and large variations exist at all ages. Masturbation is a common, normal, and completely acceptable behavior.

The similarities between female and male sexual responses far outweigh the differences. Sexual response can be divided into four phases: excitement, plateau, orgasm, and resolution. There do not appear to be any differences between "vaginal orgasms" and "clitoral orgasms." Fifteen percent of women are consistently multi-orgasmic, and at least 50 percent are capable of multiple orgasm. Males experience a refractory period after orgasm, and only 5 percent of men are multi-orgasmic. Mutual orgasm has been abandoned by most sex counselors as the ideal in lovemaking.

The most common sexual disorders are pedophilia and exhibitionism. Compulsive sexual behaviors (paraphilias) tend to emotionally handicap people. The paraphilias include pedophilia, exhibitionism, voyeurism, frotteurism, fetishism, sexual masochism, sexual sadism, and transvestic fetishism. The effects of child molestation vary greatly, depending on the severity of the molestation and the child's relationship to the molester. Exhibitionists are usually not dangerous but can escalate their sexual aggression. They can best be characterized as sexually inhibited and immature.

In the United States, a liberalization of attitudes toward sex has been paralleled by a gradual increase in sexual behavior over the last 50 years. Adolescents and young adults engage in more frequent sexual activity than they did 40 years ago. In recent years there has been a greater acceptance of female sexuality and a narrowing of differences in female and male patterns of sexual behavior. Forcible rape, acquaintance rape, and rape-supportive attitudes and beliefs are major problems in North America.

Each person must now take responsibility for practicing safer sex and for choosing when, where, and with whom to express his or her sexuality. During the last 20 years the incidence of sexually transmitted diseases has steadily increased. STDs and the spread of HIV/AIDS have had a sizable impact on patterns of sexual behavior, including some curtailment of risk taking. Many sexually active people continue to take unnecessary risks with their health by failing to follow safer sex practices.

Although solutions exist for many sexual adjustment problems, good communication and a healthy relationship are the real keys to sexual satisfaction. Communication skills that foster and maintain intimacy help to maintain successful relationships. Most sexual adjustment problems are closely linked to the general health of a couple's relationship. Problems with sexual function can involve desire, arousal, orgasm, or pain. Behavioral methods and counseling techniques have been developed to alleviate many sexual problems.

Preview: Pink and Blue?
Language Development Guide
pink and blue: the color pink is traditionally thought of as a girl color and blue for a boy
black and white: facts are clearly defined as either-or
complexity: being intricate, having multiple parts
transsexual: person with a deep conflict between his or her physical, biological sex and preferred
        psychological and social gender roles
transition: change; alteration
foundation: base on which structure is built
gay: homosexual
"natural": genetic
indicators: signs or markers
in agreement: like-minded
nevertheless: even so; yet; but
ambiguities: vagueness or uncertainties regarding interpretation

Module 10.1 Sexual Development and Sexual Orientation

Sexual Development—Circle One: *XX* or *XY*?

Survey Question: What are the basic dimensions of sex?

Language Development Guide

contrary to common belief: the opposite of what most people believe

proposition: plan; proposal

align: match, fit

conflicts: disagrees

preferred: favored; chosen

dimensions: aspects; factors

at the very least: to put it mildly

take into account: must take into account

predominance: having the highest proportion (amount of); the majority of

trace: map out

at the instant: at the moment

conception: egg from the mother unites with the father's sperm

initiate: begin

genetic makeup: the complete set of inherited characteristics

variations: differences

matures: grows up

infertile: unable to reproduce

secreted: released; given off

proportion: percentage; amount

prenatal: prior to birth

anatomy: structure; framework; makeup

embryos: early stage of prenatal development from two to eight weeks after conception

regardless: despite; no matter what

primary impulse: main goal

ambiguous: vague; unclear

masculinized: appearing boyish with male features

antimiscarriage: to prevent an unintentional early birth

superficial: outward; on the surface

puberty: the biologically defined period when a person matures sexually and becomes capable of reproduction

evident: obvious; apparent

Recite and Review

1. Genetically, Michelle is still a male, but psychologically and socially she is a female with female genitals. Michelle would be described as a(n) _____.
2. Whether you are biologically female or male is defined by the term _____.
3. All the psychological and social traits associated with being male or female is referred to as _____.
4. When a person's biological sex conflicts with his or her preferred psychological and social gender roles, the person is said to be _____.
5. At the instant of conception, one's sex chromosomes determine one's _____ sex.
6. Classifying a person as male or female based on the predominance of androgens or estrogens is called one's _____ sex.
7. If you consider a person male or female depending on whether they have ovaries or testes, then you are classifying a person based on _____ sex.

541

8. The presence of a clitoris and vagina in females and the presence of a penis and scrotum in males determine_____ sex.
9. If you have two X chromosomes, then you are genetically _____.
10. If you have an X chromosome and a Y chromosome, then you are genetically _____.
11. The parent that determines the sex of each child is the _____.
12. If a boy is born XXY, with an extra X chromosome, he may appear feminine, have undersized sexual organs, and be infertile. This condition is called _____ syndrome.
13. Being born with only one X chromosome and no Y chromosome, Marta appeared boyish as an adolescent, and she is infertile. Marta has _____ syndrome.
14. Although it alone does not determine biological sex, the dimension that stays the same throughout life is _____ sex.
15. The chemical substances secreted by the endocrine glands are called _____.
16. The primary sex organs of both males and females are referred to as _____.
17. In females, the primary sex organs are the _____.
18. The primary sex organs in males are the _____.
19. Located above the kidneys are endocrine glands that also supply sex hormones and are called the _____ glands.
20. The female hormones are called _____.
21. The male hormones, with testosterone being one of these hormones, are collectively known as _____.
22. The prenatal development of male or female anatomy is largely due to the presence or absence of _____.
23. Female development will result in a genetic male if the individual inherits an unresponsiveness to testosterone known as _____.
24. A person who has ambiguous sexual anatomy is referred to as a(n) _____ person.
25. A developing female may be masculinized by the anti-miscarriage drug _____.
26. Although Sonya is genetically female and her body produces estrogen, a genetic abnormality is causing her adrenal glands to release too much androgen so that she was born with genitals that looked more male then female. The genetic abnormality is known as _____ syndrome.
27. The sexual and reproductive organs themselves are referred to as _____ sexual characteristics.
28. The superficial physical features such as facial and body hair that appear at puberty in males are called _____ sexual characteristics.
29. The outward physical sexual characteristics in males and females that appear at puberty develop in response to hormonal signals from the _____ gland
30. Breast development in females and the deepening of the voice in males would both be considered _____ sexual characteristics.
31. Reproductive maturity is especially evident in females with the onset of menstruation that is referred to as _____.
32. Soon after the onset of menstruation, the release of ova from the ovaries occurs once a month and is called _____.
33. The end of regular monthly fertility cycles in women when they are in their late 40s or early 50s is called _____.
34. The lower end of the uterus that projects into the vagina is called the _____.
35. Located above the vaginal opening is a small, sensitive organ made up of erectile tissue referred to as the _____.
36. Once released from the ovaries, the eggs travel down the _____ to the uterus.
37. The larger outer lips of the vulva are called the _____.
38. The inner lips of the vulva that surround the vaginal opening are referred to as the _____.

542

39. The pear-shaped muscular organ in which the fetus develops during pregnancy is called the womb or _____.

40. The tube-like structure connecting the external female genitalia with the uterus is called the _____.

41. Within the male reproductive system are two small glands that secrete a clear fluid into the urethra during sexual excitement. These two structures are called the _____ glands.

42. In the male reproductive system is a gland located at the base of the urinary bladder that supplies most of the fluid that makes up semen. This gland is called the _____.

43. The duct that carries sperm from the testes to the urethra is called the _____.

44. The sac-like pouch that holds the testes is called the _____.

45. The tip of the penis is called the _____ penis.

46. Located on each side of the prostate are two small organs, which supply fluid that becomes part of the semen. These two small glands are the _____.

47. A coiled structure at the top of the testes in which sperm are stored is called the _____.

48. The tube through which urine drains as it leaves the body with semen also passing through this tube in males is referred to as the external _____.

Part 1: Connections

1. ___ genetic sex
2. ___ hormonal sex
3. ___ gonadal sex
4. ___ genital sex
5. ___ X chromosome
6. ___ Y chromosome
7. ___ gonads
8. ___ androgens
9. ___ Klinefelter's syndrome
10. ___ Turner's syndrome
11. ___ androgen insensitivity
12. ___ androgenital syndrome

a. sex as indicated by a preponderance of estrogens or androgens in the body
b. any of a number of male sex hormones, especially testosterone
c. genetic male unresponsiveness to testosterone results in female development
d. male chromosome
e. female child born with genitals that are more male than female due to a genetic abnormality of the adrenal glands
f. another name for the primary sex glands in both males and females
g. boy is born with an extra X chromosome (XXY)
h. sex as indicated by the presence of XX or XY chromosomes
i. female chromosome
j. sex as indicated by the presence of the clitoris and vagina in females and the penis and scrotum in males
k. sex as indicated by a presence of ovaries or testes
l. girl born with only one X chromosome

Part 2: Connections

1. ___ sex
2. ___ gender
3. ___ transsexual
4. ___ intersexual person
5. ___ primary sexual characteristics

a. person with a deep conflict between his or her biological sex and preferred psychological and social gender roles
b. refers to the sexual and reproductive organs themselves
c. end of regular monthly fertility cycles
d. type of androgen
e. one's biological classification as female or male

543

6. ___ secondary sexual characteristics
7. ___ estrogen

8. ___ testosterone
9. ___ menarche

10. ___ menopause
11. ___ ovulation

f. any of a number of female sex hormones
g. psychological and social characteristics associated with being male or female
h. onset of menstruation
i. sexual features, such as breasts, body shape, and facial hair
j. person who has genitals suggestive of both sexes
k. the release of ova from the ovaries

Part 3: Connections

1. ___ cervix
2. ___ clitoris

3. ___ fallopian tube
4. ___ labia majora

5. ___ labia minora
6. ___ ovary

7. ___ uterus

8. ___ vagina

a. source of hormones and eggs
b. pear-shaped muscular organ in which the fetus develops during pregnancy
c. carry eggs from the ovaries to the uterus
d. small, sensitive organ made up of erectile tissue; located above the vaginal opening
e. larger outer lips of the vulva
f. tube-like structure connecting the external female genitalia with the uterus
g. lower end of the uterus that projects into the vagina
h. inner lips of the vulva, surrounding the vaginal opening

Part 4: Connections

1. _____ pelvic bone
2. _____ urethra
3. _____ labia minora
4. _____ ovary
5. _____ vagina
6. _____ uterus
7. _____ rectum
8. _____ fallopian tube
9. _____ clitoris
10. _____ labia majora
11. _____ urinary bladder
12. _____ cervix

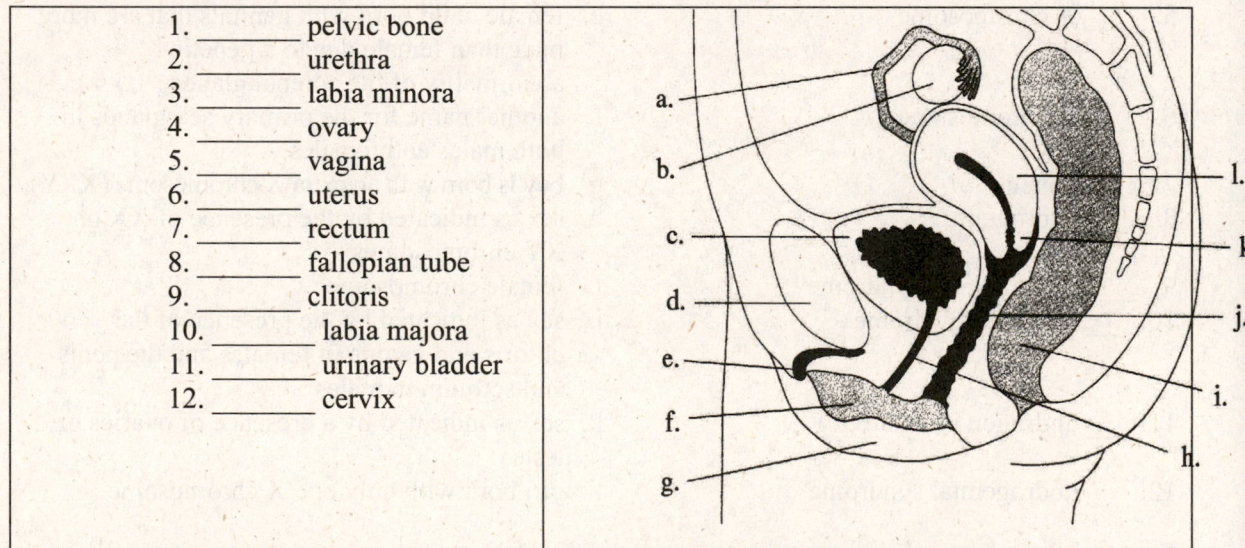

Part 5: Connections

1. ___ Cowper's glands
2. ___ epididymis

3. ___ external urethral orifice

4. ___ glans penis

a. tip of the penis
b. two small glands that secrete a clear fluid into the urethra during sexual excitement
c. duct that carries sperm from the testes to the urethra
d. two small organs on each side of the prostate that supply fluid that becomes part of semen

5. ___ prostate

6. ___ scrotum

7. ___ seminal vesicles

8. ___ testes

9. ___ vas deferens

e. opening at the tip of the penis through which urine and semen pass

f. gland located at the base of the urinary bladder that supplies most of the fluid that makes up semen

g. a coiled structure at the top of the testes in which sperm are stored

h. two glands that are the source of hormones and sperm

i. sac-like pouch that holds the testes

Part 6: Connections

1. _____ Cowper's gland
2. _____ glans penis
3. _____ urethra
4. _____ seminal vesicle
5. _____ vas deferens
6. _____ pelvic bone
7. _____ urinary bladder
8. _____ testis
9. _____ rectum
10. _____ urethral orifice
11. _____ epididymis
12. _____ prostate

Check Your Memory

1. TRUE or FALSE   Gender refers to whether you are biologically female or male.
2. TRUE or FALSE   When person's biological sex conflicts with his or her preferred psychological and social gender roles, the person is referred to as bisexual.
3. TRUE or FALSE   When a person's sex is determined by the presence of a vagina or a penis, it referred to as gonadal sex.
4. TRUE or FALSE   Genital sex is determined by whether the person has a preponderance of androgens or estrogens.
5. TRUE or FALSE   Genetic sex is determined at the instant of conception.
6. TRUE or FALSE   Two X chromosomes initiate male development, while an X chromosome plus a Y chromosome produces a female.
7. TRUE or FALSE   In Klinefelter's syndrome, a girl is born with only one X chromosome and no Y chromosome.
8. TRUE or FALSE   In Turner's syndrome, a boy is born XXY, with an extra X chromosome.
9. TRUE or FALSE   While genetic sex stays the same throughout life, it alone does not determine biological sex.
10. TRUE or FALSE   Male and female sex glands are called the gonads.

545

11. TRUE or FALSE   While the female hormones are referred to as estrogens, the male hormones are called androgens.

12. TRUE or FALSE   The parathyroid glands also supply sex hormones.

13. TRUE or FALSE   Prenatal development of male or female anatomy is largely due to the presence or absence of testosterone.

14. TRUE or FALSE   For the first six weeks of prenatal growth, genetic female and male embryos look identical.

15. TRUE or FALSE   Androgenital syndrome is an unresponsiveness to testosterone by genetic males that results in female development.

16. TRUE or FALSE   For both genetic females and males, hormonal problems before birth may produce an intersexual person, who has ambiguous sexual anatomy.

17. TRUE or FALSE   Primary sexual characteristics are features that appear at puberty, such as breast development and the broadening of the hips in females and facial hair growth and voice deepening in males.

18. TRUE or FALSE   The onset of menstruation is called ovulation.

19. TRUE or FALSE   The end of regular monthly fertility cycles in the late 40s or early 50s is called menopause.

20. TRUE or FALSE   The two tubes that carry eggs from the ovaries to the uterus are called the fallopian tubes.

21. TRUE or FALSE   The lower end of the uterus that projects into the vagina is called the clitoris.

22. TRUE or FALSE   The tube-like structure connecting the external female genitalia with the uterus is the vagina.

23. TRUE or FALSE   A gland located at the base of the urinary bladder that supplies that most of the fluid that makes up semen is called the vas deferens.

24. TRUE or FALSE   A coiled structure at the top of the testes in which sperm is stored is called the Cowper's gland.

25. TRUE or FALSE   The two small organs located on each side of the prostate and supply fluid that becomes part of semen are the seminal vesicles.

Critical Thinking Question

Why might reaching puberty be a mixed blessing for some adolescents?

Module 10.1 Sexual Development and Sexual Orientation
Sexual Orientation—Who Do You Love?
Survey Question: What is sexual orientation?

Language Development Guide

erotic: sexual desire
neatly: tidily; precisely
so too: just as
exclusively: solely; completely; totally
stable: constant
practically nil: almost zero
"converted": changed; won over; convinced
homoerotic: concerning homosexual love and desire
prospects: possibilities; likelihood
orchestrate: plan; organize
impact: influence; effect

imbalances: differences
lesbian: female homosexual
furthermore: in addition
consistent with: in agreement with
discredit: question; place in doubt
implies: means
dawn of time: beginning of time
encounter: meet; run into
inherently: naturally; essentially
more natural: more normal
understandably: as expected
stigma: disgrace
factored out: not considered
molest: abuse; mistreat
monogamous: relationships having one partner
diverse: varied
humanity: quality of being human; being civilized, kind, and caring
prejudices: negative emotional attitudes held against members of a particular group; injustices;
       biases; prejudgements
wane: decrease; fade

Recite and Review

1. Whether you are more emotionally and sexually attracted to the same sex, opposite sex, or both sexes is referred to as sexual _____.
2. Hannah is romantically and erotically attracted to members of the opposite sex. Hannah would be considered _____.
3. Tom is sexually attracted to other men, while Amy is attracted to other women. Sexually, Tom and Amy would be considered _____.
4. If a person is attracted to both men and women, the person is considered _____.
5. Sexual orientation is a deep part of one's personal _____.
6. One study found that if one identical twin is homosexual or bisexual, the chance that the other twin will also be homosexual or bisexual is _____ percent.
7. Other research points to genetic tendencies for homosexuality with sexual orientation being influenced by a gene or genes found on the _____ chromosome.
8. During the times in human evolution when there were a limited number of potential female mates, homosexuality may have developed to reduce _____ between males.
9. Some male fetuses are exposed to too little testosterone and some female fetuses are exposed to too much testosterone, which results in homosexuality according to the _____ theory.
10. The hormone levels of most gay men and lesbians are within the _____ range.
11. Research has shown that the part of the brain connected with sexual activity differs in size and neurotransmitter levels in heterosexuals and homosexuals. This part of the brain is the _____.
12. Most lesbians and gay men were raised by parents whose sexual orientation would be described as _____.
13. Regarding sexual orientation, most children raised by gay and lesbian parents become _____.
14. Based on a national survey, the percent of all adults who regard themselves as homosexual or bisexual is _____ percent.

15. Although they do not confirm their homosexuality until at a later age, most homosexual persons begin to sense that they are different during _____.
16. The problems faced by lesbians and gay men tend to be related to discrimination in hiring and housing and rejection by their _____.
17. Gay men, lesbians, and bisexuals encounter hostility not because there is anything inherently wrong with them, but because they are members of _____ groups.
18. The prejudice, fear, and dislike directed at homosexuals is referred to as _____.
19. The belief that heterosexuality is better or more natural than homosexuality is called _____.
20. Much of the rejection of homosexuals is based on oversimplified images, or false _____.

Connections

1. ___ sexual orientation

2. ___ heterosexual

3. ___ homosexual

4. ___ bisexual

5. ___ prenatal hormonal theory of homosexuality

6. ___ homophobia

7. ___ heterosexism

a. person romantically and erotically attracted to both men and women

b. explains the male fetuses are exposed to too little testosterone and female fetuses are exposed to too much testosterone, resulting in homosexuality

c. person romantically and erotically attracted to members of the opposite sex

d. belief that heterosexuality is better or more natural than homosexuality

e. one's degree of emotional and erotic attraction to members of the same sex, opposite sex, or both sexes

f. person romantically and erotically attracted to same-sex persons

g. prejudice, fear, and dislike directed at homosexuals

Check Your Memory

1. TRUE or FALSE   Your degree of emotional and erotic attraction to members of the same sex, opposite sex, or both sexes is referred to as your sex drive.
2. TRUE or FALSE   People who are bisexual are attracted to both men and women.
3. TRUE or FALSE   The chances are practically zero of an exclusively heterosexual or homosexual person being "converted" from one orientation to the other.
4. TRUE or FALSE   Apparent shifts in orientation usually involve either bisexuals or homosexual people who date or marry members of the opposite sex because of pressures to fit into heterosexual society and then realize they are not being true to themselves.
5. TRUE or FALSE   Research suggests that sexual orientation is mainly genetic and hormonal, although social, cultural, and psychological influences are also involved.
6. TRUE or FALSE   One study found that if one identical twin is homosexual or bisexual, there is a 95 percent chance that the other twin is too.
7. TRUE or FALSE   Research suggests that sexual orientation is influenced by a gene or genes found on the Y chromosome with genetic tendencies for homosexuality being passed from the father to his children.

8. TRUE or FALSE   Some researchers now estimate that sexual orientation is from 30 to 70 percent genetic.

9. TRUE or FALSE   During human evolution, homosexuality may have developed to reduce competition between males for a limited number of potential female mates.

10. TRUE or FALSE   According to the prenatal hormonal theory of homosexuality, some male fetuses are exposed to too little testosterone and some female fetuses are exposed to too much testosterone.

11. TRUE or FALSE   Research has confirmed that homosexuality is caused by a hormone imbalance in adulthood with most gay men having low testosterone levels and lesbians having low estrogen levels.

12. TRUE or FALSE   Neurotransmitter levels in the hypothalamus as well as the size of parts of the hypothalamus differ in heterosexuals and homosexuals.

13. TRUE or FALSE   Most lesbians and gay men were raised by heterosexual parents, and most children raised by gay or lesbian parents become heterosexual.

14. TRUE or FALSE   Based on a national survey, it is estimated that about 15 percent of all adults regard themselves as homosexual or bisexual.

15. TRUE or FALSE   Although most homosexual persons may begin to sense that they are different in childhood, they usually do not confirm their sexual orientation until early adolescent.

16. TRUE or FALSE   Homophobia is the belief that heterosexuality is better or more natural than homosexuality.

17. TRUE or FALSE   Gay and lesbian individuals are no more likely to have emotional problems than heterosexual people when the stresses of social rejection are factored out.

18. TRUE or FALSE   Gay and lesbian persons often try to convert others to homosexuality, especially their own children.

19. TRUE or FALSE   Gay and lesbian persons tend to hate persons of the opposite sex.

20. TRUE or FALSE   Gay and lesbian persons do have long-term, caring monogamous relationships.

Module 10.2 Gender Development, Androgyny, and Gender Variance
Gender Development—Of Manly Men and Girlie Girls
Survey Question: How does one's sense of maleness or femaleness develop?

Language Development Guide

androgyny: presence of both "masculine" and "feminine" traits in a single person

gender variance: condition in which a person's biological sex does not match his or her preferred gender

defy: challenge; resist

manly men: highly masculine men

girlie girls: highly feminine women

subtly: faintly; delicately

"sex-type": to limit one's traits or behaviors to male or female

masculinizing: causing one to show male traits

"tomboys": girls who prefer the company of boys to girls and like to play games and toys usually preferred by boys

biasing: causing a preference for

mired: stuck, slowed down

battle of the sexes: various points of argument between men and women

549

imparts: passes on

rote learning: learning by repetition and memorization

spatial reasoning: being able to mentally visualize the arrangement, change, and movement of objects within space

retaining: keep; save

shaky: uncertain, weak

sexist: discrimination based on gender

exaggerate: overstate; inflate

intuitive: without thinking

"naturally": normally; born that way

vulnerable: have a tendency or weakness

confirms: supports; proves

"turned on": sexually aroused

press: push; strongly urge

sexual passion: strong sexual feelings

"testosterone poisoning": the harmful effects of "too much" testosterone

Alzheimer's disease: age-related disease that causes memory loss, confusion, and eventually total loss of mental functions and death

albeit: even though

suited: fit, particularly able

corporate president: head of large business or company

sufficiently: adequately

dominant: forceful; able to lead

inclined: oriented; able

virtually: almost; nearly

realms: areas; fields

persist: continue

obstacle: barrier

comparable: equal; similar

professions: work that requires specialized training

measly: small; inadequate; stingy

prevail: exist; be happening

diversity: variety; range; assortment

academia: colleges and universities

running in place: making no progress

hobbled: crippled, disabled, slowed down

initiative: the lead

courting: dating

flirtatious: playful teasing, enticing to bring about a relationship

theatrics: staged shows and entertainment events

fond: like

adorning: decorating

arbitrary: random; subjective

apparent: obvious

tenderly: gently; kindly

presumed: supposed

roam: wander

errand: short trip involved in performing a specific task

tolerate: allow; accept; put up with

appropriate: proper; suitable; correct

segregated: separated

norm: standard; rule
implies: means
effeminate: having female characteristics, gestures, or behaviors
sissy: being weak or afraid, derogatory label that a boy is like a girl
mannerisms: distinctive behavioral traits
magnified: increased; enlarged
instrumental: having influence; being goal-directed
conquering: winning the battle, defeating enemies
restricted: limited
one of the costs: one of the disadvantages
burdensome: challenging, difficult, restrictive

Recite and Review

1. One's subjective sense of being male or female as expressed in appearance, behavior, and attitudes is referred to as gender _____.

2. Some psychologists believed that before birth one's chances of developing feminine or masculine traits are altered when sex hormones "_____" the brain.

3. The hypothesized effect that prenatal exposure to sex hormones has on development of the body, nervous system, and later behavior patterns is called the _____ effect.

4. Regarding the prenatal exposure to sex hormones, women are said to be more often "_____-brained.

5. Some psychologists think that biological brain differences explain why men (as a group) do slightly better on math and _____ reasoning tasks.

6. Due to these biological brain differences, women (as a group) are do slightly better at rote learning and _____ skills.

7. After a person suffers a stroke or brain injury, differences in male and female brains may affect the chances of retaining _____ abilities.

8. Female and male scores on the Scholastic Reasoning Test (SAT) are rapidly becoming more alike with this narrowing gap probably explained by male and female interests, experiences, and educational goals becoming more _____.

9. Differences that do exist between the abilities of women and men on different types of learning tasks are based on _____.

10. Most male-female performance gaps can be traced to social differences in opportunities and _____.

11. The acquiring of one's gender identity typically begins at birth when the parents _____ the child.

12. George is a preschooler who is quickly learning which gender behaviors are more appropriate for his sex in his culture. This process that George is undergoing is referred to as _____.

13. Although children are aware of gender role differences slightly earlier, gender identity is usually well formed by ages _____.

14. The favored pattern of behavior expected of each sex by their culture is called a(n) _____.

15. Oversimplified and widely held beliefs about the basic characteristics of men and women are called _____.

16. Research shows that men who are sexually aroused and have high testosterone levels are more likely to make poor decision about sexual behavior and are more likely to become _____.

17. Older men and women with too little testosterone tend to have a greater risk of developing _____ disease.

18. A major career obstacle for many jobs, which reduces a person's chances of being hired because of one's sex, are gender role _____.
19. In general, for every dollar earned by men, women in various professions earn only about _____ cents.
20. The rate for pay for women of color is worse with the least (55 cents) being earned by _____.
21. In business, academia, medicine, law, sports, and politics, women continue to earn less money and achieve lower _____ than men.
22. Regarding the gender roles in Russia, roughly 75 percent of all medical doctors are _____.
23. The gender roles of the Tchambuli people of New Guinea were studied by the famous anthropologist _____.
24. In observations of the Tchambuli men and women, it was found the ones who did the fishing, manufacturing, and took the initiative in lovemaking were the _____.
25. Regarding gender differences in North America, it was found that both parents play more roughly with _____ infants.
26. In a comparison of boys and girls during the elementary school years, the ones that are allowed to roam over a wider area without special permission and are expected to run errands earlier are the _____.
27. In comparing boys and girls, the ones that are more often urged by parents to control their emotions, except for anger and aggression, are the _____.
28. In comparing mothers and fathers, it was found that the parent that is especially likely to encourage their children to play with "appropriate" sex-typed toys is the _____.
29. TV commercials, children's picture books, and video games all show gender role _____.
30. Parents tend to encourage their sons to engage in goal-directed behaviors and to prepare for the world of work. Parents are encouraging their sons to engage in _____ behaviors.
31. Daughters are encouraged in emotion-oriented behaviors, which are referred to as _____ behaviors.
32. Differences between boys and girls are magnified because boys play mostly with boys and girls play with girls in would is described as _____ play.
33. In observing girls and boys at play, it was found that the ones that tend to play indoors and near adults, tend to cooperate more, and play games that require lots of verbal give-and-take are the _____.
34. In observing girls and boys at play, it was found that the ones that is most concerned with dominance or who is the boss are the _____.
35. The cost of adopting a masculine gender role in North America involves the restricted ability to express _____.

Connections

1. ___ gender identity a. process of learning gender behaviors considered appropriate for one's sex in a given culture

2. ___ biological biasing effect b. oversimplified and widely held beliefs about the basic characteristics of men and women

3. ___ general role socialization c. behaviors that communicate emotion or personal feelings

4. ___ gender role d. behaviors directed toward the achievement of some goal

5. ___ gender role stereotypes e. hypothesized effect that prenatal exposure to sex hormones has on development of the body, nervous system, and later behavioral patterns

552

6. ___ instrumental behaviors

    f. one's personal, private sense of maleness or femaleness as expressed in appearance, behavior, and attitudes

7. ___ expressive behaviors

    g. pattern of behaviors that are regarded as "male" or "female by one's culture

Check Your Memory

1. TRUE or FALSE   Gender identity is one's subjective sense of being male or female as expressed in appearance, behavior, and attitudes.

2. TRUE or FALSE   Female fetuses who have been exposed to male hormones have shown a masculinizing effect in which the girls were typically "tomboys" who preferred the company of boys to girls.

3. TRUE or FALSE   The hypothesized effect that prenatal exposure to sex hormones has on development of the body, nervous system, and later behavior patterns is called the hormonal processing effect.

4. TRUE or FALSE   Women are more often said to be "right-brained," while men are "left-brained."

5. TRUE or FALSE   Some psychologists think that biological differences explain why men as a group do slightly better on spatial tasks and math and why women are slightly better at language skills.

6. TRUE or FALSE   Differences in male and female brains may affect the chances of retaining language abilities after a person suffers a stroke or brain injury.

7. TRUE or FALSE   Female and male scores on the Scholastic Reasoning Test (SAT) are rapidly becoming more different.

8. TRUE or FALSE   Most male-female performance gaps can be traced to social differences in the power and opportunities given to men and women.

9. TRUE or FALSE   Men who have high testosterone levels, and who are sexually aroused, are more likely to make poor decisions about sexual behavior and are more likely to become aggressive.

10. TRUE or FALSE   Older men and women with too much testosterone tend to have equilibrium problems and a greater risk of developing Parkinson's disease.

11. TRUE or FALSE   Children are not aware of gender role differences until they are five years of age with their gender identity not being well formed until eight years old.

12. TRUE or FALSE   A gender role is the favored pattern of behavior expected for each sex within a given culture.

13. TRUE or FALSE   The process of learning the gender behaviors expected by one's culture is called gender role socialization.

14. TRUE or FALSE   Gender role stereotypes are oversimplified beliefs about what men and women are actually like.

15. TRUE or FALSE   Currently, in business, academia, medicine, law, sports, and politics, women earn the same amount of money and achieve the same status as men.

16. TRUE or FALSE   In Russia, roughly 75 percent of all medical doctors are men with men making up a significantly larger portion of the workforce.

17. TRUE or FALSE   The famous anthropologist who made classic observations of the Tchambuli people of New Guinea was Karen Horney.

18. TRUE or FALSE   The gender roles of the Tchambuli people of New Guinea are a nearly perfect reversal of North American stereotypes with the women controlling the power and economic life of the community and taking the initiative in courting and sexual relations.

553

19. TRUE or FALSE   Infant girls are held more gently and treated more tenderly than boys with both parents playing more roughly with sons than with daughters.

20. TRUE or FALSE   When they are elementary school age, girls are allowed to roam over a wider area without special permission and are expected to run errands earlier than boys.

21. TRUE or FALSE   Parents, especially fathers, tend to encourage their children to play with "appropriate" sex-typed toys.

22. TRUE or FALSE   Stereotyped gender roles are the norm in TV commercials, children's picture books, and video games.

23. TRUE or FALSE   Daughters are encouraged by their parents to engage in instrumental behaviors, while boys are encouraged to exhibit expressive behaviors.

24. TRUE or FALSE   Beginning around age three, boys start to play mostly with boys and girls play with girls.

25. TRUE or FALSE   Boys tend to play games that require lots of verbal give-and-take.

26. TRUE or FALSE   In their games, girls tend to be concerned with dominance or who is the boss.

27. TRUE or FALSE   In North American males, a restricted ability to express emotion is one of the costs of adopting a masculine gender role.

Critical Thinking Question

As children are growing up, the male emphasis on instrumental behavior comes into conflict with the female emphasis on expressive behavior. At what age do you think such conflicts become prominent?

Module 10.2 Gender Development, Androgyny, and Gender Variance
Androgyny—Are You Masculine, Feminine, or Androgynous?
Survey Question: What is psychological androgyny (and is it contagious)?

Language Development Guide

ambitious: motivated to succeed
analytical: logical
assertive: outspoken about one's will, say what you want
decisive: strong-minded; certain; determined
compassionate: kind; caring
flatterable: able to be convinced by favors or compliments
gullible: able to be tricked or lied to
sympathetic: caring for the emotions of others
yielding: willing to give up one's own needs for the sake of others' needs or wants
seminal: influential; original; creative
neutral traits: could pertain to either sex
hinge: metal hardware on which doors hang and swing
feminists: those whose aim is to establish equal rights for women and men
dust begins to settle: as the argument dies down, as time passes
the picture looks like this: this is the way it is
primarily: mainly; largely
interpersonally: interactions between individuals
oriented: leaning

Recite and Review

1. In North America, being ambitious, analytical, assertive, competitive, decisive, independent, and self-reliant are considered to be "_____" traits.
2. In North America, being cheerful, compassionate, loyal, sympathetic, and understanding are considered to be "_____" traits.
3. If a person is ambitious, analytical, assertive as well as being cheerful, loyal, and understanding, then the person would be described as _____.
4. Psychologist Sandra Bem created an assessment tool that consisted of 20 traditionally "masculine" traits, 20 traditional "feminine" traits, and 20 neutral traits and called it the Bem _____ Inventory.
5. The word androgynous literally means "_____."
6. Of those surveyed with Bem's inventory, the proportion of individuals who fell into the traditional feminine or masculine categories was _____ percent.
7. Those individuals surveyed with Bem's inventory who received high scores on both feminine and masculine items are considered _____.
8. Bem believes that men should be gentle, compassionate, sensitive, and yielding and women should be forceful, self-reliant, independent, and ambitious as the _____ requires.
9. Bem has shown that individuals are more adaptable and less hindered by images of "feminine" or "masculine" behavior if they are _____.
10. In a study in which masculine men were given the choice of doing a gender-appropriate activity, such as nailing boards, or an opposite gender activity, such as preparing a baby bottle, for more money, the masculine men consistently chose to do the _____ activity.
11. Ben has stated that masculine males have great difficulty expressing warmth, playfulness, and concern as well as accepting _____ from others.
12. Darrin tends to be very interested in sports, has mostly male friends, dislikes feminists, and sits with his knees wide apart. Darrin would be described as a(n) _____ man.
13. Women who have trouble being independent and assertive, even when these qualities are desirable, would be described as highly _____ women.
14. Individuals tend to be higher in emotional intelligence, the more _____ they are.
15. High self-esteem and being successful in many situations are related to scoring high in _____ traits.
16. People who seek and receive social support and tend to experience greater social closeness with others and more happiness in marriage usually score high in _____ traits.
17. In general, persons who are more flexible when it comes to coping with difficult situations and are more satisfied with their lives in general are people who are _____.
18. To enhance their lives and relationships, androgynous persons tend to use both their emotionally expressive and their _____ capacities.
19. When Mexican American men and European-American men were compared regarding the number of men in each group who were androgynous, more of the androgynous men were _____-American.
20. A group of men who appear to be creating a more flexible masculinity free from male dominance and linked with a capacity for caring are _____-American men.

Connections

1. ___ masculine traits
2. ___ feminine traits
3. ___ neutral traits
4. ___ androgynous

a. truthful and friendly
b. more flexible in coping with difficult situations; more satisfied with their lives
c. independent and assertive; related to high self-esteem and success in many situations
d. nurturing and interpersonally-oriented; tend to experience greater social closeness

Check Your Memory

1. TRUE or FALSE   Being ambitious, analytical, assertive, competitive, decisive, and independent are traditionally considered to be "masculine traits."
2. TRUE or FALSE   Being cheerful, loyal, sympathetic, and understanding are considered neutral traits.
3. TRUE or FALSE   By combining 20 traditionally "masculine" traits, 20 traditionally "feminine" traits, and 20 neutral traits, Sandra Bem created the Bem Sex Role Inventory (BSRI).
4. TRUE or FALSE   Of those surveyed using the BSRI, 85 percent fell into traditional feminine or masculine categories, five percent scored higher on traits of the opposite sex, and 10 percent were androgynous.
5. TRUE or FALSE   The presence of both "masculine" and "feminine" traits in a single person is referred to as psychological androgyny.
6. TRUE or FALSE   Bem believes that it is necessary for men to also be gentle, compassionate, sensitive, and yielding and for women to also be forceful, self-reliant, independent, and ambitious as the situation requires.
7. TRUE or FALSE   In one study in which people were given the choice of doing either a "masculine" activity or a "feminine" activity, masculine men and feminine women consistently chose to do gender-appropriate activities, even when the opposite choice paid more.
8. TRUE or FALSE   Masculine men find it relatively easy to accept emotional support from others, particularly from women.
9. TRUE or FALSE   Masculine men tend to be interested in sports, have mostly male friends, dislike feminists, and sit with their knees wide apart.
10. TRUE or FALSE   Androgynous individuals are more flexible when it comes to coping with difficult situations and are higher in emotional intelligence.
11. TRUE or FALSE   Androgynous individuals do not exhibit either instrumental nor emotionally expressive behaviors.
12. TRUE or FALSE   Scoring high in "femininity" is related to high self-esteem and success in many areas.
13. TRUE or FALSE   Those individuals who score high in masculinity experience more happiness in marriage.
14. TRUE or FALSE   More European-American men are androgynous than Mexican-American men.
15. TRUE or FALSE   Some Asian-American men, especially those who were born in the United States, appear to be creating a more flexible masculinity that links masculinity with a capacity for caring.

Critical Thinking Question

Could a person be androgynous in a culture where "masculine" and "feminine" traits differ greatly from those on Bem's list?

Module 10.2 Gender Development, Androgyny, and Gender Variance
When Sex and Gender Do Not Match—The Binary Busters
Survey Question: What is gender variance?

Language Development Guide

binary: consisting of two parts; dual
busters: persons who break up something
degrees: amounts; levels

shades: tints or hues of color
rainbow: multicolored; much variety in shades
significant: large; sizeable
heated: intense; fiery
controversy: disagreement; debate
pathological: evidence of a mentally disturbed condition
deserve: be worthy of; ought to have
stigmatization: to characterize one as disgraceful
trend: tendency; movement; inclination
psychiatric: dealing with diagnosis and treatment of mental illness
resolved: settled
undertaken: carried out
reconfigure: to rearrange the elements or parts
deliberate: on purpose
transform: change; alter; convert
impose: inflict; force

Recite and Review

1. The relationship between sex and gender is a rainbow of possibility ranging from psychological androgyny and childhood tomboyism to intersexuality and _____.
2. Condition in which a person's biological sex does not match his or her preferred gender is referred to as gender _____.
3. When children's preferred genders do not match their biological sex, some parents wait until they grow up to deal with the situation, while many parents try to encourage what they see as _____ behavior.
4. According to the *Diagnostic and Statistical Manual of Mental Disorders (DSM)*, person who is a transsexual would be diagnosed with a(n) _____ disorder.
5. When surgery reconfigures the external appearance of the genitals of an gender variant person, the procedure is called _____ surgery.
6. When intersexual or transsexual persons wish to change their sex, they must undergo surgery and, then, in order to shift the chemical balance in their bodies, they must undergo _____ treatments.
7. Adults who deliberately seek sex reassignment are generally _____ with the results.
8. For intersexual children, the benefits usually outweigh the long-term psychological costs, according to the supporters of early _____.
9. Rather than surgically and chemically alter their bodies as children, some psychologists believe it is better to wait until adulthood with the choice whether or not to have surgery left to the intersexual or _____ individual.

Connections

1. ___ gender variance
2. ___ gender identity disorder
3. ___ sex reassignment

a. external appearance of genitals are reconfigured by surgery and hormone treatments shift the chemical balance
b. DSM classification for transsexuals
c. condition in which a person's biological sex does not match his or her preferred gender; includes intersexual and transsexual individuals

557

Check Your Memory

1. TRUE or FALSE — Biological sex is either male or female, while gender is either masculine or feminine with no varying degrees of either.

2. TRUE or FALSE — People are referred to as gender variant if their biological sex definitely does not match their preferred gender.

3. TRUE or FALSE — When it comes to intersexual or transsexual children, many parents try to encourage what they see as gender-appropriate behavior, while others wait and see if their children will grow into more gender appropriate roles.

4. TRUE or FALSE — Regarding intersexual and transsexual individuals, if there is a trend in America today, it is towards acceptance and support.

5. TRUE or FALSE — According to the *Diagnostic and Statistical Manual of Mental Disorders (DSM)*, transsexuals suffer from a dissociative disorder.

6. TRUE or FALSE — After a sex reassignment surgery has been performed, the individual will no longer needs hormone treatments.

7. TRUE or FALSE — Adults who deliberately seek sex reassignment are generally unhappy with the results and become severely depressed.

8. TRUE or FALSE — Supporters of early sex assignment argue that the benefits usually outweigh the the long-term psychological costs.

9. TRUE or FALSE — Critics of sexual reassignment believe that it is better to wait until adulthood, when transsexual and intersexual individuals can choose for themselves whether or not to have surgery and whether to live as a man or a woman.

10. TRUE or FALSE — Because sex and gender are complex, the best course of treatment may prove to be different for different people.

Module 10.3 Sexual Behavior, Response, and Attitudes

Sexual Behavior—Mapping the Erogenous Zones

Survey Question: What are the most typical patterns of human sexual behavior?

Language Development Guide

excitement through resolution: first and last stage of the human sexual response cycle
atypical: uncommon; abnormal
erogenous zones: pleasure producing areas of the body
verified: proved; confirmed
exhibit: show
norms: widely accepted standard of conduct
restrictions: limits; controls
sex play: fooling around; making out
prostitution: having sex for money or other payment
extramarital: outside of marriage
arbitrary: random; by chance; subjective
consenting: by permission
direct stimulation: arousal through touch
urological: related to the urinary tract
gynecological: related to the female reproductive system
revulsion: disgust
script: screenplay; words and actions written for a play
plot: plan; design
"approved": agreed upon

"agendas": lists of things to do

contemporary: modern; current

what's love got to do with it: popular pop song made famous by Tina Turner; and an American
        film made in the 1990s

favoring: preferring

romance: pleasurable feeling associated with love and physical attraction

premarital: before marriage

fading: decreasing; going away

"not a big deal": no need to worry about it

casual: careless

intend: plan; expect

letdown: disappointment

He (or she) is just not that into you: meaning the other person does not feel the same way about
        you as you feel about them; also the title of a book and recent American film about
        problems that occur in dating

experimentation and exploration: refers, in this case, to the process about finding out about sex
        and other aspects of relationships through trial and error

emerge: come out; surface

unscathed: unhurt; untouched; safe and sound

encounters: meetings

"graduate": mature

potential: capability

responsive: reacts

excerpts: segments, short pieces

erotic: sexual

repulsed: wanting to have it removed

macho: stereotypically masculine; manly man

fantasy: daydream; not realistic

prop: support

initiative: lead

preferences: liking; favorite aspects

acknowledged: recognized; accepted

orgasm: climax and release of sexual excitement

peak: high point

exaggerating: overstating

comparable: similar

recency: having occurred not long ago

chats: talks

as such: by itself

inhibitions: shyness; something that restrains beahvior

no doubt: surely

accounts: explains

reputation: something a object or person is known for

seduction: luring or tempting someone into having sex

Ogden Nash: American humorist and poet

folklore: unwritten story or proverb

dandy: fine

Candy is dandy, but liquor is quicker: romance can be seductive, but a woman's defense to
having sex   can be lowered more rapidly by serving her alcohol

suppresses: holds back; blocks

reputed: supposed; presumed

impair: harm
virtually: almost; nearly
abolish: put an end to
inexperienced: have not engaged in, as yet
sex offenders: committed a crime by forcing a person to have sex against their will, ex. rape
curb: control; restrain; hold back
supplements: medication
vast: sizable
tubal ligation: surgery for permanent birth control in which a woman's fallopian tubes are cut in tied in two places
vasectomy: surgery that removes all or part of the vas deferens of a man as a birth control method
a concern: a worry
accompanies: goes together with
extended: long in duration
regularity: occurring on a normal, reliable time schedule
use it or lose it: practice or you will no longer be able to do it
fairly: somewhat
cynics: skeptic; doubter
And the other 5 percent lied!: the percentage is underestimated because the five percent that said they did not, really do masturbate, but were too embarrassed to tell the truth
feature: characteristic
substitute: alternative; replacement for
valid: suitable
compelled: forced; required
one more item on the menu: another possibility of something to do, an option
insanity: legal definition of being so mentally disturbed that one is not responsible for one's actions
acne: oily, pimpled skin
sterility: unable to reproduce
such nonsense: examples of false information; garbage
enlightened: open-minded; tolerant
well aware: recognize and understand

Recite and Review

1. The researcher that verified instances of orgasm in very young children and found that two-to five-year-old children spontaneously touch and exhibit their genitals was _____ of age.
2. Research has verified instances of orgasm in boys as young as _____.
3. In the North American culture, sex acts that are discouraged include prostitution, extramarital sex, sex between children, and sex between close relatives called _____.
4. Apart from cultural norms, it can be said that any sexual act engaged in is considered "normal" if it does not hurt anyone and is _____.
5. Areas of the body that produce pleasure and/or provoke erotic desire are referred to as the body's _____.
6. Since the touching of a person's body during a medical exam or unwanted touching does not produce sexual arousal, it can be said that human sexual arousal includes a large _____ element.
7. Jon is going on a date with his girlfriend and will follow an unspoken mental plan that defines the actions that will take place on their date. This plan is called a(n) _____.
8. Misunderstandings are almost sure to occur when two people follow very different _____.
9. For humans, the ultimate erogenous zone is the _____.

10. Sexual scripts that include having sex with friends or even strangers without any courtship or romance are examples of _____ sex.
11. The script which includes sex in a friendship, without traditional romance is called _____.
12. The more casual script in which two people having sex are more or less strangers is called the _____ script.
13. The sexual script stresses courtship, romance, and marriage is referred to as the _____ script.
14. As casual sexual scripts become more common, the focus on intercourse is fading in favor of a type of sex that is seen by young people as less risky, more acceptable, and "not a big deal," which is _____ sex.
15. Casual sex is usually associated with alcohol use and _____ sexual behaviors.
16. Young women who are having casual sex are more likely to become _____.
17. Regarding sexual arousal, women and men have a(n) _____ potential.
18. Compared to men, women tend to place more emphasis on _____ with a lover.
19. In a study in which women watched excerpts from two erotic films, one made for male viewers and the other presented from a female point of view, the women showed SIMILAR _____ arousal to both films.
20. In a study in which women watched excerpts from two erotic films, one made for male viewers and the other presented from a female point of view, the women showed DIFFERENT _____ of arousal to both films.
21. A woman's emotional response to erotic cues tends to be closely tied to her _____ of arousal.
22. Based on the frequency of orgasm (from masturbation or intercourse), the peak of male sexual activity is at age _____ .
23. The peak rate of female sexual activity appearing to occur a little _____ than men's.
24. The strength of one's motivation to engage in sexual behavior is referred to as one's _____.
25. Men's and women's sex drives are both related to the amount of a type of androgen in their bloodstream called _____.
26. Alcohol, in small doses, stimulates erotic desire by lowering inhibitions and is classified as a(n) _____.
27. Regarding the effect of large amounts of alcohol on sexual desire, arousal, pleasure, and performance, it can be said that alcohol _____ them.
28. If certain foods increased your sexual desire and pleasure, these foods would be called _____.
29. Regarding their effects on sexual desire and performance, amphetamines, amyl nitrite, cocaine, and Ecstasy tend to _____ them.
30. Regarding their effects on sexual desire and performance, barbiturates, LSD, and marijuana tend to _____ them.
31. The surgical removal of the testicles or ovaries is called _____.
32. In sexually inexperienced lower animals, the effect that surgically removing their testicles or ovaries will have on sexual activity is to _____ it.
33. Surgery to make a man or woman infertile that does not cause the person to lose interest in sex is referred to as _____ .
34. Surgery that makes a woman infertile is tubal ligation, while the surgery that makes a man infertile is called a(n _____.
35. The crucial factors for an extended sex life into one's late adulthood appear to be opportunity and _____.
36. In some instances, the sex drive in both men and women can be restored through the use of _____ supplements.

37. Self-stimulation that causes sexual pleasure or orgasm is called _____.
38. In a survey, it was found that the percent of married women and men who use sexual self-stimulation at least occasionally is approximately _____ percent.
39. For adolescents, masturbation is considered an important part of their _____ development.
40. Although now considered a normal sexual behavior at any age, masturbation was once thought to cause insanity, sterility, and acne and was referred to as "_____."

Connections

1. ___ erogenous zones

2. ___ sexual script

3. ___ sex drive

4. ___ aphrodisiacs

5. ___ castration

6. ___ sterilization

7. ___ incest

8. ___ masturbation

a. substances reputed to increase sexual desire or pleasure

b. self-stimulation that causes sexual pleasure or orgasm

c. medical procedures, such as vasectomy or tubal ligation, that make a man or a woman infertile

d. sex between close relatives

e. strength of one's motivation to engage in sexual behavior

f. areas of the body that produce pleasure and/or provoke erotic desire

g. an unspoken mental plan that defines a "plot," dialogue, and actions expected to take place in a sexual encounter

h. surgical removal of the testicles or ovaries

Check Your Memory

1. TRUE or FALSE   Researcher Alfred Kinsey verified instances of orgasm in boys as young as five months old and girls as young as four months.
2. TRUE or FALSE   Kinsey found that two-to five-year-old children spontaneously touch and exhibit their genitals.
3. TRUE or FALSE   Areas of the body that produce pleasure and/or provoke erotic desire are called temporal sensitivity points.
4. TRUE or FALSE   An unspoken mental plan that defines a "plot," dialogue, and actions expected to take place in a sexual encounter is called a sexual script.
5. TRUE or FALSE   According to one survey, only about 10 percent of all college students have been friends with benefits and engaged in this casual type of sex.
6. TRUE or FALSE   The hook-up script involves two people having sex who are more or less strangers.
7. TRUE or FALSE   Traditional sexual scripts stress courtship, romance, and marriage.
8. TRUE or FALSE   The traditional focus on intercourse is fading in favor of oral sex, which young people tend to be seen as less risky.
9. TRUE or FALSE   One study found that 20 percent of American ninth graders have already had oral sex and more than 30 percent intend to try it soon.
10. TRUE or FALSE   Casual sex is usually associated with alcohol use and unsafe sexual behaviors, such as unprotected sex.
11. TRUE or FALSE   Young women who are having casual sex are less likely to become depressed.
12. TRUE or FALSE   Men have a greater potential for sexual arousal and are more physically responsive than women.

562

13. TRUE or FALSE   Women tend to place more emphasis on emotional closeness with a lover than men do.

14. TRUE or FALSE   When women watched excerpts from two erotic films, one made from a male's point of view and one from a woman's point of view, the women's physical arousal was greater for the film made from a man's point of view than from a woman's point of view.

15. TRUE or FALSE   Based on the frequency of orgasm (from masturbation or intercourse), the peak of male sexual activity is at age 21, while the female peak occurs at age 17.

16. TRUE or FALSE   Currently in any given year, men and women ages 25 to 44 do not significantly differ in their average number of opposite sex partners or in their overall pattern of sexual activity.

17. TRUE or FALSE   When a man chats with a woman he finds attractive, his testosterone levels actually increase.

18. TRUE or FALSE   A woman's sex drive is related both to her estrogen levels and to the testosterone level in her bloodstream.

19. TRUE or FALSE   Alcohol is classified as a stimulant, which, in large doses, increases sexual desire, pleasure, and performance.

20. TRUE or FALSE   Ecstasy, amphetamines, cocaine, and LSD act as aphrodisiacs, increasing one's sexual response.

21. TRUE or FALSE   Barbiturates, amyl nitrite, and marijuana impair sexual response.

22. TRUE or FALSE   Castration of sex offenders will completely take away the sex drive in all who undergo this procedure.

23. TRUE or FALSE   Tubal ligation and vasectomy are two types of castration.

24. TRUE or FALSE   Sterilization usually decreases sexual desire and limits sexual performance.

25. TRUE or FALSE   Some people in their 80s and 90s continue to have active sex lives with the crucial factors for extended an extended sex life being regularity and opportunity.

26. TRUE or FALSE   Self-stimulation has been observed in infants under one year of age.

27. TRUE or FALSE   For adolescents, masturbation provides a healthy substitute for sexual involvement at a time when young people are maturing emotionally.

28. TRUE or FALSE   Only about 30 percent of married women and men masturbate with this self-stimulation have disastrous effects on marital relationships.

29. TRUE or FALSE   Fifty years ago, a child might have been told the myth that masturbation was "self-abuse" and would cause insanity, acne, sterility, or other such nonsense.

30. TRUE or FALSE   People are compelled to masturbate only because they lack a sexual partner.

Module 10.3 Sexual Behavior, Response, and Attitudes

Human Sexual Response—Sexual Interactions

Survey Question: To what extent do females and males differ in sexual response?

Language Development Guide

pioneering: ground-breaking; original
gynecologist: medical doctor who specializes in women's health
expanded: increased
phases: parts; stages
intensifies: made stronger

climax: high point; peak
subside: become less; settle down; decrease
ebb: fade; diminish
discharge: release
exploded: disproved
relatively: fairly; somewhat
fused together: combined
downgrade: lower; reduce
seminal fluid: thick white fluid containing spermatozoa that is ejaculated
compatibility: existing in agreement or harmony
artificial concern: a made-up, constructed worry
mutual: shared
spontaneity: to do without planning
casts: sheds; throws
contrary to popular belief: the opposite of what most people believe
sexual potency: ability to carry out sexual intercourse
flaccid: limp
undermine: weaken; damage

Recite and Review

1. Our understanding of sexual response was greatly expanded through the experiments, interviews, and controlled observations done by gynecologist William Masters and psychologist _____.
2. The human sexual response can be divided into four phases: (1) excitement, (2) plateau, (3) orgasm, and (4) _____.
3. In women, the changes in the body that include the vagina preparing for intercourse, the nipples becoming erect, the pulse rate rising, and the skin becoming flushed or reddened describes the _____ phase.
4. The phase in the human response cycle that some women skip, but that other women experience as intensification of feelings is the _____ phase.
5. Three to ten muscular contractions of the vagina, uterus, and related structures discharge sexual tension during the _____ phase.
6. Although later research has disproved this Freudian belief, Sigmund Freud claimed that an "immature" form of female response was the "_____ orgasm."
7. The inner two thirds of the vagina is relatively insensitive to touch with most sensations during intercourse come from stimulation of the _____ and other external areas
8. Orgasm is usually followed by a return to lower levels of sexual tension and arousal called the _____ phase.
9. About 15 percent of all women regularly have additional orgasms because after their first orgasm, they return to the _____ phase.
10. In the male, the phase of the human response cycle that involves the erection of the penis and nipples, a rise in heart rate, increased blood flow to the genitals, and enlargement of the testicles is the _____ phase.
11. Stimulation during the plateau phase brings about a reflex release of sexual tension, leading to the _____ phase.
12. In the mature male, orgasm is usually accompanied by the release of sperm and seminal fluid, which is referred to as a(n) _____.
13. The short period of time during which a male cannot have a second orgasm and during which many cannot have an erection is called the _____ period.
14. Compared to men, women typically go through the sexual phases more _____.

15. Although male and female sexual responses are generally quite similar, the differences that do exist can affect the couple's sexual _____.
16. During lovemaking, 10 to 20 minutes is often required for a woman to go from excitement to orgasm, while males may experience all four phases in as little as _____ minutes
17. Although now regarded as an artificial concern, it was once thought that the "goal" of lovemaking was for both parents to reach sexual climax at the same time, or have a(n) _____.
18. Couples should seek mutual satisfaction through a combination of intercourse and erotic touching, also called _____,
19. The relationship between penis size and male sexual potency is a(n) _____ correlation.
20. Forty-eight percent of all women and only five percent of men have had _____ orgasms.

Connections

1. ___ orgasm
2. ___ ejaculation
3. ___ refractory period
4. ___ plateau phase
5. ___ excitement phase
6. ___ resolution
7. ___ "clitoral orgasm"
8. ___ simultaneous orgasm
9. ___ foreplay

a. short time period after orgasm during which males are unable to again reach orgasm
b. once regarded as "goal" of lovemaking but which is now regarded as an artificial concern
c. fourth phase of sexual response, involving a return to lower levels of sexual tension and arousal for both males and females
d. first phase of sexual response, indicated by initial signs of sexual arousal
e. incorrectly referred to as an "immature" form of female response by Sigmund Freud
f. release of sperm and seminal fluid by the male at the time of orgasm
g. third phase in which climax and release of sexual excitement occur
h. erotic touching
i. second phase of sexual response during which physical arousal is further heightened

Check Your Memory

1. TRUE or FALSE   In a series of experiments, interviews, and controlled observations, Masters and Johnson directly studied sexual intercourse and masturbation in nearly 700 males and females.
2. TRUE or FALSE   According to Masters and Johnson, the sexual response phases, in order, are arousal, plateau, excitement, and sexual climax.
3. TRUE or FALSE   The physical changes and subjective feelings of arousal are more intense during the excitement phase than during the plateau phase.
4. TRUE or FALSE   Occasionally, women skip the plateau phase.
5. TRUE or FALSE   After orgasm, about 15 percent of all women regularly return to the plateau phase and have one or more additional orgasms.
6. TRUE or FALSE   The final level of sexual response, which involving a return to lower levels of sexual tension and arousal is the resolution phase.
7. TRUE or FALSE   Sigmund Freud incorrectly claimed that a "clitoral orgasm" was an "immature" form of female response and that women who experienced clitoral orgasms had not fully accepted their femininity.

8. TRUE or FALSE   The inner two thirds of the vagina are extremely sensitive to touch with most sensations during intercourse coming from stimulation of the vagina rather than the clitoris.

9. TRUE or FALSE   In males, ejaculation is followed by a short refractory period during which a second orgasm is impossible.

10. TRUE or FALSE   Men typically go through the sexual phases more slowly than women do.

11. TRUE or FALSE   Simultaneous orgasm is still considered the "goal" of lovemaking.

12. TRUE or FALSE   Only about 5 percent of males are capable of multiple orgasm, while 48 percent of women have had multiple orgasms at one time or another.

13. TRUE or FALSE   About one woman in three does not experience orgasm during the first year of marriage.

14. TRUE or FALSE   There is a significant positive relationship between penis size and male sexual potency.

15. TRUE or FALSE   Masters and Johnson found that although individual differences exist in flaccid penis size, there tends to be much less variation in size during erection.

Module 10.3 Sexual Behavior, Response, and Attitudes
Atypical Sexual Behavior—Trench Coats, Whips, Leathers, and Lace
Survey Question: What are the most common sexual disorders?

Language Development Guide

atypical: weird; abnormal
trench coats: long rain jackets often associated with exhibitionists
whips, leathers: objects commonly associated with sadists and masochists
strict: exact; narrow interpretation
deviant: abnormal; nonstandard
immense: huge; great
compulsive: irrational; uncontrollable
nonconsenting: without the permission
inanimate: non-living
humiliation: shame; disgrace
deriving: receiving; gaining
inflicting: causing or imposing something unpleasant on another
despicable: bad, evil
perverts: sexually and morally corrupt, bad people
lurking: to lie in wait; to sneak in a silent manner in the shadows
acquaintance: someone you have met but is not a friend
rapist: person who forces another to have sexual intercourse
exceed: go beyond
fondling: touching of another person in a sexual manner
rigid: unemotional and difficult to change
puritanical: very strict regarding moral or religious matters; often believes they are on the good side of a clear good and evil battle
consumers: person who buys and uses something
pornography: pictures or films of sexual behavior
witnesses: person who has seen something themselves
victims: person who has been harmed by another
incident: event; occurrence
trauma: a physical and/or emotional injury and shock

overreact: react excessively; make a big deal

hysterical: frantic; out of control

further: additionally

by no means: in no way; not at all

secretiveness: not open to the point of evading any communication

tactics: methods; tricks

convicted: found guilty

sex offenders: persons convicted of crimes involving sex, such as rape, molestation, child pornography, etc.

assaults: physical attacks

access: means of approaching

targeted: marked; aimed at

bribes: pay offs used to persuade

to lull: to calm; relax, reassure

compliance: submission; obedience

phobias: exaggerated, irrational fears

evoke: call to mind; remind

vivid: clear

repressive: overly strict; authoritarian; cruel

inadequacy: failure; incompetence

"manhood": the masculine qualities

confronted: threatened

emerges: comes out

inhibition: restrained; blocked; suppressed

infantile: child-like

victimize: make a victim of; abuse

array: selection; collection

Recite and Review

1. By strict standards, including the law in some states, any sexual activity other than face-to-face heterosexual intercourse between married adults is considered atypical or _____.
2. Public standards are often at odds with _____ behavior.
3. Psychologically, the mark of true sexual deviations is that they are destructive and _____.
4. Another name for sexual deviations is _____.
5. Sex with children, or child molesting, is called _____.
6. "Flashing" or displaying the genitals to unwilling viewers is called _____.
7. "Peeping" or viewing the genitals of others without their permission is called _____.
8. If you are in a public place, such as a subway, and another person sexually touches or rubs up against you in a sexual way without your consent, this person is engaging in _____.
9. Sexual arousal associated with inanimate objects is called _____.
10. If a person is achieving sexual arousal by wearing clothing of the opposite sex, this sexual deviation is referred to as _____.
11. If a person desires pain and/or humiliation as part of the sex act, he or she is engaging in sexual _____.
12. A person who derives sexual pleasure from inflicting pain and/or humiliation is engaging in sexual _____.
13. Between one third and two thirds of all sexual arrests are for _____.
14. Regarding their gender, child molesters are usually _____.
15. Most molestations involve the sexual act of _____.

567

16. Some signs of child molestation include secretiveness, emotional disturbance, nightmares, loss of self-esteem, unusual aggressiveness, or an act, such as riding a bicycle dangerously in traffic, which is an example of _____ behavior.

17. If an adult tries to engage a child in sexual behavior, children should be taught to shout "_____."

18. If an adult suggests to a child online that they could meet in person, the child should immediately _____ his or her parents.

19. Targeting the child with bribes or games or through the internet in chat rooms are_____ used by child molesters.

20. Most child molestations take place in the _____'s home.

21. As adults, many victims of incest or molestation develop sexual _____.

22. Most exhibitionists come from strict and repressive backgrounds and have a deep sense of inadequacy, which produces a compulsive need to prove their "_____."

23. Regarding gender, most exhibitionists are _____.

24. Regarding marital status, most exhibitionists are _____.

25. The picture of sexual deviance that most often emerges is one of sexual inhibition and _____.

26. Sexual deviations in which people tend to voluntarily associate with people who share these similar interests with their behavior not harming anyone, except when in the extreme include sadists, masochists, transvestites, and _____.

27. Unwilling participants are victimized in the sexual deviations of pedophilia, exhibitionism, frotteurism, and _____.

28. All the paraphilias, unless they are very mild, are psychologically unhealthy just like overeating, excessive gambling, and drug abuse because all of these behaviors are _____.

Connections

1. ___ paraphilias
2. ___ pedophilia
3. ___ exhibitionism
4. ___ voyeurism
5. ___ frotteurism
6. ___ fetishism
7. ___ sexual masochism
8. ___ sexual sadism
9. ___ transvestic fetishism

a. sexual arousal associated with inanimate objects
b. achieving sexual arousal by wearing the clothing of the opposite sex
c. desiring pain and/or humiliation as part of the sex act
d. compulsive or destructive deviations in sexual preferences or behavior
e. "peeping," or viewing the genitals of othes without their permission
f. "flashing," or displaying the genitals to unwilling viewers
g. deriving sexual pleasure from inflicting pain and/or humiliation
h. sex with children, or child molesting
i. sexually touching or rubbing against a nonconsenting person, usually in a public place

Check Your Memory

1. TRUE or FALSE   By strict standards, including the law in some states, any sexual activity other than face-to-face heterosexual intercourse between married adults is atypical or "deviant."

568

2. TRUE or FALSE   Psychologically, the mark of true sexual deviations is that they are compulsive and destructive.

3. TRUE or FALSE   Another name for sexual deviations is dissociative disorders.

4. TRUE or FALSE   Sex with children, or child molesting is known as frotteurism.

5. TRUE or FALSE   "Flashing," or displaying the genitals to unwilling viewers is known as voyeurism.

6. TRUE or FALSE   Sexual arousal associated with inanimate objects is called fetishism.

7. TRUE or FALSE   Whe a person achieves sexual arousal by wearing clothing of the opposite sex, it is known as sexual masochism.

8. TRUE or FALSE   Sexual sadism involves a person desiring to inflict pain or humiliation as part of the sex act.

9. TRUE or FALSE   Most child molesters are married and two thirds are fathers.

10. TRUE or FALSE   In most cases of pedophilia, the offender is a stranger to the child.

11. TRUE or FALSE   Most molestations rarely exceed fondling.

12. TRUE or FALSE   Many child molesters are rigid, passive, puritanical, or religious and are consumers of child pornography.

13. TRUE or FALSE   Many child molesters were often witnesses or victims of sexual abuse themselves.

14. TRUE or FALSE   Secretiveness, sleep problems, and unusual risk taking are all signs that a child may be experiencing child molestation.

15. TRUE or FALSE   It helps if children know the tactics typically used by molesters.

16. TRUE or FALSE   Most child molestations take place in the child's home.

17. TRUE or FALSE   Repeated molestations, those that involve force or threats, and those that involve sexual intercourse can leave lasting emotional scars.

18. TRUE or FALSE   Many victims of incest and molestation develop sexual phobias.

19. TRUE or FALSE   Exhibitionism is not a common sexual deviation and accounts for less than one percent of all sexual arrests.

20. TRUE or FALSE   Exhibitionists have a high repeat rate among sexual offenders.

21. TRUE or FALSE   Although exhibitionists were once thought to be harmless, one recent study found that up to 40 percent of exhibitionists go on to commit more serious sexual crimes and other offenses.

22. TRUE or FALSE   Most exhibitionists feel a deep sense of inadequancy, which produces a compulsive need to prove their "manhood" by frightening women.

23. TRUE or FALSE   A woman who becomes visibly upset when confronted by the exhibitionist actually discourages him from further involvement.

24. TRUE or FALSE   Many sadists, masochists, fetishists, and transvestites voluntarily associate with people who share their sexual interests with their behavior not harming anyone, except when it is extreme.

25. TRUE or FALSE   Pedophilia, exhibitionism, voyeurism, and frotterurism do victimize unwilling participants.

Module 10.3 Sexual Behavior, Response, and Attitudes
Attitudes and Sexual Behavior—The Changing Sexual Landscape
Survey Question: Have recent changes in attitudes affected sexual behavior?

Language Development Guide
landscape: scenery; view
transported: carried; moved
stunned: shocked; astonished
skimpy: small, revealing

tampons: women's menstrual protection

jock itch: a fungus in the groin area

explicit: fully and clearly expressed, leaving nothing to be implied

Victorian era: period from 1837 through 1901 when Queen Victoria reigned in Great Britain with the time period characterized by stuffy formality and strict morality

fundamental: basic

alterations: changes

liberalized: made more open and accepting

virginity: never had sexual intercourse

translated: turned into; converted

faithfulness: fidelity, monogamy; being loyal in emotionally and sexually to one partner

fidelity: faithfulness; loyalty; devotion; commitment to one partner

upheaval: turmoil; disruption

sharp: sudden, intense

encouragingly: positively

contraceptive: birth control

industrialized: developed; modern

counter-movement: a social movement opposed to another social movement

wholesale: complete

trend: tendency; development

ample: much, plenty of

promiscuity: having many sexual partners

cohabitation: living together, typically outside of marriage

preludes: coming before, introductions to

sowed some wild oats: sexually active

tacitly: expressed or carried out without words

"easy," "bad," or "promiscuous": immoral; loose; not selective with whom one is sexually active

pervade: present throughout

mores: accepted traditional customs

"separate but not equal": different and not given the same rights

counterparts: matching or corresponding individual

plight: difficulty, bad situation

oversexualized: young children, especially girls, dressing and acting in a sexual manner

antics: silly ways of behaving

equate: connect; associate

gratification: satisfaction; enjoyment; pleasure

worrisome: troubling

perpetrator: person who did it; the doer

roughly: approximately, about

"Her words were saying no, but her body was saying yes": the rape myth that she was sending mixed messages of sexual interest and consent

devastating: upsetting; distressing

persist: continue; keep it up

expression: demonstration; example

condones: excuses

depicted: describes; shows

chilling: scary; alarming; unsettling

"asking for it": wants to have sex

resistance: opposition; refusal

sexual advances: welcome or unwelcome gestures made towards another person in order to gain sex

distressingly: alarmingly
brutality: cruelty; violence
debase: humiliate; degrade; demean
impulsively: irresponsibly; hastily
harbor: maintain feelings of
resentment: anger; bitterness
outright: complete; total
sexual dysfunction: sexual adjustment problems involving desire, arousal, orgasm, or sexual pain
sodomized: forcibly anal sex
despicable: dreadful ; wicked; shameful

Recite and Review

1. Sexual behavior during the 1960s and early 1970s significantly changed due to more liberalized sexual attitudes and access to effective _____.
2. Although traditional morality calls for female virginity before marriage, even by the 1940s and 1950s, the percent of married women who had engaged in premarital sex was _____ percent.
3. In a 1959 Roper poll, 88 percent of those interviewed agreed that premarital sex is wrong; by the 1990s, the percent of young men and women that approved of premarital sex was _____ percent.
4. Compared to changes in actual sexual behavior, the changes in attitudes have been _____.
5. People tend to have greater tolerance for sexual activity, especially when the behavior is engaged in by _____.
6. Over a year, the percent of married people that have sex partners other than their spouse is only about _____ percent.
7. The 1960s led to an especially sharp rise in sexual activity among teenagers with the increase continuing into the 1980s with the rate since 1988 _____.
8. One of the highest teenage pregnancy rates among all industrialized nations is found in _____.
9. Regarding the age at which young people first engage in sexual intercourse, research confirms that sex education has the effect of _____ it.
10. Parents can encourage sexual responsibility in their children by stressing the value of delayed sexual involvement and providing close _____.
11. In recent years, a conservative counter-movement has been visible, especially among teenagers with this quieting of the sexual revolution possibly reflecting a concern regarding sexually _____.
12. Men now report having an average of seven female sexual partners in their lifetimes, while women report an average of _____ male sexual partners.
13. For most people, there still remains a strong connection between sexuality and _____.
14. Both premarital sex and cohabitation are still widely viewed as temporary substitutes for or preludes to _____.
15. In past decades, young males who "sowed some wild oats" were widely tolerated, while women who were sexually active before marriage ran the risk of being labeled "promiscuous." This illustrates the _____.
16. As the gap between female and male sexual patterns continues to close, it is increasingly likely that there will come an end to the _____.
17. In a comparison of adults in developed countries to adults in Africa where there is currently an AIDS epidemic, the adults in Africa report having _____ sexual partners.

571

18. Compared to the age at which American teenagers have their first sexual encounter, teenagers around the world have their first sexual experience, on average, at _____.
19. The high rates of venereal disease in Africa result from a lack of knowledge and access to _____.
20. For a greater acceptance of sexuality to be constructive, people must feel they have the right to choose when, where, how, and with whom they will express their sexuality and the right to _____.
21. According to many experts, beauty pageants for young girls which emphasize physical beauty to the exclusion of other characteristics may lead to these girls to become _____.
22. According to a recent American Psychological Association Task Force, a young girl who narrowly equates sexual attractiveness with being "sexy" and bases her value solely on sexual appearance or behavior is exhibiting symptoms of unhealthy _____.
23. A major point of worry is the increasing tendency for young girls to engage in risky sexual behavior, such as unprotected _____ sex.
24. Some studies have shown that sexualized girls perform more poorly on _____ activities.
25. According to the APA Task Force, parents, educators, and others should encourage young girls not to develop relationships based on how they look but on their personalities and _____.
26. At least one woman in six will be raped in her lifetime with the true figure probably being much higher since rape is _____ crime.
27. Usually accompanied by beatings, about 10 to 14 percent of all married women have experienced _____ rape.
28. Forced intercourse that occurs in the context of a date or other voluntary encounter is referred to as _____ rape.
29. Even if the person does not use a knife or become violent, forced sex is still considered _____.
30. Rape is related to traditional _____ socialization.
31. The idea that a man should take the initiative and persist in attempts at sexual intimacy even when the woman says no is a part of the traditional masculine _____.
32. Psychologists James Check and Neil Malamuth believe that attitudes that condone forced sexual intimacy exist within a society create a "_____" culture.
33. In general, research has confirmed a link between sexual violence toward women and acceptance of rape _____.
34. In a study male college students were classified as either high or low in gender role stereotyping with each student reading one of three stories, one describing voluntary intercourse, one depicting stranger rape, and one describing date rape. The college males who were most aroused by the rape stories were the ones _____ in gender role stereotyping.
35. One of the most successful ways of preventing sexual assault has been educating men about rape _____.
36. False beliefs about rape that tend to blame the victim and increase the likelihood that some men will think rape is justified are referred to as _____.
37. Rape carried out under the threat of bodily injury with rapists often inflicting more violence on their victims than was necessary to achieve their goal is referred to as _____ rape.
38. The type of brutal rape that occurs under the threat of bodily injury is now seen by most psychologists as primarily an act of aggression based on the need to _____ others.
39. For a rape victim, rage, guilt, depression, loss of self-esteem, shame, sexual adjustment problems, and a lasting mistrust of male-female relationships are some of the typical _____-effects.
40. It is important to be aware that men can also be the victims of rape, especially _____ rape.

572

Connections

1. ___ sexual revolution

2. ___ double standard

3. ___ oversexualizing (of children)

4. ___ marital rape

5. ___ acquaintance rape

6. ___ "rape supportive culture"

7. ___ rape myths

8. ___ forcible rape

a. applying different standards for judging the appropriateness of male and female sexual behavior

b. forced intercourse that occurs in the context of a date or other voluntary encounter

c. a system that condones coercive (forced) sexual intimacy

d. false beliefs about rape that tend to blame the victim and increase the likelihood that some men will think that rape is justified

e. sexual intercourse carried out against the victim's will, under the threat of violence or bodily injury

f. rapid changes in attitudes and behavior regarding sex; usually refers to changes in the 1960s and 1970s in North America

g. rape by their husband and usually includes being beaten by their husbands

h. leads children, especially young girls, to see themselves as having value only as sexual objects

Check Your Memory

1. TRUE or FALSE   Liberalized sexual attitudes and access to effective birth control significantly changed sexual behavior in the 1960s and 1970s in North America.

2. TRUE or FALSE   Although traditional morality calls for female virginity before marriage, as many as 75 percent of married women in the 1940s and 1950s had engaged in premarital sex.

3. TRUE or FALSE   In a 1959 Roper poll, 88 percent of those interviewed agreed that premarital sex is wrong with more than 70 percent of young men and women approving of premarital sex by the 1990s.

4. TRUE or FALSE   Changes in actual sexual behavior are still larger than changes in attitudes.

5. TRUE or FALSE   Over a year, about 20 percent of married people have sex partners other than their spouse.

6. TRUE or FALSE   Sexual activity among teens decreased from the 1960s until the 1980s, then began a dramatic increase up through the present day.

7. TRUE or FALSE   The United States still has one of the highest teenage pregnancy rates among all industrialized nations.

8. TRUE or FALSE   Research confirms that sex education has led young people to engage in their first sexual encounter at younger ages.

9. TRUE or FALSE   Parents can encourage sexual responsibility in their children by providing close supervision and by stressing the value of delayed sexual involvement.

10. TRUE or FALSE   People today spend as much of their adult lives (on average) alone as they do in marriage.

11. TRUE or FALSE   Men now report having an average of 12 female sexual partners in their lifetimes, while women report having eight.

573

12. TRUE or FALSE   Using different rules to judge the appropriateness of male and female sexual behavior is referred to as the opponent-process effect.

13. TRUE or FALSE   A survey of 59 nations found that a "sexual revolution" has occurred in most countries throughout the world.

14. TRUE or FALSE   On average, teenagers around the world have their first sexual experience at the same age as American teenagers.

15. TRUE or FALSE   Although Africa has a high rate of AIDS, Africans report having fewer sexual partners than their counterparts in developed countries.

16. TRUE or FALSE   Six percent of first sexual intercourse experiences are against the person's will.

17. TRUE or FALSE   Pressures to engage in sex probably come as much from the individual's own expectations as from others.

18. TRUE or FALSE   Many experts now fear that young girls are being oversexualized by influences, such as beauty pageants for very young girls.

19. TRUE or FALSE   Young boys are more likely to be oversexualized than are young girls.

20. TRUE or FALSE   Some studies have shown that sexualized girls perform more poorly on intellectual activities.

21. TRUE or FALSE   At least one woman in six will be raped in her lifetime with a rape occurring every six minutes in the United States.

22. TRUE or FALSE   Pregnancy is one result of rape in 32,000 cases every year with three percent of rape victims contracting sexually transmitted diseases.

23. TRUE or FALSE   Seventy-five percent of American women who have been sexually or physically assaulted reported that the perpetrator was a stranger to them..

24. TRUE or FALSE   Men who commit marital or date rape often believe they have done nothing wrong.

25. TRUE or FALSE   Forced sex is rape, even if the rapist does not use a knife or become violent.

26. TRUE or FALSE   Rape is related to traditional gender role socialization with these attitudes creating a "rape-supportive culture."

27. TRUE or FALSE   If a woman is sexually active, she is probably lying if she says she was raped.

28. TRUE or FALSE   A woman who appears alone in public and dresses attractively is "asking for it (sex)."

29. TRUE or FALSE   Men who believe rape myths and who have been drinking are especially likely to ignore signals that a woman wants sexual advances to stop.

30. TRUE or FALSE   Most psychologists no longer think of forcible rape as a primarily sexual act, but rather see it as an act of brutality based on the need to debase others.

31. TRUE or FALSE   The impact of rape is so great that most women continue to report fear, anxiety, and sexual dysfunction a year or two after being raped.

32. TRUE or FALSE   Men can be the victims of rape, especially homosexual rape.

Critical Thinking Question

Why do you think that fidelity in marriage is strongly encouraged by law and custom?

Module 10.3 Sexual Behavior, Response, and Attitudes

STDs and Safer Sex—Choice, Risk, and Responsibility

Survey Question: What impacts have sexually transmitted diseases had on sexual behavior?

574

Language Development Guide

compelling: convincing; persuasive

era: period

intimate: close relationship of the deepest nature

hazard: danger

virtually: almost

lethal: deadly

"opportunistic": taking immediate advantage of

invade: attack

incubation: period between the infection of a person and the appearance of the symptoms of the disease

test negative: results show no disease

"safe": non-infected

blood transfusion: receiving blood from someone else

gambling: taking a chance

abstains: go without; refrain from

mutually: jointly

intoxicated: drunk

clueless: uninformed

monogamous: having only one mate; one sexual partner

false impression: having the wrong idea

"gamblers": risk-takers

truly: really

ensure: make certain

playing Russian roulette: phrase that means the person is taking a very dangerous and unnecessary risk that could kill them just like the deadly game of Russian roulette in which a person puts one bullet in a gun and spins the chamber and pulls the trigger

befalls: happens to

precautions: preventative measures; safeguards

welfare: well-being; safety

fueled: motivated, encouraged

"the pill": birth control pill

tide: wave; flood; rush

decades: periods of ten years

Recite and Review

1. When an infection is passed through intimate physical contact from one person to another, it is referred to as a(n) _____.
2. Many people who carry sexually transmitted diseases (STDs) lack obvious symptoms, or are _____.
3. In a recent study of sexually active teenage girls, nearly 90 percent of the girls thought that they had virtually no chance of getting an STD, but, in reality, over the next 18 months the proportion of the girls who got chlamydia or gonorrhea was one in _____.
4. Curable with antibiotics, the STD that is characterized by a milky discharge from the urethra and painful, frequent urination in males and a vaginal discharge and inflammation with painful urination in females is _____.
5. A woman has painful urination, a discharge from the vagina, and abdominal pain. Her doctor will prescribe antibiotics to treat the STD that is called _____.

6. The STD in which both males and females have painless sores on their genitals, rectum, tongue, or lips; a skin rash; fever; headaches; and aching bones and joints and which responds well to antibiotics is _____.

7. Surgery or a laser is used to remove the growths that occur with the STD known as _____.

8. Although there is no cure once one is infected with this virus, there is a vaccination that can prevent one initially contracting the STD called _____.

9. The symptoms of this SDT can be treated but not cured with both males and females experiencing pain and itching in the genital area and water blisters or open sores on the genitals. This STD is _____.

10. When a person has a mild case of this STD, he or she may have no symptoms, but the infection can cause chronic liver disease, cirrhosis of the liver or liver cancer. This STD is _____.

11. With the STD, the person will have prolonged fatigue, swollen lymph nodes, fever lasting more than 10 days, night sweats, unexplained weight loss, a persistent cough, and purplish lesions on the skin. This STD is _____.

12. The symptoms of this STD are not applicable to men with women experiencing intense pain in their lower back or abdomen as well as a fever. This STD is called _____.

13. Acquired immunodeficiency syndrome (AIDS) is caused by a(n) _____ infection.

14. Other "opportunistic" diseases invade the body of the person suffering from AIDS after the person's _____ system weakens.

15. The first symptoms of AIDS may show up as little as two months after infection, but they typically do not appear for _____ years.

16. After becoming infected, a person can test negative, while carrying the AIDS virus, for at least the first _____ months.

17. Human immunodeficiency virus (HIV) infections are spread by direct contact with blood, semen, and other body _____.

18. HIV cannot be transmitted by shaking hands, social kissing, sweat, tears, sharing drinking glasses, or other types of _____ contact.

19. Around the world, HIV infection is the leading cause of death among women and men between the ages of _____ and 44.

20. In North America, some of the people at greatest risk for HIV infections are men who have had sex with other men and people who have used needles for tattoos or drug use and _____ them.

21. In North America, persons who are at greatest risk for HIV infections are individuals with hemophilia who require frequent _____.

22. Having anal sex, sex with someone you do not know well, and two or more sex partners are _____ for HIV infection.

23. Discussing contraception with partner and their sexual health prior to engaging in sex, not engaging in sex while intoxicated, and using a condom are _____ practices.

24. The proportion of sexually active teens does not know how to use a condom correctly is one in _____.

25. A study of heterosexual adults found that, with their last sex partner, the majority of the adults did not practice _____.

26. The percent of people with HIV who were infected through heterosexual sex is _____ percent.

27. A special risk that befalls people in committed relationships is that they often interpret practicing safer sex as a sign of _____.

28. Dating couples who have high levels of emotional, social, and intellectual intimacy are more likely to use _____.

Connections

1. ___ sexually-transmitted disease (STD)
2. ___ asymptomatic
3. ___ gonorrhea
4. ___ chlamydia
5. ___ syphillis
6. ___ genital herpes
7. ___ genital warts
8. ___ HIV/AIDS
9. ___ hepatitis B
10. ___ pelvic inflammatory disease

a. milky discharge for urethra or vagina; painful urination; treated with antibiotics

b. pain or itching in genital area, water blisters or open sores; symptoms treated but not cured

c. painful urination with discharge; abdominal pain in females; treated with antibiotics

d. infection can lead to chronic liver disease, cirrhosis of liver, or liver cancer; no treatment and no cure, but has a preventative vaccination

e. females experience pain in lower back and/or abdomen and fever; treated with antibiotics; symptoms applicable only to females

f. prolonged fatigue, swollen lymph nodes, night sweats, weight loss, purplish lesions on skin, and persistent cough and diarrhea; can be treated but not cured

g. painless sores on genitals, rectum, tongue, or lips; skin rash; fever; headache; aching bones and joints; treated with antibiotics

h. lacking obvious symptoms

i. growths on genitals that have to be removed by surgery or laser

j. disease typically passed from one person to the next by intimate physical contact; venereal disease

Check Your Memory

1. TRUE or FALSE — Many people who carry sexually transmitted diseases (STDs) remain asymptomatic.

2. TRUE or FALSE — Nearly 90 percent of the sexual active girls in one study thought that they had virtually no chance of getting an STD, when, in reality, one in four got chlamydia or gonorrhea over the next 18 months.

3. TRUE or FALSE — When a male or female has gonorrhea, they have painless sores on their genitals, rectum, tongue, or lips; develop a skin rash; and have headaches and aching bones and joints.

4. TRUE or FALSE — The symptoms of genital herpes can be treated but not cured.

5. TRUE or FALSE — Syphilis causes painful urination and a milky discharge from the urethra or vagina.

6. TRUE or FALSE — Mild cases of hepatitis B may have no symptoms but this infection can cause chronic liver disease, cirrhosis of the liver, or liver cancer.

7. TRUE or FALSE — There is a vaccination to prevent hepatitis B.

8. TRUE or FALSE — When a person has prolonged fatigue, a fever lasting more than 10 days, night sweats, and unexplained weight loss, the person most likely has pelvic inflammatory disease.

9. TRUE or FALSE — Most people with AIDS eventually die of multiple infections that invade the body when the immune system is weakened.

10. TRUE or FALSE   The first symptoms of AIDS may show up as little as two months after infection, but they typically do not appear for 10 years.
11. TRUE or FALSE   A person can test negative for the HIV virus for at least the first six months after becoming infected.
12. TRUE or FALSE   People can get AIDS from eating food prepared by an infected person, through sweat and tears, and by sharing drinking glasses and towels.
13. TRUE or FALSE   Recently, the AIDS epidemic has spread more quickly among heterosexuals, women, African Americans, Hispanics, and children.
14. TRUE or FALSE   Currently, around the world, only 20 percent of all HIV cases are female.
15. TRUE or FALSE   Behavioral risk factors for contracting HIV include sharing drug needles, anal sex, and having two or more sex partners.
16. TRUE or FALSE   Safer sex practices include discussing your partner's sexual healthy prior to engaging in sex, not engaging in sex while intoxicated, using a condom, and reducing the number of sexual partners.
17. TRUE or FALSE   Because of sex education, only one in 50 sexually active teens do not know how use a condom correctly.
18. TRUE or FALSE   Although AIDS initially caused a sharp decrease in risky sex by gay men, this trend is now reversing with the STD rates again rising among gay men.
19. TRUE or FALSE   Seventy-five percent of people with HIV were infected through heterosexual sex.
20. TRUE or FALSE   Practicing safer sex while in a committed relationship is a sign of mistrust.

Critical Thinking Question

Which do you think would be better suited to reducing STDs and unwanted pregnancies among adolescents: abstinence-only education programs or more comprehensive sex education programs?

Module 10.4 Psychology in Action: Sexual Problems—When Pleasure Fades

Survey Question: How can couples keep their relationship more sexually satisfying? What are the most common sexual adjustment problems?

Language Development Guide

keeping it hot: keeping long-term relationships sexually satifying
inevitable: to be expected; unavoidable
resolve: settle
takes a toll: damages; take a loss
conversely: in opposition
survive: live through
gratification: pleasure; satisfaction
mutual: joint; shared
statistics: collection and interpretation of data
sexual potency: ability to have sexual relations
superhuman: impossible or rare physical capability
exploits: feats; adventures
essence: core; real meaning
defensiveness: being excessive sensitive to criticism

whining: to complain in a childish manner
stubbornness: unreasonably inflexible
"big freeze": silent treatment
persistent: lasting; continuing
dumped: released; unloaded; thrown down
used as ammunition: saved up complaints are used like bullets or weapons during a disagreement
sensuality: expressing sexual desires
slob: messy person
mounting: beginning, preparing for battle
character attack: a hurtful verbal assault on a individual's personality
hitting below the belt: unfair, painful, unethical
resorting: turning to; choosing
seeing things through your partner's eyes: viewing a situation from the other person's perspective
"mind-reading": assuming what someone else is thinking without asking the person
muddle: mix up; put in disorder
accusatory: critical; angry; "biting"
disruptive: troublesome; upsetting; disturbing
mess up: cause problems in
interdependent: mutually supporting; co-dependent
haven: safe place
equitable: fair; just; reasonable
best-intentioned: having purpose or aim toward a good outcome
dysfunction: impaired functioning
troubled by it: causing emotional distress
repelled: wanting to escape or avoid
aversion: dislike; hate
afflicted: affected by a condition
revulsion: disgust
straightforward: clear-cut; simple
deeply rooted: firmly implanted; firmly fixed
connotations: emotional, subjective meanings
performance demands: expectation to have sexual abilities and successfully complete the sexual act
generate: produce
contribute: add to
reassurance: comfort and encouragement
vicious cycle: one trouble leads to another with that one causing more problem for the initial
        trouble; a repeating chain of problems
dejection: sad and rejected
vascular: blood circulation
prostate: gland
urological: dealing with the urethra and urinary tract
ulcers: inflamed areas of tissue like a sore
seductive: to sexually lure or entice
resentment: bitterness
hydraulics: fluid mechanics
caressing: softly touching or stroking
signaling: indicating
incestuous: incest, sex with a family member
"nondemanding": unstressed; relaxed
dynamics: interactions
abandonment: reckless freedom, relaxation, carelessness

ambivalence: mixed feelings
intellectualize: excessively reasoning
flow: course
vigorous: active, fast, energetic
with reference to: regarding
impregnating: getting a female pregnant
symbolic inability to give of oneself: person not being able to trust another in order to engage in sex
unacknowledged: not admitting to self or others
retarded ejaculation: inability or delayed release of semen during orgasm
orient: familiarize; get used to
back seat of a car: sex location, excitement caused by fear of getting caught having sex

Recite and Review

1. Most couples find that their sexual interest and passion _____ over time.
2. Within a relationship, sex is not a performance or a skill to be mastered like playing tennis, but a form of _____.
3. Marriage expert John Gottman believes that if a marriage is to survive a couple must have more positive moments than negative moments, with the ratio being only one negative for every _____ positive moments.
4. When disagreements arise over issues such as frequency of lovemaking, who initiates lovemaking or what behavior is appropriate, the role should be, "Each partner must accept the other as the final authority on his or her own _____."
5. Partners are urged to give feedback about their feelings by following what therapists call the "_____" rule.
6. When problems do arise, partners are urged to be responsive to each other's needs at an emotional level and to recognize that all sexual problems are _____.
7. Masters and Johnson believe that it is particularly important for couples to avoid being influenced by statistics on the average frequency of lovemaking, that is, they should avoid the "_____ game."
8. According to sex therapist Barry McCarthy, the four elements that are necessary for a continuing healthy sexual relationship are sexual anticipation, valuing one's sexuality, feeling that you deserve sexual pleasure, and valuing _____.
9. Looking forward to lovemaking can be inhibited by routine and poor _____ between partners.
10. The essence of satisfying lovemaking is the giving and receiving of _____.
11. Especially in long-term relationships, a sense of closeness and intimacy with one's partner helps maintain _____.
12. A study that compared happily married couples with unhappily married couples found that, in almost every regard, the happily married couples showed superior _____ skills.
13. Two of the three patterns that are almost always related to serious long-term problems in relationships are stubbornness and defensiveness, including the behavior of _____.
14. Another destructive pattern that causes problems in relationships involves a refusal to talk with one's partner, called the "_____."
15. Saving up feelings and complaints and then "dumping" them during an argument or using them as ammunition in a fight is called _____.
16. Happy couples not only talk more, they convey more personal feelings and show greater _____ to their partners' feelings.
17. Whenever possible, expressions of negative feelings should be given as statements of one's own feelings, not as statements of _____.

580

18. Constructive expression of anger involves the couples sticking to the real issues and not "hitting below the belt," or resorting to threats. In other words, it is important for couples to "fight _____."

19. Assuming that you know what your partner is thinking or feeling, rather than asking him or her can result in hostile or accusatory "_____."

20. Not talking about meaningful feelings, never showing your feelings, always being pleasant and pretending everything is okay, always winning and never compromising, making your partner guess what you want, and always taking care of your own needs first are some of the ten ways to avoid _____.

21. Sexual adjustment and loving relationships are not independent of each other; they are _____.

22. Desire disorders, arousal disorders, orgasm disorders, and sexual pain disorders are types of sexual _____.

23. In hypoactive sexual desire, the loss of desire must be persistent and the person must be _____ by it.

24. A person who feels fear, anxiety, or disgust about engaging in sex is suffering from sexual _____.

25. Vaginal dryness in women and an inability to maintain an erection for men would both be classified as _____ disorders.

26. Although psychologists now discourage the use of the term because of its many negative connotations, erectile dysfunction was once known as _____.

27. Men who have never had an erection suffer from _____ erectile dysfunction.

28. Men who previously have had erections, but then developed a problem suffer from _____ erectile dysfunction.

29. According to Masters and Johnson, the percent of lovemaking attempts on which failure must occur for an erectile problem to be diagnosed is _____ percent or more.

30. Roughly 40 percent of erectile disorders are physically caused, or _____.

31. If the erectile disorder is the result of emotional factors, it is said to be _____.

32. According to Masters and Johnson, the type of erectile disorders that are often related to harsh religious training, early sexual experiences with a seductive mother, sexual molestation in childhood, or other experiences leading to guilt, fear, and sexual inhibition are _____ erectile disorders.

33. The type of erectile disorder that occurs due to physical causes such as alcohol or drug abuse, diabetes, and aging, or to emotional causes, such as guilt because of an extramarital affair, fear of inability to perform, and concerns about STDs is _____ erectile disorders.

34. A effective technique used to treat erectile disorders directs a couple's attention to natural sensations of sexual pleasure and builds communication skills. This technique is called _____.

35. The most prevalent sexual complaint among women is a persistent inability during lovemaking to reach _____ .

36. If we focus only on the woman, the most common source of orgasmic difficulties is _____ of the sexual response.

37. The medical term for a person who does not have orgasms is _____.

38. Strict religious training, fear of impregnating, lack of interest in the sexual partner, and unacknowledged homosexuality may result in retarded ejaculation, also known as male _____ disorder.

39. When a man cannot tolerate high levels of excitement at the plateau stage of arousal, he may reach sexual climax earlier than he wanted to with this condition known as _____.

40. When a man has problems with reaching sexual climax early, treatment may involve a "stop-start" procedure called the _____ technique.

41. Pain in the genitals before, during, or after sexual intercourse is called _____.

42. A condition in which muscle spasm of the vagina prevent intercourse is called _____.
43. This condition in which vaginal muscle spasms prevent intercourse appears to be a(n) _____ response to intercourse.
44. Treatment for the muscle spasm reactions of the vagina include extinction of the conditioned muscle spasms by progressive relaxation of the vagina and the use of a behavioral procedure to alleviate the fear known as _____.
45. Sexual dysfunctions are rarely solved without professional help except for the possible exception of the dysfunction known as _____.

Part 1: Connections

1. ___ "the big freeze"
2. ___ gunnysacking
3. ___ "mind reader"
4. ___ sensate focus
5. ___ squeeze technique
6. ___ impotence
7. ___ desire disorders
8. ___ arousal disorders
9. ___ orgasm disorders
10. ___ sexual pain disorders

a. telling your partner what she or he is thinking rather than asking them
b. includes dyspareunia and vaginismus
c. term once used for what is now referred to as erectile disorders
d. usually involves vaginal dryness in women or an inability of the male to maintain an erection
e. form of therapy that directs a couple's attention to natural sensations of sexual pleasure
f. refusal to talk with your partner
g. male or female does not have orgasms or experiences orgasms too soon or too late
h. saving up feelings and complaints and "dumping" them during an argument or using them as ammunition in a fight
i. includes sexual aversion
j. method for inhibiting ejaculation by compressing the tip of the penis

Part 2: Connections

1. ___ anorgasmic
2. ___ organic
3. ___ psychogenic
4. ___ hypoactive sexual desire
5. ___ sexual aversion
6. ___ primary erectile dysfunction
7. ___ secondary erectile dysfunction
8. ___ premature ejaculation
9. ___ dyspareunia
10. ___ vaginismus

a. muscle spasms of the vagina that prevents intercourse
b. male has previously had erections, but then developed an erectile problem
c. genital pain before, during, or after sexual intercourse
d. occurs reflexively or when the man cannot tolerate high levels of excitement at the plateau stage of arousal
e. means dysfunction is caused by emotional factors
f. persistent, upsetting loss of sexual motivation
g. means dysfunction is physically caused
h. persistent feelings of fear, anxiety, or disgust about engaging in sex
i. term applied to men or women who do not have orgasms
j. male has never had an erection

582

Check Your Memory

1. TRUE or FALSE   Most couples find that their sexual interest and passion increase over time.
2. TRUE or FALSE   Sex is a performance or skill to be mastered like playing tennis.
3. TRUE or FALSE   A couple with a satisfactory sex life but a poor relationship rarely lasts.
4. TRUE or FALSE   According to marriage expert John Gottman, for a marriage to survive, a couple must have equal amounts of positive and negative moments in their marriage.
5. TRUE or FALSE   Partners are urged to give feedback about their feelings by following the technique therapists call systematic desensitization.
6. TRUE or FALSE   When sexual problems do arise, partners are urged to recognize that all sexual problems are mutual.
7. TRUE or FALSE   Masters and Johnson believe that couples should pay close attention to the statistics regarding the average frequency of lovemaking to determine whether they need to seek professional help.
8. TRUE or FALSE   Sex therapist Barry McCarthy states that partners should set aside time to spend together, should be able to deal with negative sexual experiences when they occur, and must develop a sense of closeness and intimacy.
9. TRUE or FALSE   The main difference that was found between happily married couples and unhappily married couples was that the happily married couples had more frequent sex.
10. TRUE or FALSE   Three patterns that are almost always related to serious long-term problems in relationships are defensiveness, stubbornness, and refusal to talk with your partner.
11. TRUE or FALSE   Couples are advised not to "gunnysack," or save up feelings and complaints and then use them as ammunition during an argument.
12. TRUE or FALSE   In constructive fights, anger is never shown, especially by the one who is right or who is establishing blame.
13. TRUE or FALSE   Marital harmony is closely related to the ability to put yourself in another person's place.
14. TRUE or FALSE   "Mind-reading," or assuming what the other partner is thinking, improves communication between a couple.
15. TRUE or FALSE   One way to maintain intimacy with one's partner is to always be pleasant and pretend everything is okay, even if you are upset or dissatisfied.
16. TRUE or FALSE   To maintain intimacy, one should always try to care for one's own needs first.
17. TRUE or FALSE   Sexual dysfunctions include desire, arousal, orgasm, and sexual pain disorders.
18. TRUE or FALSE   For a loss of sexual desire to be considered a dysfunction, the loss of desire must be persistent and the person must be troubled by it.
19. TRUE or FALSE   The sexual dysfunction known as hypoactive sexual desire is somewhat more common in men than in women.
20. TRUE or FALSE   A person with a sexual aversion still has some erotic feelings and may masturbate or have sexual fantasies.
21. TRUE or FALSE   Sexual desire problems may have physical causes, such as fatigue, hormonal difficulties, and the side effects of medicine as well as psychological causes, such as depression and marital conflict.
22. TRUE or FALSE   An arousal disorder in women involves vaginal dryness.

23. TRUE or FALSE   Men suffering from primary erectile disorder have previously had erections, but have developed the dysfunction due to a recent physical or emotional problem.

24. TRUE or FALSE   Sex therapists Masters and Johnson believe that an erectile problem exists when failure occurs on 10 percent or more of a man's lovemaking attempts.

25. TRUE or FALSE   Fatigue, anger, anxiety, and drinking too much alcohol can cause temporary erectile difficulties in healthy males.

26. TRUE or FALSE   About 40 percent of all cases of erectile disorders are organic with the origin of the remaining cases being psychogenic, or the result of emotional factors.

27. TRUE or FALSE   If a man can have an erection at times other than lovemaking, such as during sleep, the problem probably is not physical.

28. TRUE or FALSE   As men grow older they typically experience a decline in sexual desire and arousal and an increase in sexual dysfunction.

29. TRUE or FALSE   The squeeze technique is often used to treat erectile disorders.

30. TRUE or FALSE   Psychological factors that can cause a female sexual arousal disorder include deep-seated conflicts over being female, and extreme distrust of others, especially males.

31. TRUE or FALSE   The most prevalent sexual complaint among women is a persistent inability to reach orgasm during lovemaking.

32. TRUE or FALSE   About two-thirds of all women need direct stimulation of the clitoris to reach orgasm.

33. TRUE or FALSE   If we focus only on the woman, the most common source of orgasmic difficulties is overcontrol of the sexual response.

34. TRUE or FALSE   Approximately 50 percent of young adult men have problems with premature ejaculation.

35. TRUE or FALSE   Sensate focus is technique often used to treat premature ejaculation.

36. TRUE or FALSE   Pain in the genitals before, during, or after sexual intercourse is called the hyperphagia syndrome.

37. TRUE or FALSE   Experiencing pain in the genitals during sexual intercourse is rare in males.

38. TRUE or FALSE   A condition in which muscle spasms of the vagina prevent intercourse is known as vaginal dyskinesia.

39. TRUE or FALSE   The condition known as vaginismus involves a phobic response to intercourse and is, thus, treated like a nonsexual phobia using progressive relaxation and desensitization.

40. TRUE or FALSE   Hypnosis has also been used to treat vaginismus.

Critical Thinking Question

Who would you expect to have the most frequent sex and the most satisfying sex, married couples or single persons?

Final Survey and Review—Completion

Module 10.1 Sexual Development and Sexual Orientation

Sexual Development—Circle One: *XX* or *XY*?

Survey Question: What are the basic dimensions of sex?

1. The presence of XX chromosomes or XY chromosomes is used to determine _____ sex.

2. If Mark is genetically a female but has male genitals, and behaves psychologically and socially as a male, Mark would be described as a(n) _____.
3. If a teacher tells her class that females have ovaries and males have testes, then this teacher classifying   individuals based on _____ sex.
4. Lamont was born with a chromosome combination of XXY rather than an XY. Lamont has a condition known as _____ syndrome.
5. Besides the sex organs, another source of sex hormones is the _____ glands.
6. Jerome's voice has begun to deepen, and he is beginning to show some facial and body hair. These outward characteristics of puberty are called _____ sexual characteristics.
7. During a woman's pregnancy, her child develops in a pear-shaped muscular organ called the womb, or _____.
8. During sexual excitement, the male has two small glands that secrete a clear fluid into the urethra and are called the _____ glands.

Module 10.1 Sexual Development and Sexual Orientation
Sexual Orientation—Who Do You Love?
Survey Question: What is sexual orientation?
9. If Gary is attracted to both men and women, his sexual orientation would be described as _____.
10. According to genetic research, the tendency toward homosexuality may be carried on the _____ chromosome.
11. Dr. Malto believes that if a male fetus is exposed to too little testosterone or a female fetus is exposed to too much testosterone, the child will become homosexual. Dr. Malto supports the _____ theory.
12. Tara and Samantha are a lesbian couple who are raising three children. According to statistics, the sexual orientation of their children will most likely be _____.
13. Emma believes that being a heterosexual is better or more natural than being homosexual. Emma is exhibiting _____.

Module 10.2 Gender Development, Androgyny, and Gender Variance
Gender Development—Of Manly Men and Girlie Girls
Survey Question: How does one's sense of maleness or femaleness develop?
14. Regarding the prenatal exposure to sex hormones, men are said to be more often "_____-brained.
15. The oversimplified and widely held false belief that a woman cannot be a airplane mechanic and a man cannot be a nurse are examples of gender role _____.
16. In observations of the Tchambuli men and women, it was found the gender that was expected to be dependent and flirtatious and who adorned themselves with flowers and jewelry were the _____.
17. Regarding gender differences in North America, it was found that both parents gently held and were more delicate in handling _____ infants.
18. Greg is 10 years old, and his parents are encouraging him to set goals and prepare for the world of work. Greg's parents are encouraging him to engage in _____ behaviors.
19. Two children are playing outdoors and are arguing over "who is the boss." According to research on gender differences in play, these two children are most likely _____.

Module 10.2 Gender Development, Androgyny, and Gender Variance
Androgyny—Are You Masculine, Feminine, or Androgynous?
Survey Question: What is psychological androgyny (and is it contagious)?

585

20. The word the literally means "man-woman" and refers to having both masculine and feminine traits is _____.
21. The Bem Sex Role Inventory consists of 20 traditionally "masculine" traits, 20 traditional "feminine" traits, and 20 _____ traits.
22. Myrel, who is psychologically androgynous, will be assertive and independent at times and will be nurturing and compassionate at others, depending on the _____.
23. If a person is androgynous, they will be high in _____ intelligence.

Module 10.2 Gender Development, Androgyny, and Gender Variance
When Sex and Gender Do Not Match—The Binary Busters
Survey Question: What is gender variance?
24. Margo has a condition in which her biological sex does not match her preferred gender. Margo would be described as gender _____.
25. Even when Roger was a child, he felt like he should be a girl and preferred games and toys that girls would usually choose. According to the *Diagnostic and Statistical Manual of Mental Disorders (DSM)*, Roger would be diagnosed with _____ disorder.
26. When a person has surgery to reconfigure the external appearance of the genitals, hormone treatments to shift the chemical balance in the body, and a deliberate effort made to transform the person's sense of sexual identity, then the person is undergoing _____.

Module 10.3 Sexual Behavior, Response, and Attitudes
Sexual Behavior—Mapping the Erogenous Zones
Survey Question: What are the most typical patterns of human sexual behavior?
27. Research has verified instances of orgasm in girls as young as _____ old.
28. Jamila and Ben are college friends who engage in sex occasionally, although they do not consider themselves romantically involved. Their sexual script is known as _____.
29. Because they can produce pleasure or erotic desire, the genitals, mouth, breast, ears, anus, and to a lesser degree, the entire surface of the body, would be considered _____ zones.
30. Larry believes that alcohol can increase a person's sexual desire and performance. Larry believes the myth that alcohol is a(n) _____.
31. Surgery that makes a man infertile is the vasectomy, while the surgery that makes a woman infertile is _____.
32. The crucial factors for an extended sex life into one's late adulthood appear to be regularity and _____.
33. The normal sexual behavior that was once thought to cause insanity, sterility, and acne and was referred to as "self-abuse" is _____.

Module 10.3 Sexual Behavior, Response, and Attitudes
Human Sexual Response—Sexual Interactions
Survey Question: To what extent do females and males differ in sexual response?
34. Our understanding of sexual response was greatly expanded through the experiments, interviews, and controlled observations done by psychologist Virginia Johnson and gynecologist _____.
35. The phase in the human sexual response cycle that directly follows the excitement phase for most men and women is called the _____ phrase.
36. Sigmund Freud claimed that women who experienced clitoral orgasms had not fully accepted their _____.
37. Compared to women, men typically go through the sexual phases more _____.

Module 10.3 Sexual Behavior, Response, and Attitudes
Atypical Sexual Behavior—Trench Coats, Whips, Leathers, and Lace

Survey Question: What are the most common sexual disorders?

38. Psychologically, the mark of true sexual deviations is that they are compulsive and _____.

39. A person who views the genitals of others without their permission is engaging in the paraphilia known as "peeping" or _____.

40. Secretiveness, emotional disturbance, nightmares, loss of self-esteem, unusual aggressiveness, or risk-taking are signs that a child may be the victim of child molestation, or _____.

41. Coming from strict and repressive backgrounds and having a deep sense of inadequacy, which produces a compulsive need to prove their "manhood" describes the paraphilia known as "flashing," or _____.

Module 10.3 Sexual Behavior, Response, and Attitudes
Attitudes and Sexual Behavior—The Changing Sexual Landscape

Survey Question: Have recent changes in attitudes affected sexual behavior?

42. Sexual behavior during the 1960s and early 1970s significantly changed due to access to effective birth control and more liberalized _____.

43. Women now report having an average of four male sexual partners in their lifetimes, while men report an average of _____ female sexual partners.

44. Using different rules to judge the appropriateness of male and female sexual behavior is referred to as the _____.

45. The public antics of female role models, such as Paris Hilton and Brittany Spears, and the availability of consumer goods such as padded bras for girls as young as six has led to young girls becoming _____.

46. If a woman goes home with a man on a first date, she is interested in sex is an example of a rape _____.

Module 10.3 Sexual Behavior, Response, and Attitudes
STDs and Safer Sex—Choice, Risk, and Responsibility

Survey Question: What impacts have sexually transmitted diseases had on sexual behavior?

47. A college student has been experiencing headaches and aching bones and joints. She has a fever, a skin rash, and painless sores on her genitals. Her doctor prescribed a course of antibiotics to cure this STD, which is called _____.

48. Most people with eventually die due to the multiple infections that invade the body when the immune system is weakened by the STD known as _____.

49. Terrence is getting a vaccination as a preventative measure against the STD that can cause chronic liver disease, cirrhosis of the liver, and liver cancer. Terrence is getting a vaccination for _____.

50. A negative HIV test result is no guarantee that a person is a "safe" sex partner since a person can test negative after becoming infected at least for the first _____ months.

Module 10.4 Psychology in Action: Sexual Problems—When Pleasure Fades

Survey Question: How can couples keep their relationship more sexually satisfying? What are the most common sexual adjustment problems?

51. According to sex therapist Barry McCarthy, the four elements that are necessary for a continuing healthy sexual relationship are valuing one's sexuality, feeling that you deserve sexual pleasure, valuing intimacy, and sexual _____.

52. The three patterns that are almost always related to serious long-term problems in relationships are stubbornness, a refusal to talk with one's partner, and _____, including whining.

53. If you save up feelings and complaints and then "dump" them onto your partner during an argument, then you are engaging in a destructive practice known as _____.

54. If you have tendency to tell your partner what she or he thinks rather than asking him or her, then you are engaging in a destructive practice known as "_____."

55. In hypoactive sexual desire, the person must be troubled by the loss of desire and the loss of desire must be _____.

56. If a man has never had an erection, then he would be diagnosed with a(n) _____ erectile dysfunction.

57. The sexual pain disorder that involves vaginal muscle spasms and would be treated like a nonsexual phobia using progressive relaxation and desensitization is _____.

Final Survey and Review—Matching

Module 10.1 Sexual Development and Sexual Orientation
Part 1:
1. ____ sex
2. ____ gender
3. ____ gonadal sex
4. ____ genital sex
5. ____ transsexual
6. ____ intersexual
7. ____ bisexual
8. ____ homophobia
9. ____ heterosexism
10. ____ Turner's syndrome
11. ____ Klinefelter's syndrome
12. ____ menarche
13. ____ menopause

a. onset of menstruation
b. prejudice, fear, and dislike directed at homosexuals
c. person with a deep conflict between his or her biological sex and preferred psychological and social gender roles
d. person who has genitals suggestive of both sexes
e. end of regular monthly fertility cycles
f. person romantically and erotically attracted to both men and women
g. boy is born with an extra X chromosome (XXY)
h. psychological and social characteristics associated with being male or female
i. one's biological classification as female or male
j. belief that heterosexuality is better or more natural than homosexuality
k. sex as indicated by a presence of ovaries or testes
l. girl born with only one X chromosome
m. sex as indicated by the presence of the clitoris and vagina in females and the penis and scrotum in males

Part 2:
1. ____ vas deferens
2. ____ clitoris

a. source of hormones and eggs
b. duct that carries sperm from the testes to the urethra

588

3. ___ epididymis
4. ___ vagina
5. ___ seminal vesicles
6. ___ ovary
7. ___ Cowper's glands
8. ___ cervix
9. ___ uterus
10. ___ prostate
11. ___ fallopian tube
12. ___ testes

c. carry eggs from the ovaries to the uterus
d. two small glands that secrete a clear fluid into the male's urethra during sexual excitement
e. gland located at the base of the urinary bladder that supplies most of the fluid that makes up semen
f. tube-like structure connecting the external female genitalia with the uterus
g. lower end of the uterus that projects into the vagina
h. two glands that are the source of hormones and sperm
i. small, sensitive organ made up of erectile tissue; located above the vaginal opening
j. two small organs on each side of the prostate that supply fluid that becomes part of semen
k. a coiled structure at the top of the testes in which sperm are stored
l. pear-shaped muscular organ in which the fetus develops during pregnancy

Module 10.2 Gender Development, Androgyny, and Gender Variance

1. ___ gender identity
2. ___ biological biasing effect
3. ___ general role socialization
4. ___ gender role
5. ___ gender role stereotypes
6. ___ instrumental behaviors
7. ___ expressive behaviors
8. ___ androgyny
9. ___ gender variance

a. condition in which a person's biological sex does not match his or her preferred gender
b. oversimplified and widely held beliefs about the basic characteristics of men and women
c. behaviors that communicate emotion or personal feelings
d. presence of both "masculine" and "feminine" traits in a single person
e. hypothesized effect that prenatal exposure to sex hormones has on development of the body, nervous system, and later behavioral patterns
f. one's personal, private sense of maleness or femaleness as expressed in appearance, behavior, and attitudes
g. pattern of behaviors that are regarded as "male" or "female by one's culture
h. process of learning gender behaviors considered appropriate for one's sex in a given culture
i. behaviors directed toward the achievement of some goal

Module 10.3 Sexual Behavior, Response, and Attitudes
Part 1:

1. ___ erogenous zones
2. ___ double standard

a. substances reputed to increase sexual desire or pleasure
b. short time period after orgasm during which males are unable to again reach orgasm

3. ___ oversexualizing

    c. medical procedures, such as vasectomy or tubal ligation, that make a man or a woman infertile

4. ___ aphrodisiacs

    d. applying different rules for judging the appropriateness of male and female sexual behavior

5. ___ castration

    e. "peeping," or viewing the genitals of othes without their permission

6. ___ sterilization

    f. second stage of sexual response during which physical arousal is further heightened

7. ___ masturbation

    g. seeing oneself as having value only as sexual objects

8. ___ voyeurism

    h. sexually touching or rubbing against a nonconsenting person, usually in a public place

9. ___ frotteurism

    i. sexual arousal associated with inanimate objects

10. ___ pedophilia

    j. self-stimulation that causes sexual pleasure or orgasm

11. ___ fetishism

    k. sex with children, or child molesting

12. ___ refractory period

    l. areas of the body that produce pleasure and/or provoke erotic desire

13. ___ plateau phase

    m. surgical removal of the testicles or ovaries

Part 2:

1. ___ pelvic inflammatory disease

    a. milky discharge for urethra or vagina; painful urination; treated with antibiotics

2. ___ hepatitis B

    b. pain or itching in genital area, water blisters or open sores; symptoms treated but not cured

3. ___ gonorrhea

    c. painful urination with discharge; abdominal pain in females; treated with antibiotics

4. ___ chlamydia

    d. infection can lead to chronic liver disease, cirrhosis of liver, or liver cancer; no treatment and no cure, but has a preventative vaccination

5. ___ syphillis

    e. females experience pain in lower back and/or abdomen and fever; treated with antibiotics; symptoms applicable only to females

6. ___ genital herpes

    f. prolonged fatigue, swollen lymph nodes, night sweats, weight loss, purplish lesions on skin, and persistent cough and diarrhea; can be treated but not cured

7. ___ HIV/AIDS

    g. painless sores on genitals, rectum, tongue, or lips; skin rash; fever; headache; aching bones and joints; treated with antibiotics

Module 10.4 Psychology in Action: Sexual Problems—When Pleasure Fades

1. ___ gunnysacking

    a. muscle spasms of the vagina that prevents intercourse

590

2. ___ "mind reader"

    b. form of therapy that directs a couple's attention to natural sensations of sexual pleasure

3. ___ sensate focus

    c. male has previously had erections, but then developed an erectile problem

4. ___ squeeze technique

    d. genital pain before, during, or after sexual intercourse

5. ___ hypoactive sexual desire

    e. occurs reflexively or when the man cannot tolerate high levels of excitement at the plateau stage of arousal

6. ___ sexual aversion

    f. telling your partner what she or he is thinking rather than asking them

7. ___ primary erectile dysfunction

    g. persistent, upsetting loss of sexual motivation

8. ___ secondary erectile dysfunction

    h. saving up feelings and complaints and "dumping" them during an argument

9. ___ premature ejaculation

    i. persistent feelings of fear, anxiety, or disgust about engaging in sex

10. ___ dyspareunia

    j. used to treat premature ejaculation

11. ___ vaginismus

    k. male has never had an erection

Final Survey and Review—True or False

Module 10.1 Sexual Development and Sexual Orientation
Sexual Development—Circle One: XX or XY?
Survey Question: What are the basic dimensions of sex?

1. TRUE or FALSE   When a person's sex is determined by the presence of a vagina or a penis, it referred to as genital sex.

2. TRUE or FALSE   In Turner's syndrome, a girl is born with only one X rather than an XX combination.

3. TRUE or FALSE   The pineal gland also supply sex hormones.

4. TRUE or FALSE   Androgen insensitivity is an unresponsiveness to testosterone by genetic males that results in female development.

5. TRUE or FALSE   Secondary sexual characteristics are features that appear at puberty, such as breast development and the broadening of the hips in females and facial hair growth and voice deepening in males.

6. TRUE or FALSE   The end of regular monthly fertility cycles in the late 40s or early 50s is called menarche.

7. TRUE or FALSE   The two tubes that carry eggs from the ovaries to the uterus are called the seminal vesicles.

8. TRUE or FALSE   The two small organs located on each side of the prostate and supply fluid that becomes part of semen are the vas deferens.

Module 10.1 Sexual Development and Sexual Orientation
Sexual Orientation—Who Do You Love?
Survey Question: What is sexual orientation?

9. TRUE or FALSE   One study found that if one identical twin is homosexual or bisexual, there is a 50 percent chance that the other twin is too.

10. TRUE or FALSE   Homosexuality is not caused by hormone imbalances in adulthood with the hormone levels of most gay men and lesbians being within the normal range.

11. TRUE or FALSE   Homosexual persons confirm their sexual orientation earlier than do heterosexuals.

12. TRUE or FALSE   Gay and lesbian persons tend to molest children more often than do heterosexuals.

13. TRUE or FALSE   Gay and lesbian persons rarely have long-term, caring monogamous relationships.

Module 10.2 Gender Development, Androgyny, and Gender Variance
Gender Development—Of Manly Men and Girlie Girls
Survey Question: How does one's sense of maleness or femaleness develop?

14. TRUE or FALSE   The hypothesized effect that prenatal exposure to sex hormones has on development of the body, nervous system, and later behavior patterns is called the biological biasing effect.

15. TRUE or FALSE   Female and male scores on the Scholastic Reasoning Test (SAT) are rapidly becoming more alike.

16. TRUE or FALSE   In business, academia, medicine, law, sports, and politics in North America, women continue to earn less money and achieve lower status than men.

17. TRUE or FALSE   The gender roles of the Tchambuli people of New Guinea are a similar but more extreme version of North American stereotypes with the men doing all the fishing and manufacturing, controlling all the power within the community, and taking the lead in sexual relationships.

18. TRUE or FALSE   Since Fiona is a female, her parents will most likely encourage her to engage in instrumental behaviors, while they will encourage her brother to engage in more expressive behaviors.

19. TRUE or FALSE   When playing, girls are more cooperative and play games that require lots of verbal give-and-take.

Module 10.2 Gender Development, Androgyny, and Gender Variance
Androgyny—Are You Masculine, Feminine, or Androgynous?
Survey Question: What is psychological androgyny (and is it contagious)?

20. TRUE or FALSE   Being ambitious, analytical, competitive, and decisive are considered neutral traits on the Bem Sex Role Inventory.

21. TRUE or FALSE   Of those surveyed using the BSRI, 50 percent fell into traditional feminine or masculine categories, 15 percent scored higher on traits of the opposite sex, and 35 percent were androgynous.

22. TRUE or FALSE   Masculine men find it difficult to accept emotional support from others, particularly from women.

23. TRUE or FALSE   More Mexican-American men were found to be androgynous than European-American men.

Module 10.2 Gender Development, Androgyny, and Gender Variance
When Sex and Gender Do Not Match—The Binary Busters
Survey Question: What is gender variance?

24. TRUE or FALSE   If their biological sex definitely does not match their preferred gender, then the person would be diagnosed using the Diagnostic and Statistical Manual as having a paraphilia.

25. TRUE or FALSE   Adults who deliberately seek sex reassignment are generally happy with the results.
26. TRUE or FALSE   A sex reassignment includes both surgery to reconfigure the external genitalia and hormone treatments to shift the chemical balance in the body.

Module 10.3 Sexual Behavior, Response, and Attitudes
Sexual Behavior—Mapping the Erogenous Zones
Survey Question: What are the most typical patterns of human sexual behavior?

27. TRUE or FALSE   According to one survey, more than half of all college students have been friends with benefits and engaged in this casual type of sex.
28. TRUE or FALSE   Young women who are having casual sex are more likely to become depressed.
29. TRUE or FALSE   Based on the frequency of orgasm (from masturbation or intercourse), the peak of male sexual activity is at age 18, while the female peak occurs a little later.
30. TRUE or FALSE   Amyl nitrite, Ecstasy, LSD, and marijuana tend to increase one's sexual desire and response.
31. TRUE or FALSE   Castration of sex offenders will not completely take away their sex drive.
32. TRUE or FALSE   The earliest age that self-stimulation has been observed to occur has been in four to five year-old children.
33. TRUE or FALSE   Approximately 70 percent of married women and men masturbate at least occasionally with the masturbation usually having no effect on marital relationships.

Module 10.3 Sexual Behavior, Response, and Attitudes
Human Sexual Response—Sexual Interactions
Survey Question: To what extent do females and males differ in sexual response?

34. TRUE or FALSE   In the human response cycle, the stage that directly follows the plateau phase for both men and women is the refractory period.
35. TRUE or FALSE   Sigmund Freud claimed that a "vaginal orgasm" was an "immature" form of female response, and a woman who experience one was rejecting the role of becoming a mother.
36. TRUE or FALSE   Only about 5 percent of females are capable of multiple orgasm, while 48 percent of men have had multiple orgasms at one time or another.
37. TRUE or FALSE   There is no relationship between penis size and male sexual potency.

Module 10.3 Sexual Behavior, Response, and Attitudes
Atypical Sexual Behavior—Trench Coats, Whips, Leathers, and Lace
Survey Question: What are the most common sexual disorders?

38. TRUE or FALSE   Sexual arousal associated with inanimate objects is called sexual masochism.
39. TRUE or FALSE   Sexually touching or rubbing against a nonconsenting person, usually in a public place such as a subway is called voyeurism.
40. TRUE or FALSE   In most cases of pedophilia, the offender is a friend, acquaintance, or relative of the child.
41. TRUE or FALSE   Between one-third and two-thirds of all sexual arrests are for exhibitionism.

Module 10.3 Sexual Behavior, Response, and Attitudes
Attitudes and Sexual Behavior—The Changing Sexual Landscape
Survey Question: Have recent changes in attitudes affected sexual behavior?

42. TRUE or FALSE   Changes in attitudes are still larger than changes in actual sexual behavior.

43. TRUE or FALSE   Research confirms that sex education delays the age at which young people first engage in sexual intercourse.

44. TRUE or FALSE   A survey of 59 nations found that a "sexual revolution" has not occurred in most countries throughout the world.

45. TRUE or FALSE   People in African countries where there is an AIDS epidemic report having more sexual partners than their counterparts in developed countries.

46. TRUE or FALSE   Seventy-five percent of American women who have been sexually or physically assaulted reported that the perpetrator was a husband, intimate partner, or acquaintance.

Module 10.3 Sexual Behavior, Response, and Attitudes
STDs and Safer Sex—Choice, Risk, and Responsibility
Survey Question: What impacts have sexually transmitted diseases had on sexual behavior?

47. TRUE or FALSE   Gonorrhea causes painful urination and a milky discharge from the urethra or vagina.

48. TRUE or FALSE   Men with pelvic inflammatory disease experience intense pain in the lower back and/or abdomen and usually have a fever.

49. TRUE or FALSE   People cannot get AIDS from eating food prepared by an infected person, through sweat and tears, and by sharing drinking glasses and towels.

50. TRUE or FALSE   Only 25 percent of people with HIV were infected through heterosexual sex.

Module 10.4 Psychology in Action: Sexual Problems—When Pleasure Fades
Survey Question: How can couples keep their relationship more sexually satisfying?
What are the most common sexual adjustment problems?

51. TRUE or FALSE   Marriage expert John Gottman believes that a couple must have at least five times as many positive as negative moments in their marriage if it is to survive

52. TRUE or FALSE   A study that compared happily married couples with unhappily married couples found that the happily married couples showed superior communication skills

53. TRUE or FALSE   To maintain intimacy, a couple should try to never argue but be pleasant and pretend everything is okay, even if they are upset.

54. TRUE or FALSE   Sex therapists Masters and Johnson believe that an erectile problem exists when failure occurs on 25 percent or more of a man's lovemaking attempts.

55. TRUE or FALSE   Erectile disorders that are psychogenic are physically caused.

56. TRUE or FALSE   The most prevalent sexual complaint among women are sexual pain disorders.

57. TRUE or FALSE   Treatment for female sexual arousal disorder usually involves sensate focus.

594

Mastery Test

1. The biological classification as female or male is referred to as one's
   a. sex.
   b. gender.
   c. androgyny.
   d. intersexuality.

2. In females, the presence of ovaries determines her
   a. genital sex.
   b. gonadal sex.
   c. biological androgyny.
   d. genetic gender.

3. The presence of a Y chromosome is associated with
   a. intersexualism.
   b. prenatal testosterone.
   c. menarche.
   d. Turner's syndrome.

4. Before birth, a genetic male will develop as a female if which condition exists?
   a. excessive progestin
   b. acromegaly
   c. the androgenital syndrome
   d. an androgen insensitivity

5. In females, the broadening of the hips and breast development are
   a. primary sexual characteristics.
   b. secondary sexual characteristics.
   c. caused by the release of androgens.
   d. associated with the presence of a Y chromosome.

6. The coiled structure at the top of the testes in which sperm are stored is the
   a. seminal vesicles.
   b. epididymis.
   c. prostate.
   d. vas deferens.

7. Regarding sexual orientation, which of the following statements is TRUE?
   a. Scientific evidence suggests that sexual orientation is at least partly hereditary.
   b. Homosexuality results from an adult hormonal imbalance.
   c. Sexual orientation can be changed fairly easily with the proper therapy.
   d. Heterosexual persons tend to discover their sexual orientation at a later date than homosexual persons do.

8. Evolutionary theorists believe that homosexuality may have developed
   a. to reduce male competition for a limited number of female sexual partners.
   b. as a result of adult hormonal imbalances.
   c. to explain the different gender roles in different cultures.
   d. as a result of poor parenting practices in early cultures..

9. Regarding homosexuality, which of the following statements is FALSE?
   a. Homosexuals do have long-term, caring, monogamous relationships.
   b. Most homosexual people have at one time or another suffered verbal abuse or worse because of their sexual orientation.
   c. Parts of the hypothalamus, which is connected with sexual activity, differ in size in heterosexuals and homosexuals.
   d. Most children raised by gay and lesbian parents become homosexual.

10. Females who are exposed to prenatally to male hormones tend to be tomboys during childhood, an observation that supports the
    a. opponent-processing effect of hormones.
    b. biological biasing effect.
    c. view that gender is genetically-determined.
    d. idea that gender role socialization is dominant.

11. Some psychologists think that biological differences explain why women as a group are slightly better than men in _____ skills.
    a. spatial
    b. instrumental
    c. language
    d. math

12. Which of the following aspects is well-formed by age four?
    a. gender identity
    b. sex scripting
    c. awareness of sexual orientation
    d. psychological androgyny

13. Boys are encouraged to be strong, aggressive, dominant, and achieving through the process called
    a. neurobiological biasing.
    b. sexual orienting.
    c. gender adaptation.
    d. gender role socialization.

14. Women earn approximately $.55 to $.76 for every $1.00 men earn, which is the result of
    a. gender identity.
    b. gender role stereotyping.
    c. sexual scripts.
    d. androgen insensitivity.

15. With respect to the behaviors parents encourage in their children, which is a correct match?
    a. controlling behaviors—female
    b. goal-oriented behaviors—female
    c. expressive behaviors—male
    d. instrumental behaviors—male

16. When Bem asked people to complete the Bem Sex Role Inventory (BSRI), the percent that fell in the androgynous category was about _____ percent.
    a. 15
    b. 20
    c. 35
    d. 50

17. Timothy considers himself to be a strong man, who will not accept emotional support from others, especially women. On the Bem Sex Role Inventory (BSRI), Timothy would most likely score high in _____ traits.
    a. masculine
    b. feminine
    c. androgynous
    d. expressive

18. Regarding masculinity, femininity, and androgyny, which of the following statements is FALSE?
    a. Scoring high in "masculinity" is related to low self-esteem, causing failure in many situations.
    b. Scoring high in "femininity" tend to experience greater social closeness with others and more happiness in marriage.
    c. More androgynous individuals were found to be higher in emotional intelligence.
    d. More Mexican-American men than European-American men are androgynous.

19. Sex reassignment surgery has been used to alter the external genitalia of
    a. persons with Klinefelter's or Turner's syndromes.
    b. intersexual or transsexual persons.
    c. pedophiles or exhibitionists.
    d. sexual masochists or sexual sadists.

20. When expectations of a friendly first date clash with an attempted seduction sequence, the problem can be attributed to differences in
    a. gender roles.
    b. erogenous confrontation.
    c. gender myths.
    d. sexual scripts.

21. The strength of the sex drive in both men and women increases when there are higher levels of
    a. acetylcholine.
    b. progestin.
    c. testosterone.
    d. leptin.

22. Which condition is least likely to lower sexual performance?
    a. sterilization
    b. castration
    c. extreme alcohol intoxication
    d. sexual aversion

23. What effect does cocaine, amphetamines, and Ecstasy have on sexual desire, arousal, pleasure, and performance?
    a. increase
    b. decrease
    c. has no effect
    d. enhance a male's but not female's

24. The first two phases of the sexual response cycle are
    a. excitement and arousal.
    b. arousal and orgasm.
    c. excitement and plateau.
    d. plateau and refractory.

25. Regarding sexual response, it can be said that
   a. a short refractory period occurs just before orgasm in females.
   b. men typically go through the sexual phases more slowly than women.
   c. men are incapable of having second orgasms.
   d. some women skip the plateau phase in the sexual response cycle.

26. Sigmund Freud incorrectly believed that if a woman did not fully accept her femininity, she would experience an "immature" form of female response called a(n) "_____ orgasm."
   a. cervical
   b. vaginal
   c. clitoral
   d. uterine

27. If a person's sexual arousal is associated with inanimate objects, the paraphilia is called
   a. fetishism.
   b. voyeurism.
   c. frotteurism.
   d. pedophilia.

28. Which of the following is NOT a common tactic used by child molesters?
   a. using a chat room on the Internet to encourage children to talk about sex
   b. bribing children with gifts
   c. using threats to gain children's compliance
   d. having partners to help gain access to the child in their home.

29. Regarding exhibitionism, which of the following statements is FALSE?
   a. Exhibitionists are typically single males who grew up in overpermissive families who have a liberal view of sexuality.
   b. Exhibitionism is a common problem with exhibitionists having high repeat rates.
   c. Although once thought harmless, up to 40 percent of exhibitionists go on to commit more serious sexual crimes and other offenses.
   d. Most exhibitionists feel a sense of inadequacy, which produces a compulsive need to prove their "manhood" by frightening women.

30. One of the greatest changes in attitudes toward sex is a tolerance for
   a. teenage pregnancies.
   b. the sexual behavior of others.
   c. the double standard.
   d. STDs.

31. The decline of the double standard refers to abandoning different standards for
   a. risky sex and "safe" sex.
   b. heterosexual relationships and homosexual relationships.
   c. sexuality before and after marriage.
   d. male and female sexual behavior.

32. Which of the following is NOT a rape myth?
   a. If a woman goes home with a man on a first date, she is interested in sex.
   b. Most rapes are committed by a friend or acquaintance of the victim.
   c. Women who are sexually active are usually lying if they say they were raped.
   d. Many women who are raped secretly enjoy it.

33. Factors that increase the likelihood that a man will commit rape include
    a. drinking alcohol.
    b. being high in gender role stereotyping.
    c. belief in rape myths.
    d. all of these.

34. Which of the following sexually transmitted diseases (STDs) CANNOT be cured?
    a. gonorrhea
    b. genital herpes
    c. syphilis
    d. chlamydia.

35. In a recent study, what percent of the teenage girls who were sexually active did not believe that they would get STDs, although many got gonorrhea or chlamydia in the next 18 months?
    a. 90
    b. 75
    c. 50
    d. 35

36. The human immunodeficiency virus (HIV) can be transmitted by
    a. eating food prepared by an infected person.
    b. sharing towels or drinking glasses
    c. sweat and tears.
    d. none of these.

37. Which of the following would be POOR advice for couples who want to communicate effectively and maintain intimacy?
    a. Avoid gunnysacking.
    b. Avoid expressing anger.
    c. Do not try to win an argument.
    d. Do not be a mind-reader.

38. Which of the following is a form of therapy that directs a couple's attention to natural sensations of sexual pleasure and is used to treat arousal disorders?
    a. sensate focus
    b. hypnotic sensation
    c. sensory restriction
    d. systematic desensitization

39. The male sexual disorder that corresponds most closely to female sexual arousal disorder is
    a. sexual aversion.
    b. erectile disorder.
    c. premature ejaculation.
    d. dyspareunia.

40. The squeeze technique is typically used to treat
    a. dyspareunia.
    b. vaginismus.
    c. hypoactive sexual desire disorder.
    d. premature ejaculation.

Chapter 11: Personality

Chapter Overview

Each of us displays consistent behavior patterns that define our own personalities and allow us to predict how other people will act. Character is personality that has been evaluated, or the possession of desirable qualities. Personality traits are lasting personal qualities that are inferred from behavior. Personality types group people into categories on the basis of shared traits. Behavior is influenced by self-concept, which is a perception of one's own personality traits. A positive self-evaluation leads to high self-esteem. Low self-esteem is associated with stress, unhappiness, and depression. Personality theories combine interrelated assumptions, ideas, and principles to explain personality. Each of the four major theories of personality, trait, psychodynamic, behavioristic and social learning, and humanistic, is useful for understanding some aspects of personality.

Trait theories identify qualities that are most lasting or characteristic of a person. Allport made useful distinctions between common traits and individual traits and among cardinal, central, and secondary traits. Cattell's theory attributes visible surface traits to the existence of 16 underlying source traits. Source traits are measured by the *Sixteen Personality Factor Questionnaire* (16 PF). The five-factor model identifies five universal dimensions of personality: extroversion, agreeableness, conscientiousness, neuroticism, and openness to experience.

Like other psychodynamic approaches, Sigmund Freud's psychoanalytic theory emphasizes unconscious forces and conflicts within the personality. In Freud's theory, personality is made up of the id, ego, and superego. Libido, derived from the life instincts, is the primary energy running the personality. Conflicts within the personality may cause neurotic anxiety or moral anxiety and motivate us to use ego-defense mechanisms. The personality operates on three levels: the conscious, preconscious, and unconscious. The Freudian view of personality development is based on a series of psychosexual stages: the oral, anal, phallic, and genital stages. Fixation at any stage can leave a lasting imprint on personality.

Humanistic theories stress subjective experience, free choice, self-actualization, and positive models of human nature. Abraham Maslow found that self-actualizers share characteristics that range from efficient perceptions of reality to frequent peak experiences. Positive psychologists have identified six human strengths that contribute to well-being and life satisfaction: wisdom and knowledge, courage, humanity, justice, temperance, and transcendence. Carl Rogers viewed the self as an entity that emerges from personal experience. We tend to become aware of experiences that match our self-image, and exclude those that are incongruent with it. The incongruent person has a highly unrealistic self-image and/or a mismatch between the self-image and the ideal self. The congruent or fully functioning person is flexible and open to experiences and feelings. As parents apply conditions of worth to children's behavior, thoughts, and feelings, children begin to do the same. Internalized conditions of worth then contribute to incongruence that disrupts the organismic valuing process.

Behavioral theories of personality emphasize learning, conditioning, and immediate effects of the environment (situational determinants). Learning theorists Dollard and Miller consider habits the basic core of personality. Habits express the combined effects of drive, cue, response, and reward. Social learning theory adds cognitive elements, such as perception, thinking, and understanding to the behavioral view of personality. Social learning theory is exemplified by the concepts of psychological situation, expectancies, and reinforcement value. The behavioristic view of personality development holds that social reinforcement in four situations is critical. The situations are feeding, toilet or cleanliness training, sex training, and anger or aggression training. Identification and imitation are of particular importance in learning to be "male" or "female."

Temperament refers to the hereditary and physiological aspects of one's emotional nature. Behavioral genetics and studies of identical twins suggest that heredity contributes significantly to adult personality traits. Traits (biological predispositions) interact with situations to explain our behavior.

Techniques typically used for personality assessment are interviews, observation, questionnaires, and projective tests. Structured and unstructured interviews provide much information, but they are subject to interviewer bias and misperceptions. The halo effect may also lower the accuracy of an interview. Direct observation, sometimes involving situational tests, behavioral assessment, or the use of rating scales, allows evaluation of a person's actual behavior. Personality questionnaires, such as the *Minnesota Multiphasic Personality Inventory-2* (MMPI-2), are objective and reliable, but their validity is open to question. Projective tests ask a person to project thoughts or feelings to an ambiguous stimulus or unstructured situation. The *Rorschach Technique,* or inkblot test, is a well-known projective technique. A second is the *Thematic Apperception Test* (TAT). Projective tests are low in validity and objectivity. Nevertheless, they are considered useful by many clinicians, particularly as part of a test battery.

Shyness is a mixture of social inhibition and social anxiety. It is marked by heightened public self-consciousness and a tendency to regard one's shyness as a lasting trait. Shyness can be lessened by changing self-defeating beliefs and by improving social skills.

Preview: The Hidden Essence

Language Development Guide

rural: in the country away from the city
banged over: bumped over
brain-jarring rut: large groove (pothole) in the road that shakes the whole body as you drive over it
lurched: rocked; swayed
dilapidated: in disrepair, run down
hooting and whooping: happy screams
suited: right; well-matched
"wilds": wilderness; backwoods
resourceful: inventive; capable; practical
radical: extreme
traded: exchanged; swapped
high country: mountainous area
ranch hand: person hired to take care of cows, sheep, or other livestock usually by horseback
lumberjack, lumberjill: person who cuts down trees
decked: knocked down
harassing: upsetting; irritating
tavern: bar that sells alcoholic drinks
on the contrary: quite the opposite

more her "old self" than ever: her personality had not changed
intriguing: fascinating; very interesting
may be struck: become aware; discover
delighted: pleased; happy
semi-stranger: not completely a stranger but not well-known either
core of consistency: main part is stable or constant
without doubt: absolutely
touches: affects
zaniest: most crazy or silly
temperament: inherited part of one's personality
character: the evaluated parts of one's personality

Module 11.1 Overview of Personality
The Psychology of Personality—Do You Have Personality?
Survey Questions: How do psychologists use the term personality?

Language Development Guide
unique: one of a kind
optimistic: positive; cheerful; hopeful
charisma: charm; appeal; magnetism
style: good taste
deemed: considered
fierce: forceful; violent
Do you know any good characters?: Do you know anyone with an entertaining personality?
model: description of a complex system
keep your bearings: help you understand and stay organized
sensitive: easily upset or hurt
inferred: understood; deduced; concluded
genuine: real; true
conscientious: hard-working; reliable; careful
executive: supervisory; managerial; administrative; decision-making
hip-hop: urban youth culture associated with rap music with the dress, speech, mannerisms
        sed by residents of the inner city
techno geek: someone skilled with computers and other technology
laid-back: unhurried; relaxed
similarly: likewise; also
paranoid: mistrustful; suspicious
dependent: needy
antisocial: lacks a conscience; selfish
maladaptive: damaging, harmful
rough outlines: general ideas about
mental "picture": how you imagine yourself to be
revise: update and change
bask in the glow: enjoy the attention and recognition
brag: boast; talk about your own achievements
hotshot: person who thinks he or she is the best at a sport
boost: increase
dwells: spends time thinking about
resolves: makes up one's mind to
sketches: short stories

path: way

self-enhancement: improving one's own self-concept by focusing on one's accomplishments and minimizing one's failures

downplay: ignore, minimize, reduce the importance of

apt: ready to

think you're hot: hold a high opinion of yourself, be egotistical

bestowed: given, awarded

arrogance: overconfidence; superiority; self-importance

turns off: makes people less interested

get lost: become confused

dazzling array: variety, several

assumptions: beliefs; best guesses

sort of lens: a way of looking at something

disconfirm: to establish that a belief or claim is false

implications: something that is implied or inferred from the statement

Recite and Review

1. Psychologists regard a person's unique long-term pattern of thinking, emotions, and behavior as the person's _____.

2. Personal characteristics that have been judged to be desirable to undesirable refer to a person's _____.

3. Stable qualities that a person shows in most situations are called personality _____.

4. The consistency in who you are, have been, and will become defines your _____.

5. If you see Dan talking to strangers, first at the supermarket and later at a party, you might deduce that he is "sociable," which illustrates that traits are inferred from _____.

6. Once identified, personality traits can be used to _____ future behavior.

7. A style of personality defined by a group of related traits is referred to as a personality _____.

8. The Swiss psychiatrist who proposed that people are either introverts or extroverts was _____.

9. Maria is a bold, outgoing person whose attention is directed outward. Maria would best be described as a(n) _____.

10. Simone is a shy, reserved person. Simone would be considered a(n) _____.

11. Rather than classifying people into two or three types, it tends to be more informative to rate people on a list of _____.

12. Although types are a shorthand way of labeling people who have several key traits in common, the use of types does tend to _____ personality.

13. People who have personality traits that increase their chance of suffering a heart attack are referred to as Type _____ personalities.

14. Gary takes a laid-back approach to life, and would be described as a Type _____ personality.

15. Unhealthy personality types, such as the paranoid personality, the dependent personality, and the antisocial personality, are defined by a specific collection of _____ traits.

16. All your ideas, perceptions, stories, and feelings about who you are make up your _____.

17. The mental "picture" we have of our own personality guides what we pay attention to, remember, and think about and is built out of our daily _____.

18. If Jack has a positive evaluation of himself and regards himself as a worthwhile person, then we say that Jack has high _____.

604

19. People who suffer from poor self-knowledge with their self-concepts being inconsistent, inaccurate, and confused will also have low _____.
20. Self-esteem is based on personal success and outstanding performance in United States and other Western cultures that stress _____.
21. Japanese and other Asian cultures place a greater emphasis on the interdependence among people, referred to as _____.
22. Since people in Asian cultures believe that by correcting personal faults, one adds to the well-being of the group, people from these Eastern cultures are more apt to engage in self-_____.
23. People who think very highly of themselves and let others know it may at first seem confident, but they soon turn people off with their _____.
24. An accurate appraisal of your strengths and weaknesses is the basis for genuine _____.
25. A system of concepts, assumptions, ideas, and principles proposed to explain personality is called a personality _____.
26. The English psychologist who believed that many personality traits are related to whether you are mainly introverted or extroverted and whether you tend to be emotionally stable or unstable (highly emotional) was _____.
27. The sad and gloomy temperament described by the early Greeks was referred to as _____.
28. According to the early Greeks, a person who was hot-tempered and irritable would have a(n) _____ temperament.
29. The early Greeks described sluggish and calm persons as having a(n) _____ temperament.
30. According to the early Greeks, if you were cheerful and hopeful, you had a(n) _____ temperament.
31. The theories that attempt to learn what traits make up personality and how they relate to actual behavior are the _____ theories.
32. Psychologists who focus on the inner workings of personality, especially internal conflicts and struggles, ascribe to a group of theories described as _____.
33. Behavioristic theories place importance on the external environment and on the effects of conditioning and _____.
34. In particular, the social learning theories attribute differences in personality to socialization, expectations, and _____.
35. The theories that stress private, subjective experience, and personal growth is the _____ theory.
36. In judging a theory, it is best to evaluate the theory in terms of its _____.
37. The psychological perspective that views individuals as having free choice regarding their behavior is the _____ theory.
38. The id, ego, and superego are the personality structures within the _____ theory.
39. The conception of conscience within the social learning theories is _____.
40. The ideal self is the conception of conscience in the _____ theory.
41. In the psychoanalytic theory, the concept of conscience is part of the personality structure called the _____.
42. The role of the unconscious is maximized in _____ theory.
43. Self-actualization is the principal motive in the _____ theory.
44. The combined effects of heredity and environment make up the developmental emphasis of the _____ theories.
45. The psychosexual stages are the developmental emphasis in the _____ theory.
46. Maladaptive habits are barriers to personal growth in the social learning and _____ theories.
47. Conditions of worth and incongruence are barriers to personal growth in the _____ theory.
48. Regarding human nature, the trait, behavioristic, and social learning theories take a(n) _____ view.

605

Part 1: Connections

1. ____ personality

2. ____ character

3. ____ personality trait

4. ____ personality type

5. ____ introvert

6. ____ extrovert

7. ____ self-concept

8. ____ self-esteem

9. ____ melancholic

10. ____ choleric

11. ____ phlegmatic

12. ____ sanguine

a. a person's perception of all his or her ideas, perceptions, stories, and feelings about the person he or she is

b. attention is directed outward; a bold, outgoing person

c. early Greek's temperament described as "hot-tempered, irritable"

d. early Greeks' temperament described as "sluggish, calm"

e. a stable, enduring quality that a person shows in most situations

f. person's desirable and undesirable qualities as judged by others

g. early Greeks' temperament described as "cheerful, hopeful"

h. style of personality defined by a group of related traits

i. attention is focused inward; a shy, reserved, self-centered person

j. person's unique and relatively stable behavior patterns

k. a person regarding his or herself as a worthwhile person

l. early Greeks' temperament described as "sad, gloomy"

Part 2: Connections

1. ____ personality theory

2. ____ Early Greeks' personality theory

3. ____ Hans Eysenck's personality theory

4. ____ trait theories

5. ____ psychodynamic theories

6. ____ behavioristic theories

7. ____ social learning theories

8. ____ humanistic theories

a. focus on the inner workings of personality, especially internal conflicts and struggles

b. system of concepts, assumptions, ideas, and principles used to understand and explain personality

c. theory that views human nature as neutral; maximizes heredity, and attempts to learn how a different traits make up personality and how they relate to actual behavior

d. attribute differences in personality to socialization, expectations, and mental processes

e. included four basic types of temperament: melancholic, choleric, phlegmatic, and sanguine

f. stress private, subjective experience and personal growth

g. theory that many personality traits are related to whether you are mainly introverted or extroverted and whether you tend to be emotionally stable or unstable

h. place importance on the external environment and on the effects of conditioning and learning

606

Check Your Memory

1. TRUE or FALSE   Personality refers to the special blend of talents, values, hopes, loves, hates, and habits that make each of us a unique person.

2. TRUE or FALSE   The term character refers to the personal characteristics that have been judged or evaluated.

3. TRUE or FALSE   A stable quality that a person shows in most situations is called a personality type.

4. TRUE or FALSE   Personality traits are inferred from behavior and are used to predict future behavior.

5. TRUE or FALSE   In a study of women who appeared to be happy and had genuine smiles in their college yearbook photos, it was found that most were still happy people 30 years later.

6. TRUE or FALSE   Traits influence our health as well as our marital and occupational success.

7. TRUE or FALSE   Swiss psychiatrist Jean Piaget proposed that people are either introverts or extroverts.

8. TRUE or FALSE   An introvert is a shy, reserved person whose attention is focused inward, while an extrovert is a bold, outgoing person whose attention is directed outward.

9. TRUE or FALSE   Rating people on a list of traits tends to be more informative than classifying people into two or three personality types.

10. TRUE or FALSE   Type A personalities take a laid-back approach to life, while Type B personalities have personality traits that increase their chance of suffering a heart attack.

11. TRUE or FALSE   Unhealthy personality types, such as the paranoid personality, the dependent personality, and the antisocial personality, are defined by a specific collection of maladaptive traits.

12. TRUE or FALSE   Your self-concept is the mental "picture" you have of your own personality.

13. TRUE or FALSE   We creatively build our self-concepts out of daily experiences and slowly revise them as we have new experiences.

14. TRUE or FALSE   Your evaluation of yourself as a worthwhile person is referred to as self-esteem.

15. TRUE or FALSE   People who have low self-esteem typically also suffer from poor self-knowledge.

16. TRUE or FALSE   In the United States and other Western cultures, self-esteem is based on a secure sense of belonging to social groups called collectivism.

17. TRUE or FALSE   In Japan and other Asian cultures, self-esteem is based on the personal success and outstanding performance of the individual.

18. TRUE or FALSE   People who think very highly of themselves and let others know it may at first seem confident, but their arrogance quickly turns off other people.

19. TRUE or FALSE   Genuine self-esteem is based on an accurate appraisal of your strengths and weaknesses.

20. TRUE or FALSE   English psychologist John Locke proposed the personality theory that many personality traits are related to whether you are mainly introverted or extroverted and whether you tend to be emotionally stable or unstable.

21. TRUE or FALSE   The early Greek temperament type called phlegmatic described a person who was cheerful and hopeful.

22. TRUE or FALSE   According to the early Greeks, a person who was sad and gloomy had a sanguine temperament type.

607

23. TRUE or FALSE The early Greek temperament type called choleric described a person who was hot-tempered and irritable.

24. TRUE or FALSE Trait theories focus on the inner workings of personality, especially internal conflicts and struggles.

25. TRUE or FALSE Psychodynamic theories stress the importance of the external environment and the effects of conditioning and learning.

26. TRUE or FALSE Humanistic theories stress private, subjective experience, and personal growth.

27. TRUE or FALSE The best way to judge a theory is in terms of its usefulness.

28. TRUE or FALSE Theories often can't be fully proved or disproved.

29. TRUE or FALSE Trait, psychoanalytic, and the behavioristic and social learning theories all see our behavior as determined, while humanists believe individuals have free choice regarding their behavior.

30. TRUE or FALSE The principal motive of the psychoanalytic theory is self-actualization.

31. TRUE or FALSE The personality structures of behavioristic and social learning theories are habits and expectancies.

32. TRUE or FALSE In the humanistic theory, the personality structures are the id, ego, and superego.

33. TRUE or FALSE Psychoanalytic theory takes a negative view of human nature, while humanistic theory takes a positive view of human nature.

34. TRUE or FALSE The conception of conscience in the psychoanalytic theory is the ideal self.

35. TRUE or FALSE In humanistic theory, self-reinforcement is the conception of conscience.

36. TRUE or FALSE The role of the unconscious is maximized in psychoanalytic theory and practically nonexistent in the behavioristic and social learning theories.

37. TRUE or FALSE The developmental emphasis of the trait theorists involves critical learning situations, identification, and imitation.

38. TRUE or FALSE Incongruence and conditions of worth are the barriers to personal growth in the humanistic theory.

Critical Thinking Question

In what way would memory contribute to the formation of an accurate or inaccurate self-image?

Module 11.2 Trait Theories

The Trait Approach—Describe Yourself in 18,000 Words or Less

Survey Question: Are some personality traits more basic or important than others?

Language Development Guide

dominant: leading
underlying: core; primary
influential: important
neuroticism: negative, upsetting emotions
interrelate: connected; related
dispositions: nature; temperaments
face-to-face: in person, directly
aesthetic: artistic; view of beauty
liberal: open-minded
reflective: causing someone to think
alternative music: newest type of rock music

heavy metal music: music characterized by strong, amplified beat, distorted chords, and usually angry lyrics

conventional: conforming; predictable; traditional

conservative: traditionalist; conformist; careful; cautious

upbeat: cheerful; bubbly

soundtrack music: music from movies

pop music: contemporary music aimed at the general public, usually a light rock

rap/hip-hop: usually involves rhythmic verses spoken to a repetitive beat

soul/funk: combines jazz, blues, and soul into an earthy sound; usually involves heavy rhythmic bass

analogy: comparison

distinctions: pointed out differences

cardinal: very basic; very serious

compassion: concern; care; sympathy

overriding: overruling; dominating

Mother Teresa: Catholic nun who founded the Missionaries of Charity in Calcutta, India; won the Nobel Peace Prize

Abraham Lincoln: 16th President of the United States; president during the American Civil War

building blocks: basic elements

essence: real meaning

superficial: surface; shallow

possessive: jealous; controlling

autonomous: independent; self-directed

dramatic: intense behaviors; gains attention

clustered: grouped together

innovative: ground-breaking; pioneering

ingenious: clever; resourceful

automatically: unconsciously; unthinkingly

"picture": representation

temperamental: unpredictable; moody; volatile; high strung

space capsule: small vehicle, pod, ship, for traveling off of the planet and into outer space

answering a singles ad: dating site

open the doors... close doors: encourage certain activities and discourage others

up to a point: until a certain amount or degree is reached

cross the line: go beyond the limits of what is acceptable or helpful

authentic: real; genuine; not fake

flaw: error; mistake

intricate: complex; elaborate

costs and benefits: disadvantages and advantages

pursuing: chasing; following

Recite and Review

1. Currently, the dominant method for studying personality is the _____ approach.
2. Trait theories seek to describe personality in terms of a small number of underlying personality traits or _____.
3. Of the various trait theories, the most influential one, currently, is The _____ Personality Model.
4. To better understand personality, trait theorists attempt to analyze, classify, and _____ traits.
5. Trait theorists often think of traits as a hereditary readiness of humans to behave in particular ways, which is referred to as _____.

6. Traits are stable dispositions that a person shows in most _____.
7. Introversion and extroversion are both traits as well as _____.
8. Researchers have found that students who are more likely to prefer meeting people through the Internet than face-to-face are the students high in the trait of _____.
9. Peter Rentfrow and Samuel Gosling found the people who value aesthetic experiences, have good verbal abilities, are liberal, and tolerant of others tend to like blues, jazz, classical, and folk music, which are all complex and _____.
10. According to Rentfrow and Gosling, people who are curious about new experiences, enjoy taking risks, and are physically active prefer rock, alternative, and heavy metal music, which is intense, _____ music.
11. Marcy would be described as cheerful, extroverted, reliable, helpful, and conservative. According to Rentfrow and Gosling, she would tend to enjoy country, soundtrack, religious, or pop music, which are all types of upbeat _____ music.
12. Damien is talkative, full of energy, forgiving, and physically attractive, and he rejects conservative ideals. Damien would most likely prefer rap/hip-hop, soul/funk, and electronic/dance music, which are types of energetic, _____ music.
13. The psychologist who identified several kinds of traits, including common, individual, cardinal, central, and secondary traits was _____
14. The traits that are shared by most members of a culture are called _____ traits.
15. Traits that describe a person's unique qualities and are divided into cardinal, central, and secondary traits are the _____ traits.
16. Compassion could be said to be an overriding trait of Mother Teresa's personality, while Abraham Lincoln's personality was dominated by the trait of honesty. These overriding, dominant traits are examples of _____ traits.
17. According to Allport, the basic building blocks of personality capture the true essence of a person they are used to describe and are called _____ traits.
18. According to Allport, your food preferences, attitudes, political opinions, and other superficial personal qualities are your _____ traits.
19. According to Raymond Cattell, the numerous visible features of a person's personality are called _____ traits.
20. These numerous visible features of personality can be grouped into a few underlying dimensions of personality known as _____ traits.
21. The statistical technique used by Cattell to correlate multiple measurements and identify general underlying factors of personality is called _____.
22. The *Sixteen Personality Factor Questionnaire* (16 PF) produce a graph of a person's score on each trait so one can easily compare traits. This graph is called a(n) _____.
23. The five-factor model attempted to further reduce _____'s 16 factors.
24. The five-factor model, or "Big Five" are conscientiousness, agreeableness, extroversion, openness to experience, and _____.
25. On the five-factor model, or "Big Five," a person who is a joiner and is talkative, active and affectionate would have a high score on the factor called _____
26. If you are a cold, indifferent, self-centered, or spiteful, you would have a low score in the Big Five factor called _____.
27. Jon is self-disciplined, responsible, and achieving, while Tara would be described as irresponsible, careless, and undependable. Regarding the "Big Five" factors, Jon and Tara differ on the factor called _____.
28. People who tend to be anxious, emotionally "sour," irritable, and unhappy are high in the "Big Five" factor of _____.
29. Dancy is intelligent, creative, curious, and imaginative. According to the "Big Five," Dancy is high in the factor called _____.

30. Simon earns a great deal of money, has had many sex partners, has been divorced twice, and would be described as a risk taker. According to the research on the "Big Five" factors, Simon is most likely high in _____.

31. Janine has many friends and enjoys strong social support from others. However, Janine tends to put the interests of her friends and family ahead of her own interests, which is wearing her out. Regarding the "Big Five" Factors, Janine is most likely high in _____.

32. Jana sets unattainably high standards for herself, which causes her to feel as if she is always failing. Jana suffers from unhealthy _____.

33. Success, in the long run, is more often based not on seeking "perfection," but on seeking _____.

34. The Big Five traits have been related to different brain systems and different brain _____.

35. People who tend to perform well at work and at school, rarely have automobile accidents, and tend to live longer are the ones that score high in the "Big Five" factor of _____.

Part 1: Connections

1. ___ common traits
2. ___ individual traits
3. ___ cardinal trait
4. ___ central traits
5. ___ secondary traits
6. ___ surface traits
7. ___ source traits

a. Cattell's term for the basic underlying traits, or factors of personality
b. Allport's term for a personality trait so basic that all of a person's activities relate to it
c. Cattell's term for the visible or observable traits of one's personality
d. Allport's term for all the personality traits used to describe a single person's unique qualities
e. Allport's term for traits that are inconsistent or relatively superficial
f. Allport's term for one's core traits that characterize his or her personality
g. Allport's term for personality traits that are shared by most members of a particular culture

Part 2: Connections

1. ___ trait profile
2. ___ factor analysis
3. ___ extroversion
4. ___ agreeableness
5. ___ conscientiousness
6. ___ neuroticism
7. ___ openness to experience
8. ___ perfectionism

a. high scorers are self-disciplined, responsible, and achieving
b. high scores are talkative, active, and affectionate and are joiners
c. having negative, upsetting emotions
d. a graph of the scores obtained on several personality traits
e. having impossibly high standards
f. refers to how friendly, nurturant, and caring a person is, as opposed to cold, indifferent, self-centered, or spiteful
g. a statistical technique used to correlate multiple measurements and identify general underlying factors
h. high scorers are imaginative, creative, original, curious, and intelligent

Check Your Memory

1. TRUE or FALSE   The social learning approach is currently the dominant method for studying personality.
2. TRUE or FALSE   The Five Factor Personality Model (Big Five) is made up of the five dimensions of likability, optimism, dependence, logical, and nurturing.
3. TRUE or FALSE   Trait theorists often think of traits as biological predispositions.
4. TRUE or FALSE   Introversion and extroversion can be thought of as types and as traits.
5. TRUE or FALSE   Researchers have found that students high in the trait of extroversion are more likely to prefer to meet people through the Internet than face-to-face.
6. TRUE or FALSE   According to Rentfrow and Gosling, people who value aesthetic experiences, have good verbal abilities, are liberal, and tolerant of others tend to like music that is intense and rebellious music, such as rock, alternative, and heavy metal music.
7. TRUE or FALSE   People who are talkative, full of energy, forgiving, and physically attractive and who reject conservative ideals tend to prefer energetic, rhythmic music, such as rap/hip-hop, soul/funk, and electronic/dance music, according to Rentfrow and Gosling.
8. TRUE or FALSE   If you are cheerful, conventional, extroverted, reliable, helpful, and conservative, Rentfrow and Gosling predict that you will like music that is reflective and complex, such as blues, jazz, classical, and folk music.
9. TRUE or FALSE   Raymond Cattell identified common and individual traits, while Gordon Allport identified surface and source traits.
10. TRUE or FALSE   Common traits would tell us how people from a particular nation or culture are similar, or which traits a culture emphasizes.
11. TRUE or FALSE   Central traits are personality traits so basic that all of a person's activities are dominated by it.
12. TRUE or FALSE   Superficial personal qualities, such as food preferences and political opinions are referred to as cardinal traits.
13. TRUE or FALSE   A statistical technique used to correlate multiple measurements and identify general underlying factors is called a frequency polygon.
14. TRUE or FALSE   Source traits are one's basic underlying traits, while one's visible, observable traits are called surface traits.
15. TRUE or FALSE   Source traits can be measured by a test called the *Sixteen Personality Factor Questionnaire* (16 PF).
16. TRUE or FALSE   An adjective checklist is a graph of the scores obtained on several personality traits.
17. TRUE or FALSE   In the five-factor model, people who are high in agreeableness are self-disciplined, responsible, and achieving.
18. TRUE or FALSE   People who rate high on openness to experience tend to be intelligent.
19. TRUE or FALSE   People who are high in the factor of neuroticism tend be anxious, emotionally "sour," irritable, and unhappy.
20. TRUE or FALSE   Extroverts are more likely to divorce with extroverted men being less likely to live with their children.
21. TRUE or FALSE   Introverts tend to earn more money during their careers than extroverts.
22. TRUE or FALSE   Agreeable people often put the interests of friends and family ahead of their own.
23. TRUE or FALSE   Although college students who are perfectionists tend to get good grades, setting impossibly high standards can actually lower performance at school and elsewhere.

24. TRUE or FALSE   The Big Five traits have been related to different brain systems and chemicals.
25. TRUE or FALSE   People who score low in conscientiousness rarely have automobile accidents and tend to live longer.

Critical Thinking Question

Can you think of a Big Five trait besides conscientiousness that might be related to academic achievement?

Module 11.3 Psychoanalytic Theory
Psychoanalytic Theory—Id Came to Me in a Dream
Survey Question: How do psychodynamic theories explain personality?

Language Development Guide

probe: search; explore; investigate
animate: stimulate; bring us to life
Id came to me in a dream: play on the words, "it came to me in a dream", meaning you had a vision—joke comes from the use of Freud's concept of the Id, and the importance of dreams in understanding the unconscious
Viennese: person who lives in the city of Vienna, Austria
evolved: developed gradually
modern thought: current ideas, concepts, and theories
portrays: describes; shows
dynamic: active; self-motivating
innate: inborn; inherited
instincts: biological drives; strong natural impulses
chaotic: confused; disorganized; disordered; frenzied
underlies: bring about; triggers
offered: put forth; submitted; suggested
discharging: setting free; releasing
"executive": manager; supervisor; decision-maker
blind king or queen: a ruler who gives orders but cannot see how to carry them out or see their results, so must depend on others
awesome: great; tremendous; overwhelming
rely: to depend; to put trust in
external reality: to the world outside the person
censor: someone who suppresses or removes objectionable material
aspirations: goals; desire for advancement
"internalized parent": taking on the attitudes and beliefs of a guiding, controlling; punishing individual
delinquent: youth that breaks the law
antisocial: lacks a conscience
inhibition: restrained; blocked; suppressed
rigidity: inflexible
clash: fight; disagree
restrictions: limits
in a nutshell: briefly, to summarize
clamors: screams; cries
Go for it!: give it a try, do it
icily: in an unfriendly manner

drastic: extreme; severe

courtship: dating

seduction: luring someone into having sex

prevails: wins; succeeds; overcomes

displace: transfer feelings

sublimate: substitute; redirect; channel

push-ups: a form of exercise

rechanneled: redirecting

typify: characterize; is typical of

habitual: continual, consistent, engrained

resort: use as a way out; choose as an alternative

distort: misrepresent; falsify

repressed: unconsciously pushed out of awareness

disguised: changed in order to hide or conceal

symbolic: something that stands for or represents something else

Freudian slips: an accidental mistake of saying a word that really represents your real
        unconscious feelings

ensure: make certain

codes: set of laws

phallic: literally means resembling a penis

latency: dormant; present but undeveloped and unexpressed

unresolved: not solved; not completed

hang-up: problem, barrier

overindulgence: doing too much of something to excess

gullible: easy to fool; overly trusting

mothered: taken care of

showered with gifts: giving many, many presents

cynical: skeptical; distrustful

exploit: take advantage of

biting sarcasm: cruel humor

forte: strength or specialty; also, in music, means loud

"holding on": keeping it stubbornly; withholding it

"letting go": discharging carelessly

lenient: being tolerant; easygoing; indulgent

lock: fix permanently

obstinate: stubborn, unwilling to change

stingy: penny-pinching; ungenerous

compulsively: irrationally driven

vanity: pride; self-importance

exhibitionism: attention-seeking; could also mean to display private body parts in a revealing manner

Oedipus: (ED-eh-puss), character in a Greek tragedy who mistakenly fell in love with his mother
and killed his father

rivalry: competition

ease: calm; soothe

Electra: (eh-LECK-truh), character in a Greek tragedy who kills her mother

dormant: inactive; sleeping; undeveloped

"on hold": paused; temporary interruption

upswing: increase

upsurge: sudden increase

turmoil: confusion; unrest; uproar

bizarre: strange; odd

614

offshoot: extension, variation
wholeheartedly: entirely; enthusiastically
embrace: accept; support
portrayal: representation; description
stern: harsh; strict; demanding
verify: prove; confirm

Recite and Review

1. The theory that is the best known psychodynamic approach and grew out of the work of Sigmund Freud was _____ theory.
2. According to Freud's model the mental structure that is made up of innate biological instincts and urges is called the _____.
3. The most primitive of the mental structures has a desire for immediate satisfaction of wishes and, thus, operates on the _____ principle.
4. The mind, mental life, and personality as a whole are called the _____.
5. In Freudian theory, the force, primarily pleasure-oriented, that energizes the personality is called the _____.
6. The life instincts, which underlie our efforts to survive, are referred to as _____.
7. The death instinct that produces aggressive and destructive urges is referred to as _____.
8. The executive of the personality that directs rational behavior is the _____.
9. The rational executive part of the personality delays action until it is appropriate and is, thus, guided by the _____ principle.
10. The mental structure that acts as a judge or censor for the thoughts and actions of the ego is the _____.
11. The subpart of the judging part of the personality that reflects actions for which a person has been punished in the past is called the _____.
12. The subpart of the censoring part of the personality that reflects all the behaviors one's parents have rewarded the person for in the past is called the _____.
13. In Freudian terms, a person will become a delinquent, criminal, or antisocial personality if he or she has a weak "internalized parent," or _____.
14. When standards of the one's conscience are not met, we experience feelings of _____.
15. When the standards of the ego ideal are met, we experience feelings of _____.
16. Inhibition, rigidity, or unbearable guilt result from an overly strict or harsh _____.
17. When the ego can barely keep the id under control, these id impulses can cause _____ anxiety.
18. Threats of punishment from the superego cause _____ anxiety.
19. Mental processes that deny, distort, or otherwise block out sources of threat and anxiety are known as _____ mechanisms.
20. The region of the mind that holds repressed memories and emotions plus the instinctual drives of the id is called the _____.
21. Even if thoughts are beyond awareness, they may slip into behavior in disguised or _____ form.
22. Every thought you are aware of at any given moment resides in the _____ level of awareness.
23. Brain research has found that the unconscious emotions and memories, theorized by Freud, are processed by the brain's _____ system.
24. Someone asks you where you were when the Saints won the Super Bowl. Before you were asked this question, this information resided in your _____ level of awareness.

615

25. Your boss returns from a business trip and walks into your office; and you mistakenly say, "I'm so sad to see you" rather than "I'm so glad to see you." According to psychoanalytic theory, you unconsciously expressed your true feelings in this _____ of the tongue.

26. Freud theorized that the core of personality is formed before age six in a series of _____ stages.

27. At each of Freud's stages, a different part of the body becomes a child's primary area of producing pleasure, an area also called a(n) _____.

28. According to Freud, many adult personality traits involve unresolved conflicts or emotional hang-ups that occurred in one or more stages due to over indulgence or frustration. These unresolved conflicts are referred to as _____.

29. According to Freud, if a child is overfed or frustrated during the first psychosexual stage, the person, as an adult, may show a great deal of gum chewing, nail biting, smoking, kissing, overeating, and/or alcoholism. These behaviors would be considered adult expressions of _____ needs.

30. Fixation early in the first stage results in a personality that is gullible, passive, and needs lots of attention called a(n) _____ personality.

31. Frustrations later in the first stage may cause a personality that is cynical, sarcastic, and verbally aggressive called a(n) _____ personality.

32. Between the ages of one and three, the child's attention shifts to the process of elimination and toilet training in the psychosexual stage called the _____ stage.

33. Jeff is obstinate, stingy, orderly, and compulsively neat. According to Freud, Jeff has a(n) _____ personality.

34. Bret is often cruel, messy, disorderly, and even destructive. According to Freud, Brett has a(n) _____ personality.

35. Adult traits of vanity, exhibitionism, sensitive pride, and narcissism are often seen if fixation occurs at the _____ stage.

36. Between three and six years of age, Freud theorized that male children develop an attraction for their mothers and a rivalry with their fathers, which he called the _____ conflict.

37. Freud believed that the male child felt threatened by the father and feared _____.

38. To ease these fears of the father, the boy must identify with the father and in so doing accepts the father's values and forms a(n) _____.

39. Freud believed preschool girls love their fathers and compete with their mothers during the _____ conflict.

40. The period from age six to puberty is not so much a stage as it is a quiet time during which psychosexual development is dormant and is called the _____ period.

41. At puberty, an individual enters the stage during which sexual energies activate all the unresolved conflicts of earlier years. This stage is called the _____ stage.

42. During the last psychosexual stage, the person realizes full adult sexuality and develops a mature capacity for _____.

43. Freud is credited with pioneering the idea that development proceeds in stages and that adult personality is shaped by critical events that occur during the first few years and include feeding, early sexual experiences, and _____ training.

44. Freud's idea that the elementary school years were free from sexuality and unimportant in personality development has been challenged. Thus, these elementary school years, which encompass Freud's _____ period are really not dormant.

45. Contrary to Freud's theory, current studies show that affectionate and accepting fathers, not stern and punishing ones, are more likely to encourage their sons to develop a strong _____.

46. One criticism of Freud's theory is that in personality development, Freud overemphasized _____.

47. Freud has been criticized for his views of patients who believed they had been sexually molested as children. Freud assumed that such events were childhood _____.
48. Although Freud's theory provides numerous ways to explain almost any thought, action, or feeling after it has occurred, the theory leads to few _____.

Part 1: Connections

1. ____ id
2. ____ ego
3. ____ superego
4. ____ unconscious
5. ____ conscious
6. ____ preconscious
7. ____ oral stage
8. ____ anal stage
9. ____ phallic stage
10. ____ latency
11. ____ genital stage

a. executive part of the personality that directs rational behavior
b. region of the mind that includes all mental contents a person is aware of at any given moment
c. psychosexual stage at ages three to six when a child is preoccupied with the genitals
d. region of the mind that holds repressed memories and emotions
e. a period in childhood when psychosexual development is dormant
f. primitive part of personality that supplies energy and demands pleasure
g. period of full psychosexual development, marked by the attainment of mature adult sexuality
h. judge or censor for thoughts and actions
i. area of the mind containing information that can be voluntarily brought to awareness
j. psychosexual stage corresponding roughly to the period of toilet training ages one to three
k. period when infants are preoccupied with the mouth as a source of pleasure and means of expression

Part 2: Connections

1. ____ erogenous zone
2. ____ pleasure principle
3. ____ reality principle
4. ____ psyche
5. ____ libido
6. ____ Eros
7. ____ Thanatos
8. ____ conscience
9. ____ ego ideal

a. part of the superego that causes pride when its standards are met
b. a desire for immediate satisfaction of wishes, desires, or needs
c. death instinct
d. any body area that produces pleasurable sensations
e. the force, primarily pleasure-oriented, that energizes the personality
f. oral, anal, phallic, and genital stages during which various personality traits are formed
g. delaying action until it is appropriate
h. apprehension felt when thoughts, impulses, or actions conflict with the superego's standards
i. mental processes that deny, distort, or block out sources of threat and anxiety

10. ___ neurotic anxiety
11. ___ moral anxiety
12. ___ ego defense mechanism
13. ___ psychosexual stages

j. part of superego that causes guilt when its standards are not met
k. mind, mental life, and personality as a whole
l. apprehension felt when the ego struggles to control id impulses
m. life instincts

Part 3: Connections

1. ___ oral-dependent personality

2. ___ oral-aggressive personality

3. ___ anal-retentive personality

4. ___ anal-expulsive personality

5. ___ phallic personality

6. ___ fixation

7. ___ Oedipus conflict

8. ___ Electra conflict

a. person who is vain, exhibitionistic, sensitive, and narcissistic
b. person who wants to passively receive attention, gifts, and love
c. girl's sexual attraction to her father and feelings of rivalry with her mother
d. person who is disorderly, destructive, cruel, or messy person
e. lasting conflict developed as a result of frustration or over-indulgence
f. person who uses the mouth to express hostility by shouting, cursing, biting and openly exploits others
g. person who is obstinate, stingy, or compulsive clean
h. boy's sexual attraction to his mother, and feelings of rivalry with his father

Check Your Memory

1. TRUE or FALSE   Psychoanalytic theory is the best-known psychodynamic approach and grew out of the work of Sigmund Freud.
2. TRUE or FALSE   Freud's model of personality is directed by mental structures known as personas and archetypes.
3. TRUE or FALSE   The ego is made up of innate biological instincts and is self-serving, irrational, and impulsive.
4. TRUE or FALSE   The ego operates on the pleasure principle, while the superego operates on the reality principle.
5. TRUE or FALSE   The libido is the energy that flows from the life instincts.
6. TRUE or FALSE   The life instincts are known as Thanatos, while the death instinct is referred to as Eros.
7. TRUE or FALSE   The id is made up of the conscience and ego ideal.
8. TRUE or FALSE   The ego must meet the conflicting demands of the id and superego as well as deal with external reality.
9. TRUE or FALSE   The apprehension felt when the ego struggles to control id impulses is called moral anxiety.
10. TRUE or FALSE   Sometimes, according to Freud, the ego must displace or sublimate sexual energies into other activities, such as sports, music, dance, or exercise.
11. TRUE or FALSE   According to Freud, each person develops habitual ways of calming anxieties with many resorting to using ego-defense mechanisms.
12. TRUE or FALSE   The preconscious holds repressed memories and emotions plus the drives of the id.

13. TRUE or FALSE   The conscious level of awareness includes everything you are aware of at a given moment, including thoughts, perceptions, feelings, and memories.

14. TRUE or FALSE   Modern scientists have found that the brain's limbic system does seem to trigger unconscious emotions and memories, as theorized by Freud.

15. TRUE or FALSE   When a person feels guilty without knowing why, psychoanalytic theory credits such guilt to the unconscious workings of the superego.

16. TRUE or FALSE   Freud theorizes that the core of personality is formed by age 13 in a series of psychosocial stages.

17. TRUE or FALSE   Freud used the terms "sex" and "erotic" very broadly to refer to many physical sources of pleasure.

18. TRUE or FALSE   At each stage of development, according to Freud, a different part of the body becomes a child's primary erogenous zone.

19. TRUE or FALSE   Freud believed that many adult personality traits can be traced to fixations in one or more of his stages.

20. TRUE or FALSE   The oral stage occurs from ages one to three, while the phallic stage occurs during puberty.

21. TRUE or FALSE   Oral-dependent persons are gullible and passive and need lots of attention.

22. TRUE or FALSE   Anal-retentive personalities are disorderly, destructive, cruel, and messy.

23. TRUE or FALSE   Adult traits of the phallic personality include vanity, exhibitionism, sensitive pride, and narcissism.

24. TRUE or FALSE   According to Freud, the attraction that boys feel for their mother and the rivalry with their fathers is called the Electra conflict.

25. TRUE or FALSE   To ease the male child's fear that his father will castrate him, Freud believed that the boy must identify with his father and by so doing forms a conscience.

26. TRUE or FALSE   Freud believed that women were less effective in creating a conscience since they were less driven to identify with their mothers.

27. TRUE or FALSE   During the period of latency, psychosexual development is dormant, according to Freud.

28. TRUE or FALSE   The genital stage ends with a mature capacity for love and the realization of full adult sexuality.

29. TRUE or FALSE   Freud was among the first to propose that development proceeds in a series of stages and that the first years of life help shape adult personality.

30. TRUE or FALSE   Freud was clearly right when he portrayed the elementary school years as free from sexuality and unimportant for personality development.

31. TRUE or FALSE   Studies have shown that a son is more likely to develop a strong conscience if his father is stern and punishing.

32. TRUE or FALSE   One criticism of Freud's theory is that he underemphasized the importance of sexuality in personality development.

33. TRUE or FALSE   Freud thought that his patients who believed they were sexually molested as children were really experiencing childhood fantasies.

34. TRUE or FALSE   Freud's concepts are almost impossible to verify scientifically.

35. TRUE or FALSE   Because there is an element of truth to much of what Freud said, some clinical psychologists continue to regard Freudian theory as a useful way to think about human problems.

Critical Thinking Question

Many adults would find it embarrassing or humiliating to drink from a baby bottle. Can you explain why?

Module 11.4 Humanistic Theories

Humanistic Theory—Peak Experiences and Personal Growth

Survey Question: What are humanistic theories of personality?

Language Development Guide

mule: cross between a horse and a donkey

personal growth: self-development; improvement

fuller use of human potentials: making better use of all of one's capabilities

bring balance: humanistic theory takes a positive view of human nature, which is opposite to the psychoanalytic view of human nature as negative; thus balance is achieved

encourage our potentials to blossom: like growing a flower, to grow and develop toward our goals and hopes

pessimism: gloom; negativity

battleground: series of conflicts

inherently: innately; naturally; essentially

machine-like: behavior is controlled like the actions of a machine

overtones: implications; suggestions; hints

bundle: bunch; collection

moldable: capable of being shaped

"real worlds": each person has his or her own reality, since each views the same situation in a different way

facet: aspect; part

effective: successful

Albert Einstein: German-born physicist who proposed the theory of relativity

William James: psychologist from the United States that developed functionalism

Jane Addams: first American woman awarded the Nobel Peace Prize; opened Hull House for European immigrants

Eleanor Roosevelt: First Lady of the United States during her husband F.D. Roosevelt's terms as President; advocate of human rights; delegate to the United Nations

John Muir: naturalist and author who advocated the creation of national parks in the United States

Walt Whitman: famous American poet; often called the father of free verse

radically: totally; completely

fulfillment: contentment; satisfaction

well-schooled: being educated in many varied areas

flaws: faults; errors; defects

contradictions: inconsistencies

spontaneity: coming from natural feelings without constraint

engaged: busy

spontaneous: unplanned; impulsive; natural

mission: a calling; purpose; goal; objective

humanitarians: concern for the welfare of all persons; shows an ethic of kindness

Albert Schweitzer: French philosopher, physician, and accomplished organist who spent most of his life on a medical mission in Gabon in Africa; won Nobel Peace Prize

reliance: dependence

"innocence of vision": seeing as if for the first time

fellowship: association; friendship

620

profound: deep; thoughtful

solitude: privacy; seclusion; isolation

wry: ironic, dry humor

prodding: soft push, nudge

shortcomings: inadequacies; limitations, weaknesses

ecstasy: sudden intense feeling of joy or pleasure

harmony: pleasing orderly arrangement of parts; in agreement

empirically: scientifically; information gained from direct observation

proceed: advance; progress; continue

no magic formula: no quick, easy way

gleaned: picked up

architect of self: create in one's own self

shouldering responsibility: accepting, taking charge of

wishful thinking: the illusion that what you wish for is actually true

awe: wonder

exaltation: joy; happiness

reverence: admiration; worship

yearnings: longing; desire

community: unity; kinship; cooperation

gauge: measure

thriving: blossoming; prospering

proponents: supporters

perspective: point of view; way of regarding situations

vitality: energy; strength

prudence: carefulness

transcendence: state of being that is beyond material existence

gratitude: thankfulness

spirituality: sense of connectiveness with a higher power or with the universe

ample: lots, much

incongruent: not matching; not corresponding

discrepancy: inconsistency; difference

seething: very angry; furious

authentic: real, true

vital: very important

in accord: to be in agreement

socially poised: calm dignity in dealing with social situations

pondered: considered; thought about

carefree: not worried about appearances

party animal: person who prefers socializing to working or studying

conscientious: responsible, organized, hard-working

bookworm: person who enjoys reading

embrace: accept; welcome; take up

taller order: goal that is harder to fill

narrative: story; description

asserts: declares

alternate: different

desert: leave; abandon

elaborate: detailed; complex

enterprising: innovative, creative

entrepreneur: one who organizes a new business

grossly obese: very fat

621

anguish: torment; pain; distress; sorrow
cherished: prized; treasured
hold: possess; have
justified: reasonable; within your rights
filtering: sorting; cleaning
unshakable: firm; sure; constant; solid
"prized": valued
without...strings attached: no special demands, requirements, or limits
luxury: treat; extra
affirmation: support; encouragement

Recite and Review

1. Humanists focus on human experience, problems, ideals and _____.
2. In opposition to the view of psychoanalytic theorists, the humanists view human nature as inherently _____.
3. Humanists believe that we are creative beings capable of behavior that is not determined by genetics, learning, or unconscious forces, but instead by _____.
4. The traits, qualities, potentials, and behavior patterns most characteristic of the human species are referred to as human _____.
5. To a humanist the person you are today is largely the product of all the _____ you have made.
6. Rather than prior learning, humanists emphasize our private perceptions of reality, that is, our immediate _____.
7. Abraham Maslow became interested in people, such as Albert Einstein, Eleanor Roosevelt, and Walt Whitman, who were living or had lived unusually _____ lives.
8. According to Maslow, continuous search for personal fulfillment is at the heart of _____.
9. If you are making full use of your personal potentials, Maslow would say that you are a(n) _____.
10. Most of Maslow's subjects had a mission to fulfill in life or some problem outside themselves to pursue. Maslow referred to this quality as _____
11. Maslow referred to the wonderful capacity to laugh at oneself and never make a joke that hurt anybody as a(n) _____ sense of humor.
12. According to Maslow, self-actualizers are able to judge situations correctly and honest, thus, showing an efficient _____ of reality.
13. Self-actualizers are free from reliance on other people or on external _____.
14. Self-actualizers accept the shortcomings of others and the contradictions of the human condition with humor and _____.
15. Maslow's subjects extended their creativity into everyday activities with self-actualizers tending to be unusually alive, engaged, and _____.
16. Self-actualizers will experience a sunset or a flower intensely time after time as it were a first time experience. This tendency is known as a(n) "_____."
17. All of Maslow's subjects reported frequent, but temporary, moments of self-actualization called _____.
18. Although Maslow tried to investigate self-actualization empirically, his choice of people for study was _____.
19. Self-actualization is not a goal or an end point, but is primarily a(n) _____.
20. People will not be able to reach self-actualization if they cannot accept all kinds of information without distorting by engaging in _____ thinking.
21. With few exceptions, self-actualizers tend to have a mission or "_____" in life.

622

22. Self-actualization requires that, for every aspect of your life, you must end the habit of blaming others for your own shortcomings and instead become personally _____.
23. In recent years, the personality traits that contribute to happiness and well-being have been studied scientifically by proponents of _____ psychology.
24. Martin Seligman, Christopher Peterson, and others have identified six human strengths that contribute to well-being and life satisfaction. They are wisdom and knowledge, temperance, transcendence, humanity, courage, and _____.
25. Forgiveness, humility, prudence, and self-control make up the human strength of _____.
26. Appreciation of beauty and excellence, gratitude, hope, humor, and spirituality make up the human strength of _____.
27. One study found that the traits that are strongly associated with life satisfaction are hope, vitality, gratitude, love, and _____.
28. According to Carl Rogers, a person who lives in harmony with his or her deepest feelings and impulses is a(n) _____ person.
29. Rogers believed that a person is most likely to live in harmony with his or her deepest feelings if the person receives ample amounts of love and _____ from others.
30. Rogers called the flexible and changing perception of one's personal identity the _____.
31. One's total subjective perception of one's body and personality is referred to as one's self-concept, or _____.
32. According to Rogers, a person who thinks she is kind, but really is not, is in a state of _____.
33. When we feel that our behavior accurately expresses who we are, we are being _____.
34. The image of the person you would most like to be is referred to as the _____.
35. This image of who you would most like to be is similar to Freud's _____.
36. Researchers have found that people tended to be socially poised, confident, and resourceful when their self-image and the person they wish to become is closely _____.
37. Hazel Markus and Paula Nurius called the persons we could become and the persons we are afraid of becoming our _____.
38. Tanya, who embraces a carefree college lifestyle with lots of parties, would most likely be high in the Big Five traits of extroversion and _____.
39. Arena would be considered a "bookworm," who finds it easy to read and complete all the assignments. Arena would most likely be high in the Big Five trait of _____.
40. As we grow older, we tend to become more agreeable, conscientious, and _____.
41. Whatever possible self you choose to pursue, you are more likely to become what you imagine if you make your story more detailed, that is, _____ it.
42. Our personalities are shaped by the stories we tell about ourselves, according to the _____ approach.
43. According to Carl Rogers, mirrors, photographs, video cameras, and the reactions of others hold such and threat for many people because they provide _____ about one's self.
44. Rogers believed that positive and negative evaluations by others cause children to develop internal standards of evaluation called _____.
45. According to Rogers, thinking of oneself as a good, lovable, worthwhile person is referred to as positive _____.
46. The direct, gut-level response to life that avoids the filtering and distortion of incongruence is called _____.
47. If you are "prized" as a worthwhile human being, just for being yourself, without any "strings attached," then you are receiving _____.

Part 1: Connections

1. ___ humanism

2. ___ human nature

3. ___ subjective experience

4. ___ self-actualization

5. ___ peak experiences

6. ___ human strengths

7. ___ possible selves

8. ___ narrative approach

a. temporary moments marked by feelings of ecstasy, harmony, and deep meaning

b. include wisdom, knowledge, courage, humanity, justice, temperance, and transcendence

c. approach that focuses on human experience, problems, potentials, and ideals

d. process of fully developing personal potentials

e. those traits, qualities, potentials, and behavior patterns most characteristic of the human species

f. the person that one wants to become or is afraid of becoming

g. approach that states our personalities are shaped by the stories we tell about ourselves

h. reality as it is perceived and interpreted, not as it exists objectively

Part 2: Connections

1. ___ fully functioning person

2. ___ self

3. ___ self-image

4. ___ incongruence

5. ___ authentic

6. ___ ideal self

7. ___ conditions of worth

8. ___ positive self-regard

9. ___ organismic valuing

10. ___ unconditional positive regard

a. person living in harmony with her or his deepest feelings, impulses, and intuitions

b. internal standards used to judge the value of one's thoughts, actions, feelings, or experiences

c. thinking of oneself as a good, lovable, worthwhile person

d. total subjective perception of one's body and personality

e. a natural, undistorted, full-body reaction to an experience

f. the person you would like to become

g. unshakable love and approval given without qualification

h. a continuously evolving conception of one's personal identity

i. state that exists when there is a discrepancy between one's experiences and self-image or between one's self-image and ideal self

j. feeling that one's behavior accurately expresses who he or she is

Check Your Memory

1. TRUE or FALSE   Humanists view human nature as inherently good with people being capable of free choice.

2. TRUE or FALSE   Humanists emphasize immediate subjective experience rather than prior learning.

3. TRUE or FALSE   The humanists view personality as a battleground for instincts and unconscious forces.

624

4. TRUE or FALSE   To a humanist the person you are today is largely the product of all the choices you have made.

5. TRUE or FALSE   Maslow referred to the process of fully developing personal potentials as conditions of worth.

6. TRUE or FALSE   Most of the people whom Maslow considered to be living unusually effective lives had a mission to fulfill in life or some problem outside of themselves to pursue.

7. TRUE or FALSE   Self-actualizers rely on external authorities to judge the accuracy of their perceptions.

8. TRUE or FALSE   Despite their satisfying relationships with others, self-actualizers value solitude and are comfortable being alone.

9. TRUE or FALSE   Self-actualizers show an "innocence of vision."

10. TRUE or FALSE   All of Maslow's subjects reported frequent occurrences of peak experiences.

11. TRUE or FALSE   Self-actualization is a goal and end point, not a process.

12. TRUE or FALSE   To become self-actualized, one must be able to blame others for his or her shortcomings.

13. TRUE or FALSE   To become self-actualized, one should frequently engage in wishful thinking.

14. TRUE or FALSE   Maslow felt that everyone has a potential for "greatness," but most fear becoming what they might.

15. TRUE or FALSE   Proponents of positive psychology have tried to scientifically study positive personality traits that contribute to happiness and well-being.

16. TRUE or FALSE   Martin Seligman, Christopher Peterson, and others have identified six specific human strengths that contribute life satisfaction.

17. TRUE or FALSE   Forgiveness, humility, prudence, and self-control make up the human strength known as transcendence.

18. TRUE or FALSE   Citizenship, fairness, and leadership make up the human strength called humanity.

19. TRUE or FALSE   One study found that traits of hope, vitality, gratitude, love, and curiosity are strongly associated with life satisfaction

20. TRUE or FALSE   According to Rogers, the incongruent person lives in harmony with his or her deepest feelings and impulses.

21. TRUE or FALSE   Rogers' theory emphasizes the self, which is a flexible and changing perception of personal identity.

22. TRUE or FALSE   You would be in a state of positive regard if you believed that you are person who "never gets angry," yet you spend much of each day seething inside.

23. TRUE or FALSE   Being authentic means that you can do whatever you want, including ignoring the feelings of others.

24. TRUE or FALSE   Roger's concept of the ideal self is similar to Freud's ego ideal.

25. TRUE or FALSE   The greater the gap between the way you see yourself and the way you would like to be, the more unity and harmony you will feel.

26. TRUE or FALSE   Rogers emphasized that to maximize our potentials, we must accept information about ourselves as honestly as possible.

27. TRUE or FALSE   Researchers have found that people with a close match between their self-image and ideal self tend to be depressed, anxious, and insecure.

28. TRUE or FALSE   According to Markus and Nurius, possible selves tend to direct our future behavior.

29. TRUE or FALSE   A person high in the Big Five trait of extroversion and agreeableness will tend to embrace a carefree college lifestyle.

625

30. TRUE or FALSE   Someone high in neuroticism will be a studious "bookworm" and will make better grades.
31. TRUE or FALSE   As we grow older, we tend to become less agreeable, less conscientious, and less emotionally stable.
32. TRUE or FALSE   If you wanted to become a more studious student, you could use the narrative approach to tell yourself stories about this possible self you could become.
33. TRUE or FALSE   Rogers believed that positive and negative evaluations by others cause children to develop internal standards of evaluation called organismic valuing.
34. TRUE or FALSE   Rogers believed that congruence and self-actualization are encouraged by replacing organismic valuing with conditions of worth.
35. TRUE or FALSE   When people are "prized" as worthwhile human beings just for being themselves, without any "strings attached," they are receiving unconditional positive regard.

Critical Thinking Question

What role would your self-image and "possible selves" have in the choice of a college major?

Module 11.5 Behavioral and Social Learning Theories

Learning Theories of Personality—Habit I Seen You Before?

Survey Question: What do behaviorists and social learning theorists emphasize in their approach to personality?

Language Development Guide

Habit I Seen You Before?: play on words of "haven't I seen you before" with the learning theorists emphasis on habits to introduce this section

critics: reviewers; opponents; detractors

robots: a computer-controlled machine that is sometimes built to resemble a human; an android

not nearly: not quite

mechanistic: being controlled like a machine

mud pies: playing with wet dirt

blender: kitchen appliance used for cutting and mixing

big girl: mature woman

assert: declare; state; claim

scrupulous: careful; rigorous; thorough

assigned: designated; appointed; delegated

coming out of the pocket of the person: thought the person doing the study would have to make up the loss of money

trivial: unimportant; insignificant

armed person: person with a weapon

provoke: cause; bring about; trigger

ultimately: in the end; eventually

misplaces: loses

checkout line: a group of people waiting to pay for their purchases at a store

prone: likely

governed: ruled; directed; managed

goad: stir; stimulate; push

lust: strong desire; longing

temper tantrum: a disruptive emotional outburst

has paid off: been successful

menacing: looking dangerous

creation: formation; design

face a fact: notice, admit

"cognitive behaviorism": combination of cognitive psychology and behavioral psychology

trips: causes you to stumble and fall

or an accident: unintended

taken into account: considered

essence: real meaning

anthropology: social science that studies the origin, behavior, and the physical, social, and
cultural development of humans

ask him or her out: invite on a date

hiking: taking a long walk for exercise or pleasure

countless other: many other

efficacy: effectiveness

privileges: special benefit

"good behavior": desirable actions

with this in mind: when one considers this

counterpart: alternative

good to yourself: treating yourself well

crucial: important; key; vital

urgent: demanding; pressing

crushing frustrations: strong disappointments

imprint: mark; impression

manipulate: control and direct

aghast: horrified

smearing: spreading; smudging; coating something

feces: solid excretory waste material from the body

joyful abandon: blissful recklessness; pleasurable lack of restraint

sharp: quick and harsh

patience: capacity to good-naturedly tolerate delays and/or incompetence

asserting: emphasizing; defending

vicariously: by observing others

outcomes: results

excluding: keeping out; rejecting

rumors: gossip

as a consequence: something that naturally or logically follows from a condition or action.

intriguingly: interestingly; fascinatingly; enchantingly

popular culture: the ideas, perspectives, attitudes that are preferred within the mainstream of a
given Western culture beginning in the 1950s on.

unmistakable: instantly recognizable; clearly identifiable

neglectful: careless; inattentive

Recite and Review

1. Unlike psychoanalytic and humanistic theorists, behavioral theorists explain personality through concepts such as imitation, reinforcement, and _____.
2. Behavioral and social learning theories of personality are based on scientific _____.
3. Behaviorists have shown repeatedly that things like kindness, hostility, generosity, and destructiveness are _____ by children.

627

4. Behavioral personality theories emphasize that personality is no more (or less) than a collection of relatively stable _____ patterns.

5. Personality, like other learned behavior, is acquired through classical and operant conditioning and _____ learning.

6. Strict learning theorists reject the idea that personality is made up of the biological dispositions called _____.

7. Learning theorists are interested in the external causes of our actions referred to as _____ determinants.

8. In a study in which people were intentionally overpaid for doing an assigned task, 80 percent would be dishonest and keep the money under normal conditions. But when the participants thought the money would have to repaid by the person conducting the study, the dishonesty rate went down to _____ percent.

9. According to the behavioral theory, behavior is activated by prior learning interacting with _____.

10. What is predictable about personality, according to the behaviorists, is that we respond in consistent ways to certain types of _____.

11. John Dollard and Neal Miller proposed that the structure of personality is made up of learned behavior patterns called _____.

12. These learned behavior patterns are governed by the four elements of learning, which include a response, cue, drive, and _____

13. Any stimulus strong enough to goad a person to action is referred to as a(n) _____.

14. The signals from the environment which guide one's actions so that they are most likely to bring about reward are called _____.

15. To explain personality, learning principles, modeling, thought patterns, perceptions, expectations, and goals are combined within the _____ learning theory.

16. The "cognitive behaviorism" of personality theory is illustrated by the three concepts of the psychological situation, expectancy, and reinforcement value that were proposed by psychologist _____.

17. Our actions are affected by the anticipation that making a response will lead to reinforcement, which is called _____.

18. If a person trips you and you interpret it as an accident, you will act differently than if you interpreted it as intentional. This illustrating the importance of the _____.

19. You will be more likely to study harder if passing your courses and obtaining a degree has a high _____ value.

20. Albert Bandura believed that one of the most important expectancies we develop concerns the belief in one's capacity to produce a desired result, which is called _____.

21. You worked really hard on your psychology report and earned an A. So, you tell yourself, "Good job!" and then reward yourself with a night out with friends at your favorite restaurant. According to social learning theorists, you are engaging in _____.

22. The social learning theorist's counterpart to the superego is _____.

23. Mildly depressed college students tend to have low rates of _____.

24. John Dollard and Neal Miller agree with Freud that the years that were most crucial for personality development were the first _____ years.

25. According to Dollard and Miller, early learning experiences are so lasting because childhood is the time of powerful rewards and punishments, crushing frustrations, and urgent _____.

26. The praise, attention, or approval from others, which combine to shape the core of personality is referred to as social _____.

27. Feeding, toilet or cleanliness training, sex training, and learning to express anger or aggression are capable of leaving a lasting imprint on personality and are referred to by Dollard and Miller as the four _____.

28. A basic active or passive orientation toward the world may be created by early _____ experiences.
29. Studies have shown that undesirable effects on personality development can result from severe, punishing, or frustrating _____ training.
30. Permissiveness for sexual and aggressive behavior in childhood is linked to adult needs for _____.
31. One part of sex training involves learning socially defined "male" and "female" _____.
32. Children develop emotionally attachment to admired adults, especially those who provide love and care through a process called _____.
33. Four-year-old Ben wants to act like his father, so he carries around his own little toy tool chest and acts like he is fixing things around the house. Ben is exhibiting _____.
34. We can learn without direct reward by observing and remembering the actions of others with the learning taking place, not directly, but _____.
35. The actions we choose to imitate depend on their _____.
36. Although boys and girls have equal chances to observe adults and other children acting aggressively, girl-fighting is not a culturally-reinforced pattern, so that girls are more likely to exclude others from friendship, spread rumors, or use other _____ aggressive behavior.

Part 1: Connections

1. ____ behavioral personality theory
2. ____ situational determinants
3. ____ habit
4. ____ drive
5. ____ cues
6. ____ response
7. ____ reward
8. ____ critical situations

a. external stimuli that guide responses, especially by signaling the presence or absence of reinforcement
b. deeply ingrained, learned pattern of behavior
c. any behavior, either observable or internal
d. any stimulus strong enough to goad a person to action
e. any model of personality that emphasizes learning and observable behavior
f. anything that produces pleasure or satisfaction
g. situations during childhood that are capable of leaving a lasting imprint on personality
h. external conditions that strongly influence behavior

Part 2: Connections

1. ____ social learning theory
2. ____ psychological situation
3. ____ expectancy
4. ____ reinforcement value
5. ____ self-efficacy
6. ____ self-reinforcement

a. belief in your capacity to produce a desired result
b. an attempt to match one's own behavior to another person's behavior
c. a situation as it is perceived and interpreted by an individual, not as it exists objectively
d. praise, attention, approval, and/or affection from others
e. subjective value a person attaches to a particular activity or reinforcer
f. anticipation about the effect a response will have especially regarding reinforcement

629

7. ___ social reinforcement

8. ___ identification

9. ___ imitation

g. an explanation of personality that combines learning principles, cognition, and the effects of social relationships

h. becoming emotionally attached to admired adults and taking on characteristics of the admired person

i. praising or rewarding oneself for having made a particular response

Check Your Memory

1. TRUE or FALSE   Behavioral and social learning theories are based on scientific research.
2. TRUE or FALSE   Behavioral and social learning theorists explain personality through concepts such as classical and operant conditioning, extinction, stimulus generalization and discrimination, and imitation.
3. TRUE or FALSE   Strict learning theorists believe that one's personality is made up of traits, such as the trait of honesty.
4. TRUE or FALSE   External conditions that strongly influence behavior are called situational determinants.
5. TRUE or FALSE   What is predictable about personality is that we respond in consistent ways to certain types of situations.
6. TRUE or FALSE   In a study in which people were intentionally overpaid for doing an assigned task, 80 percent of the people were still dishonest and kept the money even when they thought the person conducting the study would have to repay the loss.
7. TRUE or FALSE   According to Dollard and Miller, learned behavior patterns are called drives, which are governed by the six antecedents of learning.
8. TRUE or FALSE   The signals that guide our responses are called rewards.
9. TRUE or FALSE   Behavioral theories have contributed greatly to the creation of therapies for various psychological problems and disorders.
10. TRUE or FALSE   The "cognitive behaviorism" of social learning theory can be illustrated by Julian Rotter's concepts of psychological situation, expectancy, and reinforcement value.
11. TRUE or FALSE   Reinforcement value is your interpretation of a situation, such as interpreting a failing grade as a challenge to work harder.
12. TRUE or FALSE   The anticipation about the effect a response will have is called the psychological situation.
13. TRUE or FALSE   Expectancy involves the attachment of different subjective values to various activities or rewards.
14. TRUE or FALSE   Albert Bandura believed that one of the most important expectancies we develop concerns self-efficacy, which is the belief in one's capacity to produce a desired result.
15. TRUE or FALSE   Believing that our actions will produce desired results influences the activities and environments we choose.
16. TRUE or FALSE   Self-reinforcement can be thought of as the social learning theorist's counterpart to the id in psychoanalytic theory.
17. TRUE or FALSE   Higher rates of self-reinforcement are associated with more depression and less life satisfaction.
18. TRUE or FALSE   Dollard and Miller agreed with Freud that the first six years are crucial for personality development.
19. TRUE or FALSE   Social reinforcement is based on praise, attention, or approval from others.

630

20. TRUE or FALSE According to Dollard and Miller, the four critical situations during childhood that are capable of leaving a lasting imprint on personality include attachment to the mother, sibling rivalry, play, and early education.
21. TRUE or FALSE A basic active or passive orientation toward the world may be created due to sibling rivalry.
22. TRUE or FALSE Studies have shown that severe, punishing, or frustrating toilet training has no effect on personality development.
23. TRUE or FALSE Permissiveness for sexual and aggressive behavior in childhood is linked to adult needs for power.
24. TRUE or FALSE Imitation refers to the child's emotional attachment to admired adults, while identification is the desire to act like the admired person.
25. TRUE or FALSE Many "male" or "female" traits come from children's attempts to imitate a same-sex parent with whom they identify.
26. TRUE or FALSE The actions we choose to imitate depend on their outcomes.
27. TRUE or FALSE Although boys and girls have equal chances to observe adults and other children acting aggressively, girls are less likely than boys to imitate directly aggressive behavior, such as shouting at or hitting another person.

Critical Thinking Question

Rotter's concept of *reinforcement value* is closely related to a motivational principle discussed in Module 9.1. Can you name it?

Module 11.5 Behavioral and Social Learning Theories
Traits and Situations—The Great Debate
Survey Question: How do traits and situations affect personality?

Language Development Guide

The Great Debate: important discussion; argument; dispute; also the title of a TV program on VH-1
grappled: struggled; wrestled
relative: comparative
"raw material": natural or original state
impact: influence
stabilize: become constant
"harden": become firm; set; solidify
"grumpy old man": stereotype of older men being bad-tempered
"cranky old woman": stereotype of older women being bitter, irritable; and complaining
reputations: status, standing
realm: are; field
tics: twitch; spasm
the Minnesota Twins?: American professional baseball team based in Minneapolis, Minnesota
diagnosed: identify the condition
preposterous: ridiculous
eerie: in this case, remarkable; usually used to mean scary, creepy, spooky, unsettling
confirmation bias: tendency to remember or notice information that fits one's expectations, while forgetting discrepancies
thank goodness: to express gratitude for something
wired in: established, permanent

long-running: has been occurring for a long time
controversy: disagreement; debate, argument
hero: brave man; champion
coward: person who shows fear
pretty much: just about
wedding reception: party held after the completion of the marriage ceremony
demeanor: attitude; manner
"someone you could easily push around": overly compliant; does not fight back
suspended: temporarily bar from a place of employment or of school
get even: settle a perceived wrong
belittlement: unfair criticism; scorn
frenzied: showing abnormal excitement
ensues: follows; develops
off-color jokes: humor that is rude or offensive, disrespectful, racist or sexist
boisterous: excited and happy

Recite and Review

1. In the shaping of personality, theorists have long debated the relative roles of nature and _____.

2. The theories that stress the role of inherited biological predispositions are the trait theory and _____ theory.

3. Since even newborn babies differ in temperament, which implies that it is _____.

4. The role of learning and life experiences are stressed by the behavioral, social learning, and _____ theorists.

5. The hereditary aspects of your personality, such as your sensitivity, irritability, distractability, and adaptability, are referred to as your _____.

6. Personality starts to stabilize at around age _____ years.

7. Personality continues to "harden" through age _____ years.

8. Personality slowly matures during old age as most people continue to become more emotionally stable, conscientious, and _____.

9. Babies who are active and happy tend to interact more easily with their parents and others than do fussy, irritable babies. This illustrates that the interaction of babies is strongly influenced by the babies' _____.

10. Serina studies people's inherited behavioral traits. Serina works in the field called _____.

11. For several decades, psychologists at the University of Minnesota have been studying individuals who have the same genetic make-up, but who grew up in different homes. These psychologists are studying reunited _____ twins.

12. Although reared apart, when these reunited twins were compared on appearance, voice quality, facial gestures, hand movements, nervous tics, and talents, they were found to be _____.

13. Similarities between people of the same age and sex occur because they select from similar societal options and live in the same _____ .

14. Many of the seemingly "astounding" coincidences shared by reunited twins may be a special case of people noticing the similarities and ignoring the differences, which is referred to as the _____.

15. Regarding variation in many personality traits, heredity is responsible for about 25 to _____ percent.

16. Personality is shaped by heredity but is also shaped as much, or more, by _____.

17. Gabe believes that most people he has known for several years have pretty much the same personalities now as they did when he first met them. Gabe tends to view behavior as strongly influenced by _____.
18. Jeremy believes that the reason people in some professions, such as teachers, lawyers, or doctors, seem so much alike is because their work requires that they act in particular ways view behavior as strongly influenced by _____.
19. If you agree that almost anyone would be polite at a wedding reception no matter what kind of personality the person has, then you are viewing behavior as strongly influenced by _____.
20. If you believe that to be comfortable in a particular job, a person's personality must match the nature of the work, then you are viewing behavior as being strongly influenced by _____.
21. Personality traits can predict such things as job performance, dangerous driving, or a successful marriage because personality traits are _____.
22. Passive, shy, and overcontrolled characterizes the individuals who become _____ murderers.
23. Usually reflecting years of unexpressed feelings of anger and belittlement, the attacks by quiet, overcontrolled individuals are usually triggered by a(n) _____.
24. Many of the passive, overcontrolled individuals who commit these violent actions have _____ for the attack.
25. The influence that external settings or circumstances have on the expression of personality traits is called _____ interaction.

Connections

1. ___ behavioral genetics
2. ___ temperament
3. ___ sudden murderers
4. ___ strongly influenced by personality traits
5. ___ strongly influenced by external situations
6. ___ trait-situation interaction

a. study of inherited behavioral traits and tendencies
b. viewing immediate circumstances as determining how people act at any given time
c. the influence that external settings or circumstances have on the expression of personality traits
d. passive, quiet, overcontrolled individuals whose attacks were especially violent
e. viewing personality as stable across situations and over a long period of time
f. the hereditary aspects of your personality

Check Your Memory

1. TRUE or FALSE Some theories, such as trait theory and psychoanalytic theory, stress the role of learning and life experiences.
2. TRUE or FALSE Behavioral and humanist theories stress the role of inherited biological predispositions.
3. TRUE or FALSE Even newborn babies differ in temperament, which implies that it is hereditary.
4. TRUE or FALSE Temperament has a large impact on how infants interact with their parents.
5. TRUE or FALSE Personality starts to stabilize around age 16 and continues to harden until age 35.

6. TRUE or FALSE Personality slowly matures during old age with most people becoming more conscientious, agreeable, and emotionally stable.

7. TRUE or FALSE The stereotypes of the "grumpy old man" and "cranky old woman" have been proven to be true.

8. TRUE or FALSE The study of inherited behavioral traits is called behavioral genetics.

9. TRUE or FALSE Medical and psychological tests reveal that identical twins are very much alike, even when they are reared apart.

10. TRUE or FALSE If one identical twin has schizophrenia, there is 100 percent chance that the other twin will also have schizophrenia.

11. TRUE or FALSE Genetic studies have shown that intelligence, language, some mental disorders, temperament, and other complex qualities are influenced by heredity.

12. TRUE or FALSE Voice quality, facial gestures, hand movements, and nervous tics, such as nail biting are learned and do not appear to be inherited.

13. TRUE or FALSE Research has shown that some identical twins reared apart appear very similar, while some identical twins reared together appear different.

14. TRUE or FALSE In a study that compared identical twins to unrelated pairs of students who were similar in age and sex, the unrelated pairs were almost as alike as the twins.

15. TRUE or FALSE Many of the seemingly "astounding" coincidences shared by reunited twins may be a special case of the Barnum effect, in which the reunited twins tended to notice their differences, while ignoring their similarities.

16. TRUE or FALSE Research points to heredity being responsible for about 75 to 90 percent of the variation in many personality traits.

17. TRUE or FALSE If you believe your friends' actions are fairly consistent from day to day and in different situations, then you are viewing behavior as being strongly influenced by external circumstances.

18. TRUE or FALSE If you believe that people can be honest or dishonest, a hero or a coward, or kind or cruel depending on the situation, then you are viewing behavior as being strongly influenced by lasting personal dispositions.

19. TRUE or FALSE Because personality traits are consistent, they can predict such things as job performance, dangerous driving, or a successful marriage.

20. TRUE or FALSE According to research by Lee, Zimbardo, and Bertholf, sudden murderers were "masculine," aggressive, undercontrolled, and impulsive.

21. TRUE or FALSE The attacks of sudden murderers are usually triggered by a minor irritation or frustration with the attack reflecting years of unexpressed feelings of anger and belittlement.

22. TRUE or FALSE Sudden murderers usually show violence out of proportion to the offense against them.

23. TRUE or FALSE Many sudden murderers have amnesia for the attack.

24. TRUE or FALSE If it a true personality trait, external circumstances will not influence the expression of that trait.

25. TRUE or FALSE When external circumstances do influence the expression of a personality trait, then it is referred to as trait-situation interaction.

Module 11.6 Personality Assessment
Personality Assessment—Psychological Yardsticks
Survey Question: How do psychologists measure personality?

Language Development Guide

painting a detailed picture: completely or thoroughly describing a person's personality

can be a challenge: can be complicated and difficult

capture: summarize

yardsticks: measuring tool used in the United States

refinements: improvements; enhancements; a sophistication

"sized up": observe someone or something to get information or to check them out

"really": in reality; in actual fact

caught off-guard: seen when they do not expect it

projection: attributing one's own feelings to others

probe: examine, explore, study

mental state: emotional and psychological well-being

personality disturbances: maladaptive pattern of habitual behaviors

contemplated: thought about

"completely calm" but trembles uncontrollably: denying how they are really feeling

insight: clear and deep understanding of a situation

swayed: influenced

preconceptions: forming an opinion without adequate information

punk: young person who is part of a rebellious counterculture

geek: intelligent but awkward person

ski bum: someone who would rather ski than work or study

accentuate: put emphasize on; highlight

deceive: mislead; trick; lie to

respected: valued; appreciated

prelude: introduction; an opening to; something that leads up to another part

supplemented: accompanied by; complemented by

bus depots: places to get tickets to ride a bus

taverns: bars, pubs, saloons

relish: enjoy; take pleasure in

extension: broadening; enlargement

"people watching": just observing the actions of people for the fun of it, not for collecting data or diagnosis

disturbed: mentally ill

withdrawn: quite; remote; inhibited; introverted

misperception: misunderstand

overlooked: failure to see

receptive: open to; interested in

simulated: faked; imitated; to pretend as if real

expose: allowed to be influenced by a particular action

temptation: enticement; lure

reality TV: placing and filming the actions and reactions of people in "real-life" settings

American Idol: real people compete to see who is the best singer

Survivor: real people are stranded on an island without supplies and compete for prizes and vote to eliminate one another from the game

The Amazing Race: pairs of people are given limited money and have to travel around the world completing tasks faster than the other teams

bear: show; display; have

account (used as a verb): explain

split-second: less than a second; very quick

armed criminals: lawbreaker that uses a weapon in doing the crime

635

high-risk: dangerous with potential for harm for the person
account (used as a noun): story
hostage: captive; prisoner
standardized: uniform; the same; consistent
ensure: make certain
yields: produces; generates
encounter: come across
reproduced: duplicated; copied
I love the smell of napalm in the morning: line spoken in the movie *Apocalypse Now*
napalm: gasoline gel-like material used in flamethrowers
Apocalypse Now: American movie with story taking place during the Vietnam war
sucks: it is worthless
absolutely: totally; definitely
satirize: make fun of, make a joke about
ridiculous: absurd; silly; nonsense
patterns: designs; arrangements
dimensions: components; features; factors
gag items: funny joke statements, fake test
legitimate: lawful; genuine; valid
discarded: thrown out; removed
second-guess: anticipate; foretell; try to tell what someone will do even before they
reassuring: comforting; encouraging
inkblot: pattern made by putting a pool of ink on a page and then folding the page
dagger: knife
elaborates: adds details
bereaved: suffering the loss of a loved one
apathetic: unconcerned; indifferent; uninterested; don't care
clinician: physician or other health or psychological professional who is involved in the treatment and observation of living patients, as distinguished from one engaged in research

Recite and Review

1. Regarding how people will behave at work, at school, or in therapy, measuring personality allows psychologists to _____ these behaviors.
2. If you use direct questioning to learn about a person's life history, personality traits, or current mental stage, then you are using a(n) _____.
3. If you are applying for a job and your potential boss asks you questions within an informal conversation with topics being taken up freely as they arise, then this boss is using the personality assessment technique specifically known as a(n) _____.
4. If you apply for a job and your potential boss asks you the same series of planned questions that she asked the other job applicants, the boss is using the personality assessment technique known specifically as a(n) _____.
5. Direct questioning makes it possible to observe a person's tone of voice, hand gestures, posture, and facial expressions, which are types of "_____" cues.
6. A person identified as a "housewife," "college student," "high school athlete," "punk," "geek," or "ski bum" may be misjudged because of an interviewer's personal _____.
7. A person who is likable or physically attractive may be rated as more mature, intelligent, or mentally healthy than she or he actually is due to the _____ effect.
8. The method of assessment that often serves as the first step in evaluating personality and as an essential beginning to therapy is the _____.

9. When used for assessment, a simple extension of our natural interest in "people watching" is _____.

10. A list of personality traits or aspects of behavior that can be used to evaluate a person is the _____.

11. As a psychologist, you are making a note of the frequency of a patient's aggression, self-care, speech, and unusual behaviors. You are using a(n) _____ assessment.

12. In one study, couples were assessed while talking with each other about their sexuality. The couples who were less likely to be receptive to discussing their sexuality and more likely to blame each other were the couples who had _____ difficulties.

13. Real-life conditions are simulated so that a person's spontaneous reactions can be observed during _____ testing.

14. The judgmental firearms training provided by many police departments is an interesting example of _____ testing.

15. Objective paper-and-pencil tests that reveal a person's personality characteristics are referred to as _____.

16. Any test that gives the same score when different people correct it, such as a multiple choice test given in your college class would be described as a(n) _____ test.

17. So that the scores are unaffected by any biases an examiner may have, the questions, administration, and scoring on personality tests are all _____.

18. If a test yields the same score each time it is given to the same person, then the test is considered _____.

19. If a test measures what it claims to measure, then the test is said to have _____.

20. The personality tests you encounter in magazines or on the Internet have little or no _____.

21. The *Guilford-Zimmerman Temperament Survey,* the *California Psychological Inventory,* the *Allport-Vernon Study of Values,* and the 16 PF are all considered to be a type of test known as a personality _____.

22. The best known and most widely used objective tests, which is composed of 567 items and measures 10 major aspects of personality, is the _____.

23. Although a single item on a personality test tells little about personality, the personality dimensions are revealed by the _____ of responses.

24. Before an item can be part of a personality test, the test item and some trait or dimension of personality would have to be shown to be highly _____.

25. After the Minnesota Multiphasic Personality Inventory-2 (MMPI-2) is scored, results are charted graphically as an MMPI-2 _____.

26. To determine whether a person's scores should be discarded, the MMPI-2 has additional scales that detect attempts by test takers to "fake good" or "fake bad." These additional scales are referred to as _____ scales.

27. The scale on the MMPI-2 that involves the person showing emotional shallowness in relationships and a disregard for social and moral standards is called _____.

28. The presence of physical complaints for which no physical basis can be established would be measured by the scale on the MMPI-2 called _____.

29. The scale on the MMPI-2 that involves emotional withdrawal and unusual or bizarre thinking and actions is called _____.

30. Test scores are informative, but they can incorrectly _____ some people.

31. Interviews, observation, rating scales, and inventories try to directly identify _____, observable traits.

32. The tests that seek to uncover deeply hidden or unconscious wishes, thoughts and needs through the use of ambiguous or unstructured stimuli are the _____ tests.

33. When you are faced with an unstructured stimulus, you must organize what you see in terms of your own _____.

34. Projective tests have no right or wrong answers, which makes them difficult to _____.
35. The test that consists of 10 standardized inkblots with the person being asked to describe what he or she sees in it is called the _____ test.
36. What parts of the inkblot are used to organize the image are more important than the _____ of the response.
37. The Thematic Apperception Test (TAT) was developed by _____.
38. When the TAT is being administered the person being assessed is shown 20 sketches, individually, and must make up a(n) _____ about each sketch.
39. The TAT is especially good at revealing feelings about a person's _____.
40. Among tests of personality, the validity of the projective tests is considered the _____.
41. For different users of the projective test, objectivity and reliability are _____.
42. Tests of personality are best used as part of a collection of assessment devices and interviews called a(n) _____.
43. A good way to detect major conflicts, to get clients to talk about upsetting topics, and to set goals for therapy is for skilled clinicians to use _____ tests.

Part 1: Connections

1. ___ interview
2. ___ halo effect
3. ___ direct observation
4. ___ rating scale
5. ___ behavioral assessment
6. ___ situational testing
7. ___ personality questionnaires
8. ___ projective tests

a. psychological tests that make use of ambiguous or unstructured stimuli
b. recording the frequency of various behaviors
c. direct questioning is used to learn about a person's life history and current mental state
d. paper-and-pencil test consisting of questions that reveal aspects of personality
e. list of personality traits or aspects of behavior on which a person is assessed
f. tendency to generalize a favorable or unfavorable first impression to unrelated details of personality
g. assessing behavior through close surveillance
h. simulating real-life conditions so that a person's reactions may be directly observed

Part 2: Connections

1. ___ unstructured interview
2. ___ structured interview
3. ___ objective test
4. ___ reliability
5. ___ validity
6. ___ Minnesota Multiphasic Personality Inventory-2 (MMPI-2)

a. ability of a test to yield nearly the same score each time it is given to the same person
b. projective test comprised of 10 standardized inkblots
c. questioning technique in which the conversation is informal and topics are taken up freely as they arise
d. ability of a test to measure what it purports to measure
e. projective test consisting of 20 different scenes and life situations about which respondents make up stories
f. collection of assessment devices and interviews

7. ___ Rorschach Technique

8. ___ Thematic Apperception Test (TAT)

9. ___ test battery

g. information is gathered by asking a planned series of questions

h. personality questionnaire composed of 567 items to which a test taker must respond "true" or "false," measures 10 major aspects of personality

i. any test that gives the same score when different people correct it

Part 3: Connections

1. ___ MMPI-2 profile

2. ___ validity scales

3. ___ hypochondriasis

4. ___ depression

5. ___ hysteria

6. ___ psychopathic deviate

7. ___ masculinity/femininity

8. ___ paranoia

9. ___ psychasthenia

10. ___ schizophrenia

11. ___ mania

12. ___ social introversion

a. extreme suspiciousness and feelings of persecution

b. feelings of worthlessness, hopelessness, and pessimism

c. graphic representation of an individual's scores on each of the primary scales of the MMPI-2

d. emotional shallowness in relationships and a disregard for social and moral standards

e. emotional excitability, elated moods or behavior, and excessive activity

f. presence of obsessive worries, irrational fears (phobias), and compulsive (ritualistic) actions

g. one's tendency to be socially withdrawn

h. exaggerated concern about one's physical health

i. emotional withdrawal and unusual or bizarre thinking and actions

j. presence of physical complaints for which no physical basis can be established

k. tells whether test scores should be invalidated for lying, inconsistency, or "faking good."

l. one's degree of traditional "masculine" aggressiveness or "feminine" sensitivity

Check Your Memory

1. TRUE or FALSE Measuring personality can help predict how people will behave at work, at school, and in therapy.

2. TRUE or FALSE Formal personality measures are refinements of more casual ways of judging a person.

3. TRUE or FALSE In an unstructured interview, information is gathered by asking a planned series of questions.

4. TRUE or FALSE Interviews are rarely used to identify personality disturbances.

5. TRUE or FALSE Interviews make it possible to observe a person's tone of voice, hand gestures, posture, and facial expressions

6. TRUE or FALSE Interviewers can be swayed by preconceptions and misjudge the interviewees because of personal biases.

7. TRUE or FALSE An interviewer's own personality, or even gender, may influence the person being interviewed.

8. TRUE or FALSE The tendency to generalize a favorable (or unfavorable) impression to an entire personality is referred to as the Barnum effect.

9. TRUE or FALSE A rating scale is used during direct observation to prevent some traits from being overlooked and others from being exaggerated.

10. TRUE or FALSE If a psychologists working with couples notes the number of times each partner blames the other, this psychologist is using a technique known as behavioral assessment.

11. TRUE or FALSE The popular "reality TV" programs, such as *American Idol*, *Survivor*, and *The Amazing Race* bear some similarity to the assessment tool known as situational testing.

12. TRUE or FALSE Situational testing involves paper-and-pencil tests that reveal personality characteristics by asking people to answer multiple choice or true-false questions regarding their personality and behavior.

13. TRUE or FALSE An objective test gives the same score when different people correct it.

14. TRUE or FALSE A test is considered valid if the test yields nearly the same score each time it is given to the same person.

15. TRUE or FALSE The questions, administration, and scoring on all personality tests are standardized so that scores are unaffected by any biases an examiner may have.

16. TRUE or FALSE Many of the personality tests you encounter in magazines or on the Internet have little or no validity.

17. TRUE or FALSE The *Allport*-Vernon *Study of Values*, the *Guilford-Zimmerman Temperament Survey*, the *California Psychological Inventory*, and the *16 PF* are considered projective techniques.

18. TRUE or FALSE The Minnesota Multiphasic Personality Inventory-2 (MMPI-2) is composed of 567 items to which a test taker must respond "true" or "false."

19. TRUE or FALSE On the MMPI-2, a single item tells little about personality with the patterns of responses revealing the personality dimensions.

20. TRUE or FALSE After the MMPI-2 is scored, results are charted graphically on what is known as an adjective checklist.

21. TRUE or FALSE The MMPI-2 subscale called hysteria is used to measure the presence of obsessive worries, irrational fears, and compulsive actions.

22. TRUE or FALSE Emotional excitability, manic moods, and excessive activity is measured by the psychasthenia subscale on the MMPI-2.

23. TRUE or FALSE The MMPI-2 subscale called schizophrenia is used to measure emotional shallowness in relationships and a disregard for social and moral standards.

24. TRUE or FALSE The MMPI-2 has additional scales that can identify substance abuse, eating disorders, Type A behavior, repression, anger, cynicism, low self-esteem, family problems, and the inability to function in a job.

25. TRUE or FALSE Personality questionnaires are only accurate if people tell the truth about themselves.

26. TRUE or FALSE The MMPI-2 has validity scales that reveal whether a person's scores should be discarded because they "faked good" or "faked bad."

27. TRUE or FALSE Psychological assessments are at least as accurate as commonly used medical tests.

28. TRUE or FALSE Interviews, observation, rating scales, and inventories try to directly identify overt, observable traits.

640

29. TRUE or FALSE   Projective tests seek to uncover deeply hidden or unconscious wishes, thoughts, and needs.
30. TRUE or FALSE   Answers on a projective test are easy to fake.
31. TRUE or FALSE   The Thematic Apperception Test (TAT) consists of 10 standardized inkblots to which the person describes what he or she sees in them.
32. TRUE or FALSE   Although obvious differences in content seen on inkblot tests can be revealing, most of the content is less important than what parts of the inkblot are used to organize the ambiguous images.
33. TRUE or FALSE   The TAT was developed by personality theorist Julian Rotter.
34. TRUE or FALSE   To score the TAT, a psychologist analyzes the content of the stories.
35. TRUE or FALSE   The TAT is especially good at revealing feelings about a person's social relationships.
36. TRUE or FALSE   The validity of projective tests is considered to be the highest among tests of personality.
37. TRUE or FALSE   The objectivity and reliability is low for different users of the TAT and the Rorschach Technique.
38. TRUE or FALSE   Projective tests are especially useful when used as part of a collection of assessment devices and interviews called a test battery.

Critical Thinking Questions

1. Can you think of one more reason why personality traits may not be accurately revealed by interviews?

2. Projective testing would be of greatest interest to which type of personality theorist?

Module 11.7 Psychology in Action
Barriers and Bridges—Understanding Shyness
Survey Questions: What causes shyness? What can be done about it?

Language Development Guide

preoccupation: worry; concern
strain: tension; stress; pressure
animation: excitement, movement
nuisance: irritation; annoyance
proficiency: skill; ability
apprehension: uneasiness; fear; dread
self-defeating: being injurious to one's own interests
unnecessarily: without cause; pointlessly
novel: new
fine: well; okay
awkward: uncomfortable; ill at ease
magnified: exaggerated; overstated
formality: ritual; ceremony
feel "naked": feeling exposed the world with everyone staring
see through them: discover their deception
outright: complete; absolute
stage fright: fear such as an actor feels when standing before an audience, fear of needing to perform well or be the center of attention in public
labeling: classifying; categorizing

641

give credit: recognize accomplishment
cover-up: an effort to conceal
needless: unnecessary; pointless
harshly: cruelly; unkindly
"innate": inborn; inherited
fancy: elaborate; imaginative
West Side: a part of city, such as Manhattan in New York City
"free information": information that is not requested

Recite and Review

1. As a personality trait, the tendency to avoid others, as well as feelings of anxiety, preoccupation, and social inhibition is called _____.
2. Characteristics of shy persons include a failure to make eye contact, retreating when spoken to, speaking too quietly, and displaying little interest or _____ in conversation.
3. Extreme shyness is often associated with depression, loneliness, fearfulness, inhibition, and low self-esteem, which may be diagnosed as _____ disorder.
4. Shy people often lack the proficiency at interacting with others, that is, they lack _____ skills.
5. A factor in shyness is a feeling of apprehension in the presence of others called _____.
6. Fears of being inadequate, embarrassed, ridiculed, or rejected are referred to as _____ fears.
7. Jasmine almost always blames herself when a social encounter does not go well. Jasmine is exhibiting a distortion in her thinking known as the _____.
8. Shyness is most often triggered by _____ social situations.
9. Shyness is magnified by formality, meeting someone of higher status, being noticeably different from others, or being in situations, such as giving a speech, where one is the _____.
10. Cheek and Buss found no connection between shyness and one's attention to inner feelings, thoughts, and fantasies, which is called _____ self-consciousness.
11. Researchers found that shyness was linked to an acute awareness of oneself as a social object, which is called _____ self-consciousness.
12. In social situations, the shy person's anxiety often causes her or him to _____ others.
13. The key difference in shy and not-shy persons is in how they _____ their anxiety.
14. Shy persons tend to consider their social anxiety as a lasting _____.
15. Not-shy persons believe that the cause of their occasional feelings of shyness is _____.
16. Because they give themselves credit for their social successes and recognize that failures are often due to circumstances, not-shy persons tend to have higher _____ than shy persons.
17. Shyness is often maintained by self-_____ beliefs.
18. "If you wait around long enough at a social gathering, something will happen" is an example of a(n) _____ belief that results in shyness.
19. Because there is nothing "innate" about knowing how to meet people or start a conversation, learning social skills takes _____.
20. Most people can learn to put more animation and skill into their self-presentations by listening to their conversations on a tape recorder and my looking at themselves in a mirror and exaggerating _____.
21. One of the simplest ways to make better conversations is by learning how to ask others _____ questions.
22. "What's it like living in a big city" is an example of a(n) _____ question.
23. At the very least, a shy person must be willing to take social _____.

642

Connections

1. ____ shyness

2. ____ social anxiety

3. ____ evaluation fears

4. ____ self-defeating bias

5. ____ private self-consciousness

6. ____ public self-consciousness

a. distortion in thinking in which person almost always blames themselves when a social encounter does not go well

b. preoccupation with inner feelings, thoughts, and fantasies

c. as a personality trait, the tendency to avoid others as well as feeling of anxiety, preoccupation and social inhibition

d. intense awareness of oneself as a social object

e. feeling of apprehension in the presence of others

f. fears of being inadequate, embarrassed, ridiculed, or rejected

Check Your Memory

1. TRUE or FALSE Mild shyness is referred to as social anxiety disorder, while excessive shyness is regarded as an obsessive-compulsive disorder.

2. TRUE or FALSE Shy people do not lack social skills and usually have no trouble carrying on a conversation with people once they overcome their initial fear.

3. TRUE or FALSE Everyone feels nervous in some social situations with this reaction typically being due to evaluation fears.

4. TRUE or FALSE Shy persons usually blame others when a social encounter does not go well.

5. TRUE or FALSE Shyness is most often triggered by novel or unfamiliar social situations.

6. TRUE or FALSE Shyness is magnified by formality and meeting someone of higher status.

7. TRUE or FALSE Shy people tend to be wrapped up in their own feelings and thoughts.

8. TRUE or FALSE Cheek and Buss found a very significant connection between shyness and private self-consciousness.

9. TRUE or FALSE People who rate high in public self-consciousness are intensely concerned about what others think of them.

10. TRUE or FALSE A shy person's anxiety often causes her or him to have a keen ability to clearly perceive others and social situations.

11. TRUE or FALSE A key difference in shy and not-shy persons is in how they label their social anxiety.

12. TRUE or FALSE Not-shy persons tend to have lower self-esteem than shy persons.

13. TRUE or FALSE Shy people tend to consider their social anxiety a lasting personality trait.

14. TRUE or FALSE When non-shy persons feel anxiety or "stage fright," they assume that almost anyone would feel as they do under the same circumstances.

15. TRUE or FALSE Shyness is often maintained by unrealistic or self-defeating beliefs.

16. TRUE or FALSE The odds of meeting someone interested in socializing are always the same, no matter where you are.

17. TRUE or FALSE If someone does not seem to like you right away, they really do not like you and never will.

18. TRUE or FALSE If people are to overcome their shyness, they cannot wait until they are completely relaxed or comfortable before taking a social risk.

19. TRUE or FALSE Even people who are very socially skillful are never successful 100 percent of the time in when interacting in social situations.

643

20. TRUE or FALSE   Learning social skills takes practice.
21. TRUE or FALSE   In order to improve your conversational style, it can be helpful to get a tape recorder and listen to several of your conversations.
22. TRUE or FALSE   Most people can learn to put more animation in their conversations by looking at themselves in the mirror and exaggerating facial expressions of surprise, interest, dislike, and pleasure.
23. TRUE or FALSE   One of the simplest ways to make better conversations is by learning to ask open-ended questions.
24. TRUE or FALSE   "Have you ever been to California?" is considered an open-ended question.
25. TRUE or FALSE   In replying to open-ended questions, people often give "free information" about themselves, which can be used to ask other questions.

Critical Thinking Question

Shyness is a trait of Vonda's personality. Like most shy people, Vonda is most likely to feel shy in unfamiliar social settings. Vonda's shy behavior demonstrates that the expression of traits is governed by what concept?

Final Survey and Review—Completion

Module 11.1 Overview of Personality
The Psychology of Personality—Do You Have Personality?
Survey Questions: How do psychologists use the term personality?
1. Once identified, personality traits can be used to predict future _____.
2. 2. If you are a bold, outgoing, sociable person, Carl Jung would have described you as a(n) _____.
3. 3. A person with a Type A personality has traits that increase his or her chance of having a(n) _____.
4. 4. People with low self-esteem typically suffer from poor self-knowledge and have inconsistent, inaccurate, and confused self-_____.
5. Self-esteem is based on personal success and outstanding individual performance in the United States and other _____ cultures.
6. The four temperaments described by the Early Greeks were melancholic, choleric, phlegmatic, and _____.
7. The theories that see our behavior has determined by outside forces are the psychoanalytic, behavioristic, social learning, and the _____ theories.
8. Social learning theories attribute differences in personality to socialization, mental processes, and _____.

Module 11.2 Trait Theories
The Trait Approach—Describe Yourself in 18,000 Words or Less
Survey Question: Are some personality traits more basic or important than others?
9. In one study, Peter Rentfrow and Samuel Gosling found people's personality characteristics were associated with their preferred types of _____.
10. According to Allport, if you describe your roommate by mentioning that his favorite food is French fries, and he likes punk rock music and votes as a Democrat, then you are mentioning your roommates _____ traits.

644

11. The personality theorist who used factor analysis to identify 16 source traits or personality factors was _____.
12. The five-factor model, or "Big Five" are neuroticism, conscientiousness, extroversion, openness to experience, and _____.
13. Janie performs well at her job work and in her college classes, and she has never had an automobile accident. Janie would most likely score high in the "Big Five" factor of _____.

Module 11.3 Psychoanalytic Theory
Psychoanalytic Theory—Id Came to Me in a Dream
Survey Question: How do psychodynamic theories explain personality?
14. Eros is the name Freud gave to the _____ instincts.
15. The rational executive of the personality that operates according to the reality principle is the _____.
16. When you feel pride, you have met the standards of a subpart of the superego known as the _____.
17. You are taking a test and read the first question. In order to answer this question, you will have to retrieve information from your _____ level of awareness.
18. According to Freud, a person who is obstinate, stingy, orderly, and compulsively neat as well as a person who is cruel, messy, disorderly, and destructive would both have been fixated during the _____ stage.
19. According to Freud, the Electra conflict occurs in girls during the _____ stage.
20. Freud is credited with pioneering the idea that development proceeds in stages and that adult personality is shaped by critical events that occur during the first few years and include early sexual experiences, toilet training, and _____.

Module 11.4 Humanistic Theories
Humanistic Theory—Peak Experiences and Personal Growth
Survey Question: What are humanistic theories of personality?
21. Psychologists who emphasize subjective experiences and free choice would be considered _____.
22. The psychologist who studied people, such as Albert Einstein, Walt Whitman, and Eleanor Roosevelt, who were living or had lived unusually effective lives was _____.
23. Self-actualizers accept the shortcomings of others and the contradictions of the human condition with tolerance and _____.
24. When a self-actualizer reports feeling at one with the universe, stronger and calmer than ever before, and filled with light, he or she is experiencing a(n) _____ experience.
25. Martin Seligman, Christopher Peterson, and others have identified six human strengths that contribute to well-being and life satisfaction. They are wisdom and knowledge, transcendence, humanity, courage, justice, and _____.
26. Jerry believes that he is a person who "never gets angry," yet he spends much of each day seething inside. Carl Rogers would say that the gulf between the Jerry's self-image and reality is _____.
27. Meg studies very hard because she wants to become a veterinarian and because she does not want to be stuck in a low-paying job, like she has now. According to Markus and Nurius, the person she wishes to become and the person she is afraid of becoming are Meg's _____.
28. A child who is told by his parents that it is wrong to feel angry toward his brother, even when the anger is justified, may develop a internal standard of evaluation that Rogers called _____.

645

Module 11.5 Behavioral and Social Learning Theories
Learning Theories of Personality—Habit I Seen You Before?

Survey Question: What do behaviorists and social learning theorists emphasize in their approach to personality?

29. Personality is no more or less than a collection of relatively stable learned behavior patterns, according to the _____ personality theories.
30. John Dollard and Neal Miller proposed that habits are governed by four elements of learning, which include rewards, responses, cues, and _____.
31. Julian Rotter's concepts that illustrate the "cognitive behaviorism" of personality theory are psychological situation, expectancy, and _____.
32. You're beginning to consider a career in psychology. If you believe that you will be able to study hard and complete the courses required, then you are exhibiting what Bandura called _____.
33. Less depression and greater life satisfaction are associated with a person showing high rates of self-_____.
34. The four critical situations proposed by Dollard and Miller are feeding, toilet or cleanliness training, learning to express anger or aggression, and _____ training.
35. When a child forms an emotional attachment to an admired adult, this is known as _____.

Module 11.5 Behavioral and Social Learning Theories
Traits and Situations—The Great Debate

Survey Question: How do traits and situations affect personality?

36. The theories that stress the role of inherited biological predispositions are the psychoanalytic theory and _____ theory.
37. If you believe that your friends' actions are fairly consistent from day to day and in different situations, then you are viewing behavior as strongly influenced by _____.
38. When the reunited identical twins met, they spent hours comparing their lives. However, many of the coincidences shared by these twins was a case of their noticing the similarities in their lives and ignoring any differences, which is referred to as the _____.
39. Sudden murderers tend to be passive, shy, and _____.
40. When your personality traits are influenced by the external settings you are in, this illustrates _____ interaction.

Module 11.6 Personality Assessment
Personality Assessment—Psychological Yardsticks

Survey Question: How do psychologists measure personality?

41. You are applying for a job. Your personality will most likely be assessed by your potential boss through direct questioning, which is a(n) _____.
42. Your are using direct observation in assessing the personality and behaviors of a group of kindergarten students. To prevent overlooking or exaggerating certain traits or behaviors, you will use a list of traits and behaviors called a(n) _____.
43. Reality shows, such as The Amazing Race and Survivor, are similar to the personality assessment technique of _____ testing.
44. Your professor's multiple choice test would be graded the same no matter whether she or her assistant graded it, since this test is a(n) _____ test.
45. A psychologist is giving a test that he claims measures creativity. If the test does measure this ability, then we say the test has _____.

46. The presence of obsessive worries, irrational fears (phobias), and compulsive (ritualistic) actions would be measured by the scale on the MMPI-2 called _____.

47. Gayla is be administered a personality test in which she is asked to tell a story about 20 different ambiguous sketches. Gayla is most likely taking the _____.

Module 11.7 Psychology in Action
Barriers and Bridges—Understanding Shyness
Survey Questions: What causes shyness? What can be done about it?

48. Characteristics of shy persons include retreating when spoken to, speaking too quietly, displaying little interest or animation in conversation, and failing to make _____.

49. Marilyn had such extreme shyness that she also exhibited depression, fearfulness, and low self-esteem. Marilyn would most likely be diagnosed with _____ disorder.

50. If you are a fancy party, and you are worrying about what people think of you, then you are showing a great deal of public _____.

51. Believing that other people who are popular are just lucky when it comes to being invited to social events or asked out is an example of a self-_____ belief.

52. "What kinds of food to you like?" would be an example of a(n) _____ question.

Final Survey and Review—Matching

Module 11.1 Overview of Personality

1. ___ character

a. focus on the inner workings of personality, especially internal conflicts and struggles

2. ___ personality trait

b. stress private, subjective experience and personal growth

3. ___ personality type

c. a stable, enduring quality that a person shows in most situations

4. ___ self-concept

d. person's desirable and undesirable qualities as judged by others

5. ___ self-esteem

e. theory that views human nature as neutral; maximizes heredity, and attempts to learn how a different traits make up personality and how they relate to actual behavior

6. ___ trait theories

f. a person's perception of all his or her ideas, perceptions, stories, and feelings about the person he or she is

7. ___ psychodynamic theories

g. a person regarding his or herself as a worthwhile person

8. ___ behavioristic / social learning theories

h. style of personality defined by a group of related traits

9. ___ humanistic theories

i. place importance on the external environment, the effects of conditioning and learning, socialization, expectations, and mental processes

Module 11.2 Trait Theories

1. ___ factor analysis

2. ___ source traits

3. ___ extroversion

4. ___ agreeableness

5. ___ conscientiousness

6. ___ neuroticism

7. ___ openness to experience

8. ___ cardinal trait

9. ___ central traits

10. ___ secondary traits

a. high scores are talkative, active, and affectionate and are joiners

b. Allport's term for a personality trait that is overwhelmingly dominant

c. high scorers are self-disciplined, responsible, and achieving

d. Allport's term for traits that are inconsistent or relatively superficial

e. having negative, upsetting emotions

f. Cattell's term for the basic underlying traits, or factors of personality

g. a statistical technique used to correlate multiple measurements and identify general underlying factors

h. refers to how friendly, nurturant, and caring a person is, as opposed to cold, indifferent, self-centered, or spiteful

i. high scorers are imaginative, creative, original, curious, and intelligent

j. Allport's term for one's core traits that characterize his or her personality

Module 11.3 Psychoanalytic Theory
Part 1:

1. ___ id

2. ___ ego

3. ___ superego

4. ___ unconscious

5. ___ conscious

6. ___ preconscious

7. ___ oral-dependent personality

8. ___ oral-aggressive personality

9. ___ anal-retentive personality

10. ___ anal-expulsive personality

11. ___ phallic personality

12. ___ latency

13. ___ genital stage

a. person who is disorderly, destructive, cruel, or messy person

b. region of the mind that includes all mental contents a person is aware of at any given moment

c. person who wants to passively receive attention, gifts, and love

d. region of the mind that holds repressed memories and emotions

e. a period in childhood when psychosexual development is dormant

f. person who expresses hostility by shouting, cursing, biting and openly exploits others

g. period of full psychosexual development, marked by the attainment of mature adult sexuality

h. judge or censor for thoughts and actions

i. area of the mind containing information that can be voluntarily brought to awareness

j. operates on the reality principle

k. person who is obstinate, stingy, or compulsive clean

l. operates on the pleasure principle

m. person who is vain, exhibitionistic, sensitive, and narcissistic

Part 2:

1. ___ erogenous zone
2. ___ fixation
3. ___ Oedipus conflict
4. ___ Electra conflict
5. ___ libido
6. ___ Eros
7. ___ Thanatos
8. ___ conscience
9. ___ ego ideal
10. ___ neurotic anxiety
11. ___ moral anxiety
12. ___ ego defense mechanism
13. ___ psychosexual stages

a. life instincts
b. mental processes that deny, distort, or block out sources of threat and anxiety
c. death instinct
d. girl's sexual attraction to her father and feelings of rivalry with her mother
e. the force, primarily pleasure-oriented, that energizes the personality
f. oral, anal, phallic, and genital stages during which various personality traits are formed
g. boy's sexual attraction to his mother, and feelings of rivalry with his father
h. apprehension felt when thoughts, impulses, or actions conflict with the superego's standards
i. lasting conflict developed as a result of frustration or over-indulgence
j. part of superego that causes guilt when its standards are not met
k. any body area that produces pleasurable sensations
l. apprehension felt when the ego struggles to control id impulses
m. part of the superego that causes pride when its standards are met

Module 11.4 Humanistic Theories

1. ___ fully functioning person
2. ___ subjective experience
3. ___ self-image
4. ___ incongruence
5. ___ authentic
6. ___ ideal self
7. ___ conditions of worth
8. ___ peak experiences
9. ___ organismic valuing
10. ___ unconditional positive regard
11. ___ self-actualization

a. person living in harmony with her or his deepest feelings, impulses, and intuitions
b. internal standards used to judge the value of one's thoughts, actions, feelings, or experiences
c. reality as it is perceived and interpreted, not as it exists objectively
d. total subjective perception of one's body and personality
e. a natural, undistorted, full-body reaction to an experience
f. feeling that one's behavior accurately expresses who he or she is
g. unshakable love and approval given without qualification
h. process of fully developing personal potentials
i. state that exists when there is a discrepancy between one's experiences and self-image or between one's self-image and ideal self
j. temporary moments marked by feelings of ecstasy, harmony, and deep meaning
k. the person you would like to become

Module 11.5 Behavioral and Social Learning Theories

1. ____ situational determinants
2. ____ habit
3. ____ drive
4. ____ cue
5. ____ temperament
6. ____ trait-situation interaction
7. ____ psychological situation
8. ____ expectancy
9. ____ reinforcement value
10. ____ self-efficacy
11. ____ self-reinforcement
12. ____ identification
13. ____ imitation

a. an attempt to match one's own behavior to another person's behavior
b. the influence that external settings or circumstances have on the expression of personality traits
c. any stimulus strong enough to goad a person to action
d. external stimuli that guide responses, especially by signaling the presence or absence of reinforcement
e. a situation as it is perceived and interpreted by an individual, not as it exists objectively
f. external conditions that strongly influence behavior
g. becoming emotionally attached to admired adults and taking on characteristics of the admired person
h. belief in your capacity to produce a desired result
i. praising or rewarding oneself for having made a particular response
j. the hereditary aspects of your personality
k. anticipation about the effect a response will have especially regarding reinforcement
l. deeply ingrained, learned pattern of behavior
m. subjective value a person attaches to a particular activity or reinforcer

Module 11.6 Personality Assessment

Part 1:

1. ____ unstructured interview
2. ____ structured interview
3. ____ halo effect
4. ____ direct observation
5. ____ rating scale
6. ____ behavioral assessment
7. ____ situational testing
8. ____ personality questionnaires
9. ____ projective tests

a. psychological tests that make use of ambiguous or unstructured stimuli
b. recording the frequency of various behaviors
c. information is gathered by asking a planned series of questions
d. paper-and-pencil test consisting of questions that reveal aspects of personality
e. list of personality traits or aspects of behavior on which a person is assessed
f. tendency to generalize a favorable or unfavorable first impression to unrelated details of personality
g. assessing behavior through close surveillance
h. questioning technique in which the conversation is informal and topics are taken up freely as they arise
i. simulating real-life conditions so that a person's reactions may be directly observed

650

Part 2:

1. ____ hysteria
2. ____ psychasthenia
3. ____ psychopathic deviate
4. ____ objective test
5. ____ reliability
6. ____ validity
7. ____ Minnesota Multiphasic Personality Inventory-2 (MMPI-2)
8. ____ Rorschach Technique
9. ____ Thematic Apperception Test (TAT)
10. ____ test battery

a. ability of a test to yield nearly the same score each time it is given to the same person

b. presence of physical complaints for which no physical basis can be established

c. projective test comprised of 10 standardized inkblots

d. presence of obsessive worries, irrational fears (phobias), and compulsive (ritualistic) actions

e. ability of a test to measure what it purports to measure

f. projective test consisting of 20 different scenes and life situations about which respondents make up stories

g. collection of assessment devices and interviews

h. emotional shallowness in relationships and a disregard for social and moral standards

i. personality questionnaire composed of 567 items to which a test taker must respond "true" or "false," measures 10 major aspects of personality

j. any test that gives the same score when different people correct it

Module 11.7 Psychology in Action: Barriers and Bridges— Understanding Shyness

1. ____ evaluation fears
2. ____ social anxiety
3. ____ self-defeating bias
4. ____ private self-consciousness
5. ____ public self-consciousness

a. distortion in thinking in which person almost always blames themselves when a social encounter does not go well

b. preoccupation with inner feelings, thoughts, and fantasies

c. intense awareness of oneself as a social object

d. feeling of apprehension in the presence of others

e. fears of being inadequate, embarrassed, ridiculed, or rejected

Final Survey and Review—True or False

Module 11.1 Overview of Personality
The Psychology of Personality—Do You Have Personality?
Survey Questions: How do psychologists use the term personality?

1. TRUE or FALSE   Personal characteristics that have been judged or evaluated are referred to as one's temperament.

2. TRUE or FALSE   Classifying people into two or three personality types tends to be more informative than rating people on a list of traits.

3. TRUE or FALSE   In Japan and other Asian cultures, self-esteem is based on a secure sense of belonging to social groups called collectivism.

4. TRUE or FALSE   English psychologist Hans Eysenck proposed the personality theory that many personality traits are related to whether you are mainly introverted or extroverted and whether you tend to be emotionally stable or unstable.

5. TRUE or FALSE   The early Greek temperament type called choleric described a person who was cheerful and hopeful.

6. TRUE or FALSE   Psychodynamic theories focus on the inner workings of personality, especially internal conflicts and struggles.

7. TRUE or FALSE   Humanistic theory takes a negative view of human nature, while psychoanalytic theory takes a positive view of human nature.

8. TRUE or FALSE   Incongruence and conditions of worth are the barriers to personal growth in the social learning theories.

Module 11.2 Trait Theories
The Trait Approach—Describe Yourself in 18,000 Words or Less
Survey Question: Are some personality traits more basic or important than others?

9. TRUE or FALSE   The trait approach is currently the dominant method for studying personality.

10. TRUE or FALSE   Gordon Allport identified common and individual traits, while Raymond Cattell identified surface and source traits.

11. TRUE or FALSE   Cardinal traits are personality traits so basic that all of a person's activities are dominated by it.

12. TRUE or FALSE   People who are high in the factor of conscientiousness tend be anxious, emotionally "sour," irritable, and unhappy.

13. TRUE or FALSE   Introverts are more likely to divorce with introverted men being less likely to live with their children.

Module 11.3 Psychoanalytic Theory
Psychoanalytic Theory—Id Came to Me in a Dream
Survey Question: How do psychodynamic theories explain personality?

14. TRUE or FALSE   The id is made up of innate biological instincts and is self-serving, irrational, and impulsive.

15. TRUE or FALSE   The superego is made up of the conscience and ego ideal.

16. TRUE or FALSE   Modern scientists have found that the brain stem near the pons does seem to trigger the preconscious emotions and memories, as theorized by Freud.

17. TRUE or FALSE   The apprehension that is felt when thoughts, impulses, or actions conflict with the superego's standards is referred to as neurotic anxiety.

18. TRUE or FALSE   Anal-retentive personalities are tend to be gullible, passive, and need lots of attention.

19. TRUE or FALSE   During the phallic stage, psychosexual development is dormant, according to Freud.

20. TRUE or FALSE   One criticism of Freud's theory is that he overemphasized the importance of sexuality in personality development, and should have given equal importance to motives and cognitive factors.

652

Module 11.4 Humanistic Theories
Humanistic Theory—Peak Experiences and Personal Growth
Survey Question: What are humanistic theories of personality?

21. TRUE or FALSE   Humanists emphasize prior learning rather than one's immediate subjective experience.
22. TRUE or FALSE   To become self-actualized, one must act as if one is personally responsible for every aspect of his or her life.
23. TRUE or FALSE   Self-actualization is a process, not a goal or end point.
24. TRUE or FALSE   Appreciation of beauty and excellence, gratitude, hope, humor, spirituality make up the human strength known as temperance.
25. TRUE or FALSE   Roger's concept of incongruence is similar to Freud's ego ideal.
26. TRUE or FALSE   Researchers have found that people with a close match between their self-image and ideal self tend to be socially poised, confident, and resourceful.
27. TRUE or FALSE   The pragmatic function approach to personality asserts that our personalities are shaped by the stories we tell about ourselves
28. TRUE or FALSE   Rogers believed that positive and negative evaluations by others cause children to develop internal standards of evaluation called conditions of worth.

Module 11.5 Behavioral and Social Learning Theories
Learning Theories of Personality—Habit I Seen You Before?
Survey Question: What do behaviorists and social learning theorists emphasize in their approach to personality?

29. TRUE or FALSE   External conditions that strongly influence behavior are called self-efficacies.
30. TRUE or FALSE   Dollard and Miller referred to the signals that guide our responses as cues.
31. TRUE or FALSE   According to Julian Rotter, the anticipation about the effect a response will have is called its reinforcement value.
32. TRUE or FALSE   Self-reinforcement can be thought of as the social learning theorist's counterpart to the superego in psychoanalytic theory.
33. TRUE or FALSE   A basic active or passive orientation toward the world may be created by early feeding experiences.
34. TRUE or FALSE   Studies have shown that severe, punishing, or frustrating toilet training can have undesirable effects on personality development.
35. TRUE or FALSE   Imitation is defined as the desire to act like the admired person.

Module 11.5 Behavioral and Social Learning Theories
Traits and Situations—The Great Debate
Survey Question : How do traits and situations affect personality?

36. TRUE or FALSE   Behavioral and humanist theories stress the role of learning and life experiences.
37. TRUE or FALSE   Personality starts to stabilize around age three and continues to harden until age 50.
38. TRUE or FALSE   The study of inherited behavioral traits is called neurobiological approach.

653

39. TRUE or FALSE   From the reunited twin studies, it appears that voice quality, facial gestures, hand movements, and nervous tics, such as nail biting appear are inherited.

40. TRUE or FALSE   When a person who is passive, shy, and overcontrolled kills in a frenzied attack that is out of proportion to the offense, the person is called a passive-aggressive murderer.

Module 11.6 Personality Assessment

Personality Assessment—Psychological Yardsticks

Survey Question: How do psychologists measure personality?

41. TRUE or FALSE   The tendency to generalize a favorable (or unfavorable) impression to an entire personality is referred to as the confirmation effect.

42. TRUE or FALSE   As a psychologist, you are making a note of the frequency of a patient's aggression, self-care, speech, and unusual behaviors. You are using situational testing.

43. TRUE or FALSE   A projective test is one that gives the same score when different people correct it.

44. TRUE or FALSE   A test is considered reliable if the test yields nearly the same score each time it is given to the same person.

45. TRUE or FALSE   The MMPI-2 subscale called psychopathic deviate is used to measure emotional shallowness in relationships and a disregard for social and moral standards.

46. TRUE or FALSE   Interviews, observation, rating scales, and inventories seek to uncover hidden or unconscious wishes and needs through the use of ambiguous stimuli.

47. TRUE or FALSE   The TAT was developed by personality theorist Henry Murray.

Module 11.7 Psychology in Action

Barriers and Bridges—Understanding Shyness

Survey Questions: What causes shyness? What can be done about it?

48. TRUE or FALSE   Cheek and Buss found no connection between shyness and public self-consciousness.

49. TRUE or FALSE   A person who does fine with family or close friends may become shy and awkward when meeting a stranger.

50. TRUE or FALSE   A shy person's anxiety often causes her or him to misperceive others in social situations.

51. TRUE or FALSE   Not-shy persons tend to have higher self-esteem than shy persons.

52. TRUE or FALSE   It is important that a person be completely relaxed and comfortable before taking a social risk.

Mastery Test

1. If you judge Jed's personality characteristics has desirable, then you are saying that he has a good
   a. character.
   b. temperament.
   c. personality type.
   d. psyche.

2. Wendy enjoys being around lots of people and would be described as assertive when standing up for her rights and the rights of others. Wendy would best be described as
   a. choleric.
   b. phlegmatic.
   c. introverted.
   d. extroverted.

3. In Asian cultures, which of the following tends to be most strongly related to group membership and the success of the group?
   a. temperament
   b. congruence
   c. self-esteem
   d. moral anxiety

4. According to the early Greeks, a person who is hot-tempered and irritable would be described as
   a. melancholic.
   b. choleric.
   c. phlegmatic.
   d. sanguine.

5. Which theory of personality places the greatest emphasis on the effects of the learning and reinforcement?
   a. trait
   b. psychodynamic
   c. behavioristic
   d. humanistic

6. The two theories that both take a neutral view of human nature are the _____ theories.
   a. trait and psychoanalytic
   b. social learning and trait
   c. psychoanalytic and humanistic
   d. humanistic and behavioristic

7. According to the research of Rentfrow and Gosling, people who prefer hip-hop, soul, and electronic music tend to
   a. be talkative and forgiving.
   b. value aesthetic experiences.
   c. be conservative.
   d. enjoy taking risks.

8. People who all grew up in the same culture would be most likely to have the same _____ traits.
   a. cardinal
   b. common
   c. secondary
   d. source

9. Allport's concept of central traits is most closely related to Cattell's
   a. surface traits.
   b. source traits.
   c. secondary traits.
   d. cardinal traits.

10. A trait profile would be used to report the results of
    a. the 16 PF.
    b. situational tests.
    c. the TAT.
    d. the inkblot test.

11. In the five-factor model, people who score high on openness to experience are
    a. intelligent.
    b. extroverted.
    c. choleric.
    d. narcissistic.

12. Regarding people who are high in the trait of conscientiousness, which of the following statements is FALSE?
    a. They tend to do well in school and perform well at work.
    b. They rarely have automobile accidents.
    c. They tend to be imaginative, curious, and creative.
    d. They tend to live longer.

13. Regarding Freud's structures of personality, the part that operates on the reality principle is the
    a. id.
    b. ego.
    c. superego.
    d. ego ideal.

14. According to Freudian theory, if your thoughts and actions conflict with the standards of the superego, you will experience _____ anxiety.
    a. social
    b. basic
    c. neurotic
    d. moral

15. The two mental structures that operate at all three levels of awareness are the
    a. id and ego.
    b. ego and superego.
    c. Thanatos and superego.
    d. Eros and Thanatos..

16. Freud theorized that there were four psychosexual stages and one latency period through which a person passes in the following order:
    a. oral, anal, latency, genital, and phallic.
    b. oral, anal, phallic, latency, and genital.
    c. anal, phallic, oral, genital, and latency.
    d. anal, oral, latency, phallic, and genital.

656

17. According to Freud, tendencies to be orderly, obstinate, and stingy are formed during the
    _____ stage.
    a. genital
    b. oral
    c. anal
    d. phallic

18. When describing a person's tendency to make full use of personal potentials, Maslow used
    the term
    a. functionally unified.
    b. self-potentiation.
    c. ego-idealization.
    d. self-actualization.

19. When a person has temporary moments of ecstasy, harmony, and deep meaning, the person is
    experiencing what Maslow called
    a. conditions of worth
    b. organismic valuing.
    c. peak experiences.
    d. congruence.

20. Which of the following is NOT a characteristic of a self-actualizer?
    a. They are able to judge situations correctly and honestly.
    b. They rely on external authorities or other people in making a decision.
    c. They value solitude and are comfortable being alone.
    d. They have a mission to fulfill in life or some task or problem outside of themselves to
       pursue.

21. Which type of psychologists believe that one's well-being and life satisfaction are influenced
    by six human strengths, including courage, temperance, and transcendence?
    a. behavioral
    b. positive
    c. psychodynamic
    d. social learning

22. According to Carl Rogers, when information or feelings do not match our self-image, they
    are said to be
    a. incongruent.
    b. fixated.
    c. actualized.
    d. authentic.

23. Which of the following is NOT part of Carl Rogers' view of personality?
    a. self-reinforcement
    b. organismic valuing
    c. conditions of worth
    d. congruence

657

24. If you wanted to join clubs and socialize more at college, you could create alternate life stories about going to parties and other social gatherings with these stories influencing your behavior. This is known as the
    a. halo effect.
    b. confirmation bias.
    c. narrative approach.
    d. projective technique.

25. In a study of honesty, 80 percent of the participants kept the extra money when they were "overpaid" in the experiment, but only 17 percent kept the money when they thought the money would be coming out of the pocket of the person doing the study. According to behavioral theory, this difference is due to
    a. temperamental differences..
    b. the differing traits of honesty.
    c. a changing habit of honesty.
    d. situational determinants.

26. Which of the following concepts is NOT part of Dollard and Miller's behavioral model of personality?
    a. drive
    b. expectancy
    c. cue
    d. reward

27. According to Albert Bandura, if you believe that you have the capacity to complete a task or to reach a particular goal, you are exhibiting
    a. expectancy.
    b. self-reinforcement.
    c. self-efficacy.
    d. the ideal self.

28. The social learning concept most closely related to the superego is
    a. the psychological situation.
    b. self-reinforcement.
    c. identification.
    d. self-concept.

29. According to Dollard and Miller, whether a person takes an active or passive orientation toward the world is linked to the critical situation of
    a. feeding.
    b. toilet or cleanliness training.
    c. sex training.
    d. learning to express anger or aggression.

30. The hereditary aspects of personality are referred to as
    a. character.
    b. temperament.
    c. the psyche.
    d. source traits.

31. Studies of reunited identical twins support the idea that
    a. personality traits are 80 percent hereditary and 20 percent learned.
    b. childhood fixations influence the expression of personality traits in adulthood.
    c. personality traits are shaped only by the environment and not heredity.
    d. personality traits reflect an interaction of both heredity and the environment.

32. According to the research of Lee, Zimbardo, and Bertholf, which of the following is NOT a characteristic of sudden murderers?
    a. quiet and shy
    b. violence triggered by minor irritation
    c. used moderate amount of violence during murder
    d. passive and overcontrolled

33. A person who is generally introverted tends to be more shy in some situations than in others. This observation supports the concept of
    a. trait-situation interactions.
    b. behavioral genetic determinants.
    c. ego-defense mechanisms.
    d. possible selves.

34. The terms "structured" and "unstructured" refer to the types of
    a. interviews.
    b. behavioral assessments.
    c. projective techniques.
    d. personality questionnaires.

35. Recording the frequency of various behaviors is done during a(n)
    a. situational test.
    b. behavioral assessment.
    c. projective assessment.
    d. interview.

36. Rating scales are primarily used in which approach to personality assessment?
    a. personality questionnaires
    b. projective testing
    c. the narrative approach
    d. direct observation

37. You give a test to the same person four times within a month and get nearly the same score each time. This test is showing
    a. objectivity.
    b. projectivity.
    c. reliability.
    d. validity.

38. Scales that rate a person's tendencies for depression, hysteria, paranoia, and mania are found on the personality questionnaire known as the
    a. MMPI-2.
    b. Rorschach Technique.
    c. TAT.
    d. 16 PF.

39. Ambiguous stimuli are used primarily in
    a. interviews.
    b. the MMPI-2.
    c. situational testing.
    d. the Rorschach Technique.

40. Regarding shyness, which of the following is a FALSE statement?
    a. Shy persons show a self-defeating bias in their thinking.
    b. Shy persons show a great deal of private self-consciousness
    c. Shy persons often lack social skills.
    d. Shy persons tend to consider their social anxiety a lasting personality trait.

Chapter 12: Health, Stress and Coping

Chapter Overview

Health psychologists are interested in behavior that helps maintain and promote health. Studies of health and illness have identified a number of behavioral risk factors and health-promoting behaviors that have a major effect on general health and life expectancy. At the minimum, it is important to maintain healthy habits with respect to diet, alcohol, exercise, and smoking. Health psychologists have pioneered efforts to prevent the development of unhealthy habits and to improve well-being through community health campaigns. Maintaining good health is a personal responsibility, not a matter of luck. Wellness is based on minimizing risk factors and engaging in health-promoting behaviors.

Stress is a normal part of life; however, it is also a major risk factor for illness and disease. Stress occurs when demands are placed on an organism to adjust or adapt. The body reacts to stress in a series of stages called the general adaptation syndrome (GAS). The stages of the GAS are alarm, resistance, and exhaustion. Bodily reactions in the GAS follow the pattern observed in the development of psychosomatic disorders. Studies of psychoneuroimmunology show that stress lowers the body's resistance to disease by weakening the immune system. Stress is more damaging in situations involving pressure, a lack of control, unpredictability of the stressor, and intense or repeated emotional shocks. Stress is intensified when a situation is perceived as a threat and when a person does not feel competent to cope with it. In work settings, prolonged stress can lead to burnout. Making a primary appraisal greatly affects our emotional responses to a situation. During a secondary appraisal, we select problem-focused coping or emotion-focused coping (or both) as a way of managing stress.

Frustration is the negative emotional state that occurs when progress toward a goal is blocked. External frustrations are based on delay, failure, rejection, loss, and other direct blocking of motives. Personal frustration is related to personal characteristics over which one has little control. Frustrations of all types become more intense as the strength, urgency, or importance of the blocked motive increases. Major behavioral reactions to frustration include persistence, more vigorous responding, circumvention, direct aggression, displaced aggression (including scapegoating), and escape or withdrawal.

Conflict occurs when one must choose between contradictory alternatives. Four major types of conflict are approach-approach, avoidance-avoidance, approach-avoidance, and multiple conflicts (double approach-avoidance and multiple approach-avoidance). Approach-approach conflicts are usually the easiest to resolve. Avoidance conflicts are difficult to resolve and are characterized by inaction, indecision, freezing, and a desire to escape (called leaving the field). People usually remain in approach-avoidance conflicts but fail to fully resolve them. Approach-avoidance conflicts are associated with ambivalence and partial approach. Vacillation is a common reaction to double and multiple approach-avoidance conflicts.

Defense mechanisms are mental processes used to avoid, deny, or distort sources of threat or anxiety, including threats to one's self-image. Overuse of defense mechanisms makes people less adaptable. A large number of defense mechanisms have been identified, including compensation, denial, fantasy, intellectualization, isolation, projection, rationalization, reaction formation, regression, repression, and sublimation.

Learned helplessness can be used as a model for understanding depression. Mastery training, optimism, and hope all act as antidotes for learned helplessness. Depression is a major, and surprisingly common, emotional problem. Actions and thoughts that counter feelings of helplessness tend to reduce depression. The college blues are a relatively mild form of depression. Learning to manage college work and to challenge self-critical thinking can help alleviate the college blues.

Work with stress scales like the *Social Readjustment Rating Scale* indicates that multiple life changes tend to increase long-range susceptibility to accident or illness. Immediate psychological and mental health is more closely related to the intensity and severity of daily hassles (microstressors). Intense or prolonged stress may cause damage in the form of psychosomatic problems. During biofeedback training, bodily processes are monitored and converted to a signal that tells what the body is doing. Biofeedback allows people to alleviate some psychosomatic illnesses by altering bodily activities. People with Type A personalities are competitive, striving, hostile, impatient, and prone to having heart attacks. People who have traits of the hardy personality seem to be unusually resistant to stress. Optimism, positive emotions, and social support tend to buffer stress.

The damaging effects of stress can be reduced with stress management techniques. A number of coping skills can be applied to manage stress. Most of these focus on one of three areas: bodily effects, ineffective behavior, and upsetting thoughts. All of the following are good ways to manage bodily reactions to stress: exercise, meditation, progressive relaxation, and guided imagery. To minimize ineffective behavior when you are stressed, you can slow down, get organized, balance work and relaxation, accept your limits, seek social support, and write about your feelings. Learning to use coping statements is a good way to combat upsetting thoughts.

Preview: Mee Jung's Amazing Race

Language Development Guide

rush: blast; hustle
make-or-break: essential to success
last leg of her race: final part
perfectly: entirely; absolutely
timed: scheduled
inflict: impose; cause
fell on: were scheduled for
Great: sarcastic reply meaning not good
traffic jam: line of cars on a highway that cannot move because of overcrowding or an obstruction
cut her off: another car pulls in front of her requiring her to put on brakes fast
one-finger salute: an offensive hand gesture
swarming: a large group moving in a disordered way
frantic: anxious; worried, hysterical
spied: saw; noticed
Mini Cooper: type of very small car
darted: rushed; dashed; moved very quickly
"her" place: her intended, not yet claimed, parking space
to honk: to blow one's car horn
impatiently: showing irritation in not wanting to wait
seized: was taken control of by an urge or desire
colossal: huge; immense
karate chop: a powerful slanting blow done by the side of an opened hand
stress: the mental and physical condition that occurs when a person must adjust or adapt to the environment
pressure: stressful condition that occurs when a person must meet urgent external demands or expectations

662

frustration: negative emotional state that occurs when one is prevented from reaching a goal
crossed the finish line: completed the task
cramming: studying too much all at one time
kick back: reduce or stop work after a period of intense work, "to sit down and put up your feet"
bronchitis: coughing illness involving inflammation in the lungs
collide: combine, interact
coincidence: accident of chance

Module 12.1 Health Psychology
Health Psychology—Here's to Your Good Health
Survey Questions: What is health psychology? How does behavior affect health?

Language Development Guide
priceless: precious; beyond price; very expensive
bedevil: cause problems; aggravate
here's to your good health: phrasing of the section title similar to a toast (raising one's beverage) in honor of someone
allied field: associated with medical specialties
diabetes: metabolic disease in which a person has high blood sugar because the body does not produce enough insulin
asthma: respirator disease caused by allergies and involves coughing, difficulty in breathing, and tightness in the chest
century: 100 years
infectious: disease usually caused by bacteria and can be passed to other people
promote: encourage; support
whereas: while
undertaker: somebody whose profession is to arrange funerals and burials
overtake: grab it; steal it
matter of fashion: how one looks
in the long run: over a long period of time
life expectancy: the number of years one can expect to live
reckless: irresponsible; out of control; careless
insufficient: inadequate; not enough
disease-prone: likely to become ill
in your mind's eye, fast-forward an imaginary film of your life: imagine what would happen in your life
add up: become more important
seething: boiling, excited; furious
assaults: attacks
squeeze: compress; jam
ravaged: worn down, damaged, broken
plaque: build-up or deposits of cholesterol in arteries
clogging: blocking; obstructing
sermonize: to lecture and point out faults or deliver moral judgments
pneumonia: inflammation of the lungs
traced: tracked; located
consuming: eating; using
fend off: keep away; repel
"silent killer": gives few warning signs before it kills
restrictive: limiting
burdensome: troublesome; difficult to deal with

tofu and wheat grass: soy protein and grass, popular foods among some vegetarians

tasty: delicious; tastes very good

Mediterranean: associated with the people living in a region that borders the Mediterranean Sea, such as Greek and Italians

*exercise like an Olympic at*hlete: physical training that takes places for several hours seven days a week 365 days a year

"lifestyle physical activity" the use of large muscles in performing routine daily activities, such as walking to work, taking the stairs, and doing household chores

teetotaler: someone who does not drink alcohol

cirrhosis: a type of illness, damaged function

fast-food junkies: one who has a great appetite or craving for quickly prepared meals, such as hamburgers, hot dogs, and fried foods

"mental virus": trend or fashion

social contagion: a mood spreading among people with people then copying others' behavior

"hang out": spend time together somewhere

to flock: to gather; to group

like-minded: people who think alike

doomed: fated; destined; condemned

social networks: group of individuals who are interconnected by common interests, friendship, business, or other types of relationships

abandoning: giving up; discarding; throwing away

take the lead: be the first one; be a leader

"immunize": make someone resistant to something

"Quitting is easy. I've done it dozens of time.": it is difficult to stop a smoking addiction; one can quit but often starts back

"uncool": not popular

lifelong pursuit: an important task that takes a long time to complete

labor of love: work you enjoy doing

bounce back: recover, heal

adversity: hardship; difficulty

Recite and Review

1. Periods of stress are frequently followed by physical _____.
2. Something that is priceless and free is your _____.
3. Many diseases and half of all deaths in North America can be traced to _____ behaviors.
4. The field of psychology that aims to use behavioral principles to prevent illness and death and to promote health is called _____ psychology.
5. Psychological principles are used to manage medical problems, such as diabetes or asthma as well as in pain control and helping people cope with chronic illnesses within the allied field of _____.
6. A century ago, people primarily died from infectious diseases and _____.
7. Today, people generally die from diseases, which are related to health-damaging personal habits, and are called _____ diseases.
8. Actions that increase the chances of disease, injury, or early death are called _____ factors.
9. Although it may soon overtake first place, the second most preventable cause of death in the United States is currently_____.
10. High levels of stress, untreated high blood pressure, cigarette smoking, abuse of alcohol or other drugs, overeating, inadequate exercise, unsafe sexual behavior, exposure to toxic substances, violence, excess sun exposure, reckless driving, and disregarding personal safety (avoidable accidents) are all major _____ factors.
11. The percentage of all American adults are overweight is roughly _____ percent.

12. Being overweight doubles the chance of dying from cancer or _____ disease.
13. Seventy percent of all medical costs are related to the following six factors: smoking, alcohol abuse, drug abuse, poor diet, risky sexual practices, and insufficient _____.
14. Your long-term health and happiness as well as your life expectancy are greatly affected by the personal habits you have by the time you are _____ years old.
15. Regarding the percentage of U.S. high school students who have engaged in health-endangering behaviors, it was found that at least 45 percent had engaged in sexual intercourse and had used _____.
16. Some people who are frequently ill, depressed, anxious, and hostile have a general _____ personality.
17. People often eat poorly, sleep poorly, rarely exercise, fail to use seat belts in cars, and smoke more when they are experiencing the emotional problem of _____.
18. Those who overeat usually do not get enough exercise and those who smoke are also likely to drink excessively, which illustrate how unhealthy lifestyles almost always create _____ risks.
19. Pneumonia tends to occur in higher rates in people who have cancer, heart disease, lung disease, or liver disease, which illustrates how behavioral risk factors of smoking, drinking, and obesity are often linked to _____ diseases.
20. To prevent disease, the removal of behavioral risk factors is usually the first step taken by _____ psychologists.
21. Often by consuming less salt, losing weight, using alcohol sparingly, and getting more exercise, one can fend off the lifestyle disease of _____.
22. Getting regular exercise, controlling smoking and alcohol use, maintaining a balanced diet, getting good medical care, and managing stress are considered _____ behaviors.
23. In one study, by being careful about diet, alcohol, exercise, and smoking, adults were able to cut the risk of dying over a 10-year period by _____ percent.
24. Marion eats a diet that is high in fruits, vegetables, and fish and low in red meat and dairy products. Marion is eating a(n) "_____ diet."
25. "Lifestyle physical activity" involves the equivalent of a brisk walk" three or four times a week for _____ minutes.
26. If the person remains alcohol free two or three days a week, moderation in drinking would mean the consumption on the other days of _____ alcoholic drinks per day.
27. According to researchers Nicholas Christakis and James Fowler the barriers to our changing unhealthy behaviors tend to involve _____ factors.
28. When one person in a group stops smoking, others in the group may follow suit, which illustrates how healthy behaviors can be spread through one's _____.
29. The growing social unpopularity of smoking may be the best explanation of why fewer and fewer American adults with those still smoking totaling only _____ percent.
30. People were found to be 57 percent more likely to become obese if they had a friend who became fat first in one study of social _____.
31. The largest preventable cause of death and the single most lethal factor is _____.
32. Programs in schools that discourage smoking with quizzes about smoking, antismoking art contests, poster and T-shirt giveaways, antismoking pamphlets for parents, and questions for students to ask their parents are referred to as _____ programs.
33. Research has shown that the long-term success for quitting smoking is _____ smoker in 10.
34. Damian is enrolled in a program at her school that teaches youths how to resist pressures to begin smoking. Damian is enrolled in _____ training.
35. Annette is enrolled in a program at her school that teaches stress reduction, self-protection, decision-making, and social skills. Annette is enrolled in _____ training.
36. Community-wide education projects designed to lessen major risk factors by informing people about stress, alcohol abuse, high blood pressure, and other topics are called _____ campaigns.

37. These community-wide education projects sometimes provide people who are positive examples of how to improve one's health and are referred to as _____.
38. People who are truly healthy enjoy a positive state of well-being, or _____.
39. People who have positive well-being are healthy both physically and _____.
40. People who enjoy a sense of well-being have supportive relationships with others, live in a clean environment, and do _____ work.

Connections

1. ___ health psychology
2. ___ behavioral medicine
3. ___ lifestyle diseases
4. ___ behavioral risk factors
5. ___ disease-prone personality
6. ___ health-promoting behaviors
7. ___ "Mediterranean diet"
8. ___ refusal skills training
9. ___ life skills training
10. ___ community health campaigns
11. ___ role models
12. ___ wellness

a. study of behavioral factors in medicine, physical illness, and medical treatment
b. includes regular exercise, maintaining a balanced diet, managing stress, avoiding sleep-deprivation, etc.
c. study of the ways in which behavioral principles can be used to prevent illness and promote health
d. community-wide education program that provides information about how to lessen risk factors and promote health
e. diseases related to health-damaging personal habits
f. program that teaches youths how to resist pressures to begin smoking or other health risks
g. high in fruit, vegetables, and fish and low in red meat and dairy products
h. a positive state of good health, more than the absence of disease
i. behaviors that increase the chances of disease, injury, or premature death
j. program that teaches stress reduction, self-protection, decision-making, self-control, and social skills
k. personality type associated with poor health, marked by persistent negative emotions, including anxiety, depression, and hostility
l. positive examples, such as used in showing people how to improve their health

Check Your Memory

1. TRUE or FALSE   Periods of stress are frequently followed by illness.
2. TRUE or FALSE   Many diseases and half of all deaths in North America can be traced to our unhealthy behaviors.
3. TRUE or FALSE   Health psychology aims to use behavioral principles to prevent illness and promote health.
4. TRUE or FALSE   Psychologists who apply psychology to manage medical problems, such as coping with chronic illnesses work in an allied field known as medical behaviorism.
5. TRUE or FALSE   A century ago, people primarily died from lifestyle diseases, while today people generally die from infectious diseases and accidents.

6. TRUE or FALSE   Some causes of illness are beyond our control, but many behavioral risk factors can be reduced.

7. TRUE or FALSE   Roughly 80 percent of all Americans adults are overweight.

8. TRUE or FALSE   A person who is overweight at age 20 can expect to lose five to 20 years of life expectancy.

9. TRUE or FALSE   Reckless driving and excess sun exposure are considered major behavioral risk factors.

10. TRUE or FALSE   Regarding health-endangering behaviors engaged in by U.S. high school students, more students have engaged in sexual intercourse than have used marijuana.

11. TRUE or FALSE   Regarding health-endangering behaviors engaged in by U.S. high school students, more students have smoked cigarettes than have been in a physical fight.

12. TRUE or FALSE   Some people have a general disease-prone personality that leaves them depressed, anxious, hostile, and frequently ill.

13. TRUE or FALSE   People who are depressed eat poorly, sleep poorly, rarely exercise, fail to use seat belts in cars, and smoke more.

14. TRUE or FALSE   Unhealthy lifestyles almost always create multiple risks.

15. TRUE or FALSE   Deaths attributed to infections are rarely traced to smoking, poor diets, or alcohol abuse.

16. TRUE or FALSE   Consuming less salt, losing weight, using alcohol sparingly, and getting more exercise can help fend off hypertension.

17. TRUE or FALSE   Health-promoting behaviors include regular exercise, maintaining a balanced diet, getting good medical care, and managing stress.

18. TRUE or FALSE   In one study, the risk of dying was cut by 65 percent during a 10-year period for adults who were careful about diet, alcohol, exercise, and smoking.

19. TRUE or FALSE   The healthiest people eat a Western diet that is high in red meat and dairy products.

20. TRUE or FALSE   "Lifestyle physical activity" involves people exercising one hour per day six days a week.

21. TRUE or FALSE   Only 38 percent of American adults still smoke.

22. TRUE or FALSE   Moderation in drinking is described as consuming only three to four drinks a day.

23. TRUE or FALSE   One study of social factors affecting health found that people were 57 percent more likely to become obese if they had a friend who became fat first.

24. TRUE or FALSE   If your spouse quits smoking, you are 67 percent more likely to quit smoking.

25. TRUE or FALSE   Currently, smoking is the largest preventable cause of death and the single most lethal factor.

26. TRUE or FALSE   Antismoking programs often include refusal skills training to help youths resist pressures to begin smoking.

27. TRUE or FALSE   The community-wide education projects designed to lessen major risk factors are known as life skills training campaigns.

28. TRUE or FALSE   Community-wide education projects often use role models who show people how to improve their health.

29. TRUE or FALSE   People who enjoy a sense of well-being have supportive relationships with others, do meaningful work, and live in a clean environment.

30. TRUE or FALSE   Wellness means being physically healthy and is not related to psychological health.

Critical Thinking Question

The general public is increasingly well informed about health risks and healthful behavior. Can you apply the concept of reinforcement to explain why so many people fail to act on this information?

Module 12.2 Stress, Frustration, and Conflict
Stress—Thrill or Threat?
Survey Questions: What is stress? What factors determine its severity?

Language Development Guide

prolonged: long-drawn-out; extended; stretched out

"happen to": occurs by chance

severity: the extent to which something is bad

woes: afflictions; troubles

wind-whipped: windy

surge: rush; flood; outpouring

your landing might, however: referring to landing on your feet after going down the ski jump, which might cause physical damage

stormy romance: passionate relationship, with both love and conflict

mobilizes: activates and organizes

dumped: put; unloaded

brilliant: wonderful

high-altitude sickness: flu-like symptoms occur in many people when they are above 8,000 feet due to lower air pressure and the loss of water vapor from the lungs

drained: used up

depleted: reduced; lessened

impending: coming; approaching; in the near future

melodramatic: overly emotional; exaggerated

endured: tolerated; suffered

microbes: germs; bacteria; viruses

dropping that into a conversation: saying that when informally talking to someone

mad dash: frantic pace in completing something

bereavement: mourning a death

"double whammy": two unpleasant things happening at the same time

worth noting: important to say

guided imagery: intentional visualization of images that are calming

boost: increase; improve

confrontations: face-to-face encounters, often with conflict involved

to issue: give out

choking: feeling like one is being suffocated

whiff: smell

"shocks": jolts; blows; upsets

cynicism: doubt; pessimism; negativity

detachment: lack of interest and involvement with other people

rock on!: keep going; good for you!-a compliment

appraise: assess, evaluate

"sized up": assessed; evaluated

invites: encourages

wreaks: causes

havoc: ruin or damage

piles on: adds on; heaps on; loads on

owe money to "Mad Dog Maddox": most likely a person who loans money and then threatens to injure or
      kill you if you do not repay
perceived: supposed; believed
competence: ability; skill
ward off: defend against; protect against
distract: divert attention
glance: quick look
clash: conflict
shortchanges: to deal with less effectively
traumatic: shocking; upsetting; distressing
torture: inflicting severe physical pain
assassination: murder of prominent or public figure
flashbacks: vivid painful memory that reoccur
emotional numbing: includes difficulty in experiencing positive emotions, lack of interest in activities
      once enjoyed, and feeling distant from others
catastrophic: disastrous; tragic; terrible
Haiti: Caribbean country
overwhelming: overpowering; devastating
witness: observe
horror: shock; awfulness; terror
elevated: increased
coupled: together
ongoing: continuing
foreseeable: near; immediate
adversity: hardship; difficulty; misfortune
resilient: ability to bounce back; quick to recover
crippling: disabling; incapacitating

Recite and Review

1. Although stress is a natural part of life, it can be a major behavioral risk factor if it is prolonged or
    _____.
2. Because stress is a matter of how we perceive events and react to them, stress can often be
    _____.
3. If one is totally without stress, one must be _____.
4. The mental and physical condition that occurs when a person must adjust or adapt to the environment
    is called _____.
5. Challenging, rewarding, and energizing activities provoke "good stress," also called _____.
6. A stress reaction begins with the same autonomic nervous system arousal that occurs during
    _____.
7. The type of stresses that can be uncomfortable, but they rarely do any damage are _____
    stresses.
8. A series of bodily reactions to prolonged stress called the General Adaptation Syndrome (GAS) was
    described by Canadian stress research pioneer _____.
9. Your body mobilizes its resources to cope with added stress during the _____ reaction of the
    GAS.
10. During the first stage of the GAS, the adrenal glands are signaled to produce more adrenaline,
    noradrenaline, and cortisol by the _____ gland.
11. People have such symptoms as headache, fever, fatigues, sore muscles, shortness of breath, diarrhea,
    upset stomach, loss of appetite, and a lack of energy during the _____ reaction of the GAS.

12. Jerrod is expressing stress, but his bodily adjustments to the stress have stabilized; and although he feels normal again, the stress really has not disappeared. In addition, Jerrod will be less able to handle any additional stress during this stage. Jerrod is in the stage of _____ of the GAS.
13. The first signs of psychosomatic disorders begin to appear during the _____ stage of the GAS.
14. When the body's resources are drained and the stress hormones depleted, then a person is experiencing the GAS stage of _____.
15. Kendra has been under a great deal of stress for a number of weeks and is exhibiting irritability, apathy, and mental fatigue. Kendra is showing the _____ signs of exhaustion.
16. When a person has been under a great deal of stress and exhibits an avoidance of responsibilities and relationships, extreme or self-destructive behavior, self-neglect, and/or poor judgment, the person is showing _____ signs of exhaustion.
17. Petra has been frequently ill over the last year, is overusing medications, and worries excessively about her health. Petra is showing the _____ signs of exhaustion.
18. When Selye examined animals in the later stages of the GAS, he found parts of body enlarged and discolored. These were the _____ glands.
19. In his examination of animals in the later stages of the GAS, Selye found that the animals had stomach ulcers and intense shrinkage of the thymus, spleen, and _____.
20. Tia is studying the links among behavior, stress, disease, and the immune system. Tia's field of study is called _____.
21. In a self-protective response to threats, stress causes the body to release substances that can prolong infections and delay healing by increasing _____.
22. Regarding their effect on the immune system response, happiness, laughter, and delight tend to _____ it.
23. Immune system functioning can actually be boosted by various psychological approaches, such as support groups, relaxation exercises, guided imagery, and _____ training.
24. Any condition or event that challenges or threatens a person is called a(n) _____.
25. Regarding the elements of stress, police officers suffer from a high rate of stress-related diseases due mainly to the nature of police work being _____.
26. In a study of students who were inhaling air and would then experience the choking effect of more carbon dioxide being added to the air supply, the students who knew in advance which trials the carbon dioxide would be added found it _____ stressful.
27. When a person must meet urgent external demands or expectations, then he or she is experiencing the element of stress known as _____.
28. People generally feel more stress in situations over which they have little or no _____.
29. Workload was found to be the number one source of stress at work, while the number two source of work stress is feeling _____.
30. Emotional exhaustion, cynicism or detachment, and feelings of reduced personal accomplishment are characteristics of the job-related condition known as _____.
31. The job-related condition of exhaustion is most likely to occur in professions, such as nursing, teaching, social work, child care, counseling, or police work, which are emotionally-demanding _____ professions.
32. The people who are the most vulnerable to burnout are the ones who are more _____ about their work.
33. This job-related condition of exhaustion can be alleviated by adjusting workloads, rewards, and the amount of _____ people have over their jobs.
34. If you have a negative attitude toward your college studies and feel that your college workload is too heavy, you may be vulnerable to _____.
35. A powerful stress reaction follows whenever a stressor is appraised as a(n) _____.
36. According to Richard Lazarus, the type of appraisal that involves deciding whether a situation is relevant or irrelevant, positive or threatening is _____ appraisal.

37. When you assess your resources and choose a way to meet a threat or challenge, you are using _____ appraisal.
38. When Greeks, who earn, on average, less than half of what Americans earn were compared on life expectancy, it was found that the group that had the longer life expectancy were the _____.
39. A study found that poorer women in California are more likely to die if they live in better-off neighborhoods than if they live in poorer neighborhoods because of the stress that occurred by being constantly reminded that they were _____.
40. We are particularly prone to feel stressed if we cannot or if we think we cannot _____ our immediate environment.
41. It is threatening to feel that we are unable to cope with life's demands because of a lack of _____.
42. When a distressed person distracts himself by listening to music or talking a walk, he is using _____ coping.
43. You are a college student, who has 10 reports due this semester. If you deal with this distressing situation by constructing a time schedule for working on each report, you are using _____ coping.
44. The type of coping that tends to be especially useful when you are facing a controllable stressor is _____ coping.
45. The type of coping that is best-suited for managing your reaction to stressors you cannot control is _____ coping.
46. Stresses, such as war, torture, rape, natural disasters, or street violence would be considered _____ stresses.
47. Victims of natural disasters or war often suffer from nightmares, flashbacks, insomnia, irritability, nervousness, emotional numbing, and _____.
48. When a person cannot stop thinking about the disturbing event, anxiously avoids anything associated with the event, and is constantly fearful or nervous, the person should seek professional help because they are showing symptoms of a(n) _____ disorder.

Part 1: Connections

1. ____ stress

2. ____ eustress

3. ____ stress reaction

4. ____ general adaptation syndrome (GAS)

5. ____ psychoneuroimmunology

6. ____ emotional signs (of impending exhaustion)

7. ____ behavioral signs (of impending exhaustion)

a. a series of bodily reactions to prolonged stress that occurs in three stages: alarm, resistance, exhaustion

b. the mental and physical condition that occurs when a person must adjust or adapt to the environment

c. avoidance of responsibilities and relationships, extreme or self-destructive behavior, self-neglect, poor judgment

d. excessive worry about illness, frequent illness, overuse of medicines, physical ailments and complaints

e. stressful condition that occurs when a person must meet urgent external demands or expectations

f. "good stress" that is usually challenging, rewarding, and energizing

g. the normal, immediate physical response to stress, consisting mainly of bodily changes related to autonomic nervous system arousal

8. ___ physical signs (of impending exhaustion)

9. ___ pressure

h. study of the links among behavior, stress, disease, and the immune system

i. anxiety, apathy, irritability, mental fatigue

Part 2: Connections

1. ___ stressor

2. ___ alarm reaction

3. ___ stage of resistance

4. ___ stage of exhaustion

5. ___ burnout

6. ___ primary appraisal

7. ___ secondary appraisal

8. ___ emotion-focused coping
9. ___ problem-focused coping

10. ___ traumatic stresses

a. deciding if a situation is relevant to oneself and if it is a threat

b. job-related condition of mental, physical, and emotional exhaustion

c. third stage of the GAS, at which time the body's resources are exhausted and serious health consequences occur

d. managing or controlling one's emotional reaction to a stressful situation

e. extreme events that cause psychological injury or intense emotional pain

f. directly managing or remedying a stressful or threatening situation

g. a specific condition or event in the environment that challenges or threatens a person

h. deciding how to cope with a threat or challenge

i. first stage of GAS, during which bodily resources are mobilized to cope with a stressor

j. second stage of the GAS, during which bodily adjustments to stress stabilize, but at a high physical cost

Check Your Memory

1. TRUE or FALSE   Stress is a matter of how we perceive events and react to them.
2. TRUE or FALSE   To be totally without stress is referred to as a positive state of well-being.
3. TRUE or FALSE   "Good stress," which is challenging, rewarding, or energizing, is referred to as eustress.
4. TRUE or FALSE   A stress reaction begins with the same autonomic nervous system arousal that occurs during emotion.
5. TRUE or FALSE   Long-term stresses can be uncomfortable but rarely do damage, while short-term stresses usually lead to physical disorders.
6. TRUE or FALSE   Richard Lazarus developed the general adaptation syndrome (GAS).
7. TRUE or FALSE   In the resistance stage of the GAS, your body mobilizes its resources to cope with stress with the person experiencing headaches, fatigue, upset stomach, and fever.
8. TRUE or FALSE   During the exhaustion phase of the GAS, the bodily adjustment to stress stabilizes and the initial symptoms disappear.
9. TRUE or FALSE   The first signs of psychosomatic disorders appear during the GAS stage of resistance.
10. TRUE or FALSE   Behavioral signs of exhaustion include apathy, irritability, excessive worry about illness, and overuse of medicines.
11. TRUE or FALSE   Animals in the later stages of the GAS have enlarged and discolored adrenal glands and intense shrinkage of the thymus, spleen, and lymph nodes with many also having stomach ulcers.

12. TRUE or FALSE The study of the links among behavior, stress, disease, and the immune system is called biopsychoimmunology.

13. TRUE or FALSE Studies show that the immune system is weakened in students during major exam times and during divorce, bereavement, job loss, and depression.

14. TRUE or FALSE Stress causes the body to release substances that decrease inflammation in the body.

15. TRUE or FALSE Happiness, laughter, and delight tend to strengthen immune system response.

16. TRUE or FALSE Stress management has not been shown to reduce the severity of colds or flu or to improve the chances of survival in people with life-threatening diseases.

17. TRUE or FALSE A stressor is a condition or event that challenges or threatens a person.

18. TRUE or FALSE Predictable stress is more anxiety-provoking than not knowing when the stress will occur.

19. TRUE or FALSE The element of stress known as conflict occurs when a person must meet urgent external demands or expectations.

20. TRUE or FALSE People generally feel more stress in situations over which they have little or no control.

21. TRUE or FALSE A lack of job satisfaction was listed as the number one work stress.

22. TRUE or FALSE Feeling undervalued was listed as the second most common work stress.

23. TRUE or FALSE When a person is emotionally exhausted, is detached from others, and feels a sense of reduced personal accomplishment, he or she is experiencing the job-related condition known as reaction formation.

24. TRUE or FALSE If you have a negative attitude toward your studies and feel that your college workload is too heavy, you may be vulnerable to burnout.

25. TRUE or FALSE Job burnout is most likely to occur in emotionally demanding helping professions, such as nursing, teaching, social work, child care, counseling, or police work.

26. TRUE or FALSE The laziest and least caring workers are the ones who tend to "burn out" on the job.

27. TRUE or FALSE Preventing job burnout involves adjusting workloads, rewards, and the amount of control people have in their jobs.

28. TRUE or FALSE To know if you are stressed, we must know what meaning you place on events.

29. TRUE or FALSE Primary appraisal of a situation involves assessing your resources and choosing a way to meet the threat or challenge.

30. TRUE or FALSE Greeks earn, on average, less than half of what Americans earn and have a shorter life expectancy than the wealthier Americans.

31. TRUE or FALSE A study found that poorer women in California are more likely to die if they live in better-off neighborhoods than if they live in poorer neighborhoods because of the stress of being constantly reminded that they are relatively poor.

32. TRUE or FALSE A perceived lack of control is less threatening than an actual lack of control.

33. TRUE or FALSE College students who feel overloaded experience stress even though their workload may not actually be heavier than that of their classmates.

34. TRUE or FALSE It is threatening to feel that one lacks competence to cope with life's demands.

35. TRUE or FALSE In problem-focused coping, one tries to control his or her emotional reactions to the situation.

36. TRUE or FALSE In general, emotion-focused coping tends to be more useful when you are faced with a controllable stressor.

37. TRUE or FALSE Extreme events that cause psychological injury or intense emotional pain are known as traumatic stresses.

38. TRUE or FALSE People cannot experience stress symptoms from just watching a trauma, such as the 9/11 attacks, on television.

39. TRUE or FALSE   When people suffer traumatic stress, they should avoid activities that they enjoyed in the past until they has completely overcome their fear and nervousness.

40. TRUE or FALSE   Symptoms of stress disorders include thinking constantly about the disturbing event, anxiously avoiding anything associated with the event, and being constantly fearful and nervous.

Critical Thinking Question

Which do you think would produce more stress: (a) appraising a situation as mildly threatening but feeling like you are totally incompetent to cope with it, or (b) appraising a situation as very threatening but feeling that you have the resources and skills to cope with it?

Module 12.2 Stress, Frustration, and Conflict

Frustration—Blind Alleys and Lead Balloons

Survey Question: What causes frustration and what are typical reactions to it?

Language Development Guide

blind alleys: a passage closed at the end so escape blocked
lead balloons: fail completely, lead balloons do not fly
impede: hinder; slow down; hold back
getting stuck: stopped, unable to proceed
finding the cupboard...dog a bone: reference to a nursery rhyme
prejudice: negative emotional attitude held against members of a particular group of people
urgency: pressing need to hurry
submerged: beneath the surface of water
trick lock: quick release lock that looks like a real lock; used in magic tricks
the straw that broke the camel's back: another negative event in a series of negative events, the one that overwhelms one's ability to cope
commutes: to travel regularly from place to place, such as from home to work
aspire: aim; desire
in the meantime: for the time being; for now
incite: provoke; stir up
persistence: determination; diligence
vigorous: characterized by forceful and energetic action
vending machine: machine in which soft drinks and snacks may be bought by putting money in and then pressing a button
small band of nomadic humans: a traveling tribe or group
parched: thirsty, very dry
menacing: threatening; scary; frightening
displaced: redirects
retaliate: hit back; get even
lashed out: burst into a verbal or physical attack
annoyance: irritation
layoffs: elimination of jobs
"foreign": unfamiliar; from another place
hitchhike: travel by getting free rides from motorists
feigned: pretend
stereotyped: fixed or set
futile: useless
gracefully: with poise; elegantly

674

"experience": in this case, work experience
overestimated: overstated the amount or degree

Recite and Review

1. Frustration is a negative emotional state that occurs when people are prevented from reaching desired _____.
2. Getting a flat tire on your way to class to take your final exam would be an example of _____ frustration.
3. Delays, failure, rejection, loss, and other direct blocking of motivated behaviors result in _____ frustrations.
4. Slow drivers, tall people in theaters, people who cut into lines are all examples of external obstacles that would be considered _____.
5. Stuck doors, dead batteries, and rain on the day of a planned outside event are all examples of external obstacles that would be considered _____.
6. If you ask friends what has frustrated them recently, most will probably mention an external obstacle, such as their supervisor being unfair or their history teacher grading too hard, both of which would be classified as _____.
7. As the strength, urgency, or importance of a blocked motive increases, there will be a dramatic increase in one's motivation and in one's _____.
8. People with long daily commutes are more likely to display "road rage" because of the accumulation of _____ frustrations.
9. If you want to earn an academic scholarship for college, but your grades are mostly C's, you frustration would be considered _____.
10. Any response made with the intent of harming a person or an object is referred to as _____.
11. Frustration is usually met first with more vigorous efforts and varied response, which illustrates _____.
12. If you are frustrated by your teacher and then you go home and lash out at your younger sibling, you are exhibiting _____ aggression.
13. If you redirect your aggression onto a target that did not originally cause the aggression, the target you choose will tend to be safer or less likely to _____.
14. When a person or group of people are habitually blamed for conditions not of their making, a pattern known as _____ is occurring.
15. Reducing discomfort by leaving frustrating situations or by psychologically withdrawing from them is referred to as withdrawal, or _____.
16. Feigned apathy and taking drugs are two common forms of psychological _____.
17. Taking drugs or feigning apathy would also be considered ineffective _____-focused coping methods.
18. Persistence that is inflexible can turn into "stupid" _____ behavior.
19. In dealing with frustration, it is first important to identify the source and determine if the frustration is external or _____.
20. In coping with frustration, it is important to distinguish between real barriers and _____ barriers.

Connections

1. ___ frustration
2. ___ external frustration
3. ___ personal frustration

a. frustration that is based on one's own characteristics and shortcomings
b. any response made with the intent of harming a person or an object
c. frustration that is based on conditions outside a person that impede progress toward a goal

675

4. ___ social obstacles
5. ___ nonsocial obstacles
6. ___ aggression
7. ___ persistence
8. ___ displaced aggression
9. ___ scapegoating
10. ___ escape
11. ___ stereotyped behavior

d. reducing discomfort by physically leaving or psychologically withdrawing from a situation
e. redirecting aggression to a target other than the actual source of one's frustration
f. external blockages that involve interactions with people, such as slow drivers
g. inflexible responding
h. habitually blaming a person or a group of people for conditions not of their making
i. external blockages that involve inanimate objects or situations and conditions outside your control, such as weather conditions
j. negative emotional state that occurs when one is prevented from reaching a goal
k. often the first response to frustration and involves more vigorous efforts and varied responses

Check Your Memory

1. TRUE or FALSE   Whenever a person must choose between contradictory needs, desires, motives, or demands, the person is experiencing the type of stress known as frustration.
2. TRUE or FALSE   Getting caught in a traffic jam on your way to work would be an example of a personal frustration.
3. TRUE or FALSE   External frustrations are based on delays, failure, rejection, loss, and other direct blocking of motivated behavior.
4. TRUE or FALSE   Raining on the day of your family picnic at the lake would be classified as a social obstacle.
5. TRUE or FALSE   A slow driver that gets in front of you when you are late to work would be a nonsocial obstacle.
6. TRUE or FALSE   If you ask friends what has frustrated them recently, most will probably mention a social obstacle, such as someone's behavior.
7. TRUE or FALSE   Frustration usually decreases as the strength, urgency, or importance of a blocked motive increases.
8. TRUE or FALSE   The effects of repeated frustrations can accumulate until a small irritation sets off an unexpectedly violent response.
9. TRUE or FALSE   If you turned in your term paper late and your professor deducted points for the report being late, your frustration was caused externally by the professor, not by your personal behavior.
10. TRUE or FALSE   Frustration does not always incite aggression.
11. TRUE or FALSE   Frustration is usually first met by displaced aggression.
12. TRUE or FALSE   When a person uses more vigorous efforts and varied responses to overcome a barrier, it is called persistence.
13. TRUE or FALSE   Targets of displaced aggression tend to be safer, or less likely to retaliate, than the original source of frustration.
14. TRUE or FALSE   The finding that unemployment and divorce are associated with increased child abuse would be an example of displaced aggression.
15. TRUE or FALSE   In a pattern known as avoidance-avoidance frustration, a person or a group is blamed for conditions not of their making.
16. TRUE or FALSE   A habitual target of displaced aggression is called a scapegoat.

17. TRUE or FALSE   When Sydney quit her job due to the frustration of her hard work never being appreciated, her response would be classified as escape.
18. TRUE or FALSE   Jacqueline is frustrated with her job, but she deals with the frustration by taking increasing amounts of tranquilizers, which would be an example of psychological escape.
19. TRUE or FALSE   Pretending that you do not care about a particular frustration would be considered an effective problem-focused coping method.
20. TRUE or FALSE   Persistence that is inflexible can lead to stereotyped behavior.
21. TRUE or FALSE   When dealing with frustration, you must determine whether persistence is futile and know when to quit and establish a new direction.
22. TRUE or FALSE   In coping with frustration, it is important to distinguish between real barriers and imagined barriers since we often create our own imagined barriers.

Critical Thinking Question

Being frustrated is unpleasant. If some action, including aggression, ends frustration, why might we expect the action to be repeated on other occasions?

Module 12.2 Stress, Frustration, and Conflict
Conflict—Yes, No, Yes, No, Yes, No, Well, Maybe
Survey Questions: Are there different types of conflict? How do people react to conflict?

Language Development Guide

Yes, No, Yes, No, Yes, No, Well, Maybe: shows the indecision that occurs with an approach-avoidance conflict

contradictory: opposing

tutti-frutti: ice cream containing chopped candied fruits

mocha: mixture of coffee, chocolate, and milk flavors

champagne: sweet, slightly acidic flavor

marmalade: jellylike preserve made from the pulp and rind of fruits, especially citrus fruits; has tangy citrus flavor

at stake: at issue; in the balance; being considered

the scales of decision are easily tipped: means the decision is easily made with decision-making being compared to a balance scale with the side of the scale dipping down because more weight on one side

"*the devil and the deep blue sea," "the frying pan and the fire," "a rock and a hard place*": choosing between two negative options

monotonous: dull; boring; repetitive

dorm food: food available in one's college dormitory

abortion: intentionally ending a pregnancy

sacred: holy; blessed; dedicated to a religious purpose

tampered: interfered with; messed with

object to: be against; protest

"*damned if you do, damned if you don't*": outcome will not be good no matter which option is chosen; both choices are negative, but not choosing may be impossible or equally undesirable

plight: dilemma; difficulty

pavement: paved surface of a road

repelled: cause to move back from

turmoil: disorder; confusion; unrest

crushing handshake: painful squeezing of the hand

ambivalent: unsure; undecided
awaits: lies ahead
intermingled: mixed together
loom: come into view; appear
hasty: too fast
regretted: feel sorry
partially: partly
in progress: underway; taking place
compromises: finding the middle ground; give and take
exact a high cost: causes a great deal of stress

Recite and Review

1. Conflict is occurring when a person must choose between needs, desires, motives, or demands that are _____.
2. The easiest conflict to resolve tends to be the _____ conflict.
3. If you must choose between eating cheesecake or chocolate fudge cake, both of which you love, you are experiencing a(n) _____ conflict.
4. A person who is caught between "a rock and a hard place" is experiencing a(n) _____ conflict.
5. A person facing two negative, or undesirable alternatives may find it impossible to decide or to take action, which is referred to as "_____."
6. A student who could not attend school unless he worked, but could not earn passing grades if he worked, eventually decided to join the navy, a reaction to avoidance conflicts called "_____."
7. A person who is "caught" by being attracted to, and repelled by, the same goal or activity is experiencing a(n) _____ conflict.
8. In cases whether one is both attracted and repelled by the same goal, a person will almost certainly feel a mixture of positive and negative feelings called _____.
9. When a person is experiencing a mixture of positive and negative feelings for a goal, they will usually deal with this situation by making a(n) _____ approach.
10. If you are offered two jobs, one involving dull work for good pay and the other being interesting work for low pay, you are faced with a(n) _____ conflict.
11. Often, when a person is faced with two alternatives, both of which have positive and negative attributes, the person will waver between the alternative, which is referred to as _____.
12. When you must choose between several brands, types, and sizes of televisions, you are faced with a(n) _____ conflict.
13. In order to make sure you did everything possible to avoid a mistake, it is good advice when making important decisions not to be too _____.
14. If you are thinking about moving to a new town, it would be best to spend a few days there first and try out this important decision _____.
15. When making decisions, it is always important to look for workable _____.
16. When all else fails, make a decision and live with it because a great deal of stress tends to result from conflict and _____.

Connections

1. ___ conflict
2. ___ approach-approach conflict
3. ___ avoidance-avoidance conflict
4. ___ "freezing"

a. being attracted to and repelled by the same goal or activity
b. experiencing mixed positive and negative feelings
c. stressful condition that occurs when a person must choose between incompatible or contradictory alternatives
d. wavering between alternatives

5. ___ "leaving the field"
6. ___ approach-avoidance conflict
7. ___ ambivalence
8. ___ partial approach
9. ___ double approach-avoidance conflict
10. ___ vacillation
11. ___ multiple approach-avoidance

e. being simultaneously attracted to and repelled by each of two alternatives
f. finding it impossible to decide or take action
g. choosing between two negative, undesirable alternatives
h. being simultaneously attracted to and repelled by each of several alternatives
i. reaction to avoidance-avoidance conflict in which person escapes by choosing a totally different alternative from the original two alternatives
j. choosing between two positive, or desirable, alternatives
k. involves committing to an alternative in a limited way

Check Your Memory

1. TRUE or FALSE   The element of stress known as pressure occurs when one must choose between contradictory needs, desires, motives, or demands.
2. TRUE or FALSE   The easiest conflict to resolve is approach-avoidance conflict.
3. TRUE or FALSE   Whether a situation is defined as a conflict is determined by one's personal needs and values with the situation being a conflict for one person but not another.
4. TRUE or FALSE   If you must choose between going to the mountains or the beach for your vacation and you love both places, you are faced with an approach-approach conflict.
5. TRUE or FALSE   If you are caught between "the frying pan and the fire," you are experiencing a double approach-avoidance conflict.
6. TRUE or FALSE   When faced with avoidance conflicts, a person may freeze, or find it impossible to decide or take action.
7. TRUE or FALSE   In approach-approach conflicts, people often become so confused that they leave the field and select an entirely different alternative.
8. TRUE or FALSE   Ambivalence is a central characteristic of approach-avoidance conflicts.
9. TRUE or FALSE   In avoidance-avoidance conflicts, people often engage in a partial approach.
10. TRUE or FALSE   Often people vacillate between choices in a double approach-avoidance conflict.
11. TRUE or FALSE   When you must choose between several brands of computer in purchasing your next computer, you are faced with a multiple approach-avoidance conflict.
12. TRUE or FALSE   People in conflict are usually faced with several dilemmas at once, so several types of conflict may be intermingled.
13. TRUE or FALSE   The best decision is usually a hasty one based on your initial gut-feeling.
14. TRUE or FALSE   In managing conflicts, one should try out important decisions partially when possible.
15. TRUE or FALSE   In managing conflicts, one should get all the available information and look for workable compromises.
16. TRUE or FALSE   Sometimes it is best to select a course of action and stick with it unless it is very obviously wrong after you have taken it.

Module 12.3 Defenses, Helplessness, and Depression
Psychological Defense—Mental Judo?
Survey Question: What are defense mechanisms?

Language Development Guide

shield: protect

helplessness: inability to overcome obstacles and avoid aversive stimuli

depression: condition characterized by feelings of sadness, powerlessness, and hopelessness

"college blues": symptoms of depression in college students due to stresses from college work, pressures to choose a career, and leaving one's support group of family and friends at home

Mental Judo: mental wrestling or mental protection; Judo is a sport similar to wrestling developed in Japan.

apprehensive: anxious

blind spots: completely unaware, many times person does not understand because they are avoiding the problem

stingy, tightwad: unwilling to spend or give money

counteracting: offsetting; canceling out

"intellectual" terms: unemotional words and ideas

"logic-tight": rigidly rational

compartments: sections; parts

justifying: explaining the reasons behind; proving oneself right

retreating: moving back; losing ground

held in check: restrained, controlled

resents: dislikes; feels bitter toward

absurdly: ridiculously

overprotective: exercise excessive control over a child's or person's activities

overindulgent: excessively giving children everything they desire, while not requiring any responsibility on their part

"smother" love: being overprotective and overindulgent

rival: opponent; challenger; competitor

infantile: childish; immature

homesick: longing to return home

discern: be aware of; detect

pillar of the community: an important, respected, and influential person

bent on: determined; fixed in one's purpose

phenomenon: occurrence; happening

incredible: hard to believe

wave of: upsurge; movement; flood

sweeps across: moves quickly

belly-up: die

as the last straw: the final irritation or trouble

"pumping iron": lifting weights

health club: place that has exercise equipment that people can use after paying a fee to join the club

bodybuilding: developing the muscles of the body through diet and physical exercise

in spite of: despite

sickly: unhealthy; weak

stutterer: person with a speech problem characterized by repetitions; pauses; or drawn-out words

working off: using exertion and effort in producing or accomplishing something

rechannel: redirect, transform

pastimes: hobbies; leisure activities

drag racing: a car race involving a fairly short, straight and level course with the winner being determined by which car can accelerate faster from a standstill and cross the finish line first.

multitude: huge number; large amount

Recite and Review

1. Apprehension, dread, or uneasiness similar to fear but based on an unclear threat is known as _____.

2. When you feel tense, uneasy, apprehensive, worried, and vulnerable, this unpleasant state can lead to a defensive type of _____-focused coping.

3. The psychologists who have identified the various defense mechanisms that allow us to reduce anxiety caused by stressful situations or our own shortcomings are the _____ psychologists.

4. When you experience a threat to your self-image, you are likely to avoid, deny, or distort this threat by using a(n) _____.

5. Many of the defenses mechanisms were first identified by the theorist named _____.

6. This theorist who first identified many of the defense mechanism assumed they operated _____.

7. When a friend or relative unexpectedly dies, a person often protects him or herself from this unpleasant reality by refusing to accept it, a defense mechanism called _____.

8. When you unconsciously prevent painful memories, such as hostility toward a family member or past failures, you are using the defense mechanism known as _____.

9. Although Jeff is not one of the popular students at his high school, he dreams of the day when he will be an important and wealthy businessman and his classmates will wish they had been nicer to him. Jeff is dealing with his anxiety and unhappiness by using the defense mechanism known as _____.

10. When a person takes on some of the characteristics of an admired person, usually as a way of coping with perceived faults, this person is using the defense mechanism called _____.

11. As an emergency room nurse, you must focus on the life-saving procedures and not on the person's pain in order to help them. Thus, by separating your emotion from your thinking, you are using the defense mechanism of _____.

12. Although you believe you are an "honest" person, you cheated on several tests and bought a term paper from an on-line source. To prevent the thoughts of "being honest" and "cheating," from coming into conflict and causing anxiety, the ego defense mechanism that will separate these contradictory thoughts into "logic-tight" mental compartments is _____.

13. Impulses are not just repressed, but are also held in check by exaggerating opposite behaviors when one uses the defense mechanism of _____.

14. Acting overly nice to a person you dislike would be an example of the defense mechanism known as _____.

15. An adult who throws a temper tantrum or a married adult who "goes home to mother" is exhibiting the defense mechanism called _____.

16. A person who tends to see his or her own feelings, shortcomings, or unacceptable impulses in others is using the defense mechanism of _____.

17. Justifying one's personal actions by giving reasonable but false reasons for them involves the defense mechanism called _____.

18. Helping to keep us from being overwhelmed by immediate threats and providing time for a person to learn to cope in a more effective, problem-focused manner are two advantages of occasionally using _____.

19. Two defense mechanisms that have a decidedly more positive quality are sublimation and _____.

20. A childhood stutterer who excels in debate in college is overcoming his initial weakness by using used the defense mechanism of _____.

21. Freud believed that art, music, dance, poetry, scientific investigation, and other creative activities could serve to rechannel sexual energies into productive behavior, illustrating the defense mechanism called _____.

22. For some players and some fans, football probably allows _____ of aggressive urges.

681

Connections

1. ___ anxiety
2. ___ defense mechanism
3. ___ compensation
4. ___ denial
5. ___ fantasy
6. ___ identification
7. ___ intellectualization
8. ___ isolation
9. ___ projection
10. ___ rationalization
11. ___ reaction formation
12. ___ regression
13. ___ repression
14. ___ sublimation

a. working off unmet desires, or unacceptable impulses, in activities that are constructive

b. preventing dangerous impulses from being expressed in behavior by exaggerating opposite behavior

c. fulfilling unmet desires in imagined achievements or activities

d. attributing one's own feelings, shortcomings, or unacceptable impulses to others

e. unconsciously preventing painful or dangerous thoughts from entering awareness

f. separating emotion from a threatening or anxiety-provoking situation by talking or thinking about it in impersonal terms

g. counteracting a real or imagined weakness by emphasizing desirable traits or seeking to excel in the area of weakness

h. justifying your behavior by giving reasonable, but false, reasons for it

i. habitual and often unconscious psychological process used to reduce anxiety

j. protecting oneself from an unpleasant reality by refusing to perceive it

k. retreating to an earlier level of development or to earlier, less demanding habits or situations

l. apprehension, dread, or uneasiness similar to fear but based on an unclear threat

m. taking on some of the characteristics of an admired person to cope with perceived weaknesses

n. separating contradictory thoughts or feelings into "logic-tight" mental compartments so that they do not come in to conflict

Check Your Memory

1. TRUE or FALSE   The behaviorists have identified various defense mechanisms that allow us to reduce anxiety caused by stressful situations or our own shortcomings.
2. TRUE or FALSE   Anxiety can lead to emotion-focused coping that is defensive in nature.
3. TRUE or FALSE   Defense mechanisms are techniques that one can use to effectively deal with pressure, frustration, and conflict.
4. TRUE or FALSE   Many of the defense mechanisms were first identified by B.F. Skinner, who assumed they were classically conditioned.
5. TRUE or FALSE   Often, defense mechanisms create large blind spots in awareness.
6. TRUE or FALSE   Every one has at one time or another used defense mechanisms.
7. TRUE or FALSE   If you were told that you had only three months to live, you would probably use the defense mechanism known as fantasy in which you would distract yourself from this reality.
8. TRUE or FALSE   Fulfilling unmet desires in imagined achievements is called intellectualization.

9. TRUE or FALSE   When you take on some of the characteristics of an admired person as a way of coping with perceived personal weaknesses, you are exhibiting the defense mechanism called identification.

10. TRUE or FALSE   Separating contradictory thoughts about yourself into "logic-tight" compartments so they do not come into conflict describes the defense mechanism known as reaction formation.

11. TRUE or FALSE   Research suggests that you are most likely to repress information that threatens your self-image.

12. TRUE or FALSE   A mother who unconsciously resents her children may, through reaction formation, become absurdly overprotective and overindulgent.

13. TRUE or FALSE   A child who becomes homesick at summer camp and wants to go home is exhibiting isolation.

14. TRUE or FALSE   Projection lowers anxiety by exaggerating negative traits in others, which justifies one's own actions and directs attention away from personal failings.

15. TRUE or FALSE   If a student give reasonable, but false reasons for not turning in his or her term paper, the student is exhibiting rationalization.

16. TRUE or FALSE   People who overuse defense mechanisms become more adaptable, because they consume smaller amounts of emotional energy in maintaining their self-image.

17. TRUE or FALSE   Defense mechanisms help keep us from being overwhelmed by immediate threats and can provide time for a person to learn to cope in a problem-focused manner.

18. TRUE or FALSE   Two defense mechanisms that have a decidedly positive quality are reaction formation and projection.

19. TRUE or FALSE   The defense mechanism of compensation is used to defend against feelings of inferiority by the person emphasizing his or her desirable traits or seeking to excel in a particular area.

20. TRUE or FALSE   If Nolan who constantly lies becomes a famous novelist, it could be said that Nolan sublimated his lying impulse into storytelling.

21. TRUE or FALSE   Sexual motives appear to be the most easily and widely sublimated.

22. TRUE or FALSE   If you use violent videogames to channel your aggressive urges, you are using the defense mechanism known as projection.

Module 12.3 Defenses, Helplessness, and Depression

Learned Helplessness—Is There Hope?

Survey Question: What do we know about coping with feelings of helplessness and depression?

Language Development Guide

spirits: mood; general feelings
soared: rose; increased
devastating: shocking; upsetting; destructive
blow: setback; painful disappointment; misfortune
deceived: lied to; tricked
lapsed: slipped; fell
concentration camps: prison camp during wartime that are known for torture
elevated: high
acquired: gained; learned
shuttle box: lab apparatus with two compartments through which an animal can move from one to the other
harness: set of leather straps fitted to an animal to restrain the animal or to attach it to a cart for pulling
crouching: squatting; bending down; stooping
resign: passively give in

fate: destiny; predetermined outcome
afflicts: badly affects; causes problems
prime: main; key
procrastinate: postpone; delay; put off
in contrast: quite the opposite
despondency: sadness; gloom
blunted: dulled; weakened
knocked down: mistreated
forcibly: by force
"safe" compartment: part of the shuttle box where no electric shocks occur
regain: get back; recover
mastery: to be in control of a situation or skill
"immunize": to make a person resistant to something
Outward Bound: an outdoor challenge program
pit: set against
rigors: harshness
fragile: easily broken; delicate
antidote: cure; remedy; solution
blues: sadness; mild depression
exert a toll: cause damage
aspirations: ambitions; goals
idealized: personal standard of perfection
"down": sad; depressed
fluctuation: variation; rise and fall; changeability
bleak: hopeless; dreary; gloomy
bouts: attacks of; short periods of
alleviate: lessen; ease
setback: a problem now that can be solved later
"blown it": ruined it; destroyed it
chip away at them: from mining, to make slow but steady progress, in small stages
progress: move forward
rational: logical; based on reason

Recite and Review

1. When researchers in San Antonio, Texas, asked older people if they were hopeful about the future and they answered "No," these older people _____ at elevated rates.
2. An acquired inability to overcome obstacles and avoid aversive stimuli is referred to as _____.
3. The researcher who studied this acquired inability to avoid aversive stimuli was _____.
4. A dog is placed in a harness from which it cannot escape and given several painful shocks, and then the dog is placed in a shuttle box in which it can escape shocks by going to the "safe" compartment. Regarding the dogs that were originally placed in the harness and shocked, and then shocked in the shuttle box, the percentage that went to the "safe" compartment to escape the shock was _____ percent.
5. Helplessness is a psychological state that occurs when events appear to be _____.
6. In humans, helplessness is a common reaction to _____ failure.
7. Helplessness often develops from unpredictable or _____ punishment.
8. In completing their assignments, college students who feel helpless about their schoolwork tend to _____.
9. Persons who are made to feel helpless in one situation are more likely to act helpless in other situations if they attribute their failure to lasting, _____ factors.

684

10. Those college students who prevent learned helplessness from spreading tend to attribute a low score on a test to _____ factors.

11. Seligman and others have pointed out that there are similarities between learned helplessness and a condition that is marked by feelings of despondency, powerlessness, and hopelessness called _____.

12. When the dogs in Seligman's research were forcefully dragged away from the shocks into the "safe" compartment, these dogs had feelings of control over the environment and regained "_____."

13. The responses are reinforced that lead to control over a threat or over one's environment in an approach known as _____.

14. Programs, in which people pit themselves against the rigors of mountaineering, white-water canoeing, and wilderness survival that help to "immunize" them against helplessness and depression by allowing them to master difficult challenges are called _____ schools.

15. The most important of all human emotions and a powerful antidote to depression and helplessness is _____.

16. In a study comparing grade point averages, the college students diagnosed with depression scored below the nondepressed students by _____ grade point(s).

17. College students may come to feel that they are missing out on fun or that all their hard work is meaningless due to the stresses from college work and pressures to choose a(n) _____.

18. When students leave their support groups behind, it is common for students to experience isolation and _____.

19. Many students start college with high aspirations and little prior experience with _____.

20. Students are especially prone to depression if they find it difficult to live up to _____ images of themselves.

21. Depressed students are more likely to abuse alcohol, a drug which is classified as a(n) _____.

22. When five conditions exist, a person is experiencing a true depression rather than a minor fluctuation in mood, according to the most notable authority on depression, Aaron _____.

23. The five conditions that indicate a depression rather than a minor fluctuation in mood include having a consistently negative opinion of yourself, placing negative interpretations on events that usually wouldn't bother you, viewing the future as bleak and negative, feeling that your responsibilities are overwhelming, and engaging in frequent _____.

24. To help alleviate mild school-related depression, students can learn to manage college work and to challenge _____ thinking.

25. College blues are common and should be distinguished from more serious cases of depression, which can lead to a major impairment of emotional functioning or even to _____.

26. Students who overreact to day-to-day disappointments are the ones who strongly link everyday events to a successful career and high income or to some other _____.

27. Cognitive psychologists Beck and Greenberg suggest that when you are feeling "blue," you should try to fill in every hour during the day with activities by making a(n) _____.

28. In order to alleviate depression, it is best to first complete the tasks on your list that are the _____.

29. By checking off each task as it is completed, one will begin to break the _____ cycle of feeling helpless.

30. Depressed students spend much of their time _____.

31. Feelings of worthlessness and hopelessness are usually supported by negative or _____ thoughts.

32. Beck and Greenberg recommend writing down negative thoughts as they occur and then writing a(n) _____ answer to each.

33. Positive events are most likely to end depression if you view them as stable and _____.

685

Connections

1. ___ learned helplessness
2. ___ depression
3. ___ mastery training
4. ___ Outward Bound
5. ___ "college blues"
6. ___ daily schedule

a. Beck and Greenberg's suggestion for dealing with the "blues"
b. reinforcement of responses that lead to control over a threat or one's environment
c. mild form of dejection and sadness common in college undergraduates
d. program in which people pit themselves against the rigors of wilderness survival or other outdoor endeavor
e. state of despondency marked by feelings of powerlessness and hopelessness
f. acquired inability to overcome obstacles or to avoid punishment

Check Your Memory

1. TRUE or FALSE   When researchers in San Antonio, Texas, asked older people if they were hopeful about the future and they answered, "No," the older people died at elevated rates.
2. TRUE or FALSE   An acquired inability to overcome obstacles and avoid aversive stimuli is referred to as pessimistic perception.
3. TRUE or FALSE   Helplessness is a psychological state that occurs when events appear to be uncontrollable.
4. TRUE or FALSE   Learned helplessness affects humans and other primates but not lower animals, such as dogs and cats.
5. TRUE or FALSE   College students who feel helpless about their schoolwork tend to procrastinate, give up easily, and drop out of school.
6. TRUE or FALSE   Persons who attribute their failure to specific factors in a situation are more likely to act helpless in other situations.
7. TRUE or FALSE   Both learned helplessness and depression are marked by feelings of despondency, powerlessness, and hopelessness.
8. TRUE or FALSE   Mastery training involves the reinforcement of responses that lead to mastery of a threat or control over one's environment.
9. TRUE or FALSE   Having positive beliefs, such as optimism, hope, and a sense of meaning and control, is closely related to overall well-being.
10. TRUE or FALSE   The Outward Bound schools are examples of programs that tend to produce learned helplessness.
11. TRUE or FALSE   Hope is a powerful antidote to depression and helplessness.
12. TRUE or FALSE   In one study, college students diagnosed with depression scored half a grade point below nondepressed students.
13. TRUE or FALSE   Stresses from college work and pressures to choose a career can leave students feeling that they are missing out on fun or that all their hard work is meaningless.
14. TRUE or FALSE   College students often develop depression because they start college with low aspirations and a great deal of experience with failure.
15. TRUE or FALSE   Depression in college students often occurs because of the isolation and loneliness that results from leaving their support groups.
16. TRUE or FALSE   Depressed college students are more likely to abuse stimulants than alcohol.
17. TRUE or FALSE   Students who find it difficult to live up to their idealized images of themselves are especially prone to depression.

686

18. TRUE or FALSE   According to Aaron Beck, if people have a consistently negative opinion of themselves, engage in frequent self-criticism, place negative interpretations on events and the future, and feel that their responsibilities are overwhelming, then they are only experiencing a mild, common, temporary fluctuation in their mood.

19. TRUE or FALSE   The "college blues" is classified as a severe depression that affects college students.

20. TRUE or FALSE   Students who fail to link every day events to long-term goals tend to overreact to day-to-day disappointments.

21. TRUE or FALSE   When one feels "blue," one should make a daily schedule and try to schedule activities to fill up every hour during the day.

22. TRUE or FALSE   In alleviating depression, one should start with the more difficult tasks on his or her list and then go to the easier items.

23. TRUE or FALSE   To alleviate depression, a depressed student should sleep as much as possible.

24. TRUE or FALSE   If you are having self-critical or negative thoughts, you should write down these thoughts as they occur and then write a rational answer to each to help alleviate depression.

25. TRUE or FALSE   Positive events are most likely to end depression if you view these positive events realistically as temporary and fragile.

Critical Thinking Question

Learned helplessness is MOST closely related to which of the factors that determine the severity of stress?

Module 12.4 Stress and Health
Stress and Health—Unmasking a Hidden Killer
Survey Question: How is stress related to health and disease?

Language Development Guide

intrepid: fearless; brave
coincidence: by chance; an accident
fast-paced: activities and communication occurs at a rapid speed
unmasking a hidden killer: identifying a cause of fatal illnesses, which is stress
stress-out: having experienced a great deal of stress and reached the exhaustion level
susceptibility: vulnerability; weakness; defenselessness
vigilant: alert, on guard, ready
on guard: to protect
subjecting myself: experiencing
graduate student: student who continues his or her college studies after graduating with a four-year degree; pursuing a masters, specialist, or doctoral degree
hazards: dangers; risks
violations: disobediences; breakings of
impact: influence; effect
rough: approximate; estimated
index: indicator; sign
deliberately: intentionally; on purpose
nothing to sneeze at: it is not something trivial, but something that is important and should not be ignored
"to be forewarned is to be forearmed.": knowing something is coming allows you to prepare
spawn: produce; generate; set off
predictors: forecaster; to make known in advance

acculturative: the changes in the culture of an individual or group due to contact with a different culture or during the process of adapting to a different culture

alienation: isolation; estrangement; distancing

identity confusion: an uncertainty about who one is and where he or she is going in life (Erikson's term)

embrace: accept; welcome; adopt

migraine headache: a severe recurring headache, usually affecting only one side of the head, which is often accompanied by sensitivity to sound and light, nausea, vomiting, and distortions in vision

dominated: controlled; governed

inflict: cause

culprit: offender; guilty party

fostering: developing; promoting; encouraging

maximize: increase; boost

hives: allergic skin reaction causing redness, swelling, and itching

rheumatoid arthritis: autoimmune disease involving swelling and deformity of the joints

ulceration: formation of bowl-shaped sores on a mucous membrane

no magic: what can explain how it works, it is not an unbelievable, unexplainable occurrence

acts as a "mirror: reflects or shows a person his or her own behavior

self-regulation: controlling one's own behavior without outside management

to a degree: in part; to a certain extent

documented: recognized; accepted

cardiologists: medical doctor who specializes in the structure, function, and disorders of the heart

glimpse: quick look; peek

landmark: breakthrough; ground-breaking; milestone

ambitious: determined; go-getter; motivated

striving: pushy; determined; go-getter

telltale: obvious, clear

chafe: become irritated; annoyed

racing the clock: trying to do things very quickly

self-imposed: voluntarily endured

"bottled up": hold back; contain it; suppress it

seethe: be furious; boil with rage

validity: truth; correctness

confirmation: proof; evidence

explosively: burst forth noisily

accentuating: putting emphasis on; stressing and making it noticeable

skim: read quickly

condensations: shortened; summarized; abbreviated

impatience: being irritated at the slow pace of something or someone

strive: try hard; make every effort

simultaneously: at the same time

vaguely: unclear; hazy

quantitative: expressed as an amount or number

clenching your fists: closing hands to form a ball with pointed down and thumb across the fingers

drumming your fingers: tapping fingertips on a flat surface, like a table or desk

allowances: amounts (of time) permitted or granted

unforeseen: unexpected

places a premium: places an unusually high value on

sacrificing: giving up; surrendering

motives: intentions; aims

indignation: righteous anger; offense; fury

considerate: thoughtful; caring; understanding

hardiness: durability; toughness
utility company: organization which provides services to the general public, such as electricity, natural
        gas, telephone, water, etc.
thriving: prospering; succeeding
commitment: dedication; loyalty; devotion; steadfastness
setbacks: delays; hindrances
contentment: satisfaction; happiness
savor: enjoy; take pleasure in
integrate: join together
adversity: hardship; misfortune
optimists: persons who tend to view situations positively
deal with problems head-on: manage or cope with difficulties directly
pessimists: persons who tend to view situations negatively
entails: brings about; causes
healthy grade: good score

Recite and Review

1. Disaster, depression, and sorrow often precede _____.
2. The susceptibility to accidents or illness is increased by both good and bad life _____.
3. The first rating scale to estimate the health hazards we face when stresses add up was Richard Rahe and _____.
4. On the Social Readjustment Rating Scale (SRRS), the impact of life events is expressed in numerical units known as _____ units.
5. According to the originators of the SSRS, there is a high chance of illness or accident when your LCU total exceeds _____ points.
6. The SRRS is at best a rough index of stress since people differ in their _____ to the same event.
7. In a study in which participants were deliberately exposed to the virus that causes common colds, the participants who were more likely to actually get a cold had a high _____ score.
8. Minor but frequent stresses are called hassles, or _____.
9. Too many things to do, not enough money for housing, driving to school, fear of losing valuables, work schedule, and parents' expectations are example of common _____ faced by college students.
10. Long-term health appears to be impacted more by major _____.
11. Immediate health and psychological well-being appears to be closely linked to daily _____.
12. Stress caused by many changes and adaptations required when a person moves to a foreign culture is referred to as "culture shock," or _____.
13. An immigrant who learns English and gets involved in American life but who also maintains his or her ties to the old cultural identity is exhibiting the pattern of adaptation known as _____.
14. Fasia and her husband are immigrants to the United States. Fasia is a homemaker and speaks only her native language and interacts only with her husband and other immigrants from her native country. Fasia is exhibiting the pattern of adaptation known as _____.
15. Maria, a teenage immigrant, has totally immersed herself in the American culture and is somewhat annoyed that her parents speak Spanish at home and want her to spend time with her other Spanish-speaking relatives rather than her new American friends. Maria is exhibiting the pattern of adaptation known as _____.
16. Ivan is a teenage immigrant who wants to be a part of his new culture, but feels rejected by the other students in his classes because of his accent. Ivan feels trapped between two cultures and is exhibiting the pattern of adaptation known as _____.

17. The patterns of adapting to a culture that usually produce a high degree of stress are separation and _____.

18. Regarding the patterns of adapting to a culture, the immigrants who tend to be only minimally stressed exhibit the _____ type of adaptation.

19. The immigrants who tend to be moderately stressed in their adaptation to a new culture are exhibiting the _____ type of adaptation.

20. People experience fewer social difficulties when they exhibit the adaptation pattern of _____.

21. One of the best antidotes for acculturative stress is a society that tolerates or even celebrates ethnic _____.

22. When one has a high stress level, a good response is to use _____ skills.

23. When psychological factors contribute to actual bodily damage, the person is experiencing a(n) _____ disorder.

24. Individuals who imagine that they have diseases would be diagnosed as _____.

25. Migraine headaches, eczema, hives, asthma, heart disease, and hypertension are examples of _____ disorders.

26. For centuries Western thinking has been dominated by a model in which health is viewed as an absence of illness and the body is seen as a complex biological machine that can break down and become ill. This model is the _____ model.

27. The model states that diseases are caused by a combination of factors and that health is a state of well-being that we can actively attain and maintain is the _____ model.

28. A person plays a role in fostering his or her own health within the _____ model.

29. The model that emphasizes that physical problems call for physical treatments is the _____ model.

30. The most common psychosomatic problems are gastrointestinal and _____ problems.

31. Sore muscles, headaches, neck aches, indigestion, chronic diarrhea, and sexual dysfunctions are health complaints that are often _____-related.

32. Psychologists have discovered that people can learn to control involuntary bodily activities by applying informational feedback to bodily control through a process called _____.

33. This informational feedback procedure holds promise as a way to treat some _____ disorders.

34. When sensors are taped to patients' hands and foreheads and the patients then learn to redirect blood flow away from the head to their extremities, they are learning to reduce the frequency of _____ headaches.

35. This technique of informational feedback through attached sensors on the body has been used with some success to control epileptic seizures and _____ in children.

36. Some researchers believe that many of the benefits of biofeedback arise mainly from general _____.

37. Other researchers stress that biofeedback acts as a "mirror" to help a person perform tasks involving _____.

38. In a landmark study of heart problems, people were classified as Type A and Type B personalities by cardiologists Meyer Friedman and _____.

39. The type that runs the greatest risk of having a heart attack is the Type _____ personality.

40. Sam would be described as hard driving, ambitious, highly competitive, achievement-oriented, and striving. Sam would be classified as a Type _____ personality.

41. The most telltale signs of the "cardiac" personality are chronic anger or hostility and _____.

42. The core lethal factor of the "cardiac personality" is _____.

43. Tanya has the habit of explosively accentuating various key words in ordinary speech, frequently finishes other people's sentences, and thinks about other things while talking to people. Tanya appears to have many of the characteristics of a(n) _____ person.

44. Although the overachieving, angry, hard-driving, hostile personality appears to promote heart disease, the factor that finally triggers a heart attack may be _____.

45. The physician who developed the three goals of reducing hostility was _____.

690

46. In order to reduce hostility, one must stop _____ the motives of others.
47. Reducing hostility involves reducing how often you feel anger and learning to be more _____.
48. Psychologist Salvatore Maddi has studied people who seemed to be unusually resistant to stress, which is referred to as a(n) _____ personality.
49. In his study of two groups of managers, Maddi found that both groups had high stress positions and both had characteristics typical of the _____ personality.
50. In the study of the two groups of managers, it was found that the group that was resistant to stress held a world view of three traits, one of which was having a personal _____ to self, work, and family.
51. The managers who were resistant to stress had a feeling of control over their lives and saw life, not as a series of threats, but as a series of _____.
52. Regarding the three traits of the hardy personality, the persons who find ways of turning whatever they are doing into something that seems interesting and important tend to be strong in the trait of _____.
53. Regarding the three traits of the hardy personality, the persons who believe that they can more often than not influence the course of events around them and not see themselves as victims of circumstance are the persons strong in the trait of _____.
54. People find fulfillment in continual growth and seek to learn from their experiences, rather than accepting easy comfort, security, and routine, when they are strong in the hardy personality trait of _____.
55. According to positive psychology, people who tend to see their lives in more positive terms, to find humor in disappointments, and look at setbacks as challenges are _____ people.
56. The emotions that tend to broaden our mental focus and tend to reduce the bodily arousal that occurs when we are stressed are _____ emotions.
57. People who expect things to turn out well, take better care of their health, and are more likely to deal with problems head-on would be classified as _____.
58. People who are more likely to ignore or deny problems would be classified as _____.

Part 1: Connections

1. ___ Social Readjustment Rating Scale (SRRS)

    a. illnesses in which psychological factors contribute to bodily damage or to damaging changes in bodily functioning

2. ___ hassle (or microstressor)

    b. personality style associated with superior stress resistance

3. ___ psychosomatic disorders

    c. person who complains about illnesses that appear to be imaginary

4. ___ hypochondriacs

    d. information given to a person about his or her ongoing bodily activities and aids voluntary regulation of bodily states

5. ___ biofeedback

    e. personality with an elevated risk of heart disease and characterized by time urgency, anger, and hostility

6. ___ medical model

    f. scale that rates the impact of various life events on the likelihood of illness

7. ___ biopsychosocial model

    g. more laid-back personality that makes it a low-cardiac risk

8. ___ Type A personalities

    h. any distressing day-to-day annoyance

9. ___ Type B personalities

10. ___ hardy personality

i. views health as an absence of illness and your body as a complex biological machine that can break down and become ill

j. views diseases as being caused by a combination of psychological, social, and biological factors

Part 2: Connections

1. ___ acculturative stress

2. ___ integration

3. ___ separation

4. ___ assimilation

5. ___ marginalization

6. ___ optimists

7. ___ pessimists

a. adopt the new culture as their own and have great deal of contact with the new culture's members

b. maintain their old cultural identity and avoid contact with the new culture

c. stress caused by the many changes and adaptation required when a person moves to a foreign culture

d. person less likely to be stopped by temporary setbacks, more likely to deal with problems head-on, and expects things to turn out well

e. reject their old culture but suffer rejection by members of the new culture

f. person more likely to ignore or deny problems and more likely to be stressed and anxious

g. maintain their old cultural identity but participate in the new culture

Check Your Memory

1. TRUE or FALSE   Disaster, depression, and sorrow often precede illness.
2. TRUE or FALSE   Life changes, both good and bad, can increase susceptibility to accidents or illness.
3. TRUE or FALSE   The Social Readjustment Rating Scale (SSRS) was developed by Salvatore Maddi.
4. TRUE or FALSE   The impact of life events is expressed in amplitudes.
5. TRUE or FALSE   Being fired from work has a higher stress rating on the SSRS than getting divorced.
6. TRUE or FALSE   Christmas has a higher stress rating on the SSRS than minor violations of the law.
7. TRUE or FALSE   Improvement in life conditions can be as costly as a decline.
8. TRUE or FALSE   There is a high chance of illness or accident when your life change unit total on the SSRS exceeds 100 points.
9. TRUE or FALSE   In a study in which participants were deliberately exposed to the virus that causes common colds, the participants that had the highest stress scores were more likely to actually get a cold.
10. TRUE or FALSE   Common hassles, or microstressors, faced by college students include driving to school, feeling discriminated against, and parents' expectations.
11. TRUE or FALSE   Frequent and severe hassles were better predictors of changes in health one or two years in the future, while major life events are better predictors of day-to-day health.
12. TRUE or FALSE   Stress caused by the many changes and adaptation required when a person moves to a foreign culture is referred to as acculturative stress.

13. TRUE or FALSE   When an immigrant maintains his or her own cultural identity but also readily participates in the new culture, the person is exhibiting the pattern of adaptation known as assimilation.

14. TRUE or FALSE   Maintaining one's old cultural identity and avoiding contact with the new culture describes the adaptation pattern known as marginalization.

15. TRUE or FALSE   The integration pattern of adaptation produces the highest amount of stress.

16. TRUE or FALSE   A big benefit of assimilating is that immigrants who embrace their new culture experience fewer social difficulties.

17. TRUE or FALSE   A person who has a psychosomatic disorder is referred to as a hypochondriac.

18. TRUE or FALSE   Psychosomatic disorders are defined as illnesses in which psychological factors contribute to bodily damage or to damaging changes in bodily functioning.

19. TRUE or FALSE   The most common psychosomatic problems involve neurological and dermatology problems.

20. TRUE or FALSE   Rheumatoid arthritis, heart disease, back aches, indigestion, and hypertension are types of psychosomatic problems.

21. TRUE or FALSE   For centuries the biopsychosocial model has dominated Western thinking and views health as the absence of illness.

22. TRUE or FALSE   The medical model states that disease are caused by a combination of factors with health being a state of well-being that we can actively attain and maintain.

23. TRUE or FALSE   Through biofeedback, people have been trained to prevent migraine headaches by redirecting blood flow away from the head to their extremities.

24. TRUE or FALSE   Biofeedback shows promise for lowering blood pressure, controlling heart rhythms, and treating insomnia.

25. TRUE or FALSE   Biofeedback was shown to have no effect in controlling epileptic seizures and hyperactivity in children.

26. TRUE or FALSE   Some researchers believe that many of biofeedback's benefits arise from general relaxation, while others believe that it acts like a "mirror" to help a person perform tasks involving self-regulation.

27. TRUE or FALSE   Genetic differences, organ weaknesses, and learned reactions to stress combine to cause psychosomatic diseases.

28. TRUE or FALSE   There appears to be "headache personalities," "asthma personalities," and "cardiac personalities."

29. TRUE or FALSE   In an eight-year follow-up of Type A and Type B personalities, it was found that the Type A's had twice the rate of heart disease than the Type B's.

30. TRUE or FALSE   Type A people believe that with enough effort they can overcome any obstacle, and they "push" themselves accordingly.

31. TRUE or FALSE   The core lethal factor of Type A behavior is time urgency.

32. TRUE or FALSE   Having a habit of explosively accentuating various key words in ordinary speech even when there is no need for such accentuation is a Type A characteristic.

33. TRUE or FALSE   When they are listening to other people talking, Type A people tend to focus intently on every word and aspect of the person's speech.

34. TRUE or FALSE   Many times, Type A people show nervous gestures or muscle twitches, such as grinding one's teeth, clenching fists, or drumming the fingers.

35. TRUE or FALSE   Although Type A behavior appears to promote heart disease, depression or distress may be what finally triggers a heart attack.

36. TRUE or FALSE   According to Redford Williams, to reduce hostility, you must stop mistrusting the motives of others, find ways to reduce how often you feel anger, and learn to be kinder and more considerate.

37. TRUE or FALSE   Hardy personalities have Type A characteristics, but seem unusually resistant to stress, so they do not develop the heart-related problems.

38. TRUE or FALSE   Competitiveness, creativity, and organization are the three characteristics that hardy personalities possess that are not shown by the Type A personalities that do develop heart disease.

39. TRUE or FALSE   When "things go wrong," hardy personalities tend to passively view themselves as victims of circumstances.

40. TRUE or FALSE   Persons strong in commitment find ways of turning whatever they are doing into something that seems interesting and important.

41. TRUE or FALSE   Happy people tend to find humor in disappointments and are strengthened by losses.

42. TRUE or FALSE   According to psychologist Barbara Fredrickson, positive emotions tend to narrow one's mental focus and increase bodily arousal.

43. TRUE or FALSE   Pessimists are less likely to be stopped by temporary setbacks and are more likely to deal with problems head-on, while optimists are more likely to ignore or deny problems.

44. TRUE or FALSE   Pessimists are less stressed than optimists because they expect problems to occur.

45. TRUE or FALSE   Pessimists tend to take better care of themselves and tend to have better health than optimists.

Critical Thinking Question

People with a hardy personality type appear to be especially resistant to which of the problems discussed earlier in this chapter?

Module 12.5 Psychology in Action
Stress Management
Survey Question: What are the best strategies for managing stress?

Language Development Guide

picture: depiction; representation
vicious: cruel; mean
"uptight": tense; anxious
sensible: reasonable; wise
remedy: cure; solution
dissipated: faded, removed, dissolved, blown away
yoga: system of breathing exercises and postures derived from a Hindu spiritual practice
outlets: means of releasing emotions
vigorous: energetic
systematically: steadily; methodically
self-generated: produced by oneself
priorities: main concerns
strike a balance: find a satisfying compromise
get blown out of proportion: to make something more important than is reasonable
"me acts": activities for oneself that you enjoy
loafing: resting
browsing: reading quickly and without effort
puttering: moving or acting aimlessly or idly
facilitates: makes possible
morale: spirit; drive; confidence
buffer: safeguard; defense
to cushion: support; to make the effect softer
befriend: take care of; help

blown it now: completely failed
knot in your stomach: nervousness
collapsing: fall to pieces emotionally
inoculation: immunization; given to prevent an illness
monologue: long, uninterrupted speech by someone
mind will go blank: person will forget the information he or she needs to remember
psyched up: excited about something
cultivating: working on; developing; improving
ups and downs: good and bad times
"Don't sweat the small stuff.": don't worry about unimportant details

Recite and Review

1. The use of behavioral strategies to reduce stress and improve coping skills is called _____.
2. A scale developed for use by college undergraduates that is similar to the Social Readjustment Rating Scale (SSRS) is the _____.
3. High scores on this scale for college students suggest that the person has been exposed to _____ levels of stress.
4. The simplest way of coping with stress is to modify the source or _____ it.
5. Stress triggers bodily effects, upsetting thoughts, and ineffective _____.
6. Once it begins, you lose, unless you take action to break the cycle of each element of stress worsening the others is the basic idea of the "_____ Game."
7. Much of the immediate discomfort of stress, which includes tight muscles and a pounding heart, is caused by _____ emotional responses.
8. Hormones, circulation, muscle tone, and a number of other aspects of physical functioning can be positively altered by regular _____.
9. For quieting the body, interrupting upsetting thoughts, and promoting relaxation, many stress counselors recommend the use of _____.
10. To improve mood and energy, one should exercise daily with the total exercise time per day that is beneficial being as little as _____ minutes.
11. Margot tightens all the muscles in a given area of her body (such as her arms) and then voluntarily relaxes them. She then does the same with other areas of her body. Margot is using the technique known as the tension-release method, or _____.
12. People visualize images that are calming, relaxing, or beneficial in other ways in a technique known as _____.
13. In using the calming images, it is important to visualize the scene as realistically as possible and to practice forming the images several times a day for about _____ minutes each time.
14. Tension and anxiety can be reduced by imagining that nearby you is a supportive friend or a loving _____.
15. Stress is often made worse by our misguided _____ to it.
16. Since stress can be self-generated, a good suggestion is to deliberately do things at a(n) _____.
17. A good suggestion to decrease stress is to try to take a fresh look at your situation, set priorities, and get _____.
18. It is important that between challenging "good stress" and relaxation you try to strike a(n) _____.
19. One should learn to say "no" to added demands or responsibilities and to set gradual, _____ goals.
20. People have better immune responses and better health when they have close, positive relationships with others, which is also referred to as _____.
21. The impact of stressful events can be cushioned by the support of family, friends, and even _____.

22. Regarding gender differences when stressed, the better use of close, positive relationships in these situations is shown by _____.
23. Regarding gender differences when stressed, the ones who tend to become aggressive or withdraw emotionally are _____.
24. Positive emotions are amplified when positive events, such as marriages, birthdays, and graduations are _____ with others.
25. Several studies have found that students, who do not have anyone to talk to about their troubles, are better able to cope with the stress of these upsetting experiences if they _____ about them.
26. Popularized by psychologist Donald Meichenbaum, the technique that involves clients learning to fight fear and anxiety with an internal monologue of positive coping statements is called

    _____.
27. Self-critical thoughts that increase anxiety are referred to as _____.
28. Reassuring and self-enhancing statements that are used to block out self-critical thoughts in stressful situations are called _____ statements.
29. The value of learning stress management skills ties back into the idea that much stress is

    _____.
30. A major antidote for stress involves knowing that a demanding situation can be _____.
31. College students who learned stress inoculation not only had less anxiety and depression, but also had better _____.
32. Anxiety and emotional distress are lowered by putting things into perspective by having a good sense of _____.

Connections

1. ___ stress management
2. ___ Undergraduate Stress Questionnaire
3. ___ "Stress Game"
4. ___ meditation
5. ___ progressive relaxation
6. ___ guided imagery
7. ___ "KIS (Keep It Simple)"
8. ___ stress inoculation
9. ___ negative self-statements
10. ___ coping statements

a. learning to let go of trivial but upsetting irritations and set realistic priorities
b. method that involves tightening all the muscles in a given area of the body and then releasing the tension
c. reassuring self-enhancing statements that are used to stop self-critical thinking
d. mental exercise for quieting the body, interrupting upsetting thoughts, and promoting relaxation
e. application behavioral strategies to reduce stress and improve coping skills
f. technique to fight fear and anxiety with an internal monologue of positive statements
g. intentional visualization of images that are calming, relaxing, or beneficial in other ways
h. designed to assess the level of stress experienced by undergraduates
i. self-critical thoughts that increase anxiety and lower performance
j. stress triggers bodily effects, upsetting thoughts, and ineffective behavior with each worsening the others in a vicious cycle

Check Your Memory

1. TRUE or FALSE Stress management involves using humanistic and psychodynamic strategies to reduce stress.
2. TRUE or FALSE The *Undergraduate Stress Questionnaire* is similar to the Social Readjustment Rating Scale (SSRS) with high scores suggesting that the person has been exposed to health-threatening levels of stress.
3. TRUE or FALSE If you are good at coping with stressors, a high score on the *Undergraduate Stress Questionnaire* may not be a problem for you.
4. TRUE or FALSE The simplest way of coping with stress is to manage the stress through relaxation.
5. TRUE or FALSE Stress triggers bodily effects, upsetting thoughts, and ineffective behavior.
6. TRUE or FALSE Much of the immediate discomfort of stress is caused by parasympathetic nervous system activating bodily arousal.
7. TRUE or FALSE As little as 30 minutes of total exercise per day, even if it occurs in short 10- to 20-minute sessions, can improve mood and energy.
8. TRUE or FALSE In a technique known as progressive meditation, people visualize images that are calming, relaxing, or beneficial.
9. TRUE or FALSE Listening to or playing music, taking nature walks, enjoying hobbies, and the like can be meditations of sorts.
10. TRUE or FALSE In progressive relaxation, a person tightens all the muscles in a given area of the body and then voluntarily relaxes them.
11. TRUE or FALSE One way to reduce stress is to try to deliberately do things at a slower pace.
12. TRUE or FALSE Getting organized and setting priorities tends to increase one's stress levels.
13. TRUE or FALSE To reduce stress, one should strike a balance between "bad stress" and "good stress."
14. TRUE or FALSE When you are "doing nothing," such as loafing, browsing, or napping, you are actually increasing your stress level.
15. TRUE or FALSE Because many of us set unrealistic and perfectionist goals, this attitude leaves many people feeling inadequate, no matter how well they have performed.
16. TRUE or FALSE People with close, supportive relationships tend to be have better immune responses and better health.
17. TRUE or FALSE Support from pets have been shown to serve as a buffer to cushion the impact of stressful events.
18. TRUE or FALSE Men tend to make better use of social support than women do.
19. TRUE or FALSE Sharing positive events in our lives tends to amplify positive emotions and to further increase social support.
20. TRUE or FALSE Studies have found that writing about one's upsetting feelings, experiences, and thoughts tends to increase one's bodily arousal rather than decreasing it.
21. TRUE or FALSE Physical symptoms and a tendency to make poor decisions are increased by negative thoughts or "self-talk."
22. TRUE or FALSE Stress inoculation involves the use of positive coping statements to control fear and anxiety.
23. TRUE or FALSE The technique of stress inoculation was developed by Hans Selye.
24. TRUE or FALSE The value of learning stress management skills ties back into the idea that much stress is self-generated.
25. TRUE or FALSE College students who learned stress inoculation not only had less anxiety and depression, but also better self-esteem.
26. TRUE or FALSE An ability to laugh at life's ups and downs is associated with better immunity to disease.

Critical Thinking Question

Steve always feels extremely pressured when the due date arrives for his major term papers. How could he reduce stress in such instances?

Final Survey and Review—Completion

Module 12.1 Health Psychology
Health Psychology—Here's to Your Good Health

Survey Questions: What is health psychology? How does behavior affect health?

1. Katie works in a field of psychology that uses behavioral principles to prevent illness and death and to promote health. Katie's field of study is called _____ psychology.
2. A century ago, people primarily died from accidents and _____ diseases.
3. Dave smokes, gets drunk on the weekend, overeats, and gets inadequate exercise. Dave is exhibiting four of the major _____ factors.
4. Detra is frequently ill, depressed, anxious, and hostile. She would be described as having a general _____ personality.
5. The Mediterranean diet is low in red meat and dairy products and high in fruits, vegetables, and _____.
6. When Garrett first went to college, he "hung out" with a group of friends who ate fast foods and played video games. After he had gained 15 pounds, he started going to the college fitness center, made friends who were into exercise and eating healthy, lost weight, and even got his couch-potato friends into healthy endeavors. Garrett's experiences illustrate how both unhealthy and healthy behaviors can be spread by _____ factors.
7. Gayle is a nurse who is helping with a community-wide education project that is designed to lessen major risk factors by informing people about stress, alcohol abuse, high blood pressure, and other topics as well as providing role models. Gayle is helping with a(n) _____ campaign.

Module 12.2 Stress, Frustration, and Conflict
Stress—Thrill or Threat?

Survey Questions: What is stress? What factors determine its severity?

8. Although stress is a natural part of life, it can be a major behavioral risk factor if it is severe or _____.
9. Stress is defined as the mental and physical condition that occurs when a person must _____ to the environment.
10. Eustress is the name given to "_____ stress."
11. Gina has just found out that she has two of her hardest exams on the same day. She feels short of breath, has an upset stomach, a loss of appetite, and a severe headache, which are symptoms of the _____ reaction of the General Adaptation Syndrome.
12. LaMecca's deadlines at work have been moved up with additional work being placed on her due to the layoffs. LaMecca is experiencing an element of stress known as _____.
13. Jimmie is a nurse in a busy emergency room. Lately, we has been feeling emotionally exhausted, detached from his fellow workers, and does not feel like he is making a "difference" even with the extra effort he puts into his work. Jimmie is experiencing the job-related stress known as _____.
14. Tommy is walking down a dark street when he hears a noise behind him. The time during which he decides whether this noise is a threat or now is called _____ appraisal.
15. When Karen lost her job due to layoffs, she immediately got her résumé together, looked through the want ads, and networked with friends. To deal with her job loss, Karen is using _____ coping.

Module 12.2 Stress, Frustration, and Conflict
Frustration—Blind Alleys and Lead Balloons

Survey Question: What causes frustration and what are typical reactions to it?

16. Having a marriage proposal rejected would be an example of a(n) _____ frustration.
17. If your sister borrows a sweater without your permission when you wanted to wear it, you are experiencing an external obstacle that would be classified as _____.
18. If you turned in your term paper late and your professor deducted points for the report being late, this would be considered a(n) _____ frustration.
19. The finding that unemployment and divorce are associated with increased child abuse would be an example of _____ aggression.
20. Stereotyped behavior occurs when persistent behavior becomes _____.

Module 12.2 Stress, Frustration, and Conflict
Conflict—Yes, No, Yes, No, Yes, No, Well, Maybe

Survey Questions: Are there different types of conflict? How do people react to conflict?

21. If you must choose between eating going swimming or playing tennis, both activities you enjoy, you are experiencing a(n) _____ conflict.
22. Dana must choose to keep coughing or take an awful tasting cough syrup that makes her feel nauseated. Having to choose between these two terrible options illustrates a(n) _____ conflict.
23. Lamont wants to ride the new rollercoaster with his friends but he is also terrified by this ride. Being both attracted and repelled by the same activity has created a mixture of feelings within Lamont, which is referred to as _____.
24. When you must choose among all the majors you could pursue in college with their strengths and weaknesses, you are experiencing (a)n _____ conflict
25. If you are thinking about going to a particular college, you may want to visit and ask if you can sit in on some classes or you may want to take a summer school course before starting in the fall. In this way, you can try out this important decision _____.

Module 12.3 Defenses, Helplessness, and Depression
Psychological Defense—Mental Judo?

Survey Question: What are defense mechanisms?

26. Research suggests that you are most likely to repress information that threatens your _____.
27. As a child, Helen Keller was unable to see or hear, but she became an outstanding thinker and writer, which illustrates the defense mechanism known as _____.
28. A student who gives logical but false reasons for turning in his assignment late is using the defense mechanism known as _____.
29. If you do not win the recent tennis competition, but you deal with this hurt by imagining the recognition that you will receive next year when you do win the competition, you are using the defense mechanism known as _____.
30. Although you are experiencing high anxiety because of a dangerous operation that your spouse is about to undergo, you deal with this anxiety by explaining the procedure and his post-surgery limitations, etc. in non-emotional terms to friends who have come to support you. You are using the defense mechanism known as _____.
31. If you channel your aggressive urges into exercises, such as kickboxing, you are using the defense mechanism known as _____.

699

Module 12.3 Defenses, Helplessness, and Depression
Learned Helplessness—Is There Hope?

Survey Question: What do we know about coping with feelings of helplessness and depression?

32. Learned helplessness is an acquired inability to avoid aversive stimuli is and to overcome _____.

33. In humans, helplessness is a common reaction to repeated _____.

34. Megan made a low test score on her first psychology test. She is less likely to experience learning helplessness if she attributes this low score to _____ factors.

35. Hal is attending a wilderness survival school that will help "immunize" him against helplessness and depression by allowing him to master difficult challenges. This program is a(n) _____ school.

36. Many times college students become depressed because they start college with little prior experience with failure but high _____.

37. When confronted with day-to-day disappointments, those students who strongly link everyday events to long-term goals, such as a successful career or high income, tend to _____.

Module 12.4 Stress and Health
Stress and Health—Unmasking a Hidden Killer

Survey Question: How is stress related to health and disease?

38. Minor but frequent stresses are called microstressors, or _____.

39. Maintaining one's old cultural identity and avoiding contact with the new culture describes an adaptation pattern with a high degree of stress known as _____.

40. Dr. Amad believes that diseases are caused by a combination of factors and that health is a state of well-being that people can actively attain and maintain. Dr. Amad supports the _____ model.

41. The most common psychosomatic problems are respiratory and _____ problems.

42. People have been able to reduce the frequency of migraine headaches through a procedure in which sensors are taped to patients' hands and foreheads and the patients then learn to redirect blood flow away from the head to their extremities. This procedure is called _____.

43. In a landmark study of heart problems, people were classified as Type A and Type B personalities by cardiologists Ray Rosenman and _____.

44. The three traits of the hardy personality are commitment, control, and _____.

45. Positive emotions tend to reduce bodily arousal and tend to _____ our mental focus.

Module 12.5 Psychology in Action
Stress Management

Survey Question: What are the best strategies for managing stress?

46. A scale developed for use by college undergraduates called the *Undergraduate Stress Questionnaire* is similar to a stress scale known as the _____.

47. Stress triggers bodily effects, ineffective behaviors, and upsetting _____.

48. Marta is visualizing images that are calming, relaxing, or beneficial in a stress management technique known as _____.

49. When faced with stress, men tend to become aggressive or to emotionally _____.

50. Merra is using a technique in which she fights fear and anxiety by using an internal monologue of positive coping statements. This technique is called _____.

Final Survey and Review—Matching

Module 12.1 Health Psychology

1. ___ health psychology
2. ___ behavioral risk factors
3. ___ disease-prone personality
4. ___ health-promoting behaviors
5. ___ refusal skills training
6. ___ life skills training
7. ___ wellness

a. personality type associated with poor health, marked by persistent negative emotions, including anxiety, depression, and hostility
b. includes regular exercise, maintaining a balanced diet, managing stress, avoiding sleep-deprivation, etc.
c. study of the ways in which behavioral principles can be used to prevent illness and promote health
d. program that teaches youths how to resist pressures to begin smoking or other health risks
e. a positive state of good health, more than the absence of disease
f. behaviors that increase the chances of disease, injury, or premature death
g. program that teaches stress reduction, self-protection, decision-making, self-control, and social skills

Module 12.2 Stress, Frustration, and Conflict

Part 1:

1. ___ stress
2. ___ pressure
3. ___ burnout
4. ___ conflict
5. ___ frustration
6. ___ scapegoating
7. ___ persistence
8. ___ psychoneuroimmunology
9. ___ general adaptation syndrome (GAS)
10. ___ psychological escape
11. ___ stereotyped behavior

a. a series of bodily reactions to prolonged stress that occurs in three stages: alarm, resistance, exhaustion
b. stressful condition that occurs when a person must choose between incompatible or contradictory alternatives
c. inflexible responding
d. stressful condition that occurs when a person must meet urgent external demands or expectations
e. Involves feigning apathy or using drugs
f. job-related condition of mental, physical, and emotional exhaustion
g. study of the links among behavior, stress, disease, and the immune system
h. habitually blaming a person or a group of people for conditions not of their making
i. the mental and physical condition that occurs when a person must adjust or adapt to the environment
j. negative emotional state that occurs when one is prevented from reaching a goal
k. involves more vigorous efforts and varied responses; usually first response when your goal is blocked

701

Part 2:

1. ___ primary appraisal
2. ___ secondary appraisal
3. ___ approach-approach conflict
4. ___ avoidance-avoidance conflict
5. ___ approach-avoidance conflict
6. ___ multiple approach-avoidance
7. ___ emotion-focused coping
8. ___ problem-focused coping
9. ___ external frustration
10. ___ personal frustration
11. ___ displaced aggression

a. being attracted to and repelled by the same goal or activity
b. your goal is blocked by conditions outside yourself that impede progress toward a goal
c. redirecting aggression to a target other than the actual source of one's frustration
d. directly managing or remedying a stressful or threatening situation
e. managing or controlling one's emotional reaction to a stressful situation
f. your goal is blocked by your own characteristics and shortcomings
g. deciding how to cope with a threat or challenge
h. choosing between two negative, undesirable alternatives
i. being simultaneously attracted to and repelled by each of several alternatives
j. deciding if a situation is relevant to oneself and if it is a threat
k. choosing between two positive, or desirable, alternatives

Module 12.3 Defenses, Helplessness, and Depression

1. ___ anxiety
2. ___ depression
3. ___ compensation
4. ___ denial
5. ___ learned helplessness
6. ___ mastery training
7. ___ repression
8. ___ sublimation
9. ___ projection
10. ___ rationalization
11. ___ reaction formation
12. ___ regression

a. justifying your behavior by giving reasonable, but false, reasons for it
b. preventing dangerous impulses from being expressed in behavior by exaggerating opposite behavior
c. acquired inability to overcome obstacles or to avoid punishment
d. attributing one's own feelings, shortcomings, or unacceptable impulses to others
e. unconsciously preventing painful or dangerous thoughts from entering awareness
f. state of despondency marked by feelings of powerlessness and hopelessness
g. counteracting a real or imagined weakness by emphasizing desirable traits or seeking to excel in the area of weakness
h. working off unmet desires, or unacceptable impulses, in activities that are constructive
i. reinforcement of responses that lead to control over a threat or one's environment
j. protecting oneself from an unpleasant reality by refusing to perceive it
k. apprehension, dread, or uneasiness similar to fear but based on an unclear threat
l. retreating to an earlier level of development or to earlier, less demanding habits or situations

Module 12.4 Stress and Health

1. ___ acculturative stress
2. ___ Social Readjustment Rating Scale (SRRS)
3. ___ hassle (or microstressor)
4. ___ psychosomatic disorders
5. ___ hypochondriacs
6. ___ biofeedback
7. ___ Type A personalities
8. ___ Type B personalities
9. ___ hardy personality
10. ___ pessimists

a. more laid-back personality that makes it a low-cardiac risk
b. illnesses in which psychological factors contribute to bodily damage or to damaging changes in bodily functioning
c. personality style associated with superior stress resistance
d. stress caused by the many changes and adaptation required when a person moves to a foreign culture
e. information given to a person about his or her ongoing bodily activities and aids voluntary regulation of bodily states
f. personality with an elevated risk of heart disease and characterized by time urgency, anger, and hostility
g. any distressing day-to-day annoyance
h. person more likely to ignore or deny problems and more likely to be stressed and anxious
i. person who complains about illnesses that appear to be imaginary
j. scale that rates the impact of various life events on the likelihood of illness

Module 12.5 Psychology in Action: Stress Management

1. ___ stress management
2. ___ Undergraduate Stress Questionnaire
3. ___ meditation
4. ___ progressive relaxation
5. ___ guided imagery
6. ___ "KIS (Keep It Simple)"
7. ___ stress inoculation

a. learning to let go of trivial but upsetting irritations and set realistic priorities
b. method that involves tightening all the muscles in a given area of the body and then releasing the tension
c. mental exercise for quieting the body, interrupting upsetting thoughts, and promoting relaxation
d. application behavioral strategies to reduce stress and improve coping skills
e. technique to fight fear and anxiety with an internal monologue of positive statements
f. intentional visualization of images that are calming, relaxing, or beneficial in other ways
g. designed to assess the level of stress experienced by undergraduates

Final Survey and Review—True or False

Module 12.1 Health Psychology
Health Psychology—Here's to Your Good Health
Survey Questions: What is health psychology? How does behavior affect health?

703

1. TRUE or FALSE   Psychologists who apply psychology to manage medical problems, such as coping with chronic illnesses work in an allied field known as behavioral medicine.

2. TRUE or FALSE   Illicit use of drugs is the second most common cause of death in the United States after smoking.

3. TRUE or FALSE   In one study, the risk of dying was cut by only about 25 percent during a 10-year period for adults who were careful about diet, alcohol, exercise, and smoking.

4. TRUE or FALSE   Maintaining a healthy diet means a person must live on a high-protein diet consisting of tofu and wheat grain.

5. TRUE or FALSE   Consuming one or two alcoholic drinks per day is generally safe for most people, especially if you remain alcohol free 2 or 3 days a week.

6. TRUE or FALSE   Only 19 percent of American adults still smoke.

7. TRUE or FALSE   Wellness can be described as an absence of disease.

Module 12.2 Stress, Frustration, and Conflict
Stress—Thrill or Threat?
Survey Questions: What is stress? What factors determine its severity?

8. TRUE or FALSE   Short-term stresses can be uncomfortable but rarely do damage, while long-term stresses can lead to physical disorders.

9. TRUE or FALSE   During the resistance phase of the General Adaptation Syndrome, the bodily adjustment to stress stabilizes and the initial symptoms disappear.

10. TRUE or FALSE   Animals in the later stages of the General Adaptation Syndrome have enlarged and discolored lymph nodes and spleens and intense shrinkage of the adrenal glands.

11. TRUE or FALSE   Predictable stress is less anxiety-provoking than not knowing when the stress will occur.

12. TRUE or FALSE   Job burnout is most likely to occur in the high pressure world of big business, such as working on Wall Street or running a company.

13. TRUE or FALSE   Secondary appraisal of a situation involves assessing your resources and choosing a way to meet the threat or challenge.

14. TRUE or FALSE   A study found that poorer women in California are more likely to die if they live in poorer neighborhoods than if they live in better-off neighborhoods because they are constantly reminded of the hope of a better life and more financial security.

15. TRUE or FALSE   People can experience stress symptoms from just watching a trauma, such as the 9/11 attacks, on television.

Module 12.2 Stress, Frustration, and Conflict
Frustration—Blind Alleys and Lead Balloons
Survey Question: What causes frustration and what are typical reactions to it?

16. TRUE or FALSE   Getting caught in a traffic jam on your way to work would be an example of a external frustration.

17. TRUE or FALSE   If you ask friends what has frustrated them recently, most will probably mention a nonsocial obstacle, such as getting caught in the rain without an umbrella or objects falling off their desk.

18. TRUE or FALSE   Excessive anger over a minor irritation is a common form of displaced aggression.

19. TRUE or FALSE   In a pattern known as scapegoating, a person or a group is blamed for conditions not of their making.

20. TRUE or FALSE   Stereotyped behavior is a type of flexible persistence that usually overcomes the barrier and ends the frustration.

Module 12.2 Stress, Frustration, and Conflict
Conflict—Yes, No, Yes, No, Yes, No, Well, Maybe
Survey Questions: Are there different types of conflict? How do people react to conflict?

21. TRUE or FALSE   The easiest conflict to resolve is avoidance-avoidance conflict.
22. TRUE or FALSE   Indecision, inaction, and freezing are typical reactions to approach-approach conflicts.
23. TRUE or FALSE   Wanting to buy a car but not wanting to make monthly payments creates an approach-avoidance conflict.
24. TRUE or FALSE   In multiple approach-avoidance conflicts, people often become so confused that they leave the field and select an entirely different alternative.
25. TRUE or FALSE   One usually regrets any decision that is tried out partially.

Module 12.3 Defenses, Helplessness, and Depression
Psychological Defense—Mental Judo?
Survey Question: What are defense mechanisms?

26. TRUE or FALSE   Many of the defense mechanisms were first identified by Sigmund Freud, who assumed they operated unconsciously.
27. TRUE or FALSE   When you take on some of the characteristics of an admired person as a way of coping with perceived personal weaknesses, you are exhibiting the defense mechanism called sublimation.
28. TRUE or FALSE   Denial is a common reaction to bad news, such as learning that a friend has died.
29. TRUE or FALSE   In reaction formation, a person fulfills unmet desires in imagined achievements.
30. TRUE or FALSE   A child who becomes homesick at summer camp and wants to go home is exhibiting regression.
31. TRUE or FALSE   Rationalization and intellectualization are the two most positive of the defense mechanisms.

Module 12.3 Defenses, Helplessness, and Depression
Learned Helplessness—Is There Hope?
Survey Question: What do we know about coping with feelings of helplessness and depression?

32. TRUE or FALSE   The researcher who studied learned helplessness in Vietnam prisoners of war and with dogs who received shocks in the shuttle boxes was B. F. Skinner.
33. TRUE or FALSE   Attributing failure to lasting, general factors, such as personal characteristics, tends to create the most damaging feelings of helplessness.
34. TRUE or FALSE   Vicarious desensitization training involves the reinforcement of responses that lead to mastery of a threat or to control over one's environment.
35. TRUE or FALSE   Making a daily schedule will only emphasize the goals that a person cannot accomplish and will push him or her deeper into depression.
36. TRUE or FALSE   Writing rational answers to self-critical thoughts can help counteract feelings of depression.
37. TRUE or FALSE   Positive events are most likely to end depression if you view these positive events realistically as stable and continuing.

Module 12.4 Stress and Health
Stress and Health—Unmasking a Hidden Killer
Survey Question: How is stress related to health and disease?

38. TRUE or FALSE   Scores on the Social Readjustment Rating Scale are expressed as life control units.
39. TRUE or FALSE   Rejecting your old culture but suffering rejection by members of the new culture describes the adaptation pattern known as integration.

40. TRUE or FALSE   People with psychosomatic disorders imagine that they have diseases.
41. TRUE or FALSE   For centuries the medical model has dominated Western thinking and views health as the absence of illness.
42. TRUE or FALSE   Biofeedback has been used with some success to control epileptic seizures and hyperactivity in children.
43. TRUE or FALSE   The core lethal factor of Type A behavior is anger or hostility.
44. TRUE or FALSE   Hardy personalities have Type B personality traits and rarely put themselves in high stressed jobs.
45. TRUE or FALSE   Optimists tend to take better care of themselves and tend to have better health than pessimists.

Module 12.5 Psychology in Action
Stress Management
Survey Question: What are the best strategies for managing stress?
46. TRUE or FALSE   The simplest way of coping with stress is to is to modify or remove its source.
47. TRUE or FALSE   Exercising for stress management is most effective when it is done daily.
48. TRUE or FALSE   Progressive relaxation involves the use of vividly visualizing realistic calming images while lying quietly with one's eyes shut and breathing deeply.
49. TRUE or FALSE   Writing down thoughts and feelings about daily events can provide some of the benefits of social support.
50. TRUE or FALSE   The technique of stress inoculation was developed by psychologist Donald Meichenbaum.

Mastery Test

1. Behavioral principles are used to prevent illness and death and promote health in the field of study known as _____ psychology.
    a. educational
    b. health
    c. community
    d. developmental

2. Jessica is a student who is frequently ill. She is often depressed or anxious, which results in her overeating, not exercising, and smoking too much. Jessica has what is referred to as a _____ personality.
    a. hypochondriac
    b. Type B
    c. behavioral-risk
    d. disease-prone

3. Petra rarely eats red meat or dairy products, but eats lots of fruits, vegetables, and fish. Petra's diet, which is considered one of the healthiest, is known as the _____ diet.
    a. Asian
    b. carb-free
    c. Mediterranean
    d. Western

4. Currently, the leading cause of preventable death in the United States is
    a. smoking.
    b. diet/inactivity.
    c. use of alcohol.
    d. infectious disease.

5. Mandy is attending a program at her high school in which she will learn techniques for stress reduction, self-protection, decision-making, goal setting, self-control, and various social skills. Mandy is enrolled in
   a. refusal skills training.
   b. life skills training.
   c. a positive psychology wellness program.
   d. a community healthy campaign.

6. For the last month at college, Martin has been pushing himself to finish various term papers and study for final exams. He has slept little and has had to eat "on the run." He finishes his exams and heads home and within two days, develops a severe cold. According to the general adaptation syndrome, Martin is in the stage known as
   a. alarm.
   b. resistance.
   c. exhaustion.
   d. recovery.

7. Asma is a researcher studying the links between a person's behavior, stress, the immune system, and disease. Asma's field of study is known as
   a. somatic immunology.
   b. psychobiological model.
   c. neuroimmunology.
   d. psychoneuroimmunology.

8. When the deadline for Jordan's presentation to the company was moved up by three days, Jordan had to work through lunch and into the evening for the next two days in order to complete the presentation. The element of stress that Jordan was experiencing is known as
   a. pressure.
   b. burnout.
   c. conflict.
   d. frustration.

9. Lately, Teresa, who is a nurse with an increased workload, has been feeling "used up" and "empty," has felt angry at her patients and her co-workers, and has felt like "she does not care anymore." Teresa appears to be experiencing the job-related condition known as
   a. pressure.
   b. burnout.
   c. conflict.
   d. frustration.

10. We answer the question "Am I okay or in trouble?" when making
    a. negative self-statements.
    b. coping statements.
    c. a primary appraisal.
    d. a secondary appraisal.

11. Shane likes to listen to his favorite music and to take long walks in the park to relax when he is stressed. Shane's method of dealing with stress involves
    a. defense mechanism.
    b. reaction formation.
    c. problem-focused coping.
    d. emotion-focused coping.

707

12. The most effective response to a controllable stressor is
    a. problem-focused coping.
    b. emotion-focused coping.
    c. leaving the field.
    d. depersonalization.

13. You are working in the lab at college, and you decide to take a break and get something to eat from the vending machine. You are so hungry and see lots of snacks you would like to eat. You put in your money and press a button, but nothing comes out. You frantically push all the buttons and the coin return and still nothing happens. Your feelings of stress are due to
    a. pressure.
    b. conflict.
    c. external frustration.
    d. personal frustration.

14. You are enjoying a movie at the theatre when two tall people sit down in front of you and begin talking to each other so that you cannot see the movie because of their heads and cannot hear the movie because of their loud chatter. In trying to view the movie, you are experiencing a
    a. nonsocial obstacle.
    b. social obstacle.
    c. double avoidance conflict.
    d. personal frustration.

15. You are laid off from your job, and you get angry at your parents and your friends at the least provocation. You are dealing with the frustration of losing your job through
    a. circumvention.
    b. sublimation.
    c. projected aggression.
    d. displaced aggression.

16. Every time the bully in third grade makes a bad grade or is punished by the teacher, he takes out his anger on the brightest, but smallest, kid in that grade by tripping or shoving him in the hall. This bully is using the small, bright kid as his
    a. projection target.
    b. scapegoat.
    c. circumvention.
    d. compensatory object.

17. When Elena's husband left her for another woman, Elena pretended that she did not care and was better off without him, even though she was deeply hurt. In dealing with her frustration, Elena's is using
    a. circumvention.
    b. displaced aggression.
    c. problem-focused coping.
    d. psychological escape.

18. A person is caught between "the frying pan and the fire" in a(n) _____ conflict.
    a. approach-approach
    b. avoidance-avoidance
    c. approach-avoidance
    d. double appraisal

708

19. Jay is offered a great job with good pay and benefits, but he will have to move a long distance from his hometown, parents, and friends. Regarding whether to take the job or not, Jay is experiencing a(n) _____ conflict.
    a. approach-approach
    b. avoidance-avoidance
    c. approach-avoidance
    d. double appraisal

20. Eduardo and Amanda are planning to purchase a new home. The realtor shows them dozens of listings on the computer as well as taking them to five of the houses. Eduardo and Amanda are experiencing _____ conflict.
    a. sublimated approach
    b. variable approach
    c. compound appraisal
    d. multiple approach-avoidance

21. You are about to teach your first class and are very nervous. In order to deal with your nervousness, you focus on the various orientation tasks on your list and on the opening to your lecture rather than on your feelings of anxiety. You are using the defense mechanism known as
    a. intellectualization.
    b. projection.
    c. rationalization.
    d. identification.

22. Sujata is often ridiculed by her boss, who also tends to give her twice as many assignments as the other employees. Although Sujata has come to hate her boss, on the surface, she acts as if she likes him very much. It is likely that Sujata is using the defense mechanism called
    a. reaction formation.
    b. Type B appraisal.
    c. problem-focused coping.
    d. sublimation.

23. A older child who reverts to infantile speech and overdependence on his parents after his younger sibling is born is showing signs of
    a. compensation.
    b. reaction formation.
    c. regression.
    d. sublimation.

24. You stayed up and watched a late movie and oversleep. When you get to work late, you tell your boss that you were late because you awoke not feeling very well but wanted to come to work to finish that important report. You are dealing with your anxiety about being late for work by using the defense mechanism known as
    a. intellectualization.
    b. rationalization.
    c. compensation.
    d. sublimation.

25. A person who monopolizes conversations and "embellishes" his stories is able to channel these irritating habits into a successful stand-up comedy act. This person is using the defense mechanism called
    a. sublimation.
    b. compensation.
    c. projection.
    d. identification.

26. Although you have tried working late, coming in early, taking on extra responsibilities, and double-checking all your work, you have never received a raise, a promotion, or a bonus for your hard work You stop trying to impress your supervisors and try to just "blend" into the work environment. You are exhibiting
    a. sublimation.
    b. reaction formation.
    c. personal frustration.
    d. learned helplessness.

27. You are helping the local high school with an Outward Bound program at the wildlife refuge. The students will be pitting themselves against difficult challenges, such as hiking, white-water canoeing, and wilderness survival. The students will learn how to face difficult challenges through this example of
    a. life skills training.
    b. mastery training.
    c. compensatory sublimation.
    d. guided imagery.

28. To combat depression, Beck and Greenberg recommend
    a. making a daily schedule.
    b. keeping a hostility log.
    c. the use of cognitive dissonance.
    d. sleeping more, including naps during the day.

29. LCUs are used to assess
    a. burnout.
    b. social readjustment.
    c. microstressors.
    d. what stage of the general adaptation syndrome a person is in.

30. Not enough money for housing, parental expectations, too many things to do, and an inflexible work schedule are examples of which of the following that are commonly faced by college students?
    a. major life changes
    b. personal frustrations
    c. hassles or microstressors
    d. acculturative stresses

31. Emilio has moved with his family to the United States. He is enjoying his new culture and his new friends and wants to be just a regular American teen. Emilio tends to get irritated with his parents when they speak Spanish at home or want him to spend all of his time with his relatives rather than his new American friends. Emilio's pattern of adaptation would be classified as
    a. marginalization.
    b. separation.
    c. integration.
    d. assimilation.

32. The pattern of adaptation that usually results in minimal stress is
    a. marginalization.
    b. assimilation.
    c. integration.
    d. separation.

33. Brent is experiencing a great deal of stress at college due to course difficulty and the amount of outside work. Brent begins to experience neck aches, stomach upset, and trouble sleeping. Brent is
    a. becoming a hypochondriac.
    b. experiencing acculturative stress.
    c. experiencing psychosomatic problems.
    d. undergoing a period of eustress.

34. Lisa's doctor views health as a state of well-being that she can attain and maintain through her lifestyle choices. Which model of explanation is her doctor relying on to diagnose and treat Lisa's disorder?
    a. medical
    b. biopsychosocial
    c. cognitive-behavioral
    d. cultural

35. Helen has been experiencing migraine headaches. In order to control these headaches, Helen's therapist attaches sensors to her forehead and hands so that Helen can learn how to voluntarily redirect the blood flow in her forehead to her extremities through a technique known as
    a. guided imagery.
    b. biofeedback.
    c. progressive meditation.
    d. mastery training.

36. There is evidence that the core lethal factor of Type A behavior involves
    a. anger and hostility.
    b. time urgency.
    c. competitiveness and ambition.
    d. accepting too many responsibilities.

37. According to Redford Williams, if you stop mistrusting the motives of others, reduce how often you feel irritated, and learn to be kinder and more considerate, you will reduce your
    a. learned helplessness.
    b. hostility.
    c. negative self-talk.
    d. pessimism.

38. Which of the following is NOT characteristic of the hardy personality?
    a. commitment
    b. a sense of control
    c. accepting challenge
    d. effective use of repression

39. The bodily effects of stress would be most effectively controlled by
    a. negative self-talk.
    b. guided imagery.
    c. mastery training.
    d. refusal skills training.

40. Coping statements are a key element in
    a. stress inoculation.
    b. the K.I.S. technique.
    c. guided imagery.
    d. progressive relaxation.

Chapter 13: Psychological Disorders

Chapter Overview

Psychopathology refers to the scientific study of mental disorders and to maladaptive behavior. Factors that typically affect judgments of abnormality include statistical abnormality, nonconformity, context, culture, and subjective discomfort. The key element in judgments of disorder is that a person's behavior is maladaptive. The result is usually serious psychological discomfort or disability and loss of control. "Insanity" is a legal term defining whether a person may be held responsible for his or her actions. Sanity is determined in court on the basis of testimony by expert witnesses.

Psychological problems are classified by using the *Diagnostic and Statistical Manual of Mental Disorders (DSM)*. Major mental problems include psychotic disorders, organic disorders, mood disorders, anxiety disorders, somatoform disorders, dissociative disorders, personality disorders, sexual or gender identity disorders, and substance-related disorders. Culture-bound syndromes are not found in the DSM and are unique to every culture. General risk factors that contribute to psychopathology include biological/physical factors, psychological factors, family factors, and social conditions. Psychiatric labels can be misused to harm and stigmatize people.

Psychosis is a break in contact with reality that is marked by delusions, hallucinations, sensory changes, disturbed emotions, disturbed communication, and personality disintegration. An organic psychosis is based on known injuries or diseases of the brain. Some common causes of organic psychosis are poisoning, drug abuse, and dementia (especially Alzheimer's disease).

Delusional disorders are almost totally based on the presence of delusions of grandeur, persecution, infidelity, romantic attraction, or physical disease. The most common delusional disorder is paranoid psychosis.

The varieties of schizophrenia all involve delusions, hallucinations, communication difficulties, and a split between thought and emotion. Disorganized schizophrenia is marked by extreme personality disintegration and silly, bizarre, or obscene behavior. Catatonic schizophrenia is associated with stupor, mutism, and odd postures. Sometimes violent and agitated behavior also occurs. In paranoid schizophrenia (the most common type), outlandish delusions of grandeur and persecution are coupled with psychotic symptoms and personality breakdown. Current explanations of schizophrenia emphasize a combination of prenatal injuries, early trauma, environmental stress, inherited susceptibility, and abnormalities in the brain. Environmental factors that increase the risk for schizophrenia include viral infection or malnutrition during the mother's pregnancy, birth complications, early psychological trauma, and a disturbed family environment. Heredity is a major factor in schizophrenia. Recent biochemical studies have focused on the neurotransmitters glutamate and dopamine and their receptor sites. The dominant explanation of schizophrenia, and other problems as well, is the stress-vulnerability model.

Mood disorders involve primarily disturbances of mood or emotion, producing manic or depressive states. Severe mood disorders may include psychotic features. In a dysthymic disorder, depression is long lasting, though moderate. In a cyclothymic disorder, people suffer from long-lasting, though moderate, swings between depression and elation. Bipolar disorders combine

713

mania and depression. In a bipolar I disorder the person swings between severe mania and severe depression. In a bipolar II disorder the person is mostly depressed but has had periods of mild mania. A major depressive disorder involves extreme sadness and despondency but no signs of mania. Major mood disorders are partially explained by genetic vulnerability and changes in brain chemistry. Other important factors are loss, anger, learned helplessness, stress, and self-defeating thinking patterns. Many women experience a brief period of depression, called the maternity blues, shortly after giving birth. Some women suffer from a more serious and lasting condition called postpartum depression. Seasonal affective disorder (SAD), which occurs during the winter months, is another common form of depression. SAD is typically treated with phototherapy.

Anxiety disorders, dissociative disorders, and somatoform disorders are characterized by high levels of anxiety, rigid defense mechanisms, and self-defeating behavior patterns. In an adjustment disorder, ordinary stresses push people beyond their ability to cope with life. Anxiety disorders include generalized anxiety disorder, panic disorder with or without agoraphobia, agoraphobia (without panic), specific phobias, social phobia, obsessive-compulsive disorders, acute stress disorder, and posttraumatic stress disorder. Dissociative disorders may take the form of amnesia, fugue, or multiple identities. Somatoform disorders center on physical complaints that mimic disease or disability. Four examples of somatoform disorders are hypochondriasis, somatization disorder, somatoform pain disorder, and conversion disorder.

Susceptibility to anxiety-based disorders appears to be partly inherited. The psychodynamic approach emphasizes unconscious conflicts as the cause of disabling anxiety. The humanistic approach emphasizes the effects of a faulty self-image. The behaviorists emphasize the effects of previous learning, particularly avoidance learning. Cognitive theories of anxiety focus on distorted thinking, judgment, and attention.

Personality disorders are persistent, maladaptive personality patterns. Sociopathy is a common personality disorder. Antisocial persons seem to lack a conscience. They are emotionally unresponsive, manipulative, shallow, and dishonest.

Suicide is a relatively frequent cause of death that can, in many cases, be prevented. Suicide is statistically related to such factors as sex, ethnicity, age, and marital status. In individual cases, the potential for suicide is best identified by a desire to escape, unbearable psychological pain, and frustrated psychological needs. People contemplating suicide narrow their options until death seems like the only way out. The impulse to attempt suicide is usually temporary. Efforts to prevent suicide are worthwhile.

Preview: Beware the Helicopters

Language Development Guide
"The helicopters. Oh no... would make good glue.": the disordered speech of a person suffering from untreated disorganized schizophrenia
survived: endured; lived through
plagued: constantly bothered, harassed
hallucinated: sensing (seeing or hearing) things that are not present
shadows of madness: gloominess of mental illness as a constant presence
incapacitated: unable to function
forged: to make or create through concentrated effort
eminent: well-known; distinguished; famous
maze of mental illness: the complex and confusing nature of mental disorders
imprisoned: held one captive; kept locked away
hint: small suggestion; trace
magnitude: large size; extent; enormity
diagnosable: able to identify

714

crazy: a slang term for a person suffering from a severe mental illness, such as psychosis

insane: a legal term meaning the inability to manage one's affairs or foresee the consequences of one's actions

cracked: broken, slang for a mental illness

lunatic: a slang term for a person with a mental illness; derived from the word "moon," since it was once believed the person was being affected by the phases of the moon

bizarre: strange; peculiar; odd

sophisticated: knowledgeable; highly developed; advanced

to draw the line: to distinguish; to show the boundary between

weigh: consider; think about

array: collection

Module 13.1 Normality and Psychopathology

Normality—What's Normal?

Survey Question: How is abnormality defined?

Language Development Guide

flagrantly: clearly, openly

lethal: deadly

reclusive: in hiding, secret

eccentric: person who is unconventional; odd; peculiar

hangs out: spend time relaxing; loafing

sanest: most mental healthy; emotionally stable

"That guy's not playing with a full deck" "Yeah, the butter's sliding off his waffle: slang expressions for a person appearing to be mentally ill

"That guy is really wacko...go postal": slang expression for being mentally ill and possibly aggressive to the point of harming others

informally: not in an official capacity

tempting: enticing; appealing

snap: quick

age-old: longstanding

impair: damage; harm

obvious: clear

tricky: difficult

deviates: differ; depart

in the same sense: similarly

where to draw the line: establish the boundary

norm: average

arbitrary: without clear rules or process

atypical: unusual; uncommon

nonconformity: Refusal or failure to abide by and follow the accepted standards of a society

prostitute: person who exchanges sex for money

"characters": odd individual; person who is significantly different in dress, mannerism, and other behaviors from average person living in that area

charming: delightful; fascinating; appealing

rigid: inflexible; unbending; stiff

conformity: abiding by or following the traditional or accepted standards of a society

social norms: unspoken rules that define acceptable and expected behavior for members of a group

offensive: disgusting; insulting

deviant: abnormal

715

kung fu: Chinese marital (warrior-type) art used for defense

stance: posture; positioning of the body

constrain: limit; hold back

facet: aspect; factor

hysterically: wildly; excitedly; uncontrollably

"bungee jumping": an activity done for entertainment that involves having a large elastic cord attached to one's feet and jumping from a tall structure, such as a bridge, crane, or hot air balloon

expose himself: show parts of one's naked body

contexts: situations; circumstances

rugby: sport similar to football

Andes: mountain range in western South America

incredibly: unbelievably

grim: bleak; harsh; horrible; gruesome

implied: suggested without being stated directly

defecate: having a bowel movement

urinate: to pass urine

housebound: confined to one's home due to physical or psychological problems

agoraphobia: an anxiety disorder in which the person is afraid to leave familiar surroundings, such as their home

virtuous: very good, moral

quite: fair amount; sizeable amount

anguish: suffering

mania: excessive excitability;

elated: overjoyed; euphoric

"on top of the world": feeling wonderful

suspect: think; believe; suppose

in practice: in reality; what actual happens

though: however

relative: compared to something else

maladaptive: problematic

dysfunction: disturbance in functioning

compulsive: irrationally driven

prime: key; major

commitment proceedings: legal actions taken in order to confine persons to a mental hospital because they are incapable of managing their affairs or are a danger to self or others due to a mental illness

declared: pronounced; stated publicly and legally

involuntarily: against their will

testimony: evidence presented

qualified: certified; licensed; an authority

Recite and Review

1. The person described in the introduction to this chapter who suffered from schizophrenia for 20 years and who became an eminent psychiatrist is _____.

2. In any given year, the percent of American adults who suffer from a diagnosable mental disorder is _____ percent.

3. Of the 33,300 Americans who committed suicide in 2006, the percent of these who had a diagnosable mental disorder was _____ percent.

4. Jim is studying mental, emotional, and behavioral disorders, which are collectively known by the term _____.
5. If you score very high or very low on some dimension, such as intelligence, anxiety, or depression, the abnormality would be defined as a(n) _____ abnormality.
6. Usually, the results of tests, such as intelligence tests, form a bell-shaped, or _____ curve.
7. On a bell-shaped curve, most people score near the _____ of the curve.
8. Drawing the line between normality and abnormality cannot be done using _____ definitions.
9. If a person's behavior does not meet the public standards for acceptable behavior, then abnormality is being defined by social _____.
10. Rather than violating accepted standards of behavior, psychopathology, in some cases, involves rigid _____.
11. Dr. Sanchez has her students perform a mildly abnormal behavior, such as walking around campus on a sunny day in a raincoat and carrying an umbrella, in order to get a sense of how "normality" in daily life is defined by social _____.
12. Before any behavior can be defined as abnormal, we must consider the behavior setting or general circumstances, in which the behavior occurs, that is, one must consider the _____ context.
13. Since what is considered normal in one country may be considered abnormal in another, one of the most influential contexts in which any behavior is judged is one's _____.
14. The idea that judgments are made with the consideration of the values of one's culture is called _____.
15. All cultures classify people as abnormal if they are consistently unpredictably in their actions and fail to _____ with others.
16. Kinsey has been experiencing panic attacks for several weeks and is very distressed by this situation. Thus, Kinsey's condition would be defined as abnormal based on _____.
17. In practice, most instances in which people voluntarily seek professional help are explained by _____.
18. The core feature of psychopathic behavior is that it is _____.
19. Psychopathic behavior often results in serious psychological discomfort, disability and an inability to maintain _____.
20. In practice, deciding that a person needs help usually occurs when the person does something (hits a person, hallucinates) that annoys or gains the attention of a person, such as a parent, teacher, or employer, who is in a(n) _____.
21. Commitment proceedings may result in the finding of _____.
22. The legal term that refers to an inability to manage one's affairs or foresee the consequences of one's actions is _____.
23. People who are declared to be not legally responsible for their actions and can be involuntarily committed to a(n) _____.
24. The determination that a person is not legally responsible for their actions is established by testimony of _____ witnesses.
25. Involuntary commitments happen most often when people are brought to _____.
26. People who are involuntarily committed are usually judged to be a danger to themselves or others, or they are severely _____.

Connections

1. ___ psychopathology

2. ___ subjective discomfort

a. failure to obey societal norms or the usual minimum standards for social conduct

b. behavior that makes it difficult to adjust to the environment or to meet the demands of day-to-day life

717

3. ___ statistical abnormality

4. ___ social nonconformity

5. ___ situational context

6. ___ cultural relativity

7. ___ maladaptive behavior

8. ___ insanity

9. ___ expert witnesses

c. scientific study of mental, emotional, and behavioral disorders; also, abnormal or maladaptive behavior

d. legal term that refers to a mental inability to manage one's affairs or to be aware of the consequences of one's action

e. recognized by a court of law as being qualified to give opinions on a specific topic

f. the idea that judgments are determined by the values of one's culture

g. private feelings of pain, unhappiness, or emotional distress

h. the behavioral setting or general circumstances in which a behavior occurs

i. abnormality defined on the basis of an extreme score on some dimension

Check Your Memory

1. TRUE or FALSE   One quarter of American adults suffer from a diagnosable mental disorder in any given year.
2. TRUE or FALSE   In 2006, about 33,300 Americans committed suicide, of whom only 20 percent had a diagnosable mental disorder.
3. TRUE or FALSE   The term psychopathology refers to both the scientific study of mental, emotional, and behavioral disorders and to the mental disorders themselves.
4. TRUE or FALSE   On a normal curve, most people score extremely high or low scores with very few people scoring near the middle of the curve.
5. TRUE or FALSE   Statistical abnormality tells us nothing about the meaning of deviations from the norm.
6. TRUE or FALSE   Statistical definitions do tell us where to draw the line between normality and abnormality.
7. TRUE or FALSE   Extreme nonconformity can lead to destructive or self-destructive behavior.
8. TRUE or FALSE   Psychopathology can involve rigid conformity.
9. TRUE or FALSE   Performing a mildly abnormal behavior is a good way to get a sense of how social norms define "normality" in daily life.
10. TRUE or FALSE   Before any behavior can be defined as abnormal, we must consider the situational context in which it occurs.
11. TRUE or FALSE   Culture is one of the most influential contexts in which any behavior is judged.
12. TRUE or FALSE   In all cultures, it is considered abnormal to defecate or urinate in public or to appear naked in public.
13. TRUE or FALSE   The idea that judgments regarding psychopathology are made relative to the values of one's culture is known as diagnostic multiculturalism.
14. TRUE or FALSE   Having a mental disorder always causes personal discomfort and anguish for the person who has the disorder.
15. TRUE or FALSE   In practice, subjective discomfort explains most instances in which people voluntarily seek professional help.

16. TRUE or FALSE The core feature of abnormal behavior is that the behavior is maladaptive.

17. TRUE or FALSE Maladaptive behavior often results in a loss of control of one's thoughts, behaviors, or feelings.

18. TRUE or FALSE In practice, deciding that a person needs help usually occurs when the person does something (hallucinates), that annoys or gains the attention of a person in a position of power (employer, teacher), and that person does something about it.

19. TRUE or FALSE Insanity is a medical diagnostic term that is applied by psychologists and psychiatrists to individuals who are in therapy.

20. TRUE or FALSE People who are declared insane are still legally responsible for their actions and are able to foresee the consequences of their actions.

21. TRUE or FALSE Within a court setting, insanity is established by testimony from expert witnesses recognized by a court as being qualified to give opinions on a specific topic.

22. TRUE or FALSE Involuntary commitments happen most often when people are brought to emergency rooms.

23. TRUE or FALSE People who are involuntarily committed are usually judged to be a danger to themselves or to others, or they are severely mentally disabled.

Critical Thinking Questions

1. Brian, a fan of grunge rock, occasionally wears a skirt in public. Does Brian's cross-dressing indicate that he has a mental disorder?

2. Many states began to restrict use of the insanity defense after John Hinkley, Jr., who tried to murder former U.S. President Ronald Reagan, was acquitted by reason of insanity. What does this trend reveal about insanity?

Module 13.1 Normality and Psychopathology
Classifying Mental Disorders—Problems by the Book
Survey Question: What are the major psychological disorders?

Language Development Guide

problems by the book: refers to the diagnosis of mental problems using the diagnostic manual of mental disorders (DSM)

billing: request for payment for debt, in this case payment for medical or counseling services

glance: quick look

"retreated from reality": moves away or withdrawn for the real world

hallucinations: imaginary sensations, such as seeing, hearing, or smelling things that don't exist in the real world

delusions: false belief held against all contrary evidence

delirium: usually a temporary state characterized by severe mental confusion and serious changes in brain function

dementia: serious mental impairment in old age caused by deterioration of the brain

agitated: state of uneasiness and violent movement

elated: overjoyed

acute: rapid and serious onset of an illness

mimic: imitate

ingrained: embedded; deeply rooted; fixed

719

borderline personality: unpredictable moods and behaviors

antisocial personality: lacking a conscience

culprits: guilty parties; problems

tic: condition characterized by abrupt, repetitive involuntary movements and sounds

Tourette's disorder: inherited disorder of the nervous system characterized by chronic motor and vocal tics

catatonic: condition characterized by a rigidness of posture and limbs alternating with catatonic excitement with constant excessive movement

schizophreniform: mental disorder with the signs and symptoms of schizophrenia but of less than six months' duration

schizoaffective disorder: mental disorder in which symptoms of a mood disorder occur along with several psychotic symptoms characteristic of schizophrenia

grandiose type: delusion or false belief that the person has some great, unrecognized talent, knowledge, or insight, such as a special relationship with an important person or with God or that they are a famous person

folie a deux: simultaneous occurrence of symptoms of a mental disorder, such as delusions, occur at the same time in two persons who are closely related, such as siblings or a husband and wife

dyssomnias: broad category of sleep disorders that involve a person having trouble getting to sleep or remaining asleep

kleptomania: obsessive need to steal without an economic reason

"unofficial": informal; not authorized; in this case not found in the official diagnostic manual

maladies: problems

folk names: informal terms used in a particular area or country for various objects, illnesses, etc.

brooding: worrying; feeling sorry for oneself; fretting

erupt: explode; lose one's temper

homicidal: murderous; killer

black magic: belief in magical spells that command evil spirits to produce supernatural effects

curse: a plea or request for misfortune to happen to someone

voodoo death: a sudden self-willed death caused by extreme fear of a curse

deceased: the dead person

futility: uselessness; pointlessness

suffocation: death due to a lack of oxygen

recede: withdraw; pull back

incites: provoke; stimulate; stir up

weeping: crying; sobbing

semen: thick white fluid containing sperm that is ejaculated from the penis by the male

nocturnal emissions: involuntary ejaculation of semen during sleep; nighttime ejaculations

empirical: gained through direct scientific observation

folk healers: unlicensed person who practices healing using herbal remedies and other methods passed down through generations

imprecise: inexact; vague; unclear

outdated: obsolete; not up to date

used loosely: not in a strict, exact sense; used informally

opponents: people who are against

bitter: resentful and angry

injustice: unfair treatment

embittered: disillusioned; resentful; angry

humiliated: disgraced; embarrassed

estranged: separated; at odds with; not speaking

melancholia: type of severe depression

apathy syndrome: lack of interest and lack of feelings and emotions

Internet addiction: compulsive use on-line

strife: conflict

social disorganization: breakdown in the structure of social relations and values resulting in the loss of social controls over individual and group behavior; has been stated as a theory that directly links high crime rates to neighborhood characteristics

Recite and Review

1. Psychological disorders are classified by using a manual called the _____.
2. The manual used by psychologists to identify mental disorders also helps them to select the best _____ for their clients.
3. A significant impairment in psychological functioning is called a(n) _____.
4. People who have "retreated from reality," suffer from hallucinations and delusions, and are socially withdrawn are suffering from _____ disorders.
5. Schizophrenia and delusional disorders are types of _____ disorders.
6. Problems caused by brain pathology, such as drug damage, diseases of the brain, brain injuries, and poisoning are referred to as _____ disorders.
7. In one type of mood disorder, people are agitated, elated, and hyperactive with these individuals being considered _____.
8. The mood disorder that involves extreme sadness and hopelessness is _____.
9. Some anxiety disorders involve feelings of panic, while others involve irrational fears called _____.
10. Two stress-related anxiety disorders are acute stress disorder and _____ stress disorder.
11. Will has been diagnosed with obsessive-compulsive disorder, which is classified as a type of _____ disorder.
12. Multiple personalities is classified as a(n) _____ disorder.
13. When people feel like they are outside of their bodies, are behaving like robots, or are lost in a dream world, they are experiencing _____.
14. Jarmon has physical symptoms that mimic disease or injury for which there is to identifiable physical cause. Jarmon has a(n) _____ disorder.
15. Paranoid, narcissistic, dependent, borderline, and antisocial are types of _____ disorders.
16. Sexual identity does not match a person's physical sex and the person may seek a sex-change operation when a person has a(n) _____ disorder.
17. Deviations in sexual behavior, such as exhibitionism, fetishism, and voyeurism, are referred to as _____.
18. Problems in sexual desire, arousal, or response are considered sexual _____.
19. A person who cannot stop using the drug and may also suffer from withdrawal symptoms, delirium, amnesia, psychosis, emotional outbursts, sexual problems, and sleep disturbances would be diagnosed with a(n) _____ disorder.
20. Tourette's disorder is classified as a(n) _____ disorder.
21. Faked disability or illness are referred to as _____ disorders.
22. Dyssomnias and parasomnias are classified as primary _____ disorders.
23. Zar, koro, and amok are examples of _____ syndromes.
24. Men in Malaysia, Laos, the Philippines, and Polynesia who believe they have been insulted are sometimes show outbursts of violence directed randomly at people and objects in a condition known as _____.
25. Among Latin Americans, insomnia, irritability, and increased sweating and heart rate due to the person being badly frightened by a black magic curse occurs during a condition known as _____.

26. Some Latin Americans also believe that when a person is frightened by the black magic curse that the fear can be so extreme that a(n) _____ death occurs.

27. When Native Americans become preoccupied with death and the deceased, a person may suffer from bad dreams, fainting, anxiety, hallucinations, and a sense of suffocation in a condition called _____.

28. In South and East Asia, when people fear that their genitals are shrinking, the folk name for this condition is _____.

29. North African and Middle Eastern societies believe that when spirits possess an individual, the person will shout, laugh, hit his or her head against a wall, sing, or weep. This folk name for this condition is _____.

30. In Indian society, the fear of the loss of semen during nocturnal emission is called _____.

31. Folk names for disturbed behavior tend to be vague. Thus, a better method for diagnosing mental disorders that is based on empirical data and clinical observations is the manual entitled _____.

32. According to American psychologists Pamela Keel and Kelly Klump, an eating disorder that is primarily a syndrome of Western cultures, such as the United states, is _____.

33. An outdated term that was once used to refer, as a group, to anxiety disorders, somatoform disorders, dissociative disorders, and some forms of depression is _____.

34. In updating the diagnostic manual in 2012, some psychologists believe that the disorder in which people's physical sex does not match their sexual identity should not be included since these individuals are well adjusted and should not be labeled as "disordered." This disorder that will probably remain a part of the diagnostic manual is _____ disorder.

35. A new mental disorder that may be added to the new edition of the diagnostic manual in 2012 is one in which a person is left so bitter after a perceived injustice that he or she cannot let it go. This proposed new disorder would be called _____ disorder.

36. Other possible disorders that may be added to the new edition of the diagnostic manual include melancholia, apathy syndrome, and _____ addiction.

37. Regarding the factors that contribute to psychopathology, inherited vulnerabilities, poor prenatal care, and exposure to toxins would be examples of _____ factors.

38. The factors that contribute to psychopathology that include stress, low intelligence, learning disorders, and lack of control or mastery are referred to as _____ factors.

39. If a person grew up in a home with severe marital strife and poor child discipline or abuse, these contributing factors to mental illness would be considered _____ factors.

40. In the development of psychopathology, poverty, stressful living conditions, overcrowding, and homelessness would be considered _____ conditions.

Part 1: Connections

1. ____ psychotic disorders
2. ____ organic mental disorders
3. ____ mood disorders
4. ____ anxiety disorders
5. ____ dissociative disorders

a. abuse of, or dependence on, psychoactive drugs
b. sexual identity does not match a person's physical sex and the person may seek a sex-change operation
c. problems caused by brain pathology, such as diseases of the brain, drug damage, injuries, or poisons
d. temporary amnesia, fugue, multiple personality, or depersonalization
e. major disturbance in emotion, such as depression or mania

722

6. ___ somatoform disorders

7. ___ personality disorders

8. ___ gender identity disorders

9. ___ paraphilias

10. ___ sexual dysfunctions

11. ___ substance-related disorders

f. sexual deviations, including exhibitionism, fetishism, and voyeurism

g. maladaptive personality pattern, such as narcissistic, dependent, or borderline

h. problems in sexual desire, arousal, or response

i. disruptive feelings of fear and apprehension with distortions in behavior, such as phobias, stress disorders, and obsessive-compulsive disorder

j. severe mental disorder characterized by a retreat from reality, by hallucinations and delusions, and by social withdrawal

k. physical symptoms that mimic disease or injury for which there is no identifiable physical cause

Part 2: Connections

1. ___ manic

2. ___ depression

3. ___ phobias

4. ___ depersonalization
5. ___ culture-bound syndromes

6. ___ biological/physical factors

7. ___ psychological factors
8. ___ family factors
9. ___ social conditions

a. people feel like they are outside their bodies, are behaving like robots, or are lost in a dream world

b. folk names for afflictions that may or may not be recognized mental disorders

c. genetic defects or inherited vulnerabilities, poor prenatal care, very low birth weight, chronic physical illness, exposure to toxic chemicals

d. characterized by sadness and hopelessness
e. severe marital strife, disordered family communication patterns, abusive parenting, or poor child discipline

f. poverty, stressful living conditions, homelessness, social disorganization, overcrowding

g. irrational fears

h. agitated, elated, and hyperactive

i. stress, low intelligence, learning disorders, lack of control or mastery

Part 3: Connections

1. ___ mental disorder

2. ___ *Diagnostic and Statistical Manual of Mental Disorders* (DSM-IV-TR)

3. ___ neurosis

4. ___ amok

a. in south and east Asia, people experience intense fear of shrinking genitals

b. Latin American affliction that includes insomnia, irritability, phobias, sweating and can result in voodoo death

c. among Native Americans, people preoccupied with death with bad dreams, weakness, dizziness, and hallucinations

d. outdated term once used to refer, as a group, to anxiety disorders, somatoform disorders,

5. ___ susto

6. ___ ghost sickness

7. ___ koro

8. ___ zar

9. ___ dhat

dissociative disorders, and some forms of depression

e. in Indian society, the fear of the loss of semen during nocturnal emissions

f. men in Malaysia who erupt in an outburst of violence randomly directed at people and objects when they feel insulted

g. helps psychologists correctly identify mental disorders and select the best therapies to treat them

h. significant impairment in psychological functioning

i. in North Africa, condition said to occur when spirits possess an individual and marked by shouting, singing, and hitting the head against the wall

Check Your Memory

1. TRUE or FALSE   Psychological problems are classified by using the Disorders and Substance-Related Manual of Diagnostic Criteria.
2. TRUE or FALSE   A significant impairment in psychological functioning is referred to as a mental disorder.
3. TRUE or FALSE   People suffering from neurotic disorders have "retreated from reality" and suffer from hallucinations and delusions.
4. TRUE or FALSE   Organic mental disorders are problems caused by brain pathology, such as drug damage, brain diseases, brain injuries, and poisons.
5. TRUE or FALSE   The diagnostic manual used to classify mental disorders does not list "organic mental disorders" as a separate category.
6. TRUE or FALSE   Some people with mood disorders alternate between mania and depression, and may also have psychotic symptoms
7. TRUE or FALSE   Multiple personalities is considered a psychotic disorder.
8. TRUE or FALSE   Obsessive-compulsive disorder is a type of anxiety disorder.
9. TRUE or FALSE   When people feel like they are outside their bodies, are behaving like robots, or are lost in a dream world, they are experiencing depersonalization.
10. TRUE or FALSE   If a person is paralyzed or blind, and there are not identifiable physical causes for these conditions, the person would most likely be diagnosed with a somatoform disorder.
11. TRUE or FALSE   Narcissistic, borderline, and antisocial are types of personality disorders.
12. TRUE or FALSE   In paraphilias, a person's sexual identity does not match a person's physical sex, so that the person may seek a sex change operation.
13. TRUE or FALSE   Sexual dysfunctions include exhibitionism, fetishism, and voyeurism.
14. TRUE or FALSE   A person with a substance-related disorder cannot stop using the psychoactive drug but may also suffer from withdrawal symptoms, delirium, dementia, amnesia, psychosis, emotional outbursts, sexual problems, and sleep disturbances.
15. TRUE or FALSE   Tourette's disorder is classified as a type of sleep disorder.
16. TRUE or FALSE   Eating inedible substances is a condition known as pica.
17. TRUE or FALSE   Dyssomnia and parasomnia are two types of factitious disorders.
18. TRUE or FALSE   Culture-bound syndromes are folk names for afflictions found in specific cultures, but which may not occur in the diagnostic manual.

724

19. TRUE or FALSE   Men in North Africa who believe they have been insulted will display random violence toward people and objects due to an affliction this culture calls koro.

20. TRUE or FALSE   In Latin America, an extreme case of susto is believed to result in voodoo death.

21. TRUE or FALSE   In the Philippines, people who suffer from zar are afraid that their genitals are shrinking.

22. TRUE or FALSE   In Indian society, dhat is the fear of the loss of semen during nocturnal emissions.

23. TRUE or FALSE   Individuals in south Asian cultures who become preoccupied with death and the deceased are said to be going amok, in which they have bad dreams, hallucinations, and a sense of suffocation.

24. TRUE or FALSE   American psychologists Pamela Keel and Kelly Klump believe that the eating disorder bulimia is primarily a culture-bound syndrome of Western cultures like the United States.

25. TRUE or FALSE   Psychosis is considered an outdated term, but was once used to describe mental disorders that would now be classified as anxiety disorders, somatoform disorders, and dissociative disorders.

26. TRUE or FALSE   New mental disorder that may also be added to the DSM-V is posttraumatic embitterment disorder, which occurs when a person is left so bitter after a perceived injustice that he or she cannot let it go.

27. TRUE or FALSE   Other possible mental disorders that may be added to the new edition of the DSM include melancholia, apathy syndrome, and Internet addiction.

28. TRUE or FALSE   Low intelligence and learning disorders are psychological conditions that have been shown to contribute to psychopathology.

29. TRUE or FALSE   Experiencing severe marital strife or extremely poor child discipline would be classified as family risk factors for a mental illness.

30. TRUE or FALSE   Poverty, homelessness, and overcrowding are classified as biological/physical risk factors for psychopathology.

Module 13.1 Normality and Psychopathology
Disorders in Perspective—Psychiatric Labeling
Survey Question: Can psychiatric labeling be misused?

Language Development Guide
maliciously: cruelly; unkindly
self-defeating personality: persistent pattern of behavior that ends of being harmful to oneself, such as being drawn to problem relationships and situations and failing to complete tasks important to life goals
penalized: punished
vain: conceited; exaggerated sense of self-importance; proud
leap to conclusions: quick to judge without having all the facts
"pseudo-patients": false patients; pretending to be a patient
pretense: deception; make-believe
phony: fake
journalist: a news reporter; writes for a newspaper or journal
jotting: brief and hurried written notes
stealth: sneakiness; secrecy
grappling: struggling; fighting
fall prey to: be harmed by

dreaded: awful; causing fear
exaggeration: overstating; greater than the actual case

Recite and Review

1. In 1840, a supposed "mental disorder" that caused slaves to run away was called _____.
2. Historically, some psychiatric terms have been applied to behaviors that are not really disorders, but only are culturally _____ behaviors.
3. The long outdated diagnosis of a type of supposed "insanity" that led one to seek a more democratic society was called _____.
4. The outdated diagnosis that was applied to a woman with a healthy sexual appetite was _____.
5. At one time, all of the following were considered disorders: childhood masturbation, lack of vaginal orgasm, homosexuality, and a personality disorder that applied mainly to women called _____ personality.
6. The most common source of bias in judging normality has been _____.
7. According to psychologist Paula Caplan, women are penalized both for conforming to and for ignoring female _____.
8. Often any woman who is emotional, irrational, and relies on others has been diagnosed with a(n) _____ personality disorder.
9. A classic study on psychiatric labeling in which several psychologists had themselves committed to mental hospitals was devised by _____.
10. The psychologists who had themselves committed feigned the symptoms of the mental disorder called _____.
11. When the psychologists, who had themselves committed to mental hospitals, started acting normally, the only people to recognize that they were phony patients were the _____.
12. To record their observations while in the mental hospital, the psychologists at first tried to jot down notes in small pieces of paper hidden in the hands. However, they soon realized their sneakiness was unnecessary and took notes on a clipboard because the hospital staff just regarded the note taking as a(n) _____ of the mental illness
13. An added problem with psychiatric labeling is that it frequently leads to prejudice and _____.
14. People who are grappling with mental illness are also harmed by being rejected and disgraced by society, which is referred to as being _____.
15. Kasey has been reading a great deal about the symptoms of the various mental disorders. She begins to notice some of these symptoms in her own behavior. Chances are, Kasey is suffering from the "_____'s disease."

Connections

1. ___ psychiatric labeling

2. ___ stigmatized

3. ___ drapetomania

4. ___ anarchia

5. ___ nymphomania

6. ___ "medical student's disease"

a. outdated term for a "disorder" that caused slaves to run away

b. outdated term for a "disorder" of women who have a healthy sexual appetite

c. outdated term for a form of "insanity" that leads one to seek a more democratic society

d. identifying people by their mental disorders

e. predictable tendency to notice in themselves the symptoms of each dreaded disease they study

f. being rejected and disgraced within one's culture

Check Your Memory

1. TRUE or FALSE   In the 1840s, slaves who ran away were said to suffer from a condition known as "anarchia."
2. TRUE or FALSE   Psychiatric terms are easily abused, and historically, some have been applied to culturally disapproved behaviors that are not really disorders.
3. TRUE or FALSE   Childhood masturbation, homosexuality, and the self-defeating personality are still considered disorders by the *Diagnostic and Statistical Manual of Mental Disorders* (DSM-IV-TR).
4. TRUE or FALSE   A woman who had a healthy sexual appetite was once said to suffer from a disorder known as nymphomania.
5. TRUE or FALSE   Gender is probably the most common source of bias in judging normality because standards tend to be based on males.
6. TRUE or FALSE   Carl Rogers and several colleagues had themselves committed to mental hospitals with a diagnosis of posttraumatic stress disorder in order to study the impact of behavioral counseling.
7. TRUE or FALSE   When the psychologists, who had themselves committed to mental hospitals, started acting normally, almost all the members of the hospital staff readily recognized the change and released them from the hospital.
8. TRUE or FALSE   An added problem with psychiatric labeling is that it frequently leads to prejudice and discrimination with the mentally ill in our culture often being stigmatized.
9. TRUE or FALSE   People who have been labeled mentally ill at any time in their lives are less likely to be hired and tend to be denied housing.
10. TRUE or FALSE   People who have been labeled mentally ill are more likely to be falsely accused of a crime.
11. TRUE or FALSE   The "paranoid delusional disorder" refers to the predictable tendency for medical and psychology student to notice in themselves the symptoms of each dreaded disease that they study.
12. TRUE or FALSE   In many cases, pathological behavior is an exaggeration of normal defenses and reactions.

Module 13.2 Psychosis, Delusional Disorders, and Schizophrenia

Psychotic Disorders—The Dark Side of the Moon

Survey Question: What are the general characteristics of psychotic disorders?

Language Development Guide

The Dark Side of the Moon: name of the rock group Pink Floyd's album with the songs having
    lyrics regarding insanity, insecurity, and death
striking: dramatic, obvious
shared views of reality: observations and beliefs regarding the real world that are held by a
    majority of the individuals within a culture
"split" from reality: withdraw from the real world through hallucinations and/or delusions
contradict: disagree with
emitting: giving off
foul: disgusting
"out to get them": trying to harm them
collide: crash; smash into
command: order; direct; demand
primitive: belonging to an earlier time in human development
garbled: mixed up, difficult to understand

chaotic: disordered; confused; muddled
word salad: using real words and perhaps some kinds of grammar but not making any sense;
        scrambled language; like a tossed salad
disintegration: breakdown
coordinated: matched; corresponding
fragmented: disjointed; split into many pieces
in a sense: in one way of looking at it
organic: involving the physical body
reserved: set aside; kept back
deterioration: diminish in function
atrophy: wasting away; withering; shriveling
mute: unable to speak
devastating: destructive; damaging; distressing

Recite and Review

1. The group of disorders that are characterized by a loss of contact with shared views of reality are the _____ disorders.
2. People who hold false beliefs that they insist are true, regardless of how much the facts contradict them, are experiencing _____.
3. If you see, hear, or smell things that do not exist in the real world, you are experiencing _____.
4. Dean has false beliefs that he has committed the "unforgivable sin" and is a horrible, awful person. Dean is experiencing _____ delusions.
5. Caden believes that her body is "rotting away" and is emitting a foul odor. Caden is experiencing _____ delusions.
6. Samuel tells everyone at the mental hospital that he is John Wayne's son and actually believes that he is, although he is not. Samuel is exhibiting a delusion of _____.
7. Tom falsely believes that his mind is completely controlled by the commercials he watches on television, so much so that he has to run out immediately and buy everything he sees on television and donate money to every charity. Tom is exhibiting a delusion of _____.
8. Roy falsely believes that his co-workers are plotting to have him fired and that they convinced his wife to leave him. Roy is exhibiting delusions of _____.
9. Dion believes that she receives special coded messages from the television that allows her to predict the future. Dion is experiencing delusions of _____.
10. The most common type of psychotic hallucination involves _____.
11. Sometimes psychotic patients display a condition in which the face is frozen in a blank expression, which is referred to as a(n) _____.
12. Many times psychotic symptoms are the only way that some patients can say, "I need help." Thus, these symptoms can be thought of as a primitive type of _____.
13. Psychotic speech tends to be so garbled and chaotic that it sounds like a "word _____."
14. When a person's thoughts, actions, and emotions are no longer coordinated, we say that _____ has occurred.
15. Withdrawing from family members, engaging in self-destructive behavior, being persistently despondent, expressing bizarre beliefs, or hearing unreal voices are all warning signs of psychotic disorders and major _____ disorders.
16. The general term that is usually reserved for problems involving clear-cut brain injuries or diseases is _____ psychosis.
17. Young children may be tempted to eat paint flakes because they taste sweet but eating these flakes can result in the children becoming psychotic or intellectually disabled due to _____ poisoning.

728

18. The Mad Hatter in Lewis Carroll's *Alice's Adventures in Wonderland* is modeled after the hat makers of the eighteenth and nineteenth centuries, who were developed brain damage and psychosis because of being heavily exposed to _____.

19. The most common organic problem is a serious mental impairment that occurs in old age and is caused by deterioration of the brain due to repeated strokes, circulatory problems, or general shrinkage and atrophy of the brain. This serious mental impairment is called

    _____.

20. The mental disorder that appears to be caused by unusual webs and tangles in the brain that damage areas important for memory and learning is _____.

21. Although psychotic symptoms can occur in some mood disorders, the two major types of psychosis are schizophrenia and _____ disorders.

Part 1: Connections

1. ___ psychosis
2. ___ delusions
3. ___ hallucinations
4. ___ flat affect
5. ___ "word salad"
6. ___ personality disintegration

7. ___ organic psychosis
8. ___ dementia

9. ___ Alzheimer's disease

a. condition in which the face is frozen in a blank expression
b. any serious mental impairment in old age caused by physical deterioration of the brain
c. speech garbled and chaotic
d. false belief held against all contrary evidence
e. any mental disorder caused by a clear-cut brain injury or disease
f. age-related disease characterized by memory loss, mental confusion, and, in its later stages, a nearly total loss of mental abilities; caused by webs and tangles in the brain
g. loss of contact with shared views of reality
h. imaginary sensation, such as seeing, hearing, or smelling things that do not exist in the real world
i. person's thoughts, actions, and emotions are no longer coordinated

Part 2: Connections

1. ___ depressive delusions

2. ___ somatic delusions
3. ___ delusions of grandeur
4. ___ delusions of influence

5. ___ delusions of persecution

6. ___ delusions of reference

a. believing your body is "rotting away" or that it is emitting foul odors
b. thinking one is extremely important
c. believing that others are "out to get them"
d. feeling as if one is being controlled by others or by unseen forces
e. giving great personal meaning to unrelated events
f. feeling that one has committed horrible crimes or sinful deeds

Check Your Memory

1. TRUE or FALSE   Psychosis reflects a loss of contact with shared views of reality.
2. TRUE or FALSE   False beliefs that a person holds to even when presented with contradictory evidence are known as cognitive hallucinations.

3. TRUE or FALSE   Delusions involve imaginary sensations, such as hearing voices or feeling "insects crawling" on one's skin.

4. TRUE or FALSE   When a person has depressive delusions, people feel that they have committed horrible crimes or sinful deeds.

5. TRUE or FALSE   A delusion of grandeur involves a person thinking that others are "out to get him or her."

6. TRUE or FALSE   A man who thinks that television programs are giving him a special personal message is experiencing a delusion of reference.

7. TRUE or FALSE   Delusions of influence involve thinking that one's body is "rotting away" or is emitting foul odors.

8. TRUE or FALSE   The most common hallucination is a sensory change, such as anesthesia or extreme sensitivity to heat, cold, pain, or touch.

9. TRUE or FALSE   When a person with psychosis displays a flat affect, they are usually hyperemotional, wildly elated, and animated.

10. TRUE or FALSE   Brain images from psychotic patients with "frozen faces" reveal that their brains are processing emotions abnormally.

11. TRUE or FALSE   Some psychotic symptoms can be thought of as a primitive type of communication and may be the only way a person with psychosis can indicate that they "need help."

12. TRUE or FALSE   Psychotic speech tends to be so garbled and chaotic that it sometimes sounds like a "word salad."

13. TRUE or FALSE   Personality disintegration occurs when a person's thoughts, actions, and emotions are no longer coordinated.

14. TRUE or FALSE   Expressing bizarre thoughts, hearing unusual voices, and engaging in self-destructive behavior are warning signs of both psychotic disorders and major mood disorders.

15. TRUE or FALSE   The general term familial psychosis is usually reserved for problems involving clear-cut brain injuries or diseases.

16. TRUE or FALSE   Children can become psychotic or intellectually disabled from eating leaded paint flakes or breathing leaded paint powder.

17. TRUE or FALSE   Children with higher levels of lead in their blood are more likely to be arrested as adults for criminal offenses.

18. TRUE or FALSE   The Mad Hatter in Lewis Carroll's *Alice's Adventures in Wonderland* is modeled after the hat makers of the eighteenth and nineteenth centuries, who were heavily exposed to mercury, which resulted in brain damage and psychosis.

19. TRUE or FALSE   A serious mental impairment in old age caused by deterioration of the brain is known as somatization.

20. TRUE or FALSE   When a person has dementia, this condition can be caused by circulatory problems, repeated strokes, general shrinkage and atrophy of the brain, or by Alzheimer's disease.

21. TRUE or FALSE   Alzheimer's disease appears to be caused by unusual webs and tangles in the brain that damage areas important for memory and learning.

22. TRUE or FALSE   Genetic factors can increase the risk of developing Alzheimer's disease.

23. TRUE or FALSE   Two major types of psychosis are somatoform disorders and dissociative disorders.

730

Module 13.2 Psychosis, Delusional Disorders, and Schizophrenia
Delusional Disorders—An Enemy Behind Every Tree
Survey Question: What is the nature of a delusional disorder?

Language Development Guide
an enemy behind every tree: those with paranoid delusions see people "out to get them" everywhere

unmistakable: obvious; instantly recognizable

erotic: concerning sexual love and desire

celebrity: famous person; movie star

stalker: person who persistently and obsessively follows, harasses, calls the person being stalked on the phone, sends unwanted mail or gifts, or watches your home creating fear in the person being stalked

grandiose: exaggerated greatness

deluded: to deceive the mind

imposter: phony; fraud; pretender

all-consuming: using all of one's time and energy

unfounded: not based on fact

unfaithful: being disloyal, in this case being sexually disloyal to one's spouse or adulterous

conspired against: plotted against; secretly plan with someone to do something bad to another person

spied on: observed; examine; search another

maligned: reputation damaged

parasites: an animal or plant that obtains its food by living in or on a host without killing the host and without the host benefiting

defective: flawed; imperfect; faulty

far-fetched: difficult to believe

self-styled: a position or talent claimed by oneself about oneself often with any justification

reformer: to improve by altering a situation, such as an organization or a government

crank letter: a hostile, usually anonymous, written message

conspiracy theorists: person who explains events as being the result of a secret plot by powerful persons, such as government officials

"UFO abductees": people who believe that they have been taken secretly against their will by nonhuman space beings and subjected to scientific procedures

and the like: and other similar delusional beliefs

on guard: protect themselves

woven: created; composed; put together

"what's really going on": the "real" truth

Mafia: criminal organization with family ties to Sicily that operates within the United States

"self-defense": attacking another person in order to protect oneself against attack

Recite and Review
1. People with delusional disorders usually do not suffer from the psychotic symptoms of emotional excesses, personality disintegration, or _____.
2. The presence of deeply held false beliefs is the main feature of _____ disorders.
3. Lenny loves the actress Sandra Bullock and has her name tattooed on his shoulder. He is convinced that she also loves him because of the picture the actress's publicity department sent him when he wrote to her. Lenny has a(n) _____ type of delusion.
4. David believes that he is a special and gifted prophet and is the only person who can save Western society from their sins. David has a(n) _____ type of delusion.

731

5. Nadine is so thoroughly convinced that her husband is "cheating" on her that she goes to his office at least three times a day, listens in on his phone conversations, and reads all his e-mail. Although her husband is at home every night and Nadine has found no evidence of his infidelity, she is consumed by this belief that he is being unfaithful. Nadine is suffering from a(n) _____ type of delusion.
6. Tony believes that the government has formed a conspiracy against "honest taxpayers" like himself and gather information about these people through the computer, television, and cell phone. He is convinced that his boss and the new secretary "they" hired for him are in on this conspiracy. Tony is suffering from _____ type delusions.
7. Although the doctors have run many tests and have assured Marian that "parasites" are not the cause of her gastrointestinal problems, Marian is still convinced that she has a parasite and keeps looking on the internet to find information to give her doctors. Marian is exhibiting a(n) _____ type of delusion.
8. People who have delusions about experiences that could happen in real-life, such as believing that someone is trying to steal their money, would be more likely to have a(n) _____ disorder.
9. People who have bizarre delusions, such as believing that space aliens have replaced all of their internal organs with electronic monitoring devices, would be more likely to have _____.
10. The most common delusional disorder that centers on delusions of persecution is _____.
11. Many self-styled reformers, crank letter writers, conspiracy theorists, and "UFO abductees," suffer from _____ delusions.
12. Because anyone suggesting that they should see a psychologist is just a part of the "conspiracy," it is difficult to treat people suffering from _____ delusions.
13. Delusional disorders are rare with the most common form of psychosis being _____.

Connections

1. ____ delusional disorders
2. ____ erotomanic type
3. ____ grandiose type
4. ____ jealous type
5. ____ persecutory type
6. ____ somatic type
7. ____ paranoid psychosis

a. having an all-consuming, but unfounded, belief that your spouse or lover is unfaithful
b. most common delusional disorder centered especially on delusions of persecution
c. delusion that your body is diseased, rotting, or infested with parasites, or parts of their bodies are defective
d. delusion that one is loved by another person, especially by someone famous or of higher status
e. psychosis marked by severe delusions of grandeur, jealousy, persecution, or similar preoccupations, but with no hallucinations
f. delusion that you are a famous person, have a special talent, or a special relationship with an important person
g. delusion that you are being conspired against, cheated, spied on, followed, maligned, or harassed

Check Your Memory

1. TRUE or FALSE   People with delusional disorders often suffer from hallucinations, emotional excesses, and personality disintegration.
2. TRUE or FALSE   A celebrity stalker who believes that a famous actress is in love with him most likely suffers from an erotomanic type of delusion.

3. TRUE or FALSE   People who believe that parts of their body are defective suffer from a persecutory type of delusion.

4. TRUE or FALSE   People who believe that their spouse or lover is being unfaithful when all evidence is to the contrary are said to being experiencing a somatic type of delusion.

5. TRUE or FALSE   People with delusional disorder tend to have delusions about experiences that could occur in real life, while people with schizophrenia have more bizarre delusions.

6. TRUE or FALSE   The most common delusional disorder is called erotomanic psychosis and centers on jealous type delusions.

7. TRUE or FALSE   People who believe in conspiracy theories and individuals who write hundreds of letters to newspapers complaining about the "government" often suffer from paranoid delusions.

8. TRUE or FALSE   It is relatively easy to treat people with paranoid delusions and consists of showing them reliable evidence that disproves their "conspiracy theories."

9. TRUE or FALSE   Although persons with paranoid psychosis are not necessarily dangerous, they may be moved to violence by their irrational fears and their attempts at "self-defense."

10. TRUE or FALSE   Delusional disorders are rare with the most common form of psychosis being schizophrenia.

Module 13.2 Psychosis, Delusional Disorders, and Schizophrenia
Schizophrenia—Shattered Reality
Survey Questions: What forms does schizophrenia take? What causes it?

Language Development Guide

shattered: broken into pieces; seriously damaged

blunted: dulled

"inserted": put in

"sensory filter": processes, identification, and separation of information

jumble: clutter; mixed up

incoherence: lack of clearness

grossly: disgustingly

bizarre: unusual, strange

stupor: in a daze; reduced ability to make any sense; reduced consciousness

posturing: adopting a statue-like posture

mutism: being unable or unwilling to speak

agitated: nervous; restless

preoccupation: fixation; obsession

prominent: major

intake interview: first session with a therapist

grotesque: distorted and unnatural; abnormal and ugly

obscenities: profane, vulgar words

Kremlin: the building where the Russian government is housed in Moscow

infernally: extremely; hellishly

Communism: form of socialistic government that abolishes private ownership

limited: small in scope

turmoil: confusion; unrest

tucked: placed; put; stuck

"reach": to be understood by someone

unconvincing: not inspiring belief

cosmic: pertaining to the universe

brutally: viciously

sensationalized: presented in a manner that is intended to arouse strong interest by including exaggerated or shocking details

intoxicated: experiencing the effects of a drug, especially alcohol (drunk)

perplexed: puzzled; hard to understand

riddle: puzzling question posed as a problem to be solved

enigma: mystery that cannot be explained

malnutrition: condition that develops when the body does not get the right amount of vitamins, minerals, and other nutrients that are needed to maintain healthy functioning of the body

complications: problems; difficulties

prevail: predominate; exist in a large amount

laden: loaded; weighed down

prying: snooping; interfering; meddling

chaotic: confused and disordered

quadruplets: four babies being born from the same mother at the same time

mutations: changes in the DNA sequence caused by viruses, radiation, or other environmental sources

alleviate: heal, relieve

tantalizing: tempting; inviting

ensuing: occurring next

fissuring: cracks, in this case in the brain

withered: shriveled up

Recite and Review

1. Schizophrenia is marked by delusions, hallucinations, apathy, and a "split between thought and _____.

2. Schizophrenic delusions may include the idea that the person's thoughts and actions are being controlled, that these thoughts have been inserted or removed, or that these thoughts can be heard by others because they are being _____.

3. Schizophrenia involves withdrawal from contact with others, a loss of interest in external activities, an inability to deal with daily events, and a breakdown of _____.

4. In any given year, the number of people who have schizophrenia is one person in _____.

5. Many schizophrenic symptoms appear to be related to the difficulty that people with schizophrenia have in focusing on one item of information at a time, or a problem with _____.

6. People with schizophrenia are overwhelmed by a jumble of thoughts, sensations, images, and feelings because their brains have an impaired "_____."

7. Schizophrenia that is marked by incoherence, grossly disorganized behavior, bizarre thinking, and flat or grossly inappropriate emotions is the _____ type of schizophrenia.

8. The type of schizophrenia that involves a stupor condition in which odd positions may be held for hours or even days is the _____ type.

9. Schizophrenia that is marked by a preoccupation with delusions or by frequent auditory hallucinations related to a single theme, especially grandeur or persecution is referred to as the _____ type of schizophrenia.

10. When prominent psychotic symptoms are present, but the person does not have specific features of the catatonic, disorganized, or paranoid types of schizophrenia, a diagnosis is made of _____ type of schizophrenia.

11. Disorganized schizophrenia is sometimes called _____ schizophrenia.

12. The disorder that comes closest to matching the stereotyped images of "madness" seen in movies is the _____ type.
13. Samuel appears to be struggling desperately to control his inner turmoil with these periods of rigidity and posturing being similar to the tendency to "freeze" at times of great emergency or panic. Samuel has the _____ type of schizophrenia.
14. The most common schizophrenic disorder is _____ schizophrenia.
15. The type of schizophrenia is rare in Europe and North American is _____.
16. Mutism, along with a marked decrease in responsiveness to the environment, makes it difficult to "reach" patients with _____ schizophrenia.
17. James Huberty, who brutally murdered 21 people at a McDonald's restaurant in San Ysidro, California had felt persecuted and cheated by life, had been hearing hallucinated voices, and told his wife he was "going hunting humans." Psychologists have diagnosed Huberty with _____ schizophrenia.
18. According to research, mentally ill individuals are no more prone to violence than are normal individuals if they are not substance abusers and are not currently experiencing _____ symptoms.
19. The risk of violence from mental patients is actually many times lower than that from persons who have the following attributes: young, male, poor, and _____.
20. Because patients may shift from one pattern to another at different times, many patients, therefore, are simply classified as suffering from _____ schizophrenia.
21. Children are more likely to become schizophrenic if their mothers, during the middle of their pregnancy were exposed to either the flu virus or to _____.
22. There is an increased risk of the infant developing schizophrenia because of disturbed brain development if the mother has complication at the time of birth or if she experienced _____ during pregnancy.
23. As children, victims of schizophrenia were often exposed to sexual abuse, divorce, and other forms of early psychological _____.
24. The families in which people with schizophrenia grow up are often laden with guilt, prying, criticism, negativity, and emotional attacks, which are considered deviant _____ patterns.
25. It appears that some individuals inherit the potential for schizophrenia, which means they are more _____ to developing it.
26. If one identical twin becomes schizophrenic, then the percent chance of the other twin becoming schizophrenic is _____ percent.
27. Since children of older fathers are more likely to develop schizophrenia because these aging male reproductive cells have genetic _____.
28. Psychotic symptoms have been alleviated by the same drugs used to treat LSD overdoses, which are called _____.
29. Research suggests that the schizophrenic brain produces some substances similar to mind-altering, or _____ drugs.
30. The flood of unrelated thoughts, feelings, and perceptions, which may account for the voices, hallucinations, and delusions of schizophrenia, appear to be due to an overabundance of the neurotransmitter called _____.
31. People who take the hallucinogenic drug PCP often have symptoms that mimic schizophrenia because PCP affects the neurotransmitter _____.
32. CT scans and MRI scans reveal that the brains of people with schizophrenia have

_____.
33. CT scans have also revealed that the schizophrenic brain has wider-than-normal surface

_____.
34. MRI scans indicate that schizophrenic people tend to have enlarged fluid-filled spaces within the brain, which are called _____.

35. Unlike normal brains, the schizophrenic brain may be unable to continually create new neurons to replace old ones that die through the process known as _____.

36. PET scans of schizophrenic brains have shown that the brain activity tends to be abnormally low in the _____ lobes.

37. The affected areas in the schizophrenic brains are crucial for regulating motivation, emotion, perception, actions, and _____.

38. The right mix of inherited potential and environmental stress brings about mind-altering changes in brain chemicals and brain structures to produce psychotic disorders as well as other forms of psychopathology, such as depression and anxiety, according to the _____ model.

Part 1: Connections

1. ___ schizophrenia

   a. schizophrenia marked by a preoccupation with delusions or by frequent auditory hallucinations related to a single theme, especially grandeur or persecution

2. ___ disorganized schizophrenia

   b. overactivity in this neurotransmitter system related to schizophrenia

3. ___ catatonic schizophrenia

   c. inability to speak

4. ___ paranoid schizophrenia

   d. schizophrenia with prominent psychotic symptoms but lacking the specific features of the other types

5. ___ undifferentiated schizophrenia

   e. psychosis characterized by delusions, hallucinations, apathy, and a "split" between thought and emotion

6. ___ mutism

   f. attributes mental disorders such as psychosis to a combination of environmental stress and inherited susceptibility

7. ___ dopamine systems

   g. schizophrenia marked by incoherence, confused behavior, bizarre thinking, and flat or grossly inappropriate emotions

8. ___ stress-vulnerability model

   h. schizophrenia marked by stupor, rigidity, unresponsiveness, posturing and, sometimes, agitated purposeless behavior

Part 2: Connections

1. ___ rubella

   a. German measles with children of mothers who contract it more likely to develop schizophrenia

2. ___ psychological trauma

   b. wider than normal surface fissuring shown on computer-enhanced X-ray images of the brains of persons with schizophrenia

3. ___ deviant communication patterns

   c. stress alters this neurotransmitter, which in turn alters dopamine systems

4. ___ psychedelic

   d. mind-altering, usually produced by drugs

5. ___ biochemical abnormalities

   e. psychological injury or shock, such as that caused by violence, abuse, neglect, and separation

736

6. ___ glutamate
7. ___ CT scans of schizophrenic brains
8. ___ MRI scans of schizophrenic brains
9. ___ PET scans of schizophrenic brains

f. enlarged ventricles in brains of persons with schizophrenia shown on these 3-D scans

g. cause related to disturbances in brain chemicals or neurotransmitters

h. abnormally low activity shown in frontal lobes of persons with schizophrenia when radioactive sugar solution is used

i. interacting in ways that are laden with guilt, prying, criticism, negativity, and emotional attacks

Check Your Memory

1. TRUE or FALSE   Persons with schizophrenia have two or more personalities.
2. TRUE or FALSE   Schizophrenic delusions may include the idea that the person's thoughts are being broadcast to the world or that their thoughts have been removed.
3. TRUE or FALSE   Schizophrenia involves withdrawal from contact with others, a loss of interest in external activities, a breakdown of personal habits, and an inability to deal with daily events.
4. TRUE or FALSE   Schizophrenia is relatively rare with only one person in 100,000 having schizophrenia in any given year.
5. TRUE or FALSE   Many schizophrenic symptoms appear to be related to problems with selective attention.
6. TRUE or FALSE   The disorganized type of schizophrenia is marked by stupor; rigidity; unresponsiveness; posturing; mutism; and, sometimes, agitated, purposeless behavior.
7. TRUE or FALSE   The catatonic type of schizophrenia is marked by a preoccupation with delusions or by frequent auditory hallucinations related to a single theme, especially grandeur or persecution.
8. TRUE or FALSE   Schizophrenia in which there are prominent psychotic symptoms, but none of the specific features of the other three types is referred to as undifferentiated schizophrenia.
9. TRUE or FALSE   The disorder known as disorganized schizophrenia is sometimes called hebephrenic schizophrenia.
10. TRUE or FALSE   The disorder that comes closest to matching the stereotyped images of "madness" seen in movies is catatonic schizophrenia.
11. TRUE or FALSE   Disorganized schizophrenia typically develops in adolescence or young adulthood.
12. TRUE or FALSE   The paranoid type of schizophrenia is rare in Europe and North America.
13. TRUE or FALSE   Chances of improvement for people suffering from disorganized schizophrenia is limited with their social impairment being usually extreme.
14. TRUE or FALSE   If a mentally ill individual is not abusing drugs or is not actively psychotic, then he or she is no more prone to violence than are normal individuals.
15. TRUE or FALSE   The risk of violence from mental patients is many times lower than that from persons who are young, male, poor, and intoxicated.
16. TRUE or FALSE   Diagnosing types of schizophrenia is fairly subjective, which is why the DSM-V may no longer make distinctions among the four subtypes of schizophrenia.

17. TRUE or FALSE   When a woman is exposed to either the flu virus or to rubella during the middle of her pregnancy, her unborn child has a greater risk of developing schizophrenia.

18. TRUE or FALSE   Psychological trauma in one's childhood, such as sexual abuse or divorce and death of family members has not been shown to increase the risk of developing schizophrenia.

19. TRUE or FALSE   The families of those who develop schizophrenia exhibit deviant communication patterns that are laden with guilt, prying, criticism, negativity, and emotional attacks.

20. TRUE or FALSE   When the children of schizophrenic parents are raised away from their chaotic home environment, their risk of developing schizophrenia is the same as children whose parents are not schizophrenic.

21. TRUE or FALSE   If you inherit a potential for developing schizophrenia, you will definitely become schizophrenic by young adulthood.

22. TRUE or FALSE   The older a man is (even if he does not suffer from schizophrenia) when he fathers a child, the more likely it is that the child will develop schizophrenia.

23. TRUE or FALSE   The same drugs called phenothiazines that are used to treat LSD overdoses tend to cause psychotic symptoms.

24. TRUE or FALSE   Many researchers believe that schizophrenia is related to overactivity in the brain's acetylcholine systems.

25. TRUE or FALSE   The neurotransmitter glutamate also appears to be related to schizophrenia.

26. TRUE or FALSE   CT scans show that the schizophrenic brain has narrower-than-normal surface fissuring.

27. TRUE or FALSE   One possibility that causes the atrophied brains of schizophrenic patients is that the schizophrenic brain is unable to continually create new neurons to replace old ones that have died.

28. TRUE or FALSE   MRI scans indicate that schizophrenia brains have enlarged ventricles.

29. TRUE or FALSE   PET scans show that brain activity tends to be abnormally high in the frontal lobes of the schizophrenic brain.

30. TRUE or FALSE   When high vulnerability combines with moderate or high stress, the person "crosses the line" and suffers from psychopathology, according to the stress-vulnerability model.

Critical Thinking Questions

1. Researchers have found nearly double the normal number of dopamine receptor sites in the brains of schizophrenics. Why might that be important?

2. Enlarged surface fissures and ventricles are frequently found in the brains of chronic schizophrenics. Why is it a mistake to conclude that such features cause schizophrenia?

Module 13.3 Mood Disorders

Mood Disorders—Peaks and Valleys

Survey Questions: What are mood disorders? What causes them?

Language Development Guide

Module 12.4

bouts: spells; attacks

bleak: miserable; gloomy

ride a wave: to be carried by
down and out: without physical strength and stamina; incapacitated
dejection: misery; unhappiness
alternates: rotates; changes back and forth
expansive: unrestrained; outgoing; extroverted
debilitating: weakening; devastating; incapacitating
subdued: passive; quiet; unresponsibe
elated: very happy
bankrupt: being unable to pay one's debts due to a lack of money
binge: a period of uncontrolled overindulgence usually in pleasurable activities, such as food, drink, shopping, or sex
promiscuous: nonselective choice of sexual partners for casual sex
despondent: hopeless; downhearted; downcast
brag: boast; show off
strain: nervous tension; stress
postpartum: occurring immediately after birth
"third-day blues": mild depression three days after giving birth
cabin fever: extreme irritability and restlessness resulting from living in isolation or within a confined indoor area for a long period
craving: intense desire for some particular thing, usually a food item
carbohydrates: sugars and starches
drowsy: sleepy
foreboding: feeling of evil or misfortune to come
secreted: released
doses: measured portions
simulates: imitates
hearty: plentiful; nourishing; substantial
tropics: part of the Earth's surface characterized by a hot climate

Recite and Review

1. Among the most serious of all psychological conditions are the major disturbances in emotion called _____ disorders.
2. Sadness and despondency are exaggerated, prolonged, and unreasonable with the person being dejected and hopeless, and unable to feel pleasure when suffering from _____ disorders.
3. People go both "up" and "down" emotionally when they are suffering from _____ disorders.
4. If a person is mildly depressed for at least two years, the problem is called a(n) _____ disorder.
5. During this two-year period if depression alternates with intervals when the person's mood is cheerful, expansive, or irritable, the problem is a(n) _____ disorder.
6. Disorders which are marked by lasting extremes of emotion and which sometimes are accompanied by psychotic symptoms are referred to as _____ disorders.
7. Aaron is experiencing feelings of failure, worthlessness, and total despair and has become extremely subdued, withdrawn, or intensely suicidal. Aaron appears to be suffering from a(n) major _____ disorder.
8. A person is loud, elated, hyperactive, grandiose, and energetic with some patients going bankrupt in a matter of days, getting arrested, or going on a binge of promiscuous sex during _____ episodes.

9. If a person experiences both extreme mania and deep depression, the person has a(n) _____ disorder.
10. If the person is mostly sad and guilt ridden, but has had one or more mildly manic episodes, then they are said to have a(n) _____ disorder.
11. Mildly manic episodes are referred to as _____
12. Major mood disorders more often appear to be produced from within, rather than being a reaction to external events. Therefore, major mood disorders are considered _____.
13. Regarding the cause of depression and other mood disorders, some scientists are interested in brain chemicals and transmitter substances, especially dopamine, noradrenaline, and _____.
14. The chemical that has been found to be effective for treating some cases of bipolar depression is _____.
15. The theory that holds that depression is caused by repressed anger with this rage being displaced and turned inward as self-blame and self-hate is the _____ theory.
16. Theories of depression that emphasize learned helplessness as the culprit are the _____ theories.
17. Self-criticism and negative, distorted, or self-defeating thoughts underlie many causes of depression, according to the _____ psychologists.
18. Life stresses trigger many mood disorders especially for people who are vulnerable to depression because of their thinking patterns and _____.
19. Persons of one gender are twice as likely to experience depression as the other. These people are _____.
20. Researchers believe that the main reason for this gender difference in rates of depression to be environmental and _____ conditions.
21. One study found that the women in the United States who were most likely to be depressed were the women of the ethnic group _____.
22. Women in the United States who were most likely to be depressed had high stress levels, were unmarried, experienced feelings of hopelessness, and lacked _____.
23. An estimated 25 to 50 percent of all women experience a mild depression that usually lasts from one to two days after childbirth and is referred to as _____.
24. Roughly 13 percent of all women who give birth develop a moderately severe depression that begins within three months following childbirth and is referred to as _____.
25. The depressions that women experience after birth are partly due to their moods being altered by the drop in the hormone _____.
26. Stress and anxiety before birth, negative attitudes toward child rearing and lack of support from the father increase the risk of _____ depression.
27. If one identical twin is depressed, the chance of the other twin suffering depression is _____ percent.
28. If one fraternal twin is depressed, the chance of the other twin suffering depression is _____ percent.
29. The difference in identical and fraternal twins in their probability for developing depression may be related to the recent finding that people are more likely to become depressed when they are stressed if they have a particular version of a(n) _____.
30. Biological factors seem to play a larger role than environment in the development of major mood disorders, especially _____ disorders.
31. Starting in the fall, Abe, who lives in Alaska tends to sleep longer and more poorly, feels tired and drowsy during the day, overeats, and become sad and irritable. Abe most likely has a condition known as _____.
32. When people are suffering from this depression that occurs in the fall and winter, they often overeat and crave sweets and _____.
33. When people are suffering this mild depression that occurs only in the fall and winter, they often show social _____.

740

34. The mild depression that only occurs during fall and winter months is especially prevalent where the days are very short during the winter, such as the _____ latitudes.
35. Seasonal depressions are related to the release of more of the hormone _____ during the winter.
36. This hormone that is related to seasonal depressions is secreted from the _____ gland.
37. The treatment for seasonal depression that involves exposing the person to one or more hours of very bright fluorescent light each day is called _____.
38. Regarding the best time of day for this light treatment, research has found that the treatment should be conducted in the _____.

Part 1: Connections

1. ___ dysthymic disorder
2. ___ cyclothymic disorder
3. ___ major depressive disorder
4. ___ bipolar I disorder
5. ___ bipolar II disorder
6. ___ postpartum depression
7. ___ maternity blues
8. ___ seasonal affective disorder (SAD)
9. ___ hypomania

a. major mood disorder in which the person has episodes of mania and also periods of deep depression
b. mild manic episodes
c. mild to moderately severe depression that begins within three months following childbirth
d. moderate depression that persists for two years or more
e. mild depression that usually lasts from one to two days after childbirth
f. major mood disorder in which a person is mostly depressed but has also had one or more episodes of mild mania
g. mild depression that occurs only during fall and winter presumable related to decreased exposure to sunlight
h. major mood disorder in which the person has suffered one or more intense episodes of depression
i. moderate manic and depressive behavior that persists for two years or more

Part 2: Connections

1. ___ major mood disorders
2. ___ endogenous disorders
3. ___ lithium carbonate
4. ___ psychoanalytic theory of depression
5. ___ behavioral theories of depression
6. ___ cognitive theory of depression
7. ___ phototherapy

a. self-criticism and negative, distorted, or self-defeating thoughts underlie many cases of depression
b. depression caused by repressed anger
c. involves exposing SAD patients to one or more hours of very bright fluorescent light each day
d. hormone secreted by the pineal gland that regulates the body's response to changing light conditions
e. excited, hyperactive, energetic, grandiose behavior
f. learned helplessness causes depression
g. disorders marked by lasting extremes of emotion and sometimes accompanied by psychotic symptoms

741

8. ___ mania
9. ___ depression

10. ___ serotonin
11.___ melatonin

h. neurotransmitter along with noradrenaline and dopamine that affect mood changes
i. produced from within (perhaps by chemical imbalances) rather than as a reaction to life events
j. chemical used to treat bipolar disorders
k. sad, despondent, guilt ridden

Check Your Memory

1. TRUE or FALSE In any given year, roughly 9.5 percent of the U.S. population suffers from a mood disorder.

2. TRUE or FALSE If a person is mildly depressed for at least two years, the problem is called a cyclothymic disorder, while if this depression alternates with periods when the person's mood is cheerful, expansive, or irritable, the condition is called dysthymic disorder.

3. TRUE or FALSE Major mood disorders include both major depressive disorder and bipolar I and bipolar II disorders.

4. TRUE or FALSE Suicide attempted during a major depression is rarely a "plea for help" with the person intending to succeed and in many cases not giving prior warning.

5. TRUE or FALSE In bipolar I disorder, the person is mostly sad and guilt ridden, but has had one or more mildly manic episodes, while people with bipolar II disorder experience both extreme mania and deep depression.

6. TRUE or FALSE Mildly manic episodes are called hypomania.

7. TRUE or FALSE Bipolar II patients usually just manage to irritate everyone around them by being excessively cheerful or aggressive or by bragging, talking too fast, interrupting conversations, or spending too much money.

8. TRUE or FALSE Sometimes, depressed individuals cannot even feed or dress themselves.

9. TRUE or FALSE In severe cases of depression and/or mania, the person may lose touch with reality and display psychotic symptoms.

10. TRUE or FALSE Major mood disorders are most often a reaction to external events rather being produced from within the person.

11. TRUE or FALSE A biological explanation for mood changes involves the brain chemicals of serotonin, noradrenaline, and dopamine.

12. TRUE or FALSE The chemical lithium carbonate has been shown to effective in treating some cases of bipolar disorder.

13. TRUE or FALSE The psychoanalytic theory emphasizes learned helplessness as the cause of depression.

14. TRUE or FALSE Cognitive psychologists believe that depression is caused by repressed anger.

15. TRUE or FALSE Life stresses trigger many mood disorders especially for people who have personality traits and thinking patterns that make them vulnerable to depression.

16. TRUE or FALSE Men are twice as likely as women to experience depression.

17. TRUE or FALSE Researchers believe that social and environmental conditions are the main reason for gender differences in depression.

18. TRUE or FALSE Women and children are most likely to live in poverty with poor women frequently suffering the stresses associated with single parenthood, loss of control over their lives, poor housing, and dangerous neighborhoods.

742

19. TRUE or FALSE   A study found that women in the United States were most likely to be depressed if they were married and highly educated.

20. TRUE or FALSE   A study found that Latina women in the United States were more likely to be depressed.

21. TRUE or FALSE   An estimated 25 to 50 percent of all women experience postpartum depression.

22. TRUE or FALSE   A depressed mother can seriously retard her child's rate of development.

23. TRUE or FALSE   Negative attitudes toward childrearing can increase a woman's risk of having postpartum depression.

24. TRUE or FALSE   After a woman gives birth, her estrogen levels can drop, altering her mood.

25. TRUE or FALSE   Educating new parents about the importance of supporting one another and groups where new mothers discuss their feelings may reduce the risk of postpartum depression.

26. TRUE or FALSE   Recently, it was found that people who have a particular version of a gene are more likely to become depressed when they are stressed.

27. TRUE or FALSE   If you suffer from mild depression only during the fall and winter months, you may be experiencing what is known as a seasonal affective disorder (SAD).

28. TRUE or FALSE   When individuals are suffering from a mild depression in the fall and winter, they often crave large amounts of proteins.

29. TRUE or FALSE   Individual suffering from a mild depression in the fall and winter often show social withdrawal during these seasons but not during the spring and summer.

30. TRUE or FALSE   Seasonal depressions are especially prevalent in the southern United States where days are longer during the winter months.

31. TRUE or FALSE   Seasonal depressions are related to the release of more thyroxin from the thyroid gland, which regulates the body's response to changing light conditions.

32. TRUE or FALSE   The treatment for seasonal depressions that involves exposure to bright, full-spectrum light is known as electromagnetic spectrology.

33. TRUE or FALSE   Light therapy used for seasonal depressions are best done late in the afternoon, when it simulates sunset in the summer.

Critical Thinking Question

How might relationships contribute to the higher rates of depression experienced by women?

Module 13.4 Anxiety-Based Disorders and Personality Disorders

Anxiety-Based Disorders—When Anxiety Rules

Survey Question: What problems result when a person suffers high levels of anxiety?

Language Development Guide

debilitating: incapacitating; devastating; unbearable
apprehension: fearfulness; worry; nervousness
signify: indicate; suggest; suggest
restrictive: limiting
elaborate: detailed; complicated
pervasive: persistent; all-encompassing
inferiority: inadequacy; weakness

constructive: positive; useful

sedation: reducing stress through medication

clammy: sweaty; moist

panic: feeling terror and a loss of control

prisoners: person held captive who cannot escape

stateroom: guest cabin on a ship

oceanliner: a ship that carries passengers

Titanic: large passenger ship that hit an iceberg and sunk in 1912

shake off: to get rid of something that is bothering you

descending order: proceed downward from largest to smallest

prevalence: the number that occurs; frequency of occurrence; incidence

garden-variety: very ordinary

humiliated: lower one's dignity or pride; feel broken; brought to a low status

endure: bear; suffer; tolerate

blushing: face becomes red due to feeling self-conscious, embarrassed, or humiliated

preoccupied: deeply absorbed

obsessional: being persistently fixed or preoccupied with a thought

jingle: song in a radio or television advertisement, used as a memory aid

immoral: violating accepted standards of right and wrong

profanities: abusive, vulgar language; curse; swear words

popping: suddenly appearing

"dirty" words: vulgar words; profanity

hoarders: person who excessively accumulates things; refuses to get rid of anything

checkers: to examine or inspect in order to make sure that everything is as it should be, such as the doors locked, stove off, etc.

cleaners: excessive tidy and neat

plunging: to thrust into; to forcefully throw into

"contaminated": impure; dirty; infected; tainted; polluted

dramatic: extraordinary; striking

orderliness: tidiness; neatness; organization

political hostages: people held captive because of their beliefs

blunted: dulled

wariness: caution; suspicion; guardedness

survival instinct: drive to stay alive

gruesome: horrible; grisly; shocking

a terrible toll: to cause damage

striking: unusual; remarkable; prominent

intolerable: unbearable; painful; impossible

perversely: wickedly; viciously

dissociations: the separation of mental processes from the rest of the personality; occurs when forming multiple identities

torture: the act of making a person suffer agony and pain

flamboyant: showy, colorful

integration: incorporating; creating links between

fusion: union; blending; synthesis

convince: prove to; persuade

dreaded: awful; something to be feared

basis: source; origin

complaints: illnesses; medical problems

curious twist: unexpected turn of events; surprise; unusual distortion

distress: suffering

744

sinus problem: inflammation of the airspaces in the bones of the face

oppositional defiant disorder: ongoing pattern of disobedient, hostile and stubborn behavior toward authority figures which goes beyond the bounds of normal childhood behavior

attention deficit disorder: persistent pattern of impulsiveness, a short attention span, and often hyperactivity

desperately: very much

"healed": cured; made physically well

"sick of being sick": was tired of being ill all the time

Ben's mother who was sick: in this case, the mother was mentally ill

fabricate: make up; produce

deliberately: intentionally

7-Up: lemon-lime soft drink

pathological: maladaptive and compulsive

health conscious: being aware of nutrition, exercise, and other practices that make one healthy

schizoaffective disorder: mental disorder in which symptoms of a mood disorder occur along with several psychotic symptoms characteristic of schizophrenia

borderline personality disorder: long-standing, maladaptive pattern in which self-image, moods, and impulses are erratic, and the person is extremely sensitive to any hint of criticism, rejection, or abandonment by others

"converted": changed; transformed

resemble: looks like; is similar to

contradict: disagree with

anesthetized: use of a drug, usually during surgery, that causes a loss of sensation

Recite and Review

1. People who suffer from extreme anxiety are miserable most of the time, and their behavior becomes distorted and self-_____.

2. To get through the day, people with anxiety-related problems tend to use avoidance responses and elaborate _____.

3. Feelings of apprehension, dread, or uneasiness are referred to as _____.

4. The term that really has no formal meaning but generally implies that the person has gone past their ability to cope with a particular situation is _____

5. Disorders that occur when ordinary stresses push people beyond their ability to cope with life, such as losing a job, increased marital strife, and chronic physical illness, are referred to as _____ disorders.

6. When ordinary stresses push people beyond their ability to cope, these problems can usually be relieved by supportive counseling, a chance to "talk through" their fears and anxieties, sedation, and _____.

7. The disorders that tend to disappear when a person's life circumstances improve are usually the _____ disorders.

8. The disorders that do not improve when a crisis has passed and which seem greatly out of proportion to the ordinary life stresses that the person was under are most likely _____ disorders.

9. The type of disorder that comes closest to the laymen's term of "nervous breakdown" is a(n) _____ disorder.

10. In any given year, the percent of the adult population that suffers from an anxiety disorder is roughly _____ percent.

11. Distress is a key ingredient in anxiety disorders and may also underlie somatoform and _____ disorders.

12. In somatoform disorders, anxiety and discomfort are actually reduced by the _____ behavior.

13. Nanette has been extremely anxious and worried about her job, marriage, and her children for at least six months and has been experiencing a racing heart, upset stomach, sweating, and poor concentration. Nanette most likely is experiencing a type of anxiety disorder known as _____ disorder.

14. Merle is always in a chronic state of anxiety but also has brief moments of sudden, intense episodes in which he becomes dizzy and cannot breathe as if he is having a heart attack. Merle most likely has a(n) _____ disorder.

15. If a person suffers from chronic anxiety but also has an intense fear that a panic attack will occur in a public place or unfamiliar situation, then the person will be diagnosed with a(n) panic disorder with _____.

16. Depending on her teenage daughters to do her shopping, Juanita has not left her house for the last six months because she fears that something extremely embarrassing will happen if she leave home or enters an unfamiliar situation. Juanita is suffering from a disorder known as _____.

17. Regarding gender, the majority of people who suffer from generalized anxiety disorders and panic disorders are _____.

18. Being afraid of heights, airplanes, or blood are examples of _____ phobias.

19. If you are fearful of strangers, then your phobia is called _____.

20. A fear of heights is called _____.

21. Being fearful of airplane travel is referred to as _____.

22. Terri is deadly afraid of storms, thunder, and lightning. Terri has a phobia called _____.

23. Sometimes people fear situations in which they can be observed, evaluated, embarrassed, or humiliated by others, which leads them to avoid certain situations, such as eating in restaurants, going to public rest rooms, or speaking in public. These people has a(n) _____.

24. Barry feels "contaminated" from touching ordinary objects because "germs are everywhere" and feels driven to wash his hands hundreds of times a day. Barry suffers from _____ disorder.

25. The disturbing thoughts or images that force their way into one's awareness are called _____.

26. To control these disturbing recurring thoughts, a person may use irrational acts that he or she feels driven to repeat, which are called _____.

27. "Checkers," "cleaners," and hoarders are three types of behaviors that people may feel compelled to repeat when they are suffering from _____ disorder.

28. Disorders, which may last a short time or years and occur when people experience trauma outside the range of normal human experience, such as floods, tornadoes, earthquakes, or horrible accidents, are called _____ disorders

29. After being in a tornado that damaged her home, Denna experiencing irritability, insomnia, nightmares, wariness, and poor concentration for the next two weeks with these symptoms disappearing within a month after the tornado. Deanna experienced a(n) _____ disorder.

30. It has been over five years since Tyron almost died in Hurricane Katrina, and he still repeatedly relives this horrible event in flashbacks and nightmares and experienced periods of irritability, insomnia, and poor concentration on his job. Tyron would be diagnosed with a(n) _____ disorder.

31. Among soldiers involved in combat in Iraq and Afghanistan, psychologists are already seeing high rates of _____ disorder.

32. A loss of memory (partial or complete) for important information related to personal identity, such as one's name, address, or past is referred to as _____ amnesia.

33. People who exhibit sudden, unplanned, travel away from their homes and who become confused about their personal identities with this fleeing appearing to be a defense against intolerable anxiety are mostly suffering from _____ .

34. In the book *Sybil*, Sybil reportedly had 16 different personality states with each identity having a distinct voice, vocabulary, posture, and talents. Sybil's condition is currently known as _____ disorder.

35. In a high percentage of persons whose personalities split into multiple identities, there is a history of childhood trauma, especially _____.

36. During therapy for a person with multiple identities, a psychologist, in order to contact the various personality states may make use of _____.

37. In order for the person to eventually have a single, balanced personality, the goal of therapy for the person with multiple personalities is integration and _____.

38. When a person interprets normal bodily sensations as proof that they have a terrible disease, this person is suffering from a somatoform disorder known as _____.

39. Sandra has numerous physical complaints, which results in her consulting many doctors and undergoing many different tests and treatments. However, no organic cause for her numerous ailments has been identified. Sandra most likely suffers from the somatoform disorder known as _____ disorder.

40. Wayne has had a backache for years, yet the doctors can find no problems with his spine, vertebrae, or muscles that can explain his problem. Wayne's disabling backache does seem to occur during times of high financial and marital stress. Wayne appears to be suffering from a somatoform _____ disorder.

41. When a mother intentionally makes her child sick in order to gain the sympathy and attention of medical professionals and others, the mother would be diagnosed with a condition known as _____.

42. Bart purposely makes himself sick in order to gain sympathy from his relatives and health professionals. Bart suffers from a condition known as _____.

43. When a person suffers from several disorders, the person is said to be _____.

44. A soldier becomes blind on the battlefield, but no physical cause can be identified that caused his blindness. This soldier is suffering from a somatoform problem known as a(n) _____ disorder.

45. A loss of sensitivity in the areas of the skin that would normally be covered by a glove with this condition contradicting known medical facts is referred to as "_____."

46. When a person exhibits uncontrollable sneezing that lasts for days or week and the person's eyes do not close when they sneeze, a doctor should suspect a somatoform problem known as a(n) _____ disorder.

47. If a person with a major physical disability does not show this limitation when he or she is asleep, hypnotized, or anesthetized and if the victim is also strangely unconcerned about suddenly becoming disabled, then a doctor should suspect a(n) _____ reaction.

Part 1: Connections

1. ___ nervous breakdown

   a. fear that something extremely embarrassing will happen if one leaves the house or enters unfamiliar situations; may refuse to go outside their home

2. ___ adjustment disorder

   b. psychological disturbance lasting more then one month following stresses that would produce anxiety in anyone who experienced them

3. ___ generalized anxiety disorder

    c. psychological disturbance lasting less than month following stresses that would produce anxiety in anyone who experiences them

4. ___ panic disorders

    d. chronic state of anxiety with brief moments of sudden, intense, unexpected dizzy, suffocating feelings

5. ___ agoraphobia

    e. intense, irrational fear of being observed, evaluated, embarrassed, or humiliated by others in social situations

6. ___ specific phobia

    f. extreme preoccupation with certain thoughts and the performance of certain behaviors (to control the thoughts)

7. ___ social phobia

    g. chronic state of tension and worries about work, relationships, ability, or impeding disaster

8. ___ obsessive-compulsive disorder

    h. intense, irrational fear of certain objects, activities, or situations

9. ___ acute stress disorder

    i. emotional disturbance caused by ongoing stressors within the range of common experience

10. ___ posttraumatic stress disorder

    j. term that has no formal meaning but implies that the person has gone past their ability to cope with a situation

Part 2: Connections

1. ___ dissociative amnesia

    a. presence of two or more distinct personalities (multiple personalities)

2. ___ dissociative fugue

    b. preoccupation with fears of having a serious disease with ordinary physical signs being interpreted as proof that the person has a disease, but no physical disorder can be found

3. ___ dissociative identity disorder

    c. affected person fakes his or her own medical problems in order to gain attention

4. ___ hypochondriasis

    d. loss of memory (partial or complete) for important information related to personal identity

5. ___ somatization disorder

    e. bodily symptom that mimics a physical disability, such as blindness or paralysis, but is actually caused by anxiety or emotional distress

6. ___ pain disorder

    f. affected person fakes the medical problems of someone in his or her care in order to gain attention

7. ___ conversion disorder

    g. sudden travel away from home, plus confusion about one's personal identity

8. ___ Munchausen syndrome

    h. pain that has no identifiable physical cause and appears to be of psychological origin

9. ___ Munchausen syndrome by proxy

    i. afflicted persons have numerous physical complaints; typically consult many doctors, but no organic cause for their distress can be identified

Part 3: Connections

1. ___ anxiety
2. ___ comorbid
3. ___ anxiety disorders
4. ___ stress disorders
5. ___ dissociative disorders
6. ___ somatoform disorders
7. ___ obsessions
8. ___ compulsions
9. ___ "glove anesthesia"
10. ___ "checkers" and "cleaners"
11. ___ integration and fusion

a. conversion reaction involving a loss of feeling in the hands

b. types of compulsive patterns shown by individuals with obsessive-compulsive disorder

c. feelings of apprehension, dread, or uneasiness

d. group of disorders in which physical symptoms have no identifiable physical cause

e. group of disorders in which fear and distress seem greatly out of proportion to a person's circumstances

f. goal of therapy for people with multiple personalities

g. suffering from more than one disorder at a time

h. irrational acts that a person feels driven to repeat

i. significant emotional disturbances caused by incidents outside the range of normal human experience, such as war or natural disasters

j. reactions include episodes of amnesia, fugue, or multiple identities

k. distressing thoughts and images that force their way into awareness against a person's will

Part 4: Connections

1. ___ acrophobia
2. ___ arachnophobia
3. ___ zoophobia
4. ___ astraphobia
5. ___ aquaphobia
6. ___ aviophobia
7. ___ claustrophobia
8. ___ ophidiophobia
9. ___ xenophobia
10. ___ hematophobia
11. ___ coulrophobia
12. ___ arachibutyrophobia
13. ___ triskaidekaphobia

a. fear of peanut butter sticking to the roof of the mouth
b. fear of closed spaces
c. fear of strangers
d. fear of airplanes
e. fear of clowns
f. fear of spiders
g. fear of storms, thunder, lightning
h. fear of being on or in the water
i. fear of blood
j. fear of the number 13
k. fear of animals (in general)
l. fear of heights
m. fear of snakes

Check Your Memory

1. TRUE or FALSE   Anxiety is a normal emotion, and only becomes a problem when the anxiety becomes so intense it prevents people from doing what they want or need to do.

2. TRUE or FALSE   In any given year, only about two percent of the adult population suffers from an anxiety disorder.

3. TRUE or FALSE   People with anxiety-related problems have a tendency to use elaborate defense mechanisms or avoidance responses to get through the day.

4. TRUE or FALSE   The term "nervous breakdown" has no formal diagnostic meaning.

5. TRUE or FALSE   A problem known as social phobia comes closest to what is meant by a "nervous breakdown."

6. TRUE or FALSE   When ordinary stresses, such as losing one's job or intense marital strife, push people beyond their ability to cope with life, the person is said to have an adjustment disorder.

7. TRUE or FALSE   Adjustment problems can often be relieved by rest, sedation, supportive counseling, and a chance to "talk through" their fears and anxieties.

8. TRUE or FALSE   In most anxiety disorders, distress seems greatly out of proportion to a person's circumstances.

9. TRUE or FALSE   The maladaptive behaviors exhibited in dissociative and somatoform disorders occur in order to reduce anxiety and discomfort.

10. TRUE or FALSE   People with generalized anxiety disorder have brief moments of sudden, intense, unexpected panic that keep them confined to their homes.

11. TRUE or FALSE   More men than women have generalized anxiety disorder.

12. TRUE or FALSE   People experiencing a panic attack often believe that they are having a heart attack, are going insane, or are about to die.

13. TRUE or FALSE   Going outside the home alone, being in a crowd, standing in line, crossing a bridge, or riding in a car can be impossible for an agoraphobic person.

14. TRUE or FALSE   People affected by phobias do not recognize that their fears are unreasonable.

15. TRUE or FALSE   Among Americans, the most common specific phobia is a fear of closed spaces.

16. TRUE or FALSE   Triskaidekaphobia is a fear of the number 13, while xenophobia is a fear of strangers.

17. TRUE or FALSE   Astraphobia is a fear of airplanes, while ophidiophobia is a fear of clowns.

18. TRUE or FALSE   Arachibutyrophobia is a fear of peanut butter sticking to the roof of the mouth.

19. TRUE or FALSE   Almost everyone has a few mild phobias, but in a true phobic disorder, the person may exhibit wild climbing or running, faint, vomit, or go to great links to avoid the feared object.

20. TRUE or FALSE   A fear of using a public restroom, writing one's name in front of others, or eating in public are all examples of a somatoform disorder.

21. TRUE or FALSE   A person who counts his or her heart beats in order to keep from thinking about saying "dirty" words in public suffers from a specific phobia.

22. TRUE or FALSE   Obsessions are irrational acts that a person feels driven to repeat, while compulsions are disturbing images and thoughts that force their way into one's awareness.

23. TRUE or FALSE   If obsessive-compulsive patterns are long-standing but less intense, they are classified as personality disorders.

24. TRUE or FALSE   A psychological disturbance lasting from one month up to several years following stresses that would produce anxiety in anyone who experienced them is referred to as an acute stress disorder.

25. TRUE or FALSE Eight percent of military veterans will suffer from post-traumatic stress disorder (PTSD) decades after they were in combat.

26. TRUE or FALSE Dissociative fugue disorder involves sudden, unplanned travel away from home and confusion about personal identity.

27. TRUE or FALSE When a person has multiple personalities, he or she is suffering from atypical schizophrenia.

28. TRUE or FALSE An example of multiple identities is the case of Sybil, who had 16 personalities with each identity having a distinct voice, vocabulary, and posture and even different talents.

29. TRUE or FALSE The majority of psychologists continue to believe that multiple personalities is a real, but rare problem.

30. TRUE or FALSE A history of childhood trauma, especially sexual abuse, is found in a high percentage of persons whose personalities split into multiple identities.

31. TRUE or FALSE When a person is in therapy for multiple identities, hypnosis is used to contact the various personality states.

32. TRUE or FALSE In conversion disorder, people interpret normal minor bodily sensations as proof that they have a terrible disease.

33. TRUE or FALSE Persons with numerous physical complaints for which no organic causes can be identified are diagnosed with a somatization disorder.

34. TRUE or FALSE An affected person who fakes his or her own medical problems in order to gain attention is suffering from Munchausen syndrome by proxy.

35. TRUE or FALSE When a person suffers from more than one disorder at a time, he or she is said to be comorbid.

36. TRUE or FALSE "Glove anesthesia" and uncontrollable sneezing are two examples of hypochondriasis.

37. TRUE or FALSE If symptoms disappear when a victim is asleep, hypnotized, or anesthetized, a conversion reaction is usually suspected.

38. TRUE or FALSE Victims of conversion reactions are strangely unconcerned about suddenly becoming disabled.

Critical Thinking Questions

1. Many of the physical complaints associated with anxiety disorders are closely related to activity of what part of the nervous system?

2. How could someone get away with Munchausen by proxy syndrome? Wouldn't doctors figure out that something was fishy with Ben long before he had 40 surgeries for a faked sinus disorder? (See "Sick of Being Sick.")

Module 13.4 Anxiety-Based Disorders and Personality Disorders
Anxiety and Disorder—Four Pathways to Trouble
Survey Question: How do psychologists explain anxiety-based disorders?

Language Development Guide

susceptibility: vulnerability; a weakness for developing

high strung: nervous and easily excitable

runs in families: a characteristic that appears in several family members

inhibited: keeping one's emotions to oneself

existential: type of humanistic therapy that focuses on issues of existence, such as meaning, responsibility, death and encourages people to make courageous choices to bring meaning into their lives

dynamics: continuous changes and activities
raging: intense; violent; uncontrolled
forbidden: not allowed; prohibited
suppress: hold back
overwhelmed: overpowered; crushed; devastated
disastrous: terrible; ruinous; devastating
end product: result
unrealistic: impractical; idealistic; unlikely; out of reach
vulnerable: weak; defenseless
contradictory: opposing
resort: choose a refuge
distortions: misrepresentations; falsehoods
provoke: cause
vicious cycle: one trouble leads to another that aggravates the first
life-enhancing: choices and activities that will improve one's life
anguish: extreme pain or suffering
crushing: powerful, strong
courageously: bravely
impersonal: distant; unfriendly
void: nothingness; hollowness
collapsed: failed
awesome: overwhelming
generalize to: apply also to
"sickness behavior": in this case imagined illness
ultimately: in the end
onset: start; beginning

Recite and Review

1. Like many other disorder, anxiety disorders may also be best explained by the _____ model.
2. Studies have shown that being high strung, nervous, or emotional runs in families; thus, susceptibility to anxiety-based disorders appears to be partly _____.
3. Sixty percent of children born to parents suffering from panic disorder will be irritable and wary as infants, shy and fearful as toddlers, and quiet and cautious introverts in elementary school; thus, these children were born with a fearful, inhibited _____.
4. The approach sees anxiety as resulting from internal motives, conflicts, unconscious forces, and other dynamics of mental life is the _____ approach.
5. Freud referred to these anxiety-based disorders as "_____."
6. Freud emphasized that intense anxiety can be caused by the forbidden impulses for sex and aggression that threaten to break through into behavior that are generated by the part of the personality called the _____.
7. According to Freud, people are tortured by the guilt that is used to suppress the forbidden impulses. This guilt is generated by the part of the personality known as the _____.
8. Freud believed that a part of the personality is caught in the middle of this conflict and is forced to use rigid defense mechanisms. This part of the personality is called the _____.
9. The theories emphasize subjective experience, human problems, and personal potentials are the _____ approach.
10. Psychologist Carl Rogers regarded emotional disorders as the end product of a faulty _____.

11. Rogers believed that anxious individuals have built up unrealistic mental images of themselves, which leaves them vulnerable to _____ information.
12. Psychologists who take an existential view stress that unhealthy anxiety reflects a loss of _____ in one's life.
13. According to the existential approach, the unavoidable anguish that comes from knowing we are personally responsible for our lives is known as _____.
14. According to existentialism, in making choices that will enhance our lives, we must show responsibility and _____.
15. Adolescents may experience considerable existential anxiety as they develop their _____.
16. From the existential view, people who are anxious and have collapsed in the face of the awesome responsibility to choose a meaningful existence, they are living in "_____."
17. Behaviorists believe that phobias can be acquired through _____ conditioning.
18. According to the behaviorists, anxiety attacks that have generalized to new situations reflect conditioned _____ responses.
19. According to the behaviorists, sympathy and attention reinforces the "sickness behavior" exhibited by people with the somatoform disorder of _____.
20. Self-defeating behavior is maintained, according to the behaviorists, because making a response delays or prevents the onset of a painful or unpleasant stimulus, which is referred to as _____ learning.
21. A behaviorist would say that the powerful reward of immediate relief from anxiety keeps self-defeating avoidance behaviors alive. This view is known as the _____ hypothesis.
22. Distorted thinking causes people to magnify ordinary threats and failures, which can lead to anxiety and distress, according to the _____ approach.
23. People with social phobias are excessively concerned about making mistakes and tend to be _____.

Connections

1. ___ genetic susceptibility

2. ___ psychodynamic approach

3. ___ humanistic approach (Rogers)

4. ___ existential approach

5. ___ behavioral approach

6. ___ anxiety-reduction hypothesis

7. ___ cognitive approach

a. distorted thinking magnifies ordinary threats and failures and leads to anxiety

b. anxiety is the end product of a faulty self-image

c. explains how immediate relief from anxiety rewards and maintains self-defeating avoidance behaviors

d. intense anxiety caused by forbidden id impulses; person uses rigid defense mechanisms to maintain control

e. unhealthy anxiety reflects a loss of meaning in one's life

f. anxiety attacks are conditioned emotional responses; self-defeating behaviors are learned

g. inherited potential for a particular condition or disorder

Check Your Memory

1. TRUE or FALSE   Anxiety disorders may be best explained by the stress-vulnerability model.
2. TRUE or FALSE   Studies show that being high strung, nervous, or emotional runs in families.
3. TRUE or FALSE   Sixty percent of children born to parents suffering from panic disorder have a fearful, inhibited temperament.
4. TRUE or FALSE   Freud was the first to propose a psychodynamic explanation for the anxiety-based disorders, which he called "neurosis."
5. TRUE or FALSE   Freud emphasized that intense anxiety can be caused by forbidden impulses for sex and aggression generated by the ego.
6. TRUE or FALSE   Freud believed that people may be tortured by guilt, which the id uses to suppress forbidden impulses.
7. TRUE or FALSE   According to Freud, the superego resorts to using rigid defense mechanisms when it is overwhelmed by the impulses of the id and ego.
8. TRUE or FALSE   The psychodynamic approach emphasizes subjective experience, human problems, and personal potentials.
9. TRUE or FALSE   Psychologist Carl Rogers regarded emotional disorders as the end product of a faulty self-image or self-concept.
10. TRUE or FALSE   Psychologists who take a cognitive view stress that unhealthy anxiety reflects a loss of meaning in one's life.
11. TRUE or FALSE   "Existential anxiety" is the unavoidable anguish that comes from knowing we are personally responsible for our lives.
12. TRUE or FALSE   Adolescents may experience considerable existential anxiety as they develop their identity.
13. TRUE or FALSE   According to the behaviorists, phobias are acquired through classical conditioning.
14. TRUE or FALSE   The behaviorists believe that self-defeating behavior begins with avoidance learning.
15. TRUE or FALSE   The anxiety reduction hypothesis states that distorted thinking causes people to magnify ordinary threats and failures.
16. TRUE or FALSE   People with social phobias tend to be perfectionists, who are excessively concerned about making mistakes.
17. TRUE or FALSE   According to cognitive theorists, changing the thinking patterns of anxious individuals can greatly lessen their fears.
18. TRUE or FALSE   To better understand the causes of anxiety-based disorders, one must combine parts of the psychodynamic, humanistic-existential, behavioral, and cognitive approaches.

Module 13.4 Anxiety-Based Disorders and Personality Disorders

Personality Disorders—Blueprints for Maladjustment

Survey Question: What is a personality disorder?

Language Development Guide

blueprints: outline or drawing of the plans for how something will look, usually of the architectural plan of a building

seclusion: privacy; isolation

mingled: mixed; blended

scars: marks left on the skin left from the healing of a previous injury

gouging: poking, prying, digging

turbulent: quarrelsome; chaotic; unstable

moody: irritable; unstable; changeable; grumpy

"emotional storms": emotional outbursts or raging

hypersensitive: touchy; overly sensitive to any criticism

dramatizing: exaggerating; overstating

submissive: passive; compliant; meek; obedient

flamboyant: showy, colorful

deceit: dishonesty; trickery

recklessness: irresponsible; carelessness

erratic: unpredictable; changeable

impulsive: hasty; reckless; irresponsible

emotionally shallow: superficial; not capable of deep emotions toward others

manipulative: calculating; scheming

socialized: acquiring a personal identity and learning the norms, values, behavior appropriate for society

delinquents: youthful offenders of the law

crazed: wild; out of control

portrayed: represented; depicted; shown

"charming": delightful; fascinating

"blind": do not choose to see; ignore

leanings: inclined to show

coldly: uncaringly; hardheartedly; unsympathetically

emotionally deprived: lack of adequate and appropriate interactions and care by others when young

grisly: horrible; gruesome; shocking

mutilations: disfigurement of people, usually involving the cutting off of various body parts

startled: upset; shocked

didn't "bat an eyelash": showed no emotional reaction; no surprise

pangs: twinges; sudden sharp feelings

"mellow": laid-back; mature; settled; calmer

exclude: leave out; keep out

dysfunction: a disturbance in functioning

groundless: unsupported; unjustified

Recite and Review

1. Julie has repeatedly lost jobs because of her turbulent relationships with other people. At times, she can be friendly and charming, while at other times she is extremely unpredictable, moody, and even suicidal. Julie has a condition called _____ personality disorder.
2. People are suspicious, hypersensitive, and wary of others when they have a(n) _____ personality disorder.
3. People who need constant admiration and are lost in fantasies of power, wealth, brilliance, beauty, or love have a(n) _____ personality disorder.
4. Carol suffers from extremely low self-confidence, allows others to run their lives, and places everyone else's needs ahead of her own. Carol most likely has a(n) _____ personality disorder.
5. The person who lacks a conscience, is impulsive, selfish, dishonest, emotionally shallow, and manipulative has a(n) _____ personality disorder.
6. Mae constantly seeks attention by dramatizing her emotions and actions, like an actress on stage. Mae most likely has a(n) _____ personality disorder.
7. Greg must follow a rigid routine at all times and demands order, perfection, and control. Greg has a(n) _____ personality disorder.

8. Leo is the classic loner, feels very little emotion, and cannot form close personal relationships with others. Leo has a(n) _____ personality disorder.
9. Initially, Ty appeared to be "charming," but people gradually become aware of his lying and self-serving manipulation and his lack of remorse. Ty has a(n) _____ personality disorder.
10. Although Mary would love to have friends, she tends to be timid, uncomfortable, and fears evaluation in social situations. Mary would be diagnosed with a(n) _____ personality disorder.
11. Sam is a loner and engages in extremely odd behavior. His thought patterns are also somewhat bizarre, although he is not actively psychotic. Sam would be diagnosed with a(n) _____ personality disorder.
12. Dependent, histrionic, narcissistic and antisocial personality disorders involve _____ impairment.
13. Borderline, paranoid, and schizotypal personality disorders involve _____ impairment.
14. The impairment for the personality disorders of obsessive-compulsive, schizoid, and avoidant is considered _____.
15. Individuals who are called sociopaths or psychopaths have a(n) _____ personality disorder.
16. One study found that psychopaths are "blind" to signs of _____ in others.
17. One finding may explain why sociopaths tend to be thrill seekers. It appears that adult sociopaths show unusual brain wave patterns that suggest _____ of the brain.
18. Sociopaths have an unusual ability to calmly lie, cheat, steal, and take advantage of others because they tend to be emotionally _____.
19. Because they manipulate therapy, it is difficult to successfully treat the _____ personality disorder.
20. Even without treatment, a sociopath's cruel and manipulative behavior does tend to decline somewhat after age _____.

Connections

1. ___ antisocial personality disorder
2. ___ dependent personality disorder
3. ___ histrionic personality disorder
4. ___ narcissistic personality disorder
5. ___ obsessive-compulsive personality disorder
6. ___ schizoid personality disorder
7. ___ avoidant personality disorder
8. ___ borderline personality disorder

a. timid, uncomfortable in social situations, and fears evaluation
b. demands order, perfection, control, and rigid routine at all times
c. deeply distrusts others and are suspicious of their motives, which are perceived as insulting or threatening
d. irresponsible, lacks guilt or remorse, reckless and deceitful, sociopath
e. loner, engages in extremely odd behavior, thought patterns are bizarre, but person is not actively psychotic
f. lacks confidence, extremely submissive to others, clinging
g. feels little emotion and cannot form close personal relationships with others
h. thinks of oneself as wonderful, brilliant, important, and worthy of constant admiration

9. ____ paranoid personality disorder

i. dramatic and flamboyant, exaggerates emotions to get the attention from others

10. ____ schizotypal personality disorder

j. self-image, moods, and impulses are erratic and person is extremely sensitive to any hint of criticism, rejection, or abandonment by others

Check Your Memory

1. TRUE or FALSE   People with borderline personality disorder are extremely sensitive to ordinary criticism and often react with anger, self-hatred, and impulsive behavior.

2. TRUE or FALSE   Noncelebrities appear to be more likely to be narcissistic than celebrities.

3. TRUE or FALSE   Histrionic personalities suffer from extremely low self-confidence, allow others to run their lives, and place everyone else's needs ahead of their own.

4. TRUE or FALSE   Personality disorders are deeply rooted with their patterns beginning during adolescence or even childhood.

5. TRUE or FALSE   Persons with an obsessive-compulsive personality disorder think of themselves as wonderful, brilliant, important, and worthy of constant admiration.

6. TRUE or FALSE   Persons with a schizoid personality disorder are sometimes called sociopaths or psychopaths.

7. TRUE or FALSE   The antisocial personality is timid, uncomfortable in social situations, and fears evaluations.

8. TRUE or FALSE   Persons with a schizotypal personality disorder demand order, perfection, control, and rigid routines at all times.

9. TRUE or FALSE   The paranoid personality is a loner who engages in extremely odd behavior and has bizarre thought patterns, but is not actively psychotic.

10. TRUE or FALSE   Impairment for the dependent, histrionic, narcissistic, and antisocial personality disorders is considered severe.

11. TRUE or FALSE   The borderline, paranoid, and schizotypal personality disorders show only a moderate impairment in functioning.

12. TRUE or FALSE   Many sociopaths are "charming" at first with people only gradually becoming aware of the sociopath's lying and self-serving manipulation.

13. TRUE or FALSE   Many successful businesspersons, entertainers, politicians, and other seemingly normal people have psychopathic leanings.

14. TRUE or FALSE   More than 65 percent of all persons with antisocial personalities have been arrested, usually for crimes, such as robbery, vandalism, or rape.

15. TRUE or FALSE   Many people with antisocial personalities were emotionally deprived and physically abused as children.

16. TRUE or FALSE   Adult sociopaths have brain waves patterns that suggest overarousal of the brain.

17. TRUE or FALSE   Psychopaths who were shown extremely grisly and unpleasant photographs of mutilations in a study exhibited no startle response to the photos.

18. TRUE or FALSE   Persons with a dependent personality disorder have been described as emotionally cold, which may explain how they can calmly lie and take advantage of others.

19. TRUE or FALSE   Sociopaths are rarely treated with success, since they manipulate therapy, just like any other situation.

20. TRUE or FALSE   Antisocial behavior does tend to decline somewhat after age 40, even without treatment, because people tend to become more "mellow" as they age.

Module 13.5 Psychology in Action
Suicide—Lives on the Brink
Survey Questions: Why do people commit suicide? Can suicide be prevented?

Language Development Guide

brink: edge; rim

distressingly: alarmingly; frighteningly

common: occurs often

"successful" suicide: ends in death

Azerbaijan: country in southwestern Asia; once part of the Soviet Union

Hungary: country in central Europe

aboriginal peoples: the original people living within an area which was later colonized by Western societies; native to an area

natural guard: built-in protection

firearm: gun

acculturative stress: stress caused by the many changes and adjustments required when a person moves to a foreign culture

bereavement: grief and sorrow at the loss of a loved one

fallacy: misleading notion; myth

prized possessions: cherished or valued belongings

death imagery in art: literal or symbolic representations that bring to mind vivid mental images of death and dying

intervene: get involved and stop

ambivalent: have mixed feelings; in this case about wanting to or not wanting to

relieved: thankful; pleased; comforted

departures: exits; ways of running away

ultimate: final

natural wish: their longing for

exceeds: goes beyond

constriction: process of narrowing or limiting

guidance: direction; advice

harmonious: agreeable

legitimate: sincere and well-founded

commitments: promises; obligations

tip the scales: change or influence a decision

deceptive: misleading

anticipation: expectation; eagerness

infeasible: not practical; difficult to achieve

Recite and Review

1. For every three people who die by homicide, the number that will kill themselves is _____.
2. Regarding gender differences with suicide, more attempts are made by _____.
3. Regarding gender differences with suicide, more completed acts of suicide ending in death are made by _____.
4. When committing suicide, males tend to use _____.
5. When committing suicide, women usually use a(n) _____.
6. When the suicide rates in the United States, Azerbaijan, and Hungary are compared, the highest suicide rate is in _____.

7. In general when Caucasians are compared to non-Caucasians, the ones with the higher suicide rate are _____.
8. Regarding ethnicity, the group with the highest suicide rate in the United States is _____.
9. The group who are particularly at risk for suicide are white males who are _____ years and older.
10. Among 15 to 24 year olds, suicide's ranking as a cause of death is _____.
11. Student suicide has been associated with the use of the drugs alcohol and _____.
12. In a comparison of married, divorced, widowed, and single person, the lowest rate of suicide was found in the _____.
13. In 90 percent of all suicides, there was a diagnosable mental disorder, which was usually either a substance abuse disorder or _____.
14. Feelings of hopelessness and worthlessness; a prior suicide attempt; depression or other mood disorder; drug or alcohol abuse; antisocial, impulsive, or aggressive behavior; severe anxiety; and the availability of a firearm are all major _____ factors for suicide.
15. Among ethnic adolescents, the factors that increased their possibility of committing suicide included a loss of face, racism, discrimination, and _____ stress.
16. The possibility of committing suicide increases dramatically when the impulse to harm others is turned _____.
17. Suicidal behavior usually progresses from suicidal thoughts, to _____, and to attempts.
18. For every 10 potential suicides, the number who give a warning beforehand is _____.
19. Withdrawal from contact with others, gift giving of prized possessions, single-car accidents, preoccupation with death, and death imagery in art are _____ signs of an impending suicide attempt.
20. When all suicide attempts are considered, the proportion of people who do not really want to die has been estimated to be _____ third(s).
21. When all suicide attempts are considered, the proportion of people who are ambivalent, or undecided about dying is almost_____ third(s).
22. The suicidal person is seeking to escape emotional _____.
23. In looking at their possible options, a suicidal person tends to _____ his or her options.
24. In talking to a suicidal person, your most important task may be to establish a harmonious connection with the person, which is referred to as establishing _____.
25. In helping a suicidal person, you should ask them to meet you for lunch, share a ride, or get some other day-by-day _____ from them.
26. A dangerous time for suicide is when a person who has had a severe depression, suddenly seems to get _____.
27. Most cities have centers for suicide prevention and mental health crisis _____ teams.
28. You should ask a person to accompany you to the emergency ward of a hospital if the person has a specific, _____ plan for committing suicide.

Connections

1. ____ suicide
2. ____ rapport
3. ____ depression or substance abuse
4. ____ acculturative stress
5. ____ warning signs of impending suicide

a. factor in ethnic adolescents' suicide
b. staff members trained to talk with suicidal persons over the phone
c. sudden swings in mood; gift giving of prized possession
d. permanent solution to a temporary problem
e. diagnosable mental disorder in 90 percent of suicides

759

6. ___ characteristics of suicidal thoughts
7. ___ crisis intervention team

f. establishing a harmonious connection
g. escape; unbearable psychological pain; frustrated psychological needs; constriction of options

Check Your Memory

1. TRUE or FALSE   Currently, for every three people who die by homicide, only one will kill themselves.
2. TRUE or FALSE   There may be as many as 25 attempts for every completed suicide.
3. TRUE or FALSE   Women complete suicide more, but men make more attempts that do not end in death.
4. TRUE or FALSE   Males typically use a gun in committing suicide, while women use a drug overdose.
5. TRUE or FALSE   The rate of suicide in the United States is 10 times higher than the suicide rate in Hungary.
6. TRUE or FALSE   Within the United States, non-Caucasians generally have a higher suicide rate than do Caucasians.
7. TRUE or FALSE   Native Americans have the highest suicide rate in the United States with the suicide rates being equally high among the aboriginal peoples of Australia and New Zealand.
8. TRUE or FALSE   Suicide rates typically decrease with advancing age.
9. TRUE or FALSE   At particular risk of committing suicide are white males who are 65 years and older.
10. TRUE or FALSE   Between 1950 and 1990, suicide rates for adolescents and young adults doubled.
11. TRUE or FALSE   Among 15 to 24 year olds, suicide is the number one cause of death.
12. TRUE or FALSE   Important factors in student suicide include not living up to their own extremely high standards, cocaine or alcohol use, chronic health problems (real or imagined), and interpersonal difficulties.
13. TRUE or FALSE   Married individuals have higher rates of suicide than the divorced, the widowed, and single persons.
14. TRUE or FALSE   A diagnosable mental disorder, usually depression or substance abuse disorder, is a factor in 90 percent of all suicides.
15. TRUE or FALSE   Major risk factors for suicide include antisocial, impulsive, or aggressive behavior and a family history of suicidal behavior.
16. TRUE or FALSE   Among ethnic adolescents, loss of face, acculturative stress, racism, and discrimination have been identified as risk factors for suicide.
17. TRUE or FALSE   Anyone may temporarily reach a state of depression severe enough to attempt suicide.
18. TRUE or FALSE   When the impulse to harm others is turned inward the risk of suicide increases dramatically.
19. TRUE or FALSE   People who talk about or threaten suicide are rarely the ones who try it.
20. TRUE or FALSE   Warning signs of an impending suicide attempt include gift giving of prized possessions, a single-car accident, and death imagery in art.
21. TRUE or FALSE   Suicide cannot be prevented because the person will find a way to do it anyway.
22. TRUE or FALSE   Two thirds of all suicide attempts are made by people who do not really want to die.
23. TRUE or FALSE   Emotional pain is what the suicidal person is seeking to escape.

24. TRUE or FALSE   In looking at their problems, suicidal persons have a tendency to over broaden their options.
25. TRUE or FALSE   In helping a suicidal person, your most important task may be to establish rapport.
26. TRUE or FALSE   It is helpful to get day-to-day commitments from suicidal persons to meet for lunch, share a ride, and the like so the person knows you expect her or him to be there.
27. TRUE or FALSE   A dangerous time for suicide is when a person suddenly seems to get better after a severe depression.
28. TRUE or FALSE   If a person seems to be suicidal, give the person the phone number of a crisis intervention center and urge them to call you or that number if she or he becomes frightened or impulsive.
29. TRUE or FALSE   One should never ask if a person is thinking about committing suicide or how the person plans to commit suicide.
30. TRUE or FALSE   The majority of suicide attempts come at temporary low points in a person's life and may never be repeated.

Critical Thinking Question

If you follow the history of popular music, see if you can answer this question: What two major risk factors contributed to the 1994 suicide of Kurt Cobain, lead singer for the rock group Nirvana?

Final Survey and Review—Completion

Module 13.1 Normality and Psychopathology
Normality—What's Normal?
Survey Question: How is abnormality defined?
1. The scientific study of mental, emotional, and behavioral disorders as well as the term that refers to mental disorders themselves is _____.
2. The results of tests, such as intelligence tests, form a normal, or _____ curve.
3. Disobeying public standards for acceptable conduct is referred to as _____.
4. All cultures classify people as abnormal if they fail to communicate with others and if they are consistently _____ in their actions.
5. A person suffering from mania might feel elated and "on top of the world." Thus, a mental problem, in this case, is revealed by a lack of _____.
6. Expert witnesses have testified that Terrence is unable to manage his affairs and is a danger to himself and others. Thus, Terrence will be placed involuntarily in a mental hospital because of these court proceedings that resulted in a legal finding of _____.

Module 13.1 Normality and Psychopathology
Classifying Mental Disorders—Problems by the Book
Survey Question: What are the major psychological disorders?
7. Barry has "retreated from reality," is hearing voices and has the delusion that he is a famous artist who lived in the 18th century. He stays in his house all day painting and wears aluminum foil hats to protect his brain from the space aliens who are projecting gamma rays through his roof. Barry is most likely suffering from schizophrenia, which is classified as a(n) _____ disorder.

761

8. People who are agitated, elated, and hyperactive, people who are extremely sad and hopeless, and people who cycle between these two states would all most likely be diagnosed as having _____ disorders.

9. Two stress-related anxiety disorders are post-traumatic stress disorder and _____ stress disorder.

10. When psychological factors appear to explain the symptoms, such as paralysis, blindness, or chronic pain where there is no physical cause, the person would most likely be diagnosed with a(n) _____ disorder.

11. Temporary amnesia, multiple personalities, and depersonalization are all types of _____ disorders.

12. You are visiting a Native American museum and read about culture-bound syndrome in which a person would become preoccupied with death and the deceased with the person suffering from bad dreams, fainting, anxiety, hallucinations, and a sense of suffocation. This culture-bound syndrome was known as _____.

13. The Diagnostic and Statistical Manual of Mental Disorders-IV-TR is a better method of diagnosing mental disorders than folk names because this manual is based on empirical data and _____.

14. Jack's wife left him 3 years ago, and he is embittered, angry, and humiliated and cannot forget or forgive her. Jack sits at home alone every night, is not seeing anyone else, is having troubles at work, and is estranged from his children. In diagnosing Jack's condition, a new disorder is being proposed that will be added to the new edition of the diagnostic manual. This disorder will be called _____ disorder.

15. Tom tells his therapist that he practically raised himself due to his mother working two jobs and his father's alcoholism. He and his mother were also on the receiving end of physical and verbal abuse. Tom's risk factors for developing a mental disorder would be classified as _____ factors.

Module 13.1 Normality and Psychopathology
Disorders in Perspective—Psychiatric Labeling
Survey Question: Can psychiatric labeling be misused?

16. In your history book, you read about runaway slaves in the mid-1800s having their toes cut off in order to treat a supposed "mental disorder" that caused slaves to run away that was called _____.

17. In the past, dissidents in totalitarian countries who were protesting to try to enact a more democratic government were confined to mental hospitals with a supposed diagnosis of _____.

18. Your psychology instructor shows the class a film clip about a classic experiment in which several psychologists had themselves committed to a mental hospital to observe the impact of psychiatric labeling. The psychologist who devised the experiment was _____.

19. Often, those who have been labeled mentally ill are denied housing and jobs as well as being rejected and disgraced, that is, _____ by society.

Module 13.2 Psychosis, Delusional Disorders, and Schizophrenia
Psychotic Disorders—The Dark Side of the Moon
Survey Question: What are the general characteristics of psychotic disorders?

20. Psychosis reflects a loss of contact with shared views of _____.

21. When a person believes that a car horn honking outside their window is sending them a personal, coded message, he or she is having a delusion of _____.

22. Feeling like "insects are crawling under your skin," tasting "poisons" in your food, or sensory changes, such as anesthesia or extreme sensitivity to heat, cold, pain, or touch, would be examples of _____.

23. Leslie, who has schizophrenia, has not changed facial expressions for day no matter what events occur when the hospital. Her "frozen face" and lack of emotions is referred to as a(n) _____.

24. The most common form of dementia is _____.

Module 13.2 Psychosis, Delusional Disorders, and Schizophrenia
Delusional Disorders—An Enemy Behind Every Tree
Survey Question: What is the nature of a delusional disorder?

25. People with delusional disorders usually do not suffer from the psychotic symptoms of emotional excesses, hallucinations, or personality _____.

26. Jed, who cannot carry a tune or dance, believes that he is really Gene Kelly, the famous Hollywood musical star. He is constantly auditioning for talent shows and putting on his "Singing in the Rain" musical number at nursing homes. Jed appears to be suffering from a(n) _____ type of delusion.

27. Belle believes that her nose, chin, and ears are badly misshapen. She has undergone three plastic surgeries, and her doctor has refused to do anymore. Belle still believes she needs more surgery to correct these hideous flaws. Belle is most likely suffering from a(n) _____ type of delusion.

28. Leo is suffering from the most common type of delusional disorder, which centers on persecutory type delusions. Leo has _____.

Module 13.2 Psychosis, Delusional Disorders, and Schizophrenia
Schizophrenia—Shattered Reality
Survey Questions: What forms does schizophrenia take? What causes it?

29. Hebephrenic schizophrenia is now referred to as _____ schizophrenia.

30. Larry is in a stupor state in which his limbs can be put in positions that he will hold for hours. He has not spoken since entering the hospital. The doctors will most likely diagnose Larry as suffering from _____ schizophrenia.

31. According to research, mentally ill individuals are no more prone to violence than are normal individuals if they are not currently experiencing psychotic symptoms and are not _____.

32. Mikka, who has schizophrenia, grew up in a family in which her parents and siblings were overly negative, hypercritical, and prying with their conversations being laden with guilt and emotional attacks. This situation illustrates one of the factors in the development of schizophrenia called _____ patterns.

33. Research on the biochemical changes that occur with schizophrenia have shown that the neurotransmitter dopamine is affected when stress alters the levels of another neurotransmitter known as _____.

34. MRI scans indicate that schizophrenic brains tend to have enlarged ventricles, which are the _____ spaces.

35. According the stress-vulnerability model, mind-altering changes in brain chemicals and brain structures produce psychotic disorders as well as other forms of psychopathology due to the right mix of environment stress and _____.

763

Module 13.3 Mood Disorders
Mood Disorders—Peaks and Valleys
Survey Questions: What are mood disorders? What causes them?

36. During this two-year period, Jessica has experienced mild to moderate depressive episodes that alternate with intervals when she is cheerful, expansive, and irritable. Jessica would most likely be diagnosed with a(n) _____ disorder.

37. David is more often withdrawn, sad, despondent, and guilt ridden, but he has on occasion displayed behavior that just managed to irritate everyone around him by being excessively cheerful, interrupting conversations, bragging, and talking too fast. David would most likely be diagnosed with _____ disorder.

38. Major mood disorders more often appear to be endogenous, rather than being a reaction to _____.

39. Regarding the cause of depression and other mood disorders, some scientists are interested in brain chemicals and transmitter substances, especially serotonin, dopamine, and _____.

40. The cause of depression, according to behavioral theories, is _____.

41. Meg having just given birth two days ago and is irritable, fatigued, tearful, and depressed. By the end of the week, she is her "old self" and is excited about being a new mother. Meg most likely had _____.

42. Doug has just moved from Memphis, Tennessee to Boston, Massachusetts in order to attend college. As fall becomes winter, Doug seems to be having a great deal of trouble sleeping, is irritable and fatigued during the day, and craves carbohydrates. Doug is most likely suffering from _____.

Module 13.4 Anxiety-Based Disorders and Personality Disorders
Anxiety-Based Disorders—When Anxiety Rules
Survey Question: What problems result when a person suffers high levels of anxiety?

43. Because Janice feels that she must be on guard against future threats that could happen at any time, she tends spend much of her day worrying and generating her own continuous tension and nervousness. Janice is most likely suffering from a(n) _____ anxiety disorder.

44. Every time that April "feels dirty" from all the germs in the office, she goes and washes her hands, which she does about fifty times a day. April is suffering from _____ disorder.

45. A person who was a prison of war for over six years during the Vietnam War still has flashbacks about the torture he received 40 years ago. This person may be suffering from _____.

46. Amnesia, fugue, and multiple identity are all part of _____ disorders.

47. In order for the person to eventually have a single, balanced personality, the goal of therapy for the person with multiple personalities is _____ and fusion.

48. Gina goes to the doctor almost every week with a new set of ailments, although the doctor has found no physical cause for her dozens of illnesses. Gina would most likely be diagnosed with the somatoform disorder known as _____ disorder.

49. It was discovered by the hospital staff that Greta was intentionally making her child sick in order to gain the sympathy and attention of other people, particularly the medical staff. Greta would most likely be diagnosed with a condition known as _____.

50. Marra was diagnosed with a dependent personality disorder, hypochondriasis, and generalized anxiety disorder. Marra's combination of disorders would be considered _____.

Module 13.4 Anxiety-Based Disorders and Personality Disorders
Anxiety and Disorder—Four Pathways to Trouble
Survey Question: How do psychologists explain anxiety-based disorders?

51. The person that first proposed a psychodynamic explanation for what he called "neurosis" was _____.
52. The psychologist who regarded emotional disorders as the end product of a faulty self-image or self-concept was _____.
53. According to existentialism, in making choices that will enhance our lives, we must show courage and _____.
54. Anxiety attacks reflect conditioned emotional responses that generalize to new situations, and the hypochondriac's "sickness behavior" is reinforced by the sympathy and attention he or she gets, according to the _____ approach.
55. Changing the thinking patterns of anxious individuals can greatly lessen their fears, according to the _____ theorists.

Module 13.4 Anxiety-Based Disorders and Personality Disorders
Personality Disorders—Blueprints for Maladjustment
Survey Question: What is a personality disorder?

56. Jeff tends to be very suspicious and wary of others and is hypersensitive regarding even the hint of criticism. Jeff appears to have a(n) _____ personality disorder.
57. The personality disorders that show a moderate impairment in functioning are the dependent, histrionic, antisocial, and _____.
58. People with a schizotypal personality disorder are loners and engage in extremely odd behavior; and although their thought patterns are also somewhat bizarre, they are not actively _____.
59. Studies have shown that the sociopath has unusual brain wave patterns that suggest under-arousal of the brain, which may explain why sociopaths tend to be _____.
60. It is difficult to successfully treat the antisocial personality disorders because just like any other situation, they will try to _____ therapy.

Module 13.5 Psychology in Action
Suicide—Lives on the Brink
Survey Questions: Why do people commit suicide? Can suicide be prevented?

61. When the suicide rates in the United States, Azerbaijan, and Hungary are compared, the lowest suicide rate is in _____.
62. Regarding age, ethnicity, and gender, the person at particular risk for suicide are 65 year old _____.
63. In 90 percent of all suicides, there was a diagnosable mental disorder, which was usually either depression or a(n) _____ disorder.
64. The possibility of committing suicide increases dramatically when a person turns inward an impulse to _____.
65. A suicidal person tends to narrow his or her _____.

765

Final Survey and Review—Matching

Module 13.1 Normality and Psychopathology
Part 1:

1. ___ psychopathology
2. ___ insanity
3. ___ neurosis
4. ___ mania
5. ___ cultural relativity
6. ___ phobias
7. ___ susto
8. ___ depersonalization
9. ___ statistical abnormality
10. ___ koro
11. ___ anarchia
12. ___ nymphomania

a. outdated term once used to refer, as a group, to anxiety disorders, somatoform disorders, dissociative disorders, and some forms of depression

b. agitated, elated, and hyperactive

c. abnormality defined on the basis of an extreme score on some dimension

d. legal term that refers to a mental inability to manage one's affairs or to be aware of the consequences of one's action

e. the idea that judgments are determined by the values of one's culture

f. in south and east Asia, people experience intense fear of shrinking genitals

g. outdated term for mental illness that leads one to seek a more democratic society

h. Latin American affliction that includes insomnia, irritability, sweating and can result in voodoo death

i. outdated term for a "disorder" of women who have a healthy sexual appetite

j. irrational fears for specific objects or situations

k. scientific study of mental, emotional, and behavioral disorders; also, abnormal or maladaptive behavior

l. people feel like they are outside their bodies, are behaving like robots, or are lost in a dream world

Part 2:

1. ___ culture-bound syndromes
2. ___ psychotic disorders
3. ___ mood disorders
4. ___ anxiety disorders
5. ___ dissociative disorders
6. ___ somatoform disorders

a. maladaptive personality pattern, such as narcissistic, dependent, or borderline

b. physical symptoms that mimic disease or injury for which there is no identifiable physical cause

c. problems in sexual desire, arousal, or response

d. temporary amnesia, fugue, multiple personality, or depersonalization

e. major disturbance in emotion, such as depression or mania

f. sexual deviations, including exhibitionism, fetishism, and voyeurism

7. ___ personality disorders

8. ___ paraphilias

9. ___ sexual dysfunctions

g. folk names for afflictions that may or may not be recognized mental disorders

h. disruptive feelings of fear and apprehension with distortions in behavior, such as phobias, stress disorders, and obsessive-compulsive disorder

i. severe mental disorder characterized by a retreat from reality, by hallucinations and delusions, and by social withdrawal

Module 13.2 Psychosis, Delusional Disorders, and Schizophrenia

Part 1:

1. ___ disorganized schizophrenia

a. psychosis marked by a preoccupation with delusions or by frequent auditory hallucinations related to a single theme, especially grandeur or persecution

2. ___ catatonic schizophrenia

b. age-related disease characterized by memory loss and mental confusion; caused by webs and tangles in the brain

3. ___ paranoid schizophrenia

c. psychosis marked by stupor, rigidity, unresponsiveness, posturing and, sometimes, agitated purposeless behavior

4. ___ undifferentiated schizophrenia

d. any serious mental impairment in old age caused by physical deterioration of the brain, repeated strokes, and/or circulatory problems

5. ___ paranoid psychosis

e. most common delusional disorder centered especially on delusions of persecution

6. ___ organic psychosis

f. psychosis with fragmented delusions and hallucinations, incoherence, confused behavior, bizarre thinking, and flat or grossly inappropriate emotions

7. ___ dementia

g. any mental disorder caused by a clear-cut brain injury or disease

8. ___ Alzheimer's disease

h. schizophrenia with prominent psychotic symptoms but lacking the specific features of the other types

Part 2:

1. ___ depressive delusions

a. feeling as if one is being controlled by others or by unseen forces

2. ___ erotomanic type delusion

b. person's thoughts, actions, and emotions are no longer coordinated

3. ___ grandiose type delusion

c. condition in which the face is frozen in a blank expression

4. ___ jealous type delusion

d. delusion that one is loved by another person, especially by someone famous or of higher status

5. ___ persecutory type delusion

e. imaginary sensation, such as seeing, hearing, or smelling things that do not exist in the real world

6. ___ somatic type delusion
7. ___ delusion of influence

8. ___ delusion of reference

9. ___ hallucinations

10. ___ flat affect

11. ___ personality disintegration

f. giving great personal meaning to unrelated events
g. delusion that you are a famous person, have a special talent, or a special relationship with an important person
h. having an all-consuming, but unfounded, belief that your spouse or lover is unfaithful
i. feeling that one has committed horrible crimes or sinful deeds
j. delusion that your body is diseased, rotting, or infested with parasites, or parts of their bodies are defective
k. delusion that you are being conspired against, cheated, spied on, followed, maligned, or harassed

Module 13.3 Mood Disorders

1. ___ dysthymic disorder
2. ___ cyclothymic disorder

3. ___ major depressive disorder

4. ___ bipolar I disorder

5. ___ bipolar II disorder
6. ___ postpartum depression

7. ___ seasonal affective disorder (SAD)

8. ___ psychoanalytic theory of depression

9. ___ behavioral theories of depression

10. ___ cognitive theory of depression

a. learned helplessness causes depression
b. moderate depression that persists for two years or more
c. mild to moderately severe depression that begins within three months following childbirth
d. self-criticism and negative, distorted, or self-defeating thoughts underlie many cases of depression
e. depression caused by repressed anger
f. major mood disorder in which a person is mostly depressed but has also had one or more episodes of mild mania
g. mild depression that occurs only during fall and winter presumable related to decreased exposure to sunlight
h. major mood disorder in which the person has suffered one or more intense episodes of depression
i. major mood disorder in which the person has episodes of mania and also periods of deep depression
j. moderate manic and depressive behavior that persists for two years or more

Module 13.4 Anxiety-Based Disorders and Personality Disorders
Part 1:

1. ___ dissociative disorders

2. ___ adjustment disorder

a. fear that something extremely embarrassing will happen if one leaves the house or enters unfamiliar situations; may refuse to go outside their home
b. psychological disturbance lasting more then one month following stresses that would produce anxiety in anyone who experienced them

768

3. ___ generalized anxiety disorder

   c. affected person fakes the medical problems of someone in his or her care in order to gain attention

4. ___ hypochondriasis

   d. bodily symptom that mimics a physical disability, such as blindness or paralysis, but is actually caused by anxiety or emotional distress

5. ___ agoraphobia

   e. intense, irrational fear of being observed, evaluated, embarrassed, or humiliated by others in social situations

6. ___ conversion disorder

   f. afflicted persons have numerous physical complaints; typically consult many doctors, but no organic cause for their distress can be identified

7. ___ social phobia

   g. chronic state of tension and worries about work, relationships, ability, or impeding disaster

8. ___ obsessive-compulsive disorder

   h. includes xenophobia, astraphobia, acrophobia, etc.

9. ___ somatization disorder

   i. emotional disturbance caused by ongoing stressors within the range of common experience

10. ___ Munchausen syndrome by proxy

   j. extreme preoccupation with certain thoughts and the performance of certain behaviors (to control the thoughts)

11. ___ specific phobias

   k. include amnesia, fugue, and multiple identities

12. ___ posttraumatic stress disorder

   l. preoccupation with fears of having a serious disease with ordinary minor physical signs being interpreted as proof that the person has a disease, but no physical disorder can be found

Part 2:

1. ___ anxiety

   a. distressing thoughts and images that force their way into awareness against a person's will

2. ___ comorbid

   b. distorted thinking magnifies ordinary threats and failures and leads to anxiety

3. ___ obsessions

   c. thinks of oneself as wonderful, brilliant, important, and worthy of constant admiration

4. ___ compulsions

   d. dramatic and flamboyant, exaggerates emotions to get the attention from others

5. ___ psychodynamic approach

   e. anxiety is the end product of a faulty self-image

6. ___ humanistic approach (Rogers)

   f. irresponsible, lacks guilt or remorse, reckless and deceitful, sociopath

7. ___ existential approach

8. ___ behavioral approach

9. ___ cognitive approach

10. ___ antisocial personality disorder

11. ___ borderline personality disorder

12. ___ histrionic personality disorder

13. ___ schizotypal personality disorder

14. ___ narcissistic personality disorder

g. intense anxiety caused by forbidden id impulses; person uses rigid defense mechanisms to maintain control

h. feelings of apprehension, dread, or uneasiness

i. anxiety attacks are conditioned emotional responses; self-defeating behaviors are learned

j. irrational acts that a person feels driven to repeat

k. unhealthy anxiety reflects a loss of meaning in one's life

l. loner, engages in extremely odd behavior, thought patterns are bizarre, but person is not actively psychotic

m. suffering from more than one disorder at a time

n. self-image, moods, and impulses are erratic and person is extremely sensitive to any hint of criticism, rejection, or abandonment by others

Module 13.5 Psychology in Action: Suicide—Lives on the Brink

1. ___ rapport

2. ___ acculturative stress

3. ___ warning signs of impending suicide

4. ___ characteristics of suicidal thoughts

5. ___ depression or substance abuse

a. escape; unbearable psychological pain; frustrated psychological needs; constriction of options

b. establishing a harmonious connection

c. diagnosable mental disorder in 90 percent of suicides

d. factor in ethnic adolescents' suicide

e. sudden swings in mood; gift giving of prized possession

Final Survey and Review—True or False

Module 13.1 Normality and Psychopathology

Normality—What's Normal?

Survey Question: How is abnormality defined?

1. TRUE or FALSE   Less than five percent of American adults suffer from a diagnosable mental disorder in any given year.

2. TRUE or FALSE   Statistical definitions do not automatically tell us where to draw the line between normality and abnormality.

3. TRUE or FALSE   Actions that are regarded as "strange" within a particular culture are often the first sign to others that a person has a problem.

4. TRUE or FALSE   Almost any imaginable behavior can be considered normal in some contexts.

5. TRUE or FALSE   Cultural relativity refers to making personal judgments about another culture's practices.

6. TRUE or FALSE   People who are declared insane are not legally responsible for their actions.

770

Module 13.1 Normality and Psychopathology
Classifying Mental Disorders—Problems by the Book
Survey Question: What are the major psychological disorders?

7. TRUE or FALSE   "Organic mental disorders" is one of the major categories in DSM-IV-TR.
8. TRUE or FALSE   Obsessive-compulsive disorder is a type of psychotic disorder.
9. TRUE or FALSE   Narcissistic, borderline, and antisocial are types of somatoform disorders.
10. TRUE or FALSE   The paraphilias include exhibitionism, fetishism, and voyeurism.
11. TRUE or FALSE   Eating inedible substances is a condition known as factitious disorder.
12. TRUE or FALSE   You are visiting a hospital in the Philippines when a man is brought in who after being insulted broke out in a fit of range aggressively attacking people and objects in the street at random. A local man tells you that this man has a condition known as dhat.
13. TRUE or FALSE   Neurosis is a legal term established in court by expert witnesses.
14. TRUE or FALSE   A new mental disorder that may be added to the DSM-V and occurs when a person is left very bitter after a perceived injustice will be called acute depersonalization disorder.
15. TRUE or FALSE   Poverty, overcrowding, and homelessness have not been shown to be risk factors for mental disorders.

Module 13.1 Normality and Psychopathology
Disorders in Perspective—Psychiatric Labeling
Survey Question: Can psychiatric labeling be misused?

16. TRUE or FALSE   A woman who had a healthy sexual appetite was once said to suffer from a disorder known as drapetomania.
17. TRUE or FALSE   David Rosenhan and several colleagues had themselves committed to mental hospitals with a diagnosis of schizophrenia in order to study the impact of psychiatric labeling.
18. TRUE or FALSE   People who have been labeled mentally ill at any time in their lives are now just as likely to be hired and to obtain housing as a person who has not been labeled mentally ill.
19. TRUE or FALSE   The predictable tendency for medical and psychology student to notice in themselves the symptoms of each dreaded disease that they study is referred to as an obsessive-compulsive disorder.

Module 13.2 Psychosis, Delusional Disorders, and Schizophrenia
Psychotic Disorders—The Dark Side of the Moon
Survey Question: What are the general characteristics of psychotic disorders?

20. TRUE or FALSE   Depressive delusions involve thinking that one's body is "rotting away" or is emitting foul odors.
21. TRUE or FALSE   The most common hallucination is hearing voices.
22. TRUE or FALSE   Brain images from psychotic patients with "frozen faces" reveal that their brains are processing emotions as normally as someone who has different facial expressions that match his or her emotions.
23. TRUE or FALSE   The general term organic psychosis is usually reserved for problems involving clear-cut brain injuries or diseases.
24. TRUE or FALSE   No genetic factor has been found that increases the risk of one developing Alzheimer's disease.

Module 13.2 Psychosis, Delusional Disorders, and Schizophrenia
Delusional Disorders—An Enemy Behind Every Tree
Survey Question: What is the nature of a delusional disorder?

25. TRUE or FALSE   In delusional disorders, people have auditory hallucinations of grandeur or persecution.
26. TRUE or FALSE   A person who believes that his body is diseased and rotting has an erotomanic type of delusional disorder.
27. TRUE or FALSE   People with schizophrenia tend to have delusions about experiences that could occur in real life, while people with delusional disorders have more bizarre delusions.
28. TRUE or FALSE   Paranoid psychosis is very difficult to treat since anyone who suggests that a person with this disorder needs help would simply becomes part of the "conspiracy" that is "out to get him or her."

Module 13.2 Psychosis, Delusional Disorders, and Schizophrenia
Schizophrenia—Shattered Reality
Survey Questions: What forms does schizophrenia take? What causes it?

29. TRUE or FALSE   In any given year, one person out of 100 will become schizophrenic.
30. TRUE or FALSE   Silliness, laughter, and bizarre behavior are common in disorganized schizophrenia.
31. TRUE or FALSE   Periods of immobility and odd posturing are characteristic of paranoid schizophrenia.
32. TRUE or FALSE   At various times, patients may shift from one type of schizophrenia to another.
33. TRUE or FALSE   If one identical twin is schizophrenic, the other twin has a 48 percent chance of also becoming schizophrenic.
34. TRUE or FALSE   MRI scans indicate that schizophrenia brains have smaller than average ventricles.
35. TRUE or FALSE   PET scans show that activity in the frontal lobes of schizophrenics tends to be abnormally low.

Module 13.3 Mood Disorders
Mood Disorders—Peaks and Valleys
Survey Questions: What are mood disorders? What causes them?

36. TRUE or FALSE   Even in severe cases of major depression or bipolar disorders, people do not lose touch with reality or display any psychotic symptoms.
37. TRUE or FALSE   Mildly manic episodes are referred to as dysthymia.
38. TRUE or FALSE   Psychoanalysts believe that self-criticism and negative, distorted, or self-defeating thoughts underlie many cases of depression.
39. TRUE or FALSE   Endogenous depression appears to be generated from within, with little connection to external events.
40. TRUE or FALSE   If one identical twin is depressed, the other has a 95 percent chance of suffering depression, too.
41. TRUE or FALSE   Overall, women are twice as likely as men to become depressed.
42. TRUE or FALSE   The treatment for seasonal affective disorder (SAD) that involves exposure to bright, fluorescent light each day is known as phototherapy.

Module 13.4 Anxiety-Based Disorders and Personality Disorders
Anxiety-Based Disorders—When Anxiety Rules
Survey Question: What problems result when a person suffers high levels of anxiety?

43. TRUE or FALSE   In any given year, only roughly 18 percent of the adult population suffers from an anxiety disorder.
44. TRUE or FALSE   For a phobic disorder to exist, the person's fear must disrupt his or her daily life.
45. TRUE or FALSE   Xenophobia is a fear of snakes.
46. TRUE or FALSE   A fear of using a public restroom, writing one's name in front of others, or eating in public are all examples of a social phobia.
47. TRUE or FALSE   "Checkers," "cleaners," and hoarders are three types of behaviors that people may feel compelled to repeat when they are suffering from somatoform disorder.
48. TRUE or FALSE   PTSD is a psychological disturbance lasting more than a month after exposure to severe stress.
49. TRUE or FALSE   Multiple personality is a dissociative disorder.
50. TRUE or FALSE   Victims of conversion reactions become overly panicked and hysterical regarding their apparent disability.

Module 13.4 Anxiety-Based Disorders and Personality Disorders
Anxiety and Disorder—Four Pathways to Trouble
Survey Question: How do psychologists explain anxiety-based disorders?

51. TRUE or FALSE   Anxiety disorders appear to be partly hereditary.
52. TRUE or FALSE   Carl Rogers believed that anxious individuals have built up unrealistic mental images of themselves, which leaves them vulnerable to contradictory information.
53. TRUE or FALSE   The humanistic approach attributes anxiety disorders to distorted thinking that leads to conditioned emotional responses .
54. TRUE or FALSE   The behavioral approach characterizes anxiety disorders as a product of id impulses that threaten a loss of control.
55. TRUE or FALSE   According to the anxiety reduction hypothesis, the powerful reward of immediate relief from anxiety keeps self-defeating avoidance behaviors alive.

Module 13.4 Anxiety-Based Disorders and Personality Disorders
Personality Disorders—Blueprints for Maladjustment
Survey Question: What is a personality disorder?

56. TRUE or FALSE   Personality disorders usually appear suddenly in early adulthood.
57. TRUE or FALSE   Celebrities appear to be more likely to be narcissistic than noncelebrities.
58. TRUE or FALSE   The histrionic personality is a loner who engages in extremely odd behavior and has bizarre thought patterns, but is not actively psychotic.
59. TRUE or FALSE   "Psychopath" is another term for the borderline personality.
60. TRUE or FALSE   Persons with a antisocial personality disorder have been described as emotionally cold, which may explain how they can calmly lie and take advantage of others.

Module 13.5 Psychology in Action
Suicide—Lives on the Brink
Survey Questions: Why do people commit suicide? Can suicide be prevented?

61. TRUE or FALSE   More men than women complete suicide.
62. TRUE or FALSE   Suicide rates steadily decline after young adulthood.

63. TRUE or FALSE   Married individuals have lower rates of suicide than the divorced, the widowed, and single persons.

64. TRUE or FALSE   For every ten potential suicides, eight give warning beforehand.

65. TRUE or FALSE   The risk of attempted suicide is high if a person has a concrete, workable plan for carrying it out.

Mastery Test

1. If you wish to specialize in a field of study that investigates the origins, symptoms, and development of mental, emotional, and behavior disorders, you will be specializing in
   a. neuropsychosis.
   b. biopsychosociology.
   c. psychopathology.
   d. psychoses.

2. If you develop a test to diagnose personality disorders based on the occurrence of extreme scores on this test, you are defining abnormality based on
   a. statistical abnormality.
   b. situational context.
   c. social noncomformity.
   d. subjective discomfort.

3. All abnormal behavior has a core feature of being
   a. statistically extreme.
   b. associated with subjective discomfort.
   c. ultimately maladaptive.
   d. marked by a loss of contract with reality.

4. Because Lorraine has purposely hurt herself in several suicide attempts over the last few weeks, Lorraine's family has gone to court to have her involuntarily committed to a mental hospital in order to help her. These commitment proceedings may result in the finding of _____ for Lorraine.
   a. psychosis
   b. neurosis
   c. insanity
   d. a nervous breakdown

5. Dr. Abbot is a clinical psychologist in private practice. In order to correctly diagnose his clients' mental and personality disorders and to select the best therapies to treat them, Dr. Abbot uses the
   a. *Annotated Diagnostic Standards for Mental and Personality Disorders, 3rd Ed.*
   b. *Diagnostic and Statistical Manual of Mental Disorders (DSM-IV-TR).*
   c. *Biochemical Diagnostic Manual (BDM-II-VR).*
   d. *Uniform Code of Mental Disorders (UCMD).*

6. Hearing voices that do not exist is an almost sure sign of a _____ disorder.
   a. psychotic
   b. dissociative
   c. personality
   d. delusional

774

7. Marcus experienced a severe head injury in a fall and since then has shown memory loss, personality changes, and impaired thinking. Marcus appears to be suffering from a(n) _____ disorder.
   a. somatoform
   b. bipolar
   c. dissociative
   d. organic mental

8. Britney has been diagnosed with obsessive-compulsive disorder, while her brother, who returned from duty in Iraq, has posttraumatic stress disorder. Both Britney and her brother are suffering from _____ disorders.
   a. anxiety
   b. somatoform
   c. psychotic
   d. dissociative

9. Marta has been under a great deal of stress and recently she has been experiencing episodes in which she feels like she is locked inside a dream world and cannot escape. Her actions during these episodes are much like a robot in which she must will herself to move. Marta is experiencing
   a. mania.
   b. somatization.
   c. conversion reaction.
   d. depersonalization.

10. Voyeurism and exhibitionism are examples of
   a. dissociative disorders.
   b. paraphilias.
   c. sexual dysfunctions.
   d. somatoform disorders.

11. Which of the following terms is no longer a recognized category of mental disorders?
   a. paraphilias
   b. somatoform disorders
   c. neurosis
   d. psychosis

12. In some cultures, it is believed that when the men have been insulted, they will erupt in random violence due to a condition known as
   a. amok.
   b. dhat.
   c. susto.
   d. koro.

13. Historically, some psychiatric terms have been applied to culturally disapproved behaviors that are not really disorders. For example, in the 1840s a slave who tried repeatedly to escape from a cruel and abusive master had the condition called
   a. anarchia.
   b. nymphomania.
   c. neurosis.
   d. drapetomania.

14. A patient feels like "insects are crawling all over his body" and also shows extreme sensitivity to heat, cold, pain, and touch. What type of symptom is he suffering from?
    a. neurosis
    b. delusions
    c. hallucinations
    d. cyclothymia

15. Which of the following is NOT a type of delusion?
    a. avoidant
    b. depressive
    c. reference
    d. influence

16. The principal problem in paranoid psychosis involves
    a. delusions.
    b. hallucinations.
    c. disturbed emotions.
    d. personality disintegration.

17. Amy believes that she is the long-lost daughter of Princess Diana and continually writes letters to Buckingham Palace informing them of her birth right. Amy is suffering from a(n)
    a. erotomanic delusion.
    b. grandiose delusion.
    c. catatonic hallucination.
    d. hebephrenic hallucination.

18. Lana's personality disintegration is almost complete with her speech sounding like a "word salad" punctuated with expletives and silly laughter. Her actions also are both bizarre and obscene. Lana most likely has which type of schizophrenia?
    a. undifferentiated
    b. paranoid
    c. catatonic
    d. disorganized

19. Which of the following would NOT be a cause of schizophrenia?
    a. the unborn child being exposed to flu virus or rubella
    b. the unborn child being exposed to X-rays or radiation
    c. early childhood psychological trauma
    d. inherited vulnerability plus stress

20. Disturbances in which brain chemicals are believed to cause the symptoms of schizophrenia?
    a. melatonin and serotonin
    b. acetylcholine and norepinephrine
    c. lithium carbonate and serotonin
    d. dopamine and glutamate

21. Research using CT, MRI, and PET scans have found that the schizophrenic brain has
    a. wider-than-normal surface fissuring.
    b. smaller than normal ventricles.
    c. abnormally high activity in the frontal lobes.
    d. all of these differences.

22. Sierta has been mildly to moderately depressed for at least two years. She would most likely be diagnosed with a _____ disorder.
    a. bipolar II
    b. dysthymic
    c. cyclothymic
    d. conversion

23. Although Greta is extremely sad and guilt ridden much of the time, she occasionally exhibits hypomania and is excessively cheerful, talks too fast, and goes on spending sprees. Greta most likely would be diagnosed with _____ disorder.
    a. bipolar I
    b. bipolar II
    c. major depressive
    d. seasonal affective

24. Cognitive theorists believe the cause of depression to be
    a. repressed anger and displaced blame.
    b. learned helplessness and conditioned responses.
    c. self-defeating thoughts.
    d. a loss of meaning in one's life.

25. After her divorce, Marie was extremely irritable and depressed. She lost her appetite and had trouble sleeping. After some supportive counseling and getting a new job and apartment, Marie's symptoms have improved significantly. Marie most likely had a(n) _____ disorder.
    a. agoraphobic
    b. adjustment
    c. obsessive-compulsive
    d. somatoform

26. Jana will only leave her house to go with her sister to the grocery store or to church once a week and never by herself. She is fearful that something extremely embarrassing will happen if she enters an unfamiliar situation, so she is essentially housebound. Jana is suffering from
    a. agoraphobia.
    b. somatization disorder.
    c. acute stress disorder.
    d. depersonalization.

27. Toni has a fear of the number 13 and does not leave the house on this day. Toni is suffering from a specific phobia known as
    a. xenophobia.
    b. astraphobia.
    c. coulrophobia.
    d. triskaidekaphobia.

28. Jasmine would be described as a frequent "checker" because she has to get up at least 20 times a night to "check" to make sure all the doors and windows are locked. She must also go back at least five times to make sure she has cut off the iron and the lights before going to work. Jasmine most likely suffers from which type of disorder?
    a. somatoform disorder
    b. obsessive-compulsive disorder
    c. panic disorder with agoraphobia
    d. dissociative disorder

29. After Edie was in a hurricane, she experienced insomnia, nightmares, poor concentration, and irritability. However, Edie's symptoms subsided within one month. Thus, Edie's initial reactions after the hurricane would be classified as a(n) _____ stress disorder.
    a. dissociative
    b. obsessive
    c. acute
    d. posttraumatic

30. A person whose personality splits into two or more identities is experiencing a type of
    a. somatoform disorder.
    b. dissociative disorder.
    c. organic psychosis.
    d. schizophrenia.

31. You find yourself in an unfamiliar town, and you cannot remember your name or address. It is likely that you are suffering from a
    a. paraphilia.
    b. borderline personality disorder.
    c. conversion reaction.
    d. dissociative fugue.

32. Ashea's family is moving across the country. Ashea is very unhappy and stressed by the upcoming move from her extended family and friends. The day of the move, Ashea awakens and is paralyzed from the waist down. She is rushed to the hospital, but no physical cause can be found for her paralysis. Interestingly, Ashea is strangely unconcerned about being disabled. Ashea would be diagnosed with a(n) _____ disorder.
    a. generalized anxiety
    b. somatization
    c. conversion
    d. dissociative fugue

33. In the past year, Kell has been to the emergency room 15 times with cuts, bruises, eye infections, vomiting, and various other ailments. He does not seem to mind waiting or undergoing the tests and treatments. In fact, Kell seems to enjoy the attention he gets from the medical staff. The doctors now realize that Kell caused all of his ailments himself. Kell is suffering from
    a. somatization disorder.
    b. hypochondriasis.
    c. Munchausen syndrome by proxy.
    d. Munchausen syndrome.

34. According to Carl Rogers, emotional disorders are the end product of
    a. conflict between the subparts of the personality.
    b. a faulty self-image.
    c. a loss of meaning in one's life.
    d. avoidance learning.

35. The most direct explanation for the anxiety reducing properties of self-defeating behavior is found in
    a. repressed anger.
    b. avoidance learning.
    c. the loss of meaning in one's life.
    d. the concept of existential anxiety.

36. Tim thinks that he is wonderful, brilliant, and worthy of constant admiration. Tim has a(n) _____ personality disorder.
    a. histrionic
    b. schizoid
    c. narcissistic
    d. paranoid

37. Sometimes Margo is friendly and charming, but at other times she is very impulsive and moody. Margo is also extremely sensitive to criticism, which interferes with her interactions with people at work. Margo most likely would be diagnosed with a(n) _____ personality disorder.
    a. avoidant
    b. borderline
    c. histrionic
    d. schizoid

38. People might describe Larry as "charming" when they first meet him, but they will gradually realize that Larry lies, is irresponsible, manipulative, and self-serving. Larry has a(n) _____ personality disorder.
    a. antisocial
    b. histrionic
    c. schizoid
    d. paranoid

39. Regarding suicide, which of the following statements is TRUE?
    a. More women complete suicide, while men make more attempts.
    b. Adolescents and young adults commit suicide more often than older adults.
    c. Married individuals have higher rates of suicides than divorced, widowed, or single persons.
    d. Caucasians generally have higher rates of suicide than do non-Caucasians.

40. Regarding suicide, which of the following statements is FALSE?
    a. People who talk about or threaten suicide are rarely the ones who try it.
    b. Suicide can be prevented if a distressed person's frustrated needs can be identified.
    c. A dangerous time for suicide is when a person suddenly seems to get better after a severe depression.
    d. It is completely acceptable and will not provoke a suicide attempt if you ask the person if he or she is planning to commit suicide and how he or she is planning to carry it out.

779

Chapter 14: Therapies

Chapter Overview

Early approaches to mental illness were dominated by superstition and moral condemnation. Demonology attributed mental disturbance to demonic possession and prescribed exorcism as the cure. In some instances, the actual cause of bizarre behavior may have been ergot poisoning. More humane treatment began in 1793 with the work of Philippe Pinel in Paris.

Psychoanalysts have become relatively rare because psychoanalysis is expensive and time intensive. However, as the first true psychotherapy, Freud's psychoanalysis gave rise to modern psychodynamic therapies. The psychoanalyst uses free association, dream analysis, and analysis of resistance and transference to reveal health-producing insights. Some critics argue that traditional psychoanalysis receives credit for spontaneous remissions of symptoms. However, psychoanalysis is successful for many patients. Brief psychodynamic therapy (which relies on psychoanalytic theory but is brief and focused) is as effective as other major therapies. One example is interpersonal psychotherapy.

All psychotherapy aims to facilitate positive changes in personality, behavior, or adjustment. Psychotherapies may be classified as insight, action, directive, nondirective, and combinations of these. Therapies may be conducted either individually or in groups, and they may be time limited.

Client-centered (or person-centered) therapy is nondirective, based on insights gained from conscious thoughts and feelings, and dedicated to creating an atmosphere of growth. Unconditional positive regard, empathy, authenticity, and reflection are combined to give the client a chance to solve his or her own problems. Existential therapies focus on the end result of the choices one makes in life. Clients are encouraged through confrontation and encounter to exercise free will and to take responsibility for their choices. Gestalt therapy emphasizes immediate awareness of thoughts and feelings. Its goal is to rebuild thinking, feeling, and acting into connected wholes and to help clients break through emotional blockages.

Cognitive therapy emphasizes changing thought patterns that underlie emotional or behavioral problems. Its goals are to correct distorted thinking and/or teach improved coping skills. Irrational beliefs are the core of many maladaptive thinking patterns. Changing such beliefs can have a positive impact on emotions and behavior. In a variation of cognitive therapy called rational-emotive behavior therapy (REBT), clients learn to recognize and challenge their own irrational beliefs.

Behavior therapists use the learning principles of classical or operant conditioning to directly change human behavior. In aversion therapy, classical conditioning is used to associate maladaptive behavior (such as smoking or drinking) with pain or other aversive events in order to inhibit undesirable responses. In desensitization, gradual adaptation and reciprocal inhibition break the link between fear and particular situations. Typical steps in desensitization are: Construct a fear hierarchy; learn to produce total relaxation; and perform items on the hierarchy (from least to most disturbing). Desensitization may be carried out with real settings or it may be done by vividly imagining the fear hierarchy or by watching models perform the feared responses. In some cases, virtual reality exposure can be used to present fear stimuli in a controlled manner. A new technique called eye movement desensitization and reprocessing (EMDR) shows promise as a treatment for traumatic memories and stress disorders. At present, however, EMDR is highly controversial.

Operant principles, such as positive reinforcement, nonreinforcement, extinction, punishment, shaping, stimulus control, and time out, are used to extinguish undesirable responses and to promote constructive behavior. Nonreward can extinguish troublesome behaviors. Often this is done by simply identifying and eliminating reinforcers, particularly attention and social approval. To apply positive reinforcement and operant shaping, tokens are often used to reinforce selected target behaviors. Full-scale use of tokens in an institutional setting produces a token economy. Toward the end of a token economy program, patients are shifted to social rewards such as recognition and approval.

Medical approaches to mental disorders, such as drugs, surgery, and hospitalization, are similar to medical treatments for physical ailments. Three medical, or somatic, approaches to treatment are pharmacotherapy, electrical stimulation therapy (including electroconvulsive therapy [ECT]), and psychosurgery. Community mental health centers seek to avoid or minimize mental hospitalization. They also seek to prevent mental health problems through education, consultation, and crisis intervention.

Effective psychotherapies are based on the therapeutic alliance, a protected setting, catharsis, insights, new perspectives, and a chance to practice new behaviors. Psychotherapy is generally effective, although no single form of therapy is superior to others. All of the following are helping skills that can be learned: active listening, acceptance, reflection, open-ended questioning, support, respect, patience, genuineness, and paraphrasing. The culturally skilled counselor must be able to establish rapport with a person from a different cultural background and adapt traditional theories and techniques to meet the needs of clients from non-European ethnic groups.

Therapy can be done with groups of people based on a simple extension of individual methods or based on techniques developed specifically for groups. In psychodrama, individuals enact roles and incidents resembling their real-life problems. In family therapy, the family group is treated as a unit. Sensitivity and encounter groups encourage positive personality change. Large-group awareness training attempts to do the same, but the benefits of such programs are questionable. Media psychologists, telephone counselors, and cybertherapists may, on occasion, do some good. However, each has drawbacks, and the effectiveness of telephone counseling and cybertherapy has not been established. Therapy by videoconferencing shows more promise as a way to provide mental health services at a distance.

Some personal problems can be successfully treated using self-management techniques, such as covert reinforcement, covert sensitization, thought stopping, and self-directed desensitization. In covert sensitization, aversive images are used to discourage unwanted behavior. Thought stopping uses mild punishment to prevent upsetting thoughts. Covert reinforcement is a way to encourage desired responses by mental rehearsal. Desensitization pairs relaxation with a hierarchy of upsetting images in order to lessen fears.

Everyone should know how to obtain high-quality mental health care in his or her community. Various psychotherapies are generally equally successful, but some therapists are more effective than others. If you need help, it is worth the effort required to find a well-qualified, highly recommended therapist. In most communities, a competent and reputable therapist can be located with public sources of information or through a referral. Practical considerations such as cost and qualifications enter into choosing a therapist. However, the therapist's personal characteristics are of equal importance.

Preview: The Duck Syndrome

Language Development Guide

blinds: type of window covering made of overlapping slats of wood, mental, plastic, or cloth that can be opened to let light in or closed to block out light

quack: sound made by ducks

losing my mind: not having control of one's mind and thinking; becoming mentally ill

personal hell: own misery; awful situation

madly: wildly; frantically

crippling: disabling; incapacitating

deathly afraid: as if one is afraid of dying; extremely frightened

absenteeism: missing school or work

got fired: lost his job

disastrous: completely unsuccessful

terrified: horrified; frightened

turning point: moment of change

existence: life; survival

nightmare: very awful like a bad dream

own worst enemy: doing things yourself that actually cause you to fail or bad things to happen to you

come to grips: begin to deal with something

regain his balance: recover completely and get back on one's feet

alleviate: lessen; ease

insight: clear perception or understanding

Module 14.1 Treating Psychological Distress

Origins of Therapy—Bored Out of Your Skull

Survey Question: How did psychotherapy originate?

Language Development Guide

fortunately: luckily

odds: chances

archaeological: involving the systematic study of the past human life and culture by examining material evidence left

dating: establishing the age of something

Stone Age: earliest period of human history in which tools and weapons were made of stone

primitive: ancient; prehistoric

superstitious: involves generally believing in a supernatural cause of events, such as being convinced that performing or not performing certain acts brings about good luck or bad luck

demons: evil spirits

witchcraft: the practice of using supposed supernatural, magical powers

magic: controlling or forecasting natural events through supposed supernatural powers; tricks and illusions that seem to cause impossible events, used for entertainment

"cures" practiced by primitive "therapists": methods of supposedly ridding a person of his or her mental illness before there were therapies based on science

bored/boring: drilled or poked a hole into something

bashing: smashing; hitting

presumably: most likely

Middle Ages: period of European history from fifth to 15th century

plagued: troubled by overwhelmed; weighed down

783

possession by Devil: mind being controlled or body occupied by evil spirits

curses: appeals to a supernatural being for harm to come to somebody

wizards: male witches that practice supernatural, magical powers

exorcism: religious rite to remove evil spirits

inhospitable: uninviting; unwelcoming

reside: exist in; live in

demonology: study of demons and belief in demons

infested: contaminated; diseased

fungus: organisms that include yeasts, molds, and mushrooms

tainted: contaminated; infected; ruined

bewitchment: affected by witchcraft or magic

madness: mental illness

spasms: tremors

doubly: twice as; even more; particularly

victimized: harmed; abused; treated unfairly

asylum: institution for the care of the mentally ill; literally means a place offering shelter and protection

squalid: unclean; dirty; filthy; neglected

"madhouse": scene of chaos and confusion; slang term for some of the early mental hospitals

compassionate: showing sympathy

humane: caring; kind

intrigued: interested; fascinated

granddaddy: either foundation, beginning, or most important or well known

Recite and Review

1. The most primitive approaches to dealing with mental illness were marked by fear and superstitious belief in demons, magic, and _____.
2. Archaeological findings dating back to the Stone Age indicate that primitive "therapists" bored, chipped, or bashed holes into a patient's head to relieve pressure or release evil spirits during a procedure known as _____.
3. During the Middle Ages, treatments for mental illness in Europe focused on the study of demons and persons plagued by spirits, which is called _____.
4. As a cure for "possession by the devil" or the "curses of evil spirits," "medieval "therapists" would "cast out evil spirits" by using _____.
5. Modern analyses of "demonic possession" suggest that many victims were suffering from epilepsy, depression, dissociative disorders, and _____.
6. In the Middle Ages, many instances of the "demonic possession" with psychotic-like symptoms was actually caused by the rye (grain) fields being infested with _____ fungus.
7. This fungus, which infested the rye fields and tainted the bread made from it, is a natural source of mind-altering chemicals, in particular, _____.
8. In 1793, compassionate care was first given to the mentally ill in the Bicêtre Asylum in Paris by a French doctor named _____.
9. The first true psychotherapy was created by a physician in Vienna named _____.
10. This first therapy that helped patients gain insight into deeply hidden unconscious conflicts was _____.
11. More than 100 years ago, this physician in Vienna was intrigued by cases in which people had physical symptoms, such as paralysis or numbness, for which no physical causes could be found. He referred to these cases as _____.
12. Today, these cases of physical symptoms with no physical causes make up a group of disorders known as _____ disorders.

784

Connections

1. ___ trepanning (or trephining)

2. ___ demonology

3. ___ exorcism

4. ___ ergotism
5. ___ Philippe Pinel

6. ___ Sigmund Freud

7. ___ hysteria

8. ___ psychoanalysis

a. in 1793 he was the first to provide compassionate treatment for the mentally ill

b. a religious ritual used to "cast out evil spirits," or make the body inhospitable place for the devil to reside

c. old term for condition in which person has physical symptoms but no physical cause, now called somatoform disorders

d. developed the first true psychotherapy

e. in medieval Europe, the study of demons and the treatment of persons "possessed" by demons

f. psychotic-like condition caused by a fungus poisoning

g. involves boring a hole in the skull to release pressure or, in ancient times, evil spirits

h. was the first true psychotherapy and involves free association, dream analysis, and analysis of resistance and transference

Check Your Memory

1. TRUE or FALSE   In ancient times, trepanning was a procedure that involved boring, chipping, or bashing holes into a person's head in order to relieve pressure or release evil spirits.

2. TRUE or FALSE   During the Middle Ages, treatments for mental illness in Europe focused on demonology.

3. TRUE or FALSE   The "casting out of evil spirits" that ranged from a religious ritual to torture was called ergotism.

4. TRUE or FALSE   Modern analyses of "possessions by the devil" suggest that many victims were suffering epilepsy, schizophrenia, dissociative disorders, or depression.

5. TRUE or FALSE   A fungus in the infested the rye fields in the Middle Ages was a natural source of LSD and other mind-altering chemicals.

6. TRUE or FALSE   People who ate the fungus-tainted bread experienced pinching sensations, muscle twitches, delirium, and hallucinations, which were misinterpreted as "demonic possessions."

7. TRUE or FALSE   In 1893, the French doctor named Jean Piaget changed the asylum in Paris into a mental hospital that provided the mentally ill with compassionate care.

8. TRUE or FALSE   The first true psychotherapy was created by Victor Frankl and was known as functionalism.

9. TRUE or FALSE   The physician who developed the first psychotherapy was intrigued by cases of what he called hysteria in which people had physical symptoms, such as paralysis with no physical causes for the symptoms.

10. TRUE or FALSE   The problems which were once referred to as hysteria are now called schizotypal disorders.

Module 14.1 Treating Psychological Distress
Psychoanalysis—Expedition into the Unconscious
Survey Question: Is Freudian psychoanalysis still used?

Language Development Guide

expedition: to explore or investigate unknown territory
reclined: to lie down; stretch out
interpretations: explanations; providing understanding
stressed: emphasized
stemming from: beginning in, growing out of
roots: to grow from
self-censorship: preventing oneself for saying or doing something
emerge: come out; appear
disguise: mask; hide
royal road: an easy or direct way
manifest: evident; plainly in view
latent: hidden; concealed; out of sight
waistband: strip of material around the top of trousers to strengthen them
target: padded disk with a marked surface that is used to shoot at to gauge accuracy
fails to discharge: misfire; a gun that does not fire when the trigger is pulled
sexual impotence: erectile dysfunction; inability to maintain an erection
roadblocks: barriers, sources of frustration
rejecting: refuse to accept
provoke: stir up; cause; bring about
playing... "games": deceiving someone about what you mean or intend to do or use to avoid
        dealing with problem
open-ended: without fixed limits, such as a completion date
contribution: gift; input
highlighting: stressing; emphasizing
switched: changed
accelerate: speed up
resume: return to; take up again
streamlined: efficient; simplified; updated
"works": is effective
critique: evaluation; review
acquaint: tell; explain to

Recite and Review

1. In order to encourage a free flow of thoughts and images from the unconscious, Freud would sit out of sight taking notes and offering interpretations, while his patients reclined on a(n) _____.
2. Freud's theory stressed that "neurosis" and "hysteria" are caused by memories, motives, and conflicts that had been _____.
3. According to Freud, these motives and conflicts that caused "neurosis" and "hysteria" stemmed from instinctual drives for sex and _____.
4. Freud believed that these hidden conflicts remain active in the personality and cause some people to develop compulsive, self-defeating behavior and rigid _____.
5. Reducing conflicts that lead to emotional suffering was the main goal of Freud's therapy called _____.

6. Having his patients say anything that came to mind, regardless of how embarrassing or unimportant it may seem was called _____.
7. When patients' thoughts are allowed to move freely from one idea to the next, without self-censorship, unconscious thoughts and feelings emerge because of this lowering of one's _____.
8. According to Freud, the "royal road to the unconscious" is through a person's _____.
9. Lora tells her therapist that she has a reoccurring dream in which she is running through a forest tangled with vines. This obvious, visible portion of her dream is called the _____ content.
10. After listening to Lora's dream, her therapist will interpret her dream for its hidden, symbolic meaning known as the _____ content.
11. In order to interpret Lora's dream, her therapist will have to analyze the images in her dream that have personal or emotional meanings, which are referred to as _____.
12. During a therapy session if the patient has blockages in the flow of ideas, Freud said that important unconscious conflicts were revealed through these _____.
13. At times, the patient may act as if the analyst is a rejecting father, an unloving or overprotective mother, or a former love. This tendency to treat the therapist similar to important persons in his or her past is called _____.
14. Because traditional psychoanalysis takes numerous years to complete, many therapists have switched to doing a time-limited therapies, which uses direct questioning to reveal unconscious conflicts, called _____ therapies.
15. A psychotherapy that utilizes this direct questioning and was first developed to help depressed people improve their relationships with others is called _____.
16. Hans Eysenck suggested that psychoanalysis simply takes so long that patients experience an improvement due to the mere passage of time, or a(n) _____ of symptoms.

Connections

1. ____ free association
2. ____ manifest content

3. ____ latent content

4. ____ dream symbols

5. ____ resistances

6. ____ transference
7. ____ brief psychodynamic therapies

8. ____ interpersonal psychotherapy

9. ____ spontaneous remissions

a. tendency of patients to treat the therapist as they do important persons in their past
b. blockage in the flow of ideas that the client talks about and can reveal important unconscious conflicts
c. improvement in one's condition due to the mere passage of time
d. technique of having a client say anything that comes to mind, regardless of how embarrassing or unimportant it may seem
e. modern therapies based on psychoanalytic theory but designed to produce insights more quickly
f. hidden, symbolic meaning of dreams
g. therapy designed to help people by improving their relationships with other people
h. images in dreams that have personal or emotional meanings
i. the obvious, visible parts of a dream

Check Your Memory

1. TRUE or FALSE   The most important element of psychoanalysis is having the patients recline on a couch during therapy to encourage a free flow of thoughts.
2. TRUE or FALSE   Freud's theory stressed that "neurosis" and "hysteria" are caused by repressed memories, motives, and conflicts, particularly those stemming from instinctual drives for sex and aggression.
3. TRUE or FALSE   In psychoanalysis, the technique of having a client say anything that comes to mind, regardless of how embarrassing or unimportant it may seem is called transference.
4. TRUE or FALSE   Freud believed that dreams provided a "royal road to the unconscious."
5. TRUE or FALSE   The obvious, visible meaning of a dream is the latent content, which must be interpreted in order to discover its manifest content.
6. TRUE or FALSE   Images that have personal or emotional meanings within a dream are called dream symbols.
7. TRUE or FALSE   When free associating or describing dreams, patients may resist talking about or thinking about certain topics with these resistances revealing particularly important unconscious conflicts.
8. TRUE or FALSE   The tendency for patients to treat their therapist similar to the way they treat important persons in lives is referred to as emotional confrontation.
9. TRUE or FALSE   Effective therapists learn to avoid reacting to their patients the way other people have in the past and resist playing the patient's habitual resistance and transference "games."
10. TRUE or FALSE   Traditional psychoanalysis called for three to five therapy sessions a week, often for many years.
11. TRUE or FALSE   Many therapists have switched to doing brief psychodynamic therapy, which uses direct questioning to reveal unconscious conflicts.
12. TRUE or FALSE   Modern psychodynamic therapists actively provoke emotional reactions that will lower defenses and provide insights.
13. TRUE or FALSE   Interpersonal psychotherapy (IPT) is an example of brief psychodynamic therapy and was first developed to help depressed people improve their relationships with others.
14. TRUE or FALSE   Although IPT has been shown to be effective for depressive disorders, it has not been effective in treating eating disorders, substance abuse, social phobias, or personality disorders.
15. TRUE or FALSE   Hans Eysenck suggested that psychoanalysis simply takes so long that patients experience a spontaneous remission of symptoms.
16. TRUE or FALSE   Research has confirmed that psychoanalysis does, in fact, produce improvement in a majority of patients.

Critical Thinking Question

According to Freud's concept of *transference,* patients "transferred" their feelings onto the psychoanalyst. In light of this idea, to what might the term *countertransference* refer?

Module 14.1 Treating Psychological Distress

Dimensions of Therapy—The Many Paths to Health

Survey Question: How do therapies differ?

Language Development Guide

dialogue: conversation; discussion; talk
depicted: shown, described, perceived

788

transformation: alteration; makeover; change
major overhaul: redone from the beginning, making totally new
viable: workable; practical; feasible
crisis: emergency; disaster
movement: interest group
autonomy: self-rule; self-sufficiency
interpersonal: between people
nurturance: physical and emotional care
genuineness: real; authentic character

Recite and Review

1. Any psychological technique that can bring about positive changes in personality, behavior, or personal adjustment is called _____.
2. To help alleviate her depression, Tanya is attending psychotherapy sessions in which she will gain a deeper understanding of her thoughts, emotions, and behavior. Tanya's psychotherapy would be considered _____ therapy.
3. Behavioral therapy is designed to bring about direct changes in behavior, while cognitive therapy is designed to directly change thought patterns. Both therapies would be classified as _____ therapies.
4. If the therapist provides strong guidance during the sessions, the therapy is considered _____ therapy.
5. A style of therapy in which clients assume responsibility for solving their own problems and the therapist assists without guiding or giving advice would be described as _____.
6. Barry attends therapy sessions in which several clients participate at the same time. Barry is participating in _____ therapy.
7. Ana attends therapy twice a week in which she and her therapist spend 50 minutes discussing her concerns. Unlike Barry who attends therapy with several other clients, Ana is in _____ therapy.
8. Elena is attending eight group therapy sessions provided by her company to deal with the company's unexpected closure. Because there will be only eight sessions, Elena's therapy would be considered _____.
9. Paul has begun therapy to deal with posttraumatic stress disorder. At this time, it is unknown how many months or even years it will take to help Paul. Therefore, Paul's therapy would be considered _____.
10. Chances for improvement through therapy are fairly good for low self-esteem, some sexual problems, marital conflicts, and irrational fears known as _____.
11. The most extreme psychological cases may not respond to psychotherapy at all; thus, leaving the only viable treatment option as _____ therapy.
12. The major benefit of therapy is that it provides comfort, support, and a way to make constructive _____.
13. Psychotherapy can be used to solve problems or end a crisis; but if a person is already doing well, therapy can be a way to promote _____.
14. Marta is attending group therapy sessions designed for minority women attending the university. Since these sessions are to enhance these women's strengths, not "fix" any weaknesses, this type of therapy was developed by _____ psychology therapists.
15. Personal autonomy and independence, a sense of identity, feelings of personal worth, skilled interpersonal communication, the capacity to forgive, and good habits of physical health are some of the elements of positive _____.

Connections

1. ____ psychotherapy
2. ____ medical therapy
3. ____ individual therapy
4. ____ group therapy
5. ____ insight therapy
6. ____ action therapy
7. ____ directive therapy
8. ____ nondirective therapy
9. ____ time-limited therapy
10. ____ open-ended therapy
11. ____ positive psychology
12. ____ elements of positive mental health

a. number of sessions determined by client's need
b. any psychotherapy whose goal is to lead clients to a deeper understanding of their thoughts, emotions, and behavior
c. therapy involving only one client and one therapist
d. includes personal autonomy, a sense of identity, feelings of personal worth, self-control, skilled interpersonal communication, capacity to forgive
e. a style of therapy in which clients assume responsibility for solving their own problems with the therapist assisting but not guiding or giving advice
f. any therapy designed to bring about direct changes in troublesome thoughts, habits, feelings, or behavior
g. therapy session in which several clients participate at the same time
h. viewpoint that advocates enhancing personal strengths, rather than "fix" weaknesses
i. any approach in which the therapist provides strong guidance
j. based on psychiatric drugs and other physical treatments
k. any psychological technique used to facilitate positive changes in a person's personality, behavior, or adjustment
l. any therapy begun with the expectation that it will last only a certain number of sessions

Check Your Memory

1. TRUE or FALSE   Any psychological technique that can bring about positive changes in personality, behavior, or personal adjustment is referred to as a somatic therapy.
2. TRUE or FALSE   Any therapy involving only one client and one therapist is called client-centered (or person-centered) therapy.
3. TRUE or FALSE   Any therapy whose goal is to lead clients to a deeper understanding of their thoughts, emotions, and behavior is called an action therapy.
4. TRUE or FALSE   A style of therapy in which clients assume responsibility for solving their own problems with the therapist assisting, but not guiding or giving advice is regarded as a nondirective therapy.
5. TRUE or FALSE   A therapy is regarded as time-limited if it is begun with the expectation that it will last only a certain number of sessions.
6. TRUE or FALSE   Psychotherapy usually involves a complete personal transformation, a sort of "major overhaul" of the psyche.

7. TRUE or FALSE   Psychotherapy has been found to be equally effective for all types of problems.
8. TRUE or FALSE   When a person enters therapy, he or she should expect to completely undo their entire past.
9. TRUE or FALSE   Techniques designed to enhance personal strengths, rather than "fix" weaknesses were developed by therapists in the positive psychology movement.
10. TRUE or FALSE   Fulfillment and satisfaction in work, a capacity to forgive, and good habits of physical health are some of the elements of positive mental health promoted by the positive psychology movement.

Module 14.2 Humanistic and Cognitive Therapies
Humanistic Therapies—Restoring Human Potential
Survey Question: What are the major humanistic therapies?

Language Development Guide
picture: imagine
restoring: bringing back; repairing
hysterical misery into common unhappiness: not made happy but less sad than you were
delve: look into; dig
"atmosphere of growth": a psychological safe environment in which one's strengths and potential will emerge and change can take place
unshakable: constant; sure; unwavering
dismay: disappointment; shock; sadness
empathy: understanding of another's feelings; showing compassion
phony fronts: masks, fake images or false impressions
armed: prepared; equipped
vast: huge; gigantic
indifferent: uncaring; unsympathetic
confront: deal with; face up to
meaninglessness: emptiness; insignificance
mortality: reality of death
Nazi concentration camp: slave labor camps and death camps where prisoners were exploited, tortured, starved, and killed
countless: numerous; too many to count
stripped: to forcibly remove or tear something of value from a person
human dignity: the rights and protection that should be given to all people
dire: terrible; awful; grim; dreadful
Buddhists: those who practice the religion, originated in India by Buddha and which later spread to China, Japan, and southeast Asia; proposes that life is filled with suffering caused by desire with this suffering ended through enlightenment
state: condition; situation
radical acceptance: only by acknowledging painful emotions and who one is alleviates suffering and allows one to make changes
reappraisal: re-evaluation; second look
rebirth: renewal; new start; new beginning
close brush with death: almost died
Marcel Proust: French novelist, critic and essayist best known for his seven volume novel *In Search of Lost Time* (also called *Remembrance of Things Past*), which focused on the time, space, and memory, and the necessity of reflection

voyage of discovery: the most important journey in which we learn
new eyes: seeing things from a different point of view
disjointed: confused and fragmented
gaps: breaks; holes
impair: damage, slow, injure, prevent
"here and now": present moment
vague: unclear; indistinct
"take care of unfinished business": deal with things you have been avoiding
impasses: blocks to progress; points at which no further progress can be made
intellectualizing: defense in which reasoning is used to ignore emotional stress and painful emotions
surrender: give in
paradoxically: in a surprising contradiction

Recite and Review

1. Like psychoanalysis, the humanistic therapies seek to help people through a deeper understanding of their thoughts, emotions, and behavior; therefore, the humanistic therapies are considered _____ therapies.
2. The type of action therapies that are concerned with helping people change harmful thinking patterns are the _____ therapies.
3. The optimistic type of therapy that believes that people have a natural urge to seek health and self-growth and assume it is possible for people to use their potentials fully and live rich, rewarding lives would be the _____ therapies.
4. Psychologist Carl Rogers believed in exploring a person's _____ thoughts and feelings.
5. Rogers preferred not to use the term "patient" because it implied that the person was "sick" and needed to be "cured." Instead, he used the term "_____."
6. Rogers' therapy is called _____ therapy.
7. Because Rogers believed that his clients must actively seek to solve their own problems without the therapist giving them advice, Rogers' therapy would be considered _____.
8. Rogers believed that the therapist must offer the client unshakable personal acceptance and not react with shock, dismay, or disapproval to anything the client says or feels. This unshakable personal acceptance is referred to as _____.
9. Lenny's therapist tries to see the world though Lenny's eyes and to feel a part of what Lenny is feeling. Lenny's therapist is attempting to achieve genuine _____.
10. Throughout therapy, when the psychologists themselves strive to be genuine and honest and not hide behind their professional roles, they are being _____.
11. A therapist that uses Rogers' techniques does not make interpretations, propose solutions, or offer advice. Instead the therapist acts as a psychological "mirror" so the clients can see themselves more clearly with the therapist _____ the client's thoughts and feelings.
12. The group of therapies that focus on the problems of death, meaning, choice, and responsibility are the _____ therapies.
13. The therapy, which seeks to uncover a "true self" hidden behind a screen of defenses, is _____ therapy.
14. The therapy, which emphasizes free will and the human ability to make choices to become the person you want to be, is _____ therapy.
15. Existential therapists try to give clients the courage to make rewarding and socially constructive _____.
16. According to existential therapists, the universal human challenges include an awareness of one's mortality, the responsibility that comes with freedom to choose, being alone in your own private world, and the need to create _____ in your life.
17. An example of existential therapy is Victor Frankl's _____.

18. Victor Frankl's therapeutic approach was based on his experiences as a prison in a(n) _____.
19. A key aspect of existential therapy involves the clients being challenged to examine their values and choices and to take responsibility for the quality of their existence. This aspect is called _____.
20. To be successful within existential therapy, the client must fully accept the challenge of changing his or her life, a state that Buddhists would call "_____."
21. The therapy that helps people rebuild thinking, feeling, and acting into connected wholes is _____ therapy.
22. Rebuilding thinking, feeling, and acting into connected wholes is achieved by expanding personal awareness; by accepting responsibility for one's thoughts, feelings, and actions; and by filling in _____.
23. Gestalt therapists believe that we often shy away from expressing or "_____" upsetting feelings.
24. Since Gestalt therapists give more guidance to their clients during their sessions, Gestalt therapy, when compared to client-centered and existential therapies, is considered to be more _____.
25. Gestalt therapists encourage their clients to become more aware of their moment-to-moment thoughts, perceptions and emotions and to have these feelings in the "_____."
26. By drawing attention to a client's posture, voice, eye movements, and hand gestures, Gestalt therapists promote _____.
27. Gestalt therapists believe that exaggerating vague feelings allows these feelings to become clear and helps clients to break through emotional impasses and to "take care of _____."
28. Gestalt therapy is often associated with the work of psychologist _____.
29. This originator of Gestalt therapy believed that by knowing what you want to do and not dwelling on what you should do, ought to do, or should want to do was the key to emotional _____.
30. Gestalt therapy emphasizes present experience and urges clients to stop talking and _____ about feelings.

Connections

1. ___ humanistic therapies
2. ___ client-centered therapy (or person-centered therapy)
3. ___ existential therapy
4. ___ Gestalt therapy
5. ___ unconditional positive regard
6. ___ empathy
7. ___ authentic

a. therapy developed by Victor Frankl and emphasizes the need to find and maintain meaning in life
b. an unqualified unshakable acceptance or another person
c. nondirective therapy based on insights gained from conscious thoughts and feeling and emphasizes accepting one's true self
d. ability of a therapist to be genuine and honest about his or her own feelings
e. process of rephrasing or repeating thoughts and feeling expressed by clients so they can become aware of what they are saying
f. trying to see the world through the client's eyes and feel some part of what the client is feeling
g. insight therapy that focuses on death, meaning, choice, and responsibility and emphasize making courageous life choices

8. ___ reflection

    h. challenging clients to examine their values and choices and to take responsibility for the quality of their existence

9. ___ logotherapy

    i. group of insight therapies that believes that people have a natural urge to seek health and self-growth

10. ___ confrontation

    j. approach that focuses on immediate experience to help clients rebuild thinking, feeling, and acting into connected wholes

Check Your Memory

1. TRUE or FALSE   Psychoanalysis and the humanistic therapies are considered action therapies.

2. TRUE or FALSE   Humanistic therapy is an optimistic approach that believes that humans have a natural urge to seek health and self-growth.

3. TRUE or FALSE   Psychologist Carl Rogers believed that it was more beneficial to explore unconscious thoughts and feelings than to explore conscious ones.

4. TRUE or FALSE   Because Carl Rogers believed that the client must actively seek to solve his or her own problems and that the client should decide what should be discussed at each session, his therapy would be considered a nondirective therapy.

5. TRUE or FALSE   In client-centered therapy, the therapist offers the client unshakable personal acceptance, which is called conditions of worth.

6. TRUE or FALSE   During client-centered therapy, the therapist strives to be authentic and not hide behind a professional role.

7. TRUE or FALSE   The chief technique of client-centered therapy involves confrontation, in which the therapist challenges the client to take responsibility for his or her own actions.

8. TRUE or FALSE   Existential therapy helps people rebuild thinking, feeling, and acting into connected wholes by expanding their personal awareness.

9. TRUE or FALSE   One example of existential therapy is Victor Frankl's logotherapy, which is based on his experiences as a prisoner in a Nazi concentration camp.

10. TRUE or FALSE   According to existential therapists, clients must fully accept the challenge of changing their lives, which is similar to the state that Buddhists call "radical acceptance."

11. TRUE or FALSE   A key aspect of existential therapy is the use of reflection, which involves destroying phony fronts and reflecting one's true self to the world.

12. TRUE or FALSE   Gestalt therapy focuses on the problems of existence, such as death, meaning, choice, and responsibility.

13. TRUE or FALSE   The German word *Gestalt* means "whole," or "complete.

14. TRUE or FALSE   Gestalt therapists believe that we must "own" upsetting feelings or else a gap will be created in one's self-awareness.

15. TRUE or FALSE   In Gestalt therapy, the therapist often promotes awareness by drawing attention to a client's posture, voice, eye movements, and hand gestures.

16. TRUE or FALSE   The Gestalt approach is less directive and more insight-oriented than client-centered or existential therapy.

17. TRUE or FALSE   Gestalt psychologists believe that it is important to discuss why clients feel guilt, anger, fear, or boredom by delving into a person's past experiences.

18. TRUE or FALSE   Clients during Gestalt therapy are asked to exaggerate vague feelings until they become clear, which will allow people to "take care of unfinished business."

19. TRUE or FALSE   Gestalt therapy is often associated with the work of psychologist Julian Rotter.

20. TRUE or FALSE   According to Gestalt therapy, emotional health comes from knowing and doing what you should do and ought to do, rather than dwelling on what you want to do.

21. TRUE or FALSE   Gestalt therapy urges clients to talk and intellectualize about their feelings.

22. TRUE or FALSE   Gestalt therapists believe that the best way to change is to become who you really are.

Critical Thinking Question

How might using the term *patient* affect the relationship between an individual and a therapist?

Module 14.2 Humanistic and Cognitive Therapies

Cognitive Therapy—Think Positive!

Survey Question: How does cognitive therapy change thoughts and emotions?

Language Development Guide

foster: promote; advance; encourage
as a consequence: as a result of
hoarder: person who acquires and keeps large amounts of objects that appear to have little value
crammed: stuffed into small spaces
remedy: cure
contamination: being unclean; having impurities that make it harmful
array: collection; group
magnify: enlarge; increase; expand
miserably: wretchedly; sadly
keep track: fully aware; informed of; monitor; watch
incompetent: useless; lacking ability
utterly: absolutely; totally
impart: pass on
stress inoculation: use of positive coping statements to control fear and anxiety
specialty: special subject of study
irrational: illogical; unreasonably
loser: someone who is a misfit, unpopular, and unlikeable
creep: weird, annoying person
pass by: go away
such a pain: very annoying
dumped: abandoned, left by a romantic partner
rotten: terrible; awful
needless: unnecessary; pointless; uncalled for
"self-talk": negative thoughts
logic: reason; judgment
"homework": activities to be completed outside of therapy
dispute: disagree; challenge; call into question
lost his shirt: lost all his money
online: on the Internet

blackjack: a card game involving gambling in which the winner is the player holding cards whose total value is closest to 21 points without going over this value

Texas Hold 'Em: a form of the card game poker that involves gambling with players each receiving two cards and sharing five cards

drop out of school: quit college; not finish his college degree

losses: in this case, money lost through gambling

ranks: body of people classed together

despite the fact: in spite of; even though

persistently: steadily

ascribe: assign; attribute

fallacy: misleading notion; myth

string of losses: losing several times in a row

"lucky": characterized by good fortune in most situations

probability: mathematical likelihood of events occurring

biases: partiality; preconceived notions

randomness: having no specific pattern

illusion: false impression

recreationally: for fun

covert sensitization: use of aversive (unpleasant) imagery to reduce the occurrence of an undesired response

thought stopping: use of aversive (unpleasant) stimuli to interrupt or prevent upsetting thoughts

covert reinforcement: use of positive imagery to reinforce desired behavior

Recite and Review

1. The therapy that helps clients change thinking patterns that lead to troublesome emotions and behaviors is called _____ therapy.

2. Changing thinking patterns has been especially successful in treating _____.

3. The psychologist who proposed that major distortions in thinking underlie depression was _____.

4. The major distortions in thinking include all-or-nothing thinking, selective perception, and _____.

5. If five good things and three bad things happen during the day, depressed people tend to focus only on the bad, which illustrates the distortion in thinking called _____.

6. If you consider yourself a total failure, or completely worthless because you failed a test, then you are applying this one upsetting event to several more unrelated situations. This tendency is called _____.

7. If you view events as either completely good or bad or totally right or totally wrong, you are engaging in _____.

8. Cognitive therapists try to correct negative thoughts by having clients recognize and keep track of their own thoughts that cause depression or anger and then gather information to _____ these beliefs.

9. Rather than looking for the presence of self-defeating thoughts, some cognitive therapists look for the absence of effective _____.

10. Cognitive therapy has been found to be at least as effective as drugs for treating many cases of _____.

11. The therapy that attempts to change irrational beliefs that cause emotional problems is called _____.

12. The psychologist who proposed the A-B-C sequence to explain how irrational beliefs lead to emotional problems was _____.

13. Regarding the A-B-C sequence that results in self-defeating habits, the A states for a(n) _____.
14. The C in the A-B-C sequence that results in self-defeating habits stands for a(n)_____.
15. Regarding this A-B-C sequence, events do not cause us to have feelings. We feel as we do because of B, which stands for our irrational and unrealistic _____.
16. "I must be loved and approved by almost every significant person in my life or it's awful and I'm worthless" is one of the ten _____.
17. Rational-emotive behavior (REBT) therapists may directly attack clients' logic, challenge their thinking, confront them with evidence contrary to their beliefs, and even assign "homework," which would make this therapy very _____.
18. Most irrational beliefs originate from the following statements: "I must perform well and be approved of by significant others;" "You must treat me fairly;" and "Conditions must be the way I want them to be," which the originator of REBT called the three _____.
19. Although you lose persistently every time you gamble, your self-confidence tends to be exaggerated, which illustrates the cognitive distortion related to gambling known as _____ skill.
20. You ascribe your wins at poker to your skill but blame your losses on bad luck. Regarding your gambling, you are making _____ errors.
21. Although you have lost the last ten hands of poker, you believe that your string of losses must be followed by some wins, so you keep playing, which illustrates the cognitive distortion known as the _____.
22. George tends to remember his wins but forgets his losses, a cognitive distortion known as _____.
23. You are walking by the roulette wheel in the casino when you get a feeling that a certain number will be the winner, so you bet $100 on this number, which loses. Your loss is due to the cognitive distortion referred to as _____ of cues.
24. Connor believes that he is a "lucky" person in general. Connor views luck as a(n) _____.
25. Your incorrect beliefs about randomness and chance events are referred to as _____.
26. Taken together, the cognitive distortions regarding gambling create an illusion of _____.
27. To help alleviate a person's gambling addiction, their beliefs about gambling would have to be cognitively _____.
28. Covert sensitization, thought stopping, and covert reinforcement are three examples of _____ approaches.

Connections

1. ____ cognitive therapy

2. ____ selective perception

3. ____ overgeneralization

4. ____ all-or-nothing thinking

a. unrealistic or faulty convictions that lead to unnecessary suffering

b. an approach developed by Albert Ellis that states that it is our beliefs that lead to our feelings

c. classifying objects or events as absolutely right or wrong, good or bad, acceptable or unacceptable, and so forth

d. blowing a single event out of proportion by extending it to a large number of unrelated situations

5. ___ rational-emotive behavior therapy (REBT)

e. therapy directed at changing maladaptive thoughts, beliefs, and feelings that underlie emotional and behavioral problems

6. ___ irrational beliefs

f. perceiving only certain stimuli among a large array of possibilities

Part 2: Connections

1. ___ magnified gambling skill

a. incorrect beliefs about randomness and chance events

2. ___ attribution errors

b. believing that a string of losses soon must be followed by wins

3. ___ gambler's fallacy

c. putting too much faith in irrelevant cues such as bodily sensations or a feeling that your next bet will be a winner

4. ___ selective memory

d. believing that one is a "lucky" person in general

5. ___ overinterpretation of cues

e. ascribe wins to skill but blame losses on bad luck

6. ___ luck as a trait

f. remembering your wins but forgetting your losses

7. ___ probability biases

g. self-confidence is exaggerated despite the fact that one loses persistently

Check Your Memory

1. TRUE or FALSE   Behavior therapy is designed to help clients change thinking patterns that lead to troublesome emotions or behaviors.
2. TRUE or FALSE   Compulsive hand-washing can be greatly reduced by changing a client's thoughts and beliefs about dirt and contamination.
3. TRUE or FALSE   Cognitive therapy has been especially successful in treating delusional disorders.
4. TRUE or FALSE   Psychologist Victor Frankl developed a cognitive therapy based on changing major distortions in thinking.
5. TRUE or FALSE   The tendency to think that an upsetting event applies to other, unrelated situations is called selective perception.
6. TRUE or FALSE   Seeing events as totally good or bad or totally right or wrong is referred to as all-or-nothing thinking.
7. TRUE or FALSE   In cognitive therapy, clients are asked to gather information to test their beliefs.
8. TRUE or FALSE   In treating depression, cognitive therapy has not been shown to be as effective as drugs.
9. TRUE or FALSE   People who have adopted new thinking patterns are less likely to become depressed again.
10. TRUE or FALSE   In an alternate approach, cognitive therapists look for an absence of effective coping skills and thinking patterns, not for the presence of self-defeating thoughts.
11. TRUE or FALSE   Stress inoculation is an example of the use of cognitive therapy.
12. TRUE or FALSE   Rational-emotive behavior therapy (REBT) is a nondirective approach that encourages people to discover their "true" selves.

798

13. TRUE or FALSE   REBT was developed by Albert Ellis, who assumed that people become unhappy and develop self-defeating habits because they have unrealistic or faulty beliefs.

14. TRUE or FALSE   In the A-B-C sequence used in REBT, A stands for acknowledging responsibility for one's actions.

15. TRUE or FALSE   According to REBT, events do not cause us to have feelings rather it is our beliefs that cause us to feel the way we do.

16. TRUE or FALSE   One of the ten irrational beliefs that therapist have identified as commonly leading to emotional upsets is "Because something once strongly affected me, it will do so forever."

17. TRUE or FALSE   Ellis said that most irrational beliefs come from three core ideas, each of which is unrealistic.

18. TRUE or FALSE   If you believe that a string of gambling losses must be followed by wins, then you have succumbed to an overinterpretation of cues.

19. TRUE or FALSE   Despite the fact that you lose persistently, your self-confidence regarding gambling is exaggerated, which illustrates the cognitive distortion known as the gambler's fallacy.

20. TRUE or FALSE   If you ascribe your wins to skill but blame your losses on bad luck, you are exhibiting probability biases.

21. TRUE or FALSE   Taken together, the cognitive distortions related to gambling create an illusion of control.

22. TRUE or FALSE   Covert sensitization, thought stopping, and covert reinforcement are three examples of cognitive approaches.

Critical Thinking Question

In Aaron Beck's terms, a belief such as "I must perform well or I am a rotten person" involves two thinking errors. What are they?

Module 14.3 Behavior Therapies
Therapies Based on Classical Conditioning—Healing by Learning
Survey Question: What is behavior therapy?

Language Development Guide

innovative: inventive; ground-breaking; pioneering
vividly: brightly; clearly
pictured: imagined
shoplifting: to steal items from a store
distressed: upset
disappointment: displeasure
covert sensitization: use of aversive (unpleasant) imagery to reduce the occurrence of an undesired response
constructive: helpful; useful; positive
probe: search; look into
broadly speaking: in general
token economies: therapeutic program in which desirable behaviors are reinforced with tokens (symbolic objects, such as money, stars, slips of paper) that can be exchanged for goods, services, activities, and privileges
hypodermic: area beneath the skin, usually refers to an injection of medicine under the skin using a needle
puffing: slang term for smoking

toxic: poisonous; deadly

forced pace: to increase or accelerate the rate of performing an activity

taking a puff: smoking

justified: defensible; acceptable; reasonable

interminable: endless; perpetual; never-ending

inhibited: unable to act; restrained

be a candidate for: in this case, a person in need of; a person who would respond well to this therapy

stage fright: fear of performing before an audience

construct: make; create

hierarchy: ranked set of items

go limp: relaxed with no tension in the muscle

abdomen: stomach area

clench: tighten

curl your toes: bend them to your foot

impractical: unreasonable; unworkable

extinguish: end something

haunt: disturb; bother; revisit

molestations: sexual touching, usually of children

ease: relieve; reduce

reprocessing: to cause to undergo special or additional course of action

dart: flit; dash; abruptly move

emerged: come into view

controversial: causing arguments

superior to: better than

breakthrough: advance; innovation; step forward

Recite and Review

1. Behavior therapy involves making constructive changes in behavior by applying _____ principles.
2. Since behavior therapy is not concerned with deep insights into one's behavior but in directly changing the behavior, it would be considered a(n) _____ therapy.
3. According to behavior therapists, if people have learned responses that cause problems, then they can change them by _____ more appropriate behaviors.
4. When a therapist uses classical or operant conditioning to directly alter human behavior, the therapist is using _____.
5. A form of learning in which simple responses (especially reflexes) are associated with new stimuli is called _____ conditioning.
6. For a child the sight of a hypodermic needle is followed by an injection, which causes anxiety or fear. The sight of the hypodermic needle will eventually produce the anxiety or fear before the child gets the injection. In this example, the sight of the hypodermic needle, which was previously neutral, has become the _____.
7. A learned dislike or negative emotional response to some stimulus is called a(n) _____.
8. An individual learns to associate a strong unpleasant stimulus to an undesirable habit, such as smoking, drinking, or gambling, in _____ therapy.
9. The realization that most emergency room doctors wear seat belts when they drive illustrates the powerful effect of this _____ type of conditioning.
10. Clients are told to smoke continuously, taking a puff every six to eight seconds until the smoker is miserable and can stand it no more during a procedure to "stop smoking" known as _____.

800

11. To take the pleasure out of drinking for alcoholics, Roger Vogler uses response-_____ shocks.
12. Drinking will begin to make the individual very uncomfortable if alcohol is linked with _____ discomfort.
13. After a diving mishap, Janice's diving instructor reduces Janice's fear of diving from the high board by having her dive several times from the side of the pool, then the low board, then the six foot platform, and so on. When Janice's fear has been reduced through this adaptation, we say that _____ has occurred.
14. The rank-ordered series of steps that allowed Janice to gradually adapt to diving from the high board is referred to as a(n) _____.
15. This procedure involving a rank-ordered series of steps combined with relaxation is used primarily to help people unlearn intense, unrealistic fears known as _____.
16. When the presence of one emotional state inhibits the occurrence of another, such as joy preventing anxiety and anxiety inhibiting pleasure, then _____ occurs.
17. To inhibit fear, one must learn to relax with one of the best ways to achieve deep relaxation of the body being the _____ method.
18. While deeply relaxed, the client will first perform the item on the list, which is the _____ disturbing.
19. Karen, who is deathly afraid of dogs, is observing a model petting a large dog. This reduction in Karen's anxiety that takes place "secondhand" by watching the model is called _____.
20. A "secondhand" reduction in anxiety can work almost as well when a person goes through each step in the hierarchy by _____ them.
21. Since people are exposed to the feared stimuli, desensitization is considered a(n) _____ therapy.
22. A procedure in which computerized fear stimuli are presented to clients in a realistic, yet carefully controlled fashion and has been used to treat fears of flying, driving, and public speaking is called _____.
23. To help ease traumatic memories and posttraumatic stress, Dr. Francine Shapiro developed a technique known as _____ therapy.
24. In Shapiro's technique, the client is asked to visualize the images that most upset her or him while in front of the client's eyes, the therapist rapidly moves from side to side a(n) _____ (or some other object).
25. Some studies suggest that Shapiro's technique has been successful because of a gradual exposure to upsetting stimuli takes place with nothing being added by the _____.

Part 1: Connections

1. ____ behavior therapy
2. ____ classical conditioning

3. ____ aversion therapy
4. ____ response-contingent shocks

5. ____ reciprocal inhibition
6. ____ systematic desensitization

a. suppressing an undesirable response by associating it with painful or uncomfortable stimuli
b. reduction in fear, anxiety, or aversion brought about by planned direct exposure to aversive stimuli
c. shocks that are linked to a response
d. form of learning in which simple responses are associated with new stimuli
e. any therapy designed to actively change behavior
f. presence of one emotional state can inhibit the occurrence of another, such as joy preventing fear

Part 2: Connections

1. ___ behavior modification

2. ___ rapid smoking

3. ___ hierarchy

4. ___ tension-release method

5. ___ vicarious desensitization

6. ___ virtual reality exposure

7. ___ eye movement desensitization and reprocessing (EMDR)

a. use of computer-generated images to present fear stimuli

b. technique for reducing fear or anxiety, based on holding upsetting thoughts in mind while rapidly moving the eyes from side to side

c. rank-ordered series of higher and lower amounts, levels, degrees, or steps

d. aversion procedure in which clients are told to smoke continuously until they become miserable and can stand it no more

e. application of learning principles to change human behavior, especially maladaptive behavior; applied behavior analysis

f. procedure for systematically achieving deep relaxation of the body

g. reduction in fear or anxiety that takes place "secondhand" when a client watches models perform the feared behavior

Check Your Memory

1. TRUE or FALSE   Behavior therapists believe that deep insight into one's problems is necessary for improvement.

2. TRUE or FALSE   According to behavior therapists, if people have learned responses that cause problems, then they can change them by relearning more appropriate behaviors.

3. TRUE or FALSE   Behavior modification refers to any use of classical or operant conditioning to directly alter human behavior.

4. TRUE or FALSE   Behavior modification is sometimes referred to as applied behavior analysis.

5. TRUE or FALSE   Aversion therapy and desensitization are two examples of the use of operant conditioning in therapy.

6. TRUE or FALSE   Operant conditioning is a form of learning in which simple responses are associated with new stimuli.

7. TRUE or FALSE   A conditioned aversion is a learned dislike or negative emotional response to some stimulus.

8. TRUE or FALSE   In aversion therapy, an individual learns to associate a strong aversion to an undesirable habit such as smoking, drinking, or gambling.

9. TRUE or FALSE   Behavior therapists have found that electric shock, nauseating drugs, and similar aversive stimuli are required, often in combination, in order to make smokers uncomfortable.

10. TRUE or FALSE   In the technique known as rapid smoking, the client is told to smoke continuously, taking a puff every six to eight seconds and continuing until the smoker is miserable and can stand it no more.

11. TRUE or FALSE   Rapid smoking is a safe technique that can be effectively utilized by anyone without the help of a therapist.

12. TRUE or FALSE   Roger Vogler used response-contingent shocks to help alcoholics stop drinking.

802

13. TRUE or FALSE   Systematic desensitization is a guided reduction in fear, anxiety, or aversion and is attained by gradually approaching a feared stimulus while maintaining relaxation.

14. TRUE or FALSE   The rank-ordered series of steps used in desensitization is called the adaptation sequence.

15. TRUE or FALSE   When one emotional state is used to block another, it is referred to as the therapy placebo effect.

16. TRUE or FALSE   Desensitization is primarily used to help people unlearn dissociative disorders.

17. TRUE or FALSE   Deep relaxation can be obtained by using the tension-release method.

18. TRUE or FALSE   Once a person is relaxed during desensitization, he or she performs the most disturbing item on his or her list of fears and then proceeds down the list to the least disturbing one.

19. TRUE or FALSE   When treating many of the phobias, desensitization works best when people are directly exposed to the stimuli and situations they fear.

20. TRUE or FALSE   For some fears, such as the fear of riding an elevator, desensitization may be completed in a single session.

21. TRUE or FALSE   Vicarious desensitization is a reduction in fear or anxiety that takes place "secondhand" when a client watches models perform the feared behavior.

22. TRUE or FALSE   Imagines each step in the hierarchy while relaxing is the most common way of doing desensitization at a therapist's office.

23. TRUE or FALSE   Desensitization is considered an exposure therapy.

24. TRUE or FALSE   Virtual reality has been used effectively to conduct desensitization in treating fears of flying, driving, heights, and public speaking.

25. TRUE or FALSE   Fritz Perls developed eye movement desensitization and reprocessing (EMDR) therapy.

26. TRUE or FALSE   In a typical EMDR session, the client is asked to visualize the images that most upset her or him while a pencil is moved rapidly from side to side in front of the person's eyes.

27. TRUE or FALSE   A number of studies suggest that EMDR lowers anxieties and takes the pain out of traumatic memories.

28. TRUE or FALSE   Research has shown that the apparent success of EMDR stems from the eye movements part of the therapy.

Critical Thinking Questions

1. Alcoholics who take a drug called Antabuse become ill after drinking alcohol. Why, then, don't they develop an aversion to drinking?

2. A natural form of desensitization often takes place in hospitals. Can you guess what it is?

Module 14.3 Behavior Therapies

Operant Therapies—All the World Is a Skinner Box?

Survey Question: What role do operant principles play in behavior therapy?

Language Development Guide

Skinner Box: operant conditioning chamber
whine: complain; moan
suppressed: held back

approximations: similar but not exactly

response cost: form of punishment in which a positive reinforcer is removed after an undesirable response is made

ward: wing or residential area of a hospital

subtler: less noticeable; more difficult to perceive

subsided: lessened

sheepishly: embarrassed

conventional: usual; established

outings: short pleasure trips, such as a walk outdoors

halfway houses: a community-based facility for individuals making the transition from an institution (mental hospital, prison, etc.) to independent living

impact: effect

full-scale use: used throughout a facility; widespread use

radically: thoroughly; completely; totally

morale: motivated state of a person that involves confidence, cheerfulness, and being willing to participate

incentive: something to encourage or motivate

manipulative: attempting to control in an unfair manner

empowers: to give power or authority to

Recite and Review

1. Learning based on the consequences of making a response is called _____ conditioning.

2. If children whine and get attention, they will whine more frequently, which illustrates _____.

3. If a response is not followed by a reward, it will occur less frequently because of this _____.

4. When you put your money in the soft drink machine at work and push a button, you get rewarded with a cold soft drink. However, today you put your money in the machine, push a button, and receive no soft drink. After pushing the button many times and still not receiving your reward of a cold soft drink, you finally walk away because your response has undergone _____.

5. If a response is followed by discomfort or an undesirable effect, the response will be suppressed through a process known as _____.

6. To reward your child for hitting a soft ball, you at first reward him or her for holding the bat correctly, then for attempting a swing, and then for a near miss. You are rewarding actions that are closer and closer approximations to the desired response through a process known as _____.

7. Removing the individual from a situation in which reinforcement occurs is called _____.

8. If you set your clock 10 minutes fast, it may be easier to leave the house on time in the morning, even if you know the clock is fast, because your departure time is under the _____ of the clock.

9. When children who fight with each other are sent to separate rooms and allowed out only when they are able to behave more calmly, the procedure being used is known as _____.

10. Nonreward can be used to produce _____.

11. In order to eliminate an undesirable response, the rewards maintaining it must be identified and _____.

804

12. By refusing to pay attention to a person who is misbehaving, you are removing the reinforcement reinforcement of your attention, with this procedure being a variation of response cost known as _____.
13. Symbolic rewards that can be exchanged for real rewards are known as _____.
14. At Tia's elementary school, the children receive printed slips of paper for every good grade or "good" behavior they exhibit. These slips of paper can be accumulated and exchanged for special privileges or for items at the "school store." These slips of paper would be considered _____.
15. The full-scale use of these printed slips of paper that can be exchanged for privileges and tangible items would make this school a(n) _____.
16. Actions or other behaviors the therapist seeks to modify are called _____ behaviors.
17. The most effective therapeutic programs gradually switch from tangible, symbolic rewards to rewards, such as praise, recognition, and approval, which are _____ rewards.

Connections

1. ____ operant conditioning
2. ____ positive reinforcement
3. ____ nonreinforcement
4. ____ extinction
5. ____ punishment
6. ____ shaping
7. ____ stimulus control
8. ____ time out
9. ____ target behaviors
10. ____ token economy
11. ____ social rewards

a. response that is not followed by reward will occur less frequently
b. responses tend to be managed or directed by the situation in which they occur
c. if response is followed by discomfort or an undesirable effect, the response will be suppressed
d. learning based on the consequences of making a response
e. therapeutic program in which desirable behaviors are reinforced with symbolic rewards that can be exchanged for goods, services, activities, and privileges
f. if response is not followed by reward after it has been repeated many times, it will go away
g. actions or other behaviors the therapist seeks to modify
h. includes praise, recognition, and approval
i. responses that are followed by reward tend to occur more frequently
j. involves removing the individual from a situation in which reinforcement occurs
k. rewarding actions that are closer and closer approximations to a desired response

Check Your Memory

1. TRUE or FALSE   Classical conditioning refers to learning based on the consequences of making a response.
2. TRUE or FALSE   If you get As in your psychology class, you may become a psychology major, which illustrates the effect of positive reinforcement.
3. TRUE or FALSE   If children whine and get attention, they will whine more frequently because of negative reinforcement.
4. TRUE or FALSE   A response that is not followed by reward will occur less frequently due to the principle of adaptive aversion.

805

5. TRUE or FALSE   After winning at a slot machine three times in a row, you pull the handle 30 more times without a payoff. You will most likely stop playing the machine because your response of handle pulling has not been followed by a reward, illustrating the process of shaping.

6. TRUE or FALSE   You always go to bed at the conclusion of the late night news. Thus, your bedtime is under the stimulus control of this news program.

7. TRUE or FALSE   Reinforcing actions that are closer and closer approximations to a desired response is know as reciprocal inhibition.

8. TRUE or FALSE   Two children are fighting on the playground, and the teacher has them sit on the sidewalk, effectively removing them from their reinforcement, which illustrates the procedure known as time out.

9. TRUE or FALSE   Nonreward tends to produce extinction of a response.

10. TRUE or FALSE   The time-out procedure is a variation of negative reinforcement because it decreases the behavior it follows.

11. TRUE or FALSE   An undesirable response can be eliminated by identifying and removing the rewards that maintain it.

12. TRUE or FALSE   Most of the rewards maintaining human behavior involve attention, approval, and concern.

13. TRUE or FALSE   By refusing to pay attention to a person who is misbehaving, you are using a form of time out.

14. TRUE or FALSE   Token economies usually are effective in changing behavior in institutional settings because a therapist can immediately reward positive responses with the tokens as well as fine clients so many tokens for undesirable behaviors.

15. TRUE or FALSE   The most effective token economies are those that gradually switch from tokens to social rewards, such as praise, recognition, and approval.

Module 14.4 Medical Therapies

Medical Therapies—Psychiatric Care

Survey Question: How do psychiatrists treat psychological disorders?

Language Development Guide

slant: viewpoint
atmosphere: environment; tone; feeling of
radically: drastically; totally
adoption: implementation
combat: contend with
mood-elevating: achieving a more cheerful emotional state
tranquilizing: soothing; relaxing
valid: suitable
robs: takes away; deprives
risk/benefit ratio: weighing the dangers of use against the help or advantages the treatment provides
cure-alls: hypothetical remedies for diseases
noteworthy: important to remember
mode: form; method
controversial: debatable; causing arguments
drastic: extreme; harsh
triggers: causes; sets off; produces
convulsion: seizure
sedative: calming; tranquilizing

soften: reduce; diminish
impact: effect
proponents: people in favor of
bad spot: uncomfortable or dangerous situation
relapse: to go back to; to worsen; setback
wildly: violently; uncontrollably
precisely: specifically; exactly
targeted: area that is the reference point for the action
enthusiastic: great excitement and interest
vegetables: alive but inactive, comatose
stupor: unresponsive; mental numbness
banned: prohibited; not allowed
sustaining: maintaining; keeping it going
temptations: appeals; enticements
clean break: completely removing the person from a bad situation
sanctuaries: safe place; shelter
refuge: place of safety
brutal: cruel
last resort: final choice or remedy to achieve some end
exhausted: used up
trend: tendency; development
chronic: long-lasting and recurrent
discharged: released
hostile: unwelcoming; adverse
supervision: direction; management
restricted: controlled; constrained; limiting
bright spot: positive, a hopeful thing
wavering: indecisive; uncertainty
accessible: easy to get to
rely: depend
capacity: ability to produce or perform
"been there": have been in that person's place before and experienced the same feelings, etc.
approachable: easy to talk to
reluctant: unwilling; hesitant

Recite and Review

1. Major mental disorders are more often treated _____.
2. Pharmacotherapy, electrical stimulation therapy, and psychosurgery are the three main types of _____ therapy.
3. Psychosurgery, electrical stimulation therapy, and pharmacotherapy are most often done in the context of psychiatric _____.
4. The use of drugs to treat psychopathology is known as drug therapy or _____.
5. The minor tranquilizers, which are used to reduce anxiety, tension, and fear, are referred to as _____.
6. Mood-elevating drugs that combat depression are called _____.
7. The major tranquilizers have tranquilizing effects as well as reduce hallucinations and delusions and are all called _____ drugs.
8. Elavil, Paxil, and Zoloft are examples of the class of psychiatric drugs known as _____.
9. Haldol, Mellaril, and Thorazine are examples of the class of psychiatric drugs known as _____.

807

10. Ativan, Valium, and Xanax are examples of the class of psychiatric drugs known as _____.

11. The psychiatric drugs that enhance the effects of the neurotransmitter GABA are the _____.

12. The effects of the neurotransmitters dopamine and serotonin are enhanced by the psychiatric drugs called _____.

13. The psychiatric group of drugs that reduce the effects of dopamine are called _____.

14. In using drugs to treat psychiatric conditions, such as schizophrenia, one must always consider the _____ ratio.

15. Fifteen percent of patients have developed a neurological disorder that causes rhythmic facial and mouth movements after long term use of _____.

16. A drug that has been effective in relieving the symptoms of schizophrenia but causes a potentially fatal blood disease in two out of 100 patients is _____.

17. A new drug that has been shown to be effective in treating schizophrenia without the potentially fatal side effects is _____.

18. For serious mental disorders, research has shown that an approach that works better than using drugs alone is to use a combination of medication and _____.

19. The treatment methods that achieve their effects by altering the electrical activity of the brain and include electroconvulsive therapy (ECT) and implanted electrodes are _____ therapies.

20. Electroconvulsive therapy (ECT) is a treatment that consists of an electric shock passed directly through the brain, which induces a(n) _____.

21. Before an ECT treatment is given, the doctors soften its impact on the patient by administering sedative drugs and _____.

22. ECT is used to treat severe _____.

23. In some patients, ECT can cause _____ losses.

24. To lower the chance of a relapse, ECT should be followed with _____ drugs.

25. Implanting electrodes allows for electrical stimulation of targeted brain regions, but, unlike ECT, requires _____.

26. Like ECT, implanted electrodes have been used to treat _____.

27. Unlike ECT, implanted electrodes have been used to treat other disorders, such as _____ disorder.

28. The most extreme medical treatment is the surgical alteration of the brain referred to as _____.

29. The frontal lobes of the brain are surgically disconnected from other brain areas in the procedure known as a(n) _____.

30. Patients suffering from a severe type of obsessive-compulsive disorder may be helped by small target areas in the brain's interior being destroyed in a procedure known as _____.

31. The placement of people with major mental disorders in a protected setting where medical therapy is provided is called mental _____.

32. Some patients spend their days in the hospital, but go home at night, while others attend therapy sessions only during the evening in an approach called _____.

33. Dependency, isolation, and continued emotional disturbance is often the result of long-term "_____."

34. The reduced use of full-time commitment to mental institutions is called _____.

35. Short-term group living facilities for people making the transition from an institution to independent living are referred to as _____.

36. A facility that offers a wide range of mental health services, such as prevention, counseling, consultation, and crisis intervention, is called a(n) _____ center.

37. The skilled management of a psychological emergency is referred to as _____.

38. Kyle, who is an ex-addict, works in a near-professional capacity at a drug rehabilitation center under the supervision of more highly trained staff. Kyle would be considered a(n) _____.

Part 1: Connections

1. ___ pharmacotherapy
2. ___ anxiolytics
3. ___ antidepressants
4. ___ antipsychotics
5. ___ electroconvulsive therapy (ECT)
6. ___ implanted electrodes
7. ___ prefrontal lobotomy
8. ___ deep lesioning

a. use of drugs to treat psychopathology
b. drugs that tend to reduce hallucinations and delusional thinking; also called major tranquilizers
c. allows for electrical stimulation of targeted brain regions
d. mood-elevating drugs
e. psychosurgery in which small target areas are destroyed in the brain's interior
f. treatment for severe depression consisting of an electric shock passed directly through the brain, which induces a convulsion
g. drugs, such as Valium that produce relaxation or reduce anxiety
h. frontal lobes are surgically disconnected from other brain areas

Part 2: Connections

1. ___ somatic therapy
2. ___ electrical stimulation therapy
3. ___ psychosurgery
4. ___ mental hospitalization
5. ___ partial hospitalization
6. ___ deinstitutionalization
7. ___ halfway houses
8. ___ community mental health centers
9. ___ crisis intervention
10. ___ paraprofessional

a. skilled management of a psychological emergency
b. approaches that achieve their effects by altering the electrical activity of the brain
c. approach in which patients usually receive treatment at a hospital during the day but return home at night
d. any bodily therapy, such as drug therapy, electroconvulsive therapy, or psychosurgery
e. reduced use of full-time commitment to mental institutions to treat mental disorders
f. any surgical alteration of the brain designed to bring about desirable behavioral or emotional changes
g. placing a person in a protected therapeutic environment staffed by mental health professionals
h. individual who works in a near-professional capacity under the supervision of a more highly trained person
i. community-based facility offering a wide range of mental health services, such as prevention, counseling, consultation, and crisis intervention
j. short-term group living facilities for people making the transition from an institution to independent living

Check Your Memory

1. TRUE or FALSE   Major mental disorders are most often treated medically.
2. TRUE or FALSE   Any bodily therapy, such as drug therapy, electroconvulsive therapy, or psychosurgery, is referred to as neurotherapy.
3. TRUE or FALSE   The atmosphere in psychiatric wards and mental hospitals changed radically for the better in the mid-1940s with the widespread adoption of electroconvulsive therapy.
4. TRUE or FALSE   Antidepressants, such as valium, are used to reduce anxiety.
5. TRUE or FALSE   Antipsychotics are also called major tranquilizers and can reduce hallucinations and delusions.
6. TRUE or FALSE   Anxiolytics, such as Elavil, are used to counteract depression.
7. TRUE or FALSE   Drugs have shortened hospital stays and made it possible for many people to return to the community, where they can be treated on an outpatient basis.
8. TRUE or FALSE   The type of drugs that reduce the effect of dopamine are the antidepresants.
9. TRUE or FALSE   Anxiolytics enhance the effects of GABA.
10. TRUE or FALSE   The drugs known as antipsychotics increase the effects of both serotonin and dopamine.
11. TRUE or FALSE   All drugs involve a trade-off between benefits and risks.
12. TRUE or FALSE   Fifteen percent of patients taking major tranquilizers for long periods of time develop a neurological disorder that causes rhythmic facial and mouth movements.
13. TRUE or FALSE   The drug Risperdal has been shown to cause a potentially fatal blood disease in two percent of patients with a safer alternative being the drug Clozaril.
14. TRUE or FALSE   For serious mental disorders, a combination of medication and psychotherapy almost always works better than drugs alone.
15. TRUE or FALSE   Electrical stimulation therapy includes ECT and implanted electrodes.
16. TRUE or FALSE   In ECT, a 500-volt electrical current is passed through the brain for three to five seconds.
17. TRUE or FALSE   ECT triggers a convulsion in the patient and causes the patient to lose consciousness for a short time.
18. TRUE or FALSE   Muscle relaxants and sedative drugs are given before ECT to soften its impact.
19. TRUE or FALSE   ECT has been shown to be effective in treating dissociative and somatoform disorders.
20. TRUE or FALSE   ECT can cause memory losses in some patients.
21. TRUE or FALSE   The implanting of electrodes does not require surgery.
22. TRUE or FALSE   Implanted electrodes has been used to treat depression by stimulating the pleasure centers in the brain as well as treating obsessive-compulsive disorder by targeting other specific brain areas.
23. TRUE or FALSE   The most extreme medical treatment is psychosurgery.
24. TRUE or FALSE   In the prefrontal lobotomy, the corpus callosum connecting the two hemispheres of the brain are cut.
25. TRUE or FALSE   After undergoing prefrontal lobotomies, some patients were calmed, some showed no change, and some went into a stupor state.
26. TRUE or FALSE   Soon after the first antipsychotic drugs became available, the lobotomy was abandoned.

810

27. TRUE or FALSE   Deep lesioning is a psychosurgery that involves destroying small target areas of the brain's interior.
28. TRUE or FALSE   Mental hospitalization can take patients out of situations that may be sustaining their problems and help them make a clean break from their self-destructive behavior patterns.
29. TRUE or FALSE   In the partial hospitalization approach, patients may spend their days in the hospital and go home at night or may come to the hospital only in the evening to attend therapy sessions.
30. TRUE or FALSE   Overall, partial hospitalization can be just as effective as full hospitalization.
31. TRUE or FALSE   Deinstitutionalization refers to the increased use of full-time commitment to mental institutions to treat mental disorders.
32. TRUE or FALSE   As a way to save money, many states have released mental patients into the community with many former patients becoming homeless or being repeatedly jailed for minor crimes.
33. TRUE or FALSE   Halfway houses are short-term group living facilities for people making the transition form an institution to independent living.
34. TRUE or FALSE   Halfway houses can reduce a person's chances of being readmitted to a hospital.
35. TRUE or FALSE   The primary aim of community mental health centers is provide preventative programs and mental health speakers for the community with counseling being a secondary role.
36. TRUE or FALSE   Skilled management of a psychological emergency is called crisis intervention.
37. TRUE or FALSE   Many mental health programs rely on paraprofessionals, such as ex-addicts, ex-alcoholics, or ex-patients, who have been through the program and who work under the supervision of the more highly trained staff.

Critical Thinking Question

Residents of Berkeley, California, once voted on a referendum to ban the use of ECT within city limits. Do you think that the use of certain psychiatric treatments should be controlled by law?

Module 14.5 Contemporary Issues in Therapy

Therapies—An Overview

Survey Question: What do various therapies have in common?

Language Development Guide

contemporary: modern; current
round out: to complete
reliance: dependence
digital technologies: electronic technology that generates, stores, and processes data in terms of binary (1's and 0's) code
cost-effectively: economically; getting the most for the least cost
tricky: difficult; complicated
take people's word for it: accept what someone says without proof
therapy placebo effect: changes in behavior due to expectations that the therapy will have some effect
clergy: group of persons in religious service, such as ministers, priests, rabbis, etc.
unethical: wrong
weed out: to remove something that is undesirable or could be harmful
fringe: on the edge; extreme

immensely: greatly; very
sampled: checked out
clarity: clearness
mending: repair; put right
therapeutic: healing
alliance: partnership; bond
rapport: understanding; connection
confidentiality: privacy
to some extent: partly; to some degree
rationale: underlying principle; reasoning; justification
distilled from: obtained from
leaping to conclusions: making a quick judgment
hassling: pestering; bothering
pressured: stressed by external demands and expectations
sort out: to study and figure out a problem
reputation: general estimation of how public view one
fantastic: unbelievable
conversationalist: someone skilled at exchanging spoken ideas with others
outpouring: expression
catharsis: a cleansing release of emotional tensions
defensive: self-protective; distrustful
heart wrenching: causing great sadness
confides: reveals in confidence
frame of reference: personal viewpoint by which experiences are perceived and evaluated
resist: fight against
imposing: forcing; inflicting
shunned: rejected
fancy: expensive; lavish
resorting: choosing the option of
acculturation: adapting to another culture
enriching: adding value; enlightening
gossip: to share personal information or secrets about someone to someone else
invitation: calling for
play "junior therapist": to try to act like a counselor or psychologist
far exceeding: significantly going beyond

Recite and Review

1. In a national survey of people who had sought mental health care, the number who said their lives improved as a result of the treatment was approximately_____ out of 10.
2. It is possible that someone who feels better after six months of therapy may just feel better because so much time has passed, that is, the person experienced a(n) _____.
3. In order to find out if therapy caused the improvement in the client and not some other source, the psychologists must compare one group of clients who received therapy to a group who did not. In other words, the psychologists must conduct a(n) _____.
4. In comparing the two groups of clients to determine the effectiveness of therapy, the group who receives therapy is called the _____ group.
5. In comparing the two groups of clients to determine the effectiveness of therapy, the group who does not receive the therapy is called the _____ control group.

6. Recently, studies have shown that some therapies are most effective for specific disorders. For example, obsessive-compulsive disorder is best treated using behavior therapy, drug therapies, and _____ therapy.

7. Psychologists are making steady progress in identifying evidence-based, also called "_____" therapies.

8. These evidence-based therapies are developed, not through intuition, but through research experiments and _____.

9. Research shows that, after 13 to 18 weekly one-hour therapy sessions, the percentage of clients who feel better is about _____ percent.

10. Because of high costs and limited insurance coverage, the number of therapy sessions that the average client receives is only _____ sessions.

11. After the number of therapy sessions attended by the average client, the percentage that felt better was only _____ percent.

12. A directive, insight-oriented group therapy whose strength is providing constructive reenactments is _____.

13. A directive group therapy that can be either insight-oriented or action-oriented and whose strength involves the shared responsibility for problems is _____ therapy.

14. A directive, action therapy that can be conducted individually or in a group and has the strength of producing observable changes in behavior is _____ therapy.

15. An individual, directive, insight therapy that may take years to complete and whose strength involves the search for honesty is _____.

16. An individual insight therapy that can be either directive or nondirective and whose strength involves personal empowerment is _____ therapy.

17. May is receiving individual, directive insight therapy, which is producing many insights into her problems very quickly through a productive use of conflict. May's therapy is most likely _____ therapy.

18. A directive insight therapy that can be conducted individually or in a group and which focuses on the client's immediate awareness is _____ therapy.

19. Tony is attending individual therapy sessions that are directive, action-oriented and provide constructive guidance in confronting his major distortions in thinking. Tony's therapy is most likely _____ therapy.

20. Al is receiving individual directive, action therapy in which he is gaining a clarity of thinking and learning to identify and confronts his irrational beliefs. Al's therapy is most likely _____.

21. A nondirective insight therapy that provides acceptance and empathy and can be used in an individual or group setting is _____ therapy.

22. All or most of the goals of restoring hope, courage, and optimism; gaining insight; resolving conflicts; improving one's sense of self; and learning to approach problems rationally are shared by the various types of _____.

23. Therapy provides a caring relationship between the client and therapist, called a(n) _____.

24. Therapy offers a protected setting in which emotional release, or _____ can occur.

25. Regarding a client's suffering, all therapies not only propose a line of action to end the suffering but also to some extent offer a(n) _____.

26. Therapy provides clients with a new perceptive about themselves and their situations and a chance to practice new _____.

27. If a friend needed to gain insight into her problems, behaviors on your part, such as judging, moralizing, placing blame, and probing painful topics would tend to _____ this process.

28. Veronica is making a sincere effort to listen to and understand her friend Beth's problem without judging or leaping to conclusions. Veronica is using the basic counseling skill called _____ listening.

29. As he listens to Jim's problems, Brett gives Jim feedback by simply restating what is said, which encourages Jim to talk. Brett is using the basic counseling technique known as _____.

30. Your best friend tells you that his boss has it in for him at work. If you reply, "Are you going to quit?" you are using a(n) _____ question.

31. If your best friend tells you that he just made a D on his report and you say, "How do you feel about it?" you are using a(n) _____ question.

32. Juanita has confided in Anna regarding a personal problem. Anna asks Juanita, "Are you saying that you feel depressed just at school? Or in general?" Anna is using the counseling skill which involves _____ the problem.

33. When discussing a problem, it is important to focus on a person's feelings, since this will encourage the outpouring of emotion that is the basis for _____.

34. The "Why don't you . . . ? Yes, but . . ." game, which follows a predictable pattern in which someone says, "I have this problem," and you say, "Why don't you do this?" and the person replying, "Yes, but….," was described by psychotherapist _____.

35. A person who feels that his or her viewpoint has been understood feels freer to question it and examine it _____.

36. A therapist who is able to adapt traditional theories and techniques to meet the needs of clients from non-European ethnic or racial groups and to establish rapport with a person from a different cultural background is referred to as a(n) _____ therapist.

37. Each of us can supply two of the greatest mental health resources available at any cost: friendship and honest _____.

Part 1: Connections

1. ___ spontaneous remission
2. ___ waiting-list control group

3. ___ therapeutic alliance

4. ___ emotional catharsis

5. ___ "empirically supported" or "evidence-based"
6. ___ active listening

7. ___ reflecting

8. ___ open-ended questions

9. ___ closed question

10. ___ frame of reference

11. ___ "Why don't you . . . ? Yes, but . . ." game
12. ___ culturally skilled therapist

a. inquiry that requires an expanded reply
b. accepting a person's message without judging it or leaping to conclusions and letting person know you are listening
c. therapist who has the awareness, knowledge, and skills necessary to treat clients from diverse cultural backgrounds
d. person's viewpoint of the world that influences their perceptions and evaluations
e. restating or paraphrasing the other person's thoughts and feelings
f. caring relationship that unites a therapist and client in working to solve the client's problems
g. pattern of verbal interaction when a person is avoiding another person's advice
h. improvement in condition only because so much time has passed
i. feeling of release that occurs in therapy when clients express their fears and anxiety
j. using research experiments and clinical practice in evaluating the effectiveness of therapies
k. participants in a group who have not yet seen a therapist but who eventually will
l. inquiry that can be answered yes or no

814

Part 2: Connections

1. ___ psychoanalysis

2. ___ brief psychodynamic therapy

3. ___ client-centered therapy

4. ___ existential therapy

5. ___ Gestalt therapy

6. ___ behavior therapy

7. ___ cognitive therapy

8. ___ rational-emotive behavior therapy

9. ___ psychodrama

10. ___ family therapy

a. involves a productive use of conflict; interpersonal therapy is an example

b. involves a search for honesty; therapy may take years

c. emphasizes a clarity of thinking and goals; confronting irrational beliefs

d. requires observable changes in behavior

e. involves a shared responsibility for problems

f. involves acceptance and empathy; nondirective therapy

g. involves constructive re-enactments

h. focuses on immediate awareness and gaps in experience

i. involves constructive guidance to test major distortions in thinking

j. emphasizes personal empowerment and meaningfulness

Check Your Memory

1. TRUE or FALSE — In a national survey, only four out of 10 people who have sought mental health care say their lives improved as a result of the treatment.

2. TRUE or FALSE — In order to find out if therapy caused the improvement in the client and not a spontaneous remission, psychologists must conduct experiments in which the experimental group receives therapy and the waiting-list control group does not receive therapy.

3. TRUE or FALSE — Studies have shown that psychoanalysis and Gestalt therapy are particularly helpful in treating obsessive-compulsive disorder.

4. TRUE or FALSE — "Empirically supported" therapies are those that rely on intuition to select the best approaches for specific types of problems.

5. TRUE or FALSE — Hundreds of studies show a strong pattern of positive effects for psychotherapy, counseling, and other psychological treatments.

6. TRUE or FALSE — Research shows that about 90 percent of all clients feel better after between 13 and 18 weekly one-hour therapy sessions.

7. TRUE or FALSE — Because of the high costs and limited insurance coverage, the average client receives only five therapy sessions, after which only 20 percent of patients feel better.

8. TRUE or FALSE — Cognitive therapy is a nondirective insight therapy that can be used as both an individual and group therapy.

9. TRUE or FALSE — Brief psychodynamic therapy is a nondirective action therapy that is most often used in group settings.

10. TRUE or FALSE — Gestalt therapy is a directive insight therapy that focuses on immediate awareness and is used both in individual as well as group therapy settings.

11. TRUE or FALSE — Psychoanalysis is considered a nondirective, action therapy whose main therapy strength is acceptance and empathy.

12. TRUE or FALSE — Family therapy can be either action or insight with its strength being the clients' sharing responsibility for their problems.

815

13. TRUE or FALSE   Psychotherapies of various types share all or most of these goals: to restore hope, resolve conflicts, change unacceptable patterns of behavior, and mend interpersonal relations.

14. TRUE or FALSE   Therapy provides a caring relationship between the client and therapist called a therapeutic alliance.

15. TRUE or FALSE   Therapy offers a protected setting in which emotional catharsis can take place.

16. TRUE or FALSE   All therapies to some extent offer an explanation or rationale for the client's suffering and propose a line of action that will end this suffering.

17. TRUE or FALSE   Therapy provides clients with a new perspective about themselves and their situations and a chance to practice new behaviors.

18. TRUE or FALSE   The basic counseling skills that would help a person gain insight into a personal problem include probing painful topics and giving advice.

19. TRUE or FALSE   When a friend is discussing a problem with you, it is important that your friend knows you are listening, through your eye contact, posture, tone of voice, and your replies.

20. TRUE or FALSE   Counselors tend to wait a longer amount of time before responding to a client than do people responding to each other in everyday conversations.

21. TRUE or FALSE   One of the best things you can do when offering support to another person is to give feedback by simply restating what is said.

22. TRUE or FALSE   If a friend tells you that she thinks the math teacher has it in for her and you reply with "Are you going to drop the class?" you are using an open-ended question.

23. TRUE or FALSE   In counseling a friend, one should never focus on feelings since this will encourage too much of an outpouring of emotion that will prevent resolving the problem.

24. TRUE or FALSE   Aaron Beck was the psychotherapist that identified the "Yes, but…" game that occurs when giving advice.

25. TRUE or FALSE   A person who feels that his or her viewpoint has been understood feels freer to examine it objectively and to question it.

26. TRUE or FALSE   A culturally skilled therapist is trained to work with clients from various cultural background and to adapt traditional theories and techniques to meet the needs of clients form non-European ethnic or racial groups.

27. TRUE or FALSE   A culturally skilled therapist must be aware of his or her own cultural values and biases.

28. TRUE or FALSE   Unless you are a licensed psychotherapist, it is not important to maintain confidentiality regarding the information that someone has confided in you regarding their problem.

Critical Thinking Question

In your opinion, do psychologists have a duty to protect others who may be harmed by their clients? For example, if a patient has homicidal fantasies about his ex-wife, should she be informed?

Module 14.5 Contemporary Issues in Therapy
The Future of Psychotherapy—Magnets and Smartphones
Survey Question: What will therapy be like in the future?

Language Development Guide

urgent: pressing; critical
devote: dedicate; give
practitioners: person engaged in the activities of a specific profession
luxury: extravagance; indulgence
transcranial: across or through the skull
noninvasive: does not involve cutting into the body
not a long stretch: not difficult
adjunct: something added; extra
disrupted: to throw into disorder
input: contributions
reenacts: pretends, acts out
incidents: situations
transfer: pass on
related: associated; connected
confrontational: exposing problems; challenging
enlarge: increase
false fronts: not showing true self; pretending
screened: checked; selected
"casualties": ones who are harmed
ambitious: grand; elaborate
versatility: able to be used for many purposes or in many places
undoubtedly: certainly
popularity: demand or desirability for something
for better or worse: whether a good or bad effect
commonplace: everyday occurrences
media: means of communication; collectively, television, radio, newspaper, magazines, and Internet
reassurance: support; hope; comfort
publicizing: to draw public attention to
tempted: persuaded; attracted to
let the consumer beware: the buyer has to make sure they aren't being cheated
caution: warning
anonymous: name withheld
intercepted: seized; obtained
misused: use wrongly; exploit
evolving: to develop by gradual changes
objections: opposition; protests
open to question: not clearly correct; debatable
to skip: leave out; miss; omit

Recite and Review

1. Regarding the future of psychotherapy, a group of experts have predicted that there will be an increase in the use of short-term therapy and solution-focused, problem-solving approaches and in the use of lower-cost telephone counseling and _____ services.
2. In the future, experts predict that there will be a greater reliance on group therapies and self-help groups run by _____.
3. In the future more therapy will be provided by practitioners with training at the _____-level.
4. Experts predict that in the future will be more precisely targeted medical therapies with fewer _____.

817

5. Many of these predicted changes are based on pressures to reduce the _____ of mental health services.
6. A new technique that uses magnetic pulses to temporarily block activity in specific parts of the brain is called _____.
7. Psychologists first tried working with groups because there was a(n) _____ of therapists.
8. In group therapy, insights are produced by the person directly experiencing or _____ problems.
9. In group therapy, other members with similar problems can offer useful input and _____.
10. Group therapy is especially good for helping people understand their personal _____.
11. One of the first group therapies was developed by Jacob L. Moreno, who called his technique _____.
12. In Moreno's group therapy, the clients re-enacts incidents that cause problems in real life through role-_____.
13. During Moreno's group therapy when a person takes the part of another person to learn how he or she feels, the technique being used is _____.
14. Jeff is participating in a group therapy originated by Moreno. During one session, another member plays Jeff and re-enact Jeff's behavior so Jeff can observe. The approach being used is the _____ technique.
15. A husband, wife, and children work as a group to resolve the problems of each family member in _____ therapy.
16. Jasmine and Colby are married and attending counseling, but their three children will not be involved in this counseling. Thus, Jasmine and Colby are participating in _____ therapy.
17. In counseling, family members work together to change destructive patterns, and to see themselves and each other in new ways, and to improve _____.
18. Although family therapists may not meet with the entire family at each session, they are concerned with the entire pattern of behavior within a family and, thus, treat the family as a(n) _____.
19. Family and couples therapy tends to be focused on specific problems, such as frequent fights or a depressed teenager and tend to be _____ limited.
20. During the 1960s and 1970s, the human potential movement led many people to seek personal _____ experiences.
21. Participants take part in exercises that gently enlarge self-awareness and understanding of others in _____ groups.
22. Participants expand their confidence in others by allowing themselves to be led around while blind-folded in an exercise known as the _____.
23. The type of groups, which are based on an honest expression of feelings, intensely personal communication, and tearing down defenses and false fronts, are called _____ groups.
24. Madeline just signed up and paid for a training program that claims to increase self-awareness and facilitate personal change. She will be attending this program with about 500 other participants at the city auditorium. Madeline is most liking attending a(n) _____ training.
25. When improvement is based on a client's belief that therapy will help, it is referred to as the _____ effect.
26. One of the criticisms of media psychologists, such as phone-in radio or television psychologists, involves whether it is reasonable to give advice without knowing anything about a person's _____.
27. Many media psychologists stress that their work is not therapeutic, but _____.

28. The well-known media psychologist, who was awarded a President's Citation from the American Psychological Association for his work in publicizing mental health issues, was _____.

29. The American Psychological Association urges media psychologists not to actually counsel anyone, but instead to discuss problems only of a(n) _____ nature.

30. A key feature of successful face-to-face therapy is the establishment of a continuing relationship between two people, which is known as the _____.

31. Distance therapies are more or less limited by a lack of interpersonal cues, such as facial expressions and _____.

32. During counseling through brief e-mails, real human interaction cannot be duplicated by the typing of emotional icons called _____.

33. There is a concern whether psychologists can legally do Internet therapy in other states if they are only _____ in one U.S. state.

34. Some advantages of online counseling and advice services include that clients can remain _____.

35. People who receive counseling through e-mail should be aware that their messages could be intercepted and misused, so e-mail counseling may not be completely _____.

36. The Internet can link psychologists living in large cities with people who live in _____ areas.

37. Compared with traditional office visits, Internet therapy is _____ expensive.

38. A two-way audio-video link which allows the client and therapist to see one another on computer monitors and to talk via speakerphones is called _____.

39. Telephone counseling helped improve success rates for smokers who wanted to quit as well as benefiting people suffering from _____.

40. Computer software has been used successfully to some relatively minor problems with clients working through ten computer-guided sessions that help them to identify a problem and then form and carry out a(n) _____.

Part 1: Connections

1. ___ transcranial magnetic stimulation (TMS)

2. ___ psychodrama

3. ___ family therapy

4. ___ couples therapy

5. ___ sensitivity group

6. ___ encounter group

a. therapy with two partners, such as husband and wife) present, but without children being present

b. includes phone-in radio psychologists and television therapists that discuss problems in a general educational way

c. uses magnetic pulses to temporarily block activity in specific parts of the brain

d. group experience consisting of exercises designed to increase self-awareness and understanding of others

e. technique in which all family members participate, both individually and as a group, to change destructive relationships and communication patterns

f. therapy in which clients act out personal conflicts and feelings in the presence of others who play supporting roles

7. ___ large-group awareness training

    g. two-way audio-video link hat allows client and therapist to see one another on computer monitors and to talk via speakerphones

8. ___ media psychologists

    h. group experience that emphasizes intensely honest interchanges among participants regarding feelings and reactions to one another

9. ___ Skype

    i. any of a number of programs (many of them commercialized) that claim to increase self-awareness and facilitate constructive personal change

Part 2: Connections

1. ___ role-playing

    a. caring relationship that unites a therapist and a client in working to solve the client's problems

2. ___ role reversal

    b. participants expand their confidence in others by allowing themselves to be led around while blindfolded

3. ___ mirror technique

    c. improvement caused not by the actual process of therapy but by a client's expectation that therapy will help

4. ___ therapeutic alliance

    d. computer icons used to denote emotions in e-mails

5. ___ "trust walk"

    e. observing another person re-enact one's own behavior, like a character in a play, designed to help person see themselves more clearly

6. ___ emoticons

    f. taking the role of another person to learn how one's own behavior appears from the other person's perspective

7. ___ therapy placebo effect

    g. client reenacts his own role within an incident that caused a problem

Check Your Memory

1. TRUE or FALSE   Regarding the future of psychotherapy, experts predict there will be a decrease in the use of short-term therapy and an increase in the use of psychiatrists and clinical psychologists.
2. TRUE or FALSE   Regarding the future of psychotherapy, experts predict that the use of lower-cost Internet services, telephone counseling, paraprofessionals, and self-help groups will grow.
3. TRUE or FALSE   A new medical therapy technique called transcranial magnetic stimulation (TMS) uses surgically implanted magnets to permanently block activity in specific parts of the brain.
4. TRUE or FALSE   Unlike surgical lesioning, TMS is noninvasive and is reversible.
5. TRUE or FALSE   Patients who suffer from compulsive gambling or obsessive-compulsive disorder have shown marked improvement when TMS disrupted brain areas involved in compulsive behavior.
6. TRUE or FALSE   Group therapy usually costs more than individual therapy does.

7. TRUE or FALSE   Psychologists first tried working with groups because there was a shortage of therapists.

8. TRUE or FALSE   Group therapy has proven to be significantly less effective than individual therapy.

9. TRUE or FALSE   In group therapy, a person can act out or directly experience problems, which often produces insights that might not occur from merely talking about an issue.

10. TRUE or FALSE   During group therapy, other group members with similar problems can offer support and useful input.

11. TRUE or FALSE   Group therapy has been shown to be effective in helping people understand their personal relationships.

12. TRUE or FALSE   One of the first group therapies was developed by António Moniz, who called his technique an encounter group.

13. TRUE or FALSE   Role-playing, role reversals, and the mirror technique are all part of a technique known as psychodrama.

14. TRUE or FALSE   In the mirror technique, a person takes the role of a significant person in his or her life and acts out this person's role in order to learn how this person's feels.

15. TRUE or FALSE   Family and couples therapy tends to be time-limited and focused on specific problems.

16. TRUE or FALSE   Family therapists believe that a problem experienced by one family member is really the whole family's problem.

17. TRUE or FALSE   Since the family is treated as a unit, the therapist meets with the entire family at each session and not with individual members.

18. TRUE or FALSE   During the 1960s and 1970s, the human potential movement led many people to seek personal growth experiences with their interest being expressed by participation in sensitivity training or encounter groups.

19. TRUE or FALSE   Sensitivity groups tend to be more confrontational than encounter groups.

20. TRUE or FALSE   Participants in encounter groups take part in exercises that gently enlarge self-awareness and understanding of others.

21. TRUE or FALSE   In a "trust walk," participants expand their confidence in others by allowing themselves to be led around while blindfolded.

22. TRUE or FALSE   Sensitivity groups are based on an honest expression of feelings and emphasize tearing down defenses and false fronts.

23. TRUE or FALSE   In business settings, psychologists still use the basic principles of sensitivity and encounter groups, such as truth, self-awareness, and self-determination, to improve employee relationships.

24. TRUE or FALSE   Large-group awareness training refers to programs, often commercialized, that claim to increase self-awareness and facilitate constructive personal change.

25. TRUE or FALSE   Although the experiences in sensitivity, encounter, and awareness groups tend to be positive, they produce only moderate benefits.

26. TRUE or FALSE   Many of the claimed benefits from sensitivity, encounter, and awareness groups may simply be the result of the therapy placebo effect.

27. TRUE or FALSE   It is perfectly reasonable and acceptable for call-in radio psychologists and television psychologists to give advice without knowing the person's background.

28. TRUE or FALSE   The well-known media psychologist Dr. Phil McGraw has been awarded a President's Citation from the American Psychological Association for his work in publicizing mental health issues.

29. TRUE or FALSE   The American Psychological Association urges media psychologists to probe the caller's personal life and to give specific advice when they counsel individuals on radio or television.

30. TRUE or FALSE   A key feature of successful face-to-face therapy is the establishment of a therapeutic alliance between two people, which is difficult for telephone, media, and Internet therapists to accomplish.

31. TRUE or FALSE   Emoticons have been used effectively during e-mail counseling to express the client's mood, voice, and simulated body language.

32. TRUE or FALSE   Internet psychologists, who are licensed in one U. S. state can legally counsel in all other states and countries.

33. TRUE or FALSE   Internet counseling allows a client to remain anonymous.

34. TRUE or FALSE   Counseling through the Internet has allowed people who live in rural areas to be linked with psychologists in large cities.

35. TRUE or FALSE   E-mail counseling has been found to be completely confidential since e-mails cannot be intercepted and misused.

36. TRUE or FALSE   Compared with traditional office visits, distance therapies tend to be more expensive.

37. TRUE or FALSE   Therapists using the telephone have been able to improve the success rates for smokers who want to quit and to help depressed people.

38. TRUE or FALSE   Skype consists of two-way audio-video links that allows a client and therapist to see one another on computer monitors and to talk via speakerphones.

39. TRUE or FALSE   Computer-guided therapy sessions in which the client works with a computer program has been successfully used to treat psychosis and other major mental disorders.

40. TRUE or FALSE   In a study of computer-guided sessions, the majority of the participants were not satisfied with the help they received from the computer.

Module 14.6 Psychology in Action
Self-Management and Seeking Professional Help
Survey Questions: How are behavioral principles applied to everyday problems? How could a person find professional help?

Language Development Guide

boosting: increasing; improving
willpower: determination; self-control
expertise: know-how; skill
straightforward: direct and uncomplicated
intensive: severe; serious
remote: distant; isolated
curb: slow; restrain; control; hold back
aversive: causing avoidance; repel
indulging: doing for pleasure
caved in: collapsed
toned down: made less strong
"grossed out": disgust someone
maggots: fly larvae
nauseating: causing sickness of the stomach; feel like vomiting
appetite: hunger; desire for food
"playing games with yourself": clever strategy against yourself

cut down: reduce; slow

put yourself down: be self-critical or insulting

conviction: confidence; passion; unshakable belief

private spot: a place where you are alone

covertly: hidden; not in the open

diaphragm: muscle below the lungs that helps breathing

comparable: similar; equal to

dismayed: alarmed; upset

employee assistance programs: benefits offered as part of one's health insurance

arbitrary: subjective

in conjunction with: jointly; connected

sliding scale: based on one's income; ability to pay for the services

mutual: shared

qualifications: meeting the proper standards and requirements

reputable: known to be good

credentials: documents that provide evidence of one's authority, expertise, etc.

consultation: conference

consult: seek advice from

referral: sent to someone else, such as a doctor sending someone to a specialist in a particular area

balanced: fair; objective

integrity: honor, reliability, honesty; adhering to moral standards

an art, not a science: involves more than just an objective procedure; in this case therapy has to be adapted for each client rather than just using a step-by-step scientific procedure each time

belittling: made to feel small or unimportant or stupid

small talk: light, informal conversation

prolonged: drawn out

absolute: total

terminate: end

Recite and Review

1. You should seek professional help when a significant problem exists, but for lesser difficulties you may want to try applying _____ principles yourself.

2. Aversive imagery is used to reduce the occurrence of an undesired response, such as smoking or overeating in a procedure known as _____.

3. In order to vividly picture the aversive imagery every day, one should take out the aversive imagery cards each time one performs a certain activity, such as getting a cup of coffee or a soft drink, thus, placing the visualization under _____.

4. Theresa is trying to lose weight, so every time she is tempted to eat a dessert, she imagines maggots crawling all over it. Theresa is using the technique known as _____.

5. Jack places a rubber band around his wrist and "pops" his wrist with this rubber band every time thinks about needless worries or "puts himself down" in his thoughts. Jack is using the technique known as _____.

6. Amy sets aside a short time each day and deliberately thinks about unwanted worries and fears. While thinking about them, she initially shouted "Stop!" but now thinks "Stop!" in her head now. Amy is using a technique known as _____.

7. The use of positive imagery to reinforce desired behavior is known as _____.

8. Learning to relax is the first step in self-directed _____.

9. Two techniques that help people relax include deep breathing and the _____ method.

10. Jeanie has a fear of public speaking. She has learned to relax through deep breathing and now will make a listing of these fearful situations with this list being referred to as a(n) _____.

11. You have a fear of closed spaces and have listed fear-producing scenes related to this fear on cards from least to highest fear producing. In order to proceed to the second card, you must vividly picture and imagine yourself in the situation listed on the first card without a noticeable increase in muscle tension _____ times.

12. When using the list of fear-producing scenes on the cards, you would stop when you reach a card that you cannot visualize without becoming tense in _____ attempts.

13. In a survey, the percent of all American households included someone who received mental health treatment during the preceding year was _____ percent.

14. You should consider seeing a psychologist or a psychiatrist if your level of psychological discomfort is comparable to a level of physical discomfort that would cause you to see a(n) _____.

15. Another signal that one should see a psychologist or psychiatrist is to watch for significant changes in behavior, such as your relationships with others, your use of drugs (including alcohol), the quality of your work (or schoolwork), and your rate of _____.

16. You should seek psychological help immediately if you have persistent or disturbing _____ thoughts or impulses.

17. Many cities have groups organized by concerned citizens that keep listings of qualified therapists and other services and programs in the community. These groups are the _____ associations.

18. In the telephone book, psychologists are listed under "Psychologist" or "Counseling Services," while psychiatrists are listed under the subheading of "_____."

19. A telephone service staffed by community volunteers who are trained to provide information concerning a wide range of mental health problems is a(n) _____.

20. Although a psychiatrist can administer somatic therapy and prescribe drugs in all 50 of the United States, psychologists are also allowed to perform somatic therapies and prescribe drugs in the states of New Mexico and _____.

21. Compared to the fees for psychologists, the fees for psychiatrists are usually _____.

22. If fees are a problem, many therapists as well as community mental health centers charge on one's ability to pay, or a(n) "_____."

23. Nonprofessionals who have learned basic counseling skills are called _____ counselors.

24. A type of group that adds valuable support to professional treatment with members sharing a particular type of problem, such as eating disorders or coping with an alcoholic parent, and offering mutual support and a chance to discuss problems describes a(n) _____ group.

25. You can usually find out about your therapist's qualifications simply by _____ him or her.

26. Far more important than the approach used by the therapist is the therapist's _____.

27. Within psychotherapy, sexual advances by the therapist or a therapist that makes repeated verbal threats, engages in excessive small talk, or encouraging prolonged dependence by the client are all _____ signals.

28. An especially important part of the therapeutic alliance is the agreement between the therapist and client about the _____ of therapy.

Connections

1. ____ covert sensitization

2. ____ thought stopping

a. use of aversive stimuli to interrupt or prevent upsetting thoughts

b. group of people who share a particular type of problem and provide mutual support to one another

3. ___ covert reinforcement

    c. groups formed by concerned citizens that keep listings of qualified therapists and other services and programs in the community

4. ___ self-directed desensitization

    d. nonprofessional persons who has learned basic counseling skills

5. ___ crisis hotlines

    e. involves using the tension release method and a hierarchy list of anxiety-provoking situations

6. ___ peer counselors

    f. using positive imagery to reinforce desired behavior

7. ___ self-help groups

    g. telephone service staffed by community volunteers trained to provide information concerning a wide range of mental health problems

8. ___ mental health associations

    h. use of aversive imagery to reduce the occurrence of an undesired response

Check Your Memory

1. TRUE or FALSE   Although the use of behavior therapy is often quite complicated and requires a great deal of expertise, people can learn to apply some behavior principles to him or herself to help alleviate minor difficulties.

2. TRUE or FALSE   In covert reinforcement, aversive imagery is used to reduce the occurrence of an undesired response.

3. TRUE or FALSE   To make sure that a person using the aversive imagery several times per day, one can place the presentation of the aversive imagery under stimulus control.

4. TRUE or FALSE   When a person is trying to lose weight and imagines maggots crawling over a dessert they are tempted to eat, the person is using covert sensitization.

5. TRUE or FALSE   Snapping a rubber band on your wrist every time you engage in negative self talk is an example of the use of self-directed desensitization.

6. TRUE or FALSE   A person who sets aside time each day to deliberately think about needless worries and while thinking about them shouting "Stop!" is using a technique known as thought stopping.

7. TRUE or FALSE   The use of positive imagery to reinforce desired behavior is called covert sensitization.

8. TRUE or FALSE   The first step in desensitization is learning to relax voluntarily by using the tension-release method or through deep breathing.

9. TRUE or FALSE   When using covert reinforcement, one constructs a hierarchy of situations related to one's fear.

10. TRUE or FALSE   In using the hierarchy of fears listed on the cards, one goes through the whole set of cards two to three times a day, attempting to relax to each one and moving on the next card when one is unable to relax to a particular card.

11. TRUE or FALSE   In a survey, half of all American households included someone who received mental health treatment during the preceding year.

12. TRUE or FALSE   If your level of psychological discomfort is comparable to a level of physical discomfort that would cause you to see a doctor or dentist, you should consider seeing a psychologist or a psychiatrist.

13. TRUE or FALSE Another signal that a person needs to seek professional psychological help is significant changes in behavior, such as the quality of one's work (or schoolwork), one's rate of absenteeism, the use of drugs (including alcohol), or one's relationships with others.

14. TRUE or FALSE If you have persistent or disturbing suicidal thoughts or impulses, you should seek help immediately.

15. TRUE or FALSE Some employers have employee assistance programs that offer confidential free or low-cost therapy for employees.

16. TRUE or FALSE Mental health associations organized by concerned citizens usually keep listings of qualified therapists and other services and programs in the community.

17. TRUE or FALSE In the phone book, psychiatrist are usually listed under "Counseling Services," while psychologists are generally listed under "Physicians."

18. TRUE or FALSE The typical crisis hotline is a telephone service staffed by community volunteers who have been trained to provide information concerning a wide range of mental health problems.

19. TRUE or FALSE Psychologists can administer somatic therapy and prescribe drugs only in California and New Hampshire.

20. TRUE or FALSE Fees for psychiatrists are usually higher than fees for psychologists.

21. TRUE or FALSE Community mental health centers almost always charge on a sliding scale.

22. TRUE or FALSE Peer counselors are nonprofessional persons who have learned basic counseling skills.

23. TRUE or FALSE Many studies have shown that paraprofessional counselors are often as effective as professionals.

24. TRUE or FALSE Awareness groups are a group of people who share a particular type of problem and provide mutual support to one another.

25. TRUE or FALSE You can usually find out about a therapist's qualifications simply by asking the therapist or by contacting local branches of organizations, such as the American
Psychological Association or the Canadian Psychological Association.

26. TRUE or FALSE A balanced look at psychotherapies and therapists suggests that all therapists can be equally successful, but all techniques are not equally successful.

27. TRUE or FALSE The most consistently successful therapists are those who are willing to use whatever method seems most helpful for a client.

28. TRUE or FALSE Former clients consistently rate the type of therapy used as more important than the person doing the therapy.

29. TRUE or FALSE Effective therapists encourage the client to have a prolonged dependence on them and demand that the client not discuss therapy with anyone else.

30. TRUE or FALSE Clients who like their therapist are generally more successful in therapy.

31. TRUE or FALSE An important part of the therapeutic alliance is the agreement between the client and therapist regarding the goals of therapy.

32. TRUE or FALSE Although clients should give their therapist a fair chance and not give up too easily, clients should not hesitate to change therapists or to terminate therapy if they lose confidence in the therapist or if they do not relate well to the therapist as a person.

Critical Thinking Question

Would it be acceptable for a therapist to urge a client to break all ties with a troublesome family member?

Final Survey and Review—Completion

Module 14.1 Treating Psychological Distress
Origins of Therapy—Bored Out of Your Skull

Survey Question: How did psychotherapy originate?

1. Any surgical procedure in which a hole is bored in the skull is referred to as _____.
2. The religious ritual, which sometimes also included physical torture to make the body an inhospitable place for the devil to reside was called _____.
3. Modern analyses of "demonic possession" suggest that many victims were suffering from epilepsy, depression, schizophrenia, and _____ disorders.
4. The French doctor, who was the first to provide compassionate care to the mentally ill in Bicêtre Asylum in Paris in 1793 was _____.
5. Somatoform disorders were originally referred to by Sigmund Freud as _____.

Module 14.1 Treating Psychological Distress
Psychoanalysis—Expedition into the Unconscious

Survey Question: Is Freudian psychoanalysis still used?

6. Dr. Rives has his patients say anything that comes into their minds, regardless of how embarrassing or unimportant it may seem. Dr. Rives is using the psychoanalytic technique known as _____.
7. The hidden, symbolic meaning of a dream is known as its _____ content
8. Amiee has started acting and talking to her therapist the same way she treats her overprotective mother. Amiee is exhibiting _____.
9. Time-limited therapies that have replaced traditional psychoanalysis and use direct questioning to reveal unconscious conflicts are called _____ therapies.
10. Hans Eysenck suggested that psychoanalysis simply takes so long that patients experience a spontaneous remission with improvement due to the mere _____.

Module 14.1 Treating Psychological Distress
Dimensions of Therapy—The Many Paths to Health

Survey Question: How do therapies differ?

11. Therapies that try to make direct changes in troublesome thoughts, habits, feelings, or behavior, without seeking insight into their origins or meanings are referred to as _____ therapies.
12. Dr. Orozco provides strong guidance during her therapy session. Her type of therapy would be described as _____.
13. Charles has schizophrenia, and although psychotherapy can help him to gain a new perspective and learn behaviors to better cope with life, his most viable option for therapy will be _____ therapy.
14. Therapists in the positive psychology movement are developing ways to help people make use of their _____.
15. Some of the elements of positive mental health include personal autonomy and independence, a sense of identity, feelings of personal worth, the capacity to forgive, and good habits of physical health, and skilled _____ communication.

Module 14.2 Humanistic and Cognitive Therapies
Humanistic Therapies—Restoring Human Potential
Survey Question: What are the major humanistic therapies?

16. Dr. Zepher does not make interpretations or give advice to her clients. Instead she acts as a "psychological mirror" and rephrases and repeats her clients thoughts and feelings. Dr. Zepher is using the technique known as _____.

17. Dr. Beckham seeks to help clients to uncover their "true selves" hidden behind a screen of defenses. Dr. Beckham is using the humanistic style of therapy known as _____ therapy.

18. Victor Frankl's logotherapy is an example of a existential type of therapy known as _____.

19. When Dr. Metiz challenges his clients to examine their values and choices and to take responsibility for the quality of their existence, he is using the technique called _____.

20. Fritz Perls is associated with _____ therapy.

Module 14.2 Humanistic and Cognitive Therapies
Cognitive Therapy—Think Positive!
Survey Question: How does cognitive therapy change thoughts and emotions?

21. The major distortions in thinking include overgeneralization, selective perception, and _____ thinking.

22. Tanya is on vacation and loves her hotel, has toured three excellent museums, had several wonderful gourmet meals, and had a great time shopping. Then, on the last day of her vacation, it begins to rain. When she gets home, she tells a friend that it was a simply awful vacation because it rained. Tanya's focus on the rain rather than the other pleasant aspects of the vacation illustrates the distortion in thinking known as _____.

23. Albert Ellis developed the cognitive therapy known as _____.

24. "It's not my fault I'm unhappy; I can't control my emotional reactions" is one of the ten _____.

25. Damon is playing a slot machine and has had a string of losses. He incorrectly reasons that he should keep playing because his luck has to change soon and a string of wins must be "just around the corner." Damon is exhibiting the cognitive distortion regarding gambling known as the _____.

Module 14.3 Behavior Therapies
Therapies Based on Classical Conditioning—Healing by Learning
Survey Question: What is behavior therapy?

26. Another name for applied behavior analysis is _____.

27. Roger Vogler and associates pioneered a procedure in which response-contingent shocks were paired with drinking alcohol. This procedure to stop drinking is an example of the use of a classical conditioning technique called _____ therapy.

28. Barry wants to stop smoking, so he undergoes a procedure with the help of a therapist in which he will smoke continuously, taking a puff every six to eight seconds until he becomes miserable. This procedure is called _____.

29. Five-year-old Kim, who is deathly afraid of putting her head under water in the pool, has her fear reduced by observing other children putting their heads under the water, splashing, and swimming, a procedure known as _____.

30. The psychologist who developed eye movement desensitization and reprocessing (EMDR) therapy is _____.

Module 14.3 Behavior Therapies

Operant Therapies—All the World Is a Skinner Box?

Survey Question: What role do operant principles play in behavior therapy?

31. If you eat lunch at 12 noon each day, then this response could be said to be under the _____ of the clock.
32. Time out involves removing the individual from a situation in which _____ occurs.
33. Extinction can be produced by _____.
34. By using tokens, the positive responses of the clients can be immediately _____.
35. Target behaviors are actions or other behaviors that the therapist is seeking to _____.

Module 14.4 Medical Therapies

Medical Therapies—Psychiatric Care

Survey Question: How do psychiatrists treat psychological disorders?

36. Samantha has been prescribed Xanax to relieve her tension and anxiety. Samantha has been prescribed a drug that belongs to the class of psychiatric drugs called _____.
37. Antidepressants tend to enhance the effects of the neurotransmitters dopamine and _____.
38. Electrical stimulation therapies include implanted electrodes and _____.
39. Simon has severe obsessive-compulsive disorder that has not responded to medication. He is undergoing a type of psychosurgery in which small target areas are destroyed in the brain's interior. Simon is undergoing _____.
40. Walt was in a mental hospital, but now is living in a short-term group living facility in the community that will help him make the transition from the hospital to independent living. Walt is living in a(n) _____.
41. Melanie works for a facility that provides short-term treatment, counseling, outpatient care, emergency services, and suicide prevention. Melanie works for a(n) _____.
42. Individuals who work in a near-professional capacity under the supervision of more highly trained staff are called _____.

Module 14.5 Contemporary Issues in Therapy

Therapies—An Overview

Survey Question: What do various therapies have in common?

43. Studies have shown that obsessive-compulsive disorder is best treated using cognitive therapy, drug therapies, and _____ therapy.
44. The "empirically-supported" therapies are developed, not through intuition, but through clinical practice and _____.
45. Jaden has been attending individual, directive, insight-oriented therapy for several years. The strength of this type of therapy is its search for honesty. Jaden's type of therapy is most likely _____.
46. Arrone is receiving therapy that provides acceptance and empathy and would be described as a nondirective, insight therapy. Arrone's therapy is most likely _____ therapy.
47. Eric Berne has described a predictable pattern of verbal interaction that occurs when a person is avoiding another person's advice. He called it the "_____" game.
48. Emil is a therapist who works in a clinic that serves a diverse ethnic population. Emil has been able to adapt traditional psychological theories and techniques to meet the needs of these clients, treats each client as an individual, and strives to not be influenced by stereotypes. Emil would be described as a(n) _____ therapist.

Module 14.5 Contemporary Issues in Therapy
The Future of Psychotherapy—Magnets and Smartphones
Survey Question: What will therapy be like in the future?

49. Regarding the future of psychotherapy, a group of experts have predicted that there will be an increase in the use of short-term therapy and solution-focused, problem-solving approaches and in the use of lower-cost Internet services and _____ counseling.
50. One of the first group therapies was called psychodrama and was developed by _____.
51. Family and couples therapy tends to be time limited and focused on specific _____.
52. In family counseling, family members work together to improve communication, to see themselves and each other in new ways, and to change _____.
53. Distance therapies are more or less limited by a lack of interpersonal cues, such as body language and _____.
54. Dr. Gordon is a clinical psychologist in a large city, who is counseling a client who lives in a remote rural area through the use of a two-way audio-video link which allows both he and his client to see one another on computer monitors and to talk via speakerphones. Dr. Gordon and his client are using the technology known as _____.

Module 14.6 Psychology in Action
Self-Management and Seeking Professional Help
Survey Questions: How are behavioral principles applied to everyday problems? How could a person find professional help?

55. Kurt is using an aversive image of a cancerous lung to reduce his smoking. Kurt is using a behavior procedure known as _____.
56. Every time that Janie starts thinking that "she is worthless and no one will ever love her," she lightly pops a rubber band she wears on her wrist. Janie is using a behavior technique known as _____.
57. The first step in desensitization is learning to relax voluntarily by using the tension-release method or through _____.
58. Although a psychiatrist can administer somatic therapy and prescribe drugs in all 50 of the United States, psychologists are also allowed to perform somatic therapies and prescribe drugs in the states of Louisiana and _____.
59. Chris would be described as a nonprofessional who have learned basic counseling skills. Chris is a(n) _____ counselor.
60. Jonas is attending a type of group that will add valuable support to his visits with a professional counselor. This group has members, like him, who are coping with an alcoholic parent. The members of this group will offer each other mutual support and a chance to discuss problems. Jonas is attending what would be described as a(n) _____ group.

Final Survey and Review—Matching

Module 14.1 Treating Psychological Distress
Part 1:

1. ___ trepanning (or trephining)

   a. any therapy designed to bring about direct changes in troublesome thoughts, habits, feelings, or behavior

2. ___ exorcism

   b. therapy designed to help people by improving their relationships with other people

3. ___ ergotism

c. viewpoint that advocates enhancing personal strengths, rather than "fix" weaknesses

4. ___ interpersonal psychotherapy

d. a style of therapy in which clients assume responsibility for solving their own problems with the therapist assisting but not guiding or giving advice

5. ___ psychoanalysis

e. psychotic-like condition caused by a fungus poisoning

6. ___ positive psychology

f. involves boring a hole in the skull to release pressure or, in ancient times, evil spirits

7. ___ action therapy

g. a religious ritual used to "cast out evil spirits," or make the body inhospitable place for the devil to reside

8. ___ nondirective therapy

h. was the first true psychotherapy and involves free association, dream analysis, and analysis of resistance and transference

Part 2:

1. ___ free association

a. tendency of patients to treat the therapist as they do important persons in their past

2. ___ manifest content

b. blockage in the flow of ideas that the client talks about and can reveal important unconscious conflicts

3. ___ latent content

c. improvement in one's condition due to the mere passage of time

4. ___ transference

d. technique of having a client say anything that comes to mind, regardless of how embarrassing or unimportant it may seem

5. ___ resistances

e. includes personal autonomy, a sense of identity, feelings of personal worth, self-control, skilled interpersonal communication, capacity to forgive

6. ___ spontaneous remissions

f. hidden, symbolic meaning of dreams

7. ___ elements of positive mental health

g. the obvious, visible parts of a dream

Module 14.2 Humanistic and Cognitive Therapies

Part 1:

1. ___ cognitive therapy

a. therapy developed by Victor Frankl and emphasizes the need to find and maintain meaning in life

2. ___ client-centered therapy (or person-centered therapy)

b. an approach developed by Albert Ellis that states that it is our beliefs that lead to our feelings

3. ___ existential therapy

c. nondirective therapy based on insights gained from conscious thoughts and feeling and emphasizes accepting one's true self

4. ___ Gestalt therapy

d. therapy directed at changing maladaptive thoughts, beliefs, and feelings that underlie emotional and behavioral problems

5. ___ logotherapy

   e. group of insight therapies that believes that people have a natural urge to seek health and self-growth

6. ___ rational-emotive behavior therapy (REBT)

   f. insight therapy that focuses on death, meaning, choice, and responsibility and emphasize making courageous life choices

7. ___ humanistic therapies

   g. approach that focuses on immediate experience to help clients rebuild thinking, feeling, and acting into connected wholes

Part 2:

1. ___ unconditional positive regard

   a. unrealistic or faulty convictions that lead to unnecessary suffering

2. ___ selective perception

   b. incorrect beliefs about randomness and chance events

3. ___ overgeneralization

   c. classifying objects or events as absolutely right or wrong, good or bad, acceptable or unacceptable, and so forth

4. ___ all-or-nothing thinking

   d. blowing a single event out of proportion by extending it to a large number of unrelated situations

5. ___ authentic

   e. challenging clients to examine their values and choices and to take responsibility for the quality of their existence

6. ___ irrational beliefs

   f. self-confidence is exaggerated despite the fact that one loses persistently

7. ___ reflection

   g. ability of a therapist to be genuine and honest about his or her own feelings

8. ___ empathy

   h. believing that a string of losses soon must be followed by wins

9. ___ confrontation

   i. process of rephrasing or repeating thoughts and feeling expressed by clients so they can become aware of what they are saying

10. ___ gambler's fallacy

   j. perceiving only certain stimuli among a large array of possibilities

11. ___ magnified gambling skill

   k. an unqualified unshakable acceptance or another person

12. ___ probability biases

   l. trying to see the world through the client's eyes and feel some part of what the client is feeling

Module 14.3 Behavior Therapies
Part 1:

1. ___ operant conditioning

   a. suppressing an undesirable response by associating it with painful or uncomfortable stimuli

2. ___ classical conditioning

   b. reduction in fear, anxiety, or aversion brought about by planned direct exposure to aversive stimuli

3. ___ aversion therapy

   c. use of computer-generated images to present fear stimuli

832

4. ___ token economy

d. form of learning in which simple responses are associated with new stimuli

5. ___ reciprocal inhibition

e. technique for reducing fear or anxiety, based on holding upsetting thoughts in mind while rapidly moving the eyes from side to side

6. ___ systematic desensitization

f. procedure for systematically achieving deep relaxation of the body

7. ___ tension-release method

g. reduction in fear or anxiety that takes place "secondhand" when a client watches models perform the feared behavior

8. ___ vicarious desensitization

h. therapeutic program in which desirable behaviors are reinforced with symbolic rewards that can be exchanged for goods, services, activities, and privileges

9. ___ virtual reality exposure

i. learning based on the consequences of making a response

10. ___ eye movement desensitization and reprocessing (EMDR) therapy

j. presence of one emotional state can inhibit the occurrence of another, such as joy preventing fear

Part 2:

1. ___ behavior modification

a. response that is not followed by reward will occur less frequently

2. ___ rapid smoking

b. includes praise, recognition, and approval

3. ___ hierarchy

c. rewarding actions that are closer and closer approximations to a desired response

4. ___ positive reinforcement

d. responses tend to be managed or directed by the situation in which they occur

5. ___ nonreinforcement

e. if response is followed by discomfort or an undesirable effect, the response will be suppressed

6. ___ extinction

f. an example of aversion therapy

7. ___ punishment

g. rank-ordered series of higher and lower amounts, levels, degrees, or steps

8. ___ shaping

h. if response is not followed by reward after it has been repeated many times, it will go away

9. ___ stimulus control

i. actions or other behaviors the therapist seeks to modify

10. ___ time out

j. application of learning principles to change human behavior, especially maladaptive behavior; applied behavior analysis

11. ___ target behaviors

k. responses that are followed by reward tend to occur more frequently

12. ___ social rewards

l. involves removing the individual from a situation in which reinforcement occurs

Module 14.4 Medical Therapies

1. ___ somatic therapy

a. community-based facility offering a wide range of mental health services, such as prevention, counseling, consultation, and crisis intervention

2. ___ anxiolytics

   b. short-term group living facilities for people making the transition from an institution to independent living

3. ___ antidepressants

   c. allows for electrical stimulation of targeted brain regions

4. ___ antipsychotics

5. ___ electroconvulsive therapy (ECT)

   d. mood-elevating drugs

   e. psychosurgery in which small target areas are destroyed in the brain's interior

6. ___ implanted electrodes

   f. treatment for severe depression consisting of an electric shock passed directly through the brain, which induces a convulsion

7. ___ prefrontal lobotomy

   g. drugs, such as Valium that produce relaxation or reduce anxiety

8. ___ deep lesioning

   h. any bodily therapy, such as pharmacotherapy, electrical stimulation therapy, or psychosurgery

9. ___ halfway houses

   i. drugs that tend to reduce hallucinations and delusional thinking; also called major tranquilizers

10. ___ community mental health centers

   j. frontal lobes are surgically disconnected from other brain areas

Module 14.5 Contemporary Issues in Therapy
Part 1: Connections

1. ___ psychoanalysis

   a. involves constructive guidance to test major distortions in thinking

2. ___ brief psychodynamic therapy

   b. two-way audio-video link hat allows client and therapist to see one another on computer monitors and to talk via speakerphones

3. ___ client-centered therapy

4. ___ existential therapy

5. ___ Gestalt therapy

6. ___ behavior therapy

   c. involves constructive re-enactments

   d. requires observable changes in behavior

   e. involves a shared responsibility for problems

   f. involves acceptance and empathy; nondirective therapy

7. ___ cognitive therapy

   g. uses magnetic pulses to temporarily block activity in specific parts of the brain

8. ___ rational-emotive behavior therapy

   h. focuses on immediate awareness and gaps in experience

9. ___ psychodrama

   i. involves a search for honesty; therapy may take years

10. ___ family therapy

   j. emphasizes a clarity of thinking and goals; confronting irrational beliefs

11. ___ transcranial magnetic stimulation (TMS)

   k. involves a productive use of conflict; interpersonal therapy is an example

12. ___ Skype

   l. emphasizes personal empowerment and meaningfulness

Part 2: Connections

1. ____ role-playing
2. ____ role reversal
3. ____ mirror technique
4. ____ therapeutic alliance
5. ____ therapy placebo effect
6. ____ spontaneous remission
7. ____ sensitivity group
8. ____ encounter group
9. ____ "trust walk"
10. ____ large-group awareness training

a. improvement in condition only because so much time has passed
b. participants expand their confidence in others by allowing themselves to be led around while blindfolded
c. group experience consisting of exercises designed to increase self-awareness and understanding of others
d. group experience that emphasizes intensely honest interchanges among participants regarding feelings and reactions to one another
e. observing another person re-enact one's own behavior, like a character in a play, designed to help person see themselves more clearly
f. taking the role of another person to learn how one's own behavior appears from the other person's perspective
g. improvement caused not by the actual process of therapy but by a client's expectation that therapy will help
h. caring relationship that unites a therapist and a client in working to solve the client's problems
i. any of a number of programs (many of them commercialized) that claim to increase self-awareness and facilitate constructive personal change
j. client reenacts his own role within an incident that caused a problem

Module 14.6 Psychology in Action: Self-Management and Seeking Professional Help

1. ____ thought stopping
2. ____ covert reinforcement
3. ____ self-directed desensitization
4. ____ covert sensitization
5. ____ peer counselors
6. ____ self-help groups

a. group of people who share a particular type of problem and provide mutual support to one another
b. using positive imagery to reinforce desired behavior
c. nonprofessional persons who has learned basic counseling skills
d. involves using the tension release method and a hierarchy list of anxiety-provoking situations
e. use of aversive stimuli to interrupt or prevent upsetting thoughts
f. use of aversive imagery to reduce the occurrence of an undesired response

Final Survey and Review—True or False

Module 14.1 Treating Psychological Distress
Origins of Therapy—Bored Out of Your Skull
Survey Question: How did psychotherapy originate?

1. TRUE or FALSE   In ancient times, the procedure that involved boring, chipping, or bashing holes into a person's head in order to relieve pressure or release evil spirits was known as ergotism.
2. TRUE or FALSE   Exorcism sometimes took the form of physical torture.
3. TRUE or FALSE   A fungus produces a natural source of LSD that when eating caused psychotic-like symptoms that were mistaken for bewitchment during the Middle Ages.
4. TRUE or FALSE   In 1793, the French doctor named Philippe Pinel changed the asylum in Paris into a mental hospital that provided the mentally ill with compassionate care.
5. TRUE or FALSE   The problem Freud called hysteria is now called a somatoform disorder.

Module 14.1 Treating Psychological Distress
Psychoanalysis—Expedition into the Unconscious
Survey Question: Is Freudian psychoanalysis still used?

6. TRUE or FALSE   Having the patient recline on a couch to encourage a free flow of thoughts is the least important element of psychoanalysis with many modern analysts having abandoned this practice.
7. TRUE or FALSE   The obvious, visible meaning of a dream is the manifest content.
8. TRUE or FALSE   When describing conflicts or dreams, patients may avoid talking about or thinking about certain topics with this tendency being referred to as transference.
9. TRUE or FALSE   Although Interpersonal psychotherapy (IPT) was developed to help depressed people improve their relationships with others, it has also been shown to be effective for treating eating disorders, substance abuse, social phobias, and personality disorders.
10. TRUE or FALSE   Research has confirmed that psychoanalysis does not produce improvement in a majority of patients with any "cures" being due to spontaneous remissions.

Module 14.1 Treating Psychological Distress
Dimensions of Therapy—The Many Paths to Health
Survey Question: How do therapies differ?

11. TRUE or FALSE   Any therapy whose goal is to lead clients to a deeper understanding of their thoughts, emotions, and behavior is called an insight therapy.
12. TRUE or FALSE   A style of therapy in which clients assume responsibility for solving their own problems with the therapist assisting, but not guiding or giving advice is regarded as an action therapy.
13. TRUE or FALSE   It is often unrealistic to expect psychotherapy to undo a person's entire past.
14. TRUE or FALSE   Psychotherapy has not been found to be equally effective for all types of problems.
15. TRUE or FALSE   Techniques designed to enhance personal strengths, rather than "fix" weaknesses were developed by psychodynamic therapists.

Module 14.2 Humanistic and Cognitive Therapies

Humanistic Therapies—Restoring Human Potential

Survey Question: What are the major humanistic therapies?

16. TRUE or FALSE   The client-centered therapist does not hesitate to react with shock, dismay, or disapproval to a client's inappropriate thoughts or feelings.
17. TRUE or FALSE   Psychologist Carl Rogers believed that it was more beneficial to explore conscious thoughts and feelings than to explore unconscious ones.
18. TRUE or FALSE   The German word *logos* means "whole," or "complete."
19. TRUE or FALSE   The Gestalt approach is more directive and less insight-oriented than client-centered or existential therapy.
20. TRUE or FALSE   Gestalt therapy may be done individually or in a group.

Module 14.2 Humanistic and Cognitive Therapies

Cognitive Therapy—Think Positive!

Survey Question: How does cognitive therapy change thoughts and emotions?

21. TRUE or FALSE   Cognitive therapy has been especially successful in treating depression.
22. TRUE or FALSE   Seeing events as totally good or bad or totally right or wrong is referred to as selective perception.
23. TRUE or FALSE   In the A-B-C sequence used in REBT, A stands for activating experience.
24. TRUE or FALSE   Rational-emotive behavior therapists are very directive in their attempts to change a client's irrational beliefs and "self-talk."
25. TRUE or FALSE   Regarding gambling, if your self-confidence is exaggerated, despite the fact that you lose persistently, you are exhibiting the cognitive distortion known as a probability bias.

Module 14.3 Behavior Therapies

Therapies Based on Classical Conditioning—Healing by Learning

Survey Question: What is behavior therapy?

26. TRUE or FALSE   If the sight of a hypodermic needle is followed by an injection that causes anxiety or fear, the sight of the hypodermic needle, which was previously neutral, will become the unconditioned response.
27. TRUE or FALSE   Aversion therapy is the guided reduction in fear and anxiety that is attained by gradually approaching a feared stimulus while maintaining relaxation.
28. TRUE or FALSE   During systematic desensitization, the person first performs the least disturbing item on his or her list of fears and then proceeds down the list to the most disturbing one.
29. TRUE or FALSE   A reduction in fear or anxiety that takes place "second hand" when a client watches models perform the feared behavior is called vicarious desensitization.
30. TRUE or FALSE   During eye-movement desensitization, clients concentrate on pleasant, calming images.

Module 14.3 Behavior Therapies

Operant Therapies—All the World Is a Skinner Box?

Survey Question: What role do operant principles play in behavior therapy?

31. TRUE or FALSE   Operant conditioning refers to learning based on the consequences of making a response.

32. TRUE or FALSE   If children whine and get attention, they will whine more frequently because of positive reinforcement.

33. TRUE or FALSE   A response that is not followed by reward will occur less frequently due to negative reinforcement.

34. TRUE or FALSE   Reinforcing actions that are closer and closer approximations to a desired response is know as shaping.

35. TRUE or FALSE   Two children are fighting on the playground, and the teacher has them sit on the sidewalk, effectively removing them from their reinforcement, which illustrates the procedure known as stimulus control.

Module 14.4 Medical Therapies

Medical Therapies—Psychiatric Care

Survey Question: How do psychiatrists treat psychological disorders?

36. TRUE or FALSE   Major mental disorders are primarily treated with psychotherapy.

37. TRUE or FALSE   Antipsychotic drugs enhance the effects of the neurotransmitter GABA.

38. TRUE or FALSE   The drug Clozaril has been shown to cause a potentially fatal blood disease in two percent of patients with a safer alternative being the drug Risperdal.

39. TRUE or FALSE   In prefrontal lobotomy, the frontal lobes are surgically disconnected from other brain areas.

40. TRUE or FALSE   To reduce a relapse, antidepressant drugs are recommended for patients with depression following ECT treatment.

41. TRUE or FALSE   In the last 50 years, the population in large mental hospitals has dropped by two thirds.

42. TRUE or FALSE   Skilled management of a psychological emergency is called partial hospitalization.

Module 14.5 Contemporary Issues in Therapy

Therapies—An Overview

Survey Question: What do various therapies have in common?

43. TRUE or FALSE   In a national survey, only nine out of 10 people who have sought mental health care say their lives improved as a result of the treatment.

44. TRUE or FALSE   Because of the high costs and limited insurance coverage, the average client receives only 10 therapy sessions, after which only 50 percent of patients feel better.

45. TRUE or FALSE   Rational-emotive behavior therapy is a nondirective insight therapy that focuses on immediate awareness and is used both in individual as well as group therapy settings.

46. TRUE or FALSE   The main strength of family therapy is a productive use of conflict.

47. TRUE or FALSE   Counselors tend to wait a shorter amount of time before responding to a client than do people responding to each other in everyday conversations.

48. TRUE or FALSE   If a friend tells you that she thinks the math teacher has it in for her and you reply with "Are you going to drop the class?" you are using an ineffective closed question.

Module 14.5 Contemporary Issues in Therapy

The Future of Psychotherapy—Magnets and Smartphones

Survey Question: What will therapy be like in the future?

49. TRUE or FALSE   Regarding the future of psychotherapy, experts predict that the use of Internet services, telephone counseling, paraprofessionals, and self-help groups will diminish.

50. TRUE or FALSE   A new medical therapy technique called transcranial magnetic stimulation (TMS) uses magnetic pulses to temporarily block activity in specific parts of the brain.

51. TRUE or FALSE   Group therapy has proven to be just as effective as individual therapy.

52. TRUE or FALSE   In psychodrama, a trust walk involves taking the part of another person to learn how he or she feels.

53. TRUE or FALSE   Family therapists treat the family as a unit, although they may not meet with the entire family at each session.

54. TRUE or FALSE   The American Psychological Association urges media psychologists to discuss problems only of a general nature, instead of actually counseling anyone.

Module 14.6 Psychology in Action
Self-Management and Seeking Professional Help
Survey Questions: How are behavioral principles applied to everyday problems? How could a person find professional help?

55. TRUE or FALSE   To do covert sensitization, you must first learn relaxation exercises.

56. TRUE or FALSE   A person who sets aside time each day to deliberately think about needless worries and while thinking about them shouting "Stop!" is using a technique known as self-directed desensitization.

57. TRUE or FALSE   Covert reinforcement should be visualized before performing steps in a fear hierarchy.

58. TRUE or FALSE   Nonprofessional persons who have learned basic counseling skills are known as therapeutic assistants.

59. TRUE or FALSE   Self-help groups are a group of people who share a particular type of problem and provide mutual support to one another.

60. TRUE or FALSE   Former clients consistently rate the person doing the therapy as more important than the type of therapy used.

Mastery Test

1. Primitive "therapists" dating back to the Stone Age bored, chipped, or bashed holes into a patient's head presumably to relieve pressure or release evil spirit. This procedure was known as
   a. trepanning.
   b. ergotism.
   c. the tension-release method.
   d. the mirror technique.

2. During the Middle Ages, it was thought that symptoms, such as pinching sensations, muscle twitches, facial spasms, delirium, and hallucinations were caused by demonology when the real reason was caused by tainted rye bread, a condition known as
   a. trepanning.
   b. ergotism.
   c. anxiolytic poisoning.
   d. exorcism.

3. The mentally ill were given humane and compassionate care for the first time in 1793 due to the efforts of
   a. Sigmund Freud.
   b. Victor Frankl.
   c. Philippe Pinel.
   d. Eric Berne.

4. The first true psychotherapy was developed by
   a. Sigmund Freud.
   b. Victor Frankl.
   c. Fritz Perls.
   d. Jacob Moreno.

5. The therapist asks Paige to say whatever comes into her mind, allowing the ideas from the unconscious to surface without censorship. This technique is known as
   a. transference.
   b. reflection.
   c. covert sensitization.
   d. free association.

6. Freddy tells his therapist about the dream he had last night in which he was being strangled by a large beast. The part of the dream that Freddy told his therapist is called the _____ content.
   a. latent
   b. manifest
   c. lucid
   d. therapeutic

7. Ernie is talking to his therapist when he begins to bully and argue with her just like he does his wife when he feels he is "being criticized." Ernie is exhibiting
   a. transference.
   b. free association.
   c. therapeutic reflection.
   d. reciprocal inhibition.

8. Tracy has been depressed for a year. She is currently receiving an individual type of brief psychodynamic therapy that will help her to improve her relationships with others and alleviate her depression. Tracy's therapy is called
   a. logotherapy.
   b. rational-emotive behavior therapy.
   c. interpersonal psychotherapy.
   d. psychodrama.

9. Although researchers did confirm that psychoanalysis does produce improvement, Hans Eysenck had once suggested that psychoanalysis simply took so long that patients experienced a(n) _____ of symptoms.
   a. reciprocal inhibition
   b. transference
   c. catharsis
   d. spontaneous remission

10. REBT, Gestalt therapy, and systematic desensitization are all types of
    a. somatic therapy.
    b. medical therapy.
    c. psychotherapy.
    d. pharmacotherapy.

11. In order to alleviate his anxiety, Gerald is receiving therapy in which he will obtain a deeper understanding of his thoughts, emotions, and behavior. Gerald is receiving _____ therapy.
    a. action
    b. insight
    c. somatic
    d. positive

12. Jasmine is receiving therapy that is designed to enhance her personal strengths, not to "fix" any weaknesses. Jasmine's type of therapy has its roots in _____ psychology movement.
    a. Gestalt
    b. psychodynamic
    c. cognitive
    d. positive

13. An element of positive mental health that therapists seek to promote is
    a. dependency on the therapist.
    b. extroversion.
    c. the capacity to forgive.
    d. the ability to disregard the demands of the work environment.

14. The therapy in which the therapist does not make interpretations or propose solutions but offers the client unconditional positive regard and genuine empathy is called
    a. psychodrama.
    b. Gestalt therapy.
    c. client-centered therapy.
    d. cognitive therapy.

15. Which of the following is a form of existential therapy that is based on its originator's experiences as a prisoner in a Nazi concentration camp?
    a. brief psychodynamic therapy
    b. logotherapy
    c. rational-emotive behavior therapy
    d. psychodrama

16. In order to increase his awareness, Carlos' therapist has Carlos exaggerate vague feelings until they become clear. His therapist also encourages him to take responsibility for his thoughts and feelings and by so doing he will be able to fill in the gaps in his experiences. The therapy Carlos is receiving would be considered _____ therapy.
    a. Gestalt
    b. brief psychodynamic
    c. client-centered
    d. rational-emotive behavior

841

17. People become depressed because of three major distortions in thinking, selective perception, overgeneralization, and all-or-nothing thinking, according to
    a. Eric Berne.
    b. Carl Rogers.
    c. Jacob Moreno.
    d. Aaron Beck.

18. "There is always a perfect solution to human problems and it is awful if this solution is not found" would be considered a(n)
    a. statement of self-awareness.
    b. irrational belief.
    c. health-promoting belief.
    d. response-contingent statement.

19. Tim is playing a slot machine and has been continually losing, but he believes that this string of losses has to soon be followed by a string of wins, so he keeps putting his money in the machine. Tim is exhibiting the cognitive distortion known as
    a. magnified gambling skill.
    b. an attribution error.
    c. the gambler's fallacy.
    d. selective memory.

20. In her therapy, Dr. Ridgewood uses procedures based on classical and operant conditioning to make constructive changes in his client's behavior. Dr. Ridgewood is using
    a. logotherapy.
    b. brief psychodynamic therapy.
    c. applied behavior analysis.
    d. existential therapy.

21. Rapid smoking that helps smokers stop smoking and the response-contingent shocks used by Roger Vogler to help alcoholics are two examples of
    a. aversion therapy.
    b. brief psychodynamic therapy.
    c. systematic desensitization.
    d. role reversal in psychodrama.

22. In order to help Santos overcome his fear of insects, his therapist first has him learn the tension-release method and then has him construct a hierarchy of his fears. Santos' therapist is using
    a. aversion therapy.
    b. brief psychodynamic therapy.
    c. systematic desensitization.
    d. existential therapy.

23. Since returning from military service in Iraq, Lance has been experiencing symptoms of posttraumatic stress syndrome. In order to alleviate his symptoms, Lance's therapist has him visualize the images that upset him and then the therapist moves a pencil rapidly from side to side in front of Lance's eyes. Lance's therapist is using
    a. brief psychodynamic therapy.
    b. hypnotherapy.
    c. dissociative therapy.
    d. eye movement desensitization and reprocessing.

842

24. If Carolyn does not receive attention when she acts silly, then her response of "acting silly" will occur less frequently. Thus, the frequency of this response decreases due to
    a. nonreinforcement.
    b. punishment.
    c. negative reinforcement.
    d. stimulus control.

25. Aiesa is learning to play the guitar. Her instructor praises her initial actions of holding the guitar correctly and her finger positions on the strings. Her instructor is rewarding Aiesa's actions as they get closer and closer to playing songs on the guitar. Aiesa's instructor is using the behavioral principle of
    a. stimulus control.
    b. shaping.
    c. operant extinction.
    d. vicarious desensitization.

26. Identification of target behaviors is an important step in designing
    a. encounter groups.
    b. activating stimuli.
    c. token economies.
    d. large group awareness training.

27. Satchel is taking Risperdal to alleviate his hallucinations and delusions. This drug is classified as a(n)
    a. antiolytic.
    b. antidepressant.
    c. major tranquilizer.
    d. minor tranquilizer.

28. Laramie underwent six sessions of electroconvulsive therapy over a period of four weeks. Laramie is most likely being treated for
    a. schizophrenia.
    b. severe depression.
    c. conversion disorder.
    d. obsessive-compulsive disorder.

29. Deep lesioning is a form of
    a. electrical stimulation therapy.
    b. EMDR.
    c. pharmacotherapy.
    d. psychosurgery.

30. To demonstrate that spontaneous remissions are occurring, you could use a
    a. patient-defined hierarchy.
    b. waiting-list control group.
    c. target behavior group.
    d. short-term dynamic correlation.

31. A good example of a directive action therapy is _____ therapy.
    a. behavior
    b. Gestalt
    c. psychoanalytic
    d. brief psychodynamic

32. The caring relationship between the client and the therapist has been shown to have a major impact on the successful of the therapy. This caring relationship is called the
    a. therapy placebo effect.
    b. therapeutic alliance.
    c. carthartic bonding.
    d. empirical support.

33. Which of the following behaviors would NOT be considered effective when counseling a person?
    a. paraphrasing
    b. judging
    c. reflecting
    d. active listening

34. Which technique is most closely related to the approach known as psychodrama?
    a. free association
    b. trepanning
    c. mirror technique
    d. ECT

35. Jonathan is participating in a group exercise in which there will be confrontations to tear down defenses and false fronts. This group exercise will most likely occur within a(n)
    a. encounter group.
    b. sensitivity group.
    c. psychodrama.
    d. token economy.

36. Which of the following is NOT a disadvantage of Internet e-mail counseling?
    a. the lack of facial expressions or body language
    b. the higher cost compared to face-to-face therapy
    c. whether e-mails are completely confidential
    d. whether therapists licensed in one state can do therapy in another state

37. Elna is receiving therapy in her rural home through a two-way audio-video link complete with computer monitors and speakerphones. This system will allow Elna's therapist in the city hundreds of miles away to have contact with Elna. This technique is called
    a. EMDR.
    b. REBT.
    c. logotherapy.
    d. Skype.

38. Judith is receiving counseling on a sliding scale at a facility that also provides crisis intervention, outpatient care, and preventive programs. This facility is a
    a. halfway house.
    b. local self-help group chapter.
    c. community mental health center.
    d. deinstitutionalization center.

39. Melissa is trying to lose weight, so she vividly imagines disturbing scenes, such as being told by a salesperson that "all the clothes in the shop are too small for her" or being asked to buy two seats by the airline because of her size. To help her lose weight, Melissa is using
    a. logotherapy.
    b. thought stopping.
    c. covert sensitization.
    d. brief psychodynamic therapy.

40. Lonny is caring for his mother who has Alzheimer's disease. Once a week he attends a group in which the members are also caring for family members suffering from dementia. The members offer each other mutual support and a chance to discuss problems. Lonny is attending a(n) _____ group.
    a. person-centered
    b. encounter
    c. sensitivity
    d. self-help

Chapter 15: Social Behavior

Chapter Overview

Social psychology studies how we behave, think, and feel in social situations. Affiliation is tied to needs for approval, support, friendship, and information. Also, affiliation can reduce anxiety. Social comparison theory holds that we affiliate to evaluate our actions, feelings, and abilities. Interpersonal attraction is increased by proximity, frequent contact, beauty, competence, and similarity. Mate selection is characterized by a large degree of similarity on many dimensions. Self-disclosure follows a reciprocity norm: Low levels of self-disclosure are met with low levels in return; moderate self-disclosure elicits more personal replies. However, overdisclosure tends to inhibit self-disclosure by others.

In comparison with liking, romantic love involves higher levels of emotional arousal and is accompanied by mutual absorption between lovers. Consummate love, involving intimacy, passion, and commitment, is the most complete form of love. Evolutionary psychology attributes human mating patterns to the differing reproductive challenges faced by men and women during the course of evolution.

Social roles, which may be achieved or ascribed, are particular behavior patterns associated with social positions. When two or more contradictory roles are held, role conflict may occur. Higher status within groups is associated with special privileges and respect. Group structure refers to the organization of roles, communication pathways, and power within a group. Group cohesiveness is basically the degree of attraction among group members. Norms are standards of conduct enforced (formally or informally) by groups. Attribution theory is concerned with how we make inferences about be. The fundamental attribution error is to ascribe the actions of others to internal causes. Because of actor–observer differences, we tend to attribute our own behavior to external causes.

Social influence refers to alterations in behavior brought about by the behavior of others. Social influence ranges from milder (mere influence, conformity, and compliance) to stronger (obedience and coercion). The mere presence of others may facilitate (or inhibit) performance. People may also engage in social loafing, working less hard when they are part of a group. The famous Asch experiments demonstrated that conformity is encouraged by group sanctions encourage conformity. Group members who succumb to groupthink seek to maintain each other's approval, even at the cost of critical thinking. Groupthink refers to compulsive conformity in group decision making.

Three strategies for gaining compliance are the foot-in-the-door technique, the door-in-the-face approach, and the lowball technique. Most people have a strong tendency to obey legitimate authority. Usually this is desirable, but it can be damaging when social power is used in misguided or unscrupulous ways. Obedience in Milgram's studies decreased when the victim was in the same room, when the victim and participant were face to face, when the authority figure was absent, and when others refused to obey. Coercion involves forcing people to change their beliefs or behavior against their will. Forced attitude change (brainwashing) is sometimes

847

used by cults and other coercive groups. Three steps in brainwashing are unfreezing, changing, and refreezing attitudes and beliefs. Self-assertion involves standing up for yourself, while aggression involves achieving your goals at the expense of another.

Attitudes are learned dispositions made up of a belief component, an emotional component, and an action component. Attitudes may be formed by direct contact, interaction with others, child-rearing practices, and group pressures. Peer group influences, reference group membership, the media, and chance conditioning also appear to be important in attitude formation.

Effective persuasion occurs when characteristics of the communicator, the message, and the audience are well matched. In general, a likable and believable communicator who repeats a credible message that arouses emotion in the audience and states clear-cut conclusions will be persuasive. Maintaining and changing attitudes is closely related to cognitive dissonance and our need to be consistent in our thoughts and actions.

Prejudice is a negative attitude held toward members of various out-groups. One theory attributes prejudice to scapegoating. A second account says that prejudices may be held for personal reasons (personal prejudice) or simply through adherence to group norms (group prejudice). Prejudiced individuals tend to have an authoritarian or dogmatic personality, characterized by rigidity, inhibition, intolerance, oversimplification, and ethnocentrism. Intergroup conflict gives rise to hostility and the formation of social stereotypes. Status inequalities tend to build prejudice. Equal-status contact tends to reduce it. Superordinate goals are a key to reducing intergroup conflict. On a smaller scale, jigsaw classrooms (which encourage cooperation through mutual interdependence) have been shown to be an effective way of combating prejudice.

Aggression is a fact of life, but humans are not inevitably aggressive. The same factors that help explain aggression can form the basis for preventing it. Ethological explanations of aggression attribute it to inherited instincts. Biological explanations of aggression emphasize brain mechanisms and physical factors that lower the threshold for aggression. According to the frustration-aggression hypothesis, frustration and aggression are closely linked. Frustration is only one of many aversive stimuli that can arouse a person and make aggression more likely. Aggression is especially likely to occur when aggression cues are present. Social learning theory has focused attention on the role of aggressive models in the development of aggressive behavior.

Four decision points must be passed before a person gives help: noticing, defining an emergency, taking responsibility, and selecting a course of action. Helping is less likely at each point when other potential helpers are present. Helping is encouraged by general arousal, empathic arousal, being in a good mood, low effort or risk, and perceived similarity between the victim and the helper. For several reasons, giving help tends to encourage others to help, too.

Multiculturalism is a recognition and acceptance of human diversity. Multicultural harmony can be attained through conscious efforts to be more tolerant of others. Greater tolerance can be encouraged by neutralizing stereotypes with individuating information; by looking for commonalities with others; and by avoiding the effects of just-world beliefs, self-fulfilling prophecies, and social competition. Cultural awareness is a key element in promoting greater social harmony.

Preview: Love and Hate

Language Development Guide
tearing: hurried leaving
wryly: matter-of-factly; dryly
naïve: immature; inexperienced
abroad: away from one's home

endlessly: seemingly without an limit; continually

harassed: pressured; hassled

Palestinian–Israeli conflict: ongoing conflict over borders, settlements, security, and control of Jerusalem

shunned: deliberately avoided; rejected

reviled: insulted with abusive language

clashes: fighting; conflicts

Catholics and Protestants in Northern Ireland: really a political conflict between those people who want Northern Ireland to become a part of Ireland (Catholics) and those in the majority in Northern Ireland who wish it to remain a part of Great Britain (Protestants)

Hutus and Tutsis in Rwanda: ethnic groups in Rwanda, a country in east central Africa, who have been in conflict over control of the government with a mass genocide of the minority Tutsis, who had once been in power, being carried out by the Hutus in 1994

"Romeo and Juliet": Shakespearean play about a pair of lovers whose love and lives end due to a feud between their families

tapestry: colorful woven rug

"sampler": checking out segments and examples taken from a larger group to get an idea about the whole group

thought provoking: challenging

Module 15.1 Affiliation, Friendship, and Love

Affiliation and Attraction—Come Together

Survey Questions: Why do people affiliate? What factors influence interpersonal attraction?

Language Development Guide

affiliation: relationship; to associate with

social animals: organisms that show a great deal of interaction with members of its own species

deprived of: being without

disorienting: loss of physical and mental bearings regarding one's surroundings

immersed: engaged deeply

clans: group of people related by blood or marriage; families with common ancestors

sects: subpart of a larger religious group

yardstick: method of measuring length; used as a metaphor for evaluating

"compared notes": to share observations

How did you do?: How well did you perform?

"Wasn't that last question hard?": asking another if he or she thought the last question on a test was Difficult

notorious: well-known

rampant: wildly; occurring in a unrestrained manner

absolute scale: totally objective; fixed; perfect way

fair scale: just; reasonable way

motive: desire; motivation for

birds of a feather flock together: people want to be with others who have similar characteristics or personalities

familiarity breeds contempt: means that when you spend too much time with people, you may begin to have negative feelings towards them

opposites attract: people are curious about people who are different

absence makes the heart grow fonder: people in a relationship have stronger love after being separated for a period of time

folklore: traditional customs, stories, or sayings of a people

affinity: natural liking; attraction to

one and only: each person has a perfect partner in the world, a "soul-mate" or best match

radius: the distance from a center point to the outside line that forms a circle; so in this case five miles straight out from the person on all sides

made in heaven: perfect, ideal

"boy-next-door" or "girl-next-door" effect…"folks-next-door" effect: stereotypes of average people, who are down-to-earth, sweet, sincere, modest, loyal; perfect mate or perfect friend, respectively

"virtual contact": interacting with people via the Internet

witty: having humor

proficiency: quality of having great skill

interesting twist: unanticipated or surprising result

revealing: informative

"college quiz bowl": verbal question-and-answer style academic matches between two teams of college students from different colleges; started on radio and later on television

clumsily: awkward; lack of physical coordination

blundered: made a mistake

more "human": having qualities like all people, who also make mistakes

clever: bright; quick; witty

"You go": phase of encouragement

acquainted: to become known to each other

freer: more free, open, able

staple: basic item

reciprocate: give back in return; mutual interaction

Recite and Review

1. The scientific study of how individuals behave, think, and feel in social situations is called _____ psychology.
2. A desire to associate with other people is referred to as our need to _____.
3. This desire to associate with other people is based on basic human desires for approval, support, friendship, and _____.
4. In evaluating our own reactions to a situation if we are ever in doubt, our behavior will tend to be guided by _____.
5. Social psychologist Leon Festinger theorized that group membership fills needs for

   _____.
6. Meaningful evaluations are based on comparing yourself with people of backgrounds, abilities, and circumstances of people who are _____.
7. The basis for most voluntary social relationships involves our affinity toward another person, or _____.
8. We look for friends and lovers who have attractive personalities, who like us in return, and who are kind and _____.
9. Attraction is promoted through the increases in frequency of contact between people that occurs because of _____.
10. More and more long-distance friendships and romances are occurring because the Internet is making it increasingly easier to stay in constant "_____."
11. When actors costarring in movies together and who are around each other every day become romantically involved, one of the reasons is _____.

850

12. People are often seen as likable, intelligence, warm, witty, mentally healthy, and socially-skilled if the people are also physically _____.
13. The tendency to generalize a favorable impression to unrelated personal characteristics is called the _____ effect.
14. In reality, almost no connection has been found between intelligence, talents, or abilities and one's physical _____.
15. A person will even start looking more attractive to you, as you discover that he or she has a good _____.
16. People who have knowledge, ability, or proficiency are referred to as _____.
17. In a classic study in which college students listened to audiotapes of candidates for a "college quiz bowl," two candidates seemed highly intelligence and two seemed to be of average ability with one "intelligence" candidate and one "average" candidate being heard to clumsily spill coffee on themselves. Later, students rated as most attractive the candidate who was clumsy and _____.
18. The candidate in the classic "college quiz bowl" who was rated as least attractive was the one who was clumsy and _____.
19. The general rule for friendships is that people are the same gender, age, and _____.
20. The term that refers to how alike you are to another person in background, age, interests, attitudes, beliefs, and so forth is _____.
21. We often select people that are similar to ourselves as friends because seeing our beliefs and attitudes being shared by others is _____.
22. In choosing a mate, we tend to marry someone who is like us in almost every way, a pattern called _____.
23. Studies show that married couples are highly similar in age, education, ethnicity, and _____.
24. To a lesser degree, married couples are also similar in attitudes and opinions, mental abilities, status, height, weight, and _____.
25. The risk of divorce is highest among couples with sizable differences in age and _____.
26. When Carrie and Sue first met, they talked about the classes at college. Now that they have known each other for a few weeks, Carrie and Sue are sharing more of their private thoughts, feelings, and other personal history with each other, a process known as _____.
27. Reciprocity is likely to occur when people share information about themselves in what would be described as _____.
28. When people share more information about themselves than is appropriate for a relationships or a social situation, then it is referred to as _____.
29. Exceeding the amount of personal information that is appropriate to be shared within a social situation tends to give rise to reduced attraction and _____.
30. People often feel freer to express their true feelings on the Internet on social networking websites, such as MySpace and _____.

Connections

1. ___ social psychology
2. ___ need to affiliate
3. ___ social comparison
4. ___ interpersonal attraction

a. tendency to generalize a favorable impression to unrelated personal characteristics
b. marriage of two people who are similar to one another
c. results in reciprocity
d. exceeds what is appropriate for a social situation and leads to suspicion and reduced attraction

851

5. ___ physical proximity
     e. how alike you are to another person in background, age, interests, attitudes, and beliefs

6. ___ physically attractive
     f. making judgments about ourselves by comparing and contrasting ourselves against others

7. ___ halo effect
     g. social attraction to another person

8. ___ competence
     h. closer people live or work to each other, the more likely they are to become friends

9. ___ similarity
     i. process of revealing private thoughts, feelings, and one's personal history to others

10. ___ homogamy
11. ___ self-disclosure
     j. desire to associate with other people

     k. scientific study of how individuals behave, think, and feel in social situations

12. ___ moderate self-disclosure
13. ___ overdisclosure
     l. regarded as good-looking by others

     m. has knowledge, ability, or proficiency

Check Your Memory

1. TRUE or FALSE   The scientific study of how individuals behave, think, and feel in social situations is called developmental psychology.

2. TRUE or FALSE   Our desire to associate with other people is referred to as a need to affiliate.

3. TRUE or FALSE   The desire to associate with other people is based on basic human desires for approval, support, security, friendship, and information.

4. TRUE or FALSE   When there are no objective standards, the only available means of evaluation is provided by social comparison with others.

5. TRUE or FALSE   Meaningful evaluations are based on comparing yourself with people of higher backgrounds, abilities, and circumstances than yourself.

6. TRUE or FALSE   A desire for social comparison provides a motive for associating with others and influences which groups we join.

7. TRUE or FALSE   Interpersonal attraction is the basis for most voluntary relationships.

8. TRUE or FALSE   Deciding whether you would like to know another person can happen very quickly, sometimes within just minutes of meeting.

9. TRUE or FALSE   The closer people live to each other, the less likely they are to become friends.

10. TRUE or FALSE   One reason why actors costarring in movies together often become romantically involved is physical proximity.

11. TRUE or FALSE   Competence promotes attraction by increasing the frequency of contact between people.

12. TRUE or FALSE   The Internet is making it increasingly easier to stay in constant "virtual contact," which is leading to more and more long-distance friendships and romances.

13. TRUE or FALSE   Beautiful people are generally rated as less intelligent and more mentally unhealthy than average-looking people.

14. TRUE or FALSE   The tendency to generalize a favorable impression to unrelated personal characteristics is called the reverse psychology effect.

15. TRUE or FALSE   Physical attractiveness has almost no connection to intelligence, talents, or abilities.

16. TRUE or FALSE   Beauty affects mainly our initial interest in getting to know others.

852

17. TRUE or FALSE   As you discover that someone has a good personality, he or she will even start looking more attractive to you.

18. TRUE or FALSE   In a classic experiment in which students listened to audiotapes of candidates for a "college quiz bowl," the students found the "average candidate" who blundered by spilling coffee the most attractive and the "intelligent candidate" who blundered by spilling coffee the least attractive.

19. TRUE or FALSE   The general rule for friendships is that you are the same age, sex, and ethnicity.

20. TRUE or FALSE   Persons who have dissimilar, or opposite, characteristics tend to have the most successful marriages.

21. TRUE or FALSE   Choosing a mate who is similar to us in characteristics is referred to as homogamy.

22. TRUE or FALSE   Homogamy rarely occurs in unmarried couples who are living together.

23. TRUE or FALSE   The risk of divorce is highest among couples with sizeable differences in age and education.

24. TRUE or FALSE   Self-disclosure is essential for developing close relationships and requires a degree of trust.

25. TRUE or FALSE   Overdisclosure tends to lead to reciprocity, while moderate disclosure leads to suspicion and reduced attraction.

26. TRUE or FALSE   On the Internet, especially on social networking websites like Facebook and MySpace, people often feel freer to express their true feelings, which can lead to genuine, face-to-face friendships.

Critical Thinking Question
How has the Internet altered the effects of proximity on interpersonal attraction?

Module 15.1 Affiliation, Friendship, and Love
Liking and Loving—Dating and Mating
Survey Question: How are liking and loving different?

Language Development Guide

angle: perspective, set of beliefs
connectedness: united; joined
mutual absorption: shared fascination or interest in one another
exclusively: solely; entirely
gaze: an intense, steady look; stare
idealized: believing someone else is perfect
blind them: make them unaware or less aware
imprint: a mark; lasting effect
infidelity: unfaithfulness to a sexual partner
evolved behavior: developed actions
preferences: more desirable choices
invest: spend; devote
consequently: as a result
resources: means of helping
fertility: producing children
prospective: potential; likely
trophy wives: a marriage to gain prestige and admiration, a wealthy but perhaps older or unattractive man with a much younger and much more attractive woman

sire: fathered
subtle: slight; mild
"polite": well-mannered; socially-acceptable
furious: angry; upset
allies: supporters

Recite and Review

1. Love that is based on interpersonal attraction and also involves high levels of passion is
   _____ love.
2. Psychologist Robert Sternberg created his influential _____ theory of love.
3. According to Sternberg, feelings of connectedness and affection are called _____.
4. Deep emotional and/or sexual feelings are referred to as _____.
5. If a couple is determined to stay in a long-term relationship with one another, then, according
   to Sternberg, they are exhibiting _____.
6. If all three components of Sternberg's love model are absence, then the person is
   experiencing _____.
7. If you feel intimacy with a person, but have no passion or commitment, then you are
   experiencing, according to Sternberg, _____.
8. Forrest and Lila have been married for forty years, enjoy spending lots of time together, and
   plan to stay married for the rest of their lives. However, the passion has cooled to the point
   that it is non-existent. According to Sternberg's theory, they are experiencing _____
   love.
9. Devin and Ramon's marriage is filled with a great deal of sexual excitement, but little else. In
   fact, they have no interests in common, except for sex and a determination to stay married.
   Their marriage is based on _____ love.
10. Love that involves passion only with no intimacy and no commitment is called _____
    love.
11. When we feel intimacy with, passion for, and commitment to another person, we are
    experiencing _____ love.
12. When you are dating a person and you enjoy being with them and feel a great deal of passion,
    but no commitment at this point, you are experiencing _____ love.
13. Marisa and Monty have been married a long time and plan to stay married for the sake of the
    children. However, they spend little time together alone together, have no other interests
    except the children, and have lost any passion they once felt for each other. According to
    Sternberg, they are experiencing _____ love.
14. In contrast to simple liking, romantic love usually involves the lovers attending almost
    exclusively to one another, that is, they are exhibiting a deep mutual _____.
15. Another characteristic of romantic love is the lovers' ability to see their partners in
    _____ ways.
16. The study of the origins of human behavior patterns is called _____ psychology.
17. In a study of gender differences in mate selection in 37 cultures on six continents, David Buss
    found that the gender that preferred slightly older partners, who are industrious, higher in
    status, or economically successful are _____.
18. According to Buss' study of gender differences in mating, the gender that was more upset by
    a partner who became emotionally involved with someone else, rather than one who is
    sexually unfaithful, are _____.
19. Buss and others believe that mating preferences evolved in response to the differing
    challenges faced by men and women involving _____.
20. According to Buss, men tend to look for health and beauty in a prospective mate because the
    reproductive success of men depends on their mates' _____.

21. According to Buss, concerns about the paternity of offspring are the basis for the male emphasis on their mates' _____.
22. Some mating patterns may simply reflect the fact that in most societies men still tend to control the resources and _____ .
23. Early research may be misleading because to questions about jealousy, women tend to give "_____" answers.
24. According to most research, potential mates are rated as most attractive if they are kind, secure, supportive, and _____.

Part 1: Connections

1. ___ romantic love
2. ___ intimacy
3. ___ passion
4. ___ commitment

5. ___ mutual absorption

6. ___ evolutionary psychology

a. the nearly exclusive attention lovers give to one another
b. feelings of connectedness and affection for another person
c. study of the origins of human behavior patterns
d. associated with high levels of interpersonal attraction, heightened arousal, mutual absorption, and sexual desire
e. the determination to stay in a long-term relationship with another person
f. deep emotional and/or sexual feelings for another person

Part 2: Connections

1. ___ liking
2. ___ fatuous love

3. ___ empty love

4. ___ romantic love
5. ___ companionate love

6. ___ nonlove

7. ___ consummate love

8. ___ infatuated love

a. based on commitment but lacking intimacy and passion
b. characterized by intimacy, passion, and commitment
c. absence of all three components: intimacy, passion, or commitment
d. consists of passion only
e. characterized by passion and commitment, but lacking in intimacy
f. characterized by intimacy and commitment but not passion
g. based on intimacy and passion but no commitment
h. based on intimacy but lacking passion and commitment

Check Your Memory

1. TRUE or FALSE   Romantic love is based on interpersonal attraction, but it also involves high levels of passion.
2. TRUE or FALSE   Psychologist Robert Sternberg created the social exchange theory of love.
3. TRUE or FALSE   According to Sternberg, intimacy refers to deep emotional and/or sexual feelings.
4. TRUE or FALSE   Commitment involves the determination to stay in a long-term relationship with another person.
5. TRUE or FALSE   If you have commitment in the relationship, but no intimacy and no passion, you are experiencing companionate love.

855

6. TRUE or FALSE   If you are experiencing passion, but no intimacy and no commitment, then you have infatuated love.

7. TRUE or FALSE   We experience romantic love when we feel intimacy with, passion for, and commitment to another person.

8. TRUE or FALSE   Liking involves intimacy only with no commitment and no passion.

9. TRUE or FALSE   Fatuous love involves intimacy and commitment but no passion.

10. TRUE or FALSE   Romantic love usually involves deep mutual absorption, in which lovers attend almost exclusively to one another.

11. TRUE or FALSE   Relationships are most likely to persist when lovers are realistic about each other's strengths and weaknesses and view their relationship objectively.

12. TRUE or FALSE   Evolutionary psychology is the study of the origins of human behavior patterns.

13. TRUE or FALSE   In a study of 37 cultures on six continents, David Buss found that men were more interested in casual sex and preferred younger, more physically attractive partners than women.

14. TRUE or FALSE   Buss found that women get more jealous than men over real or imagined sexual infidelities.

15. TRUE or FALSE   Buss and others believe that mating preferences evolved in response to the differing physical strength levels of men and women.

16. TRUE or FALSE   According to Buss, women evolved an interest in whether their partners will stay with them and whether their mates have the resources to provide for their children.

17. TRUE or FALSE   According to Buss, the reproductive success of men depends on their mates' fertility with this being the reason for some older men to abandon their first wives in favor of young, beautiful "trophy wives."

18. TRUE or FALSE   Although some evidence supports the evolutionary view of mating, it is important to remember that evolved mating tendencies are subtle at best and easily overruled by other factors.

19. TRUE or FALSE   Some mating patterns may simply reflect the fact that women still tend to control the power and resources in most societies.

20. TRUE or FALSE   In general, potential mates are rated as most attractive if they are kind, secure, intelligent, and supportive

Module 15.2 Groups, Social Influence, Mere Presence, and Conformity
Humans in a Social Context—People, People, Everywhere
Survey Question: How does group membership affect our behavior?

Language Development Guide

sects: subpart of a larger religious group

gangs: three or more people who share a common identity; more recently, referring to a gang of adolescence engaged in delinquent acts

crews: group of people working together to run a ship, aircraft, or a stage production

clans: group of people related by blood or marriage; families with common ancestors

overlapping: to lie or extend over and cover part of

attained: earned

streamline: make something easier or effortless

flunk: fail; not give a passing grade to a student

clashing: coming in conflict

tremendous: enormous; massive

network: system; arrangement
cohesive: unified
coordinated: matched, to be similar
exert: use; bring to bear
prominent: important; that stands out
nationality: belonging to a particular country; one's country of birth
predictably: as expected
exaggerate: overstate
bestows: awards, gives
pastry: sweet baked food made of dough
comply: obey; fulfill
preoccupation: concern, interest, fascination
status symbols: a possession or activity that is a mark of higher social status
checkout line: line in which you stand to pay the cashier for your groceries
littering: dropping garbage on the ground
trash: garbage; litter
flyers: an advertisement printed on a sheet of paper
lax: lenient; permissive; slack; careless
"trash" it: to make an area dirty with garbage; to destroy an area
insulted: offended; verbally abused
shreds: pieces
inferences: deductions; assumptions; conclusions
"person behind the mask": aspects of a person that are unknown
inclined: having a tendency toward; leaning toward
tuba: large brass wind instrument with the lowest bass pitch
(John Philip) Sousa: an American music composer and bandmaster known for military marches (music)
march: military marching music
fundamental: basic; important
tip: gratuity; voluntary additional payment made for services provided
cheapskates: miserly, stingy person; does not like to spend money even when necessary
Malawi: country in southeast Africa (where Madonna adopted her children)

Recite and Review

1. We all belong to many overlapping social groups, and in each, we occupy a position in the _____ of the group.
2. The patterns of behavior expected of persons in various social positions are called _____.
3. Being male or female or an adolescent or senior citizen would all be _____ roles.
4. Being a scientist, a banker, a teacher, or a spouse would all be _____ roles.
5. Roles streamline daily interactions since the behavior or others can be _____.
6. For many students, the clashing demands of work, family, and school create role _____.
7. At work the clashing demands to be a good team player versus being a strong manager can cause job burnout due to these _____.
8. The network of roles, communication pathways, and power in a group make up what is called group _____.
9. The degree of attraction among group members or the strength of their desire to remain in the group is called group _____.

857

10. Unlike informal friendship groups, organized groups, such as an army or an athletic team have a high degree of group _____.
11. The basis for much of the power that groups exert over us is due to group _____.
12. Because people tend to work better when it is present, therapy groups, businesses, and sports team seek to increase group _____.
13. Groups with which we identify are called _____-groups.
14. Groups with which we do not identify are called _____-groups.
15. We tend to attribute positive characteristics to the _____-group.
16. Negative qualities tend to be attributed to the _____-group.
17. Tony's position in the social structure of his group with respect to power, privilege, and importance is referred to as Tony's _____.
18. In an experiment, a man walked into a number of bakeries and asked for a pastry, while claiming he did not have enough money to pay for it. Half the time he was well dressed and half the time he was poorly dressed. He was equally likely to be given a free pastry no matter how he was dressed if he was _____.
19. In an experiment a man, sometimes well dressed and sometimes not, asked for a pastry in a bakery but without the money to pay for. He was much less likely to get a pastry as a poorly dressed man than as a well dressed man if he was _____.
20. In most situations, we are more likely to comply with a request made by a person who is wearing expensive clothes or other symbols showing they are of high-_____.
21. A widely accepted, but often unspoken, standard for appropriate behavior is called a(n) _____.
22. In a study in which people were handed a flyer as they entered a parking garage, it was found that the people were more likely to drop the flyer to the floor if the floor of the garage was _____.
23. Every day we must guess how people will act, often from small shreds of evidence. We do this through a process called _____.
24. If Bert salts his food before he tastes it, we would most likely infer that Ben likes salt, thus, inferring to his behavior a(n) _____ cause.
25. If Betsy tastes her food and then salts it, we would most likely infer that the food needed salt, thus inferring to her behavior a(n) _____ cause.
26. Since we seldom known the real reasons for others' actions, we tend to infer causes from _____.
27. The most common error we make in inferring the causes of behavior is to attribute the actions of others to internal causes even if they are actually caused by external forces. This error is referred to as the _____ error.
28. The tendency of people to attribute the actions of actors in television programs to the personality of the actor rather than the obvious external cause that they are playing a character is an example of the _____ error.
29. Where our own behavior is concerned, we are more likely to think that external causes explain our actions, while as observers, we attribute the behavior of others to their wants, motives, and personality traits. This difference in attribution is referred to as the _____ effect.
30. When other people do not leave a tip in a restaurant, they are cheapskates, but when you do not leave a tip, it was because the service was bad. This difference in attribution is an example of the _____ effect.

Connections

1. ___ ascribed role
2. ___ achieved role
3. ___ in-groups
4. ___ out-groups
5. ___ role conflicts
6. ___ group structure
7. ___ group cohesiveness
8. ___ status
9. ___ norm
10. ___ attribution
11. ___ fundamental attribution error
12. ___ actor-observer effect

a. tendency to attribute the behavior of others to internal causes, such as personality, even when the behavior is caused externally

b. a widely accepted (but often unspoken) standard of conduct for appropriate behavior

c. trying to occupy two or more roles that make contradictory demands on behavior

d. tendency to attribute behavior of others to internal causes while attributing one's own behavior to external causes

e. individual's position in a social situation, especially with respect to power, privilege, or importance

f. assigned to a person and not under personal voluntary control

g. people with which a person does not identify

h. process of making inferences about the causes of one's own behavior, and that of others

i. people with which a person mainly identifies

j. degree of attraction among group members or their commitment to remaining in the group

k. network of roles, communication pathways, and power in a group

l. voluntarily attained by special effort

Check Your Memory

1. TRUE or FALSE   Since being a mother, a boss, a daughter, a sibling, or a friend all involve different sets of behaviors and expectations, these positions are called social roles.

2. TRUE or FALSE   Being male or female or a middle-aged person or a child would be considered achieved roles.

3. TRUE or FALSE   Being a clerk, police officer, or a professor would be called ascribed roles.

4. TRUE or FALSE   Roles streamline daily interactions by allowing us to anticipate what others will do.

5. TRUE or FALSE   A teacher who must flunk a close friend's daughter is most likely experiencing a role conflict.

6. TRUE or FALSE   Role conflicts at work, such as being a good team player versus being a strong manager can lead to job burnout and negative health outcomes.

7. TRUE or FALSE   Group cohesiveness consists of the network of roles, communication pathways, and power in a group.

8. TRUE or FALSE   Group structure is the degree of attraction among group members or the strength of their desire to remain in the group and is the basis for much of the power groups exert over us.

9. TRUE or FALSE	An athletic team or the army would have higher degrees of group structure than an informal friendship.
10. TRUE or FALSE	Therapy groups, businesses, and sports teams seek to increase group cohesiveness because it helps people work together better.
11. TRUE or FALSE	Your own in-groups are most often defined by a combination of prominent social dimensions, such as nationality, ethnicity, age, education, religion, income, political values, gender, and sexual orientation.
12. TRUE or FALSE	We are more likely to attribute negative characteristics to our in-group than to other out-groups.
13. TRUE or FALSE	We tend to exaggerate differences between members of out-groups and our own groups, which sets the stage for conflict between groups and for racial and ethnic prejudice.
14. TRUE or FALSE	An individual's position in a social structure, especially with respect to power, privilege, or importance is referred to as leadership authority.
15. TRUE or FALSE	In an experiment in which a man asked for a pastry in a bakery but without the money to pay it, the researchers found that when the man was well-dressed and acting impolite, he was more likely to get a pastry than when poorly-dressed and acting impolite.
16. TRUE or FALSE	In general, better treatment is given to higher status persons and explains some of our society's preoccupation with expensive clothes, cars, and other status symbols.
17. TRUE or FALSE	A norm is a widely accepted, but often unspoken, standard for appropriate behavior.
18. TRUE or FALSE	In an experiment in which people were handed a flyer as they entered a public parking garage, the people were more likely to drop the flyer on the floor of the garage if the garage had very little other litter on the floor than when there was already a great deal of litter on the floor of the garage.
19. TRUE or FALSE	Every day we must guess how people will act, and why, often from small shreds of evidence.
20. TRUE or FALSE	The process of making inferences about the causes of one's own behavior, and that of others, is referred to consensus building.
21. TRUE or FALSE	If a chef adds more cayenne pepper to his dish without tasting it, we attribute his addition of pepper to the internal cause of the chef liking hot pepper.
22. TRUE or FALSE	We tend to infer causes from circumstances.
23. TRUE or FALSE	If you believe your employee is late because he is lazy, when, in reality, he stopped to help victims of a car accident, you have made the chance conditioning error.
24. TRUE or FALSE	The tendency of people to attribute the actions of actors in television programs to the personality of the actor rather than the obvious external cause of the actor playing a character is an example of the fundamental attribution error.
25. TRUE or FALSE	According to the actor-observer effect, we tend to explain our behavior based on wants, motives, and personality traits, while giving external explanations to other people's behavior.

Module 15.2 Groups, Social Influence, Mere Presence, and Conformity
Social Influence—Follow the Leader

Survey Question: What have social psychologists learned about social influence, mere presence, and conformity?

Language Development Guide

mere: simple

conformity: adjusting one's behavior to be in agreement with others

on cue: as planned to happen exactly at that moment

swayed: inclined; influenced

spontaneously: on one's own accord

induce: cause; bring about

pick up your pace: speed up

impaired: damaged

shooting pool: playing a game on a rectangular table with six openings, or pockets, two on each side and then each corner into which a person tries to hit colored numbered balls by tapping one white ball, the cue ball, with a cue stick

student union: building on college campus used for social and club activities of the student body

sharks?: person good at pool; usually wins money by playing against others

marks?: persons who are not accomplished pool players but who are selected as the intended targets or victims of pool sharks or pool hustlers in a pool match for money

loafing: idleness; putting forth less effort

solely: completely; only

tug-of-war: contest of strength in which two teams pull on opposite ends of a rope, each trying to pull the other across a dividing line in the middle, with this section of ground sometimes being a hole filled with water and mud

not shy: bold; not timid

discreet: restrained; less noticeable; tactful

increasingly: advancing in amount

conscious: aware; mindful

publicly: openly; in public; overtly; visibly

intimate: close personal relationship

thing of the past: over; no longer present

Thou shalt conform: joke, worded to sound like one of the biblical Ten Commandments, an absolute rule

uniformity: conforming to one standard; unwavering; the same each time

necessity: essential; a must

lethal: deadly

staged: planned to occur

trials: a part in a series of experiments

shock: surprise that upsets

yielding: give in; go along with

critical: important; crucial; significant

erred: made a mistake or error

denying: saying something isn't true

susceptible: inclined; prone; vulnerable

structure: highly organized

certainty: being able to confidently predict an outcome; to know without a doubt

disastrous: very bad "rock the boat": to cause trouble by questioning or disturbing a situation when situation is stable and your troubling input is unwelcome

sloppy: lack of order and precision

tolerate: to put up with; to passively permit

self-censorship: withholding of one's true opinion from an audience perceived to disagree with that opinion

misguided: bad, uninformed, poor, incorrect

Mars Climate Orbiter: a navigation error caused the spacecraft to go too low into the Martian atmosphere and be destroyed

"critical evaluator": person who will freely question and express doubts

preferences: one's best-liked choices

devil's advocate: one who argues against a position, not because this is your position but either simply for the sake of argument or to determine the validity or workability of a position

accountable: responsible

inquiry: investigation; examination

"second-chance": taking the time to reevaluate before making a final decision

deadlock: gridlock; standstill; no progress

clouded by: tarnished by; darkened by

sanctions: punishments involving rejection, isolation, exclusion

exclusion: omission; leaving out; keeping out

chill of disapproval: coolness felt upon being rejected or negatively evaluated

impressive: remarkable; noteworthy

mean looking: angry, scary, threatening

in your corner: on your side; supporting you

ally: friend; supporter

dissenting: not agreeing with the majority

rich: plentiful; abundant

diversity: variety; assortment

incidentally: by the way

Recite and Review

1. Changes in behavior induced by the actions of others are referred to as _____.
2. In the New York sidewalk experiment, as the group staring up at the sixth floor window became larger, the number of people that were swayed to look up _____.
3. The gentlest form of social influence is called _____.
4. If you spontaneously change your behavior to bring it into agreement with your friends, you are exhibiting the form of social influence known as _____.
5. Changing your behavior in response to another person who has little or no social power, or authority is called _____.
6. When you change your behavior in direct response to the demands of your boss, you are exhibiting _____.
7. The strongest form of social influence is _____.
8. You are singing your favorite song softly in your off-key voice when a stranger walks into your office, and you stop singing because of the social influence known as _____.
9. You are out riding your mountain bike when another rider pulls up beside you. You are more likely to speed up because of our general tendency to perform better in the presence of others, which is called _____.
10. The tendency to perform better when in the presence of others was the subject of the first published social psychology experiment conducted in 1898 by psychologist _____.
11. Whether the presence of others improves or impairs your performance depends on whether you have _____ in your abilities.

862

12. People tend to work less hard when they are part of a group than they do when they are solely responsible for their own work. This is known as _____.

13. A study was conducted in which people played tug-of-war while blindfolded and were led to believe they were pulling alone on some trials and pulling with a team on other trials. The participants pulled harder when they thought they were pulling _____.

14. Daily behavior is probably most influenced by group pressures for _____.

15. Bringing one's behavior into agreement or harmony with the behavior of others in a group is called _____.

16. One of the first experiments on conformity consisted of students being told they would be in a group and would be selecting the line that matched a "standard" line. This experiment was staged by psychologist _____.

17. In the classic study on conformity, the "students" who were all actors gave the wrong answer on about a third of the trials to create group pressure on the real student participants. The percent of real subjects who yielding at least once to group pressure was _____ percent.

18. People are more likely to conform if they have high needs for structure or _____.

19. People are more likely to conform if they are anxious, concerned with the approval of others and _____ in self-confidence.

20. People are more likely to conform if they live in cultures, such as in Asian cultures, which emphasize group _____.

21. An urge by decision makers to maintain each other's approval, even at the cost of critical thinking is referred to as _____.

22. In an attempt to understand a series of disastrous decisions made by government officials, a Yale psychologist proposed the theory regarding this urge by decision makers to maintain each other's approval. This psychologist was _____.

23. A misguided loyalty in which group members are hesitant to "rock the boat," question sloppy thinking, or tolerate alternative views appears to be the cause of _____.

24. To prevent this "misguided loyalty," group leaders should define each group member's role as a(n) "_____."

25. This "misguided loyalty" can be prevented by stating the problem factually, without bias and by not revealing at the beginning of the meeting any personal _____.

26. In order to prevent this "misguided loyalty," group leaders should invite a group member or outside person to play "_____."

27. To encourage critical thinking, group leaders should reevaluate important decisions by holding a(n) "_____" meeting.

28. The presence of too many alternatives in decision making can lead to _____.

29. Your group of friends, like most groups, tends to use rewards and punishments, such as approval or disapproval, to make sure its members conform to their expectations for dress and behavior, etc. These rewards and punishments are called _____.

30. The likelihood of a person being influenced by a group depends on the importance of group _____ to the person.

31. Regarding how the size of the majority affects conformity, research found that the same amount of yielding that occurred with a majority of eight occurred when there was only a majority of _____.

32. Even more important than the size of the majority is whether the group is in total agreement, or is its _____.

33. In the study involving the judgment of lines, conformity was lessened when subjects were supported by a(n) _____.

Connections

1. ___ social influence
2. ___ mere presence
3. ___ conformity
4. ___ compliance
5. ___ obedience
6. ___ coercion
7. ___ social facilitation
8. ___ social loafing
9. ___ groupthink
10. ___ group sanctions

a. changing behavior because you are forced to
b. tendency of people to work less hard when part of a group than when they are solely responsible for their work
c. rewards and punishments, such as approval or disapproval, administered by groups to enforce conformity among members
d. tendency to perform better when in the presence of others
e. changes in a person's behavior induced by the presence or by the actions of others
f. compulsion by members of decision-making groups to maintain agreement, even at the cost of critical thinking
g. changing behavior in direct response to the demands of an authority
h. changing behavior because other people are nearby
i. bending to the requests of a person who has little or no authority or other form of social power
j. spontaneously changing your behavior in to bring it into agreement with others

Check Your Memory

1. TRUE or FALSE   When people interact, they almost always affect one another's behavior.
2. TRUE or FALSE   In the New York sidewalk experiment, the more people that looked up at the sixth floor window, the less people walking on the street were influenced to look up.
3. TRUE or FALSE   The gentlest form of social influence is compliance.
4. TRUE or FALSE   When we spontaneously change our behavior to bring it into agreement with others, we are exhibiting obedience.
5. TRUE or FALSE   The strongest form of social influence is obedience.
6. TRUE or FALSE   Mere presence refers to the tendency for people to change their behavior just because of other people being nearby.
7. TRUE or FALSE   Norman Triplett found that most people tend to slow down if they are riding a bicycle and another cyclist pulls even with them due to a tendency known as social loafing.
8. TRUE or FALSE   If you are confident in your abilities, your behavior will most likely be facilitated in the presence of others, while a lack of confidence will lead to an impaired performance.
9. TRUE or FALSE   In a study, people playing tug-of-war while blindfolded pulled harder when they thought they were members of a team than when they thought they were competing alone.
10. TRUE or FALSE   Daily behavior is probably most influenced by group pressures for conformity.
11. TRUE or FALSE   When we bring our behavior into agreement with the actions, norms, or values of others in the absence of any direct pressure, we are exhibiting conformity.

864

12. TRUE or FALSE A degree of uniformity in behavior is necessary if we are to interact comfortably.

13. TRUE or FALSE One of the first experiments on conformity, which involved the judgment of lines, was staged by Robert Sternberg.

14. TRUE or FALSE In the classic study of conformity, the fake "students" who were all actors gave the wrong answer on two-thirds of the trials to create group pressure with 98 percent of the real subjects yielding at least once to the group pressure.

15. TRUE or FALSE People with low needs for structure or certainty are the most likely to conform.

16. TRUE or FALSE People who are anxious, low in self-confidence, or concerned with the approval of others are more like to conform.

17. TRUE or FALSE People in North America who tend to be individualistic are more likely to conform than the people in other cultures.

18. TRUE or FALSE Solomon Asch first proposed the concept of groupthink.

19. TRUE or FALSE The core of groupthink is misguided loyalty in which group members are hesitant to "rock the boat," question sloppy thinking, or tolerate alternative views.

20. TRUE or FALSE One analysis of 19 international crises found that groupthink contributed to most of these situations.

21. TRUE or FALSE To prevent groupthink, group leaders should make their personal preferences known at the beginning of the meeting.

22. TRUE or FALSE To reduce group think, group leaders should invite a group member or outside person to play devil's advocate.

23. TRUE or FALSE In order to reduce groupthink, group leaders should make it clear that group members will be held accountable for decisions.

24. TRUE or FALSE Defining each group member's role as a "critical evaluator" will create gridlock and will not enhance decision-making.

25. TRUE or FALSE The presence of too many alternatives can lead to deadlock, in which an inability to make a choice can delay taking necessary action.

26. TRUE or FALSE In most groups, we have been rewarded with acceptance and approval for conformity and threatened with rejection or ridicule for nonconformity with these reactions called group sanctions.

27. TRUE or FALSE The more important group membership is to a person, the less he or she will be influenced by other group members.

28. TRUE or FALSE A majority of three produces about as much yielding to conformity as a majority of eight.

29. TRUE or FALSE Having at least one person in your corner can greatly reduce pressures to conform.

30. TRUE or FALSE The size of the majority is more important than unanimity in determining conformity.

Critical Thinking Question
Is it possible to be completely nonconforming (that is, to not conform to some group norm)?

Module 15.3 Compliance, Obedience, Coercion, and Self-Assertion
Compliance—A Foot in the Door
Survey Question: What have psychologists learned about compliance?

Language Development Guide

"fit in": to be a part of; to blend in; to conform

cappuccino: drink made with strong dark coffee and foamy hot milk

honor a request: to comply or agree to a demand or appeal

notorious: well-known

lowball: undercutting, deceptively below everyone else's

bump the price up: increase the price

concluded: brought to an end

committed: pledged; having agreed to

succumbed: yielded; giving in

manipulated: controlled by someone in a devious way

game: deceptive practice

tactics: method; approach, course of action for attaining a goal

trade-in: something, such as an old car, that is used as partial payment on a new one

virtually: nearly; almost but not quite

bargaining: negotiating the price of something

hook is set: metaphor that a fish is caught when the hook is set or fixed in its mouth; in this case, the salesman has caught the customer (fish)

"hooked": snared; caught

disappointment: frustrated; feeling let down

hesitate: not eager to do something

grumble: talk about how unhappy you are

"compromise": settlement of differences in which each side must concede or yield in some way

evening the odds: making a situation fair or even

combat: oppose; fight; contend with

arm yourself: protect yourself

Recite and Review

1. Situations in which one person bends to the requests of another person who has little or no authority describes the social influence called _____.

2. Your new co-worker asks to borrow money to buy a cappuccino, and you give her the money. You have just exhibited the type of social influence known as _____.

3. If someone asks to borrow a dollar and you agree to this small request, you will be more likely to comply with a larger request to borrow ten dollars later on. This illustrates the _____ effect.

4. If a friend asked to borrow $50 and you refuse. Then, he later asks for just $10. If you give into to this smaller request after refusing the larger one, you have succumbed to the _____ effect.

5. The term for effect in which a person agrees to a smaller request after having refused a larger one was coined by psychologist _____.

6. If you ask someone to give you a ride to school in the morning; and after he agrees, you tell him that you have to be there at 6 a.m., you have used the _____ technique.

7. If a car salesperson offers you a test drive and you accept, you have given in to a small request that make you more likely to purchase a car than if you had not taken the test drive. This illustrates the compliance technique known as the _____ effect.

8. When a car dealer gets a buyer committed to buying the car at a low price but then adds on other costs that increase the price of the car, the car dealer is using the _____ technique.

9. If you are looking at a car and the salesperson asks you to go to an office and fill out some papers, "just to see what kind of a price" she or he can offer and you fill out the papers, you will be more likely to buy the car because you have succumbed to the _____ effect.

10. Salespeople once had a great advantage in negotiating because they knew exactly how much the dealership paid for each car. Now, anyone can obtain detailed automobile pricing information from the _____.

Connections

1. ____ compliance

2. ____ foot-in-the-door effect

3. ____ door-in-the-face effect

4. ____ low-ball technique

a. strategy in which commitment is gained first to reasonable or desirable terms, which are then made less reasonable or desirable

b. tendency for a person who has first complied with a small request to be more likely later to fulfill a larger request

c. tendency for a person who has refused a major request to subsequently be more likely to comply with a minor request

d. bending to the requests of a person who has little or no authority or other form of social power

Check Your Memory

1. TRUE or FALSE Pressures to "fit in" and conform are usually indirect, while compliance involves more direct pressures.
2. TRUE or FALSE If a stranger asks to borrow your cell phone and you agree, then you are exhibiting the form of social influence known as compliance.
3. TRUE or FALSE If someone asks you to put a small sign in your store window promoting the environment and you agree, you will be more likely to agree to put up a larger sign in the future, which illustrates the door-in-the-face effect.
4. TRUE or FALSE If a friend asks to borrow your car for a day and you agree and then he tells you that he forgot that he will need it a second day also, this "friend" has used the low-ball technique.
5. TRUE or FALSE If a friend asks you to keep her dogs for two weeks and you decline and she then asks if you can keep them for a couple of days and you accept, you have experienced the foot-in-the-door effect.
6. TRUE or FALSE A good way to get another person to comply with a request is to first do a small favor for the person.
7. TRUE or FALSE The foot-in-the-door effect is based on observing your own behavior of seeing yourself agreeing to a small request, which helps to convince you that you didn't mind doing what was later asked.
8. TRUE or FALSE If a car salesperson offers you a test drive and you accept, you have experienced the foot-in-the-door effect.
9. TRUE or FALSE You have agreed to purchase the computer listed in the store ad for an attractive low price, but then the salesperson adds additional costs that makes the computer more expensive, which means that you have experienced the door-in-the-face effect.
10. TRUE or FALSE If you understand the compliance tactics used by salespersons, you will be better able to critically evaluate the tactics when they are used on you and will have a far better chance of resisting their sales pressure.

Module 15.3 Compliance, Obedience, Coercion, and Self-Assertion
Obedience—Would You Electrocute a Stranger?
Survey Question: What have psychologists learned about obedience?

Language Development Guide

electrocute: injure or kill with electric shock
commands: orders; demands
slaughter: murder; kill
inhumane: cruel; brutal; heartless; sadistic
reflect: reveal; expose; indicate
character flaws: a deficiency, limitation, or imperfection in one's personality that affects one's actions and abilities
psychopaths: the antisocial personality disorder; person without a conscience, without guilt or remorse
provocative: tending to cause strong feelings
coin is flipped: throwing a coin up and which side the coin lands on (heads or tails) determines the winner or what position one will take
designated: specified; determined to be
adjacent: neighboring; next to
apparatus: equipment
escorted: accompanied and guided
corresponding: accompanying; equivalent
flip: move something with a small quick motion
moan: groan; complain
going up the scale: giving stronger shocks
chillingly: anxiously, with fear or uncertain discomfort
strapping: tie or fasten with leather bindings
polled: surveyed
astounding: very surprising
virtually: nearly; almost
dilemma: problem that requires a choice between two unfavorable alternatives
protested: objected; showed disapproval
legitimate: officially; rightful; legal
prestige: status; reputation; standing
rerun: redone; replicated; ran experiment again
shabby: untidy; dilapidated; poorly maintained
knuckle under: submit; give in to pressure
senselessly: meaninglessness; foolishly; stupidly
simulated: fake; imitation
nagging: troublesome; distressing
in this light: with the knowledge at present
substantial: important; significant; sizeable
rationalize: reason
locales: places with reference to particular events
diverse: varied; different
Cambodia: republic in southeast Asia
Rwanda: country in east central Africa
Bosnia: region in southeastern Europe
Vietnam: country in southeast Asia bordering South China Sea
Darfur: province in western Sudan in northern Africa
Sri Lanka: island country in the Indian Ocean off southeast India

Iraq: republic in southwest Asia, north of Saudi Arabia and west of Iran
sanctioned massacres: numerous people killed by order of the persons in power within that
        country; usually involves genocide (murder of an entire ethnic group)
chilling proportions: an upsetting, horrifying amount
destructive: damaging
resist: refuse to go along; oppose; defy
assertion: declaration; statement
moral: ethical; honorable
fortitude: strength; determination
misguided: bad, uninformed, poor, incorrect

Recite and Review

1. In those situations where a person has power, she or he is described as a(n) _____.
2. You are in the army, and your sergeant gives you an order. If you follow this order, you are demonstrating the social influence known as _____.
3. The psychologist who conducted the original "teacher-learner" experiment at Yale University that involved simulated electric shocks was _____.
4. When a group of psychiatrists were polled before the "teacher-learner" obedience experiment, they predicted that the percent of those tested who would obey and "shock" the learner at the 450-volt level would be less than _____ percent.
5. In the original obedience experiment, the percent of "teachers" who actually obeyed completely by going all the way to the 450-volt shock level was _____ percent.
6. Some critics of the obedience experiment argued that the subjects were convinced that no one would be hurt because of Yale University's _____.
7. When the obedience experiment was rerun away from Yale University in a shabby office building in a nearby city, the reduction was considered minor with the percent of subjects obeying being _____ percent.
8. When the subjects were close to the learner, especially face-to-face, the obedience of the subjects was _____.
9. When the experimenter gave his orders over the phone, the obedience of the subjects was _____.
10. According to the psychologist who ran the original "teacher-learner" obedience experiment, people tend to rationalize that they are not personally responsible for their actions when directions come from a(n) _____.
11. In one of the "teacher-learner" experiments, it was found that when real subjects saw two other "teachers" (both actors) resist orders and walk out of the experiment, the percent of "real subjects" who continued to obey was only _____ percent.
12. Psychologist Jerry Burger of Santa Clara University recently partially replicated the "teacher-learner" obedience study and obtained very _____ results.
13. People often find themselves obeying a legitimate authority long after that authority's demands have become _____.
14. In locales as diverse as Cambodia, Rwanda, Bosnia, Vietnam, Darfur, Sri Lanka, and Iraq, the tragic result of "blind obedience" has been "sanctioned _____."

Connections

1. ___ obedience

    a. actors who pretended to be subjects in the experiment, but were working with the experimenter

2. ___ authority

    b. performed the original obedience experiment at Yale University

3. ____ "teachers"

4. ____ "learners"
5. ____ Jerry Burger
6. ____ Stanley Milgram

c. changing behavior in direct response to the demands of an authority
d. person who has social power
e. the "real subjects" in the experiment
f. partially replicated the obedience experiment recently

Check Your Memory

1. TRUE or FALSE   A person who has social power in one situation may have very little in another.

2. TRUE or FALSE   In those situations where a person has power, she or he is described as an authority.

3. TRUE or FALSE   The pressure to conform is greater with the social influence of compliance than with obedience.

4. TRUE or FALSE   When Stanley Milgram polled a group of psychiatrist before his obedience experiment, they predicted that 20 percent of those tested would obey and "shock" the learner at the 450-volt level.

5. TRUE or FALSE   In Milgram's original obedience experiment, only 30 percent of the subjects actually obeyed completely by going all the way to the 450-volt level.

6. TRUE or FALSE   No real shocks were actually administered during the Milgram experiment.

7. TRUE or FALSE   To test whether the prestige of Yale University convinced subjects that no one would be hurt, the study was rerun in a shabby office building in nearby Bridgeport, Connecticut with the percent reduction in obedience considered minor.

8. TRUE or FALSE   Milgram found that the "teacher's" obedience increased if the teacher and learner were in the same room or were face-to-face.

9. TRUE or FALSE   When the experimenter gave his orders to the teacher over the phone, the obedience of the teacher was reduced.

10. TRUE or FALSE   Most people will obey a legitimate authority long after that person's demands have become unreasonable.

11. TRUE or FALSE   Milgram suggested that when directions come from an authority, people rationalize that they are not personally responsible for their actions.

12. TRUE or FALSE   In order to keep their jobs, many people obey orders to do things that they know
are dishonest, unethical, or harmful.

13. TRUE or FALSE   When real subjects saw two other 'teachers" (both actors) resist orders and walk out of the experiment, the majority of real subjects still maintained their obedience to the experimenter's orders.

14. TRUE or FALSE   When Milgram's study was recently partially replicated, significantly different results were obtained.

Critical Thinking Question

Modern warfare allows killing to take place impersonally and at a distance. How does this relate to Milgram's experiments?

Module 15.3 Compliance, Obedience, Coercion, and Self-Assertion
Coercion—Brainwashing and Cults

Survey Question: What have psychologists learned about coercion?

Language Development Guide

enthusiast: exciting, consuming interest in a subject

Korean War: conflict lasting from 1950 to 1953 between North Korea, and its ally China, and South Korea, supported by United Nations troops, particularly the United States; ended with a ceasefire and a truce

"thought reform": the use of outside manipulation to alter a person's basic beliefs and attitudes

false confessions: admissions of guilt to crimes not committed by the person making the confession; usually due to the "confessor" being coerced

aftermath: outcome; consequences

mass murder/suicide at Jonestown: American cult led by Jim Jones, who committed mass murder/suicide of its members in 1978 after Congressman Leo Ryan and others were killed when they came to Guyana to investigate the cult activities and take home cult members who wished to leave

Branch Davidian tragedy at Waco: American cult that grew out of a branch of the Seven Day Adventists and was led by David Koresh, who was accused of stockpiling illegal weapons and refused a search warrant by the ATF (Alcohol, Tobacco, and Firearms) and FBI in 1993; a siege resulted with the standoff ending in a fire that destroyed the compound

Heaven's Gate group suicide in San Diego: an American cult based on a UFO religion based in SanDiego, California and led by Marshall Applewhite, who along with 38 members of the group committed suicide when the Hale-Bopp Comet was at its brightest

Osama bin Laden's al-Qaeda movement: militant Islamist group founded around 1988 and eventually led by Osama bin Laden and attacked civilian and military targets in many countries, including the September 11, 2001 attack on the Trade Center in New York and the Pentagon in Washington, D.C.

heightened: increased degree of

POW camps: prison-of-war camps; captured soldiers held by the opposing side in a war

at the mercy: another person decides what will happen to you, whether you will be treated humanly or inhumanly

facilitate: make possible; make it easier to occur

humiliation: shame; dishonor; embarrassment

breaking point: moment in time when coping becomes impossible

solidify: harden

"converted": transformed; changed

reverted: went back to a previous state

recruiting: enlisting; enrolling; signing up

exhorted: urged by a strong speech

purple Kool-Aid: flavored drink mix; grape-flavored

laced: added a substance, usually poison or some drug

cyanide: colorless, extremely poisonous compound

incredible: hard to believe

inhabitants: permanent residents; people who make their home an area

intimidated: made fearful by threats

lulled: calmed; made to rest or sleep

sedatives: downers that have a strong tranquilizing effect

cut off: isolated; separated from

accustomed: in the habit of; adapted to

rigid: inflexible; strict

primed: prepared; trained

final "loyalty test": in the case of the Jim Jones' cult, being totally loyal meant following his order to kill oneself and family by drinking the poison

authoritarian: absolute obedience to an authority

allegiance: commitment and loyalty

infallible: perfect; incapable of error

dictates: orders; commands

victimized: taken advantage of

perished: died

sexual mores: socially acceptable sexual behavior

errant: misbehaving; naughty

paddled: spanked

persuaded: guided to change attitudes or beliefs through information and arguments

surrender: give up control

mistresses: women who are having a continuing sexual relationship with men, usually married ones, with the men many times providing financial support to the women

children out of wedlock: child born to parents who are not legally married to each other

absolute: total; complete

tragic: terrible; heartbreaking

aided: helped

escalating: increasing intensity

indoctrination: teaching a person to accept and follow specific beliefs without question

succumbed: submitted or given in to an overpowering force

lure: attraction

alienation: withdrawal or separation from

rebelling: opposing; resisting

drills: practice exercises that are repeated over and over

rituals: ceremonies

chanting: singing usually the same words over and over in a the same tone

devotee: committed, dedicated follower

cognitive dissonance: uncomfortable clash between self-image, thoughts, beliefs, attitudes, or perceptions and one's behavior

reference groups: any group that an individual uses as a standard for social comparison

"throne": chair occupied by a ruler

"Those who do not remember the past are condemned to repeat it": quote by author George Santayana that means if one does not study history and past events and understand why mistakes occurred, he or she will be likely to repeat these same mistakes

Recite and Review

1. If you are forced to change your beliefs or your behavior against your will, you have experienced the social influence form known as _____.
2. Forced attitude change known as brainwashing requires a(n) _____ audience.
3. Brainwashing typically begins by making the target person feel completely _____.
4. Physical and psychological abuse, lack of sleep, humiliation, and isolation serve to loosen, former values and beliefs, during the stage of brainwashing known as _____.
5. When exhaustion, pressure, and fear become unbearable, the person begins to abandon former beliefs and to undergo the stage of brainwashing known as _____.
6. When prisoners reach the breaking point and sign false confessions to gain relief, they are suddenly rewarded with praise, privileges, food, or rest, which leads to a mixture of hope and fear and serve to solidify new attitudes during the stage of brainwashing known as

   _____.

7. As shown by the returning soldiers, who had undergone brainwashing as Korean War POWs, the dramatic shifts in their attitudes brought about by the brainwashing were only _____.
8. The People's Temple in Jonestown and the Branch Davidian group in Waco, Texas, are two examples of authoritarian groups known as _____.
9. In these authoritarian groups, the most important aspect is not the beliefs preached by the leader, but the leader's _____.
10. As almost always occurs in these authoritarian type groups, the members of the People's Temple and the Branch Davidian group were _____ by their leaders.
11. Like other cult leaders, Jones and Koresh demanded absolute loyalty and _____.
12. The psychologist and pioneering brainwashing expert who aided hundreds of former cult members was _____.
13. Cult members try to catch potential converts at a time of need, especially when the converts will be most attracted by a sense of _____.
14. Rebellious adolescents are especially vulnerable to recruitment into cults because these individuals may be seeking a cause to conform to as a replacement for the _____.
15. Often cult conversion begins with intense displays of affection and understanding known as "_____."
16. After the intense displays of affection, the converts are cut off from family and friends as their _____ groups.
17. The use of all-night meditation, continuous chanting or other similar rituals wear down physical and emotional resistance, generate feelings of commitment, and discourage _____ thinking.
18. By having the recruits make small commitments, like staying an extra day, and then later they make a major commitment, such as signing over a bank account, many cults make clever use of the _____ effect.
19. Making major public commitments makes it almost impossible for converts to admit they have made a mistake because it creates a powerful _____ effect.
20. When the members of a cult think of themselves more as group members than as individuals, then _____ is complete.
21. Leaders who teach love and compassion and encourage followers to question their beliefs and to reach their own conclusions about how to live would be considered true _____ leaders.

Connections

1. ____ coercion
2. ____ brainwashing
3. ____ cult
4. ____ "unfreeze"
5. ____ "refreeze"
6. ____ "love bombing"
7. ____ cult leader
8. ____ true spiritual leader

a. has charismatic personality; expects complete obedience; victimizes his or her followers
b. intense displays of affection and understanding
c. encourage followers to reach their own conclusions about how to live
d. a group that professes great devotion to some person and follows that person almost without question
e. solidifying new attitudes
f. engineered or forced attitude change involving a captive audience
g. being forced to change your beliefs or your behavior against your will
h. to loosen former values and beliefs

873

Check Your Memory

1. TRUE or FALSE   If you are forced to change your beliefs or your behavior against your will this is known as active compliance.
2. TRUE or FALSE   Brainwashing, or forced attitude change, requires a captive audience.
3. TRUE or FALSE   Brainwashing typically begins with a process known as refreezing.
4. TRUE or FALSE   In most cases, the dramatic shift in attitudes brought about by brainwashing is permanent.
5. TRUE or FALSE   For the cult members, the cult leader's personality is more important than the beliefs that she or he preaches.
6. TRUE or FALSE   In almost all cases, cult members are victimized by their leaders in one way or another.
7. TRUE or FALSE   Cults employ high-pressure indoctrination techniques similar to those used in brainwashing.
8. TRUE or FALSE   In the United States, only a few thousand people have ever succumbed to the lure of cults.
9. TRUE or FALSE   The psychologist and pioneering brainwashing expert that studied and aided hundreds of former cult members was Joseph Wolpe.
10. TRUE or FALSE   Cult members try to catch potential converts at a time of need, especially when a sense of belonging is most needed.
11. TRUE or FALSE   Adolescents are especially vulnerable to recruitment into cults because they may be seeking a cause to conform to as a replacement for the parental authority they are rebelling against.
12. TRUE or FALSE   Cult conversion often begins with intense displays of affection and understanding known as the "broken record" technique.
13. TRUE or FALSE   Rituals are used in cult conversions to increase physical and emotional resistance and to encourage critical thinking.
14. TRUE or FALSE   By having the cult members first make small commitments, such as staying an extra day and then later making a large commitment, such as signing over their bank accounts, cults are making use of the door-in-the-face effect.
15. TRUE or FALSE   Cult members who make major public commitments to the cult experience a powerful cognitive dissonance effect.
16. TRUE or FALSE   Once in the cult, members are cut off from family and friends as their reference groups.
17. TRUE or FALSE   Conversion to a cult is complete when the recruit thinks of him or herself as an individual rather than a group member.
18. TRUE or FALSE   All cult leaders encourage their followers to question their beliefs and to reach their own conclusions about how to live.

Module 15.3 Compliance, Obedience, Coercion, and Self-Assertion

Assertiveness Training—Standing Up for Your Rights

Survey Question: How does self-assertion differ from aggression?

Language Development Guide

compliant: yielding; accommodating
assert: insist on one's rights
"making a scene": creating a disturbance that may cause embarrassment
anguish: agony; distress
poise: calmness; self-assurance; composure; dignity
backed out: decided not to do something; changed one's mind

your own behalf: in your own interests, in support of yourself
exclusively: only; solely
self-serving: interest in one own self
nonassertive: lacking self-confidence; patient; give-in to others
pent-up: held in, saved
fury: rage; anger
irresponsible: lazy; careless; not taking care of responsibilities
landlord: person who owns land, house, or apartments and rents their use to others
halted: stopped
a column of: a line of

Recite and Review

1. Because most of us were rewarded, first as children and later as adults, for compliant, obedient, or "good" behavior, many people find it difficult to _____ themselves.
2. If you have "said yes when you wanted to say no" or "backed out of asking for a raise or a change in working conditions," then you may benefit from _____ training.
3. Mel is self-denying, inhibited, and lets others make choices for him with his goals often not being achieved. Mel is exhibiting _____ behavior.
4. Barbara achieves her goals at others' expense and often makes choices for others without asking their input and even puts people down who try to disagree with her. Barbara is exhibiting _____ behavior.
5. Janie acts in her own best interests, expresses her feelings, while respecting the rights of others. Janie is exhibiting _____ behavior.
6. The first step in assertiveness training is to convince yourself of three basic rights: You have the right to refuse, to right a wrong, and to _____.
7. A direct, honest expression of feelings and desires, which is not exclusively self-serving, is the definition of _____.
8. Tim is usually patient to a fault, but sometimes his pent-up anger explodes with unexpected fury, which damages his relationships. Tim would be described as _____.
9. In assertiveness training, because each assertive action must be able to be repeated even under stress, these assertive actions must be _____.
10. In an assertiveness training exercise to return an item to a store, a person might stand in front of a mirror and rehearse the dialogue, posture, and _____ to be used.
11. Another assertive training exercise involves having a friend take the part of a really aggressive clerk and a cooperative one, while you _____ the scene.
12. A book that offers examples and techniques for using assertiveness training was written by psychologists Robert Alberti and Michael Emmons and is entitled _____.

Connections

1. ___ assertiveness training
2. ___ nonassertive behavior

3. ___ self-assertion

4. ___ aggressive behavior

a. achieves goals at others' expense
b. direct, honest expression of feelings and desires; goals achieved without hurting others

c. lets others make choices for them; goals not achieved

d. instructions in how to be self-assertive

875

Check Your Memory

1. TRUE or FALSE   Not asserting oneself is often related to anxiety about "making a scene" or feeling disliked by others.
2. TRUE or FALSE   Assertiveness training is a type of systematic desensitization that helps people adapt to conflict.
3. TRUE or FALSE   The first step in assertiveness training is to convince yourself of three basic rights: You have the right to refuse, to request, and to right a wrong.
4. TRUE or FALSE   Self-assertion is a direct, honest expression of feelings and desires, but is not exclusively self-serving.
5. TRUE or FALSE   People who are nonassertive are usually patient to a fault with their pent-up anger sometimes exploding with unexpected fury, which can damage relationships.
6. TRUE or FALSE   Assertion involves achieving one's goals at the expense of another.
7. TRUE or FALSE   A person who interacts with a nonassertive person often feels sympathy, guilt, or contempt for the nonassertive person.
8. TRUE or FALSE   A person who interacts with an assertive person feels hurt, defensive, humiliated, or taken advantage of.
9. TRUE or FALSE   Aggressive behavior is an attempt to get one's own way no matter what.
10. TRUE or FALSE   Assertion techniques emphasize firmness, not attack.
11. TRUE or FALSE   To improve assertiveness, it is recommended that people rehearse in front of a mirror the dialogue, posture, and gestures they will use in various situations requiring self-assertion.
12. TRUE or FALSE   Another assertive training exercise involves role-playing the assertive scene with a friend playing an aggressive clerk or a cooperative one.
13. TRUE or FALSE   Self-assertion supplies instant poise, confidence, and self-assurance.
14. TRUE or FALSE   Psychologists Robert Alberti and Michael Emmons' book on assertiveness training is entitled *Your Perfect Right*.

Module 15.4 Attitudes and Persuasion

Attitudes—Belief + Emotion + Action

Survey Question: How are attitudes acquired and changed?

Language Development Guide

affirmative action: policies designed to reduce discrimination, based on sex or race
euthanasia: mercy killing
death penalty: using execution as a punishment for crime
intimately: personally
woven: intertwined
predisposes: prepares
"Your attitude is showing": other people can easily tell how you feel about a subject
gun control: regulating the manufacture, sale, and use of guns
orient: make familiar
acquired: obtained; gained
take an unduly dim view: dislike
coaxed: gently urged
channeled: directed, focused
steady diet: constant exposure
smog: air pollution; mixture of fog and smoke
convenience: suited to one's comfort; ease of use

public transit: public transportation that runs on a regular schedule, such as trains, subways, buses
critical: judgmental; disapproving
vows: promises; declares
barriers: obstacles
conviction: unshakable belief
evokes: brings about; stirs up
passionate: having strong emotions; intense

Recite and Review

1. A mixture of belief and emotion that predisposes a person to respond to other people, objects, or institutions in a positive or negative way is called a(n) _____.
2. Attitudes are able to predict or direct future actions because they summarize our_____ of objects.
3. Dana is convinced that gun control laws reduce crime and violence, while her brother Darius is convinced that gun control laws will have no effect on the rate of crime. Regarding their attitudes toward gun control, these siblings have different _____ components.
4. When Jeanne says she just "loves" going to the beach, she is expressing the _____ component of an attitude.
5. Sean always donates money and supplies to the local animal shelter. This illustrates the _____ component of Sean's attitude.
6. Attitudes orient us to the social world; and in so doing, they prepare us to _____ in certain ways.
7. If you oppose pollution and support clean air and water because a nearby factory has caused smog in your community and killed all the fish in the river near your house, you acquired your attitude regarding pollution because of personal experience, or _____.
8. Although your friends rave about a particular restaurant, you received poor service and cold food on your visit to this restaurant. Thus, because of this chance event, you have a very unfavorable attitude toward this restaurant due to _____.
9. You are planning a camping trip this weekend and overhear two students in your class talking about camping and canoeing at a particular park that you have never visited. Your favorable attitude toward this park and decision to go camping at this park is due to a(n) _____ with others.
10. Although you wanted to go to the movies, your friends want to go bowling. Your now favorable attitude toward going bowling occurred because of group _____.
11. If both parents belong to the same political party, chances are that their children will belong to that same party as adults, which illustrates how attitudes are formed through _____.
12. Your favorable attitude toward and donation to an organization helping with the Haiti earthquake relief was formed through the information you saw on the television and Internet. This illustrates how your attitudes can be influenced by the _____.
13. Frequent viewers of TV violence tend to mistrust others and overestimate their own chances of being harmed. This is called the _____.
14. Although you have decided to cook healthier and eat more fruits and vegetables, you come home late from college so hungry and with two reports to write. So, you "throw a pizza" in the oven. Your attitude about eating healthier was not acted on, at least temporarily, because of the immediate _____.
15. You are out with some of your new co-workers and decide not to participate in a heated discussion regarding politics because of how your co-workers might _____ your attitude.

877

16. You decide to start walking for a half hour as soon as you get home from work. However, you soon revert back to coming home from work and eating a snack in front of the television. Thus, developing a new attitude toward exercise was affected by a long-standing _____.

17. Major changes in personal behavior can occur when attitudes are held with passionate _____.

Connections

1. ___ attitude
2. ___ belief component
3. ___ emotional component
4. ___ action component
5. ___ direct contact
6. ___ chance conditioning
7. ___ interaction with others
8. ___ group membership
9. ___ child rearing
10. ___ mean worldview
11. ___ conviction

a. attitude formed through pressures to conform
b. how one tends to act toward the object of an attitude
c. regarding the world as a dangerous and threatening place often because of being exposed to TV violence
d. acquiring an attitude through discussion with people holding a particular attitude
e. mixture of belief and emotion that predisposes a person to respond to other people, objects, or groups in a positive or negative way
f. effects of parental values, beliefs, and practices
g. unshakable belief that evokes strong emotion
h. what a person thinks about the object of an attitude
i. attitude formation due to personal experience
j. learning that takes place by coincidence
k. one's feelings toward the object of an attitude

Check Your Memory

1. TRUE or FALSE An attitude is a mixture of belief and emotion that predisposes a person to respond to other people, objects, or institutions in a positive or negative way.
2. TRUE or FALSE What you think or believe about the object of an attitude constitutes the emotional component of an attitude.
3. TRUE or FALSE Donating money or providing other support to a particular organization would constitute the belief component of an attitude.
4. TRUE or FALSE After helping out at the local food pantry and seeing how much it helps others, you buy extra can goods and other food stuffs to donate each month with your favorable attitude of the pantry being acquired through group membership.
5. TRUE or FALSE Although you have never met the candidate or heard her speak, you are planning to vote for her because your friends are supporting this candidate, which means your attitude toward the candidate was formed through direct contact.

6.   TRUE or FALSE   Although your friends love the new restaurant, your only visit to this eatery included a burned meal and the waiter spilling iced tea in your lap, which means that chance conditioning led to your unfavorable attitude toward the restaurant.

7.   TRUE or FALSE   If both parents belong to the same political party, chances are that their children will belong to that party as adults.

8.   TRUE or FALSE   Ninety-nine percent of North American homes have a television set, which is on an average of more than seven hours a day.

9.   TRUE or FALSE   Frequent viewers of TV violence develop a mean worldview, in which they regard the world as a dangerous and threatening place.

10.   TRUE or FALSE   Although Laura has decided to bike from her apartment to her college classes, she awakens late one morning and rushes to class in her car because the immediate consequence of being late weighed heavily on her transportation decision.

11.   TRUE or FALSE   Because Rachel supports a different candidate than the majority of her customers, she does not speak up during political discussions because she might lose customers to her shop, which illustrates that her attitude about speaking up is based on a long-standing habit.

12.   TRUE or FALSE   Although there are often large differences between attitudes and public behavior, the barriers to action typically fall when a person holds an attitude with conviction.

Module 15.4 Attitudes and Persuasion

Attitude Change—Meet the "Seekers"

Survey Question: Under what conditions is persuasion most effective?

Language Development Guide

Seekers: cult that developed in Chicago in 1954; its leader Marion Keech claimed that she had received messages from the planet Clarion that a flood would destroy most of North America, but her sect would be evacuated from earth by flying saucers

Bennington College: private liberal arts college in Vermont established in 1932; started out as private college for women; now co-ed

conservative: favoring traditional values; tending to oppose change

liberal: broad-minded; tolerant; favoring change and reform; protect individual freedoms; distribute wealth more evenly

typified: illustrated; demonstrated

stick to: continue believing in

deliberate: on purpose

blitz: bombardment; onslaught

clashing: conflicting; disagreeing

consistency: stability; constancy

endangers: jeopardizes; puts in danger

resolve: put an end to; settle

"don't bother me with the facts, my mind is made up": means they don't want to listen to any information, they have already decided; also a song by Shakira

bitter: very unpleasant

group break up: disband; not together as a group anymore

accomplishment: deed; triumph

environmental activist: to improve the environment would be willing to directly and openly protest through demonstrations, marches, etc.

"inherited" a car: in this case inheritance is not through death, but he got his parents' old car
    when they got a new one
barge: large car
antiquated: old-fashioned; in need of updating
gas-guzzler: a car or truck that uses a lot of gasoline
environmentalism: concern for the environment and supporter of political and social reforms to
    improve it
inefficient: uneconomical; wasteful
consonant thoughts: in agreement or harmony with something
dissonant thoughts: incompatible; conflicting
perceived choice: apparent; supposed
hectic: frantic; wild
contrary: opposite
lure: trap, draw in
reassure: comfort; support
white lie: harmless falsehood; usually told to avoid distress or embarrassment for self or others

Recite and Review

1. Any group that an individual identifies with and uses as a standard for social comparison is
    called one's _____ group.
2. In Newcomb's study of Bennington College students, both the college and the students'
    parents would be considered to be _____ groups for all the students.
3. For the Bennington College students whose views became more liberal, the college would be
    considered their _____ group.
4. Parnell is deliberately attempting to change that attitudes or beliefs of the juvenile delinquents
    he tutors through information, arguments, and discussion. Parnell's attempt at attitude change
    is called _____.
5. In deliberately attempting to change attitudes, the success or failure of this endeavor can be
    understood if we consider the message, the audience, and the _____.
6. Whether attitudes are likely to be changed depends a great deal on the likeability,
    expressiveness, trustworthiness, and expertise of the _____.
7. In changing a person's attitude, the message should appeal to a person's _____.
8. The message should provide a clear course of action that can produce personally desirable
    results or reduce the person's _____.
9. The message should state clear-cut conclusions and should be backed up by _____.
10. Both sides of the argument should be presented in the case of a(n) _____ -informed
    audience.
11. Only one side should be presented in the case of a(n) _____ informed audience.
12. We sometimes change our attitudes in response to external persuasion, while sometimes
    attitude change can occur due to the internal process of _____.
13. The influential theory that states that contradicting or clashing thoughts cause discomfort is
    _____.
14. People have a need for their thoughts, perceptions, and images of themselves to be
    _____.
15. After the predictions of Mrs. Keech and the Seekers regarding the destruction of North
    America did not come true, they had a need to convince others they were right, which
    illustrates the theory of _____.
16. LaShawn is an environmentalist but drives a gas-guzzling car. To reduce the clash between
    these two images of himself, he could decide that cars are not really a major environmental
    problem. Thus, he has dealt with the clashing images by changing his _____.

880

17. To reduce the clash between the images of himself as an environmentalist and a driver of a gas-guzzling car, LaShawn could decide that he would only drive the car when it was impossible to bike or take the bus. Thus, he has dealt with these clashing images by changing his _____.

18. The clash between his environmentalism and his use of an inefficient car could be reduced by LaShawn deciding that it was more important to support the environment through political action and donations than to worry about how he gets to his college classes. In this case, he reduced the clash of images by changing the importance of the _____ thoughts.

19. If LaShawn decides that it is a good use of the resources used when the car was manufactured for him to keep driving the old car, then he reduced the clash between his environmental image and his car driving image by adding _____ thoughts.

20. LaShawn decides that this semester is just too hectic for him to take the bus or ride his bike. So, even though it clashes with his environmental image, he plans to drive the gas guzzling car because he has reduced the amount of his _____.

21. The amount of dissonance we feel is affected by the amount of justification for acting _____ our beliefs.

22. In a classic study in which college students did an extremely boring task and then were asked to help lure others into the experiment by pretending that the task was interesting with some being paid one dollar for lying and other being paid $20 for lying. The students who changed their negative opinion and now thought the task was "pleasant" and "interesting" were the ones who were paid _____.

23. The degree to which a person's actions are explained by rewards or other circumstances is known as _____.

Connections

1. ____ reference group
2. ____ membership group
3. ____ persuasion
4. ____ cognitive dissonance
5. ____ strategies to reduce cognitive dissonance
6. ____ justification

a. uncomfortable clash between self-image, thoughts, beliefs, attitudes, or perceptions and one's behavior

b. group to which one belongs

c. degree to which a person's actions are explained by rewards or other circumstances

d. add consonant thoughts; reduce the amount of perceived choice

e. deliberate attempt to change attitudes or beliefs with information and arguments

f. group that an individual identifies with and uses as a standard for social comparison

Check Your Memory

1. TRUE or FALSE   Any group that a person belongs to is called his or her reference group.

2. TRUE or FALSE   In Theodore Newcomb's Bennington College study, the students who shifted significantly from their conservative values to the more liberal views of the college still viewed their parents and hometown friends as their primary reference groups.

3. TRUE or FALSE   Persuasion is any deliberate attempt to change attitudes or beliefs through information and arguments.

4. TRUE or FALSE   The communicator of a persuasive argument will be more successful if he or she is an expert on the topic.

5. TRUE or FALSE   The communicator of the persuasive message will be more successful if he or she appears to gain nothing if the audience accepts the message.

6. TRUE or FALSE   A message will be more persuasive if it is not backed up by a lot of facts or statistics and allows the listener to come to his or her own conclusion.

7. TRUE or FALSE   If a message is repeated frequently, it will lose its effectiveness and will not be persuasive.

8. TRUE or FALSE   Both sides of the argument should be presented if the audience is poorly informed, while only one side should be presented if the audience is well-informed.

9. TRUE or FALSE   The theory of cognitive dissonance states that contradictory or clashing thoughts cause discomfort.

10. TRUE or FALSE   Inconsistency in thoughts can motivate people to make their thoughts or attitudes agree with their actions.

11. TRUE or FALSE   Smokers who continue to smoke although they know it is dangerous may reduce the cognitive dissonance of these thoughts by changing their attitude and believing that smoking is not really that dangerous.

12. TRUE or FALSE   According to cognitive dissonance theory, after publicly committing themselves to their beliefs, people are less likely to maintain consistency in their thoughts and will be less likely to try to convince others.

13. TRUE or FALSE   If you know smoking is dangerous but tell yourself that your work and school schedule is so hectic that you cannot deal with the headaches and withdrawal symptoms right now, you have decreased your cognitive dissonance by reducing the amount of perceived choice you have.

14. TRUE or FALSE   If you had planned to take the bus or bike to classes to cut down on air pollution from your car emissions but decide that it is more important to support environmental issues politically than to worry about how you get to class, then you have reduced your cognitive dissonance by adding consonant thoughts to the issue.

15. TRUE or FALSE   The amount of justification for acting contrary to your attitudes and beliefs affects how much dissonance you feel.

16. TRUE or FALSE   In a classic study in which college students did an extremely boring task and then were asked to help lure others into the experiment by pretending that the task was interesting, the students paid $20 for lying to others changed their attitude and later rated the task as "pleasant."

Critical Thinking Questions

1. Students entering a college gym are asked to sign a banner promoting water conservation. Later, the students shower at the gym. What effect would you expect signing the banner to have on how long students stay in the showers?

2. Cognitive dissonance theory predicts that false confessions obtained during brainwashing are not likely to bring about lasting changes in attitudes. Why?

Module 15.5 Prejudice and Intergroup Conflict

Prejudice—Attitudes That Injure

Survey Question: What causes prejudice and intergroup conflict?

Language Development Guide

intergroup: occurring between two social groups
heterosexualism: the belief that heterosexuality is better or more natural than homosexuality

prevalent: common

racial profiling: the policy of some law enforcement agencies to attribute criminal intentions to specific ethnic groups and to stop and question them more often than other ethnic groups

cited: issued a traffic ticket; fined

infractions: failure to comply

cracked: broken

illegal lane change: when driving switching lanes on the highway at a time or place where it is dangerous, such as in an intersection, when a yellow line is present, on a bridge, etc.

detained: delayed; temporary in police custody

rude awakening: experiencing a severe shock when you discover the truth of a situation

debases: shames; demeans; disgraces; dishonors

accessories: those who merely know about it (the crime)

displaced aggression: redirecting the hostility to a target other than the actual source of one's frustration

"foreign": from another country

bullied: mistreating a weaker person

depiction: being shown

distinguished: famous; notable

anti-Semitism: prejudice against Jews

"at the center": as the basis for all comparisons

fascism: tendency toward strong autocratic or dictatorial control

virtues: good, desirable qualities

tireless: industrious; determined

patriotic: expressing love and loyalty to one's country

abolished: put an end to; eliminate

covet: want; long for; crave

discount: disregard

bigotry: prejudice; intolerance

runs deep: deeply rooted; entrenched; extensive

Recite and Review

1. A negative emotional attitude held toward members of a specific social group is referred to as _____.

2. Brett was not hired for a job at a government facility. It was later discovered that Brett was not hired because he was 55 years old. This illegal hiring practice is referred to as _____.

3. Santana was denied housing in an apartment complex because she is Hispanic, which illustrates an illegal practice known as _____.

4. If a person is not allowed to join a particular club due to their gender, then this illegal practice is called _____.

5. The belief that heterosexuality is better or more natural than homosexuality is called _____.

6. In general, when people treat members of various social groups differently in circumstances where their rights or treatment should be identical, the practice is referred to as _____.

7. William is an African American, who was driving from his boss' house in an unfamiliar part of the city when he was stopped by police for no reason and asked to get out of his car. William is the victim of "_____."

8. Blaming a person or a group for the actions of others or for conditions not of their making is called _____.

9. When hostilities triggered by frustration are redirected at "safer" targets, it is called _____.

10. In a classic experiment conducted at a summer camp for young men, the men were given a difficult test they all failed and which caused them to miss a trip to the movies. Attitudes toward Mexicans and Japanese were measured before the test and after the men had failed the test and missed the movie. After being frustrated by the test, the participants in this study, all European Americans, consistently rated members of the two ethnic groups _____.

11. After the September 11, 2001 terrorist attack in the U.S., people who looked "foreign" were often treated with misdirected hostility, also called _____ aggression.

12. Many children show signs of race bias by the time they are _____ years of age.

13. According to Gordon Allport, a person that perceives members of another social group as a threat to his or her own interests, such as being competition for a job, is exhibiting a source of prejudice known as _____ prejudice.

14. Your friends see you talking to a member of another social group at your college, and they tell you that they are disappointed in you for talking to "this" other person and expect you not to do it again. If you succumb to the expectations of your friends, you are exhibiting what Gordon Allport called _____ prejudice.

15. Theodore Adorno and his associates found that some people tend to have a personality marked by rigidity, inhibition, and oversimplification. Adorno and associated would describe a person with these characteristics as a(n) _____ personality.

16. Persons with the personality described by Adorno and associates tend to show prejudice towards all _____.

17. If you consider your own ethnic group to be superior to all others, then you would be exhibiting _____.

18. To measure the qualities of a prejudice-prone personality, one would use the _____ scale.

19. "People can be divided into two distinct classes, the weak and the strong" and "If people would talk less and work more, everybody would be better off" are two statements that would be found on the scale used to measure prejudice-prone personality and are considered _____ beliefs.

20. Children, who were severely punished and learned to fear authority and covet it at an early age, often grow up to have a(n) _____ personality.

Part 1: Connections

1. ___ prejudice

2. ___ discrimination

3. ___ displaced aggression

4. ___ authoritarian personality

5. ___ ethnocentrism

6. ___ F scale

a. pattern characterized by rigidity, inhibition, prejudice, and an excessive concern with power and obedience

b. redirecting aggression to a target other than the actual source of one's frustration

c. placing one's own group or race at the center and rejecting all other groups but one's own

d. measures qualities associated with fascism or authoritarian beliefs

e. negative emotional attitude held against members of a particular group of people

f. treating members of various social groups differently in circumstances where their rights or treatment should be identical

884

Part 2: Connections

1. ___ racism
2. ___ sexism
3. ___ ageism
4. ___ heterosexism
5. ___ scapegoating
6. ___ personal prejudice
7. ___ group prejudice

a. prejudicial attitudes held toward persons who are perceived as a direct threat to one's own interests
b. institutionalized tendency that affects the hiring of the young and old
c. blaming a person or a group for the actions of others or for conditions not of their making; based on displaced aggression
d. institutionalized prejudice based on race
e. prejudice held out of conformity to group views
f. belief that is reflected in prejudice toward homosexuals
g. institutionalized prejudice based solely on gender

Check Your Memory

1. TRUE or FALSE   Discrimination is defined as a negative emotional attitude held toward members of a specific social group, while prejudice refers to treating members of social groups differently in circumstances where their treatment should be identical.
2. TRUE or FALSE   The belief that heterosexuality is better or more natural than homosexuality is referred to as sexism.
3. TRUE or FALSE   If the middle-aged professors at your college are not given new computers or sent to workshops on new teaching methods, then your college is exhibiting ageism.
4. TRUE or FALSE   Discrimination prevents people from doing things they should be able to do, such as buying a house, getting a job, voting, or attending a high-quality school.
5. TRUE or FALSE   In many cities, African American drivers have been the target of "racial profiling," in which they are stopped by police without reason.
6. TRUE or FALSE   Blaming a person or a group for the actions of others or for conditions not of their making is called scapegoating.
7. TRUE or FALSE   Scapegoating is a type of reaction formation.
8. TRUE or FALSE   In a classic experiment conducted at a summer camp for young men, the European American men, who were frustrated by a difficult test and a missed outing, rated Mexican and Japanese groups lower than they did before being frustrated.
9. TRUE or FALSE   After the September 11, 2001 terrorist attacks in the U.S., people who looked "foreign" became targets for displaced anger and hostility.
10. TRUE or FALSE   Subtle influences, such as parents' attitudes, the depiction of people in books and on TV, and exposure to children of other races, can have an impact on whether prejudice develops or not.
11. TRUE or FALSE   Children rarely show race bias until they are seven or eight years old.
12. TRUE or FALSE   Once prejudices are established, they prevent us from accepting more positive experiences that could reverse the damage.
13. TRUE or FALSE   Gordon Allport concluded that there were three types of prejudice: ethnocentricity, fascism, and dogmatism.

14. TRUE or FALSE   If you viewed members of a social group as a direct threat to your own interests, you would be exhibiting group prejudice.

15. TRUE or FALSE   If your co-workers expect you to conform to their opinions regarding various social groups, you are exhibiting personal prejudice.

16. TRUE or FALSE   The authoritarian personality is characterized by rigidity, inhibition, prejudice, and oversimplification in thinking.

17. TRUE or FALSE   People who have an authoritarian personality tend to be prejudiced against all out-groups.

18. TRUE or FALSE   When a person views his or her own ethnic group as superior to all others, this person is said to be exhibiting ethnocentrism.

19. TRUE or FALSE   If you were taking a test on which you had to agree or disagree with statements, such as "People can be divided into two distinct classes: the weak and the strong," you are most likely taking the P scale with the P standing for "prejudiced."

20. TRUE or FALSE   Authoritarians tend to be rather closed-minded.

21. TRUE or FALSE   Authoritarians tend to be unhappy people.

22. TRUE or FALSE   Authoritarian personalities most often result from permissive parenting in which children did not receive enough punishment for misbehavior.

Critical Thinking Question
In court trials, defense lawyers sometimes try to identify and eliminate prospective jurors who have authoritarian personality traits. Can you guess why?

Module 15.5 Prejudice and Intergroup Conflict
Intergroup Conflict—The Roots of Prejudice

Language Development Guide
by-product: result; offshoot; side-effect
foster: encourage, cause
jarring: harsh and unpleasant
strife: bitter rivalry and conflict
exploited: used unfairly
betrayed: disloyal to; deceived; let down
amplified: made stronger
blue-collar: member of working class who typically performs manual labor
rednecks: slang term for member of white working class, rural poor from the southern U.S.; term originated from white farm laborers getting a sunburned neck from working in the fields
perpetuate: keep alive; continue; maintain
affirmations: assertions; positive statements
ethnic heritage: legacy and traditions of one's culture
abide: put up with
demeaning: humiliating; negative
aviation: having to do with aircraft
slip in his memory: minor forgetfulness
confirm: prove
memory lapses: temporary failure in remembering
"chokes": to become so tense and nervous about doing poorly during a performance that one actually does poorly
amassed: gathered; collected
"an exception to the rule": something that differs from the usual

crude: coarse; rough; offensive; vulgar

thinly veiled: only slightly disguised or hidden, as if covered by a thin scarf

raw: crude, basic

"the benefit of the doubt": choosing to take a favorable opinion of someone without any evidence

recess: break from classes

mingling: interacting

trivial: unimportant; minor; insignificant

belittle: put down; demean

viciousness: cruelty

plain: simply

unmistakable: obvious

infinitely: considerably; noticeably

simplistic: easy; straightforward

popularize: promote

witnessing: observing something personally

graphically: vividly

convey: express

American heartland: generally Midwestern or north central U.S., which consists of the twelve states: Wisconsin, Nebraska, Illinois, Indiana, Iowa, Minnesota, Missouri, North Dakota, South Dakota, Ohio, Kansas, and Michigan

urban: related to the city

coasts: those regions that border the Atlantic and Pacific Oceans

spectrum: range

highlights: emphasizes; make prominent

political persuasions: beliefs about how governments should be organized and run

tolerant: open-minded; understanding

polarizing: sharp division

intermediate: in-between; midway

equal footing: fair basis

induce: cause; generate

gang colors: particular colors, usually of clothing that identify members of particular groups of youths

vandalism: defacement or destruction of someone else's property

cooperative: working together

staked out: claimed

territory: area; region

bordered: nearly; close to

baited: tried to bring into conflict

raided: attacked and stole items or created a mess

free-for-all: impulsive, disorganized fight without rules

staged: created

we're all in the same boat: we will succeed together or all fail unity: in harmony; state of being as one

peacekeepers: division of the United Nations whose mission is to help countries in conflict to create conditions of lasting harmony or peaceful interactions

nuclear holocaust: an atomic war that makes the Earth uninhabitable

posed: put forth

religious extremism: ideology outside the norm or mainstream for that religion and often includes violent actions against those who believe differently

integrating public schools: bringing students of different racial or ethnic groups into an equal association within the school; also known as desegregation, or ending the policy of separate schools for different races

theoretically: according to theory, but not when applied in the real world

887

jigsaw puzzle: a puzzle consisting of small irregularly cut pieces that are to be fit together to form a picture

contribution: input

cross-group friendships: friendships between people from different races and ethnic groups

interdependent: providing assistance and support to each other

Recite and Review

1. Contact with people from other groups is often limited by one's group _____.
2. The bloody clash of opposing forces in the Middle East, Africa, Ireland, and Hometown, U.S.A. are reminders of the widespread occurrence of _____ conflict.
3. Common triggers for hostility between groups involve shared beliefs concerning distrust, vulnerability, distrust, and _____.
4. Oversimplified images of people in various groups are called social _____.
5. Conflicts are almost always amplified by stereotyped images of _____-group members.
6. In general, the top three categories on which most stereotypes are based are sex, race, and _____.
7. People are simplified into "us" and "them" categories by _____.
8. Stereotypes are mainly used to maintain _____ over people.
9. When a person is stereotyped, even if it is demeaning, the easiest thing for her or him to do is to abide by others' _____.
10. By placing people into a distorted category, stereotypes tend to rob people of their _____.
11. When a person fears being evaluation, negative stereotypes can actually decrease a person's performance since stereotypes tend to have a self-_____ quality.
12. Psychologist Claude Steel has found evidence that victims of stereotyping tend to feel threatened when they think they are being judged in terms of a stereotype, which is referred to as _____.
13. In an experiment when African American students were told the test they were taking was measuring academic ability, their performance as compared to European American students was _____.
14. When African American students were told the test they were taking was a laboratory problem-solving task, their performance as compared to European American students was _____.
15. Women who were reminded that "women aren't good at math" before taking a math test, tended to score _____.
16. When a prejudiced person meets a pleasant or likable member of a rejected group, the out-group member tends to be perceived as an "exception to the rule," not as evidence against the _____.
17. Some elements of prejudice are difficult to change, since they are _____.
18. Because many people realize that crude and obvious racism is socially unacceptable, they may express prejudice in thinly veiled forms known as _____ prejudice.
19. Modern racists find ways to rationalize their prejudice so that it is not based on raw racism but on _____.
20. If an African-American candidate and a European-American candidate both apply for a job and are both only moderately qualified for the position, the person most likely to be hired if the hiring decision is made by a European-American will be the _____ candidate.
21. The elementary school teacher who sought to give her pupils direct experience with prejudice by giving the blue-eyed children more privileges than the brown-eyed children was _____.
22. The "blue-eyed-brown-eyed" experiment showed that in less than one day it was possible to get children to hate each other because of eye color and differences in power, prestige, and privileges, which are referred to as _____.

23. According to a political shorthand symbolism that has developed in the U.S., people who are supposed to be Republican, conservative, middle-class, rural, religious, and live in the American heartland are symbolized by the color _____.

24. According to a political shorthand symbolism that has developed in the U.S., people who are supposed to be Democrat, liberal, upper class, urban, nonreligious, and live on the coasts are symbolized by the color _____.

25. The end result of the political shorthand that developed in the U.S. after the 2000 election is that there has been an increase in between-group prejudice because this complex American social world has been reduced to two oversimplified _____.

26. According to Conor Seyle and Matthew Newman, a better approach is to recognize that America is made up of a full spectrum of political, social, religious, and economic views and that most Americans would be better symbolized by the color _____.

27. Several lines of thought, including cognitive dissonance theory, suggest that prejudice and stereotyping can be reduced by groups in conflict having more frequent _____ contact.

28. Many school districts in the United States have begun requiring students to wear uniforms to help reduce in-group/out-group distinctions caused by _____.

29. Research in which mixed-race groups were formed at work, in the laboratory, and at schools found that personal contact with a disliked group will induce friendly behavior, respect, and liking but only if the personal contact is on an equal footing and is _____.

30. In the camp experiment on reducing intergroup conflict between the "Rattlers" and the Eagles," the conflict was finally reduced by creating emergencies that required the members of both groups to _____.

31. A goal that exceeds or overrides all others and creates a "we're all in the same boat" effect on perceptions of group membership is called a(n) _____ goal.

32. The unity that prevailed in the United States for months after the September 11 terrorist attacks shows the power of _____ goals.

33. One reason that children have trouble learning to like and understand each other is due to the _____ nature of schools.

34. The social psychologist who pioneered a way to apply superordinate goals to ordinary classrooms when he developed the "jigsaw" classroom was _____.

35. Rather than competition between students, the "jigsaw classroom" emphasizes _____.

36. Students in jigsaw classroom must depend on one another to meet each other's goals. In other words, jigsaw classrooms create _____.

37. Compared with children in traditional classrooms, children in jigsaw groups are _____ prejudiced.

38. Compared with children in traditional classrooms, children in jigsaw groups have more positive attitudes toward schools, their self-esteem increases, and their grades _____.

Connections

1. ___ social stereotypes
2. ___ stereotype threat
3. ___ symbolic prejudice
4. ___ status inequalities
5. ___ "reds" in U.S. politics

a. goal that exceeds or overrides all others
b. characterized as liberal, upper class, urban, nonreligious, and live on the coasts
c. social interaction that occurs on an equal footing, without obvious differences in power or status
d. condition in which two or more persons must depend on one another to meet each person's needs or goals
e. differences in the power, prestige, or privileges of two or more persons or groups

6. ___ "blues" in U.S. politics

7. ___ equal-status contact

8. ___ superordinate goal

9. ___ mutual interdependence

10. ___ jigsaw classroom

f. feeling vulnerable when thinking one is being judged in terms of a stereotype

g. method of reducing prejudice in which each student receives only part of the information needed to complete a project or prepare for a test

h. characterized as conservative, middle-class, rural, religious, and live in the American heartland

i. prejudice that is expressed in a disguised fashion

j. oversimplified images of the traits of individuals who belong to a particular social group

Check Your Memory

1. TRUE or FALSE A by-product of group membership is that it often limits contact with people in other groups.

2. TRUE or FALSE Shared beliefs concerning superiority, injustice, vulnerability, and distrust are common triggers for hostility between groups.

3. TRUE or FALSE Conflicts are almost always amplified by stereotyped images of out-group members.

4. TRUE or FALSE In general, the top two categories on which most stereotypes are based are sexual orientation and religion.

5. TRUE or FALSE Stereotypes are oversimplified images and often include a mixture of positive and negative qualities.

6. TRUE or FALSE When a person is stereotyped, the easiest thing for him or her to do is to angrily protest this stereotype.

7. TRUE or FALSE Negative stereotypes can have a self-fulfilling quality that is especially true in situations in which a person's abilities are evaluated.

8. TRUE or FALSE According to psychologist Claude Steele, victims of stereotyping tend to feel stereotype threat, in which the anxiety of being judged lowers their performance and seemingly confirms the stereotype.

9. TRUE or FALSE In an experiment when African American students were told the test they were taking was a laboratory problem-solving task, their performance was significantly lower than that of the European American students.

10. TRUE or FALSE In an experiment, women, who were reminded that "women aren't good at math" before a test was given, performed significantly higher on this test because of their motivation to disprove this stereotype.

11. TRUE or FALSE When modern racists find ways to rationalize their prejudice so that it seems based on issues other than raw racism, this disguised racism is referred to as personal prejudice.

12. TRUE or FALSE When a prejudiced person meets a pleasant or likeable member of a rejected group, the prejudiced person will see this person as evidence against his or her stereotype with his prejudice being significantly reduced.

13. TRUE or FALSE Because some elements of prejudice are unconscious, they are very difficult to change.

890

14. TRUE or FALSE   If an African-American candidate and a European-American candidate both apply for a job and are both only moderately qualified for the position, the person most likely to be hired if the hiring decision is made by a European-American will be the African-American candidate.

15. TRUE or FALSE   Gordon Allport conducted the experiment on prejudice that involved giving blue-eyed children more privileges than brown-eyed children in an elementary classroom.

16. TRUE or FALSE   The elementary classroom experiment on prejudice showed that in less than one day it was possible to get children to hate each other because of eye color and status inequalities.

17. TRUE or FALSE   In the elementary classroom prejudice experiment, the feelings of superiority in the blue-eyed children and inferiority of the brown-eyed children were short lived, because two days later the roles of the children were reversed with the same destructive effects occurring again, but this time in reverse.

18. TRUE or FALSE   The "red" and "blue" shorthand used to denote the two political parties in the U.S. has reduced the complex American social world into two oversimplified stereotypes, leading to an increase in between-group prejudice.

19. TRUE or FALSE   The "reds are supposed to be Democrat, liberal, upper class, urban, nonreligious, and live on the coasts, while the 'blues are Republican, conservative, middle-class, rural, religious, and live in the American heartland.

20. TRUE or FALSE   According to Conor Seyle and Matthew Newman, Americans are made up of a full spectrum of political, social, religious, and economic views and that most Americans should be considered "purple," rather than "red" or "blue.

21. TRUE or FALSE   Interacting on an equal footing without obvious differences in power or status is referred to as superordinate contact status.

22. TRUE or FALSE   The conclusion from research involving mixed-race groups being formed at work and at schools is that personal contact with a disliked group will induce friendly behavior, respect, and liking but only when personal contact is cooperative and on an equal footing.

23. TRUE or FALSE   In the experiment to reduce intergroup conflict between two groups of boys (the "Rattlers" and the "Eagles") at a camp, the researcher found that holding meetings between group leaders and having the groups eat together significantly reduced the conflict between the two groups.

24. TRUE or FALSE   Intergroup conflict between the two groups of boys at the camp significantly increased when the boys had to work together to repair the water supply system at the camp.

25. TRUE or FALSE   The power of superordinate goals can be seen in the unity that prevailed in the United States and throughout much of the rest of the world for months after the September 11 terrorist attacks.

26. TRUE or FALSE   Superordinate goals are effective because they create group individuality and group independence.

27. TRUE or FALSE   Elliot Aronson's "jigsaw" classrooms emphasize competition rather than cooperation.

28. TRUE or FALSE   In a jigsaw classroom, each child is given a "piece" of the information needed to complete a project or prepare for a test.

29. TRUE or FALSE   Compared with children in traditional classrooms, children in jigsaw groups are less prejudiced and like their classmates more.

30. TRUE or FALSE   Compared with children in traditional classrooms, children in jigsaw groups make slightly poorer grades and have a less positive attitude toward school.

Module 15.6 Aggression and Prosocial Behavior
Aggression—The World's Most Dangerous Animal
Survey Question: How do psychologists explain human aggression?

Language Development Guide

tragedy: misfortune; disaster; heartbreaking
revulsion: strong dislike; disgust
pressing: urgent
Homo sapiens: scientific classification for humans
staggering: very large, unbelievable
offer sad testimony: provide heartbreaking proof
realities: actual occurrence
"killer instinct": a capacity to kill
inhibit: restrain; holds back
dispute: clash; contest
lunge: jump at
dominance: authority; supremacy
bare its throat: lifting one's head, revealing the neck; to show vulnerability
submission: surrender; giving in
intuitive: spontaneous; insightful
appeal: charm; attraction
the Arapesh, the Senoi, the Navajo, the Eskimo: Arapesh and Senoi are tribes in Malaysia, the Navajo a Native American tribe, the Eskimo a tribe in Alaska and northern Canada
threshold: limit, starting point
indication: suggestion; sign
intoxicating: capable of making someone drunk
American Quakers: a sect of the Religious Society of Friends founded in the 1660s; tolerant of other religions; favor cooperation; committed to nonviolence
Amish: orthodox religious denomination that is a subgroup of Mennonite churches with Amish believing in simple living with little modern conveniences and committed to nonviolence (657)
nipped: bitten
insulted: verbally abused
a moment's thought will show: if you think about it for a short time you will come up with an example
spectators: those who like to watch
universal invitation: commonly provokes
trappings: tools, clothing, gear, appearances
prime: major
pipe bombing: homemade explosive devices
wielding: handling
sweltering: uncomfortable hot; very hot
bean balls: in baseball, pitches thrown to hit another player in the head
an almost nonstop parade: many; endless
arson: crime of intentionally setting a fire
villains: bad guys
problematic: posing a problem that is difficult to resolve

mugging: street robbery
sanitized: made more acceptable by removing unpleasant aspects
gross: disgusting
gut wrenching: causing mental or emotional distress; agony
graphic: vivid; detailed; lifelike
aggression begets aggression: fighting causes revenge and more fighting
mixed martial arts: use of a wide variety of fighting techniques
drain off: remove; use up; deplete
spiral of aggression: each response to aggression increases in intensity
glorify it: adore it; worship it
pulling the plug: discontinuing; in this case cutting the TV off permanently
emulate: imitate; copy
altruistic: unselfish concern for others

Recite and Review

1. For a time, the City Zoo of Los Angeles, California, had on display two examples of the world's most dangerous animal. In the cage was the species _____.
2. About 58 million humans were killed by other humans during the 125-year period ending with World War II, which works out to an average of nearly one person per _____.
3. If you intentionally harm another person, you are exhibiting _____.
4. Some theorists argue that we are naturally aggressive creatures, having inherited from our animal ancestors a(n) "_____."
5. Santos studies the natural behavior patterns of animals. He is a(n) _____.
6. Konrad Lorenz believes that the violence of humans has become different from animals because humans lack certain innate patterns found in other animals that _____ aggression.
7. In comparisons to other cultures, the Arapesh, the Senoi, the Navajo, and the Eskimo show _____ aggression.
8. Physiological studies have shown that aggressive behavior can be triggered or ended by certain _____ areas.
9. Researchers have found a relationship between aggression and such physical factors as allergies, specific brain injures and diseases, and _____.
10. For both men and women, increased aggressive behavior is associated with higher levels of the hormone _____.
11. Large percentages of murders and violent crimes have resulted from inhibitions to act aggressively being lowered by the use of _____.
12. Biological factors cannot be considered a direct cause of aggression, but instead they make hostile behavior more likely to occur by lowering one's _____ for aggression.
13. Humans are fully capable of learning to _____ aggression
14. The theory that states that having your goals blocked may lead to aggression is the _____ hypothesis.
15. Having blocked goals may not always lead to aggression. It can also cause a state of "learned helplessness" or to _____ responding.
16. Hostility and aggression can be heightened by insults, high temperature, disgusting odors, pain, and other _____ stimuli.
17. Some cues for aggression, such as angry thoughts, would be considered _____.
18. Cues for aggression, such as certain offensive words and gestures would be considered _____.
19. The fact that murders are more likely to occur in homes where guns are kept illustrate the _____ effect.

20. The theory that proposes that we learn to be aggressive by observing aggression in others is the _____ theory.
21. In the United States during 2008, a violent crime occurred every 23_____.
22. In the United States, the percent of the population who own firearms is approximately _____ percent.
23. The percent of the U.S. population who agree that 'When a boy is growing up, it is very important for him to have a few fistfights" is _____ percent.
24. To explain behavior, such as aggression, social learning theory combines learning principles with cognitive processes, socialization, and _____.
25. Children and adolescents spend about 44.5 hours a week exploring various media with the percent of popular video games that contain violent content being _____ percent.
26. The Internet not only allows children to experience media violence but also to bully or harass others in what is referred to as _____ aggression.
27. The psychologist who showed in his studies of imitation that children may learn new aggressive actions by watching violent or aggressive behavior, or they may learn that violence is "okay" was _____.
28. Watching violent TV and engaging in violent video games may result in the acting out of dangerous impulses that the viewer already has and that normally would be restrained, a process called _____.
29. Watching sanitized media violence or watching the violence in the relaxed and familiar setting of the home can lead to _____ to the violence.
30. Children who are more likely to be involved in fighting, aggressive play, and antisocial behavior at school are the ones who have witnessed violence in their communities, have suffered severe physical punishment, and have been _____ at home.
31. According to psychologist Leonard Eron, the best predictors of how aggressive a young man would be at age 19 was the violence of the television programs he preferred when he was _____ years old.
32. According to Eron, children learn aggressive strategies and actions from TV violence; and because of this, they are more prone to aggress when they face situations or cues that are _____.
33. Other researchers have found that viewers who experience violent media have more aggressive _____.
34. Violent actions are often preceded by violent _____.
35. One study found that elementary school children become less aggressive when the amount of time they spend watching TV and playing video games _____.
36. Children typically are guided by parents' reactions to media and _____ parents' media viewing habits.
37. Parents should help their children to distinguish between fantasy in media and _____.
38. As they appear on the screen, parents should reply to violence, distortions, and _____.
39. Children are more likely to be influenced by media aggression if they _____ with the media characters.
40. It is clear that we need more people who are willing to engage in helpful, altruistic, _____ behavior.

Connections

1. ___ aggression
2. ___ ethologist
3. ___ "killer instinct"
4. ___ indirect biological factors
5. ___ frustration-aggression hypothesis
6. ___ aversive stimuli
7. ___ aggression cues
8. ___ weapons effect
9. ___ social learning theory
10. ___ disinhibition
11. ___ desensitization
12. ___ prosocial behavior

a. any event that produces discomfort or displeasure and can heighten hostility and aggression
b. a reduction in emotional sensitivity to a stimulus
c. observation that guns and knives, etc. serve as strong cues for aggressive behavior
d. the removal of restraint that results in acting out behavior
e. the observation and modeling of aggression explains the occurrence of aggressive behavior
f. actions that are constructive, altruistic, or helpful to others
g. alcohol, hypoglycemia, testosterone, allergies
h. person who studies the natural behavior patterns of animals
i. internal or external signals that are associated with hostility
j. biologically-rooted tendency toward aggression
k. any action carried out with the intention of harming another person
l. having one's goals blocked leads to aggression

Check Your Memory

1. TRUE or FALSE   For a time, the City Zoo of Los Angeles, California, had on display the world's most dangerous animal, which is a gorilla.
2. TRUE or FALSE   Aggression refers to any action carried out with the intension of harming another person.
3. TRUE or FALSE   Ethologist Konrad Lorenz believed that humans lack certain innate patterns that inhibit aggression in animals.
4. TRUE or FALSE   The instinctual theory of aggression does not explain why some individuals or human cultures show little hostility or aggression.
5. TRUE or FALSE   Physiological studies have not found any brain areas that can trigger or end aggressive behavior.
6. TRUE or FALSE   Researchers have found a relationship between aggression and such physical factors as hypoglycemia and allergies.
7. TRUE or FALSE   For both men and women, higher levels of the hormone testosterone may be associated with more aggressive behavior.
8. TRUE or FALSE   Biological factors are considered a direct cause of aggression and raise the threshold for aggression, making aggressive behavior more likely.
9. TRUE or FALSE   A variety of studies show that alcohol is involved in large percentages of murders and violent crimes.
10. TRUE or FALSE   According to the frustration-aggression hypothesis, frustration always leads to aggression in humans.
11. TRUE or FALSE   Aggression can occur in the absence of frustration.

12. TRUE or FALSE   Insults, pain, and disgusting odors are examples of aversive stimuli, which can produce discomfort and heighten hostility and aggression.

13. TRUE or FALSE   Regarding aversive stimuli, there is a strong association between the temperatures at major league baseball games and the number of batters hit by a pitch during those games.

14. TRUE or FALSE   Aggression cues can be internal, such as angry thoughts, or external, such as words or gestures.

15. TRUE or FALSE   A prime example of the weapons effect is the observation that murders are more likely to occur in homes where guns are kept.

16. TRUE or FALSE   Social learning theorists predict that people growing up in nonaggressive cultures will themselves be nonaggressive.

17. TRUE or FALSE   In a national survey conducted in the U.S., only 40 percent agreed that "When a boy is growing up, it is very important for him to have a few fistfights."

18. TRUE or FALSE   Children and adolescents spend an average of 44.5 hours a week exploring various media.

19. TRUE or FALSE   The percent of the popular video games that contain violent content is 33 percent.

20. TRUE or FALSE   The Internet not only allows children to experience media violence but also allows them to directly engage in electronic aggression, through bullying or harassment of others.

21. TRUE or FALSE   Albert Bandura's studies of imitation showed that children may learn new aggressive actions by watching violent or aggressive behavior, or they may learn that violence is "okay."

22. TRUE or FALSE   Watching violent television programs or videogames tends to increase inhibition of aggression, allowing our natural aggressiveness to be restrained.

23. TRUE or FALSE   Heroes on TV are as violent as the villains, and they usually receive praise for their violence.

24. TRUE or FALSE   Media violence tends to be sanitized and unrealistic.

25. TRUE or FALSE   When Victor Cline and his associates showed a bloody fight film to a group of boys, they found that heavy TV viewers showed much more emotion than those who watched little or no TV.

26. TRUE or FALSE   Children who are physically abused at home, those who suffer severe physical punishment, and those who merely witness violence in the community are more likely to be involved in fighting, aggressive play, and antisocial behavior at school.

27. TRUE or FALSE   According to social learning theorists, watching a prizefight or sporting event drains off aggressive urges and decreases aggression behavior.

28. TRUE or FALSE   One of the best predictors of how aggressive a young man would be at age 19 was the violence of the television programs he preferred when he was eight years old.

29. TRUE or FALSE   Researchers have found that viewers who experience violent media have more aggressive thoughts with violent thoughts often preceding violent actions.

30. TRUE or FALSE   Children typically model parents' behavior, including their media viewing habits, and are guided by their parents' reactions to media.

31. TRUE or FALSE   When violent conflicts are shown in television programs, parents should not draw attention to these conflicts by discussing them with the children.

32. TRUE or FALSE   Children who identify with media characters are more likely to be influenced by media aggression.
33. TRUE or FA LSE   Research found that elementary school children become less aggressive when they decreased the amount of time they spend watching TV and playing video games.

Module 15.6 Aggression and Prosocial Behavior

Prosocial Behavior—Helping Others

Survey Question: Why are bystanders so often unwilling to help in an emergency?

Language Development Guide

bystanders: somebody nearby but not involved
fend off: repel; defend
horrifyingly: shockingly; terrifyingly
surveillance: observational
breakdown: failure; disruption
impersonality: absence of human character
dehumanizing: deprived of one's individuality or human qualities
landmark: ground-breaking; breakthrough
stalled: stopped
sparsely: thinly
freeway: multi-laned highway that has no toll or payment for driving on it
apathetic: indifferent, not caring
fainted: sudden, temporary loss of consciousness
scanned: quickly looked over
cast: gave
coolly: without emotion
fake each other out: send misleading messages
underestimated: understated
intercom system: device that allows people in different parts of a building, etc. to speak to each other, but not see each other
confidentiality: privacy
naturalistic experiment: observational study conducted in a real-life setting in which the assignment of treatments has been made "by nature" or chance, not by the experimenter
passed out: became unconscious
keyed-up: anxious or active
empathic: understanding others' feelings
plight: bad situation
norms of fairness: reciprocity; more likely to help others when we ourselves have been helped
de-victimize: helping yourself to be noticed and receive aid in an emergency
suffocation: kill by preventing access to oxygen
Peace Corps: group that sends workers to Third World countries to provide aid
Doctors of the World: physicians that volunteer to travel to other countries to provide free medical care
endeavors: undertakings
sensational: incredible
"We do well by doing good": praise for doing good work (altruistic acts of kindness)

Recite and Review

1. In the deaths of Hugo Tale-Yax in 2010 and Kitty Genovese in 1964, bystanders were unwilling to help in these emergencies and prevent these individuals' deaths. These murder cases illustrate what is known as _____.
2. According to psychologists John Darley and Bibb Latané, people are less likely to help when in the presence of _____ potential helpers.
3. If two motorists have stalled at the roadside, one on a sparsely traveled country road and the other on a busy freeway, the one most likely to receive help is the motorist on the _____.
4. People must pass through four decision points before giving help with the first decision point being to _____ something is happening.
5. Latané and Darley suggest that if you collapse on a crowded sidewalk, few people will see you because of the widely accepted norms against _____ at others in public.
6. In an experiment students were asked to fill out a questionnaire either alone or with several people. When a thick cloud of smoke was blown into the room through a vent, the quickest reaction time occurred when students were filling out the questionnaire _____.
7. In real emergencies, people often underestimate the need for action by appearing calm during the second decision point known as _____ an emergency.
8. The most crucial step in bystander intervention is _____.
9. Groups limit helping by spreading responsibility among several people, which is referred to as a(n) _____.
10. In an experiment, students took part in a group discussion over an intercom system in which students thought they were talking to one person or talking in three-person or six-person groups. During each discussion, a "student" was heard to have an epileptic-like seizure and call out for help. The quickest response time occurred when participants thought they were _____.
11. In a naturalistic experiment staged in a New York City subway, a "victim" pretended to "pass out" in a subway car, sometimes carrying a cane and sometimes carrying a liquor bottle. The "victim" received more help if he was carrying a _____.
12. Many studies suggest that when we see a person in trouble, we are motivated to give aid by a keyed-up feeling referred to as _____.
13. This keyed-up feeling can motivate us to give aid, but only if the rewards of helping outweigh the _____.
14. Potential helpers may feel compassion for the person in need or feel some of the person's pain, fear, or anguish, which is referred to as _____.
15. We will be more motivated to help when the person in need seems to be _____ to ourselves.
16. When we are feeling successful, happy, or fortune, we may feel more _____ to others.
17. The observation that we are most likely to help someone else when we feel emotions, such as empathy, sympathy, and compassion is referred to as the _____ relationship.
18. Persons who give help in one situation tend to perceive themselves as helpful people, thus encouraging them to help in other situations because of this change in _____.
19. We are encouraged to help others who have helped us by norms of _____.
20. In order to make sure you receive help during an emergency, you must "_____" yourself.
21. Since bystanders might run away from a robbery or an assault, one should, in order to be noticed shout "_____!"
22. To make sure you receive help from a bystander, you should point to a bystander and directly _____ responsibility.
23. Regarding gender differences, heroic acts, particularly those that involve physical dangers, are more likely to be performed by _____.

Connections

1. ___ bystander apathy
2. ___ bystander intervention
3. ___ diffusion of responsibility
4. ___ empathic arousal
5. ___ empathy-helping relationship
6. ___ "de-victimizing" yourself

a. involves passing through four decision points before giving help

b. making sure you get noticed and helped in an emergency

c. unwillingness of bystanders to offer help during emergencies or to become involved in others' problems

d. observation that we are most likely to help someone in need when we "feel for" that person and experience emotions such as empathy, sympathy, and compassion

e. emotional arousal that occurs when you feel some of another person's pain, fear, or anguish

f. spreading the responsibility to act among several people, which reduces the likelihood that help will be given to a person in need

Check Your Memory

1. TRUE or FALSE   The deaths of Hugo Tale-Yax in 2010 and Kitty Genovese in 1964 are examples of the bystander effect.
2. TRUE or FALSE   Darley and Latané found that the more potential helpers present in an emergency, the more likely a person is to get help.
3. TRUE or FALSE   If two motorists are stalled at the roadside, one on a sparsely traveled country road and the other on a busy freeway, the one most likely to receive help is the motorist on the busy freeway.
4. TRUE or FALSE   In giving help, people must pass through eight decision points with the first step being to assume responsibility.
5. TRUE or FALSE   Darley and Latané suggest that if you collapse on a crowded sidewalk, few people will see you because of the widely accepted norms against staring at others in public.
6. TRUE or FALSE   In an experiment in which several people in a room noticed smoke entering the room, the majority of people overreacted and ran to the doorway, blocking the exit and slowing down evacuation.
7. TRUE or FALSE   Being in a group limits helping because of a diffusion of responsibility.
8. TRUE or FALSE   In a naturalistic experiment in which a "victim passed out" in a subway car in some cases carrying a cane and in other cases carrying a liquor bottle, people gave more help when the "victim" was carrying a cane.
9. TRUE or FALSE   When a person is in a state of heightened arousal, they are more motivated to give help.
10. TRUE or FALSE   Higher costs of helping, such as great effort, personal risk, or possible embarrassment, rarely decrease helping.
11. TRUE or FALSE   Empathic arousal is especially likely to motivate helping when the person in need seems to be very different from ourselves.
12. TRUE or FALSE   Being in a good mood increases helping.
13. TRUE or FALSE   The empathy-helping relationships states that we are most likely to help someone in need when we "feel for" that person and experience emotions, such as empathy, sympathy, and compassion.
14. TRUE or FALSE   People who see others helping are more likely to offer help themselves.

15. TRUE or FALSE   When a person helps in one situation and sees himself or herself as a helpful person, that person is less likely to feel the need to help in other situations, since they have already helped in the first situation.

16. TRUE or FALSE   The norms of fairness encourage us to help others who have helped us.

17. TRUE or FALSE   To "de-victimize" yourself, you should make sure that you are noticed in an emergency in which you need help.

18. TRUE or FALSE   If you are being robbed or assaulted, it is better to shout "Fire!" since bystanders might run away from a robbery or an assault.

19. TRUE or FALSE   In an emergency situation, it is better to scream loudly than to call out "Help."

20. TRUE or FALSE   If you need help in an emergency, you should directly assign responsibility to a bystander by pointing to someone and saying, "I need YOU to call the police."

21. TRUE or FALSE   The majority of people who perform heroic acts involving physical dangers are men with as many women as men being community volunteers.

22. TRUE or FALSE   The efforts of community volunteers and blood donors contribute to these volunteers' personal growth and make them healthier and happier.

Critical Thinking Question

If media violence contributes to aggressive behavior in our society, do you think it is possible that media could also promote prosocial behavior?

Module 15.7 Psychology in Action
Multiculturalism—Living with Diversity

Survey Question: How can we promote multiculturalism and social harmony?

Language Development Guide

diversity: variety; assortment

tossed salad: metaphor for society in which people are mixed together but maintain their individual identity

melting pot: metaphor for society that is like a soup or molten metals, where materials are blended together to create something new

lingering: lasting; persistent; enduring

forsake: abandon; give up; disown

turn your back: to abandon or ignore

tolerance: open-mindedness; acceptance of different views

"prejudice habit": tendency toward being prejudice

manageable: controllable; convenient

antidotes: cures

negate: cancel out; undo; work against

fall prey to: be tricked and harmed by

in accordance: in agreement with

vicious cycle: difficult situation in which one problem causes another problem that causes the first problem again

provoke: cause

prompts: to act

rivalry: competitiveness

degrade: insult, reduce, demean

emulating: copying

buffer: cushion; shield; protect
construction: creation
intermixed: intermingled through mating
illusion: false idea
puts a premium on: values, emphasizes
fosters: encourages
vanquish: eliminate, erase, destroy
boycott: refusing to buy goods or deal with a business or organization
Confucian-steeped: where the writings of Confucius are common and well-known
sparingly: in a limited way, infrequently
ignorance: lack of knowledge; unaware
friction: conflict, difficulty
kosher: Jewish food purity practices

Recite and Review

1. Today's society is less like a cultural "melting pot" and more like a "_____."
2. If you give equal status, recognition, and acceptance to different ethnic and cultural groups, you are exhibiting _____.
3. People who are not consciously prejudiced may continue to respond emotionally to members of other ethnic groups due to lingering prejudices and _____ learned in childhood.
4. For many people, becoming less prejudiced begins by developing the ability to genuinely appreciate those who differ from us culturally, that is, accepting the value of _____ to the other.
5. When we place people into categories in order to make the social world more manageable, we are _____.
6. When we do put people in categories, we tend to see out-group members as very _____.
7. One of the best antidotes for stereotypes is _____ information.
8. When you meet individuals from various backgrounds, focus on the person, not the _____ attached.
9. In a Canadian study of English-speaking students in a French language program, these English-speaking students became more positive to the French Canadians when they spent most of their waking hours with French Canadians, a program arrangement known as being "_____."
10. Increased contact may be the best way to reduce the intergroup conflict that occurs with more subtle kinds of _____ prejudice.
11. The belief that people generally get what they deserve is called the _____ beliefs.
12. This faulty belief that people get what they deserve amounts to blaming people who are victims of prejudice and _____ for their plight.
13. A person who believes that members of another ethnic group are hostile and unfriendly will probably treat people in that group in ways that provoke hostile and unfriendly response, which reinforces the belief in the stereotype by creating a(n) _____.
14. The rivalry among groups, each of which regards itself as superior to others is called _____.
15. A person who does not need to treat others as inferior in order to feel good about himself or herself has high _____.
16. Each ethnic group has strengths that members of other groups could benefit from emulating, such as African Americans, Asian Americans, and Latinos buffer the stresses of daily life through their _____ networks.

17. From the viewpoint of modern genetics, the concept that has absolutely no meaning and which is merely an illusion based on superficial physical differences and learned ethnic identities is _____.

18. In fact, the best available evidence suggests that all people are descended from the same ancient ancestors with the origin of our species being 100,000 years ago on the continent of _____.

19. Among early human populations, the protective adaptation to sun exposure near the equator was _____.

20. We tend to share other people's joys and suffer when they are in distress, when we _____ with others.

21. Everyone knows what it feels like to be different, and when we remember these times, we tend to show greater _____.

22. Getting acquainted with a person whose cultural background is different from one's own and learning the details of their customs and beliefs are starting points in developing cultural _____.

Connections

1. ___ multiculturalism
2. ___ "openness to the other"
3. ___ individuating information
4. ___ just-world beliefs
5. ___ self-fulfilling prophecy
6. ___ social competition
7. ___ race as a social construction
8. ___ cultural awareness

a. rivalry among groups, each of which regard itself as superior to others

b. social labeling based on superficial physical differences and learned ethnic identities, not on biological reality

c. giving equal status, recognition, and acceptance to different ethnic and cultural groups

d. becoming more knowledgeable about the details and subtleties of other cultures

e. ability to genuinely appreciate those who differ from us culturally

f. information that helps define a person as an individual, rather than as a member of a group or social category

g. belief that people generally get what they deserve

h. an expectation that prompts people to act in ways that make the expectation come true

Check Your Memory

1. TRUE or FALSE   Today's society is more like a cultural "melting pot" than a "tossed salad."
2. TRUE or FALSE   Multiculturalism is a recognition and acceptance of human diversity.
3. TRUE or FALSE   A decision to forsake prejudice does not immediately eliminate prejudiced thoughts and feelings.
4. TRUE or FALSE   The ability to genuinely appreciate those who differ from us culturally is referred to as "openness to the other."
5. TRUE or FALSE   Being open to someone else means that you have to agree with that person and, to an extent, turn your back on your own culture.
6. TRUE or FALSE   Stereotypes make the social world more manageable, but also cause us to see out-group members as very much alike.

7. TRUE or FALSE   We are tempted to apply stereotypes when we have minimal information about a person.

8. TRUE or FALSE   The use of individuating information tends to make us place people into social categories and increases stereotyped thinking.

9. TRUE or FALSE   When English-speaking students in a French language program were "immersed" (spent most of their waking hours) with French Canadians, they became more negative toward the French Canadian students with intergroup conflict increasing.

10. TRUE or FALSE   The belief that people generally get what they deserve in this world is known as the self-fulfilling prophecy.

11. TRUE or FALSE   A person who believes that members of another ethnic group are hostile and unfriendly will probably treat people in that group in ways that provoke hostile and unfriendly responses, thus, reinforcing the stereotype.

12. TRUE or FALSE   Because of social competition, groups tend to view themselves as better than their rivals.

13. TRUE or FALSE   In one survey, every major ethnic group in the United States rated itself as better than any other group.

14. TRUE or FALSE   People with high self-esteem tend to treat others as inferior in order to feel good about themselves.

15. TRUE or FALSE   From the viewpoint of modern genetics, the concept of race has absolutely no meaning.

16. TRUE or FALSE   According to the best available information, the origin of the human species occurred in northern Europe about 50,000 years ago.

17. TRUE or FALSE   Among early human populations, darker skin was a protective adaptation to sun exposure near the equator.

18. TRUE or FALSE   Since everyone knows what if feels like to be different, greater tolerance comes from remembering those times.

19. TRUE or FALSE   Cultural awareness begins by getting acquainted with a person whose cultural background is different from your own and learning the details of their customs and beliefs.

20. TRUE or FALSE   Knowing more about each other's culture can prevent many conflicts in our society.

Critical Thinking Question

Why is it valuable to learn the terms by which members of various groups prefer to be addressed (for example, Mexican-American, Latino [or Latina], Hispanic, or Chicano [Chicana])?

Final Survey and Review—Completion

Module 15.1 Affiliation, Friendship, and Love

Affiliation and Attraction—Come Together

Survey Questions: Why do people affiliate? What factors influence interpersonal attraction?

1. Dr. Samuels is a psychologist who studies how individuals behave in the presence, actual or implied, of others. Dr. Samuels is a(n) _____ psychologist.

2. The human desires for approval, support, friendship, and information is the basis for our need to _____.

3. Gayle and Terrence met at work and began dating about six months later. Their interpersonal attraction was based on _____.

903

4. Because Mitzi is physically attractive, people tend to see her as intelligent, likable, and socially-skilled, which illustrates the _____ effect.

5. Moderate self-disclosure tends to a return in kind, or _____.

Module 15.1 Affiliation, Friendship, and Love
Liking and Loving—Dating and Mating
Survey Question: How are liking and loving different?

6. Romantic love that is based on interpersonal attraction and high levels of _____.

7. The triangular theory of love was developed by _____.

8. Joe and Diane have a lot of interests in common and enjoy spending time together, but they feel no passion for each other nor do they have a long-term commitment. Joe and Diane are exhibiting _____.

9. In a study of 37 cultures on six continents, the gender that was more interested in casual sex and preferred younger, more physically attractive partners were the _____.

10. David Buss believes that the differing reproductive challenges faced by men and women caused the resulting _____ preferences.

Module 15.2 Groups, Social Influence, Mere Presence, and Conformity
Humans in a Social Context—People, People, Everywhere
Survey Question: How does group membership affect our behavior?

11. Being a brother or sister or a young or older adult would all be _____ roles.

12. A soccer coach whose son is on the team but isn't a very good athlete would most likely experience a role _____.

13. Groups that tend to stand or sit close together, that pay more attention to one another, and that show more signs of mutual affection are exhibiting group _____.

14. Most people might sing loudly in the shower, but would not walk into a crowded supermarket, get in a checkout line, and begin singing loudly in their fullest voice because of the unspoken standards of behavior known as _____.

15. You chose your major in school because of what it has to offer, while other students choose their majors because of the kind of people they are. This illustrates the difference in one's attribution of cause referred to as the _____ effect.

Module 15.2 Groups, Social Influence, Mere Presence, and Conformity
Social Influence—Follow the Leader
Survey Question: What have social psychologists learned about social influence, mere presence, and conformity?

16. You have been standing at line at the coffee shop for 15 minutes when a stranger rushes in and asks can she get ahead of you because of an appointment. If you agree, you are exhibiting the type of social influence known as _____.

17. You are dancing around your dorm room to your favorite song when your roommate walks in with a stranger. You stop dancing because of the social influence known as _____.

18. A study was conducted in which people played tug-of-war while blindfolded and were led to believe they were pulling alone on some trials and pulling with a team on other trials. When the participants thought they were pulling as part of the team, they exhibited social _____.

19. People are more likely to conform if they have high needs for certainty or _____.

20. In an attempt to understand a series of disastrous decisions made by government officials, Irving Janis proposed the concept of _____.

Module 15.3 Compliance, Obedience, Coercion, and Self-Assertion
Compliance—A Foot in the Door
Survey Question: What have psychologists learned about compliance?
21. If a stranger asks to borrow your cell phone and you agree, then you are exhibiting the form of social influence known as _____.
22. The door-in-the-face effect was coined by _____.
23. If someone asks you to put a small sign in your store window promoting the environment and you agree, you will be more likely to agree to put up a larger sign in the future, which illustrates the _____.
24. If a friend asks you to keep her dogs for two weeks and you decline and she then asks if you can keep them for a couple of days and you accept, you have experienced the _____.
25. You have agreed to purchase the computer listed in the store ad for an attractive low price, but then the salesperson adds additional costs that makes the computer more expensive, which means that you have experienced the _____.

Module 15.3 Compliance, Obedience, Coercion, and Self-Assertion
Obedience—Would You Electrocute a Stranger?
Survey Question: What have psychologists learned about obedience?
26. If Sierta has social power in a situation, then she would be described as a(n) _____.
27. Stanley Milgram performed experiments designed to test the social influence known as _____.
28. Before performing his "teacher-learner" experiments, Milgram polled a group of _____.
29. Some critics of Milgram's experiment argued that the prestige of Yale University convinced the subjects that no one would be _____.
30. Milgram's experiments were recently partially replicated by a psychologist at Santa Clara University named _____.

Module 15.3 Compliance, Obedience, Coercion, and Self-Assertion
Coercion—Brainwashing and Cults
Survey Question: What have psychologists learned about coercion?
31. Brainwashing and cult conversion both involve a type of social influence known as _____.
32. During the Korean and Vietnam Wars, after prisoners of war signed false confessions to gain relief from the torture, they would be suddenly rewarded with privileges, food and rest, which served to solidify their new attitudes in the stage of brainwashing known as _____.
33. Abby was converted to a cult as a rebellious adolescent with the cult taking the place of _____ authority.
34. The use of all-night meditation, continuous chanting or other similar rituals wear down physical and emotional resistance, generate feelings of commitment, discourage critical thinking, and generate feelings of _____.
35. Conversion is complete when cult members think of themselves less as individuals and more as _____.

Module 15.3 Compliance, Obedience, Coercion, and Self-Assertion
Assertiveness Training—Standing Up for Your Rights
Survey Question: How does self-assertion differ from aggression?
36. Because Jonathan was rewarded all through life for compliant, obedient, or "good" behavior, he finds it very difficult to _____ himself.

37. When people interact with Janice, they usually find her patient to a fault, but they also feel sympathy, guilt, and even contempt for her because she is a(n) _____ person.
38. When people interact with Warren, they often feel hurt, defensive, humiliated, and taken advantage of because Warren is a(n) _____ person.
39. Juan will be asking for a raise tomorrow, so he has his brother play the part of his boss being uncooperative and rude as well as kind and considerate. Juan and his brother are practicing assertiveness through _____.
40. Your Perfect Right is a book about becoming assertive that was written by psychologists Robert Alberti and _____.

Module 15.4 Attitudes and Persuasion
Attitudes—Belief + Emotion + Action
Survey Question: How are attitudes acquired and changed?
41. Donating money or providing other support to a particular organization would constitute the _____ component of an attitude.
42. After helping out at the local food pantry and seeing how much it helps others, you buy extra can goods and other food stuffs to donate each month with your favorable attitude of the pantry being acquired through _____.
43. Although you have never met the candidate or heard her speak, you are planning to vote for her because your friends are supporting this candidate, which means your attitude toward the candidate was formed through _____.
44. Although Laura has decided to bike from her apartment to her college classes, she awakens late one morning and rushes to class in her car. Her attitude of riding her bike was not acted on because of the _____.
45. Although there are often large differences between attitudes and public behavior, the barriers to action typically fall when a person holds an attitude with _____.

Module 15.4 Attitudes and Persuasion
Attitude Change—Meet the "Seekers"
Survey Question: Under what conditions is persuasion most effective?
46. Although her parents and siblings are all Republicans, Shelia actively works for the Democratic Party. Therefore, politically, Shelia's family would be a(n) _____ group.
47. The success or failure of persuasion can be understood if we consider the communicator, the message, and the _____.
48. After publicly committing yourself to your beliefs, you will have a strong need to maintain consistency, according to the _____ theory.
49. If you know smoking is dangerous but tell yourself that your work and school schedule is so hectic that you cannot deal with the headaches and withdrawal symptoms right now, you have decreased your cognitive dissonance by reducing the amount of _____ you have.
50. In a classic study in which college students did an extremely boring task and then were asked to help lure others into the experiment by pretending that the task was interesting with some being paid one dollar for lying and other being paid $20 for lying. The students who did not changed their negative opinion and still thought the experiment was "boring" were the ones who were paid _____.

Module 15.5 Prejudice and Intergroup Conflict
Prejudice—Attitudes That Injure
Survey Question: What causes prejudice and intergroup conflict?

51. In general, prejudice is defined as a negative emotional attitude held toward members of a specific _____.
52. People are prevented from doing things they should be able to do, such as buying a house, getting a job, or attending a high-quality school, by unequal treatment referred to as _____.
53. Scapegoating is a type of _____ aggression.
54. Psychologist Gordon Allport concluded that there are two important sources of prejudice, group and _____.
55. Danny would described as rigid, ethnocentric, and prejudiced. He would be very likely to have what Adorno called a(n) _____ personality.

Module 15.5 Prejudice and Intergroup Conflict
Intergroup Conflict—The Roots of Prejudice

56. In general, the top three categories on which most stereotypes are based are age, race, and _____.
57. Barton usually rationalizes his prejudice so that it appears to be based more on the issues than on raw racism. Barton is exhibiting _____ prejudice.
58. Jane Elliot was able to create prejudice in her classroom in last that a day based on status inequalities and _____.
59. Sam would be described as conservative, middle-class, religious, and lives in rural Kansas. According to the current political shorthand symbolism in the U.S., Sam would be symbolized by the color _____.
60. Elliot Aronson developed a technique for applying superordinate goals to the classroom, which he called the _____.

Module 15.6 Aggression and Prosocial Behavior
Aggression—The World's Most Dangerous Animal
Survey Question: How do psychologists explain human aggression?

61. The famous ethologist who believed that humans lack certain innate patterns found in other animals that inhibit aggression was _____.
62. Researchers have found a relationship between aggression and such physical illnesses as hypoglycemia (low blood sugar), specific brain injures and diseases, and _____.
63. Frustration may not always lead to aggression. It can also cause stereotyped responding and a state of "_____."
64. Angry thoughts, offensive words, and gestures are examples of both internal and external _____.
65. Melanie has been bullying and harassing a fellow classmate through e-mails and on Facebook. Melanie is engaged in _____ aggression.

Module 15.6 Aggression and Prosocial Behavior
Prosocial Behavior—Helping Others
Survey Question: Why are bystanders so often unwilling to help in an emergency?

66. Many of the first bystander apathy experiments were conducted by Latané and _____.
67. The experiments on bystander apathy show that bystanders are not apathetic or uncaring, but are inhibited by the _____ of others.
68. The four decision points that a person must pass through before giving help are noticing an emergency, defining an emergency, taking responsibility, and selecting a(n) _____.

69. When there are many people present in a group, people tend to spread the responsibility for helping, which is called a(n) _____.
70. Jesse's neighbor helped him to find his dog last week. Now Jesse's neighbor is going on vacation and has asked Jesse to pick up his mail and newspaper. Jesse will be more likely to help because of the norms of _____.

Module 15.7 Psychology in Action
Multiculturalism—Living with Diversity
Survey Question: How can we promote multiculturalism and social harmony?
71. With multiculturalism, different ethnic, racial, and cultural groups are given equal _____.
72. Individuating information is one of the best antidotes for _____.
73. Jamie believes that people basically get what they deserve in this world. Jamie is exhibiting a(n) _____ belief.
74. Because Megan believes that members of another ethnic group are hostile and unfriendly, she tends to treat people in that group in ways that actually provoke hostility and unfriendliness, which creates a(n) _____.
75. To feel good about him or herself, a person with high self-esteem does not need to treat others as _____.

Final Survey and Review—Matching

Module 15.1 Affiliation, Friendship, and Love
Part 1: Connections

1. ___ social psychology
2. ___ evolutionary psychology
3. ___ need to affiliate
4. ___ social comparison
5. ___ competence
6. ___ physical proximity
7. ___ halo effect
8. ___ self-disclosure
9. ___ overdisclosure
10. ___ intimacy
11. ___ passion
12. ___ commitment

a. tendency to generalize a favorable impression to unrelated personal characteristics
b. process of revealing private thoughts, feelings, and one's personal history to others
c. closer people live or work to each other, the more likely they are to become friends
d. the determination to stay in a long-term relationship with another person
e. exceeds what is appropriate for a social situation and leads to suspicion and reduced attraction
f. deep emotional and/or sexual feelings for another person
g. making judgments about ourselves by comparing and contrasting ourselves against others
h. has knowledge, ability, or proficiency
i. study of the origins of human behavior patterns
j. desire to associate with other people
k. scientific study of how individuals behave, think, and feel in social situations
l. feelings of connectedness and affection for another person

908

Part 2: Connections

1. ___ homogamy
2. ___ mutual absorption
3. ___ liking
4. ___ fatuous love
5. ___ empty love
6. ___ romantic love
7. ___ companionate love
8. ___ nonlove
9. ___ consummate love
10. ___ infatuated love

a. based on commitment but lacking intimacy and passion
b. consists of passion only
c. based on intimacy and passion but no commitment
d. characterized by intimacy, passion, and commitment
e. absence of all three components: intimacy, passion, or commitment
f. the nearly exclusive attention lovers give to one another
g. characterized by passion and commitment, but lacking in intimacy
h. characterized by intimacy and commitment but not passion
i. based on intimacy but lacking passion and commitment
j. marriage of two people who are similar to one another

Module 15.2 Groups, Social Influence, Mere Presence, and Conformity
Part 1:

1. ___ ascribed role
2. ___ achieved role
3. ___ in-groups
4. ___ out-groups
5. ___ group sanctions
6. ___ group structure
7. ___ group cohesiveness
8. ___ groupthink
9. ___ norm
10. ___ status

a. network of roles, communication pathways, and power in a group
b. a widely accepted (but often unspoken) standard of conduct for appropriate behavior
c. rewards and punishments, such as approval or disapproval, administered by groups to enforce conformity among members
d. voluntarily attained by special effort
e. people with which a person mainly identifies
f. individual's position in a social situation, especially with respect to power, privilege, or importance
g. people with which a person does not identify
h. compulsion by members of decision-making groups to maintain agreement, even at the cost of critical thinking
i. assigned to a person and not under personal voluntary control
j. degree of attraction among group members or their commitment to remaining in the group

909

Part 2:

1. ____ fundamental attribution error

   a. bending to the requests of a person who has little or no authority or other form of social power

2. ____ mere presence

   b. tendency of people to work less hard when part of a group than when they are solely responsible for their work

3. ____ conformity

   c. tendency to attribute the behavior of others to internal causes, such as personality, even when the behavior is caused externally

4. ____ compliance

   d. tendency to perform better when in the presence of others

5. ____ obedience

   e. spontaneously changing your behavior in to bring it into agreement with others

6. ____ coercion

7. ____ social facilitation

   f. changing behavior because you are forced to

   g. changing behavior in direct response to the demands of an authority

8. ____ social loafing

   h. changing behavior because other people are nearby

Module 15.3 Compliance, Obedience, Coercion, and Self-Assertion

1. ____ authority

   a. strategy in which commitment is gained first to reasonable or desirable terms, which are then made less reasonable or desirable

2. ____ obedience

   b. engineered or forced attitude change involving a captive audience

3. ____ compliance

   c. group that professes great devotion to some person and follows that person almost without question

4. ____ coercion

   d. tendency for a person who has first complied with a small request to be more likely later to fulfill a larger request

5. ____ door-in-the-face effect

   e. lets others make choices for them; goals not achieved

6. ____ low-ball technique

7. ____ foot-in-the-door effect

   f. achieves goals at others' expense

   g. direct, honest expression of feelings and desires; goals achieved without hurting others

8. ____ brainwashing

   h. being forced to change your beliefs or your behavior against your will

9. ____ cult

   i. tendency for a person who has refused a major request to subsequently be more likely to comply with a minor request

10. ____ nonassertive behavior

   j. bending to the requests of a person who has little or no authority or other form of social power

11. ____ self-assertion

   k. person who has social power

12. ____ aggressive behavior

   l. changing behavior in direct response to the demands of an authority

Module 15.4 Attitudes and Persuasion

1. ___ attitude
2. ___ belief component
3. ___ emotional component
4. ___ action component
5. ___ conviction
6. ___ chance conditioning
7. ___ mean worldview
8. ___ reference group
9. ___ membership group
10. ___ persuasion
11. ___ cognitive dissonance
12. ___ justification

a. deliberate attempt to change attitudes or beliefs with information and arguments
b. group to which one belongs
c. regarding the world as a dangerous and threatening place often because of being exposed to TV violence
d. degree to which a person's actions are explained by rewards or other circumstances
e. how one tends to act toward the object of an attitude
f. group that an individual identifies with and uses as a standard for social comparison
g. unshakable belief that evokes strong emotion
h. what a person thinks about the object of an attitude
i. uncomfortable clash between self-image, thoughts, beliefs, attitudes, or perceptions and one's behavior
j. learning that takes place by coincidence
k. one's feelings toward the object of an attitude
l. mixture of belief and emotion that predisposes a person to respond to other people, objects, or groups in a positive or negative way

Module 15.5 Prejudice and Intergroup Conflict

1. ___ social stereotypes
2. ___ discrimination
3. ___ scapegoating
4. ___ authoritarian personality
5. ___ ethnocentrism
6. ___ personal prejudice
7. ___ group prejudice
8. ___ symbolic prejudice
9. ___ status inequalities

a. pattern characterized by rigidity, inhibition, prejudice, and an excessive concern with power and obedience
b. prejudice held out of conformity to group views
c. placing one's own group or race at the center and rejecting all other groups but one's own
d. prejudice that is expressed in a disguised fashion
e. prejudicial attitudes held toward persons who are perceived as a direct threat to one's own interests
f. goal that exceeds or overrides all others
g. condition in which two or more persons must depend on one another to meet each person's needs or goals
h. blaming a person or a group for the actions of others or for conditions not of their making; based on displaced aggression
i. oversimplified images of the traits of individuals who belong to a particular social group

911

10. ___ superordinate goal

11. ___ mutual interdependence

12. ___ jigsaw classroom

j. method of reducing prejudice in which each student receives only part of the information needed to complete a project or prepare for a test

k. differences in the power, prestige, or privileges of two or more persons or groups

l. treating members of various social groups differently in circumstances where their rights or treatment should be identical

Module 15.6 Aggression and Prosocial Behavior

1. ___ aggression

2. ___ ethologist

3. ___ bystander apathy

4. ___ diffusion of responsibility

5. ___ frustration-aggression hypothesis

6. ___ aversive stimuli

7. ___ empathy-helping relationship

8. ___ weapons effect

9. ___ social learning theory

10. ___ disinhibition

11. ___ desensitization

12. ___ prosocial behavior

a. unwillingness of people to offer help during emergencies or to become involved in others' problems

b. a reduction in emotional sensitivity to a stimulus

c. observation that we are most likely to help someone in need when we "feel for" that person and experience emotions such as empathy, sympathy, and compassion

d. the removal of restraint that results in acting out behavior

e. the observation and modeling of aggression explains the occurrence of aggressive behavior

f. spreading the responsibility to act among several people, which reduces the likelihood that help will be given to a person in need

g. observation that guns and knives, etc. serve as strong cues for aggressive behavior

h. person who studies the natural behavior patterns of animals

i. any event that produces discomfort or displeasure and can heighten hostility and aggression

j. actions that are constructive, altruistic, or helpful to others

k. any action carried out with the intention of harming another person

l. having one's goals blocked leads to aggression

Module 15.7 Psychology in Action: Multiculturalism—Living with Diversity

1. ___ multiculturalism

2. ___ "openness to the other"

3. ___ just-world beliefs

a. belief that people generally get what they deserve

b. giving equal status, recognition, and acceptance to different ethnic and cultural groups

c. becoming more knowledgeable about the details and subtleties of other cultures

4. ___ self-fulfilling prophecy

5. ___ social competition

6. ___ cultural awareness

d. ability to genuinely appreciate those who differ from us culturally

e. an expectation that prompts people to act in ways that make the expectation come true

f. rivalry among groups, each of which regard itself as superior to others

Final Survey and Review—True or False

Module 15.1 Affiliation, Friendship, and Love
Affiliation and Attraction—Come Together
Survey Questions: Why do people affiliate? What factors influence interpersonal attraction?

1. TRUE or FALSE   Meaningful evaluations are based on comparing yourself with people of similar backgrounds, abilities, and circumstances.
2. TRUE or FALSE   The closer people live to each other, the more likely they are to become friends.
3. TRUE or FALSE   In a classic experiment in which students listened to audiotapes of candidates for a "college quiz bowl," the students found the competent candidate who blundered by spilling coffee the most attractive and the average candidate who blundered by spilling coffee the least attractive.
4. TRUE or FALSE   The risk of divorce is highest among couples who are too similar in age, education, opinions, and interests.
5. TRUE or FALSE   Overdisclosure tends to lead to suspicion and reduced attraction.

Module 15.1 Affiliation, Friendship, and Love
Liking and Loving—Dating and Mating
Survey Question: How are liking and loving different?

6. TRUE or FALSE   In Sternberg's triangular theory of love, feelings of connectedness and affection are referred to as commitment.
7. TRUE or FALSE   If you are experiencing passion, but no intimacy and no commitment, then you are experiencing romantic love.
8. TRUE or FALSE   Relationships are most likely to persist when lovers idealize one another.
9. TRUE or FALSE   Buss found that men get more jealous than women over real or imagined sexual infidelities.
10. TRUE or FALSE   Some mating patterns may simply reflect the fact that men still tend to control the power and resources in most societies.

Module 15.2 Groups, Social Influence, Mere Presence, and Conformity
Humans in a Social Context—People, People, Everywhere
Survey Question: How does group membership affect our behavior?

11. TRUE or FALSE   Being a senator, a rock star, or a college student are all examples of ascribed roles.
12. TRUE or FALSE   Persons of higher status tend to receive special treatment and privileges.
13. TRUE or FALSE   The more trash that is visible in public places, the more likely people are to litter.
14. TRUE or FALSE   If someone always salts her food before eating, it implies that her behavior has an external cause.

913

15. TRUE or FALSE   Attributing the actions of others to external causes is the most common attributional error.

Module 15.2 Groups, Social Influence, Mere Presence, and Conformity
Social Influence—Follow the Leader
Survey Question: What have social psychologists learned about social influence, mere presence, and conformity?

16. TRUE or FALSE   The gentlest form of social influence is conformity.
17. TRUE or FALSE   Daily behavior is probably most influenced by obedience to authorities.
18. TRUE or FALSE   People who live in cultures that emphasize group cooperation, such as many Asian cultures, are more likely to conform.
19. TRUE or FALSE   To prevent groupthink, group leaders should avoid revealing any personal preferences at the beginning of a meeting and should just state the problem factually, without bias.
20. TRUE or FALSE   A unanimous majority of three is more powerful than a majority of eight with one person dissenting.

Module 15.3 Compliance, Obedience, Coercion, and Self-Assertion
Compliance—A Foot in the Door
Survey Question: What have psychologists learned about compliance?

21. TRUE or FALSE   While conformity tends to involve direct pressures, compliance consists of only indirect, subtle influences.
22. TRUE or FALSE   Your new co-worker asks to borrow money to buy a cappuccino, and you give her the money. You have just exhibited the type of social influence known as coercion.
23. TRUE or FALSE   If you ask someone to give you a ride to school in the morning; and after he agrees, you tell him that you have to be there at 6 a.m., you have used the door-in-the-face effect.
24. TRUE or FALSE   If you are looking at a car and the salesperson asks you to go to an office and fill out some papers, "just to see what kind of a price" she or he can offer and you fill out the papers, you will be more likely to buy the car because you have succumbed to the foot-in-the-door effect.
25. TRUE or FALSE   Salespeople once had a great advantage in negotiating because they knew exactly how much the dealership paid for each car, but now anyone can obtain detailed automobile pricing information from the Internet.

Module 15.3 Compliance, Obedience, Coercion, and Self-Assertion
Obedience—Would You Electrocute a Stranger?
Survey Question: What have psychologists learned about obedience?

26. TRUE or FALSE   When Milgram polled a group of psychiatrists before the experiment, they predicted that less than one percent of those tested would obey.
27. TRUE or FALSE   In Milgram's original obedience experiment, 65 percent of the subjects actually obeyed completely by going all the way to the 450-volt level.
28. TRUE or FALSE   Being face-to-face with the learner had no effect on the number of subjects who obeyed in the Milgram experiments.
29. TRUE or FALSE   When the experimenter gave his orders to the teacher over the phone, the obedience of the teacher increased.
30. TRUE or FALSE   People are less likely to obey an unjust authority if they have seen others disobey.

Module 15.3 Compliance, Obedience, Coercion, and Self-Assertion
Coercion—Brainwashing and Cults
Survey Question: What have psychologists learned about coercion?

31. TRUE or FALSE   Brainwashing typically begins with a process known as unfreezing.
32. TRUE or FALSE   A cult is a group in which the belief system is more important than the leader who espouses it.
33. TRUE or FALSE   The psychologist and pioneering brainwashing expert that studied and aided hundreds of former cult members was Margaret Singer.
34. TRUE or FALSE   Cult conversion often begins with intense displays of affection and understanding known as the "love bombing."
35. TRUE or FALSE   By having the cult members first make small commitments, such as staying an extra day and then later making a large commitment, such as signing over their bank accounts, cults are making use of the low-ball technique.

Module 15.3 Compliance, Obedience, Coercion, and Self-Assertion
Assertiveness Training—Standing Up for Your Rights
Survey Question: How does self-assertion differ from aggression?

36. TRUE or FALSE   Many people have difficulty asserting themselves because they have learned to be obedient and good.
37. TRUE or FALSE   Self-assertion involves the rights to react, reject, and retaliate.
38. TRUE or FALSE   Aggression involves achieving one's goals at the expense of another.
39. TRUE or FALSE   When people interact with a nonassertive person, they usually feel respect for this person and feel respected themselves.
40. TRUE or FALSE   The basic idea in assertiveness training is that each assertive action is practiced until it can be repeated even under stress.

Module 15.4 Attitudes and Persuasion
Attitudes—Belief + Emotion + Action
Survey Question: How are attitudes acquired and changed?

41. TRUE or FALSE   When Margot says she just "loves" going to the beach, she is expressing the belief component of an attitude.
42. TRUE or FALSE   If you oppose pollution and support clean air and water because a nearby factory has caused smog in your community and killed all the fish in the river near your house, you acquired your attitude regarding pollution because of personal experience, or direct contact.
43. TRUE or FALSE   Although everyone at work is talking about how wonderful a beach resort is, your two stays there were marred by crowded beaches and poor service at the hotel and restaurant, which has resulted in your unfavorable attitude toward this resort as acquired through an interaction with others.
44. TRUE or FALSE   Although you decide to start exercising 30 minutes a day, you soon revert back to watching television during your exercise time, which illustrates the effect on attitudes of long-standing habits.
45. TRUE or FALSE   Attitudes held with passionate conviction often lead to major changes in personal behavior.

915

Module 15.4 Attitudes and Persuasion
Attitude Change—Meet the "Seekers"
Survey Question: Under what conditions is persuasion most effective?

46. TRUE or FALSE   Our attitudes are more likely to match those held by members of our reference groups than our membership groups.

47. TRUE or FALSE   Persuasion is less effective if the message appeals to the emotions.

48. TRUE or FALSE   For a poorly informed audience, persuasion is more effective if only one side of the argument is presented.

49. TRUE or FALSE   Public commitment to an attitude or belief makes it more difficult to change.

50. TRUE or FALSE   The greater the reward or justification for acting contrary to one's beliefs, the greater the cognitive dissonance felt.

Module 15.5 Prejudice and Intergroup Conflict
Prejudice—Attitudes That Injure
Survey Question: What causes prejudice and intergroup conflict?

51. TRUE or FALSE   In a study in which the attitudes toward Japanese and Mexican persons was measured before or after a group of European Americans subjects were frustrated, the researchers found that the subjects unexpected rated the two ethnic groups higher after being frustrated.

52. TRUE or FALSE   Children as young as age three have begun to show signs of racial bias.

53. TRUE or FALSE   A person who views members of another group as competitors for jobs is displaying the source of prejudice known as personal prejudice.

54. TRUE or FALSE   The F in F Scale stands for fanatic.

55. TRUE or FALSE   When a person views his or her own ethnic group as superior to all others, this person is said to be exhibiting racial narcissism.

Module 15.5 Prejudice and Intergroup Conflict
Intergroup Conflict—The Roots of Prejudice

56. TRUE or FALSE   Social stereotypes can be positive as well as negative.

57. TRUE or FALSE   Symbolic prejudice occurs when people understand the causes of prejudice and do not discriminate against minorities.

58. TRUE or FALSE   Claude Steele conducted the experiment on prejudice that involved giving blue-eyed children more privileges than brown-eyed children in an elementary classroom.

59. TRUE or FALSE   Intergroup conflict between the two groups of boys at the camp significantly decreased when the boys had to work together to repair the water supply system at the camp.

60. TRUE or FALSE   Elliot Aronson's "jigsaw" classrooms emphasize cooperation rather than competition.

Module 15.6 Aggression and Prosocial Behavior
Aggression—The World's Most Dangerous Animal
Survey Question: How do psychologists explain human aggression?

61. TRUE or FALSE   Specific areas of the brain are capable of initiating or ending aggression.

62. TRUE or FALSE   Biological factors are considered an indirect cause of aggression that lower the threshold for aggression to occur.

63. TRUE or FALSE   People exposed to aversive stimuli tend to become less sensitive to aggression cues.

916

64. TRUE or FALSE   Murders are less likely to occur in homes where guns are kept.
65. TRUE or FALSE   According to Eron, children learn aggression from direct contact with other children and not from indirect contact from TV programs.

Module 15.6 Aggression and Prosocial Behavior

Prosocial Behavior—Helping Others

Survey Question: Why are bystanders so often unwilling to help in an emergency?

66. TRUE or FALSE   In an emergency, the more potential helpers present, the less likely a person is to get help.
67. TRUE or FALSE   Regarding the four decision points one must pass through before giving help, the first step in giving help is to define the situation as an emergency.
68. TRUE or FALSE   When a person is in a state of heightened arousal, they are less motivated to give help.
69. TRUE or FALSE   You are more likely to help a person who seems similar to yourself.
70. TRUE or FALSE   The majority of people who perform heroic acts involving physical dangers have been women.

Module 15.7 Psychology in Action

Multiculturalism—Living with Diversity

Survey Question: How can we promote multiculturalism and social harmony?

71. TRUE or FALSE   Multiculturalism is an attempt to blend multiple ethnic backgrounds into one universal culture.
72. TRUE or FALSE   The emotional component of prejudicial attitudes may remain even after a person intellectually renounces prejudice.
73. TRUE or FALSE   Individuating information forces us to focus mainly on the labels attached to a person.
74. TRUE or FALSE   People who hold just-world beliefs assume that people generally get what they deserve.
75. TRUE or FALSE   From a scientific point of view, race is a matter of social labeling, not a biological reality.

Mastery Test

1. Mandy and Avis, who are first-year teachers, are going to the state teaching conference and are unsure what to wear to the sessions and to the governor's reception, so they talk to several teachers at their school who have been to these conferences in the past and who are going this year. In order to make their decision regarding "what to pack," Mandy and Avis are using
    a. affiliation.
    b. social comparison.
    c. social exchange.
    d. self-disclosure.

2. Which of the following components promotes attraction by increasing the frequency of contact between people?
    a. physical attractiveness
    b. overdisclosure
    c. competence
    d. physical proximity

3. Homogamy is directly related to which element of interpersonal attraction?
   a. similarity
   b. beauty
   c. physical proximity
   d. competence

4. Suspicion and reduced attraction are associated with
   a. reciprocity.
   b. self-disclosure.
   c. competence.
   d. overdisclosure.

5. According to Robert Sternberg, if passion and commitment exist in a relationship, but with no intimacy, then the couple is experiencing _____ love.
   a. romantic
   b. infatuated
   c. consummate
   d. fatuous

6. Lovers, unlike friends, attend almost exclusively to one another, which is referred to as
   a. social exchange.
   b. mutual absorption.
   c. overdisclosure.
   d. commitment.

7. Evolutionary theories attribute mate selection, in part, to
   a. food-gathering habits.
   b. tribal customs.
   c. maternal instincts.
   d. reproductive challenges.

8. "President of the United States" is a(n)
   a. ascribed role.
   b. achieved role.
   c. structural norm.
   d. cohesive role.

9. Les is in the military, a group which has a strict network of roles, communication pathways, and power within the group. Thus, the military would be said to have a high degree of group
   a. cohesiveness.
   b. structure.
   c. attributions.
   d. goals.

10. The fundamental attribution error involves attributing the behavior of others to _____ causes.
    a. inconsistent
    b. internal
    c. external
    d. situational

11. You are talking "baby talk" to your cat on your front porch when your next door neighbor walks up. You immediately stop talking to your cat because of the social influence known as
   a. conformity.
   b. passive compliance.
   c. coercion.
   d. mere presence.

12. Janet found that when she ran in a marathon, she performed better than when she trained alone. Her better performance when around other people is an example of
   a. social facilitation.
   b. social power.
   c. social loafing.
   d. interactional attribution.

13. Darla is more likely to conform to group pressure if
   a. she has a low need for certainty.
   b. she has a low need for structure.
   c. the country she lives in emphasizes cooperation.
   d. there is a lack of group unanimity.

14. In meetings, Norris, who is the CEO of his company, tries to avoid any of his own personal preferences at the beginning of a decision-making meeting. He encourages open inquiry regarding the problem, defines each group member's role as a "critical evaluator," and makes it clear that group members will be held accountable for decisions. Norris is trying to avoid the occurrence of
   a. attribution errors.
   b. passive compliance.
   c. social loafing.
   d. groupthink.

15. A person who first agrees with a small request, such as loaning lunch money, is later more likely to comply with a larger demand, such as loaning $100. This summarizes the
   a. low-ball technique.
   b. set-the-hook technique.
   c. door-in-the-face effect.
   d. foot-in-the-door effect.

16. You just received a text message that you are eligible for a new phone on your plan. So, you go to the phone store and see the new "free" phone but then the salesperson adds additional costs, such as an activation fee and phone chargers, etc. until your "free" phone now costs $100. This compliance method is known as the
   a. low-ball technique.
   b. door-in-the-face effect.
   c. foot-in-the-door effect.
   d. sucker-punch technique.

17. When a group of psychiatrists were asked at the beginning of the obedience experiment how many subjects would "shock" the learner to the 450-volt level, the group of psychiatrists predicted only one percent would. According to the results of this experiment, the percent of subjects who administered "shocks" to the 450-volt level was _____ percent.
    a. 10
    b. 28
    c. 43
    d. 65

18. In the obedience experiment, the "teacher" was less likely to "shock" the learner when the
    a. learner complained about the pain.
    b. experimenter gave the orders to the teacher over the phone.
    c. teacher and the learner were in different rooms rather than the same room.
    d. experiment was carried out at Yale University rather than off-campus.

19. Cult conversion is an example of the strongest form of social influence known as
    a. mere presence.
    b. coercion.
    c. conformity.
    d. obedience.

20. Regarding brainwashing, which of the following statements is FALSE?
    a. Brainwashing requires a captive audience.
    b. The first step in brainwashing is called "unfreezing."
    c. The effects of brainwashing tend to be permanent.
    d. The person being brainwashed is made completely dependent on the indoctrinators.

21. Individuals often feel sympathy, guilt, or contempt for a person exhibiting _____ behavior.
    a. nonassertive
    b. assertive
    c. aggressive
    d. referent

22. Maria has strong attitudes regarding women's rights. She recently took part in a women's rights demonstration, which would illustrate the _____ component of an attitude.
    a. action
    b. belief
    c. emotional
    d. interactional

23. You decide to go to a particular movie after hearing some co-workers talking about the movie during a break. Your favorable attitude and decision to go to this movie were acquired due to
    a. chance conditioning.
    b. direct contact.
    c. an interaction with others.
    d. group membership.

24. Your political views are more similar to those of your friends than to your family. Regarding political views, your family would be considered a(n) _____ group.
    a. proxemic
    b. attribution
    c. reference
    d. membership

25. Randy is attempting to change another person's feelings, beliefs, and actions about an issue. Randy's behavior is an example of
    a. conformity.
    b. attitude.
    c. cognitive dissonance.
    d. persuasion.

26. You are trying to convince a group of people to support a local bond issue. To be most successful, you should present both sides of the issue
    a. to every audience.
    b. to none of the audiences.
    c. only to well-informed audiences.
    d. only to poorly-informed audiences.

27. You are looking over all the courses you need to take during the next two semesters to finish your degree and are feeling uneasy regarding the difficulty level of some of these courses and whether you should schedule them as day, night, or on-line courses. After you fill out your schedule, you think of your schedule more positively than you did before you filled out your schedule in order to maintain a consistency between your behavior of filling out the schedule and your attitude. This illustrates the effects of
    a. the fundamental attribution error.
    b. the actor-observer bias.
    c. groupthink.
    d. cognitive dissonance.

28. Jesse holds a negative emotional attitude toward members of another social group, and as personnel director is able to prevent members of this social group from getting jobs at his company. Jesse's unequal treatment toward members of this social group is referred to as
    a. stereotyping.
    b. discrimination.
    c. status inequality.
    d. symbolic prejudice.

29. If you blame a person or a group for the actions or for conditions not of their making, you are exhibiting
    a. scapegoating.
    b. ethnocentrism.
    c. dogmatism.
    d. reaction formation.

30. If you were degraded and criticized by a member of a particular social group, you may see all members of this group as a direct threat to you. Gordon Allport referred to this situation as
    a. group prejudice.
    b. personal prejudice.
    c. social stereotyping.
    d. discrimination.

31. Marcy is very concerned with power, authority and obedience. She would most likely score high on the
    a. Type R scale.
    b. Individuation Inventory.
    c. Status Inequalities Scale.
    d. F ("fascism") Scale.

32. The top three categories on which social stereotypes are based are
    a. employment, place of origin, and intelligence.
    b. race, intelligence, and education.
    c. gender, age, and race.
    d. sexual orientation, income, and race.

33. In Samantha's elementary classroom, the students are given only a part of the information needed for a project or to prepare for a test with the students then having to cooperate to teach this information to each other. Samantha is using a teaching method known as
    a. discovery learning.
    b. guided inquiry technique.
    c. jigsaw classroom.
    d. groupthink.

34. After watching wrestling on television, Jay puts his little brother in a "head lock." Jay's aggression toward is little brother occurred most likely because of
    a. social learning.
    b. frustration and aversive stimuli.
    c. displaced aggression.
    d. testosterone levels.

35. When shown a bloody fight film, the boys who were heavy TV viewers showed less emotion than the boys who watched little or no TV. This illustrates how the media, which is filled with violent scenes, can cause
    a. emotional catharsis.
    b. emotional disinhibition.
    c. the weapons effect.
    d. desensitization.

36. Your car breaks down on the side of a busy freeway, and you left your cell phone at home. According to Darley and Latané, the reason no one is stopping to help you is due to the
    a. lack of empathic arousal in the bystanders.
    b. bystanders' just-world beliefs.
    c. bystanders being inhibited by the presence of others.
    d. dehumanizing effects of urban life.

37. People must pass through four decision points before giving help with the first point being
    a. defining the emergency.
    b. noticing that something is happening.
    c. taking responsibility.
    d. having empathic arousal.

38. Which of the following tends to discourage a person from "helping" during an emergency?
    a. being similar to the person in need
    b. norms of fairness
    c. costs of helping outweigh the rewards
    d. seeing other people helping

39. Tanya is trying to reduce her tendency to stereotype the people she meets. To accomplish this goal, she should
    a. seek individuating information.
    b. use just-world beliefs.
    c. exhibit ethnocentrism.
    d. accept status inequalities.

40. Billy's new neighbor is from Pakistan. Because Billy wants to avoid misunderstandings and conflict when he meets and talks to his neighbor, he attends a cultural event sponsored by the Pakistani student club at his university. Billy is attempting to
    a. understand status inequalities.
    b. increase cultural awareness.
    c. increase just-world beliefs.
    d. develop superordinate goals.

Chapter 16: Applied Psychology

Chapter Overview

Applied psychology refers to the use of psychological principles and research to solve practical problems. Industrial/organizational psychologists enhance the quality of work by studying jobs to better match people to them and by studying organizational structures and culture to improve worker performance. Two basic leadership styles are Theory X (scientific management) and Theory Y (human relations approaches). Theory X is mostly concerned with work efficiency, whereas Theory Y emphasizes psychological efficiency. Theory Y methods include shared leadership (participative management), management by objectives, self-managed teams, and quality circles. Job satisfaction influences productivity, absenteeism, morale, employee turnover, and other factors that affect business efficiency. Job satisfaction comes from a good fit between work and a person's interests, abilities, needs, and expectations. Job enrichment tends to increase job satisfaction. To match people with jobs, personnel psychologists combine job analysis with selection procedures, such as gathering biodata, interviewing, giving standardized psychological tests, and using assessment centers.

To improve communication at work, state your message clearly and avoid use of obscure vocabulary, jargon, slang, and loaded words. Learn and use people's names. Be polite but not servile. Be expressive when you speak. Pay attention to nonverbal cues and messages. To be a good listener, actively pay attention, identify the speaker's purpose and core message, suspend evaluation while listening, check your understanding, and take note of nonverbal information.

Humans affect the environment and environments affect humans. Many problems can be solved by understanding both relationships. Environmental psychologists are interested in behavioral settings, physical and social environments, and human territoriality, among other topics. The study of personal space is called proxemics. Four basic spatial zones around each person's body are intimate distance (0–18 inches), personal distance (1½–4 feet), social distance (4–12 feet), and public distance (12 feet or more). The nature of many relationships is revealed by the distance you are comfortable maintaining between yourself and another person. Environmental problems such as crowding, pollution, and wasted resources are based on human behavior; they can only be solved by changing behavior patterns. Overpopulation is a major world problem, often reflected at an individual level in crowding. Animal experiments indicate that excessive crowding can be unhealthy. However, human research shows that psychological feelings of crowding do not always correspond to density. One major consequence of crowding is attentional overload. Providing feedback about resource use is an effective way to promote conservation. Research indicates that various psychological strategies can promote recycling. The origins of many environmental disasters lie in overpopulation and overconsumption (the tragedy of the commons). Environmental psychologists offer solutions to many practical problems—from noise pollution to architectural design. Their work often begins with a careful environmental assessment.

925

Educational psychologists improve the quality of learning and teaching. Educational psychologists seek to understand how people learn and teachers instruct. They are particularly interested in teaching strategies, and teaching styles, such as direct instruction and discovery learning.

The psychology of law includes studies of courtroom behavior and other topics that pertain to the legal system. Psychologists also serve various consulting and counseling roles in legal, law enforcement, and criminal justice settings. Studies of mock juries show that jury decisions are often far from objective. Scientific jury selection is used in attempts to choose jurors who have particular characteristics. In some instances, this may result in juries that have a particular bias or that do not represent the community as a whole. A bias toward convicting defendants is characteristic of many death-qualified juries.

Sports psychologists seek to enhance sports performance and the benefits of sports participation. A careful task analysis of sports skills is one of the major tools for improving coaching and performance. A motor skill is a nonverbal response chain assembled into a smooth performance. Motor skills are guided by internal mental models called motor programs. Motor skills are refined through direct practice, but mental practice can also contribute to improvement. During moments of peak performance, physical, mental, and emotional states are optimal. Top performers in sports often use a variety of self-regulation strategies to focus their attention and maintain optimal levels of arousal.

Human factors psychologist (also known as ergonomists) design tools to be compatible with our sensory and motor capacities. Successful human factors engineering uses natural design, which makes use of perceptual signals that people understand naturally. Human factors psychologists rely on usability testing to empirically confirm that machines are easy to learn and use. Human–computer interaction (HCI) is the application of human factors to the design of computers and computer software. To use tools effectively it is useful to know something about the tool and the task you are using it to complete. Be aware of satisficing. Space habitats must be designed with special attention to the numerous human factors issues raised by space flight.

Preview: In Touch with Knowledge

Language Development Guide
iPod: a personal music-playing device
podcast: pre-recorded audio program, similar to a radio broadcast posted to a website and made available for download to personal computers or mobile media devices
vodcast: on-demand video clip content posted to a website and available for download
app: abbreviation for application; computer application program
iPhone: Internet- and multimedia-enabled smartphones designed and marketed by Apple, Inc.
revolutionary: innovative; ground-breaking
hinges: relies
lay at the heart: most important part
multi-touch interface/multi-touch sensing: method of input on a touch screen that allows two or more fingers to be used on the screen at one time; replacing push buttons on phones
computer mouse: hand-held pointer control for the computer
human factors psychologists: work in a specialty concerned with making machines and work environments compatible with human perceptual and physical capacities; also called ergonomics

Module 16.1 Industrial/Organizational Psychology
Industrial/Organizational Psychology—Psychology at Work
Survey Question: How is psychology applied in business and industry?

926

Language Development Guide

live to work or work to live: enjoy working or only work in order to get enough money to live

promotion: advancement to a higher-level job

personnel: employees; workers

rabbi: Jewish religious teacher

vision: perspective, hopes and plans

time-and-motion studies: measuring the time and movements necessary in the completion of a specific job

assembly lines: product production lines in which workers, machines, and equipment are arranged so that the product is assembled in a sequence with the workers doing the same job on multiple products

job specialization: process of performing a certain task in the production of a product

cogs in the manufacturing machinery: a small and unimportant part of the overall process

task orientation: focusing on the completion of the task as a measure of success

goaded: compelled forcible

quotas: prescribed number or proportion required to complete

well-oiled machine: functions well; efficient

morale: psychological state of well-being based on self-confidence, drive, and purpose

devastatingly: overwhelmingly

autonomy: independence

meshed: woven; incorporated into; related to

"punching the clock": refers to a time clock in which a person had their time card punched with the time they came to work and when they left; used mainly for workers paid by the hour

CEOs: chief executive officer who is responsible for a company's operations

cracks are appearing in: there are signs that the concept of the glass ceiling may be weakening

labyrinth: maze, a confusing path

clash: conflict

agentic: acting on one's environment

communal: working for the good of the group, living in relationship with others

"not tough enough": would not be a strong leader

"have the right stuff": effective leadership skills

Silicon Valley: location in California known for its high number of computer technology producers

bimbo: negative stereotype of a beautiful but unintelligent woman

bitch: negative stereotype of a mean woman

scorned: disrespected; shown contempt; ridiculed

presumptuous: arrogant; conceited; going beyond what is right or proper

incongruity: clash; incompatibility

fade: weaken

Honda: a Japanese car manufacturer

outright: obvious

sabotage: intentionally do damage

egotistical: self-centered

put their suggestions into practice: to apply their ideas directly without approval

verify: confirm; prove

skyrockets: increases greatly

enlightened: progressive; open-minded; tolerant

cultivating: working on; developing; encouraging

perpetually: continually

grumpy: irritable; cranky; ill-tempered

"9 to 5": from 9:00 a.m. to 5:00 p.m.; usually business day

confining: restrictive

doom: destine
rush-hour traffic: period of heavy traffic when cars are literally bumper-to-bumper
compressed: condensed; squeezed together
trend: tendency; inclination
streamlined: simplified and well-run
ample: plenty
breed: produce
rituals: ceremonies
"flavor": general atmosphere of a place
encompasses: includes
negotiate: bargain; settle; reach a deal
pettiness: narrow-minded; small-mindedness; meanness; lack of generosity
gossiping: spreading rumors, scandal, and hearsay
erupts: explodes
empowering: giving one the confidence to do something
inspire: motivate
antidote: cure
petty: mean
optimize: get the most out of
psychological microscope: having their psychological profile examined closely
critical: important; essential
aptitudes: potential capabilities; abilities
extracurricular: outside the regular academic curriculum
civil liberty: freedom to exercise one's rights as guaranteed by law
qualifications: list of education, training, and licenses regarding one's skills and competencies
impression: first and immediate effect
cosmetics: makeup
cologne: perfume
flattering: complimenting
blatant: obvious
blowing your own horn: proudly showing or talking about your achievements
résumé: your printed summary of your education and job experiences
clerical: typing and bookkeeping, office work
enterprising: showing initiative and willingness to undertake new projects
relevant: pertinent; applicable
unfold: occur
the action freezes: the story stops
reads like a corporate Who's Who: a listing of brief biographical sketches of famous people in a
        particular field
simulated: imitation
grapples: struggles, works hard

Recite and Review

1. New words like *podcast*, *vodcast*, and *app*, have been invented to describe the ever-
   expanding range of _____ materials available.
2. Much of the iPod's success hinges on a touch-sensitive ring that enables users to quickly
   locate the desired song among thousands. This device is called a(n) _____.
3. More recent touch-based models and mobile communication devices allow easy access to the
   full range of available digital material using a(n) _____.

928

4. Whether it is the computer mouse, voice-activated computers, or computerized system that disabled users can control, the psychologists who depend on understanding human behavior to design better computer tools are the human _____ psychologists.
5. Suika is a psychologist that uses psychological principles and research methods to solve practical problems. Suika is works in the area known as _____ psychology.
6. The largest applied psychology areas are counseling and _____ psychology.
7. Community psychology, educational psychology, military psychology, space psychology, and sports psychology are specific areas in _____ psychology.
8. Absenteeism, promotion, pay schedules, labor relations, management styles, and machine design are topics of special interest to _____ (I/O) psychologists.
9. Studying jobs to identify underlying skills, which can then guide efforts to select people and train them for those jobs comprises the _____ part of I/O psychology.
10. Understanding how to create structures and company cultures that will improve worker performance comprises the _____ part of I/O psychology.
11. The key person in any organization is its _____.
12. According to family therapist and rabbi Edwin Friedman, the capacity to define oneself to others in a way that clarifies and expands a vision of the future defines _____.
13. One of the earliest attempts to improve worker efficiency was made in 1923 by an engineer named _____.
14. This engineer in 1923 speeded up production by emphasizing careful planning, control, and orderliness and by _____ work routines.
15. The type of management that uses time-and-motion studies, task analysis, job specialization, assembly lines, pay schedules, and the like to increase productivity is called _____ management.
16. Supervisors who have a task orientation and assume that workers must be goaded or guided into being productive is following Theory _____ leadership.
17. Maximum output at the lowest cost defines _____ efficiency.
18. Maintaining good morale, labor relations, employee satisfaction, and similar aspects of work behavior refers to _____ efficiency.
19. The psychologists who coined the terms Theory X and Theory Y leadership was _____.
20. The type of leadership that has a person orientation and assumes that workers enjoy autonomy and are willing to accept responsibility is Theory _____ leadership.
21. Over the last 50 years, manufacturing has declined in North America with the most common types of companies being _____ companies.
22. People who add value to a company by creating and manipulating information and include bankers, teachers, lawyers, computer engineers, writers, and scientists are called _____ workers.
23. Given the proper conditions of freedom and responsibility, many people will work hard to use their talents and gain _____.
24. Workers who have jobs manipulating information tend to view their work, not as a job, but as a(n) _____.
25. As women have begun to gain acceptance as leaders, the type of leadership style that has become more popular has been the Theory _____ leadership.
26. The percent of female CEOs found in all American organizations is nearly _____ percent.
27. Regarding gender differences in leadership, studies have shown that companies tend to perform better financially with more _____ in leadership roles.
28. The invisible barrier that has prevented women in the past from moving into leadership positions is called the "_____."

929

29. For most people, Rob would be considered a good leader because he is independent, confident, ambitious, objective, dominant, and forceful. Rob would be considered _____.

30. Like most women, Angela is expected to be dependent, caring, nurturing, tender, sensitive, and sympathetic. Angela is expected to be _____.

31. Thus, women in top executive positions are having to deal with the oversimplified images of what they expect leaders and women to be. In other words, women face a clash of _____.

32. At the Honda plant at Marysville, Ohio, employees working alongside company executives are building feelings of teamwork, which illustrates many of the features of Theory _____ leadership.

33. At the Honda plant at Marysville, Ohio, status differences are minimized because all employees hold the title of _____.

34. Two techniques that make Theory Y leadership methods effective are shared leadership and management by _____.

35. Employees at all levels are directly involved in decision making in a technique known as shared   leadership, also called _____.

36. Employees in a company, which uses shared leadership, come to see work as more of a(n) _____ effort.

37. At Jeff's company, the workers are given specific goals to meet, so they can tell if they are doing a good job, but are free to choose (within limits) how they will achieve their goals. Jeff's company is using the technique known as management by _____.

38. In making progress toward their goals, workers are especially productive when they receive _____.

39. A group of employees who work together toward shared goals by making good use of the strengths and talents of individual employees is known as a(n) _____ team.

40. Chet is in a voluntary discussion group at his company that seeks ways to solve business problems and improve efficiency. Chet is part of a(n) _____.

41. After the employees have made suggestions for solving work problems, the group that has the power to put work suggestions into practice directly are the _____.

42. Many of the methods used by enlightened Theory Y leaders ultimately improve the degree to which a person is pleased with his or her work, which is called _____.

43. More cooperation, better performance, a greater willingness to help others, more creative problem solving, and less absenteeism are associated with _____ moods.

44. The degree to which a person is pleased with his or her work comes from a good fit between work and a person's interests, abilities, needs, and _____.

45. The most productive employees are those who are _____ at work.

46. To improve worker morale, I/O psychologists recommend the use of a variety of flexible work arrangements, of which the best known is the use of flexible working hours, which is called _____.

47. Triana's works three days a week for 13 hours rather than working the regular five-day week. Triana's work schedule would be considered a(n) _____ workweek.

48. Working from his home, Tomas stays connected to the main office throughout the work day through his computer. Tomas is using a flexible work arrangement known as _____.

49. Psychologists theorize that flexible work increases productivity and job satisfaction because it lowers stress and increases feelings of _____.

50. Large corporations, such as IBM and Maytag, have attempted to make their employees' jobs more personally rewarding, interesting, and intrinsically motivating by increasing worker knowledge through an approach known as _____.

930

51. Ways of making jobs more personally rewarding may include giving employees greater freedom, choice, and authority; and in some cases, switching employees so that they are doing a complete _____ of work.

52. True job enrichment increases workers' _____.

53. Characteristics that give each organization its unique "flavor" and include how people are hired, trained, disciplined, and dismissed and how employees dress, communicate, and share power is referred to as the organizational _____.

54. Dinah is described by her supervisors and coworkers as being helpful, conscientious, and courteous. She also displays good sportsmanship by avoiding pettiness, gossiping, complaining, and making small problems into big ones at work. Dinah is displaying what is called organizational _____.

55. Job-related stresses, such as feeling that one has been treated unfairly, perceiving threats to one's self-esteem, and work-related conflicts with others can trigger workplace anger, also called "_____."

56. Most large companies now offer mental health services to troubled employees; and if violence erupts in the workplace, they provide _____ counseling.

57. Rather than always complaining and blaming, group members within organizations express sincere _____ for the efforts of others.

58. The culture in caring organizations realizes that everyone makes mistakes and, thus, includes a capacity to _____.

59. At the factory that Darrell works in, the supervisors express interest in each employee and how they and their family are doing as well as respecting their privacy. Darrell's supervisors are showing _____.

60. Healthy organizations inspire their workers and give them hope, confidence, and courage through _____.

61. A good antidote for destructive competitiveness and petty game playing within an organization is to have _____ for others.

62. Jeff is a psychologist, whose job at a large corporation involves the testing, selection, placement, and promotion of employees. Jeff's branch of I/O psychology is called _____ psychology.

63. At present, the number of people who are or will be employed in business or industry is _____ out of 10.

64. Personnel selection begins with a detailed description of the skills, knowledge, and activities required by a particular job called a(n) _____.

65. For airline pilots, the ability to deal calmly with a mechanical emergency would be a(n) _____.

66. Some psychologists are now trying to identify general characteristics that person must have to succeed in a variety of work roles, rather than in just a specific job. This broader description is known as a(n) _____.

67. Looking at a potential employee's past behavior has been shown to be a good way to predict future behavior and is the idea behind collecting detailed biographical information known as _____.

68. Job applicants are questioned about their qualifications with an impression of the applicant's personality also being obtained during a personal _____.

69. When Terrence interviews Amy for a job, he notes that Amy is a very attractive and polite individual; and, thus, he assumes that Amy is also intelligent, hardworking, and responsible. Terrence is exhibiting the _____ effect.

70. Kim is going to a job interview, so she makes sure she is well groomed, dressed appropriately, has copies of her résumé, and has practiced being interviewed. In order to portray a positive image to the interviewers, Kim is engaging in _____.

931

71. Compared to direct efforts, such as emphasizing one's positive traits and past successes, the use of indirect efforts to make a good impression, like dressing well, wearing cologne, and flattering the interviewer, have been shown to be _____ effective.

72. When a person being interviewed excessively "blows his or her own horn," the interviewers' perceptions of the person's competence and suitability for a job tends to be _____.

73. Recent studies suggest that the accuracy of interviews can be improved by asking each job candidate the same questions as well as incorporating other means of giving the interviews more _____.

74. A great deal of information about a person's chances of succeeding in various jobs can be obtained from general mental tests, also called _____ tests.

75. Tests, such as the *Strong-Campbell Interest Inventory* and the *Kuder Occupational Interest Survey* are two types of _____ tests.

76. Realistic, investigative, artistic, social, enterprising, and conventional are the six major interest themes identified by psychologist _____.

77. Ted is a business major and plans to go into sales. According to the six major interest themes, Ted would be described as _____.

78. Maggie plans to be a chemist when she finishes college. According to the six major interest themes, Maggie would be described as _____.

79. Regarding the six major interest themes, a person who would enjoy being a mechanic or a farmer would be described as _____.

80. Being a clerk or studying economics would fall under the _____ interest theme.

81. Regarding the six major interest themes, a writer or a musician would be described as _____.

82. If Laquandra wants to be a teacher or counselor, her interests, according to the six major themes, would center on _____.

83. The tests that rate a person's potential to learn tasks or skills used in various occupations, such as clerical, legal, medical, or verbal skills are called _____ tests.

84. Rather than being administered a paper-and-pencil test as part of her employment testing, Marie is seated in front of a computer to take various tests and to watch realistic work scenes. Regarding presentation, Marie is being administered _____ tests.

85. Most management and executive positions are selected through the use of _____ centers.

86. When job applicants are observed and evaluated in simulated work situations, they are taking _____ tests.

87. Chantel is taking a test in which she will be presented with several memos, requests, and various business problems and will then have to quickly read all the materials and take the appropriate actions. Chantel is taking the _____ test.

88. A test of leadership that simulates group decision making and problem solving is the _____.

Part 1: Connections

1. ___ applied psychology

    a. approach that emphasizes human relations at work and that views people as industrious, responsible, and interested in challenging work

2. ___ industrial/organizational psychology

    b. approach also known as participative management that allows employees at all levels to participate in decision making

3. ___ Theory X leadership

    c. maintenance of good morale, labor relations, employee satisfaction, and similar aspects of work behavior

4. ___ Theory Y leadership

5. ___ work efficiency

6. ___ psychological efficiency

7. ___ knowledge workers

8. ___ shared leadership

9. ___ management by objectives

10. ___ self-managed team

11. ___ quality circle

d. workers who add value to their company by creating and manipulating information

e. work group that works together to achieved shared goals and has a high degree of freedom with respect to how it achieves these goals

f. field that focuses on the psychology of work and on behavior within organizations

g. employee discussion group that makes suggestions for improvement and solving business problems

h. the use of psychological principles and research methods to solve practical problems

i. maximum output (productivity) at lowest cost

j. also known as scientific management; uses time-and-motion studies, task analysis, job specialization, assembly lines, and pay schedules to increase productivity

k. approach in which employees are given specific goals to meet in their work

Part 2: Connections

1. ___ human factors psychologists

2. ___ clickwheel

3. ___ leadership

4. ___ industrial part of industrial/ organizational (I/O) psychology

5. ___ organizational part of industrial/organizational (I/O) psychology

6. ___ agentic

7. ___ communal

8. ___ glass ceiling

9. ___ desk rage

10. ___ job satisfaction

11. ___ flextime

a. capacity to define oneself to others in a way that clarifies and expands a vision of the future

b. study structure and company cultures to improve worker performance

c. degree to which a person is comfortable with his or her work

d. invisible barrier that has prevented women from moving into leadership positions

e. dependent, caring, nurturing, tender, sensitive, and sympathetic

f. work schedule that allows flexible starting and quitting times

g. workplace anger

h. study jobs to identify underlying skills, which can guide efforts to select people and train them for those jobs

i. design better tools by understanding human behavior

j. independent, confident, ambitious, objective, dominant, and forceful

k. touch-sensitive ring that enables iPod users to locate a desired song among thousands

Part 3: Connections

1. ___ compressed workweek

2. ___ telecommuting

3. ___ job enrichment

4. ___ organizational culture

5. ___ organizational citizenship

6. ___ job analysis

7. ___ halo effect

8. ___ impression management

9. ___ personnel psychology

a. making a job more personally rewarding, interesting, or intrinsically motivating; typically involves increasing worker knowledge

b. tendency of interviewers to extend favorable or unfavorable impressions to unrelated aspects of an individual's personality

c. seeking to portray a positive image of oneself to interviewers

d. a detailed description of the skills, knowledge, and activities required by a particular job

e. approach to flexible work that involves working from home by using a computer to stay connected to the office throughout the workday

f. branch of I/O psychology concerned with testing, selection, placement, and promotion of employees

g. making positive contributions to the success of an organization in ways that go beyond one's job description

h. the blend of customs, beliefs, values, attitudes, and rituals within an organization

i. work schedule that allows an employee to work fewer days per week by putting in more hours per day

Part 4: Connections

1. ___ critical incidents

2. ___ biodata

3. ___ personal interview

4. ___ general mental abilities tests

5. ___ vocational interest tests
6. ___ aptitude tests

7. ___ computerized tests

a. presenting realistic work situations to applicants in order to observe their skills and reactions

b. test that rates a person's potential to learn skills required by various occupations

c. program set up within an organization to conduct in-depth evaluations of job candidates for executive and management positions

d. situations that arise in a job, with which a competent worker must be able to cope

e. intelligence tests

f. testing procedure that involves memos, requests, and typical business problems to simulate the individual decision-making challenges that executives face

g. detailed biographical information about a job applicant

934

8. ___ assessment centers

9. ___ situational judgment tests

10. ___ in-basket test

11. ___ leaderless group discussion

h. test that simulates group decision making and problem solving

i. formal or informal questioning of job applicants to learn their qualifications and to gain an impression of their personalities

j. test that uses a computer to present lifelike situations to test takers

k. paper-and pencil test that typically measure six major themes identified by John Holland

Part 5: Connections

1. ___ realistic
2. ___ investigative
3. ___ artistic
4. ___ social
5. ___ enterprising
6. ___ conventional

a. music; writer
b. business; sales
c. physics; chemist
d. economics; clerk
e. agriculture; mechanic
f. education; counselor

Check Your Memory

1. TRUE or FALSE — Much of the iPod's success hinges on a tiny device called a control stick that quickly locates the desired song among thousands.

2. TRUE or FALSE — More recent touch-based models of iPod's use a multi-touch interface to allow easy access to the full range of available digital materials.

3. TRUE or FALSE — Basic research refers to the use of psychological principles and research methods to solve practical problems.

4. TRUE or FALSE — The largest applied areas in psychology are educational psychology and sports psychology.

5. TRUE or FALSE — Studying jobs to identify underlying skills, which can then guide efforts to select people and train them for those jobs comprises the organizational part of I/O psychology.

6. TRUE or FALSE — Edwin Friedman stated that "Leadership can be thought of as a capacity to define oneself to others in a way that clarifies and expands a vision of the future."

7. TRUE or FALSE — Employee stress, labor relations, machine design, and pay schedules are topics of special interest to I/O psychologists.

8. TRUE or FALSE — One of the earliest attempts to improve worker efficiency was made in 1903 by Douglas McGregor, who developed what is known as Type A leadership.

9. TRUE or FALSE — Scientific management uses time-and-motion studies, task analysis, job specialization, assembly lines, pay schedules, and the like to increase productivity.

10. TRUE or FALSE — Psychological efficiency is defined as maximum output at the lowest cost.

11. TRUE or FALSE — The leadership style that emphasizes human relations at work is referred to as Theory X, while scientific management is referred to as Theory Y.

12. TRUE or FALSE — Bankers, teachers, lawyers, writers, scientists, and computer engineers are examples of knowledge workers.

13. TRUE or FALSE — Today in North America, it is estimated that only two of every five persons in the workforce are knowledge workers.

935

14. TRUE or FALSE   As Theory X leadership has become more popular, women have begun to gain acceptance as leaders.

15. TRUE or FALSE   Nearly a quarter of all American organizations have female CEOs.

16. TRUE or FALSE   Studies have shown that companies with more women in leadership roles tend to perform worse financially than do companies that have more men in leadership roles.

17. TRUE or FALSE   The invisible barrier that has prevented women from moving into leadership positions is referred to as the "glass ceiling."

18. TRUE or FALSE   According to traditional gender role stereotypes, men are seen as agentic and, therefore, better leaders.

19. TRUE or FALSE   If a woman practices communal, Theory Y leadership, she is seen as weak, while if she acts more assertive, she is scorned for "trying to be a man."

20. TRUE or FALSE   At the Honda plant at Marysville, Ohio, private offices, separate dining halls, and reserved parking spaces for executives have been abolished with company executives working alongside the other employees.

21. TRUE or FALSE   Two techniques that make Theory Y leadership methods effective are shared leadership and management by objectives.

22. TRUE or FALSE   Participative management is another name for Theory X leadership.

23. TRUE or FALSE   Workers are especially productive when they receive feedback about their progress toward goals.

24. TRUE or FALSE   Self-managed teams can typically choose their own methods of achieving results, as long as they are effective.

25. TRUE or FALSE   Workers in self-managed teams are more likely to feel that they are being overworked and not being treated fairly by their supervisors.

26. TRUE or FALSE   Quality circles usually have the power to put their suggestions into practice directly, while self-managed teams are not able to do this.

27. TRUE or FALSE   Immediate productivity can be enhanced by Theory X methods, but often results in job satisfaction being lowered.

28. TRUE or FALSE   When job satisfaction is low, absenteeism skyrockets, morale falls, and there is a high rate of employee turnover, leading to higher training costs and inefficiency.

29. TRUE or FALSE   Job satisfaction comes from a good fit between work and a person's interests, abilities, needs, and expectations.

30. TRUE or FALSE   Happy people are more often happy at work, and they are more likely to focus on what is good about their job, rather than what is bad.

31. TRUE or FALSE   The basic idea of flextime is that starting and quitting times are flexible, as long as employees are present during a core work period.

32. TRUE or FALSE   When a worker works from home by using a computer to stay connected to the office, the approach is called a compressed workweek.

33. TRUE or FALSE   Job enrichment involves assigning a person more tasks so that they are focused, busy, and working to their capacity.

34. TRUE or FALSE   Job enrichment increases workers' knowledge by encouraging them to continuously learn a broad range of skills and information related to their occupations.

35. TRUE or FALSE   Organizational citizenship refers to the blend of customs, beliefs, values, attitudes, and rituals that give each organization its unique "flavor."

36. TRUE or FALSE   Workplace anger, or "desk rage" is frequently triggered by the feelings of being treated unfairly at work, by perceived threats to self-esteem, and work-related conflicts with others.

37. TRUE or FALSE   Since everyone makes mistakes, healthy organizations show a capacity to forgive.

38. TRUE or FALSE   Healthy organizations show sensitivity to others by expressing interest in the employees and in how they are doing and also respecting their privacy.

39. TRUE or FALSE   Empirical psychology is concerned with testing, selection, placement, and promotion of employees.

40. TRUE or FALSE   At present, six out of 10 people are or will be employed in business or industry with the others self-employed or employed by the government or educational institutions.

41. TRUE or FALSE   Selection of employees begins with job analysis, which is a detailed description of the skills, knowledge, and activities required by a particular job.

42. TRUE or FALSE   Situations with which competent employees must be able to cope are called biodata.

43. TRUE or FALSE   Some psychologists are now doing a broader "work analysis," in which they try to identify general characteristics that a person must have to succeed in a variety of work roles, rather than in just a specific job.

44. TRUE or FALSE   In personnel selection, the detailed biographical information obtained from applicants is known as critical incidents.

45. TRUE or FALSE   Some of the most useful biographical information obtained from applicants include past athletic interests, religious activities, social popularity, conflicts with brothers and sisters, attitudes toward school, and parents' socioeconomic status.

46. TRUE or FALSE   College grade point averages (GPAs) do not tend to predict success in most types of work.

47. TRUE or FALSE   The Barnum effect is the tendency of interviewers to extend favorable or unfavorable impressions to unrelated aspects of an individual's personality.

48. TRUE or FALSE   Interviewees tend to actively engage in impression management, which is the process of seeking to portray a positive image to interviewers.

49. TRUE or FALSE   Indirect efforts to make a good impression, like dressing well, wearing cologne, and flattering the interviewer, are more effective in interviews than direct efforts, such as emphasizing your positive traits and past successes.

50. TRUE or FALSE   Excessive self-promotion tends to raise interviewers' perceptions of competence and suitability for a job.

51. TRUE or FALSE   When being interviewed for a job, it is important to avoid questions about salary and benefits unless a job offer is forth coming.

52. TRUE or FALSE   Recent studies suggest that interviews can be improved by giving them more structure, such as each job candidate being asked the same questions.

53. TRUE or FALSE   General mental ability tests, or intelligence tests, tell a great deal about a person's chances of succeeding in various jobs.

54. TRUE or FALSE   The *Kuder Occupational Interest Survey* and the *Strong-Campbell Interest Inventory* are two types of vocational aptitude tests.

55. TRUE or FALSE   Vocational interest inventories typically measure six major themes identified by John Holland.

56. TRUE or FALSE   If a person plans to major in economics, he or she would most likely match Holland's interest theme called realistic.

57. TRUE or FALSE   A farmer or mechanic would most likely match Holland's conventional theme.

58. TRUE or FALSE   A person showing a high score on the enterprising theme would most likely be interested in education.

59. TRUE or FALSE   In addition to screening job applicants, computerized presentations can be used to improve the job skills of current employees.

60. TRUE or FALSE   Assessment centers are primarily used to fill management and executive positions.

61. TRUE or FALSE   Situational judgment tests are used to present difficult but realistic work situations to applicants.

62. TRUE or FALSE   The in-basket test is a test of leadership that simulates group decision making and problem solving.

Critical Thinking Question

In what area of human behavior other than work would a careful task analysis be helpful?

Module 16.1 Industrial/Organizational Psychology

Communication at Work—Getting the Message Across

Survey Question: What can be done to improve communication at work?

Language Development Guide

crucial: vital; important

muddled: mixed-up; messed up; jumbled

crushed: trampled; destroyed

keep them sharp: maintain skill or practice

decisively: with certainty

give me a hand: help me

ambiguous: vague; unclear

wiggle words: words showing uncertainty

intensifiers: word modifier that increases the emphasis

awesome: overwhelming

eschew: avoid

meretricious: attractive in a superficial or vulgar manner, but based on deception

utilization: use

polysyllabic: having several syllables

locutions: phrase or style of speech

obscure: difficult to understand; little known

insecurity: lack of confidence

blur: cloud; make indistinct

pulchritude: physical beauty

solely: only

cutaneous: related to the skin

profundity: state of having great depth; profound

trendy: fashionable

buzz words: important-sounding, usually technical words often of little meaning used chiefly to impress

synergistically: in a cooperative or interactive manner so that the total effect is greater than the parts separately

proactive: taking the initiative; hand-on

networking: developing contacts to exchange information

programmatic: following a plan

megatrends: large scale changes that define present and future events, such a buying trends, etc.
purveyor: commercial supplier of goods; seller; vendor
interface: interaction
jargon: language used by a specific group, profession, or culture in which the words and phrases
        may not be understood or used by others in different groups
slang: very casual speech
specialized: particular; specific
lingo: casual speech used usually in a specific group
belittled: put down; demeaned; made to feel less important
emotionally loaded: heavy with emotionally meaning
servile: submissive, obedient, giving up power or authority
stilted: artificial, awkward, stiff or unnatural
flare: suddenly blaze or burst forth
dispute: disagreement; quarrel
amplify: make stronger
undermine: weaken; undercut
channels: paths; means
two-way street: reciprocal situation; goes both ways
digressing: deviating or wandering away from the main topic
hasty: quick
well worth cultivating: a skill that is good to have
ensuring: making certain
scratched the surface: just begun to find out about something
relevance: significance; importance; consequence

Recite and Review

1. Important messages may get lost, feelings can be crushed, trust may be damaged, and poor decisions are made, when _____ is muddled.
2. News reporters learn to be precise about the "who, what, when, where, why, and _____" of events.
3. Rather than saying, "I need someone to give me a hand sometime with some stuff," it would be better to say, "Blake, would you please meet me in the storeroom in 5 minutes? I need help lifting a box." In this way, you have stated your ideas decisively and _____.
4. One should avoid the overuse of ambiguous words and phrases, such as *I guess, I think, kinda, sort of, around, some, about, you know,* and *like,* which are sometimes referred to as "_____ words."
5. One should also avoid the overuse of words, such as *very, really, absolutely, extra, super, awesome, ultimate,* and *completely,* which are referred to as _____.
6. Overuse of big words and other obscure vocabulary is often a sign of _____.
7. Most professions have their own specialized terminology, which provides a quick, shorthand way of expressing ideas, and is referred to as _____.
8. Words can have unintended effects on the listeners if the words have strong _____ meanings.
9. Good decision making and problem solving require an atmosphere in which people feel that their ideas, even when different than yours, are _____.
10. Work relationships go more smoothly when you learn people's _____.
11. True politeness puts others at ease, while phony politeness makes people feel they are being made fun of, or manipulated, or that you are faking it to win _____.
12. If you have a dispute with someone at work, remember to use the techniques of _____.

939

13. Be aware that your behavior sends messages, too. For example, being late for a meeting tells others that they are not very _____.
14. Messages are sent by your manner of dress, personal grooming, and even the way you decorate your personal _____.
15. In addition to expressing yourself clearly, you must also be a good _____.
16. It is important to stop what you are doing, actively give the speaker your attention, and resist _____.
17. One should also communicate your interest in the speaker by your posture, body position, and by making _____ with the speaker.
18. Rather than listening for isolated facts, a good listener tries to identify the speaker's _____.
19. As you listen to a speaker, try to keep an open mind and suspend _____.
20. It is important to let the other person talk, but occasionally acknowledge and confirm what the speaker is saying and restate important parts of the message in your own words in order to _____ your understanding.
21. Listeners should also be good observers, and pay attention to gestures, facial expressions, hesitations, silences, and other types of _____ messages.
22. As a listener, it is up to you to actively search what is said for value and for _____.

Connections

1. ___ wiggle words
2. ___ intensifiers
3. ___ obscure vocabulary
4. ___ jargon
5. ___ emotionally loaded words
6. ___ phony politeness
7. ___ nonverbal messages

a. "with your permission, if you would be ever so kind"
b. specialized terminology used as a shorthand way of expressing ideas
c. words, such as stupid, dumb, and ridiculous
d. words, such as very, awesome, and ultimate
e. gestures, hesitations, and manner of dress
f. ambiguous words and phrases
g. when used tends to be a sign of insecurity

Check Your Memory

1. TRUE or FALSE   Getting a job, keeping it, and excelling in your work all depend on knowing how to communicate clearly with others.
2. TRUE or FALSE   News reporters learn to be precise about the "who, what, when, where, why, and how" of events.
3. TRUE or FALSE   *Very, really, absolutely, extra, super, awesome, ultimate,* and *completely* are examples of "wiggle words."
4. TRUE or FALSE   Overuse of obscure vocabulary is often a sign of insecurity.
5. TRUE or FALSE   To show that you are up-to-date, you should try to use trendy "buzz words" in your conversation as often as possible.
6. TRUE or FALSE   Jargon can provide a quick, shorthand way of expressing ideas.
7. TRUE or FALSE   Jargon and technical lingo should be avoided unless you are sure that others are familiar with it.
8. TRUE or FALSE   The use of slang tends to make conversation more casual and helps include more people into the conversation.
9. TRUE or FALSE   Words that have strong emotional meanings can have unintended effects on listeners.
10. TRUE or FALSE   Good decision making and problem solving require an atmosphere in which people feel that their ideas are respected, even when they disagree.

11. TRUE or FALSE   Learning names is not necessary since work relationships go much smoother if they are impersonal.

12. TRUE or FALSE   You cannot overdo politeness.

13. TRUE or FALSE   If you have a dispute with someone at work, remember to use the techniques of self-assertion.

14. TRUE or FALSE   Actions can parallel, amplify, contradict, or undermine what you are saying.

15. TRUE or FALSE   Your manner of dress, personal grooming, and even the way you decorate your personal workspace, all send messages.

16. TRUE or FALSE   The action of being late for a meeting tells others that they are not very important to you.

17. TRUE or FALSE   You communicate your interest in what the speaker is saying by your posture, body position, and eye contact with the speaker.

18. TRUE or FALSE   In listening to a speaker, it is important to focus on the facts and details, rather than the overall theme.

19. TRUE or FALSE   As you listen to a speaker, try to quickly evaluate what is being said.

20. TRUE or FALSE   As the other person talks, occasionally acknowledge and confirm what the person is saying and restate important parts of the message in your own words to check your understanding.

21. TRUE or FALSE   Good listeners are also good observers, who pay attention to the nonverbal messages being sent.

22. TRUE or FALSE   It is totally up to the speaker to convey meaning in value to the listener.

Module 16.2 Environmental Psychology

Environmental Psychology—Life on Spaceship Earth

Survey Question: What have psychologists learned about the effects of our physical and social environments?

Language Development Guide

Spaceship Earth: term expressing concern over the use of limited resources available on Earth

locker room: clothes-changing area for athletes

casino: gambling area

personal space norms: accepted standard for regulating the area surrounding the body that is regarded as private

territoriality: defining a space as one's own or protecting it from intruders

human ecology: branch of sociology that studies human communities and populations

invasion: assault

get out of my face: go away, step back, leave

spatial: related to space

exclusive: restricted

reserved: set aside; kept back

formalizes: makes official

big smelly cigar helps: the choking smell of a cigar would keep most people away

"flat": lacks three-dimension and details

"dance": movements back and forth

adjacent: next to

intruders: unwelcome persons; person who enter an area without permission or illegally

saving a place: reserving a seat for a friend

home team advantage: tendency to win when playing teams play in familiar surroundings and with supportive fans

941

"take over": claim as their own

annoyed: irritated

intrude: enter an area without being asked

adorn: decorate

prime: major

"gated communities": private, upscale residential community that is surrounded by a barrier with entry through guarded gates restricted to the residents and their guests, often has its own security force

sprung up: appeared; occurred

mark: indicate

"defensible space": secure area that can be guarded

discourages: keeps back; deters

intrusion: interference; interruption

a highly territorial bulldog may help, too: an aggressive dog will keep people away out of a fear of being bitten

vandalism: causing public damage

architects: persons who design and supervise the construction of a building or other structures

"harden": to make it stronger to withstand damage

"de-opportunize": take away that chance that a situation may occur

graffiti: writing and drawings painted on walls illegally

blights: scars; stains; blots

lure: appeal

trampling: stepping on and crushing with one's feet

twisting: winding

linger: remain; delay leaving

traffic congestion: excessive number of cars; overcrowding on the highway that makes movement slow and difficult

impersonality: being socially rude, distant, or unresponsive

overstimulation: excessive amounts of stimuli that bombard the senses increasing the amount of arousal and causing activity

urban stress: pressures and strains that occur from living in a city

exploded: greatly expanded

sustainable: able to maintain

pessimistic: those who emphasize the negative outcomes

exceeded: gone beyond

indefinitely: length of time that has no obvious end

disastrous: terrible; ruinous; devastating

teeming: swarming; abounding with

underdeveloped nations: very poor countries with very low average incomes and lack of economic growth

international: global; worldwide

demographers: study of the characteristics of human populations, such as size, growth, density

jammed: squeezed into a confined space

ample: plenty

testimony: proof; evidence

conclusive: certain; beyond question

rascals: those who behave mischievously

staked out: established boundaries or positions around an area

harems: groups of females

pathological: mentally disturbing condition

mortality: death rate

indiscriminately: unselective; lacking in judgment

rampaging: violent, frenzied behavior

rampant: spreading uncontrollably; occurring unchecked

hypersexuality: very active sexual behavior

sexual passivity: inactive or submissive role in a sexual relationship

ghettos: densely populated area lived in by a group that experiences discrimination

tempting: inviting; enticing

guarded: cautious; restrained

bombard: attack; flood; overrun

fending: ward off;

callousness: heartlessness; insensitivity; coldness

blunting: making less strong or sharp, softening

proofreading: checking for and correcting errors in a written or printed report

noise-battered: being constantly exposed to uncontrollable loud noises

intrusive: interfering; disturbing

strip...the land: clear away all the natural growth

very face of the Earth: uppermost surface of the earth

global warming: increase in the average temperature of the earth's atmosphere

extinction: destruction and disappearance of a species

ozone layer: a layer in the stratosphere at about 20 miles above the earth that contains the gas ozone in high enough concentrations to block most of the ultraviolet radiation form the sun

unchecked: not watched

descendants: all of the offspring from a specific ancestor

pesticides: bug killers

brewing: looming; threatening; gathering force

vast: much

ultimately: in the end

consumption: using up; burning up

replenish: refill; restock; make complete

regenerate: restore; renew

projected: predicted; likely; expected

squandered: wasted; misspent

prompt: timely; punctual

temptation: enticement; appeal; attraction

elusive: hard to get hold of

"master-metered": utility such as gas or electricity is sold for an apartment complex or building with the residents paying as set amount as part of rent, rather than being charged individually

magnified: made greater in size

greenhouse gases: include methane, chlorofluorocarbons and carbon dioxide with these gases acting as a shield that traps heat in the earth's atmosphere

carbon debt: the overuse of the carbon dioxide absorption capacity of the world's oceans, soil, and vegetation

"throw-away" society: country in which there is excessive production and overconsumption of short-lived, disposable products

recycle: to extract useful material from waste and, thus, reuse the original resource

refundable deposits: usually refers to giving back money for returning a glass bottle

curbside pickup: garbage and recyclables picked up by trucks in from of one's home by the border of street and homeowner's property or sidewalk

"pledge cards": making a promise in writing to do something

reiterate: repeat; say again

943

in the long run: over a long period of time in the future
intentionally: on purpose
collective: as viewed as a whole
traffic snarls: tangled situation involving numerous cars
enticed: attracted; tempted; lured
prevail: succeed; win over
inconsequential: of little importance
follow suit: continue in the same pattern; follow the example set
collective good: common good; benefits everyone
sucker: one who is easily deceived and taken advantage of
dismantle: tear down; take apart
levied: imposed (or required) and collected
rebates: partial refund following a purchase
carpooling: several people riding in the same vehicle
stagger their departure times: vary the time they leave
fall into the trap: do something which is not wise although it seemed to be a good idea when you decided to do
"crazy house": unpredictable and chaotic
clustered: group of things of the same kind that are close together
suites: group of things that together form a set, such as a group of rooms
"wanted to be alone": maybe a play on the famous movie quote, "I want to be alone" spoken by Greta Garbo in movie *Grand Hotel*

Recite and Review

1. The specialty concerned with the relationship between environments and human behavior is called _____ psychology.
2. Natural settings, such as forest and beaches as well as environments built by humans, such as buildings, ships, and cities, are referred to as _____ environments.
3. A high school reunion, a choral concert, and a baseball game would be considered _____ environments.
4. A smaller area within an environment whose use is well-defined, such as a bus depot, waiting room, or lounge would be referred to a(n) _____.
5. Human ecology, territoriality, urban planning, pollution, crowding, and architectural design are topics of interest for _____ psychologists.
6. An area surrounding the body that is regarded as private and subject to personal control is referred to as an individual's _____.
7. The fact that many train commuters prefer to stand up if it means they can avoid sitting too close to strangers illustrates the concept of _____.
8. Ramir is interested in how humans use space as well as the norms for using this space, particularly in social settings. Ramir is interested in the field of study known as _____.
9. Spatial norms that govern comfortable or acceptable distances vary according to people's relationships as well as their _____.
10. Regarding cultural differences, those people who tend to hold their faces only inches apart while talking are from many of the _____ countries.
11. In Western Europe, the English sit closer together when conversing than the French or the _____ do.
12. For the majority of people in North America, the most private and exclusive space that extends about 18 inches out from the skin is called _____ distance.
13. When you are talking with friends, you are usually 18 inches to four feet from each other, which is called _____ distance.

14. Impersonal business and casual social gathering take place in a range of about four to 12 feet, which eliminates most touching and formalizes conversation within this _____ distance.
15. Lectures by your professor and other formal speeches are usually conducted about 12 feet or more from body and are referred to as _____ distance.
16. You can learn about your relationship to others by observing the distance you comfortably hold between yourselves since spatial behavior is very _____.
17. Jean and Akram are conversing when Akram gets closer to Jean as he is talking. Jean steps back and puts her arm between them because she thinks Akram is getting to familiar, while Akram feels rejected by Jean stepping back each time he gets closer. This illustrates how misunderstandings can occur when two people of different nationalities have different norms for _____.
18. Often, we must stand within intimate distance of others in crowds, buses, subways, elevators, and other public places. At such times, privacy is maintained by standing shoulder to shoulder or back to back, by positioning a purse, bag, package, or coat as a barrier to spatial intrusions, and by avoiding _____.
19. As we move farther from the body, it becomes apparent that personal space also extends to adjacent areas that we claim as our "_____."
20. Actions that define a space as one's own or that protect it from intruders are referred to as _____ behavior.
21. In the library, you protect your space at a study table by leaving your jacket hanging on the back of the chair and your notebook on the table when you go to find another reference book. You are exhibiting _____ behavior.
22. Researchers have found that the more attached you are to an area, the more likely you are to adorn it with objects that signal your "ownership," which are referred to as _____.
23. Burglars are less likely to break into houses that have fences (even if small), parked cars, lawn furniture, exterior lights, and security signs, all of which serve as _____.
24. Small behavioral settings are defined by _____ norms.
25. Using psychological research, many architects are able to discourage vandalism and graffiti in public setting by "de-opportunizing" and "_____" these settings.
26. Shopping malls and department stores encourage shoppers to linger and wander while looking at merchandise because they are designed like _____.
27. Traffic congestion, pollution, crime, crowding, noise, overstimulation, and impersonality are s major sources of _____ stress.
28. Overpopulation ranks as one of the most serious problems facing the world today with the current world population now at more than _____ billion people.
29. By 2050, the world's population may exceed _____ billion.
30. Experts estimate that five to 20 billion persons is the maximum _____ population of the Earth.
31. When John Calhoun let a group of laboratory rats breed without limit in a confined space while providing them with enough food, water, and nesting materials, both male and female rats showed a high rate of _____ behavior.
32. In Calhoun's experiment, when the rat colony became extremely crowded, pregnancies decreased and infant mortality was _____.
33. Many of the rats in Calhoun's experiment died, apparently from _____ diseases.
34. The number of people in a given space or, inversely the amount of space available to each person is referred to as _____.
35. A subjective feeling of being overstimulated by a loss of privacy or by the nearness of others, especially when social contact with them is unavoidable is called _____.
36. Whether high density is experienced as crowding may depend on the _____ among those involved.

945

37. Stress is likely to result when crowding causes a loss of _____ over one's immediate social environment.
38. According to Stanley Milgram, living in a large city can be a stressful situation because sensory stimulation, information and social contacts make excessive demands on people's attention, a condition he called _____.
39. Milgram believed that city dwellers learn to prevent the stress that comes from so much sensory stimulation by engaging only in brief, superficial social contacts, by fending off others with cold and unfriendly expressions, and by ignoring _____ events.
40. In a study conducted in America in which a young child stood on a busy street corner in large cities and in smaller towns, the people who were more likely to help were the people in the _____.
41. One of the most serious costs of urban stresses and crowding may be a blunting of _____ to the needs of others.
42. In a comparison of children from the noisy schools near an airport and children in schools farther from the airport, it was found that children in the noisy schools had higher blood pressure and experienced difficulty on tasks requiring close attention and _____.
43. The children in these uncontrollable noisy environments often "give up" and develop a state of "_____."
44. A major source of environmental stress is annoying and intrusive noise, which is called _____.
45. Global warming; the extinction of plants and animals; a hole in the ozone layer; and polluted land, air, water, and oceans are examples of how the natural environment can be drastically changed by human _____.
46. An elevated risk of physical and mental disease occurs when people are exposed to radiation, pesticides, industrial chemicals, and other _____ hazards.
47. Since corporations and governments do much environmental damage, many of the solutions will require changes in policies and _____.
48. Most of the environmental problems we face can be traced back to the human tendency to _____ natural resources.
49. Resource consumption can be measures as the amount of land and water area required to replenish the resources that a human population consumes, which is referred to as a(n) _____.
50. Compared to Asia and Africa, North America's consumption of resources is about _____ times higher.
51. We usually find it difficult to reduce our use of resources because of a lack of prompt _____.
52. Conserving electricity is especially elusive because electricity use in some apartment complexes is not charged to individual families but is "_____."
53. Websites that allow individuals to calculate and track their individual resource consumption are called _____ calculators.
54. With growing public concern over global warming, many people are now calculating the volume of greenhouse gases individual consumption adds to the atmosphere, which is referred to as their individual _____.
55. It has also become popular for individuals to plant trees to offset some of their _____ debt.
56. Prompt and accurate information and feedback about energy use is making it possible to aspire to a lifestyle, in which one's energy consumption is reduced and the remainder offset so that the overall impact on global warming is zero. This type of lifestyle is described as _____.

946

57. One of the most effective ways to encourage pro-environmental behavior, such as recycling, is to present information on environmental problems and pro-environmental values in _____.

58. Requiring refundable deposits on glass bottles is a good example of increasing recycling by using _____.

59. Some cities have greatly increases participation in recycling programs by accepting _____ recycling materials.

60. People are more likely to follow through and actually recycle if they sign "pledge cards" or make some other public _____ to recycle.

61. Because large numbers of people in large cities want to drive for "convenience," driving becomes inconvenient with all the traffic snarls. This illustrates a(n) social _____.

62. When individuals are enticed into overuse of scarce resources that must be shared by many people and each person acts in his or her self-interest, ecologist Garrett Hardin calls such situations the _____.

63. Persuasion and education have been used to encourage conservation with effective appeals being based on self-interest (such as cost savings), on a personal desire to take better care of the planet, and to protect one's own children and future generations, also referred to as the _____.

64. By rearranging rewards and cost, it is sometimes possible to dismantle social _____.

65. To find solutions to problems like overcrowding, pollution, and overuse of resources, psychologists try to determine how environments influence the behavior and perceptions of the people using them by conducting _____.

66. Baum and Valins found that students housed in long, narrow, corridor-design dormitories often felt stressed and _____.

67. The study of the effects buildings have on behavior is called _____ psychology.

68. In a later study, Baum and Davis compared students living in a regular long-corridor dorm with those living in an altered dorm in which the corridor was divided in half with a lounge area in between. The dorm arrangement that produced less stress and more friendships was the _____ dorm.

Part 1: Connections

1. ___ personal space

   a. distance at which impersonal interaction takes place; about four to 12 feet from the body

2. ___ proxemics

   b. unspoken rules that govern the comfortable or acceptable distances maintained between individuals and which vary with relationships, activities, and cultures

3. ___ spatial norms

   c. systematic study of the human use of space, particularly in social settings

4. ___ intimate distance

   d. distance at which formal interactions, such as giving a speech, occur; about 12 feet or more from the body

5. ___ personal distance

   e. an area surrounding the body that is regarded as private and subject to personal control

6. ___ social distance

   f. distance maintained when interacting with close friends; about 18 inches to four feet

7. ___ public distance

   g. the most private and exclusive space immediately surrounding the body

Part 2: Connections

1. ___ environmental psychology
2. ___ physical environments
3. ___ social environments
4. ___ behavioral settings
5. ___ territorial behavior
6. ___ density
7. ___ crowding
8. ___ attentional overload
9. ___ noise pollution
10. ___ social dilemma

a. the number of people in a given space or the amount of space available to each person

b. environment defined by a group of people and their activities or interrelationships

c. stressful condition caused when sensory stimulation, information, and social contacts make excessive demands on attention

d. formal study of how environments affect behavior

e. stressful, annoying, and intrusive noise

f. natural settings, such as forests and beaches, as well as environments built by humans, such as building and cities

g. smaller area within an environment whose use is well defined, such as a bus depot, waiting room, or lounge

h. social situation that tends to provide immediate rewards for actions that will have undesired effects in the long run

i. any behavior that tends to define a space as one's own or that protects it from intruders

j. subjective feeling of being overstimulated by a loss of privacy or by the nearness of others

Part 3: Connections

1. ___ territorial markers
2. ___ ecological footprint
3. ___ ecological footprint calculators
4. ___ carbon footprint
5. ___ carbon-neutral lifestyle
6. ___ tragedy of the commons
7. ___ environmental assessments
8. ___ architectural psychology

a. websites that allow individual to determine and track their individual resource consumption

b. one's energy consumption is reduced and the remainder offset so that the person's overall impact on global warming is zero

c. social dilemma in which individuals, each acting in his or her immediate self-interest, overuse a scarce group resource

d. volume of greenhouse gases individual consumption adds to the atmosphere

e. the study of the effects buildings and their design have on behavior

f. measurement and analysis of the effects an environment has on the behavior and perceptions of people within that environment

g. amount of land and water area required to replenish the resources that a human population consumes

h. objects and other signals whose placement indicates to others the "ownership" or control of a particular area

948

Check Your Memory

1. TRUE or FALSE   Specific environments have a significant impact on human behavior, and people have a significant impact on environments, both natural and constructed.

2. TRUE or FALSE   Architectural design, cognitive maps, privacy, and vandalism are topics of special interest to environmental psychologists.

3. TRUE or FALSE   If you are talking to an acquaintance and move in closer, the person will either move back or if they hold their ground will turn to the side or position an arm in front of him or herself as a barrier.

4. TRUE or FALSE   Personal space extends "I" or "me" boundaries past the skin to the immediate environment.

5. TRUE or FALSE   The systematic study of norms concerning the use of personal space is called semantics.

6. TRUE or FALSE   Norms governing comfortable or acceptable distance vary according to people's relationships as well as their activities.

7. TRUE or FALSE   In many Middle Eastern countries, people hold their faces only inches apart while talking.

8. TRUE or FALSE   In Western Europe, the Dutch sit closer together when conversing than the English do with the French sitting even farther apart.

9. TRUE or FALSE   For a majority of people in North America, the most private and exclusive space is called personal distance.

10. TRUE or FALSE   The distance maintained in comfortable interaction with close friends is called social distance.

11. TRUE or FALSE   Formal speeches, lectures, and business meetings are usually conducted at public distance.

12. TRUE or FALSE   Because spatial behavior is very consistent, you can learn about your relationship to others by observing the distance you comfortably hold between yourselves.

13. TRUE or FALSE   When two people of different nationalities have different norms for personal space, this can lead to misunderstandings in which one person feels that the other is being too familiar at the same time as the person moving closer feels rejected.

14. TRUE or FALSE   If you place your book bag in the seat next to yours to "save this place" for a friend, you are exhibiting proxemic behavior.

15. TRUE or FALSE   Sports teams usually show a home team advantage by playing better on their own home territory than while playing in another team's territory.

16. TRUE or FALSE   Researchers have found that the more attached you are to an area, the more likely you are to adorn it with obvious territorial markers that signal your "ownership."

17. TRUE or FALSE   Graffiti, one of the blights of urban life, is an obvious form of territorial marking.

18. TRUE or FALSE   On the basis of psychological research, many architects now "soften" and "opportunize" public settings to discourage vandalism and graffiti.

19. TRUE or FALSE   Many shopping malls and department stores are designed like mazes to encourage shoppers to linger and wander while looking at merchandise.

20. TRUE or FALSE   Raised flowerbeds around signs have been shown to protect them because people resist trampling the flowers to get to the sign.

21. TRUE or FALSE   The world's population is currently at 20 billion people with experts estimating the maximum sustainable population of the Earth to be between 25 and 50 billion.

949

22. TRUE or FALSE   Animal studies on overcrowding are considered to be accurate and conclusive when applied to humans.

23. TRUE or FALSE   In the later phases of Calhoun's overcrowding experiment, pregnancies in the rat colony significantly increased with the rats showing less aggressive behaviors.

24. TRUE or FALSE   Most laboratory studies using human subjects have failed to produce any serious ill effects by crowding people into small places.

25. TRUE or FALSE   The number of people in a given space is called density, while crowding is a psychological condition caused by being overstimulated by social input or a loss of privacy.

26. TRUE or FALSE   Large cities tend to bombard residents with continuous input that makes excessive demands on attention with the resulting stressful condition being called sensory hyperplasia.

27. TRUE or FALSE   According to Milgram, city dwellers learn to prevent this attentional overload by engaging only in brief, superficial social contacts, by ignoring nonessential events, and by fending off others with cold and unfriendly expressions.

28. TRUE or FALSE   In an experiment in which a young child stood on a busy street corner in several large American cities and smaller nearby towns, the child was more likely to be offered help in the larger cities.

29. TRUE or FALSE   The least helpful city tested with the young child standing on the busy street corner asking for help was New York City.

30. TRUE or FALSE   Children attending noisy schools near airports did not show any more stress reactions or academic problems than children in the quieter schools because of the human ability to successfully adapt to environmental conditions.

31. TRUE or FALSE   Noise pollution is defined as a stressful, annoying, and intrusive noise.

32. TRUE or FALSE   Exposure to toxic hazards, such as radiation, pesticides, and industrial chemicals, leads to an elevated risk of physical and mental disease.

33. TRUE or FALSE   Most of the environmental problems we face can be traced back to the human tendency to overuse natural resources.

34. TRUE or FALSE   Resource consumption can be measured as an environmental echo.

35. TRUE or FALSE   According to the Global Footprint Network, humans are already consuming more than the Earth can regenerate.

36. TRUE or FALSE   North America's consumption of resources is about three times higher than that of Asia or Africa.

37. TRUE or FALSE   Psychologists have shown that lower energy bills result from simply giving families daily feedback about their use of gas or electricity.

38. TRUE or FALSE   Apartment complexes that are "master-metered" consume about 25 percent less energy than those apartments that have individual meters.

39. TRUE or FALSE   Websites known as carbon conservation calculators (CCC) allow individuals to calculate and track their individual resource consumption.

40. TRUE or FALSE   The volume of greenhouse gases individual consumption adds to the atmosphere is known as a carbon footprint.

41. TRUE or FALSE   Planting trees is one way to offset some carbon debt.

42. TRUE or FALSE   When a person's energy consumption is reduced and the remainder offset so that the person's overall impact on global warming is zero, the person is leading a carbon-neutral lifestyle.

43. TRUE or FALSE   Learning about environmental problems and pro-environmental values at school has been one of the most effective ways to encourage pro-environmental behavior including recycling.

44. TRUE or FALSE   Requiring refundable deposits on glass bottles is a good example of the use of punishment to increase recycling.
45. TRUE or FALSE   People who feel they have committed themselves to recycling are more likely to follow through and actually recycle.
46. TRUE or FALSE   When people set their own goals for recycling, they rarely ever reach these goals.
47. TRUE or FALSE   People are most likely to continue recycling if they emphasize the sense of satisfaction they get from contributing to the environment.
48. TRUE or FALSE   In a typical social dilemma, no one individual intentionally acts against the group interest, but if many people act alike, collective harm is done.
49. TRUE or FALSE   If everyone one in the community waters their lawn "just a little," this collective use of water during a drought may cause everyone to not have enough water for drinking, bathing, and washing, a situation that ecologist Garrett Hardin called the "divine tragedy."
50. TRUE or FALSE   In most social dilemmas, people are less likely to restrain themselves if they believe others in the group are restraining themselves.
51. TRUE or FALSE   It is possible to dismantle social dilemmas by rearranging rewards and costs.
52. TRUE or FALSE   The measurement and analysis of the effects an environment has on the behavior and perceptions of people within that environment is called a perceptual evaluation.
53. TRUE or FALSE   Baum and Valins found that students housed in long, narrow corridor-design dormitories formed more friendships, were more open to social contacts, and showed less stress than students housed in the divided-hall dorm design or the three-cluster dorm room design.
54. TRUE or FALSE   The study of the effects buildings have on behavior and the design of buildings using behavioral principles is called architectural psychology.

Critical Thinking Question

Many of the most damaging changes to the environment being caused by humans will not be felt until sometime in the future. How does this complicate the problem of preserving environmental quality?

Module 16.3 The Psychology of Education, Law, and Sports

Educational Psychology—An Instructive Topic

Survey Question: How has psychology improved education?

Language Development Guide

foster: promote; encourage
bribery: offering of money or other incentives to persuade somebody to do something
field trip: an outing in which something is studied
lie at the heart: at the center; most important part
classroom management: methods and strategies an educator uses to maintain a **classroom** environment that will promote student learning
curriculum: courses taught and the topics within each course that are taught
exceptional students: children or youth who require special instruction or related services due to deviating significantly from the average physical or mental ability
"breaking in": training
periodic: cyclic; recurring
rote practice: memorization using repetition

as it turns out: in the end; the result
abstract thinking: ability to understand concepts and generalizations
hand in hand: together; in cooperation
peek: quick look
ring truer: sounds even more true or likely
richly: completely; elaborately
blogs: personal journal or diary on a website
intuitive: known automatically
it won't stick to the roof of your mind: a joke comparing the Universal Design to peanut butter, which sometimes sticks to the roof of our mouth

Recite and Review

1. Effective teachers must understand learning, instruction, classroom dynamics, and _____.

2. Helena works in the field that seeks to understand how people learn and how teachers instruct, which is called _____ psychology.

3. When an instructor uses a planned method of instruction, she or he is using a specific _____.

4. Test writing, student needs, and intelligence testing are topics of special interest to _____ psychologists.

5. Whether it's "breaking in" a new coworker, instructing a friend in a hobby, or helping a child learn to read, the fact is, at times we all _____.

6. Many effective teaching strategies apply the basic principles of _____ conditioning.

7. Steps in instruction often include learner preparation, stimulus presentation, learner response, reinforcement, evaluation, and _____.

8. At the beginning of instruction, a teacher must focus attention on the topic at hand by first gaining the learner's _____.

9. During the second step in instruction, a teacher should deliberately and clearly present information, examples, illustrations, and other instructional _____.

10. The teacher should allow time for the learner to respond to the information presented by asking questions and _____ correct responses.

11. To strengthen correct responses, teachers should give positive reinforcement, such as praise or encouragement as well as giving _____.

12. Both the teacher and the learner can make adjustments when needed by assessing the learner's _____.

13. Because it helps strengthen responses to key stimuli, an important step in teaching is the _____ review.

14. Factual information is presented by lecture, demonstration, and rote practice in the teaching style known as _____.

15. Teachers create conditions that encourage students to construct knowledge for themselves when they use a teaching style known as _____.

16. Students do slightly better on achievement tests when teachers use the teaching style known as _____.

17. Students do somewhat better on tests of abstract thinking, creativity, and problem solving when the teaching strategy known as _____ is used.

18. Greg and his fellow students would be described as more independent, curious, and positive in their attitude toward school than most of the students at his school because his teacher uses the teaching strategy called _____.

19. Because educators face an increasingly diverse mix of students including "regular" students, adult learners, bilingual students, and students with disabilities, teachers have begun to apply

952

an approach in which lessons are designed so richly that most, if not all, students will benefit. This approach is called _____.

20. In using this new "richly designed teaching style," teachers may use lectures, podcasts of lectures, group activities, and Internet discussion lists. In other words, the teachers use a variety of _____.

21. We all learn better if we can choose among different ways of gaining _____.

22. Another principle of this new "richly designed teaching style" is to make learning materials simple and intuitive by removing unnecessary _____.

Connections

1. ___ educational psychology
2. ___ teaching strategy
3. ___ direct instruction
4. ___ discovery learning
5. ___ Universal Design for Instruction
6. ___ spaced review
7. ___ evaluation

a. tests and other methods are used to gauge the learner's progress

b. approach that uses a variety of instructional methods with lessons designed so richly that they benefit most, if not all, students

c. instruction based on encouraging students to construct knowledge for themselves

d. presentation of factual information by lecture, demonstration, and rote practice

e. helps to strengthen key responses during any learning process

f. field that seeks to understand how people learn and how teachers instruct

g. any planned method of instruction

Check Your Memory

1. TRUE or FALSE   Aptitude testing, language learning, and test writing are topics of special interest to educational psychologists.
2. TRUE or FALSE   Effective teachers must understand classroom dynamics.
3. TRUE or FALSE   Many effective teaching strategies apply the basic principles of classical conditioning.
4. TRUE or FALSE   A planned method of instruction is referred to as concept learning.
5. TRUE or FALSE   The first step in instruction involves gaining the learner's attention and focusing interest on the topic at hand.
6. TRUE or FALSE   Teachers should allow time for the learner to respond to the information presented by repeating correct responses or asking questions.
7. TRUE or FALSE   The use of positive reinforcement during teaching is merely a form of bribery that will prove to be ineffective.
8. TRUE or FALSE   Evaluation is done in order to assess the learner's progress so that adjustments can be made in instruction when needed.
9. TRUE or FALSE   Massed practice is an important step in teaching because it helps strengthen responses to key stimuli.
10. TRUE or FALSE   In direct instruction, factual information is presented by lecture, demonstration, and rote practice.
11. TRUE or FALSE   Students of discovery learning do slightly better on achievement tests than students in direct instruction.
12. TRUE or FALSE   Students of discovery learning do somewhat better on tests of abstract thinking, creativity, and problem solving.
13. TRUE or FALSE   Students of direct instruction tend to be more independent, curious, and positive in their attitude toward school.

953

14. TRUE or FALSE   A balanced education uses both direct instruction and discovery learning.
15. TRUE or FALSE   Because of the diversity of the students taught, educators have begun to apply an approach called *Universal Design for Instruction*, in which lessons are designed so richly that they will benefit most, if not all, students.
16. TRUE or FALSE   One principle of *Universal Design for Instruction* is to use a variety of instructional methods, such as a lecture, a podcast of the lecture, a group activity, and an Internet discussion list.
17. TRUE or FALSE   In the *Universal Design for Instruction*, learning materials are made more intricate with increasing levels of complexity.
18. TRUE or FALSE   The principles of the *Universal Design for Instruction* have been used in college and universities.

Module 16.3 The Psychology of Education, Law, and Sports

Psychology and Law—Judging Juries

Survey Question: What does psychology reveal about juries and court verdicts?

Language Development Guide

fascinating: captivating; interesting; absorbing

defendant: person on trial; person accused of breaking the law

arbitration: the hearing of a case by someone who has the power to judge and make a decision or compromise

capital punishment: death penalty

parole: early release of a prisoner on the conditions of good behavior and regular reporting to his or her parole officer

forensic: use of science to investigate and establish facts in criminal or civil cases

sentencing: final phase of a court trial; refers to the number of years the person must spend in jail as punishment

white-collar crime: general term for crimes involving fraud, cheating consumers, swindles, insider trading on the stock market, embezzlement and other forms of dishonest business schemes

twist: turn of events; development

swindling: to cheat out of one's money

swayed: inclined or bent to one side

pretrial publicity: information in the media about the case

incorporate: include; integrate it in

deliberations: discussions; debate

inadmissible: not allowed

prior conviction: was declared guilty in another case

slips out: information accidentally comes out and is heard

severity: harshness

prides itself: self-confidence in how it performs

quirks: peculiarities of behavior; whims

composition: what something consists of; the make up

all is not lost: there is some good news

demographic: characteristics of the human population

indifferent: uncaring; unmoved

justified: with good reason

necessity: required

specifically: definitely

954

disproportionate: unequal in number or amount
criminal intent: the state of mind in committing an criminal act
executed: put to death for a major crime
inevitable: unavoidable; bound to happen
ultimate: final; last
O.J. Simpson: former professional football player accused and acquitted of his ex-wife's murder
emerging: new; appearing
prosecution: lawyers for the state that pursue the formal charges against the defendant
net effect: final result after calculating the pluses and minuses
sanity hearings: to determine whether person is legally responsible for actions and is competent
       to aid in his or her defense
profile: investigating an offender's behavior, motives and background to help guide an
investigation
profile: to summarize a person's personality and behaviors
police cadets: police trainee

Recite and Review

1. The study of the behavioral dimensions of the legal system is called the _____.
2. Psychologists have begun to understand what determines how real jurors vote by studying the behavior of simulated or _____ juries.
3. In these simulated juries, volunteers are sometimes simply given written evidence and arguments to read before making a decision, while others may watch videotaped trials staged by _____.
4. Arbitration, forensic hypnosis, polygraph accuracy, and the insanity plea are topics of special interest in the psychology of _____.
5. In general when jurors are presented with attractive defendants as opposed to unattractive defendants, the jurors are more likely to find the attractive ones _____ of the crime.
6. Jurors are not very good at separating evidence from other information, such as their perceptions of the defendant, attorneys, witnesses, and what they think the _____ wants.
7. If complex scientific evidence is presented, jurors tend to be swayed more by the witness's _____.
8. Because crime-solving programs like *CSI:* and *Forensic Files* make it seem simple, today's jurors place too much confidence in _____ evidence.
9. Jurors tend to inappropriately incorporate additional information into their jury deliberations, often without being aware it has happened when they have been exposed to _____ publicity.
10. Often the jurors' final verdict is influenced by such things as the mention of a defendant's prior conviction, which is considered _____ evidence.
11. Although jurors are not supposed to let it affect their verdict, many jurors take into account the _____ of the defendant's likely punishment.
12. A jury's biases and quirks play less of a role in the verdict, the more clear-cut the evidence and the more _____ the crime.
13. Jurors typically form an opinion _____ in the trial.
14. Regarding potential jurors who may be biased, opposing attorneys, before a trial begins, are allowed a certain number which they can _____.
15. Regarding the role of gender, it has been found that the juries that are more likely to vote for conviction in child sexual assault trials are those composed of _____.
16. Psychologists help the attorneys to identify people who will favor or harm their efforts during _____ jury selection.

955

17. In jury selection, information may be collected on each juror and includes a juror's age, sex, race, occupation, education, political affiliation, religion, and socioeconomic status. This is called _____ information.
18. In order to find out how local citizens feel about the case with the assumption being that the jurors probably have similar attitudes, psychologists may conduct a(n) _____ survey.
19. In court, psychologists often watch for people who believe punishment is effective and would be more likely to vote for conviction. These people have _____ personality traits.
20. Psychologist typically watch potential jurors while they are sitting in the jury box during a trial to see which side each person is favoring by observing their _____.
21. In the United States, murder trials require a special jury made up of people who are not opposed to the death penalty and is referred to as a(n) _____ jury.
22. Regarding gender and race, the special juries for death penalty cases are disproportionately male and _____.
23. The people on the special juries for death penalty cases typically are conservative, have high incomes, and _____ personality traits.
24. Given the same facts, jurors who favor the death penalty are more likely to read into a defendant's actions _____ intent.
25. Jurors who favor the death penalty are much more likely than average to _____ a defendant.
26. In the well-publicized case of O. J. Simpson, who was accused of brutally killing his wife and her friend, people that thought Simpson was innocent tended to be _____ Americans.
27. The fact that emerging evidence and arguments had little effect on what people believed regarding the guilt or innocence of O. J. Simpson shows how the outcome of a trial can sometimes be decided by _____.
28. Unlike most people who cannot afford it, wealthy clients have the advantage of _____ jury selection.
29. If both sides in a trial have help in selecting a jury, the net effect is probably a more _____ jury.
30. Psychologists evaluate people for sanity hearings, do counseling in prisons, profile criminals in order to apprehend them, advise lawmakers on public policy, and help select and train _____ cadets.

Connections

1. ____ psychology of law
2. ____ mock juries
3. ____ scientific jury selection
4. ____ demographic information
5. ____ authoritarian
6. ____ community survey
7. ____ death-qualified jury

a. used to find out how local citizens feel about a court case and in doing so find out how the jurors who are similar feel about the case
b. personalities that tend to believe that punishment is effective and are more likely to vote for conviction
c. jury composed of people who favor the death penalty or at least are indifferent to it
d. data regarding the juror's age, sex, race, occupation, education, political affiliation, religion, and socioeconomic status
e. using social science principles to choose members of a jury
f. study of the psychological and behavioral dimensions of the legal system
g. group that realistically simulates a courtroom jury

Check Your Memory

1. TRUE or FALSE   The study of the behavioral dimensions of the legal system are referred to as comparative forensics.

2. TRUE or FALSE   Psychologists study the behavior of mock juries to help understand what determines how real jurors vote.

3. TRUE or FALSE   On the basis of the same evidence, jurors are more likely to find attractive defendants guilty than unattractive defendants, regardless of the crime being prosecuted.

4. TRUE or FALSE   Jurors are not very good at separating evidence from their perceptions of the defendant, attorneys, witnesses, and what they think the judge wants.

5. TRUE or FALSE   If complex scientific evidence is presented, jurors tend to be swayed more by the evidence than by the expertise of the witness.

6. TRUE or FALSE   Today's jurors place too little confidence in DNA evidence because of their lack of basic scientific knowledge.

7. TRUE or FALSE   Jurors who have been exposed to pretrial publicity tend to inappropriately incorporate that information into their jury deliberations, often without being aware it has happened.

8. TRUE or FALSE   Often the jurors' final verdict is influenced by inadmissible evidence, such as the mention of a defendant's prior conviction.

9. TRUE or FALSE   Although they are encouraged to do so, jurors rarely take into account the severity of the punishment a defendant faces.

10. TRUE or FALSE   Typically jurors form an opinion early in the trial and then have difficult fairly judging any evidence that contradicts their opinion.

11. TRUE or FALSE   The more severe the crime and the more clear-cut the evidence, the more a jury's biases and quirks affect the verdict.

12. TRUE or FALSE   Juries composed of men are more likely to vote for conviction in child sexual assault trials than women.

13. TRUE or FALSE   Before a trial begins, opposing attorneys are allowed to disqualify a certain number of potential jurors who may be biased.

14. TRUE or FALSE   When social science principles are applied to the process of choosing a jury, it is referred to as forensic jury profiling.

15. TRUE or FALSE   Much of the demographic information that is collected for each juror is available from public records.

16. TRUE or FALSE   Psychologists use a community survey to interview the potential jurors for a case outside the courtroom.

17. TRUE or FALSE   Jurors with authoritarian personality traits tend to believe that punishment is not effective and are less likely to vote for conviction.

18. TRUE or FALSE   Psychologists typically observe potential jurors' nonverbal behavior and try to learn from body language which side the person favors.

19. TRUE or FALSE   People in a death-qualified jury must favor the death penalty or at least be indifferent to it.

20. TRUE or FALSE   Death-qualified juries are likely to contain a disproportionate number of people who are male, white, conservative, and with high incomes.

21. TRUE or FALSE   Jurors who favor the death penalty are more likely to read criminal intent into a defendant's actions and are more likely than average to convict a defendant.

22. TRUE or FALSE   A majority of African Americans thought O.J. Simpson was guilty during the early stages of his murder trial.

23. TRUE or FALSE   Because emerging evidence and arguments had the most effect on what people believed at the end of O.J. Simpson's murder trial shows that jury makeup has very little to do in the final verdict.

24. TRUE or FALSE   Wealthy clients have the advantage of scientific jury selection, something most people cannot afford.

25. TRUE or FALSE   When both sides in a trial have help selecting jurors, the net effect in most instances is probably a more balanced jury.

26. TRUE or FALSE   Psychologists have been used to help select and train police cadets.

Module 16.3 The Psychology of Education, Law, and Sports
Sports Psychology—The Athletic Mind
Survey Question: Can psychology enhance athletic performance?

Language Development Guide

conditioning: training, preparation

spectators: those who watch an event, such as sports competitions

one-winner mentality: idea that for every contest there is one winner and everyone else is a loser; winning is everything

fair play: established standard of honesty and decency

advent: beginning; start

debatable: controversial; doubtful; questionable

homespun: created without formal training or instruction, self-taught

marksmanship: skill in shooting

bull's eye: center of a target

prone position in target shooting: lying on the front of your body holding the rifle

keen: sharp; well-developed

induced: caused

astray: off target

molded: shaped

pole-vaulting: sport where a person uses a pole to throw themselves over a high bar

shooting baskets: playing basketball

cross-country skiing: sport of skiing across the countryside rather than downhill

automated: become routine; perform without conscious attention

phenomenon: occurrence

harmonious: match, in agreement

personal bests: an individual's best level of performance, often in athletics

elusive: hard to describe

sprinter: a person who participates in track competitions in which he or she runs a short distance at top speed

choking: losing concentration at a critical moment, causing failure

watches a movie: imagines a perfect performance

berating: criticizing

savors: enjoys for a period of time

optimum: most favorable

more an art than a science: more subjective than objective

military psychology: field that applies psychological principles toward understanding and predicting the behaviors of friendly and enemy forces and civilians that may be dangerous during military operations as well as counseling and treating psychological trauma that occurs during combat

Recite and Review

1. Athletic personality, skill acquisition, team dynamics, and peak performance are topics of special interest to _____ psychologists.
2. Almost all serious athletes soon learn, peak performance requires more than physical training; it also requires mental and _____ "conditioning."
3. Dr. Jarvers seeks to understand and improve the performance of athletes and to enhance the benefits of participating in athletics. Dr. Jarvers is most likely a(n) _____ psychologist.
4. One study of adolescents found a link between sports participation and _____ self-esteem.
5. Psychologists have learned that benefits to self-esteem are more likely to occur when we minimize competition, rejection, criticism, and the "_____ mentality."
6. When working with children in sports, it is important to emphasize intrinsic rewards, self-control of emotions, independence, self-reliance, and _____ play.
7. Adults also benefit from sports through a better self-image, improved general health, and reduced _____.
8. In early studies of volleyball and gymnastics, it became clear that people teaching these sports had very little knowledge of the crucial, underlying _____.
9. Sports skills are broken into subparts by using _____.
10. Breaking down these sports skills into subparts is similar to the technique used in personnel psychology known as _____.
11. Sports psychologists have found that top marksmen consistently squeeze the trigger between _____.
12. A series of actions molded into a smooth and efficient performance, such as typing, walking, driving a car, or skiing is called a(n) _____.
13. Typically, an athletic performance involves learning a mental plan or model of what a skilled movement should be like called a(n) _____.
14. A plan that allows an athlete to perform complex movements that fit changing conditions is called a(n) _____.
15. In order to learn a particular sports skill, a person should begin by observing and imitating a skilled _____.
16. In order to back up motor learning, a person during the early phases of skill learning should learn _____ rules.
17. Later, these rules that were used during the early phases of skill learning can actually get in the way as the skill becomes more _____.
18. To prevent artificial cues and responses from becoming a part of the skill, practice of a skill should be as _____ as possible.
19. When practicing a skill, a mirror, videotape, coach, or observer can provided needed _____.
20. Whenever possible, get someone experienced in the skill to direct attention particularly to your _____ responses.
21. Rather than breaking the task into artificial parts, it is better when possible to practice _____.
22. Research has shown that learning can be aided by merely imagining a skilled performance, or _____.
23. Imagining a skilled performance tends to be most valuable after you have _____ the task.
24. Physical, mental, and emotional states are harmonious and optimal during _____ performance.

25. When their physical, mental and emotional states are harmonious and at an optimal level, many athletes report episodes during which they felt almost as if they were in a(n) _____.

26. When she is on the ice during a competition, Salina, a nationally-ranked ice skater, experiences episodes during which she feels that she is becoming one with her performance, a state known by the one word of "_____."

27. During this feeling of "being one with their performances," athletes experience intense concentration, detachment, a lack of fatigue and pain, feelings of unusual power and control, and a subjective _____ of time.

28. It is at these times when athletes are feeling at one with their performances that the athletes achieve their "personal _____."

29. For athletes who want to mentally improve their performance, a starting point is to make sure that for each task within their sport they have an appropriate _____ level.

30. For a golfer or gymnast during a big event, lowering arousal may be crucial, in order to avoid "_____."

31. One way of controlling arousal before each game or event is to go through a fixed _____.

32. To adjust their degree of arousal, athletes can learn to use imagery and _____ techniques.

33. Imaging techniques can be used to focus attention on the athlete's task and to mentally _____ it beforehand.

34. During events, athletes can avoid negative, self-critical thoughts that distract them and undermine their confidence by learning to use _____ strategies.

35. Top athletes tend to use strategies, in which they evaluate their performance and make adjustments to keep it at optimum levels. These techniques are called _____ strategies.

Connections

1. ___ sports psychology

2. ___ task analysis

3. ___ motor skill

4. ___ motor program

5. ___ mental practice

6. ___ "flow"

7. ___ controlling arousal level

8. ___ cognitive-behavioral strategies

9. ___ self-regulation strategies

a. series of actions molded into a smooth and efficient performance

b. imagining a skilled performance to aid learning

c. peak performance during which physical, mental, and emotional states are harmonious and optimal

d. used to avoid negative, self-critical thoughts that distract athletes and undermine their confidence

e. accomplished by using a fixed routine before each game or event or using imagery and relaxation

f. mental plan or model that guides skilled movement

g. evaluating one's performance and making adjustments to keep it at optimum levels

h. breaking complex skills into their subparts

i. study of the psychological and behavioral dimensions of sports performance

Check Your Memory

1. TRUE or FALSE — Peak performance by athletes requires not only physical training but also mental and emotional "conditioning."
2. TRUE or FALSE — Motor learning, mental practice, and stress reduction are three topics of special interest to sports psychologists.
3. TRUE or FALSE — In a study of adolescents, no link was found between sports participation and physical self-esteem.
4. TRUE or FALSE — Psychologists have found that the benefits of sports participation are most likely to occur when competition and the "one-winner mentality" are maximized and utilized.
5. TRUE or FALSE — When working with children in sports, it is important to emphasize fair play, intrinsic rewards, self-control of emotions, independence, and self-reliance.
6. TRUE or FALSE — Participation in sports by adults is usually not beneficial due to increased stress and the potential for injuries.
7. TRUE or FALSE — Researchers have found that running is associated with higher levels of tension, anxiety, fatigue, and depression than is found in the nonrunning population.
8. TRUE or FALSE — In early studies of volleyball and gymnastics, it was found that people teaching these sports had very little knowledge of crucial, underlying skills.
9. TRUE or FALSE — In a task analysis, sports skills are broken into subparts, so that key elements can be identified and taught.
10. TRUE or FALSE — Sports psychologists have found that top marksmen consistently squeeze the trigger during a heartbeat.
11. TRUE or FALSE — Typing, writing, and driving a car are all motor skills.
12. TRUE or FALSE — If you have learned a "bike-riding" motor program, you can easily ride bicycles of different sizes and types on a large variety of surfaces.
13. TRUE or FALSE — For optimal skill learning, you should begin by observing and imitating a skilled model and try to grasp a visual image of the skilled movement.
14. TRUE or FALSE — Learning verbal rules and using this internal speech to guide one's movements will very helpful in the later stages of learning but should not be used during the early phases of skill learning.
15. TRUE or FALSE — Practice of a new motor skill does not have to be lifelike, for example a snow skier can practice just as well on straw as on snow.
16. TRUE or FALSE — In skill learning, it is important to get feedback from a mirror, videotape, coach or observer to direct attention to correct responses when they occur.
17. TRUE or FALSE — When practicing a new motor skill, it is better to break the task into parts and learn each part, such as learning to type nonsense syllables before trying to type words.
18. TRUE or FALSE — Research has shown that mental practice can be superior to actual practice during the initial stages of motor skill learning.
19. TRUE or FALSE — During peak performances, many athletes describe these episodes as feeling like they are in a trance.
20. TRUE or FALSE — Peak performances are also called "flow" because the athlete becomes one with his or her performance and flows with it.
21. TRUE or FALSE — During "flow" athletes experience a subjective feeling that time is speeding up and their concentration and control are diffuse and scattered.

22. TRUE or FALSE   The flow state cannot be forced to happen with the flow state disappearing during a performance if the person thinks about it.
23. TRUE or FALSE   Psychologists are now seeking to identify conditions that facilitate peak performance and the unusual mental state that usually accompanies it.
24. TRUE or FALSE   Sprinters at a track meet should try to lower their arousal levels, while gymnasts and golfers should try to elevate theirs.
25. TRUE or FALSE   One way that athletes control their arousal levels is by going through a fixed routine before each game or event.
26. TRUE or FALSE   Imaging techniques that are like "watching a movie" in one's head can be used to focus attention on the athlete's task and to mentally rehearse it before the event.
27. TRUE or FALSE   During events, athletes use cognitive-behavioral strategies to increase motivation by berating themselves for being behind in points during a game and to focus on the errors made.
28. TRUE or FALSE   Top athletes tend to use self-regulation strategies, in which they evaluate their performance and make adjustments to keep it at optimum levels.

Critical Thinking Question

When an athlete follows a set routine before an event, what source of stress has she or he eliminated?

Module 16.4 Psychology in Action
Human Factors Psychology—Who's the Boss Here?
Survey Question: How are tools designed to better serve human needs?

Language Development Guide

"easy to assemble": sarcastic reference to the instructions on many items requiring assemble that are rarely, if ever "easy to assemble"

awkward: cumbersome; difficult to operate; problematic

paperweight: a desk object to hold down a pile of papers

blind spots: unable to see areas of the highway in one's rearview mirror or areas obscured by part of the car

compatible: well-matched

mimic: imitate

layout: design

resemblances: similar in form

personal computer interfaces: the means of communication between the computer and the user

culprit: guilty person, person who caused or did something

"user-friendly": easy to use

personal digital assistants (PDAs): a mobile device or palmtop computer, which connects to the Internet and manages information

fine-tune: improve and perfect

touch pad: a square on a laptop that is sensitized to touch and pressure and allows the user to point to and manipulate different information on the computer screen; functions like a mouse on a laptop

Nintendo Wii: video game system with a wand controller

remote: distant

photo editing: managing, cropping, touching up photos taken with a digital camera

get/getting by: doing just enough so as to complete the task and no more, no extra work

survival skill: way of dealing and adapting to the world to function

dive in: quickly jump in

International Space Station: internationally developed research facility in Earth's orbit

monotonous: boring; repetitive

earmuffs: covering for ears to block out cold or sound

eyeshades: covering to block out light

sensory monotony: same repetitive sights and sounds

vistas: views

diversions: distractions

one person's symphony is another's grating noise: what one person likes to listen to can be totally disliked by other people

solitary: alone; as an individual

Biosphere 2: completely enclosed three-acre structure that includes the various natural habitats found on Earth in order to conduct research on the interaction of man and the environment as well as to study the effects of confined environments

fitting: appropriate

dazzling: amazing

inevitable: inescapable; certain

famine: scarcity of food

endure: last; continue

Recite and Review

1. People who design machines and work environments so they are compatible with our sensory and motor capacities work in the field known as human factors psychology, also called _____.

2. Any dial, screen, light, or other device used to provide information about a machine's activity to a human user is referred to as a(n) _____.

3. Any knob, handle, button, lever, or other device used to alter the activity of a machine is referred to as a(n) _____.

4. Psychologist Donald Norman refers to successful human factors engineering as _____ design.

5. One way to create these successful human factors designs is to create resemblances between different subjects called _____.

6. For all current personal computers, the images of "files," "folders," and "trashcan" form what is known as the _____.

7. Effective design provides information about the effect of making a response, which is called _____.

8. The audible click designed into many computer keyboards is a good example of _____.

9. To design effective tools, human factors psychologists measure the ease with which people can learn to use a machine known as _____ testing.

10. Human factors psychologists often ask people to say everything they are thinking as they use a machine during a form of testing known as the _____ protocol.

11. Using human factors methods to design computers and software is referred to as _____.

12. Traditionally, machines, such as the automobile, were designed to make us _____.

13. In contrast, machines, such as computers, are meant to make us _____.

14. In the world of human-computer interaction, input devices are also called _____.

15. In the world of human-computer interaction, output devices are also called _____.

16. Humans communicate with computers through a set of input and output devices called a(n) _____.

17. Through hand and body movements, the Nintendo Wii game wand allows players to _____ with the game.

18. Microsoft is launching Natal in late 2010, which will allow players to play games just by moving and _____ to the computer
19. When a computer interface creates a sense of being present in a remote location, it is referred to as _____ .
20. In 2001, a surgeon in New York removed the diseased gallbladder of a patient an ocean away in France by using _____.
21. Even the best designed tools, whether for the body or the mind, can be misused or _____.
22. If you have just gotten a new digital camera, you should begin by finding out more about what specific _____ your new tool can accomplish.
23. Rather than using the full potential of the tool, it is often tempting to just get by, or to _____.
24. Although it is tempting to just dive in and use your new tool, it is important to read your new tool's _____.
25. Researchers have learned that astronauts in space prefer clearly defined "up" and "down" _____.
26. Psychologists have found that an important high point in monotonous environments is the activity of _____.
27. When in space, it is important to avoid disrupting body rhythms by carefully controlling _____ cycles.
28. Even with the magnificent vistas of Earth below, it is important to provide the astronauts with stimulating environments that use music, movies, and other diversions to prevent sensory _____.
29. Most people in restricted environments, such as in space stations or living in the Artic, find that they prefer _____ pastimes.
30. Experiences with confining environments on earth, such as Biosphere 2, suggest that stress and boredom in space habitats can be reduced by having live plants and _____.

Connections

1. ___ ergonomics

2. ___ display

3. ___ control

4. ___ natural design

5. ___ metaphor

6. ___ feedback

7. ___ usability testing

8. ___ thinking aloud protocol

9. ___ human-computer interaction (HCI)

a. empirical investigation of the ease with which users can learn to operate a machine

b. one thing used to describe another and creates a resemblance between two subjects

c. application of human factors to the design of computers and computer software

d. set of input and output devices a computer provides to allow humans to communicate with computers

e. any knob, handle, button, lever, or other device used to alter the activity of a machine

f. creating a sense of being present in a remote location

g. human factors engineering that makes use of naturally understood perceptual signals

h. problem of the restricted environments in space

i. engaging in behavior that achieves a minimum result, rather than maximizing the outcome of that behavior

10.___ interface

11.___ telepresence

12.___ satisficing

13.___ sensory monotony

j. information about the effect of making a response

k. any dial, screen, light, or device used to provide information about a machine's activity to a human user

l. people are asked to say everything they are thinking as they use a machine

m. also known as human factors psychology and is concerned with making machines and work environments compatible with human perceptual and physical capacities

Check Your Memory

1. TRUE or FALSE   The goal of human factors psychology is to design machines and work environments, so they are compatible with our sensory and motor capacities.

2. TRUE or FALSE   Another name for human factors psychology is machinistics.

3. TRUE or FALSE   A control is any dial, screen, light, or other device used to provide information about a machine's activity to a human user.

4. TRUE or FALSE   Psychologist Donald Norman refers to successful human factors engineering as divergent designs.

5. TRUE or FALSE   An example of a natural design would be the row of vertical buttons in elevators that mimic the layout of the floors in a building.

6. TRUE or FALSE   The design of all current personal computers presents a "desktop" metaphor, complete with "files," "folders," and a "trashcan."

7. TRUE or FALSE   The audible click designed into many computer keyboards is a good example of feedback.

8. TRUE or FALSE   To design useful tools, human factors psychologists do validity testing, in which they directly measure people's understanding of how a machine works.

9. TRUE or FALSE   In the thinking aloud protocol, people are asked to say everything they are thinking as they use a machine.

10. TRUE or FALSE   Using human factors methods to design computers and software is referred to as human-computer interaction (HCI).

11. TRUE or FALSE   In the past, machines were designed to make us smarter, whereas today machines are designed to make us stronger.

12. TRUE or FALSE   In the world of HCI, displays are also called input devices, while controls are called output devices.

13. TRUE or FALSE   Humans communicate with computers through the interface, or set of input and output devices a computer provides.

14. TRUE or FALSE   Microsoft is due to release an interface in 2010, currently referred to as *Natal*, which allows players to play games just by moving and speaking to the computer.

15. TRUE or FALSE   Telepresence involves computers creating a sense of being present in a remote location.

16. TRUE or FALSE   In 2001, a surgeon in New York used telesurgery to remove a diseased gallbladder in a patient in France using robotic hands to perform the surgery.

17. TRUE or FALSE   The best way to learn about the functions of a new tool, such as a digital camera, is to "dive right in" and use the new tool, rather than trying to read the instruction manual required to be sold with the product.
18. TRUE or FALSE   Many modern tools, especially electronic devices, have valuable capacities hidden several layers down in menus.
19. TRUE or FALSE   Engaging in behavior that achieves a minimum result, rather than maximizing the outcome of that behavior is called human idling.
20. TRUE or FALSE   In the weightlessness of space, researchers have learned that astronauts still prefer rooms with clearly defined "up" and "down."
21. TRUE or FALSE   Eating at least one meal together each day can help keep the crew members on a space station working as a social unit.
22. TRUE or FALSE   Problems with sleep are worsened by the constant silence on a space station, so artificial noise is often added to the environment.
23. TRUE or FALSE   Sensory monotony is rarely a problem on space stations because of the magnificent vistas of the Earth below.
24. TRUE or FALSE   Most people in restricted environments find that they prefer pastimes that involve group activities, such as socializing and game playing.
25. TRUE or FALSE   Experience with confining environments on Earth, such as Biosphere 2, suggest that including live animals and plants in space habitats could reduce stress and boredom.

Critical Thinking Question

Check out this photo of a men's urinal in Amsterdam's Schiphol Airport. Is that fly real? If not, why is it there?

Final Survey and Review—Completion

Module 16.1 Industrial/Organizational Psychology
Industrial/Organizational Psychology—Psychology at Work
Survey Question: How is psychology applied in business and industry?

1. The largest applied psychology areas are clinical and _____ psychology.
2. One of the earliest attempts to improve worker efficiency was made in 1923 by Frederick Taylor, an   engineer with versions of Taylor's approach today known as Theory X leadership or _____.
3. Two techniques that make Theory Y leadership methods effective are management by objectives and _____ leadership.
4. Becky is a college professor, while her husband is a lawyer. Both Becky and her husband would be considered _____ workers.
5. Armand's employee group typically chooses their own methods of achieving their shared goals with this group making good use of the strengths and talents of the individual employee members. Armand is most likely in a group called a(n) _____.
6. Jake is participating in a program at his company in which he will gain valuable knowledge for his career by doing a complete cycle of work involving the manufacture of the company's product. Jake is engaged in _____.
7. When an employee is seen as being helpful, conscientious, and courteous and also displays good sportsmanship by avoiding pettiness, gossiping, complaining, and making small problems into big ones at work, this employee is said to be exhibiting organizational _____.
8. Physically attractive people are often given more positive evaluations in interviews, even on traits that have no connection with appearance because of the _____ effect.

966

9. Pella took a test at the career center at her college. Her results showed that she was "social" and might enjoy a career as a teacher or counselor. Pella most likely took a(n) vocational _____ test.
10. A group of job applicants are placed in a group in which their group decision making and problem solving will be assessed. While the group deals with a real life business problem, "clerks" bring in price changes, notices about delayed supplies, and other stressful problems. These job applicants are participating in a(n) _____.

Module 16.1 Industrial/Organizational Psychology
Communication at Work—Getting the Message Across
Survey Question: What can be done to improve communication at work?

11. News reporters learn to be precise about the "who, what, when, where, how, and _____" of events.
12. Mae tells her employees, "I guess we better kinda need to get around to finishing this project like pretty soon." In this sentence Mae used a great deal of "_____ words."
13. "TR the last two lines but stet the leading" is a type of printer's _____.
14. Jacques says, "I think the supervisor's new schedule is a *dumb* idea." The word "dumb" is considered a(n) _____ word.
15. As you listen to a speaker, try to suspend evaluation and keep a(n) _____.

Module 16.2 Environmental Psychology
Environmental Psychology—Life on Spaceship Earth
Survey Question: What have psychologists learned about the effects of our physical and social environments?

16. Architectural design, cognitive maps, privacy, and vandalism are topics of special interest to _____ psychologists.
17. Your professor's office and your psychology classroom would both be considered _____.
18. Saving a seat in a theater for a friend by placing your coat in the seat would be a type of _____ behavior.
19. "Important people" in many business offices use the imposing width of their desks to maintain the type of distance that eliminates touching and formalizes speech, which is called _____ distance.
20. In Calhoun's experiment, when the rat colony became extremely crowded, pregnancies _____.
21. Jasmine is in an elevator literally inches away from people on all sides. She is beginning to feel a loss of privacy because of the nearness of others. Jasmine' uncomfortable feeling is called _____.
22. In a comparison of children from the noisy schools near an airport and children in schools farther from the airport, it was found that children in the noisy schools had difficulty on tasks requiring close attention and concentration as well as showing higher _____.
23. Ty is using a website to calculate and track his individual resource consumption. Ty is using a(n) _____ calculator.
24. If everyone one in the community waters their lawn "just a little," this collective use of water during a drought may cause everyone to not have enough water for drinking, bathing, and washing, a social dilemma that ecologist Garrett Hardin called the "_____."
25. Persuasion and education have been used to encourage conservation with effective appeals being based on a personal desire to take better care of the planet, on the collective good, such

as protecting one's own children and future generations, and on _____, such as cost saving.

Module 16.3 The Psychology of Education, Law, and Sports
Educational Psychology—An Instructive Topic
Survey Question: How has psychology improved education?

26. Effective teachers must understand learning, instruction, testing, and classroom _____.
27. Curriculum development, exceptional students, and transfer of learning are topics of special interest for _____ psychologists.
28. Besides the last step of spaced review, the steps in instruction often include learner preparation, stimulus presentation, learner response, reinforcement, and _____.
29. Gretchen is presenting information to her students through lecture, demonstration, and rote practice. Gretchen is using the teaching strategy known as _____.
30. Zoe's student have been shown to perform somewhat better than other students in the school on tests of abstract thinking, creativity, and problem solving. Zoe uses a teaching strategy in which her students actively construct knowledge for themselves called _____.
31. Kiya is using a new "richly designed teaching style" in which she uses a variety of instructional methods, such as lectures, podcasts of lectures, group activities, and Internet discussion lists so each of her students can choose among different ways of gaining knowledge. Kiya is using the teaching strategy known as _____.

Module 16.3 The Psychology of Education, Law, and Sports
Psychology and Law—Judging Juries
Survey Question: What does psychology reveal about juries and court verdicts?

32. Volunteers are sometimes simply given written evidence and arguments to read before making a decision, while others may watch videotaped trials staged by actors when they participate in simulated, or _____ juries.
33. A jury's biases and quirks play less of a role in the verdict, the severe the crime and the more clear-cut the _____.
34. Dr. DuBose is a psychologist who is helping attorneys to identify people who will favor or harm their efforts during trial. Dr. DuBose is using _____ jury selection.
35. A potential juror's age, sex, race, occupation, political affiliation, religion, and socioeconomic status is referred to as _____ information.
36. Because Gary strongly believes that punishment is effective, he will be more likely to vote for conviction if he is on a jury. Psychologists would say that Gary has _____ personality traits.
37. Jerry has just been selected for a special jury made up of people who are not opposed to the death penalty or are, at least, indifferent to it. Jerry has been selected for a(n) _____ jury.

Module 16.3 The Psychology of Education, Law, and Sports
Sports Psychology—The Athletic Mind
Survey Question: Can psychology enhance athletic performance?

38. Competition, exercise and mental health, mental practice, and peak performance are topics of special interest for _____ psychologists.
39. When working with children in sports, it is important to emphasize fair play, self-control of emotions, independence, self-reliance, and _____ rewards.

40. Dr. Carraway is breaking down various basketball skills into their subparts. Dr. Carraway is performing a(n) _____.
41. Since driving a car requires a series of actions to be molded into a smooth and efficient performance, it would be called a(n) _____.
42. During a soccer match, Mikhail suddenly feels like he is in a trance and time is slowing down. He also feels unusual power and control over his performance. Mikhail is experiencing a(n) _____ performance.
43. To adjust their degree of arousal, athletes can learn to use relaxation techniques and _____.

Module 16.4 Psychology in Action
Human Factors Psychology—Who's the Boss Here?
Survey Question: How are tools designed to better serve human needs?
44. Another name for ergonomics is _____ psychology.
45. Bob is using a knob and pushing buttons in order to alter the activity of the machine he is using in his machine shop. The knob and buttons are referred to as _____.
46. The row of vertical buttons in elevators that mimic the layout of the floors in a building is an example of a(n) _____ design.
47. Many machines are designed to provide information to the users regarding the effects of their responses. This information is referred to as _____.
48. Dr. Cierro is measuring the ease with which users can learn to use a machine. Dr. Cierro is conducting _____ testing.
49. If you figure out how to use your cell phone to call your friends, but don't know about texting, you are not using the full capacity of your cell phone. Thus, you are exhibiting _____.
50. Experiences with confining environments on earth, such as Biosphere 2, suggest that stress and boredom in space habitats can be reduced by having live animals and _____.

Final Survey and Review—Matching

Module 16.1 Industrial/Organizational Psychology
Part 1:

1. ___ applied psychology

2. ___ personnel psychology

3. ___ Theory X leadership

4. ___ Theory Y leadership

5. ___ organizational culture

6. ___ organizational citizenship

a. the blend of customs, beliefs, values, attitudes, and rituals within an organization

b. approach also known as participative management that allows employees at all levels to participate in decision making

c. a detailed description of the skills, knowledge, and activities required by a particular job

d. making a job more personally rewarding, interesting, or intrinsically motivating; typically involves increasing worker knowledge

e. work group that works together to achieved shared goals and has a high degree of freedom with respect to how it achieves these goals

f. branch of I/O psychology concerned with testing, selection, placement, and promotion of employees

7. ___ job enrichment

      g. employee discussion group that makes suggestions for improvements and solving business problems

8. ___ shared leadership

      h. the use of psychological principles and research methods to solve practical problems

9. ___ job analysis

      i. approach that emphasizes human relations at work and that views people as industrious, responsible, and interested in challenging work

10. ___ self-managed team

      j. also known as scientific management; uses time-and-motion studies, task analysis, job specialization, assembly lines, and pay schedules to increase productivity

11. ___ quality circle

      k. making positive contributions to the success of an organization in ways that go beyond one's job description

Part 2:

1. ___ jargon

      a. testing procedure that involves memos, requests, and typical business problems to simulate the individual decision-making challenges that executives face

2. ___ emotionally loaded words

      b. formal or informal questioning of job applicants to learn their qualifications and to gain an impression of their personalities

3. ___ wiggle words

      c. intelligence tests

4. ___ critical incidents

      d. words, such as stupid, dumb, and ridiculous

5. ___ biodata

      e. test that rates a person's potential to learn skills required by various occupations

6. ___ personal interview

      f. paper-and pencil test that typically measure six major themes identified by John Holland

7. ___ general mental abilities tests

      g. test that simulates group decision making and problem solving

8. ___ vocational interest tests

      h. ambiguous words and phrases

9. ___ aptitude tests

      i. program set up within an organization to conduct in-depth evaluations of job candidates for executive and management positions

10. ___ assessment centers

      j. detailed biographical information about a job applicant

11. ___ in-basket test

      k. specialized terminology used as a shorthand way of expressing ideas

12. ___ leaderless group discussion

      l. situations that arise in a job, with which a competent worker must be able to cope

Module 16.2 Environmental Psychology

1. ___ physical environments

      a. measurement and analysis of the effects an environment has on the behavior and perceptions of people within that environment

2. ___ social environments

      b. volume of greenhouse gases individual consumption adds to the atmosphere

3. ___ behavioral settings
    c. the number of people in a given space or the amount of space available to each person

4. ___ territorial markers
    d. subjective feeling of being overstimulated by a loss of privacy or by the nearness of others

5. ___ ecological footprint
    e. systematic study of the human use of space, particularly in social settings

6. ___ attentional overload
    f. social dilemma in which individuals, each acting in his or her immediate self-interest, overuse a scarce group resource

7. ___ carbon footprint
    g. stressful condition caused when sensory stimulation, information, and social contacts make excessive demands on attention

8. ___ crowding
    h. smaller area within an environment whose use is well defined, such as a bus depot, waiting room, or lounge

9. ___ tragedy of the commons
    i. environment defined by a group of people and their activities or interrelationships

10. ___ environmental assessments
    j. amount of land and water area required to replenish the resources that a human population consumes

11. ___ density
    k. natural settings, such as forests and beaches, as well as environments built by humans, such as building and cities

12. ___ proxemics
    l. objects and other signals whose placement indicates to others the "ownership" or control of a particular area

Module 16.3 The Psychology of Education, Law, and Sports

1. ___ teaching strategy
    a. breaking complex skills into their subparts

2. ___ direct instruction
    b. using social science principles to choose members of a jury

3. ___ discovery learning
    c. series of actions molded into a smooth and efficient performance

4. ___ scientific jury selection
    d. any planned method of instruction

5. ___ mock juries
    e. physical, mental, and emotional states are harmonious and optimal

6. ___ demographic information
    f. mental plan or model that guides skilled movement

7. ___ task analysis
    g. presentation of factual information by lecture, demonstration, and rote practice

8. ___ motor skill
    h. imagining a skilled performance to aid learning

9. ___ motor program
    i. evaluating one's performance and making adjustments to keep it at optimum levels

10. ___ mental practice
    j. instruction based on encouraging students to construct knowledge for themselves

11. ___ peak performance
    k. data regarding the juror's age, sex, race, occupation, education, political affiliation, religion, and socioeconomic status

12. ___ self-regulation strategies
    l. group that realistically simulates a courtroom jury

Module 16.4 Psychology in Action: Human Factors Psychology—Who's the Boss Here?

1. ___ ergonomics

2. ___ display

3. ___ control

4. ___ natural design

5. ___ metaphor

6. ___ feedback

7. ___ usability testing

8. ___ interface

9. ___ telepresence

10. ___ satisficing

a. set of input and output devices a computer provides to allow humans to communicate with computers

b. one thing used to describe another and creates a resemblance between two subjects

c. engaging in behavior that achieves a minimum result, rather than maximizing the outcome of that behavior

d. also known as human factors psychology and is concerned with making machines and work environments compatible with human perceptual and physical capacities

e. any knob, handle, button, lever, or other device used to alter the activity of a machine

f. creating a sense of being present in a remote location

g. human factors engineering that makes use of naturally understood perceptual signals

h. empirical investigation of the ease with which users can learn to operate a machine

i. any dial, screen, light, or device used to provide information about a machine's activity to a human user

j. information about the effect of making a response

Final Survey and Review—True or False

Module 16.1 Industrial/Organizational Psychology
Industrial/Organizational Psychology—Psychology at Work
Survey Question: How is psychology applied in business and industry?

1. TRUE or FALSE Studying jobs to identify underlying skills, which can then guide efforts to select people and train them for those jobs comprises the industrial part of I/O psychology.

2. TRUE or FALSE The main benefit of a Theory X management style is a high level of psychological efficiency among workers.

3. TRUE or FALSE Today in North America, it is estimated that only four of every five persons in the workforce are knowledge workers.

4. TRUE or FALSE Quality circles are typically allowed to choose their own methods of achieving results as long as the group is effective.

5. TRUE or FALSE Organizational culture refers to the blend of customs, beliefs, values, attitudes, and rituals that give each organization its unique "flavor."

6. TRUE or FALSE One way of doing a job analysis is to interview expert workers.

7. TRUE or FALSE Critical incidents are serious job applicant mistakes identified during a situational judgment test.

8. TRUE or FALSE College grade point averages (GPAs) do tend to predict success in most types of work.

972

9. TRUE or FALSE   Because of their many shortcomings, personal interviews are fading from use as a way of selecting job applicants.

10. TRUE or FALSE   Excessive self-promotion tends to lower the ratings candidates receive in job interviews.

Module 16.1 Industrial/Organizational Psychology

Communication at Work—Getting the Message Across

Survey Question: What can be done to improve communication at work?

11. TRUE or FALSE   Ambiguous messages are desirable because they leave others room to disagree.

12. TRUE or FALSE   Overuse of obscure vocabulary is often a sign of self-confidence.

13. TRUE or FALSE   Work relationships go more smoothly when you learn names and use them.

14. TRUE or FALSE   To be a good listener, learn to evaluate each sentence as it is completed.

15. TRUE or FALSE   Good listening improves communication as much as effective speaking does.

Module 16.2 Environmental Psychology

Environmental Psychology—Life on Spaceship Earth

Survey Question: What have psychologists learned about the effects of our physical and social environments?

16. TRUE or FALSE   Environmental psychologists study both physical and social environments.

17. TRUE or FALSE   The French sit closer together when talking than the English do.

18. TRUE or FALSE   Social distance basically keeps people within arm's reach (18 inches to four feet).

19. TRUE or FALSE   Burglars tend to choose houses to break into that have visible territorial markers.

20. TRUE or FALSE   In Calhoun's study of overcrowding in a rat colony, food and water rapidly ran out as the population increased.

21. TRUE or FALSE   People suffering from attentional overload tend to ignore non-essential events with their social contacts being superficial.

22. TRUE or FALSE   In an experiment in which a young child stood on a busy street corner in several large American cities and smaller nearby towns, the child was more likely to be offered help in the smaller towns.

23. TRUE or FALSE   Providing feedback about energy consumption tends to promote conservation of resources.

24. TRUE or FALSE   Direct monetary rewards have little or no effect on whether or not people recycle.

25. TRUE or FALSE   Long-corridor dormitories reduce feelings of crowding and encourage friendships.

Module 16.3 The Psychology of Education, Law, and Sports

Educational Psychology—An Instructive Topic

Survey Question: How has psychology improved education?

26. TRUE or FALSE   Many effective teaching strategies apply the basic principles of operant conditioning.

27. TRUE or FALSE   The first step in instruction involves presenting instructional stimuli, such as information, examples, and illustrations deliberately and clearly.

28. TRUE or FALSE   Spaced practice is an important step in teaching because it helps strengthen responses to key stimuli.
29. TRUE or FALSE   Students who receive direct instruction do somewhat better on tests of abstract thinking, creativity, and problem solving.
30. TRUE or FALSE   A principle of the Universal Design for Instruction is to make learning materials simple and intuitive by removing unnecessary complexity.
31. TRUE or FALSE   The Universal Design for Instruction has been used in elementary schools, but not in high schools, colleges, or universities.

Module 16.3 The Psychology of Education, Law, and Sports
Psychology and Law—Judging Juries
Survey Question: What does psychology reveal about juries and court verdicts?
32. TRUE or FALSE   In general, attractive defendants are less likely to be found guilty than unattractive persons.
33. TRUE or FALSE   If complex scientific evidence is presented, jurors tend to be swayed more by the expertise of the witness than by the evidence.
34. TRUE or FALSE   Jurors are supposed to take into account the severity of the punishment that a defendant faces, but many don't.
35. TRUE or FALSE   Scientific jury selection is only used in laboratory studies with the practice being banned in real jury trials.
36. TRUE or FALSE   The majority of the members of a death-qualified jury must be opposed to the death penalty.
37. TRUE or FALSE   A majority of European Americans thought O.J. Simpson was guilty during the early stages of his murder trial.

Module 16.3 The Psychology of Education, Law, and Sports
Sports Psychology—The Athletic Mind
Survey Question: Can psychology enhance athletic performance?
38. TRUE or FALSE   Researchers have found that running is associated with lower levels of tension, anxiety, fatigue, and depression than is found in the nonrunning population.
39. TRUE or FALSE   In early studies of volleyball and gymnastics, it was found that people using "homespun" coaching methods possessed a great deal of knowledge regarding the underlying skills within these sports.
40. TRUE or FALSE   The most accurate marksmen are those who learn to pull the trigger between heartbeats.
41. TRUE or FALSE   To enhance motor skill learning, feedback should call attention particularly to one's incorrect responses.
42. TRUE or FALSE   When learning to type, it is better to start with real words rather than nonsense syllables.
43. TRUE or FALSE   The top athletes in most sports are the ones who have learned how to force the flow experience to occur.

Module 16.4 Psychology in Action
Human Factors Psychology—Who's the Boss Here?
Survey Question: How are tools designed to better serve human needs?
44. TRUE or FALSE   Psychologist Donald Norman refers to successful human factors engineering as satisficing.

974

45. TRUE or FALSE   One form of usability testing involves having a person think aloud while using a machine.
46. TRUE or FALSE   In the past, machines were designed to make us stronger, whereas today machines are designed to make us smarter.
47. TRUE or FALSE   In the world of HCI, controls are also called input devices, while displays are called output devices.
48. TRUE or FALSE   Because a good surgeon relies on the sense of touch, it will be important to improve telepresence systems so they provide touch feedback for surgeons, who do surgery at a distance.
49. TRUE or FALSE   In weightlessness, humans don't really care about parts of the rooms being marked "up" and "down."
50. TRUE or FALSE   People in restricted environments prefer solitary pastimes to social pastimes.

Mastery Test

1. Cameron works in one of the two largest areas of applied psychology, which is _____ psychology.
    a. industrial/organizational (I/0)
    b. educational
    c. clinical
    d. social

2. Which of the following is NOT a topic of special interest for I/O psychologists?
    a. pay schedules
    b. leadership
    c. minority workers
    d. proxemics

3. Planning, control, orderliness, job specialization, and pay schedules are typical of _____ leadership.
    a. Theory X
    b. participative
    c. Theory Y
    d. enriched

4. Psychological efficiency is promoted by
    a. scientific management.
    b. Theory Y leadership.
    c. time-and-motion studies.
    d. progressive pay schedules.

5. Philip is a lawyer, and Marguetta is a teacher. Both would be considered _____ workers.
    a. agentic
    b. knowledge
    c. communal
    d. organizational

6. Joan has been given a specific sales total to meet for the month, suggesting that she works for a company that uses
   a. quality circles.
   b. job enrichment.
   c. flexi-quotas.
   d. management by objectives.

7. Which of the following would NOT be considered a flexible work arrangement?
   a. flextime
   b. compressed workweek
   c. telecommuting
   d. satisficing

8. A very important element of job enrichment is
   a. switching to indirect feedback.
   b. increasing worker knowledge.
   c. use of bonuses and pay incentives.
   d. providing closer supervision and guidance.

9. Within a company, the dress codes, hiring and firing procedures, methods of conflict resolution, and how special occasions, like employee birthdays, are handled are all a part of the
   a. organizational culture.
   b. organizational citizenship.
   c. critical incidents.
   d. biodata.

10. The company psychologist in personnel hears someone make such claims as "He was really stressed out and has been angry almost every day this past month." The psychologist would most likely say that this person is experiencing
    a. the "glass ceiling."
    b. the "business labyrinth."
    c. "desk rage."
    d. authoritarianism.

11. Greg works for a major airline with his job involving the testing, selection, placement, and promotion of employees at this company. Greg works in the field of _____ psychology.
    a. personnel
    b. human factors
    c. social
    d. counseling

12. For the job of a principal, being able to deal calmly with angry parents and to evaluate and make helpful suggestions regarding the teaching styles of teachers would be considered
    a. social dilemmas.
    b. biodata.
    c. critical incidents.
    d. satisficing.

13. The halo effect is a problem in
    a. collecting biodata.
    b. scoring interest inventories.
    c. conducting interviews.
    d. aptitude testing.

14. Which of the following identified the six major themes typically measured on interest inventories?
    a. John Holland
    b. Fredrick Taylor
    c. Douglas McGregor
    d. Stanley Milgram

15. According to the six vocational interest themes, Jed prefers to work with his hands and would like to become either a farmer or forester. Jed's interests appear to match the _____ theme.
    a. investigative
    b. realistic
    c. enterprising
    d. conventional

16. The potential for learning the skills used in various occupations is measured by
    a. interest tests.
    b. aptitude tests.
    c. in-basket tests.
    d. cognitive mapping.

17. Tomeka is applying for an executive position within a company. At the assessment center, she is placed in a simulated situation that will test her decision-making challenges. In this situation, she is given memos, requests and summaries of typical business problems to read quickly and take appropriate action. Tomeka is most likely be administered the
    a. leaderless group discussion simulation.
    b. biodata assessment.
    c. usability test.
    d. in-basket test.

18. Which of the following should be frequently used to improve communication in the workplace?
    a. emotionally loaded words
    b. intensifiers
    c. people's names
    d. jargon and obscure vocabulary

19. Which of the following is NOT recommended for persons who want to be effective listeners in the workplace?
    a. Identify the speaker's purpose.
    b. Evaluate as you listen.
    c. Check your understanding.
    d. Attend to nonverbal messages.

20. Because a classroom in a school and a locker room in a gym are smaller areas within an environment in which their use is well defined, they would be considered
    a. territorial markers.
    b. behavioral settings.
    c. proxemic applications.
    d. density fields.

21. You leave a book on a table in the library to save your place. The book is a(n)
    a. proxemic application.
    b. territorial marker.
    c. ergonomic strategy.
    d. environmental control.

22. Mandy and Carrie are at a concert where hundreds of fans are screaming and jumping up and down as the band plays. Mandy is enjoying the experience, but Carrie is uncomfortable with "all these people in her face" and touching her. Carrie is experiencing the subjective feeling known as
    a. social density.
    b. satisficing.
    c. crowding.
    d. the tragedy of the commons.

23. Resource consumption can be measured in terms of the amount of land and water area required to replenish the resources that a human population consumes, which is called a(n)
    a. environmental echo.
    b. ecological footprint.
    c. conservation demerit.
    d. carbon footprint.

24. Signs are placed on a recycling container each week showing how many aluminum cans were deposited during the previous week. This practice dramatically increases recycling and illustrates the use of
    a. feedback.
    b. public commitment.
    c. consumer symbolization.
    d. persuasion.

25. According to ecologist Garrett Hardin, when persons, each choose to satisfy their own immediate personal comfort by using a scarce resource, the whole group will suffer from what he termed the
    a. glass ceiling.
    b. ecological labyrinth.
    c. tragedy of the commons.
    d. satisficing of the environment.

26. Dividing long-corridor dormitories into two living areas separated by a lounge
    a. makes residents feel more crowded, not less.
    b. decreases social contacts.
    c. increases energy consumption.
    d. decreases stress.

27. Praise and feedback make up what part of a teaching strategy?
    a. reinforcement
    b. learner preparation
    c. stimulus presentation
    d. review

28. To encourage creative thinking by students, a teacher would be wise to use
    a. direct instruction.
    b. demonstrations as well as lectures.
    c. spaced review.
    d. discovery learning.

29. Mrs. West uses multiple instructional approaches (lectures, group activities, and Internet discussion) in her classes to ensure each student has the opportunity to find an instructional method by which he or she can best learn the material, Mrs. West is utilizing the teaching style known as
    a. Direct and Instrumental Instruction.
    b. Discovery Learning.
    c. Universal Design for Instruction.
    d. Flextime Instruction.

30. A psychologist who checks demographic information, does a community survey, and looks for authoritarian traits is most likely a(n)
    a. sports psychologist.
    b. environmental psychologist.
    c. educational consultant.
    d. legal consultant.

31. According to psychology of law studies, jurors
    a. tend to form an opinion of the guilt or innocence of a defendant early in the trial.
    b. place too little confidence in DNA evidence because of their lack of basic science knowledge.
    c. disregard the severity of the punishment in determining their verdict.
    d. are less likely to convict a defendant if they have authoritarian traits.

32. Which of the following is NOT a typical characteristic of a person on a death-qualified jury?
    a. white males
    b. opposed to the death penalty
    c. high incomes
    d. conservative and authoritarian

33. Sports psychologists were able to determine that a marksman was more accurate if he or she squeezed the trigger between heartbeats because of a(n) _____ of this sport.
    a. environmental assessment
    b. task analysis
    c. ergonomic evaluation
    d. usability test

34. Which is POOR advice for learning motor skills?
    a. Observe a skilled model.
    b. Learn verbal rules to back up motor learning.
    c. Get feedback from a mirror, videotape, or observer.
    d. Break the task into small parts and master the first before proceeding to the next.

35. When professional golfer Jack Nicklaus talks about "watching a movie" in his head before each shot, he is enhancing his sports performance by using
    a. mental practice.
    b. self-regulation.
    c. skilled modeling.
    d. task analysis.

36. Unia is in the middle of her gymnastics performance, when suddenly she feels like she is in a trance, is detached, and time has slowed down. Unia is experiencing
    a. flow.
    b. satisficing.
    c. sensory monotony.
    d. attentional overload.

37. Janine is a psychologist, who is involved in research to improve telesurgery. Janine's research is in _____ psychology.
    a. social
    b. environmental
    c. human factors
    d. architectural

38. In designing the computer to make it easier for consumers to use, engineers used
    a. satisficing.
    b. a "desktop" metaphor.
    c. a motor program.
    d. territorial markers.

39. In a computer interface, which of the following provides output?
    a. keyboard
    b. display screen
    c. touch pad
    d. voice recognition

40. Which of the following statements regarding space habitats is FALSE?
    a. Astronauts prefer rooms with clearly defined "up" and "down" even in the weightlessness of space.
    b. Problems with sleep for the astronauts are aggravated by the constant noise on a space station.
    c. Sensory monotony can be a problem in space, even with the magnificent vistas of Earth below.
    d. Most people in restricted environments, such as space stations, prefer active, group activities to solitary pastimes.

Appendix: Behavioral Statistics

Chapter Overview

Statistics are necessary in answering psychological questions. Descriptive statistics organize and summarize numbers, while inferential statistics are used to generalize information from small samples to large groups. The three types of descriptive statistics are graphical statistics, measures of central tendency, and measures of variability. Graphical statistics involve the use of frequency distributions as well as graphs, such as histograms and frequency polygons, which are used to represent numbers pictorially. Two basic questions about a group of numbers are: What is the average (central tendency)? How much do the numbers vary (variability)?

Measures of central tendency define the "typical score" in a group of scores. The mean is found by adding all the scores in a group and then dividing by the total number of scores. The median is found by arranging a group of scores from the highest to the lowest and selecting the middle score. The mode is the score that occurs most frequently in a group of scores.

Measures of variability provide a number that shows how much scores vary. The range is the difference between the highest score and the lowest score in a group of scores. The standard deviation shows how much, on average, all the scores in a group differ from the mean. To change an original score into a standard score (or z-score), you must subtract the mean from the score and then divide the result by the standard deviation. Standard scores (z-scores) tell, in standard deviation units, how far above or below the mean a score is. This allows meaningful comparisons between scores from different groups. Scores that form a normal curve are easy to interpret because the properties of the normal curve are well known.

Pairs of scores that vary together in an orderly fashion are said to be correlated. When there is a correlation, or consistent relationship, between scores on two measures, knowing a person's score on one measure allows us to predict his or her score on the second measure. The relationship between two variables or measures can be positive or negative. Correlation coefficients tell how strongly two groups of scores are related. Correlation alone does not demonstrate cause-and-effect links between variables or measures.

Inferential statistics are used to make decisions, to generalize from samples, and to draw conclusions from data. Most studies in psychology are based on samples. Findings from representative samples are assumed to also apply to entire populations. In psychology experiments, differences in the average performance of groups could occur purely by chance. Tests of statistical significance tell us if the observed differences between groups are common or rare. If a difference is large enough to be improbable, it suggests that the results did not occur by chance alone.

Module A.1 Descriptive Statistics
Preview: Why Numbers?

Language Development Guide
slumbering: sleeping; napping
premature: untimely; early
apprehension: anxiety; nervousness
design: plan
"boil down": to reduce; condense
base: establish; support
limited: incomplete; partial

Descriptive Statistics—Psychology by the Numbers
Survey Question: What are descriptive statistics?

Language Development Guide
jumble: mixture; clutter
get a clear picture: understand
pictorially: in a picture, visually
hypnotizability: the ability to be able to experience being under hypnosis
susceptibility: responsiveness to
frequency: number of occurrences
distribution: to divide in portions
overall *"picture"*: complete understanding
condensed: compressed; reduced

Recite and Review
1. The results of psychological studies are often expressed as _____ (which must be summarized and interpreted before they have any meaning).
2. The type of statistics that summarize or "boil down" data collected from research participants so the results become more meaningful and easier to communicate to others is called _____ statistics.
3. Stacy is using statistics for decision making, for generalizing from small samples, and for drawing conclusions. Stacy is using _____ statistics.
4. Statistics bring greater clarity and _____ to psychological thought and research.
5. The three basic types of descriptive statistics are graphical statistics, measures of central tendency, and   measures of _____.
6. Numbers are presented pictorially so that they are easier to visualize in the type of descriptive statistics known as _____ statistics.
7. Large amounts of information collected during research can be neatly organized and summarized by using a(n) _____ distribution.
8. Joe is breaking down the entire range of possible scores from his research data into classes of equal size and then recorde d the number of scores falling into each class. Joe is constructing a(n) _____.
9. On a graph, the X axis or horizontal line is called the _____.
10. The Y axis or vertical line on a graph is known as the _____.
11. A graph that depicts the data in vertical bars is called a(n) _____.
12. Marcia is constructing a graph of a frequency distribution in which the number of scores falling in each class is represented by points on a line. This type of graph is called a(n) _____.

982

13. The type of graph shown at the right is called a(n) _____.

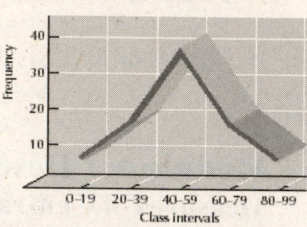

14. Regarding the various types of descriptive statistics, frequency distributions, histograms, and frequency polygons make up the type known as _____ statistics.

15. The type of graph shown below is known as a(n) _____.

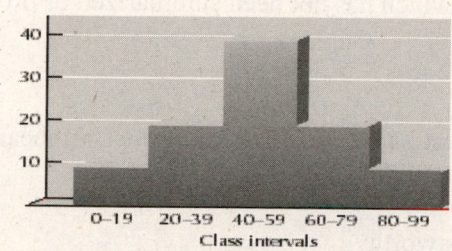

Connections

1. ____ descriptive statistics
2. ____ inferential statistics
3. ____ graphical statistics
4. ____ frequency distribution
5. ____ histogram
6. ____ frequency polygon
7. ____ abscissa
8. ____ ordinate

a. table that divides an entire range of scores into a series of classes and then records the number of scores that fall into each class
b. graph in which vertical bars are used to represent data
c. Y axis or vertical line on a graph
d. mathematical tools used for generalizing from small samples
e. X axis or horizontal line on a graph
f. group of techniques for presenting numbers pictorially
g. mathematical tools used to describe and summarize numeric data
h. graph in which data is represented by points on a line

Check Your Memory

1. TRUE or FALSE   Descriptive statistics are used to generalize from small samples to larger groups.
2. TRUE or FALSE   Psychologists must often base decisions on limited data.
3. TRUE or FALSE   It is difficult to make scientific arguments about human behavior without depending on statistics.
4. TRUE or FALSE   Measures of central tendency and measures of variability are two types of inferential statistics.
5. TRUE or FALSE   Graphical statistics are a type of descriptive statistic.
6. TRUE or FALSE   A frequency distribution is made by recording the most frequently occurring score.
7. TRUE or FALSE   Frequency distributions are often shown graphically to make them more "visual."

983

8. TRUE or FALSE   The X axis or horizontal line on a graph is called the ordinate.
9. TRUE or FALSE   A graph in which vertical bars are used to represent data is known as a frequency polygon.
10. TRUE or FALSE   A graph in which data is represented by points on a line is known as a histogram.

Module A.1 Descriptive Statistics
Measures of Central Tendency
Survey Question: How are statistics used to identify an average score?

Language Development Guide
"typical score": representative value
raw data: information collected which has not been summarized or processed in any way
assume: suppose
sensitive: are affected; responsive to
distorted: to become imprecise
Johnny Depp: American actor best known for "Pirates of the Caribbean" movies
"share" the middle spot: split the middle spot in a set of numbers
yields: produces
unreliable: undependable; untrustworthy

Recite and Review

1. A number describing a "typical score" around which other scores fall is a measure of _____.
2. The measure that is calculated by adding all the scores for each group and then dividing by the total number of scores is called the _____.
3. The most frequently occurring score in a group of scores is called the _____.
4. The measure in which half the values in a group of scores fall below it and half fall above it is the _____.
5. The measure that is sensitive to extremely high or low scores in a distribution is the _____.
6. Carlton is arranging scores from the highest to the lowest and then selecting the score that falls in the middle. For this group of scores, Carlton is determining the _____.
7. A group of nine children are asked to identify 10 alphabet letters. The number of letters correctly identified by each child was: 10, 8, 8, 8, 7, 6, 6, 5, and 5. The mean of these scores would be _____.
8. Carmen is looking at her quiz scores in psychology, which are 100, 95, 93, 90, 90, 87, 82, 75, and 62. The median of these scores would be _____.
9. A group of ten children are asked to form the past tense of ten irregular verbs. The score for each child was 10, 10, 9, 9, 8, 8, 8, 7, 6, and 6. The mode of this set of scores is _____.
10. The mean, median, and mode make up the measures of _____.

Connections

1. ____ measure of central tendency   a. most frequently occurring score in a group of scores

2. ____ mean   b. found by arranging scores from the highest to the lowest and selecting the score that falls in the middle

3. ___ median

    c. number describing a "typical score" around which other scores fall

4. ___ mode

    d. calculated by adding all the scores for each group and then dividing by the total number of scores

Check Your Memory

1. TRUE or FALSE   A measure of variability is simply a number describing a "typical score" around which other scores fall.

2. TRUE or FALSE   The mean is calculated by adding all the scores for each group and then dividing by the total number of scores.

3. TRUE or FALSE   The median is sensitive to extremely high or low scores in a distribution.

4. TRUE or FALSE   The mode is found by arranging scores from the highest to the lowest and selecting the score that falls in the middle.

5. TRUE or FALSE   If you had the scores 89, 41, 32, 30, 27, 25, and 25, the best measure of central tendency to use would be the mean.

6. TRUE or FALSE   If you had the scores 23, 23, 23, 22, 21, 20, 19, 17, 15, the mode would be 21.

7. TRUE or FALSE   For the scores 20, 20, 20, 15, 10, 10, 10, 5, 5, and 5, the mean would be 12.

8. TRUE or FALSE   If you had the scores 4, 5, 6, 6, 7, 7, 9, 12, 17, and 17, the median is 9.

Critical Thinking Question

You are asked to calculate the mean income of the following annual salaries: $2,000,000, $33,000, $27,000, $22,000, $21,000. Why might you refuse? What statistic might you propose to calculate instead?

Module A.1 Descriptive Statistics
Measures of Variability
Survey Question: What statistics do psychologists use to measure how much scores differ from one another?

Language Development Guide

agitated: active, anxious
consistently: dependably; every time
whereas: but
overall: by and large; generally
scattered: spread
"spread out": differences among the scores
variable: changeable
index: indicator
square root: a number that when multiplied by itself gives a particular quantity
"standardize": to remove variations within scores so that the scores are of the same type and can be compared
midterms: exams given halfway through the academic term
convert: change
resulting: that which occurs
illustrate: show; demonstrate
originally: at first

relatively speaking: generally
equivalent: equal
chance: unplanned; accidental
outcomes: result
probability: likelihood; odds
infrequently: occasionally
resembles: looks like
tapering: decreasing, getting smaller
traits: characteristics; features
factors: causes
roughly: approximately; about; around
match: equal
distributed: spread; scattered
fortunate: lucky
property: asset; possession
specifically: in particular
set: fixed
proportions: quantities; sections
account: story; explanation
mark: point; score
relationships: association; connection

Recite and Review

1. A single number that tells how "spread out" the scores are refers to a measure of
   _____.

2. The measure that is the difference between the highest and lowest scores is called the
   _____.

3. An index of how much a typical score differs from the mean of a group of scores is called
   a(n) _____.

4. Simpson subtracted the mean from the original score and then divided the resulting number
   by the standard deviation for that group of scores in order to convert this original score to a(n)
   _____.

5. The distribution of chance events typically resembles a(n) _____.

6. The standard deviation measures off set proportions of the normal curve above and below the
   _____.

7. Heather had a score of 120 in a class with a mean of 100 and a standard deviation of 10.
   Therefore, her z-score is _____.

8. John had a score of 90 in a class with a mean of 100 and a standard deviation of 5. His z-
   score is _____.

9. A bell-shaped distribution, with a large number of scores in the middle, tapering to very few
   extremely high and low scores is called a(n) _____.

10. The percent of all IQ scores that are between one standard deviation above and below the
    mean is roughly_____ percent.

11. The percent of all memory scores that are between two standard deviations above and below
    the mean is _____ percent.

12. The percent of all people's heights that fall between three standard deviations above and
    below the mean is _____ percent.

Connections

1. ___ variability
2. ___ range
3. ___ standard deviation
4. ___ z-score

5. ___ normal curve

a. difference between the highest and lowest scores in a group of scores
b. number that tells how many standard deviations above or below the mean a score is
c. tendency for a group of scores to differ in value
d. bell-shaped distribution, with a large number of scores in the middle, tapering to very few extremely high and low scores
e. index of how much a typical score differs from the mean of a group of scores

Check Your Memory

1. TRUE or FALSE   Measures of central tendency indicate the degree to which a group of scores differ from one another.
2. TRUE or FALSE   To find the range, you would have to know what the highest and lowest scores are.
3. TRUE or FALSE   The standard deviations can be different in two groups of scores even if their means are the same.
4. TRUE or FALSE   To find a z-score, you must know the median and the standard deviation.
5. TRUE or FALSE   When scores are widely spread, measures of variability will get smaller.
6. TRUE or FALSE   A z-score of +1.0 means a person scored exactly at the mean.
7. TRUE or FALSE   If you had a score of 70 in a class with a mean of 80 and a standard deviation of five, you would have a z-score of -2.0.
8. TRUE or FALSE   On a normal curve, the majority of scores are found near the middle of a normal curve.
9. TRUE or FALSE   Fifty percent of all scores are found below the mean in a normal curve.
10. TRUE or FALSE   Relationships between the standard deviation (or z-scores) and the normal curve do not change.
11. TRUE or FALSE   Roughly 40 percent of cases (IQ scores) fall between one standard deviation above and below the mean.
12. TRUE or FALSE   On a normal curve, 99 percent of cases (IQ scores) would be found between three standard deviations above and below the mean.

Module A.2 Correlations and Inferential Statistics

Correlation—Rating Relationships

Survey Question: How are correlations used in psychology?

Language Development Guide

inferential: not directly expressed; obtained by inference or deduction; implied
generalizations: reasoning from detailed facts to general principles
keen: sharp
phenomena: observable facts
note: observe
socioeconomic status: measure that reflects a person's work experience and his or her individual or family income and position within the community relative to others
educational status: level of education one has attained
detecting: finding out
misbehave: act badly

wealth: riches; worldly goods

exposure: experience with

hostile: aggressive; unfriendly

visualizing: seeing, imagining

construct: create; make

plots: marks

varying: differing

strength: how much or how reliably you are able to predict the association between the two events

consumed: drank

coordination: skill of muscles working together to perform some activity

correlated: associated; linked; connected

coefficient: number that serves as a measure of some characteristic

nonexistent: absent

discovered: determined; uncovered

relatively: fairly; reasonably

hypothetical: theoretical; made up to illustrate a point or to show reasoning

perfect (regarding correlations): allows one to exactly predict; to always predict

valuable: helpful; important; useful

cited: mentioned; referred to

formulas: procedures

applicants: candidates; interviewees; hopefuls that wish to join

GPA: grade point average

ratings: relative standing in a particular class; measure of their academic growth

extracurricular: activities outside the regular academic studies, such as sports, band, etc.

predictor: information that supports the likelihood of a future event occurring

screening: selecting

"trick": technique

accounted for: explained by, caused by

"squeezed": compressed

variation: difference

corresponding: having the same relationship

to vary: fluctuate; change

along the same line: in a similar way

this state of affairs: to this situation

encountered: come across; run into

sweeping: broad; nonspecific; indiscriminate

pronouncements: statements; assertions

document: record; give proof

noting: recording; taking notice of

reiterate: repeat

automatically: routinely; by design

conclude: decide; presume; deduce

solely: only

link: connection

devote: give; apply

tempting: appealing

probable: likely

origin: source; cause

humble: modest

tentative: hesitant

confidence: assurance; belief

Recite and Review

1. The descriptive statistic used to express the degree of the relationship between two variables is the _____.
2. If you wanted to find out if wealth was related to happiness or if the chance of having a heart attack was related to having a hostile personality, you would most likely use a(n) _____ study.
3. The simplest way of visualizing a correlation is to construct a(n) _____.
4. Increases in the X measure (or score) are matched by increases on the Y measure (or score) in a(n) _____ relationship.
5. Decreases in the X measure (or score) are matched by decreases on the Y measure (or score) in a(n) _____ relationship.
6. Increases in the X measure (or score) are matched by decreases on the Y measure (or score) in a(n) _____ relationship.
7. When no relationship exists between two measures, this indicates a(n) _____ correlation.
8. If students who are more susceptible to hypnosis are more likely to listen to music, then this would indicate a(n) _____ relationship.
9. If the higher a couple's socioeconomic and educational status, the smaller the number of children they are likely to have, then this would indicate a(n) _____ relationship.
10. The relationship between your hat size and your score on a memory test would yield a(n) _____ correlation.
11. The strength of a correlation can be expressed as a(n) _____ of correlation.
12. A weak relationship is indicated if the number used to express the strength of the correlation is close to _____.
13. A strong relationship is indicated if the number used to express the strength of the correlation is close to a + or - _____.
14. If the correlation is +1.00, then it is referred to as a(n) _____ positive relationship.
15. If the correlation is -1.00, then it is referred to as a(n) _____ negative relationship.

16. The graph at the right depicts a(n) _____ relationship.

17. The most commonly used correlation coefficient is called the _____.
18. Regarding its strength, a correlation of -.86 would be considered _____.
19. Regarding its strength, a correlation of +.17 would be considered _____.
20. The graph at the right depicts a(n) _____ relationship.

21. Correlations are particularly valuable for making _____.
22. In order to decide which applicants have the best chances for success, most colleges have formulas that use _____ correlations.
23. If you square the correlation coefficient, you will get a number telling the _____ accounted for by the correlation.

24. If the correlation between IQ scores and college grade point average is .5, then the amount of variation in college grades that is accounted for by knowing IQ scores is _____ percent.
25. A correlation of +1.00 or −1.00 means that the percent of the variation in the Y measure that is accounted for by knowing the X measure is _____ percent.
26. When a correlation exists, we cannot conclude that a(n) _____ relationship exists.
27. Sometimes, two correlated measures are related as a result of the influence of a(n) _____.
28. If Tamara wishes to establish causation within her research, then she must perform a(n) _____.

Connections

1. ___ correlation
2. ___ scatter diagram
3. ___ positive relationship
4. ___ zero correlation
5. ___ negative relationship
6. ___ coefficient of correlation
7. ___ perfect positive relationship
8. ___ perfect negative relationship
9. ___ percent of variance
10. ___ causation

a. mathematical relationship in which increases in one measure are matched by increases in the other (or decreases correspond with decreases)
b. mathematical relationship in which the correlation between two measures is −1.00
c. portion of the total amount of variation in a group of scores
d. existence of a consistent, systematic relationship between two events, measures, or variables
e. requires an experiment to establish this
f. mathematical relationship in which the correlation between two measures is +1.00
g. statistical index ranging from −1.00 to +1.00 that indicates the direction and degree of the relationship
h. absence of a (linear) mathematical relationship between two measures
i. graph that plots the intersection of paired measures; that is, the points at which paired X and Y measures cross
j. mathematical relationship in which increases in one measure are matched by decreases in the other

Check Your Memory

1. TRUE or FALSE   The descriptive statistic used to express the relationship to events or measures is referred to as tests of statistical significance.
2. TRUE or FALSE   If you wanted to find out if students' grades in high school are related to how well they are likely to do in college, you would most likely use a single-blind experiment.
3. TRUE or FALSE   The simplest way of visualizing a correlation is to construct a histogram.
4. TRUE or FALSE   In a positive relationship, increases in the X measure (or score) are matched by increases on the Y measure (or score).
5. TRUE or FALSE   In a negative relationship, decreases in the X measure (or score) are matched by decreases on the Y measure (or score).
6. TRUE or FALSE   With a zero correlation, increases in the X measure (or score) are matched by decreases on the Y measure (or score).
7. TRUE or FALSE   If higher alcohol levels are correlated with lower coordination scores, then a zero correlation exists.

8. TRUE or FALSE If having lower levels of education are correlated with having lower rates of pay in a particular industry, then a positive relationship exists.

9. TRUE or FALSE People's shoe sizes and IQ scores would most likely be a negative relationship.

10. TRUE or FALSE The graph at the right depicts a strong positive correlation.

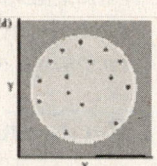

11. TRUE or FALSE Coefficients of correlation range from +3.00 to a -3.00.

12. TRUE or FALSE A coefficient of correlation of -.97 would indicate a weak relationship.

13. TRUE or FALSE If you obtained a coefficient of correlation of +1.45, you would have made a mathematical error.

14. TRUE or FALSE If the correlation is +1.00, a perfect positive relationship exists.

15. TRUE or FALSE The most commonly used correlation coefficient is called the Pearson *r*.

16. TRUE or FALSE If we know that two measures are correlated, and we know a person's score on one measure, we can predict his or her score on the other.

17. TRUE or FALSE Most colleges have formulas that use multiple correlations to decide which applicants have the best chances for success.

18. TRUE or FALSE If you find a correlation of .60 between your pretest reading scores and the students' end-of-semester scores in your class, then 60 percent of the variation in the end-of-semester scores are accounted for by knowing the students' pretest reading scores.

19. TRUE or FALSE A correlation of +1.00 or –1.00 means that 50 percent of the variation in the Y measure is accounted for by knowing the X measure.

20. TRUE or FALSE Two correlated measures may be related through the influence of a third variable.

21. TRUE or FALSE Correlation allows us to demonstrate causation.

Critical Thinking Question

Suppose it was found that sleeping with your clothes on is correlated with waking up with a headache. Could you conclude that sleeping with your clothes on causes headaches?

Module A.2 Correlations and Inferential Statistics
Inferential Statistics—Significant Numbers
Survey Question: What are inferential statistics?

Language Development Guide

meaningless fluctuation: random changes
conclusively: convincingly; decisively
depressed: condition of extreme and prolonged sadness and dejection
particular: specific
undoubtedly: certainly; definitely
promise: potential; possibility
impractical: not workable; not reasonable
terrorists: radical activist; revolutionary
status: position
cross sections: groups of individuals that differ on various characteristics, such as age, gender, etc.
meaningful: value; useful
truly: correctly

reflect: mirror
essential: necessary; critical
random: chance
estimate: approximation; educated guess
probability: likelihood; odds
certainty: assurance; confidence

Recite and Review

1. A researcher who studies the effects of a new therapy on a small group of depressed individuals and generalizes these results to the larger population is using _____ statistics.
2. An entire group of animals, people, or objects belonging to a particular category is referred to as a(n) _____.
3. Although a researcher might like to use the entire group of students to which his new reading program could be applied, this would be both impossible and _____.
4. In research, a smaller cross section of an entire group is selected, and observations of this smaller group is used to draw conclusions about the larger group with this smaller group being called a(n) _____.
5. If this smaller group reflects the membership and characteristics of the larger group, then we say that the smaller group is _____.
6. If each member of the larger group has an equal chance of being included in the smaller group, then the members of this smaller group were chosen at _____.
7. You are conducting a research project to benefit your small city, which has 10,000 citizens. You put all the citizens' names into a computer, and the computer selects 350 people for you to survey. These 350 people would be considered the _____.
8. You surveyed 350 people in order to utilize the results to help the 10,000 citizens in your city. The 10,000 citizens would be considered the _____.
9. In order to estimate how often experimental results could have occurred by chance alone, one would use tests of _____.
10. The significance of test results is stated as a(n) _____.
11. In psychology, an experimental result is considered significant if that result could have occurred by chance _____ times (or less) out of 100.
12. A value of $p = .025$ would indicate that these test results are _____.

Connections

1. ___ population
2. ___ sample
3. ___ representative
4. ___ random selection
5. ___ statistical significance

a. degree to which an event (such as the results of an experiment) is unlikely to have occurred by chance alone
b. process by which the smaller subpart is chosen so that each member of the larger group has an equal chance of being included in the smaller subpart
c. accurately reflecting the characteristics of the larger group within the smaller subpart
d. smaller subpart of a larger group under study
e. entire group of animals, people, or objects belonging to a particular category

Check Your Memory

1. TRUE or FALSE   A researcher who studies the effects of a new therapy on a small group of depressed individuals and generalizes these results to the larger population is using descriptive statistics to generalize.

992

2. TRUE or FALSE   An entire group of animals, people, or objects belonging to a particular category is referred to as a cross-sectional sample.

3. TRUE or FALSE   Observations of the sample are used to draw conclusions about an entire population.

4. TRUE or FALSE   If a sample group truly reflects the membership and characteristics of the larger population, it is referred to as a representative sample.

5. TRUE or FALSE   When each member of the population has an equal chance of being included in the sample, the sample was chosen through a process known as a double-blind assignment.

6. TRUE or FALSE   If you conduct an experiment and randomly select 100 students out of 3,000 students in the entire student body, then the 100 students would be your representative population.

7. TRUE or FALSE   Tests of statistical significance provide an estimate of how often experimental results could have occurred by chance alone.

8. TRUE or FALSE   The results of a significance test are stated as a percent of variance.

9. TRUE or FALSE   In psychology, any experimental result that could have occurred by chance 25 times (or more) out of 100 is considered significant.

10. TRUE or FALSE   In a study to determine if a drug improved memory, a probability of .025 that the group means would differ as much as they do by chance alone would allow the researchers to conclude with reasonable certainty that the drug actually did improve memory scores.

Final Survey and Review—Completion

Module A.1 Descriptive Statistics

Descriptive Statistics—Psychology by the Numbers

Survey Question: What are descriptive statistics?

1. To make the results of studies more meaningful and easier to communicate to others, descriptive statistics "boil down" or _____ data collected from research participants.

2. The three basic types of descriptive statistics are measures of central tendency, measures of variability, and _____.

3. Adam has collected large amounts of data during his research; so he is breaking it down into a range of possible scores and then recording the scores that fall into each class. Adam is constructing a(n) _____.

4. Selena is labeling the abscissa on a graph, which is the horizontal line or _____ axis.

5. Tabitha is constructing a graph in which the data is depicting in vertical bars. This type of graph is called a(n) _____.

Module A.1 Measures of Central Tendency

Survey Question: How are statistics used to identify an average score?

6. Alicia is determining the mean, median, and mode for her third grade students' last test. These measures being used by Alicia are known as measures of _____.

7. A group of ten children are asked to form the past tense of ten irregular verbs. The score for each child was 10, 10, 9, 9, 8, 8, 8, 7, 6, and 6. The median of this set of scores is _____.

8. A group of nine children are asked to identify 10 alphabet letters. The number of letters correctly identified by each child was: 10, 8, 8, 8, 7, 6, 6, 5, and 5. The mode of these scores would be _____.

9. Dr. Michel's honors class achieved the following scores on the first quiz: 100, 100, 100, 100, 90, 90, 90, 80, 80, and 70. The mean for these scores is _____.

993

Module A.1 Measures of Variability

Survey Question: What statistics do psychologists use to measure how much scores differ from one another?

10. In summarizing her research data, Krissy is utilizing the range and standard deviation, which are two measures of _____.
11. Santos' scores on his psychology quizzes so far are 90, 85, 80, and 70. The range of his scores is _____.
12. Direct measurement has shown such characteristics as height, memory span, and intelligence tend to be distributed along a(n) _____.
13. Jonas had a score of 80 in a class with a mean of 70 and a standard deviation of 5. His z-score is _____.
14. On a normal curve, 95 percent of all cases would fall between _____ standard deviations above and below the mean.

Module A.2 Correlations and Inferential Statistics

Correlation—Rating Relationships

Survey Question: How are correlations used in psychology?

15. If you wanted to find out if there is a relationship between childhood exposure to the Internet and their IQ at age 20, you would most likely use a(n) _____ study.
16. In a positive relationship, decreases in the X measure (or score) would be matched by _____ on the Y measure (or score).
17. In a negative relationship, decreases in the X measure (or score) would be matched by _____ on the Y measure (or scores).
18. If higher alcohol levels are correlated with lower coordination scores, this would be a(n) _____ relationship.
19. Regarding its strength, a correlation of -.92 would be considered _____.
20. If the correlation between the students' scores on your memory test and their GPA is .4, then the amount of variation in their GPA that is accounted for by knowing their score on the memory test is _____ percent.

Module A.2 Inferential Statistics—Significant Numbers

Survey Question: What are inferential statistics?

21. A researcher who conducts research on a new math tutoring program with a smaller group of elementary students and generalizes these results for use with all of the elementary students is using _____ statistics.
22. You randomly select 100 of the 600 psychology students on your campus and survey them about the proposed new requirement. The 600 psychology students would be the _____.
23. If you put all of the names of the registered voters in your community into a box and draw out 100 names with which to conduct a telephone interview, you have chosen the participants using a procedure known as _____.
24. The degree to which an event (such as the results of an experiment) is unlikely to have occurred by chance alone is known as _____.
25. Jay is conducted an experiment to see whether a new drug improves memory in Alzheimer's patients. In order for his results to be considered significant, his result could only have occurred by chance _____ times or less out of 100.

994

Final Survey and Review—Matching

Module A.1 Descriptive Statistics
Part 1:

1. ___ descriptive statistics
2. ___ inferential statistics
3. ___ graphical statistics
4. ___ measures of central tendency

5. ___ measures of variability

6. ___ z-score

7. ___ normal curve

a. includes the range and standard deviation
b. group of techniques for presenting numbers pictorially
c. includes mean, median, and mode
d. bell-shaped distribution, with a large number of scores in the middle, tapering to very few extremely high and low scores
e. number that tells how many standard deviations above or below the mean a score is
f. mathematical tools used to describe and summarize numeric data
g. mathematical tools used for generalizing from small samples

Part 2:

1. ___ mean

2. ___ median
3. ___ mode

4. ___ frequency distribution
5. ___ histogram

6. ___ frequency polygon

7. ___ range

8. ___ standard deviation

a. table that divides an entire range of scores into a series of classes and then records the number of scores that fall into each class
b. graph in which vertical bars are used to represent data
c. difference between the highest and lowest scores in a group of scores
d. graph in which data is represented by points on a line
e. calculated by adding all the scores for each group and then dividing by the total number of scores
f. index of how much a typical score differs from the mean of a group of scores
g. found by arranging scores from the highest to the lowest and selecting the score that falls in the middle
h. most frequently occurring score in a group of scores

Module A.2 Correlations and Inferential Statistics

1. ___ scatter diagram

2. ___ positive relationship

3. ___ zero correlation
4. ___ negative relationship

5. ___ coefficient of correlation

6. ___ percent of variance

7. ___ population

a. degree to which an event (such as the results of an experiment) is unlikely to have occurred by chance alone
b. portion of the total amount of variation in a group of scores
c. smaller subpart of a larger group under study
d. process by which the smaller subpart is chosen so that each member of the larger group has an equal chance of being included in the smaller subpart
e. mathematical relationship in which increases in one measure are matched by increases in the other (or decreases correspond with decreases)
f. statistical index ranging from −1.00 to +1.00 that indicates the direction and degree of the relationship
g. absence of a (linear) mathematical relationship between two measures

995

8. ___ sample

    h. graph that plots the intersection of paired measures; that is, the points at which paired X and Y measures cross

9. ___ random selection

    i. entire group of animals, people, or objects belonging to a particular category

10. ___ statistical significance

    j. mathematical relationship in which increases in one measure are matched by decreases in the other

Final Survey and Review—True or False

Module A.1 Descriptive Statistics
Descriptive Statistics—Psychology by the Numbers
Survey Question: What are descriptive statistics?
1. TRUE or FALSE   Graphical statistics are a type of inferential statistics.
2. TRUE or FALSE   The mean, median, and mode are types of graphical statistics.
3. TRUE or FALSE   A frequency distribution is made by breaking down the entire range of possible scores into classes of equal size.
4. TRUE or FALSE   The Y axis or vertical line on a graph is called the ordinate.
5. TRUE or FALSE   A graph in which data is represented by points on a line is known as a frequency polygon.

Module A.1 Measures of Central Tendency
Survey Question: How are statistics used to identify an average score?
6. TRUE or FALSE   A measure of central tendency is simply a number describing a "typical score" around which other scores fall.
7. TRUE or FALSE   The median is calculated by adding all the scores for each group and then dividing by the total number of scores.
8. TRUE or FALSE   The mean is sensitive to extremely high or low scores in a distribution.
9. TRUE or FALSE   If you had the scores 4, 5, 6, 6, 7, 7, 9, 12, 17, 17, and 17, the mode would be 7.

Module A.1 Measures of Variability
Survey Question: What statistics do psychologists use to measure how much scores differ from one another?
10. TRUE or FALSE   A single number that tells how "spread out" scores is a measure of statistical significance.
11. TRUE or FALSE   To calculate the range, you must put the scores in order from highest to lowest and then find the middle score in the series.
12. TRUE or FALSE   To calculate a z-score, you must know the mean and the standard deviation.
13. TRUE or FALSE   On a normal curve, a majority of scores are found near the extreme ends of the curve.
14. TRUE or FALSE   Between three standard deviations above and below the mean on a normal curve would be 68 percent of cases.

Module A.2 Correlations and Inferential Statistics
Correlation—Rating Relationships
Survey Question: How are correlations used in psychology?
15. TRUE or FALSE   The simplest way of visualizing a correlation is to construct a scatter diagram.

16. TRUE or FALSE   In a positive relationship, increases in the X measure (or score) are matched by decreases on the Y measure (or score).

17. TRUE or FALSE   Coefficients of correlation range from +1.00 to a -1.00.

18. TRUE or FALSE   A coefficient of correlation of .20 would indicate a strong relationship.

19. TRUE or FALSE   If you find a correlation of .60 between your pretest reading scores and the students' end-of-semester scores in your class, then 36 percent of the variation in the end-of-semester scores are accounted for by knowing the students' pretest reading scores.

20. TRUE or FALSE   Correlation proves that one variable causes another if the correlation coefficient is significant.

Module A.2 Inferential Statistics—Significant Numbers

Survey Question: What are inferential statistics?

21. TRUE or FALSE   A researcher who studies the effects of a new therapy on a small group of depressed individuals and generalizes these results to the larger population is using inferential statistics to generalize.

22. TRUE or FALSE   You surveyed 350 people in order to utilize the results to help the 10,000 citizens in your city. The 350 people you surveyed would be considered the population.

23. TRUE or FALSE   Choosing a sample so that each member of the population has an equal chance of being included in the sample is the process known as random selection.

24. TRUE or FALSE   The results of a significance test are stated as a standard deviation on the normal curve.

25. TRUE or FALSE   A probability of .05 or less is statistically significant.

Mastery Test

1. The type of statistics that are especially valuable for decision making and drawing conclusions are _____ statistics.
   a. graphical
   b. descriptive
   c. inferential
   d. ordinate

2. Measures of central tendency are _____ statistics.
   a. graphical
   b. descriptive
   c. inferential
   d. ordinate

3. Sorting scores into classes is a necessary step in creating a
   a. frequency distribution.
   b. correlation.
   c. scatter diagram.
   d. variability plot.

4. Vertical bars are used to indicate frequencies in a
   a. frequency polygon.
   b. scatter diagram.
   c. normal distribution.
   d. histogram.

5. Cindy is labeling the Y-axis, or vertical line on her graph, which is called the
   a. abscissa.
   b. ordinate.
   c. standard deviation.
   d. mode.

6. A group of scores must be arranged from the highest to the lowest in order and then the middle score indicated in determining the
   a. mean.
   b. range.
   c. mode.
   d. median.

7. The measure that is sensitive to extremely high or low scores in a distribution is the
   a. mean.
   b. midst.
   c. mode.
   d. median.

8. Your psychology 10-question quiz scores so far this semester are 10, 10, 10, 9, 9, 8, 8, 8. The mean of your scores is
   a. 10.
   b. 9.
   c. 8.5.
   d. 8.

9. Your history 10-question quiz scores so far this semester are 10, 10, 10, 9, 8, 8, 8, 8, 7, 7. The mode of your scores is
   a. 10.
   b. 9.
   c. 8
   d. 7.

10. In your English class, you have the following grades on your writing assignments: 95, 87, 91, 80. The range of your scores would be
    a. 88.
    b. 80.
    c. 15.
    d. 11.

11. What two statistics are needed to calculate a standard score?
    a. range and median
    b. mean and standard deviation
    c. range and mode
    d. standard deviation and z-score

12. Which is a measure of variability?
    a. Pearson r
    b. mode
    c. median
    d. range

13. If the mean on a test is 90 and the standard deviation is 10, a person with a z-score of −1.0 scored
_____ on the test.
a. 70
b. 80
c. 100
d. 110

14. On a normal curve, the largest percentage of scores falls between _____ SD.
a. 0 and +1
b. +1 and −1
c. +2 and +3
d. −3 and −2

15. What percent of all cases are found between +3 SD and −3 SD on a normal curve?
a. 50
b. 86
c. 95
d. 99

16. A good way to visualize a correlation is to plot a
a. frequency histogram.
b. polygon coefficient.
c. scatter diagram.
d. normal ordinate.

17. When measure X gets larger, measure Y gets smaller in a
a. zero correlation.
b. positive relationship.
c. variable relationship.
d. negative relationship.

18. When plotted as a graph, a zero correlation forms a cluster of points in the shape of a
a. diagonal oval to the right.
b. diagonal oval to the left.
c. horizontal line.
d. circle.

19. If higher temperatures are correlated with higher levels of hostility, this would be a
a. causal relationship.
b. positive relationship.
c. negative relationship.
d. zero correlation.

20. If you obtained a coefficient of correlation of -1.00, this would indicate that you have a
a. causal relationship.
b. weak relationship.
c. percent of variance of 50.
d. perfect negative relationship.

21. To find the percent of variance in one measure accounted for by knowing another measure, you
   should square the
   a. mean.
   b. z-score.
   c. Pearson *r*.
   d. standard deviation.

22. Correlations do not demonstrate whether
   a. a relationship is positive or negative.
   b. a cause-and-effect connection exists.
   c. knowing one measure allows prediction of another.
   d. two events are really co-relating public distance.

23. If you conduct a survey with 50 people in your small community of 200 people, these 200 people would constitute the
   a. population.
   b. sample.
   c. mean variance.
   d. median group.

24. An effective way to make sure that a sample is representative is to
   a. use random selection.
   b. calculate the correlation coefficient.
   c. make sure that the standard deviation is low.
   d. use a scatter diagram.

25. Results of an experiment that have a chance probability of which of the following are usually regarded as statistically significant?
   a. .5
   b. .05
   c. 1.5
   d. 1.05

Introduction: The Psychology of Studying—Reflective Learning

Solutions

Preview and Reflective Reading—How to Tame a Textbook

RECITE AND REVIEW

1. smarter
2. life
3. experiential
4. reflective
5. experiential
6. reflective
7. self-reference
8. related
9. meaningful
10. critical
11. review
12. survey
13. question
14. read
15. recite
16. reflect
17. survey
18. dialogue
19. glossary
20. Knowledge Builder
21. *Psychology in Action*
22. *Diversity*
23. *Brainwaves*
24. *Clinical*
25. *Summary*

CONNECTIONS

1. e
2. h
3. i
4. f
5. c
6. d
7. a
8. b
9. g

CHECK YOUR ANSWER

1. False
2. False
3. False
4. True
5. True
6. False
7. False
8. False
9. True
10. False
11. True
12. False
13. True
14. True
15. False
16. True
17. False
18. True
19. True
20. True

Critical Thinking

Both the SQ4R and the LISAN methods encourage people to be reflective and to actively seek information n as a way of learning more effectively.

Reflective Note Taking—LISAN Up!

RECITE AND REVIEW

1. active
2. LISAN
3. Lead. Don't follow
4. ideas
5. signal
6. actively listen
7. selective
8. connection
9. organize
10. test questions

1. c
2. e
3. b
4. f
5. a
6. d

CHECK YOUR MEMORY

1. True
2. False
3. False
4. True
5. True
6. True
7. False
8. True
9. False
10. True
11. True
12. True
13. True

Reflective Study Strategies—Making a Habit of Success

RECITE AND REVIEW

1. unreflective
2. place
3. cramming
4. spaced
5. massed
6. mnemonic
7. mnemonic
8. practice
9. self-testing
10. lower
11. underprepare
12. overestimate
13. overlearning
14. essay
15. effective

CONNECTIONS

1. g
2. d
3. f
4. e
5. c
6. b
7. a

CHECK YOUR MEMORY

1. True
2. False
3. True
4. False
5. True
6. True
7. False
8. True
9. True
10. False
11. True
12. True
13. True
14. True
15. False
16. True
17. False
18. False

Self-Regulated Learning—Academic All-Stars

RECITE AND REVIEW

1. self-regulated
2. objective
3. plans
4. guidance
5. self-monitoring
6. SQ4R
7. reward
8. self-praise
9. performance
10. time
11. learning environment
12. tutoring

CONNECTIONS

1. d
2. h
3. f
4. a
5. b
6. g
7. e
8. c

1. True
2. True
3. False
4. True
5. True
6. True
7. False
8. False
9. True
10. True
11. False
12. True
13. True

Procrastination—Avoiding the Last-Minute Blues

RECITE AND REVIEW

1. procrastinator
2. personal worth or self-worth
3. ability
4. all-or-nothing
5. time management
6. weekly time
7. checklist
8. term
9. guilty
10. time
11. measurable
12. day-to-day or daily
13. unpleasant
14. challenging
15. attitude

CONNECTIONS

1. c
2. a
3. d
4. g
5. b
6. f
7. e

CHECK YOUR MEMORY

1. False
2. True
3. True
4. False
5. True
6. True
7. False
8. True
9. True
10. False
11. False
12. False
13. True
14. True
15. True
16. False
17. True
18. False

Reflective Test Taking—Are You "Test Wise"?

RECITE AND REVIEW

1. clues
2. survey (look over)
3. easy (easier)
4. objective
5. partial
6. free information (cues)
7. four
8. 50-50
9. guessing
10. random
11. more
12. reflective
13. best
14. rating
15. never
16. false
17. organization
18. emphasis
19. half
20. main points (ideas)
21. grammar
22. fill in a blank
23. overlearn
24. terms
25. short answer

CONNECTIONS

1. d
2. e
3. f
4. a
5. c
6. b

CHECK YOUR MEMORY

1. False	9. True	17. True
2. False	10. False	18. False
3. False	11. False	19. False
4. True	12. False	20. True
5. True	13. True	21. True
6. True	14. False	22. True
7. False	15. True	23. True
8. True	16. True	

Using Digital Media—Netting New Knowledge

RECITE AND REVIEW

1. media	5. CengageNOW	9. abstract
2. authoritative or reliable	6. Cengage Psychology Resource	10. articles
3. skepticism	7. book companion	11. PsycPORT
4. Book Companion	8. PsycINFO	12. dead
		13. live

CONNECTIONS

1. h	5. d	9. a
2. f	6. b	10. g
3. j	7. e	
4. i	8. c	

CHECK YOUR MEMORY

1. False	6. True	11. False
2. False	7. False	12. False
3. False	8. False	
4. True	9. True	
5. True	10. True	

Final Survey and Review—Completion

Preview and Reflective Reading—How to Tame a Textbook

1. passive	4. survey	7. *Discovering Psychology*
2. self-reflection	5. reflect	
3. critical	6. running glossary	

Reflective Note Taking—LISAN Up!

8. active	9. Lead, Don't follow	11. Note taking
	10. signal	

Reflective Study Strategies—Making a Habit of Success

12. place	14. mnemonics	16. lower or poorer
13. spaced practice	15. self-testing	17. overlearn

Self-Regulated Learning—Academic All-Stars

18. self-regulated
19. self-monitoring
20. self-praise
21. distractions

Procrastination—Avoiding the Last-Minute Blues

22. high standards
23. procrastinate
24. weekly time
25. term
26. schedule
27. goals

Reflective Test Taking—Are You "Test Wise"?

28. objective
29. short answer
30. two
31. gain
32. superlatives
33. essay
34. short answer

Using Digital Media—Netting New Knowledge

35. digital
36. crossword puzzles
37. video clips
38. abstract
39. APA (American Psychological Association)
40. personal experience

Final Survey and Review—Matching

Part 1

1. i
2. c
3. d
4. f
5. g
6. h
7. e
8. b
9. j
10. a

Part 2

1. f
2. d
3. h
4. i
5. g
6. j
7. e
8. b
9. a
10. c

Final Survey and Review—True or False

Preview and Reflective Reading—How to Tame a Textbook

1. True
2. False
3. True
4. False
5. True
6. False

Reflective Note Taking—LISAN Up!

7. False
8. False
9. True
10. True

Reflective Study Strategies—Making a Habit of Success

11. False
12. False
13. True
14. False
15. False
16. False

Self-Regulated Learning—Academic All-Stars

17. True
18. True
19. True

Procrastination—Avoiding the Last-Minute Blues

20. False	23. False	26. True
21. True	24. True	
22. True	25. True	

Reflective Test Taking—Are You "Test Wise"?

27. True	30. False	33. False
28. False	31. True	
29. False	32. True	

Using Digital Media—Netting New Knowledge

34. True	37. False	40. False
35. False	38. True	
36. True	39. True	

MASTERY TEST

1. c	15. d	29. a
2. a	16. a	30. a
3. c	17. b	31. b
4. d	18. b	32. c
5. b	19. a	33. d
6. c	20. c	34. d
7. a	21. d	35. c
8. b	22. b	36. a
9. a	23. c	37. d
10. d	24. d	38. c
11. b	25. a	39. b
12. d	26. d	40. d
13. a	27. b	
14. c	28. b	

Chapter 1: Discovering Psychology and Research Methods

Solutions

Module 1.1 The Science of Psychology
Behave Yourself!

RECITE AND REVIEW

1. critical
2. mind
3. mental processes
4. overt
5. covert
6. profession
7. commonsense
8. empirical
9. systematic
10. intersubjective
11. data
12. research
13. personality
14. developmental
15. learning
16. perception
17. comparative
18. cognitive
19. biopsychologist
20. gender
21. social
22. evolutionary
23. cultural
24. forensic
25. animal
26. description
27. understanding
28. prediction
29. control

CONNECTIONS—PART 1

1. c
2. g
3. j
4. b
5. h
6. i
7. e
8. a
9. f
10. d

CONNECTIONS—PART 2

1. i
2. f
3. e
4. k
5. c
6. a
7. h
8. j
9. g
10. d
11. l
12. b

CHECK YOUR MEMORY

1. True
2. True
3. False
4. True
5. False
6. True
7. False
8. False
9. False
10. False
11. True
12. True
13. True
14. False
15. False
16. True
17. False
18. True
19. True
20. False
21. True
22. False

Critical Thinking Answer
False

Module 1.2 Critical Thinking and the Scientific Method in Psychology
Critical Thinking—Take It with a Grain of Salt (Module 1.2)

RECITE AND REVIEW

1. synthesizing
2. conventional
3. reflect
4. revising
5. empirical
6. wrong
7. authority
8. quality
9. open
10. explanation
11. conflicts

CHECK YOUR MEMORY

1. False
2. False
3. True
4. False
5. False
6. False
7. True
8. True

Critical Thinking Answer
There are many examples. Here are a few more to add to the ones you thought of: "He (or she) who hesitates is lost" versus "Haste makes waste." "Never too old to learn" versus "You can't teach an old dog new tricks."

Module 1.2 Critical Thinking and the Scientific Method in Psychology
Pseudopsychologies—Palms, Planets, and Personality (Module 1.2)

RECITE AND REVIEW

1. psychology
2. false
3. contradicts
4. phrenology
5. palmistry
6. graphology
7. astrology
8. uncritical acceptance
9. confirmation bias
10. Barnum

CONNECTIONS

1. f
2. d
3. a
4. h
5. g
6. c
7. e
8. b

CHECK YOUR MEMORY

1. True
2. False
3. False
4. False
5. True
6. True
7. False
8. True
9. True
10. True
11. False
12. False
13. True
14. False
15. False

Critical Thinking Answer
The term "Barnum statement" comes from Levy (2003), who offers the following examples: You are afraid of being hurt. You are trying to find a balance between autonomy and closeness. You don't like being overly dependent. You just want to be understood.

Module 1.2 Critical Thinking and the Scientific Method in Psychology
Scientific Research—How to Think Like a Psychologist (Module 1.2)

RECITE AND REVIEW

1. commonsense
2. systematic
3. repeatable
4. observations
5. defining
6. hypothesis
7. operational
8. hypothesis
9. theory
10. journals
11. replicate
12. abstract
13. introduction
14. method
15. results
16. discussion

CONNECTIONS

1. i
2. e
3. j
4. d
5. f
6. b
7. h
8. a
9. g
10. c

CHECK YOUR MEMORY

1. True
2. True
3. True
4. False
5. True
6. False
7. True
8. True
9. True
10. False
11. False
12. True

Module 1.3 History and Contemporary Perspectives
A Brief History of Psychology—Psychology's Family Album (Module 1.3)

RECITE AND REVIEW

1. (Wilhelm) Wundt
2. introspection
3. (Edward) Titchener
4. (William) James
5. adapt
6. (Ivan) Pavlov
7. (John B.) Watson
8. (B.F.) Skinner
9. cognitive behaviorism
10. Gestalt
11. (Sigmund) Freud
12. repression
13. Neo-Freudians
14. psychodynamic
15. humanistic
16. determinism
17. humanistic
18. self-actualization
19. reference
20. (William) James
21. (John) Dewey
22. (Margaret) Washburn
23. (Francis Cecil) Sumner
24. (Inez Beverly) Prosser
25. 70 (seventy)

CONNECTIONS

1. d
2. h
3. a
4. j
5. f
6. g
7. i
8. c
9. b
10. e

1. False	9. True	17. False
2. True	10. False	18. False
3. False	11. True	19. True
4. True	12. False	20. False
5. True	13. True	21. False
6. False	14. True	22. True
7. True	15. False	
8. False	16. True	

Critical Thinking Answer

No, it did not. The downfall of structuralism was that each observer examined the contents of his or her own mind—which is something that no other person can observe.

Module 1.3 History and Contemporary Perspectives
Psychology Today— Three Complementary Perspectives on Behavior (Module 1.3)

RECITE AND REVIEW

1. sociocultural	6. behavioristic	11. cultural relativity
2. neuroscience	7. psychodynamic	12. social norms
3. biopsychological	8. humanistic	13. eclectic
4. evolutionary	9. sociocultural	
5. cognitive	10. positive	

CONNECTIONS

1. f	5. b	9. g
2. d	6. j	10. c
3. a	7. e	
4. i	8. h	

CHECK YOUR MEMORY

1. True	6. True	11. True
2. True	7. True	12. False
3. False	8. True	13. True
4. False	9. True	
5. False	10. False	

Module 1.4 Psychologists and Their Specialties

RECITE AND REVIEW

1. psychiatrist	8. psychiatrist	16. school
2. psychologist	9. Louisiana	17. industrial-organizational (or industrial)
3. clinical	10. psychoanalyst	
4. counseling	11. licensed	18. consumer
5. scientist-practitioner	12. social worker	19. basic
6. Psy.D.	13. ethics	20. applied
7. stable (or healthy)	14. 59 (fifty-nine)	
	15. 30 (thirty)	

CONNECTIONS

1. c	5. f	9. g
2. e	6. i	10. a
3. b	7. h	
4. j	8. d	

CHECK YOUR MEMORY

1. False	8. False	15. True
2. True	9. True	16. True
3. False	10. True	17. True
4. True	11. True	18. True
5. False	12. True	19. False
6. True	13. False	20. False
7. True	14. True	

Critical Thinking Answer

Practitioners benefit from basic psychological research in the same way that physicians benefit from basic research in biology. Discoveries in basic science form the knowledge base that leads to useful applications.

Module 1.5 The Psychology Experiment
The Psychology Experiment—Where Effect Meets Cause

RECITE AND REVIEW

1. experiment	8. independent	14. alike (the same)
2. participants	9. dependent	15. deception
3. variable	10. extraneous	16. humanely
4. independent	11. control	17. ethics
5. independent	12. experimental	18. voluntary
6. dependent	13. random assignment	19. significant
7. extraneous		20. replicated

CONNECTIONS

1. f	4. b	7. d
2. h	5. g	8. e
3. a	6. c	

CHECK YOUR MEMORY

1. False	8. False	15. True
2. True	9. False	16. False
3. False	10. True	17. True
4. False	11. True	18. True
5. False	12. True	19. False
6. True	13. False	20. True
7. False	14. True	

Critical Thinking Answer

The statement implies that vitamin C prevented colds. However, not getting a cold could just be a coincidence. A controlled experiment with a group given vitamin C and a control group not taking vitamin C would be needed to learn if vitamin C actually has any effect on susceptibility to colds.

Module 1.5 The Psychology Experiment
Double Blind—On Placebos and Self-Fulfilling Prophecies

RECITE AND REVIEW

1. research participant
2. placebo
3. placebo
4. brain
5. single
6. experimental
7. control
8. researcher
9. self-fulfilling
10. double

CONNECTIONS

1. a
2. f
3. h
4. g
5. e
6. b
7. c
8. d

CHECK YOUR MEMORY

1. True
2. True
3. False
4. True
5. False
6. True
7. True
8. True
9. False
10. False
11. True
12. True

Critical Thinking Answer

Belief in astrology can create a self-fulfilling prophecy in which people alter their behaviors and self-concepts to match their astrological signs.

Module 1.6 Nonexperimental Research Methods
Nonexperimental Psychological Research—Different Strokes

RECITE AND REVIEW

1. nonexperimental
2. naturalistic observation
3. clinical
4. correlation
5. survey

CONNECTIONS

1. f
2. e
3. d
4. a
5. b
6. c

CHECK YOUR MEMORY

1. False
2. False
3. False
4. True
5. True

Module 1.6 Nonexperimental Research Methods
Naturalistic Observation

RECITE AND REVIEW
1. nonexperimental
2. tampered
3. description
4. effect
5. bias
6. anthropomorphic
7. observational record

CONNECTIONS
1. c
2. b
3. f
4. d
5. e
6. a

CHECK YOUR MEMORY
1. False
2. False
3. True
4. True
5. True
6. False
7. True

Critical Thinking Answer
Yes. It appears to be difficult for humans to resist thinking of other species and even machines in human terms.

Module 1.6 Nonexperimental Research Methods
Correlational Studies

RECITE AND REVIEW
1. correlational
2. direction
3. perfect
4. strong
5. zero
6. positive
7. positive
8. negative
9. predictions
10. third factor
11. positive

CONNECTIONS
1. c
2. g
3. d
4. b
5. f
6. e
7. a

CHECK YOUR MEMORY
1. False
2. True
3. True
4. False
5. True
6. False
7. False
8. False
9. False
10. True
11. False

Module 1.6 Nonexperimental Research Methods
The Clinical Method

RECITE AND REVIEW
1. case (clinical)
2. clinical tests
3. (Phineas) Gage
4. experiments
5. case (clinical)
6. control

1. d
2. e
3. c
4. f
5. b
6. a

CHECK YOUR MEMORY

1. True
2. False
3. True
4. True
5. False
6. True

Module 1.6 Nonexperimental Research Methods
Survey Method—Here, Have a Sample

Recite and Review

1. survey
2. sample
3. proportion
4. random
5. biased
6. web (Internet)
7. courtesy bias

CONNECTIONS

1. c
2. e
3. a
4. d
5. f
6. b

CHECK YOUR MEMORY

1. True
2. True
3. True
4. False
5. False
6. True
7. True

Critical Thinking Answer

The psychologist's coin flips *might* produce a reasonably good sample of people *at the mall*. The real problem is that people who go to the mall may be mostly from one part of town, from upper income groups, or from some other nonrepresentative group. The psychologist's sample is likely to be seriously flawed.

Module 1.7 Psychology in Action: Psychology in the Media
Psychology in the Media—Seeking Klingon Interpreter

Recite and Review

1. entertainment
2. skeptical
3. source
4. psychic
5. Barnum
6. oversimplification
7. case (or example)
8. control
9. causation
10. inference

CONNECTIONS

1. h
2. c
3. e
4. a
5. b
6. d
7. f
8. g

CHECK YOUR MEMORY

1. True	5. True	9. False
2. False	6. False	10. False
3. True	7. False	
4. True	8. False	

Critical Thinking Answer

This is another case of mistaking correlation for causation. Children who are hyperactive may eat more sugar (and other foods) to fuel their frenetic activity levels.

Final Survey and Review—Completion

Module 1.1 The Science of Psychology

1. behavior
2. covert
3. empirical
4. developmental
5. social
6. animal
7. predict

Module 1.2 Critical Thinking and the Scientific Method in Psychology
Critical Thinking—Take It with a Grain of Salt

8. reflection
9. mind

Module 1.2 Pseudopsychologies—Palms, Planets, and Personality

10. phrenology
11. forgeries
12. uncritical acceptance

Module 1.2 Scientific Research—How to Think Like a Psychologist

13. scientific method
14. operational
15. abstract

Module 1.3 History and Contemporary Perspectives
A Brief History of Psychology—Psychology's Family Album

16. structuralism
17. behaviorism
18. psychoanalytic (or psychodynamic)
19. humanistic
20. (Margaret) Washburn

Module 1. 3Psychology Today— Three Complementary Perspectives on Behavior

21. endocrine
22. eclectic

Module 1.4 Psychologists and Their Specialties

23. counseling
24. therapy
25. New Mexico
26. applied

Module 1.5 The Psychology Experiment
The Psychology Experiment—Where Effect Meets Cause

27. independent
28. extraneous
29. control

Module 1.5 Double Blind—On Placebos and Self-Fulfilling Prophecies
30. research participant 31. double 32. harm

Module 1.6 Nonexperimental Research Methods
Nonexperimental Psychological Research—Different Strokes
33. case study (or clinical) 34. survey

Module 1.6 Naturalistic Observation
35. observer effect 36. anthropomorphic

Module 1.6 Correlational Studies
37. strength 38. negative

Module 1.6 The Clinical Method
39. (Phineas) Gage 40. schizophrenia

Module 1.6 Survey Method—Here, Have a Sample
41. population 42. courtsey

Module 1.7 Psychology in Action: Psychology in the Media
Psychology in the Media—Seeking Klingon Interpreter
43. oversimplification 44. individual case (or single example) 45. inference

Final Survey and Review—Matching

MODULE 1.1 THE SCIENCE OF PSYCHOLOGY
1. h 5. j 9. g
2. f 6. i 10. d
3. e 7. c
4. b 8. a

Module 1.2 Critical Thinking and the Scientific Method in Psychology
1. g 5. b 9. f
2. d 6. e 10. a
3. j 7. i
4. h 8. c

Module 1.3 History and Contemporary Perspectives
1. g 5. i 9. c
2. a 6. d 10. f
3. b 7. k 11. e
4. h 8. j

Module 1.4 Psychologists and Their Specialties

1. f	4. b	7. c
2. a	5. g	
3. d	6. e	

Module 1.5 The Psychology Experiment

1. j	5. b	9. f
2. i	6. a	10. h
3. g	7. d	
4. e	8. c	

Module 1.6 Nonexperimental Research Methods /
Module 1.7 Psychology in Action: Psychology in the Media

1. j	5. h	9. k
2. f	6. g	10. a
3. d	7. i	11. b
4. e	8. c	

Final Survey and Review—True or False

Module 1.1 The Science of Psychology

1. True	4. False	7. True
2. False	5. True	
3. False	6. False	

Module 1.2 Critical Thinking and the Scientific Method in Psychology

Critical Thinking—Take It with a Grain of Salt

8. True	9. False

Module 1.2 Pseudopsychologies—Palms, Planets, and Personality

10. False	11. True	12. True

Module 1.2 Scientific Research—How to Think Like a Psychologist

13. True	14. False	15. False

Module 1.3 History and Contemporary Perspectives

A Brief History of Psychology—Psychology's Family Album

16. False	18. False
17. False	19. True

Module 1.3 Psychology Today— Three Complementary Perspectives on Behavior

20. False	21. False	22. True

Module 1.4 Psychologists and Their Specialties

23. True	24. False	25. True

Module 1.5 The Psychology Experiment
The Psychology Experiment—Where Effect Meets Cause
26. False 27. True 28. True

Module 1.5 Double Blind—On Placebos and Self-Fulfilling Prophecies
29. False 30. False 31. False

Module 1.6 Nonexperimental Research Methods
Nonexperimental Psychological Research—Different Strokes
32. False 33. True

Module 1.6 Naturalistic Observation
34. True 35. False 36. True

Module 1.6 Correlational Studies
37. True 38. True 39. False

Module 1.6 The Clinical Method
40. False 41. False

Module 1.6 Survey Method—Here, Have a Sample
42. True 43. False

Module 1.7 Psychology in Action: Psychology in the Media
Psychology in the Media—Seeking Klingon Interpreter
44. True 45. True

Mastery Test

1. c	15. a	29. b
2. b	16. b	30. c
3. c	17. d	31. a
4. b	18. b	32. c
5. c	19. a	33. b
6. a	20. d	34. b
7. b	21. b	35. a
8. d	22. c	36. c
9. c	23. c	37. b
10. d	24. a	38. c
11. d	25. b	39. d
12. b	26. b	40. d
13. d	27. b	
14. a	28. c	

Chapter 2: Brain and Behavior

Solutions

Module 2.1 Neurons and the Nervous System
Neurons—Building a "Biocomputer"

Recite and Review

1. brain
2. neuron
3. glial
4. dendrites
5. cell body
6. axons
7. axon terminals
8. resting
9. threshold
10. action
11. ion channels
12. sodium (Na+)
13. all-or-nothing
14. negative
15. myelin
16. saltatory
17. multiple sclerosis
18. neurotransmitters
19. receptor sites
20. dopamine
21. serotonin
22. acetylcholine
23. neuropeptides
24. glutamate
25. endorphins
26. networks
27. neuroplasticity

Part 1: Connections

1. b
2. a
3. d
4. c

Part 2: Connections

1. j
2. c
3. f
4. a
5. g
6. b
7. d
8. k
9. e
10. h
11. i

Part 3: Connections

1. e
2. f
3. b
4. a
5. c
6. d

Check Your Memory

1. True
2. False
3. True
4. True
5. False
6. False
7. True
8. False
9. False
10. False
11. True
12. False
13. False
14. True
15. False
16. True
17. True
18. True
19. True
20. False

Critical Thinking Answer

Such a drug could have wide-ranging effects, depending on which neurotransmitter(s) it blocked. If the drug blocked excitatory synapses, it would depress brain activity. If it blocked inhibitory messages, it would act as a powerful stimulant.

Module 2.1 Neurons and the Nervous System
The Nervous System—Wired for Action

Recite and Review

1. central
2. nerves
3. neurilemma
4. peripheral
5. somatic
6. autonomic
7. sympathetic
8. parasympathetic
9. white matter
10. 31 (thirty-one)
11. cranial
12. reflex arc
13. sensory
14. connector
15. motor
16. effector
17. stem
18. neurogenesis
19. constraint-induced
20. schizophrenia

Part 1: Connections

1. b
2. e
3. f
4. c
5. a
6. d

Part 2: Connections

1. f
2. g
3. b
4. c
5. j
6. e
7. a
8. i
9. h
10. d

Check Your Memory

1. False
2. False
3. True
4. False
5. True
6. True
7. False
8. True
9. False
10. True
11. False
12. True
13. False
14. True
15. False
16. True

Critical Thinking Answer

These questions, known as the mind-body problem, have challenged thinkers for centuries. One recent view is that mental states are "emergent properties" of brain activity. That is, brain activity forms complex patterns that are, in a sense, more than the sum of their parts. Or, to use a rough analogy, if the brain were a musical instrument, then mental life would be like music played on that instrument.

Module 2.2 Brain Research
Mapping Brain Structure—Pieces of the Puzzle

Recite and Review

1. biopsychologist
2. dissection
3. CT (computed tomographic)
4. MRI (magnetic resonance imaging)

Connections

1. b
2. d
3. a
4. c

Check Your Memory

1. True
2. True
3. False
4. True
5. False

Module 2.2 Brain Research
Mapping Brain Function—Figuring Out What the Parts Do

Recite and Review

1. localizing
2. clinical case
3. ESB (electrical stimulation of the brain)
4. ablation
5. deep lesioning
6. microelectrode
7. EEG (electroencephalograph)
8. glucose (sugar)
9. PET (positron emission tomography)
10. fMRI (functional MRI)
11. front

Connections

1. g
2. a
3. h
4. f
5. d
6. e
7. c
8. b

Check Your Memory

1. True
2. True
3. True
4. True
5. True
6. True
7. True
8. False
9. False
10. False
11. False
12. False

Critical Thinking Answer

Other factors might explain the apparent loss of appetite. For example, the taste or smell of food might be affected, or the rat might simply have difficulty swallowing. It is also possible that hunger originates elsewhere in the brain and the ablated area merely relays messages that cause the rat to eat.

Module 2.3 Hemispheres and Lobes of the Cerebral Cortex
The Cerebral Cortex—My, What a Wrinkled Brain You Have!

Recite and Review

1. cerebral cortex
2. gray
3. lobes
4. corticalization
5. corpus callosum
6. spatial neglect
7. neurological soft
8. split-brain
9. dollar sign
10. left
11. right
12. right
13. left
14. right
15. fissures
16. frontal
17. mirror
18. aphasic
19. Broca's
20. prefrontal
21. parietal
22. temporal
23. Wernicke's
24. autism
25. occipital
26. facial agnosia
27. women
28. frontal

1021

Part 1: Connections

1. d	4. b	7. e
2. g	5. c	
3. f	6. a	

Part 2: Connections

1. h	5. e	9. c
2. i	6. g	10. d
3. j	7. b	
4. f	8. a	

Check Your Memory

1. True	11. False	21. True
2. False	12. False	22. True
3. True	13. False	23. True
4. False	14. True	24. False
5. False	15. True	25. True
6. True	16. True	26. False
7. True	17. False	27. True
8. True	18. True	28. True
9. True	19. True	29. True
10. True	20. False	30. False

Critical Thinking Answers

1. One solution would be to gather the surface of the cortex into folds, just as you might if you were trying to fit a large piece of cloth into a small box. This, in fact, is probably why the cortex is more convoluted (folded or wrinkled) in higher animals.

2. Although there is no "correct" answer to this question, your personality, knowledge, personal memories, and self-concept all derive from brain activity—which makes a strong case for your old brain in a new body being more nearly the "real you."

Module 2.4 Subcortex and Endocrine System
The Subcortex—At the Core of the (Brain) Matter

Recite and Review

1. subcortex	6. pons	11. limbic
2. forebrain	7. cerebellum	12. amygdala
3. medulla	8. reticular activating	13. temporal
4. cerebellum	9. thalamus	14. limbic
5. reticular formation	10. hypothalamus	15. EEG

Part 1: Connections

1. d	4. g	7. h
2. e	5. i	8. f
3. a	6. b	9. c

Part 2: Connections

1. e
2. i
3. b
4. d
5. g
6. h
7. a
8. j
9. f
10. c

Check Your Memory

1. True
2. False
3. False
4. True
5. True
6. False
7. True
8. False
9. False
10. True
11. False
12. True
13. True
14. False
15. True

Critical Thinking Answer

The subcortex must be related to basic functions common to all higher animals: motives, emotions, sleep, attention, and vegetative functions such as heartbeat, breathing, and temperature regulation. The subcortex also routes and processes incoming information from the senses and outgoing commands to the muscles.

Module 2.4 Subcortex and Endocrine System
The Endocrine System—My Hormones Made Me Do It

Recite and Review

1. endocrine
2. hormones
3. sex drive
4. hypopituitary
5. acromegaly
6. pituitary
7. pineal
8. pituitary
9. thyroid
10. melatonin
11. intellectual disability
12. medulla
13. cortex
14. virilism
15. (anabolic) steroids

Connections

1. b
2. g
3. d
4. i
5. c
6. a
7. e
8. j
9. h
10. f

Check Your Memory

1. True
2. False
3. False
4. True
5. False
6. False
7. False
8. True
9. False
10. True
11. False
12. True
13. True
14. True
15. True

Module 2.5 Psychology in Action: Handedness—Are You Dexterous or Sinister?

Are You Right- or Left-Handed?

Recite and Review

1. dexter
2. Waterloo Handedness
3. handedness
4. left
5. collectivist
6. inconsistent
7. left
8. lateralization
9. ambidextrous
10. left

Connections

1. e
2. g
3. b
4. c
5. f
6. d
7. a

Check Your Memory

1. False
2. True
3. True
4. True
5. False
6. True
7. False
8. True
9. True
10. True
11. False
12. False

Critical Thinking Answer

We can't tell if handedness or average age accounts for the difference in death rates. For example, if we start with a group of 20- to 30-year-old people, in which some die, the average age of death has to be between 20 and 30. If we start with a group of 30- to 40-year-old people, in which some die, the average age of death has to be between 30 and 40. Thus, the left-handed group might have an earlier average age at death simply because members of the group were younger to start with.

Final Survey and Review--Completion

Module 2.1 Neurons and the Nervous System
Neurons—Building a "Biocomputer"

1. soma
2. resting
3. after-potential
4. myelin
5. schizophrenia
6. acetylcholine
7. neuropeptides
8. neuroplasticity

Module 2.1 The Nervous System—Wired for Action

9. spinal cord
10. axons
11. peripheral
12. somatic
13. autonomic
14. sympathetic
15. reflex arc
16. neurogenesis

Module 2.2 Brain Research
Mapping Brain Structure—Pieces of the Puzzle

17. behavior
18. CT (computed tomographic)
19. MRI (magnetic resonance imaging)

Module 2.2 Mapping Brain Function—Figuring Out What the Parts Do

20. clinical case
21. lesioning
22. EEG (electroencephalograph)
23. less
24. fMRI (functional MRI)

Module 2.3 Hemispheres and Lobes of the Cerebral Cortex
The Cerebral Cortex—My, What a Wrinkled Brain You Have!

25. cerebral cortex
26. spatial neglect
27. corpus callosum
28. question mark
29. right
30. left
31. frontal
32. Broca's
33. parietal
34. occipital
35. temporal

Module 2.4 Subcortex and Endocrine System
The Subcortex—At the Core of the (Brain) Matter

36. cerebral cortex
37. medulla
38. cerebellum
39. reticular formation
40. limbic
41. amygdala
42. hypothalamus

Module 2.4 The Endocrine System—My Hormones Made Me Do It

43. androgens
44. pituitary
45. pineal
46. norepinephrine
47. (anabolic) steroids

Module 2.5 Psychology in Action: Handedness—Are You Dexterous or Sinister?
Are You Right- or Left-Handed?

48. sidedness
49. right
50. individualist
51. immune
52. left

Final Survey and Review—Matching

Module 2.1 Neurons and the Nervous System

1. j
2. c
3. g
4. l
5. a
6. d
7. k
8. e
9. b
10. m
11. f
12. i
13. h

Module 2.2 Brain Research

1. j
2. g
3. b
4. e
5. i
6. h
7. f
8. a
9. d
10. c

Module 2.3 Hemispheres and Lobes of the Cerebral Cortex

1. f
2. g
3. d
4. a
5. e
6. c
7. b

Module 2.4 Subcortex and Endocrine System

1. i	5. a	9. b
2. d	6. l	10. e
3. j	7. f	11. c
4. h	8. k	12. g

Module 2.5 Psychology in Action: Handedness—Are You Dexterous or Sinister?

1. e	3. b	5. f
2. d	4. c	6. a

Final Survey and Review—True or False

Module 2.1 Neurons and the Nervous System
Neurons—Building a "Biocomputer"

1. False	4. False	7. True
2. True	5. True	
3. True	6. False	

The Nervous System—Wired for Action (Module 2.1)

8. True	11. False	14. False
9. True	12. True	
10. False	13. False	

Module 2.2 Brain Research
Mapping Brain Structure—Pieces of the Puzzle

15. True	16. False	17. True

Module 2.2 Mapping Brain Function—Figuring Out What the Parts Do

18. False	20. True
19. False	21. True

Module 2.3 Hemispheres and Lobes of the Cerebral Cortex
The Cerebral Cortex—My, What a Wrinkled Brain You Have!

22. True	26. False	30. False
23. True	27. False	31. True
24. True	28. True	32. False
25. False	29. True	33. True

Module 2.4 Subcortex and Endocrine System
The Subcortex—At the Core of the (Brain) Matter

34. True	37. False	40. True
35. True	38. False	
36. False	39. False	

Module 2.4 The Endocrine System—My Hormones Made Me Do It (Module 2.4)

41. True	43. False	45. True
42. False	44. True	

Module 2.5 Psychology in Action: Handedness—Are You Dexterous or Sinister? Are You Right- or Left-Handed?

46. True
47. False
48. False

49. False
50. True
51. True

52. True

Mastery Test

1. b
2. a
3. a
4. b
5. a
6. a
7. d
8. c
9. d
10. b
11. c
12. a
13. b
14. d

15. b
16. c
17. a
18. c
19. d
20. c
21. c
22. b
23. a
24. a
25. c
26. d
27. a
28. d

29. d
30. c
31. a
32. a
33. d
34. c
35. c
36. b
37. a
38. b
39. d
40. a

Chapter 3: Human Development

Solutions

Module 3.1 The Interplay of Heredity and Environment
Nature and Nurture—It Takes Two to Tango

Recite and Review

1. nurture
2. developmental
3. heredity
4. DNA
5. Human Genome
6. 46 (forty-six)
7. 23 (twenty-three)
8. genes
9. dominant
10. recessive
11. brown
12. four (4)
13. polygenic
14. maturation
15. growth sequence
16. readiness
17. three (3)
18. nurture
19. dendrites
20. synapses
21. plastic
22. blooming and pruning
23. intrauterine
24. congenital
25. genetic
26. teratogen
27. fetal alcohol syndrome (FAS)
28. oxygen
29. sensitive
30. deprivation
31. enrichment
32. cortex
33. reaction range
34. temperament
35. difficult
36. easy
37. slow-to-warm-up
38. reciprocal
39. developmental level
40. your own behavior

Connections

1. l
2. h
3. e
4. g
5. a
6. j
7. b
8. i
9. d
10. k
11. c
12. f

Check Your Memory

1. True
2. True
3. True
4. False
5. False
6. True
7. False
8. False
9. True
10. True
11. False
12. True
13. True
14. False
15. True
16. True
17. True
18. True
19. True
20. False
21. True
22. True
23. False
24. True
25. True
26. False
27. True
28. False

Critical Thinking Answer

Environmental conditions sometimes turn specific genes on or off, thus directly affecting the expression of genetic tendencies (Gottlieb, 1998).

Module 3.2 The Neonate
The Newborn—More Than Meets the Eye

Recite and Review

1. neonate
2. adaptive
3. grasping
4. rooting
5. Moro
6. order
7. cephalocaudal
8. proximodistal
9. nine (9)
10. looking chamber
11. six (6)
12. two (2)
13. (general) excitement
14. interest
15. anger
16. pleasant, unpleasant; unpleasant, pleasant
17. social

Connections

1. e
2. g
3. k
4. j
5. d
6. a
7. h
8. i
9. c
10. b
11. f

Check Your Memory

1. False
2. False
3. True
4. False
5. False
6. False
7. False
8. False
9. True
10. False
11. False
12. False
13. True
14. True
15. True

Critical Thinking Answer

In one study of the preferences of newborns, the hair color and complexion of strangers were matched to those of the mothers. Also, only the mother's or stranger's face was visible during testing. And finally, a scent was used to mask olfactory (smell) cues so that an infant's preference could not be based on the mother's familiar odor (Bushnell, Sai, & Mullin, 1989).

Module 3.3 Social Development in Childhood
Social Development—Baby, I'm Stuck on You

Recite and Review

1. social
2. attachment
3. surrogate (mothers)
4. contact comfort
5. separation anxiety
6. separation anxiety
7. (Mary) Ainsworth
8. secure
9. insecure-avoidant
10. insecure-ambivalent
11. avoidant
12. ambivalent
13. sensitive
14. high-quality
15. affectional

Connections

1. b
2. a
3. f
4. d
5. g
6. e
7. h
8. c

Check Your Memory

1. False	7. True	13. True
2. False	8. False	14. False
3. True	9. False	15. True
4. True	10. True	16. False
5. True	11. True	17. True
6. False	12. True	

Critical Thinking Answer

It certainly can for parents. When a pregnant woman begins to feel fetal movements, she becomes aware that a baby is coming to life inside of her. Likewise, prospective parents who hear a fetal heartbeat at the doctor's office or see an ultrasound image of the fetus begin to become emotionally attached to the unborn child (Santrock, 2009).

Module 3.3 Social Development in Childhood
Parental Influences—Life with Mom and Dad

Recite and Review

1. (Diana) Baumrind	6. overly permissive	11. Hispanic
2. authoritarian	7. authoritative	12. Asian
3. overly permissive	8. father	13. Arab
4. authoritative	9. mother	
5. authoritarian	10. African-American	

Connections

1. j	5. a	9. h
2. g	6. f	10. c
3. e	7. b	
4. i	8. d	

Check Your Memory

1. True	5. False	9. False
2. False	6. True	10. True
3. True	7. True	11. True
4. False	8. True	12. True

Critical Thinking Answer

Both authoritarian and permissive styles are more likely to lead to eating disorders in children. Parents who are too controlling about what their children eat OR too willing to withdraw from conflicts over eating can create problems for their children (Haycraft & Blissett, 2010).

Module 3.4 Language Development in Childhood
Language Development—Who Talks Baby Talk?

Recite and Review

1. crying
2. cooing
3. babbling
4. single-word
5. telegraphic
6. terrible twos
7. predisposition
8. Agent-Action
9. Identification
10. Nonexistence
11. psycholinguists
12. learning
13. signals
14. turn-taking
15. parentese or motherese
16. praise
17. warning
18. seven (7)

Connections

1. a
2. h
3. d
4. e
5. c
6. g
7. b
8. f
9. j
10. i

Check Your Memory

1. True
2. False
3. True
4. True
5. False
6. True
7. True
8. False
9. False
10. False
11. True
12. True
13. True
14. True
15. True
16. False
17. True
18. True
19. False
20. True

Critical Thinking Answer

Children in professional homes receive many educational benefits that are less common in welfare homes. Yet, even when such differences are taken into account, brighter children tend to come from richer language environments (Hart & Risley, 1999).

Module 3.5 Cognitive Development in Childhood
Cognitive Development—Think Like a Child

Recite and Review

1. (Jean) Piaget
2. assimilation
3. accommodation
4. object permanence
5. sensorimotor
6. preoperational
7. intuitive
8. preoperational
9. reason
10. egocentric
11. reversibility
12. concrete operational
13. conservation
14. concrete operational
15. formal operational
16. one-step-ahead
17. accommodation
18. forced teaching
19. sensorimtor
20. preoperational
21. concrete operational
22. learning
23. temporal
24. impossible
25. theory of mind
26. 18 (eighteen)
27. belief
28. (Lev) Vygotsky
29. proximal development
30. scaffolding

Connections

1. n
2. h
3. m
4. k
5. b
6. g
7. j
8. a
9. d
10. l
11. c
12. f
13. i
14. e

Check Your Memory

1. True
2. True
3. False
4. True
5. False
6. True
7. False
8. True
9. True
10. True
11. True
12. False
13. False
14. True
15. True
16. True
17. False
18. True
19. True
20. False
21. True
22. True
23. True
24. False
25. False

Critical Thinking Answer

Seventy-five percent of 4- to 6-year-olds say that a Styrofoam cup has no weight after lifting it! Most children judge weight intuitively (by the way an object feels) until they begin to move into the concrete operational stage (Smith, Carey, & Wiser, 1985).

Module 3.6 Adolescence, Young Adulthood, and Moral Development
Adolescence and Young Adulthood—The Best of Times, the Worst of Times

Recite and Review

1. adolescence
2. puberty
3. financially
4. early
5. early
6. identity
7. formal operations
8. ethnic
9. stereotypes
10. pride
11. Western
12. emerging
13. twixters
14. adolescence

Connections

1. h
2. g
3. a
4. i
5. b
6. j
7. e
8. d
9. c
10. f

Check Your Memory

1. False
2. True
3. False
4. True
5. False
6. False
7. True
8. True
9. False
10. False
11. True
12. False
13. True
14. True
15. True

Critical Thinking Answer

Environment, rather than heredity, is the better answer. Even better, the meanings of terms like "adolescence" or "adult" vary considerably from culture to culture indicating that it is really a matter of definition (Côté, 2006a).

Module 3.6 Adolescence, Young Adulthood, and Moral Development
Moral Development—Growing a Conscience

Recite and Review

1. moral
2. moral dilemmas
3. preconventional
4. conventional
5. postconventional
6. conventional
7. postconventional
8. preconventional
9. preconventional
10. conventional
11. postconventional
12. justice
13. caring
14. conventional
15. situation

Connections

1. g
2. f
3. b
4. e
5. a
6. c
7. d

Check Your Memory

1. True
2. True
3. False
4. False
5. False
6. True
7. False
8. False
9. True
10. False
11. False
12. False
13. True
14. True
15. True

Module 3.7 Challenges Across the Lifespan
The Story of a Lifetime—Rocky Road or Garden Path?

Recite and Review

1. milestones
2. task
3. psychosocial
4. trust
5. mistrust
6. autonomy
7. initiative
8. guilt
9. inferiority
10. role confusion
11. isolation
12. generativity
13. stagnation
14. integrity
15. despair

Connections

1. f
2. k
3. c
4. b
5. g
6. d
7. i
8. j
9. a
10. e
11. h

Check Your Memory

1. False	6. True	11. False
2. False	7. False	12. True
3. True	8. False	13. False
4. True	9. True	14. True
5. False	10. False	15. True

Critical Thinking Answer

Different *cohorts* (groups of people born in the same year) live in different historical times. People born in various decades may have very different life experiences. This makes it difficult to identify universal patterns (Stewart & Ostrove, 1998).

Module 3.7 Challenges Across the Lifespan
Middle and Late Adulthood: Will You Still Need Me When I'm 64?

Recite and Review

1. (Carol) Ryff	5. wake-up calls	9. empathy
2. 25 (twenty-five)	6. physical aging	10. ageism
3. correction	7. five (5)	11. fluid
4. identities	8. (Warner) Schaie	12. crystallized

Connections

1. f	4. d	7. a
2. e	5. c	
3. g	6. b	

Check Your Memory

1. False	6. True	11. True
2. True	7. False	12. True
3. False	8. True	13. True
4. False	9. False	14. True
5. True	10. True	15. False

Module 3.7 Challenges Across the Lifespan
Death and Dying—The Final Challenge

Recite and Review

1. fear	5. thanatologist	10. acceptance
2. circumstances	6. denial	11. hospice
3. denial	7. anger	
4. (Elisabeth) Kübler-Ross	8. bargaining	
	9. depression	

Connections

1. d	4. c	7. a
2. f	5. g	
3. e	6. b	

Check Your Memory

1. True	5. True	9. False
2. True	6. False	10. True
3. False	7. True	11. True
4. False	8. True	

Module 3.8 Psychology in Action: Effective Parenting—Raising Healthy Children

Recite and Review

1. authoritative	8. withdrawal of love	16. (Haim) Ginott
2. positive (parent-child)	9. management	17. (Thomas) Gordon
3. discipline	10. withdrawal of love	18. you
4. power assertion	11. overly permissive	19. I
5. withdrawal of love	12. inconsistent	20. natural
6. management	13. immediately	21. logical
7. power assertion	14. two (2)	
	15. five (5)	

Connections

1. h	4. c	7. d
2. f	5. b	8. g
3. a	6. e	

Check Your Memory

1. False	9. True	17. True
2. True	10. False	18. True
3. True	11. True	19. True
4. False	12. True	20. False
5. False	13. True	21. True
6. True	14. False	22. False
7. False	15. False	23. False
8. True	16. True	

Critical Thinking Answer

Such laws are based on the view that it should be illegal to physically assault any person, regardless of their age. Although parents may believe they have a "right" to spank their children, it can be argued that children need special protection because they are small, powerless, and dependent (Durrant & Janson, 2005).

Final Survey and Review—Completion

Module 3.1 The Interplay of Heredity and Environment
Nature and Nurture—It Takes Two to Tango

1. developmental	3. teratogens	5. slow-to-warm-up
2. recessive	4. enrichment	

Module 3.2 The Neonate
The Newborn—More Than Meets the Eye
6. Moro
7. cephalocaudal
8. (Robert) Fatnz
9. sadness

Module 3.3 Social Development in Childhood
Social Development—Baby, I'm Stuck on You
10. (Harry) Harlow
11. separation anxiety
12. secure
13. behavior

Module 3.3 Parental Influences—Life with Mom and Dad
14. authoritative
15. father
16. African

Module 3.4 Language Development in Childhood
Language Development—Who Talks Baby Talk?
17. babbling
18. terrible twos
19. (Noam) Chomsky
20. signals

Module 3.5 Cognitive Development in Childhood
Cognitive Development—Think Like a Child
21. accommodation
22. sensorimotor
23. preoperational
24. formal
25. impossible
26. mind
27. sociocultural
28. proximal development

Module 3.6 Adolescence, Young Adulthood, and Moral Development
Adolescence and Young Adulthood—The Best of Times, the Worst of Times
29. puberty
30. early-maturing
31. identity
32. emerging

Module 3.6 Moral Development—Growing a Conscience
33. (Lawrence) Kohlberg
34. postconventional
35. preconventional
36. preconventional
37. justice

Module 3.7 Challenges Across the Lifespan
The Story of a Lifetime—Rocky Road or Garden Path?
38. tasks
39. trust
40. autonomy
41. identity versus (vs) role confusion
42. intimacy

Module 3.7 Middle and Late Adulthood: Will You Still Need Me When I'm 64?
43. mastery
44. gerontologist
45. personality
46. ageism
47. fluid

Module 3.7 Death and Dying—The Final Challenge
48. circumstances
49. thanatologist
50. acceptance
51. hospice

Module 3.8 Psychology in Action: Effective Parenting—Raising Healthy Children

52. withdrawal of love
53. management techniques
54. inconsistent
55. feelings
56. I
57. logical

Final Survey and Review—Matching
Module 3.1 The Interplay of Heredity and Environment

1. h
2. e
3. g
4. j
5. i
6. f
7. b
8. d
9. a
10. c

Module 3.2 The Neonate

1. f
2. e
3. a
4. g
5. d
6. c
7. b

Module 3.3 Social Development in Childhood

1. j
2. e
3. b
4. k
5. h
6. f
7. g
8. d
9. a
10. i
11. c

Module 3.4 Language Development in Childhood

1. e
2. d
3. c
4. g
5. a
6. f
7. b

Module 3.5 Cognitive Development in Childhood

1. k
2. i
3. j
4. h
5. f
6. b
7. d
8. c
9. e
10. g
11. a

Module 3.6 Adolescence, Young Adulthood, and Moral Development

1. h
2. g
3. a
4. b
5. f
6. c
7. d
8. e

Module 3.7 Challenges Across the Lifespan

1. j
2. n
3. a
4. l
5. f
6. i
7. e
8. g
9. c
10. m
11. b
12. k
13. d
14. h

1038

Module 3.8 Psychology in Action: Effective Parenting—Raising Healthy Children

1. g	4. c	7. a
2. d	5. f	
3. b	6. e	

Final Survey and Review—True or False

Module 3.1 The Interplay of Heredity and Environment
Nature and Nurture—It Takes Two to Tango (Module 3.1)

1. False	3. True	5. True
2. False	4. False	

Module 3.2 The Neonate
The Newborn—More Than Meets the Eye

6. True	8. False
7. True	9. True

Module 3.3 Social Development in Childhood
Social Development—Baby, I'm Stuck on You

10. False	12. True
11. False	13. True

Module 3.3 Parental Influences—Life with Mom and Dad

14. True	15. True	16. False

Module 3.4 Language Development in Childhood
Language Development—Who Talks Baby Talk?

17. False	19. False
18. True	20. False

Module 3.5 Cognitive Development in Childhood
Cognitive Development—Think Like a Child

21. False	24. False	27. True
22. False	25. True	28. True
23. False	26. False	

Module 3.6 Adolescence, Young Adulthood, and Moral Development
Adolescence and Young Adulthood—The Best of Times, the Worst of Times

29. False	31. True
30. False	32. False

Module 3.6 Moral Development—Growing a Conscience

33. True	35. False	37. False
34. True	36. True	

Module 3.7 Challenges Across the Lifespan
The Story of a Lifetime—Rocky Road or Garden Path?
38.	False	40.	True	42.	True
39.	False	41.	True		

Module 3.7 Middle and Late Adulthood: Will You Still Need Me When I'm 64?
43.	True	45.	True	47.	False
44.	False	46.	False		

Module 3.7 Death and Dying—The Final Challenge
48.	False	50.	True
49.	True	51.	True

Module 3.8 Psychology in Action: Effective Parenting—Raising Healthy Children
52.	True	54.	True	56.	True
53.	True	55.	False	57.	False

Mastery Test
1.	d	15.	b	29.	b
2.	d	16.	c	30.	d
3.	c	17.	b	31.	c
4.	c	18.	d	32.	b
5.	d	19.	a	33.	a
6.	b	20.	c	34.	c
7.	c	21.	c	35.	d
8.	d	22.	b	36.	b
9.	b	23.	c	37.	d
10.	a	24.	d	38.	c
11.	c	25.	b	39.	c
12.	d	26.	a	40.	a
13.	b	27.	c		
14.	d	28.	d		

Chapter 4: Sensation and Perception

Solutions

Module 4.1 Sensory Processes
Sensory Systems—The First Step

Recite and Review

1. transducers
2. sensation
3. perception
4. data reduction
5. transduce
6. bioelectric
7. psychopsychics
8. visible spectrum
9. echolocation
10. absolute
11. unchanging
12. smell
13. analysis
14. perceptual
15. feature
16. pop-out
17. moving
18. horizontal
19. decrease
20. coding
21. difference
22. phosphenes
23. localization
24. camera

Connections

1. j
2. h
3. i
4. c
5. f
6. a
7. e
8. b
9. k
10. g
11. d

Check Your Memory

1. True
2. False
3. False
4. True
5. False
6. False
7. False
8. True
9. False
10. False
11. True
12. True
13. False
14. True
15. False
16. True

Critical Thinking Answer

The explanation is based on sensory localization: Even if a lightning flash caused rerouted messages from the eyes to activate auditory areas of the brain, we would experience a sound sensation. Likewise, if the ears transduced a thunderclap and sent impulses to the visual area, a sensation of light would occur. Amazingly, some people, called *synesthetes*, naturally experience sensory inputs in terms of other senses. For example, one synesthete experiences pain as the color orange, whereas for another the taste of spiced chicken is pointy (Dixon, Smilek, & Merikle, 2004).

Module 4.2 Vision
Vision—Catching Some Rays

Recite and Review

1. visible spectrum
2. purple or violet
3. hue
4. white
5. saturated
6. brightness
7. lens
8. photoreceptors
9. retina
10. cornea
11. accommodation
12. hyperopia
13. myopia
14. astigmatism
15. presbyopia
16. bifocals
17. cones
18. rods
19. blind spot
20. fovea
21. 20/20
22. Snellen
23. Landolt rings
24. peripheral
25. tunnel
26. night
27. trichromatic
28. opponent-process
29. afterimages
30. opponent-process
31. cones
32. weakness
33. eight (8)
34. Ishihara
35. yellow
36. blue
37. dark adaptation
38. bleach
39. recombine
40. red

Part 1: Connections

1. c
2. h
3. d
4. b
5. g
6. a
7. e
8. f

Part 2: Connections

1. a
2. e
3. j
4. c
5. i
6. f
7. d
8. b
9. h
10. g

Part 3: Connections

1. b
2. j
3. d
4. f
5. a
6. h
7. e
8. i
9. k
10. c
11. g

Check Your Memory

1. False
2. True
3. True
4. True
5. False
6. False
7. False
8. False
9. False
10. True
11. False
12. False
13. True
14. True
15. True
16. False
17. True
18. True
19. True
20. True
21. False
22. True
23. False
24. False
25. True
26. False
27. False
28. False
29. False
30. False
31. True
32. True
33. True
34. False

1042

Critical Thinking Answer

False. While the cornea and lens prepare incoming light rays by bending them and focusing them on the retina, they do not change light to another form of energy. No change in the *type* of energy takes place until the retina converts light to nerve impulses.

Module 4.3 Hearing, the Chemical Senses, and the Somesthetic Senses
Hearing—Good Vibrations

Recite and Review

1. compression
2. rarefaction
3. sound waves
4. vacuum
5. frequency
6. pitch
7. amplitude
8. loudness
9. pinna
10. tympanic membrane
11. ossicles
12. incus
13. oval window
14. organ of Corti
15. stereocilia
16. frequency
17. place
18. frequency
19. base
20. outer tip
21. place
22. conductive
23. sensorineural
24. conductive
25. high
26. noise-induced
27. 85 (eighty-five)
28. 10 (ten)
29. 150 (one hundred-fifty)
30. cochlear implant

Part 1: Connections

1. e
2. g
3. h
4. a
5. d
6. f
7. c
8. i
9. b
10. j

Part 2: Connections

1. f
2. a
3. b
4. d
5. c
6. e

Part 3: Connections

1. f
2. h
3. c
4. j
5. b
6. e
7. g
8. i
9. a
10. d

Check Your Memory

1. True
2. False
3. False
4. False
5. False
6. False
7. False
8. False
9. True
10. True
11. False
12. False
13. False
14. True
15. False
16. False
17. True
18. True
19. False
20. True
21. True
22. True
23. True
24. True

Critical Thinking Answer

The answer lies in another question: How else might vibrations from the voice reach the cochlea? Other people hear your voice only as it is carried through the air. You hear not only that sound, but also vibrations conducted by the bones of your skull.

Module 4.3 Hearing, the Chemical Senses, and the Somesthetic Senses
Smell and Taste—The Nose Knows When the Tongue Can't Tell

Recite and Review

1. olfaction
2. gustation
3. chemical
4. airborne
5. dysosmia
6. etherish
7. lock and key
8. number
9. anosmia
10. olfactory nerves
11. bitter
12. sweet
13. sour
14. umami
15. glutamate
16. pain
17. taste buds
18. bitter
19. sour(ness)

Connections

1. b
2. c
3. i
4. d
5. g
6. a
7. f
8. h
9. e

Check Your Memory

1. False
2. True
3. True
4. False
5. True
6. True
7. True
8. False
9. True
10. False
11. True
12. True
13. True
14. True
15. False
16. False

Critical Thinking Answer

Both smell and hearing can detect stimuli (including signals of approaching danger) around corners, behind objects, and behind the head.

Module 4.3 Hearing, the Chemical Senses, and the Somesthetic Senses
The Somesthetic Senses—Flying by the Seat of Your Pants

Recite and Review

1. somesthetic
2. kinesthetic
3. pressure
4. free nerve endings
5. density (concentration)
6. warning
7. pain insensitivity
8. reminding
9. gate control
10. spinal
11. central biasing
12. acupuncture
13. phantom limb
14. neuromatrix
15. counterirritation
16. increase
17. decrease (lower)
18. control
19. counterirritation
20. distraction
21. vestibular
22. otolith
23. semicircular canals
24. crista
25. sensory conflict
26. poison
27. motion sickness

1044

Connections

1. d
2. i
3. c
4. g
5. m
6. l
7. a
8. b
9. e
10. k
11. n
12. f
13. j
14. h

Check Your Memory

1. True
2. True
3. True
4. False
5. False
6. True
7. False
8. True
9. True
10. False
11. False
12. False
13. False
14. True
15. True
16. False
17. True
18. True
19. True
20. True
21. False
22. True
23. False
24. True
25. False
26. False
27. True
28. True
29. True
30. False

Critical Thinking Answer

1. Experiments that cause pain must be handled with care and sensitivity. Participation must be voluntary; the source of pain must be noninjurious; and subjects must be allowed to quit at any time.

2. Drivers experience less sensory conflict because they control the car's motion. This allows them to anticipate the car's movements and to coordinate their head and eye movements with those of the car.

Module 4.4 Perceptual Processes
Perception—The Second Step

Recite and Review

1. perceive
2. perceptual construction
3. illusion
4. Ames
5. hallucination
6. illusion
7. reality testing
8. hallucinations
9. reality testing
10. Charles Bonnet
11. sane hallucinations
12. bottom-up
13. top-down
14. bottom-up
15. top-down
16. figure-ground
17. reversible
18. Gestalt
19. nearness
20. similarity
21. continuity or continuation
22. closure
23. illusory
24. contiguity
25. common region
26. top-down
27. figure-ground
28. hypothesis
29. ambiguous
30. ambiguous
31. impossible
32. familiar
33. size constancy
34. native
35. empirical
36. constancy
37. shape constancy
38. brightness constancy

Part 1: Connections

1. i
2. f
3. e
4. a
5. h
6. j
7. d
8. b
9. g
10. c

Part 2: Connections

1. c
2. e
3. d
4. a
5. f
6. b

Part 3: Connections

1. m
2. j
3. i
4. a
5. h
6. b
7. f
8. d
9. l
10. c
11. g
12. e
13. k

Check Your Memory

1. True
2. True
3. False
4. False
5. True
6. True
7. True
8. True
9. False
10. False
11. True
12. False
13. False
14. False
15. True
16. False
17. False
18. True
19. True
20. True
21. False
22. True
23. True
24. True
25. False
26. True
27. True
28. True
29. True
30. True

Critical Thinking Answer

Perceptual constancies (size, shape, and brightness).

Module 4.4 Perceptual Processes
Selective Attention—Tuning In and Tuning Out

Recite and Review

1. selective
2. cocktail party
3. selective attention
4. inattentional blindness
5. selective attention
6. inattentional blindness
7. selective attention
8. attention
9. repetition
10. contrast

Connections

1. g
2. f
3. e
4. a
5. b
6. c
7. d

Check Your Memory

1. True
2. True
3. False
4. False
5. True
6. True
7. False
8. True
9. False
10. True

Module 4.5 Depth Perception
Depth Perception—What If the World Were Flat?

Recite and Review

1. depth
2. visual cliff
3. deep
4. two (2)
5. six (6)
6. coordination
7. binocular
8. monocular
9. retinal disparity
10. stereoscopic
11. disparity
12. convergence
13. 10 (ten)
14. accommodation
15. binocular
16. monocular
17. pictorial
18. linear
19. relative size
20. size
21. height in the picture plane
22. shadow
23. interposition
24. texture
25. aerial
26. motion parallax
27. motion parallax or relative motion
28. moon illusion
29. apparent-distance
30. smaller

Part 1: Connections

1. e
2. g
3. f
4. c
5. a
6. b
7. h
8. d

Part 2: Connections

1. d
2. b
3. i
4. l
5. g
6. a
7. m
8. h
9. k
10. e
11. c
12. f
13. j

Check Your Memory

1. True
2. True
3. False
4. True
5. False
6. False
7. True
8. True
9. False
10. False
11. False
12. False
13. False
14. True
15. True
16. False
17. False
18. True
19. True
20. False
21. False
22. False

Critical Thinking Answer

1. If you close your eyes, you can usually tell the direction and perhaps the location of a sound source, such as a hand-clap. Locating sounds in space is heavily dependent on having two ears, just as stereoscopic vision depends on having two eyes.

2. The most popular answers range from a quarter to a softball. Actually, a pea held in the outstretched hand will cover a full moon (Kunkel, 1993). If you listed an object larger than a pea, be aware that perceptions, no matter how accurate they seem, may distort reality.

Module 4.6 Perception and Objectivity
Perceptual Learning—Believing is Seeing

Recite and Review

1. perceptual expectancy (or set)
2. expectancy (set)
3. motives
4. anxiety
5. negative
6. positive
7. other-race
8. positive (good)
9. sets
10. individualistic
11. collectivist
12. internal
13. social
14. figure
15. (back)ground
16. narrow
17. broad(er)
18. top-down
19. learning
20. perceptual learning
21. perceptual habits
22. constancy
23. Müller-Lyer
24. size-distance invariance
25. Zulus

Connections

1. i
2. e
3. d
4. b
5. g
6. c
7. a
8. f
9. h

Check Your Memory

1. True
2. True
3. False
4. True
5. True
6. False
7. True
8. False
9. True
10. False
11. True
12. False
13. False
14. False
15. True
16. True
17. False
18. False
19. True
20. False
21. True
22. False
23. True

Critical Thinking Answer

Advertisers place health warnings in the corners of ads, where they attract the least possible attention. Also, the labels are often placed on "busy" backgrounds so that they are partially camouflaged. Finally, the main images in ads are designed to strongly attract attention. This further distracts readers from seeing the warnings. Over time, perceptual learning renders these warnings practically invisible.

Module 4.7 Extrasensory Perception
Extrasensory Perception—Do You Believe in Ghosts?

Recite and Review

1. extrasensory perception (ESP)
2. parapsychology
3. psi
4. extrasensory perception (ESP)
5. telepathy
6. mediumship
7. clairvoyance
8. precognition
9. psychokinesis
10. (J.B.) Rhine
11. Zener
12. five (5)
13. coincidence
14. stage
15. cold
16. Barnum
17. fraud
18. double
19. reinterpreted
20. replicated (reproduced or repeated)
21. fewer
22. run of luck
23. decline effect
24. fragile
25. psi missing
26. (James) Randi
27. skeptic
28. not

Connections

1. i
2. k
3. f
4. c
5. g
6. a
7. m
8. b
9. l
10. h
11. d
12. e
13. j

Check Your Memory

1. True
2. True
3. False
4. False
5. True
6. True
7. False
8. True
9. True
10. False
11. True
12. True
13. True
14. True
15. False
16. False
17. True
18. True
19. True
20. True
21. False
22. False

Critical Thinking Answer

1. Most people assume that this would be a relatively rare event. Actually there is a 71 percent chance that two people will share a birthday in a group of 30. Most people probably underestimate the natural rate of occurrence of many seemingly mysterious coincidences (Alcock, Burns, & Freeman, 2003).

2. When psychologists handled watches awaiting repair at a store, 57 percent began running again, with no help from a "psychic." Believing the psychic's claim also overlooks the impact of big numbers: If the show reached a large audience, at least a few "broken" watches would start working merely by chance.

Module 4.8 Psychology in Action: Becoming a Better Eyewitness to Life

Recite and Review

1. 25 (twenty-five)
2. accuracy
3. worded
4. decrease
5. the same
6. weapon focus
7. transference
8. monochromatic
9. DNA
10. reality
11. (Abraham) Maslow
12. present
13. habituation
14. dishabituation
15. habituate
16. top-down
17. expectancies or sets
18. reality testing
19. perspective
20. pay attention

Connections

1. c
2. b
3. f
4. d
5. g
6. e
7. a

Check Your Memory

1. True
2. False
3. False
4. True
5. True
6. False
7. False
8. True
9. True
10. True
11. False
12. True
13. False
14. True
15. False
16. False
17. False
18. False
19. True
20. True

Critical Thinking Answer

The girl's misperception, communicated so forcefully to one of your textbook authors, created a powerful expectancy that influenced what he perceived. Also, the event happened quickly (the exposure time was brief) and the stressful or emotional nature of the incident encouraged his own misperception.

Final Survey and Review--Completion

Module 4.1 Sensory Processes
Sensory Systems—The First Step

1. perception
2. adaptation
3. vertical
4. phosphenes

Module 4.2 Vision
Vision—Catching Some Rays

5. astigmatism
6. Snellen
7. blind spot
8. opponent-process
9. rods

Module 4.3 Hearing, the Chemical Senses, and the Somesthetic Senses
Hearing—Good Vibrations

10. pinna
11. eardrum
12. cochlea
13. sensorineural

1050

Module 4.3 Smell and Taste—The Nose Knows When the Tongue Can't Tell

14. shapes
15. anosmia
16. glutamate
17. lock and key

Module 4.3 The Somesthetic Senses—Flying by the Seat of Your Pants

18. kinesthetic
19. reminding
20. counterirritation
21. semicircular canals

Module 4.4 Perceptual Processes
Perception—The Second Step

22. Ames
23. hallucinations
24. bottom-up
25. closure
26. ambiguous
27. constancy

Module 4.4 Selective Attention—Tuning In and Tuning Out

28. selective attention
29. inattentional blindness
30. increase (or gain)

Module 4.5 Depth Perception
Depth Perception—What If the World Were Flat?

31. visual cliff
32. binocular
33. retinal disparity
34. linear perspective
35. aerial perspective
36. larger

Module 4.6 Perception and Objectivity
Perceptual Learning—Believing is Seeing

37. broad(er)
38. individualistic
39. learning
40. Müller-Lyer

Module 4.7 Extrasensory Perception
Extrasensory Perception—Do You Believe in Ghosts?

41. mediumship
42. Zener
43. cold
44. decline

Module 4.8 Psychology in Action: Becoming a Better Eyewitness to Life

45. the same
46. transference
47. habituation
48. reality

Final Survey and Review—Matching

Module 4.1 Sensory Processes

1. c
2. g
3. a
4. e
5. d
6. f
7. b

Module 4.2 Vision

1. f	5. b	9. j
2. g	6. c	10. k
3. i	7. h	11. a
4. d	8. e	

Module 4.3 Hearing, the Chemical Senses, and the Somesthetic Senses

1. d	7. h	13. f
2. m	8. n	14. g
3. k	9. b	15. i
4. c	10. o	16. j
5. a	11. p	17. q
6. e	12. l	

Module 4.4 Perceptual Processes

1. e	6. k	11. g
2. d	7. i	12. a
3. l	8. c	13. h
4. m	9. f	
5. j	10. b	

Module 4.5 Depth Perception

1. d	5. f	9. c
2. b	6. g	10. a
3. h	7. e	
4. j	8. i	

Module 4.6 Perception and Objectivity

1. f	3. a	5. d
2. c	4. b	6. e

Module 4.7 Extrasensory Perception

1. g	4. f	7. c
2. d	5. a	
3. e	6. b	

Module 4.8 Psychology in Action: Becoming a Better Eyewitness to Life

1. c	3. e	5. a
2. b	4. d	

Final Survey and Review—True or False

Module 4.1 Sensory Processes
Sensory Systems—The First Step

1. True	3. False
2. True	4. False

1052

Module 4.2 Vision
Vision—Catching Some Rays

5. False	7. False	9. False
6. True	8. True	

Module 4.3 Hearing, the Chemical Senses, and the Somesthetic Senses
Hearing—Good Vibrations

10. True	12. True
11. False	13. True

Module 4.3 Smell and Taste—The Nose Knows When the Tongue Can't Tell

14. False	16. True
15. True	17. False

Module 4.3 The Somesthetic Senses—Flying by the Seat of Your Pants

18. False	20. False
19. True	21. True

Module 4.4 Perceptual Processes
Perception—The Second Step

22. False	24. False	26. False
23. True	25. False	27. False

Module 4.4 Selective Attention—Tuning In and Tuning Out

28. True	29. True	30. False

Module 4.5 Depth Perception
Depth Perception—What If the World Were Flat?

31. False	33. False	35. True
32. True	34. True	36. False

Module 4.6 Perception and Objectivity
Perceptual Learning—Believing is Seeing

37. True	39. False
38. True	40. True

Module 4.7 Extrasensory Perception
Extrasensory Perception—Do You Believe in Ghosts?

41. False	43. True
42. False	44. True

Module 4.8 Psychology in Action: Becoming a Better Eyewitness to Life

45. True	47. False
46. True	48. False

Mastery Test

1. d	15. a	29. b
2. d	16. c	30. c
3. c	17. d	31. b
4. d	18. c	32. a
5. c	19. b	33. b
6. b	20. a	34. d
7. d	21. a	35. a
8. a	22. b	36. c
9. b	23. a	37. b
10. d	24. a	38. c
11. a	25. b	39. c
12. d	26. a	40. a
13. c	27. b	
14. c	28. d	

Chapter 5: States of Consciousness

Solutions

Module 5.1 States of Consciousness and Sleep
States of Consciousness—The Many Faces of Awareness

Recite and Review
1. consciousness
2. first-person
3. introspection
4. third-person
5. waking consciousness
6. altered state
7. sweat lodge
8. altered states
9. altered state
10. cultural

Connections
1. d
2. c
3. e
4. b
5. a

Check Your Memory
1. True
2. False
3. True
4. False
5. True
6. True
7. True
8. True
9. False
10. True
11. False

Sleep—Catching a Few ZZZ's

Recite and Review
1. 25 (twenty-five)
2. biological rhythm
3. death
4. (Randy) Gardner
5. deprivation
6. increased
7. hypersomnia
8. complex
9. microsleep
10. sleep-deprivation psychosis
11. sleep need
12. 24 (twenty-four)
13. external time markers
14. short sleepers
15. long sleepers
16. six (6)
17. 20 (twenty)
18. two (2)

Connections
1. c
2. b
3. d
4. f
5. e
6. a

Check Your Memory
1. False
2. False
3. True
4. True
5. True
6. False
7. True
8. False
9. False
10. True
11. False
12. True
13. True
14. True
15. False
16. False
17. True
18. False
19. True
20. True
21. False

1055

Critical Thinking Answer

Sleep experts theorize that the 25-hour average leaves a little "slack" in the cycle. External time markers can then retard the body cycle slightly to synchronize it with light-dark cycles. If the body cycle were shorter than 24 hours, we all might have to "stretch" every day to adjust.

Stages of Sleep—The Nightly Roller-Coaster

Recite and Review

1. balance
2. pattern
3. EEG (electroencephalo graph)
4. beta
5. alpha
6. sleep stages
7. light
8. hypnic jerk
9. sleep spindles
10. delta
11. deep
12. REM
13. NREM (non-REM)
14. NREM (non-REM)
15. REM
16. REM
17. NREM (non-REM)
18. REM
19. REM
20. REM behavior
21. hypnopompic hallucinations

Connections

1. e
2. f
3. i
4. j
5. b
6. a
7. k
8. g
9. d
10. l
11. c
12. h

Check Your Memory

1. True
2. False
3. True
4. False
5. False
6. False
7. False
8. False
9. True
10. False
11. False
12. True
13. False
14. True
15. True
16. False

Critical Thinking Answer

Lowering body activity and metabolism during sleep may help conserve energy and lengthen life. Also, natural selection may have favored sleep because animals that remained active at night probably had a higher chance of being killed. (We'll bet they had more fun, though.)

Module 5.2 Sleep Disturbances and Dreaming
Sleep Disturbances—The Sleepy Time Blues

Recite and Review

1. sleep disorders (sleep disturbances)
2. insomnia
3. limb movement
4. restless legs
5. sleep drunkenness
6. sleep terror (night terror)
7. sleep-wake schedule
8. temporary
9. chronic
10. drug-dependency
11. 4 (four)
12. stimulus control
13. sleep restriction
14. paradoxical intention
15. relaxation
16. exercise
17. tryptophan
18. serotonin
19. stimulant
20. somnambulists

21. NREM (non-REM)
22. sexsomnia
23. nightmare
24. night terror
25. nightmare
26. imagery rehearsal
27. sleep apnea
28. CPAP (continuous positive airway pressure)
29. SIDS (sudden infant death syndrome)
30. backs
31. overlaying
32. narcolepsy
33. cataplexy
34. REM
35. hereditary (genetic)
36. sodium oxybate

Part 1: Connections
1. e
2. a
3. b
4. i
5. g
6. k
7. j
8. c
9. h
10. d
11. f

Part 2: Connections
1. g
2. j
3. a
4. f
5. i
6. k
7. b
8. h
9. e
10. c
11. d

Check Your Memory
1. True
2. False
3. True
4. False
5. True
6. True
7. True
8. True
9. False
10. True
11. False
12. True
13. False
14. True
15. False
16. False
17. False
18. True
19. True
20. True
21. False
22. False
23. True
24. False
25. False
26. True
27. True
28. False
29. False
30. True
31. False
32. False
33. True
34. True
35. True
36. True

Critical Thinking Answer
Because people are immobilized during REM sleep and REM sleep is strongly associated with dreaming. This makes it unlikely that sleepwalkers are acting out dreams.

Dreams—A Separate Reality?
Recite and Review
1. 1952
2. 90 (ninety)
3. (William) Dement
4. REM rebound
5. (total) amount
6. REM
7. psychodynamic
8. (Sigmund) Freud
9. dream symbols
10. manifest
11. latent
12. activation-synthesis
13. (Robert) McCarley
14. neurocognitive (dream)
15. (William) Domhoff
16. frontal
17. more
18. neurocognitive (dream)

Connections

1. h
2. d
3. f
4. e
5. a
6. g
7. c
8. b

Check Your Memory

1. False
2. True
3. False
4. False
5. True
6. True
7. False
8. True
9. True
10. False
11. True
12. True
13. True
14. False
15. True
16. False
17. True
18. False
19. True

Module 5.3 Hypnosis, Meditation, and Sensory Deprivation
Hypnosis—Look into My Eyes

Recite and Review

1. (Franz) Mesmer
2. (James) Braid
3. sleep
4. different
5. suggestion
6. (Ernest) Hilgard
7. dissociative
8. hidden observer
9. nonstate
10. autosuggestion
11. autosuggestion
12. imagination
13. basic suggestion
14. immoral
15. four (4)
16. susceptibility
17. *Stanford Hypnotic Susceptibility Scale*
18. false (pseudo-)
19. sensory
20. stage hypnosis

Connections

1. i
2. c
3. d
4. g
5. a
6. h
7. b
8. f
9. e

Check Your Memory

1. False
2. False
3. False
4. True
5. False
6. True
7. True
8. True
9. True
10. False
11. False
12. False
13. False
14. True
15. True
16. False
17. True
18. True
19. True
20. True
21. True
22. False
23. True
24. True
25. False

Critical Thinking Answer
Most experiments on hypnosis include a control group in which people are asked to simulate being hypnotized. Without such controls, the tendency of subjects to cooperate with experimenters makes it difficult to identify true hypnotic effects.

Meditation—Chilling, the Healthy Way

Recite and Review
1. relaxation
2. frontal
3. concentrative
4. mindfulness
5. mindfulness
6. mantra
7. relaxation
8. immune
9. mindfulness
10. sensory deprivation (SD)
11. monotonous
12. REST (Restricted Environmental Stimulation Therapy)
13. isolation
14. suggestion
15. concentrative
16. mindfulness
17. mindfulness

Connections
1. e
2. d
3. b
4. a
5. c

Check Your Memory
1. True
2. False
3. False
4. False
5. True
6. False
7. True
8. True
9. True
10. True
11. False
12. True
13. True
14. True
15. False
16. False
17. True

Critical Thinking Answer
Studies on the effects of meditation must control for the placebo effect and the fact that those who choose to learn meditation may not be a representative sample of the general population.

Module 5.4 Psychoactive Drugs
Drug-Altered Consciousness—The High and Low of It

Recite and Review
1. psychoactive drug
2. stimulant
3. depressant
4. neurotransmitters
5. receptor
6. reward
7. nucleus accumbens
8. adolescents (teenagers)
9. controlled
10. punishment (negative consequences)
11. physical
12. withdrawal symptoms
13. drug tolerance
14. psychological
15. compulsive
16. experimental
17. socio-recreational
18. situational
19. intensive
20. compulsive
21. polydrug
22. interactions
23. physical
24. psychological
25. intravenously

Connections
1. j
2. m
3. g
4. k
5. l
6. c
7. a
8. i
9. f
10. d
11. e
12. h
13. b

Check Your Memory

1. True	9. True	17. True
2. True	10. True	18. False
3. True	11. True	19. False
4. False	12. True	20. False
5. True	13. True	21. False
6. False	14. False	22. False
7. False	15. False	23. True
8. False	16. True	24. True

Uppers—Amphetamines, Cocaine, MDMA, Caffeine, Nicotine

Recite and Review

1. amphetamines	10. noradrenaline (norepinephrine)	22. 15 (fifteen)
2. depressant	11. cocaine	23. 90 (ninety)
3. ADHD (attention deficit/ hyperactivity disorder	12. anhedonia	24. carcinogens
	13. cocaine	25. smokeless
4. creativity	14. MDMA	26. oral
5. methamphetamine	15. serotonin	27. second-hand (secondary)
6. tolerance	16. hyperthermia	28. cold turkey
7. crash	17. orgasm	29. scheduled gradual reduction
8. amphetamine psychosis	18. depression	
	19. caffeine	30. withdrawal
9. cocaine	20. caffeinism	
	21. nicotine	

Connections

1. j	6. b	11. l
2. g	7. h	12. i
3. m	8. d	13. f
4. a	9. k	
5. e	10. c	

Check Your Memory

1. True	13. False	25. True
2. False	14. False	26. False
3. False	15. True	27. False
4. False	16. True	28. True
5. True	17. True	29. False
6. True	18. False	30. True
7. False	19. False	31. True
8. False	20. False	32. True
9. False	21. True	33. True
10. False	22. True	34. False
11. True	23. True	35. False
12. False	24. True	36. False

Critical Thinking Answer
Neither can we.

Downers—Sedatives, Tranquilizers, and Alcohol

Recite and Review

1. alcohol
2. barbiturates
3. GHB (gamma-hydroxybutyrate
4. three (3)
5. gag
6. (benzodiazepine) tranquilizers
7. Rohypnol
8. alcohol
9. depressant
10. binge
11. 10 (ten)
12. negative emotions
13. paced
14. overestimate
15. detoxification
16. Alcoholics Anonymous (AA)
17. Rational Recovery
18. deny

Connections

1. c
2. e
3. g
4. a
5. h
6. i
7. b
8. d
9. f

Check Your Memory

1. True
2. True
3. True
4. False
5. False
6. False
7. True
8. True
9. True
10. False
11. False
12. True
13. False
14. True
15. True
16. False
17. False
18. False
19. False
20. True

Hallucinogens—Tripping the Light Fantastic

Recite and Review

1. hallucinogens
2. marijuana
3. LSD (lysergic acid diethylamide)
4. THC (tetrahydrocannabinol)
5. mescaline
6. psilocybin
7. PCP (phencyclidine)
8. marijuana
9. hashish
10. reproductive
11. psychological
12. short-term
13. (50 percent) more
14. lowers (decreases)
15. immune
16. cerebellum

Connections

1. c
2. f
3. h
4. b
5. d
6. e
7. g
8. a

Check Your Memory

1. True
2. True
3. True
4. False
5. True
6. False
7. True
8. True
9. True
10. True
11. False
12. True
13. True
14. False
15. True
16. False
17. True
18. True

1061

Critical Thinking Answer

Drug laws in Western societies reflect cultural values and historical patterns of use. Inconsistencies in the law often cannot be justified on the basis of pharmacology, health risks, or abuse potential.

Module 5.5 Psychology in Action: Exploring and Using Dreams

Recite and Review

1. REM
2. closed
3. diary
4. decrease
5. increase
6. no
7. dream processes
8. condensation
9. displacement
10. symbolization
11. secondary elaboration
12. (Calvin) Hall
13. (Rosalind) Cartwright
14. (Fritz) Perls
15. (Fritz) Perls
16. waking fantasy
17. imagery rehearsal
18. creative
19. inhibitions
20. set
21. lucid
22. (Stephen) LaBerge
23. paralysis
24. lucid
25. vestibular

Connections

1. a
2. f
3. b
4. d
5. h
6. e
7. i
8. c
9. g

Check Your Memory

1. True
2. False
3. True
4. False
5. True
6. False
7. True
8. False
9. False
10. False
11. False
12. True
13. False
14. False
15. True
16. True
17. True
18. False
19. False
20. False
21. False
22. True
23. False

Critical Thinking Answer

In waking consciousness, our actions have consequences that produce immediate sensory feedback. Dreams lack such external feedback. Thus, trying to walk through a wall or doing similar tests would reveal if you were dreaming.

Final Survey and Review—Completion

Module 5.1 States of Consciousness and Sleep
States of Consciousness—The Many Faces of Awareness

1. third-person
2. waking
3. altered state

Module 5.1 Sleep—Catching a Few ZZZ's

4. hypersomnia
5. microsleep
6. short sleepers

Module 5.1 Stages of Sleep—The Nightly Roller-Coaster

7. 2 (two)
8. delta
9. REM
10. hypnopompic hallucinations

1062

Module 5.2 Sleep Disturbances and Dreaming
Sleep Disturbances—The Sleepy Time Blues

11. chronic
12. tryptophan
13. night terror
14. sleep apnea
15. narcolepsy

Module 5.2 Dreams—A Separate Reality?

16. REM rebound
17. manifest
18. (Sigmund) Freud
19. neurocognitive (dream)

Module 5.3 Hypnosis, Meditation, and Sensory Deprivation
Hypnosis—Look into My Eyes

20. attention
21. hidden observer
22. autosuggestion
23. *Stanford Hypnotic Susceptibility Scale*
24. waking

Module 5.3 Meditation—Chilling, the Healthy Way

25. concentrative
26. fight-or-flight
27. sensory deprivation (restriction)

Module 5.4 Psychoactive Drugs
Drug-Altered Consciousness—The High and Low of It

28. stimulant
29. neurotransmitters
30. withdrawal
31. polydrug

Module 5.4 Uppers—Amphetamines, Cocaine, MDMA, Caffeine, Nicotine

32. hyperactivity (or ADHD)
33. amphetamine psychosis
34. caffeine
35. Ecstasy or MDMA
36. caffeine
37. scheduled gradual reduction

Module 5.4 Downers—Sedatives, Tranquilizers, and Alcohol

38. depressant
39. barbiturate
40. GHB (gamma-hydroxybutyrate)
41. (benzodiazepine) tranquilizers
42. binge
43. detoxification

Module 5.4 Hallucinogens—Tripping the Light Fantastic

44. PCP (phencyclidine)
45. psilocybin
46. brain
47. immune

Module 5.5 Psychology in Action: Exploring and Using Dreams

48. decrease
49. displacement
50. (Rosalind) Cartwright
51. lucid

Final Survey and Review—Matching

Module 5.1 States of Consciousness and Sleep

1. l
2. k
3. e
4. f
5. i
6. j
7. b
8. a
9. g
10. d
11. c
12. h

Module 5.2 Sleep Disturbances and Dreaming

1. f
2. a
3. l
4. k
5. c
6. e
7. b
8. i
9. h
10. g
11. d
12. j

Module 5.3 Hypnosis, Meditation, and Sensory Deprivation

1. j
2. g
3. i
4. b
5. h
6. a
7. f
8. e
9. c
10. d

Module 5.4 Psychoactive Drugs

1. l
2. n
3. i
4. k
5. m
6. g
7. b
8. j
9. e
10. h
11. c
12. d
13. f
14. a

Module 5.5 Psychology in Action: Exploring and Using Dreams

1. a
2. e
3. d
4. c
5. b

Final Survey and Review—True or False

Module 5.1 States of Consciousness and Sleep
States of Consciousness—The Many Faces of Awareness

1. True
2. True
3. False

Sleep—Catching a Few ZZZ's (Module 5.1)

4. True
5. True
6. False

Module 5.1 Stages of Sleep—The Nightly Roller-Coaster

7. False
8. True
9. True
10. False

Module 5.2 Sleep Disturbances and Dreaming
Sleep Disturbances—The Sleepy Time Blues

11. False
12. False
13. False
14. True
15. False

Module 5.2 Dreams—A Separate Reality?

16. False
17. False
18. False
19. False

Module 5.3 Hypnosis, Meditation, and Sensory Deprivation
Hypnosis—Look into My Eyes

20. False
21. True
22. True
23. False
24. True

Module 5.3 Meditation—Chilling, the Healthy Way

25. False
26. True
27. False

Module 5.4 Psychoactive Drugs
Drug-Altered Consciousness—The High and Low of It

28. True
29. False
30. False
31. False

Module 5.4 Uppers—Amphetamines, Cocaine, MDMA, Caffeine, Nicotine

32. True
33. True
34. False
35. True
36. False
37. True

Module 5.4 Downers—Sedatives, Tranquilizers, and Alcohol

38. True
39. True
40. False
41. True
42. True
43. False

Module 5.4 Hallucinogens—Tripping the Light Fantastic

44. True
45. True
46. False
47. False

Module 5.5 Psychology in Action: Exploring and Using Dreams

48. False
49. True
50. False
51. True

Mastery Test

1.	d	21.	a
2.	a	22.	c
3.	c	23.	c
4.	d	24.	a
5.	c	25.	b
6.	a	26.	d
7.	d	27.	a
8.	b	28.	c
9.	a	29.	d
10.	c	30.	b
11.	d	31.	a
12.	a	32.	d
13.	b	33.	d
14.	b	34.	a
15.	c	35.	b
16.	b	36.	a
17.	d	37.	d
18.	b	38.	c
19.	c	39.	d
20.	a	40.	a

Chapter 6: Conditioning and Learning

Solutions

Module 6.1 Learning and Classical Conditioning
What Is Learning—Does Practice Make Perfect?

Recite and Review

1. vicarious
2. learning
3. associative
4. associative
5. cognitive
6. wise
7. reinforcement
8. response
9. antecedents
10. consequences
11. classical (Pavlovian, respondent)
12. reflex
13. classical (Pavlovian, respondent)
14. classical (Pavlovian, respondent)
15. operant (instrumental)
16. reinforcement
17. punishment

Connections

1. c
2. i
3. f
4. j
5. a
6. e
7. d
8. g
9. h
10. b

Check Your Memory

1. False
2. True
3. True
4. True
5. False
6. True
7. False
8. True
9. False
10. False
11. True
12. False
13. True
14. True
15. True

Module 6.1 Learning and Classical Conditioning
Classical Conditioning—Does the Name Pavlov Ring a Bell?

Recite and Review

1. classical
2. digestion
3. food (meat powder)
4. bell
5. unconditioned
6. response
7. conditioned
8. bell
9. conditioned
10. conditioned
11. cerebellum
12. minimally conscious

Connections

1. c
2. g
3. a
4. e
5. b
6. d
7. f

1067

Check Your Memory

1. True
2. False
3. False
4. False
5. True
6. False
7. True
8. False
9. False
10. True
11. False

Module 6.1 Learning and Classical Conditioning
Principles of Classical Conditioning—Here's Johnny

Recite and Review

1. acquisition
2. respondent
3. unconditioned
4. conditioned
5. five (5)
6. higher order
7. higher order
8. informational
9. expectancies
10. informational
11. extinction
12. spontaneous recovery
13. generalization
14. decline (decreases)
15. generalization
16. discrimination
17. discrimination

Connections

1. a
2. g
3. c
4. f
5. d
6. h
7. e
8. i
9. b

Check Your Memory

1. True
2. False
3. True
4. False
5. False
6. False
7. False
8. True
9. True
10. True
11. False
12. False
13. True
14. True

Critical Thinking Answer

Door handles have become conditioned stimuli that elicit the reflex withdrawal and muscle tensing that normally follows getting a shock. This conditioned response may also have generalized to other handles.

Module 6.1 Learning and Classical Conditioning
Classical Conditioning in Humans—An Emotional Topic

Recite and Review

1. reflex
2. conditioned emotional
3. autonomic
4. conditioned
5. phobia
6. conditioned emotional
7. generalization
8. amygdala
9. cognitive
10. desensitization
11. emotional
12. vicarious (secondhand)
13. vicarious (secondhand)

Connections

1. b   3. e   5. c
2. d   4. a

Check Your Memory

1. True   5. True   9. False
2. False   6. False   10. True
3. False   7. False   11. True
4. True   8. True   12. False

Module 6.2 Operant Conditioning
Operant Conditioning—Ping-Pong Playing Pigeons?

Recite and Review

1. instrumental
2. consequences
3. effect
4. (Edward L.) Thorndike
5. operant (instrumental)
6. classical (Pavlovian, respondent)
7. before
8. after
9. classical (Pavlovian, respondent)
10. operant (instrumental)
11. emitted
12. reward
13. reinforcer
14. Skinner
15. (B. F.) Skinner
16. informational
17. contingent
18. 50 (fifty)
19. chaining
20. superstitious
21. response chaining
22. superstitious
23. shaping
24. successive approximations
25. extinction
26. spontaneous recovery
27. attention-seeking
28. positive reinforcement
29. negatively
30. punishment
31. aversive
32. punishment
33. punishment
34. time out
35. response cost
36. increases
37. decreases
38. decreases

Connections

1. h   6. d   11. b
2. l   7. m   12. g
3. a   8. c   13. j
4. f   9. e
5. k   10. i

Check Your Memory

1. True	11. False	21. False
2. False	12. True	22. True
3. False	13. True	23. False
4. True	14. True	24. False
5. False	15. False	25. True
6. False	16. True	26. True
7. True	17. False	27. True
8. True	18. True	28. True
9. False	19. True	29. False
10. True	20. False	

Module 6.2 Operant Conditioning
Operant Reinforcers—What's Your Pleasure?

Recite and Review

1. operant (instrumental)	12. social	20. feedback (knowledge of results, KR)
2. cognitive	13. social	21. ecological footprint
3. primary	14. feedback (knowledge of results, KR)	22. carbon footprint
4. primary	15. feedback	23. detailed
5. limbic	16. consequences	24. programmed
6. nicotine	17. response cost	25. computer-assisted instruction (CAI)
7. secondary	18. (positive) reinforcement	26. serious
8. primary	19. mother	27. simulations
9. token		
10. primary		
11. token economies		

Connections

1. j	5. h	9. d
2. k	6. a	10. e
3. b	7. f	11. g
4. i	8. c	

Check Your Memory

1. True	10. True	19. False
2. False	11. False	20. False
3. False	12. True	21. False
4. True	13. True	22. False
5. True	14. False	23. False
6. False	15. False	24. True
7. True	16. True	25. False
8. True	17. False	26. True
9. False	18. False	

Critical Thinking Answer

Knowledge of results means you find out if your response was right or wrong. Knowledge of correct response also tells you what the correct response should have been. Elaboration feedback adds additional information, such as an explanation of the correct answer. Adding knowledge of correct response and/or some elaboration is more effective than knowledge of results alone.

Module 6.3 Partial Reinforcement and Stimulus Control

Partial Reinforcement—Las Vegas, a Human Skinner Box?

Recite and Review

1. schedule
2. continuous
3. partial
4. partial reinforcement
5. extinction
6. continuous
7. partial
8. cumulative
9. steep
10. horizontal
11. tick marks
12. fixed ratio
13. variable ratio
14. fixed ratio
15. variable ratio
16. variable
17. variable ratio
18. fixed interval
19. cognitive time
20. fixed interval
21. passage
22. fixed interval
23. variable interval
24. variable interval

Connections

1. g
2. d
3. h
4. f
5. e
6. b
7. a
8. c
9. i

Check Your Memory

1. False
2. False
3. True
4. False
5. True
6. True
7. False
8. False
9. True
10. True
11. False
12. False
13. False
14. True
15. False
16. True
17. True
18. True
19. True
20. False

Critical Thinking Answer

Continuing to use fixed interval rewards (hourly wage or salary) would guarantee a basic level of income for employees. To reward extra effort, the owner could add some fixed ratio reinforcement (such as incentives, bonuses, commissions, or profit sharing) to employees' pay.

Module 6.3 Partial Reinforcement and Stimulus Control

Stimulus Control—Red Light, Green Light

Recite and Review

1. stimulus control
2. stimulus control
3. generalization
4. generalization
5. discrimination
6. discriminative
7. discriminative
8. generalization
9. nonreinforcement (nonreward)
10. discrimination
11. discrimination
12. discriminative

Connections

1. e	3. c	5. d
2. a	4. b	

Check Your Memory

1. True	5. False	9. True
2. True	6. False	10. True
3. False	7. True	
4. True	8. True	

Critical Thinking Answer

An excellent way to train a pet to come when you call is to give a distinctive call or whistle each time you feed the animal. This makes the signal a secondary reinforcer and a discriminative stimulus for reward (food). Of course, it also helps to directly reinforce an animal with praise, petting, or food for coming when called.

Module 6.4 Punishment

Punishment—Putting the Brakes on Behavior

Recite and Review

1. punishment	15. escape	28. danger
2. punisher	16. avoidance	29. incompatible
3. reinforce	17. escape	30. response cost
4. contingent	18. avoidance	31. counter
5. response cost	19. aggression	32. physical
6. timing	20. positive	punishment
7. immediately	21. reinforcement	33. respect (esteem,
8. consistency	22. punishment	worth)
9. intensity	23. nonreinforcement	34. punishment
10. mild	24. combination	35. reward
11. severe	25. (positive)	(reinforcement)
12. classical	reinforcement	36. negative
13. escape	26. extinction	
14. avoidance	27. punishment	

Connections

1. c	5. i	9. e
2. g	6. b	10. f
3. h	7. d	
4. a	8. j	

Check Your Memory

1. True	12. True	23. False
2. True	13. True	24. False
3. False	14. False	25. True
4. False	15. False	26. True
5. True	16. True	27. True
6. True	17. True	28. False
7. False	18. True	29. True
8. False	19. True	30. False
9. True	20. True	31. True
10. True	21. False	32. False
11. True	22. True	33. True

Critical Thinking Answer

1. An inconsistently punished response will continue to be reinforced on a partial schedule, which can make it even more resistant to extinction.

2. Many automobiles have an unpleasant buzzer that sounds if the ignition key is turned before the driver's seat belt is fastened. Most drivers quickly learn to fasten the belt to stop the annoying sound. This is an example of escape conditioning. Avoidance conditioning is evident when a driver learns to buckle up before the buzzer sounds.

Module 6.5 Cognitive Learning and Imitation
Cognitive Learning—Beyond Conditioning

Recite and Review

1. cognitive	5. latent	9. discovery
2. cognitive map	6. discovery	10. guided discovery
3. latent	7. rote	
4. cognitive map	8. discovery	

Connections

1. d	3. f	5. a
2. c	4. b	6. e

Check Your Memory

1. True	5. False	9. False
2. True	6. True	10. True
3. True	7. True	
4. False	8. True	

Critical Thinking Answer

Your cognitive map of the campus has undoubtedly become more accurate and intricate over time as you have added details to it. Your drawings should reflect this change.

Module 6.5 Cognitive Learning and Imitation
Modeling—Do as I Do, Not as I Say

Recite and Review

1. observational
2. (Albert) Bandura
3. observational
4. trial-and-error
5. model
6. attention
7. reproduce
8. rewarded (reinforced)
9. imitated
10. feedback
11. Bo-Bo the Clown
12. cartoon
13. prepares
14. does
15. television (TV)
16. aggressively (violently)
17. desensitizes
18. practiced
19. cause
20. solve problems
21. realistic (real)
22. identify
23. fantasies
24. Canada

Connections

1. e
2. d
3. c
4. b
5. f
6. a

Check Your Memory

1. False
2. False
3. True
4. True
5. False
6. True
7. True
8. False
9. True
10. False
11. False
12. True
13. True
14. True
15. False
16. False
17. False
18. True
19. False
20. False
21. True
22. True
23. True
24. False
25. True
26. True

Critical Thinking Answer

The observation is based on a correlation. Children who are already aggressive may choose to watch more aggressive programs, rather than being made aggressive by them. It took experimental studies to verify that televised aggression promotes aggression by viewers.

Module 6.6 Psychology in Action: Behavioral Self-Management—A Rewarding

Recite and Review

1. self-management
2. operant (instrumental)
3. target behavior
4. baseline
5. shaping
6. reinforcers
7. Premack
8. Premack
9. feedback
10. observe
11. alternate responses
12. extinction
13. response chains
14. antecedents
15. behavioral contract

Connections

1. f
2. d
3. h
4. b
5. a
6. c
7. i
8. e
9. g

1074

Check Your Memory

1. False	5. True	9. True
2. False	6. True	10. False
3. True	7. False	11. True
4. False	8. True	

Critical Thinking Answer

Daily performance goals and rewards reduce the delay of reinforcement, which maximizes its impact.

Final Survey and Review—Completion

Module 6.1 Learning and Classical Conditioning

What Is Learning—Does Practice Make Perfect?

1. associative
2. before
3. reinforcement

Module 6.1 Classical Conditioning—Does the Name Pavlov Ring a Bell?

4. respondent
5. food
6. conditioned
7. eye-blink

Module 6.1 Principles of Classical Conditioning—Here's Johnny

8. expectancies
9. extinction
10. generalization
11. discrimination

Module 6.1 Classical Conditioning in Humans—An Emotional Topic

12. emotional response
13. desensitization
14. vicarious

Module 6.2 Operant Conditioning

Operant Conditioning— Ping-Pong Playing Pigeons?

15. (Edward L.) Thorndike
16. operant (instrumental)
17. contingent
18. chaining
19. superstitious
20. negative reinforcement
21. response cost

Operant Reinforcers—What's Your Pleasure?

22. primary
23. token economy
24. social
25. knowledge of results (KR)
26. frequent

Module 6.3 Partial Reinforcement and Stimulus Control

Partial Reinforcement—Las Vegas, a Human Skinner Box?

27. continuous
28. variable ratio
29. time travelers
30. fixed interval

Module 6.3 Stimulus Control—Red Light, Green Light

31. stimulus control
32. discriminative
33. generalization

Module 6.4 Punishment
Punishment—Putting the Brakes on Behavior

34. punishment
35. nonreinforcement
36. avoidance

37. counter-conditioning

38. negative reinforcement

Module 6.5 Cognitive Learning and Imitation
Cognitive Learning—Beyond Conditioning

39. cognitive map

40. latent

41. guided discovery

Module 6.5 Modeling—Do as I Do, Not as I Say

42. observational
43. reinforcement

44. reproduce
45. desensitizes

46. identifies

Module 6.6 Psychology in Action: Behavioral Self-Management—A Rewarding

47. self-management
48. Premack

49. alternate responses

50. behavioral contract

Final Survey and Review—Matching

Module 6.1 Learning and Classical Conditioning
Part 1:

1. c
2. h
3. b

4. a
5. e
6. i

7. g
8. f
9. d

Part 2:

1. c
2. d
3. f

4. g
5. a
6. h

7. e
8. i
9. b

Module 6.2 Operant Conditioning

1. h
2. f
3. b

4. g
5. a
6. c

7. i
8. e
9. d

Module 6.3 Partial Reinforcement and Stimulus Control

1. b
2. d
3. c

4. a
5. g
6. e

7. f
8. h

Module 6.4 Punishment

1. e
2. c

3. f
4. a

5. b
6. d

Module 6.5 Cognitive Learning and Imitation

1. d
2. h
3. f
4. a
5. g
6. e
7. b
8. c

Module 6.6 Psychology in Action: Behavioral Self-Management—A Rewarding

1. e
2. c
3. a
4. f
5. b
6. d

Final Survey and Review—True or False

Module 6.1 Learning and Classical Conditioning

What Is Learning—Does Practice Make Perfect?

1. False
2. True
3. False

Module 6.1 Classical Conditioning—Does the Name Pavlov Ring a Bell?

4. False
5. True
6. False
7. True

Module 6.1 Principles of Classical Conditioning—Here's Johnny

8. True
9. False
10. False
11. False

Module 6.1 Classical Conditioning in Humans—An Emotional Topic

12. True
13. True
14. False

Module 6.2 Operant Conditioning

Operant Conditioning— Ping-Pong Playing Pigeons?

15. False
16. False
17. True
18. False
19. True
20. False
21. False

Module 6.2 Operant Reinforcers—What's Your Pleasure?

22. True
23. True
24. False
25. True
26. True

Module 6.3 Partial Reinforcement and Stimulus Control

Partial Reinforcement—Las Vegas, a Human Skinner Box?

27. True
28. False
29. True
30. True

Module 6.3 Stimulus Control—Red Light, Green Light

31. False
32. True
33. True

Module 6.4 Punishment

Punishment—Putting the Brakes on Behavior

34. True
35. True
36. True
37. False
38. False

Module 6.5 Cognitive Learning and Imitation
Cognitive Learning—Beyond Conditioning

39. True   40. True   41. False

Module 6.5 Modeling—Do as I Do, Not as I Say

42. False   44. False   46. True
43. True   45. True

Module 6.6 Psychology in Action: Behavioral Self-Management—A Rewarding

47. True   49. False
48. False   50. False

Mastery Test

1. a	15. d	29. a
2. a	16. c	30. c
3. b	17. d	31. a
4. b	18. b	32. b
5. c	19. a	33. c
6. d	20. c	34. c
7. a	21. b	35. a
8. c	22. c	36. c
9. b	23. d	37. d
10. c	24. a	38. c
11. a	25. b	39. d
12. d	26. b	40. b
13. b	27. c	
14. d	28. a	

Chapter 7: Memory

Solutions

Module 7.1 Memory Systems
Stages of Memory—Do You Have a Mind Like a Steel Trap? Or a Sieve?

Recite and Review

1. mnemonist
2. forget
3. forget
4. memory
5. Atkinson-Schiffrin
6. encoding
7. storage
8. retrieval
9. sensory
10. iconic
11. echoic
12. selective attention
13. phonetically
14. (maintenance) rehearsal
15. interference
16. working
17. long-term
18. easier
19. meaning
20. short-term
21. encode
22. American
23. Chinese
24. self-
25. historical

Part 1: Connections

1. c
2. g
3. a
4. e
5. b
6. d
7. f

Part 2: Connections

1. g
2. i
3. d
4. b
5. f
6. j
7. c
8. a
9. h
10. e
11. k

Check Your Memory

1. True
2. True
3. False
4. False
5. False
6. False
7. True
8. True
9. False
10. True
11. False
12. True
13. True
14. False
15. True
16. True
17. False
18. True
19. True
20. False
21. True
22. False
23. False

Critical Thinking Answer

Without sensory memory, a movie would look like a series of still pictures. The split-second persistence of visual images helps blend one motion-picture frame into the next.

Module 7.2 STM and LTM
Short-Term Memory—Do You Know the Magic Number?

Recite and Review

1. short-term
2. digit span
3. seven (7)
4. bit
5. chunk
6. chunking
7. chunking
8. four (4)
9. maintenance rehearsal
10. repeated
11. rote
12. elaborative encoding
13. reflective
14. (maintenance) rehearsal

Connections

1. d
2. f
3. b
4. g
5. a
6. c
7. e

Check Your Memory

1. True
2. False
3. True
4. False
5. True
6. True
7. False
8. True
9. False
10. False
11. True
12. True

Module 7.2 STM and LTM
Long-Term Memory—A Blast from the Past

Recite and Review

1. (Wilder) Penfield
2. dreams
3. constructive processing
4. memory jamming
5. false memories or pseudomemories
6. false or pseudo-
7. source
8. cognitive interview
9. cues
10. orders
11. memory index
12. memory structure
13. bird
14. network
15. associations
16. redintegration
17. elaborative encoding
18. rote
19. long-term
20. procedural
21. cerebellum
22. declarative
23. semantic
24. semantic
25. episodic
26. semantic
27. episodic
28. episodic

Part 1: Connections

1. c
2. a
3. e
4. b
5. d

Part 2: Connections

1. j
2. e
3. l
4. h
5. b
6. i
7. c
8. k
9. a
10. d
11. g
12. f

Check Your Memory

1. False
2. False
3. True
4. True
5. False
6. True
7. True
8. True
9. True
10. False
11. True
12. True
13. True
14. False
15. False
16. False
17. False
18. False
19. False
20. True
21. False
22. False
23. False
24. False
25. True
26. False
27. False
28. False
29. False
30. True

Critical Thinking Answer

Because the more information you have in long-term memory, the greater the possibilities for linking new information to it. Generally, the more you know, the more you can learn—even if some of what you know is "junk."

Module 7.3 Measuring Memory
Measuring Memory—The Answer Is on the Tip of My Tongue

Recite and Review

1. tip-of-the-tongue (TOT)
2. feeling of knowing
3. déjà vu
4. details
5. relearning
6. recall
7. serial position
8. short-term
9. rehearsal
10. recall
11. recognition
12. recognition
13. recall
14. recognition
15. distractors
16. poor
17. false positive
18. sequential
19. relearning
20. relearning
21. savings
22. explicit
23. implicit
24. explicit
25. implicit
26. priming

Connections

1. b
2. e
3. g
4. i
5. h
6. a
7. m
8. f
9. l
10. j
11. d
12. k
13. c

Check Your Memory

1. True
2. False
3. True
4. True
5. True
6. False
7. False
8. False
9. True
10. True
11. True
12. False
13. False
14. True
15. False
16. False
17. False
18. True
19. True
20. False
21. True
22. True
23. False
24. True
25. True
26. True

Critical Thinking Answer

It is possible to have an implicit memory that cannot be consciously recalled. Memories like these (*available* in memory even though they are not consciously *accessible*) show that failing to recall something does not guarantee it is no longer in memory (Landau & Leynes, 2006).

Module 7.4 Forgetting
Forgetting—Why We, Uh, Let's See; Why We, Uh . . . Forget!

Recite and Review

1. (Herman) Ebbinghaus
2. nonsense syllables
3. curve of forgetting
4. slow
5. cramming
6. encoding
7. 30 (thirty)
8. encoding failure
9. older adults
10. encoding failure
11. general
12. elaborative
13. traces
14. decay
15. disuse
16. disuse
17. accessible
18. cue
19. cue-dependent
20. state-dependent
21. interference
22. slept
23. retroactive
24. proactive
25. positive transfer
26. negative transfer
27. negative
28. repression
29. suppression
30. repression
31. recovered
32. Amytal
33. false memory

Part 1: Connections

1. d
2. a
3. i
4. e
5. b
6. c
7. h
8. f
9. g

Part 2: Connections

1. h
2. d
3. g
4. b
5. a
6. c
7. f
8. e

Check Your Memory

1. True
2. False
3. False
4. True
5. True
6. False
7. False
8. True
9. True
10. True
11. True
12. False
13. True
14. False
15. True
16. True
17. True
18. True
19. True
20. False
21. True
22. False
23. True
24. False
25. True
26. False
27. True
28. True
29. False
30. True
31. True
32. False
33. True
34. True
35. False
36. True
37. False
38. True

Critical Thinking Answers

1. Music tends to affect the mood that a person is in, and moods tend to affect memory (Miranda & Kihlstrom, 2005).

2. Any order that separates French from Spanish and psychology from biology would be better (for instance: French, psychology, Spanish, biology).

Module 7.4 Forgetting
Memory and the Brain—Some "Shocking" Findings

Recite and Review

1. retrograde
2. anterograde
3. consolidation
4. consolidation
5. retrograde
6. hippocampus
7. anterograde
8. consolidation
9. flashbulb
10. limbic
11. confidence
12. procedural
13. declarative
14. episodic
15. semantic
16. snail
17. transmitter chemicals or neurotransmitters
18. learning
19. long-term potentiation
20. decreased

Connections

1. f
2. i
3. b
4. k
5. j
6. c
7. a
8. g
9. e
10. h
11. d

Check Your Memory

1. False
2. False
3. True
4. True
5. False
6. False
7. True
8. True
9. True
10. False
11. False
12. False
13. True
14. True
15. True
16. False
17. True

Module 7.5 Exceptional Memory and Improving Memory
Exceptional Memory—Wizards of Recall

Recite and Review

1. mental image
2. distances
3. eidetic
4. mental
5. eidetic
6. eidetic imagery
7. selective
8. short-term
9. chunking
10. interests
11. mnemonics
12. natural

Connections

1. c
2. b
3. a
4. e
5. d

Check Your Memory

1. True
2. True
3. False
4. True
5. True
6. False
7. True
8. False
9. True
10. False
11. True
12. False

Critical Thinking Answer

Mr. S's memory was so specific that faces seemed different and unfamiliar if he saw them from a new angle or if a face had a different expression on it than when Mr. S last saw it.

Module 7.5 Exceptional Memory and Improving Memory
Improving Memory—Keys to the Memory Bank

Recite and Review

1. encoding
2. retrieval
3. elaborative encoding
4. selective
5. chunks
6. encoding
7. whole
8. part
9. progressive-part
10. meaningful
11. serial position
12. middle
13. cues
14. elaborative
15. overlearning
16. overlearning
17. spaced
18. massed
19. feedback
20. recitation
21. reviewing
22. search
23. partial
24. cognitive interview
25. extending
26. reduces
27. lower

Connections

1. e
2. g
3. j
4. i
5. h
6. a
7. f
8. b
9. c
10. d

Check Your Memory

1. True
2. True
3. False
4. True
5. False
6. False
7. True
8. True
9. False
10. True
11. True
12. False
13. True
14. True
15. False
16. False
17. True
18. True
19. False
20. True
21. True
22. False
23. True
24. False
25. False

Critical Thinking Answer

Note-taking is a form of elaborative encoding and recitation; it facilitates the organization and selection of important ideas, and your notes can be used for review.

Module 7.6 Psychology in Action: Mnemonics—Memory Magic

Recite and Review

1. mnemonic
2. acrostics
3. meaningful
4. images or visual pictures
5. distinctive
6. simple
7. rote
8. keyword
9. initial
10. fragile
11. images
12. story or chain
13. mental walk
14. system

Connections

1. b
2. a
3. d
4. e
5. c
6. f

Check Your Memory

1. False
2. False
3. True
4. True
5. True
6. True
7. False
8. True
9. True
10. False
11. True
12. False
13. True
14. True

Critical Thinking Answer

Both attempt to relate new information to information stored in LTM that is familiar or already easy to retrieve.

Final Survey and Review—Completion

Module 7.1 Memory Systems
Stages of Memory—Do You Have a Mind Like a Steel Trap? Or a Sieve?

1. short-term
2. iconic
3. working
4. culture

Module 7.2 STM and LTM
Short-Term Memory—Do You Know the Magic Number?

5. digit span
6. chunking
7. rote
8. elaborative

Module 7.2 Long-Term Memory—A Blast from the Past

9. constructive processing
10. cognitive interview
11. redintegration
12. procedural or skill
13. episodic

Module 7.3 Measuring Memory
Measuring Memory—The Answer Is on the Tip of My Tongue

14. tip-of-the-tongue (TOT)
15. feeling of knowing
16. middle
17. recall
18. priming

Module 7.4 Forgetting
Forgetting—Why We, Uh, Let's See; Why We, Uh . . . Forget!
19. encoding failure
20. state-dependent
21. decay
22. most
23. proactive
24. positive
25. false memory

Module 7.4 Memory and the Brain—Some "Shocking" Findings
26. retrograde
27. anterograde
28. consolidation
29. flashbulb
30. cerebellum

Module 7.5 Exceptional Memory and Improving Memory
Exceptional Memory—Wizards of Recall
31. mental
32. eidetic
33. selective
34. short-term

Module 7.5 Improving Memory—Keys to the Memory Bank
35. selective
36. progressive-part
37. serial position
38. overlearning
39. spaced
40. partial
41. viewpoints

Module 7.6 Psychology in Action: Mnemonics—Memory Magic
42. mnemonics
43. bizarre
(outrageous,
exaggerated)
44. keyword
45. mental walk

Final Survey and Review—Matching

Module 7.1 Memory Systems
1. g
2. c
3. a
4. e
5. b
6. h
7. d
8. f

Module 7.2 STM and LTM
1. j
2. e
3. a
4. h
5. f
6. i
7. c
8. b
9. k
10. d
11. g

Module 7.3 Measuring Memory
1. d
2. f
3. a
4. e
5. h
6. i
7. c
8. g
9. b

Module 7.4 Forgetting
1. c
2. a
3. j
4. i
5. f
6. h
7. e
8. b
9. g
10. d

Module 7.5 Exceptional Memory and Improving Memory

1. b
2. h
3. f
4. g
5. a
6. e
7. c
8. d

Module 7.6 Psychology in Action: Mnemonics—Memory Magic

1. b
2. a
3. d
4. e
5. c
6. f

Final Survey and Review—True or False

Module 7.1 Memory Systems
Stages of Memory—Do You Have a Mind Like a Steel Trap? Or a Sieve?

1. True
2. True
3. False
4. True

Module 7.2 STM and LTM

Module 7.2 Short-Term Memory—Do You Know the Magic Number?

5. False
6. True
7. False
8. True

Module 7.2 Long-Term Memory—A Blast from the Past

9. False
10. False
11. True
12. True
13. False

Module 7.3 Measuring Memory
Measuring Memory—The Answer Is on the Tip of My Tongue

14. True
15. False
16. True
17. True
18. False

Module 7.4 Forgetting
Forgetting—Why We, Uh, Let's See; Why We, Uh . . . Forget!

19. False
20. False
21. True
22. False
23. True
24. True
25. False

Module 7.4 Memory and the Brain—Some "Shocking" Findings

26. False
27. False
28. False
29. True
30. False

Module 7.5 Exceptional Memory and Improving Memory
Exceptional Memory—Wizards of Recall

31. True
32. False
33. True
34. True

Module 7.5 Improving Memory—Keys to the Memory Bank

35. False	38. True	41. False
36. True	39. True	
37. True	40. True	

Module 7.6 Psychology in Action: Mnemonics—Memory Magic

42. True	44. True
43. False	45. True

Mastery Test

1. c	11. d	21. a
2. a	12. b	22. b
3. d	13. c	23. c
4. b	14. c	24. b
5. b	15. b	25. c
6. c	16. a	26. a
7. d	17. d	27. b
8. a	18. a	28. c
9. a	19. b	29. c
10. b	20. d	30. d
31. c	34. d	37. d
32. a	35. d	38. a
33. c	36. a	39. b
		40. c

Chapter 8: Cognition, Language, Creativity, and Intelligence

Solutions

Module 8.1 Imagery, Concepts, and Language
What Is Thinking?—Brains over Brawn

Recite and Review

1. thinking
2. wise
3. cognition
4. cognition (or thinking)
5. thinking (or thoughts)
6. plan
7. images
8. concepts
9. language

Connections

1. e
2. d
3. c
4. b
5. a

Check Your Memory

1. False
2. False
3. True
4. False
5. True
6. True
7. False
8. False
9. True
10. True

Module 8.1 Imagery, Concepts, and Language
Mental Imagery—Does a Frog Have Lips?

Recite and Review

1. auditory
2. movement
3. synaesthesia
4. images
5. flat
6. rotate
7. rotation
8. reverse vision
9. stored
10. created
11. creativity
12. three (3)
13. three (3)
14. small
15. oversized (or enlarged)
16. kinesthetic
17. kinesthetic
18. kinesthetic

Connections

1. c
2. e
3. d
4. a
5. f
6. b

Check Your Memory

1. False
2. False
3. False
4. True
5. False
6. True
7. True
8. False
9. False
10. True
11. False
12. True
13. False
14. True
15. True

Module 8.1 Imagery, Concepts, and Language
Concepts—I'm Positive, It's a Whatchamacallit

Recite and Review

1. concept
2. details
3. concept formation
4. negative
5. rules
6. conceptual rule
7. conjunctive
8. disjunctive
9. relational
10. relational
11. prototype
12. faulty (or inaccurate)
13. stereotypes
14. all-or-nothing
15. denotative
16. connotative
17. connotative
18. semantic differential

Connections

1. c
2. i
3. a
4. j
5. g
6. f
7. b
8. e
9. k
10. d
11. h

Check Your Memory

1. False
2. True
3. False
4. True
5. False
6. False
7. True
8. True
9. False
10. True
11. True
12. False
13. False
14. True
15. True

Critical Thinking Answer

If they both assume the word refers to a form of government, not a political party or a candidate.

Module 8.1 Imagery, Concepts, and Language
Language—Don't Leave Home Without It

Recite and Review

1. encoded
2. semantics
3. context
4. Stroop Interference
5. languages
6. bilingualism
7. subtractive
8. additive
9. two-way
10. symbols
11. phonemes
12. morpheme
13. grammar
14. syntax
15. syntax
16. (Noam) Chomsky
17. transformation
18. transformation
19. productive
20. gestural
21. spatial
22. identity
23. productive
24. operant
25. (David) Premack
26. conditional
27. gestures
28. syntax
29. lexigram
30. two (2)

Connections

1. d
2. l
3. j
4. b
5. e
6. n
7. c
8. m
9. f
10. h
11. g
12. a
13. i
14. k

Check Your Memory

1. True
2. True
3. False
4. True
5. True
6. False
7. True
8. False
9. True
10. False
11. False
12. False
13. True
14. True
15. False
16. True
17. True
18. False
19. False
20. True
21. True
22. False
23. False
24. False
25. True
26. True
27. False
28. True
29. True
30. False
31. True
32. True
33. True
34. True

Critical Thinking Answer

The problem of anthropomorphizing (ascribing human characteristics to animals) is especially difficult to avoid when researchers spend many hours "conversing" with chimps.

Module 8.2 Problem Solving
Problem Solving—Getting an Answer in Sight

Recite and Review

1. mechanical
2. algorithm
3. algorithm
4. understanding
5. general
6. functional
7. trial-and-error
8. rote
9. general properties
10. random search
11. heuristic
12. heuristic
13. heuristics
14. patterns
15. automatic processing
16. 10 (ten)
17. insight
18. encoding
19. comparison
20. encoding
21. combination
22. encoding
23. comparison
24. combination
25. comparison
26. culture
27. fixation
28. functional fixedness
29. flexible
30. preconceptions
31. emotional
32. cultural
33. learned
34. perceptual
35. learned

Part 1: Connections

1. k
2. g
3. h
4. l
5. e
6. j
7. i
8. f
9. c
10. a
11. d
12. b

Part 2: Connections

1. f
2. d
3. g
4. b
5. e
6. a
7. c

Check Your Memory

1. True
2. False
3. True
4. True
5. False
6. True
7. True
8. False
9. True
10. True
11. True
12. False
13. False
14. True
15. True
16. False
17. True
18. False
19. False
20. True
21. True
22. True
23. False
24. True
25. False
26. True
27. False
28. False

Critical Thinking Answers

1. Although this might be an overstatement, it is true that clearly defining a starting point and the desired goal can serve as a heuristic in problem solving.

2. Psychologist Donald Griffin believes it does because thinking is implied by actions that appear to be planned with an awareness of likely results.

Module 8.3 Creative Thinking and Intuition
Creative Thinking—Down Roads Less Traveled

Recite and Review

1. inductive
2. deductive
3. logical
4. illogical
5. creativity (or divergent thinking)
6. fluency
7. flexibility
8. originality
9. divergent
10. convergent
11. divergent
12. Unusual Uses
13. Anagrams
14. Consequences
15. practical
16. orientation
17. preparation
18. incubation
19. illumination
20. verification
21. incubation
22. orientation
23. illumination
24. incremental
25. personality
26. positive
27. greater (larger)
28. sets
29. consciousness
30. divergent

Part 1: Connections

1. d
2. g
3. b
4. a
5. i
6. f
7. c
8. e
9. h

Part 2: Connections

1. f
2. c
3. a
4. g
5. h
6. b
7. d
8. e

Check Your Memory

1. False	11. True	21. True
2. False	12. True	22. False
3. True	13. True	23. True
4. False	14. False	24. True
5. False	15. False	25. True
6. False	16. False	26. False
7. True	17. True	27. True
8. False	18. True	28. False
9. False	19. False	
10. True	20. True	

Module 8.3 Creative Thinking and Intuition
Intuitive Thought—Mental Shortcut? Or Dangerous Detour?

Recite and Review

1. creative
2. intuition
3. high (or strong)
4. thin-slicing
5. cognitive unconscious
6. (Daniel) Kahneman
7. representativeness heuristic
8. representativeness
9. emotions (or feelings)
10. base rate (or underlying odds or underlying probability)
11. base rate (or underlying odds or underlying probability)
12. framing
13. broadest
14. framing

Connections

1. b	3. e	5. a
2. f	4. d	6. c

Check Your Memory

1. True	6. True	11. True
2. False	7. False	12. False
3. True	8. True	13. False
4. False	9. True	14. True
5. True	10. True	

Critical Thinking Answer

The chance of getting heads on the fifth flip is the same in each case. Each time you flip a coin, the chance of getting a head is 50 percent, no matter what happened before. However, many people intuitively think that *b* is the answer because a head is "overdue," or that *c* is correct because the coin is "on a roll" for heads.

Module 8.4 Intelligence
Human Intelligence—The IQ and You

Recite and Review

1. (Alfred) Binet
2. rationally
3. g-factor
4. operational
5. (Lewis) Terman
6. age-ranked
7. two (2)
8. verbal
9. nonverbal
10. fluid reasoning
11. knowledge
12. quantitative reasoning
13. visual-spatial processing
14. working memory
15. nonverbal
16. (David) Wechsler
17. WAIS (Wechsler Adult Intelligence Scale)
18. perceptual reasoning
19. working memory
20. processing speed
21. mental age
22. chronological age
23. mental
24. IQ (or intelligence quotient)
25. 90 (ninety)
26. 130 (one hundred and thirty)
27. seven (7)
28. 109 (one hundred and nine)
29. above (or higher than)
30. below (or less than)
31. 100 (one hundred)
32. deviation
33. 50th (fiftieth)
34. 50th (fiftieth)
35. individual
36. group
37. group
38. SAT Reasoning Test (SAT)
39. flexibility
40. artificial
41. rules
42. artificial
43. simulations
44. expert

Part 1: Connections

1. g
2. c
3. i
4. e
5. a
6. j
7. f
8. d
9. b
10. h

Part 2: Connections

1. f
2. h
3. d
4. a
5. i
6. b
7. e
8. c
9. g

Check Your Memory

1. True
2. True
3. False
4. True
5. True
6. False
7. True
8. False
9. False
10. False
11. True
12. True
13. True
14. False
15. False
16. True
17. True
18. True
19. False
20. False
21. False
22. True
23. True
24. False
25. False
26. True
27. True
28. False
29. True
30. True
31. True
32. False
33. False
34. True
35. True
36. False

Critical Thinking Answer

Rule-driven expert systems may appear "intelligent" within a narrow range of problem solving. However, they are "stone stupid" at everything else. This is usually not what we have in mind when discussing human intelligence.

Module 8.4 Intelligence
Variations in Intelligence—Curved Like a Bell

Recite and Review

1. normal
2. middle
3. gifted
4. genius
5. (Lewis) Terman
6. successful
7. .50
8. creativity
9. potential
10. intellectual determination
11. talents
12. memory
13. giftedness
14. ethnic minority
15. savant
16. left
17. practice
18. 70 (seventy)
19. adaptive
20. feelings (emotions)
21. moderate
22. profound
23. organic
24. teratogens
25. birth
26. metabolic
27. familial
28. mild

Connections

1. f
2. b
3. a
4. i
5. e
6. h
7. d
8. c
9. g

Check Your Memory

1. True
2. False
3. False
4. True
5. True
6. False
7. False
8. False
9. True
10. True
11. False
12. True
13. True
14. True
15. False
16. False
17. True
18. False
19. True
20. True
21. False
22. False
23. False
24. True
25. True

Module 8.4 Intelligence
Questioning Intelligence—How Intelligent Is the Idea of Intelligence?

Recite and Review

1. function
2. fool
3. visual
4. navigational
5. culture-fair
6. visual
7. real-world
8. eight (8)
9. multiple intelligences
10. spatial
11. intrapersonal
12. interpersonal
13. bodily-kinesthetic
14. naturalist
15. heredity (or nature or genetics)
16. fraternal
17. identical
18. fraternal
19. 50 (fifty)
20. environmental (or nurture)
21. 29 (twenty-nine)
22. 26 (twenty-six)
23. 15 (fifteen)
24. complex
25. 15 (fifteen)
26. 13 (thirteen)
27. Obama
28. practical
29. analytic
30. no significant
31. wisdom

Connections

1. f
2. d
3. h
4. i
5. c
6. g
7. j
8. a
9. e
10. b

Check Your Memory

1. False
2. False
3. True
4. True
5. True
6. False
7. False
8. True
9. True
10. True
11. True
12. True
13. False
14. True
15. False
16. True
17. True
18. False
19. False
20. True
21. True
22. True
23. True
24. False
25. False
26. True
27. False
28. True
29. False
30. True

Critical Thinking Answer

Because one's IQ depends on the intelligence test used to measure it: Change the test and you will change the score. Also, heredity establishes a range of possibilities; it does not automatically preordain a person's intellectual capacities.

Module 8.5 Psychology in Action: Enhancing Creativity—Brainstorms

Recite and Review

1. perspiration
2. persistence
3. set
4. sets
5. broadly
6. divergent
7. decrease (or lower)
8. increase
9. increase
10. (Edward) de Bono
11. decrease (lower)
12. well
13. enjoy (like)
14. relaxing

Connections

1. d
2. f
3. g
4. e
5. b
6. a
7. c

Check Your Memory

1. True
2. False
3. True
4. False
5. False
6. False
7. True
8. True
9. False
10. True
11. False
12. True

Critical Thinking Answer

In general, more intense moods are associated with higher creativity (Davis, 2009).

Final Survey and Review—Completion

Module 8.1 Imagery, Concepts, and Language
What Is Thinking?—Brains over Brawn

1. cognition (or thinking)
2. language
3. concepts

Module 8.1 Mental Imagery—Does a Frog Have Lips?

4. synaesthesia
5. rotate
6. reverse vision
7. created
8. kinesthetic

Module 8.1 Concepts—I'm Positive, It's a Whatchamacallit

9. rules
10. conjunctive
11. disjunctive
12. prototype
13. denotative
14. connotative

Module 8.1 Language—Don't Leave Home Without It

15. semantics
16. context
17. bilingual
18. morphemes
19. transformation
20. gestures
21. productivity

Module 8.2 Problem Solving
Problem Solving—Getting an Answer in Sight

22. trial-and-error
23. algorithm
24. heuristic
25. expert
26. comparison
27. functional fixedness
28. cultural

Module 8.3 Creative Thinking and Intuition
Creative Thinking—Down Roads Less Traveled

29. deductive
30. flexibility
31. convergent
32. Anagrams
33. sensible
34. preparation
35. metaphors

Module 8.3 Intuitive Thought—Mental Shortcut? Or Dangerous Detour?

36. intuition
37. thin-slicing
38. representativeness heuristic
39. base rate (or underlying odds or underlying probability)

Module 8.4 Intelligence
Human Intelligence—The IQ and You

40. (Lewis) Terman
41. operational
42. fluid reasoning
43. verbal comprehension
44. 12 (twelve)
45. deviation
46. SAT Reasoning Test (SAT)
47. expert

Module 8.4 Variations in Intelligence—Curved Like a Bell

48. bell
49. 130 (one hundred and thirty)
50. intellectual determination
51. savant
52. adaptive
53. familial

Module 8.4 Questioning Intelligence—How Intelligent Is the Idea of Intelligence?

54. Western
55. culture-fair
56. interpersonal
57. heredity (or genetics)
58. environmental (or nurture)
59. analytic

Module 8.5 Psychology in Action: Enhancing Creativity—Brainstorms

60. set
61. broadly
62. divergent
63. thinking

Final Survey and Review—Matching

Module 8.1 Imagery, Concepts, and Language
Part 1:

1. h
2. i
3. a
4. j
5. g
6. e
7. b
8. c
9. f
10. d

Part 2:

1. b
2. d
3. h
4. a
5. g
6. c
7. e
8. f

Module 8.2 Problem Solving

1. g
2. i
3. j
4. c
5. h
6. a
7. k
8. d
9. b
10. e
11. f

Module 8.3 Creative Thinking and Intuition
Part 1:

1. i	4. a	7. f
2. g	5. e	8. c
3. b	6. h	9. d

Part 2:

1. a	4. g	7. d
2. c	5. h	8. e
3. f	6. b	

Module 8.4 Intelligence
Part 1:

1. g	5. a	9. d
2. f	6. l	10. h
3. i	7. j	11. c
4. e	8. k	12. b

Part 2:

1. j	5. a	9. b
2. d	6. c	10. h
3. g	7. i	
4. f	8. e	

Module 8.5 Psychology in Action: Enhancing Creativity—Brainstorms

1. d	3. c	5. b
2. f	4. e	6. a

Final Survey and Review—True or False

Module 8.1 Imagery, Concepts, and Language
What Is Thinking?—Brains over Brawn

1. False	2. True	3. False

Module 8.1 Mental Imagery—Does a Frog Have Lips?

4. False	6. True	8. False
5. True	7. True	

Module 8.1 Concepts—I'm Positive, It's a Whatchamacallit

9. True	11. True	13. True
10. False	12. False	14. False

Module 8.1 Language—Don't Leave Home Without It

15. False	18. True	21. False
16. True	19. True	
17. False	20. False	

1099

Module 8.2 Problem Solving
Problem Solving—Getting an Answer in Sight

22. True
23. False
24. True

25. True
26. False
27. False

28. True

Module 8.3 Creative Thinking and Intuition
Creative Thinking—Down Roads Less Traveled

29. False
30. False
31. False

32. False
33. False
34. True

35. True

Module 8.3 Intuitive Thought—Mental Shortcut? Or Dangerous Detour?

36. False
37. False

38. True
39. True

Module 8.4 Intelligence
Human Intelligence—The IQ and You

40. False
41. True
42. True

43. False
44. False
45. False

46. False
47. True

Module 8.4 Variations in Intelligence—Curved Like a Bell

48. True
49. True

50. True
51. False

52. True
53. False

Module 8.4 Questioning Intelligence—How Intelligent Is the Idea of Intelligence?

54. False
55. True

56. True
57. False

58. False
59. True

Module 8.5 Psychology in Action: Enhancing Creativity—Brainstorms

60. False
61. True

62. True
63. False

Mastery Test

1. a
2. b
3. c
4. d
5. a
6. b
7. d
8. c
9. c
10. a
11. a
12. b
13. b
14. c

15. b
16. d
17. b
18. c
19. c
20. b
21. b
22. c
23. d
24. b
25. a
26. c
27. a
28. c

29. b
30. d
31. d
32. b
33. c
34. b
35. d
36. a
37. a
38. b
39. c
40. d

1100

Chapter 9: Motivation and Emotion

Solutions

Module 9.1 Overview of Motivation

Motivation—Forces that Push and Pull

Recite and Review

1. alexithymia
2. move
3. terminated or ended
4. need
5. drive
6. response
7. goal
8. response
9. drive
10. incentive
11. incentive
12. incentives
13. biological
14. stimulus
15. learned
16. homeostasis
17. automatic
18. thermostat
19. circadian
20. peak or high point
21. circadian rhythms
22. two (2)
23. west
24. melatonin
25. preadaptation

Part 1: Connections

1. e
2. a
3. f
4. g
5. b
6. h
7. c
8. d

Part 2: Connections

1. e
2. d
3. a
4. b
5. f
6. c

Check Your Memory

1. False
2. True
3. False
4. True
5. True
6. True
7. True
8. False
9. True
10. False
11. True
12. True
13. False
14. True
15. False
16. True
17. False
18. False
19. True
20. False

Critical Thinking Answer

Because of homeostasis: Blood sugar is normally maintained within narrow bounds. While blood sugar levels fluctuate enough to affect hunger, true hypoglycemia is an infrequent medical problem.

Module 9.2 Hunger, Thirst, Pain, and Sex
Hunger—Pardon Me, My Hypothalamus Is Growling

Recite and Review

1. Cannon
2. digestive
3. sexual
4. sugar or glucose
5. lateral
6. ventromedial
7. lateral
8. ventromedial
9. ghrelin
10. ghrelin
11. paraventricular
12. paraventricular nucleus
13. large
14. marijuana
15. glucagon-like peptide 1 (GLP-1)
16. 10 (ten)
17. fat
18. set point
19. leptin
20. diet
21. 65 (sixty-five)
22. obesity
23. external eating
24. leptin
25. less
26. taste aversion
27. classical
28. emotional
29. incentive
30. diet
31. supermarket
32. 25 (twenty-five)
33. lowering, reducing, or slowing
34. Yo-yo
35. raising
36. behavioral
37. 200 (two hundred)
38. diet diary
39. anorexia (nervosa)
40. bulimia (nervosa)
41. dysmorphia
42. body
43. anorexia (nervosa)
44. reinforcing
45. cognitive-behavioral

Part 1: Connections

1. b
2. a
3. c

Part 2: Connections

1. c
2. b
3. f
4. h
5. a
6. g
7. d
8. e

Part 3: Connections

1. f
2. h
3. e
4. a
5. b
6. g
7. c
8. d

Check Your Memory

1. False
2. False
3. False
4. False
5. True
6. True
7. False
8. True
9. False
10. True
11. True
12. True
13. True
14. False
15. True
16. True
17. False
18. True
19. True
20. True
21. False
22. True
23. False
24. True
25. True
26. True
27. False
28. False
29. True
30. True
31. False
32. False
33. True
34. False
35. False
36. True
37. True
38. True
39. True
40. False
41. True
42. True
43. False
44. True
45. True
46. False

Critical Thinking Answer

The time of day can influence eating, especially for externally cued eaters, who tend to get hungry at mealtimes, irrespective of their internal needs for food.

Module 9.2 Hunger, Thirst, Pain, and Sex
Biological Motives Revisited—Thirst, Pain, and Sex

Recite and Review

1. hypothalamus
2. extracellular
3. intracellular
4. extracellular
5. intracellular
6. extracellular
7. intracellular
8. episodic
9. learned
10. sex drive
11. hormones
12. estrus
13. estrogen
14. castration
15. androgens
16. androgens
17. inhibitions
18. decreasing or impairing
19. aphrodisiacs
20. impair or decrease
21. impair or decrease
22. nonhomeostatic
23. deprivation

Connections

1. i
2. f
3. h
4. b
5. g
6. c
7. a
8. e
9. d

Check Your Memory

1. True
2. True
3. False
4. False
5. True
6. False
7. False
8. True
9. True
10. False
11. True
12. True
13. True
14. True
15. False
16. True
17. False
18. True
19. False
20. True

Module 9.3 Arousal, Achievement, and Growth Needs
Stimulus Drives—Skydiving, Horror Movies, and the Fun Zone

Recite and Review

1. stimulus
2. arousal
3. arousal
4. arousal
5. stimulation or arousal
6. high
7. low
8. high
9. moderate
10. inverted-U
11. complexity
12. high
13. low
14. Yerkes-Dodson
15. low
16. high
17. worry
18. hard work
19. overpreparation
20. relaxation
21. emotional (social) support
22. rehearse
23. coping

Connections

1. a
2. e
3. h

4. b
5. f
6. i

7. d
8. c
9. g

Check Your Memory

1. True
2. False
3. False
4. False
5. True
6. True
7. True

8. False
9. True
10. True
11. False
12. False
13. True
14. True

15. True
16. False
17. True
18. True
19. False
20. True

Module 9.3 Arousal, Achievement, and Growth Needs
Learned Motives—The Pursuit of Excellence

Recite and Review

1. social
2. achievement
3. determination
4. ability
5. effort
6. achievement

7. self-confidence
8. attainable
9. visualize
10. progress
11. self-confidence
12. achievement

13. power
14. (lots of) money
15. expert instructor or coach
16. 10 (ten)

Connections

1. d
2. a

3. c
4. b

Check Your Memory

1. True
2. False
3. False
4. False
5. True

6. True
7. True
8. True
9. False
10. True

11. False
12. True
13. True
14. True
15. False

Module 9.3 Arousal, Achievement, and Growth Needs
Motives in Perspective—A View from the Pyramid

Recite and Review

1. self-actualization
2. (Abraham) Maslow
3. physiological or biological
4. prepotent
5. safety and security
6. basic
7. love and belonging
8. esteem and self-esteem
9. deficiency
10. growth
11. meta-needs
12. decay
13. lower
14. security (or safety)
15. intrinsic
16. extrinsic
17. self-determination
18. extrinsically
19. intrinsic
20. intrinsically
21. intrinsic
22. extrinsic

Part 1: Connections

1. d
2. g
3. c
4. a
5. e
6. b
7. f

Part 2: Connections

1. c
2. f
3. e
4. g
5. d
6. a
7. b

Check Your Memory

1. False
2. True
3. False
4. True
5. False
6. True
7. True
8. True
9. False
10. True
11. True
12. False
13. True
14. True
15. False
16. True
17. True
18. False

Critical Thinking Answer

None of the meta-needs are fulfilled by "making more money."

Module 9.4 Emotion and Physiological Arousal
Inside an Emotion—How Do You Feel?

Recite and Review

1. emotion
2. move
3. adaptive
4. physiological changes
5. sympathetic
6. adrenal
7. emotional expressions
8. emotional feelings
9. emotional expressions
10. primary
11. intensity
12. guilt
13. jealousy
14. moods
15. good (happy, positive) mood
16. circadian rhythms
17. (cerebral) hemispheres
18. left hemisphere
19. right hemisphere
20. amygdala
21. amygdala
22. eyes

Connections

1. j
2. h
3. d
4. b
5. k
6. f
7. e
8. a
9. g
10. i
11. c

Check Your Memory

1. False
2. True
3. False
4. False
5. False
6. True
7. False
8. True
9. True
10. True
11. False
12. False
13. True
14. True
15. False
16. False

Module 9.4 Emotion and Physiological Arousal
Physiology and Emotion—Arousal, Sudden Death, and Lying

Recite and Review

1. innate
2. (endocrine) glands
3. sympathetic
4. parasympathetic
5. sympathetic
6. parasympathetic
7. parasympathetic
8. parasympathetic
9. parasympathetic rebound
10. sympathetic
11. 25 (twenty-five)
12. polygraph
13. (William) Marston
14. emotional arousal
15. galvanic skin response (GSR)
16. guilty knowledge
17. 95 (ninety-five)
18. (self-inflicted) pain
19. five (5)
20. (actively) challenge
21. functional MRI (fMRI)
22. a lie

Connections

1. f
2. c
3. g
4. h
5. e
6. a
7. d
8. b

Check Your Memory

1. True
2. False
3. False
4. True
5. False
6. True
7. True
8. True
9. True
10. True
11. False
12. False
13. True
14. True
15. False
16. True
17. False
18. False
19. False
20. True

Critical Thinking Answer

In cultures where there is deep belief in magic or voodoo, a person who thinks that she or he has been cursed may become uncontrollably emotional. After several days of intense terror, the stress of sympathetic arousal may produce a heart attack. Regardless, a parasympathetic rebound is likely. If the rebound is severe enough, it can also lead to physical collapse and death.

Module 9.5 Emotional Expression and Theories of Emotion
Expressing Emotions—Making Faces and Talking Bodies

Recite and Review

1. (Charles) Darwin
2. emotional expressions
3. angry
4. surprise
5. interest
6. smile
7. blend
8. activation (or arousal)
9. learning
10. surprise
11. context
12. anger
13. Asian
14. Western
15. individuals
16. men
17. male
18. anger
19. kinesics
20. emotional tone
21. tension
22. relaxation
23. liking
24. concealed (hidden)

Connections

1. f
2. h
3. e
4. b
5. i
6. c
7. d
8. a
9. g

Check Your Memory

1. True
2. True
3. False
4. True
5. False
6. True
7. True
8. False
9. True
10. False
11. False
12. False
13. True
14. False
15. True
16. False
17. False
18. True
19. True

Module 9.5 Emotional Expression and Theories of Emotion
Theories of Emotion—Several Ways to Fear a Bear

Recite and Review

1. commonsense
2. James-Lange
3. Cannon-Bard
4. thalamus
5. cognitive
6. attribution
7. attributed
8. attribution
9. (Richard) Lazarus
10. emotional appraisal
11. feedback
12. autonomic
13. teeth
14. suppress
15. James-Lange
16. Cannon-Bard
17. (Richard) Lazarus
18. contemporary
19. emotional appraisal
20. adaptive
21. autonomic

Connections

1. d
2. b
3. h
4. f
5. a
6. i
7. c
8. g
9. e

Check Your Memory

1. False	8. True	15. False
2. True	9. True	16. True
3. False	10. True	17. True
4. True	11. True	18. False
5. False	12. False	19. False
6. True	13. True	20. True
7. False	14. True	

Critical Thinking Answer

The James-Lange theory and Schachter's cognitive theory are contradicted by this observation regarding people with spinal injuries. The facial feedback hypothesis helps explain the observation.

Module 9.6 Psychology in Action
Emotional Intelligence—The Fine Art of Self-Control

Recite and Review

1. Aristotle	5. using	10. empty
2. emotional intelligence	6. understanding	11. emotional intelligence
3. intelligence	7. manage	12. learned
4. perceive	8. negative	
	9. positive	

Connections

1. f	4. a	7. e
2. d	5. g	8. c
3. h	6. b	

Check Your Memory

1. True	5. False	9. True
2. False	6. True	10. True
3. True	7. True	11. False
4. True	8. False	12. True

Critical Thinking Answer

There's no single right answer. Rather than being angry, it might be better to reflect on whether friendship or money is more important in life. If you appreciate your friend's virtues, accept that no one is perfect, and reappraise the loan as a gift, you could save a valued relationship and reduce your anger at the same time. Alternately, if you become aware that your friend persistently manipulates other people with emotional appeals for support, it may be worth reappraising your friendship.

Final Survey and Review—Completion

Module 9.1 Overview of Motivation
Motivation—Forces that Push and Pull
1. motivation
2. learned
3. homeostasis
4. east
5. pineal

Module 9.2 Hunger, Thirst, Pain, and Sex
Hunger—Pardon Me, My Hypothalamus Is Growling
6. Washburn
7. satiety
8. ghrelin
9. marijuana
10. set point
11. taste aversion
12. behavioral
13. bulimia (nervosa)

Module 9.2 Biological Motives Revisited—Thirst, Pain, and Sex
14. extracellular
15. episodic
16. androgens
17. nonhomeostatic

Module 9.3 Arousal, Achievement, and Growth Needs
Stimulus Drives—Skydiving, Horror Movies, and the Fun Zone
18. stimulus
19. sensation seeker
20. Yerkes-Dodson
21. coping

Module 9.3 Learned Motives—The Pursuit of Excellence
22. conditioning
23. achievement
24. specific
25. power

Module 9.3 Motives in Perspective—A View from the Pyramid
26. dominant
27. personal appearance
28. self-actualization
29. intrinsically

Module 9.4 Emotion and Physiological Arousal
Inside an Emotion—How Do You Feel?
30. physiological changes
31. (Robert) Plutchik
32. moods
33. amygdala

Module 9.4 Physiology and Emotion—Arousal, Sudden Death, and Lying
34. sympathetic
35. parasympathetic rebound
36. polygraph or lie detector
37. functional MRI (fMRI)

Module 9.5 Emotional Expression and Theories of Emotion
Expressing Emotions—Making Faces and Talking Bodies (Module 9.5)
38. fear
39. attention-rejection
40. Asian
41. kinesics

Theories of Emotion—Several Ways to Fear a Bear (Module 9.5)
42. commonsense
43. hypothalamus
44. cognitive
45. (Paul) Ekman
46. emotional feeling

Module 9.6 Psychology in Action
Emotional Intelligence—The Fine Art of Self-Control
47. (John) Mayer
48. using
49. negative
50. rational

Final Survey and Review—Matching

Module 9.1 Overview of Motivation
1. d
2. i
3. c
4. a
5. g
6. f
7. h
8. b
9. e

Module 9.2 Hunger, Thirst, Pain, and Sex
Part 1:
1. i
2. b
3. f
4. c
5. k
6. a
7. e
8. d
9. l
10. m
11. h
12. g
13. j

Part 2:
1. e
2. d
3. a
4. g
5. f
6. b
7. c

Module 9.3 Arousal, Achievement, and Growth Needs
1. d
2. f
3. h
4. b
5. c
6. i
7. e
8. j
9. a
10. g

Module 9.4 Emotion and Physiological Arousal
1. h
2. j
3. f
4. e
5. a
6. k
7. i
8. c
9. l
10. d
11. g
12. b

Module 9.5 Emotional Expression and Theories of Emotion
1. e
2. b
3. g
4. f
5. a
6. d
7. c

Module 9.6 Psychology in Action: Emotional Intelligence—The Fine Art of Self-Control
1. b
2. d
3. a
4. c

Final Survey and Review—True or False

Module 9.1 Overview of Motivation
Motivation—Forces that Push and Pull (Module 9.1)

1. True
2. False
3. False
4. False
5. False

Module 9.2 Hunger, Thirst, Pain, and Sex
Hunger—Pardon Me, My Hypothalamus Is Growling

6. True
7. False
8. True
9. True
10. True
11. False
12. True
13. False

Module 9.2 Biological Motives Revisited—Thirst, Pain, and Sex

14. True
15. False
16. False
17. True

Module 9.3 Arousal, Achievement, and Growth Needs
Stimulus Drives—Skydiving, Horror Movies, and the Fun Zone

18. True
19. True
20. False
21. True

Module 9.3 Learned Motives—The Pursuit of Excellence

22. False
23. False
24. True
25. True

Module 9.3 Motives in Perspective—A View from the Pyramid

26. False
27. False
28. False
29. True

Module 9.4 Emotion and Physiological Arousal
Inside an Emotion—How Do You Feel?

30. True
31. False
32. True
33. False

Module 9.4 Physiology and Emotion—Arousal, Sudden Death, and Lying

34. True
35. False
36. True
37. True

Module 9.5 Emotional Expression and Theories of Emotion
Expressing Emotions—Making Faces and Talking Bodies

38. True
39. False
40. True
41. True

Module 9.5 Theories of Emotion—Several Ways to Fear a Bear

42. False
43. True
44. True
45. False
46. True

Module 9.6 Psychology in Action
Emotional Intelligence—The Fine Art of Self-Control

47.	True	49.	False
48.	True	50.	False

Mastery Test

1.	b	21.	d
2.	d	22.	a
3.	d	23.	d
4.	c	24.	c
5.	b	25.	a
6.	c	26.	c
7.	b	27.	b
8.	d	28.	c
9.	a	29.	c
10.	b	30.	d
11.	a	31.	c
12.	a	32.	a
13.	b	33.	a
14.	a	34.	d
15.	b	35.	a
16.	a	36.	c
17.	a	37.	a
18.	b	38.	d
19.	d	39.	c
20.	c	40.	a

Chapter 10: Sex, Gender, and Sexuality

Solutions

Module 10.1 Sexual Development and Sexual Orientation
Sexual Development—Circle One: *XX* **or** *XY***?**

Recite and Review

1. transsexual
2. sex
3. gender
4. transsexual
5. genetic
6. hormonal
7. gonadal
8. genital
9. female
10. male
11. father
12. Kleinfelter's
13. Turner's
14. genetic
15. hormones
16. gonads
17. ovaries
18. testes
19. adrenal
20. estrogens
21. androgens
22. testosterone
23. androgen insensitivity
24. intersexual
25. progestin
26. adrogenital
27. primary
28. secondary
29. pituitary
30. secondary
31. menarche
32. ovulation
33. menopause
34. cervix
35. clitoris
36. fallopian tube
37. labia majora
38. labia minora
39. uterus
40. vagina
41. Cowper's gland
42. prostate
43. vas deferens
44. scrotum
45. glans
46. seminal vesicles
47. epididymis
48. urethral orifice

Part 1: Connections

1. h
2. a
3. k
4. j
5. i
6. d
7. f
8. b
9. g
10. l
11. c
12. e

Part 2: Connections

1. e
2. g
3. a
4. j
5. b
6. i
7. f
8. d
9. h
10. c
11. k

Part 3: Connections

1. g
2. d
3. c
4. e
5. h
6. a
7. b
8. f

Part 4: Connections

1. d
2. h
3. f
4. b
5. j
6. l
7. i
8. a
9. e
10. g
11. c
12. k

Part 5: Connections

1. b
2. g
3. e
4. a
5. f
6. i
7. d
8. h
9. c

Part 6: Connections

1. d
2. g
3. i
4. a
5. j
6. k
7. l
8. e
9. c
10. f
11. h
12. b

Check Your Memory

1. False
2. False
3. False
4. False
5. True
6. False
7. False
8. False
9. True
10. True
11. True
12. False
13. True
14. True
15. False
16. True
17. False
18. False
19. True
20. True
21. False
22. True
23. False
24. False
25. True

Critical Thinking Answer

When girls reach puberty early, they may experience heightened social anxiety about their new bodies and increased sexual pressure. When boys reach it late, they may also experience social anxiety.

Module 10.1 Sexual Development and Sexual Orientation
Sexual Orientation—Who Do You Love?

Recite and Review

1. orientation
2. heterosexual
3. homosexual
4. bisexual
5. identity
6. 50 (fifty)
7. X
8. competition
9. prenatal hormonal
10. normal
11. hypothalamus
12. heterosexual
13. heterosexual
14. four (4)
15. childhood
16. families
17. minority
18. homophobia
19. heterosexism
20. stereotypes

Connections

1. e
2. c
3. f
4. a
5. b
6. g
7. d

Check Your Memory

1. False
2. True
3. True
4. True
5. True
6. False
7. False
8. True
9. True
10. True
11. False
12. True
13. True
14. False
15. True
16. False
17. True
18. False
19. False
20. True

Module 10.2 Gender Development, Androgyny, and Gender Variance
Gender Development—Of Manly Men and Girlie Girls

Recite and Review

1. identity
2. sex-type
3. biological biasing
4. left
5. spatial
6. language
7. language
8. similar (alike)
9. averages
10. power
11. label
12. gender role socialization
13. three (3) or four (4)
14. gender role
15. gender role stereotypes
16. aggressive
17. Alzheimer's
18. stereotypes
19. 76 (seventy-six)
20. Latinas
21. status
22. women (female)
23. (Margaret) Mead
24. women (females)
25. male (boy)
26. boys (males)
27. boys (males)
28. father
29. stereotypes
30. instrumental
31. expressive
32. sex-segregated
33. girls (females)
34. boys (males)
35. emotions

Connections

1. f
2. e
3. a
4. g
5. b
6. d
7. c

Check Your Memory

1. True
2. True
3. False
4. False
5. True
6. True
7. False
8. True
9. True
10. False
11. False
12. True
13. True
14. True
15. False
16. False
17. False
18. True
19. True
20. False
21. True
22. True
23. False
24. True
25. False
26. False
27. True

Critical Thinking Answer

Children segregate themselves into same-sex groups during much of childhood, which limits conflicts between male and female patterns of behavior. However, as children move into adolescence they begin to spend more time with members of the opposite sex. This brings the dominant, competitive style of boys into conflict with the nurturing, expressive style of girls, often placing girls at a disadvantage.

Module 10.2 Gender Development, Androgyny, and Gender Variance
Androgyny—Are You Masculine, Feminine, or Androgynous?

Recite and Review

1. masculine
2. feminine
3. androgynous
4. Sex Role
5. man-woman
6. 50 (fifty)
7. androgynous
8. situation
9. androgynous
10. gender-appropriate
11. emotional support
12. masculine (or manly)
13. feminine (or girlie-girl)
14. androgynous
15. masculine
16. feminine
17. androgynous
18. instrumental
19. Mexican
20. Asian

Connections

1. c
2. d
3. a
4. b

Check Your Memory

1. True
2. False
3. True
4. False
5. True
6. True
7. True
8. False
9. True
10. True
11. False
12. False
13. False
14. False
15. True

Critical Thinking Answer

Yes. Being androgynous means having both masculine and feminine traits as they are defined within one's culture.

Module 10.2 Gender Development, Androgyny, and Gender Variance
When Sex and Gender Do Not Match—The Binary Busters

Recite and Review

1. transsexuality
2. variant
3. gender-appropriate
4. gender identity
5. sex reassignment
6. hormone
7. happy
8. sex (re)assignment
9. transsexual

Connections

1. c
2. b
3. a

Check Your Memory

1. False
2. True
3. True
4. True
5. False
6. False
7. False
8. True
9. True
10. True

Module 10.3 Sexual Behavior, Response, and Attitudes
Sexual Behavior—Mapping the Erogenous Zones

Recite and Review

1. (Alfred) Kinsey
2. five (5) months
3. incest
4. consensual
5. erogenous zones
6. mental
7. sexual script
8. sexual scripts
9. mind (or brain)
10. casual
11. friends with benefits
12. hook-up
13. traditional
14. oral
15. unsafe
16. depressed
17. equal
18. emotional closeness
19. physical
20. subjective feelings
21. subjective feelings
22. 18 (eighteen)
23. later
24. sex drive
25. testosterone
26. depressant
27. reduces (decreases, impairs)
28. aphrodisiacs
29. impair (decrease, reduce)
30. impair (decrease, reduce)
31. castration
32. abolish (end)
33. sterilization
34. vasectomy
35. regularity
36. testosterone
37. masturbation
38. 70 (seventy)
39. psychosexual
40. self-abuse

Connections

1. f
2. g
3. e
4. a
5. h
6. c
7. d
8. b

Check Your Memory

1. True
2. True
3. False
4. True
5. False
6. True
7. True
8. True
9. True
10. True
11. False
12. False
13. True
14. False
15. False
16. True
17. True
18. True
19. False
20. False
21. True
22. False
23. False
24. False
25. True
26. True
27. True
28. False
29. True
30. False

Module 10.3 Sexual Behavior, Response, and Attitudes
Human Sexual Response—Sexual Interactions

Recite and Review

1. (Virginia) Johnson
2. resolution
3. excitement
4. plateau
5. orgasm
6. clitoral
7. clitoris
8. resolution
9. plateau
10. excitement
11. orgasm
12. ejaculation
13. refractory
14. slowly
15. compatibility
16. three (3)
17. simultaneous orgasm
18. foreplay
19. zero
20. multiple

Connections

1. g
2. f
3. a
4. i
5. d
6. c
7. e
8. b
9. h

Check Your Memory

1. True
2. False
3. False
4. True
5. True
6. True
7. True
8. False
9. True
10. False
11. False
12. True
13. True
14. False
15. True

Module 10.3 Sexual Behavior, Response, and Attitudes
Atypical Sexual Behavior—Trench Coats, Whips, Leathers, and Lace

Recite and Review

1. deviant
2. private
3. compulsive
4. paraphilias
5. pedophilia
6. exhibitionism
7. voyeurism
8. frotteurism
9. fetishism
10. transvestic fetishism
11. masochism
12. sadism
13. exhibitionism (or flashing)
14. male
15. fondling
16. risk-taking
17. No
18. tell
19. tactics
20. abuser's
21. phobias
22. manhood
23. male
24. married
25. immaturity
26. fetishists
27. voyeurism
28. compulsive

Connections

1. d
2. h
3. f
4. e
5. i
6. a
7. c
8. g
9. b

Check Your Memory

1. True
2. True
3. False
4. False
5. False
6. True
7. False
8. True
9. True
10. False
11. True
12. True
13. True
14. True
15. True
16. False
17. True
18. True
19. False
20. True
21. True
22. True
23. False
24. True
25. True

Module 10.3 Sexual Behavior, Response, and Attitudes
Attitudes and Sexual Behavior—The Changing Sexual Landscape

Recite and Review

1. birth control (or contraception)
2. 75 (seventy-five)
3. 70 (seventy)
4. larger (or greater)
5. others
6. four (4)
7. declining (or decreasing)
8. the United States
9. delaying
10. supervision
11. transmitted diseases
12. four (4)
13. love (or affection)
14. marriage
15. double standard
16. double standard
17. fewer
18. the same age
19. condoms
20. say no
21. oversexualized
22. sexualization
23. oral
24. intellectual
25. interests
26. underreported
27. marital
28. acquaintance (or date)
29. rape
30. gender role
31. stereotype
32. rape-supportive
33. myths
34. high
35. myths
36. rape myths
37. forcible
38. debase
39. after
40. homosexual

Connections

1. f
2. a
3. h
4. g
5. b
6. c
7. d
8. e

Check Your Memory

1. True
2. True
3. True
4. False
5. False
6. False
7. True
8. False
9. True
10. True
11. False
12. False
13. False
14. True
15. True
16. True
17. True
18. True
19. False
20. True
21. True
22. True
23. False
24. True
25. True
26. True
27. False
28. False
29. True
30. True
31. True
32. True

Critical Thinking Answer

Through marriage laws and customs, human societies tend to foster enduring bonds between sexual partners to help ensure that children are cared for and not just produced.

Module 10.3 Sexual Behavior, Response, and Attitudes
STDs and Safer Sex—Choice, Risk, and Responsibility

Recite and Review

1. sexually transmitted disease (STD)
2. asymptomatic
3. four (4)
4. gonorrhea
5. chlamydia
6. syphilis
7. genital warts
8. hepatitis B
9. genital herpes
10. hepatitis B
11. HIV/AIDS
12. pelvic inflammatory disease
13. HIV
14. immune
15. 10 (ten)
16. six (6)
17. fluids
18. casual
19. 25 (twenty-five)
20. shared
21. blood transfusions
22. (behavioral) risk factors (or risky behaviors)
23. safer sex
24. three (3)
25. safer sex
26. 75 (seventy-five)
27. mistrust
28. contraceptives

Connections

1. j
2. h
3. a
4. c
5. g
6. b
7. i
8. f
9. d
10. e

Check Your Memory

1. True
2. True
3. False
4. True
5. False
6. True
7. True
8. False
9. True
10. True
11. True
12. False
13. True
14. False
15. True
16. True
17. False
18. True
19. True
20. False

Critical Thinking Answer

More comprehensive programs are actually more effective at reducing STDs and unwanted pregnancies among adolescents.

Module 10.4 Psychology in Action: Sexual Problems—When Pleasure Fades

Recite and Review

1. decline
2. communication
3. five (5)
4. feelings
5. touch and ask
6. mutual
7. numbers
8. intimacy
9. communication
10. pleasure
11. sexual desire
12. communication
13. whining
14. big freeze
15. gunnysacking
16. sensitivity
17. blame
18. fair
19. mind-reading
20. intimacy
21. interdependent
22. dysfunctions
23. troubled
24. aversion
25. arousal
26. impotence
27. primary

28. secondary	35. orgasm	41. dyspareunia
29. 25 (twenty-five)	36. overcontrol	42. vaginismus
30. organic	37. anorgasmic	43. phobic
31. psychogenic	38. orgasmic	44. desensitization
32. primary	39. premature	45. premature
33. secondary	ejaculation	ejaculation
34. sensate focus	40. squeeze	

Part 1: Connections

1. f	5. j	9. g
2. h	6. c	10. b
3. a	7. i	
4. e	8. d	

Part 2: Connections

1. i	5. h	9. c
2. g	6. j	10. a
3. e	7. b	
4. f	8. d	

Check Your Memory

1. False	15. False	29. False
2. False	16. False	30. True
3. True	17. True	31. True
4. False	18. True	32. True
5. False	19. False	33. True
6. True	20. True	34. True
7. False	21. True	35. False
8. True	22. True	36. False
9. False	23. False	37. True
10. True	24. False	38. False
11. True	25. True	39. True
12. False	26. True	40. True
13. True	27. True	
14. False	28. True	

Critical Thinking Answer

Contrary to mass media portrayals of sexy singles, married couples have the most sex and are most likely to have orgasms when they do. Greater opportunity, plus familiarity with a partner's needs and preferences probably account for these findings.

Final Survey and Review—Completion

Module 10.1 Sexual Development and Sexual Orientation
Sexual Development—Circle One: *XX* or *XY*?

1. genetic	4. Kleinfelter's	7. uterus
2. transsexual	5. adrenal	8. Cowper's
3. gonadal	6. secondary	

Module 10.1 Sexual Orientation—Who Do You Love?

9. bisexual
10. X
11. prenatal hormonal
12. heterosexual
13. heterosexism

Module 10.2 Gender Development, Androgyny, and Gender Variance
Gender Development—Of Manly Men and Girlie Girls

14. right
15. stereotypes
16. men (males)
17. female (girl)
18. instrumental
19. male (boys)

Module 10.2 Androgyny—Are You Masculine, Feminine, or Androgynous?

20. androgyny
21. neutral
22. situation
23. emotional

Module 10.2 When Sex and Gender Do Not Match—The Binary Busters

24. variant
25. gender identity
26. sex reassignment

Module 10.3 Sexual Behavior, Response, and Attitudes
Sexual Behavior—Mapping the Erogenous Zones

27. four (4) months
28. friends with benefits
29. erogenous
30. aphrodisiac
31. tubal ligation
32. opportunity
33. masturbation

Module 10.3 Human Sexual Response—Sexual Interactions

34. (William) Masters
35. plateau
36. femininity
37. quickly

Module 10.3 Atypical Sexual Behavior—Trench Coats, Whips, Leathers, and Lace

38. destructive
39. voyeurism
40. pedophilia
41. exhibitionism

Module 10.3 Attitudes and Sexual Behavior—The Changing Sexual Landscape

42. sexual attitudes
43. seven (7)
44. double standard
45. oversexualized
46. myth

Module 10.3 STDs and Safer Sex—Choice, Risk, and Responsibility

47. syphilis
48. HIV/AIDS
49. hepatitis B
50. six (6)

1122

Module 10.4 Psychology in Action: Sexual Problems—When Pleasure Fades

51. anticipation
52. defensiveness
53. gunnysacking
54. mind-reading
55. persistent
56. primary
57. vaginismus

Final Survey and Review—Matching

Module 10.1 Sexual Development and Sexual Orientation
Part 1:
1. i
2. h
3. k
4. m
5. c
6. d
7. f
8. b
9. j
10. l
11. g
12. a
13. e

Part 2:
1. b
2. i
3. k
4. f
5. j
6. a
7. d
8. g
9. l
10. e
11. c
12. h

Module 10.2 Gender Development, Androgyny, and Gender Variance
1. f
2. e
3. h
4. g
5. b
6. i
7. c
8. d
9. a

Module 10.3 Sexual Behavior, Response, and Attitudes
Part 1:
1. l
2. d
3. g
4. a
5. m
6. c
7. j
8. e
9. h
10. k
11. i
12. b
13. f

Part 2:
1. e
2. d
3. a
4. c
5. g
6. b
7. f

Module 10.4 Psychology in Action: Sexual Problems—When Pleasure Fades

1. h	5. g	9. e
2. f	6. i	10. d
3. b	7. k	11. a
4. j	8. c	

Final Survey and Review—True or False

Module 10.1 Sexual Development and Sexual Orientation
Sexual Development—Circle One: *XX* or *XY*?

1. True	4. True	7. False
2. True	5. True	8. False
3. False	6. False	

Module 10.1 Sexual Orientation—Who Do You Love?

9. True	11. False	13. False
10. True	12. False	

Module 10.2 Gender Development, Androgyny, and Gender Variance
Gender Development—Of Manly Men and Girlie Girls

14. True	16. True	18. False
15. True	17. False	19. True

Module 10.2 Androgyny—Are You Masculine, Feminine, or Androgynous?

20. False	22. True
21. True	23. True

Module 10.2 When Sex and Gender Do Not Match—The Binary Busters

24. False	25. True	26. True

Module 10.3 Sexual Behavior, Response, and Attitudes
Sexual Behavior—Mapping the Erogenous Zones

27. True	30. False	33. True
28. True	31. True	
29. True	32. False	

Human Sexual Response—Sexual Interactions

34. False	36. False
35. False	37. True

Module 10.3 Atypical Sexual Behavior—Trench Coats, Whips, Leathers, and Lace

38. False	40. True
39. False	41. True

Module 10.3 Attitudes and Sexual Behavior—The Changing Sexual Landscape

42. True	44. True	46. True
43. True	45. False	

1124

Module 10.3 STDs and Safer Sex—Choice, Risk, and Responsibility

47. True
48. False
49. True
50. False

Module 10.4 Psychology in Action: Sexual Problems—When Pleasure Fades

51. True
52. True
53. False
54. True
55. False
56. False
57. True

Mastery Test

1. a
2. b
3. b
4. d
5. b
6. b
7. a
8. a
9. d
10. b
11. c
12. a
13. d
14. b
15. d
16. c
17. a
18. a
19. b
20. d
21. c
22. a
23. b
24. c
25. d
26. c
27. a
28. d
29. a
30. b
31. d
32. b
33. d
34. b
35. a
36. d
37. b
38. a
39. b
40. d

Chapter 11: Personality

Solutions

Module 11.1 Overview of Personality
The Psychology of Personality—Do You Have Personality?

Recite and Review

1. personality
2. character
3. traits
4. personality
5. behavior
6. predict
7. type
8. (Carl) Jung
9. extrovert
10. introvert
11. traits
12. oversimplify
13. A
14. B
15. maladaptive
16. self-concept
17. experiences
18. self-esteem
19. self-esteem
20. individualism
21. collectivism
22. criticism
23. arrogance
24. self-esteem
25. theory
26. (Hans) Eysenck
27. melancholic
28. choleric
29. phlegmatic
30. sanguine
31. trait
32. psychodynamic
33. learning
34. mental processes
35. humanistic
36. usefulness
37. humanistic
38. psychoanalytic
39. self-reinforcement
40. humanistic
41. superego
42. psychoanalytic
43. humanistic
44. trait
45. psychoanalytic
46. behavioristic
47. humanistic
48. neutral

Part 1: Connections

1. j
2. f
3. e
4. h
5. i
6. b
7. a
8. k
9. l
10. c
11. d
12. g

Part 2: Connections

1. b
2. e
3. g
4. c
5. a
6. h
7. d
8. f

Check Your Memory

1. True	14. True	27. True
2. True	15. True	28. True
3. False	16. False	29. True
4. True	17. False	30. False
5. True	18. True	31. True
6. True	19. True	32. False
7. False	20. False	33. True
8. True	21. False	34. False
9. True	22. False	35. False
10. False	23. True	36. True
11. True	24. False	37. False
12. True	25. False	38. True
13. True	26. True	

Critical Thinking Answer

Memory is highly selective; and long-term memories are often distorted by recent information with such properties adding to the ability of self-concept to be molded.

Module 11.2 Trait Theories
The Trait Approach—Describe Yourself in 18,000 Words or Less

Recite and Review

1. trait	13. (Gordon) Allport	26. agreeableness
2. factors	14. common	27. conscientiousness
3. Five Factor	15. individual	28. neuroticism
4. interrelate	16. cardinal	29. openness to
5. biological	17. central	experience
predispositions	18. secondary	30. extroversion
6. situations	19. surface	31. agreeableness
7. types	20. source	32. perfectionism
8. introversion	21. factor analysis	33. excellence
9. reflective	22. trait profile	34. chemicals
10. rebellious	23. (Raymond) Cattell	35. conscientiousness
11. conventional	24. neuroticism	
12. rhythmic	25. extroversion	

Part 1: Connections

1. g	4. f	7. a
2. d	5. e	
3. b	6. c	

Part 2: Connections

1. d	4. f	7. h
2. g	5. a	8. e
3. b	6. c	

Check Your Memory

1. False
2. False
3. True
4. True
5. False
6. False
7. True
8. False
9. False
10. True
11. False
12. False
13. False
14. True
15. True
16. False
17. False
18. True
19. True
20. True
21. False
22. True
23. True
24. True
25. False

Critical Thinking Answer

In one study conscientiousness was positively related to academic performance, as you might expect. Students high in neuroticism were also better academic performers, but only if they were not too stressed.

Module 11.3 Psychoanalytic Theory
Psychoanalytic Theory—Id Came to Me in a Dream

Recite and Review

1. psychoanalytic
2. id
3. pleasure
4. psyche
5. libido
6. Eros
7. Thanatos
8. ego
9. reality
10. superego
11. conscience
12. ego ideal
13. superego
14. guilt
15. pride
16. superego
17. neurotic
18. moral
19. ego defense
20. unconscious
21. symbolic
22. conscious
23. limbic
24. preconscious
25. Freudian slip
26. psychosexual
27. erogenous zone
28. fixations
29. oral
30. oral-dependent
31. oral-aggressive
32. anal
33. anal-retentive
34. anal-expulsive
35. phallic
36. Oedipus
37. castration
38. conscience
39. Electra
40. latency
41. genital
42. love
43. toilet
44. latency
45. conscience
46. sexuality
47. fantasies
48. predictions

Part 1: Connections

1. f
2. a
3. h
4. d
5. b
6. i
7. k
8. j
9. c
10. e
11. g

Part 2: Connections

1. d
2. b
3. g
4. k
5. e
6. m
7. c
8. j
9. a
10. l
11. h
12. i
13. f

Part 3: Connections

1. b
2. f
3. g
4. d
5. a
6. e
7. h
8. c

Check Your Memory

1. True
2. False
3. False
4. False
5. True
6. False
7. False
8. True
9. False
10. True
11. True
12. False
13. True
14. True
15. True
16. False
17. True
18. True
19. True
20. False
21. True
22. False
23. True
24. False
25. True
26. True
27. True
28. True
29. True
30. False
31. False
32. False
33. True
34. True
35. True

Critical Thinking Answer

A psychoanalytic theorist would say that it is because the bottle rekindles oral conflicts and feelings of vulnerability and dependence.

Module 11.4 Humanistic Theories
Humanistic Theory—Peak Experiences and Personal Growth

Recite and Review

1. potentials
2. good (or positive)
3. free choice
4. nature
5. choices
6. subjective experience
7. effective
8. self-actualization
9. self-actualizer
10. task centering
11. nonhostile
12. perceptions
13. authorities
14. tolerance
15. spontaneous
16. innocence of vision
17. peak experiences
18. subjective
19. process
20. wishful
21. calling
22. responsible
23. positive
24. justice
25. temperance
26. transcendence
27. curiosity
28. fully functioning
29. acceptance
30. self
31. self-image
32. incongruence
33. authentic
34. ideal self
35. ego ideal
36. matched
37. possible selves
38. agreeableness
39. conscientiousness
40. emotionally stable
41. elaborate
42. narrative
43. information
44. conditions of worth
45. self-regard
46. organismic valuing
47. unconditional positive regard

Part 1: Connections

1. c
2. e
3. h
4. d
5. a
6. b
7. f
8. g

Part 2: Connections

1. a
2. h
3. d
4. i
5. j
6. f
7. b
8. c
9. e
10. g

Check Your Memory

1. True
2. True
3. False
4. True
5. False
6. True
7. False
8. True
9. True
10. True
11. False
12. False
13. False
14. True
15. True
16. True
17. False
18. False
19. True
20. False
21. True
22. False
23. False
24. True
25. False
26. True
27. False
28. True
29. True
30. False
31. False
32. True
33. False
34. False
35. True

Critical Thinking Answer

Career decisions almost always involve, in part, picturing oneself occupying various occupational roles. Such possible "future selves" play a role in many of the major decisions we make.

Module 11.5 Behavioral and Social Learning Theories
Learning Theories of Personality—Habit I Seen You Before?

Recite and Review

1. learning
2. research
3. learned
4. learned behavior
5. observational
6. traits
7. situational
8. 17 (seventeen)
9. situations
10. situations
11. habits
12. reward
13. drive
14. cues
15. social
16. (Julian) Rotter
17. expectancy
18. psychological situation
19. reinforcement
20. self-efficacy
21. self-reinforcement
22. self-reinforcement
23. self-reinforcement
24. six (6)
25. drives
26. reinforcement
27. critical situations
28. feeding
29. toilet
30. power
31. gender roles
32. identification
33. imitation
34. vicariously
35. outcomes
36. indirectly

Part 1: Connections

1.	e	4.	d	7.	f
2.	h	5.	a	8.	g
3.	b	6.	c		

Part 2: Connections

1.	g	4.	e	7.	d
2.	c	5.	a	8.	h
3.	f	6.	i	9.	b

Check Your Memory

1.	True	10.	True	19.	True
2.	True	11.	False	20.	False
3.	False	12.	False	21.	False
4.	True	13.	False	22.	False
5.	True	14.	True	23.	True
6.	False	15.	True	24.	False
7.	False	16.	False	25.	True
8.	False	17.	False	26.	True
9.	True	18.	True	27.	True

Critical Thinking Answer

Rotter's concept of *reinforcement value* is closely related to a motivational principle of incentive value.

Module 11.5 Behavioral and Social Learning Theories
Traits and Situations—The Great Debate

Recite and Review

1. nurture
2. psychoanalytic
3. hereditary (inherited)
4. humanistic
5. temperament
6. three (3)
7. 50 (fifty)
8. agreeable
9. temperaments
10. behavioral genetics
11. identical
12. similar
13. historical times
14. confirmation bias
15. 50 (fifty)
16. environment
17. personality traits (or lasting personal dispositions)
18. external situations (circumstances)
19. external situations (circumstances)
20. personality traits (or lasting personal dispositions)
21. consistent
22. sudden
23. minor irritation or frustration
24. amnesia
25. trait-situation

Connections

1.	a	3.	d	5.	b
2.	f	4.	e	6.	c

Check Your Memory

1. False
2. False
3. True
4. True
5. False
6. True
7. False
8. True
9. True
10. False
11. True
12. False
13. True
14. True
15. False
16. False
17. False
18. False
19. True
20. False
21. True
22. True
23. True
24. False
25. True

Module 11.6 Personality Assessment
Personality Assessment—Psychological Yardsticks

Recite and Review

1. measure
2. interview
3. unstructured interview
4. structured interview
5. body language (kinesics)
6. biases
7. halo
8. interview
9. direct observation
10. rating scale
11. behavioral
12. sexual
13. situational
14. situational
15. personality questionnaires
16. objective
17. standardized
18. reliable
19. validity
20. validity
21. questionnaire
22. Minnesota Multiphasic Personality Inventory (MMPI-2)
23. patterns
24. correlated
25. profile
26. validity
27. psychopathic deviate
28. hysteria
29. schizophrenia
30. label
31. overt
32. projective
33. life experiences
34. fake
35. Rorschach Inkblot
36. content
37. (Henry) Murray
38. story
39. social relationships
40. lowest
41. low
42. test battery
43. projective

Part 1: Connections

1. c
2. f
3. g
4. e
5. b
6. h
7. d
8. a

Part 2: Connections

1. c
2. g
3. i
4. a
5. d
6. h
7. b
8. e
9. f

Part 3: Connections

1. c
2. k
3. h
4. b
5. j
6. d
7. l
8. a
9. f
10. i
11. e
12. g

Check Your Memory

1. True
2. True
3. False
4. False
5. True
6. True
7. True
8. False
9. True
10. True
11. True
12. False
13. True
14. False
15. True
16. True
17. False
18. True
19. True
20. False
21. False
22. False
23. False
24. True
25. True
26. True
27. True
28. True
29. True
30. False
31. False
32. True
33. False
34. True
35. True
36. False
37. True
38. True

Critical Thinking Answers

1. Because of trait–situation interactions, a person may not behave in a normal fashion while being evaluated in an interview.

2. Psychodynamic theorist would be most interested because projective testing is designed to uncover unconscious thoughts, feelings, and conflicts.

Module 11.7 Psychology in Action
Barriers and Bridges—Understanding Shyness

Recite and Review

1. shyness
2. animation
3. social anxiety
4. social
5. social anxiety
6. evaluation
7. self-defeating bias
8. novel or unfamiliar
9. focus of attention
10. private
11. public
12. misperceive
13. label
14. personality trait
15. external situations
16. self-esteem
17. defeating
18. self-defeating (or unrealistic, unproductive)
19. practice
20. facial expressions
21. open-ended
22. open-ended
23. risks

Connections

1. c
2. e
3. f
4. a
5. b
6. d

1134

Check Your Memory

1. False	10. False	19. True
2. False	11. True	20. True
3. True	12. False	21. True
4. False	13. True	22. True
5. True	14. True	23. True
6. True	15. True	24. False
7. False	16. False	25. True
8. False	17. False	
9. True	18. True	

Critical Thinking Answer

Trait-situation interactions explain Vonda's shyness.

Final Survey and Review—Completion

Module 11.1 Overview of Personality
The Psychology of Personality—Do You Have Personality?

1. behavior
2. extrovert
3. heart attack
4. concept
5. Western
6. sanguine
7. trait
8. expectations

Module 11.2 Trait Theories
The Trait Approach—Describe Yourself in 18,000 Words or Less

9. music
10. secondary
11. (Raymond) Cattell
12. agreeableness
13. conscientiousness

Module 11.3 Psychoanalytic Theory
Psychoanalytic Theory—Id Came to Me in a Dream

14. life
15. ego
16. ego ideal
17. preconscious
18. anal
19. phallic
20. feeding

Module 11.4 Humanistic Theories
Humanistic Theory—Peak Experiences and Personal Growth

21. humanists
22. (Abraham) Maslow
23. humor
24. peak
25. temperance
26. incongruent
27. possible selves
28. conditions of worth

Module 11.5 Behavioral and Social Learning Theories
Learning Theories of Personality—Habit I Seen You Before?

29. behavioral
30. drives
31. reinforcement value
32. self-efficacy
33. reinforcement
34. sex
35. identification

Module 11.5 Traits and Situations—The Great Debate

36. trait
37. personality traits
    (or lasting
    personal
    disposition)
38. confirmation bias
39. overcontrolled
40. trait-situation

Module 11.6 Personality Assessment
Personality Assessment—Psychological Yardsticks

41. interview
42. rating scale
43. situational
44. objective
45. validity
46. psychasthenia
47. Thematic
    Apperception Test
    (TAT)

Module 11.7 Psychology in Action
Barriers and Bridges—Understanding Shyness

48. eye contact
49. social anxiety
50. self-consciousness
51. defeating
52. open-ended

Final Survey and Review—Matching

Module 11.1 Overview of Personality

1. d
2. c
3. h
4. f
5. g
6. e
7. a
8. i
9. b

Module 11.2 Trait Theories

1. g
2. f
3. a
4. h
5. c
6. e
7. i
8. b
9. j
10. d

Module 11.3 Psychoanalytic Theory
Part 1:

1. l
2. j
3. h
4. d
5. b
6. i
7. c
8. f
9. k
10. a
11. m
12. e
13. g

Part 2:

1. k
2. i
3. g
4. d
5. e
6. a
7. c
8. j
9. m
10. l
11. h
12. b
13. f

Module 11.4 Humanistic Theories

1. a	5. f	9. e
2. c	6. k	10. g
3. d	7. b	11. h
4. i	8. j	

Module 11.5 Behavioral and Social Learning Theories

1. f	6. b	11. i
2. l	7. e	12. g
3. c	8. k	13. a
4. d	9. m	
5. j	10. h	

Module 11.6 Personality Assessment

Part 1:

1. h	4. g	7. i
2. c	5. e	8. d
3. f	6. b	9. a

Part 2:

1. b	5. a	9. f
2. d	6. e	10. g
3. h	7. i	
4. j	8. c	

Module 11.7 Psychology in Action: Barriers and Bridges—Understanding Shyness

1. e	3. a	5. c
2. d	4. b	

Final Survey and Review—True or False

Module 11.1 Overview of Personality

The Psychology of Personality—Do You Have Personality?

1. False	4. True	7. False
2. False	5. False	8. False
3. True	6. True	

Module 11.2 Trait Theories

The Trait Approach—Describe Yourself in 18,000 Words or Less

9. True	11. True	13. False
10. True	12. False	

Module 11.3 Psychoanalytic Theory

Psychoanalytic Theory—Id Came to Me in a Dream

14. True	17. False	20. True
15. True	18. False	
16. False	19. False	

Module 11.4 Humanistic Theories
Humanistic Theory—Peak Experiences and Personal Growth

21. False	24. False	27. False
22. True	25. False	28. True
23. True	26. True	

Module 11.5 Behavioral and Social Learning Theories
Learning Theories of Personality—Habit I Seen You Before?

29. False	32. True	35. True
30. True	33. True	
31. False	34. True	

Module 11.5 Traits and Situations—The Great Debate

36. True	38. False	40. False
37. True	39. True	

Module 11.6 Personality Assessment
Personality Assessment—Psychological Yardsticks

41. False	44. True	47. True
42. False	45. True	
43. False	46. False	

Module 11.7 Psychology in Action
Barriers and Bridges—Understanding Shyness

48. False	50. True	52. False
49. True	51. True	

Mastery Test

1. a	15. b	29. a
2. d	16. b	30. b
3. c	17. c	31. d
4. b	18. d	32. c
5. c	19. c	33. d
6. b	20. b	34. a
7. a	21. b	35. b
8. b	22. a	36. d
9. b	23. a	37. c
10. a	24. c	38. a
11. a	25. d	39. d
12. c	26. b	40. b
13. b	27. c	
14. d	28. b	

Chapter 12: Health, Stress, and Coping

Solutions

Module 12.1 Health Psychology
Health Psychology—Here's to Your Good Health

Recite and Review

1. illness
2. health
3. unhealthy
4. health
5. behavioral medicine
6. accidents
7. lifestyle
8. behavioral risk
9. obesity (or being overweight)
10. behavioral risk
11. 65 (sixty-five)
12. heart
13. exercise
14. 18 or 19 (eighteen or nineteen)
15. alcohol
16. disease-prone
17. depression
18. multiple
19. infectious
20. health
21. hypertension (high blood pressure)
22. health-promoting
23. 65 (sixty-five)
24. Mediterranean
25. 30 (thirty)
26. one or two (1 or 2)
27. social
28. social networks
29. 19 (nineteen)
30. contagion
31. smoking
32. prevention
33. one (1)
34. refusal skills
35. life skills
36. community health
37. role models
38. wellness
39. psychologically
40. meaningful

Connections

1. c
2. a
3. e
4. i
5. k
6. b
7. g
8. f
9. j
10. d
11. l
12. h

Check Your Memory

1. True
2. True
3. True
4. False
5. False
6. True
7. False
8. True
9. True
10. True
11. False
12. True
13. True
14. True
15. False
16. True
17. True
18. True
19. False
20. False
21. False
22. False
23. True
24. True
25. True
26. True
27. False
28. True
29. True
30. False

Critical Thinking Answer

Many of the health payoffs are delayed by months or years, greatly lessening the immediate rewards for healthful behavior.

1139

Module 12.2 Stress, Frustration, and Conflict
Stress—Thrill or Threat?

Recite and Review

1. severe
2. managed or controlled
3. dead
4. stress
5. eustress
6. emotion
7. short-term
8. (Hans) Selye
9. alarm
10. pituitary
11. alarm
12. resistance
13. resistance
14. exhaustion
15. emotional
16. behavioral
17. physical
18. adrenal
19. lymph nodes
20. psychoneuro-immunology
21. inflammation
22. strengthen
23. stress management
24. stressor
25. unpredictable
26. less
27. pressure
28. control
29. undervalued
30. burnout
31. helping
32. passionate
33. control
34. burnout
35. threat
36. primary
37. secondary
38. Greeks
39. relatively poor
40. control
41. competence
42. emotion-focused
43. problem-focused
44. problem-focused
45. emotion-focused
46. traumatic
47. depression
48. stress

Part 1: Connections

1. b
2. f
3. g
4. a
5. h
6. i
7. c
8. d
9. e

Part 2: Connections

1. g
2. i
3. j
4. c
5. b
6. a
7. h
8. d
9. f
10. e

Check Your Memory

1. True
2. False
3. True
4. True
5. False
6. False
7. False
8. False
9. True
10. False
11. True
12. False
13. True
14. False
15. True
16. False
17. True
18. False
19. False
20. True
21. False
22. True
23. False
24. True
25. True
26. False
27. True
28. True
29. False
30. False
31. True
32. False
33. True
34. True
35. False
36. False
37. True
38. False
39. False
40. True

Critical Thinking Answer

There is no correct answer here because individual stress reactions vary greatly. However, the secondary appraisal of a situation often determines just how stressful it is. Feeling incapable of coping is very threatening.

Module 12.2 Stress, Frustration, and Conflict
Frustration—Blind Alleys and Lead Balloons

Recite and Review

1. goals
2. external
3. external
4. social
5. nonsocial
6. social
7. frustration
8. repeated
9. personal
10. aggression
11. persistence
12. displaced
13. retaliate
14. scapegoating
15. escape
16. escape
17. emotion
18. stereotyped
19. personal
20. imagined

Connections

1. j
2. c
3. a
4. f
5. i
6. b
7. k
8. e
9. h
10. d
11. g

Check Your Memory

1. False
2. False
3. True
4. False
5. False
6. True
7. False
8. True
9. False
10. True
11. False
12. True
13. True
14. True
15. False
16. True
17. True
18. True
19. False
20. True
21. True
22. True

Critical Thinking Answer

If a response ends discomfort, the response has been negatively reinforced. This makes it more likely to occur in the future.

Module 12.2 Stress, Frustration, and Conflict
Conflict—Yes, No, Yes, No, Yes, No, Well, Maybe

Recite and Review

1. contradictory or incompatible
2. approach-approach
3. approach-approach
4. avoidance-avoidance
5. freezing
6. leaving the field
7. approach-avoidance
8. ambivalence
9. partial
10. double approach-avoidance
11. vacillation
12. multiple approach-avoidance
13. hasty
14. partially
15. compromises
16. indecision

Connections

1. c
2. j
3. g
4. f
5. i
6. a
7. b
8. k
9. e
10. d
11. h

Check Your Memory

1. False
2. False
3. True
4. True
5. False
6. True
7. False
8. True
9. False
10. True
11. True
12. True
13. False
14. True
15. True
16. True

Module 12.3 Defenses, Helplessness, and Depression
Psychological Defense—Mental Judo?

Recite and Review

1. anxiety
2. emotion
3. psychodynamic (or psychoanalytic)
4. defense mechanism
5. (Sigmund) Freud
6. unconsciously
7. denial
8. repression
9. fantasy
10. identification
11. intellectualization
12. isolation
13. reaction formation
14. reaction formation
15. regression
16. projection
17. rationalization
18. defense mechanisms
19. compensation
20. compensation
21. sublimation
22. sublimation

Connections

1. l
2. i
3. g
4. j
5. c
6. m
7. f
8. n
9. d
10. h
11. b
12. k
13. e
14. a

Check Your Memory

1. False
2. True
3. False
4. False
5. True
6. True
7. False
8. False
9. True
10. False
11. True
12. True
13. False
14. True
15. True
16. False
17. True
18. False
19. True
20. True
21. True
22. False

Module 12.3 Defenses, Helplessness, and Depression
Learned Helplessness—Is There Hope?

Recite and Review

1. died
2. learned helplessness
3. (Martin) Seligman
4. zero
5. uncontrollable
6. repeated
7. unavoidable
8. procrastinate
9. general
10. specific
11. depression
12. hope
13. mastery training
14. Outward Bound
15. hope
16. half of a (1/2)
17. career
18. loneliness
19. failure
20. idealized
21. depressant
22. Beck
23. self-criticism (or self-blame)
24. self-critical
25. suicide
26. long-term goal
27. daily schedule
28. easiest
29. self-defeating
30. sleeping
31. self-critical
32. rational
33. continuing

Connections

1. f
2. e
3. b
4. d
5. c
6. a

Check Your Memory

1. True
2. False
3. True
4. False
5. True
6. False
7. True
8. True
9. True
10. False
11. True
12. True
13. True
14. False
15. True
16. False
17. True
18. False
19. False
20. False
21. True
22. False
23. False
24. True
25. False

Critical Thinking Answer

Feelings of incompetence and lack of control are the factors.

Module 12.4 Stress and Health
Stress and Health—Unmasking a Hidden Killer

Recite and Review

1. illness
2. changes
3. (Thomas) Holmes
4. life changes
5. 300 (three hundred)
6. reactions
7. stress
8. microstressors
9. hassles (or microstressors)
10. life events
11. hassles (or microstressors)
12. acculturative stress
13. integration
14. separation
15. assimilation
16. marginalization
17. marginalization
18. integration
19. assimilation
20. assimilation
21. diversity
22. stress management
23. psychosomatic
24. hypochondriacs
25. psychosomatic
26. medical
27. biopsychosocial
28. biopsychosocial
29. medical
30. respiratory
31. stress
32. biofeedback
33. psychosomatic
34. migraine
35. hyperactivity
36. relaxation
37. self-regulation
38. (Ray) Rosenman
39. A
40. A
41. time urgency
42. anger (or hostility)
43. Type A
44. depression (or distress)
45. (Redford) Williams
46. mistrusting
47. considerate (or kind)
48. hardy
49. Type A
50. commitment
51. challenges
52. commitment
53. control
54. challenge
55. happy
56. positive
57. optimists
58. pessimists

Part 1: Connections

1. f
2. h
3. a
4. c
5. d
6. i
7. j
8. e
9. g
10. b

Part 2: Connections

1. c
2. g
3. b
4. a
5. e
6. d
7. f

Check Your Memory

1. True	16. True	31. False
2. True	17. False	32. True
3. False	18. True	33. False
4. False	19. False	34. True
5. False	20. True	35. True
6. True	21. False	36. True
7. True	22. False	37. True
8. False	23. True	38. False
9. True	24. True	39. False
10. True	25. False	40. True
11. False	26. True	41. True
12. True	27. True	42. False
13. False	28. True	43. False
14. False	29. True	44. False
15. False	30. True	45. False

Critical Thinking Answer

They are especially resistant to learned helplessness.

Module 12.5 Psychology in Action
Stress Management

Recite and Review

1. stress management	11. progressive relaxation	22. women (or females)
2. Undergraduate Stress Questionnaire	12. guided imagery	23. men (or males)
3. health-threatening	13. five (5)	24. shared
4. remove	14. pet	25. write
5. behavior	15. responses (or reactions)	26. stress inoculation
6. stress	16. slower pace	27. negative self-statements
7. fight-or-flight	17. organized	28. coping
8. exercise	18. balance	29. self-generated
9. meditation	19. achievable	30. managed
10. 30 (thirty)	20. social support	31. self-esteem
	21. pets	32. humor

Connections

1. e	5. b	9. i
2. h	6. g	10. c
3. j	7. a	
4. d	8. f	

Check Your Memory

1. False	10. True	19. True
2. True	11. True	20. False
3. True	12. False	21. True
4. False	13. False	22. True
5. True	14. False	23. False
6. False	15. True	24. True
7. True	16. True	25. True
8. False	17. True	26. True
9. True	18. False	

Critical Thinking Answer

The stress associated with doing term papers can be almost completely eliminated by breaking up a long-term assignment into many small daily or weekly assignments. Students who habitually procrastinate are often amazed at how pleasant college work can be once they renounce "brinkmanship" (pushing things off to the limits of tolerance).

Final Survey and Review—Completion

Module 12.1 Health Psychology
Health Psychology—Here's to Your Good Health

1. health	4. disease-prone	7. community health
2. infectious	5. fish	
3. behavioral risk	6. social	

Module 12.2 Stress, Frustration, and Conflict
Stress—Thrill or Threat?

8. prolonged	11. alarm	14. primary
9. adjust or adapt	12. pressure	15. problem-focused
10. good	13. burnout	

Module 12.2 Frustration—Blind Alleys and Lead Balloons

16. external	18. personal	20. inflexible
17. social	19. displaced	

Module 12.2 Conflict—Yes, No, Yes, No, Yes, No, Well, Maybe

21. approach-approach	22. avoidance-avoidance	24. multiple approach-avoidance
	23. ambivalence	25. partially

Module 12.3 Defenses, Helplessness, and Depression
Psychological Defense—Mental Judo?

26. self-image	28. rationalization	30. intellectualization
27. compensation	29. fantasy	31. sublimation

Module 12.3 Learned Helplessness—Is There Hope?

32. obstacles
33. failure
34. specific
35. Outward Bound
36. aspirations (or goals)
37. overreact

Module 12.4 Stress and Health
Stress and Health—Unmasking a Hidden Killer

38. hassles
39. separation
40. biopsychosocial
41. gastrointestinal
42. biofeedback
43. (Meyer) Friedman
44. challenge
45. broaden

Module 12.5 Psychology in Action
Stress Management

46. Social Readjustment Rating Scale (SSRS)
47. thoughts
48. guided imagery
49. withdraw
50. stress inoculation

Final Survey and Review—Matching

Module 12.1 Health Psychology

1. c
2. f
3. a
4. b
5. d
6. g
7. e

Module 12.2 Stress, Frustration, and Conflict
Part 1:

1. i
2. d
3. f
4. b
5. j
6. h
7. k
8. g
9. a
10. e
11. c

Part 2:

1. j
2. g
3. k
4. h
5. a
6. i
7. e
8. d
9. b
10. f
11. c

Module 12.3 Defenses, Helplessness, and Depression

1. k
2. f
3. g
4. j
5. c
6. i
7. e
8. h
9. d
10. a
11. b
12. l

Module 12.4 Stress and Health

1. d
2. j
3. g
4. b
5. i
6. e
7. f
8. a
9. c
10. h

Module 12.5 Psychology in Action: Stress Management

1. d
2. g
3. c

4. b
5. f
6. a

7. e

Final Survey and Review—True or False

Module 12.1 Health Psychology
Health Psychology—Here's to Your Good Health

1. True
2. False
3. False

4. False
5. True
6. True

7. False

Module 12.2 Stress, Frustration, and Conflict
Stress—Thrill or Threat?

8. True
9. True
10. False

11. True
12. False
13. True

14. False
15. True

Module 12.2 Frustration—Blind Alleys and Lead Balloons

16. True
17. False

18. True
19. True

20. False

Module 12.2 Conflict—Yes, No, Yes, No, Yes, No, Well, Maybe

21. False
22. False

23. True
24. False

25. False

Module 12.3 Defenses, Helplessness, and Depression
Psychological Defense—Mental Judo?

26. True
27. False

28. True
29. False

30. True
31. False

Module 12.3 Learned Helplessness—Is There Hope?

32. False
33. True

34. False
35. False

36. True
37. True

Module 12.4 Stress and Health
Stress and Health—Unmasking a Hidden Killer

38. False
39. False
40. False

41. True
42. True
43. True

44. False
45. False

Module 12.5 Psychology in Action
Stress Management

46. True
47. True

48. False
49. True

50. True

Mastery Test

1. b	15. d	29. b
2. d	16. b	30. c
3. c	17. d	31. d
4. a	18. b	32. c
5. b	19. c	33. c
6. c	20. d	34. b
7. d	21. a	35. b
8. a	22. a	36. a
9. b	23. c	37. b
10. c	24. b	38. d
11. d	25. a	39. b
12. a	26. d	40. a
13. c	27. b	
14. b	28. a	

Chapter 13: Psychological Disorders

Solutions

Module 13.1 Normality and Psychopathology
Normality—What's Normal?

Recite and Review

1. (Carol) North
2. 25 (twenty-five)
3. 90 (ninety)
4. psychopathology
5. statistical
6. normal
7. middle
8. statistical
9. nonconformity
10. conformity
11. norms
12. situational
13. culture
14. cultural relativity
15. communicate
16. subjective discomfort
17. subjective discomfort
18. maladaptive
19. self-control
20. position of power
21. insanity
22. mental hospital
23. expert
24. emergency rooms
25. mentally disabled

Connections

1. c
2. g
3. i
4. a
5. h
6. f
7. b
8. d
9. e

Check Your Memory

1. True
2. False
3. True
4. False
5. True
6. False
7. True
8. True
9. True
10. True
11. True
12. False
13. False
14. False
15. True
16. True
17. True
18. True
19. False
20. False
21. True
22. True
23. True

Critical Thinking Answers

1. Probably not. Undoubtedly, Brian's cross-dressing is socially disapproved by many people. Nevertheless, to be classified as a mental disorder it must cause him to feel disabling shame, guilt, depression, or anxiety. The cultural relativity of behavior like Brian's is revealed by the fact that it is fashionable and acceptable for women to wear men's clothing.

2. It emphasizes that insanity is a legal concept, not a psychiatric diagnosis. Laws reflect community standards. When those standards change, lawmakers may seek to alter definitions of legal responsibility

Module 13.1 Normality and Psychopathology
Classifying Mental Disorders—Problems by the Book

Recite and Review

1. Diagnostic and Statistical Manual of Mental Disorders-IV-TR (DSM-IV-TR)
2. therapies
3. mental disorder
4. psychotic
5. psychotic
6. organic mental
7. manic
8. depression
9. phobias
10. posttraumatic
11. anxiety
12. dissociative
13. depersonalization
14. somatoform
15. personality
16. gender identity
17. paraphilias
18. dysfunctions
19. substance-related
20. tic
21. factitious
22. sleep
23. culture-bound
24. amok
25. susto
26. voodoo
27. ghost sickness
28. koro
29. zar
30. dhat
31. Diagnostic and Statistical Manual of Mental Disorders-IV-TR (DSM-IV-TR)
32. bulimia
33. neurosis
34. gender identity
35. posttraumatic embitterment
36. Internet
37. biological/physical
38. psychological
39. family
40. social

Part 1: Connections

1. j
2. c
3. e
4. i
5. d
6. k
7. g
8. b
9. f
10. h
11. a

Part 2: Connections

1. h
2. d
3. g
4. a
5. b
6. c
7. i
8. e
9. f

Part 3: Connections

1. h
2. g
3. d
4. f
5. b
6. c
7. a
8. i
9. e

Check Your Memory

1. False
2. True
3. False
4. True
5. True
6. True
7. False
8. True
9. True
10. True
11. True
12. False
13. False
14. True
15. False
16. True
17. False
18. True
19. False
20. True
21. False
22. True
23. False
24. True
25. False
26. True
27. True
28. True
29. True
30. False

1152

Module 13.1 Normality and Psychopathology
Disorders in Perspective—Psychiatric Labeling

Recite and Review
1. drapetomania
2. disapproved
3. anarchia
4. nymphomania
5. self-defeating
6. gender
7. stereotypes
8. dependent
9. (David) Rosenhan
10. schizophrenia
11. (real) patients
12. symptom
13. discrimination
14. stigmatized
15. medical student's

Connections
1. d
2. f
3. a
4. c
5. b
6. e

Check Your Memory
1. False
2. True
3. False
4. True
5. True
6. False
7. False
8. True
9. True
10. True
11. False
12. True

Module 13.2 Psychosis, Delusional Disorders, and Schizophrenia
Psychotic Disorders—The Dark Side of the Moon

Recite and Review
1. psychotic
2. delusions
3. hallucinations
4. depressive
5. somatic
6. grandeur
7. influence
8. persecution
9. reference
10. hearing voices
11. flat affect
12. communication
13. salad
14. personality disintegration
15. mood
16. organic
17. lead
18. mercury
19. dementia
20. Alzheimer's disease
21. delusional

Part 1: Connections
1. g
2. d
3. h
4. a
5. c
6. i
7. e
8. b
9. f

Part 2: Connections
1. f
2. a
3. b
4. d
5. c
6. e

1153

Check Your Memory

1. True	9. False	17. True
2. False	10. True	18. True
3. False	11. True	19. False
4. True	12. True	20. True
5. False	13. True	21. True
6. True	14. True	22. True
7. False	15. False	23. False
8. False	16. True	

Module 13.2 Psychosis, Delusional Disorders, and Schizophrenia
Delusional Disorders—An Enemy Behind Every Tree

Recite and Review

1. hallucinations	6. persecutory	10. paranoid
2. delusional	7. somatic	psychosis
3. erotomanic	8. delusional	11. paranoid
4. grandiose	9. schizophrenia	12. paranoid
5. jealous		13. schizophrenia

Connections

1. e	4. a	7. b
2. d	5. g	
3. f	6. c	

Check Your Memory

1. False	5. True	9. True
2. True	6. False	10. True
3. False	7. True	
4. False	8. False	

Module 13.2 Psychosis, Delusional Disorders, and Schizophrenia
Schizophrenia—Shattered Reality

Recite and Review

1. emotion
2. broadcast
3. personal habits
4. 100 (one hundred)
5. selective attention
6. sensory filter
7. disorganized (or hebephrenic)
8. catatonic
9. paranoid
10. undifferentiated
11. hebephrenic
12. disorganized (or hebephrenic)
13. catatonic
14. paranoid
15. catatonic
16. catatonic
17. paranoid
18. psychotic
19. intoxicated
20. undifferentiated
21. rubella (or German measles)
22. malnutrition
23. trauma (or injury or shock)
24. communication
25. vulnerable
26. 48 (forty-eight)
27. mutations
28. phenothiazines
29. psychedelic
30. dopamine
31. glutamate
32. shrunk (or atrophied)
33. fissuring
34. ventricles
35. neurogenesis
36. frontal
37. attention
38. stress-vulnerability

Part 1: Connections

1. e
2. g
3. h
4. a
5. d
6. c
7. b
8. f

Part 2: Connections

1. a
2. e
3. i
4. d
5. g
6. c
7. b
8. f
9. h

Check Your Memory

1. False
2. True
3. True
4. False
5. True
6. False
7. False
8. True
9. True
10. False
11. True
12. False
13. True
14. True
15. True
16. True
17. True
18. False
19. True
20. False
21. False
22. True
23. False
24. False
25. True
26. False
27. True
28. True
29. False
30. True

Critical Thinking Answers

1. Because of the extra receptors, schizophrenics may get psychedelic effects from normal levels of dopamine in the brain.

2. Because correlation does not confirm causation. Structural brain abnormalities are merely correlated with schizophrenia. They could be additional symptoms, rather than causes, of the disorder.

Module 13.3 Mood Disorders
Mood Disorders—Peaks and Valleys

Recite and Review

1. mood
2. depressive
3. bipolar
4. dysthymic
5. cyclothymic
6. major mood
7. depressive
8. manic
9. bipolar I
10. bipolar II
11. hypomania
12. endogenous
13. serotonin
14. lithium carbonate
15. psychoanalytic
16. behavioral
17. cognitive
18. personality traits
19. women (or females)
20. social
21. Latinas
22. education
23. maternity blues
24. postpartum depression
25. estrogen
26. postpartum
27. 67 (sixty-seven)
28. 19 (nineteen)
29. gene
30. bipolar
31. seasonal affective disorder (SAD)
32. carbohydrates
33. withdrawal
34. northern
35. melatonin
36. pineal
37. phototherapy
38. early morning

Part 1: Connections

1. d
2. i
3. h
4. a
5. f
6. c
7. e
8. g
9. b

Part 2: Connections

1. g
2. i
3. j
4. b
5. f
6. a
7. c
8. e
9. k
10. h
11. d

Check Your Memory

1. True
2. False
3. True
4. True
5. False
6. True
7. True
8. True
9. True
10. False
11. True
12. True
13. False
14. False
15. True
16. False
17. True
18. True
19. False
20. True
21. False
22. True
23. True
24. True
25. True
26. True
27. True
28. False
29. True
30. False
31. False
32. False
33. False

Critical Thinking Answer

Women tend to be more focused on relationships than men are. When listing the stresses in their lives, depressed women consistently report higher rates of relationship problems, such as loss of a friend, spouse, or lover, problems getting along with others, and illnesses suffered by people they care about. Depressed men tend to mention issues such as job loss, legal problems, and work problems.

Module 13.4 Anxiety-Based Disorders and Personality Disorders
Anxiety-Based Disorders—When Anxiety Rules

Recite and Review

1. defeating
2. defense mechanisms
3. anxiety
4. nervous breakdown
5. adjustment
6. rest
7. adjustment
8. anxiety
9. adjustment
10. 18 (eighteen)
11. dissociative
12. maladaptive
13. generalized anxiety
14. panic
15. agoraphobia
16. agoraphobia
17. women
18. specific
19. xenophobia
20. acrophobia
21. aviophobia
22. astraphobia
23. social phobia
24. obsessive-compulsive
25. obsessions
26. compulsions
27. obsessive-compulsive
28. stress
29. acute stress
30. posttraumatic stress (PTSD)
31. posttraumatic stress (PTSD)
32. dissociative
33. dissociative fugue
34. dissociative identity
35. sexual abuse
36. hypnosis
37. fusion
38. hypochondriasis
39. somatization
40. pain
41. Munchausen by proxy syndrome
42. Munchausen syndrome
43. comorbid
44. conversion
45. glove anesthesia
46. conversion
47. conversion

Part 1: Connections

1. j
2. i
3. g
4. d
5. a
6. h
7. e
8. f
9. c
10. b

Part 2: Connections

1. d
2. g
3. a
4. b
5. i
6. h
7. e
8. c
9. f

Part 3: Connections

1. c
2. g
3. e
4. i
5. j
6. d
7. k
8. h
9. a
10. b
11. f

Part 4: Connections

1. l
2. f
3. k
4. g
5. h
6. d
7. b
8. m
9. c
10. i
11. e
12. a
13. j

1157

Check Your Memory

1. True	14. False	27. False
2. False	15. False	28. True
3. True	16. True	29. True
4. True	17. False	30. True
5. False	18. True	31. True
6. True	19. True	32. False
7. True	20. False	33. True
8. True	21. False	34. False
9. True	22. False	35. True
10. False	23. True	36. False
11. False	24. False	37. True
12. True	25. True	38. True
13. True	26. True	

Critical Thinking Answers

1. The autonomic nervous system (ANS), especially the sympathetic branch of the ANS.

2. No one doctor tolerates false symptoms for long. Once a doctor refuses further treatment, the Munchausen sufferer will move on to another. Also, often more than one doctor is being seen at one time.

Module 13.4 Anxiety-Based Disorders and Personality Disorders
Anxiety and Disorder—Four Pathways to Trouble

Recite and Review

1. stress-vulnerability	9. humanistic	17. classical
2. inherited	10. self-image (or self-concept)	18. emotional
3. temperament	11. contradictory	19. hypochondriasis
4. psychodynamic	12. meaning	20. avoidance
5. neurosis	13. existential anxiety	21. anxiety-reduction
6. id	14. courage	22. cognitive
7. superego	15. identity	23. perfectionists
8. ego	16. bad faith	

Connections

1. g	4. e	7. a
2. d	5. f	
3. b	6. c	

Check Your Memory

1. True	7. False	13. True
2. True	8. False	14. True
3. True	9. True	15. False
4. True	10. False	16. True
5. False	11. True	17. True
6. False	12. True	18. True

1158

Module 13.4 Anxiety-Based Disorders and Personality Disorders
Personality Disorders—Blueprints for Maladjustment

Recite and Review

1. borderline
2. paranoid
3. narcissistic
4. dependent
5. antisocial (or psychopathic)
6. histrionic
7. obsessive-compulsive
8. schizoid
9. antisocial (or psychopathic)
10. avoidant
11. schizotypal
12. moderate
13. severe
14. high
15. antisocial
16. disgust
17. under-arousal
18. cold
19. antisocial (or psychopathic)
20. 40 (forty)

Connections

1. d
2. f
3. i
4. h
5. b
6. g
7. a
8. j
9. c
10. e

Check Your Memory

1. True
2. False
3. False
4. True
5. False
6. False
7. False
8. False
9. False
10. False
11. False
12. True
13. True
14. True
15. True
16. False
17. True
18. False
19. True
20. True

Module 13.5 Psychology in Action
Suicide—Lives on the Brink

Recite and Review

1. five (5)
2. women (or females)
3. men (or males)
4. guns (or lethal methods)
5. drug overdose
6. Hungary
7. Caucasian
8. Native Americans
9. 65 (sixty-five)
10. third (3rd)
11. cocaine
12. married
13. depression
14. risk
15. acculturative
16. inward
17. threats
18. eight (8)
19. warning
20. two (2)
21. one (1)
22. pain
23. narrow (or constrict or reduce)
24. rapport
25. commitment
26. better
27. intervention
28. workable

Connections

1. d
2. f
3. e
4. a
5. c
6. g
7. b

1159

Check Your Memory

1. False	11. False	21. False
2. True	12. True	22. True
3. False	13. False	23. True
4. True	14. True	24. False
5. False	15. True	25. True
6. False	16. True	26. True
7. True	17. True	27. True
8. False	18. True	28. True
9. True	19. False	29. False
10. True	20. True	30. True

Critical Thinking Answer

Drug or alcohol abuse and availability of a firearm are the two major risk factors.

Final Survey and Review—Completion

Module 13.1 Normality and Psychopathology
Normality—What's Normal?

1. psychopathology
2. bell-shaped
3. (social) nonconformity
4. unpredictable
5. discomfort
6. insanity

Module 13.1 Classifying Mental Disorders—Problems by the Book

7. psychotic
8. mood
9. acute
10. somatoform
11. dissociative
12. ghost sickness
13. clinical observations
14. posttraumatic embitterment
15. family

Module 13.1 Disorders in Perspective—Psychiatric Labeling

16. drapetomania
17. anarchia
18. (David) Rosenhan
19. stigmatized

Module 13.2 Psychosis, Delusional Disorders, and Schizophrenia
Psychotic Disorders—The Dark Side of the Moon

20. reality
21. reference
22. hallucinations
23. flat affect
24. Alzheimer's disease

Module 13.2 Delusional Disorders—An Enemy Behind Every Tree

25. disintegration
26. grandiose
27. somatic
28. paranoid psychosis

Module 13.2 Schizophrenia—Shattered Reality

29. disorganized
30. catatonic
31. substance (drug) abusers
32. deviant communication
33. glutamate
34. fluid-filled
35. inherited potential

Module 13.3 Mood Disorders
Mood Disorders—Peaks and Valleys
36. cyclothymic
37. bipolar II
38. external events
39. noradrenaline
40. learned helplessness
41. maternity blues
42. seasonal affective disorder (SAD)

Module 13.4 Anxiety-Based Disorders and Personality Disorders
Anxiety-Based Disorders—When Anxiety Rules
43. generalized
44. obsessive-compulsive
45. posttraumatic stress disorder (PTSD)
46. dissociative
47. integration
48. somatization
49. Munchausen by proxy syndrome
50. comorbid

Module 13.4 Anxiety and Disorder—Four Pathways to Trouble
51. (Sigmund) Freud
52. (Carl) Rogers
53. responsibility
54. behavioral
55. cognitive

Module 13.4 Personality Disorders—Blueprints for Maladjustment
56. paranoid
57. narcissistic
58. psychotic
59. thrill seekers
60. manipulate

Module 13.5 Psychology in Action
Suicide—Lives on the Brink
61. Azerbaijan
62. white males
63. substance abuse
64. harm others
65. options

Final Survey and Review—Matching

Module 13.1 Normality and Psychopathology
Part 1:
1. k
2. d
3. a
4. b
5. e
6. j
7. h
8. l
9. c
10. f
11. g
12. i

Part 2:
1. g
2. i
3. e
4. h
5. d
6. b
7. a
8. f
9. c

Module 13.2 Psychosis, Delusional Disorders, and Schizophrenia
Part 1:
1. f
2. c
3. a
4. h
5. e
6. g
7. d
8. b

1161

Part 2:

1. i	5. k	9. e
2. d	6. j	10. c
3. g	7. a	11. b
4. h	8. f	

Module 13.3 Mood Disorders

1. b	5. f	9. a
2. j	6. c	10. d
3. h	7. g	
4. i	8. e	

Module 13.4 Anxiety-Based Disorders and Personality Disorders

Part 1:

1. k	5. a	9. f
2. i	6. d	10. c
3. g	7. e	11. h
4. l	8. j	12. b

Part 2:

1. h	6. e	11. n
2. m	7. k	12. d
3. a	8. i	13. l
4. j	9. b	14. c
5. g	10, f	

Module 13.5 Psychology in Action: Suicide—Lives on the Brink

1. b	3. e	5. c
2. d	4. a	

Final Survey and Review—True or False

Module 13.1 Normality and Psychopathology

Normality—What's Normal?

1. False	3. True	5. False
2. True	4. True	6. True

Module 13.1 Classifying Mental Disorders—Problems by the Book

7. False	10. True	13. False
8. False	11. False	14. False
9. False	12. False	15. False

Module 13.1 Disorders in Perspective—Psychiatric Labeling

16. False	18. False
17. True	19. False

Module 13.2 Psychosis, Delusional Disorders, and Schizophrenia
Psychotic Disorders—The Dark Side of the Moon

20. False
21. True

22. False
23. True

24. False

Module 13.2 Delusional Disorders—An Enemy Behind Every Tree

25. False
26. False

27. False
28. True

Module 13.2 Schizophrenia—Shattered Reality

29. True
30. True
31. False

32. True
33. True
34. False

35. True

Module 13.3 Mood Disorders
Mood Disorders—Peaks and Valleys

36. False
37. False
38. False

39. True
40. False
41. True

42. True

Module 13.4 Anxiety-Based Disorders and Personality Disorders
Anxiety-Based Disorders—When Anxiety Rules

43. True
44. True
45. False

46. True
47. False
48. True

49. True
50. False

Module 13.4 Anxiety and Disorder—Four Pathways to Trouble

51. True
52. True

53. False
54. False

55. True

Module 13.4 Personality Disorders—Blueprints for Maladjustment

56. False
57. True

58. False
59. False

60. True

Module 13.5 Psychology in Action
Suicide—Lives on the Brink

61. True
62. False

63. True
64. True

65. True

Mastery Test

1.	c	15.	a	29.	c
2.	a	16.	a	30.	b
3.	c	17.	b	31.	d
4.	c	18.	d	32.	c
5.	b	19.	b	33.	d
6.	a	20.	d	34.	b
7.	d	21.	a	35.	b
8.	a	22.	b	36.	c
9.	d	23.	b	37.	b
10.	b	24.	c	38.	a
11.	c	25.	b	39.	d
12.	a	26.	a	40.	a
13.	d	27.	d		
14.	c	28.	b		
41.					

Chapter 14: Therapies

Solutions

Module 14.1 Treating Psychological Distress
Origins of Therapy—Bored Out of Your Skull

Recite and Review

1. witchcraft
2. trepanning (or trephining)
3. demonology
4. exorcism
5. schizophrenia
6. ergot
7. LSD
8. (Philippe) Pinel
9. (Sigmund) Freud
10. psychoanalysis
11. hysteria
12. somatoform

Connections

1. g
2. e
3. b
4. f
5. a
6. d
7. c
8. h

Check Your Memory

1. True
2. True
3. False
4. True
5. True
6. True
7. False
8. False
9. True
10. False

Module 14.1 Treating Psychological Distress
Psychoanalysis—Expedition into the Unconscious

Recite and Review

1. couch
2. repressed
3. aggression
4. ego defenses (or defense mechanisms)
5. psychoanalysis
6. free association
7. defenses
8. dreams
9. manifest
10. latent
11. dream symbols
12. resistances
13. transference
14. brief psychodynamic
15. interpersonal psychotherapy (IPT)
16. spontaneous remission

Connections

1. d
2. i
3. f
4. h
5. b
6. a
7. e
8. g
9. c

Check Your Memory

1. False	7. True	13. True
2. True	8. False	14. False
3. False	9. True	15. True
4. True	10. True	16. True
5. False	11. True	
6. True	12. True	

Critical Thinking Answer

Psychoanalysts (and therapists in general) are also human. They may transfer their own unresolved, unconscious feelings onto their patients. This sometimes hampers the effectiveness of therapy.

Module 14.1 Treating Psychological Distress
Dimensions of Therapy—The Many Paths to Health

Recite and Review

1. psychotherapy	6. group	11. medical
2. insight	7. individual	12. changes
3. action	8. time-limited	13. personal growth
4. directive	9. open-ended	14. positive
5. nondirective	10. phobias	15. mental health

Connections

1. k	5. b	9. l
2. j	6. f	10. a
3. c	7. i	11. h
4. g	8. e	12. d

Check Your Memory

1. False	5. True	9. True
2. False	6. False	10. True
3. False	7. False	
4. True	8. False	

Module 14.2 Humanistic and Cognitive Therapies
Humanistic Therapies—Restoring Human Potential

Recite and Review

1. insight
2. cognitive
3. humanistic
4. conscious
5. client
6. client-centered (or person-centered)
7. nondirective
8. unconditional positive regard
9. empathy
10. authentic
11. reflecting
12. existential
13. client-centered (or person-centered)
14. existential
15. choices
16. meaning
17. logotherapy
18. (Nazi) concentration camp
19. confrontation
20. radical acceptance
21. Gestalt
22. gaps in experience (or awareness)
23. owning
24. directive
25. here and now
26. awareness
27. unfinished business
28. (Fritz) Perls
29. health
30. intellectualizing

Connections

1. i
2. c
3. g
4. j
5. b
6. f
7. d
8. e
9. a
10. h

Check Your Memory

1. False
2. True
3. False
4. True
5. False
6. True
7. False
8. False
9. True
10. True
11. False
12. False
13. True
14. True
15. True
16. False
17. False
18. True
19. False
20. False
21. False
22. True

Critical Thinking Answer

The terms "doctor" and "patient" imply a large gap in status and authority between the individual and his or her therapist. Client-centered therapy attempts to narrow this gap by making the person the final authority concerning solutions to his or her problems. Also, the word "patient" implies that a person is "sick" and needs to be "cured." Many regard this as an inappropriate way to think about human problems.

Module 14.2 Humanistic and Cognitive Therapies
Cognitive Therapy—Think Positive!

Recite and Review
1. cognitive
2. depression
3. (Aaron) Beck
4. overgeneralization
5. selective perception
6. overgeneralization
7. all-or-nothing thinking
8. test
9. coping skills
10. depression
11. Rational-emotive behavior therapy (REBT)
12. (Albert) Ellis
13. activating experience
14. emotional consequence
15. beliefs
16. irrational beliefs
17. directive
18. core ideas
19. magnified gambling
20. attribution
21. gambler's fallacy
22. selective memory
23. overinterpretation
24. trait
25. probability biases
26. control
27. restructured
28. cognitive

Part 1: Connections
1. e
2. f
3. d
4. c
5. b
6. a

Part 2: Connections
1. g
2. e
3. b
4. f
5. c
6. d
7. a

Check Your Memory
1. False
2. True
3. False
4. False
5. False
6. True
7. True
8. False
9. True
10. True
11. True
12. False
13. True
14. False
15. True
16. True
17. True
18. False
19. False
20. False
21. True
22. True

Critical Thinking Answer
Overgeneralization and all-or-nothing thinking are the two thinking errors.

Module 14.3 Behavior Therapies
Therapies Based on Classical Conditioning—Healing by Learning

Recite and Review

1. learning
2. action
3. relearning
4. behavior modification (or applied behavior analysis)
5. classical
6. conditioned stimulus
7. conditioned aversion
8. aversion
9. aversive
10. rapid smoking
11. contingent
12. immediate
13. desensitization
14. hierarchy
15. phobias
16. reciprocal inhibition
17. tension-release
18. least
19. vicarious desensitization
20. imagining
21. exposure
22. virtual reality exposure
23. eye movement desensitization and reprocessing (EMDR)
24. pencil
25. eye movements

Part 1: Connections

1. e
2. d
3. a
4. c
5. f
6. b

Part 2: Connections

1. e
2. d
3. c
4. f
5. g
6. a
7. b

Check Your Memory

1. False
2. True
3. True
4. True
5. False
6. False
7. True
8. True
9. False
10. True
11. False
12. True
13. True
14. False
15. False
16. False
17. True
18. False
19. True
20. True
21. True
22. True
23. True
24. True
25. False
26. True
27. True
28. False

Critical Thinking Answers

1. Committed alcoholics may actually "drink through it" and learn to tolerate the nauseating effects.

2. Doctors and nurses learn to relax and remain calm at the sight of blood and other bodily fluids because of their frequent exposure to them.

Module 14.3 Behavior Therapies
Operant Therapies—All the World Is a Skinner Box?

Recite and Review

1. operant
2. positive reinforcement
3. nonreinforcement (or nonreward)
4. extinction
5. punishment
6. shaping
7. time out
8. stimulus control
9. time out
10. extinction
11. removed
12. time out
13. tokens
14. tokens
15. token economy
16. target
17. social

Connections

1. d
2. i
3. a
4. f
5. c
6. k
7. b
8. j
9. g
10. e
11. h

Check Your Memory

1. False
2. True
3. False
4. False
5. False
6. True
7. False
8. True
9. True
10. False
11. True
12. True
13. True
14. True
15. True

Module 14.4 Medical Therapies
Medical Therapies—Psychiatric Care

Recite and Review

1. medically
2. somatic
3. hospitalization
4. pharmacotherapy
5. anxiolytics
6. antidepressants
7. antipsychotics
8. antidepressants
9. antipsychotics (or major tranquilizers)
10. anxiolytics (or minor tranquilizers)
11. anxiolytics (or minor tranquilizers)
12. antidepressants
13. antipsychotics (or major tranquilizers)
14. risk/benefit
15. major tranquilizers (or antipsychotics)
16. Clozaril (or clozapine)
17. Risperdal (or risperidone)
18. psychotherapy
19. electrical stimulation
20. convulsion (or seizure)
21. muscle relaxants
22. depression
23. memory
24. antidepressant
25. surgery
26. depression
27. obsessive-compulsive
28. psychosurgery
29. prefrontal lobotomy
30. deep lesioning
31. hospitalization
32. partial hospitalization
33. institutionalization
34. deinstitutionalization
35. halfway houses
36. community mental health
37. crisis intervention
38. paraprofessional

Part 1: Connections

1. a
2. g
3. d
4. b
5. f
6. c
7. h
8. e

Part 2: Connections

1. d
2. b
3. f
4. g
5. c
6. e
7. j
8. i
9. a
10. h

Check Your Memory

1. True
2. False
3. False
4. False
5. True
6. False
7. True
8. False
9. True
10. False
11. True
12. True
13. False
14. True
15. True
16. False
17. True
18. True
19. False
20. True
21. False
22. True
23. True
24. False
25. True
26. True
27. True
28. True
29. True
30. True
31. False
32. True
33. True
34. True
35. False
36. True
37. True

Critical Thinking Answer

The question of who can prescribe drugs, perform surgery, and administer ECT *is* controlled by law. However, psychiatrists strongly object to residents, city councils, or government agencies making *medical* decisions.

Module 14.5 Contemporary Issues in Therapy
Therapies—An Overview

Recite and Review

1. nine (9)
2. spontaneous remission
3. experiment
4. experimental
5. waiting list
6. cognitive
7. empirically supported
8. clinical practice
9. 50 (fifty)
10. five (5)
11. 20 (twenty)
12. psychodrama
13. family
14. behavior
15. psychoanalysis
16. existential
17. brief psychodynamic
18. Gestalt
19. cognitive
20. rational-emotive behavior therapy (REBT)
21. client-centered (or person-centered)
22. psychotherapy
23. therapeutic alliance
24. catharsis
25. explanation (or rationale)
26. behaviors
27. hinder
28. active
29. reflecting (or reflection)
30. closed
31. open-ended
32. clarifying
33. catharsis
34. (Eric) Berne
35. objectively
36. culturally skilled
37. communication

Part 1: Connections

1. h
2. k
3. f
4. i
5. j
6. b
7. e
8. a
9. l
10. d
11. g
12. c

Part 2: Connections

1. b
2. a
3. f
4. j
5. h
6. d
7. i
8. c
9. g
10. e

Check Your Memory

1. False
2. True
3. False
4. False
5. True
6. False
7. True
8. False
9. False
10. True
11. False
12. True
13. True
14. True
15. True
16. True
17. True
18. False
19. True
20. True
21. True
22. False
23. False
24. False
25. True
26. True
27. True
28. False

Critical Thinking Answer

According to the law, there is a duty to protect others when a therapist could, with little effort, prevent serious harm. However, this duty can conflict with a client's rights to confidentiality and with client-therapist trust. Therapists often must make difficult choices in such situations.

Module 14.5 Contemporary Issues in Therapy
The Future of Psychotherapy—Magnets and Smartphones

Recite and Review

1. Internet
2. paraprofessionals
3. master's
4. side effects
5. cost
6. transcranial magnetic stimulation (TMS)
7. shortage
8. acting out
9. support
10. relationships
11. psychodrama
12. playing
13. role reversal
14. mirror
15. family
16. couples
17. communication
18. unit
19. time
20. growth
21. sensitivity
22. trust walk
23. encounter
24. large-group awareness
25. therapy placebo
26. background
27. educational
28. (Phil) McGraw (or Dr. Phil)
29. general
30. therapeutic alliance
31. body language
32. emoticons
33. licensed
34. anonymous
35. confidential
36. rural
37. less
38. Skype
39. depression
40. plan (of action)

Part 1: Connections

1. c
2. f
3. e
4. a
5. d
6. h
7. i
8. b
9. g

Part 2: Connections

1. g
2. f
3. e
4. a
5. b
6. d
7. c

Check Your Memory

1. False
2. True
3. False
4. True
5. True
6. False
7. True
8. False
9. True
10. True
11. True
12. False
13. True
14. False
15. True
16. True
17. False
18. True
19. False
20. False
21. True
22. False
23. True
24. True
25. True
26. True
27. False
28. True
29. False
30. True
31. False
32. False
33. True
34. True
35. False
36. False
37. True
38. True
39. False
40. False

Module 14.6 Psychology in Action
Self-Management and Seeking Professional Help

Recite and Review

1. behavioral
2. covert sensitization
3. stimulus control
4. covert sensitization
5. thought stopping
6. thought stopping
7. covert reinforcement
8. desensitization
9. tension-release
10. hierarchy
11. two (2)
12. three (3)
13. 50 (fifty)
14. (medical) doctor (or dentist)
15. absenteeism
16. suicidal
17. mental health
18. Physicians
19. crisis hotline
20. Louisiana
21. higher
22. sliding scale
23. peer
24. self-help
25. asking
26. personal qualities
27. danger (warning)
28. goals

Connections

1. h
2. a
3. f
4. e
5. g
6. d
7. b
8. c

1173

Check Your Memory

1. True	12. True	23. True
2. False	13. True	24. False
3. True	14. True	25. True
4. True	15. True	26. False
5. False	16. True	27. True
6. True	17. False	28. False
7. False	18. True	29. False
8. True	19. False	30. True
9. False	20. True	31. True
10. False	21. True	32. True
11. True	22. True	

Critical Thinking Answer

Such decisions must be made by clients themselves. Therapists can help clients evaluate important decisions and feelings about significant persons in their lives. However, actively urging a client to sever a relationship borders on unethical behavior.

Final Survey and Review—Completion

Module 14.1 Treating Psychological Distress
Origins of Therapy—Bored Out of Your Skull

1. trepanning or trephining
2. exorcism
3. dissociative
4. (Philippe) Pinel
5. hysteria

Module 14.1 Psychoanalysis—Expedition into the Unconscious

6. free association
7. latent
8. transference
9. brief psychodynamic
10. passage of time

Module 14.1 Dimensions of Therapy—The Many Paths to Health

11. action
12. directive
13. medical
14. (personal) strengths
15. interpersonal

Module 14.2 Humanistic and Cognitive Therapies
Humanistic Therapies—Restoring Human Potential

16. reflection
17. client-centered (or person-centered)
18. logotherapy
19. confrontation
20. Gestalt

Module 14.2 Cognitive Therapy—Think Positive!

21. all-or-nothing
22. selective perception
23. Rational-emotive behavior therapy (REBT)
24. irrational beliefs
25. gambler's fallacy

Module 14.3 Behavior Therapies
Therapies Based on Classical Conditioning—Healing by Learning

26. behavior modification
27. aversion
28. rapid smoking
29. vicarious desensitization
30. (Francine) Shapiro

Module 14.3 Operant Therapies—All the World Is a Skinner Box?

31. stimulus control
32. reinforcement (or reward)
33. nonreward (or nonreinforcement)
34. rewarded (or reinforced)
35. modify (or change)

Module 14.4 Medical Therapies
Medical Therapies—Psychiatric Care

36. anxiolytics (minor tranquilizers)
37. serotonin
38. electroconvulsive therapy (ECT)
39. deep lesioning
40. halfway house
41. community mental health center
42. paraprofessional

Module 14.5 Contemporary Issues in Therapy
Therapies—An Overview

43. behavioral
44. research experiments
45. psychoanalysis
46. client-centered (person-centered)
47. "Why don't you…? Yes, but"
48. culturally skilled

Module 14.5 The Future of Psychotherapy—Magnets and Smartphones

49. telephone
50. (Jacob) Moreno
51. problems
52. destructive patterns
53. facial expressions
54. Skype

Module 14.6 Psychology in Action
Self-Management and Seeking Professional Help

55. covert sensitization
56. thought stopping
57. deep breathing
58. New Mexico
59. peer
60. self-help

Final Survey and Review—Matching

Module 14.1 Treating Psychological Distress
Part 1:

1. f
2. g
3. e
4. b
5. h
6. c
7. a
8. d

Part 2:

1. d
2. g
3. f
4. a
5. b
6. c
7. e

Module 14.2 Humanistic and Cognitive Therapies
Part 1:
1. d
2. c
3. f
4. g
5. a
6. b
7. e

Part 2:
1. k
2. j
3. d
4. c
5. g
6. a
7. i
8. l
9. e
10. h
11. f
12. b

Module 14.3 Behavior Therapies
Part 1:
1. i
2. d
3. a
4. h
5. j
6. b
7. f
8. g
9. c
10. e

Part 2:
1. j
2. f
3. g
4. k
5. a
6. h
7. e
8. c
9. d
10. l
11. i
12. b

Module 14.4 Medical Therapies
1. h
2. g
3. d
4. i
5. f
6. c
7. j
8. e
9. b
10. a

Module 14.5 Contemporary Issues in Therapy
Part 1:
1. i
2. k
3. f
4. l
5. h
6. d
7. a
8. j
9. c
10. e
11. g
12. b

Part 2:
1. j
2. f
3. e
4. h
5. g
6. a
7. c
8. d
9. b
10. i

Module 14.6 Psychology in Action: Self-Management and Seeking Professional Help
1. e
2. b
3. d
4. f
5. c
6. a

Final Survey and Review—True or False

Module 14.1 Treating Psychological Distress
Origins of Therapy—Bored Out of Your Skull
1. False
2. True
3. True
4. True
5. True

Module 14.1 Psychoanalysis—Expedition into the Unconscious
6. True
7. True
8. False
9. True
10. False

Module 14.1 Dimensions of Therapy—The Many Paths to Health
11. True
12. False
13. True
14. True
15. False

Module 14.2 Humanistic and Cognitive Therapies
Humanistic Therapies—Restoring Human Potential
16. False
17. True
18. False
19. True
20. True

Module 14.2 Cognitive Therapy—Think Positive!
21. True
22. False
23. True
24. True
25. False

Module 14.3 Behavior Therapies
Therapies Based on Classical Conditioning—Healing by Learning
26. False
27. False
28. True
29. True
30. False

Module 14.3 Operant Therapies—All the World Is a Skinner Box?
31. True
32. True
33. False
34. True
35. False

Module 14.4 Medical Therapies
Medical Therapies—Psychiatric Care
36. False
37. False
38. True
39. True
40. True
41. True
42. False

Module 14.5 Contemporary Issues in Therapy
Therapies—An Overview
43. True
44. False
45. False
46. False
47. False
48. True

Module 14.5 The Future of Psychotherapy—Magnets and Smartphones
49. False
50. True
51. True
52. False
53. True
54. True

Module 14.6 Psychology in Action
Self-Management and Seeking Professional Help

55. False
56. False
57. False
58. False
59. True
60. True

Mastery Test

1. a	15. b	29. d
2. b	16. a	30. b
3. c	17. d	31. a
4. a	18. b	32. b
5. d	19. c	33. b
6. b	20. c	34. c
7. a	21. a	35. a
8. c	22. c	36. b
9. d	23. d	37. d
10. c	24. a	38. c
11. b	25. b	39. c
12. d	26. c	40. d
13. c	27. c	
14. c	28. b	

Chapter 15: Social Behavior

Solutions

Module 15.1 Affiliation, Friendship, and Love
Affiliation and Attraction—Come Together

Recite and Review

1. social
2. affiliate
3. information
4. social comparison
5. social comparison
6. similar
7. interpersonal attraction
8. understanding
9. physical proximity
10. virtual contact
11. physical proximity
12. attractive
13. halo
14. attractiveness
15. personality
16. competent
17. intelligent or competent
18. average
19. ethnicity
20. similarity
21. reinforcing
22. homogamy
23. religion
24. eye color
25. education
26. self-disclosure
27. moderate self-disclosure
28. overdisclosure
29. suspicion
30. Facebook

Connections

1. k
2. j
3. f
4. g
5. h
6. l
7. a
8. m
9. e
10. b
11. i
12. c
13. d

Check Your Memory

1. False
2. True
3. True
4. True
5. False
6. True
7. True
8. True
9. False
10. True
11. False
12. True
13. False
14. False
15. True
16. True
17. True
18. False
19. True
20. False
21. True
22. False
23. True
24. True
25. False
26. True

Critical Thinking Answer

As mentioned earlier, today's widespread Internet interactions between people make actual proximity less crucial in interpersonal attraction. Internet romances are a good example of this possibility.

Module 15.1 Affiliation, Friendship, and Love
Liking and Loving—Dating and Mating

Recite and Review

1. romantic
2. triangular
3. intimacy
4. passion
5. commitment
6. nonlove
7. liking
8. companionate
9. fatuous
10. infatuated
11. consummate
12. romantic
13. empty
14. absorption
15. idealized
16. evolutionary
17. women (or females)
18. women (or females)
19. reproduction
20. fertility
21. sexual fidelity
22. power
23. polite
24. intelligent

Part 1: Connections

1. d
2. b
3. f
4. e
5. a
6. c

Part 2: Connections

1. h
2. e
3. a
4. g
5. f
6. c
7. b
8. d

Check Your Memory

1. True
2. False
3. False
4. True
5. False
6. True
7. False
8. True
9. False
10. True
11. False
12. True
13. True
14. False
15. False
16. True
17. True
18. True
19. False
20. True

Module 15.2 Groups, Social Influence, Mere Presence, and Conformity
Humans in a Social Context—People, People, Everywhere

Recite and Review

1. structure
2. social roles
3. ascribed
4. achieved
5. predicted
6. conflicts
7. role conflicts
8. structure
9. cohesiveness
10. structure
11. cohesiveness
12. cohesiveness
13. in
14. out
15. in
16. out
17. status
18. polite
19. impolite (or rude)
20. status
21. norm
22. littered (or dirty, messy)
23. attribution
24. internal
25. external
26. circumstances (or situations)
27. fundamental attribution
28. fundamental attribution
29. actor-observer
30. actor-observer

Connections

1. f	5. c	9. b
2. l	6. k	10. h
3. i	7. j	11. a
4. g	8. e	12. d

Check Your Memory

1. True	10. True	19. True
2. False	11. True	20. False
3. False	12. False	21. True
4. True	13. True	22. True
5. True	14. False	23. False
6. True	15. True	24. True
7. False	16. True	25. False
8. False	17. True	
9. True	18. False	

Module 15.2 Groups, Social Influence, Mere Presence, and Conformity
Social Influence—Follow the Leader

Recite and Review

1. social influence
2. increased (or become larger)
3. mere presence
4. conformity
5. compliance
6. obedience
7. coercion
8. mere presence
9. social facilitation
10. (Norman) Triplett
11. confidence
12. social loafing
13. alone
14. conformity
15. conformity
16. (Solomon) Asch
17. 75 (seventy-five)
18. certainty
19. low
20. cooperation
21. groupthink
22. (Irving) Janis
23. groupthink
24. critical evaluator
25. preferences
26. devil's advocate
27. second-chance
28. deadlock
29. group sanctions
30. membership
31. three (3)
32. unanimity
33. ally

Connections

1. e	5. g	9. f
2. h	6. a	10. c
3. j	7. d	
4. i	8. b	

Check Your Memory

1. True	11. True	21. False
2. False	12. True	22. True
3. False	13. False	23. True
4. False	14. False	24. False
5. False	15. False	25. True
6. True	16. True	26. True
7. False	17. False	27. False
8. True	18. False	28. True
9. False	19. True	29. True
10. True	20. True	30. False

Critical Thinking Answer

A person who did not follow at least some norms concerning normal social behavior would very likely be perceived as extremely bizarre, disturbed, or psychotic.

Module 15.3 Compliance, Obedience, Coercion, and Self-Assertion
Compliance—A Foot in the Door

Recite and Review

1. compliance
2. compliance
3. foot-in-the-door
4. door-in-the-face
5. (Robert) Cialdini
6. low-ball
7. foot-in-the-door
8. low-ball
9. foot-in-the-door
10. Internet

Connections

1. d
2. b
3. c
4. a

Check Your Memory

1. True
2. True
3. False
4. True
5. False
6. True
7. True
8. True
9. False
10. True

Module 15.3 Compliance, Obedience, Coercion, and Self-Assertion
Obedience—Would You Electrocute a Stranger?

Recite and Review

1. authority
2. obedience
3. (Stanley) Milgram
4. one (1)
5. 65 (sixty-five)
6. prestige (or reputation)
7. 48 (forty-eight)
8. reduced (or decreased)
9. reduced (or decreased)
10. authority
11. 10 (ten)
12. similar
13. unreasonable
14. massacres (or killings)

Connections

1. c
2. d

3. e
4. a

5. f
6. b

Check Your Memory

1. True
2. True
3. False
4. False
5. False

6. True
7. True
8. False
9. True
10. True

11. True
12. True
13. False
14. False

Critical Thinking Answer

There is a big difference between killing someone in hand-to-hand combat and killing someone by lining up images on a video screen. Milgram's research suggests that it is easier for a person to follow orders to kill another human when the victim is at a distance and removed from personal contact.

Module 15.3 Compliance, Obedience, Coercion, and Self-Assertion
Coercion—Brainwashing and Cults

Recite and Review

1. coercion
2. captive
3. helpless
4. unfreezing
5. change
6. refreezing
7. temporary
8. cults

9. personality
10. victimized (or exploited)
11. obedience
12. (Margaret Singer)
13. belonging
14. parental authority

15. love bombing
16. reference
17. critical
18. foot-in-the-door
19. cognitive dissonance
20. conversion
21. spiritual

Connections

1. g
2. f
3. d

4. h
5. e
6. b

7. a
8. c

Check Your Memory

1. False
2. True
3. False
4. False
5. True
6. True

7. True
8. False
9. False
10. True
11. True
12. False

13. False
14. False
15. True
16. True
17. False
18. False

Module 15.3 Compliance, Obedience, Coercion, and Self-Assertion
Assertiveness Training—Standing Up for Your Rights

Recite and Review

1. assert
2. assertiveness
3. nonassertive
4. aggressive
5. assertive
6. request
7. self-assertion
8. nonassertive
9. practiced
10. gestures
11. role play
12. <u>Your Perfect Right</u>

Connections

1. d
2. c
3. b
4. a

Check Your Memory

1. True
2. False
3. True
4. True
5. True
6. False
7. True
8. False
9. True
10. True
11. True
12. True
13. False
14. True

Module 15.4 Attitudes and Persuasion
Attitudes—Belief + Emotion + Action

Recite and Review

1. attitude
2. evaluations
3. belief
4. emotional
5. action
6. act
7. direct contact
8. chance conditioning
9. interaction
10. membership
11. child rearing
12. (mass) media
13. mean worldview
14. consequence
15. evaluate
16. habit
17. conviction

Connections

1. e
2. h
3. k
4. b
5. i
6. j
7. d
8. a
9. f
10. c
11. g

Check Your Memory

1. True
2. False
3. False
4. False
5. False
6. True
7. True
8. True
9. True
10. True
11. False
12. True

Module 15.4 Attitudes and Persuasion
Attitude Change—Meet the "Seekers"

Recite and Review

1. reference
2. membership
3. reference
4. persuasion
5. communicator
6. communicator
7. emotions
8. fear (or anxiety)
9. facts (or statistics)
10. well
11. poorly
12. cognitive dissonance
13. cognitive dissonance
14. consistent
15. cognitive dissonance
16. attitude
17. behavior
18. dissonant
19. consonant
20. perceived choice
21. contrary
22. one dollar ($1)
23. justification

Connections

1. f
2. b
3. e
4. a
5. d
6. c

Check Your Memory

1. False
2. False
3. True
4. True
5. True
6. False
7. False
8. False
9. True
10. True
11. True
12. False
13. True
14. False
15. True
16. False

Critical Thinking Answers

1. Cognitive dissonance theory predicts that students who sign the banner will take shorter showers to be consistent with their publicly expressed support of water conservation. This is exactly the result observed in a study done by social psychologist Elliot Aronson.

2. There is strong justification for such actions. As a result, little cognitive dissonance is created when a prisoner makes statements that contradict his or her beliefs.

Module 15.5 Prejudice and Intergroup Conflict
Prejudice—Attitudes That Injure

Recite and Review

1. prejudice
2. ageism
3. racism
4. sexism
5. heterosexism
6. discrimination
7. racial profiling
8. scapegoating
9. displaced aggression
10. lower
11. displaced
12. three (3)
13. personal
14. group
15. authoritarian
16. out-groups
17. ethnocentrism
18. F (fascism)
19. authoritarian
20. authoritarian

Part 1: Connections

1. e
2. f
3. b
4. a
5. c
6. d

Part 2: Connections

1. d
2. g
3. b
4. f
5. c
6. a
7. e

Check Your Memory

1. False
2. False
3. True
4. True
5. True
6. True
7. False
8. True
9. True
10. True
11. False
12. True
13. False
14. False
15. False
16. True
17. True
18. True
19. False
20. True
21. True
22. False

Critical Thinking Answer

Because authoritarians tend to believe that punishment is effective, they are more likely to vote for conviction.

Module 15.5 Prejudice and Intergroup Conflict
Intergroup Conflict—The Roots of Prejudice

Recite and Review

1. membership
2. intergroup
3. injustice
4. stereotypes
5. out
6. age
7. stereotypes
8. control
9. expectations
10. individuality
11. fulfilling
12. stereotype threat
13. lower (or worse, poorer)
14. the same (or equal)
15. lower (or worse, poorer)
16. stereotype
17. unconscious
18. symbolic
19. issues
20. European-American
21. (Jane) Elliot
22. status inequalities
23. red
24. blue
25. stereotypes
26. purple
27. equal-status
28. status inequalities
29. cooperative
30. cooperate (or work together)
31. superordinate
32. superordinate
33. competitive
34. (Elliot) Aronson
35. cooperation
36. mutual interdependence
37. less
38. improved

Connections

1. j
2. f
3. i
4. e
5. h
6. b
7. c
8. a
9. d
10. g

Check Your Memory

1. True	11. False	21. False
2. True	12. False	22. True
3. True	13. True	23. False
4. False	14. False	24. False
5. True	15. False	25. True
6. False	16. True	26. False
7. True	17. True	27. False
8. True	18. True	28. True
9. False	19. False	29. True
10. False	20. True	30. False

Module 15.6 Aggression and Prosocial Behavior
Aggression—The World's Most Dangerous Animal

Recite and Review

1. Homo sapiens
2. minute
3. aggression
4. killer instinct
5. ethologist
6. inhibit (or restrain)
7. little (or less)
8. brain
9. hypoglycemia (or low blood sugar)
10. testosterone
11. alcohol (or intoxicating drugs)
12. threshold (or inhibitions)
13. inhibit
14. frustration-aggression
15. stereotyped
16. aversive
17. internal
18. external
19. weapons
20. social learning
21. seconds
22. 38 (thirty-eight)
23. 70 (seventy)
24. modeling (or observational learning)
25. 90 (ninety)
26. electronic
27. (Albert) Bandura
28. disinhibition
29. desensitization
30. physically abused
31. eight (8)
32. frustrating
33. thoughts
34. thoughts
35. decreased
36. model
37. reality
38. stereotypes
39. identify
40. prosocial

Connections

1. k
2. h
3. j
4. g

5. l
6. a
7. i
8. c

9. e
10. d
11. b
12. f

Check Your Memory

1. False
2. True
3. True
4. True
5. False
6. True
7. True
8. False
9. True
10. False
11. True

12. True
13. True
14. True
15. True
16. True
17. False
18. True
19. False
20. True
21. True
22. False

23. True
24. True
25. False
26. True
27. False
28. True
29. True
30. True
31. False
32. True
33. True

Module 15.6 Aggression and Prosocial Behavior
Prosocial Behavior—Helping Others

Recite and Review

1. bystander apathy (or the bystander effect)
2. many (or more)
3. (sparsely traveled) country road
4. notice
5. staring
6. alone
7. defining

8. taking responsibility
9. diffusion of responsibility
10. alone
11. cane
12. heightened arousal
13. costs
14. empathic arousal
15. similar

16. connected
17. empathy-helping
18. self-image
19. fairness
20. de-victimize
21. Fire
22. assign
23. men (or males)

Connections

1. c
2. a

3. f
4. e

5. d
6. b

Check Your Memory

1. True
2. False
3. False
4. False
5. True
6. False
7. True
8. True

9. True
10. False
11. False
12. True
13. True
14. True
15. False
16. True

17. True
18. True
19. False
20. True
21. True
22. True

Critical Thinking Answer

Yes. Media could be used to promote helping, cooperation, charity, and brotherhood in the same way that it has encouraged aggression. Numerous studies show, for example, that prosocial behavior on TV increases prosocial behavior.

Module 15.7 Psychology in Action
Multiculturalism—Living with Diversity

Recite and Review

1. tossed salad
2. multiculturalism
3. stereotypes
4. openness
5. stereotyping
6. similar
7. individuating
8. label
9. immersed
10. symbolic
11. just-world
12. discrimination
13. self-fulfilling prophecy
14. social competition
15. self-esteem
16. family
17. race
18. Africa
19. darker skin
20. cooperate
21. tolerance
22. awareness

Connections

1. c
2. e
3. f
4. g
5. h
6. a
7. b
8. d

Check Your Memory

1. False
2. True
3. True
4. True
5. False
6. True
7. True
8. False
9. False
10. False
11. True
12. True
13. True
14. False
15. True
16. False
17. True
18. True
19. True
20. True

Critical Thinking Answer

Labels might have negative meanings that are not apparent to persons outside the group. People who are culturally aware allow others to define their own identities, rather than imposing labels on them.

Final Survey and Review—Completion

Module 15.1 Affiliation, Friendship, and Love
Affiliation and Attraction—Come Together

1. social
2. affiliate
3. physical proximity
4. halo
5. reciprocity

Module 15.1 Liking and Loving—Dating and Mating

6. passion
7. (Robert) Sternberg
8. liking
9. men (or males)
10. mating

Module 15.2 Groups, Social Influence, Mere Presence, and Conformity
Humans in a Social Context—People, People, Everywhere
11. ascribed
12. conflict
13. cohesiveness
14. norms
15. actor-observer

Module 15.2 Social Influence—Follow the Leader
16. compliance
17. mere presence
18. loafing
19. structure
20. groupthink

Module 15.3 Compliance, Obedience, Coercion, and Self-Assertion
Compliance—A Foot in the Door
21. compliance
22. (Robert) Cialdini
23. foot-in-the-door effect
24. door-in-the-face effect
25. low-ball technique

Module 15.3 Obedience—Would You Electrocute a Stranger?
26. authority
27. obedience
28. psychiatrists
29. hurt
30. (Jerry) Burger

Module 15.3 Coercion—Brainwashing and Cults
31. coercion
32. refreezing
33. parental
34. commitment
35. group members

Module 15.3 Assertiveness Training—Standing Up for Your Rights
36. assert
37. nonassertive
38. aggressive
39. role playing
40. (Michael) Emmons

Module 15.4 Attitudes and Persuasion
Attitudes—Belief + Emotion + Action
41. action
42. direct contact (or personal experience)
43. group membership
44. immediate consequence
45. conviction

Module 15.4 Attitude Change—Meet the "Seekers"
46. membership
47. audience
48. cognitive dissonance
49. perceived choice
50. $20 (twenty dollars)

Module 15.5 Prejudice and Intergroup Conflict
Prejudice—Attitudes That Injure
51. social group
52. discrimination
53. displaced
54. personal
55. authoritarian

Module 15.5 Intergroup Conflict—The Roots of Prejudice
56. sex
57. symbolic
58. eye color
59. red
60. jigsaw classroom

1190

Module 15.6 Aggression and Prosocial Behavior
Module 15.6 Aggression—The World's Most Dangerous Animal
61. (Konrad) Lorenz
62. allergies

63. learned helplessness

64. aggression cues
65. electronic

Module 15.6 Prosocial Behavior—Helping Others
66. Darley
67. presence

68. course (or plan) or action

69. diffusion of responsibility
70. fairness

Module 15.7 Psychology in Action
Multiculturalism—Living with Diversity
71. status
72. stereotypes
73. just-world

74. self-fulfilling prophecy
75. inferior

Final Survey and Review—Matching

Module 15.1 Affiliation, Friendship, and Love
Part 1:
1. k
2. i
3. j
4. g

5. h
6. c
7. a
8. b

9. e
10. l
11. f
12. d

Part 2:
1. j
2. f
3. i
4. g

5. a
6. c
7. h
8. e

9. d
10. b

Module 15.2 Groups, Social Influence, Mere Presence, and Conformity
Part 1:
1. i
2. d
3. e
4. g

5. c
6. a
7. j
8. h

9. b
10. f

Part 2:
1. c
2. h
3. e

4. a
5. g
6. f

7. d
8. b

Module 15.3 Compliance, Obedience, Coercion, and Self-Assertion
1. k
2. l
3. j
4. h

5. i
6. a
7. d
8. b

9. c
10. e
11. g
12. f

Module 15.4 Attitudes and Persuasion

1. l	5. g	9. b
2. h	6. j	10. a
3. k	7. c	11. i
4. e	8. f	12. d

Module 15.5 Prejudice and Intergroup Conflict

1. i	5. c	9. k
2. l	6. e	10. f
3. h	7. b	11. g
4. a	8. d	12. j

Module 15.6 Aggression and Prosocial Behavior

1. k	5. l	9. e
2. h	6. i	10. d
3. a	7. c	11. b
4. f	8. g	12. j

Module 15.7 Psychology in Action: Multiculturalism—Living with Diversity

1. b	3. a	5. f
2. d	4. e	6. c

Final Survey and Review—True or False

Module 15.1 Affiliation, Friendship, and Love
Affiliation and Attraction—Come Together

1. True	3. True	5. True
2. True	4. False	

Module 15.1 Liking and Loving—Dating and Mating

6. False	8. True	10. True
7. False	9. True	

Module 15.2 Groups, Social Influence, Mere Presence, and Conformity
Humans in a Social Context—People, People, Everywhere

11. False	13. True	15. False
12. True	14. False	

Social Influence—Follow the Leader (Module 15.2)

16. False	18. True	20. True
17. False	19. True	

Module 15.3 Compliance, Obedience, Coercion, and Self-Assertion
Compliance—A Foot in the Door

21. False	23. False	25. True
22. False	24. True	

Module 15.3 Obedience—Would You Electrocute a Stranger?

26. True
27. True
28. False
29. False
30. True

Module 15.3 Coercion—Brainwashing and Cults

31. True
32. False
33. True
34. True
35. False

Module 15.3 Assertiveness Training—Standing Up for Your Rights

36. True
37. False
38. True
39. False
40. True

Module 15.4 Attitudes and Persuasion
Attitudes—Belief + Emotion + Action

41. False
42. True
43. False
44. True
45. True

Module 15.4 Attitude Change—Meet the "Seekers"

46. True
47. False
48. True
49. True
50. False

Module 15.5 Prejudice and Intergroup Conflict
Prejudice—Attitudes That Injure

51. False
52. True
53. True
54. False
55. False

Module 15.5 Intergroup Conflict—The Roots of Prejudice

56. True
57. False
58. False
59. True
60. True

Module 15.6 Aggression and Prosocial Behavior
Aggression—The World's Most Dangerous Animal

61. True
62. True
63. False
64. False
65. False

Module 15.6 Prosocial Behavior—Helping Others

66. True
67. False
68. False
69. True
70. False

Module 15.7 Psychology in Action
Multiculturalism—Living with Diversity

71. False
72. True
73. False
74. True
75. True

Mastery Test

1. b	15. d	29. a
2. d	16. a	30. b
3. a	17. d	31. d
4. d	18. b	32. c
5. d	19. b	33. c
6. b	20. c	34. a
7. d	21. a	35. d
8. b	22. a	36. c
9. b	23. c	37. b
10. b	24. d	38. c
11. d	25. d	39. a
12. a	26. c	40. b
13. c	27. d	
14. d	28. b	

Chapter 16: Applied Psychology

Solutions

Module 16.1 Industrial/Organizational Psychology
Industrial/Organizational Psychology—Psychology at Work

Recite and Review

1. downloadable
2. click wheel
3. multi-touch interface
4. factors
5. applied
6. clinical
7. applied
8. industrial/organizational
9. industrial
10. organizational
11. leader
12. leadership
13. (Fredrick) Taylor
14. standardized
15. scientific
16. X
17. work
18. psychological
19. (Douglas) McGregor
20. Y
21. knowledge
22. knowledge
23. competence
24. career
25. Y
26. 25 (twenty-five)
27. women (or females)
28. glass ceiling
29. agentic
30. communal
31. stereotypes
32. Y
33. associate
34. objectives
35. participative management
36. cooperative
37. objectives
38. feedback
39. self-managed
40. quality circle
41. self-managed team
42. job satisfaction
43. positive
44. expectations
45. happy
46. flextime
47. compressed
48. telecommute
49. independence
50. job enrichment
51. cycle
52. knowledge
53. culture
54. citizenship
55. desk rage
56. trauma
57. gratitude (or thanks)
58. forgive
59. sensitivity
60. encouragement
61. compassion
62. personnel
63. nine (9)
64. job analysis
65. critical incident
66. work analysis
67. biodata
68. interview
69. halo
70. impression management
71. less
72. lowered
73. structure
74. intelligence
75. vocational interest
76. (John) Holland
77. enterprising
78. investigative
79. realistic
80. conventional
81. artistic
82. social
83. aptitude
84. computerized
85. assessment
86. situational judgment
87. in-basket
88. leaderless group discussion

Part 1: Connections

1. h
2. f
3. j
4. a
5. i
6. c
7. d
8. b
9. k
10. e
11. g

Part 2: Connections

1. i	5. b	9. g
2. k	6. j	10. c
3. a	7. e	11. f
4. h	8. d	

Part 3: Connections

1. i	4. h	7. b
2. e	5. g	8. c
3. a	6. d	9. f

Part 4: Connections

1. d	5. k	9. a
2. g	6. b	10. f
3. i	7. j	11. h
4. e	8. c	

Part 5: Connections

1. e	3. a	5. b
2. c	4. f	6. d

Check Your Memory

1. False	22. False	43. True
2. True	23. True	44. False
3. False	24. True	45. True
4. False	25. False	46. False
5. False	26. False	47. False
6. True	27. True	48. True
7. True	28. True	49. False
8. False	29. True	50. False
9. True	30. True	51. True
10. False	31. True	52. True
11. False	32. False	53. True
12. True	33. False	54. False
13. False	34. True	55. True
14. False	35. False	56. False
15. True	36. True	57. False
16. False	37. True	58. False
17. True	38. True	59. True
18. True	39. False	60. True
19. True	40. False	61. True
20. True	41. True	62. False
21. True	42. False	

Critical Thinking Answer

One such area is sports psychology. As described later in this chapter, sports skills can be broken into subparts, so key elements can be identified and taught. Such methods are an extension of techniques first used for job analyses. To a large extent, attempts to identify the characteristics of effective teaching also rely on task analysis.

Module 16.1 Industrial/Organizational Psychology
Communication at Work—Getting the Message Across

Recite and Review

1. communication
2. how
3. clearly
4. wiggle
5. intensifiers
6. insecurity
7. jargon
8. emotional
9. respected
10. names
11. approval
12. self-assertion
13. important
14. workspace
15. listener
16. distractions
17. eye contact
18. purpose
19. evaluation (or judgment)
20. check
21. nonverbal
22. meaning

Connections

1. f
2. d
3. g
4. b
5. c
6. a
7. e

Check Your Memory

1. True
2. True
3. False
4. True
5. False
6. True
7. True
8. False
9. True
10. True
11. False
12. False
13. True
14. True
15. True
16. True
17. True
18. False
19. False
20. True
21. True
22. False

Module 16.2 Environmental Psychology
Environmental Psychology—Life on Spaceship Earth

Recite and Review

1. environmental
2. physical
3. social
4. behavioral settings
5. environmental
6. personal space
7. personal space
8. proxemics
9. activities
10. Middle Eastern
11. Dutch
12. intimate
13. personal
14. social
15. public
16. consistent
17. personal space
18. eye contact
19. territory
20. territorial
21. territorial
22. territorial markers
23. territorial markers
24. personal space
25. hardening
26. maze
27. urban
28. six (6)
29. 10 (ten)
30. sustainable
31. pathological
32. (very) high
33. stress-caused
34. density
35. crowding
36. relationships
37. control
38. attentional overload
39. nonessential
40. smaller towns
41. sensitivity
42. concentration
43. learned helplessness
44. noise pollution
45. activities
46. toxic
47. politics
48. overuse
49. ecological footprint
50. 10 (ten)
51. feedback
52. master-metered
53. ecological footprint
54. carbon footprint
55. carbon
56. carbon-neutral
57. school
58. incentives (or monetary rewards)
59. unsorted
60. commitments
61. dilemma
62. tragedy of the commons
63. collective good
64. dilemmas
65. environmental assessments
66. crowded
67. architectural
68. altered dorm

Part 1: Connections

1. e
2. c
3. b
4. g
5. f
6. a
7. d

Part 2: Connections

1. d
2. f
3. b
4. g
5. i
6. a
7. j
8. c
9. e
10. h

Part 3: Connections

1. h
2. g
3. a
4. d
5. b
6. c
7. f
8. e

Check Your Memory

1. True	19. True	37. True
2. True	20. True	38. False
3. True	21. False	39. False
4. True	22. False	40. True
5. False	23. False	41. True
6. True	24. True	42. True
7. True	25. True	43. True
8. False	26. False	44. False
9. False	27. True	45. True
10. False	28. False	46. False
11. True	29. True	47. True
12. True	30. False	48. True
13. True	31. True	49. False
14. False	32. True	50. False
15. True	33. True	51. True
16. True	34. False	52. False
17. True	35. True	53. False
18. False	36. False	54. True

Critical Thinking Answer

A delay of consequences (rewards, benefits, costs, and punishments) tends to reduce their impact on immediate behavior.

Module 16.3 The Psychology of Education, Law, and Sports
Educational Psychology—An Instructive Topic

Recite and Review

1. testing	9. stimuli	17. discovery learning
2. educational	10. repeating	18. discovery learning
3. teaching strategy	11. feedback	19. Universal Design for Instruction
4. educational	12. progress	20. instructional methods
5. teach	13. spaced (or periodic)	21. knowledge
6. operant	14. direct instruction	22. complexity
7. spaced (or periodic) review	15. discovery learning	
8. attention	16. direct instruction	

Connections

1. f	4. c	7. a
2. g	5. b	
3. d	6. e	

Check Your Memory

1. True	8. True	15. True
2. True	9. False	16. True
3. False	10. True	17. False
4. False	11. False	18. True
5. True	12. True	
6. True	13. False	
7. False	14. True	

Module 16.3 The Psychology of Education, Law, and Sports
Psychology and Law—Judging Juries

Recite and Review

1. psychology of law
2. mock
3. actors
4. law
5. innocent
6. judge
7. expertise
8. DNA
9. pretrial
10. inadmissible
11. severity
12. severe (or serious)
13. early
14. disqualify
15. women (or females)
16. scientific
17. demographic
18. community
19. authoritarian
20. nonverbal behavior (or body language)
21. death-qualified
22. white
23. authoritarian
24. criminal
25. convict
26. African
27. jury makeup (or jury composition)
28. scientific
29. balanced
30. police

Connections

1. f
2. g
3. e
4. d
5. b
6. a
7. c

Check Your Memory

1. False
2. True
3. False
4. True
5. False
6. False
7. True
8. True
9. False
10. True
11. False
12. False
13. True
14. False
15. True
16. False
17. False
18. True
19. True
20. True
21. True
22. False
23. False
24. True
25. True
26. True

Module 16.3 The Psychology of Education, Law, and Sports
Sports Psychology—The Athletic Mind

Recite and Review

1. sports
2. emotional
3. sports
4. physical
5. one-winner
6. fair
7. stress
8. skills
9. task analysis
10. job analysis
11. heartbeats
12. motor skill
13. motor program
14. motor program
15. model
16. verbal
17. automated
18. lifelike
19. feedback
20. correct
21. natural units
22. mental practice
23. mastered
24. peak
25. trance
26. flow
27. slowing
28. bests
29. arousal
30. choking
31. routine
32. relaxation
33. rehearse
34. cognitive-behavioral
35. self-regulation

Connections

1. i
2. h
3. a
4. f
5. b
6. c
7. e
8. d
9. g

Check Your Memory

1. True
2. True
3. False
4. False
5. True
6. False
7. False
8. True
9. True
10. False
11. True
12. True
13. True
14. False
15. False
16. True
17. False
18. False
19. True
20. True
21. False
22. True
23. True
24. False
25. True
26. True
27. False
28. True

Critical Thinking Answer

As discussed in Module 12.2, stress is reduced when a person feels in control of a situation. Following a routine helps athletes maintain a sense of order and control so that they are not overaroused when the time comes to perform.

Module 16.4 Psychology in Action
Human Factors Psychology—Who's the Boss Here?

Recite and Review

1. ergonomics
2. display
3. control
4. natural
5. metaphors
6. desktop metaphor
7. feedback
8. feedback
9. usability
10. thinking aloud
11. human-computer interaction (HCI)
12. stronger
13. smarter
14. controls
15. displays
16. interface
17. interface
18. speaking
19. telepresence
20. telesurgery
21. underused
22. tasks
23. satisfice
24. instruction manual
25. rooms
26. eating
27. sleep
28. monotony
29. solitary
30. animals

Connections

1. m
2. k
3. e
4. g
5. b
6. j
7. a
8. l
9. c
10. d
11. f
12. i
13. h

Check Your Memory

1. True
2. False
3. False
4. False
5. True
6. True
7. True
8. False
9. True
10. True
11. False
12. False
13. True
14. True
15. True
16. True
17. False
18. True
19. False
20. True
21. True
22. False
23. False
24. False
25. True

Critical Thinking Answer

Men tend aim at the "fly" and hence are more accurate when they urinate. The result is much cleaner men's washrooms.

Final Survey and Review—Completion

Module 16.1 Industrial/Organizational Psychology
Industrial/Organizational Psychology—Psychology at Work

1. counseling
2. scientific management
3. shared
4. knowledge
5. self-managed team
6. job enrichment
7. citizenship
8. halo
9. interest
10. leaderless group discussion

Module 16.1 Communication at Work—Getting the Message Across

11. why
12. wiggle
13. jargon
14. emotionally loaded
15. open mind

Module 16.2 Environmental Psychology
Environmental Psychology—Life on Spaceship Earth

16. environmental
17. behavioral settings
18. territorial
19. social
20. decrease
21. crowding
22. blood pressure
23. ecological footprint
24. tragedy of the commons
25. self-interest

Module 16.3 The Psychology of Education, Law, and Sports
Educational Psychology—An Instructive Topic

26. dynamics
27. educational
28. evaluation
29. direct instruction
30. discovery learning
31. Universal Design for Instruction

Module 16.3 Psychology and Law—Judging Juries

32. mock
33. evidence
34. scientific
35. demographic
36. authoritarian
37. death-qualified

Module 16.3 Sports Psychology—The Athletic Mind

38. sports
39. intrinsic
40. task analysis
41. motor skill
42. peak
43. imagery

Module 16.4 Psychology in Action
Human Factors Psychology—Who's the Boss Here?

44. human factors
45. controls
46. natural
47. feedback
48. usability
49. satisficing
50. plants

Final Survey and Review—Matching

Module 16.1 Industrial/Organizational Psychology
Part 1:

1. h
2. f
3. j
4. i

5. a
6. k
7. d
8. b

9. c
10. e
11. g

Part 2:

1. k
2. d
3. h
4. l

5. j
6. b
7. c
8. f

9. e
10. i
11. a
12. g

Module 16.2 Environmental Psychology

1. k
2. i
3. h
4. l

5. j
6. g
7. b
8. d

9. f
10. a
11. c
12. e

Module 16.3 The Psychology of Education, Law, and Sports

1. d
2. g
3. j
4. b

5. l
6. k
7. a
8. c

9. f
10. h
11. e
12. i

Module 16.4 Psychology in Action: Human Factors Psychology—Who's the Boss Here?

1. d
2. i
3. e
4. g

5. b
6. j
7. h
8. a

9. f
10. c

Final Survey and Review—True or False

Module 16.1 Industrial/Organizational Psychology
Industrial/Organizational Psychology—Psychology at Work

1. True
2. False
3. True
4. False

5. True
6. True
7. False
8. True

9. False
10. True

Module 16.1 Communication at Work—Getting the Message Across

11. False
12. False

13. True
14. False

15. True

Module 16.2 Environmental Psychology
Environmental Psychology—Life on Spaceship Earth (Module 16.2)

16. True
17. False
18. False
19. False
20. False
21. True
22. True
23. True
24. False
25. False

Module 16.3 The Psychology of Education, Law, and Sports
Educational Psychology—An Instructive Topic

26. True
27. False
28. True
29. False
30. True
31. False

Module 16.3 Psychology and Law—Judging Juries

32. True
33. True
34. False
35. False
36. False
37. True

Module 16.3 Sports Psychology—The Athletic Mind

38. True
39. False
40. True
41. False
42. True
43. False

Module 16.4 Psychology in Action
Human Factors Psychology—Who's the Boss Here?

44. False
45. True
46. True
47. True
48. True
49. False
50. True

Mastery Test

1. c
2. d
3. a
4. b
5. b
6. d
7. d
8. b
9. a
10. c
11. a
12. c
13. c
14. a
15. b
16. b
17. d
18. c
19. b
20. b
21. b
22. c
23. b
24. a
25. c
26. d
27. a
28. d
29. c
30. d
31. a
32. b
33. b
34. d
35. a
36. a
37. c
38. b
39. b
40. d

Appendix: Behavioral Statistics

Solutions

Module A.1 Descriptive Statistics
Descriptive Statistics—Psychology by the Numbers

Recite and Review
1. numbers
2. descriptive
3. inferential
4. precision
5. variability
6. graphical
7. frequency
8. frequency distribution
9. abscissa
10. ordinate
11. histogram
12. frequency polygon
13. frequency polygon
14. graphical
15. histogram

Connections
1. g
2. d
3. f
4. a
5. b
6. h
7. e
8. c

Check Your Memory
1. False
2. True
3. True
4. False
5. True
6. False
7. True
8. False
9. False
10. False

Module A.1 Descriptive Statistics
Measures of Central Tendency

Recite and Review
1. central tendency
2. mean (or average)
3. mode
4. median
5. mean (or average)
6. median
7. 7 (seven)
8. 90 (ninety)
9. 8 (eight)
10. central tendency

Connections
1. c
2. d
3. b
4. a

Check Your Memory
1. False
2. True
3. False
4. False
5. False
6. False
7. True
8. False

Critical Thinking Answer
The single large salary in this small group will distort the mean. In cases like this, the median is a better measure of central tendency.

Module A.1 Descriptive Statistics
Measures of Variability

Recite and Review
1. variability
2. range
3. standard deviation
4. z-score
5. normal curve
6. mean
7. +2.0
8. -2.0
9. normal curve
10. 68 (sixty-eight)
11. 95 (ninety-five)
12. 99 (ninety-nine)

Connections
1. c
2. a
3. e
4. b
5. d

Check Your Memory
1. False
2. True
3. True
4. False
5. False
6. False
7. True
8. True
9. True
10. True
11. False
12. True

Module A.2 Correlations and Inferential Statistics
Correlation—Rating Relationships

Recite and Review
1. correlation
2. correlation
3. scatter diagram
4. positive
5. positive
6. negative
7. zero
8. positive
9. negative
10. zero
11. coefficient
12. 0.00 (zero)
13. 1.00 (one)
14. perfect
15. perfect
16. positive
17. Pearson r
18. strong
19. weak
20. (perfect) negative
21. predictions
22. multiple
23. percent of variance
24. 25 (twenty-five)
25. 100 (one hundred)
26. cause-and-effect (causal)
27. third variable
28. experiment

Connections
1. d
2. i
3. a
4. h
5. j
6. g
7. f
8. b
9. c
10. e

Check Your Memory
1. False
2. False
3. False
4. True
5. False
6. False
7. False
8. True
9. False
10. False
11. False
12. False
13. True
14. True
15. True
16. True
17. True
18. False
19. False
20. True
21. False

Critical Thinking Answer

No. To reiterate, correlation does not prove causality. It is more likely here that a third factor is causing *both* the sleeping with the clothes on at night *and* the headaches (too much alcohol, anyone?).

Module A.2 Correlations and Inferential Statistics
Inferential Statistics—Significant Numbers

Recite and Review

1. inferential
2. population
3. impractical
4. sample
5. representative
6. random
7. (representative) sample
8. population
9. statistical significance
10. probability
11. 5 (five)
12. significant

Connections

1. e
2. d
3. c
4. b
5. a

Check Your Memory

1. False
2. False
3. True
4. True
5. False
6. False
7. True
8. False
9. False
10. True

Final Survey and Review—Completion

Module A.1 Descriptive Statistics
Descriptive Statistics—Psychology by the Numbers (Module A.1)

1. summarize
2. graphical statistics
3. frequency distribution
4. X
5. histogram

Measures of Central Tendency (Module A.1)

6. central tendency
7. 8 (eight)
8. 8 (eight)
9. 90 (ninety)

Measures of Variability (Module A.1)

10. variability
11. 20 (twenty)
12. normal curve
13. +2.0
14. two (2)

Module A.2 Correlations and Inferential Statistics
Correlation—Rating Relationships (Module A.2)

15. correlation
16. decreases
17. increases
18. negative
19. strong
20. 16 (sixteen)

Inferential Statistics—Significant Numbers (Module A.2)

21. inferential
22. population
23. random selection
24. statistical
25. 5 (five)
significance

Final Survey and Review—Matching

Module A.1 Descriptive Statistics
Part 1:

1. f
2. g
3. b

4. c
5. a
6. e

7. d

Part 2:

1. e
2. g
3. h

4. a
5. b
6. d

7. c
8. f

Module A.2 Correlations and Inferential Statistics

1. h
2. e
3. g
4. j

5. f
6. b
7. i
8. c

9. d
10. a

Final Survey and Review—True or False

Module A.1 Descriptive Statistics
Descriptive Statistics—Psychology by the Numbers

1. False
2. False

3. True
4. True

5. True

Module A.1 Measures of Central Tendency

6. True
7. False

8. True
9. False

Module A.1 Measures of Variability

10. False
11. False

12. True
13. False

14. False

Module A.2 Correlations and Inferential Statistics
Correlation—Rating Relationships (Module A.2)

15. True
16. False

17. True
18. False

19. True
20. False

Module A.2 Inferential Statistics—Significant Numbers

21. True
22. False

23. True
24. False

25. True

Mastery Test

1. c	10. c	19. b
2. b	11. b	20. d
3. a	12. d	21. c
4. d	13. b	22. b
5. b	14. b	23. a
6. d	15. d	24. a
7. a	16. c	25. b
8. b	17. d	
9. c	18. d